JOHNSTON PUBLIC LIBRARY
IJOH 00 0 074199 M

D1265224

JOHN F. KENNEDY

ALSO BY MICHAEL O'BRIEN

No Ordinary Joe: The Biography of Joe Paterno

Hesburgh: A Biography

Senator Philip Hart: The Conscience of the Senate

Vince: A Personal Biography of Vince Lombardi

McCarthy and McCarthyism in Wisconsin

B
KENNEDY

Michael O'Brien

JOHN F. KENNEDY

A BIOGRAPHY

THOMAS DUNNE BOOKS

St. Martin's Press

New York

WITHDRAWN

JOHNSTON PUBLIC LIBRARY
JOHNSTON IOWA 50131

THOMAS DUNNE BOOKS.
An imprint of St. Martin's Press.

JOHN F. KENNEDY. Copyright © 2005 by Michael O'Brien. All rights reserved. Printed in the United States of America. No part of this book may be used or reproduced in any manner whatsoever without written permission except in the case of brief quotations embodied in critical articles or reviews. For information, address St. Martin's Press, 175 Fifth Avenue, New York, N.Y. 10010.

Excerpts from "The Exner File" by Michael O'Brien, which appear here in a slightly revised version from the original, reprinted with permission of *The Washington Monthly*. Copyright © by Washington Monthly Publishing, LLC, 733 15th St. NW, Suite 520, Washington, D.C. 20005. (202) 393-5155. Web site: www.washingtonmonthly.com

www.stmartins.com

Design by Kathryn Parise

Maps on pages 144–146 by Mark Stein Studios

Library of Congress Cataloging-in-Publication Data

O'Brien, Michael, 1943-
    John F. Kennedy : a biography / Michael O'Brien.—1st U.S. ed.
    p. cm.
    Includes bibliographical references (p. 909).
    ISBN 0-312-28129-3
    EAN 978-0312-28129-8
    1. Kennedy, John F. (John Fitzgerald), 1917-1963. 2. Presidents—United States—Biography.   I. Title.
E842.O23 2005
973.922'092—dc22

2004056209

First Edition: March 2005

10 9 8 7 6 5 4 3 2 1

To friends and colleagues, past and present,
at the University of Wisconsin–Fox Valley

CONTENTS

ACKNOWLEDGMENTS

D uring the nearly ten years that this book has been in progress, I have
incurred many debts, and I am delighted to express my deep gratitude. Several librarians and archivists generously assisted me during
my visits to their institutions. They are Carol Bowers at the American Heritage Center at the University of Wyoming; Chris Carberry of the Massachusetts Historical Society; Patrick Quinn and Janet Olson of Northwestern
University; and Ellen Burke of the State Historical Society of Wisconsin.
Teresa Hornbrook of the National Park Service provided information on
John Kennedy's birthplace, and Nancy Kaufmann rendered the same service
for the Riverdale Country School.

The professional staff at the John F. Kennedy Library in Boston efficiently
processed all my requests, guided me through their voluminous collections,
and patiently answered all my questions. For this I am indebted to Megan
Desnoyers, Allan Goodrich, William Johnson, Sharon Kelly, June Payne,
Stephen Plotkin, and Maura Porter.

I owe special thanks to staff members at the University of Wisconsin–Fox
Valley who provided exceptional assistance over several years. They are Becky
Hoffman, Patricia Warmbrunn, and Christine Chamness. Almost daily for five
years, Kathy Skubal expertly processed mountains of written drafts, always doing the work with patience and humor. Dean Jim Perry kindly endorsed my

project from the beginning. Dave Huehner, my History Department chair, also graciously supported my project for many years.

My lasting gratitude to James Giglio, who took time to expertly critique a large portion of the book. Thanks to several colleagues and friends who critiqued parts of the manuscript within their expertise: Jane Garton, Rex Hieser, Jeff Kuepper, Marc Potash, Dan Putman, and George Waller. Several members of the Fox Valley Writers Club—Curtis Brown, Don Derozier, Earl Gates, and Helen Gray—made valuable stylistic suggestions. My son Jeremy O'Brien read the entire manuscript and offered his advice and encouragement.

This is not an authorized study. I did not ask permission of anyone to write this biography. Nonetheless, thanks to Robert F. Kennedy Jr. for granting me permission to use the K. LeMoyne Billings Papers. Thanks also to the John Fitzgerald Kennedy Library Foundation for a generous two-week travel grant.

During an early stage of my research on this project I was granted a wonderful nine-month fellowship by the Institute for Research in the Humanities at the University of Wisconsin–Madison. I am particularly indebted to Paul Boyer, the institute's director at the time. The University of Wisconsin–Fox Cities Foundation provided several timely travel grants, and the University of Wisconsin awarded me a sabbatical during the last stage of my writing.

Ten years ago, at the beginning of my research, six former students volunteered to scour local libraries and photocopy important articles. No, I have not forgotten your assistance. Thanks to Jeanne Dempsey, Anne Palm, Scott Plach, JoAnn Weiss, and especially Carol Anne VanDenHeuvel.

Thanks to Dr. David S. Sandock of Milwaukee, who shared his wisdom about John Kennedy's medical history. I am especially indebted to the expert team of physicians who graciously joined me in studying the recently opened Kennedy medical files at the Kennedy Library. They are Edwin Cassem, professor of psychiatry at Harvard Medical School and consulting psychiatrist at Massachusetts General Hospital; Gilbert Daniels, endocrinologist, associate professor of medicine at Harvard Medical School, and physician at Massachusetts General Hospital; and Robert Boyd, retired, formerly assistant clinical professor of orthopedic surgery at Harvard Medical School and chief of the Orthopedic Spine Service of Massachusetts General Hospital.

I would also like to thank my agent, Scott Waxman, my editor, Thomas Dunne, and Sean Desmond and Katherine Carlson at Thomas Dunne Books, and my superb copy editor, Adam Goldberger.

My wife, Sally, graciously endured her husband's sixth book with patience, encouragement, and love. Once again, thanks to my children, Tim, Sean, Jeremy, and Carey, for all the love and enjoyment they bring me.

INTRODUCTION

———————•———————

In May 1963, Jacqueline Kennedy arranged a small dinner party in the White House for her husband, President John F. Kennedy. In addition to close friends—the Chuck Spaldings, the Ben Bradlees, Bill Walton, and others—the featured guest was Frederick Loewe. The Austrian-born composer had teamed with lyricist Alan Jay Lerner to create several of America's most popular stage musicals.

After dinner the group adjourned to the private quarters of the White House, where a piano waited. Loewe played several of his compositions from *My Fair Lady* and from the President's current favorite, *Camelot.* Always curious about other people's expertise, Kennedy queried the composer. "How do you go about writing a piece of music?" he asked. "Do you write the music first and then put the words to it?" He flattered Loewe by confessing he went to sleep many nights listening to tapes of *Camelot.* Later Kennedy told friends how much he enjoyed the evening.[1]

The musical *Camelot* focuses on King Arthur's later years and the love triangle between Arthur, Queen Guinevere, and Sir Lancelot. It opened on Broadway on December 3, 1960, and closed January 5, 1963, after 873 performances. The play's music album rose to number one in the country and remained there for over sixty weeks.

As a youth Kennedy had read and enjoyed the stories of King Arthur and the Knights of the Round Table. He was attracted by the adventure, the courtliness, and the heroes. The song he loved best in the musical appears at the end, when King Arthur sings "Camelot (Reprise)." The last four lines are:

> *Don't let it be forgot,*
> *That once there was a spot*
> *For one brief shining moment that was known*
> *As Camelot.*[2]

In late November 1963, a few days after President Kennedy's funeral, Jackie Kennedy phoned journalist Theodore H. White. He was flabbergasted to hear there was something she wanted *Life* magazine to report to the country, and that he must write the article. She would send a Secret Service car to bring him to Hyannis Port.

White was a friend who happened to be a journalist, someone reliable, who could report Jackie's thoughts. On Friday evening, November 29, 1963, White arrived with his tape recorder, but left it unopened; instead, he sat, listened, and took notes as Jackie poured out her heart. "She was without tears; drained, white of face," the journalist later wrote.

She asked him to Hyannis Port wanting White to make sure that her husband was not forgotten in history. ("The thought that it was up to me to make American history remember John F. Kennedy was so unanticipated that my pencil stuttered over the notes," said White later.) He thought his first duty was to let "this sad, wan lady talk out her grief."

Interspersed with her memories, spoken softly, was her concern about how historians would treat her husband. Her message was simple: She believed, as had John Kennedy, that history belongs to heroes; and heroes must not be forgotten.

"There'll be great Presidents again," she told White, "and the Johnsons are wonderful, they've been wonderful to me—but there'll never be another Camelot again.

"For a while I thought history was something that bitter old men wrote. But then I realized history made Jack what he was. You must think of him as this little boy, sick so much of the time, reading in bed, reading history, reading the Knights of the Round Table, reading Marlborough. For Jack, history was full of heroes. And if it made him this way—if it made him see the heroes—maybe other little boys will see. . . . Jack had this hero idea of history, the idealistic view."

She insisted that White feature her emphasis on Camelot in the *Life* magazine article. She kept returning to the Camelot image: "Don't let it be forgot, that once there was a spot, for one brief shining moment that was known as Camelot, and it will never be that way again."

"Camelot, heroes, fairy tales, legends, were what history was all about,"

White wrote in summarizing her views. "So the epitaph on the Kennedy administration became Camelot," White wrote years later, "a magic moment in American history when gallant men danced with beautiful women, when great deeds were done, when artists, writers and poets met at the White House, and the barbarians beyond the walls held back."[3]

White's story appeared in the *Life* magazine issue of December 6, 1963. Because of America's grief, the article immediately attracted enormous attention. At the time, *Camelot* was on the road, playing at the Opera House in Chicago, a huge theater with over three thousand seats. At an evening performance shortly after White's article appeared in *Life,* the theater was packed. Alan Jay Lerner described what happened when "Camelot (Reprise)" was sung:

> Louis Hayward was playing King Arthur. When he came to those lines, there was a sudden wail from the audience. It was not a muffled sob; it was a loud, almost primitive cry of pain. The play stopped, and for almost five minutes everyone in the theatre—on the stage, in the wings, in the pit, and in the audience—wept without restraint. Then the play continued.

When Robert Kennedy played home movies of Jack at the 1964 Democratic National Convention, the music of *Camelot* played in the background.[4]

For some supporters of John Kennedy the Camelot image rang true. The idealistic President had tried to inspire people to cross new frontiers in human history. His followers were his knights—youths excited by adventures in the Peace Corps, for example, "fighting the dragons of poverty and helping populations in distress, enduring hardships for noble causes in foreign lands."

Since late 1963, when pundits have needed a metaphor to describe the Kennedy years, they have settled on Camelot. Compared to the events following Kennedy's death—the Vietnam War, domestic strife, violence, Watergate— the image of Kennedy's Camelot has looked positively utopian.

All of Kennedy's aides, though, have derided the notion that Kennedy's presidency in any way resembled Camelot. For Larry O'Brien, the White House liaison with Congress, the Kennedy administration was exhaustingly hard work, seven days a week. "If at any time Camelot existed, it eluded me," he reflected. "I never saw it or felt it." Kennedy's secretary, Evelyn Lincoln, accused Jackie of creating a Camelot fantasy. "You know what [the President] would have said about it—'Oh not *that* trash!' [Jackie] said 'Camelot' was his favorite song. His favorite song was 'Bill Bailey, Won't You Please Come Home?' "

"No one while J.F.K. was alive thought of his Washington as Camelot," commented Kennedy adviser and historian Arthur Schlesinger Jr. "Had those of us around the President ever proposed such a fancy, no one would have kidded us more swiftly or decisively than Kennedy himself. Certainly J.F.K. listened to the Camelot record late at night. So did we all. This did not implicate us in its plot."[5]

Historians and others who have written in praise of President Kennedy have come to be designated "Camelot" historians, a label they detest, but one that has stuck with them nonetheless. In the noteworthy accounts by historian Schlesinger and JFK's aide Theodore Sorensen, written shortly after the President's assassination, Kennedy had flair, panache, aspirations to great deeds, and contagious confidence. A leader with superior intelligence, imagination, and curiosity, he wielded power with grace, verve, and civility. Above all, John Kennedy had courage, a trait he displayed in the South Pacific during World War II and as President. He wrote a Pulitzer Prize–winning book on political courage, and bore pain and personal tragedy with stoic forbearance. As President he took considerable political risks, as he did in promoting civil rights starting in June 1963, a courageous and principled decision, resulting in loss of support among white Southern segregationists.[6]

Because of Kennedy, Americans reexamined religious bigotry, poverty, racial discrimination, and selfish corporate power. Economic growth averaged 5.6 percent per year during his presidency; unemployment went down, and inflation was only 1.3 percent. His administration was also remarkably free of financial scandal and incompetence.

The caution Kennedy displayed at times stemmed not from fear but prudence. His minuscule election margin in 1960 and the conservative-dominated Congress imposed practical restrictions on him. Skeptical of ideology, he approached problems rationally.[7]

In foreign policy his most compelling desire was to reduce the risk of nuclear holocaust by miscalculation, or as Richard Neustadt observed, "to outlast [the Cold War] with American society intact and nuclear risks in check." In Schlesinger's account of the Cuban missile crisis it was Kennedy's combination of "toughness and restraint, of will, nerve and wisdom, so brilliantly controlled, so matchlessly calibrated, that dazzled the world."

He grew in office. The Kennedy of 1963 was a different, more mature, more capable leader than the Kennedy of 1961. "What was killed in Dallas was not only the President but the promise," wrote *The New York Times*'s James Reston.

Kennedy served as President for only two years and ten months—1,037 days. He had so little time. "It was as if Jackson had died before the nullification controversy and the Bank War, as if Lincoln had been killed six months after Gettysburg or Franklin Roosevelt at the end of 1935 or Truman before the Marshall Plan," Schlesinger reminded us.[8]

Kennedy deserves credit for major domestic legislation passed after his death. In the summer of 1964 a reporter for *Look* magazine questioned congressional leaders about whether Kennedy would have been successful in passing civil rights and tax-reduction bills. The response was overwhelming. Republican senator Everett Dirksen: "This program was on the way before November 22, 1963. Its time had come." Democratic congressman Carl Albert: "The pressure behind the program had become so great that it would have been adopted in essentially the same form whether Kennedy lived or died." Republican congressman Charles A. Halleck: "The assassination made no difference. The program was already made."

In memory John F. Kennedy remains forever young. He was the first president born in the twentieth century, with a young wife and two small children. One time the President was overheard saying to his daughter, "Hurry up, Caroline, I want to use the phone." Heart-wrenching photographs, appearing shortly after the President's death, showed Kennedy at his desk in the White House while John-John peered through a cubbyhole beneath him.[9]

Kennedy was a catalyst for activism among youth. The Peace Corps is the primary example cited to prove his capacity to inspire young people. In the highly publicized agency volunteers unselfishly served the cause of humanity throughout the world. "The Peace Corps will always belong to John F. Kennedy and share the splendor of his memory," said one commentator. "It was an adventure, so like the man, bold and young, warm and gallant."

A young volunteer in Africa wrote shortly after the President's death: "Being in the Peace Corps we all here felt we had a special attachment to him. Hell, most of us felt we were working for him and would refer to him as Jack—as if he were a Peace Corps Volunteer."[10]

Kennedy's major addresses in mid-1963 on civil rights, détente, and the nuclear test ban were brilliant. In his American University speech he said in reference to U.S.-Soviet relations, "In the final analysis, our most basic common link is that we all inhabit this small planet. We all breathe the same air. We all cherish our children's future. And we are all mortal."

Kennedy had an almost "existential" impact on the social imagination. He set in motion a "new set of moods" in the country "galvanized by his words and actions." American idealism, dormant during the complacent Eisenhower presidency, revived because Kennedy "invoked a spirit of sacrifice, commitment, and vision," touching a responsive chord within Americans. He literally asked Americans to reach for the moon, and, by insisting that we try, he inspired a feeling that we could do it. "The energies he released, the standards he set, the purposes he inspired, the goals he established would guide the land he loved for years to come," Schlesinger wrote in praise of Kennedy's intangible qualities.[11]

Most revisionist writers, though, disdain the views of the Camelot historians. Their critical accounts, published mainly since the mid-1970s, exposed Kennedy's alleged links to the Mafia, his covert operations in Cuba and Vietnam, his secret and life-threatening health problems, and his stunning—nearly pathological—sexual philandering.

The Kennedy family was an emotional wasteland in revisionist accounts. Jack's mother, Rose, was cold, unmotherly, and often unavailable; his father, Joe, was a ruthless, ignoble, philandering reprobate. Recent accounts of John's early life portray him as privileged, pampered, often irresponsible and insensitive, and emotionally cold. Critics challenge Kennedy's reputation as a war hero. Had he been more alert and responsible, *PT 109* would never have been sunk by a Japanese destroyer in 1943.[12]

Revisionists contend that the Kennedys, particularly John, benefited from a mythmaking machine, "an apparatus of publicists, friendly journalists and starry-eyed academics, all inspired by the family's wealth and charm." There were many myths and lies. Ted Sorensen and other ghostwriters, for example, actually wrote *Profiles in Courage,* a fact Kennedy covered up, thereby "perpetuating his image as a prize-winning author and historian." Because he courted intellectuals, he created the myth of an intellectual president. "One almost forgets how carefully his father had cultivated this image for him, getting his two books published, and securing a Pulitzer Prize for one of them," said Bruce Mazlish. Kennedy's favorite reading, say critics, was Ian Fleming's superficial spy thrillers about James Bond, "the debonair, womanizing, rule-breaking cold warrior."[13]

Advised by the "best and the brightest"—McGeorge Bundy, Robert McNamara, Walt Rostow, and Maxwell Taylor—Kennedy's foreign policy was dangerous and mostly a failure. He was an orthodox cold warrior, a dogmatic anticommunist, whose policies of flexible containment and counterinsurgency sank the United States deeply into the disastrous Vietnam War. In dealing with European countries Kennedy never developed a "coherent and purposeful strategy and oscillated between hardline and conciliatory approaches with little apparent rationale."

Kennedy's Alliance for Progress in Latin America failed because New Frontiersmen exaggerated their ability to bring about change and "underestimated the daunting nature of Latin America's socioeconomic problems." Ironically, the Kennedy administration ended up bolstering regimes that were "undemocratic, conservative, and frequently repressive."[14]

In domestic affairs, Kennedy's legislative efforts came to little. To be sure, he succeeded in passing minor bills, but important measures—in education, health care, urban affairs, civil rights, tax reform—all failed or were drastically weakened. That he was unable to produce a domestic record of any consequence stemmed from his inability to relate to legislators, his half-hearted efforts, and his poor leadership. He temporized on a variety of issues which needed concerted pushing, civil rights being the most conspicuous example. "His public position on civil rights was, almost always, simply a reflection of his perception of its strategic value to him in his pursuit of office," claimed one historian.[15]

Revisionist accounts claim that Kennedy's presidency rested mostly on style, not on substance. He had wit, charm, grace, and beauty, but he "was pragmatic to the point of amorality"; his character lacked a "moral center." He was unwilling to risk position, power, and career for the sake of an abiding conviction; his sole standard seemed to be political expediency.

At times he was petty and vindictive toward unfriendly journalists and toward politicians he didn't respect, like Adlai Stevenson.

In his best-selling book on the Kennedy presidency, Richard Reeves portrayed JFK as an egocentric, a person who brandished his charm to manipulate people for his own ends. Kennedy was "an artist who painted with other people's lives. He squeezed people like tubes of paint, gently or brutally, and the people around him—family, writers, drivers, ladies-in-waiting—were the indentured inhabitants serving his needs and desires."

He was reactive rather than proactive, Reeves contended. He reacted to events that he often didn't understand or anticipate. He was impatient, easily bored, addicted to excitement, and "dangerously disorganized."[16]

While Kennedy's reputation among historians has declined, he remains the most popular Cold War President in opinion polls. In 1975, when a Gallup poll asked Americans whom they considered their greatest president, Kennedy was rated highest with 52 percent. In 1991, after a period of Kennedy debunking, Abraham Lincoln managed to edge him out, but just barely—40 percent to 39 percent. If Americans could pick a president, any president, which one would they choose to run the country today? a *New York Times*/CBS News poll asked in 1996. The answer: John F. Kennedy.

"There's a tremendous difference in how Kennedy is viewed by historians and the public," mused historian Michael Beschloss. "It should make historians modest." Modest or confused. James MacGregor Burns, the eminent early biographer of Kennedy, was perplexed by Kennedy's high ratings in the opinion polls. "His actual tangible material impact on history was not enough to justify this," Burns insisted. "After all, he was not a Churchill, he was not a Roosevelt. He didn't have a chance to be these people. . . . Why did he have this kind of impact on the world? Was it a fabrication? Was it that

he was handsome, and his wife and his kids? One statesman who had cute little kids? Was it civil rights?"[17]

So who was John F. Kennedy? What influenced his development? How
should history judge his personality, his character, and his presidency?

JOHN F. KENNEDY

1

KENNEDYS AND FITZGERALDS

All of John Kennedy's great-grandparents were born in Ireland, probably the poorest and most backward country in Europe in the mid-nineteenth century. Having endured famines and agonizing defeat in war, Ireland had fallen into utter subjection. In the 1640s the Irish allied with the Stuart kings during an eight-year civil war. After Oliver Cromwell's conclusive victory in England, he executed Charles I in 1649 and led a ruthless invasion of Ireland resembling a religious crusade. After capturing an Irish army at Drogheda, he ordered them massacred, killing 2,800. By 1652 all of Ireland had been taken over by Cromwell's efficient army.

One-third of Ireland's population had died in the wars, plague, and famine of the previous ten years. Cromwell, the hated Puritan, sold thousands of Irishmen into slavery in the West Indies, confiscated two-thirds of Ireland's land, and redistributed the property to his anti-Catholic, Protestant soldiers and retainers, making the Irish farmers landless peasants with no rights to the soil, paying exorbitant rents to absentee landlords.[1]

To maintain the English Protestant ascendancy the English implemented new penal codes which deprived the Irish of civil and political rights. The

s forbade the Irish language and banished the Catholic hierarchy and religious orders. No Irish Catholic could enroll at a university, work for the
government, become a lawyer, or teach school. Nor could Catholics vote or
serve on juries. To keep the Irish docile, the British enforced illiteracy.

Although battered, beaten, and impoverished, the stubborn Irish would
not allow the English to crush them completely. "They mustered their aggressiveness," wrote historian William Shannon,

> rolled and twisted their anger into a knot, and tried to hold on to what
> was theirs: . . . their family identity, their memories, their pattern of
> speech, their way of looking at the world. Rebellion had failed, social
> movement was blocked, individual talent brought no reward, social
> wrongs no relief, and appeals for understanding no quarter. Then let the
> outsiders, the government, and the world be damned, and let each man
> look to his own and his family's interest.[2]

The Irish subsisted on a diet of potatoes because the crop was easy to cultivate; a small plot of land could feed a large family. The typical tenant farmer
and his family lived in a windowless mud hut with a thatched roof and a dirt
floor. "Cottages were dirty and smoky from turf fires, constant rains turned
floors into mud holes, and thatched roofs hosted a variety of vermin," noted
historian Lawrence McCaffrey. These farmers shared their hovels with pigs
and chickens—the animals being valuable to pay rent—and the dreadful
conditions caused diseases and a high rate of infant mortality.

Because most Irishmen could not read or write, the Irish came to prize
oratory and storytelling. "Out of this tradition emerges one of the arche-
types of Irish character—the man with the gift for words," Shannon observed. Ambitious Irish youths dreamed of winning fame as orators and
admiration as good talkers.

Ireland was the most Catholic country in the world. Directed and guided
from Rome, the Catholic Church was the one Irish institution to survive despite persecution. Its dogma, sacraments, and rituals sustained the Irish
through their tribulations. Their faith was a common bond, the heart of Irish
identity, comforting the wretched and, as McCaffrey pointed out, adding "a
touch of beauty to miserable existences." The Church helped release "pent-
up emotions," dampened "violent tendencies," and offered "a hope of salvation and justice in another world if not in this one."[3]

There had been frequent famines in Ireland, but they were usually brief.
In 1845, however, a fungus devastated nearly the entire potato crop. The catastrophe returned the following year. The year 1847 was fungus free, but the
blight returned devastatingly in 1848. By then the blight had already de-

stroyed morale and brought hunger, scurvy, typhoid, and cholera; eight hundred thousand people died.

Between 1845 and 1854, 1.5 million Irish immigrants fled to the United States. The British subsidized the Cunard shipping line, and when a government report in 1841 determined that the most efficient way to get mail from England to its colony of Canada was via Boston's port, Cunard established its terminus there. Other shipping lines followed. So when the Irish emigrated to America, many arrived in Boston.

They were herded like cattle into the "coffin ships," with little sanitation or ventilation, and about 6 percent died during the six- to eight-week voyage. Others were stricken with ship fever, derisively nicknamed "famine fever" or "hunger typhus."[4]

Unlike earlier American settlers, who sought freedom and opportunity, the desperate Irish came to America to escape hunger and oppression. What's more, the fiercely Catholic Irish arrived in an overwhelmingly Protestant country founded by the hated Englishmen and still dominated by their descendants.

Because the impoverished Irish were unfit for the pioneer life, disillusioned with agriculture, and comfortable with communal living, they tended to live in large cities like Boston. Unhealthy living conditions predominated in Irish-American neighborhoods. Overcrowding, vermin, and poor ventilation and sanitation were the norm, leading to outbreaks of tuberculosis, cholera, and smallpox. "Living in filth and hunger in their reeking Paddyville and Mick alleys and rookeries," wrote one observer, "they created the first urban mass slums of America." In Boston the Irish immigrant could expect to live about fourteen years after arrival.[5]

The unskilled Irish had trouble gaining employment in Boston's urban and commercial setting. Employers were reluctant to hire them except for lowly positions as longshoremen, hod carriers, and railroad workers. The Irishman's reputation for hard drinking and fighting was detrimental in securing excellent jobs. On the eve of World War I the Irish remained locked mostly in low-status blue-collar jobs.

Prejudice was a constant irritant. In the late nineteenth century, journalists who supported urban reform stereotyped the newly arrived Irish as corrupt, drunken, illiterate, and priest-ridden. The prominent cartoonist Thomas Nast caricatured the Irish, castigating their violence, mocking their loyalty to the Democratic Party, and making them appear subhuman.

Help-wanted advertisements in newspapers blatantly discriminated, requesting "Protestants only"—"No Irish need apply." Newspapers divided the Sunday social section into one for the Proper Bostonians and the other for the Irish. While listening to an admiring description of the cobblestone pavement on Yankee Protestant Beacon Hill, an Irish woman bitterly re-marked, "Those aren't cobblestones. Those are Irish heads." Hatred of the Irish was unusually intense partly because the Irish bitterly resisted denigra-tion and took to politics as an avenue to express their grievances.

Historian Albert Bushnell Hart wrote in defense of the Irish-Americans that they

> were thought to be too clannish, flocking by themselves and cutting themselves off from the life of the community like an alien element; al-though one wonders what else could have been expected in view of the attitude of mingled dislike, distrust, and contempt which they so fre-quently encountered from the natives. In fact, they could usually find real friendliness and help only from people of "their own kind" and from their priests.[6]

The Irish formed their own society within Boston's society, an emerging Catholic bloc of voters in opposition to the Protestant Yankee oligarchs. Block by block, the Irish organized politically until they captured control of precincts, wards, and, finally, city government. Fortunately for Irish political success, Anglo-Protestants gradually withdrew from politics, regarding it as a third-rate occupation compared to business and the professions.

Politics fascinated the Irish. An election was a game that must be won; a moral victory was no victory at all. Irish politicians became skilled concilia-tors and compromisers. Gregarious, they enjoyed people. "Conversation is one of their most attractive gifts," noted McCaffrey. "They prefer to con-vince by argument than by force."[7]

The Irish-American politician loved to make speeches. It was an art, much as it had been in the mother country. Historian Dennis Ryan noted that the nineteenth-century Irish-American politician, "with his penchant for flamboyant rhetoric, vivid metaphors, witty anecdotes, and personal invec-tive, inherited the responsibility of entertaining a people who came to value the way a public figure said something almost as much as what he said."

The Irish were conspicuous in the large cities for their taverns and sa-loons, which provided a five-cent beer, a meager lunch, a convivial atmo-sphere, and an informal meeting place. Ward-boss politics flourished in the saloons; proprietors circulated nomination papers and corralled votes from their customers on election day.

The liquor business became a means of upward mobility—if not socially, at least economically and politically. Irish politicians profited from their close affiliation with the saloons and liquor trade, but they were often teetotalers themselves, not wanting to impair their abilities.[8]

The Irish were so closely linked with the Democratic Party that Irish,

Catholic, and Democrat "composed a trinity of associations," observed Mc-Caffrey. "In their political quest for power, Irish politicians used Catholic solidarity as a voting base, saloons as political clubs, and police and fire department appointments as patronage sources to recruit votes and party workers."

There was no single citywide machine in Boston. "Each ward boss was a feudal lord, and city politics was an unfolding drama of temporary alliances interspersed with bitter infighting," noted Martin Kaufman. The ward boss was the labor agent for people in his ward, and his primary role was to secure public jobs for his supporters. "The average laboring man lives not two weeks away from starvation," remarked a contemporary newspaper. The ward boss who secured quality jobs won gratitude, a warm following, and votes.

At Thanksgiving and Christmas, the Irish ward boss distributed baskets of food, helped needy neighbors pay their rent, and "made sure he was within camera focus when he handed a basket to a crippled child or a blind old man."

Irish-American political leaders used government to improve the lives of the urban poor. Their method was inefficient and graft-ridden social justice, "but the Irish approach rather than that of Anglo Protestants was the precursor of communal liberalism in the United States," observed McCaffrey.[9]

John Kennedy's maternal great-grandfather was Thomas Fitzgerald of County Wexford in Ireland. His wife, Rose Mary Murray, also came from Wexford. Both had escaped Ireland in the 1840s and settled in Boston's North End. Thomas worked as a farm laborer for a while, but by the mid-1860s he owned a grocery and liquor store. The Fitzgeralds were better off than most Irish families and always had food on the table. Thomas and Rose Mary had eleven children. Their third child, John Fitzgerald, was born in a tenement near the Old North Church in Boston on February 11, 1863. Most Irish youths completed only grammar school, but young Johnny continued his education at the elite Boston Latin School. Short, stocky, and agile, he was an outstanding football and baseball player and a good student. Listing other talents, a contemporary account described him as the "swiftest sprinter in the North End, the fastest swimmer, the best dancer, the most tuneful singer and the most eloquent speaker." Even as a youth, he refused to smoke tobacco, or to drink liquor or even coffee. Following graduation, he enrolled in Harvard Medical School, but after his father died during his first year, his mother having died earlier, he quit to help take care of his family.[10]

For several years he worked as a clerk in the customhouse, then resigned to establish his own insurance and investment business in the North End.

Setting his professional sights on politics, he joined scores of organizations that would advance his career: the Massachusetts Order of Foresters, the Ancient Order of Hibernians, the Knights of St. Rose, the Red Berry Club, the Heptasophs, the Royal Arcanum, the Charitable Irish Society, the Dorchester Catholic Club, the St. Alphonsus Association, the Catholic Union of Boston, the Young Men's Catholic Association of Boston College, and the Knights of Columbus.

He talked his way into a job as ward heeler with North End's ward boss, Matthew Keany. "Ward heelers shanghaied voters for the ballot boxes by promising jobs to those who played ball and blacklisting those who didn't," noted Charles Higham.[11]

Tireless, unabashed, full of blarney and cunning, "Honey Fitz"—so called for his sweet tooth and his syrupy speeches—was elected to the city council in 1892, and moved up to the Massachusetts state senate the following year. As a state senator he advocated measures to establish maximum hours for workers and workmen's compensation insurance, and was an early supporter of old-age pensions. From 1895 to 1901, he served as U.S. congressman from Boston's Eleventh District.

After leaving Congress, he purchased a weekly newspaper, *The Republic,* giving him a public forum to enhance his political career. In 1905 he was elected Boston's mayor, and in 1910 he was reelected to a four-year term under a new reform charter.

The story goes that Honey Fitz could talk to a person for fifteen minutes, at the rate of two hundred words a minute, without letting the person cut in more than two or three times, then pat the fellow on the back and say how much he had enjoyed the conversation.

Every morning he studied the obituary notices in *The Boston Globe* and handed out assignments for his "wake-house campaigns." Either he or one of his retainers expressed his sorrow at each home in the ward where someone had died. "He was highly emotional—Johnny Fitz—with an extraordinary trick of weeping when he chose," wrote one commentator. "His 'wake-house campaigns' have never yet been equaled in the ward."[12]

An energetic publicist, he often visited the office of the Associated Press to make sure the office reported his speeches. While he was in Congress, a Boston newspaper correspondent led a tour of constituents through the Capitol.

"Let's go to the House and hear Fitz," said the correspondent.

"What, does he speak to-day?" asked a constituent.

"He will when he sees us," said the correspondent.

A popular song, "Sweet Adeline," being sung by countless barbershop quartets throughout the country, became his theme song. On hundreds, perhaps thousands, of occasions—in assembly halls and beer gardens, on bandstands—

people listened as Honey Fitz, "straw hat perched rakishly on his head, hand pressed to heart," would belt out the lyrics. In the summer of 1911, during a European tour, he even sang "Sweet Adeline" for Kaiser Wilhelm in Berlin.[13]

Although he attacked contemporary Yankees, he was proud of Boston's Yankee past. He urged his fellow Irish Catholics to attend the public schools in order to mix "with the superior men, read their words, listen to them, talk to them." Like his fellow Hibernians, Fitzgerald detested the Brahmins, but he wanted Irishmen to learn from their superior talents.

Fitzgerald was incredibly energetic; one account estimated that in his first two years as mayor he attended 1,200 dinners, 1,500 dances, 200 picnics, and 1,000 meetings, and delivered 3,000 speeches. Critics dismissed him as a lovable old windbag—"Fitzblarney." "The only reason he had a head was to give him a place to park his hat," said one.[14]

Although he campaigned against rascality and corruption, his own administration was badly tainted with unscrupulous practices. The evils of the spoils system were never more glaring. He appointed a saloonkeeper to replace a physician on the board of health; liquor dealers held sway as superintendent of public buildings and wire commissioner; and he divided the Street Department into six divisions with separate directors. He created a peculiar office, city dermatologist, and awarded the four-thousand-dollar job to the son of a leader in Ward Six.

Appointing bartenders, undertakers, and politicians, he increased the number of tax collectors from sixty-two to eighty-three. Eight additional deputy sealers were added to the Department of Weights and Measures. He invented new job categories—tea warmers, tree climbers, rubber-boot repairers, watchmen to watch other watchmen. Graft was blatant. A single coal company defrauded the city of two hundred thousand dollars.

Fitzgerald was never indicted for graft or corruption, but suspicion followed him for the rest of his life. He had entered politics poor, and left it rich. "He was a classic politician of his age, and in all probability his hands had left the till with coins sticking to them," biographer Lawrence Leamer concluded.[15]

Yet his accomplishments were impressive. His administration built the City Hall Annex, the aquarium at South Boston, and the Franklin Park Zoo. Libraries, gymnasiums, and playgrounds in poorer areas, a measles hospital, and a child hygiene system to protect the health of the city's children were all part of his legacy.

"Everyone can't be a scholar and a white-collar worker," he said. "Some have aptitudes for other things, and those aptitudes must be given a chance to develop." Supporting continuing education that would teach a trade, he helped create the Girls' High School of Practical Arts, the Trade School for Girls, and the School for Bookbinding and Printing. He made himself an authority on the history of the people, places, and events of Boston's North End, becoming an articulate booster of the city of Boston.[16]

On September 18, 1889, Honey Fitz wed Mary Josephine "Josie" Hannon, a marriage that lasted sixty-one years. Josie was a slender, petite beauty with a fine complexion whose attractiveness the Kennedy clan would inherit. The couple had six children, of whom Rose, born on July 22, 1890, was the oldest and her father's favorite.

The daughter of a poor Irish-American Massachusetts farmer, Josie lacked sophistication and social skills, and couldn't entertain Fitzgerald's guests. In some ways Honey Fitz and Josie were opposites. He was an extrovert; she was shy and reserved. He loved the stage, loved being with people; she contented herself with close friends and family, and needed time for solitude and prayer.[17]

Rose Fitzgerald Kennedy described her mother as an immaculate housekeeper, prudent with money, devoted to her family, and deeply religious. Josie loved taking vacation trips with her husband, "leaving us children . . . in the care of a nursemaid and housekeeper," said Rose.

A strict disciplinarian, Josie made certain her children behaved, studied in school, learned their religious lessons, and were punctual, neat, and well-mannered. If the children didn't obey the rules, she spanked them. The Catholic faith was a pervading and abiding presence in Josie's life, and she instilled the Church's tenets into her children. "She drilled us in our catechism and other religious lessons," Rose recalled, "and talked to us about the fasts and feasts and special seasons of the Church." The Fitzgeralds had a shrine in their house with a statue of the Blessed Virgin. "Every night during Lent my mother would gather us in one of the rooms of the house, turn out the lights—the better to concentrate—and lead us in reciting the Rosary."[18]

Some people disliked Josie. Her niece, Geraldine Hannon, described her aunt as a dissatisfied person. "I didn't like her very well. She froze and was aloof when she met people." Others described Josie as "really a pill," a woman who "brought gloom into the house."

Rose resembled her mother in appearance, in loving travel and fine clothes, in needing solitude and prayer, in stoically facing adversity, and in devotion to her family. But she was more intelligent than her mother, was not shy, and would perform brilliantly on the public stage.[19]

John Kennedy's paternal great-grandfather, Patrick Kennedy, grew up in Dunganstown in County Wexford, about six miles from New Ross, a seaport town of fifteen thousand. Unlike most of the Irish, Patrick's family was not destitute, fortunate to have been located in a part of Ireland spared the worst of the potato blight. Patrick's father, also named Patrick, was a tenant farmer, and the family lived in a two-room stone cottage with a dirt floor and a straw-thatched roof. The family cultivated twenty-five acres of potatoes, sugar beets, and barley, and raised cattle and sheep.

Although less affected by the famine, the Kennedys were menaced by high rents. Money that landlords lost in the famine regions were made up by raising the rents on tenants who survived—like the Kennedy family. At age twenty-five, his prospects bleak, young Patrick decided to emigrate to America.[20]

In October 1848, Patrick booked passage on the SS *Washington Irving,* making the dangerous voyage to Boston in forty days. No one knows for sure how he met his wife, Bridget Murphy, also a native of Wexford. Bridget and Patrick named their fourth child, born on January 14, 1858, Patrick Joseph Kennedy. Known as P.J. to distinguish him from his father, he was John Kennedy's grandfather.

Exhausted at thirty-five after working for a decade as a cooper making barrels, Patrick Kennedy died of cholera less than a year after the birth of P.J. Left alone to support her family, Bridget Kennedy purchased a small notions shop in East Boston, leaving P.J. to be raised mostly by his sisters.

Lawrence Leamer described Bridget as a crafty, acquisitive woman "who had climbed out of nearly indigent widowhood by selling thread and needles, bread and milk, measuring out her ascent in dimes, nickels, and pennies." P.J. attended the neighborhood parochial school, and assisted his mother at the store in the afternoons and on Saturdays. In his early teens he left grammar school to work as a stevedore in East Boston.[21]

Later, with financial assistance from his mother, P.J. purchased a dilapidated saloon and made it a success. "Year by year, he plowed back the profits, expanding into retail and wholesale whiskey distribution," observed biographer Richard Whalen.

On November 23, 1887, P.J. married Mary Augusta Hickey, who was better educated, more genteel and cultivated than he was. She was the daughter of another saloonkeeper, but from a more successful and prominent family. One of her brothers was the mayor of Brockton, Massachusetts; another was a physician. "To wed Mary Augusta was to gain entry into an assembly of the cultured and social elite of East Boston," noted Leamer.[22]

Like many bartenders, P.J. moved into politics, becoming one of the shrewdest and most powerful ward bosses in Boston. He offered discreet counsel, free drinks, a small loan before payday, and coal in the winter, and smoothed over people's problems with the police. Elected by a landslide to the Massachusetts House of Representatives in 1886, he moved up to the state senate six years later. But he disliked campaigning, was a poor public speaker, and had little interest in officeholding. "Elective office, with all its demands for public appearances and speeches, was not his style," recalled Rose Kennedy in her autobiography. "He preferred to work quietly, behind the scenes."

P.J. had blue eyes, reddish hair, and a swooping handlebar mustache. A mild-mannered man of moderate habits, a nondrinker, P.J. was unassuming, generous, kind, and widely respected. Old-timers often found fault with Boston's political leaders, but seldom was a bad word said about Pat Kennedy. He was the "salt of the earth," "a good man," "a decent man." Nonetheless, he was not averse to election-day shenanigans. His son Joseph recalled two ward heelers showing up on election day at his father's house. "Pat," one said, "we voted one hundred twenty-eight times today."[23]

Although contemporaries, Honey Fitz and P.J. were never close. Pat Kennedy privately thought Honey Fitz was insufferable. Of the two Pat was the more successful businessman. In the mid-1880s he entered the wholesale liquor business, eventually owning two dealerships. He also bought a coal company, and in 1895 helped establish a bank, the Columbia Trust Company, and subsequently became its president. "He accumulated a substantial estate by contemporary standards," noted biographer David Koskoff, "and when he died in May 1929, his assets were valued at $57,000."[24]

In 1913, one of the great demagogues in American history viciously undermined Honey Fitz's reelection bid. A product of poor immigrant parents, with little formal education, James Michael Curley, a U.S. congressman, also sought the mayor's office. The inspiration for Edwin O'Connor's novel *The Last Hurrah* (1956), Curley was an unscrupulous exploiter of ethnic and religious tensions. His demagoguery infuriated his opponents but endeared him to many of the powerless. Part of the Boston community regarded him as a hero—good-willed, charitable, a keen student of government; others despised him as a devious, cold-blooded charlatan.

During campaigns Curley vilified his opponents, referring to Yankee reformers as "Goo Goos." He and Honey Fitz had similar talents, but they differed markedly in their physical presence, speaking ability, and personality. The broad-shouldered, six-foot, two-hundred-pound Curley dwarfed Honey Fitz. "Although an effective orator, Fitzgerald was not in the same spellbinding class as the magna vox of Roxbury," observed John Cutler. Curley "could turn a jeering, hooting assembly into a wet-eyed or cheering audience."[25]

Fitzgerald had been expected to win easily until he faced the Curley-inspired "Toodles" scandal. "Toodles" was the nickname for Elizabeth Ryan, the well-known cigarette girl and harlot at the Ferncroft Inn whom Honey Fitz had met several years earlier.

In the course of a legal case, Toodles volunteered to her lawyer the names of several men who had shown a sexual interest in her. One of the suitors she cited was none other than the mayor of Boston, John Francis Fitzgerald.

When Curley learned about Ryan's sensational story, he arranged for an anonymous poison-pen letter to be sent to Fitzgerald's home describing his adulterous affair with Toodles, stressing that the mayor's reprehensible behavior would be made public unless Honey Fitz withdrew from the mayor's race.

Soon a ditty circulated in Boston:

> *A whisky glass and Toodles' ass
> made a horse's ass out of
> Honey Fitz.* [26]

When the letter arrived at Fitzgerald's home, Josie opened it and shared its contents with Rose. The two women were horrified. When Fitz arrived home, Josie confronted him. "An ugly scene followed," observed Charles Higham. "Mother and daughter talked of shame and disgrace; he of blackmail, lies, and the need to ignore the letter. Josie and Rose refused to accept his explanations. He must withdraw from the race at once."

Then Curley raised the stakes. Kennedy biographer Nigel Hamilton described the new ploy:

With the help of a university president he announced a forthcoming series of public lectures devoted to corruption in history, the first entitled "Graft in Ancient Times Versus Graft in Modern Times." The second lecture was to be called "Great Lovers in History: From Cleopatra to Toodles." A third—"Libertines in History from Henry the Eighth to the Present Day"—was to follow.

For Mrs. Fitzgerald this was intolerable. "Her daughter Rose would be twenty-four next birthday. A dirty campaign, involving further 'revelations' by Congressman Curley, might do irreparable harm to Rose's marriage prospects, as well as her younger sister's." On December 17, 1913, the mayor's assistant, Edward Moore, announced that the mayor would not seek reelection. "Acting under the advice of my physician," the mayor's statement read, "who urged upon me the necessity for a prolonged rest in my present condition resulting from overwork, I withdraw my name from the mayoralty contest." [27]

Curley won the mayor's race in 1914 and would later win three more terms as mayor, one as governor, and one more as a congressman. "Curley failed to transcend the boundaries of his own personal ambition and ultimately did both Massachusetts and himself a disservice by squandering his talent and debasing the moral tone of political life," concluded William Shannon.

As for Honey Fitz, he ran for U.S. Senator against Henry Cabot Lodge in 1916, for governor of Massachusetts in 1922, and in several subsequent elections, but he never won elective office again.[28]

2

JOE AND ROSE

On September 6, 1888, while Pat Kennedyof served his third term in the Massachusetts legislature, his wife gave birth to their first child, Joseph. There followed another son, who died in infancy, and two daughters, Loretta and Margaret.

Compared to most of the Irish who lived in impoverished East Boston, the Kennedy family was well-to-do. A conscientious father, Patrick showed keen interest in his son's development. When young Joe was ten, his father was a banker, one of Boston's most powerful politicians, and the family lived in a stately mansion at 165 Webster Avenue.[1]

His father's example taught Joe that with perseverance and determination a man could take the world as he found it, improve himself, and be successful. Ambitious and energetic, young Joe enjoyed making money. He hawked newspapers after school hours to sailors, passengers, and shopkeepers on the Cunard Line docks in East Boston and sold candies and peanuts to excursion-boat passengers and sightseers at the wharfs in Boston's harbor. His cousin Joe Kane remembered that whenever he met his childhood friend on the street, young Kennedy would always broach the question, "How can we make some money?"

Joe Kennedy attended Catholic grade school, but his parents wanted their son to have a secular education. Deliberately throwing Joe into the company of the Protestant Brahmins, they enrolled him at Boston Latin School, a public institution, where the sons of New England's leading families had been educated for almost three hundred years. The school's celebrated alumni included Cotton Mather, Ralph Waldo Emerson, Charles Sumner, Henry Adams, and George Santayana.[2]

At Boston Latin, Joe was an indifferent student. Because of his poor grades—he flunked elementary physics, elementary French, and advanced Latin—the school forced him to repeat one year to make up his deficiencies. But while not a good student, he excelled at sports and extracurricular activities. As colonel of the school's cadet regiment, he led it to victory in a citywide drill competition, winning accolades from the school's six hundred students. Classmates elected him president of his senior class, and he captained the baseball team for two years.

Joe graduated in June 1908. In those days few Irish youths attended college, and the ones who did usually attended Catholic schools like Boston College or Holy Cross. But Pat Kennedy preferred that his son attend secular Harvard. Based on his academic record at Boston Latin, Joe should never have been admitted to Harvard, but the admissions committee bent its standards and accepted him, probably because he was the son of an influential politician.[3]

Harvard's upper-crust students never granted Kennedy full admittance into campus life, never admitted him to the exclusive Brahmin strongholds of the Fly and Porcellian clubs. Unfriendly and cold, the Brahmins balked at accepting the cocky Irish Catholic from Boston. Being blackballed from the prestigious "final" clubs stung and angered Joe, and partly explained his subsequent drive and ambition to upstage the Boston elite. He could go much further than the best of them, and make them regret they had ever closed their doors on him.

Because his academic work held little fascination, Joe remained an indifferent student. "As a financier, he would one day penetrate the mysteries of a balance sheet in a moment's study," said his biographer Richard Whalen, "but as an undergraduate he could not cope with a course in accounting and was forced to drop out before he failed."

He was far more interested in making money. For three summers Joe and a partner managed a tourist business in Boston. Holding forth with a microphone while his partner drove a sightseeing bus, Joe presented a glib history of Boston. "And now," Joe would say, "we come to the Paul Revere House, the oldest frame building in Boston, having been built around 1660. . . . It was from the doorway of this house that he set out on his famous midnight ride." The venture netted Joe $5,000, part of which he immediately invested in real estate. He was cut out for a career in business.[4]

After graduating from Harvard in June 1912, he failed to secure a job in any major Yankee-dominated business or bank. But his father found him employment as a bank examiner for the Massachusetts commissioner of banks at a salary of $1,200 a year.

Probably through his job as a bank examiner, Joe learned that the First Ward National Bank planned to take over Columbia Trust Company, the bank in which his father held a minority interest. "Afraid that other stockholders would vote to sell," said another of Joe's biographers, Ron Kessler, "Joe borrowed $45,000 from family members and friends to obtain control of the bank and keep it independent." On January 20, 1914, the directors of Columbia Trust elected Joe president. At twenty-five, he was the youngest bank president in Massachusetts.[5]

Rose Fitzgerald spent her childhood in a big rambling home in West Concord, near Acton, until 1904, when Honey Fitz purchased a fifteen-room home in the Boston suburb of Dorchester. Inspired by her father's history lessons and tours of Boston's rich heritage, Rose grew to love history, especially New England's history. She loved the novels by Louisa May Alcott, who had lived and written in nearby Concord, especially *Little Women*.

Every summer Rose's family spent several weeks at a cottage on the shore at Old Orchard Beach, Maine. One of her abiding pleasures was swimming, though she never progressed beyond the dog paddle and breaststroke.

On June 23, 1906, a month before her sixteenth birthday, Rose graduated from Dorchester High School. One of the youngest graduates in the school's history, she ranked in the top three academically in a class of 285. She was also voted Boston's prettiest high school senior.[6]

Since Mrs. Fitzgerald hated the glare of publicity, Honey Fitz brought along his beautiful and articulate oldest daughter to act as his official hostess. Rose assumed a full round of political and social duties, smiling through banquets and rallies, appearing at the mayor's side for wakes and funerals, dedicating public buildings, and hosting prominent visitors at city hall. Having met Presidents McKinley and Taft, she took celebrities in stride.

At sixteen she presided over the launching of a ship, and made her first major speech—at welcoming ceremonies for German students visiting Boston. Her speech, in German, was a "big hit," reported a Boston newspaper.

At age seventeen Rose seemed to be blessed with everything a girl could want. Historian Doris Kearns Goodwin described her as having "an open, ardent nature filled with wonder and belief; a radiant complexion and eyes filled with laughter; a fine, slim figure and plenty of new clothes, a strong active mind and abundant opportunity to engage it in stimulating conversation."[7]

Rose longed to attend Wellesley, the distinguished women's college at Lake Waban, west of Boston. At first her father agreed. But the archbishop of Boston, William H. O'Connell, strongly objected to Honey Fitz letting his daughter attend a Protestant college. Worried about the archbishop's influence and the reaction of Catholic voters, the mayor changed his mind.

Rose was packed and ready to leave for Wellesley when her father informed her of his new plan. She was "too young" for Wellesley, he told her; instead, he had arranged for her to attend the Convent of the Sacred Heart on Commonwealth Avenue, where the archbishop was a patron.

Until late in her life, Rose never publicly complained about her father's decision to derail her college ambition. At the time, though, she was enraged. "There was screaming and yelling, absolute madness," she remembered. "I was furious at my parents for years. I was angry at my church. As much as I loved my father, I never really forgave him for not letting me go . . . It is something I have felt a little sad about all my life."

On September 16, 1907, Rose entered the Convent of the Sacred Heart, a stern, repressive, and cheerless place, but a college she claimed to like. There she learned to "guard herself against feelings that were childish, visionary, sensual or exuberant." Penance and self-renunciation were the order of the day, and laughter was forbidden.[8]

In July 1908, Rose sailed to Europe with her parents and her sister Agnes. Commencing a lifetime of wanderlust and global curiosity, she toured most of Europe for a hectic two months. At the end Honey Fitz enrolled his two daughters in the cloistered Academy of the Sacred Heart in Blumenthal, Holland, where they remained for two difficult years.

Repressive, regimented, and cheerless, the school aimed to guide young women on a spiritual journey, teach them self-control, and make them "very strong, very innocent and determined to do something for God in their life." The austere setting created a powerful psychological atmosphere that drew in most of the young women.

Rose received an excellent classical education, specializing in French and German, but the transcendent drama at the school emphasized development of the Catholic spirit. The convent tolerated no frivolity, not even friendships; the women couldn't touch or hug each other. The nuns regulated every moment of the day. "Study. Class. Recreation. Study. Writing lesson. Luncheon. Recreation. Recitation."

"There were sins of pride and vanity that the world outside treated at most as blemishes, scratches on the soul that here the nuns magnified into monstrous proportion," noted Lawrence Leamer. "Rose learned that self-sacrifice, self-abnegation, and suffering were the crosses that her sex carried through life." Returning home, Rose attended the Sacred Heart Convent at Manhattanville in New York, graduating on June 10, 1910.[9]

Rose resented the "proper Bostonians." "Their main citadel and symbol was the region known as Back Bay where wealthy and distinguished families such as the Cabots and Lodges lived serenely amid ancestral portraits and mahogany sideboards and silver tea services in spacious houses on large grounds," she reflected in her autobiography. "With the advantages of inherited wealth and status and close-knit interfamily ties, they controlled the banks, insurance companies, the big law firms, the big shipping and mercantile enterprises . . . They had many admirable qualities. But they were a closed society." Overt hostility had declined by the early part of the twentieth century, but mistrust and resentment remained.

Despite the resentment, Rose and many of her fellow Irish Catholics patterned themselves after the Brahmin elite. They were earnest, self-conscious imitators. Rose did not drink or smoke and tried to match the Brahmins in her sense of propriety. "I remembered my father saying that the typical picture of an Irish politician was a man with a glass of whiskey in his hand and a pipe in his mouth. So my father never took a drink in public, and he never smoked anyway."[10]

Back in Boston, Rose joined the Cecilian Guild, the Irish counterpart of the exclusive Junior League. Now a socially prominent young lady, her outlook broadened by her political background and her European travel and study, she became interested in public affairs. She countered the elite Protestant clubs by founding the Ace of Clubs for bright young women who spoke French and had studied abroad. At their meetings they discussed national and international affairs. "Thanks to my father, we were able to get all sorts of visiting dignitaries to address us," Rose later wrote.

Aimless frivolity never appealed to her. "What does anyone get out of it? A life of partying and socializing would have bored me to death." Instead, she studied French, German, and art at Boston University; took music and piano lessons at the New England Conservatory; and joined a theater group, appearing in a few plays. She became the youngest member of the Boston Public Library's examining committee, which selected books for children. She taught Sunday school in Dorchester and catechism in the North End slums. Her former catechism pupils remembered her as a painstaking instructor, who prodded the youngsters to win prizes in annual competitions. "Life with father," said one observer, "had taught her to take winning very seriously."[11]

A contemporary article in *Cosmopolitan* magazine cited Rose's "vivacious manner" and thought she displayed "depth and strength of mind rarely found in so young a woman. Undoubtedly her father's influence upon her life has broadened her outlook, so that she lives much more vividly than most girls of her age."

One winter her father led the Boston Chamber of Commerce to Panama to study the possible effects on Boston of the recently opened Panama Canal. She went along as "hostess-companion-helper." On another trip Honey Fitz took a chamber delegation to Europe to examine Hamburg and other ocean port cities, and the inland waterways that carried goods to and from those ports. "Agnes and I accompanied him, and with our fluent German and French, and our basic knowledge of Europe, we performed valuable services for the group."

In one area of life Rose remained mostly ignorant. In the only college course that touched on the human body, she studied good posture, proper diet, and the evils of liquor, morphine, and tobacco. She learned almost nothing about sex. She and other young women "entered adulthood as woefully ignorant about this aspect of life as were their mothers and their grandmothers before them," noted Leamer.[12]

Joe Kennedy and Rose Fitzgerald met as children while Rose accompanied her father on his visits to East Boston. But Honey Fitz disliked Pat Kennedy and hoped to lure a more suitable beau for his daughter. While at Boston Latin, Joe dated Rose, but both kept their relationship secret.

In the spring of 1906, Joe invited Rose to a dance at Boston Latin, but Honey Fitz refused to let her attend, claiming she was too young. The following spring, though, her father allowed Rose to invite Joe to a graduation dance at Dorchester High. Their romance slowly blossomed, which Rose's father suspected and continued to oppose.

As they talked, the young couple discovered they had much in common. Catholics, the offspring of Boston Irish politicians, they both lived in a world of comfort and well-being. Tall, thin, wiry, blue-eyed, with sandy blond hair tinged with red, Joe was a heartthrob. "His face was open and expressive, yet with youthful dignity, conveying qualities of self-reliance, self-respect, and self-discipline," said Rose. He didn't drink or smoke. "He smiled and laughed easily and had a big, spontaneous, and infectious grin that made everybody in sight want to smile, too."[13]

They attended concerts, walked hand in hand through the grounds of Harvard, and explored museums and art galleries. Charles Higham, one of Rose's biographers, observed that she became increasingly infatuated "not only by Joe's cheeky, cheerful good looks, lithe, athletic figure and ease of manner, but by the fact that he listened to her when most young men failed to take her, as a female, seriously. He had the knack of making her feel the center of the universe."

Throughout his courtship with Rose, Joe still remained a ladies' man. He had a special fondness for chorus girls. Before his Harvard graduation, he and a friend dated two young women from *The Pink Lady,* a musical comedy. "For Joe, it was important not only to conquer shapely young women, but to be seen with them. It gave him a feeling of power and success," noted biographer Ron Kessler.[14]

In June 1914, the young couple announced their engagement. Four months later, on October 7, 1914, William Cardinal O'Connell married Joe, twenty-five, and Rose, twenty-four, in a quiet ceremony in the private chapel connected to the cardinal's residence. A few days later the couple boarded a train south to their honeymoon resort: the luxurious Greenbrier Hotel at White Sulphur Springs, West Virginia.

Shortly before their marriage, Joe and Rose had purchased a nine-room, three-story gray frame home at 83 Beals Street in Brookline, a pleasant middle-class Boston suburb of thirty-eight thousand, a half-hour trolley ride from Boston. With no houses across the street or to the east, Rose envisioned plenty of space for her children to play when they grew up.[15]

On July 25, 1915, Rose delivered their first child, Joseph Patrick Kennedy Jr. Immediately after the birth of his first grandson, Honey Fitz informed the press. "His mother and father have already decided that he is going to be President of the United States," he exuberantly reported.

In the last week of May 1917, Rose felt the first contractions indicating the approaching birth of her second child. Dr. Frederick Good and his assistant arrived at the home on Beals Street. Kettles of hot water were boiled as Rose tried to control her discomfort. At 3:00 P.M. on May 29, she delivered her second son. Since the first child had been named after a Kennedy, Joe and Rose decided their second son should be named after her beloved father. So they named him John Fitzgerald Kennedy. Three weeks later, on June 19, 1917, at nearby St. Aidan's Roman Catholic Church, Monsignor John T. Creah baptized the infant.[16]

In April 1917, the United States entered World War I. As a million men trained to fight in Europe, including Joe's Harvard friends, Joe didn't enlist and avoided the draft, sparking deep resentment from some former classmates. Instead, in the fall of 1917, Joe resigned his position at Columbia Trust and accepted a fifteen-thousand-dollar-a-year position as assistant general manager of the Bethlehem shipyards at Fore River in Quincy, Massachusetts. This calculated decision allowed him to avoid serving in the war.

After the war, in June 1919, Joe became the manager of the Boston office of the brokerage firm Hayden, Stone and Company, a position he held until 1922. There he came under the tutelage of Galen Stone, one of the smartest speculators of the era, who schooled him in the intricacies of the stock market—and the ways to manipulate it.[17]

Richard Whalen described a typical pool, one of the techniques Joe learned:

> A few traders would take options on, say, one hundred thousand shares of an idle stock at a price of twenty dollars a share. . . . The pool would "advertise" the stock by trading shares back and forth across the tape until the public, seeing this activity, leaped at a seeming good thing. At the likely top price, perhaps thirty or forty dollars, the pool would "pull the plug," selling the gullible public all it wanted of the overvalued stock and pocketing the profits above the option price of twenty dollars.

Galen Stone also taught his protégé how to make huge sums by trading on inside information, and in the process often ruining unsuspecting investors. Biographer Kessler explained:

> Stone sat on the boards of twenty-two companies whose securities he sponsored. One was the Pond Coal Company, of which he was chairman. Stone was about to agree to acquisition of the company by Henry Ford. . . . Before the public was told about the plan, Joe bought fifteen thousand shares at $16, later selling the stock for $45 a share. In nine months, he made a profit of $675,000.

After three years with Hayden, Stone, Joe struck out on his own, establishing a firm in Boston. "It's easy to make money in this market," he told a friend. "We'd better get in before they pass a law against it."[18]

Many people who conducted business with Joe complained of treachery, deceit, a bitter parting of the ways. An anguished stockholder who lost her life savings because of Joe's stock manipulation criticized him in a letter. "This seems hardly Christian like, fair or just for a man of your character," she wrote. "I wish you would think of the poor working women who had so much faith in you."

Fiercely independent, Joe had a flair for organization and management. The telephone was his Stradivarius. "He could do business on a telephone in a few minutes that took his supposed peers a day or a week to accomplish across a desk in an office and conference room," said his friend Morton Downey.

Joe had a lifelong talent for soliciting expert advice. He asked questions and listened carefully. "What do you hear?" "What do you know?" "What do you think?" From associates and advisers he culled what he needed and applied it.[19]

Gathered around him was a tight protective circle of lawyers, advisers, retainers, agents, and hangers-on. "If Joe liked you, you were tops—no matter what anybody else thought," said the family's financial adviser, Jim Fayne. "If he stopped liking you, you simply didn't exist anymore." Edward Moore, a former assistant to several Boston mayors, including Honey Fitz, became Joe Kennedy's primary assistant and confidential secretary.

Always have a plan, Joe preached, and then follow through. "Always have an immediate objective and an ultimate objective. Keep your ultimate objective always in mind, but be sure you achieve the immediate."

"Know people who are in key spots and you can get things done."

"Success is not the money you make or the position that you obtain, but how your family turns out. If your family is a success you are a success."[20]

Kind to his loyal staff, he sent condolences to employees after a personal tragedy, made available to them his own physicians and other specialists at times of serious illnesses, and rented Cadillacs to drive his office girls home safely during an approaching hurricane.

In 1926, at age thirty-seven, Joe Kennedy was on his way to making his second million. Still thin and athletic, he inadvertently masked his handsome features with prim dark-rimmed spectacles that made him look like a "disapproving schoolmaster."

Joe viewed the burgeoning motion picture industry as "another telephone," and tried to secure an early advantage in the infant business. A group he headed bought control of thirty-one movie theaters in New England. In the mid-1920s he acquired the Film Booking Office of America, and by the end of the decade he was splitting time between Hollywood and Wall Street. But in the early 1930s Joe left the movie business except for loose ties with several firms. His brief career making movies netted him a profit of five million dollars.[21]

By midsummer 1933, enough states had ratified the Twenty-first Amendment to ensure the end of Prohibition in the United States. Joe had maneuvered successfully to take advantage of the liquor boom when it came. British distillers appointed him as the U.S. agent for Haig and Haig, John Dewar and Sons, and Gordon's Dry Gin Company. "He arranged for his newly organized Somerset Importers to import and stockpile thousands of cases of liquor, the whiskey coming into the legally dry U.S. under 'medicinal' licenses issued in Washington," said Whalen. Months before Prohibition had officially ended, Kennedy had filled his warehouses to overflowing with Haig and Haig and John Dewar scotch. In a few years his liquor business earned him a fortune.[22]

By the time Prohibition ended in 1933, he had already plunged deeply into a new field. His political experience dated to childhood, when he watched his father artfully scheme with Boston's ward politicians. He assisted Honey Fitz in his campaign for Congress in 1917 and for governor in 1922. In the second half of the 1920s he took a hiatus to concentrate on making money, but when he reentered politics he did so on a grand scale, joining the circle surrounding New York's Democratic governor, Franklin D. Roosevelt.

The eagerness of men to enter public life, Joe once said, was "due almost entirely to that psychological element of honor and prestige." Near the end of his life, when asked why he became involved in politics, he offered another explanation. "I wanted power," he replied. "I thought money would give me power and so I made money, only to discover that it was politics—not money—that really gave a man power. So I went into politics."

Joe believed that government should merely defend individual rights from chaos and oppression. He didn't adhere to, or even understand, the positive notion of liberty which sought to expand personal rights and promote the values of justice and equality.[23]

As Roosevelt prepared to run for President in 1932, he flattered Joe by listening to his views. They had known each other during World War I, and in the course of their mutual reappraisal, they formed a political partnership. "Kennedy offered the governor a valuable conduit to Wall Street, financial support, and counsel on practical economics and the folkways of the urban machines," said historian Michael Beschloss, who studied their relationship. "Roosevelt offered Kennedy an entrée into national politics and a style of leadership that would quell his fears of social upheaval [caused by the depression]."

After winning the 1932 presidential election, FDR appointed Joe chairman of the new Securities and Exchange Commission (SEC), created to develop rules and regulations for the stock market. Joe's own nasty practices on Wall Street caused some pundits to denounce the President's nominee. Columnist John T. Flynn, an impassioned critic of Wall Street's way of handling other people's money, exploded in disbelief: "I say it isn't true. It is impossible. It could not happen."[24]

But Joe handled the chairmanship admirably, earning accolades for his administrative ability, public relations, political acumen, and conflict mediation. "Kennedy has done one of the best jobs of anyone connected with the New Deal," said *The Washington Post,* "and has done it without bluster or publicity seeking and without leaving anyone angry at him." Columnist Flynn ate crow and confessed that the chairman was the most useful member of the commission.

While working in Washington, Joe leased an opulent estate, Marwood, but departed most weekends to join his family. After resigning as chairman of the SEC in 1935, he campaigned vigorously for FDR's reelection in 1936, and was named chairman of the U.S. Maritime Commission the following year. Journalists often praised his public service. Marquis Childs of the *St. Louis Post-Dispatch* described him as an astute and purposeful man.

Joe cultivated friendships with prominent journalists, columnists, and press barons—Westbrook Pegler, Louella Parsons, William Randolph Hearst, Hedda Hopper, Arthur Hays Sulzberger, Henry Luce, Walter Lippmann, and Walter Winchell. He was profiled in the *Saturday Evening Post,* the *American Magazine,* and *Fortune.* Later, he used his contacts in the media to advance the political career of his second son.[25]

Rose Kennedy always stayed as slim as the day she married. A short woman with dark chestnut hair and gray-green eyes, she usually sported a healthy outdoor tan. An incessant shopper, she estimated that in one year (1940) she bought two hundred suits and dresses.

She read extensively in theology, philosophy, Catholic Church history, and current events. She accumulated scrapbooks and looseleaf notebooks filled with inspirational thoughts, a hobby she maintained all her life. A reporter described one of her notebooks as jammed with "bits of information and homilies, neatly divided into sections: definitions, phrases, men, women, politics, religion, quotes from writers like Emily Dickinson, George Eliot, Camus, Solomon." She titled one page "distillation of sublime wisdom." Example: "Emotionalism in front of people is a great sign of immaturity."

"If we have a choice to make, what shall it be? Serenity, normality, contentment and possible mediocrity [NEVER, she annotated] . . . or challenge, stimulation."[26]

Rose could be generous, kind, and outgoing; also stingy, selfish, and withdrawn. Louella Hennessey, who worked for the Kennedys for several decades, described her as "kind" and "considerate." A close female companion said of Rose, "I've never heard her say an unkind word about anybody, and how many women are like that?" As an act of charity and thoughtfulness, Rose wrote letters to people she didn't know who had suffered a serious setback.

She constantly worked to improve herself—by listening to French records, by strolling on the lawn reading her inspirational sayings. "Every little walk with Mother [was] an educational experience," recalled her son Edward.[27]

Although dedicated to motherly duties, Rose did not let motherhood consume her. She stood slightly aloof from the whirlwind of family activities, preserving her separate identity. She was an intrepid world traveler, and when her children accompanied her on European trips, she provided them with full exposure to museums, art galleries, and concerts. A few of her journeys were trailblazing: It took courage for an American woman to travel to Russia in 1936 with only daughter Kathleen as companion. "She approached Moscow with characteristic matter-of-factness, as if Communist Russia were all in a day's travel for a former debutante," commented a reporter. During her travels she reported back to her family about all the fascinating people she met. "Tea at [American] Embassy today. Lunch with Winston Churchill tomorrow."[28]

At Hyannis Port she insisted on having a place for herself. She put a prefabricated shack on the property, away from the bustling activity, where she could meditate and read her books and mail. "All her life she would hold a part of herself back from the children," Goodwin commented, "keeping intact a mysterious region of her soul into which she did not consider it necessary to admit [anyone]."

Despite the heartbreaking tragedies she would have to endure, she would remain remarkably stoic, seldom shedding tears. "Nobody's ever going to have to feel sorry for me," she would say, putting her chin up.[29]

Rose had several unattractive traits, and several of the children's friends laughed at her idiosyncrasies. Occasionally a nag, she would bring up a problem in an unexpectedly irritating manner. "Why did you take the white towels on the boat? You know you're supposed to take the yellow ones." Or, "You're eating too many cookies." "I suppose [family members] did what I did up there—try to avoid her," said a Hyannis Port guest. "I think she made them all very nervous."

Sometimes she caked "pasties" on her face all day to avoid wrinkles. Because she developed the habit of pinning her "to-do lists" to her blouse or dress, in the morning she looked like a walking notice board. "As she finished with one reminder," said a member of the household staff, "she would tear it off and go on to the next." At the end of the day, her paper corsage plucked clean, she was proud of having systematically accomplished all her tasks. These peculiar habits led some visitors to judge her as dull-witted.[30]

Although she bought expensive clothes—the latest Paris fashions—she was extremely frugal in mundane household matters. She lectured an in-house nurse about the rising cost of coffee: "So would you post a note on the bulletin board to the effect that I would appreciate it if the nurses would please confine themselves to, say, one cup of coffee a shift? Or perhaps it might be a good idea if they would fix themselves a little thermos at home."[31]

By 1919 the Kennedys' wealth allowed them to hire a governess for the older children and a nurse for the younger ones. The family grew rapidly. Rosemary (1918) and Kathleen (1920) were born while the family lived on Beals Street. In 1921, when the Kennedys outgrew the Beals Street residence, they moved a few blocks away to a twelve-room house on Naples Road in a more fashionable section of Brookline. John Kennedy lived in the home on Naples Road from age four through ten. Eunice (1921), Patricia (1924), and Robert (1925) were all born on Naples Road. In 1927 the family moved to Riverdale, New York, where Jean (1928) and Edward (1932) joined the clan.

Joe Jr. had been a healthy infant and became a strong, healthy child. Jack was a healthy infant as well, but as a child he suffered numerous illnesses. The most serious, diagnosed on February 20, 1920, when Jack was two years old, was scarlet fever, a dreaded disease, sometimes fatal, often crippling in its aftereffects. The disease swept through the Boston area, closing schools and decimating colleges. "It was highly contagious," Rose recalled, "and Rosemary was only a year and a half, and Kathleen had just been born." Rose worried that Joe Jr., Rosemary, and Kathleen might come down with the disease, "and so might I."[32]

Jack's temperature rose to 105 degrees, and he suffered from a sore throat, vomiting, severe headache, and coated tongue. A blistering rash spread over his body. For the safety of his family, Jack was quarantined in the Boston City Hospital, which had the best infectious-disease wing in New England. Doctors and nurses entered his room only after thoroughly scrubbing their hands and donning disinfected gowns.

In the third week of March 1920, the illness subsided and Jack slowly improved, but he still couldn't return home. Instead he was moved to the Mansion House Hotel in Poland Springs, Maine, where he could recuperate with the healing mineral water.[33]

Emotionally distraught, Joe Kennedy pledged to God that if his son recovered he would donate half of all his fortune to charity. When Jack did fully recover, his grateful father wrote a heartfelt letter thanking Jack's doctor.

I would indeed be an ingrate if I let this chance pass by without telling you how much I appreciate your wonderful work for Jack during his recent illness. I had never experienced any very serious sickness in my family previous to this case of Jack's, and I little realized what an effect such a happening could possibly have on me. During the darkest days I felt that nothing else mattered except his recovery, and you must have some notion of what the gratitude of a parent can be to have his boy returned in the wonderful shape that Jack seems to be now.

Fulfilling his pledge, Joe sent a $3,750 check to the Guild of St. Apollonia, an organization of Catholic dentists who provided dental care to children in Catholic schools. According to Rose, the amount represented exactly half of Joe's fortune at that time. (She considerably underestimated his wealth.)[34]

In the hospital sick little Jack projected such an appealing sweetness and vulnerability that he won the nurses' affection. "He is such a wonderful boy," nurse Sara Miller wrote Joe during Jack's hospital stay. "We all love him very dearly." So ingratiating and powerful was his charm that two nurses later visited him at his home; one wrote to his father requesting a photo of Jack.

The bout with scarlet fever was one in a long series of illnesses and disabilities for John Kennedy. In addition to the expected childhood ailments—bronchitis, whooping cough, chicken pox, mumps, and German measles—Jack suffered from diphtheria, allergies, frequent colds and flus, hives, an irritable colon, a sensitive stomach (which required a bland diet most of his life), and asthma. More sickness followed in his adult years. "He went along for many years," Rose accurately observed, "thinking to himself—or at least trying to make others think—that he was a strong, robust, quite healthy person who just happened to be sick a good deal of the time."[35]

Partly because he was so often convalescing, reading became Jack's major entertainment. A natural reader, he devoured books. He enjoyed reading Thornton Burgess's nature stories in the newspaper, but his favorite was an illustrated series of children's books by Frances Trego Montgomery about the fictional adventures of a mischievous goat named Billy Whiskers. In a role Jack himself sometimes played as a youth, "the trickster protagonist would instigate chaos in an ordered environment and then bemusedly watch the resulting crisis," said one critic.

As Jack grew older he read virtually all of the PTA- and library-approved books that Rose stored in the family library: A. M. Hadfield's *King Arthur and the Round Table,* Rudyard Kipling's *The Jungle Book, Kidnapped* and *Treasure Island* by Robert Louis Stevenson, *Uncle Tom's Cabin* by Harriet Beecher Stowe, *Wing and Wing* by James Fenimore Cooper, and the *Arabian Nights.*

He loved stories of adventure and chivalry, biographies of famous and fascinating people, subjects having to do with history, "so long as they had flair, action, and color," said Rose. A romantic and idealistic streak inclined him to daydreaming. "I often had a feeling his mind was only half occupied with the subject at hand, such as doing his arithmetic homework or picking his clothes up off the floor, and the rest of his thoughts were far away weaving daydreams."[36]

As a young adult Jack habitually misspelled words. His sister Kathleen corrected the spelling in one of Jack's letters: "Such mistakes as neice for niece . . . resemblence for resemblance, agression for aggression, afriad for afraid."

Jack had a narrow face, his ears stuck out a bit, and his hair wouldn't stay put, giving him an elfin appearance. "I was enchanted and amused," said Rose. "He was a funny little boy, and he said things in such an original, vivid way."

Rose kept a diary during 1923. "Took care of children," she noted on

January 7. "Miss Brooks, the governess, helped. Kathleen still has bronchitis and Joe sick in bed. Great life."

February 25, 1923: "Joe Jr. and Jack have a new song about the Bedbugs and the Cooties. Also a club where they initiate new members by sticking pins into them."

December 5, 1923: "Jack said, 'Daddy has a Sweet Tooth, hasn't he? I wonder which one it is?' His teacher is coming over to tell on him. He says, 'You know I am getting on all right and if you study too much, you're liable to go crazy.' "[37]

Rose kept the children's allowances small, and Jack chafed under the character-building restriction. At age ten he addressed a solemn—sometimes misspelled—plea to his father for an increase in his allowance:

A PLEA FOR A RAISE
by Jack Kennedy
Dedicated to my
Mr. J. P. Kennedy

Chapter I

My recent allowance is 40¢. This I used for areoplanes and other play-things of childhood but now I am a scout and I put away my childish things. Before I would spend 20¢ of my 40¢ allowance and in five min-utes I would have empty pockets and nothing to gain and 20¢ to lose. When I am a scout I have to buy canteens, haversacks, blankets search-liagts ponchos things that will last for years and I can always use it while I cant use a chocolate marshmellow Sunday with vanilla ice cream and so I put in my plea for a raise of thirty cents for me to buy scout things and pay my own way more around.

Finis
John Fitzgerald Francis Kennedy

Whether Joe Kennedy granted the appeal is not known.[38]

A few blocks away from Naples Road was Devotion School, a religious-sounding name but a public school. Joe Jr. started there in kindergarten, and Jack followed a year later. Although fine academically, Devotion School had no organized sports. Joe wanted his boys to compete in sports with the sons of Beacon Hill. Not far from Naples Road stood the lower branch of Noble and Greenough School, a six-year elementary school for boys. Known for its outstanding classical education, the school had an excellent reputation. In the fall of 1924, Joe Jr. and Jack started school there, studying English, Latin, math, history, and geography. "[Noble and Greenough] provided early train-ing in the mores of private-school life for those born to positions of wealth and influence," Goodwin noted.

After Christmas 1925, as Joe and Jack started the new semester, the school's board of trustees advised parents that it planned to accept an offer for the purchase of the property and would close the school. Surprised and indignant, Joe Kennedy and eight other parents conferred and arranged to buy the school for $188,000. They renamed the institution Dexter and re-opened without disruption.[39]

Joe Jr. and Jack played both baseball and football at Dexter School. Despite his slight build, Jack was the only catcher who could come close to holding on to his older brother's blazing pitches. "Jack hung on," said Hank Searls, Joe Jr.'s biographer, "mitt stinging and tears in his eyes, sometimes knocked down by the whiplash delivery and often, to Joe's disgust, dropping the ball."

In the fall of 1926, Joe Jr., eleven, and Jack, nine, played tackle football for Dexter. Strong, muscular, and heavier than the other boys, young Joe played fullback; lean but "brainy," and a better athlete than his brother, Jack was quarterback. "They were both outstanding," recalled their head coach, Willard Rice, then a senior at Harvard. Rice thought the Kennedy boys were "good fun" and "easy to work with."[40]

Coach Rice appreciated the enthusiastic backing he received from Joe and Rose. "Well, Coach," Joe told Rice, "you're going to have quite a problem, because here are two young 'micks' who need discipline, and Mrs. Kennedy and I will give you carte blanche for any disciplinary measures that you need to take to get them into line and to teach them to play, and to teach them to be good sportsmen." Joe encouraged both of his sons. "Good luck to the team in your game with Rivers this afternoon and hope you all play well," he telegraphed Jack.

The Dexter team always played on Fridays; on Saturdays Rice took his squad to Harvard Stadium to watch Harvard's varsity play. Because Dexter wore the same color uniforms and ran the same offensive system as Harvard, they looked like a miniature Harvard team.[41]

At the end of the season undefeated Dexter played Browne and Nichols of Cambridge, also undefeated, for the Greater Boston Private School championship (lower division). Dexter's parents were nervous soon after play began because Dexter couldn't get untracked. Browne and Nichols quickly ran up a 13–0 lead. In the second half, quarterback Jack Kennedy helped pull the boys together. Jack ran some, passed a little, and, whenever he badly needed yards, gave the ball to big Joe Jr. The touchdowns began to come, and Dexter ran away with the game, 31–13. Everybody agreed that Jack had done an outstanding job of quarterbacking for a nine-year-old. Because of Jack's poor health, however, the game was one of the last times he could excel in any sport except swimming and sailing.[42]

Augustus Soule, a contemporary of the Kennedy boys at Dexter, remembered the two Kennedys being the targets of derision and taunts:

> Almost everybody was a Protestant . . . I think there was a sort of snobbery, which the children adopted. I think that in those days the upper crust Boston families, of which there were a great number sending their children to the school, were very down on the Irish. . . . To be an Irish Catholic was a real, real stigma.

As for Joseph P. Kennedy, Soule continued, "A lot of the parents wouldn't even speak to him because he was so disliked. The view was: Mr. Kennedy had made his money in ways that were known, in banking circles, to be unsavory; Mrs. Kennedy's father, Honey Fitzgerald, was a scalawag if ever there was one, and everybody put these two things together and they said, 'This couple's up to no good.' "

Discrimination against the Kennedys infuriated Joe. "I was born here," he exclaimed in an interview. "My children were born here. What the hell do I have to do to be an American?"[43]

"Boston is no place to bring up Catholic children," Joe said in disgust. With that he relocated his family to New York in September 1927. Boston was also an unpromising place to pursue Joe's financial ambitions. "This city was a small, clear puddle," recalled banker Ralph Lowell. "New York was a big muddy one, and that's what Joe wanted." Joe hired a private railroad car to move the family—Rose, Joe Jr., Jack, Rosemary, Kathleen, Eunice, Pat, Robert, plus the family's nurse, chauffeur, and cook—to 5040 Independence Avenue, a stately twenty-room Georgian-style mansion in exclusive Riverdale, located a few miles up the Hudson from New York City.[44]

Jack attended fifth, sixth, and seventh grades at the excellent private Riverdale Country Day School. At Riverdale Jack's teachers described him as bright, confident, and personable; friends remembered him as popular, athletic, and girl crazy. In sixth grade Jack received excellent grades in his history bimonthly report and earned a school award for best composition. "Far be it from the Kennedys to spoil their children," recalled Harold Klue, one of his social studies teachers. "They were taught to do for themselves and think for themselves."

In seventh grade Jack was less successful. In the first-half grade report he maintained a C+ average, which the headmaster labeled "creditable," adding "now for honors." "His main interest was getting a date for the Saturday afternoon movie," recalled classmate Manuel Argulo.[45]

Meanwhile, as Joe Kennedy's wealth increased, so did the number and size of his homes. In the spring of 1929, he moved the family from Riverdale to the exclusive Westchester County community of Bronxville, New York (population 4,040 in 1925). The Kennedys' estate at 294 Pondfield Road, costing $250,000, offered not only elegance but, with twenty-one rooms, plenty of space for the children. The property included an opulent redbrick colonial mansion with towering white columns, a curving driveway, and six acres of elm trees, manicured lawn, and well-tended gardens. They owned the home for twelve years.

When Joe Jr. and Jack brought friends home after school, they played kickball, baseball, and football on the lawn or listened to music on the Victrola. Thomas Schriber, a friend of the boys in Bronxville, played football on the Kennedy lawn. "I always ran looking for the trees and the ball at the same time. But Joe and Jack . . . never did, and WHANG! that was that. They were always knocking themselves out. I can remember many occasions when one or the other of the boys would be picked up unconscious; they were always bandaged and bruised all over."[46]

In 1922 the Kennedys had rented a cottage overlooking the rocky beach at Cohasset, Massachusetts, where many of Boston's wealthiest, most patrician families sought summer refuge. Hostile to interlopers and reserving particular scorn for Irish newcomers, Cohasset residents shunned the Kennedys. When Rose and Joe applied for membership at the Cohasset Country Club, their application languished and was never accepted. The Brahmin Protestants had taught Joe and Rose another nasty lesson. "It was petty and cruel," recalled Ralph Lowell. "The women of Cohasset looked down on the daughter of Honey Fitz, and who was Joe Kennedy but the son of Pat, the barkeeper?"

Giving up on Cohasset, in the fall of 1928 the Kennedys bought a large cottage in Hyannis Port, Massachusetts, one they had rented for the previous three summers. The community of three hundred homes about sixty-five miles southeast of Boston was populated by wealthy Republican blue bloods from the Boston area and the scions of Pittsburgh steel money. The Kennedys' sprawling white clapboard, green-shuttered house sat on a bluff overlooking Nantucket Sound, and included two and one-half acres of lawn sloping to a wide stretch of beach.[47]

A few weeks before the family moved in, workmen built an addition to the fourteen-room house in the basement: a thirty-by-fifteen-foot private theater with a fifteen-thousand-dollar RCA sound movie projector. Boston newspapers described it as "probably the first private installation of talking pictures apparatus in New England or in the country."

At the cottage the children spent most of the day in T-shirts, shorts, and sneakers. Young Joe and Jack shared a room reflecting their two great interests: literature and sports. Books overflowed their enormous bookcase; their trophies for sailing, swimming, and tennis filled a large cabinet. Neighborhood playmates frequently crowded the lawn surrounding the home.

Some Hyannis Port neighbors sharply disapproved of the Kennedys. Kennedys "never said thank you" and treated an employee as "just a machine to work." Journalist Leo Damore claimed that "Western Union messengers who delivered telegrams to the Kennedy house were warned in advance not to expect large tips."[48]

When Jack was sixteen, the Kennedys added a third home. Following the births of Joe Jr and Jack, the young Kennedy family had made yearly pilgrimages to Palm Beach, Florida, to escape the harsh New England winters. Among Joe's most pleasant memories was playing with his infant sons on the beach.

In 1933 Joe and Rose bought a Palm Beach vacation home on North Ocean Boulevard, known locally as "Millionaires' Row." Purchased from Rodman Wanamaker, the Philadelphia department store magnate, the white stucco pseudo-Spanish-style villa faced the ocean, and included tall royal palms, front-shaded patios, a swimming pool, and tennis courts. In a secluded solarium, dubbed the Bullpen, with cushioned benches and wicker furniture, Joseph Kennedy sunned himself in the nude and conducted his business by telephone in privacy. Although impressive, the Palm Beach home had narrow boundaries and was modest compared to its neighbors.

The Kennedys initially felt the sting of prejudice in Palm Beach as well. When Joe applied for a golf membership at the Everglades Club, he was turned down. In order to play golf, he applied to the Jewish-dominated Palm Beach Country Club, which accepted him.

After 1933 the Kennedy family moved three times a year—to Palm Beach for Christmas and Easter holidays, to Hyannis Port for the summer, and to Bronxville during school sessions.[49]

In some ways Joe and Rose had a satisfactory relationship. Each was considerate, respectful, complimentary, and affectionate with the other. But one critical feature of their marriage was dysfunctional.

Rose was brought up to believe that the husband worked hard, encountered many difficulties during his working day, and had a right to expect comfort, peace, and love when he returned home. "He didn't want to be bothered [by] . . . a complaining wife," Rose observed. Because Joe was "very generous" and "thoughtful," and was "very dear to me and all the children," she said, "I was quite happy to do everything I could to make him happy." Rose had great faith in Joe's judgment about the children's education, household matters, and moneymaking. "It gave her a lot of security," said daughter Eunice.

Joe complimented his wife for wearing the prettiest dress at the party or for being the "belle of the ball." He surprised her with flowers and jewelry for their anniversaries and her birthdays. "The constant compliments and encouragement which he always gave me for my efforts great and small in the household made life so easy," said Rose.[50]

Their correspondence radiated affection. "Joe dearest," she wrote her husband in about 1936, "Just a short note, my darling, to tell you again that I love you very, very much—more all the time and more than I can ever write." Following the outbreak of World War II, with Joe living in besieged London, they wrote each other heartfelt letters. "Well darling, I've dictated the news but I want you to know that I love you and miss you terribly," he wrote. "My darling, I am wondering when I shall see you and what is happening," Rose remarked in one of her letters. "I just hope and pray daily that you are taking care of yourself and are not too terribly lonely. . . . All I can do is to pray very hard that I shall see you soon. All my love always."[51]

When Joe traveled on business or golfed with friends in Florida, Rose managed the children, knowing that when he returned she would be off on a trip of her own and Joe would manage the household. Neither seemed bitter when the other was gone.

Over the years the foundation of their marriage changed to more of a collaboration based on their intense love for their children and their respect for each other as parents. They were partners in the common enterprise of raising their children with the highest standards. "They made the family the object of their concord, the instrument of their togetherness," noted Goodwin. "Instead of living for each other as they had done as young lovers, they now lived for the children and for themselves." Joe had his world of business and his golfing buddies—a world Rose didn't impose on; she had her clubs, friends, travel, reading, solitude, and prayer.

Rose was like many Irish-American women who were "chaste to the point that some came to denigrate sex even within marriage." She read books by Catholic priests and physicians who offered sexual advice for married couples. In *Marriage and Parenthood: The Catholic Ideal* (1911), Father Thomas Gerrard stated that sexual intercourse should be completed quickly. "To let it have its full fling" was "to lessen its keenness, destroy its power, and to render it disgusting." The book recommended abstinence from sex during Advent and Lent.[52]

Rose took the advice to heart, but Joe became a notorious philanderer. While working in Hollywood he rented a large house on Rodeo Drive in Beverly Hills, where he often beguiled dazzling young women. With one screen idol he had an extended sexual affair. Petite, chic, always perfectly coiffed, Gloria Swanson enjoyed a natural screen presence, and in 1925, she was Hollywood's premier sex goddess, earning about one million dollars a year. For five years in the late 1920s Swanson periodically came east to visit Joe, and even accompanied Joe and Rose on a trip to Europe. Joe belonged to the Bronxville Field Club, and the local newspaper reported that Swanson and Joe played tennis together at the club.

In August 1929 Swanson flamboyantly arrived near the Kennedys' home in Hyannis Port aboard a Sikorsky amphibious aircraft as people gaped from the beach. On several occasions Hyannis Port residents watched Joe chauffeur Swanson around town in his Rolls-Royce after Rose had left on a trip. "After Mrs. Kennedy left for Europe . . . then sooner or later Gloria Swanson would swing by," recalled a Kennedy neighbor. Because Joe flaunted himself and his women in front of townspeople in Hyannis Port, many residents detested him.

In Hollywood, away from his family for long periods, Joe enjoyed Swanson's companionship. She was far more interested in Joe's business activities than Rose was, and engaged his mind; her humor, wit, and sharp tongue also kindled the warmth of their relationship.[53]

The singer and ladies' man Morton Downey, one of Joe's closest friends, passed along gorgeous women to Joe. "Mort did him favors in the department Joe liked best—girls," a confidant said. "[Downey] knew chorus girls."

When Kennedy appeared with provocative young women at a stylish New York nightspot, he didn't even try to hide them. Rejecting more private tables, he dined with his female companions openly in the center of the dining room.

Like Hyannis Port's residents, many people in Bronxville detested Joe and took their feelings out on Rose by snubbing her. Almost every woman of good station belonged to the Bronxville Women's Club, where they shared gossip about Rose's husband. "The Kennedys were treated just awfully by the town's socially prominent people," said a Bronxville resident. "It was her husband. He was just so blatant about his affairs."[54]

Later Joe Kennedy even tried to date and bed his sons' girlfriends. Alone in the darkened theater in the Hyannis Port home, he pinched his daughters' girlfriends. Many were bewildered by Joe's lechery. "One night I was visiting Eunice at the Cape," said Mary Pitcairn, "and he came into my bedroom to kiss me good night! I was in my nightgown, ready for bed. Eunice was in her bedroom. We had an adjoining bath. The doors were open. He said, 'I've come to say good night,' and kissed me. Really kissed me. It was so silly. I remember thinking, 'How embarrassing for Eunice!'"

"I think all this confused Jack," Pitcairn speculated. "He was a sensitive man and I think it confused him. What kind of object is a woman? To be treated as his father treated them? . . . There was always a young, blonde, beautiful secretary around. I think it was very confusing to Jack. When he did get involved with someone, what kind of a woman was she? Like his mother or like his father's girls?"

Knowledge of Joe's womanizing filtered down to his children's friends.

"The story around school was that the old man would go away on a trip with another gal once he had gotten his wife pregnant," recalled Alan Gage, a classmate of Jack's. "Whether that was truth or fiction I don't know, but that was the word around the school."[55]

The Kennedy children knew about their father's affairs and simply accepted them. Later Jack joked with close friends about his father's womanizing. "He was totally open about what a wicked old man he'd been," said one confidant.

On one occasion, socialite Kay Halle joined the Kennedy party at a posh restaurant in Washington. "It was Joe and his two sons, Jack and Bobby. Jack was a congressman then. When I joined them the gist of the conversation from the boys was the fact that their father was going to be in Washington for a few days and needed female companionship. They wondered whom I could suggest, and they were absolutely serious."[56]

"Yes, he was amoral, sure he was," said Joe's friend Arthur Krock of *The New York Times.* "I think only a Roman Catholic could possibly describe how you could be amoral and still religious. That is, how you can carry an insurance policy with the deity and at the same time do all those other things . . . It was a way of the world as far as I knew it and the way of *his* world."

Franklin D. Roosevelt's son personally experienced Joe's wretched side. "I was on a plane with him when I was a kid," Franklin D. Roosevelt Jr. said of Joe, "and he was telling me foul stories in loud language until a woman behind us leaned forward and said she would appreciate it if he would have the decency to keep quiet in a place where other people couldn't walk away from him if they didn't want to listen. He simply laughed and went right on. I think Jack's father was one of the most evil, disgusting men I have ever known . . . He was a rotten human being."[57]

Joe's brazen relations with women conflicted with his cultivated public image of moral rectitude. Popes and cardinals honored him. He always postured as a strong advocate of decency in public entertainment. "You can entertain the public as well and as profitably with moral pictures as you can with immoral ones," he once said.[58]

How much Rose knew about her husband's intimacy with Swanson and other women is still in question. Late in life, she spoke confidentially about Swanson with the writer who assisted in preparing her autobiography. "I stepped aside," said Rose about the European trip Swanson took with her and Joe. "Afterwards the story got around that Joe and Gloria had gone on a trip to Europe together." She deplored the rumor that Joe had fathered a child with Swanson. In public Rose always referred to the actress as Joe's business associate. "Throughout her life," noted Goodwin, "Rose spoke about Gloria with a strange solicitude, never publicly giving the slightest hint of jealousy, fear or rage."

Gullible about rumors of her husband's infidelities and his denials, Rose said, "There was never any deceit in our relations." She privately insisted that her husband told her that he purposely arranged for his secretary Eddie Moore to accompany him almost everywhere as a potential witness, particularly when he had to meet "dames." That way no woman could "frame" him.[59]

Rose repressed or blocked out the unpleasant reality of her husband's lechery. She based her formula for survival on seeing what she wanted to see and hearing what she wanted to hear. "Mrs. Kennedy had this amazing knack for shutting out anything she did not want to know or face or deal with, and conversely of actually believing whatever she wanted to believe," said a Kennedy employee.

Rose acted as if the other women didn't exist. She willed the unpleasant knowledge of her husband's affairs out of her mind. "After all, Rose seemed to have what she wanted in her marriage: children, wealth and privilege," Goodwin observed. "At the same time, the marriage satisfied what may have been her own desire for sexual distance." Better to suffer privately in silence than risk public disgrace or a divorce that would shatter the Kennedy family.[60]

3

THE KENNEDY SYSTEM

Because of their wealth, the Kennedys could have become dilettantes or beachcombers, but Joe and Rose had a special vision for their family, plus the drive and the determination to achieve it. Over the years, the parents spent many hours together discussing the children, going over each youngster's activities and planning the child's future. Neither parent had much social life apart from their family. They didn't play bridge or host large parties. "Years ago," Rose told an interviewer in the late 1930s, "we decided that our children were going to be our best friends and that we never could see too much of them. Since we couldn't do both, it was better to bring up our family than to go out to dinners."[1]

With an almost mystical faith in himself, Joe Kennedy tried to instill in his children that the Kennedys were an exceptional family. Away from his work, the children preoccupied him. In most respects he was an excellent child psychologist, insightfully appraising the strengths and weaknesses of each child. After measuring the child's potential, he relentlessly encouraged its fulfillment. With a troubled or discouraged youngster Joe invariably offered support. "That may be one of the *best* things that ever happened to you!" he often declared. Jack and the other children felt bolstered by their father's infectious optimism.

Joe usually took a roundabout way to motivate his children but only so long as it yielded results. If necessary he played the drill sergeant, issuing blunt, direct commands. "His children responded out of love tinged with an element of fear," said Richard Whalen, "the latter not so much dread of his tongue lashings, although these were colorful and memorable, but rather fear of failing to measure up to his expectations. He was the supreme arbiter whose approval the children constantly sought."[2]

When Alice Cahill Bastian ("Keela"), the family's nurse, was introduced to Joe in the late 1920s, Mr. Kennedy's first words to her were, "Miss Cahill, don't hesitate to interrupt me, whether I am at a meeting, in conference, or visiting with friends, if you wish to consult me about my children."

Of Joe's exceptional devotion to his children, Rose wrote in her memoirs, "He loved them and let them know it . . . in the most outgoing demonstrative ways. In business and politics people found him hardheaded and tough, but they should have seen him at home, warm and gentle with the little ones." He swept them into his arms, hugged them, grinned and teased. As a young one became old enough to talk, Joe took the child into bed with him for a little while each morning and "the two of them would be propped up on pillows with perhaps the child's head cuddling on his shoulder and he would talk or read a story or they would have conversations," Rose recalled.[3]

While the family lived in Bronxville, Joe took the youngsters on Saturday excursions to New York City for a roast beef lunch at a restaurant and to the movies—*Pinocchio* and *Huckleberry Finn*—at the Radio City Music Hall.

He kissed the children good-bye when he left for his office or on a trip, and was never too hurried to ask them about their progress in school or their plans for the day. Oftentimes the younger ones accompanied him to the train depot. He played games and sports with them—croquet, golf, and tennis; jaunted to the water's edge to watch a beginner swim; and stood on the pier awaiting the start of a sailboat race.

Wisely, Joe always sought out experts to assist the family—highly respected physicians, lawyers, and teachers. His children had to have the finest athletic equipment, schools, hospitals, and travel experiences. "Joe automatically went to the expert," said his friend Kay Halle. "[The children] were trained by their father to go to the best source available for anything they sought. Look for the best. Look for the person that was the most skilled and the most expert."

After listening to a discussion about another wealthy family, whose children seemed confused and unmotivated, Joe remarked, "Yes, they do have money—but no *direction*."[4]

"Mr. Kennedy was somehow able to do it right," said LeMoyne "Lem" Billings, Jack's friend; "not to spoil his children and yet not to make them resentful with his strictness. He was able to follow a very fine line . . . make them want to improve themselves and please him, and he did this without undue force. He did it with love, and yet with strictness."

Even those vehemently hostile to Joseph P. Kennedy for his boorish behavior and unethical and immoral conduct admired his extraordinary relations with his children. "Most fathers in those days simply weren't that interested in what their children did," said a Hyannis Port resident. "But Joe Kennedy knew what his kids were up to all the time."

When Joe moved his career to Hollywood, young Joe and Jack, ages eleven and nine, avidly followed the glamorous life their father was leading. Goodwin observed of this period:

> What boy was there in whose mind the prospect of meeting face to face with cowboy movie star Tom Mix or baseball great Babe Ruth or football hero Red Grange, all of whom were negotiating with Kennedy for different FBO movies, would not conjure up irrepressible feelings of awe and delight at the richness of their father's world? . . .
>
> When Joe was at home, the boys would listen intently to his every word; to be with him, to talk with him, to do things with him—all that was pleasure beyond imagining. And while he was away, they would write him spirited misspelled letters in which the details of their daily lives are suffused with powerful feelings of affection. And almost always, reserving the warmest side of his character for his family, Joe would respond by return mail to each letter from every child.

For all the attention and love Joe showered on his children when he was home, the fact remained that he was often gone—in Hollywood, New York, or Washington, D.C. Grandpa Fitzgerald often stepped in to watch their games or to take them to Fenway Park. "Yet, in spite of his long absences," noted Goodwin, "Kennedy managed to make his children feel they were always on his mind; somehow he was the one—being all the more idealized, perhaps, in his absence—who held the enchantment for them."[5]

Rose dedicated herself to fulfilling her ideal of a Catholic mother. By striving to create an exemplary family, she hoped to provide her husband and her children with a sense of belonging to something greater than themselves. She wanted to instill excellent values, traditions, and habits that would sustain her children for their entire life. Use your mind to the fullest; discover the world through reading, study, and travel; welcome new adventures. Life was exciting.

"When I held my newborn baby in my arms," Rose once said, "I used to think that what I said and did to him could have an influence not only on him but on all whom he met, not only for a day or a month or a year, but for all eternity—a very challenging and exciting thought for a mother."

Rose kept the peace when necessary, exercising a soothing influence on the arguments and debates among her rambunctious brood. Because Joe often traveled, Rose assumed most of the burden of rearing the children. "They owe much of what they were and are to their mother," observed journalist and family friend Arthur Krock. "She's the one who put the family spirit in them," said a friend of Rose. "She would leave any party early to be home in time for a baby's feeding," added another friend.[6]

Knowing nothing about Sigmund Freud or Dr. Benjamin Spock, Rose avidly studied the most respected and popular child experts of her era. Profound changes in American child-rearing advice and practices took place from 1900 to 1930. Instead of the thoughtless, haphazard practices of the past, child-care experts promoted new, progressive, systematic methods. They urged strict feeding and sleeping schedules and early toilet training, and warned mothers not to fondle, play, or display affection with their children.

Mothers turned to doctors, home economists, government pamphlets, and popular women's magazines for child-rearing advice. A survey of magazine articles focusing on motherhood between 1910 and 1935 found that the writers considered the greatest threat to the child to be "too much love." Dr. John B. Watson's scientific bible of child care, *The Psychological Care of Infant and Child* (1928), warned of the "danger lurking in the mother's kiss."

Watson practiced behaviorist psychology and promoted a stern and regimented line of advice for parents. "Children," he wrote, "are made not born." Mothers had a huge responsibility to mold their offspring through a process of positive and negative reinforcement. Parents should reward behavior they wanted to encourage and punish behavior they hoped to discourage, thereby producing a properly socialized child.

Watson deplored unsystematic parenting. He criticized parents who coddled their children and smothered them with affection. Nothing disturbed him more than the possibility of irrational and emotional elements in the mother's relationship with her child. Don't hug or kiss the child; never let him or her sit on your lap. "If you must, kiss them once on the forehead when they say good night. Shake hands with them in the morning."[7]

Watson based his ideas on the writings of L. Emmett Holt Jr., a pediatrician whose book *The Care and Feeding of Children,* first published in 1894, was still being used in the 1940s. Enormously influential, Holt was the Dr. Spock of his day, consulted by millions of mothers, including Rose Kennedy.

Holt stressed that children should be weighed at standardized intervals; trained to eat a variety of foods (not making an entire meal of one or two articles); dine at established hours; and get plenty of fresh air. Good teeth were essential to health and good looks, said Holt. Bad teeth were a menace to the general health, and no amount of dentistry in later life could compensate for the effects of early neglect.

"Babies under six months old should never be played with," Holt firmly declared, because "they are made more nervous and irritable, sleep badly, and suffer from indigestion and cease to gain weight." Don't express affection either. "Tuberculosis, diphtheria, syphilis, and many other grave diseases may be communicated in this way," he warned. "The kissing of infants upon the mouth by other children, by nurses, or by people generally, should under no circumstances be permitted. Infants should be kissed, if at all, upon the cheek or forehead, but the less even of this the better."[8]

Although Rose nursed her first four babies, she followed Holt's advice and did not normally express affection with her children. She cared deeply about them, but she remained reserved and emotionally distant. "She wasn't a bring-them-to-the-bosom kind of mother," said a former neighborhood youth.

"Mrs. Kennedy didn't say she loved her children," observed Luella Hennessey, the nurse who worked with the Kennedys for four decades. "It just wasn't said. It was all about respect. She respected them and they respected her. They weren't touchy people. Jack never was, not when he was a young man, not ever. Never."

Early in her marriage, on the recommendation of child experts, Rose walked into a stationery store and purchased three-by-five-inch file cards and index tabs. Following the birth of each new baby Rose filled out a card with the child's name, birthplace, and baptism. Every Saturday night she weighed each child and entered the result on the card. Through the years she listed all their illnesses, medical and dental appointments, and eye exams.

Superior achievements, making the most of one's abilities, grew out of excellent, ingrained habits. While the maids helped dress and prepare the children for breakfast, Rose was downstairs supervising the first meal of the day. As Holt and the other experts advised, she saw to it that the children ate what they were supposed to eat, in the proper quantity. "If they were a mite too thin, she plied them with fats, sugars, and creams," noted Lawrence Leamer. "If they looked plump, she cut down on sweets and breads. Scrawny little Jack was certain to get something extra." When they were old enough for school, she inspected their clothes, looking for spots and dirt. "We were really organized," Eunice remembered. "It was an extraordinary thing the way she had us all . . . disciplined."[9]

The Kennedys not only had dentists; they had orthodontists as well. "People think they were born with that smile," Rose explained. "They all had their teeth straightened. That was hard work, getting them to the dentist." Indeed, it was hard work. Once every three weeks, for five years, Rose drove several of her daughters from Boston to New York and back for appointments with an excellent orthodontist. (The local one wasn't good enough.)

Rose monitored her children's intake of sweets. She kept a box of assorted candies in her bedroom, and after dinner each of the children could select a favorite piece. Only one piece, not two. After every meal they brushed their teeth. "Dentists have always recommended it but we actually did it," said Eunice.

Rose had a natural desire to keep a tidy home, but the hired help performed most of those duties. Her children had more important things to do than housekeeping chores. They should be batting tennis balls, sailing, reading, and playing games. Consequently, cleaning up after themselves was never a priority for any of the children, which bred in them a casual attitude. There would always be someone to clean up their mess.[10]

The Catholic Church was the center of Rose's life, and she tried to make its tenets the foundation for her children's moral training. She took the little ones into church for a visit almost daily because children should form the habit of making God a part of their daily lives, not just on Sundays. The family said grace before meals—a different daughter or son leading the prayer each time. On Sunday mornings Rose stood at the bottom of the stairs, checking off her children one by one, making sure they were spick-and-span, properly attired, and all clutching their prayer books and rosaries. When the children marched into church with their nursemaid, they looked, recalled one observer, "like a little tribe dressed up in their velvet-collar wool Chesterfield coats." They listened attentively and remembered well mostly because Rose quizzed them about the sermon and the Gospel at Sunday's lunch.[11]

On a holy day or a notable saint's day, Rose discussed the meaning of the special event or the saint's life. At Easter she quizzed them about the Resurrection and life everlasting. "Why did Jesus accept crucifixion and suffer and die for us?" "What was He doing for us, and by His example telling all of us?" Faith, she explained, was a great living gift from God intended to sustain our lives on earth, to guide us in our activities, and to act as a source of solace and comfort. A daily communicant, Rose prayed that in her own life, faith would sustain her, guide her activities, and offer solace and comfort.

Sometimes she was too intense in her faith. When daughter Pat was ill, Rose walked up and down in Pat's room, praying, holding a crucifix, and saying, "Remember how Christ suffered and died on the cross."

Young Jack's somewhat unorthodox attitude toward his religion was a minor irritant for his devout mother. On one occasion, when Rose attended church with the children, she urged them all to wish for a happy death. They all complied except Jack, who irreverently wished for two dogs. When Rose told the children the story of Palm Sunday, she explained that Christ rode to

Jerusalem on a donkey, amid admirers waving palms, and shortly after, he was crucified. Following the Easter lesson, Rose waited for the children's questions. Jack looked up and said, "What became of the donkey?"[12]

Overall, however, Rose seemed successful in making religion a part of her children's daily life. Her five daughters attended Catholic schools, and by 1938, observed Lynne McTaggart, Kathleen Kennedy's biographer, "Joe Jr. had been the head of the Catholic Club at Harvard, thirteen-year-old Bobby was an altar boy, and Eunice was displaying missionary zeal about converting their Protestant friends."

The media increasingly portrayed the Kennedys as exemplars of the modern American Catholic family, lauded them for their precocious children, praised them for their faith, and honored them for their philanthropy to the church.

Although Rose didn't sweep the floor, cook, or serve meals, she tried to teach and inspire. She carefully monitored her children's reading, homework, and skating lessons. "There was a lot of pressure all the time," said Eunice. Rose wouldn't accept excuses. She would help Eunice with her homework, but if Eunice didn't catch on, Rose became angry and said, "You just sit there and learn that verb!" "[She] sounds like an ogre," Eunice recalled. "But you never felt that she was doing it for her. She felt you had more in you than you thought you did."[13]

Rose spurred on the children. "Mother always urged, cajoled and prodded us on our way," said Eunice. So did Joe. His letters to his children often contained messages urging self-improvement. He exhorted them, noted Kennedy family historian Amanda Smith, "to work on their handwriting, their grades, their attitudes or their eating habits."

Preaching a fierce stoicism, Joe and Rose expected their children to tolerate pain, distress, and disappointment without whining or complaining. Joe would clap his hands and say, "No-crying-in-this-house! No-crying-in-this-house!"

Normally all the children were to be outdoors playing because Rose wanted everybody healthy and robust. It didn't matter if they had a slight cold or a touch of the flu. "You took care of yourself, but then you hustled right along," said Eunice. If Eunice had an upset stomach, she would take her medicine and read a book, but when dinner was ready, she came downstairs like everyone else. "You must realize my mother was never sick," Eunice observed. "She never sat and dwelled on negative things, like being sick or having a tummy ache."[14]

Joe Kennedy may have spanked his children occasionally, but nobody seems to remember him doing it. "I can't remember a single time that he ever spanked any of them," said Rose. Bobby Kennedy, whom Rose spanked regularly, could not recall ever being turned across his father's knee.

Joe enforced discipline by the strength of his personality—an almost physical emanation of energy, power, mental quickness, and forthrightness. He did not suffer fools gladly. If one of his children upset him, he could show ferocious displeasure merely with his eyes. That was usually enough. "All it took was a look," Rose said.

Ordinarily Rose enforced the discipline. "Hot water was my department," she said. "Business was Joe's department." When the children misbehaved, they got a good old-fashioned spanking, which Rose believed was one of the very effective means of instruction. In general, though, neither parent imposed harsh or lockstep discipline.[15]

As the family's financial fortunes soared, the parents made a halfhearted effort to keep their children unspoiled. They purposely handed out allowances about equal to those of the neighborhood children. Sometimes, though, they spoiled and overprotected the children. Rose, for example, took her child's side in disputes with outsiders, even though she didn't know the facts or the circumstances. When young Teddy, "the little angel," got into a water fight at school and was disciplined, she immediately took his side. "It seems quite unfair," she wrote family members, "because I am sure the [older] boys who were there . . . provoked him to mischief."[16]

Although seventeen years separated the first child from the last, the Kennedy children grew up with a sense of mutual responsibility, learning to help and to depend on each other. At the children's request the older children served as godparents to the younger ones. Starting with Joe Jr. who was carefully trained as a substitute father, Joe and Rose encouraged the older children to teach their juniors and to act as exemplars. An older child taught swimming to the beginner and gave advice on sailing, tennis, and study methods for school.

The Kennedys stuck together. "No matter what anyone else had done, the Kennedy children always praised each other's accomplishments to the skies," one childhood playmate recalled. "While it was amusing and touching for a time, it got to be rather tiresome after a while."

Rose took the children on long walks and historic tours—to the Bunker Hill Monument, the *Constitution,* Old North Church, and the Boston Common. Remembering her own love of history, cultivated by her father, she wanted her children to understand and "feel" the past. She also brought them into Boston for civic festivities—the parades, public ceremonies, and political rallies.[17]

"We went to dancing lessons once a week, which bored us, but we did turn out to be good dancers," said Eunice. Eunice estimated that the children attended two swimming classes each week, all summer long, for eight consecutive summers. Rose arranged lessons to teach them to sail, and to play tennis and golf. The children sometimes complained about the regimen, but, Eunice observed, "we did develop the skills and they've been assets."

Rose also coordinated family picnics, usually at one of the excellent Cape beaches. The standard menu became a big thermos jug of creamed chicken, a large container of ice cream (and a package of cones), lollipops, and fresh fruit. "As the crowning glory and favorite of all," said Rose, "a white cake . . . iced with thick, gooey chocolate frosting."[18]

Most of the children were reasonably prompt, but Jack was usually the exception. Frequently the family drove to a beach club a few miles from Hyannis Port in a station wagon loaded with children. Rose instructed them to reassemble at the car at twelve forty-five so the family could be home for one o'clock lunch. At the agreed-upon time Jack would be nowhere in sight. To teach him a lesson, Rose drove off without him. Jack always managed to "hook a ride home" with somebody and would show up late at the luncheon table. Because Rose had decreed that tardiness meant starting in the middle of the meal, Jack faced a meager lunch. "Afterward," said Rose, "he would slip into the kitchen and charm the cook into filling him up. I knew what he was doing. And he knew that I knew." She allowed him to subvert her rule because "I felt he needed the nourishment more than the discipline."

On cold, windswept days at Hyannis Port the children stayed inside, nestling in the warmth of the veranda, playing Monopoly, backgammon, checkers, twenty questions, or charades—anything, said Luella Hennessey, "that would keep the Kennedy wits sharpened to razor edge." In the evening Rose occasionally played the piano and the clan gathered around her and sang in voices "almost universally off-key." Thanks to Joe's film business, on many evenings the children watched a Hollywood film, often a first-run exclusive not yet appearing in theaters.[19]

Every Thursday Rose took the youngsters to the public library to select books. During the summer she required all the Kennedy children to read an hour per day, and the books had to be approved by Rose. When they were toddlers, she read them bedtime stories; when they were ill and bedridden, she read to them several hours at a time. She carefully selected the books from the PTA, the Boston Women's Exchange, and library lists—books with educational and inspirational value, not just entertainment.

Rose didn't think she wasted her college education on motherhood. "I have found my education of inestimable value even when I stayed at home rocking the cradle," she said. She intelligently discussed world events, and her knowledge of French and German gave her a new appreciation of operas, symphonies, and literature. In the public forum, "I can express my ideas coherently and forcibly." She later did speak effectively on behalf of the disadvantaged, the mentally retarded, and her sons' political careers.[20]

Besides the morning walks, the historical tours, the visits to church, and the reading program, Rose insisted on regular family mealtimes. Meals were a time for family communication. As the family grew larger, Rose instituted two separate meal sittings, one for the young children, a later time for the older children and adults. At the early one Rose sat at the little table supervising the eating and directing the conversation.

A cook and kitchen maid prepared the meals; a butler and waitress set the food on the table. The kitchen help served up enormous helpings of simple, healthy food, washed down with milk, sometimes twenty quarts a day or more. Providing for so many people with healthy appetites was like operating a small hotel. Consequently, Rose established a fixed time every day for the evening meal and demanded prompt adherence to the schedule. Schoolwork, sport, and play were important, but none of these activities took precedence over the ritual of the family meal.[21]

When Joe traveled on a business trip, Rose directed the family's conversation, presenting lessons on geography, history, patriotism, manners, and religion. At Thanksgiving she discussed the Pilgrims and their difficult journey to America in search of religious freedom.

Joe and Rose decreed that the children read the newspapers, with special attention to the "News of the Week in Review" in the Sunday *New York Times*. Then the children discussed news items at Sunday's lunch. Rose also hung a bulletin board—where the children were sure to see it—and tacked up news items. The youngsters who could read and reason were to study the items and express their opinions, comments, or questions during the mealtime conversations.

A Florida item cued Rose to ask how the state got its name. "What does the word mean, what language is it from? Think of Spanish names of towns there. Sarasota, Tampa—no, not Miami, that's Indian. Where else in the country are there a lot of Spanish names? Yes, California. What about San Francisco?—what does that mean, who was it named after? You know about that from church? Think of some other saints' names out there. San Diego, San Gabriel, Santa Barbara. And what about Los Angeles?"[22]

In turn, the Kennedy youths quizzed an Irish dinner guest about Irish culture, painting, and writers. "It was very stimulating, very interesting conversation because they were all terribly intelligent and well educated and very enthusiastic about everything," said Dorothy Tubridy, a visitor from Ireland.

Prominent guests—foreign dignitaries, politicians, actors, and musicians—often visited the Kennedy household. "It was Joe's idea to expose his young brood to men and women of accomplishment, hoping, I think, that their elements of greatness would be seen and studied by the children," said Joe's friend Supreme Court justice William O. Douglas.[23]

When Joe presided, sparks flew during the evening meals. "It was something!" said Lem Billings, a frequent dinner guest. "It wasn't like any other dinner table," added a family friend. "The . . . father kept the conversation on a high level. If you didn't talk about world affairs, you just didn't talk." Never frivolous, the discussions were nonetheless usually exhilarating and fun. If a youngster asked him a question about a public policy, Joe went to great lengths to explain its strengths and weaknesses. Because he wanted his children to argue and debate, he didn't force his views on them, and often purposely played the devil's advocate. If he had anything to say, the boys waited for him to say it; then they all felt perfectly free to express, in respectful terms, a completely different opinion. He didn't try to restrain them, although he sometimes said he thought they didn't have "any sense" or were "idiots." "He never wanted them to agree with him," said Billings. "All this talk about [John Kennedy] being influenced by his father is crazy because he was raised *not* to be."[24]

"The truth," commented one dinner-table visitor, "is that they couldn't possibly be around the old man without being interested in damn near everything. Some [of his notions] are sound, some are preposterous. But everything he says tends to be interesting."

At the dining-room table Joe always insisted that his children treat their mother with deference, but he wasn't interested in Rose's opinions, or those of his daughters. "He paid more attention to the boys," Louella Hennessey said. "With the boys it was talking about world events, politics, long conversations. With the girls it was 'What are you doing tonight?' 'How was the party?' kind of fluffy talk."

If one of his children's friends—an outsider—interjected, Joe responded curtly, as if he didn't want to be bothered. Jack's friends were always welcome in the Kennedy home, but Joe Kennedy practically ignored their opinions at the dinner table. They were not permitted to penetrate the exclusive inner circle Mr. Kennedy drew around his family.[25]

Both parents tried to inspire an intense competitive spirit. In every competitive activity their children should strive to be first. "Even in school games and races, we always took an interest," said Rose. "We went, and watched, and then talked about it afterwards. If they didn't win, we tried to find out why."

Joe was passionate—sometimes obsessed—about excellence, winning, and the virtues of competition. Life was a contest in which the winner took all, Joe often preached; the runner-up was merely a loser. On the evidence of his own rise, he believed that the Kennedys were destined to win, and could accomplish anything they resolved to do. Seldom introspective, he spoke in the simple imperatives of the pep talk, giving powerful emphasis to platitudes and clichés ("When the going gets tough, the tough get going"), and influencing his children with the force of his personality.

Intense competition improves self-discipline, initiative, perseverance, and determination. Few aspects of life are free from competitive struggle; business, politics, law, sports are all intensely competitive. Unfortunately, competition often causes collateral damage leading to a host of destructive consequences, including the moral evils of deceit, lying, and hypocrisy. Though serious problems can follow in its wake, competition provides a means for assigning position, place, power, productive ability, and excellence. Without competition's powerful stimulant, potentialities fail to develop. Because athletics often provides the purest form of competitive struggle, Joe expected huge benefits to flow from his children's participation in sports.

Despite Joe's limited insight and unimaginative expression, the platitudes and clichés he preached were important. The remarkable feature of Joe's teaching was the passion, persistence, and skill with which he successfully transmitted virtues necessary to succeed. His children knew that he deeply believed every platitude and every cliché.

Joe expected his children to have a winning attitude, but this in itself wasn't measurable. It was impossible to have a winning attitude and still lose with regularity. Losing was evidence of poor planning, concentration, strategy, organization, preparation, and attitude.[26]

Joe encouraged his boys to play football, and he thrust each child into individual sports—swimming, sailing, golf, and tennis—in the hope that they would learn to compete, win, and excel. Whether running a race, catching a football, or competing in school, the Kennedys were to try—try harder than anyone else. "We might not be the best, and none of us were, but we were to make the effort to be the best," said Robert Kennedy.

If his youngster didn't win, Joe expressed his disappointment. "He didn't like his children to be second best," said Billings. "Of course, the children were aware of this constant pressure. They knew that everything he did was because he loved them . . . so they automatically felt that they wanted to win."

Jack's friend Paul Chase visited Hyannis Port, where he crewed for Jack in several racing contests. "Once we lost badly," said Chase, "and caught a half hour lecture from the 'old man' on our return to shore. He said he had watched the race and that he was disgusted with both of us. There was no sense, he claimed, in going into a race unless you did your damndest to win, an endeavor at which we had failed miserably. He was really angry with us."[27]

When the children were about seven, Joe entered them in public swimming races, in the different age categories so they wouldn't have to compete against each other. He did the same with sailing races. "And if we won, he got terribly enthusiastic," observed Eunice. "The thing he always kept telling us was that coming in second was just no good. The important thing was to win." Eunice continued: "I was twenty-four before I knew I didn't have to win something every day."

Jack hated to lose as well. "He hates to lose at anything," said Eunice. "That's the only thing Jack gets really emotional about—when he loses. Sometimes he even gets cross." Even in a game of checkers, said a close friend, "If I win and don't want to play anymore, [Jack] insist[s] that we keep on playing, until he finally wins more games than I do."

Because Joe Kennedy's approach to winning was strident and extreme, several Kennedys, including Jack, subsequently tried to soften their father's image as a tyrant about winning. Win or lose, they knew their father loved them, and if they failed, he would pick them up. "The main point of the whole exercise was not 'winning' *per se*," Rose claimed. "It was rather that we wanted them to do their absolute best. Always give their maximum effort." Robert Kennedy recalled his father saying, "After you have done the best you can, the hell with it."[28]

Joseph Kennedy encouraged his sons to have stimulating intellectual encounters so they could compete with the "bright guys." But because of Joe's own mental limitations, he was forever barred from the intellectual world except on a superficial level. The children devoted intense efforts to athletic competition, but displayed only modest interest in academic competition, mostly because Joe stressed competition in athletics far more than he did in academics. The schoolboy athlete was a hero; the schoolboy scholar was not. Jack became the most intellectually inclined member of the family partly because he wasn't strong and healthy enough as a youngster to compete effectively in athletics like his older brother.

Joe Kennedy stressed winning, excellence, and competition, but he taught little about ethics and morals. He regularly attended Sunday Mass and usually received Communion; he became agitated when a friend neglected to have her son baptized. Overall, though, he was not a religious or moral person. Rose believed religion was the finest molder of character; Joe put his faith in experience.[29]

Joe and Rose strongly discouraged the use of tobacco and alcohol. Neither of the parents smoked, and they seldom drank. In Rose's circle any girl or young wife who smoked a cigarette was typecast as a scarlet woman. Rose's father had deeply resented the Boston Brahmin image of the drunken Irish and tried to dispel it. Honey Fitz drank with friends in private, but he never took alcohol in public, because, said Rose, "he believed it would contribute to the caricature of 'drunken Irish politicians—a glass of whiskey in one hand, a pipe in the other.'"

Only when they entertained did the Kennedys serve cocktails. The standard nightcap was milk. Joe offered each of his children a thousand dollars for not smoking and another thousand for not drinking until they reached the age of twenty-one. He didn't spy on them or question them; it was all done on the honor system. On each child's twenty-first birthday, Joe wrote out two checks and handed them to the birthday celebrant. It was up to the new twenty-one-year-old to decide whether to keep the checks. "Two of the kids handed the checks back to me," Joe said. One of them was Jack; still, he seldom drank or smoked.[30]

Joe was a superb moneymaker, but he never pushed his children toward careers in business and never successfully taught them about money. Over the years he created several trust funds for his children so they would never have to worry about money. The children received income from the trusts at the age of twenty-one, and one-half their share of the principal at forty-five. By 1961 each Kennedy was worth about ten million dollars. Joe boasted to a friend, "I fixed it so that any of my children, financially speaking, could look me in the eye and tell me to go to hell."

During an interview in the late 1940s Joe explained why he steered his boys toward careers in public service rather than in business. "The country's got plenty of businessmen," he said. "What [the nation] needs is some sound, informed, well-qualified representation in its contacts with other nations and in the handling of its own affairs . . . We chance to be in a position in which they can be spared the necessity of supporting themselves. Spared that, why shouldn't they better try to qualify to serve their country in some needed capacity?"

Money was a matter of indifference to Jack, who seldom carried any. He reached maturity almost innocent of the meaning of money as appreciated by most working people. But wealth allowed Jack and his brothers and sisters to enjoy the luxury of spacious homes in magnificent settings, access to superb health care and excellent schools, extensive domestic and foreign travel, exposure to the social and intellectual elite, stimulating work, and a variety of material advantages.[31]

"The Kennedys lived at the vanguard of the new and novel," noted Clay and Joan Blair, who studied John Kennedy's life. When commercial air travel started in the United States, and later in Europe, the Kennedys were among the first to use it. The youngsters enjoyed the newest radios and phonographs, and later the first tape recorders and television sets. They viewed the newest movies at home. Jack grew up traveling between Hyannis Port and Palm Beach, between Europe and America; he was exposed to new gadgets, stimulating entertainment, and novel ideas.

There were, however, gaps in their experiences. Except for Rose, none of the Kennedys developed any serious interest in the arts. They didn't acquire fine paintings, antiques, or rare books, and seldom listened to classical music. They enjoyed Broadway musicals but not opera.

Overall, Jack entered the race of life serene and secure from money worries, and, noted journalist William Shannon, with a "self-confident style that inherited wealth and family prestige can provide."[32]

One constant burden disrupted Joe and Rose's idealistic plans for their family and caused enormous worry and strain. Their third child, daughter Rosemary, was retarded. At first she seemed normal. "She was a very pretty baby," Rose recorded in her memoirs, "and she was sweet and peaceable and cried less than the first two had, which at the time I supposed was part of her being a girl." During infancy, though, ominous signs appeared. She was slower to crawl, to walk, and to speak than her brothers.

When Rosemary followed her two older brothers to the Devotion School for kindergarten, she did poorly, and the teachers could not recommend her for promotion to the first grade. Although sweet and gentle, she couldn't grasp even the simplest tasks which the other children in the class routinely accomplished. "The teachers' report confirmed in her mother all the lurking suspicions she had harbored about her five-year-old daughter from the first year of her life," Goodwin said.

"I am trying to get [Rosemary] going which always takes a lot of planning," Rose wrote her husband. With the problem of her oldest daughter constantly on her mind, Rose later admitted that she probably didn't spend as much time as she wanted to with the other children, including Jack, "who was so ill so much of the time as a little boy that he needed a lot of attention." She gave Rosemary most of the attention, thinking she could circumvent her daughter's affliction by finding the right school and the best psychologist. She never heard Jack complain about being neglected.[33]

Rosemary's behavior was unpredictable. If the other youngsters walked to the post office, Rosemary would impulsively tag along, but then forget to come home. "So it was a great worry," Rose said.

Desperately, the Kennedys kept seeking a solution. For a while Joe hoped a "gland" specialist could cure Rosemary. "We do not want to leave a stone unturned if there is anything possible to be done," he wrote the family's physician, Dr. Frederick Good.

That the experts differed in their recommendations about Rosemary confused Joe and Rose. There was no consensus. The parents bridled at advice to place Rosemary in an institution. "What can they do in an institution that we can't do better for her at home—here with her family?" Joe commented.

So the Kennedys kept Rosemary at home. To develop her capacities to the utmost, Rose hired a special governess and private tutors to teach her how to print, play tennis, dance, and read. For a while it seemed to be working, and Rosemary slowly improved.[34]

Jack was tender with Rosemary and tried to help her. As an adolescent, he was at the age when most boys would have cringed at the idea of escorting a sister to a dance, especially a sister perceived as "different." But Jack and Joe Jr. escorted Rosemary to dances on Cape Cod and elsewhere. "She was *their* sister, a member of *their* family," observed Lawrence Leamer, "and they danced with her, waltzed her around the ballrooms, brought her punch, stood with her and shared a quiet laugh, stayed with her so that she appeared not different at all."

Later, when Jack was in college, he took Rosemary out on the town and reported back excellent results: "Rose seemed to enjoy the Stork Club and acted *very* well," he wrote his mother. "She seems to be much better when alone and when the attention is chiefly on her. Her dancing was *much* better."

The Kennedy family formed a closed circle around Rosemary, protecting her from the outside world. But her disability continued to haunt them, leading to a disastrous decision in the early 1940s.[35]

Because of Rosemary's retardation, Kathleen—nicknamed "Kick"— assumed the status of oldest daughter in the family. Three years younger than Jack, with reddish brown hair, deep-set blue-gray eyes, and rosy skin, small and dainty like her mother, she was Jack's favorite.

A fine all-around student, Kathleen applied herself to her studies and never needed tutoring, as her sisters did. She was a great dancer, had excellent taste in clothes, and could ski, sail, and play tennis as well as her brothers. Vivacious and high-spirited, she was "sunshine," one of her friends said. "Wherever she stood, there would be warmth, fun, gaiety and charm."[36]

Kathleen and Jack shared the same self-deprecating humor, free-spiritedness, and unharnessed energy. They showed up together at all the activities on the Cape—the barn dances and the Saturday matinees at the Idle Hours movie theater in Hyannis Port. After Jack received his driver's license, the two often went for leisurely drives.

Kathleen adored Jack, but she could express her love only by teasing and joking with him. To her father she confided her intense feeling for her brother. "She really thinks you are a great fellow," Joe wrote to Jack in February 1935. "She has a love and devotion to you that you should be very proud to have deserved. It probably does not become apparent to you, but it does to both Mother and me. She thinks you are quite the grandest fellow that ever lived and your letters furnish her most of her laughs."[37]

Joe Jr. was the golden child, the mentor for his siblings, but one who often tormented young Jack. Disciplined, hardworking, and mature for his age, young Joe was, in Goodwin's words, "reverent the way the mother wanted, ambitious the way the father wanted. He was clearly the favorite child of both his parents."

It was assumed that young Joe would succeed his father as the family's standard-bearer. "I think a lot depends on the oldest one, and how he turns out," the elder Kennedy reflected. "The younger ones follow his example. . . . If the oldest one tries to set a good example, the other ones try to live up to it."

Joe treated his oldest son like an adult and seldom scolded him; instead of demanding, he suggested, quietly, "man to man." The father gave few orders, but those he did issue young Joe obeyed instantly.[38]

Kind and patient with his young brothers and sisters, Joe Jr. willingly accepted his role as family exemplar, spending many hours with the young ones teaching them to ride a bicycle, throw a football, play tennis, and sail. Jack was like a pal to the little Kennedys; Joe Jr. acted like a father.

Both brothers were handsome, charming, and athletic; both had warm smiles and easily made friends. But Joe Jr. was taller, broader, stronger, and more aggressive and intense. "While Joe was an orderly child at home and a serious student at school, even tackling things he did not like," said Goodwin, "Jack was unpardonably sloppy at home and lazy at school, interested only in the things that pleased him."

While not an introvert, young Jack was more withdrawn, quiet, and shy; Joe was dynamic, sociable, an extrovert. Jack had the best sense of humor in the family; young Joe's humor was often sarcastic and biting.

"He had a pugnacious personality," Jack reflected on his older brother. "Later on it smoothed out, but it was a problem in my boyhood." Refusing to obey and emulate his brother-paragon, Jack determined to resist the submersion of his personality, but he quickly learned that determination was no substitute for brute muscle.[39]

With Jack, the rival for his throne, a challenge to his status in the family, Joe Jr. was often sarcastic, overbearing, disapproving, a taunting bully. The younger children scattered or cowered in terror upstairs as their brothers wrestled on the first floor. Young Joe usually pinned his brother, leaving Jack humiliated again. Joe Senior refused to mediate the fighting, apparently believing that the stronger should teach the weaker.

Young Joe would lob a football to Rosemary or Eunice, but would smash the ball into Jack, and laugh when Jack dropped it or had the wind knocked out of him. While racing around the block on their bicycles in opposite directions, both boys stubbornly refused to veer, and they collided head-on. Joe emerged unscathed; Jack required twenty-eight stitches.

Using impishness to even the odds, Jack struck back. At dinner young Joe savored the cook's chocolate pie. When the pie was served for dinner, young Joe flashed a grin and asked for his piece early. He placed it on display by his plate so he could look at it. "One noon Jack snatched it, stuffed it into his mouth, and took off at a dead run," wrote Hank Searls, Joe Jr.'s biographer. "With Joe in pursuit, he dived off the breakwater into Lewis Bay. Joe waited in implacable anger until his brother finally emerged, shivering with cold, and then there was a free-swinging brawl, for keeps. The lesson was clear to Jack: to embarrass Joe Kennedy before an audience was a dangerous affair."[40]

Having an older brother was a convenience for Jack, though, because it relieved him of his father's pressure to excel, achieve, and lead. In high school and college Jack would tell close friends, "Thank God Joe Kennedy's there so that my father's not on my back."

Despite the friction between the two brothers, they still shared a fundamental closeness. They joked, golfed, and sailed together. When young Joe attended a sleepover camp in the summer of 1926, Jack initially relished the freedom from harassment, but after two weeks he began to miss his older brother. Jack was "really very lonesome for you," the father wrote young Joe, "and he wants me to be sure and promise him that he will go to camp next summer."

"Forming a family within the family, Joe Jr., Jack and Kathleen were the golden trio who shared all the inestimable advantages of being wealthy, good-looking, confident and intelligent," Goodwin observed.

The Kennedys had much for which to be thankful. "Most of our relationships were so wonderful within the family and with our parents," said Eunice. "If you had a little problem, so what? That's what comes with a large family. It's a great advantage. You can see other people's problems and they don't complain. You don't see your mother complaining. My brother Jack was the same. He didn't complain, so what's to complain?"[41]

For many years Joe and Rose were praised as model parents for creating such a celebrated family. *Reader's Digest* described the Kennedys as "one of the most interesting family groups in the world"; *Parents Magazine* judged them "the natural expression of a fundamentally happy family, each youngster a personality at peace with himself."

Recently, though, a new, critical perspective has emerged. Several authors, most notably Nigel Hamilton in his best-selling and influential book *J.F.K.: Reckless Youth* (1992), judge both Kennedys as far from admirable. According to Hamilton, Joe Kennedy was a "Boston-Irish braggart"; "a foul-mouthed, controlling, frightening, evil-eye his children could not escape." He was "bigoted, almost psychotic . . . ignoble"; a "sniveling," "cowardly," "swindling" "despot" whose life Hamilton summarized as "odious."

At times Joe displayed most of these traits, particularly in his business career, and his philandering had a profoundly detrimental impact on his second son. Nonetheless, Hamilton's assessment ignores Joe's deep love for his family and his admirable fatherly traits.

Joe Kennedy inspired in Jack and his other children some of his own qualities—his doggedness, perseverance, and ambition, his interest in public affairs, love of the limelight, and flaming competitive spirit. He overly intervened in his children's social life and was too controlling, but he encouraged his children to think for themselves and provided superb opportunities for them to grow and succeed. Even President Franklin Roosevelt admired Kennedy's fierce paternal pride and his determination to spur on his children.

Hamilton thought Joe Kennedy's tyrannical approach to winning damaged his children. "To win, for the Kennedy children," said Hamilton, "meant to gain their father's love; to lose, conversely, was to forfeit it—hardly a recipe for relaxed and self-confident children." The young Kennedys did feel pressured and did worry about temporarily losing their father's respect, but Hamilton exaggerated the resulting damage. The children didn't think they forfeited their father's love by losing. Nor did his admonitions make them, in the long run, noticeably less self-confident and less relaxed. Besides, they learned important lessons in self-discipline, initiative, perseverance, and determination.[42]

"What nobody should ever forget," Senator George Smathers of Florida later said, "was that Jack had a tremendous respect for his father, just a *tremendous* respect."

Despite serious flaws in his character, Joe Kennedy lifted his children out of the ordinary human experience of living and gave them the opportunity to make history. "When he conceived the ambition of seeing a son enter the White House, there seemed to be no chance of a Roman Catholic being elected to the Presidency," observed Richard Whalen. "Yet Kennedy believed, with unshakable certainty, that his unattainable ambition would be a reality for his son."

Although historian Arthur Schlesinger Jr. was no admirer of Joe Kennedy, he compared him favorably as a parent with two other famous fathers. "Winston Churchill and Franklin Roosevelt were incontestably greater men than Joseph P. Kennedy," Schlesinger observed. "Yet Randolph and Franklin Jr., both men of talent and charm, seemed to have lived lives beneath their promise and capacity, while the sons of Joseph Kennedy, endowed somewhere with a capacity for self-discipline, had risen beyond their father, and no doubt, because of him."[43]

Recent biographers and historians have disparaged Rose. "A theme in the recent literature on the Kennedys," said one historian, "is that Rose was not the model mother depicted in earlier writings."

Critics charge that Rose dealt with her husband's philandering by isolating herself from the family. Later in life, Jack reflected bitterly that his mother was "either at some Paris fashion house or else on her knees in some church. She was never there when we really needed her. . . . My mother never really held me and hugged me. Never! Never!" Angry over this maternal frostiness, he allegedly told a friend: "My mother is a nothing."[44]

Hamilton's Rose Kennedy was a pathetic figure, a maternal monster— "cold," "unmotherly," "severe," "distant," "sanctimonious," crippled by an "Irish-Catholic mindset," and guilty of a "vengeful piety" toward her children. She was "an often ridiculed Boston-Irish Roman Catholic concealing her failed marriage behind a façade of proper manners, proper attire, proper talk, proper religious observance, proper reading, and proper film-viewing."

Compulsive and trite, she railed "against the children's bad grammar, insisting on the proper usage of *who* and *whom, I* and *me, shall* and *will, may* and *can*. Her zeal was extraordinary, but love, like a candle, had gone out of her life."

Hamilton's most telling point focuses on Rose's extensive travel, particularly while Jack attended high school at Choate and was often ill. "If Rose Kennedy was anxious in Palm Beach, she had a strange way of showing it. She had ventured abroad seventeen times in four years, but could not manage the journey to Connecticut, where Jack lay in the hospital a further month."

According to Hamilton, Rose caused one of Jack's major character flaws. "Jack's lifelong need not simply to flirt with women but compulsively to lie with them—obsessively, maniacally, to the point of sexual addiction—would owe much to his twin obsessions: sexual revenge against his mother and, quite simply, the need for a quality of physical touching denied him from infancy."

Recent critics have underestimated Rose's strengths. She supervised a variety of family matters, from visiting the orthodontist to arranging picnics, from meals to swimming lessons. She taught, inspired, and disciplined nine children, a daunting task. Considering the burden of raising her brood—and providing special care for Rosemary—she needed a leisure outlet, and her favorite was travel.[45]

Rose's critics often take out of context, distort, and emphasize a comment about Rose's traveling that Jack made to his mother when he was only five years old. "Jack . . . thought about why his mother was not there much of the time," Hamilton observed. "Rose's announcement that she was departing on another six-week vacation with her sister, Agnes, earned the five-year-old's memorable rebuke: 'Gee, *you're* a great mother to go away and leave your children all alone!' "

Critics don't indicate, however, that the source for Jack's comment was Rose herself in her diary entry of April 3, 1923. An example of her self-deprecating humor, she included the remark in her autobiography to highlight Jack's precociousness and wit. Still, the comment stung Rose at the time, leading to her explanation—never quoted by critics—in her autobiography:

> I must say that Jack's comment made me feel I was a little hard-hearted. And the next day, April 4, [1923,] when I said good-bye to the children on the porch, I felt miserable. They looked so forlorn, and when I kissed them good-bye I had tears in my eyes. After I was down the street a way I suddenly realized there was something I had forgotten and I came back—to find them all, laughing and playing on the porch, apparently not missing me much at all. I resumed my journey with an easy conscience.

Although Rose traveled extensively, she and Joe made arrangements for Joe to be home when she was gone, and a governess, a nurse, Honey Fitz and his wife, and others helped supervise. Perhaps Rose traveled too much, but the children seldom complained. Some hardly noticed. "She was there all the time," Eunice later said.[46]

Rose was pregnant with her ninth child during part of the time Jack was at Choate. Joe visited Choate several times. In any case, as one observer noted, Joe and Rose both "rained down upon the headmaster at Choate a constant barrage of letters, telegrams, and notes, a correspondence unprecedented in the history of the school." Harold Tinker, an English teacher at Choate, praised Rose's concern for Joe Jr. and Jack. "She was marvelous all the time they were there," said Tinker. "She kept track of everything about all of her children, checked on the diseases, was on the phone whenever anything happened, medically she was alert and carried it all."

Rose's surviving diaries do not suggest coldness or lack of tenderness. In any case, hands-on mothering was not fashionable in her day; nurses, governesses, and tutors were at the center of the children's life.[47]

Chuck Spalding, who became Jack's friend, is often cited by critics of Rose's approach to mothering. "I never saw her with her arms up, outstretched," said Spalding. "I never saw her in any easy, sophisticated position— by sophisticated I mean a woman who knew that her son needs some fondling and so she rumples his hair or something like that. That is not Mrs. Kennedy. I doubt if she ever rumpled the kid's hair in his whole life." Spalding's insights on the quality of Rose's maternal care of Jack are highly questionable, however, considering that he didn't come to know the Kennedys until Jack was twenty-three years old.

Columnist Arthur Krock, a family friend, described Rose as "a marvelous mother, calm, serene, reserved, extremely well educated but nothing stuffy about her." The Kennedy children may have been hobbled by too much prescribed behavior and regulated activity. But as Goodwin contended, "Living in the shadow of the disintegrating twenties—the dizzying decade of flappers and bootleggers, of sensuous music, scandals and fads—Rose believed that adherence to daily ritual offered the best hope for the family's survival." The only way to hold a family together, Rose believed, was to impose upon all the children time-tested ideals, uplifting Christian virtues, and excellent daily habits. In this way she hoped to resist the pressures of moral and social drift.[48]

Critics often quote the caustic remarks others heard Jack express about his mother, but they ignore his comments in praise of her. Inga Arvad Fejos, Jack's lover at the start of World War II, realized how deeply Jack felt about his mother. A "mother will always be a mother," she wrote him. "I am happy you love yours so much, and I understand why she is so fond of you." "She's not as forceful as my father, but she was the glue," he often said. "I thought she was a very model mother for a big family." He specifically credited her with stimulating and encouraging his interest in reading, and appreciated that she spent many hours reading to him as a boy. "She was great on self-improvement," he said. "She always saw to it that we read good books, had good conversation." Jack thought he inherited curiosity from his mother. During foreign trips together, he watched her face light up as she experienced a new city. "Whenever Mother traveled anywhere," Jack told Billings, "her eyes were so bright and so gay and her enthusiasm so contagious that she could not help but attract everyone who came in contact with her."[49]

Although subsequent critics mocked Rose, Dr. L. Emmett Holt and Dr. John Watson might have selected her as an exemplar of their approach to modern and progressive child care.

4

CHILDISH, IRRESPONSIBLE BOY

Throughout Jack's childhood, Joe and Rose worried about his health, but they worried about something else as well: his lack of diligence in his studies. "Or, let us say," Rose pointedly observed, "lack of 'fight' in trying to do well in those subjects that didn't happen to interest him."

In his teenage years Jack was impulsive and undisciplined, yet witty and charming; although a poor student, he displayed intellectual promise. Careless and untidy, he nonetheless had a winning way with friends and young women.

When Joe Jr. was ready for high school, his father selected Choate, an exclusive college-preparatory school attended by the sons of many upper-class Yankee families. In 1930 thirteen-year-old Jack entered eighth grade at Canterbury, a Catholic boys' boarding school in New Milford, Connecticut, the only Catholic school he ever attended. Perhaps Rose insisted on some Catholic training for her second-oldest. In any case, Jack could escape the squabbling with his overbearing older brother; for a while at least, the two Kennedys went their separate ways.[1]

Canterbury required each student to write a weekly letter home, and Jack wrote often. Shortly after school started, on September 24, 1930, he scrawled to grandfather Honey Fitz: "Its [sic] a pretty good place but I was pretty home sick the first night. You have a whole lot of religion and the studies are pretty hard."

Feeling isolated at Canterbury, he asked his father for a subscription to *Literary Digest* because he wanted to learn more about the "market slump." "Please send me some golf balls," he added.[2]

The religious atmosphere of the school didn't seem to bother him. He had chapel every morning and evening. "I will be quite pius [sic] I guess when I get home." One sermon particularly stimulated him. "We had Mass said this morning by a missionary who gave us one of the most interesting talks that I ever heard about India."

Playing football on the school's "small team," he displayed quickness and spunk and performed well enough to warrant mention in the school's newspaper. "Football practice is pretty hard and I am the lightest fellow about on the squad," he wrote his mother. "My nose my leg and other parts of my anatomy have been pushed around so much that it is beginning to be funny."[3]

Academically he didn't fare well. He did well in English and math, but nearly flunked Latin. When his Latin marks fell below passing, the headmaster informed the Kennedys what they already knew: "He can do better than this." Although lackadaisical and absentminded, Jack enjoyed reading. "We are reading *Ivanhoe* in English," he wrote to his father, "and though I may not be able to remember material things such as tickets, gloves and so on I can remember things like *Ivanhoe*, and the last time we had an exam on it, I got ninety-eight."

At choir practice he thought he sounded increasingly like the family's pet dog. "My voice must be changing, because when I go up it sounds as if Buddy was howling. I go up another note and Buddy is choking. Another note and Buddy and me have gasped our last."[4]

Mysteriously, he was often tired and sick and wasn't gaining weight. He had hives, and complained about an eye problem and a cold. "I was weighed yesterday and I have lost one pound and have not grown at all." Nelson Hume, the headmaster at Canterbury, made a mission of improving Jack's health. He wrote Joe Kennedy that he was taking "immediate charge" of Jack's weight. The headmaster added more milk to Jack's diet, increased "digestible fats and vitamins," and required him to rest for three quarters of an hour in the late afternoon.

During Mass, Jack wrote on one occasion, "I began to get sick, dizzy and weak. I just about fainted and everything began to get black." In the infirmary he was placed on a diet of rice and potatoes, "which ain't too appetizing."[5]

In late April 1931, he suffered an attack of appendicitis and underwent an appendectomy, and he was withdrawn from school on May 2 to recuperate at home. He never returned to Canterbury, but the school gave him credit for the full year.

For Jack's freshman year in high school the Kennedy's decided to change schools. Joe Jr.'s growing maturity and success at Choate impressed his father, who decided to send Jack there as well, hoping for similar results. Rose wrote Choate's headmaster, George St. John, that Jack hated routine work but loved English and history and that he had a very attractive personality. So for the next four years, Jack would attend Choate. Trying to measure up to his brother's standard proved frustrating, though, leading Jack to seek less acceptable means of gaining attention and earning respect from friends.[6]

Founded in 1896, Choate was a boys boarding school located in Wallingford, Connecticut, a few miles north of New Haven, and sixty miles from the Kennedy home in Bronxville, New York. Its beautiful, spacious, elm-shaded campus included athletic fields, a chapel, a gymnasium, an infirmary, classrooms, and rooming houses. The school's graduates usually went on to prestigious universities, including Harvard, Yale, and Princeton.

Among Choate's distinguished alumni were novelist John Dos Passos ('11) and lyricist Alan Jay Lerner ('36). Choate was also the alma mater of two people John Kennedy came to know well: Chester Bowles Jr. ('19), a congressman, governor of Connecticut, State Department official, and ambassador to India; and Adlai E. Stevenson ('18), governor of Illinois, two-time Democratic nominee for President, and U.S. ambassador to the United Nations.[7]

Choate had Episcopalian roots, and two of its headmasters had been ordained priests of the Episcopal Church. Its most famous director—or "head"—was the Reverend George St. John, who served in that capacity for forty years. He and his wife, Clara, made Choate one of the country's foremost private schools. St. John immersed himself in the life of the school, down to the smallest, trivial detail. Most students found him scary and inscrutable. The enforcer of rules, his punishment of transgressors was reputed to be harsh, inflexible, and final.

Divided into groups of fifteen to twenty, the boys lived in tree-shaded shingled cottages which served as their sleeping quarters, study rooms, and social centers. Housemasters, living in close community with the students, served as tutors and advisers to their charges—as well as disciplinarians.

If a boy didn't cooperate or work up to his potential, Choate informed parents of the reasons, and the strategy the school would use to solve the problem. Each teacher (or "master") wrote a report about each boy in his class, in his house, in athletics, and in all outside activities. Stern warnings might be issued, but the tone was supposed to be optimistic and hopeful. Then George St. John, assisted by his wife, laboriously collated and edited the four thousand reports on the five hundred young men, added his personal summaries, and mailed them to the parents.[8]

In Jack's freshman year (the third "form" in the parlance of Choate) his housemaster was Earl Leinbach. Blond, blue-eyed, athletic, "Cap" Leinbach had been a World War I military intelligence captain in France and Germany, and was one of Choate's most respected and admired faculty members. He taught a full schedule of math classes and coached three different sports.

Jack's roommate as a freshman was Godfrey Kauffmann. At loggerheads within a few weeks, the two boys drew a chalk line down the middle of their room, creating an invisible wall which neither crossed. Because of their different temperaments, Jack and Godfrey frequently asked to be separated, but when the rooming committee agreed to separate them, the boys changed their minds and remained together.[9]

Leinbach quickly realized that Jack had much potential but little self-discipline. On his IQ test Jack had scored 119, placing him in the top 20 percent of Choate students, but the test measured only capacity, not achievement.

Leinbach required Jack to attend a conference every day on a course he was failing. For a while, Leinbach went over Jack's French and Latin vocabularies with him every night, and didn't allow him to leave his room during the study period. Leinbach thought Jack's trouble stemmed from immaturity and inability to concentrate. More positively, he reported, "What makes the whole problem difficult is Jack's winning smile and charming personality. It is an inescapable fact that his actions are *really* amusing and evoke real hilarity."

Jack's antipathy for rules surfaced almost immediately. At the end of Jack's first week, Leinbach sounded the refrain that Joe and Rose would hear often during the next four years: "Rules bother him a bit."[10]

In December 1931, during Jack's first trip back to Bronxville, he wrote exultantly to his father, who was out of town, that while his older brother roughhoused in the hall at school, several sixth formers (seniors) caught and paddled him. "Did the sixth formers lick him. O Man he was all blisters, they almost paddled the life out of him. What I wouldn't have given to be a sixth former."

At the end of his freshman year Jack had failed both French and Latin and barely passed algebra. Mr. Davis, his French teacher, was fond of Jack, but couldn't inspire him to learn French. "There is actually very little except physical violence that I haven't tried!" Davis reported. "His papers are chaotic, and he invariably forgets books, pencil or paper."[11]

In his report Cap Leinbach wrote, "Jack is emotionally willing and really wants to do a good job. Until he came here, I do not think he was held strictly to well-defined tasks or well-regulated routine. Mentally Jack is well-equipped and will in time be able to cope efficiently. Impulsive actions characterize every move, but very rarely are any of them malicious—just adolescent whims and fancies. This habit lends inconsistency to his scholastic drive with resultant mediocrity."

Leinbach inspected Jack's room twice every day, and always found the floor cluttered with articles of every description. "When he sees me enter the room, he will at once start to put everything in order. He does it willingly and often remarks, 'I never get away with anything in this house.'"

Headmaster St. John broke the bad news to Joseph Kennedy. "We have a real job on our hands, one bigger than we could accomplish in one year," he wrote. He urged that Jack attend summer school. Joe Kennedy agreed, and Jack attended the summer session from August 7 to September 15, 1932, to review his Latin, French, and algebra.[12]

Jack's sophomore year was his best at Choate. Eugene Musser, his housemaster, concluded in his final report: "An ever-increasing maturity and sense of responsibility. His improvement in the house has been really remarkable. Very much on the job—most friendly and anxious to cooperate. This extends even to the neatness of his room."

Academically Jack enjoyed his first taste of success. In English he displayed a flair for reading and writing, although he was still plagued by work that demanded close attention. His English teacher commended his "splendid final examination," while pointing out his terrible spelling: "attemp, jelousy, comming, and sieze." At the end of that year Jack earned an 81 in English, a 71 in algebra, a 69 in Latin, and a 73 in French.[13]

Jack's antics, wit, and personality had broad appeal among his classmates. Most of his friends were athletes, but his closest friend and lifelong companion was not. Jack took on some of the reflected glory of Texans Bob Beach and Butch Schriber, both outstanding athletes. New Yorker Ralph Horton, the son of a beer distributor, was also a good athlete and a Catholic. (Horton and Jack went off campus to attend Mass on Sunday and seldom missed.)

Olive Cawley, Jack's first serious girlfriend, often attended Choate dances with Jack and knew his friends. She first met Jack when she was invited to a Choate dance by one of Jack's friends. When the friend fell ill, Jack agreed to pick her up at the Wallingford train station. The tousle-haired youth who met her in khakis and sneakers stated in his Bostonian twang: "I'm Jack Kennedy and I have to take care of you for the weekend. But I'm in love with Ruth Moffett, so don't fall in love with me." Cawley commented: "I promptly did!"

Cawley described Jack as witty, clever, and mischievous. "He was always surrounded by excitement. In the group that traveled together, Jack called the shots: where they would go, what they would do. His friends were the satellites, especially LeMoyne."[14]

Jack met LeMoyne Billings in the spring of 1933 while Jack served on the business board of *The Brief,* the school yearbook, and Billings was the advertising manager. Billings was Jack's first intimate friend, and they remained friends until Kennedy died. They roomed together during their final two years at Choate.

Billings came from Pittsburgh, where his father, a physician, had lost heavily in the 1929 crash and died early in 1933. His family impoverished, Billings went to Choate as a lowly scholarship student. With his high forehead, grizzly-bearish appearance, and awkward manner, Lem was physically unattractive.

Lem shared a major burden with Jack. Both were second sons who had for years submitted to bullying, patronizing older brothers who were highly successful and admired. Young Joe Kennedy, '33, had been vice president of the St. Andrews Society (a charitable organization), a letterman on the undefeated football team of 1932, and the winner of the Harvard Football Trophy for the Choate football player who best combined "scholarship and sportsmanship."

At Choate, F. Tremaine "Josh" Billings Jr., '29, captained the varsity football team, was president of his class, and served as editor in chief of *The Brief.* Later an academic and football star at Princeton, Josh earned a Rhodes Scholarship and went into medicine. "He was pretty tough to follow," said Lem. "It was a constant concern to try to keep up with him."[15]

Billings often double-dated with Jack, but he never married. His voice—a high, nasal whine—contributed to the belief among some of Jack's friends that Billings was gay. Ralph Horton assumed Billings was a homosexual. Horton claimed that for those friends of Jack's who disdained homosexuality, Billings complicated their relationship with Jack because Billings was so often with him. Horton assumed that Jack knew Billings was gay and simply accepted it. "Jack was a hell of a forgiving guy. He was terribly understanding." No other reliable evidence, though, indicates that Billings was a homosexual or that JFK knew of it. Their extensive correspondence makes no reference to Billings being gay.

Some of Jack's friends disliked Billings, judging him shallow and simply a foil to Jack. "Billings is one of the guys that never grew up," said one of Jack's friends. "He was just a clown." Joseph P. Kennedy, however, believed that Billings's dedication to Jack—and subsequently to other Kennedy children—was strong, enduring, and beneficial.[16]

In the summer of 1933 Billings spent several weeks with the Kennedys at Hyannis Port amidst the extraordinary commotion of nine Kennedy chil-

dren and their parents, nurses, governesses, cousins, and pets. The daily schedule of vigorous activity was far more rigorous than anything he had ever encountered. He swam, ran, and sailed, played tennis, softball, and touch football.
He learned that winning was necessary to be invited back. He had

> dropped passes (Jack's); rushed in too fast on the enemy quarterback
> (Jack's older brother, Joe); run some more (faster this time, away from
> Joe); been teased (by Jack's sister Kathleen); joked about (by Jack's nine-
> year-old brother, Robert); teased again (by Jack's thirteen-year-old sister,
> Eunice); teased some more (by Jack's ten-year-old sister, Patricia); pawed
> over (by a variety of more or less friendly dogs); and, finally, allowed to
> take a shower.[17]

During the summers, sailing was Jack's favorite sport. The Kennedys
owned a series of sailboats—the first in 1927, christened by Joe Jr. and Jack
the *Rose Elizabeth* for their mother. That summer at Cohasset the two boys,
relaxing on the veranda of their father's cottage after a sailing race, noticed
an overturned boat in the harbor. Dashing back to the *Rose Elizabeth,* they
sailed out into the open sea again and managed, after some difficulty, to pull
an exhausted man, one Ralph Russell, into their boat, and brought him safely
to shore.

Probably prodded by the boys' doting grandfather, Honey Fitz, the *Boston
Post* described the rescue as "daring" and referred to the boys as "champions." Their action did indicate early signs of initiative, self-reliance, and
courage. At the time Joe Jr. was twelve and Jack only ten.

Joe and Rose ordered the two youngsters to stay inside the breakwater,
where watchful eyes could see them in case they capsized or fell overboard.
Joe Sr. used his powerboat to observe them during some races, all the while
prodding them to improve. Why was your sail not as large as the other boat's?
Why was it flapping while the other boat's sail was straight? The other boat
won the race and you didn't. Why? On one occasion, when the two
Kennedy boys countered that their sails were three years old, Joe Sr. firmly
told them they should have tended to that problem earlier. "If you're in a
race, do it right," he bellowed. "Come in a winner; second place is no
good."[18]

Joe Jr. and Jack criticized and kidded each other about their sailing competition, claiming to be "out for blood." "If one brother's sail was a bit wrin-
kled or not properly trimmed, it seldom escaped the critical eye of the
other," said J. Julius Fanta, a student of Jack's sailing career. If Jack or Joe
made a mistake in a race, inadvertently letting an opponent take advantage,
the erring skipper faced the music afterward.

As a racing skipper, Jack was clever at the helm, often outwitting his opponents in maneuvers and catching his rivals flat-footed. Hank Searls, Joe Jr.'s biographer, described the Kennedy boys' approach to racing: "The goal was victory, the style wild: split-second timing at the start, recklessness at the windward buoy, disregard for the risk of a tiny misjudgment." Both Joe and Jack carried full canvas while others reefed, expertly sensed the hint of breeze in light winds, and developed an uncommon touch on the tiller. Parents of other racers were leery of having their children race the Kennedys; it seemed futile to have their own children get beat again by Joe Jr., Jack, or Eunice.

As the children became more proficient sailors, Joe Sr. added to the fleet. The Wianno junior class of rugged sixteen-foot sloops was a local favorite, and the Kennedy family soon had two swinging at anchor: the *Tenovus* and the *One More*. Joe Sr. bought secondhand a twenty-five-foot Wianno senior with a small cuddy for overnight trips which Jack named the *Victura* ("Something to do with winning," he said). With the *Victura* Jack enjoyed his greatest competitive successes. The Kennedys hired a series of "skippers," usually older men and skilled sailors who maintained the boats and supervised the children's sailing activities.[19]

Fanta described one extraordinary race during Jack's teenage years. The summer had been scorching hot with little breeze. Fed up with the light winds and calms, Jack yearned for a brisk wind to provide plenty of action. "He got it shortly before school opened when the vanguard of Fall blustered in with a healthy blow out of the sou'east," said Fanta. "The wind-swept waters of Nantucket Sound were thrashed into frothing seas that piled through the unprotected opening in the Hyannis Port breakwater."

Jack had personally crafted a new mahogany tiller, and was anxious to experiment with it. (Proud of making his own sailing equipment, he kept his boats shipshape, maintaining their appearance with paint and varnish he applied himself.)

When officials called off the race because of the danger, Jack dissented. "What are you going to do when it [really] blows?" Jack protested. "C'mon, fellas, let's have a race of our own."

"Are you nuts?" said brother Joe.

"We've been out in worse weather. What are we, a bunch of sissies?"

All twelve of his fellow skippers expressed their willingness to race, despite the weather and the protests of their elders, but only five remained undaunted and showed up at the starting line.

Before hoisting his sail, Jack unbolted the old tiller and installed his sleek new one. He tossed the discarded one through the companionway into the cabin, expecting to throw it in the garbage later. While maneuvering the *Victura* near the starting line, though, Jack suddenly heard a crack, and discovered his new tiller had broken.

Falling behind at the start, he reattached his old tiller and tore after his rivals, including Joe Jr. Despite his poor start, "Jack ran through the fleet and was fighting it out tooth and nail. . . . Foot by foot and yard by yard, Jack crashed through wave after wave as he gained steadily with only a hundred yards to go. Battling equally hard, Joe inched ahead to increase his lead; but Jack countered every move until he finally nosed ahead with a mere over-lap, or a half-boatlength, to win."

Afterward, instead of the usual hazing and criticism, Jack found himself basking in congratulations from his admiring rivals. Even brother Joe pounded him on the back. "The race," concluded Fanta, "was not only long talked about but also well-remembered."[20]

In the fall of 1933, Jack started his junior year at Choate, the first without his brother Joe, who was studying in London. The year inaugurated a struggle between the demands of John Maher, a strong and disciplined housemaster, and the immature behavior of two fun-loving, self-centered young trouble-makers, Kennedy and Billings. An Irish-Catholic bachelor and history teacher, John Maher was highly respected by the school's administration as a leader of men. "I am glad Jack is with Mr. Maher," St. John wrote Joe Kennedy. "There is no finer man on earth."

Jack disagreed. Writing his father that he and Billings were on Mr. Maher's corridor, Jack said, "We are practically rooming with him which is more then [sic] we bargained for." Jack grew to despise Maher, whom he considered short-tempered, bullying, and a constant nag.[21]

Jack was full of practical jokes. After lights were out, he entered the room of the student council president and turned his radio to full blast, then dashed out of the room before the tubes warmed up. One winter Rose sent a crate of oranges from Florida, but instead of savoring the fruit, he opened his window and pegged them at fellow students. On another occasion, he led a gang of students in collecting hundreds of pillows and put them in a student's room, filling it from top to bottom. When the boy returned to his room and opened his door, he faced a solid wall of pillows.

In November 1933, Joe Kennedy visited Choate to watch Jack play football. Jack was a tackle and, according to Coach Leinbach, was aggressive, alert, and a "tower of strength on the line."

During his visit Joe became deeply disturbed with Jack's overall attitude. "I can't tell you how unhappy I felt in seeing and talking with Jack," he wrote George St. John. "He seems to lack entirely a sense of responsibility. His happy-go-lucky manner with a degree of indifference does not portend well for his future development." The father conceded that he and Rose may have been partly responsible by spoiling him, "by having secretaries and maids following him to see that he does what he should do, and he places too little confidence on his own reliance." Joe asked young Joe to write Jack setting forth "some ideas that will give him a sense of responsibility."[22]

St. John boldly advised Joe on better parental relations. "I asked Jack if he had a good chance to talk with you when you were here," St. John replied, "and he said that there really wasn't much time. He said that you had more time to talk with some of the masters than him, and that when you talked with him, you were of course 'rather peeved.' "

St. John recommended two strategies: "One, follow him up and check him all the time; two, treat him as a man and show that we have confidence in him."

As always St. John concluded with a note of optimism. "I would be willing to bet that within two years you will be as proud of Jack as you are of Joe."

Jack intensely disliked math and physics and refused to apply himself in those courses. In English he enjoyed poems and short essays; novels and biographies took too much of his time. He had a flair for phrasemaking and style. But his teachers complained of the gap between his high potential and his daily performance. "He was not very studious," agreed a classmate. He "was continually trying to get me to do his trigonometry."[23]

Brown graduate Harold Tinker, a specialist on the English poet and novelist Thomas Hardy, was another of Jack's English teachers. He liked Jack and saw potential in him. Tinker judged Jack's spelling and punctuation erratic, but his vocabulary exceptionally good. When Tinker explained something, Jack was often gazing out the window, apparently daydreaming. But after class Jack asked trenchant questions showing depth of understanding. "He learned not what you wanted him to learn, but what he wanted to learn."

Jack enjoyed the poetry of Robert Frost. His face lit up when Tinker quoted a line from Frost, "Happiness makes up in height for what it lacks in length." The English teacher contrasted Frost's view with the pessimistic perspective of Thomas Hardy, who said, "Happiness is but the occasional episode in the general drama of pain." Kennedy preferred the optimism of Frost.[24]

In one fascinating essay, written in April 1934 for advanced English composition, Kennedy addressed the problem of justice. How can a Christian God allow evil in the world? Specifically, how can God be just when people are born into widely different circumstances?

Justice is always linked with God, he began. "But should this be so? To quote Webster, justice means 'The rendering to everyone his just due.' But does God render to everyone his just due?"

He alluded to his own grand upbringing when he continued:

A boy is born in a rich family, brought up in [a] clean environment with an excellent education and good companions, inherits a foolproof business from his father, is married and then eventually dies a just and honest man. Take the other extreme. A boy is born in the slums, of a poor family, has evil companions, no education, becomes a loafer, as that is all there is to do, turns into a drunken bum, and dies, worthless. Was it because of the [rich] boys abylity [*sic*] that he landed in the lap of luxery [*sic*], or was it the poor boys fault that he was born in squalor? The answer will often come back "The poor boy will get his reward in the life hereafter if he is good." While that is a dubious prospect to many of us, yet [there is] something in it. But how much better chance has [the] boy born with a silver spoon in his mouth of being good than the boy who from birth is surrounded by rottenness and filth. This even to the most religious of us can hardly seem a "square deal." Thus we see that justice is not always received from "The Most Just" so how can we poor mortals ever hope to attain it.

Kennedy doubted that the unfortunate, living in poverty and squalor, would benefit much from the traditional Christian notion that things will even out in heaven, where they will get their reward. Heaven is supposed to reward those who live a good life on earth. Yet the disparities of environment and upbringing make living a morally good life much more daunting for those born into poverty and squalor. So the problem of injustice remains.

Given the problem, if people on earth didn't strive to overcome injustice, no one else would. More than just the guilt of a young rich boy who sympathized with the downtrodden, his perspective showed a spark of social conscience, his awareness of the metaphysical injustice in life for which Christianity had no answer.[25]

Jack loved the American history course he took from Harvard graduate Russell Ayers. "He read a great deal of history," Billings recalled. "As a matter of fact he read a great deal generally while he was at school. . . . He had a tremendous interest in history, and I think he carried this all the way through his life."

While reading, he seemed oblivious of anything else, deeply concentrating in a way he seldom did with the classes he didn't like or the rules he didn't choose to obey. "It was a real source of irritation to me," said Billings, "that, if he were reading and I [was] talking to him, it was honestly just the same as if he had earplugs. He really didn't hear. . . . I learned to never talk to him while he was reading, because there was no point in doing so."[26]

Kennedy also enjoyed reading about current events. Rose's tenacious insistence that her children keep up with the news took hold with Jack. "In those days, it wasn't the ordinary boy who subscribed to *The New York Times* in prep school," said a classmate. "But Jack did, and as far as I know, he was the only one who did." At sixteen, said Tinker, Jack knew more about the world than most men of thirty. He read the editorial pages of newspapers rather than just the sports sections. Tinker thought that the Kennedy family dinner table was Jack's classroom in political and international affairs; it was Jack's parents, not Choate, who most effectively stimulated Jack's mind.[27]

Jack probably missed more classes because of illness than any other boy at Choate. In four years Rose Kennedy wrote scores of letters to school officials, particularly to Clara St. John, the headmaster's wife, most of them focusing on the many ailments afflicting her son. Repeatedly in the infirmary, Jack suffered from chronic colds, pinkeye, flu, swollen glands, boils, scraped legs, injured knees, and fallen arches. There were ten letters alone focusing on the fallen arches. "Regarding the condition of Jack's feet," Rose wrote in March 1933, "his fallen arches are . . . [an] inherited weakness and he has persisted in wearing cheap, rubber soled shoes during the last two or three years."

Jack also had major orthodontic work, and in the fall of 1934, an eye doctor found a small degree of nearsightedness in his right eye and a little farsighted astigmatism in his left.[28]

In January 1932, a cold put Jack in the infirmary, resulting in another flurry of letters between school officials and Rose. "Mr. St. John would give him a high A for taking all his study books with him," Clara St. John wrote Rose. "Jack is picturesque in his lavender bathrobe and green and lavender pajamas!" Rose suggested that the school give him Kepler's malt and cod liver oil.

Throughout his bouts with illness, Jack remained stoic, like his mother, and never complained except jokingly. His wry sense of humor endeared him to the medical staff. When hives covered his entire body, doctors told him that they were delighted to have the trouble come to the surface. Jack responded, "Gee! The doctors must be having a happy day today!"[29]

There was nothing funny about the mysterious and frightening disease Jack developed in January 1934. No one at Choate could diagnose it, and he was losing weight. On February 6, 1934, Jack had his first meal in a long time and said, "It was just as well that they decided to give me breakfast; if they hadn't, I think the nurse would have come in pretty soon and looked in my bed and not been able to see me at all." St. John wrote to Rose, "We are still puzzled as to the cause of Jack's trouble." He was hospitalized in New Haven, missed several months of school, and recuperated in Palm Beach. He returned to Choate after Easter.

Doctors initially feared he had leukemia and regularly checked his blood count. They never diagnosed the illness conclusively, but Dr. William Murphy of Boston settled on agranulocytosis, a rare disease that impairs the production of granulated white blood cells by bone marrow. The depletion of granulocytes resulted in severe respiratory infections, ulcers in the mouth and colon, high fever, and physical and mental exhaustion. Left untreated, the fatality rate was high. Dr. Murphy strongly urged that Jack be injected with liver extract every eight hours.

When Jack arrived at Palm Beach, he weighed only 125 pounds. Joe wrote young Joe that Dr. Murphy planned to prepare an article about Jack's illness "because it is only one of the few recoveries of a condition bordering on leuchemia [sic], and it was the general impression of the doctors that his chances were about five out of one hundred that he ever could have lived. He is still taking the treatments, and I am going to have him go to the Mayo Clinic at the close of school."[30]

Once Jack returned to Choate, his behavior again deeply irritated Maher. "Jack is such a complete individualist in theory and practice that the ordinary appeals of group spirit and social consciousness (even to the plea of not walking on the other fellow's feet) have no effect," Maher lamented. "When he discovered that no one was getting particularly excited about his silly game, or that he was playing the simpleton to his own amusement, the game lost its zest. And now for the first time I'm beginning to hope a little that Jack has learned to distinguish between liberty and license."[31]

Jack spent most of June 1934 at the Mayo Clinic in Rochester, Minnesota, undergoing a battery of tests. When he entered the hospital, he complained of cramping, abdominal pain, and alternating bouts of diarrhea and constipation. Jack wryly reported to Billings that all the staff thought he was an "interesting case," but continued, "Nobody [is] able to figure what's wrong with me." He added, "God, what a beating I'm taking. I've lost 8 lbs. and still going down." In another letter he wrote nonchalantly, "I've got something wrong with my intestines—in other words I shit blood."

One of Joe Kennedy's friends, Kay Halle, visited Jack in the hospital and discovered him among a pile of books. "He was so surrounded by books I could hardly see him. I was very impressed, because at that point this very young child was reading *The World Crisis* by Winston Churchill."[32]

In late June Jack worried that he wouldn't be out of the hospital until July 4. "Shit!!!" He told Billings that his "penis looks as if it has been run through a wringer. The poor beaten red lethal implement." He claimed to have had "18 enemas in 3 days!!! I'm clean as a whistle. They give me enemas till it comes out like drinking water which they all take a sip of." Then he described the "most harassing experience of my life," an incident that happened the previous day. Doctors had given him five enemas.

I was white as snow inside. They then put me on a thing like a barber's chair. Instead of sitting in the chair I kneeled on something that resembles a foot rest with my head where the seat is. Then [a blonde] took my pants down!! Then they tipped the chair over. Then surrounded by nurses the doctor first stuck his finger up my ass. I just blushed because you know how it is. He wiggled it suggestively and I rolled 'em in the aisles by saying 'you have a good motion'!! He then withdrew his finger. And then, the shmuck stuck an iron tube 12 inches long and 1 inch in diameter up my ass. They had a flashlight inside it and they looked around. Then they blew a lot of air in me to pump up my bowels. I was certainly feeling great as I know you would having a lot of strangers looking up my asshole. . . . I was a bit glad when they had their fill of that. My poor bedraggled rectum is looking at me very reproachfully these days.[33]

Tests of his colon were normal. Paul O'Leary, his primary physician at the Mayo Clinic, didn't mention agranulocytosis in his report. O'Leary concluded that Jack had a blood infection and a decrease in the number of white cells. "When the bone marrow was stopped, the white cells dropped to 3400 but picked up again to 5800 when he started it again." In addition, "We found Jack to be an allergic type of boy." He was allergic to dogs, cats, horses, and house dust. O'Leary recommended that Jack be treated with bone marrow, receive plenty of rest, and avoid strenuous exercise.

Some accounts assume that the 1934 illness was the onset of Addison's disease, diagnosed thirteen years later, but the doctor who later treated his Addison's disease categorically ruled out that possibility.

Just before Jack's senior year, Joe updated St. John about Jack's condition, and added, "If there is the slightest tendency to a relapse, he would have to be taken out of school for a year." Throughout his senior year the medical staff at Choate closely monitored his blood count and always found it normal.[34]

During Jack's junior year the inevitable Mae West movie arrived in Wallingford. When the theater placed a life-size cardboard cutout of Mae's famous figure on display in front of the movie house, Jack and Billings swiped it, transported it back to school, and put it under the covers in one of their beds.

At the age of seventeen, Ralph Horton related, Jack lost his virginity. Horton already had some experience with sex; now it was time for Kennedy and Billings. All three took a cab to a whorehouse in Harlem, and after watching a "dirty show," for three dollars Jack had sexual relations with a white prostitute in a room. Billings followed suit. Billings and Jack returned in a panic to the apartment of Horton's parents in New York. "They were frightened to death they'd get VD," said Horton. "So I went with them to a hospital . . . where they got these salves and creams and a thing to shove up the penis to clean it out." Subsequently, though, Jack would adopt a far more casual attitude toward venereal disease.[35]

During his stay at the Mayo Clinic for most of June 1934, Jack filled his letters to Billings with sexual bravado. "I had an enema given by a beautiful blonde. That, my sweet, is the height of cheap thrills." "I have not [had an] orgasm for 6 days so feel kind of horny which has been increased by reading one of the dirtiest books I've ever seen."

During Jack's hospitalization in Minnesota, Billings badly scalded himself in a defective shower at the Kennedys' home in Hyannis Port. After three weeks of hospitalization, he recuperated at the Kennedy compound. For a while Billings's mother stayed at the Kennedys' home, nursing her son back to health. Alluding to his father's lechery, JFK warned Billings to "watch your mother and my father with an eagle eye."[36]

Jack hoped to go to Europe following his senior year and had apparently reached an understanding with his parents that he could make the trip if his grades improved. By the end of the first quarter of his senior year, though, Jack evidently worried that he couldn't fulfill his portion of the understanding. On December 4, 1934, he wrote to his father: "LeMoyne and I have been talking about how poorly we have done this quarter, and we have definitely decided to stop any fooling around. I really do realize how important it is that I get a good job done this year if I want to go to England. I really feel, now that I think it over, that I have been bluffing myself about how much real work I have been doing."[37]

Considering how much worry their underachieving son caused them, Rose thought that Joe's response was a model of reasonableness, which indeed it was. In reply to Jack's letter, Joe expressed "great satisfaction" over the "forthrightness and directness that you are usually lacking." He didn't want to nag, but after "long experience in sizing up people I definitely know you have the goods and you can go a long way. Now aren't you foolish not to get all there is out of what God has given you?. . . . I will not be disappointed if you don't turn out to be a real genius, but I think you can be a really worthwhile citizen with good judgment and good understanding."[38]

Unfortunately, Jack didn't have the self-discipline to follow through on his good intentions, and was nearly kicked out of Choate for his shenanigans.

In October 1934, Maher reported that after a "poor" start Jack was "improving." "Works best . . . if not hammered too hard or too often." But by January 1935, Maher was ready to throw in the towel. After a conference with Jack and Lem, Maher wrote to St. John: "I'm afraid it would be almost foolishly optimistic to expect anything but the most mediocre from Jack. He'd like to be a 'somebody' in school, but as in practically everything else, he wants to sit back and have it all fall into his lap, standing off on the sidelines catcalling and criticizing those who do things. . . . I'm afraid I must admit my own failure as well as his."

After reading one of Maher's despairing reports on Jack, George St. John pondered his next approach. "See Jack and LeMoyne and give them thunder," he wrote in a memo. "They need it. Can we separate them? Not feasible. Would a gland specialist help overcome this strange childishness?" In a letter to Jack's father, St. John took up the idea: "Jack is the most childish, irresponsible sixth form boy in his house. If Jack were my son, I believe I should take him to a gland specialist."[39]

Part of the daily schedule at Choate was compulsory evening chapel, which started about twenty minutes after supper. Seniors could have radios and phonographs, and Jack and Billings had excellent ones, making their room a popular and convenient meeting spot for their friends to visit between supper and chapel. Jack and Billings decided to form a club—and only club members could be in the room during that period. Thirteen boys eventually became members.

"Ten percent of the boys at Choate are *muckers*," St. John had thundered during a sermon in evening chapel in the fall of 1934. The typical "mucker" was a "bad apple," a boy who misbehaved in class, acted impiously in chapel, and made a general nuisance of himself. St. John would not tolerate muckers.[40]

Reflecting on the headmaster's sermon, Billings and Kennedy mischievously decided to call their gang the Choate Muckers Club. For twelve dollars each member purchased a small gold charm designed in the shape of a shovel and engraved with the initials "C.M.C." All members were seniors, and very hostile to the student council, which they apparently thought was too officious; most were athletes, including the captains of four varsity sports. They shared another characteristic: "We liked to bug people," said Ralph Horton.[41]

One plan they half joked about was to bring gold shovels and a pile of horse manure to Spring Festivities and have photographs taken on the dance floor. When George St. John got wind of the club's activities, he devised a draconian solution. On February 11, 1935, at lunch in the school's dining hall, St. John read off the names of the thirteen offenders and demanded their presence in his study immediately after lunch. There he expelled the boys and ordered them to pack their trunks and make arrangements to leave Choate immediately. He would notify their parents. Then he dismissed them.

St. John contacted all their parents. "Will you please make every effort to come to Choate on Saturday for a conference we think a necessity," he wired

Joe Kennedy. Although busy as chairman of the Securities and Exchange Commission, Kennedy wired back that he would arrive at Choate on February 18.[42]

Joe, Jack, and St. John met together in the head's study, where St. John recited chapter and verse of all the offenses. Jack's attitude turned "to considerable sorrow," St. John recalled. Joe Kennedy completely supported the headmaster. "I've always been very grateful to him," said St. John.

After the expulsions, a compassionate assistant headmaster apparently persuaded St. John to reduce the sentence to strict probation. What's more, St. John kept the boys at school a few extra days during the Easter vacation. The boys, including Jack, had been duly chastened.[43]

After the Muckers incident, Choate gave three of the offenders the chance to visit the psychologist Prescott Lecky of Columbia University, and Jack took advantage of the opportunity. Lecky subsequently described Jack's psychological condition. Jack was very able, "but definitely in a trap, psychologically speaking," Lecky wrote. "He has established a reputation in the family for thoughtlessness, sloppiness, and inefficiency, and he feels entirely at home in the role. Any criticism he receives only serves to confirm the feeling that he has defined himself correctly. In fact the definition is the best possible defense that could be devised."

Lecky asked him, "How are you going to amount to anything if you have to be thoughtless and sloppy to be true to your role?" This stumped Jack. When Lecky pointed out the great handicap he would be under in the business world, Jack responded, "Yes, that is true enough."

Lecky continued his report: "He thinks of himself as a self-reliant, intelligent, and courageous boy, but he has never recognized the difficulty he will have in maintaining those definitions unless he sacrifices the defense devices that he has built up through the years."

In probing Jack's sibling rivalry with Joe Jr., Lecky struck a bull's-eye. "A good deal of his trouble is due to comparison with an older brother. Jack remarked, 'My brother is the efficient one in the family, and I am the boy that doesn't get things done. If my brother were not so efficient, it would be easier for me to be efficient. He does it so much better than I do.'" Lecky concluded, "Jack is apparently avoiding comparison and withdraws from the race, so to speak, in order to convince himself that he is not trying."[44]

At the end of Jack's senior year his classmates voted him "Most Likely to Succeed." Presumably, this astounded the administration, but the honor came only because of extensive lobbying by his friends. Classmate Paul Chase recalled that Jack's friends divided up the senior class, then pressured people on their list to vote for Jack. "The result was a one-sided victory for Jack." Chase continued that "it did not seem to me so astounding because even in

1935 Jack, although a mediocre student, had charm and a lot of drive and ambition."

In late April 1935, on Jack's application to Harvard, George St. John pointed out that Jack's illness in his junior year partly explained his mediocre academic record. "Jack has rather superior mental ability," St. John reported, "without the deep interest in his studies or the mature viewpoint that demands of him his best effort all the time." Still, St. John suggested that Jack would establish "a record in college more worthy [of] his natural gifts of intelligence, likableness, and popularity."[45]

Out of 110 students in his senior graduating class, Jack ranked sixty-fifth. He didn't win any literary or scholastic honors. Despite the widespread feeling that Joe Jr. outperformed Jack by a wide margin at Choate, their academic records were nearly identical. Joe Jr. graduated with a four-year average of 75; Jack had a 73.

By commencement in June 1935, there was evidence that Jack was becoming more mature. The crackdown by school and his parents, the discussion with the psychologist, and perhaps simply his growing older had had an effect. He completed the year with passing grades. In his final report, Maher wrote that recently Jack had been "meticulously punctual" and "as neat as his nature permitted." Jack, he continued, "has lost some of the feeling that every master is an enemy who has to be outwitted at every turn."[46]

In June Jack took the Harvard University entrance examinations and received an 85 percent in English and the same in history, both honors grades. "For a boy so often sick and who had been dramatically expelled from school only three months before," concluded Hamilton, "this . . . was no mean achievement."

Twenty-five years after graduating from Choate, John Kennedy somberly reflected on his high school years. "I didn't know what I wanted to do and I didn't do much of anything. I was just a drifter. I didn't really settle down seriously to study until the last couple years at Harvard. Why? I don't know."[47]

5

BROADENING
HORIZONS

To enhance the education of his two oldest boys, Joe Kennedy sought advice from one of America's great intellects, Felix Frankfurter of the Harvard Law School. Frankfurter privately detested Joe Kennedy, but nevertheless gave him excellent advice. "If they were mine," Frankfurter told Joe, "I know what I would do. I would send them to London to spend a year with Harold Laski, who is the greatest teacher in the world."

A political scientist and British Labour Party leader, Laski taught at the London School of Economics. By the mid-1930s Laski and the London School had become almost synonymous. He was such a brilliant lecturer, writer, and academic adviser that students from the United States, Asia, and Africa came to London to study under him. A prolific author and an active socialist politician, he advocated a modified form of Marxism and held a strong belief in personal freedom.[1]

Young Joe Kennedy had studied under Laski in 1934–1935. "I am a socialist," Laski would say, "though from time to time I shall prescribe other books as an antidote to my poison. If you disagree, come along to my study and tell me where I am wrong." Laski's real teaching took place in his home at the famous Laski Sunday teas. Laski developed deep affection for young Joe, later remarking, "He has often sat in my study and submitted with that smile that was pure magic to relentless teasing about his determination to be nothing less than President of the United States."

Remarkably, Joe and Rose allowed their two oldest sons to study abroad with a socialist professor whose prominent wife was an ardent leader of the birth-control movement. Later, asked about his open-minded decision, the capitalist Joe Kennedy responded, "I was confident that they were both mature enough and sensible enough to be able to hear the other side and still make a choice for themselves." His sons, he made clear, "are going to have a little money when they get older, and they should know what the have-nots are thinking and planning. . . . They should be exposed to someone of intelligence and vitality on the other side."[2]

In the fall of 1935, Joe, Rose, and Kathleen accompanied Jack to London aboard the *Normandie.* Joe had always stressed with his children the importance of teamwork and cooperation, so when he met Lawrence Fisher, one of the brothers who had founded Fisher Body, a division of General Motors, he sent word to "find Jack." Jack came running up to his father's deck chair, hair tousled, necktie flying, and said, "Dad, I've been playing deck tennis." Joe responded, "Jack, I want you to meet Mr. Lawrence Fisher, a top official of General Motors, because I want you to see what brothers can do who work together."

Jack had other concerns on board besides deck tennis and meeting prominent businessmen. "There is a fat Frenche aboard who is a 'homo,'" Jack wrote Billings on September 29. "He has had me to his cabin more than once and is trying to bed me."

After he arrived in London, Jack studied under Laski only briefly—no more than a week—before becoming ill, apparently with hepatitis. "He was a sick man," Frida Laski recalled. Later, to bolster his academic credentials, Jack would lie about the length of time he studied under Laski, telling reporters that following his graduation from Choate he attended the London School of Economics as a special student of Laski for "three months." (Sometimes he said "six months.")[3]

Joe and Rose decided that he should return home to be closer to his doctors. Meanwhile, Jack had convinced his father to let him enroll at Princeton instead of Harvard because Billings and Ralph Horton were both enrolled there. On October 21, 1935, Billings received a wire: ARRIVING PRINCETON THURSDAY AFTERNOON. HOPE YOU CAN ARRANGE ROOMING—KEN.

Billings, who was rooming with Horton, could afford his share of cheap housing only on campus, a dumpy two-bedroom apartment with a living room on the fourth floor of South Reunion Hall. Seventy-two steps separated the bedroom from the bathroom below.

When Jack arrived, he agreed that the apartment was awful, but none of the three seemed to mind. They often joked about it, counting off loudly each of the seventy-two steps as they ascended from the bathroom.

Shortly after Jack enrolled at Princeton, his father wrote him an affectionate letter, urging him to monitor his health until Thanksgiving, when they would reassess his condition and his ability to remain in school.

> After all, the only consideration I have in the whole matter is your happiness, and I don't want you to lose a year of your college life (which ordinarily brings great pleasure to a boy) by wrestling with a bad physical condition and a jam in your studies. A year is important, but it isn't so important if it's going to leave a mark for the rest of your life. So let's give it a try until Thanksgiving and see if you are showing any improvement, then you and I will discuss what's best to do.
>
> You know I really think you are a pretty good guy and my only interest is in doing what is best for you.

It was a happy but brief autumn for the three roommates of South Reunion. After only two months at Princeton, Jack's illness forced him to withdraw from school during the Christmas holiday.[4]

When he left Princeton, Jack entered Peter Bent Brigham Hospital in Boston for two months of observation and tests. "My blood count this morning was 3500," he wrote Billings on January 18, 1936. "When I came it was 6,000. At 1500 you die. They call me '2,000 to go Kennedy.'" He was allowed to leave the hospital on weekends, but his social life bored him. He was "getting rather fed up with the meat [women] up here," he told Billings at the end of January; he was anxious to get down to Palm Beach.

"They haven't found out anything as yet," he told his friend, adding about his misdiagnosed condition, "except that I have leukemia, and agranalecencytosis [sic]. Took a peek at my chart yesterday and could see that they were mentally measuring me for a coffin. Eat, drink, and make Olive, as tomorrow or next week we attend my funeral."[5]

When he recovered sufficiently, he went to Palm Beach to convalesce. Meanwhile, Joe Kennedy had asked his journalist friend Arthur Krock if he knew of any place Joe Jr. and Jack could spend the summer of 1936 in useful manual labor. Krock contacted an old New Jersey friend who had moved to Benson, Arizona, to run a large cattle ranch he had purchased in the early thirties. "Work hell out of them," Krock suggested, ignoring Jack's fragile health.

Located halfway between Tucson and Naco on the Mexican border, the Jay Six Cattle Company, owned by J. G. F. Speiden, had about a thousand head of commercial and registered Herefords. The two Kennedys served as paid ranch hands, the first time either of them had earned any money.

Speiden was constructing permanent ranch offices which he intended to build the old-fashioned way—with indigenous adobe mud and strong backs. The Kennedys bunked with the other ranch hands, who never knew about the brothers' wealthy father. With a Mexican, an alcoholic Scotsman, and Speiden himself, the crew labored all day six days a week for one dollar a day erecting the adobe complex.

On several Saturday nights they traveled to the Mexican border town of Nogales, where Jack enjoyed his favorite leisure pastime. "I have just had an escapade," he proudly wrote Billings from Arizona on May 9, 1936. "Got a fuck and a suck in a Mexican hoar-house [sic] for 65¢ so am feeling very fit and clean. . . . They say that one guy in *four* years has gotten away *without* just the biggest juiciest load of claps." Upholding the principle of always getting "your piece of arse in the most unhealthy place that can be found," he signed the letter your "gonnerrichal roomie." Two weeks later Jack claimed he had visited Hollywood and "got tail" with a Hollywood extra.

When the Kennedys left the ranch after four months of labor, the ranch offices were finished. The pair returned home tanned, lean, and, Speiden recalled, "like leather." Meanwhile, his health restored, Jack had decided to transfer from Princeton to Harvard and to try out for football.[6]

"I really like Harvard pretty well," Jack wrote Billings early in his freshman year. "They work you much harder here than at Princeton," he continued. "There are also plenty of shits!" Jack, though, still took a lackadaisical approach to his studies. "Freshman year [at Harvard] was mostly sports, football and swimming," he remembered. He listed government as his primary field of concentration, followed by a combination of history and literature. His freshman adviser reported that he was "planning to work in government."[7]

"Exam to-day so have to open my book and see what the fucking course is about," he told Billings. Jack's early academic record at Harvard reflected his attitude and resulted in the gentleman's C. As a freshman he received a B in economics and Cs in English, French, and history. No better his sophomore year, he managed one B, four Cs, and a D.

Some professors could barely remember him. Professor Carl Friedrich recalled only a "bright young face," and William Langer, who gave Jack a C+ and a D+ in two European history courses in Jack's sophomore year, could remember even less.[8]

In a class for history or political science Jack wrote a ten-page research paper on Jean-Jacques Rousseau, the Swiss-born eighteenth-century philosopher. Jack's mundane analysis approved of Rousseau's contention that "we too readily accept what we read without subjecting it to our own personal criticism." He also credited Rousseau with properly interpreting the purpose of education, "that is formation of judgment and character."

But JFK disagreed with two of Rousseau's ideas. He deplored the philosopher's call for a return to a primitive nature. "[It] is preposterous to consider ourselves going back to primitive days," Jack wrote. He also mostly disagreed with the philosopher's contention that "material progress" had corrupted society. "[The] evils of such progress have certainly been offset by definite advantages," Jack wrote, such as a "higher standard of living and [an] improvement in social conditions."[9]

One professor saw potential in Jack as early as his sophomore year. In addition to offering classes, Harvard maintained a tutorial system in which the student tutored with a professor to discuss the student's research and readings. During the fall of 1937, Payson Wild, assistant professor of government and acting master of Jack's dorm, Winthrop House, tutored both Jack and Joe Jr. once a week. He remembered vividly his first contact with Jack. The young sophomore came to Wild's office in Winthrop House, sat down on the sofa, and said candidly, "Dr. Wild, I want you to know I'm not bright like my brother Joe." Wild thought Jack obviously had an inferiority complex in relation to his older brother. Gradually, though, Wild became more impressed with Jack than with his brother because Jack's work was more substantial.

"I felt at the time that he was a person who probably would go into law or might go into the Foreign Service," said Wild; "he was a . . . genuine intellectual." The professor also tutored Joe Jr. whose personality and political acumen, Wild thought, earmarked him for politics. Joe was more flamboyant. "[Joe Jr.] would call out under my window, 'Hi, Dr. Wild. I'm coming.' But Jack would never do that. He'd come up in a much quieter way."[10]

At Harvard Jack joined several organizations, competed in football and swimming, but didn't gain eminence at anything. He helped the college sailing team to victory, but the sport was a minor one at Harvard and his success gained little notice. He joined the staff of the *Harvard Crimson* (but was barely active) and the Hasty-Pudding Institute of 1770 (a social club, best known for staging an annual musical comedy). For four years he belonged to St. Paul's Catholic Club (and consistently attended Sunday Mass).

He lost his first election. On February 23, 1937, the freshmen held their class elections. A student could be nominated by submitting a petition bearing the signatures of thirty-five students. Twenty-nine were nominated, including Jack. Six of them made the final runoff, but Jack was not among them.[11]

He did better in his second election. Students selected him to chair the committee to arrange the freshman smoker, an event held on May 4, 1937. Responsible for the evening's entertainment, Jack booked Gertrude Niesen, twenty-six, the sultry New York singer and recent movie star, backed up by a band of forty musicians. A classmate labeled the smoker simply a "high class beer party," but it was an honor to be elected to arrange it.

Jack's primary goal was to make Harvard's freshman football team, a daunting task at his weight of only 156 pounds. He became a sure-hand end, but he was too small to block effectively on the line.

In the locker room he met Torbert Macdonald, an outstanding running back, who later captained the varsity team, and Macdonald agreed to throw him passes after practices. Often he snagged passes for an extra hour—hundreds of passes—until darkness made it impossible to see the ball. "You couldn't help being impressed by the way he drove himself," Macdonald later said.[12]

"The most adept pass catcher was John Kennedy, but his lack of weight was a drawback," reported the *Harvard Freshman Red Book*. "He played for keeps," commented his freshman coach, Henry Lamar. The next year Jack played occasionally on the junior varsity and earned his minor letter, but he quit football after his sophomore season.

He injured his knee playing football, and several people remember a serious back injury as well. Exactly how he hurt his back is still unclear. One account said he suffered a "spinal injury" in a junior varsity scrimmage. Willard Rice, Jack's grade-school football coach, thought he suffered an injury to his "right hip" in his freshman year. Nigel Hamilton reported that in late October 1937, during Jack's sophomore year, the family's chauffeur playfully tackled him after a junior varsity game, causing a serious back injury. "He wore a corset all the time," fellow player and roommate Charles Houghton remembered. "It was real bad. If I'd been [in] anywhere near the kind of shape he was in, I wouldn't have gone out for football or anything else."[13]

Somehow the injury did not noticeably affect Jack's ability to swim the backstroke for the Harvard swimming team. The swimming season lasted from late fall until spring, with training sessions running as long as four hours a day. Illness prevented Jack from doing well in competition. "Beat the number one man in backstroke for 100 yards," Jack boasted to Billings on January 20, 1937. "Supposed to swim in a meet today but have a fucking cold."

For three years Harold Ulen coached Jack on his Harvard varsity teams. "He was a fine kid, frail and not too strong, but always giving it everything he had," said Ulen. "I'd put a stop watch on him. His time didn't satisfy him. He'd look a little depressed, but that's all. He was the kind of kid who'd bounce right back strong."[14]

After his freshman season illnesses continued to disrupt his swimming. In his sophomore year, shortly before Jack was slated for the runoff trial for the number two backstroke spot for a crucial contest with Yale, he caught a cold. "Have a slight cold contracted swimming at Dartmouth so it looks as though my swimming career may be finished," he wrote his mother. "I don't think I can get back in shape quick enough for the Yale meet which is only two weeks away. This is an awful pain as it means whole season gone to waste." The slight cold turned into nasty flu and sent him to the infirmary.[15]

When the doctor told him to forget about swimming against Yale, because he wouldn't be out of the infirmary in time, Jack quietly rejected the advice. Torb Macdonald visited Jack the next day. Although his fever had subsided, Jack still looked pale and could scarcely prop himself up. "I'm going to make that Yale meet if it kills me," he told Macdonald.

The following day, when Macdonald again visited the infirmary, Jack was more perky. "Get me a steak, Torb. Get me a couple of malteds," he said. "What for? You get good food here," Torb remembered replying. "I'll need all the energy I can get," Jack said, grinning.

Torb understood immediately what Jack had in mind. For the next several days Macdonald smuggled steaks and malteds into Jack's room to rebuild his friend's strength. He also smuggled Jack out of the infirmary to practice in the pool when no one was there. But the steaks, the malteds, and the practice couldn't counteract the weakening effects of the flu. On the afternoon of the tryouts for the Yale meet, Jack lost to teammate Richard Tregaskis (who later gained prominence for his book *Guadalcanal Diary*).

"I can see where it might be dismissed as college rah-rah stuff," Macdonald later concluded of Jack's determination.

"But the important thing was that he had once again made the maximum effort."[16]

In the fall of 1937, Jack's sophomore year, he was admitted to the Spee Club, located in a large building in Cambridge. "Was it important to Jack Kennedy? You bet it was!" fellow member Jim Rousmanière emphasized. "In those days, the Spee served three meals a day, five or six days a week—which was important because Jack had a diet problem." The club even installed an ice-cream-making machine because Jack's doctor recommended he put on more weight. Above all, admittance to the Spee Club gave Jack a social standing which his brother never enjoyed. "Jack and Joe were good friends," said Rousmanière, "but I think that Jack always felt happy that he was able to do some things that Joe couldn't do. And the Spee Club was the means of doing it."

Intercollegiate sailing was in its infancy and a minor sport at Harvard. In June 1938 Jack helped Harvard sail to victory in the 1938 McMillan Cup race, competing against the Naval and Coast Guard academies and the other

Ivy League schools. In the race Jack outsailed two skippers who subsequently defended the America's Cup, Robert N. Bavier Jr. and Bus Mosbacher.[17]

During a summer vacation, though, a joyous racing weekend turned sour after an Edgartown, Massachusetts, summer regatta degenerated into a bout of drinking and rowdiness. A victory celebration hosted by Jack and Joe Jr. came to an abrupt end when vandalism prompted the management at an Edgartown hotel to alert police. Both Kennedys were incarcerated in the village's cramped jail. When called to grant bail, Joseph P. Kennedy refused, telling his sons to "stay where you are" in order "to teach you a lesson." The police didn't press charges, and released the boys the next morning.[18]

Despite the intense political agitation at Harvard in the 1930s, Jack stayed out of politics and away from campus politicians.

Whenever Jack read about his father in the newspaper, the story was usually linked to Franklin Roosevelt's presidency. "I can hardly remember a mealtime," Robert Kennedy later said, "when the conversation was not dominated by what Franklin D. Roosevelt was doing or what was happening around the world." During the 1936 campaign, Joe Kennedy stumped for Roosevelt's reelection, but Jack, then a freshman at Harvard, remained aloof.

A friend, Charles Spalding, thought Jack studied FDR and the New Deal, but "I don't recall that there was any idolatry on the part of . . . Kennedy for President Roosevelt, as a young man, the way there was for so many people." Spalding added, "There just wasn't anything about President Roosevelt that stirred . . . Kennedy emotionally, as there was [later] about Churchill."

Most likely Jack remained subdued because his father's private attitude toward Roosevelt was inconsistent—sometimes supportive, other times critical. Historian William Leuchtenburg has observed that "If Jack Kennedy felt even intermittent excitement about FDR, it found no public expression. Though Harvard in these years was churning with discussions of the New Deal, he shunned the Harvard Liberal Union and the Young Democrats and never spoke out in favor of the Roosevelt reforms."

Asked in 1960, "What do you remember about the Great Depression?" JFK responded candidly. "I have no first-hand knowledge of the depression," he answered. "My family had one of the great fortunes of the world and it was worth more than ever then. We had bigger houses, more servants, we traveled more. About the only thing that I saw directly was when my father hired some extra gardeners just to give them a job so they could eat. I really did not learn about the depression until I read about it at Harvard." (Then he took his feet off his desk, leaned forward, and said to the interviewer, "My experience was the war. I can tell you about that.")[19]

Like his father, who esteemed athletes, Jack surrounded himself with rugged football players and other athletes. "I think he . . . had this hero worship of athletes as a result of him not being a tremendous athlete himself," a friend speculated. Never physically fit enough to play football well, Jack gravitated to men who did. He loved touch football, and games with friends were often a major part of weekend activities.

After living alone his freshman year, Jack roomed the following year with Torbert Macdonald. The next year the pair shared a four-room suite in Winthrop House with two other football players, Charlie Houghton and Ben Smith. (During his senior year Jack roomed only with Macdonald.) Jack's other close friends were also athletes—Jim Rousmanière (squash champion at Harvard) and Ralph Horton (golf).[20]

The illness that kept Jack out of school put him in the class behind Billings, who remained at Princeton. They exchanged scores of telegrams about weekend activities in New York, dances in Boston, and parties at the Kennedy's Hyannis Port cottage.

Meeting in New York became a way of life. Kennedy would fly from Boston while Billings hitchhiked from Princeton. They would often meet at the Roosevelt Bar, pick up their dates—sometimes with one of Joe Kennedy's cars—and go to the Stork Club for a night of dancing. Lem was self-conscious about his lack of spending money, so Jack Kennedy matter-of-factly solved the problem by not spending much himself. Kathleen Kennedy often joined Jack and his friends for an evening in Manhattan.[21]

"I have a bit of bad news," Jack began a letter to Billings on February 10, 1938. As it turned out, Jack had bad news for Billings, whom Jack wanted to shoulder the blame for an auto accident. It was the worst case of Jack Kennedy exploiting his friendship with LeMoyne Billings.

On the evening of the previous fall's Harvard-Yale football game, Jack had come in "unpleasant contact" with a woman in a car who was a "shit." Therefore Jack gave her "a lot of shit." She claimed that his car bumped her car "four or five times" (which Jack admitted to Billings had "some truth"). Unfortunately, she had taken down his license number and reported the incident to the Registry of Motor Vehicles in Massachusetts.

When the police contacted Jack, he lied and told them that he had loaned his car to a friend. Now a police official in Boston wanted the friend's name. "I am contemplating giving [him] yours so you can in your inimitable style carry on communication with him." JFK advised Billings to tell the official "you're sorry and realize you should not have done it." Jack would write the official naming Billings "as the culprit"; then "you write him a gracious letter and admit [it]." JFK helpfully provided the police official's name and address. Whether Billings complied or if anything developed from the incident is unknown. (There is a slight possibility that Jack's letter was an elaborate practical joke.)[22]

Whatever Billings thought about being asked to shoulder the blame for

Jack's auto accident, the pair remained close friends until Jack's death. Jack seldom expressed emotion or affection, but was extremely loyal to his friends. "If you needed him," said Billings, "he was sensitive enough to understand it and he'd spend whatever time was necessary in helping you." Jack would do everything in his power to hide his emotions, Billings thought, but "I certainly don't think he was cold in any way. He had a very warm personality. I think he cared a great deal about people and his feelings of loyalty were far above average. I'd even go further; I never knew anyone with stronger feelings of loyalty."[23]

Normally disdaining a suit, Jack's formal attire consisted of gray slacks, a sport coat, and sometimes a tie. "He was just a carefree individual," said his black valet, George Taylor, whom Jack's father had assigned to assist Jack at Harvard.

Of the roommates in Jack's junior year, Jack was the messiest and the most absentminded about his clothes. After thanking Billings for mailing Jack's tuxedo, Alice Cahill, the Kennedys' governess, explained that "[a] package arrives for him almost daily containing various articles of wearing apparel he has dropped some where."

"He never hung up anything," said his roommate Charles Houghton; "he just dropped it." George Taylor picked up after all of the roommates, not just Jack, and he pressed all of their clothes as well.[24]

For the most part, Joe Jr. and Jack stayed on good terms at Harvard during their undergraduate days. They led separate lives, enjoyed different friends, and had interests of their own. Yet they often saw each other, exchanged family news, and attended movies together.

Torbert Macdonald thought the two Kennedys had a normal, brotherly relationship. "The amount of [reported] rivalry, I think, has been overdone," said Macdonald. Joe Jr. tried to encourage his younger brother. "How's it going, Jack? . . . Come on, you can do this." Young Joe watched swimming practices and chatted with Coach Ulen about Jack. How was Jack getting along? Would he make a good swimmer?[25]

Family loyalty remained paramount. Joe Jr. approached Jack after a football practice and offered some advice. "Jack," he said, "if you want my opinion, you'd be better off forgetting about football. You just don't weigh enough and you're going to get yourself banged up."

Macdonald watched Jack closely as his brother was talking and saw Jack's face flush with anger. Macdonald decided to interject. "Come off it, Joe. You're making too much out of nothing. Jack doesn't need any looking after."

Now Jack was furious at Macdonald. "Jack whirled on me and told me off in no uncertain terms for butting into a family affair," Macdonald recalled. "I never did it again."

Jack was popular at Harvard primarily because he was fun. "That's one thing that always stood out," Jim Rousmanière said. "Anytime you were with Jack Kennedy you would laugh. He was a laugh a minute." Lem Billings agreed. "Jack was more fun than anyone I've ever known, and I think most people who knew him felt the same way about him."[26]

Most of the women in Jack's life during college were intelligent, bright, beautiful, and amusing. Being from a prominent Catholic family, he couldn't marry a Protestant or afford to make a mistake in marriage. He dated mostly "safe" girls whom he had no intention of marrying or could not marry because they were not Catholics. Several of his girlfriends were also friends of Kathleen's. When he entered Harvard, he was still taking out his high school sweetheart, Olive Cawley. In 1938–1939 he dated Frances Ann Cannon, daughter of the wealthy Cannon Mills family, who was intelligent and exceptionally attractive, but happened to be Protestant. (She later married the prominent writer John Hersey.) By 1940 his new "serious" girl was Charlotte McDonnell. When he took her to the Princeton game, he wrote his father that she "will be my first taste of a Catholic girl so will be interested to see how it goes."

He had three favorite girlfriends in college, but he casually dated many others. "Jack was always very successful with girls," said Rousmanière. "Very. All he had to do was snap his fingers. He never had only one girlfriend at a time; he had many."

Jack romped with coeds, models, stewardesses, nurses, showgirls, and prostitutes. He had an endless supply. "Every time he went to New York for a weekend, he returned with ten new names," said Rousmanière.[27]

"I can now get my tail as often and as free as I want which is a step in right direction," Jack proudly wrote Billings on January 13, 1937. (Through 1937 Jack's letters to Billings were filled with sexual bravado and his conquests of women. Thereafter, while still sometimes referring to sex and women, his letters usually explored other subjects, particularly his travel and observations on the coming of World War II and on the war itself.)

Spencer Klaw, the *Crimson*'s editor for part of Jack's years at Harvard, told of being at an after-hours Boston bar and meeting several hookers. When the women discovered his Harvard connection, they asked, "Do you know Jack Kennedy and Torby Macdonald?"

Jack tried to shield Kathleen from the seamier side of his approach to women. When he expressed a desire for "something that likes lovin," he advised Billings "preferably therefore not Kick this weekend."

Despite his own vulgar and insincere attitude toward many women, Jack sometimes tried to act as Kathleen's counselor. He would lecture her sternly about her alleged "insincerity" with his friends. She had difficulty accepting Jack's advice, knowing her brother's cavalier attitude toward women.[28]

During Jack's Harvard years he made three trips to Europe: a two-month sightseeing excursion in the summer of 1937, a brief vacation in the summer of 1938, and a major seven-month tour in 1939.

Billings was his partner during the summer of 1937. Jack's father loaned the impoverished Billings five hundred dollars for the trip, which Billings agreed to repay after graduating from college. They departed for Europe on July 1 and returned in mid-September. To keep within Billings's budget, the two Americans stayed in cheap lodging—paying one dollar for a double room, sixty cents for another, and a dime at a youth hostel.[29]

The pair toured France, Italy, Germany, Holland, and England. During the jaunt through France they visited Paris, Versailles, the Loire Valley, Saint-Jean-de-Luz, Biarritz, Marseilles, Lourdes, Cannes, and Monte Carlo. After crossing the border into Italy, there were visits to Genoa, Milan, Pisa, and Rome. With Rome as their base they toured Tivoli, Naples, and Capri. On the way to Germany the pair stopped in Florence and Venice. Crossing into Germany, they visited Munich, Nuremburg, Frankfurt, and Cologne. Then it was on to Amsterdam and London, and back home. During their excursion they looked in on museums, castles, palaces, and cathedrals and hiked over mountains, ruins, and battlefields.

Throughout the trip Jack dashed off long letters to his father and kept a daily diary. "Very smooth crossing," he noted in the diary after landing at the port of Le Havre on the northern coast of France. "Looked pretty dull the first couple of days but investigation disclosed some girls."

Jack intended to rush to Paris after his Ford sedan was hauled off the ship, but before reaching the capital, Billings insisted that they visit every cathedral town from Rouen to Beauvais. At Princeton, Billings had taken architectural courses that covered the history of European cathedrals, and he was keen on personally seeing them. Jack had never studied architecture, but he became fascinated with them as well, and willingly drove at "cathedral pace." "Jack's mind was always receptive," said Billings. "He was [as] terribly interested as I was. I think my being so interested affected him and he spent just as much time [touring the cathedrals]."[30]

Jack's diary entries were irreverant, witty, and sometimes incisive: "The distinguishing mark of the Frenchman is his cabbage breath and the fact that there are no bath tubs."

They watched several movies during the trip, including *The Plainsman*. "Gary Cooper speaking French as well as the Indians is worth the price of admission."

After a visit to Lourdes to see where the Virgin Mary had appeared to

Saint Bernadette, Billings became ill and ran a temperature of 103 degrees. Two days later they stopped at Carcassonne, a medieval town in perfect condition, which, Jack wrote, "is more than can be said for Billings."

On July 26, they attended a bullfight near the Spanish border. "Very interesting, but very cruel, especially when the bull gored the horse." That the crowd seemed most pleased with the scenes of cruelty disturbed Jack. "They thought funniest sight was when horse ran out of the ring with his guts trailing."[31]

His diary contained little mention of the women he met or his sexual exploits. One reason was native custom. "Was out with [a] French girl," he wrote. "Their customs [are] very strict requiring a chaperone until 21 or so."

He had more luck in Rome in early August. He and Billings arranged dates with two "very beautiful girls," but the Americans were handicapped by not speaking Italian. This caused a "temporary damper," but they concocted some "parlor tricks" that broke the ice. That night, Jack wrote in his diary, he went to bed "tired but happy!"[32]

Most of the sites dazzled. "Went to Mass at St. Peters which was terribly impressive, being by far the most beautiful building we had yet seen."

Always inquisitive, Jack insisted on picking up hitchhikers, many of whom were students who spoke English. Then he grilled these new traveling companions about European politics and current events, especially about fascism in Franco's Spain, Mussolini's Italy, and Hitler's Germany. He compared these thoughts with the book he read during the journey, John Gunther's *Inside Europe*. Then he pondered the often conflicting judgments, and mused about them in his diary and in letters to his father.

Before he embarked on his European trip, Jack had asked if his father could pull strings to get him and Billings into war-torn Spain for three weeks "as newspaper correspondents or as members of the Red Cross." Because Joe Kennedy couldn't or wouldn't make the arrangements, the two Americans didn't get near the fighting in Spain. Jack had to educate himself by reading and questioning.

As he and Billings approached the Spanish border with France, he heard an earful about the Spanish civil war, which had been raging for a year. Since 1931, when Spain established a republic, the situation had been tense and unstable. The efforts of the republic's first government to enact reforms— freedom of action for trade unions, separation of church and state—led conservatives to believe the country was turning to the left. When the Left won new elections in February 1936, the Right feared imminent social revolution. In July 1936, General Francisco Franco led a military revolt against the government that plunged Spain into civil war. Fascist Germany and Italy provided substantial assistance to Franco, while the Soviet Union sent far fewer supplies and advisers to the republican forces, who were increasingly dominated by Spanish Communists. (In 1939 Franco's victory would end the bloody fighting.)[33]

At first, Jack found convincing the arguments of Franco supporters, but after reading Gunther's critical assessment of the Spanish fascist leader and his followers, he wasn't so sure. "Not quite as positive now about Franco victory," he wrote. "Shows that you can be easily influenced by people around you if you know nothing and how easy it is for you to believe what you want to believe, as the people of St. Jean [France] do."

He wrote to his father, "While I felt that perhaps it would be far better for Spain if Franco should win—as he would strengthen and unite Spain—yet at the beginning the [elected] government was in the right morally speaking as its program was similar to the New Deal."

On August 7 Jack dined with the Italian Fascist Count Enrico Galeazzi, secretary to Cardinal Eugenio Pacelli (later Pope Pius XII). "[Galeazzi] gave me quite a [talk] about the virtues of fascism and it really seemed to have its points—especially the corporate system which seems quite an interesting step forward."[34]

In Munich, the proprietor of his rooming house was a fan of Hitler. "There is no doubt about it that these dictators are more popular [inside their own country] than outside due to their effective propaganda."

"All the towns are very attractive," he wrote on August 21 while touring Germany, "showing that the Nordic races certainly seem superior to the Latins. The Germans really are too good—it makes people gang [up] against them for protection." In his diary Jack made no mention of Hitler's persecution of Jews or Germany's totalitarian system.

Overall, though, both Jack and Billings detested the attitude of the Germans. The Germans "were so anti everything and so snotty," Billings recalled. "They were insufferable. We just had awful experiences there." Everywhere in Germany they sensed contempt for Americans. When Germans saluted and said, "Heil Hitler!" Lem and Jack were expected to do the same. Instead, the two Americans practiced casually throwing back their hands, waving, and saying, "Hi ya, Hitler."[35]

On their way to Nuremberg, Jack purchased a dachshund for eight dollars as a gift for Olive Cawley, and named him Offie. Almost immediately the dog aggravated Jack's hay fever, so that, he noted, "it looks like the odds are about 8–1 towards Offie getting to America." The next day Jack wrote, "Offie is quite a problem because when he's got to go—he goes." By the time the two American tourists arrived in London, ending their trip, Jack had broken out with hives. "Went home and was damn sick," he wrote.[36]

On January 5, 1938, President Roosevelt appointed Joe Kennedy as ambassador to Great Britain. Delighted and proud, the Kennedys packed for London in time for Joe to assume his official duties on March 8.

At first the British delighted in their new ambassador, dubbing him "Jolly Joe" and, in a reference to the size of his attractive, often-photographed family, hailing him as the "father" of his country. Joe responded with ebullience and good humor. "Hardly a day passed without a photograph in the papers of little Teddy, taking a snapshot with his Brownie held upside down," said Lynne McTaggart, "or the five Kennedy children lined up on a train or bus." Columnists marveled at Rose's slim profile, and Kathleen often appeared in the society pages. Next to Jack's presidency, Rose would consider her stay in London the best time of her life.

The American embassy at 14 Prince's Gate was a huge complex of thirty-six rooms, elaborately furnished in the Louis XVI style. Operating the residence like a luxury hotel, Rose directed a permanent staff of twenty-three house servants and three chauffeurs, and an additional reserve of twenty part-time employees for official functions.[37]

As war clouds darkened Europe, the thought of war horrified Joe Kennedy, partly because of his deep sense of foreboding for the safety of his children. "I have four boys," he said with visible emotion to a colleague, "and I don't want them to be killed in a foreign war." He believed war would reduce Europe to rubble, destroy capitalism, and probably accelerate the triumph of communism. Considering the gloomy consequences of war, Nazism, despite its objectionable features, seemed clearly preferable. Hitler's anticommunism seemed authentic; most likely his expansionist dreams lay to the east and would bring the Germans into conflict with the Soviet Union.

Joe steadfastly opposed American intervention in Europe, and had no faith that the British could survive a war with the Nazis. Bewildered by the British, he couldn't understand why they would plunge into war on an idealistic whim. In 1939 and 1940, as Franklin Roosevelt inched toward aid to Britain, the President began to distrust Kennedy's judgment and surreptitiously shifted his major diplomatic business from Kennedy to personal envoys and the British ambassador in Washington. Angry at being circumvented, Kennedy disparaged Roosevelt before London friends and recklessly boasted that he could "put twenty-five million Catholic votes behind [Republican] Wendell Willkie to throw Roosevelt out [in the 1940 election]."

Kennedy's disloyalty quickly found its way back to FDR. The White House kept receiving reports that Kennedy spoke savagely about the President in private and to hostile American publishers. "Roosevelt gave full credence, too," said historian William Leuchtenburg, "to information that Kennedy was telling people in England that the Jews were running America and that FDR would be beaten in 1940."[38]

Throughout the years of Hitler's dictatorship neither John Kennedy nor his father expressed any empathy for the horrible plight of Jews in Germany. Once in power in 1933, Hitler and the Nazis excluded Jews from public life and business activity, and eventually from life itself. In 1935 Hitler used the occasion of the Nazi rally in Nuremberg to issue the Nuremberg Laws, which, among other things, removed Jewish equality before the law and prohibited marriage or sexual relations between Jews and non-Jews.

After the assassination of the third secretary in the German embassy in Paris by a young Jewish student, the Nazis used the incident as a pretext for an orgy of violent reprisals against German Jews. On November 9–10, 1938, the so-called Kristallnacht, or night of glass, Nazis burned synagogues, destroyed seven thousand Jewish businesses, killed a hundred Jews, and sent twenty-five thousand more to concentration camps.

On FDR's orders, Kennedy had several long conversations with the German envoy to London, Herbert von Dirksen. Kennedy's private remarks to Dirksen later came back to haunt him. Dirksen sent reports on these talks to the German foreign office, and when the Allied armies seized them after the war, they became public. According to Dirksen, Kennedy expressed sympathy for the Nazi cause and claimed that "a large portion of the [American] population had an understanding of the German attitude toward the Jews."[39]

After the war Joe Kennedy vehemently denied ever being anti-Semitic. He correctly pointed to his many Jewish friends and business associates, his membership in a Jewish golf club in Palm Beach, and his philanthropic efforts on behalf of Jewish groups as evidence of his open-mindedness.

Nonetheless, Joe privately referred to Jews as "sheeny" or used a code phrase, "Canadian geese" (because of the stereotype that Jews have long noses). He bragged that in his Hollywood years "he'd made more money beating Jews in deals than could fit into the building." He said he loved besting the Jewish "pants pressers" who ruled Hollywood. His frequent derogatory remarks about Jews indicated he had not overcome many years of Boston Irish anti-Semitism. Yes, he had Jewish friends and associates, but they existed apart from his often-expressed anti-Semitism. Still, he shared his anti-Semitism with millions of his contemporaries in America.[40]

In October 1938, Joe spoke to the annual Trafalgar Day Dinner sponsored by the British Navy League in London, and his neutralist views sparked a firestorm. He cast the debate between democracy and fascism as one between two equally valid political systems. It was "unproductive" for democracies and dictatorships "to widen the division now existing between them by emphasizing their differences," he said. There was "simply no sense, common or otherwise, in letting these differences grow into unrelenting antagonisms. After all, we have to live together in the same world whether we like it or not."

Chancelleries throughout the world interpreted Kennedy's speech as a sharp turnabout in American diplomacy. "The proposal directly contradicted Franklin Roosevelt's view, delivered a year earlier in an electrifying address at Chicago, that a quarantine should be imposed upon the bandit nations," noted Michael Beschloss. People "whispered that Kennedy favored the fascists and doted on dictators." Because of his arrogance and poor judgment, the man who had once enjoyed mostly flattering press coverage in America now had to weather the most critical.

Throughout the wrangling, Jack remained loyal to his father. "[Your] Navy Day speech, while it seemed to be unpopular with the Jews" and others, he wrote from Harvard, "was considered to be very good by everyone who wasn't bitterly antifascist."[41]

In August 1938 and in the winter of 1939, Jack vacationed with his family in Europe. During the long English winter holiday, the Kennedys went to St.-Moritz, Switzerland, where the children skied and improved their skating. They spent summers in a villa high in the hills in back of Cannes in southeastern France, with a spectacular panoramic view of the Riviera and the Mediterranean.

Louella Hennessy recalled that when Jack joined the family after one of his jaunts through Europe, he would come looking for her and everyone else, bounding up the stairs at breakneck speed. "Hi!" he'd call out. "Have they been treating you all right around here? Heard from home lately? Isn't that a new dress?" Jack seemed to sense that Hennessy—in Europe, far from home—might sometimes feel lonely.

Hennessy's most poignant memory of life near Cannes was of a stormy afternoon when Jack sat in front of a blazing fire and presented a history lesson to his younger brothers and sisters. Gathered around him on a big sofa, Jack mused about Hannibal, Caesar, Napoleon, and the rise and fall of nations.

Different nations had had their moment of greatness, he explained. One leader usually ruled and controlled all the power and the wealth, while the common people received little or nothing from their country's glory. Eventually the ruler was overthrown, and a succession of new rulers gained control, until the country lost everything and either ceased to exist or became unimportant.

The United States, Jack told them, was now among the most powerful nations in the world. The United States was unique, though, because it was a democracy, where the people held the real power. The daunting dilemma for America was how to keep its exalted position, avoid the mistakes that had led to the fall of other nations, and at the same time preserve its freedom.

"As I listened to Jack," Hennessy said, "I thought with amazement, 'Why, he's only 21. Imagine his caring about these things!' "[42]

When Joe Kennedy suggested that he take a semester's leave of absence from Harvard to work in the London embassy, Jack jumped at the chance. Harvard granted him permission to withdraw during the spring semester of 1939, and he stayed in Europe for seven months, until the following September.

To make sure that everywhere Jack traveled he would get "superior entry," Joe Kennedy arranged letters of introduction from the State Department. Everywhere Jack traveled a telegram preceded him: "Will appreciate any courtesy my son Jack arriving [Belgrade] today."

During the spring and summer of 1939, Jack traveled throughout Europe, the Soviet Union, the Balkans, and the Middle East. From each capital he reported to his father on the political and economic situation. "For a twenty-two-year-old American," said Richard Whalen, "it was a unique opportunity to look behind the scenes as the stage was set for the Second World War."

Although he was provided with superior entry, third-class trains and dumpy hotels didn't faze Jack. Not content with official answers, he aimed an endless stream of questions at peasants, students, soldiers, businessmen, American reporters, diplomats—anyone who'd speak with him.

Soon after his arrival in London he met the king and queen and Princess Elizabeth. To greet the royalty he wore silk knee breeches, "which are cut to my crotch tightly and in which I look mighty attractive," he wrote Billings.[43]

Jack accompanied the Kennedys to Italy, where on March 12, 1939, the ambassador was President Roosevelt's special representative at the coronation of Pope Pius XII. After returning to England, Jack reported to Billings that the new pope "gave Dad and I communion with Eunice at the same time at a private mass and all in all it was very impressive."

After the coronation in Rome, Jack began a serious regimen of work, study, and travel. He spent several weeks in the Paris embassy under the guidance of ambassador William Bullitt. Carmel Offie, Bullitt's close adviser, recalled Jack "sitting in my office and listening to telegrams being read or even reading various things which actually were none of his business but since he was who he was we didn't throw him out."

The European situation was so "damn complicated," Jack explained to Billings in late March.

For example: In trying to get Russia in the peace front, they have to be able to have her bring troops to help in case Germany attacks Poland, or Romania. However, Poland and Romania have a defense alliance against Russia which they fear almost as much as Germany as Russia has claims on their territories and they feel that once Russian troops get in they couldn't get them out. The situation is even worse because due to the Seigfried [*sic*] line ⅓ of the German army can hold [off] the whole French army—meanwhile Germany can march its other ⅔ into Romania or Danzig. And what the hell can the English fleet do about it[?] So until they can iron out problems like these—they can't get started.

And, in a remark he was to make often in 1939, he concluded, "The whole thing is 'damn interesting.' "[44]

In May Jack was in Danzig, an ancient Baltic seaport at the mouth of the Vistula River. In re-creating the Polish nation after World War I, the Treaty of Versailles designated Danzig a demilitarized free city under a League of Nations commissioner. The treaty also gave Poland a strip of land with a coastline, which had been part of prewar Germany, the so-called Polish Corridor. Local elections in 1933 gave the indigenous Nazi Party control of Danzig. In 1939, Hitler demanded the political reunification of the city with the German Reich, and an extraterritorial passageway through the Polish Corridor.

Jack discussed the tense situation with Nazi officials in Danzig. The Germans didn't care what happened to Poland. "They told me frankly that the best thing for Poland would be to come into a customs union with Germany," he wrote Billings. "Poland is determined not to give up Danzig and you can take it as official that Poland will not give up Danzig."

He predicted accurately that the Germans would try to make Poland appear the aggressor "and then go to work." "Poland has an army of 4,000,000 who are damn good—but poorly equipped," he noted, and then he further predicted—inaccurately—that Poland's poor roads would "nullify Germany's mechanical advantage." Since neither France nor Great Britain could help, Poland would have to fight alone. "But they are tough," he concluded, "and whether they get help or not they will fight."[45]

After Danzig, Jack traveled through the Soviet Union—Leningrad, Moscow, Kiev, and the Crimea. Charles Bohlen, the U.S. consul in Moscow, and several others had lunch with Jack. "We were all struck by Kennedy's charm and quick mind, but especially his open-mindedness about the Soviet Union, a rare quality in those pre-war days. He made a favorable impression."[46]

After the Soviet Union, Jack traveled to Hungary, Lithuania, Latvia, Estonia, Romania, Turkey, Egypt, and Palestine. In a four-page single-spaced typed report to his father, Jack perceptively grasped the complex history and current status of the Arab-Jewish conflict in Palestine.

He described Britain's policy in the region since World War I, Jewish immigration to Palestine in the 1930s, the current bitterness between Jews and Arabs, and the political divisions within each group.

On the Jewish side there is the desire for complete domination, with Jerusalem as the capital of their new land of milk and honey, with the right to colonize in Trans-Jordan. They feel that given sufficient opportunity they can cultivate the land and develop it as they have done in the Western portion. The Arab answer to this is incidentally that the Jews have had the benefit of capital, which had the Arabs possessed, equal miracles could have been performed by them. Though this is partly true, the economic set up of Arabic agricultural progress with its absentee landlords and primitive methods of cultivation, could not under any circumstances probably have competed with the Jews.

Unlike many British officials, Jack refused to blame all Jews for the difficulties in the region; instead, he attributed the problems to "reactionary" zealot elements among the Jews.

For the first time we see evidence of Jack's anticolonialism. "After all," he reminded his father, "Palestine was hardly Britain's to give away."

Several times he stressed the need for a realistic, pragmatic solution. It "is useless to discuss which has the 'fairer' claim. The important thing is to try to work out a solution that will work."[47]

In July Jack was joined by Torbert Macdonald, who had come to Europe with the Harvard track team. During their travels Jack and Macdonald met Byron "Whizzer" White, a recent all-American halfback from Colorado, then a Rhodes scholar at Oxford, and the three Americans visited Berlin, Munich, Danzig, Budapest, and Italy.

Ambassador Kennedy had sternly warned Jack and Macdonald to stay away from trouble. While in Berlin, White borrowed a car and the three of them drove to Munich to see the tomb of the Nazis' hoodlum-martyr, Horst Wessel. "We parked near the tomb and got out to look at the perpetual flame inside the monument," Macdonald later explained. Suddenly, a gang of local bullies engaged them with rough heckling and started throwing rocks at them and the car. "Our first reaction was to lay into them, but Jack, even though he was as sore as the rest of us, led us in a diplomatic retreat."

White later speculated that they had become targets because the car they drove had English license plates. Kennedy seemed to realize, Macdonald thought, that war was unavoidable "if this is the way these people feel."[48]

With war imminent, Jack was in Prague in late August 1939. Unlike Charles Bohlen in Moscow, George Kennan, the U.S. consul in Prague, wasn't pleased with either the timing or the importance of Jack's visit. "We were furious," Kennan recalled. The embassy staff disliked Joe Kennedy. John Kennedy had no official diplomatic status and was "in our eyes, obviously an upstart and an ignoramus." That busy foreign service officers needed to arrange Jack's tour seemed outrageous. Nonetheless, Kennan managed to get Jack escorted around Prague, "saw to it that he was shown what he wanted to see, expedited his departure, then, with a feeling of 'that's that,' washed my hands of him."[49]

In August 1939, with the Germans planning to invade Poland on September 1, Hitler secured the noninterference of the Soviet Union. On August 23, the two longtime enemies signed the Nazi-Soviet Non-Aggression Pact, temporarily at least ending the animosity between the two nations. The pact isolated Poland and put it in mortal danger. Great Britain and France remained steadfast in their commitments to Poland, but could not assist her directly in the event of a German attack. The stage was set for the beginning of World War II.

In the last ten days of August 1939, John Kennedy had a front-row seat at the riveting drama as he hustled between Prague and the German cities of Munich, Berlin, and Hamburg.

The pervasive, incredibly powerful propaganda of Hitler's totalitarian regime shocked him.

> The anti-Polish campaign is beyond description. Every edition of the newspapers has a more gruesome tale to tell of Polish outrages against the Germans, of planes being attacked and of German soldiers tortured. In the news reel about two minutes was given over to showing the real German background of the city of Danzig. The Nazi banners, the fascist salute, and the goose-stepping soldiers were all featured. After this they showed the women and children who had been turned out of their homes by the Poles. With tears streaming down their cheeks they bawled into the microphone their tale of grief. Even children told theirs.

The Germans had the "most powerful propaganda I have seen anywhere," he wrote, and when the war broke out, "the Poles will be shown to be the aggressors, and it will be the duty of every German to stop them."[50]

Germany invaded Poland on September 1, 1939, commencing World War II. By then Jack had maneuvered his way back to London. On September 3, Rose, Kathleen, Joe Jr., and Jack ventured forth into the gloomy streets to hear Neville Chamberlain's speech to Parliament. "As they walked toward the Palace of Westminster," observed Lawrence Leamer, "a photographer snapped a photograph of the three young Kennedys, Kathleen in her white gloves, pearls, and big hat, and the two men in impeccably tailored double-breasted suits, the threesome marching forward with a jaunty air as if they had good seats at the Royal Opera, rather than being observers at the beginning of World War II."[51]

On September 3, 1939, the very day the British declared war, a German U-boat sank the SS *Athenia* near the Herbrides off the coast of Scotland. The British passenger liner bound for Montreal carried 1,417 passengers, including over three hundred Americans. One hundred and twenty-eight, including eighty-five women and children, lost their lives. Twenty-eight American citizens were among the victims.

A destroyer delivered several hundred survivors to Ireland; most were brought to Scotland. On the evening of September 6, 1939, Ambassador Kennedy sent Jack to Glasgow to represent the American embassy in London, whose staff was swamped with work. Joe thought the assignment would be routine, but it turned out to be a formidable challenge for a twenty-two-year-old.

The "schoolboy diplomat," as the press described Jack, explained to the *Athenia*'s American survivors that their government would help alleviate their distress and get them safely home. "I talked to my father this morning, and he has spoken to America since," Jack told a group of anxious survivors. "He asked me to tell you that the government has plenty of money for you all." Ten thousand dollars had been allocated for their immediate needs, new tickets would be provided, and a ship was on its way from New York. All the survivors would be returned on the same ship.

Before Jack had arrived on September 7, Glasgow officials had most of the situation in hand. Jack went from hotels to hospitals in Glasgow, visiting the ship's American survivors, helping to reunite families, and speeding up their processing through the London embassy.[52]

The faces of many survivors turned to joy at seeing a benevolent link to their homeland. "Mr. Kennedy displayed a wisdom and sympathy of a man twice his years," reported a British newspaper.

Many of the American survivors still had wounds and burns from the disaster; some were hysterical. When Jack explained to one group in the Beresford Hotel in Glasgow that an American vessel was coming to take them home, they vented their frustration and anger.

"Will it have a convoy?" an elderly lady asked.

"You cannot trust the Goddamned German Navy! They fired on us," yelled another woman.

A reporter described the scene:

> Mr. Kennedy again attempted to reason with the crowd, but was interrupted by grey-haired Thomas McCubbin of Montclair, N.J., who said: "A convoy is imperative. Ninety destroyers have just been commissioned by the United States Navy and surely they can spare us a few. Six billion dollars of United States Navy and they cannot do this for us!" Another survivor cried, "Two years ago the whole Pacific fleet was sent out

for one woman flyer [Amelia Earhart]." One college girl declared: "We defiantly refuse to go until we have a convoy. You have seen what they will do to us."

Young Kennedy was taken aback, but managed to shout above the din. "You will be safe in a ship flying the American flag under international law; a neutral ship is safe."

The survivors looked unimpressed. Jack looked tense. "I will tell my father all you say," he told them. "I know he will consider all aspects."[53]

When a reporter asked about Jack and his brothers and sisters, Jack replied, "We must get back to school, but we shan't go until all other American citizens have gone."

Afterward, back in London, Jack made four recommendations to his father: that a convoy accompany the ship taking the survivors back to America; that the boat depart from Glasgow; that the United States officially thank the men in the destroyer who picked up the survivors; and that the United States extend a similar expression of appreciation to the city of Glasgow for its assistance.

Joe Kennedy thanked the city of Glasgow and the Royal Navy, but turned down his son's suggestion for a convoy. (President Roosevelt had announced that a U.S. convoy would not be provided for returning refugees.)

Jack continued to work on repatriating the ship's survivors until he returned by air to New York on September 21, 1939. It was his first transatlantic flight, and he was hooked. "It's really the way to come, and it's very difficult for me to realize that I was in England two days ago," he told his father.

During his assignment in Scotland, Jack displayed kindness, compassion, diplomacy, and a natural flare for handling the thorny problems. Newsreels in movie theaters throughout the United States showed Jack consoling the survivors. "The *Athenia* story got a big spread here and the newsreel was all over," Jack delightedly wrote his father upon his return.[54]

Within three weeks the Polish armies collapsed in the face of the ferocious German blitzkrieg, and by the end of September 1939, Poland had been defeated.

"I am enclosing an editorial I had written in the *Crimson*," Jack, back at Harvard, reported to his father in October 1939. In the editorial, called "Peace in Our Time," Jack appealed to his fellow students to ignore the defeat of Poland. President Roosevelt should "exert every office he possesses to bring about . . . peace." Germany and England, he argued, were "both painfully eager to end the fight after the first preliminary round. It would be the saddest event in all history if their peace hopes were frustrated merely because neither is in a position to make direct overtures." A third power, obviously the President of the United States, must bring them together through secret diplomatic channels.

Jack wanted Roosevelt to secure peace at any price rather than allow Britain and France to be destroyed. The editorial reflected his father's defeatism. "There is every possibility—almost a probability—of English defeat," Jack predicted. "At the best, Britain can expect destruction of all her industrial concentrations and the loss of the tremendous store of invested wealth. . . . At the worst she can expect extreme political and economic humiliation." Peace was the wisest choice, a peace based "on solid reality."

Jack's "solid reality" was as dishonorable as his father's views. Restoring the old Poland was "an utter impossibility, come what may," Jack contended. The war should be ended immediately "not in the light of what should be done but in the light of what can be done." Unfortunately, Jack said, this would entail "considerable concessions to Hitlerdom": a puppet Poland, a free economic hand for the Nazis in Eastern Europe, and a redistribution of colonies. "But if Hitler could be made to disarm, the victory would be likewise great for the democracies. Hitlerism—gangsterism as a diplomatic weapon—would be gone, and Europe could once more breathe easy. The British and French Empires would be reasonably intact." Then there would be "peace for our time."

To believe Hitler would disarm was exceptionally naive. Fortunately, editorials in the *Crimson* were unsigned, so few people knew that Jack wrote it. "It was, after a studiously apolitical career at Harvard, Jack's first major statement on Hitler and appeasement, and one he would soon wish he'd never made," Nigel Hamilton noted.[55]

A lull in the war followed the defeat of Poland, but the lull ended in May 1940. In England, Chamberlain's poor handling of the war crisis aroused much opposition, leading to a loss of parliamentary and public confidence. On May 10, 1940, he resigned, and Winston Churchill formed a national coalition government. A longtime advocate of a tough policy toward Nazi Germany, Churchill proved to be the inspiring leader the British needed, and eventually became one of Jack's heroes.

On the same day Churchill assumed power, the Germans struck in the West. A German force invaded the Netherlands, knocking out the Dutch army in five days, brushed aside the Belgians, and continued its assault into France. The German spearheads crushed the resistance and forced France to capitulate on June 22. Suddenly, Hitler was triumphant, and the British were left to resist alone. In August 1940, the German Luftwaffe began sustained night bombardment of English cities; the Battle of Britain lasted until mid-May 1941. The shocking German success and the dire threat to England forced Jack, like many Americans, to revise his thinking about the war and America's role in it.[56]

Meanwhile, in his junior and senior years Jack took his courses far more seriously. Because he intended to join his father in Europe during the spring semester, in the fall of 1938 he took six courses instead of the usual four, and did remarkably well—five Bs and one C, earning him a spot on the dean's list.

Professor A. Chester Hanford taught Jack in "State Government in the United States," a course that studied state constitutional development, the governor, the legislature, the state judiciary, problems of administrative organization, federal-state relations, and a small dose of state politics. "He was regular in attendance and took an active part in classroom discussion in which he made pertinent remarks," Hanford recalled, even though the subject of state government didn't fascinate Jack. The long essays Jack wrote on optional readings impressed Hanford, "They were well organized, and gave evidence of independent thinking."[57]

In his junior year Jack produced a paper in his U.S. politics class which his professor judged "superb." Arthur Holcombe taught political science at Harvard for forty-six years. (Among his students were Henry Kissinger and Henry Cabot Lodge Jr.) A scholar with far-ranging interests, he wrote books on state government, the constitutional system, political parties, international human rights, and China. Aware that Jack was a Democrat, the Republican Holcombe purposely assigned him to study Congressman Bertram Snell, an influential upstate New York Republican who often spoke on behalf of private utilities. "I figured he'd learn more if he studied a Republican," said Holcombe.

Holcombe instructed each student to study a congressman using the official publications available in public libraries. He assigned a specific task each week. First week, how did the congressman vote? Students discovered the answer in the *Congressional Record*. Next week, what did he have to say? Third week, what did he do in his committee? Holcombe challenged them to grasp the congressman's purpose. Was he serving the public interest? Or some local or private interest? There were other challenges. What methods did the congressman use? Did he speak out often? Did he accomplish his purposes in his committee work, or out of sight? Finally, Holcombe wanted each student to evaluate the congressman's performance. Did he seem to accomplish his purposes? Did he influence the form of any measure coming out of his committee? Did he vote? "[Jack] did a very superior job of investigating, and his final report on his congressman was a masterpiece," Holcombe recalled.[58]

In his senior year Jack received a B+ in "Elements of International Law" taught by Payson Wild. Wild maintained that Jack thought deeply and theoretically; fundamental political questions intrigued him. Why do people obey? Given a few people at the top and masses below, why do the masses obey? What's the explanation? "As we went through . . . the Aristotelian theory of the state, then the Platonic [theory] and then coming to the contract theory and so on, he did discuss those with acumen and thoroughness," said Wild; "he understood and he was interested."[59]

Jack took two stimulating international-relations classes from Bruce Hopper, one focusing on contemporary Europe and the other on Asia. (He received a B+ in the first class and a B in the second.) In 1931 Hopper had written *Pan-Sovietism: The Issue Before America and the World,* a balanced, informed, and original study of the Soviet Union. In one section he compared the Soviet and American systems, socialist and capitalist, and speculated that in the future the great economic battleground of the two would be in the Far East.

Hopper also tutored Jack. They met once a week in the professor's cozy room, with its oak walls and fireplace. Near his chair Hopper had placed a plaque whose Latin inscription meant "It will give you pleasure to look back on the scenes of this suffering."

In his tutorial comments on May 13, 1939, at the end of Jack's junior year, Hopper wrote that "Kennedy took six courses the first half, and is following a course of reading I laid out for him while away in Europe this second half. I have been in correspondence with him regarding the gathering of thesis material, and should very much like to have him next year."

A year later Hopper was still mostly impressed with Jack's ability. "He is surprisingly able, when he gets down to work. His preparation may be spotty, but his general ability should bolster him up. A commendable fellow."[60]

As Jack completed his college career, friends and other observers were increasingly impressed with the quality of his intellect. He liked to probe a person's mind. Donald Thurber, who also studied government at Harvard, reflected:

> He was a person who would ask questions of you, who would challenge your assumptions, not unpleasantly, but he'd say, "Why do you feel that way? What makes you think so?" And then he'd continue a line of questioning as long as it interested him—and then, having sucked the orange dry, he would go on to another piece of fruit. You got the impression that here was a mind that was learning from other people, and that longed to learn from other people—he would regard them as sources of information and knowledge to fill out his own. The questioning was never ruthless.

History professor William G. Carleton of the University of Florida spent an evening of conversation with the Kennedys at Palm Beach and was most impressed with Jack: "It was clear to me," Carleton recalled, "that John had a far better historical and political mind than his father or his elder brother; indeed, that John's capacity for seeing current events in historical perspective and for projecting historical trends into the future was unusual."[61]

Jack's European trips had deepened his interest in political problems and international affairs, and given him a solid basis for understanding the coming of World War II. "He could be very concrete and very specific about issues because he'd been there," observed Payson Wild; "he'd met people, and he knew firsthand what the issues were."

"Jack Kennedy grew every single year of his life," Billings later emphatically stated. "If you'd gone to Europe with him in 1937 and then gone in 1939, you would have seen an entirely different man." "We all were either restless or more serious after war broke out in Europe," another classmate recalled, "but Jack seemed to mature faster than the rest of us."

Having witnessed events in Europe firsthand made all of Jack's studies at Harvard more meaningful. "My courses are really interesting this year," he wrote his father early in 1940. "That year [in Europe] is really standing me in good stead as I am quite a seer around here." For his senior thesis he was studying Great Britain's controversial appeasement policy up to the Munich Conference of September 1938, a conference that shamelessly dismembered Czechoslovakia.[62]

Created in 1918 following World War I, democratic Czechoslovakia comprised seven million Czechs, two million Slovaks, and three and a quarter million Germans living in the Sudetenland, a mountainous region between Bohemia and Silesia, bordering Germany. Hitler exploited nationalist sentiment in Germany by demanding the return of the Sudetenland to the Reich. In 1938, aided by his agents in the Sudetenland, Hitler manipulated complaints by Sudeten Germans over high unemployment and repressive security measures to manufacture a crisis.

To solve the crisis, Mussolini suggested a conference, which took place in Munich in September. England, France, Italy, and Germany attended; neither the Czechs nor the Russians were invited. To "appease" Hitler, Czechoslovakia's democratic friends abandoned her and forced the country to surrender the Sudetenland to Germany, mortally wounding the new Czech state.

After he returned to England, Chamberlain boasted that the Munich agreement meant "peace in our time." Hitler had promised him, Chamberlain said, that the Sudetenland was his final demand and that all future problems would be settled by talks. Chamberlain's mistake was to believe Hitler's promises. But the Munich settlement was wildly popular in Great Britain.

In the beginning of 1939, Hitler and his agents started creating disorder in the rest of Czechoslovakia, trying to justify German occupation of the country under the pretense of preventing anarchy. Demoralized and browbeaten by Hitler, the President of Czechoslovakia, Emil Hácha, capitulated, and on the morning of March 15, 1939, German troops marched into Prague. Independent, democratic Czechoslovakia ceased to exist.

Hitler's takeover of Czechoslovakia went far beyond simply rectifying the Treaty of Versailles. Evidently Hitler's promises made at Munich were worthless, causing public opinion in France, Great Britain, and the United States to be far more critical of him.

The Munich agreement subsequently gave the word "appeasement" a new and disagreeable meaning. No longer was "soothing or pacifying" an adequate definition; appeasement now implied "moral inadequacy and a lack of determination to defend one's rights against aggression." Munich stood as a symbol for national humiliation and betrayal. When Jack began his thesis, it had been fifteen months since Chamberlain had negotiated the Munich Pact, and ten months since Hitler had ripped up the agreement by taking over all of Czechoslovakia.[63]

In the first two months of 1940, at Jack's request, James Seymour, Joe Kennedy's aide in London, sent a steady stream of materials—scores of books, articles, pamphlets, and booklets—to Jack at Harvard.

The thesis rejected the opinion, prevalent in both Britain and the United States, that British unpreparedness was primarily the fault of a group of appeasers, led by Stanley Baldwin, Britain's Conservative prime minister from 1935 to 1937, and his successor, Chamberlain. Jack contended that the critics of Munich had been firing at the wrong target. The Munich Pact itself should not be the object of criticism; rather, "underlying factors" had made " 'surrender' inevitable."[64]

He traced the British appeasement policy and the country's lag in rearmament to varying moods and interests in England in the 1930s: blind faith in the weak League of Nations, petty and self-indulgent political partisanship, foolish pacifism, obsession with a balanced budget, the feeling that specific German claims were legitimate, self-seeking business, trade union opposition to rearmament, and the fear that social services would be trimmed to provide money for rearmament. Jack blamed the failure on almost everything—except British leaders. Explaining this omission, Jack argued weakly that "leaders are responsible for their failures only in the governing sector and cannot be held responsible for the failure of a nation as a whole."

A dictator like Adolf Hitler had superior power to control his country's foreign policy, Jack argued. Hitler could change its direction overnight by bringing the power of a unified nation into any issue, whether his followers liked it or not. In the long run, under a democratic system, the people unite in support of policy once a war begins. But before the war starts, a democracy suffers strategic defeats which may jeopardize its ultimate hope of victory. That is the price that must be paid for living in a democracy. "In the end it is felt the democratic way is the best way," Jack wrote.[65]

Unlike a dictatorship, a democracy does not take the long-range view. In the final two pages of his thesis, Jack pointedly used the word "sacrifice" three times. A democracy must sacrifice when confronted by aggressive dictatorial regimes:

> Instead of speaking of the glories of democracies in regard to its superiority in domestic affairs, we should realize the disadvantages in the international field. . . . If you decide that the democratic form is the best, be prepared to make certain great sacrifices.

Be realistic, he urged:

> Try to see things as they are. Instead of looking at Munich as the result of one man's weakness or misjudgment, try to look at it as it really was, the penalty England had to pay for her year of grace. Instead of blaming the condition of British rearmament on Baldwin, try to realize the factors really responsible. On this basis then, be prepared to make the necessary sacrifices to save the system. England was fortunate in having the period after Munich, we are fortunate in having a broad ocean. But if the dictators win the present war, we are going to have to be prepared to make the same type of sacrifices that England made during the last year.
> . . . We can't afford to misjudge situations as we misjudged Munich. We must use every effort to form accurate judgments—and even then our task is going to be a difficult one.

Munich, he concluded, was the price England had to pay for enjoying the luxury of democracy during the preceeding six years.[66]

Many historians subsequently agreed with Jack's insightful thesis. Neville Chamberlain had no other realistic choice at Munich; the pact was the best he could have negotiated under the circumstances, considering that Britain was in no position to fight in 1938. Following the seizure of all of Czechoslovakia, the British became more united, determined, and prepared than they had been at the time of Munich. The Commonwealth was now behind

them, and Hitler had exposed for the first time his determination to dominate all Europe, whether German or non-German.

Yet the Munich Pact was still dishonorable, a point Jack's thesis did not
address. One scholar characterized it as "the nadir of diplomacy—a personal
deal between two men at the expense of a third party." The commitment to
peace on which Chamberlain's appeasement rested also displayed a moral
blindness to the evils and the dangers of fascism in Europe.[67]

"Finished my thesis," Jack wrote exultantly to his father in early spring.
Titled "Appeasement at Munich: The Inevitable Result of the Slowness of
the British Democracy to Change from a Disarmament Policy," the thesis
"represents more work than I've ever done in my life," Jack said.

Joe Kennedy later took credit for inspiring the thesis. But he was brag-
ging; he had nothing to do with Jacks's selecting the topic. Jack credited his
European travel for his interest in Munich. "I wouldn't say that my father got
me interested in it," he said. "They were things that I saw for myself."

After Munich, American opinion turned against Chamberlain, an attitude
Jack thought unjustified, since America wasn't prepared to stop Hitler at Munich. What right did Americans have to criticize when they weren't rearming themselves?

Joe Jr. wrote his father in the spring 1940 that Jack was working "madly"
on his thesis. With the aid of five stenographers, Jack turned it in on the last
day, just under his deadline. Young Joe conceded that the thesis had "some
good ideas," but passed along his own literary judgment that "It seemed to
represent a lot of work but did not prove anything."[68]

In the Harvard system a senior thesis could receive a grade of summa cum
laude, magna cum laude, cum laude, or nondistinction. Professor Henry Yeo-
mans judged the thesis magna cum laude, saying, "Badly written; but a labo-
rious, interesting and intelligent discussion of a difficult question."

Professor C. J. Friedrich's report gave it a cum laude–plus. He remarked:
"Fundamental premise never analyzed. Much too long, wordy, repeti-
tious. . . . Yet thesis shows real interest and reasonable amount of work. . . .
Many typographical errors." The end result added up to an award of magna
cum laude, bettering the thesis grade of cum laude that Joe Jr. had received
for his thesis.[69]

Meanwhile Jack was changing his position about the war. Until the fall of
France in the spring of 1940, Jack believed, along with his father, that the
United States should not become entangled in another European war. But he
never shared the ambassador's tolerant view of Hitler's Germany. "He was
very much disturbed by Nazism," observed Payson Wild. "He was somewhat
embarrassed by his father's position, but he didn't get on any stands or pulpits
to declare his difference of opinion. He was a very loyal son." Jack's friends

agreed. "I think he was rebelling [against his father], but he did it rather discreetly," said Jim Rousmanière.

After France's collapse, Jack worried about England's ability to survive. In his private tutorial conferences Bruce Hopper thought Jack showed an "appreciation of the gallantry of the British people under fire, and a sensitivity to the meaning of their example for our own country."

On June 9, 1940, the *Crimson* printed Jack's letter criticizing a neutralist editorial the newspaper had printed a week earlier. The *Crimson* had stated that "there is no surer way to war, and a terribly destructive one, than to arm as we are doing." Jack responded:

> This point of view seems to overlook the very valuable lesson of England's experience during the last decade. . . . If anyone should ask why Britain is so badly prepared for this war or why America's defenses were found to be in such shocking condition . . . , this attitude toward armaments is a substantial answer. The failure to build up her armaments has not saved England from a war, and may cost her one. Are we in America to let that lesson go unlearned?[70]

In late spring of 1940, after turning in his thesis, Jack organized a student committee to raise funds for the Red Cross to help refugees in war-torn Europe. In a statement printed in the *Boston Herald* on May 20, Jack pointed out that "the desperate needs of Europe's invaded population require no more argument than the familiar facts reported in the daily papers." In a letter to his father in London, Jack expressed satisfaction about the drive's success. "[We] . . . raised $1700.00 which was five hundred over the quota that was set for us."

Despite Jack's mediocre academic record in his first two years, he did well enough in his junior and senior years to graduate cum laude, placing him above 70 percent of his classmates. In June 1940, Rose, Rosemary, Eunice, and Bobby attended Jack's Harvard graduation ceremony. From London, Ambassador Kennedy sent Jack a cable: "TWO THINGS I ALWAYS KNEW ABOUT YOU ONE THAT YOU ARE SMART AND TWO THAT YOU ARE A SWELL GUY."[71]

Before Jack graduated he had already begun revising his thesis for publication. Normally a college senior thesis isn't good enough to lure a publisher. Jack wrote to his father in London, "I thought I could work on rewriting it and make it somewhat more complete and maybe more interesting for the average reader—as it stands now—it is not anywhere polished enough although the ideas etc. are O.K."

His father's friend Arthur Krock liked the thesis and encouraged Jack to publish it. It was Krock who came up with the arresting title, *Why England Slept,* which deliberately paraphrased the title of an earlier Churchill book, *While England Slept.* (Jack asked his father if Churchill would mind.)

Joe Kennedy strongly encouraged publication. Even if Jack didn't make a cent, the book would do him an "amazing" amount of good, particularly if critics praised it.

> You would be surprised how a book that really makes the grade with high-class people stands you in good stead for years to come. . . . I remember that in the report you are asked to make after twenty-five years to the Committee at Harvard, one of the questions is "What books have you written?" and there is no doubt you will have done yourself a great deal of good.

But contrary to conventional wisdom, cynical calculation wasn't the only motivation for Joe's encouragement. He admired his son's ability to turn out a respected piece of scholarship.[72]

On May 20, 1940, Joe offered his son astute criticism. A friend Joe had consulted thought Jack's manuscript had let "[Stanley] Baldwin off too easily." Then Joe added his own insights into the responsibilities of leadership:

> The basis of your case—that the blame must be placed on the people as a whole—is sound. Nevertheless, I think that you had better go over the material to make sure that, in pinning it on the electorate, you don't give the appearance of trying to do a complete whitewash of the leaders. I know that in a democracy a politician is supposed to keep his ear to the ground; he is also supposed to look after the national welfare, and to attempt to educate the people when, in his opinion, they are off base. It may not be good politics but it is something that is vastly more important— good patriotism. . . . Why not say that British national policy was the result of British national sentiment and that everyone, leaders and people alike, must assume some share of the responsibility for what happened. It is not fair to hang it all onto the leaders; it is equally unfair to absolve them of all responsibility. For some reason, Britain slept. That means pretty much all Britain, leaders and people alike.

Roosevelt had difficulty awakening the United States to the dangers of aggression, Joe pointed out.

> To say that democracy has been awakened now by the horrible events of the past few weeks does not prove anything; any system of government would awaken at a time like this. Any person will wake up when the

house is burning down. What we want is a kind of government that will wake up when the fire first starts or, better yet, one that will not permit a fire to start at all.

Jack immediately agreed with his father's excellent critique. "Will stop white washing Baldwin." Jack incorporated portions of his father's letter almost verbatim into the book's concluding pages.[73]

Harvey Klemmer, Joe Kennedy's speechwriter and publicist in London, claimed he helped revise the manuscript. Jack, with Arthur Krock, worked together in the journalist's library in Georgetown, editing and polishing as well. "He brought the stuff to me and we worked over it," said Krock. "I may have supplied some of the material as far as prose is concerned, but it was his book." Krock contacted a literary agent, who found a publisher.

From London Joe Kennedy phoned Henry Luce, the prominent publisher of *Time, Fortune,* and *Life* magazines, and asked him to write a foreword. After reading proofs of Jack's book, Luce was impressed and agreed to write it.

Both the thesis and the book were objective and detached, but the book's conclusion turned into a warning for America. Written with becoming modesty, the book had an appealing quality of freshness and understanding. Most reviewers found it dispassionate, clear, scrupulously objective, and, above all, timely. *Time*'s review called it "startlingly timely, strenuously objective," and added, "To Americans who believe that democracy always triumphs because of its moral superiority over fascism, *Why England Slept* is a warning and challenge." The *London Times Literary Supplement* described it as "a young man's book" but one that "contains much wisdom for older men."[74]

In London Harold Laski registered a strong dissent. Writing to Joe Kennedy, Laski regretted "deeply" that Jack published the thesis because it was so immature, poorly structured, and superficial.

> In a good university, half a hundred seniors do books like this as part of their normal work in their final year. But they don't publish them for the good reason that their importance lies solely in what they get out of doing them and not in what they have to say. I don't honestly think any publisher would have looked at that book of Jack's if he had not been your son, and if you had not been Ambassador. And those are not the right grounds for publication. . . .
>
> Thinking is a hard business and you have to pay the price for admission to it. Do believe that these hard sayings from me represent much more real friendship than the easy price of "yes men" like Arthur Krock.

Although Laski didn't like the book, a man of almost equal stature sang its praises. Liddell Hart, the defense correspondent of the *London Times* and one of the greatest military analysts in the world, wrote Jack an incredible letter of congratulation. "I would like to express my admiration for the outstanding way it combines insight with balanced judgement, in a way that nothing that has yet been written here approaches," Hart said. "It is all the more impressive by comparison with other recent books which I have read, by both English and American writers, who were apt to get led astray by superficial appearances."[75]

During a revealing radio interview in August 1940, Jack deplored the fact that the United States was so unprepared for war. "We must always keep our armaments equal to our commitment," he said. "Munich should teach us that. We must realize that any bluff will be called. . . . There must be no doubt in anyone's mind. The decision must be automatic. If we debate, if we question, if we hesitate, it will be too late."

Why England Slept sold eighty thousand copies in the United States and England. Delighted, the ambassador sent copies to the queen, Churchill, and other English officials. In addition to winning modest fame, Jack earned forty thousand dollars in royalties. He bought a classy green Buick convertible with his American royalties and donated the English portion to the bombed city of Plymouth, England.[76]

By 1940 isolationism had become a major political movement in the United States, advocated by influential figures like William Randolph Hearst and Charles Lindbergh. In September, isolationists formed the primarily anti-British America First Committee, which included leading politicians of both major parties and remained in the forefront of U.S. domestic affairs until late 1941. In contrast, after the German attack on France, interventionists, who sought to aid England and France, formed the Committee to Defend America by Aiding the Allies.

The same division polarized Harvard. The isolationist American Independence League claimed seven hundred members in 1939, and the pacifist Student Union had five hundred. Several anti-Nazi groups formed to aid refugees and to support England and France.

"In the minds of the 3,500-odd undergraduates now beginning a new year at Harvard, as in the minds of most American citizens, one thought is uppermost," wrote William Frye (class of '40), the Harvard *Alumni Bulletin's* undergraduate correspondent: " 'Will the United States enter the European war?' The undergraduates know only too well that if such a tragedy ever does occur, they will be in the first draft."

Roosevelt's reelection victory in November 1940 increased his leverage with the powerful isolationist lobby in the Senate. After several months of vigorous debate, Congress passed the Lend-Lease Act in March 1941, allowing Roosevelt to aid the British. FDR also embarked on an aggressive buildup of U.S. military strength, and Congress approved the nation's first peacetime conscription law. The country inched closer to war.[77]

Meanwhile, Ambassador Kennedy remained perplexed about the war and continued to underestimate the diabolical nature of Hitler's system and its dire threat to democracies. "I can't make head or tail out of what this war's all about," he said after the start of hostilities. "If you can find out why the British are standing up against the Nazis you're a better man than I am," was his comment to American reporters. In his speeches he continued to compare democracy to totalitarianism, and while he always concluded that the democratic system was preferable, he did so halfheartedly. Certainly, Germany was no paradise, but was the Reich really as bad as the interventionists made her out to be?

Back in the United States in early November 1940, after the third-term reelection of FDR, Joe Kennedy's rash statements during an interview with three reporters severely damaged his reputation and cast his political career into oblivion. He told the newsmen what he had been saying in cables and in off-the-record conversations for several years, only this time he didn't take the precaution of setting the ground rules.[78]

On November 10, 1940, the interview story ran on page one of the Sunday *Boston Globe,* and the Associate Press spread it worldwide. "There's no sense in our getting in. We'd just be holding the bag," he said in the interview. "Democracy is finished in England. It may be here. Because it comes to a question of feeding people. It's all an economic question. . . . It's the loss of our foreign trade that's going to threaten to change our form of government. We haven't felt the pinch of it yet. It's ahead of us." It was "nonsensical" to say the United States would not trade with Europe if Hitler won the war. England wasn't fighting to save democracy, Joe said. That was "bunk." "She's fighting for self-preservation, just as we will if it comes to us."

What did he think of Eleanor Roosevelt? She was a "wonderful woman," he said, "marvelously helpful" and "full of sympathy." Joe should have stopped there, but he unwisely continued. She "bothered" him more than anyone during his New Deal jobs, always wanting him and others "to take care of the poor little nobodies who hadn't any influence." Later, when he was ambassador, she was "always sending me a note to have some little Susie Glotz to tea at the embassy." (Joe probably thought he used generic slang when he referred to "Glotz," but the term was commonly applied to Jews and was taken by some to mean that Eleanor Roosevelt wanted him to meet with Jews.)

At a time when the U.S. government had pledged to give every possible aid to England short of war, when popular opinion overwhelmingly sympathized with Britain's heroic fight, Ambassador Kennedy's interview caused an international storm.[79]

When the story became controversial, Kennedy weakly claimed that all his comments were supposed to be off the record, but that one of the reporters had violated his confidence. But he didn't deny the substantial accuracy of his remarks.

The interventionist *New York Herald Tribune* charged that he was encouraging the enemies of democracy, and discouraging democracy's defenders. His attitude contributed to the destruction of democracy by assuming that it had already been destroyed. "There is a world of difference between the realism that recognizes unpleasant facts [about England's dire predicament] and fights to overcome them and the emotional despair that concedes a fight before it is put to the test. . . . Despair can stab democracy in the back quite as fatally as treason."[80]

On December 5, 1940, Jack gingerly, lovingly advised his father on how to extricate himself from his public relations nightmare. Jack urged his father to counter the popular misconception that he was a defeatist and an appeaser by writing an article that emphasized the courage and sacrifice the British had displayed. Putting words into his father's mouth, Jack wrote,

> I am gloomy and I have been gloomy since September, 1938. It may be unpleasant for America to hear my views but let me note that Winston Churchill was considered distinctly unpleasant to have around during the years from 1935 to 1939. It was felt he was a gloom monger. In the days of the Blitzkrieg the optimist does not always do his country the best service. It is only by facing squarely reality that we can hope to meet it successfully. . . .
>
> I have seen the English stand with [their] backs to the wall and not whimper. I have seen the grim determination with which the man in the street met the news of the disasters of May and June. I have seen the soldiers coming back from the hell that was Dunkirk with their thumbs still up. . . . I have seen the boys who were friends of my children die in the air. I have seen the spirit of the Londoners through 244 air raids.

Jack plotted out for his father the best way to rebut newspaper critics: "I take serious issue with some of the [latest] stories which brand me as an appeaser and a defeatist on the basis of a newspaper interview which I later denied. The original storie [*sic*] was given an entire column, the denial not a single line."

Jack wanted his father to express his views more subtly, but Jack's advice was too transparent, and badly underestimated British antipathy toward the ambassador:

In showing how you always looked out for America's interest you might show that at Munich you agreed closely with British policy, and were very popular, yet during this last winter you became quite unpopular because of your firm stand against America's entry and your statements that America would never come in and couldn't if she wanted to. You felt that while it hurt you temporarily in the long run you feel and felt before you left that the British appreciated that you had played fairly with them by telling them the truth as you saw it. In the same way you think that in the long run this country will be glad you are telling them the truth.

Jack concluded that his father's "best angle" would be to say he "hates" dictatorships: "You have achieved the abundant life under a democratic capitalistic system—you wish to preserve it. But you believe that you can only preserve it by keeping out of Europe's wars, etc. It's not that you hate dictatorship less—but that you love America more."[81]

While advising his father, Jack clarified his own evolving thoughts about the war. Two weeks later he followed his initial advice with another letter. This one specifically advised his father to support U.S. rearmament and aid to Great Britain. "As Munich awakened England, so the events of the month of May [1940] awakened us," he wanted his father to say. "But like England we are rearming in much the same leisurely fashion."

In advising America to stay out of the war, the ambassador should not make the plea at the expense of minimizing aid to Britain. "If England is defeated America is going to be alone in a strained and hostile world. In a few years, she will have paid out enormous sums for defense yearly to maintain her armaments—she may be at war—she even may be on the verge of defeat or defeated by a combination of totalitarian powers. . . . We should see that our immediate menace is not invasion, but that England may fall—through lack of our support." He delicately urged his father not to express gloom. Rather, he should say that the situation is dangerous for America. "America must get going. . . .

"The reason I am advocating strength [at] this point is that while you believe in aid for Britain, there is [a] most popular fancie [sic] that you are [an] appeaser and against aid. This you have to nip."[82]

Throughout most of World War II Joe Kennedy remained gloomy and defeatist, ignoring his son's advice.

During his years at Harvard and after his graduation, two health problems continued to bother Jack. Since 1934, during his junior year at Choate, he had had intermittent abdominal pain, usually of a dull nature. When the pain became acute for two months in 1938, Dr. Sara Jordan suspected that he was suffering from "mild colitis" or "irritation of the duodenum," a precursor to an ulcer, but she left her diagnosis tentative. Jack described the acute pain as a burning sensation in his upper abdomen. Under Jordan's supervision, he used discretion in his diet—avoiding roughage and highly seasoned foods—and sometimes took antispasmodic medication prescribed by Jordan.

Jack's many ailments disturbed his father. Twice in September 1938, in letters to Dr. Jordan, Joe Kennedy expressed fear that his second-oldest child was becoming a hypochondriac. "He may get to thinking he is a sick boy— I see some signs of this—and I want him to get away from that idea as quickly as possible." Three weeks later he wrote, "I constantly have in mind not letting him become a hypochondriac. I want him to think he is a well boy with just a little upset, which isn't any different from what his father had at his age."[83]

Between 1938 and 1940 Jack was often hospitalized: in February 1938 at the Mayo Clinic, two weeks in June at New England Baptist Hospital, and another trip to the Mayo Clinic in February 1939. Biographer Robert Dallek observed, "It was the same old routine: a diet of bland foods three times a day and another inspection of his colon and digestive system."

In February 1939, Dr. Walter Alvarez of the Mayo Clinic hinted that Jack's stomach pain might, indeed, stem from hypochondria. All the major tests of Jack's stomach were negative. There was "nothing significant except tenderness on both sides of the abdomen," Alvarez reported. He suggested that Jack's stomach problems might be caused by "an inherited nervousness or sensitiveness of the nervous system. We see this sort of thing commonly in college students who get over it as they grow older and as responsibilities come upon them." There was "no doubt" that some of Jack's "loose [bowel] movements are due to emotion."[84]

Jack seemed to understand that part of his stomach ailment stemmed from emotional stress. His awareness was a major reason he did not immediately go on to law school after graduating from Harvard. Law school would be more difficult than college, he wrote in June 1940 to Dr. Paul O'Leary at the Mayo Clinic. Perhaps a year off from the academic pressure would rid him of his stomach ailment. He didn't want to waste time, but "I don't want to have this thing the rest of my life, and if I thought that one year of solid rest would hold a good chance of getting rid of it, then I think that I should do it."[85]

In 1938 Jack began experiencing back pain. When the pain subsided, he continued to swim, golf, and play touch football. Then in August 1940 he felt "something" pull in his back while he was serving at tennis, and the pain recurred the next time he played. He often felt something "slip out" in his back; if he sat in a certain position for a while, it would "go in again."

Gradually his back became stiffer and more painful. After getting out of bed in the morning, his left sacroiliac region would hurt, forcing him to walk stiff-legged. Occasionally the soreness crossed over to the region of the right sacroiliac.

In 1940, an orthopedist at Boston's Lahey Clinic thought, incorrectly, that Jack had a "very unstable . . . lumbo-sacral joint." He urged that conservative measures—"manipulative" treatment and exercises—be tried first. If those failed, Jack should undergo a fusion operation "which will completely fix his joint." It is uncertain whether Jack underwent the treatment and exercises, but he did decide, for the moment, not to have surgery.[86]

Following his graduation from Harvard, Jack thought about attending Yale Law School or following his father into business. Actually, he didn't know what he wanted to do, and was worried about his health. Because 1940 was not a good time for making long-term plans, Jack waited. "We were so damn close to going to war," said Billings. "There was no depth to the future. You didn't know what you were going to do so what was the point of getting into any life-long thing. I think every boy at that time was just sort of marking time."[87]

Why not head west and audit some graduate classes at Stanford? It would be an adventure—meeting new people, especially attractive coeds. He explained to friends and to interviewers that he planned to study business law, first taking courses at Stanford's business school, and later entering Yale Law School.

Located in Palo Alto, California, Stanford had a student body that was mostly middle-class, white, and Protestant. It was also politically conservative; in straw polls throughout the 1920s and 1930s students voted Republican by about a two-to-one margin; in 1932 they voted more than three-to-one for Hoover over Roosevelt.

For sixty dollars a month Jack rented a small cottage on campus behind the home of Gertrude Gardiner of 624 Mayfield Avenue. She described him as "standing out head and shoulders above the other [students]."[88]

"Have become very fond of Stanford," Jack wrote Billings on November 14, 1940; "everyone is very friendly—the gals are quite attractive—and it's a very good life." A month earlier he had registered for the draft. "They will never take me into the army—and yet if I don't [get into military service] it will look quite bad—I may be able to work out some sort of thing."

"As you may have heard went down to Hollywood and took it by storm," he wrote Billings. "I have many glowing reports to tell you." During several jaunts to Hollywood he met Clark Gable, Spencer Tracy, Lana Turner, and Margaret Sullavan.[89]

At a Hollywood studio Jack also met the young actor Robert Stack, who introduced him to several women and a new technique of womanizing.

Near the Hollywood Hills, Stack had a hideaway that included his prized "Flag Room." "The room itself was no bigger than a full-size bed," Stack wrote in his autobiography; "the ceiling was too low to allow an adult to stand fully upright." On the walls and the ceiling Stack had plastered flags from every nation. "I devised a game that required the lady of the evening to memorize the flags on the ceiling in a given time or pay the penalty. Since she was already in a horizontal position, paying the penalty was usually no problem." Stack introduced Jack to his flag game. "I am happy to say that Jack Kennedy found occasion to further his geopolitical studies and gain future constituents at our little pad."

Stack left little doubt as to Kennedy's prowess with women. "I've known many of the great Hollywood stars, and only a very few of them seemed to hold the attraction for women that JFK did, even before he entered the political arena. He'd just look at them and they'd tumble."

A male friend from his days at Stanford remembered that one of Jack's favorite phrases was "Slam, Bam, Thank You, Ma'am." He allegedly told the same friend, "I'm not interested in carrying on, for the most part. I like the conquest. That's the challenge. I like the contest between male and female—that's what I like. It's the chase I like—not the kill!"[90]

Jack took dates to the popular Stanford hangouts—Dinah's Shack, a steak house with a bar and a fireplace, and L'Omlette, where students congregated to listen to the jukebox and drink beer. "Jack was never a drinker, he rarely took anything," said Harriet "Flip" Price, Jack's steady girlfriend at Stanford. Jack escorted Price (class of 1942), a stunningly beautiful sorority girl, to dances and to Stanford football games in his new Buick convertible.

"I wanted to tell you that I hadn't 'cooled' in the way I feel," she wrote Jack after one date. "You are difficult at times and those last two nights were a good example. But you make up for that in a hundred other ways."

Their relationship eventually fizzled. "Yes, I was in love with him," Price recalled. "Of course, I was wildly in love with him. He was extremely attractive. We never talked about the possibility of marriage seriously, a little bit, but not seriously."[91]

The author of *Why England Slept* was a person of note on the Stanford campus. "Photographers were always taking his picture," said Price. "He was sort of a minicelebrity." Jack told some people he met at Stanford that he had not only graduated from Harvard but had spent "six months" at the London School of Economics.

Since he contemplated a career in business, he audited a business economics course in the Graduate School of Business. Professor Theodore J. Kreps, who taught the course, remembered him as "a very able lad, with a good, independent mind."

Because his interest in politics remained acute, Jack audited courses from two of Stanford's most eminent professors of political science, Thomas S. Barclay and Graham H. Stuart. Barclay taught a graduate seminar in politics where eight students discussed the presidential campaign of 1940 and other political issues. Jack took part in the discussions and came to know the other students. "He had a very friendly and charming manner at all times," Barclay recalled. "I considered him well-informed and intelligent in the field of politics and international relations. He had had a splendid background both at Harvard and in London."[92]

Jack met Bruce Jessup, a mild-mannered campus politician just beginning his term as Stanford's new student body president. Complaining to Jack about the failure of student government at Stanford, Jessup worried that his new administration was becoming as ineffective as its predecessors. What could he do about the problem? Jack responded sensibly that any government without power will be ineffective; Jessup would have to overthrow the university's administration to get power.

Another acquaintance, Harry Muheim, recalled accompanying Jack to a get-together for two dozen faculty and students at the home of Edgar Eugene Robinson, a Stanford history professor. "I had never before heard one of my contemporaries allude to so many things," Muheim said about Jack.

At the Robinsons', Muheim recalled, "We listened to one person, then another, and as the evening went on, we listened mostly to Kennedy. . . . He didn't force himself upon us. The talk just seemed to move easily to him, and he responded." Because Jack knew more about why England slept than anybody in the room, he held the floor on the current status of World War II. "I got the feeling that even Edgar Eugene Robinson was picking up a couple of points," Muheim recalled.

> Jack Kennedy did not seem to be depressed by the news that he brought us. Even though the subject was solemn, he kept tossing bright humor into the exchanges, and several times he had the place roaring with laughter. Not only the students laughed. The faculty men were laughing, too.[93]

The news from Europe and the predicament in which the Battle of Britain had put his father captivated Jack. "He was interested in this one thing only," recalled Professor Kreps of Jack's preoccupation with World War II. Defending the ambassador, he told the *Stanford Daily* on October 15, 1940, "I understand they're calling Dad 'America's most bombed ambassador' now. That's a helluva title, isn't it?" He listened to every radio broadcast. "I turned it off once when we were driving around San Francisco, and he was furious," said Harriet Price. "He was really angry."

On May 7, 1941, he set sail aboard the *Argentina* for a tour of South America. After landing in Rio de Janeiro he flew to Argentina to spend two weeks. Following visits to Montevideo, Uruguay, and Santiago, Chile, on June 14 he boarded the USS *Santa Lucia* bound for New York. By then U.S. military preparedness for war was almost in full swing; it was time for him to enlist.[94]

6

THE DANISH SPY

Despite his medical problems, Jack was determined to enter military service. "It was an impressive act of courage," said Robert Dallek. "His intestinal and back problems would make a military regimen a constant struggle and seemed likely to further undermine his health." But Jack failed the physical exams for both the army's and the navy's officer candidate schools. In desperation he allowed his father to use his connections. "Only a denial of his medical history would allow [Jack] to pass muster, and he was able to ensure this through Captain Alan Kirk, his father's former naval attaché at the American embassy in London and current head of the Office of Naval Intelligence (ONI) in Washington, D.C.," noted Dallek. "I am having Jack see a medical friend of yours in Boston tomorrow for physical examination and then I hope he'll become associated with you in Naval Intelligence," Joe wrote Kirk in August 1941.

A month later, the board of medical examiners declared him "physically qualified for appointment" as an officer in the naval reserve and assigned him to Naval Intelligence. "It was a complete whitewash," said Dallek, "that would never have been possible without his father's help. . . . True, being in intelligence made it unlikely that he would be exposed to physical danger, but once in the service almost anything could happen."[1]

Jack officially joined the navy in October 1941 and was immediately assigned to the Foreign Intelligence Branch of the ONI in Washington. He rented a small apartment in Washington only a few blocks away from his sister Kathleen, who had recently moved to Washington to work as a reporter at the *Washington Times-Herald*. Kick had become a close friend of twenty-eight-year-old Inga Arvad Fejos, who wrote a daily column, "Did You Happen to See," in the *Times-Herald*. Inga interviewed lower-echelon government officials for her uncritical personality sketches.

When Jack became a member of Kathleen's active social group, he naturally met Inga. In fact, Inga wrote a personality profile of Jack for the *Times-Herald* on November 27, 1941. By late November they had become passionate lovers.[2]

Born on October 6, 1913, in Copenhagen, Inga had studied in England, captured a Denmark beauty contest at age sixteen, and competed for the Miss Europe title at age seventeen. Still in her teens, she eloped with Kamal Abdel Nabi, an Egyptian diplomat, but quickly divorced him. In 1936 she married Paul Fejos. The Hungarian-born Fejos was a naturalized U.S. citizen who according to Arvad worked as an archaeologist and motion picture director. For the past two years he had been in charge of a scientific expedition in South America, and Inga was in the process of seeking a divorce from him. She had arrived in the United States in 1940. She attended the Columbia University School of Journalism in New York City before securing the job on the *Times-Herald*.

Worldly, multilingual, well traveled, sophisticated, sexually experienced, Inga was also stunningly beautiful. "Luscious, luscious is the word," remarked Kathleen Kennedy's friend John White. "Like a lot of icing on a cake."[3]

Her life and Jack's life changed dramatically after December 7, 1941. Following the Japanese attack on Pearl Harbor, the United States declared war on Germany, Italy, and Japan. With rumor and paranoia permeating the atmosphere in Washington, Inga's past soon attracted suspicion.

One morning a few days after the Pearl Harbor disaster and America's entry into the war, a reporter for the *Times-Herald* discovered an old photo of a smiling Inga sitting alongside Adolf Hitler at the 1936 Olympics in Berlin. The reporter informed his colleague Page Huidekoper about the discovery. Thinking Inga might be a German spy, Huidekoper told Kathleen Kennedy and her boss, Frank Waldrop, and Kathleen told Inga.

On December 12, 1941, Inga, Waldrop, and Huidekoper marched to the Washington Field Office of the FBI to try to clear her reputation. She volunteered background information about herself because it had been "rumored" she was working for the German propaganda ministry. Inga claimed she never had a close association with Hitler or Hermann Göring. Meeting them was simply part of her brief European journalistic career. After she learned that Göring was to be married, she secured an exclusive interview with him and sold the story to a Danish newspaper. Impressed by her article, the Danish newspaper sent her to Berlin to get more exclusives. She met Hitler at Göring's wedding. Impressed, the führer referred to Inga as a "perfect example of Nordic beauty." Afterward she interviewed him, and he invited her to sit with him at the Berlin Olympic Games of 1936.

She denied she was an intelligence agent, claiming her interviews with Hitler and his henchmen were nonpolitical. She only wrote human interest stories—their views on marriage, and "what they ate for breakfast, etc." Although polite, the FBI official gave Inga no satisfaction.[4] "Miss Arvad heatedly denied the accusations and professed to detest the Germans," an FBI official wrote to J. Edgar Hoover the same day. "Miss Arvad stated that she wanted an investigation made and then wanted a letter from the Federal Bureau of Investigation, stating that she was not a spy." The FBI refused to grant her wish.

In fact, the FBI had already begun to investigate her. On June 7, 1941, her "friendship" with Hitler had been reported by the FBI's New York office. So when the photo was discovered at the *Times-Herald,* the FBI's Washington office swung into action.[5]

The FBI's suspicions went beyond Inga's alleged friendship with Nazi leaders. Her husband, Paul Fejos, was currently employed by Axel Wenner-Gren, reputed to be the Axis "super-agent for the Western hemisphere," sent to soften up Latin America. One of the wealthiest men in the world, the Swedish businessman owned the *Southern Cross,* a spectacular yacht fitted with machine guns, rifles, and sophisticated radio equipment. U.S. Naval Intelligence suspected that the yacht was being used to refuel German submarines. Since December 1941, Wenner-Gren had been formally blacklisted by the U.S. government.[6]

Biographer Nigel Hamilton has provided the most richly detailed account of Kennedy's courtship with Arvad. "Why the Washington Field Office of the FBI did not simply reinterview Inga, a compliant citizen, is incomprehensible," observed Hamilton. "Instead, for the remainder of 1941 and the first few weeks of 1942, it resorted to surveillance, interception of mails, phone tapping, burglary, and information from janitors and postmen to piece together its own picture of Inga's past and present, guaranteeing a comic mishmash of distortion, paranoid speculation, and plain ignorance."

Despite the innumerable details he needed to handle, the fate of massive armies on his mind, even President Roosevelt briefly focused on the alleged Danish spy. "In view of the connection of Inga Arvad . . . with the Wenner-Gren Expeditions' leader, and in view of certain other circumstances which have been brought to my attention, I think it would be just as well to have her specially watched," he wrote J. Edgar Hoover.[7]

Jack and Inga's affair quietly flourished until January 12, 1942, when the gossip columnist Walter Winchell publicly exposed their relationship in the *New York Mirror*. "One of Ex-Ambassador Kennedy's eligible sons is the target of a Washington gal columnist's affections. So much so she has consulted her barrister about divorcing her exploring groom. Pa Kennedy no like." Winchell apparently had gathered his information from the FBI's reports on Inga and Jack.[8]

The day after the column's appearance Jack abruptly received telephone orders transferring him from Washington to a desk job in Charleston. What's more, Joe Sr. soon arrived at Waldrop's newspaper office to gather the details of Jack's new love affair, now so publicly exposed. Joe saw a huge problem with the relationship: Inga was four years older than Jack, was about to be divorced for the second time, and was suspected of being a German spy.

"Jack is here only until Friday, when he is to be stationed at Charleston," Rose Kennedy wrote the children on January 20. "He said he was completely mystified as to why he was changed and he was quite stunned by the suddenness of the news." Jack probably was mystified and stunned, but he must have known that his sudden transfer had a lot to do with the Winchell gossip item, a story Rose apparently hadn't read.[9]

Jack soon grew alarmed about a rumor—unfounded as it turned out—that the Winchell column was inspiring a *Life* magazine article about his relationship with Inga. "I'll try to get up this weekend," he told Inga. "You didn't hear any more about *Life*, did you?" Inga had not.

Before the appearance of the Winchell column, Joe Sr. acted cavalier about Jack's fling with Inga, not knowing her background or Jack's thoughts of marriage. Afterward, Joe had several conversations with his son about Inga, pressuring him to break their relationship. "Jack, she's *already* married!" he exclaimed on one occasion.

John White dated Kathleen Kennedy at the time, and she often told him that her father was getting ready to "drag up his big guns" because of Jack's relationship with Inga. "We used to go out, the four of us, fairly regularly because it was such a good cover for everybody," White recalled.

> We'd part immediately and go about our businesses and then join again. Kathleen said we might have to give up these pleasant foursomes because her father was disapproving of Inga. We had to sort of sneak around because he wasn't even supposed to be seen with her because her reputation was so dubious. The combination of possible marriage and [her] dubious reputation frightened the old man.

"I am not going to try and make you change," Inga told Jack on January 27, 1942; "it would be without result anyway—because big Joe has a stronger hand than I."[10]

When FBI agents broke into Arvad's apartment, they discovered, among other things, letters written by Jack to Inga. In one Jack wrote, "I've returned from an interesting trip, about which I won't bore you with the details, as if you are a spy I shouldn't tell you and if your [*sic*] not you won't be interested. But I missed you."

In the demented view of FBI agents, Inga had supposedly saluted Hitler and been assigned as chief of Nazi propaganda in Denmark. When Inga spent the first weekend in February with Jack in Charleston, at the request of the FBI the Fort Sumter Hotel's management had assigned them to a pre-bugged room. The FBI overheard a little Washington gossip, no discussion of military secrets, and a lot of sex. "Technical surveillance coverage disclosed that they engaged in sexual intercourse on a number of occasions in the hotel room during this period," stated the FBI's report.[11]

"For the FBI, sex could only be associated with criminality or espionage," noted Nigel Hamilton. "Such conversations were thus laboriously transcribed, pored over, analyzed for indications of spying." But to the two lovers, "sex was part of love—a kind of love Jack had never known before." Inga "tormented Jack with a depth of maternal, womanly affection he would never experience again in his starlet-studded life—an appreciative, forgiving, understanding, tantalizing, humorous, intuitive, feminine love that made every other relationship seem small and artificial." He would "confide hopes, ambitions, and fears he never told another mortal soul, and to her he exhibited a quality of strutting, boyish, witty candor no other man in Inga's career would ever match."

By early February Jack knew that they were both under suspicion.

"I hear the hotel clerk at the Fort Sumter is an investigator," he told Inga on February 9 (with the FBI listening).

"For what?"

"The Navy." . . .

"Wonderful. You'll soon be kicked out."

"There is more truth than poetry to that," Jack replied.[12]

Hamilton provided concrete evidence that Jack Kennedy had presidential ambitions as early as 1941, and discussed them with Inga. He told her that he was torn between his postwar dreams of moving to a ranch out west or pursuing an extraordinary political ambition—as she rephrased it, "to be a White-House-Man."

Inga was serious when she referred to Jack's secret presidential ambitions. "Jack had known Inga would not expose him to ridicule," said Hamilton. "Nor did she, for she was quite convinced he had it in him to become president if he set his mind to it."

"Put a match to the smoldering ambition, and you will go like wild fire," she advised him. ("It is all against the ranch out West, but it is the unequalled highway to the White House.) And if you can find something you really believe in, then my dear you caught the biggest fish in the ocean."[13]

According to an FBI surveillance report, she called him "honey, darling, honeysuckle," and "honey child Wilder," and often told him, "I love you." In her letter of January 26, 1942, she offered encouragement and advice: "Go up the steps of fame. But—pause now and then to make sure that you are accompanied by happiness. Stop and ask yourself. 'Does it sing inside me today.' . . . Look around and don't take another step till you are certain life is as you will and want it."

She thought he feared expressing his innermost feelings: "Maybe your gravest mistake handsome is that you admire brains more than heart, but then that is necessary to arrive."

She was motherly, fretting about his ailing back. "It is because you are dearer to me than anybody else that I would want to be with you when you are sick," she wrote. "Maybe it is the maternal instinct."[14]

Inga's teasing tantalized him. When he praised a recent column she had written, Inga dissented, claiming it was "terrible work." Jack thought she didn't know "what is good and what is bad." Inga responded wickedly: "I know that you are good—and damned bad too." No woman in Jack's life, said Hamilton, "would ever come close to Inga's mix of licentiousness and wit. . . . She could turn a phrase or witticism as quick or quicker than Jack."

"To you I need not pretend," Jack told her. "You know me too well." Inga agreed. "I do, not because I have put you on a pedestal—you don't belong there, nobody does—but because I know where you are weak, and that is what I like."

Jack was kind to her. When Inga's mother had surgery, he took Inga to visit her every evening, always bringing flowers, always with a few cheerful words.

Jack's feelings were so intense that he briefly explored the possibility of an annulment for Arvad's two marriages so he could marry her within the Catholic Church.

Inga alternated between wanting to carry Jack's baby and worrying about becoming pregnant. The thought of carrying Jack's child delighted her because "you are the kind the world ought to swarm with." Later, though, she accused Jack of "taking every pleasure of youth but not the responsibility."[15]

Meanwhile, when Rear Admiral Theodore Wilkinson, the director of Naval Intelligence, got wind of the FBI's information about Jack cavorting with a possible spy, and read Winchell's column, he became frantic. According to Captain S. A. D. Hunter, Jack's section chief in the Office of Naval Intelligence, Wilkinson "wanted to get Kennedy out as quickly as possible." The assistant director, Captain Howard Kingman, was equally alarmed, fearing Inga was a Mata Hari. "Captain Kingman called me in and said we have a very serious problem on our hands and we would have to get rid of Kennedy as soon as possible," Hunter recalled. Apparently Joe Kennedy intervened, made phone calls, and persuaded the navy brass to reassign Jack to Charleston, rather than cashier him.

Inga was no spy, and Jack was not privy to any important confidential information. "The information at [Jack's] disposal was just laughable," Hunter said. "Most of our information we got out of the newspapers—like *The New York Times*."[16]

In late February 1942, Jack phoned Inga and told her that his father had just called and convinced him what he must do about their relationship. Jack obtained special permission to fly to Washington on February 28 for one night, where the couple discussed their relationship and agreed to separate. Jack returned to Charleston the next day. (Also in late February Inga had received a phone call from a former Danish boyfriend, then living in New York. Almost immediately they began a sexual relationship. So while Jack visited Inga on February 28, he was being two-timed.)

But the lonely ensign couldn't persevere in his decision to break off their relationship.

"Surprised to hear from me?" Jack inquired when he phoned Inga a week after they had agreed to end their affair.

"A little maybe," Inga answered.

"It's about time," Jack said.

"Kathleen says every day that you will call me," Inga remarked.

"I've been in bed with a bad back," Jack apologized. "Why didn't you come [to Charleston]?"

"What a question. Don't you remember that we talked it over on Sunday?"

"I know it."

"Oh, you don't think it's going to stay?"

"Life's too short."

"Oh, Kennedy!" Inga cried out. Was Jack going back on their agreement to separate?

"No," Jack answered, "not till the next time I see you. I'm not too good, am I?"

"Did you think I was coming to Charleston?" she asked a little later.

"I had big hopes."[17]

After the breakup, they occasionally wrote each other. She wondered "how you are getting on, how that back of yours is behaving, and what you think of life in general," she wrote him on April 23. "It won't ever be like the old days . . . but you have a great future, don't ever let anybody make you believe anything different."

On June 3, 1942, Inga obtained a divorce from Fejos in Reno, Nevada. She resigned from her *Times-Herald* job and moved to New York City and subsequently to California.

After Jack returned from the war he visited Inga once or twice. Arvad later married the former cowboy actor Tim McCoy, who was thirty years her senior, and moved to Arizona. Six months after the marriage she gave birth to a son, Ronald McCoy. Not until twenty years later, according to Ronald McCoy, did Inga inform her son that she had been pregnant when she married McCoy. She added, "I don't know who your father was for sure. . . . I really don't know if it was Jack or Tim. I don't know."[18]

In Charleston Jack was frustrated with his desk job at the headquarters of the Sixth Naval District. Encoding and deciphering mundane messages and signals bored him. The dramatic progress of his older brother's military career rekindled their sibling rivalry. In May 1942, Joe Jr. graduated from flight training at Jacksonville, Florida, received his commission as an ensign in the Naval Reserve, and was named "outstanding" cadet in his class. While attending the graduation ceremony, Ambassador Kennedy proudly pinned the wings on his son's chest. How could Jack compete with that success?

"He was *very* unhappy" in Charleston, Billings recalled. Jack's correspondence referred to "tired old Charleston." In a letter to his sister Jean, he mocked his inactivity: "I am fighting on the beaches and the landing places of the Isle of Palms, located 'in easy driving distance of the city of Charleston.'"[19]

He kept lobbying for sea duty. "He has become disgusted with the desk jobs and all the Jews," Joe Sr. wrote young Joe, "and as an awful lot of the fellows that he knows are in active service, and particularly with you in the fleet service, he feels that at least he ought to be trying to do something. I quite understand his position, but I know his stomach and his back are real deterrents—but we'll see what we can do." (In his reference to Jews, Joe Sr. was probably expressing his own opinion, not Jack's.)

In his offhand use of the phrase "we'll see what we can do," the ambassador revealed the extraordinary degree of his involvement with his children's lives. Doris Goodwin wondered: "Was it simply, as he liked to say, that he enjoyed being with his children and doing things for them more than anything else in the world, especially now that his public career had been brought to a halt?" This was part of his motivation, but not all of it, "for it would seem that by investing in his children's future as deeply as he did, Kennedy was able to balance the frustrations in his own life and to hide the fact that he had nothing else to do."[20]

When Billings visited Jack in Charleston, he witnessed his friend's first public speech. Jack spoke on incendiary bombs to an audience of 350 factory workers. He knew very little about the subject, but delivered a good speech. "I was impressed," said Billings. Afterward, though, Jack asked for questions, a potentially fatal error. "You have told us about these two kinds of bombs," asked the first questioner. "If one lands, how do you tell which is which?" Jack hadn't the faintest idea, but, thinking fast on his feet, he responded, "I'm glad you asked that question, because a specialist is going to be down here in two weeks, and this is the kind of thing he wants to talk about."

Billings didn't hear Jack's second speech in Charleston, one with insight into Jack's values and views. He was asked to deliver an address at the induction ceremony for navy recruits in Charleston, part of an Independence Day celebration on July 4, 1942. His speech, "For What We Fight," praised the founding fathers and lauded the Declaration of Independence. "Some may argue that the ideals for which we fight now, those embodied in the Atlantic Charter and the Four Freedoms, are . . . impossible to achieve. Indeed, some men argue that Christianity itself has failed. They point to a world aflame with war, and they say that the principles that Christ taught are too high, that men will never live their lives according to his precepts."

The pessimists might be correct, he suggested. Perhaps the world could never live according to those exemplary principles. "But that does not mean we should throw these principles aside. They represent ideals and goals worth working for—worth fighting for. A world which casts away all morality and principle—all hopeless idealism, if you will—is not a world worth living in."

America's current enemies could never be accused of idealism. "We say that all men are created equal. They deny it. They believe in the theory of the Master Race, in government by the elite—a government of a chosen few, by a chosen few, for a chosen few."

Jack worried about America's attitude following the current conflict. "Weary of war, we may fall ready victims to post-war cynicism and disillusionment, as we did at the end of the last war." Americans should not allow that to happen again, should not become discouraged or disheartened. "Even if we may not win all for which we strive—even if we win only a small part—that small part will mean progress forward and that indeed makes our cause a worthy one."

Americans must sacrifice, like our ancestors, for high ideals which may appear difficult or impossible. "The sacrifice is not too great," he concluded. "As young men, it is, after all, for our own future that we fight. And so with a firm confidence and belief in that future, let us go forward to victory."

It was a surprisingly stirring speech, reflecting a strong faith in democratic values and the need to sacrifice and fight for ideals, and yet to temper faith with practical realism.[21]

While performing his boring administrative chores in Charleston and chafing to get out to the war zone, Kennedy spent much of his time reading and writing his impressions of current events. In February 1942, he became infuriated with Congress for wasting precious time on an acrimonious debate about a trivial issue. On February 6, 1942, the House of Representatives exploded with indignation at the appointments of screen actor Melvyn Douglas and dancer Mayris Chaney to the Office of Civilian Defense. Critics suspected Eleanor Roosevelt, the president's controversial wife, of pushing the appointments to "get jobs for her friends."

From both the Republican and Democratic sides of the House came bitter assertions and sarcastic comments. The "parasites and leeches" should be stricken from the payroll, one congressman declared. Member after member pointed out that enemy air raids on the United States were to be expected, and then demanded to know what actors and dancers could do to eliminate the threat. Another congressman rebutted critics of Mrs. Roosevelt, declaring that the House was "putting on a burlesque show." The ludicrous "debate" continued throughout the rest of February.

For the most part the United States was mobilizing effectively for the war, but in sarcastic letters to several friends Jack bemoaned the dawdling of Congress, using it as evidence that Americans weren't taking the war seriously. Wars were only won by "fighting them," he told a friend.[22]

In the fall of 1941, the pain and stiffness in his back increased, and by April 1942, Jack felt miserable. Following tests at the U.S. Naval Hospital in Charleston, doctors sent him to the U.S. Naval Hospital in Chelsea, Massachusetts, where he was admitted on May 18 for what a Chelsea medical report described as a "dislocation, chronic, recurrent, sacroiliac, right side." "He now feels that he is not getting ahead," the report stated, "and, as [he] wants to get duty he came in here for a checkup."

By June 15 Jack's condition had dramatically improved. He was suffering less pain, walking fine, and completing leg raises to 90 degrees, with good back motion. "Diagnosis changed to strain, muscular, lower back," doctors reported. Eight days later doctors discharged him to duty. Periodically, though, his pain would return.[23]

Throughout World War II Jack continued to suffer simultaneously from the two debilitating health problems, his stomach and his back. Scores of tests at several different clinics and hospitals, plus two torturous operations, hadn't improved his condition by the war's end. That he could still function effectively during the war testified to his fortitude and courage.

7

PT 109

Finally, in late July 1942, Jack received a long-awaited telegram transferring him to midshipmen's school at Northwestern University. On his way to his new assignment he stopped off in Washington to see Inga, who was dismayed with the condition of his back. She explained in a telephone call to a friend (monitored by the FBI) that "he is going on active sea duty. Only you know, his back—he looks like a limping monkey from behind. He can't walk at all. That's ridiculous, sending him off to sea duty."[1]

"Am out at this sea school in Chicago—sleeping eight in a room—and B.O. can be exceedingly dismal," he complained in a letter to Billings. "However there is a good bunch here."

Shortly after arriving at Northwestern, Jack became mesmerized by one of America's heroes in the early part of World War II. During a grave moment in the Pacific war, as the Philippines were about to fall to the Japanese, Lieutenant John D. Bulkeley commanded a motor torpedo boat squadron that plucked General Douglas MacArthur off the U.S. fortress at Corregidor. Beginning on March 11, 1942, the squadron wound its way through Japanese-patrolled water on a 560-mile voyage to bring the general to safety. Afterward, Bulkeley was brought back to the States to receive a hero's welcome. President Roosevelt personally presented him with the Medal of Honor, after which Bulkeley spent a year crisscrossing the nation speaking at bond rallies and recruiting patrol torpedo (PT) boat skippers. *They Were Expendable,* the book about Bulkeley's exploits, became a best-seller and glamorized PT boats and their courageous crews.[2]

A powerful public speaker, Bulkeley extolled the gallantry of PT skippers and the virtues of PT boats, and in the process greatly exaggerated the prowess of the boats. If two hundred new PTs were rushed to the Pacific, he argued, Americans would win the war against the Japanese. Before Jack's class at Northwestern, Bulkeley repeated his fantasies, boasting, "The PT boat is a great weapon. The enemy has not yet won a brush with one. Our little half squadron sank one Jap cruiser, one plane tender and one loaded transport, badly damaged another cruiser, set a tanker on fire and shot down four planes." Bulkeley, whose assertions have never been confirmed, fabricated a myth about the effectiveness of PT boats in the Pacific, and in the process ignored the huge contributions of marines, aircraft, warships, and submarines.

Under the headline BULKELEY ASKS 50—1,024 VOLUNTEER! the *New York Herald American* reported that Bulkeley wanted "50 young men of surpassing courage to enter the dangerous service in which he distinguished himself, and when he issued his invitation at the Naval Officers School [in Chicago], he practically was swept off his feet as 1,024 young Ensigns . . . stepped forth and asked for the job." One was Jack Kennedy.

Alvin Cluster, later Jack's squadron commander in the Pacific, knew Bulkeley well and deplored his arrogance and exaggerations. Americans desperately needed heroes after the Pearl Harbor disaster and seized on any exploit, any success, that showed the greatness of the United States. "The only reason PT boats ever got the attention they did was that we had nothing else!" said Cluster.

Because Bulkeley could select only a small fraction of the men who applied for PT boat training, Joe Kennedy worried that his son might not be among them. To tip the balance in Jack's favor, the older Kennedy invited Bulkeley to lunch at the Plaza Hotel in New York. Bulkeley recalled the meeting fifty years later: "Joe wanted to know if I had the clout to get Jack into PT boats, and I said that I did, and would interview his son the next time I was at Northwestern. If I thought Jack could measure up, I would recommend his acceptance, I told Joe." Joe Kennedy was pleased, but told Bulkeley he hoped Jack could be sent someplace that "wasn't too deadly."[3]

As it turned out, Jack had ample qualifications. Together with Bulkeley, Lieutenant Commander John Harllee had a major role in selecting candidates for PT boat training. He first met Jack at Northwestern:

> I recall him as a young man of very boyish appearance and great enthusiasm and desire to get into combat. . . . Many Ivy League graduates came from families which owned sailing craft or cabin cruisers or power boats,

and they were familiar with small boats and therefore appeared to be good material for PT boats. Also they had good educations and mental qualifications as well as physical qualifications.

Harllee later commented that he saw nothing wrong with the Kennedys' lobbying effort with Bulkeley. "There's a lot of people in America who use political influence to keep *out* of combat, but Jack Kennedy used it to get *into* combat!"

After Bulkeley and Harllee recommended Jack as a PT officer, on October 1, 1942, he started an eight-week training course at Melville, Rhode Island. (When they selected Jack, neither Harllee nor Bulkeley knew anything about Jack's weak back or abdominal pain.) He was going to torpedo boat school under Lieutenant Bulkeley, Jack told Billings, adding, "The requirements are very strict physically—you have to be young, healthy and unmarried—and as I am young and unmarried, I'm trying to get in."[4]

Low, squat, eighty feet long, the high-speed PT boats were powered by three 12-cylinder Packard engines, each with 1,350 horsepower. The boat carried four 21-inch torpedoes and mounted four .50-caliber machine guns in two twin turrets. Her normal complement was three officers and nine men.

PT boats fought in every major theater of war: in the English Channel and the North Sea, off Burma, Malaya, and the Philippines, and across the Pacific islands. In the ideal torpedo attack, PTs silently lay in wait in the path of a convoy, then idled unseen toward the target, launched their torpedoes, and quickly slipped away. Unlike any other naval ship, PT boats offered the exhilaration of speed, a feature that enticed Jack. The PTs' greatest weakness was the Mark VIII torpedoes fitted in the boats. Designed in the 1920s, the outmoded torpedoes frequently malfunctioned and had to be launched through tubes which often caught fire.[5]

Opinions differ on the effectiveness of PT boats. In *Tales of the South Pacific* (1949), author James Michener belittled them as "rotten, tricky little craft for the immense job they were supposed to do. They were improvised, often unseaworthy, desperate little boats." On the other hand, Richard Keresey, a PT boat skipper and colleague of Jack's in the Solomons, described PT boat fighters as ferocious, tough, and versatile. "Superb rescuers, they saved hundreds from death or capture: downed fliers, sunk sailors, trapped Marines, coast watchers, stranded nuns, and Gen. Douglas MacArthur."

Kennedy and fifty others in his class at Melville studied guns, torpedoes, engines, navigation, and boat handling. In October 1942 he was promoted to lieutenant, junior grade.[6]

After the day's classes, Jack helped organize the touch football game, the kind where players could pass anywhere on the field. Jack called all the plays.

Paul "Red" Fay, who played opposite him, "saw nothing but elbows, shoulders and knees, and acquired a collection of bumps and bruises. The game itself became almost secondary to the battle between the skinny kid and myself at the line of scrimmage."

At Melville the students didn't learn how to fire torpedoes and received no night training, drills that would be critical for their work in the Pacific. "The training was very poor," Alvin Cluster admitted. "A lot of the things we did at Melville were, in hindsight, ridiculous. . . . The main purpose was to teach you to handle boats, to be able to come alongside a pier, how to take care of your engines, torpedoes, radios—things like that."[7]

At the end of November, when Jack finished his courses at Melville, John Harllee, the senior instructor, graded him as superior in boat handling, good in engineering, and "very willing and conscientious." Jack was such an outstanding student that Harllee selected him as an instructor at Melville, meaning Jack would remain stateside and not get a combat assignment. Jack was depressed with the news. "He yearned with great zeal to get out to the war zone and do his share of the fighting," Harllee recalled. Arguing vehemently with Harllee, Jack insisted that he be sent overseas to one of the squadrons in combat. "I told him that we needed people of his ability for instructors," Harllee said. "I absolutely insisted that he remain, which made him extremely unhappy." Kennedy must stay at least six months, an eternity to Jack.

With the assistance of grandfather Honey Fitz, in late November 1942, Jack quietly arranged an interview with the influential U.S. Senator from Massachusetts David I. Walsh, chairman of the Senate Naval Affairs Committee. "Frankly, I have not met a young man of his age in a long time who has impressed me more favorably," Walsh later wrote Honey Fitz. "He has a fine personality, energetic and outstanding qualities of leadership, and with all a becoming modesty."

On January 8, 1943, after only five weeks as an instructor, Jack was delighted to learn that he had orders to take four of the training squadron's boats on a thousand-mile trip to Jacksonville, Florida, where the boats were to be shipped to Panama.[8]

On the trip through the Atlantic Intracoastal Waterway, one of the boats ran aground. Jack went to her assistance, throwing a line to tow the other boat, but the rope tangled in his own propellers. He dived overboard into freezing water to clear it. Several hours later he became ill and, on January 12, was treated by a private physician in Aurora, North Carolina, for "acute gastro-enteritis." Weak, nauseated, with a temperature of 103, he was transferred to a navy medical facility in Morehead City, North Carolina. Within two days, though, his temperature returned to normal, he felt better, and he resumed his duties. Jack rejoined his flotilla on January 16 in Jacksonville.

On January 22, 1943, the navy ordered him to report to Squadron 14 in

Norfolk, Virginia. Two weeks later he received awful news. Instead of going to the combat zone, Squadron 14 was being sent to guard the Panama Canal.[9]

Jack immediately appealed the assignment, requesting of the navy's Bureau of Personnel in Washington that he "be reassigned to a Motor Torpedo Squadron now operating in the South Pacific." He also telephoned Senator Walsh, who agreed to grease the wheels of the navy's personnel department. The formal written request, together with Walsh's influence, succeeded in getting Jack detached from Motor Torpedo Boat Squadron 14 and reassigned to Motor Torpedo Boat Squadron 2 in the Pacific.

Kennedy's voyage to the Pacific war zone began in San Francisco on March 6, 1943, aboard the troop carrier *Rochambeau*. Together with a group of transient navy officers (like himself) bound for combat assignments, the transport picked up fifteen hundred navy enlisted personnel in San Diego, then embarked on a journey to the New Hebrides, a thousand miles northeast of Australia.[10]

James Reed first met Kennedy while both were shipmates aboard the *Rochambeau*. Reed and two other officers debated Neville Chamberlain and Munich while Jack listened.

> I was taking the position against Chamberlain. . . . [Kennedy] took the other side and argued on behalf of Chamberlain. He brought to it not only a great deal of knowledge but a great aura of humility. He always made the listener feel that he, the listener, knew a great deal more about the subject than he really did.

After disembarking from the *Rochambeau,* Jack weaved his way to Tulagi, the prewar capital of the British Solomon Islands, near Guadalcanal, now controlled by the Americans. For two decades before the war, the Solomon Islands, stretching for six hundred miles, had slumbered as a backwater of the British Empire, ignoring the outside world and being ignored in turn. The government of the protectorate focused on collecting taxes and reducing the incidence of head-hunting and intertribal war.[11]

After their sudden attack on Pearl Harbor in December 1941, the Japanese captured island after island in the Pacific, including the Solomons, which lay in the path of the Japanese advance on Australia and New Zealand. Moving almost unopposed, in May 1942 they occupied Tulagi and north Guadalcanal in the Solomons.

The Solomons were ideally suited for the first Allied counterattack, a fact recognized by the U.S. Chiefs of Staff in March 1942, when they decided that an assault on Japanese-held New Guinea would have to be launched from a little-known island in the Solomons. American troops landed on Guadalcanal on August 7, 1942, commencing a ferocious battle lasting six months. The eventual American victory was the first penetration of the Japanese defense perimeter; in the next two years the perimeter steadily eroded.

After the victory at Guadalcanal, Admiral William Halsey's amphibious forces leapfrogged up the Solomons, bypassing and isolating Japanese strongholds, and building new airfields and bases to cover the next landing. In February 1943, the U.S. troops took the next step up, landing unopposed in the Russells, a group of islands lying between Guadalcanal and New Georgia. By the end of July 1943, the Americans had more than fifty PT boats operating from two bases in the Solomons.[12]

At Tulagi on April 24, 1943, Jack was assigned to *PT 109*, a dirty, battle-scarred veteran of the Guadalcanal campaign. Together with his mostly inexperienced crew, Jack cleaned the dirt and grime, eliminated the rats and cockroaches, and began repairs and training.

While at Tulagi, Jack made a brief trip to nearby Guadalcanal to visit a grave. Several of Jack's friends had died in combat. One was George Mead, whose father had founded the Mead Paper Company. In the spring of 1942, young Mead had been assigned to the Fifth Marine Regiment, about to embark for Guadalcanal in the South Pacific. In April Kathleen Kennedy and Jack joined several others for a farewell party at the Meads' winter plantation in Aiken, South Carolina. The partygoers rode horses, played badminton, and engaged in a spirited scavenger hunt. "One night George pulled out his tape recorder, and they amused themselves by mimicking a popular radio show, each pretending to be a commentator on the war," wrote Lynne McTaggart.[13]

On August 7, 1942, Mead was one of thousands of marines who landed on Guadalcanal. Twelve days later, during the marines' first major assault on the entrenched Japanese, a bullet struck him in the face, killing him.

A year later, Jack sought out Mead's grave, finding it in the first row of a makeshift military cemetery. He felt moved by the epitaph on the simple aluminum plate:

LT. GEORGE MEAD, AUGUST 20, 1942.
A GREAT LEADER OF MEN—GOD BLESS HIM.

"The whole thing was about the saddest experience I've ever had and enough to make you cry," he stated in a letter. Later Jack wrote to the Meads and described George's grave.[14]

On Tulagi, Jack passed his free time reading and writing scores of letters. Occasionally he played poker or cribbage and participated in the debates on current events. He had purchased a record player, and repeatedly played his favorite tune:

Blue skies
Smiling at me,
Nothing but blue skies
Do I see. . . .

On patrol Jack quickly learned that his boat was vulnerable to Japanese aircraft and surface warships. PTs in the Solomons were restricted to base during the day, being too vulnerable to the enemy. They did their hunting at night, relying on speed, stealth, and surprise. Kennedy's ship log gave a concise, though uneventful, account of his patrols from Tulagi. In mid-May he saw flares and gunfire at a distance, investigated suspicious objects, and practiced firing at floating oil drums.

When fellow PT skipper Lieutenant Richard Keresey ran aground on a reef in PT 105, Jack went to his assistance, skillfully towing the helpless 105 into a floating dry dock. "I mistook him for an old hand," Keresey recalled; "he was also the only boat captain at Tulagi who did not make a funny remark about my running aground."[15]

As the commander of *PT 109*, Jack had his first real taste of leadership, and by all accounts his peers and his crew respected him. "I thought he was a real good officer," recalled Ensign Johnny Iles. "His boat was shipshape and his crew was well organized, orderly. . . . He was a fellow who made you feel good to be with—and you would never have known about his personal, privileged life by visiting with him. He was always a genuine person."

From the Pacific in May 1943, Jack reported to his parents that he felt fine. His back had stood up "amazingly well and gives me scarcely no trouble." But his brief respite from pain wouldn't last long.

On May 30 the navy ordered him to report to a new forward base in the Russell Islands, where his and several other boats were to provide support for the upcoming invasion of the island of New Georgia in the Western Solomons. His six-week stay at the Russells was uneventful, though, except for one incident not involving the enemy.[16]

When the boats returned from patrol at dawn, the skippers raced to the refueling dock because the crew that arrived first was serviced first, ate breakfast first, and got to bed before the others. (It took several hours to refuel all the boats.) Exhilarated by the contest, which he often won, Jack thundered toward the dock at high speed, then reversed engines at the last second, just in time to brake his momentum and glide to the dock. In doing so, he ignored his engine crews' warning that someday the engines might conk out.

One morning *PT 109* and another boat were leading the race, prow to prow, and the outcome depended on which skipper could maintain his speed the longest. In the end, Kennedy held out and pulled ahead.

In 1961 newspaperman Robert Donovan published *PT 109*, the most detailed, accurate, and unbiased account of Jack's naval career in the Pacific. Donovan described the conclusion of the race:

> Immediately he ordered the engines into reverse. All three conked out, and *PT 109* went streaking at the dock like an eighty-foot missile on the loose.
>
> On the dock, the fueling crew had reported and a work party under a warrant officer had entered the shed to get out the tools when the whole world came crashing down on them.
>
> Tools flew in all directions. Wrenches, jacks, screwdrivers and hammers plopped into the water. Some of the men who were still outside toppled off the dock. Those on the inside who weren't too terrified to move clawed their way out. When they burst through the door, however, they beheld not the expected formation of Japanese dive bombers overhead, but a single PT boat sliced into a corner of the dock. . . .
>
> The warrant officer howled at Lt. Kennedy, who was his senior. Shaken-up enlisted men stamped about the dock cussing out 109 and everyone aboard. A gale of indignation was blowing, and beyond uttering a word of quiet apology here and there, Kennedy could do little but wait for the storm to blow itself out.

Kennedy might have gotten into serious trouble with his superiors had it not been discovered at the same time that two or three PT boats had broken away from their moorings. Everyone's attention shifted to the greater emergency while Kennedy slunk away, docking in a small stream out of sight until the commotion subsided.

Small mishaps often occurred with the PT boats. They ran aground, smashed into buoys, dinged a propeller, and banged into each other. "If it hadn't been a serious war, you'd have had a *McHale's Navy* type of operation," recalled Lieutenant Alvin Cluster. "In the early days while learning how to operate PT boats, we were like novice wranglers trying to tame wild horses—we all got thrown a couple of times," said Keresey.

Still, Jack's crash was more reckless than the norm, reflecting his foolhardy, daredevil attitude about speed. For the rest of his life he drove automobiles with the same reckless abandon. He was lucky no one was killed or seriously injured.[17]

In mid-July Jack received orders to move *PT 109* to Rendova, where the navy had established a new forward base in the middle of the current battle zone, bringing Jack the closest he would come to tangling with the enemy.

Rendova Harbor was five and a half miles away from New Georgia, where U.S. Marines were engaged in a savage battle to wrest the Munda airstrip from the Japanese. Jack's new boss, Lieutenant Commander Thomas Warfield, had established his command post at Lumberi Island, a small base next to Rendova.

PT 109 ventured out many successive nights with little rest, scouting for Japanese warships and barges. During the early fighting in the Solomons, the Japanese often used cruisers and destroyers to support their bases, providing the PTs with tantalizing targets. But after losing their larger warships to the American preponderance of air and sea power, the Japanese resorted to armed coastal barges to transport troops and supplies to their island bases. By the time Jack arrived in the Pacific, the armed barges, hugging the shore and making their runs mostly at night, had become the prime target for the PTs.[18]

From their powerful base at Rabaul the Japanese moved soldiers and supplies at night down the New Georgia Sound, known since Guadalcanal days as "the Slot." Usually they transported by motorized barges, but when the Japanese needed to execute a major reinforcement they organized an "Express," consisting of several destroyers, and rammed it down the Slot. The primary responsibility of the PT boats was to intercept nightly Japanese shipments.

The Tulagi base had offered movies and an officers club, but no luxuries existed at Rendova. "For months war had seemed comfortably distant most of the time," Donovan observed. "Now the air was heavy with it. Uneasiness and fear lay just below the surface everywhere. Like an ocean current that cannot be seen, this fear conditioned the air above. Men became tense."

At anchor the PT boat smelled of engines, damp life jackets, stale coffee, and sweat. Jack lived on the boat, ate canned army rations (beans, fried Spam), and went out nearly every night.

He wrote to his sister Kathleen: "That bubble I had about lying on a cool Pacific Island with a warm Pacific maiden hunting bananas for me is definitely a bubble that has burst. You can't even swim—there's some sort of fungus in the water that grows out of your ears—which will be all I need. With pimples on my back, hair on my chest and fungus in my ears I ought to be a natural for the old sailors home in Chelsea, Mass."[19]

By midday the crew's quarters were hot and airless, making sleeping belowdecks unbearable. Despite the burning sun, the crew preferred to sleep on the deck. Kennedy slept next to a torpedo tube or sometimes on the plywood canopy of the dayroom. Sleeping in the heat produced stupor; no one could sleep for very long.

After returning to base, exhausted, there was still work to do. Refueling from fifty-gallon drums was a long, cumbersome process because the boats needed two thousand gallons. The engines, torpedoes, guns, and radio all needed cleaning and adjustment after a night of bouncing around on patrol.

There were barely enough men to man the PT boats at Rendova, as weary, malnourished crews fell prey to malaria, dengue fever, and dysentery.

Japanese airplanes posed the greatest danger to the PT boats. Often the PT skipper couldn't tell in the dark if an approaching plane was friend or foe. The pilots had the same problem with the boats. (PTs operating out of Rendova suffered several casualties from American planes and, in turn, shot down several American pilots.)[20]

One evening in July 1943, *PT 109* had a close call. Suddenly Jack heard a plane above. "The next minute I was flat on my back across the deck," he wrote home.

[The plane] had straddled us with a couple [of bombs]. The boat was full of holes and a couple of the boys were hit, but are doing O.K. . . . [The Japanese pilots] usually drop a flare of terrific brilliance—everything stands out for what seems miles around. You wait then as you can't see a thing up in the air. The next minute there's a heck of a cr-aaa-ck—they have dropped one or two. All in all, it makes for a certain loss of appetite.

The nerves of men tightened as they neared Ferguson Passage. Beyond the passage the Japanese surrounded them—on Gizo, on Vella Lavella, on Kolombangara, and on New Georgia.[21]

Jack's letters gave his impressions of conditions in the Solomons and his views on the Pacific war. Within Jack's circle of navy and marine personnel, army general Douglas MacArthur was very unpopular. But Jack sensed their judgment was probably unfair. "His nickname is 'Dug-out-Doug' which seems to date back to the first invasion of Guadalcanal. The Army was supposed to come in and relieve the Marines after the beach-head had been established. In ninety-three days no Army. Rightly or wrongly (probably wrongly) MacArthur is blamed." The one commander who had everyone's confidence was the brusque, dynamic Admiral William Halsey. "He rates at the very top," Jack reported.[22]

Jack was pessimistic that the Pacific war would end soon. Sure, eventually the Japanese would be licked because U.S. pilots and planes were superior and U.S. resources seemed inexhaustible. Nonetheless, "this island to island stuff isn't the answer." Moreover, the Japanese were the greatest jungle fighters in the world,

perhaps not the most skillful but they make up for this by an unbelievable determination to die rather than quit. Supremacy in the air does not hold the whole answer in the land warfare here as I've seen the Japs absorb an unbelievable amount of punishment from the air for days and then when we move in and it appeared as though there couldn't be a leaf left alive,

they kick the hell out of us. . . . The one bright gleam on the dark horizon is that we are knocking them stiff in the air.

He criticized the military leadership for logistical bottlenecks.

A great hold-up seems to me to be the lackadaisical way they handle the
unloading of ships. They sit in ports out here weeks at a time while they try
to get enough Higgins boats to unload them. . . . Don't let any one sell the
idea that everyone out here is hustling with the old American energy. They
may be ready to give their blood but not their sweat, if they can help it, and
usually they fix it so they can help it. They have brought back a lot of old
Captains and Commanders from retirement and stuck them in as the heads
of these ports and they give the impression of their brains being in their
tails as Honey Fitz would say. The ship I arrived on—no one in the port
had the slightest idea it was coming. It had hundreds of men and it sat in
the harbor for two weeks while signals were being exchanged.

The navy screwed up everything it touched: "Even the simple delivery of
a letter frequently overburdens this heaving puffing war machine of ours.
God save this country of ours from those patriots whose war cry is 'what this
country needs is to be run with military efficiency.'"

Few of his comrades had any interest in politics. "They wouldn't give a
damn whether they could vote or not and would probably vote for Roosevelt just because they knew his name."[23]

Although uninterested in politics, at Tulagi some of the men congregated
at Jack's tent before dinner to discuss the war and current events. "Jack always emphasized that we had no right to complain about political decisions
unless we exercised some leadership in local or national politics," recalled
Red Fay, Jack's friend from Melville who had also been assigned to PT boats
in the Solomons.

Jack didn't spend his leisure time drinking or playing cards. He preferred
to sit around and chat or lie on his bunk reading and writing. Many of his
letters were unusually thoughtful and eloquent.

Before being assigned to the Pacific, Jack had asked an employee of the
Kennedys to scour the family's library in Hyannis Port and send him any
books on government and economics, biographies, any "really good novels,"
plus any books by P. G. Wodehouse, the light comic fiction writer. One book
Jack praised was Franz Werfel's *The Forty Days of Musa Dagh,* the account of
the stand the Armenians made against the Turkish campaign of annihilation
during World War I. He told anyone who asked, though, that his favorite
book was John Buchan's *Pilgrim's Way.*[24]

"Going out every other night for patrol," he wrote home in May 1943.

"On [a] good night it's beautiful—the water is amazingly phosphorescent—flying fishes which shine like lights are zooming around and you usually get two or three porpoises who lodge right under the bow and no matter how fast the boat goes keep just about six inches ahead of the boat."

His letters were often hilarious. Joe Kennedy Sr. had "plenty of laughs" reading them. "Admiral Halsey inspected us yesterday," Jack wrote the family in June 1943, "and I tried to look broken-down so he would send me home—but he said we were a 'fine looking crowd'—which was obviously a lie—and said it was a 'privilege for us to be where we are' which made me edge away from him in case God hit him with lightning."[25]

"I myself am completely and thoroughly convinced that nothing is going to happen to me," he wrote home in a more serious vein. "As the real curse of war is being stuck in some isolated spot with nothing to relieve the monotony for months—I feel I'm lucky to have this chance."

During the war years Kennedy seemed on the verge of renouncing his Catholic faith. In the Pacific Johnny Iles discussed religion with his navy comrade. "He had kind of lost his religion," Iles recalled. When Iles teased him about dropping his Catholic faith even while coming from a prominent Catholic family, Kennedy jocularly responded, "I'll work it out some day. I'll go see Fulton Sheen and get it all straightened out when I get back home." (Fulton Sheen was the popular priest on the radio's *Catholic Hour*.)[26]

Religion was a recurring theme in Jack's letters home. Usually his remarks were funny: "[It is good] to know that all nuns and priests along the Atlantic Coast are putting in a lot of praying time on my behalf. . . . I hope it won't be taken [as] a sign of lack of confidence in you all or the Church if I continue to duck."

"Mother, you will be pleased to know that there is a priest nearby who has let all the natives go and is devoting all his energies to my salvation." Jack was stringing him along. "I'm not going over [too] easy—as I want him to work a bit—so he'll appreciate it more when he finally has me in the front row every morning screaming hallelujah."

Jack challenged Rose's traditional Catholic views in an unusually sarcastic letter, cutting close to the bone.

They want me to conduct a Bible class here every other Sunday for about ½ hour with the sailors. Would you say that that is un-Catholic[?]

I have a feeling that dogma might say it was—but don't good works come under our obligations to the Catholic Church[?] We're not a completely ritualistic, formalistic hierarchical structure in which the Word, the truth, must only come down from the very top—a structure that allows for no individual interpretation—or are we[?][27]

After Jack and Inga Arvad split up, Jack still longed for her. Before he went to the Pacific, he talked for hours with Kathleen about Inga. For a while Jack thought she had remarried. "You probably have not heard—Inga Binga got married—and not to me," Jack wrote Billings. "Anyway she's gone and that leaves the situation rather blank." Actually Inga had not remarried, but had moved to Los Angeles to work for the North American Newspaper Alliance.

By the time Jack reached the Pacific, he had learned that the account of Inga's marriage was incorrect and that she had resumed her career as a journalist. He wrote her, but she didn't respond. He then wrote her an angry second letter: "You won't write a damn word unless you are paid and paid well. . . . This I refuse to do."

When Inga finally did respond, Jack replied that "while I'm still [mad] as hell that you didn't answer before, this will keep me for awhile. You still have the knack of making me feel one hundred per cent better after talking with you or hearing from you."

With Inga he shared his intimate thoughts. His display of sensitivity and vulnerability may also have been a ploy to win her back:

> You said that you figured I'd go to Texas, and write my experiences—I wouldn't go near a book like that, this whole thing is so stupid, that while it has a sickening fascination for some of us, myself included, I want to leave it far behind me when I go.
>
> Inga Binga, I'll be glad to see [you] again. I'm tired now, we are riding every night, and the sleeping is tough in the daytime. . . . I used to have the feeling that no matter what happened I'd get through. It's a funny thing that as long as you have that feeling, you seem to get through. I've lost that feeling lately, but as a matter of fact don't feel badly about it. If anything happens to me I have this knowledge that if I had lived to be a hundred, I could only have improved the quantity of my life, not the quality. This sounds gloomy as hell. I'll cut it. You are the only person I'd say it to anyway. As a matter of fact knowing you has been the brightest point in an extremely bright twenty-six years.[28]

When he returned from the Pacific, Jack and Inga would briefly resume their relationship.

While scrounging about the army base on Rendova, Jack discovered an unused 37-millimeter antitank gun. After getting permission to take it, he hauled the gun back to the PT base and announced to his astonished crew that he would fasten the gun to the forward deck, giving *PT 109* substantially more firepower. By the afternoon of August 1, 1943, the crew had completed part of the fastening process but still needed to attach planks to stabilize the legs of the gun. That afternoon Japanese dive bombers attacked the Rendova Harbor PT boat base, disrupting Kennedy's plan for mounting the gun. As a temporary expedient the crew lashed the gun and the planks to the deck with a rope. It was "a small chore," said Donovan, "for which they would give large thanks later."

The attack on the base, which destroyed two boats and caused several casualties, was part of the Japanese plan to knock out PT boats before that evening's large express. In Rabaul the Japanese had decided to ferry nine hundred men and supplies to Kolombangara on three destroyers, with a fourth, the *Amagiri,* as an escort.

Meanwhile, on the afternoon of August 1, after Lieutenant Commander Warfield received a message warning him to expect the Express that night, he called an emergency meeting of the skippers. To meet the Express he organized the remaining fifteen boats into four divisions, each to operate independently. He assigned *PT 109,* not scheduled to patrol that night, to a group of four boats under the command of Lieutenant Henry Brantingham, a twenty-six-year-old graduate of Annapolis.[29]

As *PT 109* set out that evening, the crew consisted of Torpedoman Raymond Starkey; Motor Machinist Mate Gerard Zinser; Seaman Raymond Albert; Gunner Harold Marney; Gunner's Mate Charles Harris; Seaman Edgar Mauer; Radioman John Maguire; Motor Machinist Mate William Johnston; and, at thirty-seven the oldest crew member, the stoic, uncomplaining Motor Machinist Mate Patrick McMahon.

Another crew member, Torpedoman Andrew Kirksey, initially had seemed as brave, bold, and steady as any of the others. But since the last week of July, he had become convinced he was going to be killed, and no one could dispel his premonition of death.

Kennedy relied most on his second-in-command, Ensign Leonard Thom of Sandusky, Ohio. A blond-haired giant, Thom had played left tackle at Ohio State in 1939 and 1940. "He had no fear," Charles Harris said of Thom. "[He] could rule anybody. You'd just look at him and do what he told you; he was that big. He was an awful nice man."

During the afternoon of August 1, Jack had run into an acquaintance from Melville days, Ensign George "Barney" Ross, whose PT boat had been sunk twelve days earlier. "How about letting me ride with you tonight, Jack?" Ross asked. Jack readily agreed, so Ross also joined the crew that evening.[30]

All the boats were ordered to maintain radio silence. "When the leading boat saw something and attacked, the other boats were to follow right along without further ado and no further conversation," Lieutenant Brantingham later stated. "That was the practice in our squadron." He conceded, though, that it may not have been the practice in other squadrons. Unfortunately for Jack, this was the first time he had ever patrolled with Brantingham, and the Annapolis graduate never informed Kennedy of his procedures.

Unknown to all the PT boats, the four Japanese destroyers were going to arrive at Vila an hour earlier than expected. Of the four boats in Jack's division only Brantingham's had radar. Shortly after midnight, when Brantingham saw blips on his radar screen, he thought they were Japanese barges and tore off after them. A second boat, *PT 157* under the command of Lieutenant William Liebenow, followed him. Confused and left behind were *PT 109* and *PT 162,* commanded by Lieutenant John Lowrey. Shocked to be greeted by salvos from the Japanese destroyers, Brantingham and Liebenow fired their torpedoes, which all missed their targets, and then fled the scene, never rejoining the two boats they had left behind. Since Kennedy and Lowrey had no radar and heard only garbled, panicked radio transmission, they were left in a quandry. At 12:30 A.M. the three destroyers arrived at Vila with the *Amagiri* patrolling offshore. Forty-five minutes later, unloaded, the destroyers started their return trip.[31]

Meanwhile, Kennedy resumed his patrolling, paired with Lowrey in *PT 162.* While they eased their way up Blackett Strait, a third boat, *PT 169* under the command of Lieutenant Phil Potter, emerged out of the darkness and joined them. Potter had lost contact with his division leader the same way as Lowrey and Kennedy.

At about 2:30 A.M. on August 2, a ship suddenly appeared on *PT 109's* starboard bow about 250 yards away.

"Ship at two o'clock!" Marney shouted to Kennedy from the forward gun turret, commencing thirty to forty seconds of terror.

Kennedy glanced off his starboard bow at the same moment Ross was pointing to a shape suddenly appearing out of the darkness. For a moment Kennedy thought it might be one of the other PT boats. So did Mauer. But as the shape became clearer they both realized that it wasn't a PT boat. It was the *Amagiri,* a new gray two-thousand-ton Japanese destroyer, carrying thirteen officers and 245 men under the command of Lieutenant Commander Kohei Hanami.

"Lenny," Kennedy said, "look at this."

When Kennedy realized the ship was a destroyer, he instinctively spun his wheel to make a torpedo attack. (His torpedoes would have been ineffective anyway because they could not explode at such a short distance.) He had turned thirty degrees when the *Amagiri* slashed through *PT 109.*[32]

Harold Marney was immediately crushed to death. Kirksey, the quiet Georgian with the premonition of death, also perished. Neither man's body was ever found. Ensign Thom, Mauer, Maguire, McMahon, Johnston, Albert, Harris, Starkey, Zinser, and Ensign Ross floated amid the fire and debris, some of them unconscious. The engine portion sank immediately; the bow stuck out of the water at a steep angle.

"So this is how it feels to die!" was the first thought that flashed through Jack's mind. Once he realized he was still alive, he developed an implacable desire to survive, and his indomitable spirit over the next six days sustained him and bolstered his crew.

"Mr. Kennedy! Mr. Kennedy!" Harris shouted in the darkness. "McMahon is badly hurt." On the floating bow Kennedy removed his shoes, his shirt, and his sidearm, then dived in and swam toward Harris's voice. McMahon and Harris were a hundred yards away.

When Kennedy reached them, he found McMahon in serious condition with terrible burns.

"How are you, Mac?"

"I'm all right. I'm kind of burnt."

Kennedy shouted out, "How are the others?"

Harris said softly, "I hurt my leg."

Jack helped Harris out of his heavy sweater and jacket and coaxed him to swim back to the bow, then took McMahon in tow. With a breeze blowing the bow away from the swimmers, it took forty-five minutes to swim what had earlier been an easy hundred yards. During the ordeal, Harris complained, "I can't go any farther." Kennedy shot back sharply, "For a guy from Boston, you're certainly putting up a great exhibition out here, Harris." Harris cursed his skipper, but completed the swim and didn't complain anymore. Having successfully towed in McMahon and prodded Harris, Kennedy swam from one man to another, checking their condition. All of those who had survived the crash were still afloat, thanks to their life preservers.[33]

Maguire rescued Zinser; Thom hauled in Johnston, who had inhaled gasoline fumes and could barely move. Finally, eleven men were accounted for.

They had a Very pistol, which shot a pyrotechnic signal, but they feared using it in Japanese-controlled water. Fortunately, the Japanese never came; unfortunately, neither did the Americans.

"We were waiting for the other PT boats to come back," Maguire recalled with some bitterness. "Those sons of bitches ran away from us. We were left."

The skippers of the other two boats later claimed that they thought the entire crew of *PT 109* had perished in the crash and flames. Fearing the destroyers, they returned to base.

The men were conspicuous on the water, only a few miles from enemy garrisons on Kolombangara and Gizo.

"What do you want to do, fight or surrender?" Kennedy asked.

"Fight with what?" someone asked.

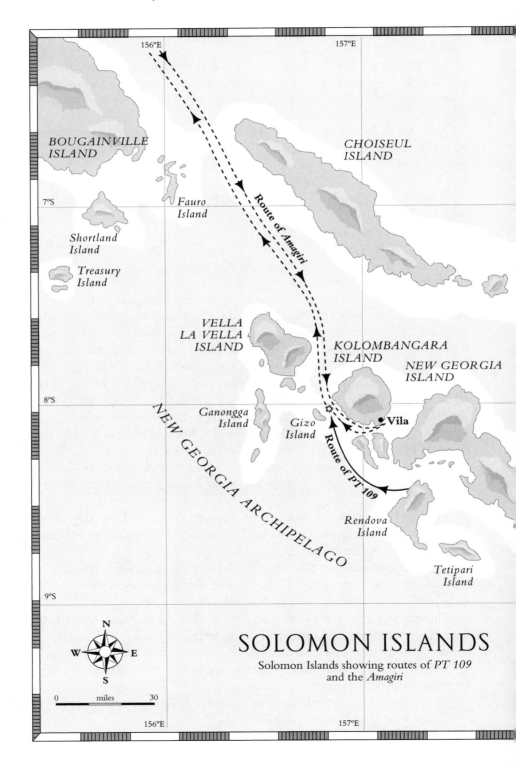

156°E   157°E

BOUGAINVILLE
ISLAND

CHOISEUL
ISLAND

7°S

*Fauro
Island*

Route of Amagiri

*Shortland
Island*

*Treasury
Island*

VELLA
LA VELLA
ISLAND

KOLOMBANGARA
ISLAND

NEW GEORGIA
ISLAND

8°S

*Ganongga
Island*

*Gizo
Island*

● **Vila**

NEW GEORGIA ARCHIPELAGO

Route of PT 109

*Rendova
Island*

*Tetipari
Island*

9°S

N
W   E
S

SOLOMON ISLANDS

Solomon Islands showing routes of *PT 109*
and the *Amagiri*

0   miles   30

156°E   157°E

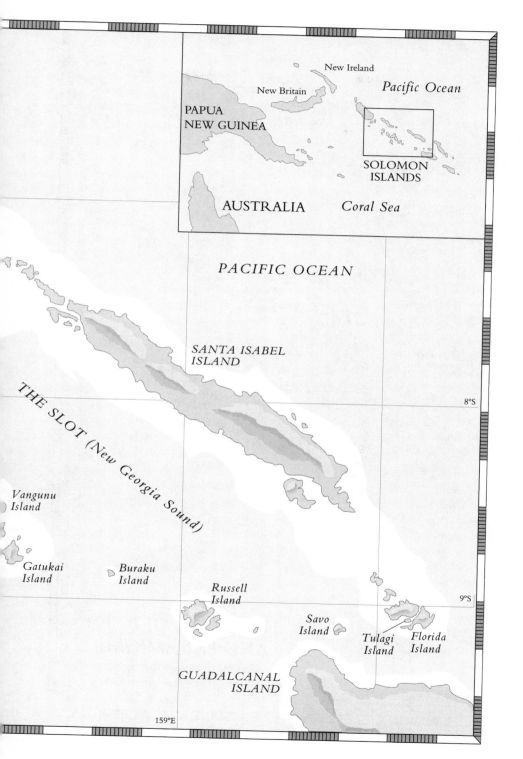

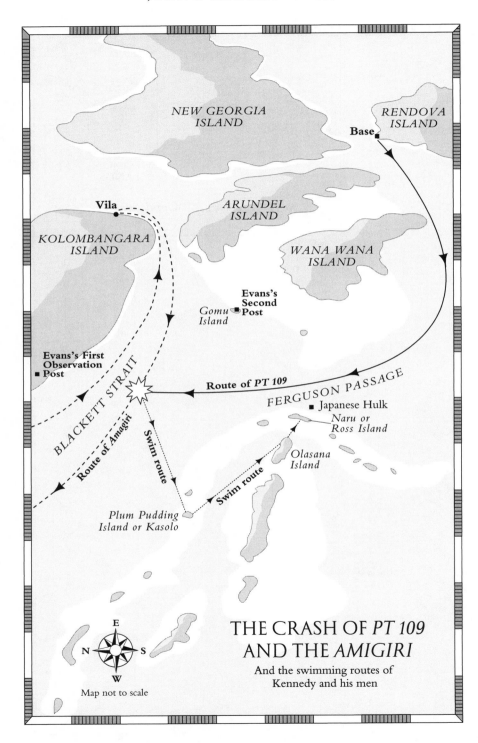

THE CRASH OF *PT 109*
AND THE *AMIGIRI*

And the swimming routes of
Kennedy and his men

"There's nothing in the book about a situation like this," Kennedy said. "A lot of you men have families and some of you have children. What do you want to do? I have nothing to lose." (Maguire thought Jack's last remark incongruous. With his wealth and advantages, Kennedy seemed to have the most to lose.)

They took stock of their weapons. The 37-millimeter gun was still tied to the deck, but it had fallen overboard and hung in the water. Among them they had one Thompson submachine gun, six .45s (and Kennedy had a .38), and three knives—not much firepower. Their first-aid kit had been lost during the crash.

They had heard horror stories about how the Japanese tortured prisoners. Still, how could they put up a fight? Would their sidearms even fire after so many hours in the water? Zinser suggested that they put off a decision until they could gauge the size of any Japanese force that tried to attack them. Nobody had a better idea, so they deferred the decision.[34]

When the bow of the boat turtled, Kennedy knew that he soon needed to make a crucial decision. If the hulk sank with the men still clinging to it, some would become separated in the dark and drown. If the bow remained afloat, they might drift into the arms of the Japanese. If help did not come soon, they would have to abandon the boat and swim to shore before dark. Which direction should they go? Toward which island?

Shortly after 1:00 P.M., still on August 2, Kennedy ordered the men to abandon ship. They must try to reach land before dark. He directed them toward a group of islands east of Gizo, his best guess of land not occupied by the Japanese.

"I'll take McMahon with me," he said. Under Thom's direction, the others tied their shoes and a battle lantern to a two-by-eight-foot plank which they detached from the 37-millimeter gun. They would cling to the plank.

"Will we ever get out of this?" someone asked.

"It can be done," Kennedy replied. "We'll do it."

They gathered themselves about the plank, four on one side and four on the other. The ninth man, Thom, moved from back to front, back and forth, pushing and pulling the plank.

Jack put the straps of McMahon's life jacket between his teeth and began swimming. He and McMahon were back to back with Kennedy low in the water underneath McMahon. It was an epic swim.[35]

Jack did the breaststroke for ten to fifteen minutes, rested briefly, then resumed swimming.

"How far do we have to go now?" McMahon occasionally inquired. Kennedy kept assuring him they were making progress.

"How do you feel, Mac?"

McMahon always replied, "I'm okay, Mr. Kennedy, how about you?"

Near sundown Jack and McMahon arrived on the shore of Plum Pudding Island. It had taken nearly four hours for Kennedy to make the three-and-a-half-mile swim across Blackett Strait. As Kennedy and McMahon stumbled onto the island, the coral spikes and spurs lacerated their feet and shins and bruised their thighs.

Kennedy lay panting, his feet in the water, his face on the sand. His feet blistered, his burns painful, McMahon crawled out of the water on his knees and feebly helped Kennedy up. Donovan observed:

> Swimming with the strap in his teeth Kennedy had swallowed quantities of salt water. When he stood he vomited until he fell again in exhaustion. McMahon's hands were swollen grotesquely. Every move he made tortured him. . . . He tried to drag Kennedy across the ten feet of sand, yet he could scarcely drag himself. He found he could crawl, and as Kennedy's strength returned he too crawled across the beach in stages with McMahon until the two of them collapsed under the bushes. After a while Kennedy was strong enough to sit up and watch the others as they neared the beach on their two-by-eight plank.

Plum Pudding Island was about a hundred yards long and seventy yards wide. A few minutes after the eleven arrived on the island, a Japanese barge patrolled slowly by their hiding place in the bushes. The men watched tensely as the barge continued straight ahead for the enemy garrison at Gizo Anchorage four miles away.

The sight of the barge deeply frightened the men, making them keenly aware of their dangerous predicament. For all the men knew, there were Japanese on Plum Pudding. They spoke only in hushed tones.[36]

From his hideaway on Kolombangara several hundred feet above Blackett Strait, the Australian coast watcher Lieutenant Arthur Reginald Evans looked over the Japanese base at Vila. One of a network of courageous coast watchers engaged in intelligence work throughout the Solomon Islands, Evans used his binoculars and a telescope to report by radio to his superiors on Guadalcanal all the Japanese movements he detected or that were reported by the native scouts assisting him.

At 9:30 A.M. on August 2, Evans was notified that *PT 109* had been lost in action. "Request any information." Now alerted, Evans kept a watchful eye out for any signs of survivors. Late in the afternoon he told his native scouts to be on the lookout for the survivors of the PT boat wreck.

On Plum Pudding, McMahon couldn't be moved; Johnston was in better shape but was also in poor condition, coughing and retching. Jack decided that he would swim alone into Ferguson Passage that evening, hoping to signal a patrolling PT boat.[37] Nobody attempted to stop their determined skipper. He stripped down to his skivvies. Carrying the battle lantern, wearing a rubber life belt around his waist and shoes to protect his feet on the reefs, and with his .38 revolver hanging from a lanyard around his neck, he entered the water at dusk.

His trek in the dark over the coral reefs, a distance of about two and a half miles, was eerie. Strange creatures flitted through the water; he worried about mutilation by sharks or barracuda. In Ferguson Passage he treaded water, looking for PT boats, ready to signal to them with his lantern.

He didn't know that instead of patrolling in Ferguson Passage that night, the boats operated farther north. While he was swimming back to Plum Pudding Island, the current running through Ferguson Passage carried him sideways. At dawn he crawled up on the tiny islet of Leorava, a mile and three-quarters from Plum Pudding, where he collapsed on the sand and fell into a deep slumber.

Waking up in broad daylight, cold and exhausted, he still needed to swim back to Plum Pudding. Having discarded his shoes the night before, he waded back into the water, where the coral again cut his feet.

Late in the morning of August 3, he arrived on Plum Pudding. When Thom and Ross went to meet him, Jack fell to the ground, retching. Sick for a while longer, he then fell asleep.

The survivors on the island were hungry, but their main problem was thirst. They even tried to dig for water. While it rained one night, they laid on their backs and caught drops in their mouths. The next morning they gathered large leaves and licked a few drops of water off them only to discover unpalatable bird droppings on the leaves. "Our wounds were bad but thirst was our main discomfort," said Zinser. "Hunger didn't seem to bother me too much." Jack never joked about their predicament, but occasionally he made light remarks that would evoke a laugh. "What I would give for a can of grapefruit juice!"[38]

Hoping to secure more coconuts for his hungry crew, and wanting to be closer to Ferguson Passage and possible rescue, on Wednesday August 4 Kennedy moved his crew to Olasana Island, only one island removed from Ferguson Passage.

At midday the men dragged the plank into the water, and Kennedy again towed McMahon, this time for a distance of a mile and three-quarters. Several hours later, as the eleven men gathered in the trees behind the curved beach of Olasana, Kennedy could see another island, Naru, a half-mile away.

The following day, Kennedy consulted with Thom and Ross. What should they do now? They had swum into Ferguson Passage at night, changed islands, and posted lookouts for boats or planes. Was there anything they had overlooked? Restless, Kennedy didn't want to just sit and wait. To bolster the morale of his men, he felt he must keep striving for rescue. He looked across to the far side of Naru Island, which faced Ferguson Passage. From there it might be easier to flag down friendly boats. Considering his earlier, exhausting efforts, swimming the half-mile to Naru would be easy.

Shortly after noon on Thursday Kennedy and Ross crawled up on Naru, a narrow, four-hundred-yard-long island. They quickly crossed to the side facing Ferguson Passage. On the reef, about a mile away, they spotted the wreckage of a small Japanese ship. Exploring the vessel, they found nearby a crate containing hard candy. They ate a few pieces and saved the rest for the crew on Olasana. Twenty yards farther they discovered a dugout canoe with a large tin of precious rainwater.

While Kennedy and Ross quenched their thirst, two of Evans's native scouts, Biuku Gasa and Eroni Kumana, happened to stop at Naru to explore the Japanese wreck. Both pairs of men spotted each other at the same time from a mile away. Afraid that Kennedy and Ross were Japanese from the wreckage, the two scouts paddled furiously away in their canoe.[39]

Instead of returning immediately to their base, Biuku and Eroni made a fateful decision. They would stop at Olasana. "I was thirsty, so I told [Eroni] to leave me at the island so I could get a coconut," recalled Biuku. "[While] I was going ashore, I saw a white man crawling out from the bushes near the shore. I said '[Eroni], a Japanese here'. They pushed their canoe out to get away. Neither scout spoke English. The white man tried to communicate with them, but failed.

Then Lenny Thom emerged from the bushes.

"Navy, navy," Thom pleaded. "Americans, Americans."

Eroni and Biuku were far enough away to stop and listen. "Me no Jap," said Thom, rolling up his sleeve to show his white skin. Biuku and Eroni were still dubious. Thom tried several other approaches. "Me know Johnny Kari," he blurted out. John Kari was a prominent native scout known to the PT men.

"At this point I began to believe the soldiers and to understand what had happened," said Biuku. The natives went ashore and hid their canoe in the bushes. It was about 4:00 P.M.

Meanwhile, on Kolombangara, Evans had decided that because he couldn't see enough of Ferguson Passage and the west side of Blackett Strait, he would move to a new station, Gomu, more in the center of the area.

Using his newfound canoe, Kennedy returned to Olasana before dusk with the candy and water, leaving Ross to sleep on Naru. When Kennedy arrived, crewmen yelled to him, "We're saved! Two locals have found us!" Kennedy put down the water and candy and ran over and embraced the two natives.[40]

Shortly after, he again canoed back to Naru. He had a new plan. He and Ross would venture into Ferguson Passage in the canoe in hopes of hailing a

PT boat. Huge waves put them in trouble almost immediately. When Ross complained of the danger, Kennedy replied, "Barney, I think we ought to go on." Once the canoe was beyond the reef, the waves splashed over the gunwales until a five-foot wave capsized them.

"Sorry I got you out here, Barney," Kennedy said as they thrashed about in the dark.

"This would be a great time to say I told you so, but I won't," Ross responded.

They gripped the overturned canoe until an enormous wave hurled them across a reef onto jagged coral. With new lacerations on their feet, they made their way to the shore of Naru, where they lay down in exhaustion and slept.

On Friday, August 6, new excitement animated the stranded Americans. With two canoes, and the natives assisting them, perhaps they could now help themselves.

Kennedy awoke early on Naru and made his way back to his men on Olasana. Without a definite plan, Kennedy persuaded Biuku to paddle him back to Naru for another look at Ferguson Passage. There he had Biuku quarter a coconut.

Using his sheath knife, Kennedy scrawled on the coconut the message:

Nauro Isl
Native knows posit
He can pilot 11 alive need
Small boat
Kennedy

hom, still on Olasana with the men, had a similar plan. Using the stub pencil and a blank invoice which Maguire found in his pocket, Thom wrote a message. When Kennedy returned to Olasana, he entrusted u and Eroni with both messages and sent them by canoe to Rendova bor, thirty-eight miles away.[41]

The two natives set off but wisely stopped at a nearby island to tell Benjamin Kevu, an English-speaking scout, about the survivors. In turn, Kevu sent another scout to inform Evans of the news. With Evans's resources—a radio and the native scouts—the rescue effort accelerated. The coast watcher immediately dispatched seven of his scouts in a large war canoe to Naru with a message:

On His Majesty's Service
To Senior Officer, Naru Is.

Friday 11 p.m. Have just learnt of your presence on Naru Is. and also that two natives have taken news to Rendova. I strongly advise your return immediately to here in this canoe and by the time you arrive here I will be in Radio communication with authorities at Rendova and we can finalize plans to collect balance your party.

A R Evans Lt.

Seven scouts, led by Kevu, made their way to Olasana, followed footprints into the underbrush, and found the survivors.

The arrival of Evans's scouts on Olasana seemed like a miracle. The canoe itself was a cornucopia, Donovan reported.

Before the gluttonous eyes of eleven famished sailors, yams, pawpaws, rice, potatoes, boiled fish, Chelsea cigarettes and C rations with roast-beef hash poured ashore. Some of the natives scampered up palm trees like monkeys to fetch coconuts. Others collected palm fronds and built a hut for McMahon. Still others lighted three kerosene burners for cooking.

On Saturday morning, August 7, Biuku, Eroni, and John Kari reached Rendova Harbor. Lumberi was already thrilled by the radio message the base had just received from Evans. At 9:20 A.M. the coast watcher had radioed to headquarters that there were "eleven survivors" of *PT 109*.[42]

Back on Olasana, after finishing their feast, Kennedy and the natives began the journey to Gomu to meet Evans. Covering Kennedy with dead palm fronds to conceal him from the Japanese, they paddled into Blackett Strait. Evans, watching anxiously from Gomu, spotted them shortly before 6:00 P.M. When the canoe came ashore, Kennedy stuck his head through the palm fronds, smiled at Evans, and said, "Hello, I'm Kennedy."

Over tea at Evans's new hideout they discussed the rescue plan. Two PT boats would meet Kennedy at 10:00 P.M. near Patparan Island. Kennedy insisted that he accompany the rescue boats to Olasana. Well after 10:00 P.M., the PT boats arrived and hauled Jack aboard. Commander Cluster, Biuku, and Eroni were there to share the jubilation. Then the party made its way to Olasana, arriving shortly after midnight.

Using a rubber raft Kennedy guided one of the PT boats safely through the reef. Exultantly, he shouted through the darkness to Thom, "Lenny! Hey, Lenny!"

"The boats are here!" came a shout from a man on the beach. Using a shuttle service, all the survivors were aboard within a short time.[43]

The rescue party and the eleven survivors reached Rendova at dawn on Sunday, August 8. The injured crewmen were immediately taken to sick bay. Several war correspondents had heard the news about the rescue and rushed to interview the son of the wealthy and prominent former ambassador. After debriefing by Rendova intelligence officers, Jack talked with the correspondents in a tent.

After the interview Jack strode outside and walked to a broken-down army cot under a tree, and Commander Cluster squatted next to him. The accumulated strain of Jack's weeklong ordeal exploded. Clenching his fists, tears running down his cheeks, he bitterly told Cluster that the two lost crewmen, Kirksey and Marney, might have been saved if the other boats had tried to rescue the crew of *PT 109*. Trying to calm Jack's emotions, Cluster explained that the other boats had seen the crash but assumed that all the crewmen had been killed.

At Lumberi, Jack, the crew, and the natives consumed a small feast. Kennedy toasted Biuku and Eroni for saving his life and the lives of the crew. He told them that if he survived the war, he promised to see them again. "What he wanted to get was command of another PT boat and join the fight again," Biuku recalled.[44]

Some commentators have condemned Warfield for not making a determined effort to locate and rescue the survivors. Warfield probably could have tried harder, but for the most part, the accusation is unfair. During a discussion at the base at Rendova Harbor, at 6:00 A.M. on August 2, someone asked, "Commander [Warfield], do you want to send some boats back to look?" Warfield turned his eyes to Lowrey and Potter, who'd been with Kennedy, and asked, "What do you think?" "Commander, there was nothing left," one of them responded. "The boat went up in a ball of flames." That ended the discussion. A daytime rescue attempt with PT boats was too dangerous, the boats too vulnerable. "We weren't about to just send boats out scurrying around looking for survivors up there," said Cluster. "We depended on the planes and there were specific searches made by [airplanes] and they reported nothing. So we had to assume that the whole damn boat had exploded and sunk."

James Woods, Warfield's aide, insisted that rescue attempts were made after the crash. Headquarters notified coast watcher Evans and launched an airplane search.

Headquarters informed Evans that U.S. planes had searched the area on August 2 but found no one. Why didn't the planes locate the survivors? The reason was the search wasn't made until dusk on August 2. By the time the aircraft searched the Gizo area, Kennedy and his crew were hiding in the bushes on Plum Pudding Island.[45]

A larger issue is why didn't Lieutenant Lowrey and Lieutenant Potter come to the rescue immediately after the crash? Both were spooked by the *Amagiri* and the fiery crash. Lowrey in *PT 162* sped away from the site, convincing himself that everyone aboard *PT 109* was lost. He returned to base without bothering to search for survivors. Potter claimed that he spent thirty to forty-five minutes patrolling the crash site looking for survivors, but found nothing in the darkness.

Potter probably lied. While everyone aboard *PT 109* was presumed lost, a distraught Paul Fay asked Potter if he tried to search for survivors. According to Fay, Potter became irritated and replied, "Listen, Fay, we went back and thoroughly searched the scene of the accident and there wasn't a trace of anything." Subsequently several members of Potter's crew contradicted their skipper, telling Fay that no serious effort had been made to press the search.[46]

For many years journalists, historians, and biographers lauded Kennedy's wartime leadership and heroics after the sinking of *PT 109*. The story became one of Kennedy's greatest political assets and a major theme in his early campaign literature. His exploits were proof of his courage, tenacity, resourcefulness, and coolness under pressure. At the height of his political career there were visual reminders of his intrepidity: documentary films, a Hollywood motion picture, the coconut shell on Kennedy's desk, former crew members campaigning for him, and *PT 109* tie clasps given to campaign workers.

Critics, though, have minimized and criticized his actions. *PT 109* was the only PT boat ever hit by a Japanese destroyer during the Pacific war, they argued. Kennedy was told to expect Japanese destroyers. Why wasn't he more vigilant? "Kennedy had the most maneuverable vessel in the world," recalled one PT squadron leader. "All that power and yet this knight in white armor managed to have his PT boat rammed by a destroyer. Everybody in the fleet laughed about that."[47]

The primary source for the new version of the *PT 109* story is Joan and Clay Blair's *The Search for JFK* (1976). Clay Blair, a former editor in chief of *The Saturday Evening Post,* and his wife performed groundbreaking research for their book, most notably interviewing 150 people who knew Kennedy.

Before the crash, the Blairs contended, Kennedy ignored "prescribed procedure" by not following his section leader, Lieutenant Brantingham, when he attacked. "Moreover, when the section leader suffered a 'flash' in his torpedo tube, drawing heavy enemy fire, Jack left him to his fate."

More important, several people the Blairs interviewed, including Warfield, laid the blame for the collision on the fact that Kennedy was running with his engines muffled. When Jack saw the *Amagiri,* he instinctively rammed on full power, and the engines either choked severely from exhaust backup or conked out altogether. Kennedy should have been expecting the enemy destroyers, and therefore should have been unmuffled, as ready as possible to move to full power. Warfield told the Blairs:

He knew the destroyers were coming out. He saw this thing coming at him and got bugged a little bit and shoved his throttles forward. And I think he killed his engines. Actually, it doesn't matter if he had the engines muffled or not; if he shoved the throttles forward too fast, it would still have killed the engines. And that's what I think he did.[48]

Kennedy should have known that Japanese destroyers were in the area. When the Express came down Blackett Strait, there was pandemonium for about thirty or forty minutes. The destroyers fired almost without interruption, using their searchlights and firing star shells. Japanese planes dropped flares and bombs, and made strafing runs. The PT boats raced everywhere, firing torpedoes. By all accounts, the Blairs contended,

the VHF radio during the period carried an almost continuous (if confused) load of messages relating to the destroyers. There were many contact reports, movement reports, queries, and exhortations from Warfield, and reports from some of the skippers who had fired torpedoes. In the hour or so following, Warfield was busy relaying information to the boats remaining on station, redeploying them on picket lines to intercept the destroyers when they withdrew from Vila.

Didn't Kennedy hear any of this? the Blairs wondered. Donovan had written that Kennedy did hear a few messages on his radio—"I am being chased through Ferguson Passage" . . . "have fired fish" . . . "Well, get the hell out of there." Those galvanizing messages "should have been enough to tell Kennedy that the Express had gone through—and would be coming back," said the Blairs.

The authors asked several of the other PT boat skippers if it was possible that Kennedy did not know the destroyers had come through. Lieutenant Arthur Berndsten, Warfield's executive officer and the leader of another division on the night of the crash, replied, "I find it very difficult to believe from my experience that night, with all the shooting and everything else that took place, and all the messages that were sent back to the base. If that was true, everybody had to have his mind in neutral and be half asleep."[49]

Potter, who joined Kennedy and Lowrey, said Kennedy did know the destroyers were expected. He told the Blairs:

I had talked to Warfield on the VHF. He told me to stay in the area. I found Lowrey and Kennedy. We talked back and forth on the VHF. We all knew then that four or five destroyers had gotten through to Vila. . . . We'd called Warfield and he'd said stay there in the area and try to intercept them on the way back. . . .

We decided to form a three-boat picket line. Since I was the senior officer, I led it. Lowrey was on my port quarter and Kennedy was on *his* port quarter. . . . Back and forth across the strait on a diagonal. We patrolled at slow speed, with mufflers in, with about one mile between each of us.

The Blairs didn't think Kennedy had his crew properly alert. He should have had everyone at general quarters. "It seemed incomprehensible that at a tense moment like this, two of the thirteen men who could have served as lookouts were asleep and that Thom and Kirksey were lying down. Four out of thirteen unalert. The radioman, Maguire, was in the cockpit with Kennedy. . . . Why didn't Kennedy have him in the chart house monitoring the radio?" Why didn't anyone aboard *PT 109* see the *Amagiri*'s wake until the last seconds? Potter had seen the wake from an estimated two miles. Lowrey had seen it from about a half mile.

"The 109 had had two separate contacts with the Express, about two and a quarter hours apart," the Blairs contended. "In the first, when the Express was southbound, the 109 failed to follow its leader to attack, and 'bugged out' toward Gizo Strait. In the second, when it was northbound, the 109 was rammed and sunk. On the basis of this performance—Jack's first contact with enemy surface ships—we had to agree with Warfield, who told us, 'He wasn't a particularly good boat commander.' "[50]

Earlier writers praised Jack's heroism for swimming into Ferguson Passage on August 2 to try to flag down a friendly boat. But the Blairs disagreed. It was impulsive, reckless, a failure, and Jack could have been killed. "The crew was at a point when reflection might have been called for, 'estimating the situation,' as military men say; calmly conceiving an escape plan or signaling devices; or reconnoitering. But reflection and careful planning were not Jack Kennedy's strong suits. He was an 'action' man."

Finally, the Blairs charged, contrary to most published reports of the six-day survival episode, Jack did not "save" his crew. The PT base alerted coast watcher Evans, who with his native rescue apparatus ultimately rescued the survivors. Kennedy's famous coconut message was useless. He had been "stubbornly courageous" in saving the life of McMahon, but his efforts at rescue came to naught. "Evans, with the help of the Lumbari base and many other people, rescued the castaways."

Jack, in short, "was not a war hero." As evidence the Blairs cited Leonard Nikoloric (often cited by other critics as well), who stated, "There was a lot of criticism in the Navy about the loss of the 109. MacArthur is supposed to have said that Jack should have been court-martialed, but I think he denied it. Jack was actually in a lot of trouble over that, so we never said a word about it. . . .

"Nobody could understand how he could get rammed," Nikoloric continued. "We used to say that he was the only PT boat skipper who got rammed by the target. It was a bright moonlit night and it was calm. Out there on that kind of a night, you could see for miles and miles. Nobody who knows anything about these boats can really understand how it happened."[51]

On one point, the Blairs were probably correct. After the rescue, Kennedy briefly shared quarters with Rich Pedroncelli, another PT boat skipper. Pedroncelli recalled that Kennedy admitted that just before the crash his engines were idling with the mufflers closed. When he saw the destroyer he pushed the throttle forward, and the engines stalled. He had neglected to open his flaps first.

The Blairs' challenge to conventional wisdom provided needed correction, but on several major points of contention their evidence was flawed, and so was their judgment.

All the witnesses agree that on the night of the crash it was as dark as the inside of a well—no moon, no stars. It was "so dark that night you couldn't hardly see a foot and a half in front of your nose," observed Gerard Zinser. The *Amagiri* "had the island of Kolombangara for a background and that's what made it that much more difficult for our lookout to spot it."

Barney Ross agreed: "People have often asked me, how could you get sunk in a PT boat by a destroyer? And I have to always say that it was as dark as if you were in a closet with the door shut."[52]

PT boat commanders in the same division were often strangers to each other, but on this occasion Jack's division leader, Lieutenant Brantingham, didn't communicate with the skippers in his division. He never explained his procedures or tactics to Kennedy, who was riding with him for the first time. Jack didn't follow when Brantingham attacked, because he had no idea what the division leader saw or intended. Lieutenant Lowrey in *PT 162* had the same problem as Kennedy. It was too dark for Kennedy to identify the distant fire in Brantingham's torpedo tube. Jack was also too far away from the "pandemonium" caused by the enemy destroyers coming down Blackett Strait.

The radios on PTs often lost their frequencies. Richard Keresey, who patrolled in another division the same evening, later remarked, "I believe this was Kennedy's problem, his radio was off frequency, so he couldn't hear everybody. He didn't know what was going on. I can bear that out because neither did I."

The only clear message Radioman John Maguire heard that evening was "Let's get the hell out of here." "There were no instructions at all," Maguire recalled. "Once we got out there we never heard from anybody . . . about the destroyers."

Jack's boat, joined by *PTs 162* and *169,* formed a picket line. Given the chaos, Kennedy, Lowrey, and Potter behaved intelligently and responsibly.[53]

Only the division leaders had radar on their boats; the others had to depend on regular vision. "The division leaders were the ones who fired, and left the rest of us out there with no radar," said Keresey.

"We didn't know the Express had gone down to Vila," Harris stated. "We thought it was shore batteries firing. Our lead boat, the radar boat, picked something up but they didn't tell us anything about it. They took off after it and left us sitting there. . . . When we got back we were really going to look up that skipper and give him the business for leaving us high and dry like that. We were kind of mad. He had the eyes and we didn't."

Biographer Nigel Hamilton castigated Brantingham for his irresponsibility and cowardice: "How Brantingham imagined that his own trailing team, in pitch dark and without radar or even the license to communicate by radio, would be able to first follow him and then sight the enemy defies explanation."

After their encounter with the destroyer, Brantingham and Liebenow fled the scene. "We zigzagged for ten or fifteen miles, I have no idea what direction we went," said Liebenow. Hamilton observed:

> In fact they . . . had fled the wrong way, ending up in the Gizo Strait. Meanwhile no attempt at communication with the remaining two boats in their division was made by either Liebenow or Brantingham. By the time Liebenow finally came alongside Brantingham's flagship, behind Gizo Island, it was clear that they had lost all trace of Lieutenant Kennedy on *PT 109* and Lieutenant Lowrey on *PT 162.* Brantingham later blamed Warfield, claiming that Warfield "ordered all boats who had fired their torpedoes back to the base." But PT-boat skippers in other theaters of the war, such as Jack's friend Fred Rosen, considered it a gross dereliction of duty for a division leader's boat ever to leave the battle area without its fellow vessels. "It was unheard of in the Mediterranean," Rosen later declared, "like leaving your own family."[54]

Did Kennedy have his crew sufficiently alert? Two of the men were asleep; two others were lying down. That still left nine other crewmen. At least five served as lookouts at the time of the crash: Albert, Mauer, Marney, Ross, and Kennedy himself. "The lookouts were out," said Ross. "I was up on the bow, I was a lookout. . . . We weren't all laying around sleeping." More lookouts probably wouldn't have seen the *Amagiri* any sooner than Marney did.

Operating at slow speed with only the center engine engaged was a common practice—indeed, both Lowrey and Potter were also idling on one engine at the time of the crash. It saved fuel and reduced the wake and the noise, making the boat less likely to be spotted by Japanese planes, the greatest nemesis to PT boats. Seen from the air, a big wake led enemy planes to a boat like a road map. The procedure also made it easier to keep station with the other PT boats.[55]

With hindsight Jack had advice for his colleagues when enemy destroyers posed the most imminent danger. On September 15, 1943, the Flotilla One newsletter, *Mosquito Bites,* summarized Jack's advice to other PT boat skippers: "Jack Kennedy believes that the reason that he was unable to get out of the way of the Jap destroyer which rammed him was because only one of his engines was in gear. He strongly advises that, whenever enemy destroyers are known to be in a patrol area, all engines should be in gear." At the moment of the crash, however, Jack, and the captains of the two boats with him, were focused primarily on keeping station and avoiding Japanese planes.

Jack's swim into Ferguson Passage was dangerous and didn't accomplish its goal, but it wasn't reckless or impulsive. Risk was involved, but in his judgment there was a good possibility of success. If a boat appeared, he would be astute enough to assess the situation and judge whether it was friend or foe. That the PT boats didn't patrol that night in Ferguson Passage was simply bad luck.[56]

Warfield, who had never trained his crews in night patrolling and never went out on patrol himself, had devised an incredibly poor plan of attack; nor did he understand the conditions on the night of the crash. Yet he was quick to criticize his crews for cowardice and later stated to the Blairs that Jack "wasn't a particularly good boat commander."

The PT boat action on the night of the crash was a story of misfortune and incompetence, the most poorly conceived and executed PT boat action during the entire Pacific campaign. Half of the fifteen PT boats never fired their torpedoes. The rest fired over thirty torpedoes without scoring a single hit. The chief fault, a naval historian contended, was that the PTs "didn't pass the word. Each attacked independently, leaving the others to discover the enemy for themselves."

"The four radar-equipped division leaders had all abandoned their comrades," observed Hamilton of the futile operation. "The Tokyo Express had brought sufficient supplies and men to Kolombangara to keep the battle for New Georgia going for another month and had escaped to Rabaul with impunity after sinking a PT boat."

The Blairs correctly set the record straight on the rescue of the eleven survivors. Contrary to the view of countless reporters, historians, and biographers, Jack did not "save" his crew. Coast watcher Evans and his native scouts, assisted by PT boat headquarters, rescued the castaways. Jack Kennedy agreed and consistently praised his rescuers.[57]

Nonetheless, was Jack a hero? The Blairs and others chose to believe Leonard Nikoloric, possibly an acquaintance of Kennedy's while both were briefly assigned to Miami in the spring 1944. (Jack never mentioned Nikoloric and may not have known him at all.) Not an eyewitness and apparently never stationed in the Solomons, Nikoloric based his assessment on speculation, gossip, and hearsay. All of his observations remain unverified. It was hokum that "a lot" of people criticized Jack within the navy, that MacArthur wanted him court-martialed, and that Kennedy was in "a lot of trouble."

With a much better perspective on their skipper's leadership, the crew of *PT 109* were unanimous in their judgment. Long after the ordeal Gerard Zinser insisted that Kennedy was a hero: "None of us felt the base did enough to save us but Kennedy done everything he possibly could to save us. . . . He had extraordinary energy, he just wouldn't give up. . . . That's what made him go out and try to flag down a PT boat. He was exhausted each morning when he got back in."

Charles Harris agreed:

> He saved our lives. I owed him my life. I tell everybody that. If it wasn't for him I wouldn't be here. I really feel that. I venture to say there are very few men who would swim out in that ocean alone without knowing what was underneath you. Brother, I wouldn't do it. You could give me a million dollars and I wouldn't swim out there. That took a lot of guts. I thought he was great. Everybody on the crew thought he was top-notch.[58]

The day after his rescue, on August 9, Jack was treated at the thatched hospital in Tulagi for fatigue and for many deep abrasions and lacerations of his entire body, especially his feet. Hospital personnel treated him with hot soaks, alcohol and glycerine dressings, and bed rest, and fed him multiple vitamin tablets and a high-calorie diet. Seven days later, on August 16, he left the hospital, seemingly much improved.

While in the hospital, Jack brooded over the fate of *PT 109*. Commander Cluster told him it was navy custom to allow shipwrecked survivors to be reassigned back home. Jack replied that he did not want to return home, because he hadn't accomplished anything yet. He wanted reassignment to another PT boat. (To get the assignment he disguised the seriousness of the back and stomach problems aggravated by the crash and its aftermath.)

Cluster recommended Jack for the Silver Star for his performance after the crash, but Jack received the less prestigious Navy and Marine Corps Medal. "It kind of burned me," Cluster later remarked, because "one squadron out there . . . handed out Silver Stars like they were popcorn prizes."[59]

Back home in Hyannis Port eleven-year-old Teddy Kennedy was buying a newspaper for Honey Fitz at the newsstand when he glanced at the *Boston Herald*. Drawings on the newspaper's front page depicted the ramming of a PT boat, and an accompanying story described the eventual rescue of Jack Kennedy and his crew. "I was dumbfounded," Teddy said. "I hadn't been told anything about it." Nor had Rose or the other Kennedy children. Joseph Kennedy knew that Jack was missing, but, not wanting to worry the family, hadn't told anyone. Rose rushed toward Joe, crying: "I just turned on a news broadcast. They say Jack's been saved. Saved from what?"

News of the *PT 109* rescue made the front pages of America's major newspapers. The stories focused on Lieutenant Kennedy because he was the officer in charge and his name was the best known. "Kennedy's Son Is Hero in Pacific as Destroyer Splits His PT Boat," read the headlined account in *The New York Times* on August 20. Young Kennedy had blazed a "new saga in PT boat annals," wrote the *New York Herald Tribune*. In *The Boston Globe* James Morgan praised Jack's resourcefulness and described the incident as "one of the great stories of heroism in this war."[60]

"This is just a short note to tell you that I am alive and *not* kicking," Jack wrote home on August 12. "It was believed otherwise for a few days—so reports or rumors may have gotten back to you. Fortunately, they misjudged the durability of a Kennedy—and am back at the base now and am O.K."

Shortly after, he offered his parents more extended observations on his ordeal. On the bright side of an otherwise depressing time, he wrote, was the way most of his crew had stood up to it. It was a tragedy, though, to lose two men. "One had ridden with me for as long as I had been out here. He had been somewhat shocked by a bomb that had landed near the boat about two weeks before. He never really got over it; he always seemed to have the feeling that something was going to happen to him. He never said anything about being put ashore—he didn't want to go—but the next time we came down the line I was going to let him work on the base force."[61]

After Jack's rescue his family expected him to be transferred back to the United States, probably around Christmas. "I am so delighted I can hardly think of anything else," Rose wrote the children. Throughout the war Joe Kennedy remained exceptionally devoted to his two war-weary sons. When it became obvious that logistics made it impossible to send Jack a Christmas present in 1943, Joe Sr. tenderly informed Jack, "We're all heartbroken that we can't get anything out to you by Christmas as they tell me they just won't guarantee anything. We had planned on your being here and we had made our plans accordingly, so if you'll just forgive us and remember that we'll make it up to you when we can."

Although Jack didn't inform his superiors about the real state of his health, his stomach and his back now ached. "[Dr.] Jordan will have a bit of work and am going to get my back fixed once and for all," he wrote home on September 1.

"Please don't do anything till I let you know," Jack wrote his father, trying to head off a lobbying campaign by Joe to pull strings in Washington to get his son sent home. Indeed, Joe Kennedy was in the process of doing just that. "I'm trying to pull what wires I can to get Jack back home because I imagine he's pretty well shot to pieces by now," the ambassador wrote young Joe on August 31.

After receiving Jack's letter, the ambassador backed off and agreed not to intervene. "I know you'd hate to have anybody mix into your schedule so I'm leaving it at that until I hear from you further."[62]

As U.S. forces advanced across the Solomons, the PT boats kept moving to new forward bases. When Jack returned to duty on September 1, his base had moved to Lambu Lambu Cove on the northeast coast of Vella Lavella.

Jack's insistence on staying on the job even though he had a legitimate reason to return home impressed everyone. "I was counting the weeks before I got to go home and he was volunteering for everything," recalled new crewman Edward Servatius. Jack's "devotion" was as important as his "courage," thought Alvin Cluster. He had a "mature dedication to service not often seen by any of us."

Jack was assigned to *PT 59*, an old seventy-seven-footer being converted from a torpedo boat to a heavily armed gunboat. The navy in the South Pacific no longer needed the high-speed torpedo missions for which PT boats were originally designed. The Japanese had few destroyers left in the area; most of the remaining enemy ships were the armed supply barges operating close to shore.

PT 59 and similar boats were stripped of their torpedoes and tubes, and reequipped with extra .50-caliber machine guns and 40-millimeter automatic weapons. Kennedy and his crew had to install much of the new gear themselves, and Jack plunged into the work like a stevedore.[63]

In October the navy promoted Jack to full lieutenant. He was now a mature, wise warrior, a veteran, but he hadn't lost any of his dogged aggressiveness. He also had a veteran crew. Robert L. Rhoads became executive officer. Four veterans of the original *PT 109* crew were under his new command. Cluster gave Kennedy three veterans who had served under him. On October 18, following a month of reconversion, *PT 59* arrived at the new advance base at Lambu Lambu Cove.

Jack wrote home that the new PT boat commander in the Solomons was Edward "Mike" Moran. "He's fresh out from six months in the States and full of smoke and vinegar and statements like—'it's a privilege to be here' and 'we would be ashamed to be back in the States,' and 'we'll stay here ten years if necessary.' That all went over like a lead balloon. However, the doc told us yesterday that Iron Mike was complaining of head-aches and diarrhea—so we look for a different tune to be thrummed on that harp of his before many months."[64]

"Feeling fine," Jack assured his father on October 20, trying to relieve his family's anxiety, "but after this present fighting is over will be glad to get home. When I do get out of here you'll find that you have a new permanent fixture around that Florida pool. I'll just move from it to get into my sack."

Jack repeatedly volunteered for missions, some of them dangerous. "He had guts," said Servatius. "No matter how dangerous the mission was, he'd always volunteer." Jack's superiors wanted to send a PT boat through Blackett Strait to draw enemy shell fire so that U.S. aircraft overhead could spot the guns. Kennedy immediately volunteered. "He said he'd go if they could find somebody else to go with him," Servatius recalled. Since nobody else volunteered, they scrapped the mission.[65]

Chief Petty Officer Glen Christiansen was horrified at one of Jack's suggestions. Kennedy wanted to enter the Warrior River at Choiseul with *PT 59* and wreck havoc on Japanese barges there. The river narrowed as it went up, and another squadron's boat had earlier suffered many casualties in a firefight with Japanese forces. "I couldn't see risking everybody's lives," Christiansen later said. "I felt let's do something, let's bomb them or something, but let's don't do *that*." They argued until Cluster sided with Christiansen. Kennedy's plan was too risky.

"We had the firepower," Christiansen concluded. "We could have raised hell up there, but I think they'd have had us. . . . [Kennedy] just wasn't thinking real clearly at the moment. It was a vengeance thing, which is fine, but I don't think he quite realized what the repercussions would be."

It got to the point where some of Jack's crew didn't want to go out with him because he took too many chances. "I think it was the guilt of losing his two crewmen, the guilt of losing his boat, and of not being able to sink a Japanese destroyer," Al Cluster said. "Jack felt *very strongly* about losing those two men and his ship in the Solomons. He . . . *wanted to pay the Japanese back.* I think he wanted to recover his own self-esteem—he wanted to get over this feeling of guilt which you would have if you were sitting there and had a destroyer cut you in two."[66]

Although leery of Kennedy's occasional impulsiveness, Jack's new crew deeply respected their skipper. The crew always came first for him, said Servatius. "I'd ride with him anywhere."

Ensign John Mitchell came aboard *PT 59* at the same time as Jack. "Everyone knew his station in life, except him. Unless you knew it yourself, you'd never find it out from him. He was very gracious, very considerate."

"He was a good officer in that he knew how to handle men," said Christiansen. "His disciplinary abilities were very, very tactful. He could tell you something and mean it, but he didn't offend you. . . . He was an excellent navigator. He took us in and out of places I couldn't believe. We'd have our run-ins every once in a while, but he was always a hell of a man about it."[67]

In midafternoon on November 2, 1943, an urgent radio message arrived at headquarters. A patrol of marines, eighty-seven officers and men, was caught in a fight with the Japanese on the Warrior River on Choiseul and desperately needed PT boats to help extricate it.

Because Kennedy's boat was less than one-half refueled at that point, not nearly enough for a round-trip across the Slot at the high speed that would be required, it was agreed that a second boat, fully fueled, would accompany *PT 59* and tow her back after the rescue mission.

"Get going, then," Lieutenant Arthur Berndsten ordered.

"Let's go get them," Kennedy said, hopping aboard. "Wind her up!"

Two landing craft at the Warrior River had struggled to rescue the marines; one had sprung a leak after hitting a coral reef and begun to sink. "The exultation of escape was snuffed out by the terrible realization that the waves were delivering the Marines back to the Japanese waiting on the shore," said Donovan.

At the height of their despair, a marine shouted almost hysterically, "Here's a PT boat!"

The terrified men saw *PT 59* and the other boat rushing toward them. Jack's helmeted men scurried about the deck getting ready to come along-side the sinking landing craft. Exposing his boat to the Japanese fire from the shore, Jack edged *PT 59* against the landing craft, and his crew hauled aboard the soaked marines.

One marine was critically wounded.

"We'll find a place for him," Kennedy said.

About forty-five marines were plucked to safety, occupying every foot of space on the boat. "[Kennedy] saw to it we had coffee and warm shirts," re-called one of those rescued.[68]

Jack was ordered to bring the marines to Voza, where they were trans-ferred to another landing craft. The critically wounded marine remained on *PT 59* for the return trip, but at 1:00 A.M. on November 3, he died in Kennedy's bunk. Two hours later, when *PT 59* had consumed its last drop of gasoline, the other PT boat towed her back to Lambu Lambu Cove.

For the next two weeks, while marines fought the Japanese on Bou-gainville, *PT 59* kept searching out enemy barges, ferrying troops in and out of battle zones, and firing at Japanese float planes. However, the arduous duty, constant strain, and primitive living conditions took their toll. Three of Jack's crewmen entered sick bay during the first half of November. Finally, on doctor's orders, Jack was relieved of his command.

His last action in the war occurred on the night of November 16–17, when *PT 59* uneventfully patrolled across the Slot. On November 18 he entered the final entry into his log: "Lt. J. Kennedy left boat as directed by Dr. at Lambu Lambu. (Ensign J. Mitchell took over as Capt. of *PT 59*.)"

Looking emaciated, Jack walked quietly along the deck of *PT 59* shaking hands with his crew and saying good-bye. "If there is ever anything I can do for you, ask me," he told them. "You will always know where you can get in touch with me." Then he walked down the path that led to the airstrip for the trip back home.[69]

Kennedy emerged from the war wiser, mentally tougher, and with self-respect for having done his duty. During his extraordinary adventure, he had mingled and worked with men from different classes, backgrounds, regions, and religions, and he enjoyed the camaraderie. Unlike many officers, whose men hated them for their cowardice, insensitivity, or arrogance, Kennedy was respected by his crews for his modesty, initiative, fortitude, and bravery, and for accepting the responsibility for the safety of his men.

While patriotic, Kennedy never naively believed that World War II was the war to end all wars. Having witnessed war's horror, its death and destruction, he emerged with an intense interest in maintaining peace in the postwar era. In a world of tyrants, he believed, peace could be maintained only by vigilance and continued military preparedness.

8

FAMILY TRAGEDIES

On January 7, 1944, Jack arrived in San Francisco. He later wrote Red Fay that he didn't have time to visit his San Francisco friend and had, instead, "headed Southward where I spent my next four days in a Mexican Bordello in lower California." Jack was joking; he first stopped to visit Inga Arvad in Beverly Hills. Inga, who thought Jack had arrived with his "health wrecked," had a new beau, making the visit awkward. Still, Inga interviewed Jack and wrote an article that was prominently featured in *The Boston Globe* on January 11, 1944.

Touchingly diffident about his Pacific exploits, Jack seemed slightly embarrassed by all the fuss made over him. To reporters he repeatedly praised his crew and denied being a hero. "None of that hero stuff about me," Arvad quoted Jack as saying. "Real heroes are not the men who return, but those who stay out there like plenty of them do, two of my men included."[1]

Rose was overcome with emotion at her son's safe return. "He is really at home," she wrote in her diary,

the boy for whom you prayed so hard—at the mention of whose name your eyes would become dimmed—the youngster who you would think dead some nights and you would wake up with sorrow clutching at your heart. What a sense of gratitude to God to have spared him.

What joy to see him—to feel his coat and to press his arms [and know he's here,] to look at his bronze tired face which is thin and drawn.

Things returned to normal. "He is just the same," Rose told the children about Jack's return to his sloppy personal habits. He "wears his oldest clothes, still late for meals, still no money. He has even overflowed the bathtub, as was his boyhood custom, and I was the one who discovered it as the water came trickling down through the ceiling to my bath house below."

Together with Governor Leverett Saltonstall and Boston mayor Maurice Tobin, Jack was a featured speaker at a large bond rally in Boston on February 11, 1944. Nine hundred people heard Jack warn that the Pacific war would not be over soon. "Lots of fellows overseas won't be able to get back for a long time, and they're depending on your support by buying bonds," Jack told the crowd. "The boys [would] like to know they won't have to pay for the war they have to fight."[2]

On March 8, 1944, the navy assigned Jack to the Submarine Chaser Training Center in Miami. He had little to do there and returned to Palm Beach most weekends. For many of the men assigned to Miami a typical day was eighteen holes of golf, swimming at the Bath Club, and carousing at night.

"Once you've got your feet upon the desk in the morning the heavy work of the day is done," he quipped in a letter. The people of Miami "wait anxiously for D-day and you can find the beaches crowded every day with people all looking seaward and towards the invasion coast."

Following Jack's return from the Pacific, he took on the responsibility of relieving the anxiety of friends and relatives of his comrades still in the war zone. He wrote Barney Ross's father, and visited Pat McMahon's wife, giving her an account of the collision and assuring her that Pat was recuperating from his burns. (McMahon eventually did recover.) Afterward Mrs. McMahon, with tears in her eyes and a shaky voice, commented that "my husband wrote home to me that Lt. Kennedy was wonderful, that he saved the lives of all the men and everybody at the base admired him greatly and had the greatest respect for him."

Jack also phoned Leonard Thom's wife, Kate, who later reflected:

One day, right after Jack came home, the telephone rang. I answered and a voice said, "Kate? This is Jack Kennedy." It was just like we had known each other. We talked for quite a while and he told me everything that had been going on out there, how he had left Lennie. Everything was fine. Lennie had developed an ear infection, a fungus from being in the water so long, but there was nothing else physically wrong with him.[3]

Jack's immediate goal was to regain his health. He spent a large portion of 1944 in hospitals and clinics. When the *Amagiri* rammed *PT 109*, Jack smashed his back against the rear wall of the cockpit with a steel reinforcing brace. His extraordinary physical effort to swim to safety while towing the injured McMahon probably compounded the strain on his back.

In early August 1943, while Jack was being treated for lacerations and malnutrition at the Tulagi hospital, he never told the doctors that he had injured his back and only briefly alluded to his sore stomach—all to make sure he would not be denied assignment to another boat.

Kate Thom recalled that her husband greatly admired Jack for his stoic courage in working through his pain. "That seemed to be the thrust of Lenny's letters, that Jack was feeling ill but a team of horses couldn't get him to report to sick bay. He was always working under a sort of duress."

On January 12, 1944, before he headed home to Palm Beach from the Pacific, Jack entered the Mayo Clinic. He wanted tests for his gastrointestinal pain and for his aching lower back. In his finding, Dr. Paul O'Leary reported that Jack's "activities in the South Pacific with irregular and limited food caused him several episodes in which he had gastric pain. In addition, he has had some lower abdominal pain usually aggravated by a bowel movement. During the last few months he has had a return of the mild diarrhea of which [he] complained several years ago. He has tended to overcome it by limiting his bowel movements to every two or three days." Jack had lost eighteen pounds since his previous visit to Mayo. Again, tests of his colon were normal and no ulcer was found. O'Leary concluded that he suffered from "diffuse duodenitis."

The orthopedic physician who examined him at the clinic found some "sagging" of the left gluteal muscles and "mild" atrophy and weakness of the back muscles, but the evidence was "not sufficient" to warrant an "operation at the present time."

O'Leary concluded that Jack had no specific illness or injury, but that his overall condition was terrible:

> In other words, it would seem that with the duodenitis, the weight loss, the backache, and the anemia, Lieutenant Kennedy at the present time is in a state of fatigue and nervous exhaustion which [I] believe would require more than a month for him to recuperate. He seemed anxious to return to the South Pacific at the completion of his leave of one month, but it was the impression of all the men who saw him here that a month's time would not be sufficiently long for him to recuperate from his present difficulty.

Three months later, reporting on the results of spinograms of Jack's back, O'Leary wrote to confirm that Jack did not have a protruded disk and did not need back surgery. "Unless a diagnosis of a disk is very obvious then the results from surgical intervention are none too good."

Meanwhile, Jack had also had his back examined by orthopedists at the Lahey Clinic, who came to the opposite conclusion. Jack probably had a protruded disk and needed an operation.

Joe Kennedy, who read the conflicting reports and wanted to advise his son wisely, was understandably frustrated. "Where this leaves us now I haven't the slightest idea," he wrote Dr. Frank Lahey on April 7, 1944. "In the meantime Jack suffers tremendously from his back, and I believe that the stomach keeps bad because of the constant worry about the back. . . . I admit now that I don't know how to proceed."

JFK's back pain up to 1944 was never satisfactorily explained. It may have stemmed from his football injury, and was probably a back strain, aggravated by his war experiences.

Orthopedists at the Lahey Clinic pushed for back surgery; orthopedists at the Mayo Clinic dissented and urged nonsurgical, conservative treatment.

Tragically, Jack and his father made the wrong decision. They opted for surgery. Dr. Lahey, who was closer to the Kennedy family than the physicians at the Mayo Clinic, intervened and convinced them that it was "worth while operating." He suggested an "exploratory operation" to see if there was a disk protruding.[4]

On June 23, 1944, Dr. James L. Poppen of the Lahey Clinic operated on Jack's back to explore herniation of his fifth lumbar intervertebral disk. But the operation proved a dismal failure. Poppen removed "degenerative . . . cartilage," but the surgeon did not find a protruded disk. "The patient did well following the operation for a period of two weeks," the mortified Dr. Poppen explained in his medical report. "Upon having the patient get up and about, however, severe muscle spasms in the low back took place. These necessitated fairly large doses of narcotics in order to keep him comfortable. . . . I have had nine other patients in a series of over five hundred ruptured intervertebral disks with a similar experience. They have all subsided in a few days or few weeks. I am indeed sorry that this had to happen with Lieutenant Kennedy."

When Torbert Macdonald visited the Chelsea naval hospital, he found Jack "lying in bed all strapped up as part of the treatment to mend his back. . . . When I came into his room, he raised a bony wrist and gave me a shaky wave. I asked him how he felt. He tried to lift his head. I had to lean over to hear him. 'I feel great,' he said. 'Great?' Macdonald replied. 'Well,' he smiled, 'great considering the shape I'm in.' "

After the operation Jack convalesced in Hyannis Port, often sitting in a wicker chair on the veranda of his father's house, gazing out at the busy harbor.[5]

Jack's stomach also bothered him again. It felt "different," he said, from what he had experienced years earlier. By July 1944, the pain was constant and could be relieved only by codeine.

On August 1, 1944, Dr. Sara Jordan summarized Jack's condition for Captain Frederic Conklin at the Chelsea hospital:

> Lt. Kennedy has continued to have low abdominal distress rather constantly, accentuated always by either an enema or by a spontaneous bowel movement. The pain has been quite severe at times. We have used the antispasmodic medicines such as pavatrine, trasentin, as well as a mixture of belladonna, phenobarbital and elixir of pepsin, and while I think there may be some improvement in his condition, I feel that he is still far from completely relieved of symptoms referable to the spastic colitis.

Sixteen days later, on August 17, 1944, Jack underwent rectal surgery by a Dr. Hensen at the Chelsea naval hospital. Once more the operation failed. While the "back pain and leg pain [were] less," and the patient could "walk with less discomfort," Hensen reported, the abdominal symptoms remained. Shortly after the doctor's report, Jack's back pain returned as well.[6]

While Jack struggled with his health and the two failed operations, the story of his gallantry in the South Pacific was trumpeted to the entire nation after a chance encounter with one of America's most prominent writers. John Hersey had first met Jack in 1939 when Frances Ann Cannon, one of Jack's girlfriends, introduced him as her new fiancé. (Jack was astounded.) On February 9, 1944, they met again in New York, and over drinks at the Stork Club, Jack described the ordeal of *PT 109* and its crew.

"Right away I said I'd like to do a piece on it if he'd be willing," Hersey recalled. Jack postponed a decision, but when they met a second time, he agreed, provided that Hersey would first interview Jack's crew. Hersey worked for *Time* and *Life* and told Jack that he expected to publish the story in *Life*.

Acclaimed for his direct style and eye for detail, John Hersey was a journalist, novelist, and eventually the author of two dozen books. His *Into the Valley* described the fierce fighting in the Solomon Islands during the early part of World War II; in 1944 he won the Pulitzer Prize for his novel *A Bell for Adano*. His most famous nonfiction book, *Hiroshima* (1946), evoked the horrors of the first atomic firestorm by relating the experiences of six innocent civilians who lived through it.[7]

As Jack had requested, Hersey traveled to the motor torpedo boat training center at Melville, Rhode Island, and interviewed William Johnston, Patrick McMahon, and John Mcguire. On February 23, 1944, he interviewed Jack at the New England Baptist Hospital in Boston, where Kennedy was having his back examined. "He asked if the crew had given a decent account of him and I assured him they had," recalled Hersey. "His insistence that I see the crew first struck me very favorably. It didn't seem to me to be self-serving. There was a real kind of officer's modesty about it. . . . He had a kind of diffidence about himself that seemed to be quite genuine at that time. So in a joking way he wondered how he looked to them. They were wildly devoted to him, all of them."

From the three crewmen Hersey had pieced together part of his narrative. While he was interviewing Jack all afternoon and part of the evening, Jack drew him a map of the accident area, and went over the story step by step. Afterward, Hersey returned to New York and finished writing the article.[8]

"Needless to say—you did a great job with the story," Jack wrote Hersey after reading a draft of the article; "even I was wondering how it all would end." Jack offered several suggestions. He thought that Thom's contributions had been slighted. "Thom did a splendid job," Jack wrote, giving examples. "He did so much to hold the group in a disciplined body that I think you might credit him more." Hersey agreed.

Jack also succeeded in urging Hersey not to mention one member of the crew who had acted dishonorably during the ordeal, and who was later killed in action. His "fate is ironic and dramatic," Jack explained, and "is so well-known both to men in the boats and to his family and friends that the finger would be put too definitely on his memory and after all he was in my crew."

When Hersey submitted his essay to *Life,* the magazine surprised him by turning it down. After *The New Yorker* accepted it, it appeared under the title "Survival" in the magazine's issue of June 17, 1944.

When Hersey told Jack that *The New Yorker,* a prestigious but small-circulation magazine, would publish the story instead of the large-circulation *Life* magazine, Jack was disappointed. "*Life* would have been a better vehicle for him," recalled Hersey. To get wider readership Joe Kennedy—and probably Jack—lobbied editors at the *Reader's Digest* to reprint the essay in condensed form. Following extensive negotiations, *The New Yorker* granted rights to the *Reader's Digest,* and the condensed article, appearing in August 1944, made Jack a national hero.[9]

After the article appeared in *The New Yorker,* Jack replied to a letter he had recently received from Lem Billings: "What you said about the break I got when Hersey did the article is extremely true I guess and it was such an accident that it rather makes me wonder if most success is merely a great deal of fortuitous accidents. I imagine I would agree with you that it was lucky the whole thing happened if the two fellows had not been killed which rather spoils the whole thing for me."[10]

During World War II the Kennedy family suffered a series of profound tragedies. One in particular dramatically altered Jack's position in the family.

By the late 1930s Rosemary's retardation was giving rise to troubling behavior, probably associated with delayed puberty. Easily frustrated and avid for sexual experience, she became difficult to manage. "Every day there would be fights where Rosemary would use her fists to hit and bruise people, long absences at night when she'd be out wandering the streets and violent verbal exchanges," recalled Lem Billings. Once the sweetest-natured of the Kennedys, Rosemary was now the most rebellious. Rose worried that her daughter would run away, be enticed and flattered by someone, and end up sexually assaulted or kidnapped.

Always impressed by innovations and modern technology, Joe Kennedy thought he had discovered the solution to Rosemary's problems. In 1935, at the University of Lisbon, Dr. Egas Moniz, a Portuguese psychiatrist, performed the first lobotomy for relief of severe mental disorder (and later won the Nobel Prize for his work). Within four years his procedure and its modifications had attracted worldwide attention as an effective, innovative therapy for chronically ill patients who had previously been untreated or hospitalized for long periods.

"Few surgical events can top the dramatic simplicity of a typical frontal lobotomy as performed in an up to date hospital," reported Marguerite Clark in *The American Mercury* in 1941. "Until about seven years ago the pre-frontal lobes of the brain were the least understood region of the cerebral hemispheres. Today it is a different story. Scientists have learned that the frontal lobes are the organs of imagination and anticipation." However, in an unhealthy brain, the theory contended, these frontal lobes caused frustration and worry. "These unfortunates may, in some cases, be brought back to useful life by the surgical removal of the frontal lobes of the brain," Clark wrote.

In the United States Dr. Walter Freeman and Dr. James Watts of the George Washington University School of Medicine reported successful operations on the frontal lobes to the American Medical Association. Freeman, who performed thousands of lobotomies in the 1940s, would plunge a gold-plated ice pick through the base of the eye socket, severing the frontal nerve connections.[11]

With hindsight it is clear that performing a lobotomy on Rosemary, who was only mildly retarded and had ill-defined emotional problems, was extremely risky. At the time, though, Joe convinced himself that a lobotomy was a progressive innovation, sanctioned by the medical community and perfectly suited for his daughter. The operation could control Rosemary's sexual drive and violent moods, permitting her to remain with the family for the rest of her life. In the fall of 1941, therefore, he decided to go ahead, convincing doctors that his daughter would be an ideal candidate.

The operation turned out to be an unqualified disaster. Rosemary emerged far worse than she had been before. "They knew right away that it wasn't successful," Ann Gargan later said. After the operation Joe told Rose it was time to place their retarded daughter in an institution, and chose St. Coletta in Jefferson, Wisconsin. Friends and relatives were mystified. For a long while they were told nothing about the operation—only that the family simply couldn't take care of Rosemary anymore.

For Rosemary's sisters and brothers, Doris Goodwin observed, "her sudden disappearance must have been met by dozens of questions that were never fully answered, surrounding the incident with the aura of forbidden mystery. . . . [Why] after all these years, did she have to be institutionalized now? And why couldn't any of the family see her? And most ominously, why wouldn't anyone really talk about what was happening?"[12]

Embarrassed by her condition, Joe and Rose concocted several fictional explanations for her disappearance. Inquiring reporters were told that she was "studying to be a kindergarten instructor" or had "an interest in social welfare work" or "harbored a secret longing to go on the stage." The fabrications worked, and her condition remained private.

Not until John Kennedy's presidential campaign in 1960 did the Kennedy family openly acknowledge that Rosemary was retarded and living at St. Coletta's. (They still said nothing about the lobotomy.) Perhaps the family hoped to head off ugly rumors. In any case, the decision was made easier because by 1960 the public attitude toward mental retardation was more enlightened. Even Joseph Kennedy discussed it openly. "I used to think it was something to hide, something not to talk about," he told a reporter. "But then I learned that almost everyone I know has a relative or good friend who has the problem of a mentally retarded child somewhere in the family."[13]

Four decades after the operation, Goodwin interviewed Rose and asked about Rosemary. Goodwin reported:

After [the operation] turned out so badly, [Joe] simply sent Rosemary to St. Coletta's and explained to his wife that the time had come to put their daughter away. He also said it was important for Rose not to see her so that she could get accustomed to being in the institution. What seemed to me inexplicable was that Rose Kennedy did not question that. It was not until many years later that Rose finally uncovered the truth about the lobotomy.

As Goodwin walked with Rose, they passed a picture of Rosemary on the wall. Rose turned to Goodwin and said, "I will never forgive Joe for that awful operation he had performed on Rosemary. It is the only thing I have ever felt bitter towards him about."

Prompted perhaps by his guilt over Rosemary, Joe later donated huge sums of money to fund research on mental retardation. Rosemary's condition also sensitized the Kennedy children to the misfortunes of the underprivileged and the retarded. Eunice subsequently became a leading force in the field of retardation.[14]

The next tragedy involved Joe and Rose's oldest son. At Harvard Joe Kennedy Jr. had been extremely active, playing football and rugby, chairing the Freshman Smoker Committee, serving three years on the student council, and chairing his house committee in his senior year.

After graduation in 1938, he toured Europe and was in Madrid when the city fell to Franco. In the summer of 1939 he worked as the secretary to his father at the London embassy. The following year he resumed his studies at Harvard Law School, completing two years before he joined the navy.

Handsome and charming, an excellent orator with a fine platform presence, young Joe had a natural flair for politics. He candidly admitted his ambition to be president of the United States. Kathleen Kennedy wrote Jack that she had recently "had dinner with future Pres. of the United States."

Most people liked young Joe and many admired him. "Adorably unsophisticated," said Harold Laski, characterizing him as a man who took criticism with "disarming friendliness" and had a "smile that was pure magic."[15]

But young Joe had a dark side as well. Quick-tempered and sometimes cruel, he was the kind of person "who could shove somebody aside so he could catch the ball," said one observer. A pugnacious brawler at Harvard, he and his burly friends would provoke fights at lower-class bars for sport.

Early on and continuing throughout his life, Joe Jr. knew the pleasures of the flesh. His biographer filled a book with strippers and showgirls, but concluded that deep down young Joe was emotional, vital, and honest with women when he really cared.

In 1940 young Joe was elected as a Massachusetts delegate to the Democratic National Convention in Chicago. He was pledged to James Farley, and when Franklin Roosevelt decided to seek a third term, the President's agents considered a unanimous vote for Roosevelt to be crucial. "They applied excruciating pressure to the last few delegates pledged to Farley, clustered mainly in the delegation from Massachusetts," noted Michael Beschloss. Roosevelt's agents warned the young Kennedy that ingratitude to Roosevelt might damage his future political career. After consulting several of his father's friends, young Joe, with admirable courage, kept his pledge to Farley at the convention, one of the few dissenters who denied Roosevelt unanimous renomination.[16]

Before World War II young Joe walked in his father's ideological footsteps. His opinions about Roosevelt and the coming of war were almost identical with his father's isolationist views. At a time when he should have known better, he expressed admiration for Adolf Hitler. At Harvard Law School he organized noninterventionist activities on campus. America must remain neutral, he insisted in speeches delivered around the Boston area.

Young Joe's career in the navy started off well but stalled. Jack's heroism in the Solomons put pressure on his older brother to be heroic. Rose later noted that "in their long brotherly, friendly rivalry, I expect this was the first time Jack had won such an 'advantage' by such a clear margin."

Young Joe only halfheartedly praised his brother's heroism in the South Pacific. "I read the piece in *The New Yorker*, and thought it was excellent," he wrote, but added acidly, "What I really want to know is where the hell were you when the destroyer hove into sight, and exactly what were your moves, and where the hell was your radar?"[17]

An extraordinary mission Joe volunteered for involved flying a navy Liberator bomber loaded with ten tons of high-explosive TNT from England to within a few miles of a purported German V-bomb base, where he was supposed to eject and let the plane guide itself the rest of the way to the target by remote control.

Shortly before 6:00 P.M. on August 12, 1944, he took off. His plane was in the air only twenty minutes when there were two huge explosions, and the aircraft disintegrated. Not even a particle of young Joe's body—or the body of his copilot—was ever found.

The Kennedys received the news at 2:00 P.M. on a Sunday afternoon at Hyannis Port. While Joe Sr. napped upstairs and Rose read the Sunday newspaper, two priests knocked at the front door. When Rose opened the door, the priests asked to speak with Mr. Kennedy. It was urgent. The priests told Rose and the ambassador that their oldest son was missing in action and presumed lost. "We sat with the priests in a smaller room off the living room, and from what they told us we realized there could be no hope, and that our son was dead," Rose later wrote.[18]

After hearing the awful news, Joe walked out to the sunporch and said, "Children, your brother Joe has been lost. He died flying a volunteer mission." In a muffled voice, with tears in his eyes, he continued, "I want you all to be particularly good to your Mother." Jack took a long walk on the beach in front of the house.

An army transport plane flew Kathleen home from London on August 16. Jack met her on the tarmac at Boston's Logan Airport, where she raced into his arms, weeping. That evening Jack and Kick visited the pastor of St. Francis Xavier Church in Hyannis Port.[19]

"Rose was hit hardest at first," said Doris Goodwin, "but eventually, as letters poured in to her from priests and nuns and friends, she began to accept in her mind that God had his reasons even if she could not fully comprehend them, and that gave her solace." Joe Kennedy, though, never fully recovered from the tragedy and was overwhelmed with tears anytime he attempted to talk about it.

For as long as he could remember, Jack told Billings, the competition with his older brother had defined his own identity. In the following months Jack felt exposed and vulnerable. "For twenty-seven years," Goodwin observed, "he had lived with a protective shield, since everything was expected of his older brother. . . . But with Joe's death came an abrupt removal of the protection he had enjoyed and he felt an 'unnamed responsibility' both to his parents and to his brothers and sisters."[20]

Jack decided that the best way to memorialize his brother was to collect material for a book honoring Joe. He set about writing and phoning people, gathering tributes and reminiscences from family members, friends, classmates, former teachers, his commanding officer, a girlfriend, even his valet.

He hoped to present the book to his mother and father as a Christmas present in 1944, but it proved to be a more demanding project than anticipated. "The book on Joe is going slower than I had hoped," he wrote Billings on February 20, 1945, "but it should be out in another month or so and I think will be pretty good. The piece I wrote for it is the best writing I ever did."

While the family discussed how nice it would be to have someone write a book about Joe, Eunice later remarked, "it was Jack who disappeared every evening from five to seven-thirty and wrote letters and made calls, and collected information, and wrote the book while the rest of us were still playing games."[21]

The result was a slim but moving book, *As We Remember Joe*. "The book, I am afraid—may make you sad," Jack wrote his parents on May 21, 1945, shortly after publication. "I hope that that sadness will be mitigated by the realization—clearly brought out in the book—of what an extraordinarily full and varied life Joe had." Five hundred copies were privately printed and distributed.

Early in life, Jack wrote in the introduction, Joe Jr. "acquired a sense of responsibility towards his brothers and sisters, and I do not think that he ever forgot it. Towards me who was nearly his own age, this responsibility consisted in setting a standard that was uniformly high." Jack only halfheartedly listed Joe's "defects": a hot temper and "an intolerance for the slower pace of lesser men." Jack thought he mostly understood his brother, but "I sometimes wonder whether I ever really knew him. He had always a slight detachment from things around him—a wall of reserve which few people ever succeeded in penetrating."

Jack stated that young Joe was an excellent role model for his brothers and sisters. "I think that if the Kennedy children amount to anything now or ever amount to anything, it will be due more to Joe's behavior and his constant example than to any other factor." The future had held the promise of great accomplishments, making his death all the more tragic. "His worldly success was so assured and inevitable that his death seems to have cut into the natural order of things."[22]

Many years after his brother's death Jack explained the high standards his brother set:

In college I had something of a mediocre record, you might say, until that first book [*Why England Slept*]. The book, which I might well not have written except for pressure to do well, brought out latent ability that I had. . . . So if you say what was Joe's influence, it was pressure to do your best. Then the example that Joe and I had set put pressure on Bobby to do his best.

Referring to Joe's death, Jack wrote to a former teacher at Choate that the war "makes less sense to me now than it ever made and that was little enough—and I should really like—as my life's goal—in some way and at some time to do something to help prevent another."

A few years later, after leaving Sunday Mass, Jack startled a friend by saying, "Will you wait a minute? I want to go up and light a candle for Joe."[23]

On the heels of young Joe's death came another dreadful tragedy, the culmination of a heartbreaking struggle within the family for the soul of Kathleen Kennedy. Living in London during the war, Kathleen had decided to marry William "Billy" Cavendish, the Marquess of Hartington, one of the most eligible young bachelors in England. Wealthy and prominent, the Cavendish family had an impeccable lineage back to the seventeenth century. Upon the death of his father, Billy would become the Duke of Devonshire. With the marriage Kathleen would one day become the mistress of several sumptuous mansions in England, a gigantic hunting estate in Scotland, and the wonderful Lismore Castle in Ireland.

From the Kennedys' standpoint, though, there was one huge stumbling block to the proposed marriage: The Cavendish family was Protestant and had gained its prominence in large part by its intense opposition to Catholicism. In the seventeenth century the first duke, William, fought the Catholic king, James II, in bloody rebellion.

For Billy to convert to Catholicism was unthinkable because the Catholic Church required that the children of a mixed marriage be brought up Catholic, which would betray three centuries of his family history. On the other hand, observed Lawrence Leamer, the Kennedys, one of the great Catholic families of America, "could not abide their daughter marrying into such a notoriously anti-Catholic family, breaking the laws of Rome by allowing her children to be raised in the Church of England."[24]

"I want to do the right thing so badly and yet I hope I'm not giving up the most important thing in my life," Kathleen wrote her parents in late February 1944. She was going to consult a Catholic bishop to request a dispensation. "I suppose it will [be] practically impossible." Indeed, all the attempts by Kathleen, Joe, and Rose to secure a dispensation proved futile.

Rose schemed to break up the impending wedding, confiding in her diary:

> Joe phoned me said he hadn't slept—Naturally I was disturbed horrified—heartbroken—Talked for a minute on our responsibility in allowing her to drift into this dilemma then decided we should think of practical way to extricate her. I said I would think it out and then call him later.
>
> Later we decided we would send a cable about like this Heartbroken—think-feel you have been wrongly influenced—Sending Archie Spell's [Archbishop Spellman's] friend to talk to you. Anything done for Our Lord will be rewarded hundredfold.

Just before the marriage Rose entered New England Baptist Hospital in Boston for what newspapers were told was "a routine physical checkup." Actually, Rose was on the verge of a nervous breakdown. On the day before the wedding, *The Boston Traveler* wrote that the marriage would bring Kathleen into "a family prominent in the defense and spread of Protestantism throughout the British realm." Observed Leamer: "This was the kind of commentary that was a stake through Rose's heart, a public airing of her shame."[25]

"I thought it would have such mighty repercussions in that every little young girl would say if Kathleen Kennedy can, why can't I," Rose later admitted. "Everyone pointed to our family with pride as well-behaved, level-headed and deeply religious. What a blow to family prestige."

On May 6, 1944, Kathleen and Billy married in a civil ceremony at the Chelsea Registry Office. Joe Jr., in England during the turmoil, staunchly backed his sister's marriage, giving solace to Kathleen. Across the Atlantic, Joe Sr. secretly supported his daughter, sending the soothing message, "Remember you are still and always will be tops with me."[26]

"Last week was most difficult," Kathleen wrote to her mother three days after the marriage. "The clergy of both churches were after me and now every morning letters arrive condemning my action. . . . I only hope and pray that things will not be too difficult for you and the rest of the family with the McDonnells etc." (The McDonnells were prominent New York Catholics, and friends of the Kennedys.) Rose should not blame herself for

Kathleen's decision. "You did your duty as a Roman Catholic mother. You have not failed, there was nothing lacking in my religious education. Not by any means am I giving up my faith, it is most precious to me."

Two months after the wedding Rose partially reconciled herself to the marriage. Magnanimous and kind, she wrote Kathleen, explaining that the wedding had surprised and "stunned" her. "However, that is all over now, dear Kathleen, and as long as you love Billy so dearly, you may be sure that we will all receive him with open arms. I guess I told you that Joe [Jr.] liked him better every time that he saw him, which was a great satisfaction to all of us."

After the marriage, Billy, an officer in Britain's Coldstream Guards, returned to his battalion to prepare for the D-day invasion. On September 9, 1944, a month after Joe Jr.'s death, Billy was killed, a bullet through his heart. "So ends the story of Billy and Kick," Kathleen wrote in her diary on September 20. "I can't believe that the one thing I feared most should have happened. . . . Life is so cruel."[27]

In their last report on Jack's health, in late November 1944, the doctors at the Chelsea Naval Hospital stated that Jack's recovery depended on a "long period of rest in a secluded outdoor environment." Jack and his father agreed; Jack should spend an indefinite period, perhaps as long as a year, resting in Arizona.

In Arizona, Jack stayed at the Castle Hot Springs Hotel in Castle Hot Springs, where he became close friends with Pat Lannan, another resident of the hotel. "The air is wonderful," Jack wrote his parents, "and the [hot] springs are amazing."

Jack wrote Billings on February 20, 1945: "I've been out here for about a month—but the back has been so bad that I am going to go to Mayo's . . . about the first of April unless it gets a little better."[28]

Jack took one brief trip to Phoenix. "Their [sic] was some pumping which interested me," he informed Billings, "and I did take [actress] Veronica Lake [for] a ride in my car. . . . I don't mean by all this that I pumped her or that if you should ever see her you should get a big hello. You would get the usual blank stare you get under similar circumstances."

At five o'clock every afternoon Jack's father phoned, always asking if his son needed anything. "I just don't know many fathers," said Lannan, "who I have ever run into that at 5 o'clock, like you'd set your clock, the phone would ring. How are you? What did you do today? How are things going? Is there anything I can do for you?" Joe sent steaks and lamb chops, and after Jack talked to his father about the issue of organized labor, Joe sent a huge crate of books on labor and labor law. Jack sat up until early in the morning reading the books until he finished the whole crate.

By late March Jack's health hadn't improved, and Joe Kennedy was worried. "It is very difficult to get anything from him, as you know," he wrote Paul Fay, "but Dr. Lahey saw him in Phoenix and didn't think he was getting along well at all."[29]

When Lannan asked Jack about his career plans, Jack seemed agitated. He answered vaguely that he wanted to go into "public service." Lannan had never heard of the phrase. "He said that his father had made a considerable amount of money and had set up a trust for him, and he didn't see any point in his making more money or going into business so he thought he'd go into public service. I couldn't get him to say politics to save his life."

When Lannan and Jack became bored, they vacationed in Los Angeles. While staying in a suite at the Beverly Hills Hotel, they ran into Chuck Spalding, and the three of them "bummed around." They met actress Olivia de Havilland at her home in Hollywood. "Jack was just fascinated," Spalding recalled, and "he put himself out to be just as attractive as he could be. He leaned toward her and fixed her with a stare and he was working just as hard as he could, really boring in . . . So finally we got up to leave and he is still working on her to come out to dinner and he walked into a closet. Tennis rackets and tennis balls and everything came down on top of his head."

Later that same evening, Jack wryly mused about the reasons for his failure. "I just can't understand it," he said. "Do you think it was me walking into the tennis closet? Do you think that's what really did it?"[30]

In April, through his friend William Randolph Hearst, Joseph Kennedy secured Jack a temporary assignment as a Hearst reporter. The position would give Jack something stimulating to do, keep his name before the public, probably grant him credentials to travel in Europe, and expose him to journalism as a possible career. Initially Jack was only going to write for Hearst's *Chicago Herald American,* but Joe Kennedy lobbied the Hearst organization to secure wider coverage. "I'm arranging to have the articles printed in some of the other Hearst papers," he wrote Kathleen on May 1, 1945. For whatever reason, Jack's articles were published in other major Hearst newspapers.

Jack's first assignment was to report on the founding of the United Nations in San Francisco, covering the conference, read his byline, from a GI's viewpoint. His initial articles, published in the first two weeks of May 1945, were cliché-ridden, inconsequential, and boring. An article on the World Court, appearing in the *New York Journal-American* on May 2, used sports references and trite phrases: "an international football game . . . carrying the ball . . . tried to tackle him all over the field." Two days later he began his article with this cliché: "The word is out more or less officially that Molotov is about to pick up his marbles and go home." There were awkward expressions: "As we were discussing the legal end—let's look at that."[31]

His articles didn't quote his sources, and read more like columns than straight reporting. They were full of his opinions. (Today his pieces would appear on the editorial page or the op-ed page.)

Unlike most reporters, he logically built up to his major point instead of using the inverted-pyramid style. Journalists learn to place the most important news at the beginning of the article so people will read that first, become interested, and continue with the story. Journalists do not expect to have patient readers willing to wade through a step-by-step report to reach the important news. Also, particularly in his early pieces, Jack presumed that the reader knew exactly what he was writing about. Journalists normally do not presume there is a constant reader; each article requires some explanation to set the stage or to identify the players. Jack didn't do this. Joan and Clay Blair judged Jack's reporting a "dismal performance, on a par with the output of any cub reporter."[32]

But Jack noticeably improved. By the end of May he wrote with more confidence and skill. On May 23, 1945, he effectively explained the veto power given the Big Five nations in the new world organization:

> Briefly it means that the new world organization can do nothing to stop an attack unless each of the Big Five gives its approval. In other words, any one of them can prevent any diplomatic economic or military pressure being applied to any aggressor. They can, in fact, even prevent any investigation of the attack being made.
>
> For example: Supposing Yugoslavia seized a portion of Greece. The Greeks might protest to the world organization and ask that steps be taken to stop Yugoslavia.
>
> Before any action could be taken by the Security Council, the Big Five would all have to agree on a course of action. Supposing, however, that Russia had sympathy with Yugoslavia. By voting against any action being taken, by voting against the matter even being investigated, she could absolutely prohibit any aid being given to Greece by the world organization.
>
> Thus, any of the Big Five can effectively veto assistance for an attacked nation. With this grave weakness in the new world organization, it is little wonder that the smaller countries have attempted to make treaties with the neighbors for protection against aggressors.

Throughout the San Francisco conference he took a sympathetic but realistic view of the emerging UN. He often reported on the "belligerent Russian attitude." The Russians would never entrust their safety and security to any organization other than the Red Army. Any "organization drawn up here will be merely a skeleton," Jack concluded. "Its powers will be limited. It will reflect the fact that there are deep disagreements among its members."

His personal notes summed up his thoughts about the UN:

> *Danger of too great a build-up.*
> Mustn't expect too much.
> A truly just solution will leave every nation somewhat disappointed.
> There is no cure all.

"It would be very easy to write a letter to you that was angry," he wrote a PT boat friend who had asked his views on the UN. When he thought about the deaths of people he knew, "it would be a very easy thing to feel disappointed and somewhat betrayed." The conference lacked moral force, he said; self-interest held sway. "You have seen battlefields where sacrifice was the order of the day and to compare that sacrifice to the timidity and selfishness of the nations gathered at San Francisco must inevitably be disillusioning."[33]

After Prime Minister Winston Churchill decided to call a general election for July 6, 1945, before the defeat of Japan, Jack was assigned to fly to London to cover the campaign. In June he interviewed scores of British politicians, sampled public opinion, listened to Churchill's speeches, and hosted intimate political gatherings.

Shortly after Jack's arrival in London Pat Lannan, reporting for the *Chicago Journal of Commerce,* joined him, and they roomed together at the Grosvenor House hotel. Every afternoon about five o'clock Kennedy invited a small group of young English political figures over for refreshments and political discussion. The group exchanged views about the British election, the impending arms race, Russian aggression in Eastern Europe, the threat of a Communist takeover of exhausted Western Europe, and the prospects for building the peace.[34]

Kathleen Kennedy asked an acquaintance, Barbara Ward, to introduce Jack to some British political leaders. Ward took him to visit the politician Herbert Morrison. Ward recalled:

> [Jack] . . . asked every sort of question of what were the pressures, what were the forces at work, who supported what, what was Mr. Morrison's significance in the London scene; and you could see already that this young lieutenant was political to his fingertips. So my chief first memory is of a very young man, still hardly with the eggshell off his back—he seemed so young—but with an extraordinarily, I would say, well—informed interest.

Jack had his own opinions, but he wanted to understand everyone else's. "He always asked an enormous number of questions," echoed another British political friend. "For every one question I asked him he asked two, at least. 'Why?' He always wanted to know why things were and how things worked, the root cause of things. . . . He had an inquisitive mind."

From London on June 23, less than two weeks before Britain's election, Jack wrote a startling article forecasting the defeat of Churchill and his Conservative Party. "This may come as a surprise to most Americans, who feel Churchill is as indomitable at the polls as he was in war," he wrote.[35]

The opposition Labour Party, composed of "leftwing doctrinaires, trade unionists and simple men with high ideals," had a radical platform:

Socialism—state ownership and control of industry and land, commencing with the mines, steel and iron works, transportation, the Bank of England and down through the list.

There is no genuflection to private enterprise that even our most liberal politicians in America feel they must make.

Capitalism must go and private enterprise must go.

Why were people in England willing to accept the controls the Labour Party would impose? He clearly described three reasons.

Most importantly, they are tired after 10 years of Tory government and they feel it is time for a change.

Second, the Tory government has been the object of an intense and clever attack during the last five years.

There has been firmly fixed in people's minds that in the years before the war, it was the Tory government that carried the umbrella of appeasement.

Third, was its treatment of the depression during the '30's.

The Conservative government, instead of indulging in a broad program of public spending as we did, tightened the country's belt and advanced its budget with consequent hardship for the people and political unpopularity for themselves.

If Labour won, England would carry through major changes "that many people in America and England feel cannot be made without an important limitation on democratic government. By watching England we will have much to learn."

At *The New York Times* Arthur Krock thought Jack's articles had become "very professional, very good and very clear." Kennedy's insight into the

British election gave Krock the "only intimation I got from anyone that Churchill would be defeated. Churchill was defeated, and I made up my mind that this boy had the makings of a very good political observer."

Krock must have overlooked Jack's subsequent articles. During the following two weeks, Jack felt compelled to tone down his forecast so that by election day he predicted a close contest.[36]

Because of the need to count the ballots of British soldiers overseas, the results of the July 6 election were not announced until July 26. After Churchill's government suffered a crushing defeat, Jack offered another reason for the upset. Living conditions in England "have always been difficult for the working man," he wrote. Enemy bombings, high prices, and standing in long queues had taken their toll on the temper and the patience of ordinary citizens.

> The Socialists promised that "things will be better for the working man," and to the Socialist party just about everyone is a working man.
>
> Churchill, on the other hand, took the same line in this campaign that had been so successful in 1940.
>
> He offered them nothing but "toil and sweat" and said that the Conservative party would make no glib promises that it could not keep.
>
> Unfortunately for the Conservatives, the people of this island have been on a diet of toil and sweat for the past five years.
>
> The British people will take that diet in an emergency but they feel that the emergency has passed.[37]

Throughout July and August Jack maintained a diary of his thoughts, typing most on a small manual typewriter, then gathering his pages into a loose-leaf notebook. His reflective and literate entries, written mostly in complete sentences, were too polished for an ordinary reporter's notebook. He probably intended to use his material in the future as the basis for a book.

Journalist Hugh Sidey, who analyzed the diary, thought Kennedy displayed the instincts of a good journalist, "the unflagging curiosity, the eyes, the ears." But, wrote Sidey, Jack searched for news "in the salons and country homes of too many dukes and lords and the airplanes of too many VIP's for my taste." Sidey conceded, though, that it was among the elite that the "political power struggle was being waged in those days. It also was about the only way a novice journalist could get around and gain entry to the authorities and particularly the Potsdam Conference, the most critical power meeting of the moment."

On two topics Jack was far more critical in his private diary than in his published articles. Not having experienced the Depression himself, oblivious of the poverty and the anger of the dispossessed, Jack accused President Franklin

Roosevelt of having inadequately handled the economic crisis (Roosevelt had died on April 12, 1945):

> Mr. Roosevelt has contributed greatly to the end of Capitalism in our own country, although he would probably argue the point at some length. He has done this, not through the laws which he sponsored or were passed during his Presidency, but rather through the emphasis he put on rights rather than responsibilities—through promises like, for example, his glib and completely impossible campaign promise of 1944 of 60,000,000 jobs.

He attacked socialism as he saw it exemplified by Britain's Labour Party. "Socialism is inefficient," he wrote. "I will never believe differently, but you can feed people in a socialistic state, and that may be what will insure its eventual success."

> The great danger in movements to the Left is that the protagonists of the movement are so wrapped up with the end that the means becomes secondary and things like opposition have to be dispensed with as they obstruct the common good.
> When one sees the iron hand with which the Trade Unions are governed, the whips cracked, the obligatory fee of the Trade Unions Political representatives in Parliament, you wonder about the liberalism of the Left. They must be most careful. To maintain Dictatorships of the Left or Right are equally abhorrent no matter what their doctrine or how great their efficiency.[38]

On July 23, while waiting for the results of the British election, Jack left for Ireland to report on the nation's political situation. Ambassador Kennedy arranged the visit through the State Department, hoping it would be valuable should Jack decide on a political career.

"Think it most important as do important people here that you go and cover the situation minutely," Joe cabled his son. "All papers and magazines will be vitally interested I know."

Jack's clearly written, balanced article explained Ireland's complicated politics and constitutional status. (For the first time, he quoted his sources.) He focused on the dispute between Prime Minister Eamon de Valera and his political opponent, James Dillon.

Ireland, Jack explained, was divided into two distinct political entities: the twenty-six counties of the south, which make up present-day Eire, and the six counties of the north, known as Ulster, which was still attached directly to the British Crown.

De Valera was determined to unify Ireland, the cause for which he had dedicated his life.

> In this cause, all Irishmen of the south are united.
> On this there is no dispute between Dillon and De Valera.
> The dispute concerns the method to be followed.
> Dillon and General Mulcahy, leader of the Fine Gael Party, Ireland's second largest political party, argue it is time to bury old hatchets. . . .
> By cooperating and the building of mutual trust, the partition can be broken and all Ireland united.
> So argue Dillon and a substantial section of the Irish populace.
> But ranged against this group is the powerful Fianna Fail Party, led by the brilliant, austere figure of De Valera, born in New York, the son of a Spanish father and an Irish mother.
> De Valera . . . feels that everything Ireland has ever gained has been given grudgingly and at the end of a long and bitter struggle.
> Always it has been too little and too late.

De Valera and his close associates fought in the abortive uprising of 1916, struggled against the Black and Tans in the civil war of 1922, and spent years in English and Irish prisons. They had not forgotten or forgiven.

> The only settlement they will accept is a free and independent Ireland, free to go where it will be the master of its own destiny.
> Only on these terms will they accept the ending of the partition. . . .
> The other is willing to compromise in view of present world circumstances and willing to join the commonwealth and work with it.
> Thus we begin to see behind the debate of De Valera and Dillon these two viewpoints.
> Dillon is attempting to pin De Valera to being completely in or completely out of the British Commonwealth and thus make political capital, no matter what decision he makes.
> In the north, Sir Basil Brooke, head of the government of Ulster, listened to the debate and roared down to the gentlemen in Dublin that "not an inch" will he give up of the six counties.
> And in the south, De Valera hurled back the challenge that from his present position he will retreat "not an inch."

Jack concluded that the problem of partition "seems very far from being solved."

Jack's article appeared in the Hearst papers, but did not garner the attention his father had anticipated.[39]

Thanks to arrangements made by Joe Kennedy, Jack flew to Paris at the end of July to meet Secretary of the Navy James Forrestal and his party on their way to the Potsdam Conference, the Allied summit with Stalin. On July 30, Jack accompanied the Forrestal party on a tour of German ports and cities, and Nazi landmarks.

In Frankfurt, Kennedy toured a salt mine where the Nazis had stored millions in looted gold, silver, and securities. He viewed the ruins of Berchtesgaden, Hitler's onetime mountain chalet, and inspected Hitler's Eagle's Nest.

The Soviet army had behaved horribly in Germany, raping and looting, he wrote in his diary. Still displaying fairness in judgment, he noted that the "British and ourselves" had also been guilty of looting and destruction, if not rape and other cruelties.

He took an analytical, dispassionate view of the poverty and misery he witnessed in postwar Germany.

> On some of the streets the stench—sweet and sickish from dead bodies—is overwhelming.
>
> The people all have completely colorless faces—a yellow tinge with pale tan lips. They are all carrying bundles. Where they are going, no one seems to know. I wonder whether they do.
>
> They sleep in cellars. The women will do anything for food. One or two of the women wore lipstick, but most seem to be trying to make themselves as unobtrusive as possible to escape the notice of the Russians.

Neither his newspaper articles nor his diary mentioned Jews or the Holocaust. "Had he not heard of the death chambers yet?" Sidey wondered. "It is hard to believe." At that time Kennedy's mind was focused elsewhere; perhaps he was simply callous.

Jack's manner of analyzing Hitler was peculiar: "He had boundless ambition for his country which rendered him a menace to the peace of the world, but he had a mystery about him in the way that he lived and in the manner of his death that will live and grow after him. He had in him the stuff of which legends are made."

That Hitler "had in him the stuff of which legends are made" is true but obviously incomplete. In fairness, there is no indication in his diary, or any of his other writings, of sympathy for Hitler or Nazi Germany.[40]

After returning to London from Germany, Jack mysteriously fell ill at the Grosvenor House, and was hospitalized at the U.S. Naval Dispensary in London. "He scared the hell out of me," said Pat Lannan. "I'd never seen anybody go through the throes of that fever before. I saw the bed clothes ringing wet, and this guy just burning up."

"Was well until yesterday afternoon when he had a chill, became nauseated, vomited several times, had vague abdominal discomfort," said Jack's medical report. As mysteriously as it began, the fever, nausea, and stomach pain ended. The report concluded that he had suffered from "Gastro-Enteritis, Acute."

"The larger question of Jack's susceptibility to such fevers went unaddressed," Nigel Hamilton perceptively noted. On August 6, the day the atomic bomb was dropped on Hiroshima, Jack felt good enough to fly back home aboard Forrestal's plane.[41]

Kennedy's brief journalism career, from May to August 1945, had been an extraordinary experience for a twenty-eight-year-old. He had closely observed international leaders—Winston Churchill, Clement Attlee, Ernest Bevin, Eamon de Valera, Andrey Gromyko, and Vyacheslav Molotov. He discussed world affairs with British political figures Anthony Eden, Hugh Fraser, Herbert Morrison, and Harold Laski. And he met and became acquainted with senior U.S. State Department officials Averell Harriman, John McCloy, Robert Murphy, Joe Davies, and Will Clayton. On August 1, after accompanying Forrestal on a visit with General Dwight Eisenhower, Jack noted in his diary: "It was obvious why [Eisenhower] is an outstanding figure. He has an easy personality, immense self-assurance, and gave an excellent presentation of the situation in Germany."

Afterward Kennedy told friends that he enjoyed journalism, but often felt frustrated. Reporting was too passive. "Instead of doing things," he said, "you were writing about people who did things. . . . I really would like to weigh in a little heavier." Politics offered a chance to do just that.[42]

9

KENNEDY FOR CONGRESS

After his ambassadorial career, Joe Kennedy never served the nation again in a major capacity. Instead, he turned his attention to the business world, partly to occupy his time, but also because he enjoyed making money and did it easily.

In 1945 he arranged a staggering real estate coup by purchasing the Merchandise Mart in Chicago, a building with twenty-four stories and ninety-five acres of rentable floor space. It was previously a spectacular money-loser, so he paid only $12.5 million; fifteen years later it was worth almost $100 million.

As the war was coming to an end, Joe also focused on family business—specifically, helping to plan the political future of his two oldest sons. He still had contacts in Boston and kept a mental inventory of people who could be helpful to him. In the spring of 1944, before the death of young Joe, Joe Kennedy had asked Joe Kane, his second cousin and a veteran Boston political operative, to assess the political potential in Massachusetts for both young Joe and Jack.[1]

Since young Joe was still in Europe, and Jack at the time was in the hospital in Boston, Kane became much better acquainted with Jack. He was very impressed. "There is something original about your young daredevil," Kane wrote Kennedy on February 14, 1944, after several visits with Jack. "He has poise, a fine Celtic [face]. A most engaging smile." At a Boston dinner for Honey Fitz's birthday, Kane reported, Jack "spoke with perfect ease and fluency but quietly, deliberately and with complete self-control, always on the happiest terms with his audience. He was the master, not the servant of his oratorical power. He received an ovation and endeared himself to all by his modesty and gentlemanly manner."

But when Kane raised the possibility to Jack of running as a candidate for office, Jack replied simply, "My brother Joe has priority in aspiring for public office." Kane concluded that Jack probably preferred an appointment to a governmental commission.

After young Joe died, the question of priority was removed, and father and son began to reassess their options. Initially apprehensive about his father viewing him as the heir to the family's political traditions, Jack told Paul Fay, "I can feel Pappy's eyes on the back of my neck."

Fay intended to work in his father's California construction business after the war. "Red," Jack said with no enthusiasm, "when the war is over and you are out there in sunny California giving them a good solid five and a half inches for a six-inch pavement, I'll be back here with Dad trying to parlay a lost PT boat and a bad back into a political advantage. I tell you, Dad is ready right now and can't understand why Johnny boy isn't 'all engines ahead full.' "[2]

As Doris Kearns Goodwin pointed out, the process by which Joe Kennedy came to see Jack as a surrogate for young Joe was complicated. Having focused almost exclusively on his eldest's political talents, Joe senior had never carefully evaluated the considerable political potential that Jack possessed. "Jack in those days . . . was rather shy, withdrawn and quiet. His mother and I couldn't picture him as a politician. We were sure he'd be a teacher or a writer."[3]

Gradually Jack came to agree with his father that maybe he should consider running for political office. After all, he had been taught since childhood that he should do something worthwhile with his life, and maybe politics was the right choice. He enjoyed reading about current events and had enjoyed his political science courses in college. Some of the practical aspects of Boston's politics he had absorbed from "Grampa" Fitzgerald. "Jack always considered Grampa fabulous," said Rose Kennedy. "He never tired of listening to him, and he soaked it all in."

"I got Jack into politics," Joe Kennedy later bragged. "I was the one. I told him Joe was dead and that it was therefore his responsibility to run for Congress. He didn't want to. He felt he didn't have the ability, and he still feels that way. But I told him he had to."

Jack remembered it differently. "It was the other way around," he said. "We all like politics, but [young] Joe seemed a natural to run for office. Obviously, you can't have a whole mess of Kennedys asking for votes. So when Joe was denied his chance, I wanted to run and was glad I could."

"I am returning to Law School at Harvard . . . in the Fall," Jack wrote Billings on February 20, 1945, but suggested that if a political opportunity arose in Massachusetts, "I will run for it." He added, "I have my eye on something pretty good now if it comes through."[4]

What looked pretty good and what both Jack and his father eyed was a possible congressional race. Jack's letter alluded to the political intelligence gathered by his father on the political plans of James Curley, then congressman from the Eleventh District in Massachusetts. In the spring of 1945, Curley announced his candidacy for mayor of Boston in the fall election. He was expected to win, and if he did, he would have to vacate his congressional seat. Joe Kennedy eyed the seat for his second son. (Rumors spread that Joe Kennedy paid Curley to vacate.)

Still, Jack had doubts. He disliked the style of politics associated with Boston: the exuberant backslapping and handshaking, the exaggerated claims and denunciations, the inflated rhetoric. Jack also wondered if he had the talent for public speaking. Obviously, he would need expert advisers if he jumped into the race.

For a neophyte speaker, a good place to begin was the Hyannis Port Rotary Club, where Jack appeared in September 1945. His speech, "England and Germany: Victor and Vanquished," was neither appropriate nor memorable. "Jack Kennedy more closely resembled a high-school senior chosen as Boys' State representative . . . than a young man on the threshold of his political career," said local historian Leo Damore. Because the collar of his white shirt gaped at the neck, and his gray suit hung slackly, a Rotarian described him as "a little boy dressed up in his father's clothes."

In a scratchy voice Jack projected an earnestness that masked his discomfiture. No humor enlivened his talk, and he seldom diverged from his prepared text. But his personality shone through. "Stumbling over a word, he flashed a quick, self-deprecating grin that, a member of his audience remembered, 'could light up the room,'" reported Damore. Jack's waiflike quality and his winning sincerity impressed his audience more than his high-flown language.[5]

In November 1945, Curley was elected mayor of Boston, and the primary election to fill his vacant seat was set for June 18, 1946. Overwhelmingly Democratic, the Eleventh District included businessmen and Harvard intellectuals, but the district was one of the state's poorest, brimming with slums and serving primarily Italian and Irish Catholics who worked in the shipyards, markets, and factories. Among the few people Jack knew in Boston were eighty-two-year-old Honey Fitz and his wife, who lived at the Bellevue Hotel. So when Jack moved to Boston he rented a two-room suite at the Bellevue, just down the hall from his grandparents.

The Kennedys had deep roots in the Eleventh. The area included East Boston, Joe Kennedy's birthplace, and the North End, where John F. Fitzgerald and Rose Kennedy had both been born. Patrick Kennedy, father of the ambassador, at one time represented part of the Eleventh District in the state house of representatives and senate. The district encompassed Cambridge, where the Kennedys had gone to Harvard, and the strongly Irish sections of Brighton, Somerville, and Charlestown, where the family was highly respected.[6]

Although Joe Kennedy's reputation had diminished outside Massachusetts, Boston still regarded him as the patriarch of a legendary family. The Kennedys' achievements, triumphs, and sorrows were well known in the community. They were "Catholic Brahmins," as sophisticated and worldly as any of the old Yankee families. "They were people with whom the socially aspiring identified," observed Lawrence Leamer, "hoping to rub shoulders with members of this exalted family, if only in a political house party or at a campaign rally."

In the fall of 1945, while Jack and his father quietly planned the congressional race, the ambassador was recruited by Governor Maurice Tobin to chair the Governor's Committee on Commerce, which conducted an economic survey of Massachusetts. Crisscrossing the state, Joe met influential people in government, politics, and the media who could assist Jack's campaign.

To win office Jack needed to build a loyal personal organization. He and his father constructed one that blended seasoned professionals with energetic amateurs.[7]

One professional recruit, the clever Joe Kane, became Joe Kennedy's primary consultant. He had the ambassador's ear anytime he wanted it. White-haired, perfectly groomed, with his fedora pulled down over one eye in the manner of movie star Edward G. Robinson, Kane was one of the wisest and most cunning political operators in the Boston area. Kane coined Jack's campaign slogan, "A New Generation Offers a Leader."

Another of Joe Kennedy's confidants was his longtime secretary, Eddie Moore. If anyone in Jack's campaign needed money, Moore was the person to see. Each month, when volunteer Dave Powers needed forty dollars to pay the rent for Jack's Charlestown headquarters, he contacted Moore. "It was the strangest experience," Powers recalled. "I would meet Moore at the campaign's central headquarters . . . and he would then lead me into the men's room, where, putting a dime into the slot, he would take me into a closed toilet. There, with no one able to watch us, he would hand me the cash, saying, 'You can never be too careful in politics about handing over money.' "8

Joe Kennedy and Jack made all of the major decisions, but campaign director Mark Dalton wrote speeches, advised on strategy, and coordinated Jack's appearances. A newspaper reported that "a lot of politicians are trying to get on the Kennedy gravy train, no matter what he runs for." Indeed, the appeal of Kennedy money convinced some of the other candidates' supporters to jump ship because they wanted a large paycheck. When Billy Sutton first laid eyes on Jack Kennedy, he said to himself, "150 lbs. of pure cash!"

A student of politics, Sutton became a paid staff member for the campaign, and often guided Jack around the district. He spent more time with the candidate than anyone else. He was clever, funny, and likable, and his humor often broke tension within the campaign organization before it reached a boiling point.

Several court jesters lightened the tone around Jack. One was Irish Patsy Mulkern, who always looked drunk but never touched liquor, an old-line pol who somehow got on Joe Kennedy's payroll for the campaign. "Patsy used profanity instead of pauses," said one observer. His swearing shocked reporters and some of Jack's friends. But Jack enjoyed him. Paranoid about strangers—usually Jack's friends—tagging along with the candidate, Patsy said to Jack, "All these guys. You don't know who's witcha and who's not witcha but I want to tell you one thing. If you weren't a millionaire I wouldn't be witcha." Jack laughed uproariously at Mulkern.9

More than Joe Kennedy's money attracted people to Jack's campaign. Because he was decent and fair—a war hero who seemed to have a great political future—Jack motivated people to want to work for him. Together with the savvy Boston professionals, a large contingent of amateur enthusiasts energized the campaign. "It was a marvelous combination, a very effective one that continued throughout Jack's political career," said Rose Kennedy.

Dave Powers, an unemployed air force veteran, lived with his sister in a Charlestown three-decker tenement when he met Jack. The son of immigrants from County Cork, Ireland, Powers served as campaign manager in Charlestown and directed a voter-registration drive for Jack among returning veterans. An exceptionally funny storyteller, Powers remained a close friend and supporter for the rest of Jack's life.

Several family members, college chums, and other friends also worked on Jack's behalf. Red Fay came from San Francisco and campaigned for two months; Torbert Macdonald, Jack's Harvard roommate, worked in Cambridge and in Somerville; Ted Reardon, young Joe Kennedy's former college roommate and friend, took over the Somerville headquarters; LeMoyne Billings spent most of the campaign in the Cambridge headquarters; brother

Bobby Kennedy, just out of the navy, knocked on doors in east Cambridge for three months; and sister Eunice pitched in at the Boston headquarters.[10]

Rose was another campaign asset. An exceptional campaigner, she stumped for Jack during the last few weeks of the race. With her distinctive glamour and style, Rose represented an unreachable dream for thousands of Irish matrons. "Women came as much to see her and her clothes as they did to see Jack," said Billy Sutton. Spurning the conventional political speech, Rose delighted crowds with stories about her family and the challenge of raising her children.

A timely change in the leadership of Boston's Catholics proved another benefit for Jack's campaign. When William Cardinal O'Connell died in April 1944, Pope Pius XII named Bishop Richard Cushing as the new archbishop of Boston. The future cardinal quickly befriended the Kennedy family and assisted Jack in the 1946 campaign. He introduced Jack at parochial school meetings and Holy Name and Communion breakfasts. With his blossoming ecumenical spirit, Cushing also arranged Jack's appearances before Jewish groups and at bar mitzvahs.[11]

Joe Kennedy briefly considered having Jack run for lieutenant governor instead of Congress. In February 1946, Governor Tobin discussed the state office with Joe because Tobin needed a well-known veteran to prop up the Democratic state ticket. But most of Jack's friends didn't think his talents were suited for either governor or lieutenant governor because he had no experience in administration or in haggling with a fractious legislature. His interest in national affairs and foreign policy pointed toward Congress. Joe Kane adamantly opposed the governor's invitation, and Kane's view prevailed.[12]

Arrayed against Jack in the Democratic primary were nine other candidates, a few of them prominent. Included in the mix were two with the same name: Joe Russo. An old political trick in Boston was to place another person with the same name on the ticket to weaken the strong one. A veteran member of the Boston City Council, Joe Russo claimed publicly during the campaign that someone had "seen fit to buy out a man who has the same name as mine . . . so the voters of this district will be confused and deceived." Russo obviously meant someone in the Kennedy camp. The evidence points to Joe Kane as the trickster. Billy Sutton claimed Kane did it intentionally and that Jack was unaware of it. Joe Kennedy probably approved the move.

Candidate Mike Neville, former Democratic leader in the Massachusetts legislature, had his base of support in his home city of Cambridge and in the adjoining Somerville wards. Among veteran politicians Neville was the best-liked and seemed the most capable candidate.

Another potentially strong candidate was John F. Cotter, secretary to former congressman James Curley. Some of Jack's advisers feared that women voters might send Catherine Falvey to Washington. A veteran, Major Falvey, thirty-five, a slim, hazel-eyed lawyer, had twice been elected a Democratic member of the state legislature from Somerville. "We thought there was a little danger . . . because she was a woman," recalled John Droney, one of Jack's aides. "We didn't know how the women would react. They [might] go for her."[13]

The anti-Kennedy forces accused Jack of being too young and inexperienced, a carpetbagger, a rich Harvard graduate. Too British, he favored a postwar loan to England, and his sister had even married a descendant of the hated Irish nemesis, Oliver Cromwell.

Tip O'Neill, a young Democrat who would later succeed Jack as congressman in the Eleventh District, summed up the skeptical view of veteran politicians: "Here was a kid who had never run for anything in his life. . . . Kennedy for Congress? It was hard not to see it as a lark. So young Jack Kennedy had thrown his diaper into the ring? He didn't stand a chance."

A newspaper ad declared:

CONGRESS SEAT

FOR SALE

NO EXPERIENCE NECESSARY

APPLICANT MUST LIVE IN

NEW YORK OR FLORIDA

ONLY MILLIONAIRES NEED APPLY

Boston columnist Dante O'Shaughnessy, the most scathing critic, lampooned Jack for having an English-style valet (George Taylor). "No wonder he favors the loan to England, out of your taxes, of course," said the columnist. "Kennedy's candidacy is the nerviest thing ever pulled in local politics. . . . He moves in, valet and all, and demands that because of his family you send him to Congress. If you can beat that for bold, brazen gall, I'll quit and campaign for deah Jawn, and fly the British Union Jack from my flagpole." There was one fundamental question, the columnist concluded: "Is the Congressional seat in the Eleventh Congressional District for sale?"[14]

Jack was dazed by the bitterness and the assaults that came from every side, but he remained outwardly calm. He did not try to discredit or disparage the other candidates. On occasion, when an opponent assailed him from the same platform, he replied, but not with obvious ill temper.

Overall, Jack's critics made little headway. Because the Kennedy family was so prominent and admired throughout the district, voters treated the carpetbagger accusation as sheer nonsense. Of course he was a local boy. His father and grandfathers had all been local boys. Even if they felt Jack had not

spent much time in the district, they were still proud to have a young returning war hero run as a candidate in their district.[15]

To win a political office, Joe Kane maintained, three things were necessary: "The first is money and the second is money and the third is money."
Joe Kennedy provided all three. He spent about three hundred thousand dollars on the campaign, far more than the combined expenditures of all of
Jack's opponents.

Today, of course, candidates routinely employ advertising agencies in their
campaigns, but in 1946 doing so was uncommon. The ambassador hired the
John Dowd Advertising Agency in Boston to handle Jack's public relations.
The Dowd Agency assisted Jack with position statements, press releases, and
interviews, the goal being to get the candidate's name in the newspaper day
after day.

The Kennedy organization saturated the district with Kennedy billboards,
posters, car cards, leaflets, and radio spots. A campaign volunteer remembered
that voters "saw Kennedy, heard Kennedy, ate Kennedy, drank Kennedy, slept
Kennedy, and Kennedy talked and we talked Kennedy all day long."[16]

Jack's campaign dominated the spotlight of newspaper publicity. The free
coverage was partly a natural result of having a war hero with a prominent
name as the candidate. It also stemmed from Joe Kennedy's energetic efforts
to court political writers and editors. Spending many hours on the phone, he
flattered them, traded confidences, and asked favors.

Joe urged Jack to court journalists. "I would suggest," he wrote his son,
"that from now on you write a personal note to any magazine or newspaper
making a kind reference to you. . . . These fellows are like everyone else;
they will appreciate hearing from you."[17]

At the Ritz-Carlton, Joe met with Jack almost daily to analyze recent
events and to plan for the future. Joe also summoned key workers to his suite
to report on the campaign's progress, comparing each report with others.
"Generally there'd be somebody with him—a secretary or somebody," said
campaign worker Peter Cloherty. "He'd ask you how you thought the campaign was going and if you had any suggestions. He would ask you three or
four very pointed questions." Then Joe dismissed the individual. "He was all
business," Cloherty said. "Not severe, but [he] didn't spend a lot of time on
amenities."

Cloherty claimed that Joe Kennedy didn't intimidate him, but others
were petrified of the old man. During Dave Powers's meeting, Joe asked him
how many votes there were in Charlestown. "Oh, about ten thousand,"
Powers answered. "I know about," Joe replied sharply. "I want to know exactly."

"Was he scary!" Powers recalled. "Yet the next morning when I saw him
again and told him the figure was 10,637, he patted me on the back and

made me feel great. And from then on I always made sure I had my numbers straight."[18]

Joe's influence extended beyond just approval of staff and the outlay of money. "The Ambassador was the essential, real campaign manager," Mark Dalton claimed. In a letter to Kathleen, Rose explained that Joe was remaining behind the scenes "so whatever success there is will be due entirely to Jack and the younger group."

From Palm Beach on February 11, 1946, the ambassador wrote Kane that he knew Jack was working diligently, but "I hear from some other people up there that they think he should visit more Jewish organizations." Within two weeks Kane reported that he had lined up three Jewish organizations for Jack to address.[19]

Unlike his key opponents, Jack didn't hold down a full-time job and could campaign all day. He had obviously lived his life differently than had voters in his district, but few seemed to resent his wealth, and he treated his differences with humor and grace.

His political style contrasted with the traditional Boston pol, who smoked a cigar and sported a wide-brimmed fedora, a splashy necktie, and a chesterfield coat with a black velvet collar. Refusing to wear a hat, seldom smoking in public, and wearing a dark two-button suit, Jack looked different, more refined.

He disdained the overblown rhetoric and corny style of Boston's hard-boiled politicians. "Compared to the Boston Irish politicians we grew up with," Billy Sutton said, "Jack Kennedy was like a breath of spring. He never said to anybody, 'How's Mother? Tell her I said hello.' He never even went to a wake unless he knew the deceased personally." One evening, as he sat at a rally with dozens of other candidates, the moderator's introduction kept hailing each candidate as "a young fellow who came up the hard way." When Kennedy's turn came, Jack said, "I seem to be the only person here tonight who didn't come up the hard way." The audience roared.[20]

At first Jack found it difficult to approach people on the street, introduce himself, and strike up a conversation. His demeanor betrayed self-consciousness. Whether on the rostrum, on the streets, or in homes, he struck people as shy. But he was aggressively shy. He forced himself to go into firehouses, police stations, saloons, and poolrooms. "It must have been a tremendous effort of will," said Mark Dalton.

"There was a basic dignity in Jack Kennedy," Dave Powers said, "a pride in his bearing that appealed to every Irishman who was beginning to feel a little embarrassed about the sentimental, corny style of the typical Irish politician. As the Irish themselves were becoming more middle-class, they wanted a leader to reflect their upward mobility."

On a typical day Jack rose at 6:30 A.M., rushed over the bridge to

Charlestown, stood outside the Charlestown Navy Yard from seven to eight o'clock, and shook thousands of workmen's hands as they entered the gate. Then he would stop for breakfast.[21]

From about nine to noon, he and Sutton (or another aide) walked the streets in the district, going into stores, firehouses, tailor shops, factories, drugstores, post offices—anywhere they could find people. "I'm glad to see you," Jack would say. "How's it going? Have you got any suggestions?" At lunchtime Jack would speak to a gathering, then grab a hamburger and malt. Early in the afternoon he returned to his hotel room, soaked his back in a hot bath, received a rubdown from a former boxing trainer, and took a nap.

Later in the afternoon he knocked on doors in a three-decker neighborhood—the Sullivans on the first floor, the Doughertys on the second, and the Murphys on the third. At four o'clock, he was back at the navy yard shaking more hands. In the evening, he spoke at a dinner or rushed to a half dozen house parties.

Even late at night Jack would ask, "Is there anyplace else we have to go?" Sutton would say, "Well, do you want to go to . . . ?" Jack responded, "Yes!" Then the two of them dashed off to a tavern, a legion hall, or an Italian club. "We'd get home about, maybe one forty-five and then we'd go to sleep," said Sutton. "He got no more than four and a half hours' sleep every night for four months."

"He wore me out," said Sutton. "As tired as you would be," Powers added, Jack made "you try harder because he was trying so hard, doing his best all the time."[22]

He was often jovial and good-humored. One evening Bob Morey, a campaign aide, Billy Sutton, and Jack drove to a speaking engagement. As usual they were late, and since Morey didn't like being blamed for tardiness, he reluctantly agreed to Jack's backseat prodding to drive faster. As they sped along, Jack turned to Sutton and said: "Billy, if we get into an accident, you'll have to remain conscious so that you can give our names, but more important than that, don't forget to tell the reporters that I was in the state of grace."

"All the girls wanted to marry him, and all the mothers wanted to mother him," said Sutton. He was acquiring political sex appeal. At an appearance at East Boston High School young girls gathered around him chanting "Sinatra! Sinatra!"[23]

"I am rather surprised to find that the candidate is not a snob, and has not the least bit of uppishness about him for this is rather unusual for one who has been brought up with plenty," wrote Boston columnist Clem Norton. "He has everything that is necessary for success in Boston's politics," Norton continued. "Youth, money, personality and ability, and he is not lazy . . . His future looks better to me than that of any other young man in Boston politics today."

While canvassing door-to-door in Cambridge for Mike Neville, young Tip O'Neill quickly discovered that the Kennedy avalanche was about to smother his candidate. O'Neill listened to a housewife praise Jack. "What a wonderful boy. We have all the literature, that beautiful story of the PT boat and how he got lost on the islands and all." After hearing similar stories at several more homes, O'Neill told Neville, "We're in trouble, make no mistake about it. This young fellow has captivated everybody."

Jack found himself enjoying the daily give-and-take of life as a congressional candidate, absorbing gossip about rivals, plotting strategy, writing new speeches, and kibitzing at his busy campaign headquarters. Although he often campaigned fourteen hours a day, he could still relax in his apartment, put on a sweatshirt, throw a football around, or engage in chitchat. "He had this tremendous flexibility and the ability to relax on a dime," said Anthony Gallucio, a campaign worker.[24]

Altogether Jack made about 450 speeches during the campaign. For a while, after his speech to the Hyannis Port Rotary Club, Jack's speaking continued to be nervous, hesitant, and self-conscious. At first he delivered only one speech. He described the sinking of the *PT 109*, focusing attention on the grim heroism of crew member Patrick McMahon, and on his own heroism only by indirection. He referred to himself in the third person. ("The commanding officer of the *PT 109*, believing it to be a Japanese destroyer . . . turned the bow of his PT to make a torpedo attack.") He used the word "I" only when he said, "Patrick McMahon was assigned to *PT 109*, of which I was in command."

Then he expressed praise for the personal qualities he had observed in McMahon. "I felt that his courage was the result of his loyalty to the men around him," Kennedy said of McMahon. "Most of the courage shown in the war came from men's understanding of their interdependence on each other. Men were saving other men's lives at the risk of their own simply because they realized that perhaps the next day their lives would be saved in turn. And so there was built up during the war a great feeling of comradeship and fellowship and loyalty."[25]

Returning veterans desperately missed those feelings, Jack said. "They miss the close comradeship . . . that sense of working together for a common cause." The challenge of politics, he suggested vaguely, was to re-create that sense of common effort, making people recognize they were as dependent upon each other in peacetime as they were in the war.

After the *PT 109* story Jack made an awkward transition—"We face critical times"—followed by a ponderous and mostly irrelevant account of the defeat of the British Conservative Party in 1945. Concluding, he urged Americans to take a deeper interest in their government and politics.

Gradually the Kennedy team helped Jack develop a new speech focused on bread-and-butter issues: more jobs, better housing, tougher price and rent controls, a higher minimum wage, veterans' benefits, and Social Security.

Eunice Kennedy later recalled her brother being discouraged with the quality of his speeches, and her father's ever-present reassurance. "Many a night when he'd come over to see Daddy after a speech, he'd be feeling rather down, admitting that the speech hadn't really gone very well or believing that his delivery had put people in the front row fast asleep." But Joe encouraged him. "Why, I talked to Mr. X and Mrs. Y on the phone right after they got home and they told me they were sitting right in the front row and that it was a fine speech. And then I talked with so and so and he said last year's speaker at the same event had 40 in the audience while you had 90.

"And then," Eunice continued, "and this was the key, Father would go on to elicit from Jack what he thought he could change to make it better the next time. I can still see the two of them sitting together, analyzing the entire speech and talking about the pace of delivery to see where it had worked and where it had gone wrong."

Jack slowly developed a comfortable style—simple, direct, and informal—avoiding any bombastic rhetoric. Although he sometimes stumbled over his words, audiences responded warmly to his determination, his self-deprecating humor, and his sincerity.[26]

Dave Powers first heard Jack speak to hundreds of Gold Star Mothers in Charlestown, a community that had lost many young men in the war. Powers was unimpressed until the candidate said, awkwardly but sincerely, "I think I know how you feel because my mother is a gold-star mother too." Powers recalled the impact: "I could hear them—where I was sitting on the fringe—saying, 'He reminds me of my own': the John, Joe, Peter they had lost. When he finished his little ten-minute talk he was surrounded by these wonderful Charlestown ladies. In all my years in politics I've never seen such a reaction."

"I have an obligation as a rich man's son to people who are having a hard time of it," he told the reporter from *Look,* which did a feature on him that appeared in June 1946, a few days before the primary election. "He was sort of a novelty," said Billy Sutton, "a millionaire guy speaking for the poor." *Look* labeled him a "conservative," but in a newspaper interview he called himself a "liberal" Democrat.[27]

Jack said he didn't endorse all the policies of the Democrats, "but most things done by the Democratic Party have made us stronger at home and abroad. This has been the great contribution of the Democratic Party, and I am proud to be found among its members."

Jack sounded more like a maverick when Gilbert Harrison (later the editor of *The New Republic*) interviewed him for the *Harvard Crimson.* If it was necessary to tag him, Jack told Harrison, "make it 'Massachusetts Democrat.' I'm not doctrinaire. I'll vote them the way I see them."[28]

Some government controls were necessary, he declared, because the Republican philosophy of laissez-faire, "with underproduction and inflation, overproduction and depression never will work." The public would not tolerate the cycles of prosperity and starvation.

Although he supported some restrictions on labor's right to strike, "If it's too hard on labor when it comes out of a Republican committee, I'll vote against it." He thought, though, that "industry should have some kind of protection against jurisdictional strikes and things like that."

His constituency included thousands of returning veterans susceptible to being courted by a fellow vet, particularly one with a heroic combat record. In newspaper ads and on billboards a banner, KENNEDY FOR CONGRESS, displayed a veteran and his father gazing at a photo of Jack. Pointing at the photo, the father said, "There's our man, son."

The nation should use the same ingenuity and energy in meeting the postwar housing shortage that it employed in overcoming the problems of World War II. "Why can't this ingenuity solve the housing problem and solve it now? We did it for war; we can certainly do it for peace."

He endorsed low-cost housing that was "really both low cost and housing." The returning veteran often faced a cruel dilemma: "buying a new home at an inflated price he cannot honestly afford, or . . . on the other hand, [being] forced to buy a makeshift structure that can never be a real home and will ultimately end up in the loss of almost his entire investment."[29]

After Joe Kennedy arranged a poll that found greater interest in Jack as a war hero than as a congressional candidate, the ambassador insisted that Jack run primarily as a veteran and war hero. The Kennedy organization mailed a condensation of Hersey's New Yorker article to almost every home in the district.

Advertisements, and nearly every press release, stressed the veteran-hero angle:

Men who pushed back the Japs, island by island in the Pacific, men who stormed into blazing Normandy on D-Day and who hammered their way across France and Germany to blunt the Nazi military might are now fighting a different kind of campaign—a political battle on behalf of a young man who at one time during the war was reported missing in action. . . . One of the impressive features of his campaign has been the manner in which veterans of all branches have rallied behind his candidacy.

William Johnston of Jack's *PT 109* crew stated in a campaign press release that if the Eleventh District wanted a "congressman with real ability, with great qualities of leadership and with unusual courage," then Kennedy was their man.

> I know something of what Kennedy can do under stress in an emergency. I saw him go into water burning with flaming oil to rescue two men who had been injured when our boat was hit. I saw him rally the members of our crew when they thought they were lost and were going to die. Though Kennedy was as sick and as tired as any of us.
>
> Somebody has talked about the need for a seasoned Congressman. Kennedy was seasoned enough to command a PT boat in action. He was seasoned enough for the lives of his crew to be entrusted to him, and it wasn't a trust that he regarded lightly.

The *PT 109* story became the primary theme of Jack's campaign. "By the time the preliminary election day rolled around, 'Kennedy the war hero' and 'PT-109' were household phrases in the Eleventh District," said Sutton.[30]

House parties were an old campaign technique. What distinguished the Kennedy parties was their large number, careful planning, and efficient scheduling. Jack's sisters Eunice and Pat helped coordinate the volunteer hostesses, and provided them with cups and saucers, coffee and cookies, silver and flowers. The pair started off in one home overseeing arrangements, then moved to the next, with Jack following shortly behind. Tight scheduling allowed Jack to appear at six tea parties in an evening. Volunteers took down the names of all the people who attended and forwarded them to headquarters, where other volunteers solicited their help.

Jack's personality sparkled at the house parties. He arrived a bit timidly but, as biographer James Burns noted, "with his flashing, picture-magazine smile, charming the mothers and titillating their daughters, answering questions with a leg draped over an arm of his chair, wandering into the kitchen for a word with proud grandparents about news from the 'old country,' a final round of handshaking before leaving for the next affair."

Coordinated by Eunice Kennedy, a team of volunteers arranged a huge reception three days before the June primary. Thousands of women in the congressional district received engraved invitations. Probably most of them had never received an engraved invitation to anything in their lives.

On the evening of the reception, held at the Commander Hotel in Cambridge, the Kennedys and the volunteers arrived early to arrange flowers, stack dainty sandwiches, and fill silver urns of tea—like a wedding reception or a fiftieth wedding anniversary party.

Before the scheduled hour, guests began strolling into the hotel's lobby. Taking their places in the reception line, they shook hands with Rose, Jack, and finally Eunice, who quickly directed the women into the ballroom. "On and on they came," said one account, "garrulous, stout old ladies in bifocals and flowered hats; stunning Irish-American women, wearing up-to-the-minute dresses with padded shoulders; matrons in stylish suits; a full cross section of Boston's womanhood." About fifteen hundred guests jammed the ballroom. Hundreds more, unable to gain entrance to the ballroom, crowded into the hotel lobby and overflowed into the street, snarling traffic on Harvard Square—all waiting patiently for a glimpse of the Kennedys.[31]

As the campaign drew to a close Jack turned more and more hollow-eyed and anemic-looking. His back bothered him, causing worried aides to wonder if he could get through the day. He often put his hands in his pants pockets to adjust the strap of his back brace. Climbing steps in apartment houses particularly aggravated his back.

After Jack had climbed up and down three flights of stairs, his face expressed pain. "You don't feel good?" inquired his aide Thomas Broderick. Jack replied, "I feel great." "He would never admit that he felt the least bit tired or anything," said Broderick. Jack's refusal to give in to his pain strengthened his heroic persona among intimates and at the same time added an appealing vulnerability.

At his apartment he found some relief by soaking in a hot bath. In the tub he continued working, often consulting about the campaign with key aides. Red Fay described the bathroom as an "inner sanctum," where Jack enjoyed the therapy of the hot bath while his campaign aides stood by perspiring.[32]

On Monday, June 17, 1946, the day before the primary, Jack walked five miles in the annual Bunker Hill parade through Charlestown, waving at the enthusiastic crowd that lined the streets. The grueling campaign, though, combined with the drawn-out parade in blistering heat, left him exhausted.

When the parade ended, Jack collapsed. He was assisted to the nearby home of State Senator Robert Lee, who had been helping Jack's campaign. Lee claimed that Jack turned "yellow and blue. . . . He appeared to me as a man who probably had a heart attack."

Lee and others took off his clothes and sponged him down. Jack swallowed pills in his pocket. Meanwhile, Joe Kennedy was informed of his son's condition. "That was one of the questions his father asked, did he have his pills with him," said Lee.

Jack spent the final evening of the campaign recuperating. Fortunately, the public hadn't witnessed his frightening and mysterious collapse, and knew nothing about his health problems. A year later Jack would finally learn what was wrong.[33]

The next day, primary election day, Jack felt better. As he awaited the returns, he squeezed in a movie—the Marx Brothers in *A Night in Casablanca*. Then he drove to several of his campaign headquarters to thank his workers.

The election results were a landslide for Kennedy. He collected 22,183 votes, almost doubling the vote for Neville. He defeated Cotter by more than three to one. (Major Falvey took fifth.) Kennedy ran ahead of all his opponents in Boston and Charlestown; Neville defeated him only in Cambridge. In the ten-person race his share of the vote was an impressive 42 percent.

That evening at the Boston headquarters Honey Fitz had tears in his eyes as he sang "Sweet Adeline." As Jack thanked his supporters, he choked up and had to fight back his own tears.[34]

After the primary Jack rested for two weeks at Hyannis Port. His campaign pace slowed considerably after the June primary, since winning the Democratic primary in the Eleventh was tantamount to final victory in November. He did some campaigning for the rest of the state Democratic ticket, but there was no need to campaign in his own contest.

Reporters sought more information about him. Did the handsome eligible bachelor have a steady girlfriend? "I don't know when I'd have time for much social life just now," he said with a smile, "and if I get a Sunday free I like to get home and see the family. That doesn't leave any time for parties." What were his future political plans? He emphasized his desire to help the veterans, especially with jobs and homes. "I've got to think it out and look for a solution."[35]

What were his views on the economy? He worried about another depression. "There is danger that in four or five years, with our productive capacity and with 15,000,000 men back [from the war] who have not been available for industry, there will be over-production and a consequent letdown." He wouldn't hazard a guess as to the solution. "That is the great problem of our capitalistic system," he said.

He made plain, though, that he opposed a socialistic solution. "Socialism can be democratic, as it is in England," he said, "but I think it is inefficient and tends toward more and more control. It is, of course, difficult to say at what point socialism comes in, whether it begins with public health provisions, workmen's compensation, or what."

In speeches and interviews he worried about Joseph Stalin, and America's unwillingness to stand up to him. The lesson of Munich still burned in his mind. "If we had had such a determination and had been prepared to back it up in '14 and '39, we might have saved ourselves a couple of wars." The Soviet Union was our greatest foreign danger. "She can cause us great unhappiness."

In what one newspaper described as a "dramatic" address for the Independence Day ceremonies at Faneuil Hall, Jack said the basic religious ideas that had inspired the nation over the years were being challenged "at home in the cynical philosophy of many of our intellectuals"—whom he didn't identify—and "abroad by the doctrine of collectivism which sets up the twin pillars of atheism and materialism as the official philosophical establishment of the State."[36]

In August Jack presented Archbishop Cushing with a check for $650,000—at the time the largest contribution in the history of the Boston diocese. Everyone understood that the gift came from the huge wealth earned by Joe Kennedy. During his presentation, Jack praised the Franciscan nuns who were to staff the proposed Joseph P. Kennedy Jr. Memorial Hospital in Brighton, a $2 million project toward which the Kennedys had donated the money. (After giving the archbishop the check, Jack had to borrow money from Cushing for taxi fare to get to his next stop.) The first of the Kennedys' spectacular charitable contributions, the gift earned praise and banner headlines in all the Boston newspapers, which reported that a Joseph P. Kennedy Jr. Foundation was to be established to make other charitable contributions in the future.[37]

In early October 1946, Jack received horrible news: Lennie Thom, his reliable *PT 109* shipmate, had died in an automobile accident in Ohio on Friday night, October 4. On Monday, Jack flew to Youngstown for the funeral, staying with one of Thom's neighbors and serving as a pallbearer. Kate Thom, Lennie's wife, later said that Jack was a great comfort to her. "He really helped me through it," she said. "His philosophy was the living go on living. There was much more to life. He encouraged me to go back to school after I had the baby and get into teaching. He said that Lennie's friends would be my friends for life." In Jack's case, that was true, as he remained a comfort to Kate right up to his own death.

While addressing the American Legion post in Charlestown in the fall, Jack suffered an unusual loss of composure. He was doing fine until he came to "No greater love has a man than he who gives up his life for his brother." The thought of his brother Joe's death caused a brief emotional breakdown and an inability to finish his speech.[38]

As expected, on November 5, 1946, John Kennedy easily beat Republican Lester A. Bowen, 69,093 to 26,007. Both Joe Kennedy and Jack, in different ways, contributed about equally to the victory. The father masterminded the campaign from afar, funded it abundantly, recruited excellent professional assistance, and constantly encouraged his son.

Jack clearly understood the role his father played and how his father's assertiveness needed to be handled. When a campaign aide questioned the ambassador's judgment on an issue, Jack responded, "I know you're right about this, but [my father is] putting up the money and we have to let him win a couple."

But Jack wasn't merely a puppet, manipulated by his father. During the campaign he worked hard and displayed persistence, dedication, and sacrifice, reflecting a deeper ambition and drive than early observers had thought he possessed. He motivated people to want to work for him. Growing in political acumen and self-confidence, he became convinced that he could make wise political decisions, sometimes against the advice of his elders and the professionals.[39]

One thing is certain: His victory transformed him into a major force in Massachusetts politics.

10

PLOTTING HIS OWN
COURSE

Jack was twenty-nine, and his youthful appearance caused misunderstanding on Capitol Hill. "Well, how do you like that?" he declared with mock indignation as he burst into his office one morning. "Some people got into the elevator and asked me for the fourth floor!"

In January 1947, Eunice accompanied Jack to Washington, where the two Kennedys moved into an attractive three-story row house at 1528 Thirty-first Street in Georgetown. Eunice had taken a job as an executive secretary with the Juvenile Delinquency Committee of the Justice Department. Billy Sutton, who also lived at the house, remembered the place as virtually "a Hollywood hotel," with guests popping in unexpectedly at any moment.[1]

One guest was a young Republican congressman from California. Jack thought Richard Nixon was a very capable legislator, who displayed his ability during the debate on what became the Taft-Hartley Act. "I was glad . . . to see Nixon win by a big vote," he wrote a friend in November 1950, after Nixon defeated Democratic incumbent Helen Gahagan Douglas in California's U.S. Senate race.[2]

Margaret Ambrose, who had worked for the Kennedy family for many years, became Jack's cook and housekeeper, and she tried to fatten up the skinny congressman. From journalist Arthur Krock, Jack had obtained the services of George Thomas, thirty-nine, a heavyset, cherubic-looking black domestic servant.

Enjoying the luxury of others taking care of most of his practical needs, Jack seemed to be leading a charmed life. He didn't have to worry about money, because all of his personal expenses were paid by Paul Murphy, who worked in Joe Kennedy's New York office. Jack's Capitol Hill secretary, Mary Davis, simply collected the bills and sent a note to Murphy: "Here are [the] bills Jack's accumulated over the past week. Would you please pay them?" And they were paid. His father's accountants in New York also paid his rent, telephone, and utilities. The domestic help cooked his meals, did his laundry, made his bed, sent out his dry cleaning, and packed his bags. His office staff arranged his travel and picked up his tickets; often he was chauffeured from place to place.[3]

A millionaire, Jack lived off the interest of his trust fund. In 1951 this amounted to $50,000 a year after taxes. He also received a congressman's salary of $20,000, which he donated to charity. Still, he needed to watch his spending. In the first half of 1951, Jack had spent $31,070.73. The New York office warned him of a problem: "We have been thinking that your total income [from the trust] for 1951, after payment of income taxes, will be about $50,000. You can see that at the present rate of expenditure you will soon be dipping into capital."

He rarely carried any money on him and only casually showed interest in his own investments.

"Jack has absolutely no understanding of his own finances," an exasperated Joe Kennedy complained to an associate. When Jack's staff and friends loaned him money for a restaurant tab or cab fare, he habitually "forgot" to pay them back. Dates were dumbfounded when they were forced to pick up the evening's tab because he had no money.[4]

At his congressional office Mary Davis typed his correspondence, answered his phone, and welcomed visitors. Ted Reardon, the administrator of the office, acted as liaison with Jack's supporters in Massachusetts. He also did research, monitored legislation that interested Jack, and contributed to Jack's speeches and statements. In the Washington office Billy Sutton was a jack-of-all-trades. He drove the congressman to engagements, personally delivered messages, and befriended other congressmen and their staffs. "He did a thousand and one different things," said Davis. "He was a terrific asset to the boss."

Jack graciously met with his constituents. Sometimes he returned from the House to find a group of constituents whose names he couldn't remember. "Oh, hi, how are you? Give me a minute, give me a minute, will ya? Be right with ya." After retiring into his office, he buzzed Davis on the intercom. "Come in here, quick." After Davis entered and closed the door, Jack said, "Who the hell are those guys? Tell me, what are their names?" After Davis's briefing, Jack returned to the delegation with cheery first-name greetings. "Hello Jack. Hello Joe. Hi Bert. It's good to see you."

Hardworking and pleasant Grace Burke directed Jack's Boston office, and Francis X. Morrissey handled political matters in the district. Overall, Jack's staff of assistants provided careful, conscientious, and efficient service to constituents. They gave Jack the free time to meet people, adapt to the House, and educate himself about issues.[5]

During his evening leisure in Washington, Jack often read at home. Or he attended movies, often three a week, usually musicals and Westerns—his favorite being the Western *Red River* starring Montgomery Clift and John Wayne.

Still fond of football, he sometimes left his office early, slipped on an old sweatshirt and tennis shoes, and hurried over to a Georgetown playground for a touch football game. "Soon he would be the center of a gang of boys, white and colored," Burns observed, "who had no idea that they were catching passes from a congressman." During Easter, long weekends, and recesses he flew to Palm Beach, often with Congressman George Smathers.

But Jack's primary leisure activity was pursuing beautiful women. At the end of World War II he met brown-eyed, dark-haired Florence "Flo" Pritchett, a former model and a divorcée, then working as fashion editor at the *New York Journal-American*. Their on-again off-again romance lasted until 1963. In the late 1940s Jack often spent weekends with Flo in New York.

In a letter to Jack from New York on June 5, 1947, Flo offered a suggestion: "Instead of making history with the Knights of Columbus, why not make something of your nights. The summer will be long and hot. So [I] think you should adjourn occasionally and help make [June] hotter. . . . I hope you will be [heading] up this way again, and that when you do, we can play."[6]

Flo had already been married, foreclosing the possibility that Jack would ever marry her. It was impossible for the Catholic Kennedy to marry a divorcée without ruining his political career. Flo Pritchett epitomized the type of woman Jack usually squired. Bright, beautiful, and amusing, all were "safe" girls whom he could not or would not marry.

Ralph Horton recalled visiting Congressman Kennedy in Georgetown:

We went to his house for dinner and shortly after dinner, a lovely-looking blonde from West Palm Beach joined us to go to a movie. After the movie, we went back to the house and I remember Jack saying something about, well, I want to shake this one. She has ideas. Shortly thereafter, another girl walked in. . . . I went to bed figuring this was the girl for the night. The next morning a completely different girl came wandering down for breakfast. They were a dime a dozen.

When Mary Pitcairn dated Jack, she thought he wasn't interested in a serious relationship with one woman. "I felt that his commitment would never be a profound one because he wasn't ready. Not because he was playing games or deceitful. He was flirtatious, and he liked flirtations. If the lady or the girl succumbed, that was part of it. . . . I was more interested in more serious relationships."

Pitcairn dated Jack in 1950 when Robert Kennedy married. "He wouldn't get over the seriousness of the vows Bobby had taken," she recalled. "Jack kept commenting [that his brother had] really made a commitment. . . . The fact that his little brother had agreed to do all these things and had committed himself for life to this girl. He just couldn't leave it alone, all evening."[7]

After he returned from the Pacific in 1945 and again following his 1946 primary victory, Kennedy visited California and consorted with Hollywood actresses and would-be actresses. There he had brief flings with Welsh actress Peggy Cummins and skating star and actress Sonja Henie.

With one Hollywood star he developed a serious relationship. In the spring of 1946, while visiting a movie studio in Hollywood, he met actress Gene Tierney, who was performing in a scene for the movie *Dragonwyck*. As she turned to the camera, she found herself staring into "the most perfect blue eyes I had ever seen on a man." When Kennedy smiled at her, "My reaction was right out of a ladies' romance novel," she said. "Literally, my heart skipped."[8]

Soon they met again at a party, danced, lunched together, and began a romance. Tierney had just separated (and later divorced) from her husband, Oleg Cassini, later an international fashion designer.

Three years younger than Kennedy, Tierney had broken into Broadway in 1939 and subsequently signed with 20th Century–Fox, where she settled into a film career consisting mostly of routine feminine leads. Lonely, troubled, and unhappy, Tierney suffered from depression and worried about the propensity for mental illness that ran in her family. In addition, her first child, three-year-old Daria, was retarded, blind, and deaf.

Jack sympathized with her problems, especially with Daria, who was about to be put into an institution. They talked about the Kennedy family's problem with Rosemary. "The subject was awkward for him," said Tierney. The Kennedys did not like to dwell on their imperfections. "Gene," he said, after a silence had passed between them, "in any large family you can always find something wrong with somebody."

They dined together in New York, and Jack met her family. She visited him in Washington as well, and sat quietly in the guest balcony during a congressional session. "Still," Tierney said, "we tried to keep our romance out of the gossip columns, and for the most part we succeeded."

When she visited friends on Cape Cod, Jack met her wearing patched blue jeans. "I thought he looked like Tom Sawyer," she said. They spent an enjoyable week together swimming, sailing, and walking on the beach in the moonlight.

"He made you feel very secure," she said. "He was good with people in a way that went beyond politics, thoughtful in more than a material way. Gifts and flowers were not his style. He gave you his time, his interest. He knew the strength of the phrase 'What do *you* think?'"

But Tierney was in the process of divorcing. As they ate lunch one day, Jack said, "You know, Gene, I can never marry you." Shortly thereafter they mutually agreed to end their romance.

Kennedy's friends thought that Tierney brought out his best side, his chivalry, concern, and compassion. "I think he felt great sympathy for her," Lem Billings later said. "She had gone through a terrible tragedy with her retarded daughter, and Jack told me he had talked with her a lot about it and reminded her of his retarded sister Rosemary and counseled her on bearing what had to be borne."

Tierney consistently defended Kennedy. She denied that he ever used her, then dumped her. "No one really broke up our relationship, not Jack's father nor his mother nor my family. . . . In truth, ours was a sweet but short-lived romance."[9]

In the first few years after the war a bevy of women moved in and out of Jack's life—Pam Farrington, Ann Marie Ostergren, Anne McGillicuddy, Kay Stammers, Bunny Walters, Angela Greene, Durie Malcolm. One of his flings was with seventeen-year-old stripper Blaze Starr, who later became a queen of burlesque, nearly in the same league as Gypsy Rose Lee. "I'm a 38 double-D," she boasted, and "they all come to see me." In Baltimore she was known as the "Queen of the Block," an area of strip joints and porn clubs. A few weeks a year she worked at the Crossroads in Bladensburg, Maryland, near the D.C. line. In 1949, while she promenaded on stage at the Crossroads, she met Congressman Kennedy. Over the next four years they saw each other every time she played the Crossroads. She claimed that he gave her a pair of diamond earrings for Christmas.

Several women had painful memories of their sexual relationships with Kennedy. "I was fascinated by him at the time," said one woman, "but our lovemaking was so disastrous that for years later I was convinced I was frigid. He was terrible in bed, which I assumed was my fault. It wasn't until I had a loving relationship with someone else that I realized how awful my affair with Jack had been."

Jack's social life was a subject of constant speculation. Yes, he told an inquiring reporter, he was on the lookout for a prospective wife. "Something nice—intelligent but not too brainy."[10]

Six months into his first congressional term Jack found himself in the middle of a tense, career-threatening political dilemma brought about by the imprisonment of Boston's Mayor James Curley.

Convicted in 1947 for using the mails to defraud in war contracts, Curley was imprisoned in Danbury Penitentiary. He had pleaded with the judge that he suffered from nine separate ailments. Still mayor of Boston and pulling strings to get out of prison, he wanted Democratic leaders in Massachusetts and Washington to urge President Truman to pardon him. Congressman John McCormack led the move to free Curley, drawing up a petition to the President. McCormack promptly gathered signatures from all leading Massachusetts Republicans and Democrats. All except Kennedy. On the floor of the House, McCormack handed him the petition and asked him to sign. The two men eyed each other tensely.

"If you don't want to sign it, don't sign it," said McCormack.

"Well, I'm not going to sign it," Kennedy replied.

The easiest thing to do would have been to sign the petition. Everyone who counted had, and Curley had a fanatically devoted following in Boston who might seek revenge. But Jack refused, for two reasons. First, Jack apparently checked with the U.S. surgeon general and other health officials, who convinced him that Curley was not seriously ill.[11]

"If I don't honestly believe he's sick and I don't honestly believe that he should be pardoned on the basis of what he said, do you think I should do it?" Jack asked a supporter. "It isn't worth being in Congress if I can't do what I feel." Jack had received many appeals from people asking his office for help to free loved ones from jail, some pathetically sad, and he'd had to refuse. So how could he sign the petition for Curley?

But the primary reason he refused to sign stemmed from Honey Fitz's long-standing grievances against Curley. Jack felt loyalty to his grandfather. "It would have been politically expedient not to have the Curley crowd against you," said Sutton. "It wasn't [Jack's] hatred for Curley. It was his love for his grandfather."

Everybody called, trying to get Jack to sign it—Archbishop Cushing,

Jack's father, Congressman McCormack. Most of Jack's aides wanted him to sign the petition as well. But he still refused.

It was a courageous stand, but not taken without trepidation. As Jack walked into his office after making his final decision, he waved his hands and said, "Well, I'm dead now. I'm politically dead, finished." He told a supporter, "I guess I'm going to be a one-term congressman."[12]

Several state newspapers praised Jack for exposing himself to political vengeance, for refusing to do something his conscience told him not to do. "Currently the air is filled with threats of what the Curley group will do to Mr. Kennedy in the 1948 primary election," said the *Boston Herald*.

President Truman eventually commuted Curley's prison term to the five months he had already served, and Curley went back to being the mayor of Boston. Fortunately for Jack, the promise of political revenge by Curley's forces didn't materialize, and the incident never became a political liability.[13]

Meanwhile, Kennedy was learning the ropes in Washington. He didn't have fully developed positions on every major issue. Like many new members of Congress, he was not informed on some topics; on others he was unsure. But on bread-and-butter issues—like improved economic conditions for labor, better wages, Social Security, housing, prices, rents, and aid to veterans and the aged—he had formed definite opinions. Because of the needs of his urban constituents, his campaign promises, the social-welfare tradition in the Kennedy-Fitzgerald family, and his own Democratic views, he chose to fight for social-welfare programs.

Republicans had scored a stunning victory in the 1946 congressional election, winning control of both houses of Congress for the first time since 1928. The Eightieth Congress was not a hopeful arena for any liberal reform. Democrats could barely salvage New Deal welfare programs from the conservative onslaught, much less extend them.

After World War II a huge demand arose for inexpensive housing. Millions of returning soldiers, plus the shortage of building materials during the war, had made the housing shortage acute. Jack thought his constituents needed low-cost public housing. He had seen firsthand during the 1946 campaign the drab and crowded tenements in Charlestown and East Boston, the seedbed for apathy, delinquency, and despair.

From 1945 to 1948 Congress debated a housing bill sponsored by Senators Robert Wagner, Robert Taft, and Allen Ellender. Its provisions included extensive federal aid for urban redevelopment and construction of a half million units of public housing. Critics, led by the powerful real estate lobby, branded the bill socialistic.[14]

In May 1947 at a housing rally sponsored at Faneuil Hall by the Massachusetts Allied Veterans Housing Council, Kennedy charged the American

Legion with obstructing public housing for veterans. The Legion was the "legislative drummer boy for the real estate lobby." He preferred a more advanced bill that would provide "really low-cost housing."

Boston columnist Clem Norton praised Jack's stand on the housing issue. "Watch this young fellow," said Norton. "Here is wealth standing up for what is right. Here is one of the very very few young men in the political life of our state for many a year, who has had the fortitude and the courage and the independence, to come right out and name names."

Jack also became involved in debate on a major new labor law. The Taft-Hartley Act of 1947, passed over President Truman's veto, amended the prounion Wagner Act of 1935. It reduced the political and economic power of unions by outlawing the closed shop (the practice of hiring only union workers) and specifying unfair labor practices. It also required unions to give sixty days' advance notification of a strike; authorized eighty-day federal injunctions when a strike threatened to imperil national security; restricted union political contributions; and required union officers to deny under oath any Communist affiliations. Labor leaders denounced the act as the "slave labor" bill. Like most Northern Democrats, Jack voted against the measure, but he wasn't entirely impressed with labor's lament.[15]

Jack's primary committee assignment was the House Committee on Education and Labor, chaired by Republican Fred Hartley, the House sponsor of the new labor bill. During deliberations on the Hartley bill, Jack and two assistants, Mark Dalton and Joe Healey, a labor official, diligently worked an entire weekend preparing Jack's position on the complex legislation. Healey later observed that Jack displayed "great depth of thinking and analytical ability" and was "not afraid to speak out and take an independent position."

When the Hartley bill passed his committee, Kennedy voted against the measure and wrote an independent minority report. "If repressive and vindictive labor legislation is enacted at the behest of management," he said, "a tide of leftwing reaction will develop which may well destroy our existing business system. At the same time, if labor continues to insist on special privileges and unfair advantage in its relations with management, I have grave doubts as to the future of the trade union movement."[16]

In April 1947, during the House floor debate on the bill, Jack was a jumble of nerves. A reporter described him: "Strums a pencil on his knee for minute after minute. Stops it. Taps left foot. Taps it, taps it. Hair awry. The labor bill is out of his committee and he knows its seams and stitches. Up on his feet and down again. Perpetual motion."

For several years after passage of the Taft-Hartley Act, Jack joined the insistent chorus of organized labor in urging its repeal. Nonetheless, he repeatedly lectured labor groups on two weaknesses he perceived in the labor movement. Unions must reform themselves and stop asking for special privileges. The Taft-Hartley Act was no political accident. It showed "distinctly that somewhere along the road, labor has lost the public support it enjoyed in the 30's—and without public support the American labor movement cannot survive."

Because the public believed that Communists had gained positions of power in some unions, he urged labor "to remove Communists from positions of control." He deplored the action of a New York union official who allegedly pointed to a Soviet flag hung over the speaker's platform and said, "This is the flag the union will follow from now on."[17]

In March 1947, while the House Committee on Education and Labor held hearings on Communist influence in labor unions, one witness was Harold Christoffel, the president of UAW-CIO Local 248 in Milwaukee, Wisconsin. Under oath Christoffel unequivocally denied being a Communist. Subsequently, Louis F. Budenz, a former Communist, testified before the committee that Christoffel was indeed a member of the Communist Party, and had taken orders from the Communist Party in 1941 to call a lengthy strike at the Allis-Chalmers plant in Milwaukee.

For three days in mid-March 1947, Kennedy and two House colleagues took extensive testimony in Milwaukee about Christoffel's Communist connections and his leadership of the seventy-six-day strike at the Allis-Chalmers plant, which severely damaged defense production in 1941. Kennedy introduced a motion in the committee to start the process of indicting Christoffel for perjury.

Various appeals brought Christoffel's case to the U.S. Supreme Court, which reversed his conviction on a technicality: The majority of committee members had not been present when Christoffel denied being a Communist, meaning the committee lacked a quorum.

Kennedy was furious with the Court's ruling: "What a travesty on justice, that a Communist witness testifies untruthfully before a recognized committee of the House and then escapes the consequences of perjury by a technical claim that a specified number of Congressmen were not present at a particular moment."

The case was then retried. Christoffel was again convicted, then sentenced to prison and not released until 1956.[18]

Jack's approach to his legislative duties impressed Esther Peterson, a legislative lobbyist for the Amalgamated Clothing Workers of America. She met him while both worked on the minimum-wage issue in 1947. He asked intelligent questions, she thought. "He didn't pretend to know what he didn't know, and you knew always that he'd make up his mind for himself on a lot of these issues. He was not well versed in the labor field at that time, but he was certainly learning."

She found him less political than most legislators on Capitol Hill. His priority was to understand pending labor legislation. Wouldn't additional minimum-wage coverage cause more unemployment? he asked. "He kept coming back at me very hard," Peterson said. " 'But why? But why?' "[19]

As a member of the House Education and Labor Committee Jack almost immediately became embroiled in the intracommittee maneuvering over the explosive issue of federal aid to education. In January 1947, Archbishop Cushing's office informed Jack that it supported federal aid to parochial schools and urged Jack to support parochial aid. Taking his guidance primarily from the National Catholic Welfare Conference, Jack contended that if the federal government spent money for education, parochial-school children—as distinct from parochial schools—should receive funds for such personal services as bus transportation. The committee defeated his amendment, and the House did not pass a federal aid-to-education bill. Billy Sutton claimed Jack worked exceptionally hard on the issue. "Jack wanted to get federal aid for parochial [school children]."

The *Boston Pilot,* Boston's Catholic weekly, effusively praised Jack for his efforts. "Mr. Kennedy has already proved himself to be a statesman in the best sense of the word, one whom it is a pleasure to salute as 'Honorable.' "[20]

A major Jewish issue also attracted his interest. Lewis Weinstein, a lawyer with a strong interest in Jewish issues, had met Jack during the 1946 campaign. After the election he asked the congressman to address the opening session of a Zionist convention to be held on June 14, 1947, at Boston's Hotel Bradford. At first Jack rejected the invitation. "I'm afraid, Lew, that I can't make a pro-Zionist speech. I hate to say 'no' to you, but I believe the Arabs have rights under the McMahon letters, and I doubt that Great Britain had the power to issue the Balfour Declaration. In addition, I don't believe that a Jewish homeland can exist and be self-sufficient in a huge Arab sea."

Trying to convince his friend, Weinstein sent Kennedy books, articles, and a twelve-page letter. They exchanged phone calls and agreed to meet for lunch on May 29. "It was clear that he read everything in the big bundle I had sent," Weinstein recalled.

Jack, Weinstein, and several others met for five hours. Jack had prepared almost four pages of questions. "He raised one issue after another," said Weinstein, "usually with detailed notes in front of him; he had done his homework well."

What about the rights of Arabs? How could a Jewish Palestine exist with Arabs and the Mediterranean completely surrounding it? The questions continued one after another; Weinstein and his associates provided detailed answers.

At five o'clock that afternoon Jack commented: "I've spent a lot of time on this. I read everything you sent me. I'm convinced that you're right. I think that a democratic Jewish state is what America needs in the Middle East. I'll give the speech. I've concluded that I was wrong."

On June 14, before one thousand delegates, Kennedy opened the convention by reading from the speech he had prepared himself, stressing the international mandate for Palestine signed by fifty-two nations, and America's responsibility for leadership in carrying out that mandate. He called for "dynamic action" by the United States to bring about a just solution: "It is my conviction that a just solution requires the establishment of a free and democratic Jewish commonwealth in Palestine [and] the opening of the doors of Palestine to Jewish immigration. . . . If the United States is to be true to its own democratic traditions, it will actively and dynamically support this policy."

He closed to thunderous applause and embraces on the platform. Boston's *Jewish Advocate* praised his high-mindedness. "His stand on the Palestine question has endeared him to all fair-minded citizens. . . . Congressman Kennedy not only preaches but practices the great American principle of tolerance and good-will."[21]

Jack's record in the House is not easily pigeonholed. On some issues he was conservative; on others, liberal. What is usually overlooked, however, is that on most *important* issues he voted with President Truman and with liberal northern Democrats for New Deal–Fair Deal policies.

Jack accepted some of his father's advice on issues related to economics and business, often expressing a "doom and gloom" philosophy representative of Joseph Kennedy's views. On most issues he didn't echo his father. Friends and critics of the Kennedys talked often about the old man's powerful personality, his strongly held positions on public issues, and his tendency to meddle in his children's lives. All true. But Jack and his father differed on most issues, and the father never pressured the son to conform.

From the father's perspective the United States should not commit itself abroad but should withdraw into strong continental defenses; from the son's perspective the United States should make commitments abroad provided that our allies shared some of the burden. On domestic matters they also differed. Jack endorsed most of Truman's Fair Deal—more welfare and reform; the ambassador opposed most of the Fair Deal proposals.[22]

At a cocktail party one afternoon early in Jack's congressional career, Joe Kennedy said to his friend Kay Halle, "Kay, I wish you would tell Jack that he's going to vote the wrong way. . . . I think Jack is making a terrible mistake." At this point Jack turned to his father and said: "Now, look here, Dad, you have your political views and I have mine. I'm going to vote exactly the way I feel I must vote on this. I've got great respect for you, but when it comes to voting, I'm voting my way."

Joe turned to Halle and said, "Well, Kay, that's why I gave them each a million dollars—so they could spit in my eye if they wished."

The biggest difference with his father involved foreign policy. "We don't even discuss it anymore," Jack told a reporter, "because we're just so far apart, there's no point in it. I've given up arguing with him. I make up my own mind and [make] my own decisions."

Father and son exchanged information about issues and family matters, but that was all. On January 30, 1950, Jack sent his father a copy of the speech he had recently delivered at the University of Notre Dame. Joe's encouraging response arrived four days later. "I enjoyed your talk very much. I thought it had real class and distinction."

Joe rarely called Jack's office either. "So many people said that the ambassador was pulling the strings for Jack, and he certainly was not," said Mary Davis. "Jack was his own man."[23]

On important bread-and-butter domestic legislation Jack usually aligned with President Truman and northern Democrats. The same was true of foreign policy and military aid programs. Jack supported the Truman Doctrine, the Marshall Plan, and NATO. On issues of little concern to his constituents, he departed from Democratic Party policy, as when he voted for cuts in Interior and Agriculture Department spending programs.

Jack sounded like a New Deal–Fair Deal liberal in late 1947 when he said the United States must adopt "a sensible and fair tax policy, which will be in accordance with Jefferson's wise saying that 'widespread poverty and concentrated wealth cannot long endure side by side in a democracy.'"

Congress must raise the minimum wage, extend unemployment compensation and Social Security, continue the great power and reclamation projects started in the 1930s, and provide federal aid to education and health.

Legislators should represent their constituencies, and Kennedy's district was very poor. "Naturally the interests of my constituents led me to take the liberal line," he later said; "all the pressures conveyed towards that end."

Jack also supported most positions endorsed by organized labor. The *CIO News*'s rating system showed him voting "wrong" only twice out of fifty-seven opportunities during his six years in the House.[24]

Some historians later criticized him, claiming that his liberalism conveyed "no passion, no heart, no force," but this critique misrepresents his intentions. He associated political passion with demagogues who exploited the public's emotions, fears, and prejudices. The responsible politician should be wary of passion and strive for reasonableness. Actually he conveyed his views on most issues with considerable sincerity, reasonableness, and force.

He wasn't submissive to powerful economic pressure groups, sometimes defying them openly. He criticized the leadership of the American Legion and the Veterans of Foreign Wars in housing fights and on a bonus for World War II veterans. "At one time or another," James M. Burns noted, "he took on real-estate interests, oil interests, processors of farm commodities, airlines (in a hard fight for separation of airlines' subsidies from airmail payments), and various agricultural and other producer interests."

Some people who knew Jack privately grumbled that he had a carefree attitude. "He never seemed to get into the midstream of any tremendous political thought, or political action," said William Douglas, Supreme Court justice and Kennedy family friend. "He didn't seem to be caught up in anything, and he was sort of drifting. And when he started drifting, then I think he became more of a playboy."

Others thought his speeches were inadequate. Occasionally a Massachusetts newspaper found something to fault. "All we hear about him is canned publicity put out by an advertising agency in Boston," complained a Boston weekly newspaper in 1949.

Tip O'Neill remembered that Jack hated any criticism:

> He had such a thin skin! If a group of politicians were talking and somebody said something mean about Jack and it got back to him, he'd be over to see me. "Why doesn't so-and-so like me?" he'd ask. "Why can't he and I sit down and straighten this thing out?" . . .
>
> He hadn't grown up in the school of hard knocks. Politically he had lived an easy life and was used to people loving him.[25]

For the most part, though, Jack was rarely criticized in public in his home state. His boyish good looks and fascinating family made him a curiosity and brought him extensive—and mostly favorable—publicity. Most newspapers judged his speeches as intelligent, forceful, and often courageous, and they praised his early record in the House. Claiming to have taken soundings among competent observers in Washington, on October 6, 1947, a columnist in the *Boston Post* pronounced him "the outstanding veterans' leader." Democrats looked to "Kennedy's views on all matters concerning veterans, as well as on other major party policies, more particularly housing, labor and foreign affairs."

Columnist Clem Norton repeatedly lauded him. On May 25, 1947, Norton wrote:

> How did we ever have the good fortune to produce at this time, a champion for the people? A champion for the common man? A champion for the children of the slums? Do you think for one minute that Mayor Cur-

ley of Boston or former Governor Maurice J. Tobin, or former Attorney
General Paul A. Dever, would dare oppose the American Legion?[26]

The *Worcester Sunday Telegram* reported that Democrats loved him:

A great many Democrats will tell you that young Mr. Kennedy is the
grand hope of the Democrats in this state. . . . He "has everything," they
will tell you. He is young, able, of high integrity, personally attractive, and
modest. He has never been an exhibitionist or a prima donna. . . . He is
sanely progressive and wisely cautious.

The best-selling book *The Truman Merry-Go-Round* (1950), by Robert
Allen and William Shannon, singled Jack out for high praise. Although
sharply critical of most congressmen of both parties, the authors wrote that
"[Foster] Furcolo and [John] Kennedy are two of the most attractive young
men to emerge in New England politics in many years." In 1947 acerbic
columnist Drew Pearson included Jack among fifteen freshmen congressmen
he judged as outstanding. "[Kennedy] shows that same brilliance as his father,
though steadier. Should have a great future."

After only seven months as a congressman, Jack had become a political
phenomenon in Massachusetts, a refreshing change from the stodgy leadership in the state.[27]

"We want Kennedy!" clamored state Democrats.

On July 31, 1947, cheering delegates to the convention of the Massachusetts Federation of Labor overwhelmingly adopted a motion calling on him
to run against incumbent Republican Leverett Saltonstall for the U.S. Senate
in 1948. (Saltonstall had voted in favor of the Taft-Hartley Act.) And that he
might run against Saltonstall was a real possibility, reporter James Colbert
wrote. Yes, the congressman was young, but "you can mature pretty fast . . .
looking down the Jap guns as Kennedy did"; and Kennedy had "tremendous
appeal for the younger voters."

By late 1947 newspapers constantly speculated whether he would run for
mayor of Boston, for governor, or for senator. There were reports that veteran Democrats, especially former governor Maurice Tobin and former attorney general Paul Dever, were holding back their announcements of
candidacy for governor in expectation of a declaration by Kennedy. "It was
known that a poll conducted throughout the state proved Kennedy's overwhelming popularity," reported the *Boston Advertiser*.[28]

Although Jack usually sided with the positions taken by President Truman,
northern Democrats, and organized labor, in some ways he was a maverick.

During a speech to a Boston audience, he announced himself flatly and forcefully opposed to any tax cuts. Asserting that lowering taxes would gamble with America's future, he charged both Democrats and Republicans with playing politics on the tax-reduction issue.

When he finished, his listeners gave him a rousing ovation even though they undoubtedly favored a tax cut and differed sharply with his view. "What they were applauding and what apparently fired their enthusiasm was Kennedy's willingness to take a bold and forthright stand on a highly controversial matter," observed reporter James Colbert in the *Boston Post.* "Kennedy's political courage," said Colbert, "his disregard of election year expediency, his readiness to stand up and be counted on any measure, have contributed to making him the No. 1 political glamour boy of the Democratic party in Massachusetts. . . . He declares that his job is to tell people what he believes is the truth even if it's unpleasant to take."

"He never straddles anything," a veteran congressman and seasoned politician declared in commenting on Kennedy's record, but it was unclear whether the seasoned politician's tone reflected admiration or concern for his younger colleague.

While the media in Massachusetts extolled his independence and courage, some leading House Democrats found him exasperating because they thought he impeded smooth progress of the party's goals in Congress. He was decidedly not a wheeler-dealer who prided himself on hammering out compromises to get bills passed. He struck veteran Democratic legislators as a lone wolf, not inclined to play the get-along, go-along game, and seemed to take pride in his independence. "I never had the feeling I needed Truman," Jack later conceded.[29]

Jack's reputation in Congress as a maverick, though, was more a matter of style and attitude than of voting record. He always seemed in a rush, was always late to meetings and appointments. Traditionalists in the House disdained his informality and his casual dress, as when he appeared in the House wearing old khaki pants and addressed the House with his shirttail out and clearly visible from the galleries. He enjoyed fun-filled three- or four-day weekends, especially trips to Florida. The long weekends, plus illness and his extensive campaigning throughout Massachusetts, resulted in a high absentee rate in the House.

Mary Davis thought her boss seemed lost in his early years in the Congress. "I don't think he really knew if he wanted politics, if he was going to remain with it, or what politics was going to do with him."[30]

He found most of his fellow congressmen boring, preoccupied only with advancing their careers and their narrow political agendas. The arcane House rules and customs, which slowed legislation, exasperated him. "All his life he had had troubles with rules externally imposed and now here he was, back once again in an 'institutional setting,' " Billings insightfully observed. Jack suggested two changes: a revised system of seniority and a faster method of taking roll calls. But he knew such changes were only a pipe dream.

The routine of the House of Representatives didn't challenge him. Even when he was not sick, he appeared underwhelmed by his position. "We are just worms here," he told a friend as if to suggest his insignificance. "[The House] totally failed to fascinate him," said another close friend. "I think his father may have made one mistake which was to give him an air travel credit card so that he was on the plane to Palm Beach every Friday night during the winter and of course up to the Cape in the summer."

He wasn't a lazy congressman, although some House leaders thought he was. "You can't get anywhere," he often said privately. "You have to be here twenty years." He was too impatient and unwilling to wait the twenty years to have any influence in the House.

Occasionally he turned cynical. He told journalist Charles Bartlett that one thing he liked about George Smathers was that the Florida congressman didn't give a damn. "I think he found that rather refreshing. I think that all these sort of hustling freshmen—that just wasn't his temperament," said Bartlett.[31]

Jack steadfastly resolved to plot his own course in the House with no guidance from his party's leaders. He kept influential and highly respected House leaders at arm's length, including the senior member of the Massachusetts delegation, Democrat John W. McCormack. The white-haired congressman from South Boston was a confidant of President Truman and a member of the inner circle of the Democratic Party. "I think he was one of the kindest men I ever met, in or out of politics," said Billy Sutton. "If he'd been against us, he could have really screwed us, but he never did."

An elder statesman, McCormack's approval was usually sought by ambitious freshmen congressmen. A prominent Boston politician who met Kennedy on the steps of the Capitol a few days after he had taken his seat in the House advised Jack to "marry" John McCormack. "I'd hang around with him in the House, eat dinner with him a couple of nights a week, listen to every thing he had to say and ask for his advice." But Jack looked unimpressed. "He backed away from me in horror as if I had pointed a gun at him," said the Boston politician.

In 1949 Jack led a group of young Massachusetts Democratic congressmen to protest to President Truman about McCormack's dominance of patronage. The group felt he hadn't approached the state's Democratic congressmen on the matter of political plums. Of special concern was who would parcel out the federal jobs in the state for the 1950 census. "He hogged all the patronage," Jack later said. "He wouldn't give us anything."

But when the Kennedy-led group went to the White House, President Truman ignored their complaint.[32]

Jack made a poor impression on Sam Rayburn, the powerful Democrat from Texas and Speaker of the House. Rayburn probably sensed that Jack disdained his own party's leaders—Truman, McCormack, and himself. Rayburn privately referred to him as a"sickly little fellow" and a "cipher," a person who didn't do his homework, didn't accomplish anything, and didn't consistently show up for committee hearings and floor debate.

Rayburn was irritated when Jack's floor speeches garnered media coverage while other House members, who had worked tirelessly on a measure, didn't even get their names in the paper. Lazy John Kennedy seemed to be stealing the headlines. "He resented it and it was a resentment that he built up against [Kennedy] through the years," said Tip O'Neill.

Whether or not they judged Jack as lazy, a playboy, or too independent, most of his House colleagues liked his personality and invariably found him pleasant and charming. "He was pleasant and attractive," said Congressman Richard Bolling of Missouri. "He just wasn't much of a House member." He was very much the maverick, Bolling thought. "He voted the way he damn well pleased."[33]

"I was quite brash [and] independent," Jack mused to biographer Burns in 1959, seven years after he completed his House career. Being independent at times was fine, but Jack thought he had made a mistake by not being more friendly with the Democratic leadership in the House and by not following their lead. This was particularly true of John McCormack, who was so helpful to Jack and his staff. Later McCormack, who had intimate ties with the Massachusetts Jewish community, boosted Jack's career by campaigning for him among Jewish voters. McCormack was the "greatest Democrat that I've ever met in my life," Jack reflected. "He had no reason in the world to do that for me because . . . I never followed his leadership. I voted the way I felt like. . . . I took some bad advice when I first came down here. If I had my life to live over, I wouldn't have been a maverick. . . . I think I would have followed along and been far more friendly." Jack advised Tip O'Neill never to "get into the position that I got myself into with the leadership."[34]

Despite Jack's respect for McCormack, circumstance and misunderstanding would cause further tension in the future. Yet neither man would ever allow the friction to lead to permanent estrangement.

On August 1, 1947, Jack announced that he would travel to Ireland in September to make a personal study of food and fuel shortages. He said he planned to meet with Prime Minister Eamon de Valera to discuss the situation. Another reason for going to Ireland was to search for his Irish relatives. "I'm going to find out where the Kennedys and the Fitzgeralds came from," he said.

The trip Jack took was not a congressional junket; he took it on his own initiative and paid for it himself. After Ireland he intended to join two other members of the House Committee on Education and Labor, Representatives Charles Kersten and Richard Nixon, to investigate the extent of Communist control of the French and Italian labor movements. But he never completed that portion of the trip.[35]

He arrived at Shannon airport on September 1 and spent most of his three weeks in Ireland with his sister Kathleen at Lismore Castle in County Waterford in southern Ireland. Owned by the Devonshires, the parents of Kathleen's late husband, the moss-covered eleventh-century castle commanded a high bluff. Kathleen had organized a monthlong house party, including among her guests several writers, Conservative British politicians, and Kick's friend Pamela Digby Churchill, the beautiful ex-wife of Randolph Churchill, Winston's son. Kick and her companions played golf, took long walks, rode horses, and at night talked politics.

Only Jack's persistent and mysterious illness marred the idyllic holiday. He couldn't take part in the daily strenuous activities, but on September 10, he did manage to travel to Dublin and spend an hour discussing economic and financial problems with de Valera.[36]

One morning, when Jack felt well enough, he quietly asked Pamela, "Would you mind coming on an expedition with me to find the original Kennedys?" She agreed, and the two of them spent several hours driving to Dunganstown in Kathleen's new American station wagon.

First directed to the home of James Kennedy, Jack met Jim, his wife, and their four children. Jim could recall only a Patrick Kennedy from Boston who had visited about 1912. "That was my grandfather," Jack declared. Jack stayed for an hour and took photos. The Jim Kennedys remembered Jack as "a frail, thin young man of most unassuming disposition."

He was then directed down the road to the thatched cottage of Mary Ryan, Jim's sister, who lived in the original Kennedy home. Mary Ryan, the granddaughter of Patrick Kennedy's brother James, had married her second cousin, James Ryan, a grandson of another brother, John. They treated Jack to the luxury of fresh butter and eggs, partly because their visitor appeared in need of nourishment. "He didn't look well at all," Mary later said. Amid the chickens, ducks, and pigs, Jack peppered the Ryans with questions about ancestors who had gone to America. He could never make a definite link, but they decided they were third cousins.[37]

Jack left in a glow of nostalgia, jarringly interrupted when Pam Churchill declared, "Just like *Tobacco Road*." Jack was insulted by her remark, and later complained to friends that Pam had not understood the magical moment. "I felt like kicking her out of the car."

Why was he upset? The novelist and short story writer Erskine Caldwell had published *Tobacco Road* in 1932. The novel depicts a degraded, poor white family living in a decrepit shack on eroded land in Georgia. Illiterate, dehumanized, hopeless, the pitiful characters are in no condition to help themselves, and the story describes the family's continuing degeneration.

Intending no insult by her remark, Pam Churchill probably had a superficial familiarity with the novel. The Irish families she had just seen were poor and rural—like those in Caldwell's novel. But Jack had a better understanding of Caldwell's characters, and the people he enjoyed meeting in Dunganstown were not hopeless, dehumanized, or degraded. Like his own ancestors, they were hardworking, hopeful, and decent.

When they arrived back late for dinner at Lismore Castle, Jack exclaimed, "We found the original Kennedys!" Kathleen, apathetic about her Irish ancestors and obviously irritated by her brother's tardiness, simply inquired, "Did they have a bathroom?" At dinner Jack surveyed the plush castle surroundings, thought about the humble cottage where his cousins lived, and said to himself, "What a contrast."[38]

On September 21 Jack arrived in London, accompanied by Pam Churchill. On the same day he became so ill he couldn't get out of his hotel bed. He phoned Pam and asked if she knew of a London doctor. He looked "an awful color," she later said. She called her doctor, Sir Daniel Davis, a prominent semiretired physician, who had Kennedy admitted to a hospital, where Davis diagnosed him as suffering from Addison's disease. Shortly after Jack's crisis, Dr. Davis told Pam, "That young American friend of yours, he hasn't got a year to live."[39]

The family arranged for Anne McGillicuddy, the American nurse who had taken care of Jack at the Chelsea naval hospital in 1944, to fly to London to help care for Jack. She accompanied him back to the United States aboard the *Queen Mary*. After the ship docked in New York on October 16, an ambulance transported him to LaGuardia Airport, and a chartered plane flew him to Boston, where he was admitted to the Lahey Clinic.

Rose and Joe made the decision to withhold information about the true nature of his illness. The media were told that he had suffered from another bout with malaria—a much less ominous disease than Addison's—which he had contracted three years earlier in the South Pacific. Ironically, a common symptom of both diseases was a brownish yellow skin, making the cover-up easier to sell.[40]

The Boston Globe reported that Kennedy had been "Invalided Home." He looked drawn and pale as he was carried off the ship on a stretcher. "Although looking wan, Kennedy appeared to be in good spirits as he entered the hospital for observation and treatment," said the newspaper. "He grinned at reporters as he was wheeled to his room and said 'I'm feeling better.'" The *Globe* gave what became the standard explanation for Jack's illness. "Kennedy came down with malaria last month while visiting in Ireland. He has suffered from the disease since 1945 when he first contracted it while serving with the Navy in the Pacific."[41]

In 1855, an English physician, Thomas Addison, first described the disease which impacted Jack's life. He studied patients who were thin and weak, and suffered from low blood pressure, anemia, and brownish pigmentation of the skin. After autopsies, he found that the size of their adrenals had been greatly reduced.

The two adrenal glands, one sitting atop each kidney, produce more than half a dozen hormones, the most important being cortisol and aldosterone. Cortisol ensures that the bloodstream has enough glucose, a form of sugar essential to brain function. It also maintains appetite, blood pressure, a sense of well-being, and response to stress. Aldosterone averts the loss of large quantities of sodium, a mineral necessary to maintain blood pressure. Modern scientists presume that Addison's is the result of autoimmune disease, in which antibodies attack and destroy the glands.

Addison's disease was incurable, and before 1930, 90 percent of victims died within five years. In the late 1930s, scientists developed a synthetic substance, desoxycorticosterone acetate (DOCA), a weak adrenal hormone, which substantially reduced the mortality rate.[42]

"Kennedy was not in the crisis stage when I saw him," said endocrinologist Dr. Elmer Bartels, who cared for him at the Lahey Clinic. Bartels speculated that in London Jack had episodes of nausea and vomiting, plus low blood pressure, and those symptoms led to Dr. Davis's diagnosis. Bartels judged that Jack's illness was of recent origin and not related to the many ailments he had suffered from earlier in his life.

Before the advent of adrenal replacement, the patient usually died from infection—often after simply having a tooth pulled out. "That's the way most Addison's patients used to die, by way of minor dental things," said Bartels.

In 1947, when Kennedy was diagnosed, treatment was still cumbersome and limited in its benefits. A pellet containing DOCA was implanted through an incision into Jack's thigh. This allowed slow absorption of the compound, but the procedure needed to be repeated several times a year. Such treatment could not prevent death, but it could extend life expectancy from about six months to between five and ten years. Jack must have been haunted by the prospect that he would almost certainly be dead by 1957.[43]

Bartels's treatment helped Jack stave off his Addisonian crisis, but Jack suffered emotionally, and it affected the quality of his performance in the House of Representatives. Was there any point to beating his brains out in Washington if he would shortly be dead? Could he ever hope to realize his own and his father's ambitions for him? What about a family and children?

After the onset of the disease, Jack had one of the highest absentee rates of any member of Congress. He sponsored no major legislation, garnered less press coverage for his congressional work, and conducted no major congressional investigations. Later, political commentators, even those sympathetic to him, admitted that his performance in the House was "unspectacular," "lackluster," or "undistinguished." His mediocre performance in the House partly stemmed from his illness.

The public remained ignorant of Jack's precarious condition; newspapers soon reported that his health had been restored. On February 1, 1948, reporter James Colbert claimed that contrary to widespread belief, Jack's health would not be a factor in determining his political future, for "he has overcome the malaria he brought back from the South Pacific with him and he is in better physical condition now than at any time since his discharge from the Navy. In fact, according to his supporters, his health is almost as robust as his political courage."[44]

Eight months after Jack learned he had Addison's disease, another family tragedy sent him and the other Kennedys into a tailspin. After Billy Cavendish's death in 1944, the widowed Kathleen had plunged into war work to assuage her grief. A familiar figure in London in the austere robin's-egg blue of the American Red Cross, she served coffee and doughnuts to servicemen. Following the war she continued to live in England, rarely returning home.

In May 1948, Kathleen died in an airplane crash in France. Her death was not only a terrible tragedy, but was potentially scandalous as well because she was in the company of her not-yet-divorced Protestant lover, the dashing millionaire playboy Earl Fitzwilliam, who also died in the crash.

After Jack returned from a dinner engagement, a reporter for *The Boston Globe* phoned him at his Georgetown home to inform him of the wire service report of Kathleen's accident. Initially there was no positive identification of her body. Jack thought his sister might possibly have made a trip, but he wasn't sure. "What does the dispatch say? Can you read it to me?" he asked.

About ten minutes later the reporter called back to confirm that Kathleen's body had been positively identified. In a broken voice Jack asked the reporter to read the news release to him again. Upon hearing it the second time, he said: "I'll be right here by the telephone for the rest of the night if you hear anything else."[45]

Ted Reardon made arrangements to get Jack and Eunice up to Hyannis Port. There, grief stricken, Jack closeted himself in a back room, admitting only servants delivering food.

Deeply despondent, Joe Kennedy later wrote his British friend and newspaper magnate Lord Beaverbrook, "The sudden death of young Joe and Kathleen within a period of three years has left a mark on me that I find very difficult to erase. . . . I am afraid I see very little hope on the horizon."

Kathleen's death remained a "closed subject" within the Kennedy household. The explanation put out by the Kennedys and reported in newspapers was that Kathleen had "casually encountered" her "friend" Fitzwilliam, and he had offered to fly her to the South of France. A chance meeting became the official explanation for Kathleen's flight with her married lover.[46]

For a while after Kathleen's death, Jack suffered severe insomnia. "Just as he started to close his eyes," Billings recalled, "he would be awakened by the image of Kathleen sitting up with him late at night talking about their parties and dates. He would try to close his eyes again, but he couldn't shake the image. It was better, he said, when he had a girl in bed with him, for then he could fantasize that the girl was Kathleen's friend and that when morning came the three of them would go for breakfast together."

Since the Kennedy family considered grief a weakness, Jack had no outlet for his feelings. "For Jack, losing Joe and Kathleen was losing a part of his past, his common experiences, his identity," said Billings. "Yet there was no one in his family with whom he could share this huge loss. As a result, he seemed to lose his *raison d'être*. He just figured there was no sense in planning ahead anymore. The only thing that made sense, he decided, was to live for the moment, treating each day as if it were his last, demanding of life constant intensity, adventure and pleasure."

In the months after the tragedy his thoughts often morbidly turned to death. He became preoccupied by what runs through the mind in the moments before death. Would a person think about the wonderful things that had happened, or would he have regrets for all the things he hadn't done? Walking together on a spring day, Jack said to Ted Reardon, "Tell me, Teddy boy, what's the best way to die?" Reardon thought old age was probably best, but Jack disagreed. "You're wrong, wrong as hell. In war—that's the best way to die. The very best way. In war." Jack asked another friend a similarly morbid question. "He asked me how did I think I'd die," said John Galvin. "He said he thought he'd get killed in an automobile accident."[47]

Death seemed ever present. It had taken young Joe and Kick, and it was awaiting him. Gradually he adjusted and accepted the fact that he was the sole survivor of the golden trio. "Slowly," Billings recalled, "he began to fight back, knowing that to stand still was to stay in sorrow, that to live he had to move forward. . . . The interesting thing is that once he focused on what *he* really wanted to do with his life, he realized that it really might be politics after all."[48]

In the summer of 1948, several of Jack's supporters sparked an effort to collect enough signatures to place him on the ballot for governor. "We did this on orders, probably from Mr. Kennedy," Billy Sutton later explained. "I don't think that Jack approved of this too much, but the father did. I don't think Jack ever wanted to be governor. . . . But it made enough publicity and we frightened a few of the heavies." Indeed, a Roper poll conducted in May and June 1948 showed Kennedy's support for governor at 33.0 percent, Tobin's at 32.2, and Dever's at 15.9.

The goal was to test Jack's strength and stimulate interest. "It doesn't hurt providing you pull your papers out on time," said Sutton. At the last minute, Jack's organization did withdraw his papers; Paul Dever was nominated and won the governorship in 1948.

Later Jack conceded he considered running against Senator Saltonstall in 1948, but it didn't look like a promising year for a Democrat to run. Besides, Jack said of his attitude at the time, "Senators look rather formidable to Congressmen."[49]

He thought of running in 1950 as well, but by then Dever was the state's incumbent governor, and Jack couldn't challenge a fellow Democrat. There was no U.S. Senate election in the state in 1950. So his next best opportunity would be 1952. (Jack easily won reelection to Congress. In 1948 he ran unopposed; two years later he defeated Republican Vincent Celeste 87,699 to 18,302.)

After 1948, he focused most of his efforts on advancing the liberal domestic agenda on bread-and-butter issues. The welfare of all the people was far more important than the special privileges of any individual or small group, he argued. "Jobless men must be able to collect unemployment compensation for a longer period. They cannot be told that they are to pay the full price for other people's blunders."

In May 1949 he boldly chided New England businessmen for not supporting legislation advocated by the Democratic administrations of the previous sixteen years. Those measures were designed to improve the economic condition of the country and to stave off depressions. The haunting specter in the United States was unemployment, he told the business leaders. "I wonder if any of you New England businessmen has supported any of the legislation which has been advanced to help check and cure unemployment growing out of the depression which set in 20 years ago. I fear you have opposed and are still opposing such measures. If you come out against everything, you are not doing anything constructive." The businessmen should separate what is good from what is bad in the legislative program and support the good.[50]

In March 1949, during a House debate on a veterans' pension bill, Jack interrupted to declare that the leaders of the American Legion had not "had a constructive thought for the benefit of this country since 1918." Such heresy against the country's elite veterans organization shocked and angered many of his fellow congressmen, several of whom rose to defend the Legion. The remark worried Kennedy as well.

"Well, Ted," he said to his assistant Reardon as he walked back to his office, "we're gone." Fortunately, Jack had referred to the "leadership" of the Legion and not to the entire organization.

One Massachusetts newspaper defended the Legion from the "glib wisecrack of an oversmart sophomore Congressman." For the most part, though, home-state newspapers praised Jack for speaking out. The *Fitchburg Sentinel* lauded his "courage" and "intrepidity." "Mr. Kennedy seems to be functioning as a congressman in the manner in which the founding fathers and their Constitution intended to have congressmen function."[51]

Although he supported federal measures for public housing, veterans, education, and the like, he worried about going to an extreme, turning over too many "major problems into the all-absorbing hands of the great Leviathan—the state." It was dangerous to allow the expanding power of the federal government to absorb functions that states and cities once considered their own responsibilities.

On one issue Jack joined Republicans in harsh criticism of the Roosevelt-Truman policies. As the Soviets rolled back the Nazis in 1944–1945, they treated ruthlessly the people and the governments which lay in their path. After the war the Soviets set up Communist governments in Eastern Europe, and those governments suppressed opposition parties, extinguished civil liberties, and gagged the media. Stalin ignored his commitment made at Yalta to hold free elections in Poland. In February 1948, the Czech Communists, with Soviet assistance, seized control of the government. All of these events horrified Americans, horrified residents in Massachusetts's Eleventh Congressional District, and horrified John F. Kennedy.[52]

Understandably, Americans developed a profound aversion to communism; unfortunately, they tolerated some unsavory methods of attacking it. "It was this detestation that gave politicians broad leeway to pursue anti-Communist endeavors," observed historian Richard Fried of the red scare following World War II.

Massachusetts and the Eleventh Congressional District had a high percentage of Roman Catholics who considered communism the Antichrist. The church condemned the atheism, materialism, and violent methods of the Marxist movement. The Communist desire to abolish private property challenged the church's assumption that property was integral to an orderly society.

On February 7, 1949, after Joszef Cardinal Mindszenty, the Catholic primate of Hungary, was arrested by Hungary's Communist government, then beaten and humiliated, Jack paid tribute to him for "being faithful to his country, his church and his God." President Franklin Roosevelt was to blame for a large part of America's Cold War predicament, Jack often argued. In June 1948, he told a Polish-American audience in Roxbury that Roosevelt "did not understand the Russian mind."[53]

Following a twenty-year civil war, in December 1949 Chiang Kai-shek's Nationalist forces fled to the island of Formosa, leaving the mainland to Mao Tse-tung's Communists. In the aftermath, Republicans castigated the Truman administration for "losing" China to the Communists. Jack joined the chorus of the Republican opposition, charging that the blame for the catastrophe should fall squarely on the shoulders of the Truman administration.

In the House of Representatives on January 25, 1950, shortly after Mao's victory, Jack requested unanimous consent to address the chamber for one minute. Nobody objected. In this instance Jack did not display his usual calm and detached manner.

He blamed the Chinese "disaster" on "the White House and the Department of State."

"The continued insistence that aid would not be forthcoming, unless a coalition government with the Communists were formed, was a crippling blow to the National Government.

"So concerned were our diplomats and their advisers, the Lattimores and the Fairbanks, with the imperfection of the democratic system in China after 20 years of war and the tales of corruption in high places that they lost sight of our tremendous stake in a non-Communist China."

Owen Lattimore, an expert on China, would subsequently become a major target of Senator Joe McCarthy's red-hunting crusade. John Fairbank was one of Jack's constituents. A highly respected China scholar, the Harvard history professor had criticized Chiang Kai-shek in his 1948 book, *The United States and China.*[54]

Jack's outburst was irrational. The blame fell squarely on the Chiang Kai-shek government. Corrupt, inefficient, and obtuse, it had ignored the just aspirations of the masses of Chinese people. Nothing the United States could have done within the reasonable limits of its capabilities would have changed the result. Still, China was lost. Now the Communist leaders of the Soviet Union and China ruled more than a quarter of the world's people.

Weakness breeds aggression, Jack kept preaching, repeating the theme of *Why England Slept*. England's failure to prepare in the early 1930s had been based on the false premise that more armaments would lead to war. To learn from the valuable lesson of Munich, the United States must maintain a strong national defense and contain the spread of aggressive communism. A strong national defense would result in diplomatic strength.[55]

In June 1950, Truman did take a vigorous stand in Asia, sending U.S. troops to stop the North Korean invasion of South Korea. Yet Jack showed little enthusiasm. He worried about spreading U.S. troops too thin, preventing our ability to counter Communist expansion in other danger zones. (He worried particularly about Germany.) "It is idle now to discuss whether we should have gone into Korea," he said in mid-August 1950. "We are in—and according to the President, we are in to stay." But he hoped our effort in Korea would not drain troops from other areas that had more strategic importance.[56]

New treatment for Addison's disease proved enormously encouraging for Jack. In 1949, two years after he had been diagnosed, researchers discovered cortisone, and new hope suddenly blossomed for victims of the disease. By 1951 cortisone could be taken orally, and Kennedy ingested 25 milligrams daily. He also continued to receive periodic implants of 150 milligrams of DOCA pellets in his thighs.

With this new treatment nearly mimicking the natural function of the adrenal glands, Kennedy's health and stamina improved dramatically. As his health improved, so did his emotional outlook and his ambition, leading him to consider running for governor or the Senate in 1952.[57]

In 1951 Jack took two major foreign trips primarily to establish his credentials to address foreign-policy issues if he sought a Senate seat the following year. In January, accompanied by Torbert Macdonald, Kennedy visited England, Turkey, Italy, Spain, Yugoslavia, and France, and had a private audience with Pope Pius XII. The trip's highlight was his hour-long visit with Marshal Tito at the premier's luxurious villa on the outskirts of Belgrade. The Yugoslavian dictator had broken with the Soviets and Stalin's iron-fisted methods, and had established an independent Communist nation. Tito's independence was a hopeful sign to the West, leading the United States to send military and economic assistance to Yugoslavia. The premier told Jack to discount the rumor that some of Stalin's satellite nations—Bulgaria, Hungary, and Romania—intended to attack Yugoslavia in the spring. Kennedy quoted Tito as saying, "My people are confident of the future. But I am no prophet and we are preparing for any eventuality."

Jack conferred with defense ministers in each country he visited and left reassured. "I don't believe that the communists have any chance now of taking over Western Europe politically, unless there is an economic collapse," he announced upon his return.[58]

Far more important was his second trip. In the fall of 1951, the Kennedy party, which included Jack, his brother Robert, and his sister Patricia, flew almost twenty-five thousand miles during seven weeks of constant movement—to Israel, Iran, Pakistan, India, Singapore, Thailand, to embattled Indochina, then north to war-torn South Korea. Jack consulted with U.S. generals Collins and Ridgway, and with the flamboyant French general Jean de Lattre de Tassigny, the commander in chief of the French troops in Indochina. He met Prime Ministers Ben-Gurion of Israel, Nehru of India, and Liaquat Ali Khan of Pakistan (only hours before he was assassinated). He also talked with scores of ambassadors, ministers, consuls, businessmen, journalists, Communists, and ordinary people on the street. Before returning home, though, Jack suffered a severe Addisonian crisis which almost killed him.

Jack was impressed with Israel. After arriving in Tel Aviv, he wrote in his diary: "On every side signs of tremendous construction, clearing, growing, transporting. . . . Soldiers appeared tough, rugged, and cocky." After his discussions with Jews and Arabs, he noted: "Emphasis is on necessity from the American point of view of reconciliation between Arabs and Jews but present prospects dim. Jews very aggressive—confident. Arabs fear expansion. Says it is inevitable result of Jews encouraging immigrants."[59]

On October 8, 1951, the Kennedys arrived in Iran, where the controversial Mohammad Mossadegh, an outspoken advocate of Iranian nationalism, had recently nationalized the British-owned Anglo-Iranian Oil Company. Jack's discussions in Iran left him pessimistic: "Feeling among most Americans here is country is hopeless—poor, ignorant, sick, with rich landowners and corruption rampant. . . . [The] rich [are] irresponsible, and any money we spend would probably go down the drain. No middle classes or liberal groups to appeal to."[60]

India, which had received its independence from great Britain in August 1947, was led by Prime Minister Jawaharlal Nehru, who showed little interest in being interviewed by an obscure U.S. congressman. As Jack talked to him, Nehru kept looking at the ceiling, not paying attention, but the prime minister was very attracted to Patricia Kennedy, directing most of his conversation at her. "My brother always remembered that," said Robert Kennedy. "We really laughed about it." Perhaps the personal slight, plus Jack's perception that Nehru was arrogant and offensive, led to his permanent distaste for the Indian prime minister.

India was Jack's first encounter with a government not aligned with either the U.S. or the Soviet bloc. After conferring with various Indian ministers and studying India, Jack adopted a live-and-let-live attitude. "Russia and America are nations [of] whose quarrels India wishes no part," he later declared. "She can neither be bribed or cajoled to join either our or the Russian camp. She will deal and has dealt with communism in her own way, but not in ours."[61]

On October 19, 1951, the Kennedy party arrived in Saigon, but they couldn't leave the city alone for fear of the Vietminh guerrillas. "People seem sullen and resentful," Robert Kennedy wrote in his diary. "If free election held throughout the country Ho Chi Minh would probably win."

Jack loathed the colonialism he saw in Indochina. Taking seriously his role as inquiring congressman, he was determined to gain a better understanding of the Indochina situation.

After Japan surrendered in August 1945 and pulled its troops out of Indochina, the Communist and nationalist forces led by Ho Chi Minh filled the vacuum. But the French, who had controlled Indochina for more than half a century, decided to resume their colonial empire, which had been interrupted by World War II. War broke out in 1946 between the French and Ho's Vietminh forces, and the fighting lasted until 1954.[62]

The French military position became more precarious each year of the war. France refused the Vietminh's demand for immediate self-government and eventual independence, believing instead in assimilation and full French citizenship. The French could not militarily defeat the Vietminh, but in 1949 they tried to undercut their enemy politically by forming native governments in Laos, Cambodia, and Vietnam, and giving them the status of "free states" within the French Union. The French selected Bao Dai to rule in Vietnam.

The French continued to remain dominant, though, controlling Vietnam's treasury, commerce, and foreign and military policies. The Bao Dai government, composed mostly of wealthy southern landowners, didn't attract much support from native Vietnamese. Nationalists of any stature refused to support Bao Dai. But the Truman administration recognized the Bao Dai government because it at least avoided the appearance of endorsing blatant French colonialism.

The increasingly tense Cold War confrontation with the Soviets, the Communist victory in China in 1949, and the onset of the Korean War the following year all led to greater urgency among U.S. policymakers to prevent a Communist victory in Southeast Asia. By early 1950, the United States had embraced the "domino theory," the belief that the fall of Indochina would lead to the rapid collapse of the other nations in the region. In March 1950 the United States began furnishing France with military and economic assistance to help the French crush the Vietminh.

"In retrospect," observed historian George Herring, "the assumptions upon which American policy-makers acted in 1950 appear misguided. The Southeast Asian revolutions were not inspired by Moscow. . . . Although a dedicated Communist, Ho was no mere tool of the Soviet Union, and while he was willing to accept help from the major Communist powers, . . . he was not prepared to subordinate Vietnamese independence to them." Ho had captured the standard of Vietnamese nationalism, and by supporting France the United States had attached itself to colonialism and to a losing cause.[63]

In his first extended remarks on the Indochina situation, Jack told a gathering of Legionnaires in May 1950 that Communists in Southeast Asia deceived the native people in promoting nationalism. They rarely sold communism. "They sell nationalism, but their purpose in so doing is to secure control of the nationalist movements and use them to the advantage of world communism."

The United States had been placed in an awkward position, he said, showing more insight than most U.S. policymakers of the time. Faced with the choice of supporting the French or the Communists, "we have had by necessity to choose the French and have thus become involved with a colonial power which is opposed by a majority of the people."

On October 19, 1951, French officials and soldiers met the Kennedy entourage at the airport, ready to persuade Congressman Kennedy of the ultimate French victory. Jack listened to the official briefings, but he also sought out newspaper reporters and others who had informed judgments. Often he showed up unannounced at their apartments, grilled them with questions, and received different answers than he did from the French officials. Seymour Topping, an AP reporter in Saigon, watched Kennedy disembark from his plane at the Saigon airport, consult notes in his wallet, and seek him out shortly after. Upsetting social plans arranged by U.S. ambassador Donald R. Heath, Jack showed up at Topping's flat, where he submitted the reporter to hours of searching questions. "He really wanted to know," recalled Topping, impressed by Kennedy's attitude.[64]

What Jack learned left him deeply pessimistic. The Vietminh were winning the war, and the French had not granted any real independence to the Vietnamese. He detested the callousness and vulgarity of the French colonialism, the harshness of their regime, and their attempt to hold on to an empire in a world which had already changed. "They were bad politicians and they were living in the past," observed David Halberstam of Jack's attitude; "by contrast, he was impressed with what the British had done in India, leaving when they should, with none of the worst predicted consequences taking place."

Communism was spreading, Jack noted in his diary while in Vietnam, because advocates of democracy had failed to explain the theory of democracy in terms the ordinary person could understand. "This especially true in Far East which does not have same experience and tradition in personal liberty, etc. that Westerners do—therefore, do not miss it. . . .

"Remarkable that Communists can keep British fighting in Malaya, French [in] Indochina, and U.S. in Korea without one Russian soldier being engaged."[65]

After leaving Indochina, Jack headed for Korea, but he became deathly ill from a severe Addisonian crisis and was flown instead to a hospital in Okinawa, where his temperature one evening soared to 106 or 107. "They didn't think he could possibly live," Robert Kennedy later said.

Medical officials on Okinawa telephoned Dr. Elmer Bartels, who prescribed penicillin and adrenal hormones. Boston newspapers reported that Jack had cut short his trip, and once again misreported his illness, speculating that it was probably a recurrence of malaria.

The rigors of his long trip and his failure to consistently take his medicine had brought on Jack's crisis. "Jack just wasn't taking care of himself," said Dr. Bartels. "He had to take medicine. He'd forget to take it, or not take [it] with him on trips."[66]

When Jack recovered and returned home, he and his staff sent out a blizzard of news releases explaining Congressman Kennedy's conclusions from his seven-week tour. In a radio broadcast over station WOR in New York on November 14, 1951, he expressed views he would develop over the next decade. U.S. policymakers did not understand that Arab nationalism was the dominant force in the Middle East, and its origins were not simply a vengeful reaction to the rise of Israel to nationhood.

> The true enemy of the Arab world is poverty and want. . . . We have appeared too frequently to the Arab world as being too ready to buttress an inequitable status quo, whether it be the imposition of foreign controls, the safety of foreign investment not too equitably made, or a domestic regime heedless of the crying need for reforms. The central core of our Middle Eastern policy [should] not [be] the export of arms or the show of armed might but the export of ideas, of techniques, and the rebirth of our traditional sympathy for and understanding of the desires of men to be free. Our intervention [on] behalf of England's oil investments in Iran, . . . our failure to deal effectively after these years with the terrible human tragedy of the more than 700,000 Arab refugees, these are things that have failed to sit well with Arab desires and make empty the promises of the Voice of America.[67]

Jack also charged that France's arrogant colonialist mentality had blinded it to the nationalistic aspirations of the native peoples of Indochina. "To check the southern drive of communism makes sense but not only through reliance on the force of arms. The task is, rather, to build strong native non-Communist sentiment within these areas and rely on that as a spearhead of defense."

He attacked the U.S. Foreign Service for failing to understand the real hopes and desires of the peoples to which they were accredited. With a few exceptions, U.S. representatives "seem to be a breed of their own, moving mainly in their own limited circles, not knowing too much of the people to whom they are accredited, unconscious of the fact that their role is not tennis and cocktails but the interpretation to a foreign country of the meaning of American life and the interpretation to us of that country's aspirations and aims."[68]

As one congressman among 435, Jack found it difficult to win the spotlight or dramatize issues. House rules and customs frustrated him. To strike out on his own in the House meant facing one barrier after another. Bored by his insignificance in the House, stymied by the body's rigid seniority system, and impelled by ingrained self-expectation, Jack decided to abandon his congressional seat and seek higher office in 1952. He would rather "take the shot," he told a friend, than serve another term in Congress. "The [1950] campaign came through alright," Jack wrote Paul Fay on November 14, 1950. "I am all set for the big run in 1952."[69]

11

TWO BRAHMINS

Before Jack could run for any statewide office, he needed a statewide name. Starting in 1949 he delivered so many speeches throughout Massachusetts that in three years he visited almost all of the 351 cities and towns in the state.

To accommodate legislators who had other business or wanted to return to their district, key House votes were usually cast on Tuesdays, Wednesdays, and Thursdays. On the other four days many congressmen, especially those who lived near the capital, scattered to their other pursuits. That allowed Kennedy to fly to Massachusetts on long weekends to make speeches.

On his tours of the state he quietly evaluated potential Kennedy loyalists. At a communion breakfast or a testimonial dinner he took notes on key officials at the event ("Good speaker" or "Active in electrical workers' union"). He particularly wanted to attract younger professional people, whose loyalty to John Kennedy would be paramount.[1]

In 1950 the surprising Senate victories of Richard Nixon in California and Jack's friend George Smathers in Florida gave him the extra impetus he needed to target Massachusetts senator Henry Cabot Lodge Jr. The 1952 election was a presidential contest, and Massachusetts had gone Democratic in every presidential election since 1928. Seven of the last eleven gubernatorial elections had been won by Democrats. Since 1944, though, both Massachusetts senators had been Republicans, and since 1948 eight of the state's fourteen congressmen had been Republicans.

Although Jack craved Lodge's seat, his decision to run depended on the plans of a prominent Democratic Party colleague. In 1951 Democratic governor Paul Dever, forty-eight, approached a crossroads in his political career. Should he run for a third term as governor or try for the Senate seat held by Lodge?

Actually, Dever was exhausted and would have preferred not to run for anything, but he was driven by his deep sense of obligation to public service. He worried about his health. Several members of his family had died young from heart disease (which Dever later died from himself).[2] Privately Dever told Tip O'Neill, "I'm not interested in running for reelection to Governor. It's a killing job. It's a sickening job. I've had it. I've made too many enemies." Nonetheless, Dever persevered and decided to stay in politics for a while longer. But for which office should be run?

While Dever pondered his options, Jack fidgeted. He had to wait for Dever, the senior statesman, to make up his mind. Jack may have considered running against Dever, but not seriously. Such internecine warfare among state Democrats would spark enormous enmity that might ruin Jack's career. Besides, the Massachusetts governorship had been hard on the political fortunes of Democrats. It was only a two-year term, and Jack had no experience in state government, not even in the state legislature. Jack viewed the governorship as a mundane administrative post. "I don't look forward to sitting over there in the governor's office and dealing out sewer contracts," he told an associate.[3]

Acting as an intermediary between Dever and Kennedy was Joseph Healey, who arranged for the two to meet at the Ritz-Carlton Hotel in the spring of 1951. Although cordial, the meeting proved inconclusive. Dever would let Jack know when he made up his mind. Two more inconclusive meetings followed. "[Kennedy] showed signs of growing impatience," said Healey. "I pleaded with him to be patient, counseling him that I felt a split between the Dever-Kennedy organizations . . . would hurt him substantially."

On Palm Sunday, 1952, Dever and Kennedy met for the fourth time. "Jack, I'm a candidate for reelection," Dever simply announced. "Well, that's fine," Jack replied. "I'm a candidate for the Senate." Jack got the race he wanted.[4]

Jack's opponent, Henry Cabot Lodge Jr., had an enviable reputation as a champion vote getter. He and his fellow Republican, Senator Leverett Saltonstall, both Protestants, had repeatedly defeated Catholics running on the Democratic ticket. In 1936, the high-water mark of New Deal voting strength, Lodge defeated James Curley by 142,000 votes to capture the Senate seat. After winning reelection six years later, Lodge, then forty-one, resigned from the Senate in 1944 to enter the military, serving with distinction in Libya, Italy, and France. When he returned from the war, he defeated the supposedly unbeatable isolationist Senator David I. Walsh in 1946.

Heir to a patrician Yankee name, Lodge had inherited the goodwill earned by his famous grandfather, the first Senator Henry Cabot Lodge. "Rarely in American politics have hunter and quarry so resembled each other," noted biographer Burns. Both candidates were tall, handsome, and self-assured. Both were veterans of World War II. Both had graduated from Harvard and worked briefly in journalism before entering politics at an early age. Both possessed noted isolationist forebears. Each acted composed under pressure. Lodge was more suave, polished, and mature; Kennedy more frail looking, rumpled, and boyish.

Both men were Brahmins in their own way. The astute Paul Dever summed up Kennedy in six words: "Jack is the first Irish Brahmin." Kennedy met Lodge as a self-confident equal.

Many Massachusetts politicians judged Jack's challenge as foolhardy, likely to end in humiliating defeat. But they underestimated his competitive fire and political acumen, not to mention the powerful backing of his family and his legion of campaign supporters.[5]

The Kennedy campaign in 1952, observed journalist Ralph Martin, "was the most methodical, the most scientific, the most thoroughly detailed, the most intricate, the most disciplined and smoothly working state-wide campaign in Massachusetts history."

The state's campaign finance laws were antiquated and unworkable. By law a candidate could spend no more than $20,000 on his own contest, and a supporter could contribute no more than $1,000 to the candidate. But the law had two giant loopholes, and both were exploited in the 1952 Senate race. One loophole allowed the state party to spend unlimited sums from which a candidate benefited but for which he was not held accountable. This was the avenue the Lodge forces used. The second allowed the candidate to set up multiple committees on his behalf, making it possible for supporters to contribute $1,000 to each committee.

The Massachusetts Republican state organization spent a record $1,058,501 on all its candidates, most going to Lodge and his gubernatorial running mate, Christian Herter.

Kennedy set up six paper committees to receive contributions. His parents, two brothers, and three sisters all reported giving the legal limit of $1,000 to five different committees for a total of $35,000. Kennedy's committees spent a total of $349,626, about the same as Lodge did, using the other loophole.

Joe Kennedy provided constant encouragement for his son. "Jack, you knocked them dead in Somerville. What a great week you've had. Now let's take a look at what we should do to get more Independents and Republicans lined up."[6]

The ambassador worked tirelessly on Jack's behalf, bringing in talented speechwriters and advisers, consulting businessmen and politicians, and studying reports. A troubleshooter, he meshed a thousand and one details into a unified and energetic campaign.

Joe intuitively understood that the new medium of television could project his telegenic son into people's living rooms. "He figured that television was going to be the greatest thing in the history of politics," observed Sargent Shriver, assistant manager of the Kennedy enterprises in Chicago, who was engaged to Eunice Kennedy. (They married in 1953.) "He knew how Jack should be dressed and how his hair should be, what his response should be and how to handle Lodge."

One evening about eight campaign advisers met in Joe Kennedy's apartment to watch Jack make a television speech. Shriver described the scene:

> After it was all over, Mr. Kennedy asked what they thought of it. They gave these mealymouthed answers and all of a sudden Mr. Kennedy got ferocious, just *ferocious*. He told them it was the worst speech he'd ever heard and they were destroying Jack and he never wanted to see his son have to get up on TV and make such a fool of himself again. The guy who wrote the speech said he couldn't talk to him like that and Mr. Kennedy got red and furious and told him if he didn't like it to get out. He told them they would have a meeting in the morning and come up with a whole new concept because they were ruining this precious commodity they had and he gave a long speech about how wonderful Jack was. Then Jack called and Mr. Kennedy said, "Boy, Jack, you were great."

Jack had marvelous political abilities, Shriver contended, but the campaign operation was orchestrated by Joe Kennedy. "Nobody ever saw him," said Shriver. "He was always in the background."[7]

The millions of dollars Joe Kennedy had contributed to various charities, especially Catholic charities in Massachusetts, had earned deep gratitude and opened many doors. "When Archbishop Cushing baptized the baby of Bobby and Ethel in a special weekday ceremony just before the election, that cut our hearts out," said a Lodge aide.

"Sometimes you couldn't get anybody to make a decision," said a Kennedy worker. "You'd have to call the old man. Then you'd get a decision."

Joe Kennedy's explosive temper and erratic behavior also caused anger and confusion. Many were afraid to confront him. Nobody dared fight back when the ambassador stubbornly settled on a course of action. In those in-stances, said a campaign official, "the only time the campaign got any direction was when John Kennedy . . . was able to get up to Massachusetts to overrule his father."[8]

Joe Kennedy recruited a strategy team made up of Joe Healey, James Landis, and John Harriman. Healey had worked for Jack in North Cambridge in 1946; Landis, a longtime friend of Joe Kennedy's, had been dean of the Harvard Law School; and Harriman was recruited from the staff of *The Boston Globe*. "We were concerned mainly with the development of issues, basic strategy, the reply to statements that might be made by the opposition," said Healey. They wrote most of the speeches Jack delivered in the campaign.

Joe Kennedy met with the trio practically every morning. "If Jack was in town," said Healey, "we sat down, reviewed the status of the campaign as far as issues were concerned [and] decided in effect what the basic approach ought to be." In the spring of 1952, Joe Kennedy hired a high-priced press agent, Ralph Coghlan, former editorial writer for the *St. Louis Post-Dispatch*.

Despite Joe Kennedy's major role in 1952, the Senate campaign marked a transition between the ambassador's dominance of Jack's campaigns and Jack's insertion of his own people onto his staff. One of the newcomers was Kenneth O'Donnell, a native of Worcester, Massachusetts, and the son of the football coach at Holy Cross College. After World War II he and Robert Kennedy were teammates on Harvard's football squad. (O'Donnell was the team captain in his senior year.) Bobby asked O'Donnell to help Jack, and he joined the campaign in 1951. Wiry, tight-lipped, and blunt, O'Donnell proved to be a natural politician and gained valuable experience during the 1952 campaign.[9]

Another addition was burly, crew-cut Larry O'Brien. A friendly but tough Irishman from Springfield, Massachusetts, O'Brien had formerly worked in advertising and public relations, and had been the administrative assistant to Massachusetts congressman Foster Furcolo. O'Brien was politically astute, and his genius lay in voter registration and precinct organization.

During the 1952 contest Dave Powers became Jack's booking agent, and he would remain one of Jack's closest friends. "No town was too small or too Republican for him," said Powers. "He was willing to go anywhere, and every group was glad to have him, not only because he was an interesting political figure and a well-known war hero, but because he never charged a dime for expenses."[10]

The most critical new recruit was Jack's own brother, Bobby. Initially Mark Dalton served as campaign manager. But the complex challenge of a statewide senate campaign apparently overwhelmed him, and his easygoing manner irritated Joe Kennedy. "The old man wants performance," said a campaign aide. "He's a taskmaster, hard-driving." Dalton wasn't a taskmaster or hard-driving.

The campaign seemed to be floundering under Dalton's direction. At a meeting, probably in late May 1952, Joe Kennedy flew into a rage and vented his spleen on Dalton. His tirade ranged from an attack on the campaign's strategy to the lapel buttons it should adopt. Why wasn't the campaign attacking labor unions? Joe foolishly wondered. "We've got to hit the Jews," he madly insisted. As an aside he bragged to the group that he made more money in Hollywood besting Jew "bastards" in business deals than could fit into the building. Throughout his father's rage Jack said little.

Fed up with Joe's abuse and constant meddling, Dalton rose from his chair and left the room. "I thought he had gone to the john," said one witness. But Dalton had quit. "Mark didn't like the old man's style," recalled John Galvin; "he resented the old man, who was a son of a bitch." With no manager the Kennedy campaign seemed in serious trouble. An emergency call went out to Robert Kennedy to come and straighten out the mess.[11]

Twenty-six years old, Robert had graduated from Harvard in 1948 and received his law degree in 1951 from the University of Virginia. On June 17, 1950, he married Ethel Skakel. Currently working in New York as an attorney with the Criminal Division of the U.S. Department of Justice, he was reluctant to abandon his job, and doubted his ability to help Jack's campaign. "I don't know anything about Massachusetts politics," he told O'Donnell. "I don't know any of the players, and I'll screw it up. I just don't want to come." O'Donnell replied, "Unless you come, I don't think it's going to get done." Bobby finally agreed.

On June 2, 1952, RFK officially became the new campaign manager. Well tanned, ruggedly handsome, with a big shock of unruly hair, he arrived at the Boston headquarters every morning at eight-thirty to unlock the door. For the next five months he worked every day, laboring longer and harder than anyone else.

From the time he assumed control, the campaign began humming on all cylinders. He unleashed his ferocious energy, tapped his dormant organizational genius, and motivated thousands of volunteers. "He could stand up to his father, and he could stand up to the powers," said Ken O'Donnell. "We didn't have that capacity until he came, we didn't have any real muscle. He supplied it, which began the controversy about his ruthlessness."[12]

RFK disdained the "politicians" and "elder statesmen" who wandered into headquarters wanting to chat, give advice, and pose for pictures. "The main difference between our campaign and others is that we did work. You can't get any work out of a politician."

Because of his brusque manner, he stepped on toes and alienated some

VIPs. One evening, when a state labor leader visited Kennedy's Boston head-quarters, Bobby walked by him and said, "If you're not going to work, don't hang around here!" Late one evening Dave Powers suggested to Bobby that he was unpopular with the Democratic pols in Boston. "I don't care if any-body around here likes me, as long as they like Jack," he replied.

Normally political campaigns in Massachusetts did not accelerate until af-ter summer, but the Kennedy machine started early. "We had to do work in the summer if we wanted to win the campaign," observed Robert Kennedy. "We couldn't rely on the older people who said that you don't ever get started until after Labor Day. We wouldn't win under those circumstances."[13]

The campaign again exploited Jack's heroic war record. About nine hun-dred thousand copies of an eight-page tabloid featured a series of artist's conceptions of Kennedy rescuing his shipmates after the *PT 109* sinking. On the facing page was a photograph of brother Joe with his fatal mission described under the heading "John Fulfills Dream of Brother Joe Who Met Death in the Sky Over the English Channel." Inserted in each tabloid was the *Reader's Digest* reprint of John Hersey's account of Jack's Pacific heroism. Volunteers hand-delivered the tabloid to dwellings throughout the state; other copies they strategically placed on bus seats and in cabs.

"I am today delivering to you approximately 10 thousand of the *Reader's Digest* reprint of an article written in 1944 about . . . John F. Kennedy," Robert Kennedy wrote Vincent Pace. "We would very much like to get full distribution of this article in the barber shops [and] beauty parlors . . . in Boston." The crafty campaign manager asserted that the material was *not* po-litical advertising. "It is simply objective reporting by a world famous news-man," he claimed. "The article is just plain 'good reading.' "[14]

The Kennedy organization laboriously created a statewide network of 286 local Kennedy secretaries. They sought out political novices, people well respected in the community—businessmen, lawyers, doctors, accountants, in-surance agents. Eventually they recruited twenty-one thousand volunteers to work under the secretaries' direction.

The title of "secretary" was significant. "We could have called them Kennedy chairmen," Larry O'Brien observed, "but that might have offended the local [Democratic] party chairmen, who in theory were still chairmen of everything—our campaign included—so we settled on the more modest ti-tle of secretary." There was a second reason for the title. "Secretary" was a nonpolitical term and connoted work; "chairman" suggested somebody go-ing through the motions.

Each secretary received a letter of appreciation from Jack. Each issued a press release about his appointment, according to a form supplied him; the opening of a local headquarters meant another press release, again according to a prepared format.

"We went into towns where Democrat was a dirty word," Ken O'Donnell said. "Places where nobody had ever tried to start an organization of any kind. And we found people with enthusiasm, people who liked Kennedy, people who worked their heads off for free."

Robert Kennedy kept touring the state, speaking constantly to secretaries and their assistants. "Our object was to get a little work out of as many people as possible, instead of a lot of work out of a few," said Bobby. The secretaries grew more sophisticated and by the end of the campaign made weekly reports to Larry O'Brien.[15]

The Kennedy campaign understood that it was a serious mistake to gather a horde of supporters, eager to help, and have little for them to do. Sending out thank-you letters made them feel needed. Later, teams of volunteers personally delivered Kennedy literature door-to-door even though the campaign could have sent the literature through the mail.

Kennedy needed only about 5,000 signatures on his nomination papers to run for the Senate. Partly to provide work for thousands of campaign workers, the Kennedy organization astonished pundits by turning in 262,324 signed papers, and then had volunteers send each signer a thank-you letter.

Besides the elaborate system of secretaries, the organization formed groups for various occupations and ethnic groups. Doctors, dentists, lawyers, and taxi drivers each had a committee; so did Italians, Canadians, Frenchmen, and Greeks.[16]

The campaign letter sent by the Polish-American Committee promised that Senator Kennedy would wage a fight to force the nonunion, low-wage areas of the South to raise wages and end their threat to Massachusetts industry. "John F. Kennedy stands for Poland," the letter continued. "He knows her tragic history and her valiant people. In 1948 he protested Poland's betrayal at the Teheran Conference, when Russia was allowed to grab nearly half of Poland's territory."

The Albanian American Citizens Committee for John F. Kennedy urged fellow Albanians to vote for Jack because he had consistently voted against the McCarran bill, which discriminated against immigrants from Albania, and because Jack had a deep hatred for atheistic communism. In the sidebar of the letter were the names of Albanian leaders in the state who endorsed Kennedy.

One Sunday afternoon and evening Jack went from an Albanian-American picnic to a Greek-American picnic to a Polish-American meeting to a Portuguese-American banquet to an Italian-American banquet, and ended the day at an Irish-American dinner at a country club.[17]

The campaign strategically purchased ads in the state's foreign-language newspapers. In return, the Kennedy camp requested—and expected—each paper to print Jack's press releases and statements. Joseph Lola, who organized the Kennedy effort with foreign-language papers, paid $627 for an ad in a Polish-language newspaper. "After 5 visits we hit it off very well and they agreed to releases and space," Lola reported. "J.F.K. got an excellent full column write-up on veteran's page. They let me see opponent's stuff before it was printed. J.F.K. making a very favorable impression on the Polish people." Negro newspapers in Massachusetts complained bitterly that they did not receive their fair share of advertising money. "To keep peace and to conserve time I gave in," wrote Lola. "Humph!!!"[18]

One group needed a delicate touch. For the first time in Jack's political career, his father's anti-Semitism proved burdensome. Lodge supporters distributed copies of Ambassador Dirksen's prewar dispatches in predominantly Jewish wards. The Kennedy camp cried foul.

Lodge had a strong pro-Israel record, and Jack had introduced a foreign-aid amendment interpreted as harmful to Israel. Ralph Martin explained:

> The amendment reduced aid to Middle East countries from $175,000,000 to $140,000,000. Kennedy felt that his cuts could be applied to selected specifics of which he disapproved, although Congressmen Javits and Ribicoff both tried to explain to him on the floor that his cuts would be across the board. The general acceptance is that Kennedy misunderstood the language of the original bill, but still his defeated amendment was construed by some as an anti-Israel effort.

To counter the handicaps, the Kennedy organization put on a massive effort to capture Jewish votes. Kennedy's visit with Ben-Gurion in Israel was widely publicized, as was his support of subsequent aid-to-Israel legislation. Congressman John McCormack, popular with Jewish voters, campaigned for Kennedy in Jewish areas. The campaign solicited endorsements from Jewish congressmen.

A pamphlet sent to Jewish voters emphasized the Kennedy family's solidarity, the excellent schools Jack had attended, his religious orthodoxy, and his family's philanthropy—all in the hope of appealing to the well-known Jewish love of family, education, religion, and philanthropy. The campaign publicized the Kennedys' charitable efforts, particularly the donation of fifty thousand dollars to the Massachusetts Jewish Philanthropies. The appeal to Jewish voters succeeded, and Jack swept the Jewish wards.[19]

While Dwight Eisenhower remained in Europe, claiming that "under no circumstances" would he resign his NATO command to seek the presidency, Lodge led the pro-Eisenhower forces back home. As a spokesman for East Coast Republicans, Lodge urged Ike to allow political experts to take control of the Citizens for Eisenhower organization, and to permit the use of Ike's name in the Republican primaries. Speed was essential, Lodge argued; otherwise Senator Robert Taft would soon sew up the nomination. Eventually Eisenhower moved to active candidacy.

At the Republican convention in Chicago in the summer of 1952, Taft thought he had a firm hold on the Southern delegations. "Lodge set out to steal them for Eisenhower," observed Ike's biographer Stephen Ambrose. "Through a complex parliamentary process, Lodge got the convention to vote on a 'Fair Play' amendment that almost no one understood, except for the point that counted—a vote for 'Fair Play' was a vote for Ike." By a narrow margin, Lodge succeeded in getting the amendment passed, and Eisenhower went on to sweep the nomination on the first ballot.

Afterward, bitter over the tactics used to defeat their hero, Taft delegates and their supporters in Massachusetts vented their wrath on Lodge. Kennedy, after all, might not be so bad, they reasoned. True, he was a Fair Dealer on domestic matters, but he had criticized Truman's foreign policy more often than Lodge had. Besides, Joe Kennedy was a personal friend and admirer of Taft.[20]

At a press conference shortly after the Republican convention, Basil Brewer, the influential publisher of the *New Bedford Standard Times* and a diehard Taft supporter, expressed the resentment felt by many backers of Taft. He announced his full support for the Eisenhower-Nixon ticket and some local Republican candidates, but he refused to endorse Lodge, whom he blamed for "crooking" Taft out of the nomination.

While the Taft camp turned against Lodge, Joe Kennedy worked behind the scenes to exploit their resentment. During the rest of the Senate race, Brewer lambasted Lodge in his editorials and worked closely with the Kennedy camp. T. Walter Taylor, a former office employee in the state Taft headquarters, opened an "Independents for Kennedy" office.

"We engaged in a very ardent campaign on behalf of Senator Kennedy," recalled Charles Lewin, who worked for the *New Bedford Standard-Times*. "We distributed thousands of copies of texts of the press conference in which Mr. Brewer answered questions. . . . And we carried on a considerable consultation campaign with the Kennedy leadership." Jack inherited many of the votes of the disaffected Taft supporters, clustered mainly in the ring of Republican suburbs surrounding Boston.[21]

Lodge's own campaign was brief and surprisingly ineffective. The senator busily campaigned throughout the nation for Eisenhower's nomination during the first six months of 1952. Then he took a vacation. He didn't start his own campaign until mid-September. Robert Kennedy thought Lodge had become lazy, insisting on his afternoon nap. "He was . . . a very, very lazy man as a campaigner."

Meanwhile, Jack impressed everyone with his exceptional diligence. "He would wear out three shifts of men a day," said Jackson Holtz, the vice chairman of Kennedy's Senate campaign. "Jack Kennedy was the hardest-working candidate that I ever saw in my life," echoed Tip O'Neill. "He was really a prodigious worker."[22]

He doggedly shook hands day and night. He trudged up and down assembly lines, scrambled over fishing boats to greet returning fishermen at the Boston wharves, and tramped through deep mud and foul smells to meet tannery workers. Using a blanket and pillow in the backseat of his car, Jack rested while his driver headed for the next engagement.

He was warm and gracious to guests who filed past him in a reception line. Larry O'Brien described people as seeming nervous or hesitant as they approached him, but "loosening up as he took their hand, and finally beaming with pleasure as they walked away from their first encounter with one of the famous Kennedys."[23]

Once again, Jack motivated people to want to help him. After watching young female volunteers hand out pamphlets for Kennedy at the entrance to an Eisenhower rally, an Ike supporter lamented, "What is there about Kennedy that makes every Catholic girl in Boston between eighteen and twenty-eight think it's a holy crusade to get him elected?"

Like most campaigns of the time, women did not have a leadership role, having been stereotyped as best suited for clerical work. But political campaigns needed armies of volunteers who would telephone voters, update voting lists, prepare folders, distribute flyers, type letters, and seal envelopes.

Some of the young women volunteers were afraid to miss an evening of work because that might be the night Jack visited the campaign office. "It really lit up the place when he'd come in," said a woman volunteer. "He just had such a nice way with everybody, and he always made every girl feel that he was really interested in talking to them."[24]

Once Jack's path was clear to run for the Senate, Joe Kennedy mobilized the rest of the Kennedy clan, intending to turn the campaign into a family crusade. "Jack is going to run for the United States Senate," he told his children. "All of you think of what you can do to help him."

In late May 1952, the far-flung Kennedys began to gather. From Chicago came Eunice and Sargent Shriver. The more reserved Jean Kennedy, who had been working for her father at the Merchandise Mart, also arrived from Chicago. From New York came Patricia, who was beginning her career in television production. And from Paris, where she was vacationing, came Rose Kennedy, still so small and svelte that she could pass for one of her daughters.

A reporter observed that when an outsider threatened to thwart the ambition of a Kennedy, "the whole family forms a close-packed ring, horns lowered, like a herd of bison beset by wolves." Lodge and his camp respected the remarkable solidarity of the Kennedy family. "I don't worry about Jack Kennedy. I don't worry about Kennedy's money," moaned a Lodge supporter. "It's that family of his . . . they're all over the state." "Poor old Lodge never had a chance," said another commentator. "The Kennedys were like a panzer division mowing down the state."

Bobby's wife, Ethel, delivered a speech in Fall River one evening, then drove to Boston, entered the hospital, and delivered a baby before morning.[25]

The Kennedy campaign put on thirty-three formal receptions. Each elegant gathering, complete with lace tablecloths and candelabras, resembled an exclusive party. The turnouts were exceptional: a thousand women in Brockton, two thousand in Springfield, a thousand in Salem, seventeen hundred in Fitchburg. All together, seventy-five thousand persons—almost all women—attended the receptions.

The receptions were an obvious ploy to exploit the Kennedys' charm. They were often staged at an elegant local hotel; the women guests got new hairdos, dressed themselves in fashionable outfits, and stood in a reception line to meet Rose, three of her daughters, and her bachelor son, the Senate candidate. Sometimes the women got so carried away that they bussed the candidate on the cheek. Like the receptions during the 1946 campaign, the guests drank tea, ate small sandwiches, and listened to Rose and Jack give good-humored talks.[26]

Amazed by the awe inspired by the Kennedys' glamour and wealth, a veteran newsman observed:

> Kennedy's career is a curious reversal of the law of the log cabin. . . . That family behaved like royalty at their rallies. Whoever heard of reception lines in politics, as though to meet the king and queen. They fancy themselves in that role, and it was all they could do to keep those old gals who came to the affairs from curtsying. They had every tendency to drop one knee.

At each reception the visitors signed a guest book, later passed on to the local Kennedy secretary for appropriate follow-up. "Often today's reception guest became tomorrow's volunteer," said Larry O'Brien.

Besides appearing at the teas, Rose Kennedy made other speeches on Jack's behalf. She always knew exactly what to wear and what to say. Between appearances she would change clothes and accessories in the car. "Mrs. Kennedy carefully selected her accessories and tailored her remarks," wrote a New York Times reporter. "Thus to a group of Italian women in the North End, she was the mother of nine children, one of whom died in the war. Perhaps a single pearl necklace over a black dress would be worn. Before a Chestnut Hill group of matrons, she might don a mink stole and a few rings and certainly a different hat."

"Rose wowed them everywhere," Dave Powers recalled. "In Dorchester, she talked about her days in Dorchester High School. She showed them the card index file she kept when her kids were little to keep track of the vaccinations and medical treatments and dental work. At a high-toned gathering of women, she'd talk for a few minutes about Jack and then she'd say, 'Now let me tell you about the new dresses I saw in Paris last month.' They loved her."[27]

A television program, "Coffee with the Kennedys," proved a successful innovation. On the morning of October 15, 1952, forty-five thousand women in Massachusetts opened their homes to friends and neighbors to watch Jack, Rose, Pat, and Eunice on WNAC-TV. Exceptionally telegenic, Jack and his mother and two sisters presented an enchanting image of family. "It was an unrehearsed, homey little affair," a reporter observed, "in which the Kennedys chattered on a sofa, then invited the viewers to telephone the station—collect—any questions they wanted Jack to answer during the program." Viewers phoned in questions, which Jack answered with aplomb.[28]

There was one issue, though, that Jack Kennedy didn't feel comfortable with and preferred to avoid.

Sargent Shriver, sent as an intermediary to Democratic presidential nominee Adlai Stevenson, advised the Illinois governor on what to say during his campaign swing through Massachusetts. Shriver wanted Stevenson to emphasize that "Jack Kennedy is Stevenson's kind of a man" and had fought for minimum-wage laws, decent housing, and civil rights. Kennedy was courageous and "independent of special interest groups." "Up here this anti-Communist business is a good thing to emphasize," Shriver also told Stevenson. Nonetheless, he urged Stevenson to avoid the specific subjects of Senator Joe McCarthy and isolationism.

Shriver didn't explain further, but isolationism might remind voters of the discredited stand Jack's father had taken before World War II. And the issue of Joe McCarthy was too awkward, too sensitive for Jack to handle.

In early July 1949 Republican senator Joseph McCarthy of Wisconsin arrived at Cape Cod on a Northeast Airlines flight and proceeded to Hyannis Port for an unpublicized Fourth of July holiday weekend at the Kennedy home. The senator was warmly received by Joe Kennedy, who enjoyed McCarthy's affability and bonhomie. "[McCarthy] went out on my boat one time and he almost drowned swimming behind it," Joe Kennedy later said, "but he never complained." McCarthy played the infield during the

Kennedy family's softball game on the lawn, but was allowed to retire after committing four errors.

Seven months later, Senator McCarthy delivered the most famous speech of his life, commencing his five-year red-hunting career and sparking furious partisan debate over the effectiveness of President Truman's anticommunist policies. On February 9, 1950, at Wheeling, West Virginia, McCarthy charged that 205 people, known to the secretary of state to be members of the Communist Party, were still working in the State Department and shaping American foreign policy. The Cold War atmosphere of the time made McCarthy's sensational accusation seem believable. During 1949–1950 various events—the explosion of a nuclear bomb by the USSR, the takeover of China by Mao Tse-tung, the conviction of the spy Alger Hiss for perjury, and the Korean War—all served to catalyze popular fears about communism. In the paranoid world of McCarthyism, the mistakes and failures of U.S. foreign policy were due to deliberate disloyalty—or at least the willingness to tolerate deliberate disloyalty—not to misjudgment, error, or unforeseen events.[29]

In Cold War America, both liberals and conservatives shared and seldom questioned a broad anticommunist consensus. Many liberals searched for a way that would contain communism and guard against Communist subversion but still protect civil liberties. But moderation had only limited appeal in the hysterical atmosphere. "The argument of those on the Right, that there should be no compromise in the war against Communism, easily prevailed," noted historian Richard Fried.

Millard Tydings, a Democrat from Maryland, chaired the subcommittee of the Senate Committee on Foreign Relations that conducted an inquiry into McCarthy's accusations and eventually branded them a "fraud and a hoax." Although Democrats nationwide deplored McCarthy, few powerful senators were willing to take him on. Fear explained the dearth of volunteers. In the 1950 election the media credited McCarthy's campaign efforts with the defeat of Senator Tydings and other Democratic senators. The defeat of Tydings stemmed from several factors, but the media reported only one, Joe McCarthy, thereby turning the Wisconsin senator into a giant-killer.[30]

McCarthy's unique personal qualities—his exaggerated sense of drama, willingness to gamble, and talent for political invective and press-agentry—contributed to his political success, but McCarthyism was preeminently a partisan weapon used by Republicans to hammer Democrats.

McCarthy described the five terms of Democratic Presidents Roosevelt and Truman as "twenty years of treason." Secretary of State Dean Acheson was a Kremlin lackey who should seek asylum in the Soviet Union. McCarthy's attack on General George Marshall was the most seditious of his career. A man of enormous stature and prestige, noted for his integrity and public service, Marshall had coordinated the Normandy invasion in 1944, served as secretary of state, and initiated the Marshall Plan. But in his lengthy indictment on the Senate floor on June 14, 1951, McCarthy, in so many words, labeled the general a traitor for participating in "a conspiracy so immense and an infamy so black as to dwarf any previous such venture in the history of man." According to McCarthy, Marshall had marched "side by side" with Stalin in war and peace, had been party to the "sellout" of China, and had "stood at Roosevelt's elbow at Yalta" when Poland was delivered to the Soviets.

In his "slip of the tongue" during a television speech against Adlai Stevenson in the 1952 presidential campaign, McCarthy referred to "Alger—I mean Adlai." The vicious innuendo, with its introduction of the first name of the hated Hiss, was supposed to suggest Stevenson's close relationship with Communist spies.

Liberal Democrats denounced McCarthy's ethics and tactics. Before he became the nation's preeminent anticommunist, McCarthy had been censured twice by the Wisconsin Supreme Court for judicial misconduct; had distorted his military record in World War II to advance his political career; had failed to pay his Wisconsin taxes; and, as senator, had accepted money from a corporation he was supposed to be investigating for corruption.[31]

During his anticommunist campaign McCarthy repeatedly lied, distorted, and slandered. His irresponsible attacks damaged the morale of government employees, threatened traditional American liberties, and created a witch-hunt atmosphere. But many people viewed McCarthy as a noble, courageous crusader, rooting atheistic Communists out of the temples of government. In Massachusetts many Catholics revered him. Devoted to his every cause, the *Boston Post* printed most of his accusations and treated him with the veneration due a saint.

Not one prominent Massachusetts Democrat had spoken out against McCarthy up to 1952. "Attacking him in this state," said the *Boston Post,* "is regarded as a certain method for committing political suicide."[32]

Many of Kennedy's constituents loved McCarthy. And Jack's own family was close to the Wisconsin senator. In Chicago, McCarthy became social friends with Eunice Kennedy and Sargent Shriver. Both Eunice and Pat Kennedy had friendly chats with the senator in his Washington office; McCarthy dated Pat. Robert Kennedy was also enamored of McCarthy and would later join the senator's staff.

Joe Kennedy, though, was the most adamant and loyal supporter of McCarthy, and donated several thousand dollars to his reelection campaign in 1952. Since his falling-out with Franklin Roosevelt, Joe Kennedy had grown increasingly cranky, conservative, and conspiratorial. "Kennedy liked Mc-

Carthy's slash-and-burn attacks on liberal Democrats," observed writer Ronald Steel.

Jack made no speeches supporting McCarthy and didn't attempt to appease the passions of the McCarthyites in his state. On the other hand, he made no speeches attacking McCarthy either. As an Irish Catholic with an excellent war record, he could have been an influential critic of the Wisconsin senator. "McCarthy symbolized everything Kennedy personally detested," noted Burns. "Vulgar, bullying, crude, cynical, dishonest. . . . McCarthy sneered at the traditions, orderly procedures, and senatorial good manners that Kennedy valued so highly." Still, Jack wouldn't publicly criticize him, and cautiously answered constituent mail about McCarthy.[33]

This thorny problem placed both Lodge and Kennedy in a quandary during the 1952 election. Lodge disliked McCarthy and opposed his tactics, but McCarthy was a Republican colleague, and most Republican leaders and partisans backed his anticommunist crusade. With pro-McCarthy sentiment strong in Massachusetts, especially among Irish Catholics, Lodge had to be careful. He hoped that McCarthy would not campaign in the state. Nonetheless, what if he did come? "Kennedy asked the same question," observed Burns of the dilemma McCarthy posed. "Lodge was being attacked in Boston for his coolness toward McCarthy. What if McCarthy came and endorsed Lodge? What if he endorsed Kennedy?" There was no way to know what McCarthy would do.

"Whether [or not] McCarthy comes here," campaign adviser Edward Dunn wrote Robert Kennedy, "our speakers should be coached to keep driving home the fact that Jack moved in on the Communists and really did something about it before McCarthy and others." Citing the Harold Christoffel case of 1947, Dunn urged the campaign to stress that Jack had obtained the first citation of anybody in Congress against an alleged Communist.

Jack rejected the advice. During the campaign he often addressed the danger of Communist expansion, but he did not focus on internal subversion or advertise himself as a Communist hunter.[34]

One evening, Gardner "Pat" Jackson, a diehard liberal and McCarthy opponent, then on loan to the Kennedy campaign from the CIO, prepared a strong statement condemning McCarthyism which he hoped Kennedy would agree to sign. "So I took it up to Jack's apartment the next morning," said Jackson. Sitting at a card table in the center of the room were Joe Kennedy and the three speechwriters: Jim Landis, John Harriman, and Joe Healey.

Jackson started to read the statement, but he had gone only two sentences when Joe Kennedy jumped to his feet and began shouting at Jackson, "You're trying to ruin Jack!" Yelling obscenities, Joe said he was not opposed to McCarthy and had even contributed to McCarthy's campaign. Jackson, liberals, union people, and the Jews were only trying to ruin Jack's career. "I can't estimate how long he poured it out on me," Jackson recalled. "I have never had a working over like that in my life. It was just a stream of stuff—always referring to 'you and your sheeny friends.'"

Jack appeared briefly during his father's harangue, but acted cravenly, and hardly spoke. Then Jack and Ted Reardon slipped out for the day's campaigning.

A few days later, Jackson sat in the same living room while the candidate dressed in the bedroom.

"They gave you a bad time, Pat?" Kennedy called casually through the half-open door.

"How do you explain your father, Jack?" Jackson asked.

Kennedy was silent for a few moments. "Just love of family." He paused and then corrected himself: "No. Pride of family."[35]

The liberal wing of the Democrat Party continued to place strong pressure on Jack to take an anti-McCarthy position. The Kennedy camp wondered why their candidate was the one expected to take a position on McCarthy. What about Senator Lodge? "It [was] one in which we really [couldn't] win," Joe Healey remembered; "it was one that we wanted to avoid, regardless of what might be the basic feelings in the matter." In effect, the Kennedy campaign adopted the position that when Lodge took a position on McCarthy, Kennedy would take a position on the Wisconsin senator. And since Lodge did not issue a public statement on McCarthy, neither did Kennedy. In the end McCarthy did not speak or intervene in the Massachusetts Senate campaign, and both Kennedy and Lodge pretended he didn't exist. The prickly issue, though, would continue to haunt Jack Kennedy.[36]

Both Kennedy and Lodge tried, with only limited success, to formulate issues giving the impression of deep differences. In fact, the two candidates seldom differed. Slogans dominated billboards and advertisements. Kennedy's slogan was "Kennedy Will Do *More* for Massachusetts." Lodge's advisers countered with "Lodge Has Done—and Will Do—the *Most* for Massachusetts."

Lodge voted for and Kennedy against the Taft-Hartley Act in 1947. Lodge favored a bill to reduce income taxes in 1948, the first reduction in twenty years; Jack voted against it in the House. Kennedy took a slightly stronger position in favor of federal programs for housing, labor, price controls, and economic aid for the Northeast. He attacked Lodge for taking contradictory positions on several issues—trade with Communist countries, civil rights, price control, China, troops to Europe, rent control.[37]

Lodge accused Kennedy of absenteeism in the House; Jack accused Lodge of being absent from the Senate. "Both charges were true," noted reporter

Fletcher Knebel. "Kennedy had been home campaigning for Kennedy, and Lodge had been off campaigning for Eisenhower." In fact, Kennedy's record of absenteeism in the last session of Congress was the worst of any of the fourteen-person Massachusetts delegation.[38]

Unlike his isolationist grandfather, Lodge was an internationalist. He supported the Truman Doctrine, the Marshall Plan, and NATO. Jack focused on insights he had gained during his 1951 trips. "The Middle East and Southeast Asia is [sic] where the Communists really hope to seize control," Jack stated. "French Indo-China, Burma, Malaya, Indonesia, and India, where reports are 20,000,000 are starving and where the status quo is so bad—though we always are defending it—these areas are a threat as important as the military threat to us of Russia." The United States overemphasized the threats to Western Europe. "I was the first congressman to visit French Indo-China in more than three years," he noted to prove his point; "while I was there, 187 members of Congress were visiting Rome."

Jack stressed the regional problems of the Massachusetts and New England economy, and the need to regenerate the economic strength of the region. Massachusetts needed a senator who not only worried about national and international issues, but focused on state problems, like the unemployment caused by the flight of the textile and leather-manufacturing industries. Because New England faced increasingly tough competition from the Icelandic fishing industry and cheap Southern labor, Jack promised to organize a bloc of New England senators to act in a cooperative effort for the entire region.[39]

He candidly admitted errors. As a congressman he had voted for a substantial cut in Point Four funds for the Middle East. After he made his trip there in 1951, he judged that the technical-assistance program was vitally important. "So I made a mistake," he said during the campaign. "I've since changed my mind."

A critic writing in *The New Republic* accused him of practicing the political art of "popularism"—that is, a willingness to give people what they wanted in specific situations, but shunning the generalities of a liberal ideology. Kennedy readily acknowledged that this might be accurate.[40]

Jack peppered his advisers with queries and suggestions. "We should have prepared my position on reciprocal trade," he wrote Ted Reardon in late August 1952. "I will be for it in principle but want reasonable protection given to Massachusetts industries, such as fishing."

He searched for specific information to use as leverage against Lodge. On one issue he accepted the advice of his conservative advisers. He wanted to portray Lodge as more in agreement with Truman's foreign policy than Kennedy himself. "I would like to get Lodge's record as compared to mine on the administration's foreign policy," Jack asked Reardon. "Can we show that there was no stronger supporter of the administration's foreign policy than Senator Lodge?"

Jack instructed Reardon to study Lodge's pre-1946 record on issues important to the AFL and CIO. "We could perhaps increase [Lodge's] percentage of wrong votes." In the last month of the campaign, he urged his advisers to turn out a "newsworthy . . . thought" each day. "Whip these into shape now," he insisted.[41]

The candidates debated twice. The most noteworthy was the one on September 16, 1952, to an overflow crowd at South Junior High School in Waltham. Three thousand people tried to enter the 640-seat auditorium. Spectators watched from the stage, sat on the floor in front of the stage, and stood along the sides and rear of the auditorium; a public address system carried the debate to a large throng outside who spread out over the lawn in front of the school.

Like most of the campaign, it was a gentlemanly debate. Kennedy's manner was relaxed, unhurried, and direct. He stated that he did not agree with everything the Democratic Party had done during the past two decades. Mistakes and miscalculations had been made. But the party's efforts should be judged against the vastness and turmoil of a depression, the rise of Hitler, World War II, and the postwar period. "It is against this vast panorama that our actions must be judged—and not merely through the trick binoculars of hindsight—which makes all things easy, all men wise. To claim our successes were bipartisan, our failures Democratic is good politics perhaps, but not good sense."

The challenger called labor the field in which the Democratic Party had made the most substantial contribution. He mentioned the rights to unionize and bargain collectively, and stopping the exploitation of women and children. Democrats had enacted the minimum-wage law. Kennedy won both loud boos and cheers for his statement that he would try to repeal the Taft-Hartley Act.

Reporter Mary McGrory of the *Washington Star* covered the debate and judged Kennedy the clear winner. "He was totally self-possessed, had all the facts at his command, and charmed everybody."[42]

Joe Kennedy may have offered a bribe to an influential newspaper publisher. Brought to light inadvertently six years after the election during an unrelated House investigation, the incident sparked a flurry of gossip but caused no long-term damage to Jack's career. John Fox, owner of the *Boston Post* and a diehard Republican, had supported Lodge during most of the campaign, but suddenly, just before the election, he switched his editorial backing to Kennedy. Fox's newspaper had been losing money, and he was apparently in serious financial straits. In 1958 he testified that he felt Lodge "had been soft on Communism" and claimed he switched "without any knowledge of anybody in the Kennedy family." However, Fox conceded that the night after the endorsement, Joe Kennedy called on him, and that following the election, Kennedy loaned him five hundred thousand dollars.

Was this a quid pro quo? Did Fox testify truthfully that the huge loan had nothing to do with his switch to Kennedy? After Fox's revelation, Joseph Kennedy's New York office issued a statement declaring that no loan had been discussed before the endorsement. "The loan, as mentioned," said the statement, "was made after the election as a purely commercial transaction— for sixty days, with full collateral, at full interest, and was fully repaid on time—and was simply one of many commercial transactions in which this office has participated."

Though not conclusive, evidence suggests that the loan *was* directly related to the endorsement. Joseph Timilty, a personal assistant to the ambassador, remembered receiving information that Fox's *Post* was about to endorse Lodge. "So I immediately told Joe and he didn't waste any time," Timilty recalled. "[He got in] touch with Mr. Fox. . . . I never knew what took place, I never asked, I heard rumors, but the next day the *Post* came out for Jack Kennedy."[43]

When asked about the incident in 1964, Robert Kennedy claimed he couldn't remember details, but generally supported the notion that the endorsement was linked to the loan. "We needed [the *Boston Post*'s] support," he said. "My father went down to see [Fox], and I don't know whether he arranged for him to get a loan or got him a loan or what. I don't remember the details, but the *Boston Post* supported John Kennedy. And there was a connection between the two events."

In 1960, at the conclusion of a lengthy discussion about the incident with Fletcher Knebel, who had publicized Fox's testimony in 1958, John Kennedy said, "You know we had to buy that fucking paper or I would have lost the election." Knebel understood Jack's comment to be an admission that Joe Kennedy had bribed Fox. But Jack could have been joking. Most likely, though, before the election Joe Kennedy promised to loan Fox five hundred thousand dollars if the publisher endorsed Jack for the Senate, and Fox agreed to the deal.[44]

The last thing the campaign needed was any suggestion that Jack had health problems. Yet during the grueling 1952 election campaign Kennedy suffered numerous ailments: headaches, respiratory infections, stomach pain, urinary-tract discomfort, and his sore back. During the period, as historian Robert Dallek has pointed out, Kennedy "consulted an ear, nose, and throat specialist about his headaches; took anti-spasmodics and applied heat fifteen minutes a day to ease his stomach troubles; consulted urologists about his bladder and prostate discomfort; had DOCA pellets implanted and took daily oral doses of cortisone to control his Addison's disease; and struggled unsuccessfully to find relief from his back miseries."

On one of his visits to Springfield, he stopped at a local fire station to shake hands. While up on the third floor, he playfully grabbed the fire pole and slid down to the first floor. Landing with a jolt, he doubled up with pain. A doctor later confirmed that he had aggravated his back problem and would have to use crutches.

For many weeks afterward he suffered excruciating pain. When he used crutches, the pain lessened, but he hated to appear in public with them. When he arrived at an appearance, he concealed the crutches in his car. As he walked from his car to the hall, he'd grit his teeth. Once he entered the room where the crowd waited, he smiled and walked as erect as a West Point cadet. After he completed his speech, answered questions, and shook hands, he practically collapsed in the car, leaning back on the seat and closing his eyes in pain. Dave Powers said: "When we got to the hotel, out would come the crutches from the floor of the back seat, and he would use them to get upstairs." Powers filled the bathtub with hot water, and Jack soaked himself for an hour before going to bed.[45]

In the final weeks of the campaign, friction developed between Kennedy's massive, finely tuned personal organization and those working for Governor Dever's reelection. Dever's people insisted on a combined effort—joint appearances and advertisements.

All over the state, perennial ward heelers expressed irritation with what they thought was the Kennedy campaign's aloofness. Pittsfield's Democratic Party regulars, sitting on chairs in an abandoned greeting card shop, peered enviously at the plush Kennedy headquarters in the lobby of a local hotel.

Why were the regular Democrats being bypassed? they asked. Why weren't they invited to sit in on the Kennedy meetings? Why did Pittsfield's mayor, Robert T. Capeless, Kennedy's local campaign manager, give party regulars the brush-off?

"We had in fact cooperated with Dever in Boston, where the party organization was strong, but we knew that association with Governor Dever beyond that would hurt us," said Larry O'Brien. "Yet we didn't want an angry, public break with the regular organization, so we had to handle the situation with extreme care." Kennedy declared that he was too tightly scheduled to allow for more than a few appearances with Dever.[46]

Several days before the election, Joe Kennedy convened a top-level meeting at his rented apartment in Boston. He had arranged chairs in a circle. Standing in the middle, he dramatically announced: "Gentlemen, I think that the campaign is over and we have won. The only way that we can lose it is if we make a mistake, and we are not going to make any mistakes from here on because I'm going to make all the decisions."

With Jack physically and emotionally exhausted, the primary concern was to make him look healthy in an upcoming fifteen-minute live television broadcast. Appearing drained and exhausted on live television might be the dreaded big mistake. Instead of exposing him to the danger, the strategists agreed to splice together film clips of Jack earlier in the campaign. The ploy proved effective.

Jack was confident that he would win, and that Eisenhower would defeat Stevenson. On the evening of election day, but before the ballots were counted, Jack said to Torbert Macdonald, "I wonder what sort of job that Ike will give Cabot."[47]

Kennedy beat Lodge by 1,211,984 to 1,141,247, a margin of over 70,000 votes. Eisenhower won the presidency, and in Massachusetts defeated Stevenson by 208,800 votes. Dever narrowly lost the governor's race to Christian Herter. "Like a sapling, left standing amid uprooted oaks, Kennedy was suddenly the dominant political figure in the state, eclipsing even [John] McCormack," said Burns.

Later, when critics suggested that his millionaire father had bought his Senate election, Jack grew indignant. "It wasn't the Kennedy name and the Kennedy money that won that election. I beat Lodge because I hustled for three years. I worked for what I got. I worked for it."

Political commentators repeatedly commented on the high level of the campaigns conducted by both Kennedy and Lodge. One of Jack's publicity agents noted late in the campaign that Kennedy took a firm stand on veracity: "He is tough to do publicity for because he insists that no corners be cut and is meticulous as far as truth and honesty are concerned." Lodge held no animosity toward his opponent. He later said that Jack "had a tremendous and well-deserved popularity" and was an extraordinarily likable man. "In fact, I liked him," said Lodge. "So often in a campaign, you look for a man's faults and then campaign on them. Well, in his case, you didn't do that."[48]

During the campaign Larry O'Brien spent a few days at the Kennedy home in Hyannis Port. At breakfast one morning Joe Kennedy looked O'Brien in the eye and said, "Larry, Jack is a man of destiny. He is going to defeat Lodge and serve with distinction in the Senate and eventually he is going to be President of the United States."[49]

12

ROOKIE SENATOR, ROOKIE HUSBAND

In Kennedy's transition from congressman to senator, his staff underwent two major changes. In 1951, following a dispute with Kennedy, Eddie Sutton left the staff. Mary Davis resigned as Jack's personal secretary after the 1952 election because she was unhappy with her salary.

To replace Davis, Jack hired Evelyn Lincoln, who remained his personal secretary for the next eleven years. The daughter of a Methodist minister, the unsophisticated Lincoln was pleasant, tactful, competent, and loyal.

The heavy workload in the office often frustrated Lincoln. She tried to take on too much responsibility, and often felt overwhelmed. "She was worried about whether his clothes had come back from the dry cleaners or whether the barber shop would be open at the time he wanted his appointment," a staff member remarked. By the end of the week a pile of mail had built up on her desk, but rather than let others help her, she insisted on doing the work herself.

Jack appreciated Lincoln, but occasionally grew impatient with her and even pondered her dismissal. In turn, she found the condition of the senator's desk maddening. "It seemed as if someone had taken a waste paper basket and turned it upside down on top of the desk." Each time he left the office "I would rush in, straighten up his desk, and file the papers." When Kennedy returned from the Senate chamber, he was dismayed by Lincoln's cleanup efforts. "How can you ever expect me to find anything? Why don't you leave my desk alone?"[1]

While Kennedy was seeking a new legislative assistant, one young applicant's exceptional academic background and success in publishing articles impressed him. After two brief interviews, he hired Theodore Sorensen, commencing one of the most important political partnerships in modern American history.

Sorensen grew up in Lincoln, Nebraska, where his father, C. A. Sorensen, was prominent in Nebraska politics. A staunch supporter of Senator George Norris, Nebraska's maverick progressive Republican, C.A. managed several of the senator's campaigns and also won two terms as Nebraska's attorney general. His four sons came to share their father's liberalism and avid interest in politics. Young Ted's mother, Annis Chaikin, a descendant of Russian Jews, had been a suffragette and was an activist in the League of Women Voters. "The Sorensens," a family friend commented, "came campaigning from the womb."

Ted Sorensen starred on his high school debate team, earned Phi Beta Kappa at the University of Nebraska, graduated first in his class at the university's law school, and edited the *Law Review*. In 1949, while still in law school, he married a college classmate, and they soon had three children, but his obsession with advancing Kennedy's career would later ruin his marriage.[2]

When they started their partnership, Kennedy was thirty-five, Sorensen only twenty-four. Ascetic-looking, with plastic-rimmed glasses, Sorensen would come closer than anyone to being Kennedy's political alter ego. Kennedy was to be his work of art.

Kennedy immediately assigned his new aide to fulfill the campaign promise, "I'll do More for Massachusetts." Needing a concrete legislative program to live up to the slogan, he challenged Sorensen to create one. Sorensen, who had never set foot in Massachusetts, toured the state, listened, and learned. After meeting with journalists, businessmen, bankers, and economists, he prioritized problems, searched for answers, and began framing them into bills. With Kennedy's assistance, he organized New England's senators into a group to work on regional legislative problems.

Soon Jack extolled the talents of his new assistant. "I finally got some brains into my office," he told Tip O'Neill. "I heard a compliment about you a couple of weeks ago," Eunice Shriver wrote Sorensen. "Jack said you are the smartest man he has ever met—including the Senator from Massachusetts."[3]

Sorensen provided a sounding board for Kennedy's ideas, offered advice, and clarified and simplified policies. "What do you think, Ted?" became one of Kennedy's most frequent questions at staff meetings during their eleven years together.

Kennedy and Sorensen both enjoyed ideas, books, and intellectual argument; both were tireless workers, and easily bored by pointless small talk. Nonetheless, they seldom socialized together.

Sorensen's role evolved rapidly—from legislative problems, to speeches, to a book, to general policy, and finally to national politics. At the end of Jack's Senate career Sorensen handled all the political correspondence, scheduled trips and speeches, arranged receptions and meetings, supervised publicity, and researched and wrote speeches and magazine articles.

Although he performed many functions for the senator, his primary task was to paint in words. Kennedy's speeches up to 1953 were workmanlike efforts, but lacked flair. Sorensen provided flair. When Jack delivered a speech, Sorensen faced him in the front row, watching every gesture and listening to the audience reaction. Then he collected comments, digested them, and offered suggestions.[4]

He deluged the Library of Congress with requests for books and other information. (Later, the library staff reported that Kennedy's office signed out more books than any other on Capitol Hill.) He researched topics for speeches and articles that Jack suggested, organized the ideas into a rough draft, incorporated Jack's corrections and additions, and added the final touches, bringing major points into critical focus.

Ambitious, he expected big things from his association with Kennedy. "Stick with me and we'll go places," Sorensen told Gloria Sitrin, his personal secretary. Stories later circulated about tension, real or imagined, between Sorensen and Ted Reardon, but neither allowed friction to surface. What's more, Sorensen quickly superseded Reardon as Kennedy's top staff member. "It seemed to me that there was an effort on Ted Sorensen's part to be closer to the senator . . . and to sort of push Ted Reardon aside," observed office secretary Jean Mannix. If Reardon was resentful, he never showed it. In any case, after 1954 Reardon played a sharply reduced role in Jack's career.[5]

To some senatorial aides Sorensen seemed dour, abrasive, and abrupt. He rarely took time to lunch with other aides, chat in the hall, or trade gossip. They complained that he wouldn't even nod as he passed them in the hall.

Shy and reserved, Sorensen never learned the art of small talk, and his brusqueness struck others as arrogance. "He has to go to the heart of the matter," a colleague asserted. "You can call this arrogance, or you can call it efficiency."

Evelyn Lincoln later remarked that Sorensen was a Rock of Gibraltar in the office. Time meant nothing to him. "He gave it all to the Senator."

Both Kennedy and Sorensen ended up being pragmatic liberals although they arrived at their views from different paths. "Theirs was a gradual intellectual coming-together," said one observer, "with Kennedy moving toward the liberalism that was Sorensen's heritage, and Sorensen moving toward the realism that was Kennedy's heritage."[6]

Kennedy worked at a furious pace. "If he got to an airport ten minutes early," Burns wrote, "he rushed to a phone booth to shower Mrs. Lincoln with instructions or even squeeze in a couple of long-distance calls." When Jack took the wheel of his car, he drove fast and recklessly, oblivious of the danger he posed to himself and others. With a reporter in tow, he sped sixty miles per hour down Washington's city streets. When a policeman pulled Jack's car over, he looked at Jack and said, "Oh, Senator Kennedy. Listen, take it a little easy will you, I don't want to have . . ." "Okay, thanks, Officer." On Jack went, racing down a narrow road. "It would scare you to death," the reporter reflected. "He [was] talking all the time."[7]

Many mornings Kennedy seemed to be bursting with new ideas. "I have several things for you to do," he would say to Lincoln as soon as he entered his office. "First . . . second . . . third . . ." Enthusiastically grabbing his mail, he raced through the letters, laughing as he read one from a friend. While dictating letters, he usually paced back and forth in his office; sometimes he stared out the window, or picked up a golf club and swung at an imaginary ball—all the while spewing forth a stream of words and ideas.

Kennedy was assigned three small offices in a suite in the Senate Office Building. He used one himself. A second was split up into two small cubbyholes, one for Ted Reardon, the other for Sorensen and Lee White, another new staff member. Evelyn Lincoln and several other secretaries sat in a third small office where visitors entered.[8]

The senator still insisted that the mail be given immediate attention. "Each person in the office had to make up a little folder indicating how many pieces of mail came in that . . . day, how many of those pieces of mail had been answered [and] what the backlog was," said Helen Lempart, one of the secretaries. "I thought that we had a very smooth-running office at the time, despite the constant tracking of people in and out and the great volume of mail we always got. It was always handled [expeditiously]."

Kennedy's office gained a reputation for responding quickly to requests from constituents. As the reputation grew, so did the volume of requests. Biographer James Burns analyzed constituent relations in Kennedy's office:

Some [requests] were routine: requests for copies of government documents, for help on application for veterans' benefits, for information on passports, and the like. Some were more troublesome: a professor's request for study space in the Library of Congress, a small businessman needing guidance through Washington's bureaucratic maze, a disappointed father anxious to know why his son was turned down at Harvard or George-town. Could the Senator do anything about it?

In a surprising number of cases, the senator and his staff could.

"We had a very warm office, a very friendly office," recalled Jean Man-nix. "We were very anxious to be liked and to be nice to everybody. And we had a very busy office."

Jack seldom raised his voice or expressed anger with a staff member. Al-though usually patient, he disliked inefficiency and incompetence. Sorensen thought that Jack had only one serious weakness as an administrator of his office: He couldn't personally fire anyone. "I keep calling her in for that pur-pose," Jack said to Sorensen of one inefficient female assistant, "but when she comes in looking so hopeful and vulnerable, I give her another assign-ment. . . . You do it."[9]

Kennedy once said to his friend Paul Fay, "I've known a lot of attractive women in my lifetime before I got married, but of all of them there was only one I could have married—and I married her."

In 1951 Jack met that woman, Jacqueline Bouvier, at a small dinner party at the home of journalist Charles Bartlett. A Chicago native and Yale gradu-ate, Bartlett had met Kennedy in Palm Beach after the war. Playing match-maker, Bartlett's wife, Martha, pushed Jack and Jackie together on the couch, trying to ignite a relationship.[10]

Jackie Bouvier was born on Long Island on July 28, 1929, to John "Jack" Bouvier, a stockbroker who had lost most of his money in the Wall Street crash, and Janet, his society-conscious wife. After divorcing her hus-band, Janet was remarried to Hugh D. Auchincloss, who was much wealth-ier and more successful than Jack Bouvier. Jackie attended the fashionable Chapin School in New York and the prestigious Miss Porter's School in Farmington, Connecticut. She and her younger sister Lee spent their child-hood shuttling between Merrywood, the Auchincloss home outside Wash-ington, and Hammersmith Farm, the three-hundred-acre estate in Newport, Rhode Island. Jackie attended Vassar for two years and studied another year at the Sorbonne in Paris before finishing college at George Washington University.

She had a breathless voice, like the Hollywood star Marilyn Monroe, that was not an affectation. Hers was a gilded world of servants, trips to Europe, horse shows, and elegant eighteenth-century French furniture. Fluent in French and Spanish, she cultivated tastes for ballet, opera, fine art, and expen-sive furniture and antiques. "Her genteel life," said one observer, "unlike

Eleanor Roosevelt's, never included exposure to poverty, hardship, or injustice, so she never developed a social consciousness."[11]

Like most young women, Jackie was attracted by Jack's handsome features, charm, wit, and wealth. He was exceptionally eligible and conveniently Catholic, like her. Both enjoyed reading, both were writers, and both had lived abroad.

Joe Kennedy worried that a failed marriage could destroy Jack's political future. Many Catholic voters disdained Adlai Stevenson because he was divorced. And Stevenson was a Protestant. Far worse to be a divorced Catholic politician. Jackie, on the other hand, seemed to have all the vital features that Joe thought would advance his son. Refined and cultured—Jackie had the right religion and was pretty and charming besides.

Their dates consisted of movies and evening games of Chinese checkers and Monopoly with friends. There were evenings, according to Billings, "when they would simply neck in the back seat of Jack's car." Afterward he would drive her home to Merrywood.[12]

Jackie described their courtship as very spasmodic:

> We didn't see each other for six months, because I went to Europe again, and Jack began his summer and fall campaigning in Massachusetts. Then came six months when we were both back. Jack was in Congress, and I was in my last year at George Washington University. But it was still spasmodic, because he spent half of each week in Massachusetts. He'd call me from some oyster bar up there, with a great clinking of coins, to ask me out to the movies the following Wednesday in Washington. . . . He was not the candy-and-flowers type, so every now and then he'd give me a book.

He gave her *The Raven,* a biography of Sam Houston by Marquis James, and *Pilgrim's Way* by John Buchan.

In the summer of 1952, during Jack's campaign for the Senate, Jackie appeared at several speeches and teas. "I guess I'm a Democrat now," she announced. In January 1953, she attended the inaugural ball as Jack's date.[13]

Billings immediately judged Jackie to be different from the other women Jack had dated. "She was more intelligent, more literary, more substantial." Billings added that "Joe Kennedy not only condoned the marriage, he ordained it." A politician needed a wife, and a Catholic politician needed a Catholic wife. She should have class, and Joe Kennedy thought Jackie had more class than any of Jack's previous girlfriends.

That Jack was twelve years older didn't noticeably bother her. She knew generally—not specifically—about Jack's reputation with women, but she remained undaunted. She idolized her father, who was also a womanizer. It bothered her that she differed so much from the seductive, sensual, full-bodied women Jack seemed to prefer; she was highly conscious of her flat figure.[14]

She felt that Jack was a deeply private person, like herself. Both were like "icebergs" with the greater part of their selves invisible. That they both sensed this in each other may have created a special bond.

On June 24, 1953, the couple announced their engagement. On the day of the announcement Jack wrote his friend Red Fay:

> I gave everything a good deal of thought—so am getting married this fall. This means the end of a promising political career as it has been based up to now almost completely on the old sex appeal. . . . I need you to come down the aisle with me. Your special project is the bride's mother—one fine girl—but who has a tendency to think I am not good enough for her daughter, and to talk just a bit too much.

The wedding would take place September 12.[15]

While Jack courted Jackie Bouvier and became engaged, he still pursued other women. When she started work in Jack's Senate office early in 1953, one of Evelyn Lincoln's most unusual secretarial duties was calling her boss's girlfriends to ask them for a date to go to the movies. "The mood seemed to strike him suddenly. We would go through the entire operation, sometimes spending an hour or more of constant telephoning to locate the girl. He always seemed very anxious to see her that evening and no one else would do. Then, as often as not, I would never hear her name mentioned again. . . .

"The women chased him," Lincoln continued. "I had seen nothing like it in my whole life. Half my telephone calls were women." Even after the engagement announcement, women continued to phone him at his office.[16]

One woman who saw his worst side was Margaret Coit. A distinguished writer, she met the senator in the early spring of 1953 while researching her biography of Bernard Baruch. Three years earlier she had published *John C. Calhoun, American Portrait,* which met with critical acclaim and earned her the Pulitzer Prize for biography.

Phi Beta Kappa in college, single, two years younger than Kennedy, Coit was working as a Massachusetts newspaper columnist. She had already interviewed fifteen senators about Baruch, and spoke with Kennedy three times. Following the third interview he offered to drive her to her run-down rooming house in the southeast section of Washington. "I had designs on John F. Kennedy," she later frankly admitted. "Everybody in Massachusetts did. . . . He was the golden boy, the most eligible bachelor in New England."

As they drove by the White House, Kennedy turned unusually serious, almost solemn. "One day that's going to be my home," she said he told her.

He was impressed to learn that Coit had won a Pulitzer Prize. "He found it hard to believe that a woman had any intellect," she recalled. Later he asked her, "Why don't you write a book about me? What I am interested in is me. Why don't you write a book about me?"[17]

She invited him into her rooming house, and as they sat on her sofa, he began to seduce her. He tried to drag her down beside him, and they struggled.

"Wait a minute," said Coit. "I made up my mind that I was not going to kiss you on the first date."

"This isn't a first date," he answered. "We have been making eyes at each other three times now." Then he lunged for her.

"Let me talk to you," she said. "I have standards, just like your sisters. You wouldn't want me to do anything you wouldn't want your sisters to do, would you?"

Kennedy said he didn't care what his sisters did. He grabbed her again.

"What about your priest?" Coit asked. "What will you tell him?"

"Oh, he'll forgive me," said Kennedy, grinning as he pressed her to the couch.

"This is only our first date," she repeated. "We've got plenty of time."

Kennedy raised his head and looked deeply into her eyes. "I can't wait," he said in a cold, mechanical, robotlike voice. "I'm going to grab everything I want. You see, I haven't any time."

When she persisted in rejecting his advances, he turned wild. "I'm sad; I'm gay; I'm melancholy; I'm gloomy—I'm all mixed up, and I don't know how I am!"

His demeanor frightened Coit:

> He was so cold. It was as if he had shifted gears. We had been talking about books and ideas and my concepts of the books on Baruch, and then he had seen me as one kind of person. He had seen me as a mind; and now he saw me just as something female. He couldn't fit the two together, and it was as if he were two parts. He was like a fourteen-year-old high school football player on the make; and he was like an elder statesman of sixty in his intellectual process.

Throughout their encounter Kennedy had been restless and impatient. "Everything he did was sudden and abrupt with me," she recalled. "When he jumped at me, it was just as if he shifted a gear going from one thing to another with no time, no buildup, no preparation."

The next time she saw Kennedy was five years later, in 1958, and he was warm and charming, acting as if nothing unusual had happened earlier.[18]

In August 1953, a few weeks before his marriage to Jackie, Kennedy vacationed on the French Riviera. There a friend introduced him to Gunilla Von Post, a twenty-one-year-old Swedish woman, sparking a bittersweet romance lasting two years. The story of their relationship comes entirely from Von Post's recollections in her autobiography, *Love Jack* (1997).

"His eyes were intensely blue," she noticed, "sparkling with joy." As they were introduced, Kennedy "looked straight into my eyes."

Kennedy moved fast, overwhelming Von Post. When she asked the whereabouts of a woman friend he had earlier been with, he replied with a smile and downcast eyes, "I don't know. I don't care, actually. I'm here with you now." By nightfall they were dancing together. "I feel as though I'm dancing with one of the most exciting, enchanting women in the world," he said, "and I'm very happy."

He kissed her tenderly, and "my breath was taken away," she said. She found conversation easy with him. "When he asked questions, he really seemed interested in the answers."

After one evening of intense romance, Jack informed her that he had something important to tell her. He rubbed his cheek nervously. Von Post recalled their conversation:

> "I'm going back to the United States next week to get married," he said.
>
> My shiver turned to a chill. I pulled my silk shawl tightly around my shoulders.
>
> "If I had met you one week before," Jack continued, "I would have canceled the whole thing."
>
> I glanced at him. His expression was one I hadn't seen before then that night. He looked defeated and sad. There were no words to describe the emotional tension in the air.

Soon after, Jack returned to the United States, but his relationship with Von Post had only begun.[19]

Before the wedding on September 12, Hugh Auchincloss hosted a bachelor dinner at the Clambake Club, an exclusive Newport retreat. Jack quizzed Paul Fay about the protocol for such an affair.

"There is really only one thing to keep in mind," Fay told him. "That is for you to be sure to offer the first toast to the bride. And when the glasses are drained, no one should drink out of them again. They should be thrown into the fireplace."

Jack nodded.

At the dinner Jack stood up and said solemnly, "Gentlemen I want you all to rise and drink a toast to my lovely bride." All the guests stood and drained their glasses.

Then Jack said, "Into the fireplace. We will not drink out of these glasses again."

All the guests tossed their glasses into the fireplace.

The shaken Hugh Auchincloss called the waiter to replace the glasses.

As soon as the new crystal was set on the table, Jack rose again from his chair.

"Maybe this isn't the accepted custom," he said, "but I want to again express my love for this girl I'm going to marry. A toast to the bride."

Everyone toasted a second time, and once again smashed the expensive glasses into the fireplace.

By this time the stunned Auchincloss had seen enough damage.

"When the next set of glasses came in, they could have fitted very nicely into the rack at Healy's ten-cent restaurant," said Fay.[20]

Robert Kennedy served as best man; brother Ted, Charles Bartlett, Senator George Smathers, LeMoyne Billings, and Torbert Macdonald were among the fourteen ushers. Two thousand onlookers outside St. Mary's Catholic Church in Newport waited to get a glimpse of the couple through the open doors of the church. The guests, who included the nation's political, social, and economic elite, filled every pew, and some stood in the back of the church.

One hitch marred the wedding day. The bride's father, John Bouvier, who was to give away his daughter and had gone through the rehearsal the day before, was reported ill. Instead, Hugh Auchincloss walked his step-daughter down the aisle. Archbishop Richard J. Cushing celebrated the nuptial Mass and read a special blessing from the pope. To the accompaniment of "Ave Maria" and "Panis Angelicus," the couple knelt at the flower-decorated altar and recited their vows.[21]

As Jackie appeared before the crowd for the first time as Mrs. John Kennedy, Jack gently tugged on her arm to stand for a while on the top of the church steps to pose for news photos. She grimaced, but complied. Tired of having their view blocked by the photographers, the throng of onlookers surged forward, knocking over police barricades and No Parking signs. The crowd "nearly crushed the bride," *The New York Times* reported.

Twelve hundred guests attended the reception at Hammersmith Farm overlooking Narragansett Bay. A buffet was served in the house and on the terraces and lawns outside. The newlyweds distributed pieces of the five-tiered, four-foot-tall wedding cake as white-jacketed waiters served trays of champagne to guests.

Following a few days in Acapulco, the newlyweds flew to Los Angeles, where they stayed for a week in the Beverly Hills mansion of Marion Davies, the mistress of the late William Randolph Hearst. Next it was on to San Francisco to spend several days with Red Fay and his wife, Anita. After returning to Washington, the couple moved into a rented home at 3321 Dent Place in Georgetown.[22]

Back at the capital, Kennedy faced a controversial vote. His adviser and former speechwriter, Joseph Healey, remembered Kennedy pacing the floor agonizing about his stance. It was early January 1954. "Joe, I just don't know what to do on this one. It's one of the toughest that I've had to decide. I'm trying to balance the national good against the interest of my own state and the New England area." He had spent many hours trying to decide the position he should take on building the St. Lawrence Seaway.[23]

The vast, controversial seaway project had been kicked around for over fifty years. In 1895, recognizing the possible need for a deep waterway into the interior of North America, the United States and Canada established a Deep Waterway Commission, commencing one of the longest political battles in United States history. The goal was to build a series of locks and dams through the impassable sections of the International Rapids in the St. Lawrence River, opening the North American heartland to ocean shipping and unleashing an enormous flow of new electric power.

The project proved a daunting engineering challenge, but the most formidable obstacle during the next fifty years of weary debate was the antiseaway lobby. "The coalition," said one account of the controversy, "has managed to frustrate the efforts of every U.S. President since Wilson and every New York governor since Al Smith to push the seaway through Congress."

Chambers of commerce, coal companies, railroad labor unions, miners, many private utilities, sundry industries, towns large and small, and many states worried about competition with the Midwest—all opposed the project. The national St. Lawrence Project Conference, an umbrella organization that lobbied on behalf of all the opponents of the seaway, distributed antiseaway literature with such titles as "Iceway" and "The Great Delusion."

The seaway project had obvious advantages. It would transform Chicago, Detroit, Cleveland, and Toronto into deepwater ports; provide a low-cost inland route for shipment of iron ore to Midwestern steel mills; speed overseas shipment of U.S. and Canadian farm products; and pump electric energy into New York, Ontario, and Quebec.[24]

Early in 1954 the proposal came before the Senate again. On six different occasions over the previous twenty years, not one senator or congressman from Massachusetts had ever voted in favor of building the seaway. New England shipping, dockworkers, railroads, and other commercial interests were convinced it would hurt them. After World War II Senator Lodge led the opposition to the seaway in the Senate. Kennedy had gone on record against it during his 1952 Senate campaign. Massachusetts's other senator, Leverett Saltonstall, in one of his few disagreements with President Eisenhower, also opposed the project.

Kennedy assigned Sorensen to conduct an objective study of the project. Sorensen reported that the seaway would not do severe harm to Massachusetts, as often alleged, and was unquestionably in the national interest. In all probability Canada would build it alone if the United States continued to dally.[25]

On January 5, 1954, Sorensen sent Jack a memo outlining possible legislative projects for the upcoming year. Included among Sorensen's observations was the following: "I have assumed that you would have no hesitation in tackling issues with a responsible and/or bipartisan, although not necessarily popular and vote-getting, approach, including at least one issue with presumably little or no direct vote-getting appeal in Massachusetts."

Highlighted as the primary issue in this category was the upcoming debate on the St. Lawrence Seaway. Jack ordered a speech drafted to endorse the project, but withheld a final decision.[26]

Debate on the Senate floor started on January 13, 1954, and lasted one week. Jack was to take the floor on the second day. According to Sorensen, on January 14 he still hesitated. "Then, with a shake of his head—a shake I would often see, meaning 'Well, this is what I must do, for better or worse'— he walked over to the Senate floor and delivered the speech."

He focused primarily on two questions. Would the St. Lawrence Seaway be built regardless of the Senate's action? He answered yes. Was it in the national interest to participate in building it? Again, he answered in the affirmative.

Foreign trade would be lost by the port of Boston, but only "an extremely small percentage." Nor would New England railroads seriously suffer from the project. Would the St. Lawrence Seaway help Massachusetts? He admitted that it probably would not. "I know of no direct economic benefit to the economy of Massachusetts or any segment thereof from the Seaway, and I have been urged to oppose the Seaway on these grounds, inasmuch as the initial investment, even though repaid, will come in part from Massachusetts tax revenues."

But, he concluded, he couldn't take a narrow view of his functions as a United States senator:

> I have sought the support of Senators from all sections of the country in
> my efforts on behalf of New England, pointing out to them not only the
> concern which they should have for an important region in our country,

but also the fact that an increase in economic activity in New England would benefit the nation as a whole. For these reasons, I cannot oppose the seaway because the direct economic benefits will go largely to the Great Lakes and Middle Western areas.[27]

A "fine and very thoughtful speech," commented New York's Democratic senator Herbert Lehman. It was indeed, but in his effort to be thoughtful, fair, and statesmanlike, he seemed, as James Burns observed, "deliberately to drain any element of drama out of his action." The speech was dry and logical, but remarkably candid. Sorensen stood proudly at the back of the Senate chamber as Kennedy spoke. Afterward he distributed copies of the address to reporters who crowded around him.[28]

The anger against Kennedy was not as intense as had been anticipated. The *Boston Post* blamed him for "ruining New England," and a friend on the Boston City Council warned him not to march in the upcoming St. Patrick's Day parade because of potential harassment. (He marched anyway.) Critics charged that Kennedy's vote was influenced by his father's ownership of the Merchandise Mart in Chicago. (The Merchandise Mart would inevitably benefit from the expected economic boom in the Great Lakes region.) But there is no evidence to support the contention. Kennedy wanted "to recognize what was right and speak up for it," said Sorensen, who conceded that the speech "certainly had the effect of making [Kennedy] a national figure."

The defection of Kennedy, from a key antiseaway state, weakened the opposition and gave the bill a better chance for passage. On May 13, 1954, President Eisenhower signed the legislation. The St. Lawrence Seaway and Power Project, finally completed in 1959, ranks among the greatest engineering feats of all time. "If ever I saw a person make a decision in conscience and on the merits," said Joe Healey, "it was the St. Lawrence Seaway decision made by Jack Kennedy."[29]

In February 1954, Kennedy started to fulfill one of his major campaign promises. He visited Senator Saltonstall's office and proposed that all the New England senators, Democrats and Republicans, meet periodically to discuss economic problems facing New England. Regional economic problems might be alleviated by mutual consultation and planning. The region's Washington representatives could discuss federal policies on employment, taxation, government contracts, transportation rates, power development, and water projects. Saltonstall liked the idea, and the two agreed to ask Senator Henry Styles Bridges, New Hampshire Republican, and Senator Theodore Greene, Rhode Island Democrat, the region's senior senators, to invite the other senators to a luncheon. Greene and Bridges agreed to preside. On

March 5, 1954, eight of New England's twelve senators met over lunch to discuss their plans.[30]

Being in the spotlight as an advocate for New England bolstered Jack's political stock in the region. The New England Conference of Senators earned plaudits from newspapers throughout the area. New England "has many problems common to all six states, but the individual states are too small to solve them separately," wrote a newspaper in Maine in praise of the conference. "It would seem that a great deal might be accomplished through this cooperative approach."

The group met with representatives of the New England fishing, textile, rubber, and electronics industries. At one meeting in Kennedy's office to improve the port of Boston, said Tip O'Neill, "We had every department head from the government who had anything to do with shipping United States materials overseas."[31]

The conference pushed legislative projects on the price of wool, a minimum wage in the woolen industry, a lower tariff on raw wool imports, wage studies of southern textile manufacturing, shipbuilding contracts at the Fore River Shipyard in Quincy, funds to rehabilitate the Boston Army Base Pier, and a longshoremen safety bill.

Kennedy delivered several Senate speeches on conference issues. When colleagues quizzed him, Jack's articulate responses displayed complete mastery of the complex subjects. His performance impressed Senator Hubert Humphrey, Democrat of Minnesota. "He'd make [the speeches] late in the day. They were very well documented, . . . very well developed, thought out speeches."

All in all, the New England Conference of Senators was impressive. "For a freshman, traditionally expected to be properly passive during his senatorial nonage, [Kennedy's] performance was bold," said historian Herbert Parmet.[32]

The conference cemented a warm friendship between Massachusetts's two senators. "[Kennedy] was very instrumental in the organization of the New England Conference of Senators," Senator Leverett Saltonstall recalled. "He really stimulated that conference."

The Harvard-trained Saltonstall, a lawyer and liberal Republican, had first been elected senator in 1944, after serving five years as governor of Massachusetts. He delighted Kennedy's friends by referring to his new Senate colleague as "Johnny." "I liked him and trusted him," Saltonstall later said. "When he gave me his word, he lived up to it. . . . In fact I don't remember that he ever went back on his word to me in any shape, way, form, or manner."

Despite the efforts of the conference, the region's economy continued to slump. "It was a very depressing experience for the senator," said Harvard economist Seymour Harris, who was advising Kennedy.[33]

13

---❖---

McCARTHYISM, AGONY,
AND COURAGE

K ennedy's difficulty with the McCarthy dilemma resurfaced after the
1952 election, and Robert Kennedy's new job was part of the
problem. Early in 1953, probably at the request of Joseph Kennedy,
the newly reelected Senator McCarthy created a position on his staff for
Bobby, who eagerly accepted. From January to July 1953, Bobby served as
assistant counsel to the Permanent Subcommittee on Investigations, which
McCarthy chaired. (Thanks to Republican control of the Senate, Mc-
Carthy also chaired the subcommittee's parent committee, the Committee
on Government Operations, to which Jack had been assigned.) After seven
months Robert quit following a bitter dispute with McCarthy's aide G.
David Schine and chief counsel Roy Cohn. He worked the rest of the year
for the Hoover Commission, and in 1954 he joined the Democratic opposition as minority counsel for the permanent subcommittee.

RFK passionately agreed with McCarthy about the dangerous threat of
communism and would not speak ill of him. McCarthy's role as an underdog appealed to him. Both Joe Kennedy and Robert attended McCarthy's

wedding in 1953, and Bobby remained on friendly personal terms with McCarthy until the senator's death in early May 1957.[1]

During 1953, when constituents queried Jack about McCarthy, his reply was cautious and legalistic:

> As you know, the Senate Election Subcommittee has recently completed a full report on various questions which have been raised about Senator McCarthy. This report must necessarily be approved by the full Rules Committee prior to its coming to the Senate for action. . . .
>
> I assure you that I am giving attention to this situation, and I am hopeful that the outcome will be the one most desirable for the good of the Senate and the country.

He never explained the "attention" he gave the matter, the "hopeful . . . outcome" he wanted, or what he thought was "most desirable."

Throughout the McCarthy controversy Jack remained preoccupied with other problems and issues—organizing his office, adjusting to married life, focusing on the St. Lawrence Seaway and the problems of the New England economy. At times neither Jack nor Sorensen seemed troubled by McCarthy's shenanigans. On December 11, 1953, Sorensen casually wrote Jack that the office had received only a few letters on a recent spat between McCarthy and Eisenhower. "I am enclosing one exchange of correspondence which we have had with one of my 'liberal' friends, who takes a rather intolerant view of first your reply and then mine. You may wish to dictate an answer to this, or file the whole lot in the well-known circular file."[2]

Although Kennedy remained cautious and didn't criticize the Wisconsin senator, he did publicly go on record against certain McCarthy practices and positions. Joining with the Democratic Party's liberals, in 1953 Kennedy supported the confirmation of Jack's former Harvard president, James Conant, as high commissioner to West Germany, even though McCarthy and his supporters objected to Conant's criticism of parochial education and claimed that Harvard's president held opinions contrary to "the prevailing philosophy of the American people." Kennedy also disregarded McCarthy's opposition in voting to approve Charles Bohlen as ambassador to the Soviet Union.

Again in 1953, Jack voted against the appointment of McCarthy's friend Robert E. Lee to the Federal Communications Commission because he didn't think he was qualified. The story goes that McCarthy was so irritated that he never again spoke with Kennedy. During the confirmation hearing on Lee, Jean Mannix, a secretary in Jack's Senate office, overheard Kennedy say to himself, "John Fox [of the *Boston Post*] and McCarthy are going to be wild about this, but I can't vote for this confirmation. This Bobby Lee's a good Catholic, but I just can't . . . vote for his confirmation."[3]

When Jack voted against McCarthy crony R. W. Scott McLeod as security officer for the State Department, the *Boston Post* lashed out at him. McLeod had been cleaning the "communist coddlers" out of the State Department, the newspaper charged. Kennedy "wasn't elected for the purpose of conducting a sniping campaign against anti-Communists from a bullet-proof pillbox . . . or for acquiring merit with the oh-so-superior liberals." Later Jack also voted against the confirmation of McLeod as ambassador to Ireland.

None of the positions Jack took, though, placed him in the national spotlight as a leading opponent of either McCarthy's methods or his mission.

"I never had the feeling that Jack was a great admirer of Joe McCarthy," said Senator George Smathers. "Jack was not pugnacious, not belligerent." "I know that [JFK] didn't approve of the majority of things McCarthy did," added Jean Mannix, "but I think there was a friendship there and I think that was the problem."[4]

Joe Kennedy counseled Jack not to believe the accusation that McCarthy's anticommunist crusade was damaging relations between the United States and Europe. "I am sending you some clippings from the *SUNDAY OBSERVER,*" he wrote Jack from Paris on July 19, 1954. "It's the only mention I have seen or heard of McCarthy either in France or in Rome. The public isn't the slightest bit interested. . . . As far as strained relations which we have heard so much about, that's a lot of bunk."[5]

After weeks of bitter contention, on March 11, 1954, the army officially filed twenty-nine charges against McCarthy; his subcommittee counsel, Roy Cohn; and the subcommittee's staff director, Francis Carr. The army accused McCarthy and Cohn of seeking preferential military treatment for G. David Schine, a McCarthy staff member who had been drafted into the army. The following day, McCarthy countered that the army had tried to divert his investigation of the army to other branches of the service and that Schine had been held hostage to compel McCarthy to stop his investigation. As a result the Senate established an investigative committee to weigh the charges, and the Army-McCarthy hearings began on April 22, 1954. During thirty-six days of public hearings, millions of television viewers witnessed the arrogant, rude, and bullying McCarthy destroy himself. During the tumult Jack Kennedy said nothing publicly that warranted attention.

On Friday evening, July 30, 1954, Republican senator Ralph Flanders of Vermont introduced a resolution to censure McCarthy. Ninety senators were assembled; the galleries were packed. Jack was also present, holding his speech. Because questions arose about orderly procedure and the absence of formal charges, the Senate set up a special committee headed by Republican senator Arthur Watkins to study the McCarthy censure issue. After the Senate changed its approach, Kennedy took his undelivered speech back to his office and filed it.[6]

On October 21, 1954, Jack underwent spinal surgery in New York, and didn't resume his Senate duties until May 24, 1955. On December 2, 1954, five weeks after Jack entered the hospital, the Senate voted 67 to 22 to censure McCarthy for obstructing the Senate's business, impairing its dignity, and bringing the entire Senate into dishonor and disrepute. Forty-four Democrats voted yea. Recuperating from his back surgery, Kennedy was the only Democrat not present or recorded.

Ted Sorensen later claimed that Kennedy "hoped that the [Watkins] report would be made and final action taken before his scheduled back operation." Sorensen took personal responsibility for not recording Jack on the censure vote, insisting that the senator's failure to be recorded was not due to Jack's indifference. Had the senator been present, Sorensen said, Jack would have voted for censure. "I guessed that my failure to record him would plague him for years to come. But I had been trained in the discipline of due process and civil liberties. An absent juror, who had not been present for the trial or even heard the indictment (which in this case was amended in the course of debate), should not have his predetermined position recorded."[7]

It is impossible to believe that Jack "hoped" he could vote on the Watkins censure report. Of course, Jack was not indifferent to the McCarthy censure; nobody assumed he was. The issue was why he didn't record his vote. Sorensen's argument based on due process and civil liberties has merit, but would have been more convincing if Jack had championed the Bill of Rights during McCarthy's five-year rampage. Later Sorensen conceded that the senator "was sufficiently conscious" in the hospital to send a message that he wanted to be paired with an absent senator who opposed censure. "I think he deliberately did not contact me."

Two years after McCarthy's censure, Jack's undelivered speech resurfaced and was given to reporters; Kennedy's office used it to prove that Jack had been prepared to vote in favor of censure. But the speech did not get Kennedy off the hook with critics of McCarthy. "It may hang him even higher," said a reporter in *The Progressive,* "because he so pointedly refused to criticize McCarthy except on a single narrow ground, and then only because it involved the honor of the Senate."[8]

"This issue involves neither the motives nor the sincerity of the junior Senator from Wisconsin," Jack had intended to say.

Many times I have voted with Senator McCarthy, for the full appropriation of funds for his Committee, for his amendment to reduce our assistance to nations trading with the Communists, and on other matters. I have not sought to end his investigations of Communist subversion, nor is the pending matter related to either the desirability or continuation of these investigations. . . . We are not asked to vote for or against Senator McCarthy, but for or against a motion censuring certain practices in which he acquiesced. . . . I do not feel free to base my vote upon the long past misconduct of Senator McCarthy to which I registered no public objection at that time.

Reflecting Ambassador Kennedy's argument denying alleged international damage caused by McCarthy, Jack said he disagreed "with those who would vote to censure Senator McCarthy in order to conciliate foreign opinion in regard to the United States." Instead, Kennedy based his stand for censure on a narrow technical point. Influenced by Bobby Kennedy's animus, Jack contended that evidence brought out during the Army-McCarthy hearings showed that McCarthy condoned the improper conduct of Cohn and Schine. "The misconduct and abuse of power by a Committee counsel is not merely the concern of his chairman or his Committee," Jack argued.

If his behavior brings disrespect and dishonor, it falls upon the entire Senate. . . . The Senate is faced again with the necessity of reasserting its honor and dignity in the face of an abuse of those privileges affirmed by one of its members. . . . It is an action which serves as a warning to all Senators to guard the dignity of the Senate whenever they entrust Senatorial prerogatives to members of their staff. . . . It is for these reasons and these reasons only, that I shall vote to censure the Junior Senator from Wisconsin.[9]

Why did Kennedy take such a narrow position on a matter that for many Americans—especially liberal Democrats—was the most momentous moral issue of the time? Never answering directly, Jack merely restated his legal reasoning. If there was any objection to McCarthy's conduct prior to 1953, the fight should have been made in January 1953, when the Senate seated McCarthy. McCarthy was entitled to a specific indictment, not just disapproval. "Hell, if you get into the question of just disapproving of Senators, you're going to be in some difficulty. . . . We have never exercised our judgment on our peers very vigorously, and it's probably just as well."

Privately Jack knew his argument for not recording his vote was unconvincing. Aware of the sensitive nature of the issue in Massachusetts, pressured by his father's and his family's wishes, he took advantage of being hospitalized and remained silent.

Shortly before Christmas in 1954, as Jack left his hospital room for his family's home in Palm Beach, he joked with Charles Spalding. "When I get downstairs, I know exactly what's going to happen. Those reporters are go-ing to lean over my stretcher. There's going to be about ninety-five faces bent over me with great concern, and everyone of those guys is going to say, 'Now, Senator, what about McCarthy?' " Jack continued, "Do you know what I'm going to do? I'm going to reach back for my back and I'm just go-ing to yell, 'Oow,' and then I'm going to pull the sheet over my head and hope we can get out of there." Unfortunately for Jack, covering his head from reporters couldn't solve his difficulty with the issue. The ghost of Joe McCarthy continued to plague his career.[10]

After Jack's election to the Senate, his back pain became excruciating. Early in 1954, when he participated in floor debate, he leaned on crutches. Be-cause of the pain, he didn't return to his Senate office between roll calls, choosing instead to remain all day at his seat in the Senate chamber. Evelyn Lincoln carried his appointment book and his mail over to the Senate floor. "Let's keep the appointments down to a minimum," he occasionally told her. "Cancel everyone you possibly can." By the end of May 1954, he used crutches all the time. Senator Saltonstall secured the Senate's permission for him to deliver his remarks while sitting on the arm of his chair.[11]

After Congress adjourned in late August, Jack rested in Hyannis Port, where a team of doctors assessed his condition and his options. Jack's best hope was a complicated operation, they told him, a double fusion of his spinal disks. However, because his Addison's disease lowered his resistance to infections, the operation was extremely dangerous. That same year, noted Doris Goodwin, "in the same hospital where Jack would be admitted, a forty-seven-year-old man with Addison's disease underwent an appendec-tomy and died three weeks later from a massive infection that antibiotics were unable to treat."

Dr. Elmer Bartels, who managed Jack's Addison's disease, recommended conservative treatment—physiotherapy and exercise. "We didn't want him to have any stress other than what was positively necessary," said Bartels, who was "not sold on the need for the operation."

Bartels thought that Jack hadn't taken enough precautions with his back. "It just wasn't his temperament to take care of himself. He played touch football, and you can certainly injure your back playing that." The public still knew nothing about his Addison's disease.[12]

On one occasion Jack glanced at his crutches, punched them with his fist, and said to a friend, "I'd rather die than spend the rest of my life on these things." He insisted on going forward with the surgery, telling his father that he wanted the operation even if his odds of surviving were only fifty-fifty. He would rather be dead than spend the rest of his life hobbling on crutches, paralyzed by pain. At first Joe Kennedy tried to convince him to change his mind. Even confined to a wheelchair, Joe argued, Jack could lead a fairly normal life, like President Franklin Roosevelt, who managed an incredible political career despite his paralysis. But when Jack remained adamant, Joe conceded. "Don't worry, Dad," Jack said. "I'll make it through."

Jack decided to go ahead with the surgery under the care of two prominent New York physicians. One was Dr. Ephraim Shorr, an endocrinologist at the Cornell University Medical College Complex, who was in the forefront of the clinical application of the hormones used to treat Addison's disease, and would mastermind the management of the disease during Jack's surgery. The other was Dr. Philip D. Wilson, a surgeon at the New York Hospital for Special Surgery.

On October 9, 1954, Larry O'Brien and JFK had lunch at the Ritz-Carlton Hotel in Boston. "This is it, Larry," Jack told O'Brien. "This is the one that cures you or kills you."

Lunch over, Jack hauled himself up on his crutches, grinned at O'Brien, and said, "I'll be seeing you." Then he hobbled out to his car. The following day, October 10, he entered the New York Hospital for Special Surgery. Following tests, the operation took place on October 21.[13]

The team of surgeons who operated on Jack described the operation in an article for the *Archives of Surgery* (November 1955). The article explained the unique feature of Jack's surgery and the dilemma it posed. The authors identified Jack as a thirty-seven-year-old man who had had Addison's disease for seven years.

Orthopedic consultation suggested that he might be helped by a lumbosacral fusion together with a sacroiliac fusion. Because of the severe degree of trauma involved in these operations and because of the patient's adrenocortical insufficiency due to Addison's disease, it was deemed dangerous to proceed with these operations. However, since this man would become incapacitated without surgical intervention, it was decided, reluctantly, to perform the operations by doing the two different procedures at different times if necessary and by having a team versed in endocrinology and surgical physiology help in the management of this patient before, during, and after the operation.

Doctors performed the lumbosacral fusion and the sacroiliac fusion at the same time, since Jack's condition remained good. Dr. Wilson was a respected orthopedic surgeon, but his operation on Kennedy was an experimental procedure which turned out to have a low success rate. To stabilize Jack's lower back, Wilson used three screws to bolt a plate onto bone. The operation lasted more than three hours, and required four pints of blood to replenish the amount lost during the surgery. That evening Jack returned to his room in fair condition, but he had a gaping, sickly-looking hole in his back.[14]

A major discrepancy exists in accounts of Jack's condition on the third postoperative day. In their article in the *Archives of Surgery* Dr. Wilson and the other surgeons reported no serious complications following the operation. "The postoperative course was satisfactory in that no Addisonian crisis developed at any time during the next 2 months," said the article. Only "minor complications" occurred—a urinary tract infection on the third postoperative day, a transfusion reaction, and a mild wound infection. "In each instance increased cortisone and salt were given," resulting in a "smooth postoperative course."

Other evidence indicates that the infection on the third day after the operation was a staph infection that nearly killed Jack. Most accounts of his life say he slipped into a coma, was placed on the critical list, and received the last rites of the church. "He nearly died," said Rose. Journalist Arthur Krock later said that during the dark time the ambassador came to his office at *The New York Times*. "He told me he thought Jack was dying and he wept sitting in the chair opposite me in the office."

It is impossible to ignore the testimony of friends and family who reported that Jack was critically ill on the third day following his surgery. Too many people related the same story. Most likely the infection that so worried Dr. Bartels was not managed as successfully as the New York team of doctors reported in the *Archives of Surgery*. The authors probably downplayed his critical condition after the operation to make their work appear more impressive to their peers.[15]

On December 21, Kennedy left the hospital to recuperate at his father's home in Palm Beach. During his long absence, his office staff tried to pick up the slack. "It was months before we would ever bother him with anything because he was so seriously ill," said Jean Mannix. Still receiving tons of mail, his staff usually replied to letter writers, "In the absence of the senator, who is recuperating . . ." Sorensen and Reardon assumed the burden of the senator's legislative work, keeping an eye on legislation in his committees, answering correspondence, and placing the senator's name on bills he endorsed.

Sorensen worked on state problems and consulted with Senator Saltonstall. "We never had any real differences of opinion regarding Massachusetts questions," said the senior senator, "and I found Sorensen very helpful." (After Kennedy returned to work, Saltonstall remarked about his excellent relations with Sorensen. Jack replied with a smile, "Oh, you dealt with Senator Sorensen.")[16]

For months after his operation, persistent rumors in the Senate cloakroom raised doubts whether Kennedy would ever walk again unaided. Racked with constant pain—with the scar on his back over eight inches long—Jack thought the operation had failed. His spirits sagged. "It was a terrible time," Billings recalled. "He was bitter and low. We came close to losing him. I don't just mean losing his life. I mean losing him as a person."

In January Robert Kennedy phoned Paul Fay and asked him to come to Florida. "The doctor felt that [Jack] was losing interest," Fay recalled, "and a visit from someone closely associated with happier times might help him regain his usual optimism and enjoyment of life." Fay spent ten days in Palm Beach. Billings took a monthlong leave of absence from his marketing job to be with Jack.[17]

In mid-February 1955, Kennedy was flown back to New York, where Dr. Wilson performed another operation to remove the metal plate installed during the first one. The plate had probably been infected. In any case, doctors had to remove the three screws and the plate and added bone graft. On February 25, 1955, he left the hospital and resumed his convalescence in Palm Beach.

After the two operations there was evidence of erosion and loss of bone in the center portion of the left sacroiliac joint where Wilson had operated. Moreover, the fusion Wilson attempted apparently never became solid.

After Wilson's operations the problem of explaining Jack's continuing back pain was complicated by the surgical trauma, scarring, and wound infection, all of which caused mechanical vulnerability of the lower lumbar spine, and no doubt contributed to ongoing chronic recurrent low back and leg symptoms.

There is no orthopedic evidence that JFK ever had a ruptured intervertebral lumbar disk or a congenitally weak or unstable back. The most appropriate management overall for his low back pain would have been exercises and other conservative measures rather than operative treatment.

In Palm Beach, at first a hired nurse changed Jack's dressings; after several weeks Jackie assumed the responsibility. "The incision was very large, it was still draining, and the dressings had to be changed several times a day," recalled Rose Kennedy. "She did this skillfully and gently and calmly, and made no comment about it to anyone."

"Jackie was magnificent with him," said Charles Bartlett. "She had this almost uncanny ability to rise to the occasion. She sat with him for hours, held his hand, mopped his brow, fed him, helped him in and out of bed, put on his socks and slippers for him, entertained him by reading aloud and reciting poems she knew by heart, bought him silly little gadgets and toys to make him laugh, played checkers, Categories and Twenty Questions with him." One day she gave him a popgun and balloons for him to shoot at. When his condition improved, she encouraged friends to visit, hoping to distract him from the pain. "Jack is feeling lousy. Come on down."[18]

At a dinner party the beautiful young actress Grace Kelly met Jackie and her sister Lee for the first time. "They asked me to go to the hospital with them to pay a visit and help cheer him up. They wanted me to go into his room and say I was the new night nurse." She reluctantly agreed. Embarrassed, she hesitated before entering his room. "Eventually I was sort of pushed into his room by the two girls. I introduced myself, but he had recognized me at once, and couldn't have been sweeter or more quick to put me at ease."

Because of his discomfort, Jack couldn't sit or lie down in one position for long. While confined to his bed during the day, he worked on his book about political courage and talked by telephone with his office. In the evening he watched television or read for pleasure.

On March 1, 1955, he gingerly walked without crutches for the first time. The next day, dressed in shorts and a baseball cap, he managed to walk to the beach with Jackie and Dave Powers steadying him. "He stood there," Powers recalled, "feeling the warm salt water on his bare feet, and broke into a big smile."[19]

On May 24, seven and a half months after entering the hospital for his first back operation, Jack returned to the Senate. As he got off the elevator near his third-floor office a swarm of newsmen and photographers met him. He walked through his office shaking hands, greeting his smiling secretarial staff. As he entered his inner office, he found a camera crew had already set up its floodlights. On his desk was a large basket of fruit and candy with a note saying, "Welcome home, Dick Nixon."

He was to observe his thirty-eighth birthday on May 29.

"I'm looking forward to it," he said. "I'll certainly be glad to get out of my thirty-seventh year."

Reporters peppered him with questions.

Will Ike run again?

"I don't know," Kennedy responded, laughing.

Wasn't the president's strength just as strong everywhere as it had been since he entered the White House?

"Well," replied Kennedy, smiling, "I've been in a pretty limited area. I'll say that he seems to be standing up well in Palm Beach." Everyone laughed.

How had he found reading the *Congressional Record* each day?

"An inspiring experience," replied Kennedy, again evoking laughter.

Had he really read it through all the way?

"Well, I hit the highlights."

Jack planned to make every roll call, he said, starting with a vote to override President Eisenhower's veto of the bill increasing postal workers' pay. Senator Harry Byrd, Democrat of Virginia, offered him the use of a private office near the Senate floor.[20]

Upon his return he embarked on an ambitious schedule of activities. His engagements started June 3 with a commencement address at the Assumption College graduation in Worcester, another address at Boston College's graduation on June 5, and the Jefferson-Jackson Day dinner on June 9.

On June 10, Kennedy entertained about three hundred state legislators and legislative assistants, both Republicans and Democrats, at the Kennedy compound in Hyannis Port. Following a luncheon at the Hyannis Port Golf Club, guests played golf, baseball, and touch football, and even did some trap shooting. Then on June 16 he attended the fifteenth-year reunion of his Harvard class.[21]

All in all, it was a joyous homecoming. Friends sensed a more serious tone in the months following his return. "He had gone through the valley of the shadow of death," said one.

"I wasn't afraid of dying when I was in the hospital," Jack later observed, one of the few times he talked about his feelings during his ordeal. "In fact, I almost welcomed it. Because I didn't want to live the rest of my life the way I was living. The pain was so bad. I could [temporarily] stand the pain, but couldn't bear the thought of living the rest of my life with that kind of pain."

There was a surreal quality about Jack's return to the Senate. He looked relatively healthy, and was embarking on an ambitious schedule. As far as the public knew, his back surgery had succeeded and his recovery was complete. In fact, he still suffered excruciating back pain, and physicians would soon discover a host of other ailments as well.[22]

In the spring of 1954, Ted Sorensen walked into Kennedy's office while the senator was reading historian Herbert Agar's *A Time for Greatness*. Kennedy showed him a page describing when John Quincy Adams courageously voted against the Louisiana Purchase and in favor of Jefferson's Embargo Act, both unpopular votes in Adams's Massachusetts. Like the senator, Sorensen found the passage fascinating. "How about using this one and some other examples [of political courage] and put it together for *Harper's* or *Atlantic Monthly*?" suggested Kennedy. Sorensen liked the idea. Several others were recruited to assist with the project, including Joe Kennedy's associate Jim Landis, and Jules Davids, a history professor at Georgetown. (Davids, Jackie Kennedy's recent instructor for a college history course, thought that a lecture he gave on political courage may have led her to mention the subject to her husband.)

In early 1955 the idea of expanding the material into a book gained momentum. Sorensen worked with several clerical assistants, who took dictation, transcribed from Dictabelts, and typed. Instead of an article suitable for a magazine, they visualized a short book, possibly titled "Patterns of Political Courage."[23]

Harper and Brothers came through with a book contract in April 1955 (which included a five-hundred-dollar advance). The publisher assigned Evan Thomas, the son of the famous American socialist, as the book's editor. Thomas suggested that Kennedy consider such alternative titles as "These Brave Men" and "The Patriots." Subsequently the publisher settled on *Profiles in Courage*.

From Washington Sorensen mailed a steady stream of material to the senator's bedside in Palm Beach. He claimed that JFK sent instructions almost daily by letter and sometimes telephone about "books to ship down, memoranda to prepare, sources to check, materials to assemble."[24]

During the first half of 1955, Sorensen spent most of his time on the book, often putting in twelve-hour days. Sorensen and Davids checked out about six hundred items from the Library of Congress. In February 1955, Sorensen wrote his boss that the "monumental work" was the "most gigantic undertaking we have ever gigantically undertaken; and I doubt whether Gibbon could have produced 'The Decline and Fall of the Roman Empire' in a proportionately brief time."

Sorensen traveled to Palm Beach in March and again in May, each time for about ten days. "I brought a secretary with me, and he had his secretary, and we divided the work," said Sorensen; "he dictated to his secretary and I dictated to mine."

"The way Jack worked," continued Sorensen, "was to take all the material, mine and his, pencil it, dictate the fresh copy in his own words, pencil it again, dictate it again—he never used a typewriter."[25]

Instead of a strictly historical and chronological approach, the book focused on eight political leaders—their backgrounds, personalities, motives, and courageous acts. "This does not mean," Sorensen advised the senator, "that we will ignore the historical context in which these individuals performed their acts of political courage, but that primary emphasis will be on the personalities, their courageous acts and the consequences of these acts, rather than on any thorough explanation of the historical background."

Kennedy and Sorensen strove to produce an excellent book and welcomed candid criticism. Davids suggested that the emphasis upon the calamity which followed in the wake of displays of political courage might weaken the inspirational tone; the book would be more inspiring if it *pretended* that justice always triumphed. But Sorensen and JFK rejected the phony intrusion. "I indicated my belief that we not only were willing to admit that political courage often resulted in tragedy," Sorensen wrote the senator, "but that we believed the drama and significance—and probably the inspirational value—of each story was heightened by a description of the difficulties which followed [each senator's courageous decision]."[26]

JFK wrote his former teacher Arthur Holcombe on June 23, 1955, "I hope you will be ruthlessly frank in giving me your criticisms, comments and suggestions, however major or however petty—not only on the historical accuracy of these chapters, but also on the general theme, style, interest and overall contribution." If any or all of the chapters were inadequate, "I would prefer to hear that from you now." Later, when one segment was about to go into production for *Kraft Television Theatre,* Kennedy insisted on the final right of approval on any program arrangements or advertising materials because he worried about his name being associated with a "second rate, cheap or badly commercialized production."

The book became a collection of stories about eight political leaders whose courage at critical moments had led them to resist their constituents and defy their colleagues in order to serve a broader or national good, much as Kennedy thought he had done on the St. Lawrence Seaway issue.

John Quincy Adams defied the interests of Massachusetts by supporting both the Louisiana Purchase and Jefferson's Embargo Act. Daniel Webster pleaded for tolerance and spoke—not as a Massachusetts man, nor as a Northern man, but as an American—in favor of the Compromise of 1850. Thomas Hart Benton struggled to keep Missouri from joining the Southern confederacy. Sam Houston aroused opposition by voting for the Kansas-Nebraska Act of 1854. Republican senator Edmund Ross of Kansas defied his state and party to vote against convicting President Andrew Johnson of impeachment charges. After Reconstruction, Lucius Q. C. Lamar of Mississippi eulogized the late Northern abolitionist Charles Sumner, a hated foe of the South, because Lamar wanted to promote national unity rather than continue sectional strife. The book praised young insurgent George Norris for opposing the tyrannical rule of House Speaker Joe Cannon of Illinois. It cited Senator Robert Taft of Ohio for courage in opposing the Nuremberg Trials of Nazi war criminals because the U.S. Constitution prohibited ex post facto laws.[27]

The book was uncomplicated, but clearly, vividly, sometimes dramatically written. Subjects were chosen partly to give political balance—three from the South, three from the Midwest, two from New England. The book judiciously included two Republicans, noted one critic, "lest the Democratic Senator from Massachusetts be accused of making courage a . . . party monopoly." All eight heroes were white males.

In *Profiles* what mattered most was the act of courage, not the individual's ideology. The book praised progressive George Norris and conservative Robert Taft. Daniel Webster was courageous because he supported the Compromise of 1850, while Senator Thomas Hart Benton was courageous because he opposed it. One man exposed himself to damaging criticism in Massachusetts; the other, to damaging criticism in Missouri. Any philosophy or ideology could produce an act of courage. "I make no claim that all those who staked their careers to speak their minds were right," Kennedy wrote.[28]

Profiles found the courage of its subjects not in war, where it is usually featured, but in the intellectual and moral struggles of politics. Often private, undramatic, with no admiring audience to applaud, the courage displayed resulted in the loss of a career or the scorn of the public.

The book portrayed the clay feet of some of the heroes—their venality, ambition, and crudeness. All of them have the "smell of mortality," making their acts of political courage all the more credible and impressive.

The stories were inspirational in tone, as if delivering a civics lesson. Each story reinforced the confident belief that one person with fortitude counted. Kennedy hoped readers would act like the heroes in his book, "for the same basic choice of courage or compliance continually faces us all, whether we fear the anger of constituents, friends, a board of directors or our union, whenever we stand against the flow of opinion on strongly contested issues."[29]

Beneath the surface, though, was a strain of pessimism. Despite the optimistic and inspirational tone, in the twentieth century, as the techniques of government become more complex and impersonal, individual acts of courage were less noticeable, more difficult, and less decisive. "Our political life is becoming so expensive, so mechanized and so dominated by professional politicians and public relations men," Kennedy wrote, "that the idealist who dreams of independent statesmanship is rudely awakened by the necessities of election and accomplishment."

Historian Alonzo Hamby thought *Profiles* "formulated a theory of democracy and political leadership that was more fully developed and more clearly expressed than that of any of [Kennedy's] rivals, including Adlai Stevenson."

Some have assumed that the book was Kennedy's "personal catharsis," a substitute for his uncourageous role in the McCarthy censure controversy. But there is no evidence to support the conjecture, and the book's theme predated the McCarthy censure proceedings.[30]

Kennedy focused most of his attention on an introductory chapter, a vivid and perceptive analysis of the complex forces a political leader faces in acting courageously. In the popular view senators advance politically only as they "placate, appease, bribe, seduce, bamboozle, or otherwise manage to manipulate" the insistent demands of their constituents. "The decisive consideration is not whether the proposition is good but whether it is popular," Kennedy contended.

The path of the conscientious insurgent is usually a lonely one because of the enormous pressure to conform, to get along with fellow legislators, to be a polite member of the club and abide by the clubhouse rules. Pursuing a unique and independent course might embarrass or irritate the other members. "We realize, moreover, that our influence in the club—and the extent to which we can accomplish our objectives and those of our constituents—are dependent in some measure on the esteem with which we are regarded by other Senators." When Kennedy entered Congress, he was told, "The way to get along is to go along."

Legislators want to be reelected and must pay attention to all the forces and pressures which might ruin their careers. "It should not automatically be assumed that this is a wholly selfish motive," JFK observed. Those who have chosen politics as their profession naturally want to continue their careers. "Senators who go down to defeat in a vain defense of a single principle will not be on hand to fight for that or any other principle in the future."

In no other profession except politics do people expect a person to sacrifice honors, prestige, and chosen career to take an unpopular stand on a single issue. "Lawyers, businessmen, teachers, doctors, all face difficult personal decisions involving their integrity—but few, if any, face them in the glare of the spotlight as do those in public office."

Some think there is no problem. "Always do what is right, regardless of whether it is popular. Ignore the pressures, the temptations, the false compromises." But that solution is too simplistic. A senator has obligations to his state, his political party, and, above all, his constituents. "Are we rightfully entitled to ignore the demands of our constituents even if we are able and willing to do so?"

Compromise should not be equated with cowardice. It is "frequently the compromisers and conciliators who are faced with the severest tests of political courage as they oppose the extremist views of their constituents. It was because Daniel Webster conscientiously favored compromise in 1850 that he earned a condemnation unsurpassed in the annals of political history."[31]

In the end Kennedy returned to the primary dilemma: Should a political leader defy his constituents and colleagues in order to serve the national good? According to one school of thought, "If I am to be properly responsive to the will of my constituents, it is my duty to place their principles, not mine, above all else. . . . To be sure, the people will make mistakes—they will get no better government than they deserve—but that is far better than the representative of the people arrogating for himself the right to say he knows better than they what is good for them."

But Kennedy rejected this argument. The legislator should disagree if an issue is great enough to be a matter of conscience. It is not the function of the representative "to serve merely as a seismograph to record shifts in popular opinion." At moments of crisis, democracy requires independent leaders willing to take chances.

The voters select political leaders, in short, because they have confidence in the leaders' judgment and ability. "This may mean that we must on occasion lead, inform, correct and sometimes even ignore constituent opinion, if we are to exercise fully that judgment for which we were elected." Constituents will be the final judges of the wisdom of the course. But political leaders "have faith that those constituents—today, tomorrow or even in another generation—will at least respect the principles that motivated their independent stand."[32]

The book officially appeared on January 1, 1956. Kennedy had instructed the publisher to reinvest 10 percent of all subsidiary earnings for additional promotion and to do the same with his share of the royalties. The book served double—sometimes triple—duty. Prepublication arrangements were made with major magazines and newspapers: *Harper's, Reader's Digest, Collier's, The New York Times Magazine,* and *The Boston Globe.* Usually the senator was pictured along with his courageous heroes.

The book received prominent reviews, most of them containing high praise. A smashing popular success, *Profiles* rose to the top of best-seller lists and remained there for several months. By early June 1957, over one hundred thousand copies had been sold. It was eventually translated into many other languages. "Readers seemed delighted and surprised that a politician—even a politician in the United States Senate—could be so literate," observed James Burns.[33]

"That a United States Senator, a young man of independent means with a gallant and thoughtful background, should have produced this study is as remarkable as it is helpful," wrote editor Erwin D. Canham of *The Christian Science Monitor.* "It is a splendid flag that Senator Kennedy has nailed to his mast. May he keep it there!"

In *The New York Times Book Review* Cabell Phillips expressed satisfaction at having a "first-rate politician write a thoughtful and persuasive book about political integrity." Kennedy's book, concluded Phillips, was "the sort to restore respect for a venerable and much abused profession."

The book proved more popular and politically valuable than Kennedy could ever have imagined. It boosted his stature considerably within the Democratic Party, making him the spokesman for the politics of integrity, and enhanced his image as an insightful student of American history and democratic theory. He became the unofficial historian of the Senate, placed in charge of a subcommittee to honor five outstanding senators from history. On February 7, 1956, he was the featured speaker at the annual National Book Awards dinner in New York City, and was photographed in the illustrious literary company of W. H. Auden and John O'Hara.[34]

Profiles, though, had one unforeseen negative consequence: His position on controversial political issues would from now on be compared to the courageous heroes he had profiled. The book particularly drew attention to what many considered his greatest failure as a senator: his equivocal position on the searing issue of McCarthyism. When historian Arthur Schlesinger Jr. suggested to Kennedy that he had paid a heavy price for giving his book that title, Kennedy replied drily, "Yes, but I didn't have a chapter in it on myself."[35]

14

MARRIED LIFE AND OTHER WOMEN

In 1955 Jack and Jackie paid $125,000 for Hickory Hill in McLean, Virginia, acquired from the estate of the late Supreme Court justice Robert H. Jackson. An old Georgian house of large white brick, with six acres of beautifully landscaped grounds across the Potomac River from Washington, Hickory Hill was only a short distance from the Merrywood estate of Jackie's mother and stepfather. But Hickory Hill proved too large and inconvenient. It was seven miles from the Capitol, and Jack's morning and evening commutes in slow and heavy traffic drove him to distraction.

In 1956, after selling Hickory Hill to Ethel and Bobby, Jack and Jackie rented a smaller home in Georgetown, near their Washington friends and Jack's work, and within walking distance of the movies. In June of the following year they purchased for seventy-eight thousand dollars a redbrick town house at 3307 N Street NW, Georgetown. Built in 1812, the home was similar to other narrow, three-story Georgian houses on the quiet, tree-bordered street. Determined to make their new home look gorgeous, Jackie redid the double living room downstairs at least three times. For a while Jackie decorated almost everything—walls, curtains, upholstery—in different shades of beige. As he looked around, Jack remarked to Mrs. Auchincloss, "Do you think we're prisoners of beige?"[1]

Earlier, in October 1956, the young Kennedys had become Cape Cod taxpayers after purchasing for forty-six thousand dollars the Irving Avenue property in Hyannis Port destined to become the "Summer White House." The home was within the same compound as Joe and Rose's home, only a few hundred feet away. Several years later Bobby and Ethel Kennedy acquired a third home within the compound. The three houses formed a triangle with the back yards adjoining, separated only by shrubs and outbuildings.[2]

The marriage of Jack and Jackie was loving, but distant and sometimes strained. Few ever saw Jack kiss or embrace his wife. Jacqueline's world had not included politics; she had not even bothered to vote. Since Jack seldom discussed political matters with her, she had little sense of participation in his work. Although reserved in public, Jackie did try to assume the proper role of senatorial wife. She followed the Senate debates, joined the gallery whenever Jack gave an important speech, read the *Congressional Record,* answered some of her husband's office mail, and attended political rallies, receptions, luncheons, and a few cocktail parties.

In April 1954, she watched from the Senate gallery as Jack addressed the Indochina situation. Later she told a reporter, "The more I hear Jack talk about such complex problems, the more I feel like a complete moron. So now I am taking courses at the Georgetown University School of Foreign Service—among them a grounding [in] American history."[3]

Duke Zeller, a Senate page, occasionally delivered notes between Jack on the Senate floor and Jackie in the gallery. "They had to be clever and romantic," said Zeller, "because I waited to see if she had a message for him, and as soon as she got them she read them, and they always made her immediately break into a smile."

Sometimes the political ground rules confused her. Historian Arthur Schlesinger Jr. related a story in which Jack complained about a fellow politician. Judging this man an enemy, Jackie glared across the reception room at the offender. Later, when Jack spoke favorably about the same person, she exclaimed, "Are you saying nice things about [him]? I've been hating him for three weeks." Her husband replied, "No, no, that was three weeks ago." In politics, he told her, there rarely are foes, only colleagues. The politician should never get in so heated a quarrel as to lose all chance of conciliation. On a future issue he might have to work with the other fellow again.[4]

Jackie wanted her husband to become more refined, more cultivated, a person with superior taste, style, and manners. She only partially succeeded, but friends and observers noticed an improvement.

When Jack and Eunice shared their house together, they both lived like bachelors, tossing their clothes in a heap, devouring hurried dinners, and rushing to engagements. Ted Reardon had always shown up at the office meticulously dressed and well groomed, but the senator's clothes were often unpressed. Occasionally he asked someone to use Scotch tape to collect the lint off his suit jacket.

If bachelor Jack entertained, he served no wine with dinner, no after-dinner liqueur. A colleague recalled a dinner for three at Kennedy's bachelor quarters: "We had chicken, and we drank Scotch before, during and after dinner." (If Jack hosted a large dinner party, the affair was catered.) "Until he married Jackie he really had no idea about how you should decorate a room or what was the difference between a pretty house and an ugly house, and he certainly had no great feeling about good food or good wine," said Jack's British friend David Ormsby-Gore. Jackie helped make him more refined. Jack now wore sharply cut and perfectly pressed suits, becoming an immaculate dresser.[5]

"I brought a certain amount of order to Jack's life," Jackie later said. "We had good food in our house—not merely the bare staples that he used to have. He no longer went out in the morning with one brown and one black shoe on. His clothes got pressed, and he got to the airport without a mad rush, because I packed for him." She also directed Jack's manservant, George Thomas, to take hot lunches to his Senate office, consisting of chops, potatoes, peas, and Jack's favorite, New England chowder.

The early years of their marriage were hard on Jackie because of the exceptionally busy schedule of her ambitious husband. During the week Jack usually arrived home from his office exhausted. The pain of separation was most acute on weekends when Jack traveled to speaking engagements throughout the country, and she remained alone. "I was alone almost every weekend," she said of the first year of marriage. "It was all wrong. Politics was sort of my enemy and we had no home life whatsoever."

"Sometimes, when he is at home, he is so wrapped up in his work that I might as well be in Alaska," she candidly told a reporter, as if she wanted to send her husband a message. "He rushes to finish dinner so we can turn on TV or get to a movie on time," Jackie told another reporter.[6]

Jack often vacationed without Jackie, usually accompanied by Torby Macdonald, Lem Billings, or George Smathers. For a while he spent Tuesday evenings in Baltimore taking a speed-reading course. He never seemed to understand—or to care—about the damaging effect of his absences on Jackie or on his marriage. He told Billings that his parents had often been separated, and yet their marriage had survived.

Besides Jack's work and his travel, other sources of tension emerged. She disliked some of Jack's old friends and new political pals. Why, for instance, was Lem Billings forever present? The answer was that Jack was easily bored.

"Jack got bored with people—male or female," said Ralph Horton. "His attention span with people was brief. . . . He got bored with Jackie."[7]

Soon after their marriage, Jack began complaining about Jackie's spending habits. He judged them to be almost pathological. "Jack was livid when it came to her spending," George Smathers recalled. "He'd wave the bills in the air and yell, 'Goddammit, she's breaking my ass!' He'd get really worked up about it, turn purple with rage."

"I have to dress well, Jack, so I won't embarrass you," Jackie countered. "As a public figure, you'd be humiliated if I was photographed in some saggy old housedress. Everyone would say your wife is a slob and refuse to vote for you."[8]

"I feel that I have very inadequate control over my own expenses," Jack wrote in 1956 to Tom Walsh, one of the battery of accountants his father employed in New York to manage the family's finances. "Therefore, I think I should sign all of my checks and no one in the New York office should sign any of my checks. As it is now, major expenditures are made and I don't hear about them for several months." He wanted all bills and requests for essential expenditures to be sent to his Senate office, where Evelyn Lincoln would write out the checks and he would sign them. "I do this only because I feel that I have no real knowledge of my month to month disbursements." The New York office agreed, although it continued to manage his federal and state income taxes, and to pay his airline bills and the rent for his Boston office.[9]

Why spend so much money on furniture? After Jackie had purchased several eighteenth-century French chairs, Jack told Ormsby-Gore, "What's the point of spending all this money? I mean a chair is a chair and it's perfectly good the chair I'm sitting in. What's the point of all this fancy stuff?"

Jack merely wanted familiar food and a comfortable, unchanging place in which to read in peace and quiet. But Jackie replaced the wallpaper in Jack's study three times in just a few months. While Jackie changed furnishings, Jack furiously hunted for a comfortable nook. One day he hollered in disgust, "Dammit it, Jackie, why is it that the rooms in this house are never completely livable all at the same time?"

Jackie's primary weapon in her marital arsenal was to sulk. "Jack hated it when people sulked," Charles Spalding said. True, Jack had a temper, but after he blew up, he seldom held a grudge. "He couldn't stand it when somebody gave him the silent treatment."

In Washington, whispered cocktail conversation proclaimed the Kennedy marriage in trouble. In his newspaper column Drew Pearson reported gossip of a divorce.[10]

The dynamic, frenzied pace of the Kennedy clan also caused stress for Jackie, but she eventually adjusted. She had less resilience and energy, and far less athletic prowess, than the other Kennedy women. She enjoyed sports—horseback riding and water skiing—but not the ferociously competitive games and group athletic contests the Kennedys preferred.

"They never relax even when they're relaxing," she marveled. "After dinner they all play guessing games like Categories or Charades or Twenty Questions—you're doing mental somersaults all the time." Usually all the Kennedys were on one side and all their friends and in-laws were on the other.

She once remarked to Jean Smith, her closest friend among the Kennedy women, "You all play Monopoly as if you really owned the property." Describing an evening when all the Kennedys were playing Monopoly after an exhausting day of outdoor sports, Jackie said, "I get so sleepy that I make a mistake deliberately to end the game."

A reporter asked, "Does Jack mind?"

"Not if I'm on the other side."

She didn't want to exhaust herself playing tennis or touch football, preferring instead to paint or read. Rather than move in a convoy, she preferred to move by herself. The conversation she enjoyed was not necessarily the normal Kennedy family fare.[11]

At first Jackie tried to maintain the blistering Kennedy pace, but eventually she reverted to her own tranquil and reflective manner. "It's enough for me to enjoy a sport without having to win, place or show," she told Jack. "You had to be strong not to be captured and absorbed by the Kennedys," observed Ormsby-Gore, "and Jackie was."

Jackie's relations with Rose Kennedy were mixed. On the one hand, she reportedly thought Rose was self-centered, selfish, and scatterbrained. At times she rudely mimicked her. Mary Gallagher, who worked for Rose, recalled one morning when Rose stopped at her desk and sarcastically inquired, "Do you know if Jackie is getting out of bed today?"

> When I responded that I couldn't be sure, she added, "Well, you might remind her that we're having some important guests for lunch. It would be nice if she would join us."
>
> I immediately went in to relay the message to Jackie, but she took it gaily. She imitated her mother-in-law's manner of speech and singsonged, "You might remind her we're having important guests for lunch . . ."
>
> The luncheon guests arrived and departed without any sight of Jackie.

On reflection, though, Jackie praised her mother-in-law as a "thoroughbred." She emphasized that Rose went out of her way to be nice to her daughter-in-law. "She was terribly sweet to me," said Jackie. "I liked [Rose] enormously. I saw that this woman did everything to put one at one's ease."[12]

Joe Kennedy appreciated Jackie, and the two developed a warm bond. Accustomed to deference from his children and his employees, he found Jackie's independence refreshing, and he enjoyed her teasing. "Joe soon became Jackie's most ardent supporter," said Billings. "He admired her because of her individuality. She wasn't afraid of him. She cajoled him, teased him, talked back to him."

"I used to tell [Joe] he had no nuances," Jackie later explained, "that everything with him was either black or white, while life was so much more complicated than that." While other Kennedys played touch football, Joe and Jackie sat on the porch, discussing classical music and movies.

At Hyannis Port she insisted on eating dinner at their own home, not always at the family dinners at her father-in-law's house. "Once a week is great," she told Jack. "Not every night."

Backed by the ambassador and Jack, the Kennedy family gradually came to accept Jackie into the family, despite her differences. Their love and loyalty for each member of the clan made it impossible for them to hold a grudge against her. "They seem proud if I read more books, and of the things I do differently," Jackie later remarked. "The very things you would think alienate them brings you closer to them."[13]

Soon after his marriage, Jack began corresponding with Gunilla Von Post, and he phoned her several times. "I see your face everywhere," he said during a transatlantic call in August 1954, "and sometimes you come to me in dreams. I can't tell you how badly I want to see you, but you will understand how much when we meet." Von Post was overwhelmed with his seemingly sincere romantic interest.

In August 1955, two years after their first brief encounter, Jack and Torby Macdonald arrived at Von Post's home in Bastad in southwestern Sweden. There Jack and Gunilla engaged in a week of whirlwind passion.

Kennedy asked Macdonald to take care of the bags as Kennedy and Von Post went to his room. "Inside, he swung the door shut so eagerly that it banged," she said, "and I fell into his arms."

> I gave in totally to my emotions. He kissed me so that it seemed as if we had seen each other only yesterday. . . .
>
> From the very beginning, I could tell he wanted desperately to please me, and I felt the same. Jack was gentle and caring, and his love was as sweet as his kisses and caresses had been on the Riviera. . . .
>
> I was relatively inexperienced, and Jack's tenderness was a revelation. He said, "Gunilla, we've waited two years for this. It seems almost too good to be true, and I want to make you happy." For the first time, I

could let go and luxuriate in the attentions of a man who not only respected and cared for me but clearly loved me. I fully trusted him.[14]

They met her friends, swam, toured the countryside, strolled in gardens, and ate lazy lunches and festive dinners. They both felt a "special pulse" all day, Von Post recalled, "because we knew that soon, after nightfall, we would be in each other's arms again."

"I can't believe this is happening—that I'm with you again," he told her. (She saw tears in his eyes.) "I feel as though I've been set free." During his visit Jack never mentioned Jackie, but Macdonald gave Von Post the impression that their marriage was unhappy.

At one festive dinner Jack charmed all her friends and relatives. "He positively radiated warmth . . . He rarely missed a chance to flirt with all the women, our mothers included. But he cast a spell on people that I've never quite seen before or since. And everyone—man, woman, child—was smitten, and happy to be near him."

After Jack and Macdonald returned to the United States, Kennedy told her on the phone that he intended to talk to his father about "us." Shortly after, he phoned her again. Von Post recalled their conversation:

"I talked to my father."
I did a slow-breathing exercise to calm down.
"It wasn't a very pleasant conversation," he said.
"What happened?"
"You don't know him. But he can be—he's very harsh . . . It's impossible to bring up my troubles with my wife to him. He doesn't even want to hear about it, because she likes him and he responds to that."
"But you told him about me?"
"I said that I'd fallen in love with you, and I didn't think I could go on the way things are now. That I wanted to end my marriage so that I could be with you."
"What did he say?"
"He didn't just say it. He yelled at me, 'You're out of your mind. You're going to be president someday. This would ruin everything. Divorce is impossible. Look at what happened with me and Gloria Swanson!' He also said that whether I had a happy marriage or not wasn't the point. He repeated something he's been telling us all our lives. He said, 'Can't you get it into your head that it's not important what you really are? The only important thing is what people *think* you are!'"
My heart was sinking. "Oh, Jack, I don't know. This is getting complicated."
"I know. It sounds that way. Look. I feel terrible. I can't stand talking

about this—talking about us—without being near you. I'm going to think of something."

Whether Jack *actually* consulted his father about Von Post is unknown. Her story about Jack's conversation with the ambassador sounds at least partly contrived, and may be mostly fiction. In any case, shortly afterward Jack and Von Post ended their relationship.[15]

There were many other women in Jack's life. In 1955 the famed stripper Tempest Storm was performing at the Casino Royale in Washington, D.C., when Senator Kennedy and his entourage arrived to spend the evening. In her 1987 autobiography Storm wrote about her relationship with Jack.

After her performance one of Kennedy's aides came backstage and asked if she would like to meet Senator Kennedy.

"Not particularly," she answered.

The man persisted.

"Is he married?" she asked.

"Well, yes, he is, but that doesn't matter."

"It matters to me," Storm retorted, and firmly rejected the request.

However, she did sneak a look past the curtains. Expecting to see an older man, she was captivated by Kennedy's "stunning good looks." The following night Kennedy returned with his entourage. After the show the same aide again invited Storm to meet the senator. This time she agreed, and conversed alone with Kennedy at his table.

They started seeing each other the next evening. The relationship was never smooth, and her habit of being late clashed with his desire for punctuality. "Goddamn it, you kept me waiting!" he barked angrily when she had kept him cooling his heals in his car.

But Kennedy was usually charming, and, said Storm, "he melted me like butter over an open flame. In many ways, he was like a little boy who wouldn't grow up. In other ways, he was one of the most mature men I've ever known."

Kennedy's youthful side emerged during a balmy evening drive through Washington, D.C. As the car approached a park near the Potomac River, he ordered his driver to stop.

"Come on, let's get out and walk around," he said; moments later he challenged her to a race to the river. Storm pulled off her high heels, tossed them back into the limousine, pulled up her evening gown, and ran.

Less than a hundred yards from the riverbank, she fell. He collapsed beside her and said, "I hope you're all right."

"Yes," I said, "I'm fine."

"Yes, by God, you are all right," he said, and he kissed her passionately.

Then he picked her up and carried her to the car. He told his driver to take them to the Mayflower Hotel, where she had a suite.

"Later that evening," she recalled, "he told me that he was not happily married, that Jackie was cold toward him. I held my finger to his lips to silence talk about his home life." In her memory Kennedy's sex drive lived up to the legend that developed around it since his death. "The man just never wore out," she said.[16]

In the fall of 1956, while Kennedy was in Malibu, California, he stopped into the Sip 'n' Surf bar accompanied by Ted Sorensen and Jack's new brother-in-law, the actor Peter Lawford, who had recently married Pat Kennedy. One of the bar patrons was Joan Lundberg (later Hitchcock), a twenty-four-year-old ex–airline stewardess, ex–cocktail waitress, and a divorcée with two children. Lundberg was at the bar with another man.

She was aggressively determined to meet the handsome senator she'd seen on television. As she was about to play a song on the jukebox, Kennedy began chatting with her. When he asked what she intended to play, she answered, "Elvis Presley, but what would you like to hear?" He looked into her eyes and said: "I would like to hear something soft so I can concentrate on you."

She gushingly expressed her admiration for him and his political views. They bantered back and forth, ignoring the rest of the bar patrons, engaging in small talk. Finally she returned to her date. As Kennedy and his party left, he gave her a gentlemanly smile. A few minutes later the bar owner told Lundberg her brother was on the telephone. "What are you doing in town and how did you know I was here?" she inquired.

But it wasn't her brother. Instead a distinctive Boston accent crackled out of the telephone, "How-a-ya?" Realizing she was with a date, Kennedy was too discreet to make a play in the bar. "Shall we say he was too much of a politician?" Lundberg recalled. "What an operator."[17]

Two weeks later at a Malibu hotel they began their affair. During the next three years they had whirlwind trysts at restaurants, bars, motels, rallies, and parties in the California home of the Peter Lawfords. "From that wonderful night in Malibu, we just started to see each other whenever and wherever we could," she said. Washington, New York, the West Coast—"He arranged and paid for me to travel to these places." Because Lundberg earned only $250 per month, Kennedy also sent her money.

How was Kennedy as a lover? "He was rather quick," she said. "In fact, he was just a little bit slower than a rabbit." She continued: "Jack loved to fuck, loved getting head. He used to hold my head down there forever. But he would never go down on me—that's the kind of uptight Irish Catholic he was. He thought oral sex was dirty. But he loved threesomes—himself and two girls. He was also a voyeur."

She had no illusions that she was the only woman in his life besides Jackie. "Jack was a very busy boy," she said. "I don't remember him making a great secret of it. He was fairly straightforward in things like that. He was just a very healthy male." It was no use for her to get jealous. "As far as I was concerned, I could hardly expect more."

Then she got pregnant. "I didn't like wearing a diaphragm, and Jack wouldn't wear a rubber," she said. "I don't think I was the only girl he knocked up." Outwardly Kennedy remained poised at the news. She claimed he sent her four hundred dollars in cash to have an abortion, but the money was lost in the mail, probably stolen. When she told him the money had never arrived, he exploded. "You have never heard anybody use expletives so much in the whole history of Washington," she said. "He ranted and stormed and raved and sent the money straight over with a messenger."

At the Lawford home Lundberg had been a welcome guest. But as Kennedy intensified his drive for the presidency, their affair received more attention, becoming the talk of the beach community there. Pat Lawford, protective of her brother's ambition, decided to slam the door on her brother's lover, cutting Lundberg off from the Lawfords. "I just wasn't allowed in the house again," claimed Lundberg; "it had become too well known."

"It was good to have the pleasure of his company," said Lundberg. "I was very much in love."[18]

Kennedy's cohort in philandering was George Smathers. Ruggedly handsome, a high school and college athlete, Smathers was first elected as a Democratic congressman from Florida in 1946, the same year as Kennedy's first congressional victory. In a bitter Senate primary contest in 1950, Smathers upset Florida's incumbent Democratic senator Claude Pepper, then went on to victory in the general election.

Although married with two children, Smathers behaved like a bachelor. His friendship with Kennedy was based primarily on the acquisition of women together. At a night session in the Senate, an elderly senator watched Kennedy and Smathers in the gallery sneaking out with a couple of women. "[We] were still in there working while they went on the town," said the senator.

"Jackie never particularly liked me because she felt I was a bad influence on her husband," Smathers observed. "He told her stories about me moving in circles maybe I shouldn't have been moving in at the time. He was always using me as a cover for himself. . . . I was catching hell for his running around and God knows he was a far worse influence on me than I ever could have been on him. I had trouble protecting my own limited territory from the guy."[19]

Kennedy's sexual adventurism frequently led him into orgies at the Carroll Arms Hotel across the street from the Senate Office Building. There he amused himself with several women. "That kind of thing was probably his favorite pastime," said Smathers.

JFK and Smathers had another hideaway where they romped with their girlfriends. "I remember once," said Smathers,

> I went down with this pretty little thing and Jack was already there with someone. He went into another room to make a phone call, and a few minutes later Evelyn Lincoln called and said I was wanted back on the Hill. So I left and was driving towards Washington when it dawned on me that I couldn't be wanted back there because the Senate was in recess. I knew then that old Jack had pulled a fast one on me. So I turned around and drove back and entered the place just like I'd left it. What do you suppose I found when I walked in? There was the old rascal chasing both of the girls around, having himself a fine old time. He liked that sort of thing, you know. He was something, let me tell you.

"Jack had the most active libido of any man I've ever known," said Smathers. "He was really unbelievable—absolutely incredible in that regard, and he got more so the longer he was married." Smathers added that his friend "was like a rooster getting on top of a chicken real fast and then the poor little hen ruffles her feathers and wonders what the hell happened to her. . . . Just in terms of the time he spent with a woman, though, he was a lousy lover. He went in more for quantity than quality. I don't know how the women ever tolerated it."[20]

Smathers introduced his disreputable friend Bill Thompson to Senator Kennedy in the mid-1950s, and Kennedy served as best man when Thompson remarried in 1958. Thompson was a railroad lobbyist from Florida and a notorious seducer of women. Kennedy and Thompson developed a "very special relationship," reflected Thompson's daughter Gail Laird. "I think it was somewhat on the sleazy side. My father was a terrible womanizer." Thompson had such an uncanny power over women, claimed an observer, "that friends said he could actually fondle strange women on the street and get away with it."

Bobby Baker, secretary to the Democratic majority in the Senate, revealed in his autobiography that he had "helled" around with Smathers and Thompson. On one occasion Baker searched for Senator Kennedy in the Senate restaurant and found him in the company of Thompson and a beautiful woman.

> I had no more than approached their table when Thompson said, "Bobby, look at this fine chick. She gives the best head in the United States." I couldn't believe my ears. . . . I attempted to sputter out my message to

Senator Kennedy and, at the same time, sneak glances at the beautiful, smiling lady who was being so highly advertised. JFK saw my discomfort and laughed: "Relax, Bobby. She's from Paris and she doesn't understand a word of English. But what Bill's saying is absolutely right!"[21]

Whether by accident or design, Thompson's friendship with Kennedy remained unknown to the media throughout Kennedy's life. Thompson did service while remaining invisible, and the service he provided was mostly beautiful women. "He was a pimp for Jack," said Charles Bartlett.

In the late 1950s Kennedy continued to pursue Hollywood actresses. Apparently some were only friends or acquaintances, such as actress Audrey Hepburn, who visited his Senate office. Actress-singer Judy Garland established a bond with Kennedy, who occasionally phoned her and requested she sing "Over the Rainbow" for him. "Just the last eight bars," he would say. Rumor circulated that he also developed relationships with actresses Jean Simmons and Lee Remick.[22]

One attempt to seduce a prominent actress failed miserably. In the late 1950s Italian actress Sophia Loren came to the United States to make the movie *Houseboat* with Cary Grant. Reporter Maxine Cheshire was assigned to cover Loren's visit to Washington. By the time the actress ended up at the Italian embassy for a late-afternoon party, Cheshire had been shadowing her for so long that Loren assumed she was a studio employee.

Kennedy and George Smathers arrived at the embassy party with only one purpose in mind: to seduce Loren. "Instead of approaching her directly," Cheshire recalled, "Kennedy sent Smathers, who poured on the charm, explaining that Senator Kennedy, who was surely going to be the next President of the United States, wanted Loren to join him at his Georgetown home for a late dinner, where the butler already had the champagne chilling."

Twice Loren sent Smathers away. Cheshire watched Kennedy out on the patio, impatiently rocking back and forth on his heels, refusing to take no for an answer. Smathers made a third attempt. "This time Sophia looked at me imploringly," said Cheshire, "as if beseeching me to help Smathers understand her lack of interest in him or his friend." Senator Smathers had gotten the impression that Cheshire was a chaperone who'd been assigned by the studio to accompany Loren. Finally, in desperation, Smathers declared in an exasperated tone, "Oh, what the hell, bring her too. We'll make it a twosome." That approach didn't work either. Cheshire recalled: "She looked at me, I shook my head no; she looked at Smathers and shook her head no, also." Kennedy and Smathers left disappointed.[23]

———————

"[Jack] was a lousy husband," Charles Bartlett bluntly concluded. Billings speculated that Jackie never suspected the depth of Jack's need for other women.

> Nor was she prepared for the humiliation she would suffer when she found herself stranded at parties while Jack would suddenly disappear with some pretty young girl. Before the marriage, I think she found Jack's appeal to other women tantalizing—I suspect it reminded her of the magic appeal her handsome, rakish father had had with women all his life—but once she was married and once it was happening to her, it was much harder to accept.

Jack was not so foolish as to flaunt his infidelities in front of Jackie. He wouldn't intentionally hurt her. "Jack would never intentionally hurt anyone, most of all Jackie," observed Smathers. "He was never rude or cruel to her; he respected her too much. . . . There is no doubt that she was crazy about him, and there is no doubt that he loved her. I just don't think he was capable of being monogamous, and he handled it the best way he could."[24]

15

LEAPING TO
PROMINENCE

The young Kennedy boys had often heard their father and grandfather talk about the perils of state and local politics. "It's an endless morass from which it is very difficult to extricate oneself," Robert Kennedy remembered learning. Much better for an aspiring national politician to avoid having to choose the ward committeeman or the sheriff of Middlesex County. Meddling in local political squabbles always made enemies and "sucked away" strength. "You're either going to get into the problems of Algeria, or you're going to get into the problems of Worcester," said Robert Kennedy.

Although his roots lay in the rough-and-tumble world of Massachusetts politics, John Kennedy had tried to avoid the factionalism and petty bickering. Throughout his fourteen years in the House and Senate, he played almost no part in Democratic Party affairs in Massachusetts—with two notable exceptions.[1]

One was a nasty incident in 1954 involving the only major Democratic political figure in Massachusetts whom Kennedy disliked. The other was a brief but intense effort to capture control of the state Democrats in 1956.

Catholic, a graduate of Yale Law School, Foster Furcolo served from 1948 to 1952 as Massachusetts's Second District congressman. After being elected state treasurer in 1952, he won the Democratic Senate nomination in 1954 to challenge incumbent Republican Leverett Saltonstall in the November 2 election.

Furcolo detested Jack. One source of his ill feeling was his belief that the Kennedys had socially snubbed the Furcolos by not inviting them to a Kennedy cocktail party (maybe several parties). "He thinks he's too good for you," Furcolo complained to Tip O'Neill. After O'Neill was elected to fill Jack's vacant congressional seat in 1952, Furcolo warned him to expect to be socially embarrassed by the Kennedys. "Every ambassador and every general and every admiral will be [at the cocktail party] and every big shot in the town. But you'll not be invited. And, boy, will your wife suffer embarrassment." (Subsequently O'Neill and his wife were always invited to the Kennedy parties.) "It seethed Kay, Furcolo's wife," said O'Neill. "It used to get under her skin. She felt as though she had been snubbed . . . by the Kennedys."[2]

During his 1954 Senate campaign against Saltonstall, Furcolo fumed when Kennedy and Saltonstall issued a joint statement in September detailing a long list of legislative achievements by the New England Conference of Senators. Kennedy should have been trying to defeat the Republican incumbent, not cooperating with him, Furcolo believed. After all, Furcolo had been a reliable Fair Deal Democrat whose vote the Truman administration could always count on.

Jack's animosity against Furcolo stemmed from the meeting with Truman in 1949 to protest Congressman John McCormack's alleged dominance of patronage. When the Kennedy-led group of state Democratic congressmen arrived at the White House, President Truman already knew the purpose of their visit. Tipped off, McCormack had already consulted with the president. All the disaffected congressmen had showed up except one—Foster Furcolo. And Furcolo had been one of the prime instigators. President Truman gave the delegation no satisfaction whatsoever. "Jack was furious at Foster," observed Tip O'Neill, "because he felt that the President was well prepared and had his answers ready for them when they had arrived and that he had already talked to McCormack about it. There could only be one leak, and the leak had to be Foster."[3]

Jack complained privately that he didn't like the "bums" hanging around Furcolo. Competing ambitions played a role as well. "A lot of Jack's cronies and associates looked on Foster Furcolo as somebody who was rather new on the political scene and who could, in the future, possibly be a [rival] to Jack in his ascendancy," observed Mary Davis, Jack's congressional secretary. Jack undoubtedly agreed.

In 1952, when Furcolo sought the Democratic nomination for state trea-surer, Kennedy had joined with Paul Dever in openly supporting him in the primary so Italian-Americans would have representation on the party ticket. But Jack felt that Furcolo didn't actively support him in his race against Lodge in the same election.[4]

In the 1954 election race for Massachusetts governor, the Democratic candidate, Robert Murphy, faced incumbent Republican Christian Herter. Kennedy's supporters worked hard for Murphy, but many were unenthusias-tic about Furcolo. Kennedy also assisted Murphy but privately preferred that Saltonstall remain with him in the Senate. (Jack later told friends he voted for Saltonstall.)

Still, Kennedy could not afford an open break with Furcolo; otherwise he might alienate Furcolo's Italian-American supporters and be accused of di-viding the party. Knowing Jack's awkward predicament, Furcolo insisted that Kennedy appear prominently with him on television, attack Saltonstall, and give Furcolo a firm endorsement.

Massachusetts Democrats had scheduled a major television program for October 9, 1954, the night before Kennedy entered the hospital for his back operation. An advance script had been agreed to by all three participants—Kennedy, Furcolo, and Murphy. Feeling miserable, Kennedy showed up at the studio on crutches and in considerable pain. When Furcolo insisted on changing the script—demanding that Kennedy not only endorse Furcolo but strongly attack Saltonstall—Jack was miffed. ("I didn't know whether to take a swing at the guy or clout him with my crutch," he later told Larry O'Brien.) As Jack began to hobble out of the studio, aides persuaded him to return. That was the tense situation as the state's three leading Democrats went on the air ostensibly to display the Democratic Party's grand unity.

On the live program Kennedy did revise the prepared script but not the way Furcolo had insisted. The key line in the script had Jack turning to Robert Murphy and saying, "Thank you, Bob, and I want to wish you and Foster and the entire Democratic ticket every success." But on the live show, Jack said, "Thank you, Bob, I want to wish you and the entire Democratic ticket every success." He left out just two words, "and Foster."[5]

At first the omission went unnoticed. No one complained. But on Octo-ber 11, two days after the broadcast, while Jack lay in the hospital, his refusal to endorse Furcolo exploded with delayed action. Kennedy's aide, Francis X. Morrissey, confirmed to an inquiring Associated Press reporter that the sena-tor had purposely omitted a personal endorsement of Furcolo. The friction, Morrissey explained, developed when Furcolo insisted that Kennedy make a personal attack on Saltonstall's record.

Suddenly the Kennedy-Furcolo feud was front-page news all over Massachusetts; *The New York Times* and *The Christian Science Monitor* also published lengthy accounts. State Republican leaders reacted with glee. Furcolo wouldn't comment.

In retaliation John D'Agostino, president of the eight-hundred-member Italian-American Club, bitterly withdrew his club's endorsement of Torbert Macdonald, Jack's friend and a Democratic candidate for Congress in Massachusetts. The action was taken, he said, because of Kennedy's "attack" on Furcolo. (Macdonald won anyway.) When Furcolo lost to Saltonstall by only twenty-nine thousand votes, his supporters bitterly blamed Kennedy for the defeat.[6]

After Jack returned to the Senate following his long convalescence, he and Furcolo mended their fences. A highlight of the state Democratic Party's annual Jefferson-Jackson Day dinner on June 9, 1955, was the joint appearance of Kennedy and Furcolo. Each praised the other. "Relationships take turns," Jack told the audience, "and our relationship did last fall. But [Furcolo] remains as one of the leaders of our party and one of the leaders in the state. I hope you won't hear any more about Furcolo and Kennedy." And in a television appearance in Boston before the 1956 election, Jack endorsed Furcolo for governor, describing him as "an outstanding Congressman" and "an excellent State Treasurer."

After Furcolo won the gubernatorial election in 1956, he and Kennedy maintained a surface cordiality and a practical working relationship. But ill will remained beneath the surface—at least on the part of Furcolo. When JFK ran for reelection to the Senate in 1958, he asked for the support of Governor Furcolo. "I got a telegram from Jack Kennedy wanting me to endorse him," Furcolo told Tip O'Neill. "I'll endorse him. I'll endorse him [at] 12 o'clock midnight, the night before the election, when it's too late for him to use it."[7]

In almost every city and town in Massachusetts Jack relied on his own loyalists—his Kennedy secretaries—and didn't go through Democratic Party channels. The local secretary was always notified when Kennedy was in the area. "He made the secretaries feel that they were a part of [his] organization," said the Massachusetts political figure William Hartigan. "No contribution, time-wise or effort-wise, was too small for recognition." Every city and town in the commonwealth had a clearly identified Kennedy organization. "And believe me," said O'Neill, "they were resented, for the most part, by the regular Democratic Party. But they were effective."

The secretaries provided major assistance in 1956 when Ken O'Donnell and Larry O'Brien dragged Jack into the middle of a ferocious party squabble. To Kennedy's dismay, the effort inadvertently turned into a power struggle between himself and John McCormack, then the prominent House majority leader. The end result pleased Jack, though, because his victory over McCormack gave him more power and prestige leading up to the 1956 Democratic National Convention.

Annoyed with the meager efforts of the state Democratic Committee, O'Brien and O'Donnell thought Kennedy had a responsibility to improve the party. Bored, seeking political excitement, the pair had "idle hands," said Robert Kennedy.

Their focus was the state Democratic Committee and its chairman, William Burke. Composed of eighty members elected every four years, the Democratic Committee normally had few people contest the election vacancies. Kennedy could control the committee if he elected a few dozen of his own loyalists. "Once we had a majority we could elect our own chairman and control the organization," said Larry O'Brien. Although instinctively dreading internal party conflict, Kennedy granted cautious approval. "Ken [O'Donnell] and I kept pushing him," O'Brien recalled, "but he also told us to keep him out of direct involvement." Keeping him uninvolved proved impossible.[8]

Chairman Burke, a rotund Hatfield onion grower and warehouse man, was an ally of Congressman McCormack. Both men opposed the presidential candidacy of Adlai Stevenson, who had lost to Eisenhower in 1952 and was the leading contender for the Democratic nomination again in 1956. (Neither indicated whom he did support.) Backed by the *Boston Post*, Burke initiated a write-in campaign to elect McCormack as the state's favorite son in the Democratic presidential primary on April 24, 1956. The move succeeded, as McCormack trounced Stevenson.

In deference to McCormack, neither Kennedy nor Paul Dever, both Stevenson supporters, took any active part in the primary campaign once the favorite-son movement for McCormack gained momentum, but they worried about the alliance of Burke, McCormack, and the normally conservative *Post*. The preferential results were not binding on the Massachusetts delegates, but it seemed likely that McCormack would at least receive a complimentary vote on the first ballot.

Upon reflection Kennedy became convinced that Burke and McCormack were attempting to control the state delegation to the Democratic National Convention, and damage Stevenson's presidential nomination.

Burke's statements and behavior during the primary campaign irritated Kennedy. Early in Stevenson's career, while working in various federal positions during FDR's presidency, Stevenson had crossed paths with Alger Hiss, later exposed as a Communist spy and sent to prison for perjury. With no evidence except guilt by association, Senator Joe McCarthy and other Republicans had tried to smear Stevenson's reputation because he knew Hiss. Now, during the Massachusetts primary campaign in 1956, Burke joined the chorus of witch-hunters, saying that Stevenson supporters in the state should have been at Princeton University listening to a speech by Hiss. The statement infuriated Jack and other Stevenson supporters.[9]

Kennedy expected the state chairman to be neutral during intraparty campaigns for state or federal office. But Burke had turned over the party's resources and machinery to only one candidate. He sent out McCormack's literature and letters on state committee stationery, used the party's mailing list, and denied the same privileges to Stevenson.

Moreover, Kennedy knew that he might be put forward as a vice-presidential candidate to run with Stevenson. To remain a prospect, Kennedy needed firm control of the party machinery in his home state to deliver the votes of the Massachusetts delegation to Stevenson at the national convention. So Jack wanted at least some Massachusetts delegates who were Kennedy loyalists. "Lightning might strike out there," he told Tip O'Neill, referring to the national convention. "I may be a candidate for vice president, and I certainly don't want to be shut out of delegates and friends that would be operating for me." Burke, he believed, wouldn't give him any support.

"Although the *Post* has made it clear that they will use every weapon possible to reelect Burke, we are hopeful of being able to elect a new State Chairman more favorably disposed to us," Jack told Stevenson's lieutenant, James Finnegan, on May 2, 1956. "We have already contacted all newly elected State Committeewomen and men, and I plan to follow this up with personal contacts between now and the State Committee meeting in mid-May."[10]

On May 7, 1956, while on a tour of the Berkshires, Kennedy said it would be a "serious mistake" to reelect Burke as chairman of the state committee. After that simple statement, the fur began to fly.

Two days later Burke countered with a statement of his own charging that Senator Kennedy had tried to get him to step down because he "supported Congressman McCormack as the favorite-son candidate" and was "too close to Congressman McCormack."

From Washington Kennedy issued a statement branding Burke's account as "wholly untruthful." Burke was just attempting to drive a wedge between McCormack and Kennedy. Burke next embarrassed Jack by asserting that the senator had offered to buy him out of the chairmanship by giving him James Curley's seat on the Democratic National Committee, an accusation Kennedy also denied.

During the public squabble with Burke, McCormack insinuated that he regarded the fight as an attack upon himself as well. Burke, he asserted, would be unopposed for reelection to the chairmanship if he had not helped McCormack win the state presidential primary.

In his appeal for Burke's reelection, McCormack delivered an unmistakable slap at Kennedy for not supporting Furcolo in 1954. "Mr. Burke, as I did, vigorously supported the party nominees for 1954," said the Democratic majority leader. "It is through no fault of Burke or myself that Foster Furcolo was not elected United States Senator in 1954." When state newspapers played up the contest as a Kennedy-McCormack fight, Jack was upset. "What the hell are you guys doing to me?" he demanded of O'Brien and O'Donnell.[11]

Most major newspapers in the state blamed Burke for setting off the pyrotechnics and said the problems could have been solved discreetly if Burke hadn't been so rash. "[Kennedy has] been subjected to back alley abuse, accusations of bribery, character assassination and misrepresentation that would wither a less determined man," wrote the *Boston Herald*. "And Kennedy is at a disadvantage because he can't drop to the level of his opponents and still maintain his integrity."

The *Boston Post* and McCormack supported Burke; Dever, Kennedy, and the Massachusetts chapter of Americans for Democratic Action were on the other side, backing Pat Lynch, their candidate to oppose Burke. In mid–May 1956, Lynch won the election 47 to 31.[12]

Afterward Jack quickly tried to mend his relations with McCormack. "I never felt that [Kennedy] was ever very bitter personally towards John," said *Boston Globe* reporter Thomas Winship. For his part, McCormack insisted that the differences he'd supposedly had with Kennedy were "completely exaggerated."

In retrospect, O'Brien thought he erred in leading Kennedy into the state committee battle. "Kennedy's forces won, but the victory never revitalized the Democratic Party in Massachusetts. The party was too diverse for any superficial unification." After 1956 Kennedy and his advisers were too preoccupied with the national political scene to pay close attention to the Massachusetts Democrats.[13]

In the spring of 1956, the veteran journalist Theodore H. White visited Kennedy as part of his research for an article about the national Democratic Party. White took notes on his visit. "Senator Kennedy . . . Boyish, open face, bronzed, hair almost golden with sun bleaching. Easy talk. Good ideas, frank about himself. Gracious. The easy slurring of consonants of all northeasterners."

Kennedy told White that he admired Adlai Stevenson's stands on major issues, and thought the former Illinois governor "lifts politics above the humdrum." White broached a subject that would dominate Kennedy's thinking for most of 1956. If the Democrats again nominated Stevenson to face Eisenhower, the Stevenson camp had told White that they were considering Jack and three others for the vice-presidential nomination. (The others were Senator Albert Gore and Governor Frank Clement, both of Tennessee, and the Catholic mayor of New York, Robert Wagner.)[14]

What did Kennedy think about the second spot on the ticket? Jack replied that he had difficulty picturing himself as vice president. It was a hell of a job, he joked, greeting people at the airport and going to banquets. But, he supposed, if it came his way he wouldn't turn it down, even though he was unenthusiastic. He suggested that being a senator was the height of his ambition and all the ambition he rightfully ought to have. Having said that, if the offer was made, maybe he should take it.

In 1956 the race for the Democratic presidential nomination pitted Senator Estes Kefauver of Tennessee against Stevenson. Kefauver, an independent liberal, a supporter of labor, civil liberties, and—most unusual for a Southern senator—civil rights, had waged a strong battle for the presidential nomination in 1952, but finally lost to Stevenson.

Discerning, eloquent, and witty, Stevenson had served as governor of Illinois for four years before carrying the Democratic standard against Eisenhower in 1952. That his wife had divorced him in 1949 hung like an albatross around his presidential ambitions.

Kefauver surprised Stevenson by winning the Minnesota primary on March 20, 1956. But when Stevenson narrowly captured primaries in Florida and Oregon, and then won an overwhelming victory in California, Kefauver ended his bid. On the eve of the Democratic convention in Chicago in August, therefore, Stevenson was in firm control. The only drama left was who would be his running mate.[15]

Of the various possibilities only Senator Hubert Humphrey of Minnesota publicly announced he was seeking the office. Senator Gore, Governor Clement, and Mayor Wagner were also prominently mentioned. After Kefauver withdrew from the presidential race and urged his pledged delegates to swing their votes behind Stevenson, he indicated that he would accept the second spot if asked.

Some pundits judged Kennedy as a logical choice. "As a Catholic, he would offset the disadvantage of Stevenson's divorce," Newsweek reported; "moreover, he's from the industrial East and would therefore appeal to the big-city labor and minority vote."

In June 1956 at the annual governors' conference in Atlantic City, Governor Abraham Ribicoff of Connecticut promoted Jack for vice president, making front-page news. So did Governor Dennis Roberts of Rhode Island. Kennedy would be acceptable to the South, added Governor Luther H. Hodges of North Carolina.[16]

Whenever Kennedy endorsed Stevenson, Sorensen advised his boss, he should do it at a Washington press conference because it would get "a little more attention," and, "more important, provide an opportunity to clear up all doubts about your health, which is the one question I still hear frequently raised around here when your name is discussed as a possibility for the ticket."

Kennedy curried favor with the Stevenson camp. Stan Karson, an aide to Stevenson, scouted Massachusetts in May 1956 and consulted with Kennedy. After the ouster of Burke, Jack told Karson, it was agreed that McCormack would get the first-ballot favorite-son vote and that Stevenson would receive the majority of the votes on the second ballot. However, McCormack would not get a first-ballot endorsement if that ballot was crucial to Stevenson's nomination. "In other words," Karson reported to the Stevenson camp, "if Kennedy is told that the Governor feels it important to have Massachusetts on the first ballot, Kennedy will see to it that this is done." Karson added: "My strongest feeling upon leaving Kennedy was that for the first time since I have known him over the past few years, he appears to be in control of [the] political situation, knows it, and likes it."

Kennedy, of all people, wanted Stevenson to exploit Kefauver's absentee record in the Senate. In late March Sorensen phoned Newton Minow, an adviser to Stevenson, and relayed Kennedy's suggestion to capitalize on Kefauver's absenteeism "in a vigorous way." "Senator Kennedy's judgment was that we should use this just as hard as we can," Minow wrote Stevenson.[17]

Harvard historian Arthur Schlesinger Jr., who was close to the Stevenson camp and a supporter of Kennedy for vice president, warned Sorensen not to promote Jack actively for the nomination. Sorensen agreed. "In keeping with your advice," he wrote the historian on August 1, 1956, "this office has not attempted to obtain public endorsements from anyone, nor engaged in any extensive private campaign by mail or otherwise." Actually, Sorensen had been feverishly lining up endorsements for several months, and would continue to seek them despite his promise to Schlesinger.

On July 6 Sorensen had urged a Kennedy supporter in Detroit "to get some pro-Kennedy declarations from farm-district Congressmen, farm newspapers and local farm organizations." Letters of support from influential people should be sent to "Governor Stevenson and his group." To all his correspondents, Sorensen urged secrecy. "I know you will understand, too, the Senator's desire to stay at arm's length from this activity and not to appear to be pushing himself for a place on the ticket."[18]

The day after he told Schlesinger he wouldn't solicit endorsements for Jack, Sorensen urged Boston's black leader Belford Lawson to write Stevenson encouraging him to make Kennedy his running mate. To make it easier for Lawson, Sorensen drafted the letter for him: "The first step, of course, is your selection of a Vice-Presidential running-mate," Sorensen had Lawson say. "No man can speak for fifteen million Negro Americans—but as one who has worked with them, for them and as one of them for many years, I want to tell you how much it would mean to see Senator John F. Kennedy selected for the Vice-Presidential nomination."

Sorensen instructed Lawson on the next step. "Your secretary should re-type the letter for your signature on your office letterhead stationery, send the original to Governor Stevenson in Chicago, and letterhead copies, if possible, to the following. . . ." Sorensen then listed seventeen newspapers and news organizations.[19]

Sorensen's devious promotion of his boss for second spot on the ticket was too improvised to ignite a bandwagon for Jack. More successful was his surreptitious effort to suggest that a Catholic running mate would propel Stevenson into the White House. For months Sorensen planted stories in newspapers and magazines that Kennedy's religion would actually help the Democratic ticket, not hurt it, if he was nominated as Stevenson's running mate.

On the surface Sorensen's forceful sixteen-page memo made a com-pelling argument. Catholics left the old Democratic alliance in droves to vote for Eisenhower in 1952. The key to a Democratic victory in 1956, therefore, was to nominate as Stevenson's running mate a Catholic who could win back the states with a high percentage of Catholic voters. These were heav-ily populated industrial states; fourteen of them—from Rhode Island (60 percent Catholic) to Ohio (20 percent)—had 261 electoral votes, just 5 short of the majority needed for victory. Sorensen's memo pointed out that the Democrats had carried twelve of those fourteen states for Roosevelt in 1944, and eight for Truman in 1948, but in 1952 none of those states had gone Democratic. Eisenhower had won all 261 of their electoral votes.

"Has the Democratic era ended? Has the party permanently lost its politi-cal base among the Catholics and immigrants of the large Northern cities that made a Democratic victory possible in 1940, 1944, and 1948? . . . A Catholic Vice-Presidential nominee could refashion this base as Al Smith did [in 1928] and begin a new era of Democratic victories."[20]

"I am extremely reluctant to let this personal study out of my hands," Sorensen wrote reporter Fletcher Knebel in April 1956. "I would not want it known that Senator Kennedy's assistant, even on his own, was preparing such material or circulating it to newsmen." In truth, Sorensen was delighted when Knebel and other journalists published the Catholic memo without identifying it as having come from Kennedy's office. (During the rest of 1956 the memo became known as the "Bailey Report" after the national Democratic Party leader, John Bailey of Connecticut, a friend of Kennedy, agreed to front for it.)

In June Knebel prominently featured Sorensen's study in an influential ar-ticle for *Look*. Democratic leaders keenly felt the loss of these crucial

Catholic voters and the need to regain them. "Instead of the question, 'Is a Catholic a liability on the ticket?' many Democrats have begun to ask, 'Would a Catholic on the ticket be an asset?'"

Sorensen's memo exaggerated the impact a Catholic vice-presidential candidate could have on the election of a Democratic presidential nominee. Voters of Irish Catholic ancestry, presumably most attracted to a candidate named Kennedy, were already comparatively loyal to Stevenson and the Democrats. Only Jews and blacks exceeded the Irish in their loyalty to Stevenson in 1952.[21]

Some aspects of Kennedy's career peeved Democrats. A Stevenson supporter from San Francisco wrote the former governor strongly objecting to the "weak sister" Kennedy because he had weaseled on the McCarthy issue. "If we can't win with the two top candidates *unequivocally* opposed to Joe McCarthy let's not run this time."

Farm leaders, led by Governor Orville Freeman of Minnesota, a backer of Senator Hubert Humphrey, opposed the selection of Kennedy for a very practical political reason: his opposition to high price supports for farmers. In June Freeman declared that Kennedy would not be "acceptable" to the Midwest because of his farm record. "I felt that his addition to the ticket would have meant, without any doubt, the loss of the Midwest farm states," Freeman reflected.

Schlesinger wrote Jack in late June about another thorny problem, a rumor circulating among prominent Democrats "that in 1950 you contributed to the Nixon campaign against Helen Douglas. If this is so, it might be worthwhile giving some thought about how this could best be handled."[22]

For the most part, though, magazines and newspapers extolled Jack's virtues. A writer in the liberal *New Republic* praised his serious purpose and outstanding command of issues:

> His preparation for a Senate speech or public statement . . . only begins with his personal study of the issue involved. The subsequent research is apt to exhaust both the subject and his aides . . . and the resulting documentation gives compelling weight to his arguments. Among his colleagues in the Senate, this sort of preparation has won Kennedy a reputation for "doing his homework," a phrase that might be extended without strain to the whole of his political activity. He seems to have pondered a wide range of foreign and domestic topics. . . .
>
> In the coming campaign, this ready command of the issues, this force of argument and appealing manner of speaking, might make Kennedy a match—and rather more than a match—for the Republicans' forensic Mr. Nixon.

On June 29, 1956, Jack summarized the favorable developments for his father—the public endorsements by Ribicoff, Roberts, and Hodges; the private support of Arthur Schlesinger Jr., who was about to spend a month in Stevenson's headquarters—and added some bad news: "Competition is mostly from Hubert Humphrey," he wrote, "who had his Governor make a statement that I would not be acceptable because of my vote on the farm bill." Overall, Jack anticipated beneficial results. "While I think the prospects are rather limited, it does seem of some use to have all of this churning."[23]

A month later Joe Kennedy advised his son what to tell the media if he decided not to seek or to accept the vice-presidential nomination, or if it wasn't offered to him.

> You should get out a statement to the effect that representing Mass. is one of the greatest jobs in the world, and there is lots to be done for your state and her people, and while you are most grateful for the national support offered you for the Vice Presidency, your heart belongs to Massachusetts. In your own words this should get out in order to have the proper effect for your candidacy [for reelection to the Senate] two years from now, if nothing happens on the V.P.

In mid-July Sargent Shriver flew from Boston to Chicago on the same plane with Adlai Stevenson and managed to speak with him for ten minutes. Afterward Shriver excitedly reported the results of his lobbying to his boss, Joe Kennedy, and Joe informed Jack.

Stevenson expressed concern about Jack's health, Shriver wrote. "This was obviously his number one point." Shriver tried to reassure. "I cited [Jack's] hard 'campaigning' in connection with [the] recent Massachusetts battle for control of [the] state committee. I mentioned his swimming, his discard of crutches, etc."

But Stevenson wasn't convinced; ominously, he continued to probe. (Stevenson had probably heard rumors that Kennedy had Addison's disease.) What was the nature of Jack's war injuries? What about the malaria? What really happened to Jack in the war? What is his real condition now? Aside from reassuring Stevenson of Jack's robust health, Shriver had no specific answers. (At the time, Shriver probably did not know about Jack's Addison's disease.)

Stevenson changed the subject to the "Catholic Issue." The Al Smith experience had been misinterpreted, Stevenson thought; Smith had not been defeated solely or even primarily because he was a Catholic. When Shriver brought up the much-publicized "Bailey Report," it was obvious that Stevenson had read it and was impressed.

"Finally, you will be interested to know that Stevenson thinks Jack would make 'a splendid contrast to Nixon,'" Shriver reported. "He contrasted Jack's clean appearance to Nixon's heavy, almost swarthy, thick look so he mentioned that Jack is certainly the 'All American Boy' type candidate, and commented on his excellent TV personality."[24]

In late July Jack was still ruminating. "I think he wants it," Eunice reported to her father after spending time with Jack in Hyannis Port:

> He thinks, first of all, that he would handle Nixon as you suggest. Secondly, he reasons that they wouldn't select him as a presidential candidate any other time in the future. Third, he feels he would become better known throughout the country if he conducts a good campaign and, therefore, this would help him in the future.

If Jack had any serious intention of actively campaigning to win the second spot at the convention, his closest advisers knew nothing about it. The ambassador was in Europe. When Jack discussed with Larry O'Brien whether his aide should go to Chicago, both agreed there was nothing for O'Brien to do there. So Kennedy's brilliant organizer stayed home. Both Robert Kennedy and Dave Powers expected to relax in Chicago and watch the convention as spectators. All the lobbying was over. Either Stevenson would select Jack or he wouldn't.[25]

"Kennedy in Movie Star Role," read the caption in the *Boston Herald* reporting on the opening day of the Chicago convention. On Monday, August 13, Jack had appeared on a screen in the amphitheater as narrator of a documentary history of the Democratic Party, *The Pursuit of Happiness*. The short film, put together by Hollywood writer and producer Dore Schary, extolled the party's virtues from Thomas Jefferson to Harry Truman. The voice of William Jennings Bryan bellowed "You shall not crucify mankind upon a cross of gold." There were lengthy passages from Franklin Roosevelt, with FDR saying at the finale, "I propose to sail ahead. For to reach port we must sail, sail, not lie at anchor—sail, not drift!"

While making the documentary, Schary had personally filmed Kennedy's introduction. Jack rehearsed a few times, then grasped his lines quickly. "Then we did the actual voice dubbing, and he was very good at it," said Schary. "All of us who were in contact with him immediately fell in love with him because he was so quick and so charming and so cooperative, and obviously so bright and so skilled." There were a few problems, particularly with Jack's pace and tone. "We asked him to get pauses in and in some instances [to] speed up his speaking, and then in other instances to slow down." Jack responded well. The "personality of the senator just came right out," Schary recalled. "It jumped at you on the screen."

After the film was shown at the convention, Jack made an appearance on the platform and received a long standing ovation. "Suddenly there seemed to be this feeling that Jack Kennedy was the man to be vice president," Ken O'Donnell recalled. Delegates asked O'Donnell, "Where is he? Can I meet him? Isn't he attractive? Can I get an autograph—he's so good-looking." Surprisingly, Kennedy was a force at the convention.[26]

The Stevenson camp had informed Jack that he might be asked to give the nominating speech for Stevenson. From past practice at conventions Jack assumed that if Stevenson did ask him to present the nominating speech, it meant he was eliminated from consideration as Stevenson's choice for running mate. The final word on Kennedy's selection for the speech didn't come until 1:30 A.M. on Thursday. Because the speech was the first order of business nine and a half hours later, Sorensen labored all night to get it ready.

Before the speech Jack sat on the stage next to Governor Luther Hodges. "Why don't you run for the nomination for vice president?" Hodges asked. Kennedy responded, "No, Governor, they have paid me off by letting me make this nominating speech for Governor Stevenson."[27]

After his easy nomination Stevenson made an unexpected announcement, a decision that electrified the convention, providing its wildest, most dramatic moments. Without a hint of his own personal preference, he broke precedent and left the nomination of his running mate entirely up to the will of the convention delegates. He and his advisers hoped to stimulate interest and generate publicity by having a competitive contest; his decision also avoided offending the prominent prospects who would have to be turned down if Stevenson anointed his choice.

Kefauver had a huge advantage in an open contest because so many delegates from his presidential bid were still in attendance ready to vote him the consolation prize. Most of them were from the Farm Belt and the West. The South and most big-state, big-city machines desperately wanted to settle on a candidate to stop Kefauver. John Kennedy was one possibility.[28]

After Stevenson's announcement, Jack's brothers and sisters, in-laws and friends, advisers and staff gathered in Jack's room. Should Jack be a candidate? Robert Kennedy started writing down delegate information on various states. Jack would say, "I think I can get four or five of those delegates." "I can bring in that state," remarked John Bailey.

Then someone rushed in to announce the shocking news that Georgia had held an early caucus and had came out for Kennedy. Shriver recalled: "We all knew how anti-Catholic they were in Georgia, and Jack said, just like that, 'Gee, if Georgia went for me, then I may really have a chance. O.K. then, I'm a candidate.' And that's when he really decided." Soon the suite was filled with confused, chaotic action as Kennedy's supporters burst forth with amateurish enthusiasm.

The vice-presidential contest stirred the deep competitive instincts within Jack and others in the Kennedy camp. Eunice Shriver worked on Delaware. Jack had breakfast with part of the California delegation, then attended the caucuses of several other delegations. "We got Virginia because Governor Battle's son was in the Navy with me," Jack later said. "And we got Louisiana because their delegation sat right next to ours and they had a lot of bright young fellows with whom we got real friendly."[29]

Clumsily organized, with poor communications, the Kennedy camp inadvertently slighted some major Democratic leaders and tactlessly pressured others. "Bobby and I ran around like a couple of nuts," Ken O'Donnell recalled. "It was a joke; we didn't know two people in the place. It was John Kennedy by himself."

"It's true we didn't sleep that night," said Sorensen, "but frankly we didn't accomplish very much. It was hectic, not very well organized, too many people packed into my bedroom who were just like me—green, completely green. I couldn't have been greener. I didn't talk to many people because I didn't know too many people."

On the first ballot Kefauver jumped off to a quick lead. The earliest indication of a dramatic contest occurred when Georgia awarded its 32 votes to Kennedy. Soon after, Louisiana and Virginia added 56 more votes to Kennedy's total.

Delegates had to keep score on the backs of envelopes and scraps of paper—because no one had anticipated a contest for the second spot, someone had dismantled the scoreboard which had electronically kept score during the presidential balloting. In any case, the balloting confused the delegates—everyone had a different score.[30]

At the end of the first ballot, Kennedy and Kefauver seemed to be the only two major contenders:

Kefauver	483½
Kennedy	304
Gore	178
Wagner	162½
Humphrey	134½

Kennedy had drawn his strength from New England, the South, and Illinois; the West and Midwest had mainly supported Kefauver.

The second ballot turned into a nail-biting duel between Kefauver and Kennedy. Alaska and Arizona gave Kefauver an early lead, but Kennedy went ahead 26 to 22 when Arkansas switched from Gore to Kennedy. The lead seesawed. By Illinois, Kennedy was up 155 to 82; but by New Hampshire his lead had narrowed to 271½ to 229½. New Jersey and New York, which had earlier supported Wagner, switched 128 of their 134 votes to Kennedy.

During the balloting Kennedy stayed in his small room at the Stock Yard Inn about five hundred feet from the amphitheater. Watching the balloting on television with the senator were Sorensen and Tom Winship of the *Boston Globe*. Kennedy lay on his bed in undershorts, with a pillow supporting his shoulders, his bare toes twitching, his face serious. His bathtub water was running.

Momentarily Kennedy jumped to a lead of 402½ to 245½. Then four state delegations went for Kefauver, narrowing the margin to 416½ to 387.[31]

Texas continued the Southern surge for Kennedy as Lyndon Johnson announced his state's 56 votes for "the fighting Senator who wears the scars of battle, that fearless Senator . . . John Kennedy of Massachusetts."

As Jack approached a majority of votes, the Kennedy camp became jubilant, thinking he was going to win. Shriver burst into Jack's room and exclaimed, "Jack you've got it!" But Kennedy wasn't nearly as certain as his brother-in-law.

At the end of the second ballot, with all the states recorded, Kennedy led Kefauver, 618 to 551½, only 69 votes away from 687, the magic number to win the nomination. When Kentucky switched its 30 votes from Gore to Kennedy, only 39 votes separated Jack from a majority.

What happened next became the subject of intense discussion and controversy. Sam Rayburn, the permanent chairman of the convention, recognized Tennessee. Given unanimous consent to make a statement, Senator Gore requested that his name be withdrawn as a candidate "in favor of my colleague, Senator Estes Kefauver." Kefauver supporters were ecstatic.

After Tennessee, Rayburn recognized Oklahoma, which changed its 28 votes to Kefauver. Minnesota gave Kefauver all 30 of its votes. Next, following Gore's endorsement, Tennessee switched its 32 votes to Kefauver.[32]

Missouri gave Kefauver 37 of its 38 votes. Suddenly, Kefauver surpassed Kennedy, 662 to 645½. After more switches, the final vote stood at Kefauver 755½ to 589 for Kennedy. Jack had lost.

As Kefauver was sweeping to victory, Kennedy turned away from the television screen and abruptly told Sorensen, "That's it. Let's go." Entering the amphitheater through a rear door, Jack was recognized by Rayburn and assumed the rostrum. The crowd roared.

Kennedy spoke without notes; his remarks were brief, gallant, and touching.

> I want to take this opportunity first to express my appreciation to
> Democrats from all parts of the country, north and south, east and west,

who have been so generous and kind to me this afternoon. I think it proves, as nothing else can prove, how strong and united the Democratic party is.

Secondly what has happened today bears out the good judgment of our Governor Stevenson in deciding that this issue should be taken to the floor of the convention. Because I believe that the Democratic party will go from this convention far stronger for what we have done here today. And therefore, ladies and gentlemen, recognizing that this convention has selected a man who has campaigned in all parts of the country, who has worked untiringly for the party, who will serve as an admirable running mate to Governor Stevenson, I hope that this convention will make Estes Kefauver's nomination unanimous. Thank you.

Then he moved away. "Go back and make a motion," whispered Rayburn. "Make a motion." Jack returned to the rostrum, made his motion, and the convention nominated Kefauver by acclamation.[33]

During the contest Kennedy had received scant support in the West and Midwest. But the South's backing for Kennedy was the talk of the convention. "It seemed to defy all logic that the most fundamentalist Protestant area of the country would fall into line behind a New England Roman Catholic and reject fellow Southerner and Baptist Kefauver," said Joseph Gorman, Kefauver's biographer. The reason was simple. The conservative Southern delegates detested the liberal Kefauver so intensely that they were willing to support anyone who might beat him. On the other hand, some Catholic delegates, recalling the bitter attacks against Catholic Al Smith in 1928, worried that a Catholic vice-presidential candidate might stir up religious prejudice again and help defeat Stevenson. David Lawrence, the powerful Catholic governor of Pennsylvania, opposed Kennedy because he feared a replay of 1928.

After Jack turned away from the podium, he looked drained, his smile gone, his shoulders sagging. He remained distressed for several hours. "He's like all the Kennedys—once they're in something, they don't like to lose," said a friend. Kennedy told several people, "I feel like the Indian who had a lot of arrows stuck in him and, when he was asked how he felt, said 'It only hurts when I laugh.' "[34]

He glared at advisers who tried to console him by telling him that he was lucky because the Stevenson-Kefauver ticket would undoubtedly go down to defeat anyway. "This morning all of you were telling me to get into this thing," he responded, "and now you're telling me I should feel happy because I lost it."

"We did our best," Jack told his father during a transatlantic phone call to France. "I had fun and I didn't make a fool of myself."

By the time Arthur Krock ran into Jack at the Drake Hotel in Chicago, Jack was in a better mood. Elated over the support he, a Catholic, had received from delegates in the Protestant South, he jocularly told Krock, "I'll be singing 'Dixie' the rest of my life."[35]

In a widely discussed article published after the convention, *Time* blamed Congressman McCormack for undercutting Jack at a decisive moment. The magazine reported that Missouri's Senator Tom Hennings was seen "whispering" with McCormack, who then rushed through the crowd toward the chairman's platform where Sam Rayburn presided. "Sam! Sam! Missouri!" yelled McCormack. Rayburn, who had been pondering which state to recognize next, called on Missouri. Hennings then announced Missouri's crucial switch from Humphrey to Kefauver. Because Kefauver was so close to winning, Missouri's votes all but settled the matter. By directing Rayburn's attention to Missouri, said *Time*, McCormack "had settled a score" with Jack for the beating McCormack took in the fight for control of the Massachusetts state Democratic organization. Several Kennedy aides believed *Time*'s version, permanently souring them on McCormack.

Several Massachusetts Democrats who witnessed the congressman's strong lobbying efforts on behalf of Kennedy among New York and Texas delegates challenged the *Time* article. McCormack later insisted that *Time*'s reporter got the story wrong. "I didn't know where Missouri was seated in 1956," he pleaded. "It was Kentucky that I sent word up to Rayburn to recognize, because Kentucky had told me that they were going to shift their vote to Kennedy, and they did." For some reason, in the confusion, said McCormack, Rayburn recognized Missouri.

Did Jack believe what *Time* reported? He remained suspicious. "[McCormack] would be delighted to have me go down the drain," Jack later told biographer James Burns. "I wouldn't have considered it unreasonable if he had, but I have no evidence he did." Indeed, there is little evidence. Why would McCormack work diligently for Jack among delegates in New York and Texas, and then undercut Kennedy at the last moment? *Time*'s reporter was probably mistaken.[36]

For a while, Jack incorrectly believed that his experience in Chicago demonstrated that being a Catholic was no longer a major liability in presidential politics. He won the Protestant South, he pointed out, and lost in heavily Catholic Ohio, Michigan, and Pennsylvania. "The American people have gone beyond the point where religion would be held for or against a candidate for political office."

Biographer Gorman critically assessed Kennedy's Southern support. "Kennedy had the dubious distinction of having almost the unanimous support of the reactionary, racist delegations." He won South Carolina, Mississippi, Georgia, Louisiana, and Virginia. Other than the Southern states of Texas and Arkansas, the only state west of the Mississippi River to give Jack over half of its votes on the second ballot was Nevada.

Jack recovered quickly from his defeat. "I was, of course, disappointed at the time," he told reporters in early September. "But, like everything in life, you cannot tell how it will be reflected in the future. After all, we came much closer than I thought we were going to."[37]

"If there was a hero, it was you," Stevenson graciously wrote Jack shortly after the convention, "and if there has been a new gallantry on our horizon in recent years, it is yourself." Stevenson's remarks were not just currying favor with Kennedy; he was deeply impressed. "I have a feeling that he was the real hero of the hour and that we shall hear a great deal more from this promising young man," Stevenson wrote Dore Schary.

The huge outpouring of mail into Kennedy's Senate office showed clearly that he had captured the heart of America. Especially young America. The largest proportion of letters came from people under twenty.

The Democratic convention in Chicago was the critical turning point in Jack's national ambitions. He passed through a kind of "political sound barrier," observed James Burns, indelibly registering on the nation's memory. "The dramatic race had glued millions to their television sets. Kennedy's near-victory and sudden loss, the impression he gave of a clean-cut boy who had done his best and who was accepting defeat with a smile—all this struck at people's hearts in living rooms across the nation. In this moment of triumphant defeat, his campaign for the presidency was born."[38]

During the Chicago convention Jackie had stayed with Eunice Shriver. "I never saw [Jack] except when he wandered by our box," she later said of her busy husband.

Anticipating his need for a vacation after the Chicago convention, Jack had instructed Evelyn Lincoln to charter a sailboat and a crew for a Mediterranean cruise. Starting in the South of France, he planned to sail with Ted Kennedy and Torby Macdonald. Rather than remain by herself while Jack was gone, Jackie decided to stay with her mother and stepfather at Hammersmith Farm.

Jack and his companions stopped in Paris for a night on the town, then visited his father on the French Riviera. "Jack arrived here very tired," Joe Kennedy wrote to his friend Morton Downey, "but I think very happy because he came out of the convention so much better than anyone could have hoped . . . His time is surely coming!"[39]

At Cannes, Jack boarded the forty-foot boat and sailed off into the Mediterranean with his brother and MacDonald. A reporter for the *Washington Star* later interviewed the crew, who reported several young women aboard. (George Smathers had also gone to Europe with Jack, but decided against the boat trip.)

Jack's trip was poorly timed. Jackie was expecting a baby in October. Because she'd had a miscarriage in the first year of their marriage, this was her second pregnancy, and she was tired after her hectic week at the convention. She apparently had asked Jack not to leave her, but he had decided to go anyway.

Shortly after Jackie arrived at Hammersmith Farm, she suffered severe cramps and began to hemorrhage. Rushed to the Newport hospital, on August 23, 1956, she underwent an emergency cesarean section. But it was hopeless. The fetus, a girl, was stillborn. Robert Kennedy immediately flew to Newport to be near Jackie while Eunice Shriver tried frantically to contact Jack in the Mediterranean.[40]

"Sen. Kennedy at Sea, Lacks News of Wife," screamed a news caption in the *Boston Herald*. It took three days to contact Jack, cruising off Capri. He took the news calmly, and after learning that Jackie was in good condition, he initially intended to resume his leisurely sail. Only after Smathers forcefully interjected was he persuaded to return home. "If you want to run for president, you'd better get your ass back to your wife's bedside or else every wife in the country will be against you," Smathers insisted. "Why the hell should I go now?" Jack asked. Smathers remained adamant, and when Joe Kennedy agreed, Jack and Smathers returned.

Lawrence Leamer has offered the best judgment on Jack's attitude about the family tragedy:

> Jack in his terrible obtuseness, his awesome, willful insensitivity had defined the emotional parameters of his marriage. He had shown what he truly felt, more accurately what he did not feel. Even after he heard about the miscarriage, he had initially wanted to stay on the boat, to enjoy himself, to relax. He had little apparent regard for Jackie and her anguish.[41]

By the time Jack arrived back in the United States, his attitude appeared to have changed. He seemed upset and worried. He flew directly into Boston's Logan Airport, then jumped into a waiting private plane that sped him to Newport. At Logan, when a reporter asked him a question about Adlai Stevenson, he snapped, "I'd rather talk politics with you some other time."

"Can you get me to Newport Hospital in ten minutes?" he asked his driver. Only by breaking traffic laws came the reply. "He was nervous," said his driver, "and if the light would be yellow, he'd say, 'Go through it. I'll pay for all the tickets.'"

Thousands of well-wishers responded sympathetically to the tragedy. A flood of letters, on top of those from people who had earlier been touched by Jack's convention appearances, descended on his office. "People wrote of how they cried and how their children cried and how they prayed for him," Evelyn Lincoln later said.

The death of the baby placed added strain on Jack and Jackie's marriage.

"Jackie worried about whether she'd ever be able to have a baby," Billings recalled, "and she blamed her problem on the crazy pace of politics and the constant demands to participate in the endless activities of the Kennedy family."[42]

After Jack returned from vacation, he spent part of every day for two weeks with Jackie. Then he was on the campaign trail again, promoting the Stevenson-Kefauver ticket. For the next two months Jackie seldom saw him. He was in constant demand, his office reporting that he had received 1,500 speaking invitations from throughout the country in the six weeks after the Democratic convention.

He cooperated fully with Stevenson's campaign organizers, willingly accepting assignments. On September 21, he spoke to six hundred of the party faithful at the Fairmont Hotel in San Francisco. The *San Francisco Examiner* tagged him the "fast rising star" of the Democratic Party. "The grinning Kennedy, his boyish charm belying his noted political aggressiveness, got a standing ovation when he entered the hotel's Gold Room, another when he was introduced . . . and still another when he finished speaking."

Jack's appearance in Louisville, Kentucky, on October 4, 1956, nearly caused a riot. Ursuline College students gave him a standing ovation when he was introduced as a "Catholic and a statesman." After his speech he virtually had to fight his way through admiring coeds on his way to his waiting auto. Young women lined the driveway and stopped his car repeatedly to ask for his autograph. "We love you on TV," the women screamed. "You're better than Elvis Presley."[43]

Throughout the fall his speeches stressed two themes: one on domestic issues, the other on foreign policy.

Voters were disappointed in Eisenhower's "lack of courage and determination" in meeting domestic problems, he said repeatedly. Republicans boasted of peak prosperity, but the profits of the largest corporations had risen some 61 percent, while factory wages had gone up only 10 percent and farm prices and small business profits were down 18 percent and 52 percent, respectively.

The country needed new social programs. "We can build the schools and the hospitals and the homes and the highways that our nation needs. We can wage relentless war against slums and poverty and illiteracy and illness and economic insecurity."

In foreign policy, a field Kennedy said Adlai Stevenson would excel in as President, Republicans practiced "drift, inaction and vacillation." He appealed for an honest, unemotional discussion of foreign policy issues, completely free from what he called "partisan distortion, exaggeration or oversimplification."[44]

The Eisenhower attitude toward anticolonialism received his sharpest rebuke. U.S. policy had been too closely linked to the interests of our Western allies—the British, French, Belgian, and Dutch nations. While concentrating on the dangers of communism, the United States had virtually ignored the Asian-African upsurge of nationalism and the struggle for self-determination. Consequently the United States had allowed itself to appear in the eyes of millions of uncommitted people as no longer the champion of independence.

Meanwhile, nothing clicked in Stevenson's campaign. The former Illinois governor campaigned less effectively than he had four years earlier. His speeches were not as witty, urbane, or eloquent. On television he appeared tired, and sometimes his delivery was stumbling and awkward.

The campaign came down to personality. Eisenhower impressed voters with his sincerity, his patriotism, his earnestness, in short, with his extreme likability. Voters disapproved of Stevenson's divorce and were less impressed by his personality. On election day the Democrats consolidated their majorities in both houses of Congress, but Stevenson was trounced by Eisenhower, winning only Missouri and six Southern states.[45]

Of all the Democrats in 1956, Kennedy emerged the biggest winner. He had leaped to prominence while being spared the handicap of association with the humiliating Stevenson-Kefauver defeat.

16

IMAGE AND STATURE

D uring Thanksgiving at Hyannis Port in 1956, Kennedy told Dave Powers, "With only about four hours of work and a handful of supporters, I came within thirty-three and a half votes of winning the vice presidential nomination. If I work hard for four years, I ought to be able to pick up all the marbles."

In the first six months of 1957 Kennedy delivered eighty-five speeches in thirty states. (He turned down about fifteen hundred other invitations.) From memory he gave his advisers a complete rundown on every state he visited, rattling off the names of local politicians who were friendly, hostile, or neutral and specifying the number of convention delegates each was likely to control in 1960. He detailed the states that had primaries, the delegations with the unit rule, the ones that would come to the convention under instruction from a state convention, and those free to vote openly for their favorite candidates. "He knew, for example," said Ken O'Donnell, "that the Democratic chairman in Puerto Rico, José Benitez, controlled more delegates than Governor Muñoz-Marin, and he had already enlisted key contact men in several states who were comparatively unknown before 1960 but turned out to be invaluable during the campaign."[1]

Publicly Jack did all he could to dampen speculation about a run for the presidency. He had no intention of announcing his plans until after his Senate reelection in 1958. "I'm not thinking about 1960, I'm tremendously interested in my Senate job and want to stay there."

With friends and reporters he often discussed other potential presidential challengers. Since Stevenson had already had two shots at the presidency, Democrats didn't owe him a third. Jack didn't believe that Hubert Humphrey would make a better President than he would; besides, the South would never support the Minnesota senator because of his strong support for civil rights. Senator Stuart Symington was experienced, but lazy. "The man we owe the nomination to is Lyndon," Jack said. "He wants the same things for the country that I do. But it is too close to Appomattox for him to get the nomination."

Pollsters consistently reported him well out in front of potential rivals in the opinion of Democratic voters. Still, he did not presume that the office would seek the man; nobody would hand him the nomination. "In every campaign I've ever been in," he told Sorensen, "they've said I was starting too early—that I would peak too soon or get too much exposure or run out of gas or be too easy a target. I would never have won any race following that advice."

Meanwhile his Senate staff had grown. Myer Feldman, a tall Pennsylvanian and seasoned government lawyer, handled most legislative matters and drafted legislation. Fred Holborn, an expert on international affairs, kept watch on several areas and helped draft foreign-policy statements. From the staff of the Senate Education and Labor Committee, Kennedy acquired Ralph Dungan to handle labor and social-welfare issues.[2]

During the campaign of 1956 Robert Kennedy, then thirty, traveled with Adlai Stevenson's entourage as an assistant to James Finnegan, Stevenson's campaign manager. But he wasn't assigned any duties. "Nobody asked me anything, nobody wanted me to do anything, nobody consulted me," said Bobby. Bored, he took reams of notes about how to organize—and not organize—a national presidential campaign.

There were problems to overcome, skeptics to convert. His father, his ambiguous stand on civil rights, his silence on the McCarthy issue, his youth, and his Catholicism all concerned Democrats. "He'll never make it with that haircut," said a New York political figure. A politician in the Midwest thought Kennedy's youth a bigger liability than his religion. "It makes no difference how mature Kennedy may be," the man said; "if the bosses and the voters decide that he *looks* immature."

Why was Kennedy in such a rush? "If I were his father," said James Reston in *The New York Times* in 1957, "I would tell him to slow down . . . His age is against him now; in another few years it won't be. He has time."[3]

A writer in the *Progressive* thought Kennedy did not "have the grand manner of Franklin Roosevelt, the wit of Adlai Stevenson, the rough and tumble of Harry Truman, the brilliant flow of ideas of Hubert Humphrey, or the brutal force of Vice President Nixon. He has, instead, a high degree of sex appeal and 'sincerity.'"

Whatever it was, the media and the public found him fascinating. By 1957 he was Washington's "hottest tourist attraction." Reporter Rowland Evans found it impossible to lunch with him in the Senate Dining Room because well-wishers and autograph seekers engulfed him.

"Everything he did seemed to get attention," marveled Senator Humphrey. People contrasted him with the passive, aging President Eisenhower, who, while still popular, lacked Kennedy's vibrant qualities. Jack's youth, war heroism, handsome features, large energetic family, great wealth, and stunning wife made excellent copy. In the summer of 1957, *Look* featured Jack and Bobby in an eight-page article, complete with sixteen photographs of the two brothers at work, with their families, and meeting the public.[4]

In September Harold Martin in *The Saturday Evening Post* described "The Amazing Kennedys." Jack was the clean-cut, smiling American boy, "trustworthy, loyal, brave, clean and reverent, boldly facing up to the challenges of the Atomic Age." Nor was Jack the only amazing member of the amazing Kennedy family. Beginning with father Joe, Martin described the accomplishments of every child—from heroic Joe Jr. to young Edward.

The *American Mercury* called Jack the "perfect politician"; *Catholic Digest* focused on the entire Kennedy family; and *McCall's* and *Redbook* did feature stories on Jackie.[5]

"Senator Kennedy, do you have an 'in' with *Life*?" asked a high school newspaper editor. In fact, he did. Henry Luce, the conservative Republican publisher of *Time* and *Life,* had known John Kennedy since the publisher had endorsed *Why England Slept* in 1940. He was also a close friend of the ambassador's. A cover story in *Life* in July 1953 featured Jack and Jackie sailing in the waters off Hyannis Port, "breathlessly attractive and casual, with toothy smiles and windblown hair, adventurous and gay." A *Life* cover story in March 1957 portrayed Jack as "the voice of the future in the Democratic Party." *Time*'s cover story in December 1957 said, "Jack Kennedy has left panting politicians and swooning women across a large spread of the U.S." *Time*'s piece received more letters and favorable comment than any feature story in the magazine's history.

Senator Humphrey, a potential rival in 1960, complained privately about Kennedy's lavish coverage in the popular magazines. "I don't know how he does it," said Humphrey. "I get into *Photoplay* and he gets into *Life*."[6]

Most of the feature stories were initiated by the magazines themselves, not by Kennedy or his staff. Reporters and photographers were constantly at his office, always requesting his time.

"Should I try to discourage them so you won't be interrupted so much?" Evelyn Lincoln asked.

"By no means, Mrs. Lincoln. If I know one thing, it is that a politician can kill himself faster by playing hard-to-get with the press than he can by jumping off the Capitol dome. . . . As long as they want to talk to me, I want to talk to them. Maybe longer."

When Rowland Evans teased him about the extravagent publicity, Jack responded, "If somebody comes to your office . . . and they say, 'My editor sent me down here to do a story,' what am I going to say? I don't want you to do my story? I wouldn't make a good story, beat it! I can't say that. I have to be nice to these people." And besides, he said, "this publicity does one good thing. It takes the V out of VP." He meant that the attention made him a viable presidential candidate instead of just a vice-presidential prospect.[7]

The Kennedy image in the mass media was superficial and one-dimensional, paying scant attention to his political views. The media mainly portrayed a captivating politician, a radiant celebrity. Photographers from national magazines took hundreds of photos of him. Jack Gould, the *New York Times*'s television columnist, called him "the most telegenic personality of our times."

Jack valued the exposure in popular magazines, but complained about the mostly mindless stories. "They are all writing about my glamorous wife and me, personality stuff," he said. "Why doesn't anybody ever report what I think about issues?" To Fletcher Knebel of *Look* he said, "You did not spell out my qualifications as a candidate."

Several reporters judged him exceptionally candid. "It was miraculous to me that nobody seemed to break the trust, or print these off-the-cuff remarks," said journalist Laura Bergquist. She thought reporters felt honor-bound not to abuse his confidence. But an old friend of Jack's thought he was more often calculating than candid. "All the time he's beaming at reporters, he's cautiously doling out only the news that will create the exact impression he wants the public to get."[8]

Despite his mostly warm and solicitous feeling for reporters, some stories irritated him. "Get Sorensen," he would tell Evelyn Lincoln after reading a critical item. "Ted, look at what this fellow has said about me. Let's give him the facts and blast him." The two then sent off a rebuttal. If the offending writer ignored the rebuttal, or continued criticizing, Jack didn't repeat the process. "His mind's made up and facts won't change it," he would say.

The image he projected in polls was almost entirely favorable. Asked to describe Kennedy, voters answered "energetic . . . intelligent . . . good-looking . . . strong character . . . good family . . . aggressive . . . dynamic . . . outspoken."

Before 1956 Kennedy had to submit articles to journals like any other fledgling author; after 1956, editors solicited articles from him. A favorite theme requested by magazines was still political courage; he and Sorensen even wrote a piece on three women of courage for *McCall's*.

Kennedy's byline appeared above more than three dozen articles. Some appeared in mass-circulation magazines; others, in high-brow journals like *Foreign Affairs*. Several focused on legislative issues that interested him—military policy (*Reporter*), admission to the military academies (*Saturday Evening Post*), regulation of lobbying (*The New York Times Magazine*). Foreign policy was another favorite theme: "A Democrat Looks at Foreign Policy" (*Foreign Affairs*), "Algerian Crisis" (*America*), "If India Falls" (*Progressive*).[9]

The public didn't know, though, that Ted Sorensen did most of the research and writing. (Kennedy usually critiqued Sorensen's drafts and provided intellectual inspiration.) After sending Jack the draft of an article for *This Week Magazine* ("Who Should We Vote For"), Sorensen added: "If you could give me your corrections over the phone we should be able to meet this deadline very easily."

Historian Herbert Parmet studied the "backstage" operation of producing the articles:

> When, for example, Sorensen forwarded to Kennedy the draft of an article that ultimately appeared in the October 1957 issue of *Foreign Affairs* as "A Democrat Looks at Foreign Policy," there was little doubt about how it had been put together. . . . Sending it on to Kennedy, Sorensen added the hope that it was "reasonably satisfactory, and won't interfere too much with your enjoying your trip to California." When *Foreign Affairs* editor Hamilton Fish Armstrong received it, the article came with a cover letter over Kennedy's signature stating that "it has been a pleasure for me to write it and to ponder some of the issues which it treats."[10]

Usually cogently written and thoughtful, the Kennedy-Sorensen literary efforts succeeded in portraying Jack as a serious student of politics and current affairs. But it was the glamorous photos, stories, and articles *about him* that attracted the most potential voters. And this fact bothered a few critics.

The most profound early criticism of Kennedy's presidential ambition focused on his glamorous image. In November 1957, columnist William V. Shannon pointed out that the ideal president should have long and diverse experience in politics—administrative experience and foreign-policy expertise. "Presidents do not always measure up to this ideal, but at the present juncture in history it is by this ideal they must be measured."

Kennedy didn't measure up. He had virtually no executive experience, and had not bossed any operation larger than his own Senate office. With more experience he would be wiser and more accomplished. He might be an excellent prospect for the nomination in 1972, but not 1960.

That Kennedy was so "attractive" was precisely one of the major difficulties. "There is a growing tendency on the part of Americans to 'consume' political figures in much the same sense we consume entertainment personalities on television and in the movies," Shannon wrote.

> Month after month, from the glossy pages of *Life* to the multicolored cover of *Redbook,* Jack and Jackie Kennedy smile out at millions of readers; he with his tousled hair and winning smile, she with her dark eyes and beautiful face. We hear of her pregnancy, of his wartime heroism, of their fondness for sailing. But what has all this to do with statesmanship? . . . Meanwhile ballistic missiles are being tested in Siberia, children are going to sleep hungry in Bombay, and Communist rioters are marching in the streets of Jakarta.

Voters should make their choices in terms of "considered judgment of men and issues," not "on marginal personality differences." To do otherwise was unpolitical and escapist. Kennedy and others "have responded to this problem by downgrading issues and upgrading charm."[11]

Shannon made one crucial error in his otherwise persuasive argument. For the most part, it wasn't John Kennedy who downgraded issues and upgraded charm. He had a highly refined grasp of issues and articulately addressed them. It was the media and the public that downgraded issues and upgraded charm.

On May 7, 1957, the Pulitzer Prize Advisory Committee announced its list of winners in the field of letters for 1957. Together with awards for such distinguished works as Eugene O'Neill's play *Long Day's Journey into Night,* George Kennan's historical account *Russia Leaves the War: Soviet-American Relations, 1917–1920,* and a volume of verse by Richard Wilbur, *Things of This World,* went a prize in biography to John F. Kennedy for *Profiles in Courage.*

The prestigious award was marvelous publicity for JFK. Unknown at the time was the division among the judges about Kennedy's book. What's more, the prize sparked rumors about whether Kennedy actually wrote *Profiles* or merely benefited from the superb ghostwriting of Theodore Sorensen.

Normally the Pulitzer Prize's Advisory Committee accepted the recommendation of its jury of experts—as it did in 1957, except for *Profiles in Courage*. The biography jury, composed of Professor Julian Boyd, editor of the Thomas Jefferson Papers at Princeton, and Professor Bernard Mayo of the University of Virginia, had ranked Kennedy's book third. Their first choice was Alpheus T. Mason's *Harlan Fiske Stone: Pillar of the Law;* their alternate recommendation was *Roosevelt: The Lion and the Fox* by James M. Burns of Williams College.

The advisory committee was ready to accept Mason's book when a member unexpectedly intervened. Donald Ferguson, the editor of the *Milwaukee Journal,* had become enchanted with *Profiles.* Raising his hand hesitantly, Ferguson told his colleagues how much he admired Kennedy's book and how he had tested its inspirational value. "I read it aloud to my 12-year-old grandson and the boy was absolutely fascinated," said Ferguson. "I think we should give the prize to *Profiles in Courage.*"

Suddenly, the atmosphere changed. Others agreed with Ferguson, and the advisory committee proceeded to override the recommendations of the jury of historians and award the biography prize to Kennedy.[12]

Shortly after learning the news, Kennedy informed his friend Ralph Horton. "I never heard Jack Kennedy boast about any accomplishments or anything he had ever done," Horton recalled, "but I could see that he was extremely proud and extremely touched by . . . [the] Pulitzer Prize award."

Some observers contend that the Kennedy circle lobbied for the award, pulling strings to secure it. At the beginning of 1957 JFK sent his father a list of the members of the advisory committee, presumably so the ambassador could contact the members on behalf of *Profiles.* Several years after Kennedy's honor, Arthur Krock boasted that he had lobbied committee members, implying that his role was decisive in convincing members to grant the award to Kennedy.[13]

John Hohenberg, a distinguished journalist, was professor of journalism at Columbia, and from 1954 to 1976 served as administrator of the Pulitzer Prizes and secretary of the Pulitzer board. Krock did lobby for Kennedy, he said, but Hohenberg stressed that Krock's advocacy was not instrumental. Krock had such a well-known reputation as a "drumbeater" that his efforts may have been counterproductive. Nor was there any sign that Ambassador Kennedy had intervened. Joseph Pulitzer Jr. later emphatically declared that there was "not a chance in a million" that the ambassador could have had any kind of influence even if he had tried.[14]

After winning the Pulitzer Prize, Kennedy was besieged by offers for articles in prominent journals. But the prize also sparked rumors that he did not deserve the honor because he was not the book's real author. The first published account suggesting fraudulent authorship appeared on May 15, 1957, when Gilbert Seldes claimed in the *Village Voice* that not only was *Profiles* a book for adolescents but was written with a collaborator. Seldes's accusation received little publicity. Far more serious was an accusation made seven months later.

On December 7, 1957, during ABC television's *The Mike Wallace Interview,* correspondent Wallace interviewed Drew Pearson, one of the country's most widely read political columnists. In the course of the interview Pearson referred to Kennedy and his recent book:

PEARSON: Jack Kennedy is . . . the only man in history that I know who won a Pulitzer Prize on a book which was ghostwritten for him, which indicates the kind of public-relations buildup he's had.

WALLACE: Do you know for a fact, Drew—

PEARSON: [speaking over Wallace] Yes, I do—

WALLACE: . . . that the book, *Profiles in Courage,* was written for Senator Kennedy—

PEARSON: I do.

WALLACE: . . . by somebody else—and he has never acknowledged the fact?

PEARSON: No, he has not. You know, there's a little wisecrack around the Senate about Jack, who is a very handsome man, as you know. Some of his colleagues say, "Jack, I wish you had a little bit less profile and more courage."

The following Monday morning, December 9, 1957, Kennedy phoned attorney Clark Clifford and asked to meet with him immediately. When Kennedy arrived, very dejected, he asked Clifford for assistance. "Did you see *The Mike Wallace Interview* Saturday night?" he asked. Clifford had not, so Kennedy described Pearson's comments. "I cannot let this stand," he told Clifford. "It is a direct attack on my integrity and my honesty."

The best solution, Clifford thought, was to obtain a quick retraction from ABC and Pearson before the story spread and generated a life of its own. During the conversation in Clifford's office, Joe Kennedy phoned with a different strategy. "I want you to sue the bastards for fifty million dollars," he told Clifford. "Get it started right away. It's dishonest and they know it. My boy wrote the book. This is a plot against us."

Throughout his father's tirade the senator remained calm. When the phone conversation ended, JFK said to Clifford, "Well, that's just Dad. Let's deal with this thing."[15]

Clifford quickly arranged a meeting with executives and lawyers at ABC, who contacted Pearson. On the television program Pearson had been unable to recall the name of the "ghostwriter," but now he remembered. Theodore Sorensen, Pearson said, had written *Profiles in Courage.*

Brilliantly prepared for Pearson's charge, Clifford pointed out that in the book's preface Kennedy had acknowledged his "greatest debt" to his "research associate, Theodore C. Sorensen." Kennedy conceded that Sorensen had been paid six thousand dollars, but stressed that this admission did not mean that Sorensen had written the book.

The crafty Clifford had stashed Sorensen in a nearby hotel, waiting to be called. Therefore when ABC asked to interrogate Sorensen, the senator's assistant rushed to ABC from the hotel and expertly rebutted efforts by ABC's lawyers to break down his story.

Shortly after, Sorensen signed an affidavit which Clifford sent to ABC. In it Sorensen said:

> The author of Profiles in Courage is Senator Kennedy, who originally conceived its theme, selected its characters, determined its contents, and wrote and rewrote each of its chapters. The research, suggestions and other materials received by him in the course of writing the book from me and the others listed in the Preface were all considered by the Senator along with his own material, and in part rejected by him and in part drawn upon by him in his work. To assert that any one of us who supplied such materials "wrote the book" for the Senator is clearly unwarranted and in error.

After Clifford threatened legal action, ABC caved in and agreed to a retraction. On Saturday evening, December 14, at the beginning of *The Mike Wallace Interview*, Oliver Treyz, an ABC vice president, read a statement prepared by Clifford:

> This company has inquired into the charge made by Mr. Pearson and has satisfied itself that such charge is unfounded and that the book in question was written by Senator Kennedy. We deeply regret this error and feel it does a grave injustice to a distinguished public servant and author and to the excellent book he wrote, and to the worthy prize that he was awarded. We extend our sincere apologies to Senator Kennedy, his publishers, and the Pulitzer Prize Committee.[16]

A month after ABC's retraction, JFK visited Pearson. "He didn't ask me for a retraction, but I think I shall give him one," Pearson wrote in his personal diary on January 14, 1958. Kennedy "showed enough knowledge of the book, had lived with the book, made the book so much a part of him, that basically it is his book. Furthermore, it is quite an inspiring book. I don't think it deserves a Pulitzer prize, but nevertheless it is good." Shortly after their meeting Pearson issued a brief retraction in his column.

Trying to squelch the rumors, Kennedy wrote several media sources who had repeated the reports that he had not written *Profiles*. His letter to John Oakes of *The New York Times* was typical:

> I have on many occasions, directly and indirectly, formally and informally, stated unequivocally that I was the sole author of the book—when I signed a contract with the publishers, filed a copyright, accepted the royalties (all of them) and accepted the Pulitzer Prize. . . . The question was very thoroughly investigated by ABC before the attached statement was issued; and, in addition, I have had a recent conversation with Mr. Drew Pearson. I would welcome the opportunity to review the notebook and other evidence with you when you are next in Washington, should you think this desirable or necessary.

Part of Kennedy's letter misrepresented the truth. He may have accepted all the royalties for *Profiles,* but Davids and Sorensen were paid for their contributions. Nor did ABC "thoroughly" investigate the matter before issuing its retraction.

Despite Kennedy's efforts, and despite the retractions by ABC and Pearson, doubts and rumors persisted. On December 24, 1957, John Fischer of *Harper's* magazine advised Sorensen of "wide-spread rumors" that the book was produced by a ghostwriter. "These rumors appear to predate the Pearson broadcast, although, of course, that gave them impetus—and the network's apology did not help to squelch them."[17]

Martha MacGregor, the book editor of the *New York Post,* pressed the senator about the rumors. They still persisted even though "they've gone underground," she wrote him:

> There is a rumor that you wrote the first and last chapters and that the rest of the book was worked on by various people. Then there's the rumor that Mr. Sorensen did the whole book and that he collects 50% of the royalties. . . . I mention all this to show you that the official denial on Mike Wallace's [program] has not stopped the rumors. . . . Would you be willing to tell me for publication exactly how the book was written and what the acknowledgments in the foreword imply? In other words, exactly what did Messrs. Sorensen, Davids and Landis do in connection with the book? Is or isn't Mr. Sorensen collecting a royalty? Would it be possible to examine the notebooks?

In a despairing tone Kennedy replied that, yes, he wrote the book, adding that "most of us who are active in public affairs have become accustomed to many rumors about many things which have no factual basis whatsoever."[18]

The crucial question remains: Was Kennedy the real author of *Profiles in Courage* or was it ghostwritten? Did he manufacture a writing talent to enhance his image as an exceptionally imaginative and perceptive young senator, distinctively different from conventional politicians, and then, while denying that the book was principally the work of others, accept a Pulitzer Prize?

In the book's preface JFK generously thanked those who aided him. Besides two secretaries and editor Evan Thomas, he acknowledged Jules Davids for assisting "materially in the preparation of several chapters, as did my able friend James M. Landis, who delights in bringing the precision of the lawyer to the mysteries of history." Criticism by Arthur Holcombe and Arthur M. Schlesinger Jr., both of Harvard, and Walter Johnson of the University of Chicago "greatly improved" the book. "The greatest debt," Kennedy wrote, "is owed to my research associate, Theodore C. Sorensen, for his invaluable assistance in the assembly and preparation of the material upon which this book is based."[19]

Pulitzer Prize official John Hohenberg thought Kennedy more than adequately acknowledged assistance on the book. "From my experience with writers and as the author of a number of books," he reflected, "I have seldom seen so complete a characterization of sources and assistance as Senator Kennedy offered the public for his *Profiles in Courage.*"

Evan Thomas claimed that Kennedy was the real author. Plenty of people witnessed Jack working on the book. Rose Kennedy reported seeing her son at Palm Beach "in his sea-wall alcove with his writing board and a thick writing pad clamped to it, and a folding table or two piled with books and notebooks and file folders—paperweights or perhaps some rocks from the beach to hold things down against the sea breezes—and his head would be forward, and he would be writing away on that book."[20]

Gloria Sitrin, Sorensen's secretary, later said, "I personally took dictation from Senator Kennedy on the book . . . in Florida." Another secretary, Jean Mannix, saw Kennedy's handwritten drafts after Sorensen returned from Palm Beach, and later typed for the senator when he returned to Washington. "There's no doubt in my mind that Ted did a great deal of the research," said Mannix, "but the book was written by [Kennedy]."

"I recalled seeing him lying flat on his back on a board with a yellow pad on which he was writing the book," said Arthur Krock, "and . . . I read enough of those pages at the time to know that the product was his own."[21]

Some of Sorensen's letters to the senator convey the impression that Kennedy was a major contributor. "All of the corrections which you have suggested in your various letters . . . have been incorporated, along with several fairly minor corrections that I have made from time to time," Sorensen wrote on September 12, 1955. He added that the editor Evan Thomas didn't want any further editing for style because Thomas preferred to "keep the manuscript in your original words."

Sorensen has consistently and repeatedly denied ghostwriting the book. "I can look in the book and find words and even sentences of mine," he reflected. "I worked damn hard on that book, and I don't want to underestimate what I did. But [Kennedy] gave me proper credit in the preface, just as he gave all the others proper credit. But the basic conception, direction, decisions on what materials to use, digestion of all the research reports and the dictation of the final drafts, the penciling of the final drafts, the rewriting of the final first draft—that was all his."

"I have no doubt that had the book been a total failure," Sorensen added, Kennedy "would have received all the blame."[22]

The foremost expert on the writing of *Profiles in Courage* is Professor Herbert Parmet, who closely studied the controversy for his book, *Jack: The Struggles of John F. Kennedy* (1980). Because Parmet's book is well researched, thoughtful, and usually evenhanded, his judgment on *Profiles* has influenced a generation of historians and other students of Kennedy's life. Parmet's conclusion? *Profiles* was essentially ghostwritten, mostly by Theodore Sorensen.

The chronology of Kennedy's life in 1954 and 1955, and the materials accumulated in the preparation of the book, "do not even come close to supporting the contention that Jack could have been or was its major author," said Parmet. Besides his work in the Senate, Kennedy underwent two major spinal operations, and when not convalescing, he frequently made appearances throughout the country to advance his political career. He also made an extensive European tour from August to October of 1955.

"The evidence is now available," said Parmet, "perhaps as detailed as will ever be known. Relevant handwritten drafts, typescripts, and recorded tapes have been deposited with the Kennedy Library." In his close inspection of the files Parmet found that what Kennedy personally wrote were "very rough passages without paragraphing, without any shape, largely ideas jotted down as possible sections, obviously necessitating editing." JFK's portion of the handwritten material "in no way resembles the final product." Parmet added:

> There is no evidence of a Kennedy draft for the overwhelming bulk of the book; and there is evidence for concluding that much of what he did draft was simply not included in the final version. The inescapable impression is that Kennedy's own interest, other than the question of representing one's conscience rather than merely reflecting constituent desires, largely related to John Quincy Adams, and he bogged down in that area, completely out of proportion to the needs of the book. Those who took over the project, headed by Sorensen, rescued him and helped fill out the material.

If the handwritten evidence is scant, dictation could have justified his claim to authorship. The existing tapes, however, duplicate the pattern of the nearly illegible scrawls on those canary sheets.

For practical reasons—limitations of time, health, and appropriate talent—Kennedy served "principally as an overseer or, more charitably, as a sponsor and editor, one whose final approval was as important for its publication as for its birth," Parmet said. "At the working level, research, tentative drafts, and organizational planning were left to committee labor, with such talents as Professor Davids making key contributions." The burdens of time and literary craftsmanship, said Parmet, "were clearly Sorensen's, and he gave the book both the drama and flow that made for readability."[23]

Parmet laid out the group's division of labor:

During the senator's hospitalization . . . Sorensen carried books and documents to his bedside in New York. Then, at Palm Beach, they worked together with the assistance of secretaries, and additional material was dictated. From his Washington office Sorensen performed multiple functions as coordinator of the structure and director of the flow of paperwork to and from the various contributors and critics. After the Webster chapter, Davids submitted twenty-six pages on Sam Houston, twenty-four on Lucius Q. C. Lamar, a twenty-six-page chapter on George W. Norris, and a thirteen-page essay on "The Meaning of Political Courage" for the closing section. Sorensen himself drafted the chapters on John Quincy Adams, Thomas Hart Benton, and Edmund Ross, plus the section on "Additional Men of Courage." Landis . . . wrote a chapter on Robert A. Taft and helped rework the Webster material. Kennedy then combined Davids's and Sorensen's work on "The Meaning of Courage" and completed Chapter XI by adding his own personal comments and observations.

The final phase of writing hardly involved Kennedy at all, Parmet claimed. "Sorensen's talents gave the manuscript its lucid and dramatic readability, which included the important function of providing for stylistic consistency."

Influenced by Parmet's analysis, most students of Kennedy's life have referred to Kennedy as the author only in a limited sense. Kennedy authorized the book, observed Garry Wills. He "directed the writing; delivered nothing he did not accept; had final right to delete anything or add anything. His authority could not be overruled. It was all done in his name. But Theodore Sorensen . . . along with Jules Davids and others, wrote *Profiles in Courage*."

History, though, may have cast too harsh a judgment on Kennedy's role in writing *Profiles*. Although Parmet's research was extensive, it was not exhaustive. Some evidence seems to have disappeared, evidence which might have shown additional Kennedy contributions. New tape recordings with Kennedy's dictation were made on top of old recordings, Parmet conceded, "so that the existing reels do not represent the full extent of [Kennedy's] dictation."[24]

Missing are the notebooks—to which Kennedy often referred—which impressed Drew Pearson and others, convincing them that Kennedy did write major portions of *Profiles*. In Sorensen's correspondence at the time and in subsequent interviews, he repeatedly referred to letters and phone calls from the senator concerning the book. Yet none of these sources appear in Parmet's analysis.

It is incorrect to assume that the chronology of Kennedy's life in 1954–1955 made it unlikely that he could substantially contribute to writing the book. In fact, while convalescing from his two surgeries, he had little else to do *except* work on the book. He may also have done some writing during his tour of Europe from August to October of 1955.

Even if additional information shows that Kennedy deserves more credit for writing the book, historians may still conclude that Sorensen actually wrote most of *Profiles in Courage*. Nonetheless, one thing is clear: Kennedy deeply believed he wrote enough of *Profiles* to claim real authorship. He may have been mistaken in his judgment, but there is no evidence he tried to deceive. He could accept the Pulitzer Prize with a clear conscience.

The difficult process of writing the book created remarkable synergy between Kennedy and Sorensen, a dynamic working relationship that resulted in the strikingly memorable speeches Kennedy subsequently delivered. In the end, that creative working partnership may have been the most important consequence of *Profiles in Courage*.

17

COPING WITH PAPA
AND PAIN

In the fall of 1957, as the senator crisscrossed the country giving speeches, he worried about Jackie, who was awaiting the birth of their much-anticipated first child. He cautioned Evelyn Lincoln to "keep in close touch with Jackie in case you need me in a hurry." As it turned out, Jackie's New York obstetrician decided to deliver the baby by cesarean section, and set the date for November 27, 1957. On that day Jackie gave birth to a seven-pound baby girl, Caroline Bouvier Kennedy.

While Jackie was in the operating room, the nervous senator paced the hospital corridor. After Jackie was wheeled out of the operating room, re-called Louella Hennessey, Jack "seemed to take that corridor in one great giant step. When he reached her side, his face lit up. I'm sure it was the happiest moment of his life." Janet Auchincloss also remembered the "sweet expression on [Jack's] face and the way he smiled" when the doctor told him the baby had arrived and Jackie was fine. While viewing Caroline in the nursery through the glass window, he said to the nurses, "She's easily the prettiest baby in the room, don't you think?"[1]

Three weeks after Caroline's birth, the Kennedys moved into a new home at 3307 N Street, Georgetown, along with Maud Shaw, the British nanny hired to take care of Caroline. The new father, according to Shaw, wanted to give Caroline a bottle but was apprehensive. "He asked me to stand quite near him in case he dropped her." After a few moments, the fidgety senator said, "Miss Shaw, how have you got the patience to feed the child all this bottle? You take the bottle and finish her."

Neither Rose Kennedy nor Janet Auchincloss had ever been troubled by mundane child-rearing matters, and Jack and Jackie saw no reason to break with that tradition. Jackie never had to sweep floors, launder clothes, prepare meals, or wash dishes. She delegated routine household and child-rearing matters to the nanny, maid, laundress, and cook. Jackie gave them directions. When Caroline awoke crying at 2:00 A.M., Maud Shaw, not Jackie, shuffled down two flights of stairs to heat up a bottle of formula to feed her. Nonetheless, Jackie cared for Caroline in other ways. She dressed her, took her for walks, played with her in the garden, and splashed with her in an inflatable pool in the backyard.

Caroline Kennedy stirred strong emotions in both parents. "For Jackie, being a mother seemed to validate her sense of self," observed Goodwin. "It gave her an inner peace and security which nothing else ever had. It opened her heart." As for the forty-year-old father, he seemed more emotional about Caroline's birth than anything his friends had ever seen. "His voice cracked when he called to tell the news," said Lem Billings, "and when he showed me the baby he looked happier than I had seen him look in a long time. With this child, he finally had a family of his own."[2]

The late 1950s was the heyday of the Kennedy clan's raucous athletic contests. Because of his fragile back, Jack usually watched as his brothers, sisters, in-laws, and friends engaged in the ferocious touch football games on his father's lawn at Hyannis Port. Energy, pride, strident competition, raw guts were all on display—sometimes with photographers capturing the action.

One guest, David Hackett, a friend and aide to Robert Kennedy, later wrote his "Rules for Visiting the Kennedys":

> Prepare yourself by reading the Congressional Record, US News & World Report, Time, Newsweek, Fortune, The Nation, How to Play Sneaky Tennis and The Democratic Digest. Memorize at least three good jokes. Anticipate that each Kennedy will ask you what you think of another Kennedy's a) dress, b) hairdo, c) backhand, d) latest public achievement. Be sure to answer "Terrific." This should get you through dinner. Now for the football field. It's "touch" but it's murder. If you don't want to play, don't come. If you do come, play, or you'll be fed in the kitchen

and nobody will speak to you. Don't let the girls fool you. Even pregnant, they can make you look silly. If Harvard played touch, they'd be on the varsity. Above all, don't suggest any plans, even if you played quarterback at school. The Kennedys have the signal-calling department sewed up, and all of them have A-pluses in leadership. If one of them makes a mistake, keep still. . . . But don't stand still. Run madly on every play, and make a lot of noise. Don't appear to be having too much fun though. They'll accuse you of not taking the game seriously enough. Don't criticize the other team, either. It's bound to be full of Kennedys, too, and the Kennedys don't like that sort of thing. To become really popular you must show raw guts. To show raw guts, fall on your face now and then. Smash into the house once in a while, going after a pass. Laugh off a twisted ankle, or a big hole torn in your best suit. They like this. It shows you take the game as seriously as they do.

But remember. Don't be too good. Let Jack run around you now and then. He's their boy.[3]

In 1957 *Fortune* magazine estimated Joe Kennedy's wealth at between $200 million and $400 million. Only eight other Americans ranked higher. Despite his diverse and extensive business holdings, Joe didn't encourage any of his children to go into business, or even to carry on for him after his retirement. He did bring into his businesses two of his sons-in-law—Sargent Shriver and Steve Smith, Jean's husband—but not his sons. Rather than have Jack, Bobby, or Ted become "just another businessman," he pushed them toward political careers. As a consequence, the Kennedy brothers—particularly Jack—remained innocent about business or money in general. "When they talked about business they really were just naïve," Jack's friend Charles Spalding observed. "Listening to them talk about money was like listening to nuns talk about sex. It was awkward."

Generous and sympathetic, Joe routinely sent money to the widow and children of the navy pilot killed with young Joe in 1944. When his close aide Eddie Moore became too old to work, Kennedy continued to support him in a comfortable retirement.[4]

By 1960 the Kennedy Foundation had given $43 million to charities. Joe's philanthropy naturally won lasting gratitude and valuable publicity for Jack and the family. In 1956 the *Boston Pilot* praised Joe Kennedy's recent "immensely gracious gesture," which revealed the "character of a great Christian family." Instead of donating to traditional recipients of philanthropy—health organizations, universities—the Kennedy Foundation used its vast resources for causes and organizations that personally appealed to Joe and Rose: the Catholic Church and mental retardation.[5]

Often Joe squeezed every last ounce of publicity value out of his bequest, especially publicity that would advance Jack's political career. What's more, Jack kept an eye out for politically advantageous philanthropy. "You asked me if I could discreetly inquire about a Greek organization that the Kennedy Foundation could contribute several thousands of dollars [to] . . . which would give us some [political] advantage," Francis X. Morrissey wrote the senator in March 1957. Morrissey named one. Three days later Jack wrote his father: "It might be worthwhile if we would give the Holy Cross Orthodox Theological School, a worthy Greek School, a nominal contribution. Perhaps around $2500."[6]

In his middle age Joe hired a secretary who also served as his mistress for nine years. He started his affair with Janet Des Rosiers in December 1948, three months after he hired her. "Very few suspected that I was anything to him," she later said. "I was not a sex bomb. I didn't wear sexy clothes. No one would suspect my other nature." But an associate of Joe's claimed it was widely assumed at Kennedy's New York office that they were having an affair, since she was "always available."

Joe and Des Rosiers had sexual relations in her apartment in Hyannis, in a rented house in West Palm Beach, in Joe's apartments in New York and Boston, and at Joe's vacation villa on the French Riviera. When Rose traveled, Joe moved Des Rosiers into the Hyannis Port home and had sex with her in his bedroom.

Des Rosiers decided that Rose knew about her relationship with Joe, and simply tolerated it because it took pressure off Rose. "She must have known I was around all the time and not unattractive," Des Rosiers said. "I used to massage Joe's scalp and neck with Rose in the living room. . . . I feel she must have known." But Rose never uttered one word.[7]

There were other women in Joe's life as well. When he vacationed in Nevada, he often stayed at the Cal-Neva Lodge, a gambling haven in Lake Tahoe. There and elsewhere he continued his womanizing, often associating with Frank Sinatra, who procured women for him. Late in the evening at Hyannis Port, a member of the household staff accidentally encountered Joe and a young woman Sinatra had brought along. Joe had the woman backed against a hallway wall and was fondling her breasts. When the flustered staff member explained that he had just shined Kennedy's riding boots, Joe laughed. "My riding boots! Just in time!"[8]

Joe Kennedy continued to meddle in Jack's life. Joe had a special arrangement with Grace Burke, the secretary in Jack's Boston congressional office, and with Frank Morrissey, the office manager. Both were to report to Joe. "They kept a log of every visitor so Joe could be sure his son wouldn't be swayed by anybody with a bad reputation who showed up with a hard-luck story," said Tip O'Neill.[9]

Joe furnished money for Jack to hire additional staff, and fully intended to help finance Jack's campaign for the White House. He also expected to capitalize on his valuable contacts in the media and among big-city bosses, like Mayor Richard Daley of Chicago.

One evening in 1958, LeMoyne Billings, then vice president of Lennen and Newell, a New York advertising firm, dined privately with Ambassador Kennedy at the Pavilion restaurant in New York. Jack was not present. When Lem made a light joke about Jack, Joe Kennedy was not amused. Billings listened as the ambassador sharply upbraided him, then explained that he should never again talk that way about Jack in public. "LeMoyne," he said, "you are one of the people who must understand this. You can never know who might be listening. From here on, you must think of Jack less as a friend and more as a potential candidate for President of the United States." Lem sat speechless, totally unprepared for the ambassador's final remark: "I will tell you right now that the day is going to come when you will not call Jack 'Jack.' You will call him 'Mr. President.' "[10]

As well as anybody, Joe Kennedy understood that he had to remain far offstage; otherwise his unsavory reputation would damage Jack's career. His philandering and vicious business practices were not widely known yet, but influential people knew he was a lecher and sometimes a ruthless predator (or they had heard stories and rumors that he was). More widely known were his prewar isolationism, British defeatism, anti-Semitism, toleration of Nazism, and political conservatism.

Many liberals judged Jack's father the most reactionary person in the Democratic Party. Liberal, wealthy Jewish Democrats in New York City, led by former Democratic senator Herbert Lehman, nervously (and correctly) viewed Joe Kennedy as anti-Semitic. Public-spirited and generous, leaders in the city, they worried that the father had influenced his son.[11]

Other prominent Democrats also detested Joe Kennedy. "I never liked Joe Sr.," said New Dealer and Supreme Court justice Felix Frankfurter. "Does anybody like Joe Sr.? Have you ever met anybody, except his family?"

"He was a domineering and dominating bastard," said Abraham Ribicoff, the Democratic governor and later the senator from Connecticut.

"I disliked and mistrusted [Joseph P. Kennedy]," said foreign-policy expert George Ball.

"Joseph P. Kennedy's reputation was secure as a womanizing robber baron, who had been anti-war and seen as pro-German while he was Ambassador to Britain during World War II, and pro-McCarthy during the fifties," observed Jack's journalist friend Ben Bradlee.

The media widely reported the wisecrack "It's not the Pope but the Pop."[12]

Although he was usually offstage, Joe Kennedy's large ego and propensity for irresponsible chatter occasionally undermined Jack's effort to appear independent. "What's a hundred million dollars if it'll help Jack?" Joe once said, causing Jack to cringe.

While Jack attempted to minimize his father's influence and effect on his career, Joe maximized it. "I got Jack into politics. I was the one," Joe boasted. "The rest of the family was in Boston helping me," Jack said of his 1952 campaign, "but my father stayed up at the Cape the whole time." But the father told the same reporter, "I was in Boston throughout."

For the most part, in the late 1950s Joseph Kennedy curtailed his public statements and remained quiet so as not to hinder or embarrass his son. "Jack and Bob will run the show, while Ted's in charge of hiding Joe," ran a favorite Republican gibe. He withdrew from public life, sold business interests some considered disreputable (Somerset Importers and the Hialeah racetrack), and kept his money in more respectable enterprises.[13]

It pained Jack that his father was so widely disliked. He loved his father and thought Joe's achievements had been underestimated. "[Critics] really beat him up and knock him for this and knock him for that," Jack told friends. "But you can't knock him for what he's done. Think of what he's done!" Jack meant the high positions his father had held, the business success, the money made.

While interviewing the senator, journalist Theodore White frankly told him "that no matter what he said, I just didn't like his father, old Joe Kennedy." White explained why. Saddened by White's remarks, Jack leaned forward and said, "Teddy, you must meet my father someday; he's not like that at all." But Jack made no further attempt to persuade White to like his father.[14]

After Eleanor Roosevelt criticized Jack's father, the senator vented his feelings to Brandeis University professor Lawrence Fuchs in a Honolulu hotel room. "It's just a matter of prejudice; it's an argument she had with my father thirty years ago," he said. "She hates my father." Storming around the room, Jack continued: "Don't you love your father? I love my father. But that doesn't mean I have to agree with him. We hardly agree on anything. Why, he's to the right of Herbert Hoover. Do you agree with your father on everything in politics?" No, said Fuchs. "Then why the hell are they so prejudiced?" Jack wondered.[15]

Joe Kennedy's political assistance, while still significant, was no longer central, as it had been through 1952. He sat out the 1956 Democratic convention in the South of France, and took little part in Jack's Senate reelection race in 1958. Jack had cultivated his own political instincts and surrounded himself with bright young advisers. The ambassador was invited to strategy sessions at his estates at Palm Beach and Hyannis Port, but mostly as a courtesy, and campaign organizers often disregarded his advice. During one planning session, the senior Kennedy expressed his views with "characteristic pungency." Afterward Jack said: "Well, we've heard from the Ambassador. Now, let's discuss what we're going to do."

The Kennedy camp expected Joe Kennedy to pay the campaign bills, cajole his friends throughout the country to support Jack, but otherwise remain invisible—no speeches, no interviews, no statements that would embarrass Jack. For the most part, Joe played his role perfectly.[16]

Jack's charm, wit, and personality reminded people of his grandfather Honey Fitz. His curiosity, his stoic and gentle nature, his love of travel, and his remarkable courage came more from his mother.

In 1957 Arthur Krock wrote Jack inquiring on behalf of a fellow journalist if the senator was less willing than his father to stand "four-square on an unpopular position."

Jack replied:

> I do not "enjoy" taking "unpopular" stands as much as my father did. This is partly a matter of glands and partly a matter of my profession. Politicians are as slow to seek out unpopular causes as financiers like my father to seek out unprofitable investments. And for the same reason. Political security is as essential to a politician and as attractive as economic security is to the businessman.
>
> Nevertheless, whether we like it or not, unpopularity does come, and I hope I bear it with normal equanimity.[17]

Jack shared several traits with his father, but differed in important ways. Each had intense loyalty to family, a deep concern for public service, and a flair for publicity. Like his father, Jack was self-confident and had boundless energy, intense competitive drive, and the will to win. Each managed to compartmentalize his life, showing different sides of his personality to different people in different circumstances. Both father and son were unrestrained womanizers and adulterers.

Both Kennedys possessed natural charm, Ted Sorensen insightfully observed,

> but the father, though very emotional underneath, was often dour and gruff while his son kept outwardly calm. Both had a winning Irish smile—but the father was capable of more angry outbursts than his infinitely patient son. Both had a tough inner core, capable of making hard decisions and sticking to them—but the father had a more aggressive exterior compared to his son's consistently gentle composure. The father's

normal conversation was often filled with hyperbole—his son's speech, in private as in public, was more often characterized by quiet understatement.[18]

While Joe grew more conservative, Jack became more liberal. "You and I are prehistoric, antediluvian," Joe told a friend in the late 1950s. "The kind of conservative thinking that we have had is out of style. It's the new generation, the more progressive type of thinking that motivates Jack and the people who are with him."

Jack saw a far more complex world than his father. Alluding to a discussion with his dad on foreign policy, Jack rolled his eyes and said, "Different time and different conditions."[19]

From May of 1955 until October of 1957, Kennedy spent forty-five days in hospitals, all while he was campaigning for the vice presidency and planning his campaign for the presidency in 1960.

All but one of his hospitalizations were in New York City, safely away from the glare of the New England and Washington media. Back miseries, abdominal pain, a real bout with malaria, and problems in managing his Addison's disease accounted for the confinements.

So did a new major ailment. Since the 1940s Jack had felt a burning sensation when he urinated, which by the early 1950s had become chronic prostatitis, an inflammation of the prostate. That Jack became fixated on bladder infections may indicate that he thought he had a sexually transmitted disease, but none was explicitly recorded by his doctors.

Although he seemed upbeat when he returned to the Senate in May 1955, in private his back was causing him excruciating pain. On May 26, only two days after Jack's triumphant return, Dr. Ephraim Shorr, the endocrinologist who had taken care of Kennedy during his back surgery, secretly brought him to see Dr. Janet Travell at her office on West Sixteenth Street in New York City. Again on crutches, he could barely manage to enter Travell's office. He complained about pain in his left lower back with radiation to the left lower extremity. He couldn't put weight on his left leg without intense pain. When seated he could not reach his left foot to put on his sock. He had difficulty seating himself in a low chair and in turning over in bed. Flexion of his right knee was limited; he could raise his left leg only twenty to twenty-five degrees. (Jack also told Travell that an old Harvard football injury made his right knee stiff and painful.)

A native of New York and a graduate of Cornell University's medical school, Travell began her career as a heart specialist, but had moved into the field of pharmacology. By the mid-1950s she had gained a reputation in New

York City for her expertise in the study and treatment of pain, particularly muscle spasms. Because of her reputation, Dr. Shorr brought Jack to see her.[20]

Deeply resentful, Kennedy told Travell that he had now undergone three back operations and his back still felt terrible. Travell started him on injections of procaine to relax his spinal muscles, and he seemed to improve. She kept treating him until August when Jack left for Europe.

While Jack was visiting Gunilla Von Post in Sweden in August, his back throbbed. "Please, Gunilla, you have to get me some painkillers," he pleaded. "I've run out, and I can't go on without some medication."

Travell designed a new mattress for him made of hair—tightly tied and firm—and installed a heavy bed board underneath his mattress. From then on when Evelyn Lincoln made hotel reservations for him, she specified his new bed requirement: "It will be appreciated," she wrote a Beverly Hills hotel clerk, "if you will place a mattress which is made of felt or hair and does not [have] innersprings on his bed. Likewise, he would appreciate it if you would place a board under this mattress."[21]

At Jack's request Travell redesigned some of his household furnishings, particularly his chairs. She had a rocking chair in her New York office. After Jack sat in it, he said, "This is so comfortable, why can't I have one of these?" She arranged for several.

In late September 1957, he developed a fever, plus back pain and redness and swelling along the scar from his last surgery in 1955. Another virulent staph infection was diagnosed, and Dr. Preston Wade removed an abscess in the scar.[22]

Kennedy left the hospital two days after the surgery but remained on high doses of antibiotics. The incision healed quickly, but he had no faith that the recent operation would give him long-term relief. "This was the only time when I knew him when he was really discouraged," said Travell. She was far more optimistic. On October 5, 1957, a chilly and windy day, she visited him at Hyannis Port.

"I don't feel great," he said.

"Senator, what you need right now is a long soak in a hot bath."

"Oh, I couldn't do that," he replied.

"Why not?"

"Not with that big hole in my back." (He hadn't been in a tub since he entered the hospital in October 1954.)

"But, Senator, you don't *have* a hole in your back! The abscess is practically healed—there's hardly any discoloration on the gauze."

Jack didn't know that the "hole" in his back was almost completely healed. Nor had anyone told him he could resume his baths.

The senator's eyes began to twinkle.

"I couldn't use soap, could I?"

"Of course you can," Travell answered. To convince him, she phoned Dr. Wade, who confirmed Travell's judgment. Yes, he could resume hot baths and use soap.[23]

Travell treated several other ailments as well. He was "extremely anemic," she found. He was put on a course of vitamin B_{12}, and B-complex injections, and his anemia responded to treatment. Tests also indicated that he had shockingly high cholesterol and an underactive thyroid, two more problems that Travell medicated.

She treated his allergies—to dog hair, horse hair, household dust, and various foods. He loved dogs, but whenever he encountered one, he suffered a severe breathing attack. Travell referred him to Dr. Anne M. Belcher, a nose and throat specialist at the New York Hospital, who prescribed antihistamines and other medication. On one occasion, after encountering a dog at Merrywood, Jack had difficulty breathing. "He would go off and use whatever spray he had to try to get himself breathing again," said Janet Auchincloss.

Travell convinced him to bring in a professional household cleaner to clean the drapes and rugs and wash the walls at his home and at his father's apartment on Park Avenue in New York.[24]

To counter the house-dust problem, Travell concocted an autogenous household-dust vaccine made from a sample of his own environment. "I believe that this course of vaccine therapy was of inestimable benefit to him," she claimed. "Prior to that time he had not only asthma, but following exposure and congestion of the mucous membranes in the nose and throat he would develop head colds and sinus trouble."

Managing Jack's illnesses was becoming a pharmaceutical nightmare. Dallek described the various treatments he was receiving:

> Ingested and implanted DOCA for the Addison's, and large doses of penicillin and other antibiotics to combat the prostatitis and the abscess. He also received injections of procaine at "trigger points" to relieve back pain; anti-spasmodics—principally Lomotil and trasentine—to control the colitis; testosterone to keep up his weight (which fell with each bout of colitis and diarrhea); and Nembutal to help him sleep.

Usually nobody except intimates knew Jack was in the hospital. "I told Senator Kennedy that if he didn't tell anybody . . . and didn't have visitors coming, that I would put an assumed name on his door," Travell later explained. "This was my idea, not his." Kennedy agreed.

He worried that news of his ailments might become public. In 1960, after a speech in Waterbury, Connecticut, he flew to Boston. Early the next morning Governor Ribicoff of Connecticut received a frantic phone call from Jack. "Jesus, Abe, the bag with all my medications, we can't find it. I don't want anybody to find that bag and see what's in it." Ribicoff contacted the state police and ordered them to find that "goddamn bag." The next day the police found it, and Ribicoff phoned Jack with the good news. "Keep it, don't send it," Jack instructed. "I don't want anybody to see it."

Dr. Travell always publicly referred to Kennedy's Addison's disease as merely an "adrenal insufficiency." Kennedy "maintained considerable secrecy about his health," Sorensen later admitted, adding that both he and Travell "were given some responsibility for coordinating what health information would be given to the press."[25]

In 1955, shortly after his recent back surgeries, Jack attended a party in a restaurant and was talking with Kay Halle, a family friend. As he leaned against the back of another chair, the person sitting in the other chair suddenly rose. Jack tumbled backward, hitting the bottom of his spine on the floor. White as a sheet, he rose, righted himself, and resumed conversing with Halle. "The understandable pallor was finally replaced by his normal ruddiness," Halle recalled. "I was absolutely staggered, because when he landed, I could hear his spine hit the floor. I thought that was the most remarkable demonstration of his iron courage and power to dominate the physical with his will."

Joe and Rose taught their children to be self-reliant, tough, and stoic. "Kennedys don't cry," the children were taught. "Be as good as the spirit is."[26]

Indomitable, with astonishing willpower, John Kennedy refused to surrender to his own debilities. "Jack was a very brave fellow," said George Smathers. "He could withstand pain about as well as anybody I ever saw in my life. He never talked about it. He never would complain about it and yet [when] that poor guy would get out of the chair, he couldn't even straighten up for thirty minutes or so."

As far as the public knew, Kennedy was a picture of robust health—young, trim, physically active, with family and friends who enjoyed rigorous sports. The public admired his vigor, but his friends, who knew the pain he endured much of his life, found him to be an inspiration.[27]

18

COMMUNISM AND COLONIALISM

The Senate Foreign Relations Committee was a prized appointment for a senator with presidential ambitions. It afforded the opportunity to gain expertise in foreign affairs, an essential qualification for any aspirant to the modern presidency. When a vacancy opened after the 1956 election, Kennedy eagerly sought the appointment. He believed that his study of international relations at Harvard, experience at the London embassy, European travel, and keen observations of Munich and the coming of World War II, and his strong interest in foreign policy while in the House and the Senate—all qualified him to shape foreign policy.

Blocking Jack's path to the prestigious committee was Estes Kefauver, who had more seniority and also coveted the vacancy. But Kefauver was widely disliked among his Senate colleagues. Despite his seniority, the Democratic Steering Committee, dominated by Senator Lyndon Johnson, ignored the Tennessee senator's wish; instead, it awarded the Foreign Relations opening to Kennedy.[1]

Although he found foreign relations engrossing, Kennedy had a poor at-

tendance record on the Foreign Relations Committee. Senator William Fulbright, chairman of the committee, constantly complained about the difficulty of getting members to attend committee meetings. He growled at the
staff to phone an absent member and "Get him over here!" "He used to have
us chasing Kennedy to get him to a committee meeting, with no success or
even much hope of any success," recalled Pat Holt, consultant to the committee. Campaigning nationwide at the time, Jack attended only 24 out of
117 committee meetings in 1959, and in 1960, only 3 out of 96. Fulbright
complained privately that when Kennedy did come to meetings, he sat at the
table and autographed posters of himself.[2]

Kennedy pondered several controversial dilemmas of U.S. foreign policy.
How far could we trust the Soviet Union? Under what conditions should we
stop nuclear tests? "We need a new approach to the Russians," he said, "one
that is just as hard-headed and just as realistic as Mr. Khrushchev's, but one
that might well end the frozen, belligerent, brink-of-war phase of the long
Cold War." Neither country wanted a nuclear war, "a war that would leave
not one Rome intact but two Carthages destroyed." Neither wanted nuclear
weapons to proliferate. Finally, neither the Americans nor the Soviets wanted
to breathe radioactive air. Both nations would benefit, he said, "by a much
greater exchange and pooling of goods, ideas, and personnel."

He deplored Secretary of State John Foster Dulles's simplistic phrases:
"godless Communism," "Soviet master plan," "liberation of enslaved peoples," the "immorality" of neutralism. "Public thinking is still being bullied
by slogans which are either false in context or irrelevant to the new phase of
competitive coexistence in which we live," he observed in 1957.

At one hearing focusing on the appointment of wealthy Republican
campaign contributors to ambassadorships, Kennedy learned that affluent
people had to be appointed because of the high social costs of an embassy.
Kennedy denounced the social demands. "I really don't see any reason why
United States ambassadors should be obliged by custom to give a party for
tourist Americans and visiting Americans, two or three thousand of them,
who come and eat up in one day his whole representation allowance for the
year," he said. The State Department should prohibit the practice.

Secretary Dulles emphasized the need for military foreign aid to counter
internal Communist subversion. Jack wanted more emphasis on economic
assistance. "I think the economic assistance that is proposed in this bill is inadequate," he said to Dulles at a hearing, "in view of the very serious nature
of the problems within those underdeveloped countries, the population increase and the effort that the Soviet Union is making."[3]

After touring Vietnam in 1951, Kennedy stepped up his brash but clear-sighted criticism of U.S. policy in the Far East. He rebuked the French for their colonialism, and urged the United States not to involve itself in the Vietnam quagmire.

"Senator Kennedy suspects the French have not been spending as much as they say they have on the economic welfare of French Indochina," a Kennedy aide wrote privately in the spring of 1953, reflecting the senator's views. Kennedy "suspects the French are still too much in control of the Government and that is one reason for the trouble. . . . The U.S. should insist on reforms being made there *before* [U.S.] aid is given."[4]

In the spring of 1954, while the French tried to fend off Vietminh forces at Dien Bien Phu, Admiral Arthur Radford, chairman of the Joint Chiefs of Staff, advocated U.S. intervention in Indochina, and Secretary Dulles talked of "united action" with allies to assist the French.

Jack dissented. On April 6, 1954, in a major Senate speech, he conceded that eventually the United States might have to commit manpower to save Southeast Asia. "But to pour money, material, and men into the jungles of Indochina without at least a remote prospect of victory would be dangerously futile and self-destructive."[5]

Jack listed all the top U.S. military and State Department officials who had been painting roseate pictures of the French action in Vietnam: "the military situation appears to be developing favorably" (Acheson, 1952); "in Indochina we believe the tide now is turning" (Assistant Secretary of State Walter Robertson, 1953); "the French are going to win" (Admiral Radford, 1954). Kennedy contrasted the official optimism with the grim reality. "I am frankly of the belief," he said, "that no amount of American military assistance in Indochina can conquer . . . 'an enemy of the people' which has the sympathy and covert support of the people."

> Until political independence has been achieved, an effective fighting force from the associated states cannot be expected. . . . The apathy of the local population to the menace of Vietminh communism disguised as nationalism is the most discouraging aspect of the situation. That can only be overcome through the grant of complete independence to each of the associated states.

Every year America had received three sets of assurances:

First, that the independence of the Associated States is now complete; second that the independence of the Associated States will soon be completed under steps "now" being undertaken; and, third, that military victory of the French Union forces in Indochina is assured, or is just around the corner, or lies 2 years off.

None of the three had occurred. The United States should "recognize the futility of channeling American men and machines into that hopeless internecine struggle."[6]

On May 7, 1954, after fifty-five days of futile resistance, the battered French forces at Dien Bien Phu surrendered to the Vietminh. In July France relinquished its colony and signed the Geneva accords, ending the Indochina War.

What happened during the next two years had an enormous impact on the future of Southeast Asia, on the policies of the United States, and on the career and reputation of John F. Kennedy. The Geneva accords imposed a cease-fire and divided Vietnam at the seventeenth parallel. To separate the forces, the French withdrew from the northern part of Vietnam and the Vietminh from the southern part. The temporary division, the agreement said, should not be "interpreted as constituting a political or territorial boundary." Free democratic elections were to take place in 1956 to reunify the two parts of Vietnam. The United States only reluctantly participated at Geneva because negotiation with any Communist nation was anathema.[7]

As the French were leaving Vietnam, the Eisenhower administration adopted a momentous change in policy. The United States would replace the departing French as the defender of Laos, Cambodia, and the southern part of Vietnam (which the United States now recognized as the independent nation of South Vietnam with its capital in Saigon). Historian George Herring noted:

> The first essential was to draw a line which the Communists would not cross and then to "hold this area and fight subversion within it with all the strength we have" by providing military and economic assistance and building a strong military force. The United States would also have to take the lead in forming a strong regional defense grouping "to keep alive freedom" in Southeast Asia.

The Eisenhower administration and other U.S. leaders helped maneuver Ngo Dinh Diem to power in South Vietnam. While living in the United States, Diem had met Richard Cardinal Spellman of New York, Supreme Court justice William O. Douglas, and Senators Mike Mansfield of Montana, Lyndon B. Johnson of Texas, and Kennedy. They and others in the American Friends of Vietnam became Diem's patrons and helped establish him in power.

In 1955 Diem became the president of the Republic of Vietnam. From the U.S. standpoint he had two major strengths: He was anticommunist, and as a nationalist, he had opposed the French. Unfortunately, he had several major shortcomings as well, weaknesses U.S. policymakers badly underestimated. An elitist, he was insensitive to the needs and problems of the Vietnamese people. He had no blueprint for building a modern nation. "Introverted and absorbed in himself, he lacked the charisma of Ho Chi Minh," said Herring. Nor did Diem believe in democracy. A Confucian mandarin, he thought of himself as an enlightened sovereign with the "mandate of heaven" to govern.[8]

With various interests and sects contending for power, South Vietnamese politics became chaotic. A new influx of Catholics from northern Vietnam brought the Catholic population in the South to 1.5 million people. Diem favored the Catholics. A northern Catholic himself, he provided Catholics with special services and favors. What's more, he refused to promote land reform, and by 1960 about 50 percent of cultivated land in the Mekong Delta was owned by 2 percent of the people.

Diem, said Herring, violated "the spirit and sometimes the letter of the Geneva Accords." He canceled the scheduled elections for 1956 with the blessing of the Eisenhower administration. Meanwhile, the administration committed itself to Diem's fragile government, using its economic and military resources to construct in South Vietnam a strong non-Communist nation.

Diem crushed his opponents, but he successfully restored order, earning American praise. "Premier Diem is the best hope that we have in South Vietnam," said Senator Hubert Humphrey. "He deserves and must have the wholehearted support of the American government." John Kennedy—and almost everyone else in America who followed the Vietnam struggle—agreed.[9]

On June 1, 1956, when Jack addressed the conference of the American Friends of Vietnam, his speech revealed how quickly he had lost touch with the actual conditions in Vietnam. South Vietnam was the "cornerstone of the Free World in Southeast Asia, the keystone to the arch, the finger in the dike." He accepted the new domino theory: Burma, Thailand, India, Japan, the Philippines, Laos, and Cambodia would all be threatened "if the Red Tide of Communism overflowed into [South] Vietnam."

Diem's government was a "democratic experiment," and South Vietnam's political liberty was "an inspiration to those seeking to obtain or maintain their liberty in all parts of Asia—and indeed the world."

The United States had special obligations in South Vietnam because we were "directly responsible" for this "experiment." The United States must not allow the experiment to fail.

If we are not the parents of little Vietnam, then surely we are the godparents. We presided at its birth, we gave assistance to its life, we have helped to shape its future . . . This is our offspring—we cannot abandon it, we cannot ignore its needs. And if it falls victim to any of the perils that threaten its existence—Communism, political anarchy, poverty and the rest—then the United States, with some justification, will be held responsible; and our prestige in Asia will sink to a new low.

Instead of colonialism and communism struggling for supremacy, Diem had proclaimed "a free and independent republic" and the people had elected a constituent assembly. Social and economic reforms had "vastly improved" the living conditions of the peasants.

The United States made the correct decision to back Diem's refusal to allow elections called for by the Geneva Agreement of 1954, he said. Neither the United States nor "Free Vietnam" was a party to that agreement—and neither the United States nor Free Vietnam was ever going to be party to an election "obviously stacked and subverted in advance." The Communists offered the Vietnamese an alluring kind of revolution, "glittering and seductive in its superficial appeal," Jack concluded. "The choice between the two can be made only by the Vietnamese people themselves."[10]

Kennedy's address summed up the rationale for the American policy in Vietnam, shared by almost all U.S. policymakers of the time. In it he showed the limitations of his support for nationalism. Staunch commitment to containing communism had priority in his thinking.

Kennedy was once an informed, insightful critic of the U.S. and French policies in Indochina; but his views after 1954 were less informed, less thoughtful. He left several serious problems unanalyzed. By asserting U.S. power and influence in Vietnam, wouldn't the United States be perceived as colonial imperialists in the same way as the recently ousted French? He knew little about Diem, except that he was a nationalist and an anticommunist. Could Diem lead a "democratic experiment" in South Vietnam when he lacked key leadership traits and didn't believe in democracy? Was Western-style democracy a priority for impoverished Vietnamese peasants?

Kennedy didn't anticipate the quagmire the United States might be entering. Earlier, while keenly perceiving the French mistakes, he had argued that pouring money and material into Indochina was a hopeless attempt to save for the French a land that did not want to be saved, in a war in which the enemy was "everywhere and nowhere at the same time." Perhaps the South Vietnamese did not want to be saved by the United States either. Perhaps the United States was entering a conflict in which the enemy would be everywhere and nowhere at the same time.

Ho Chi Minh believed that the first Indochina War had been a political war in which his Vietminh forces outlasted the French. Maybe he could outlast the Americans as well.[11]

Kennedy wanted the United States to demonstrate to all "under colonial bondage that we are a freedom loving people who want all people free." We should take a "moral stand" on foreign policy, he said; then the United States would be on the "side of angels." On the issue of Algeria he didn't think the United States was on the side of the angels.

On July 2, 1957, in his role as chairman of the Foreign Relations Subcommittee on United Nations Affairs, Kennedy indicted France, a U.S. ally, for its policies in Algeria. He criticized the Eisenhower administration as well, for refusing to condemn the French action in Algeria and resisting efforts to bring about an international settlement, thus effectively aligning the United States with French colonialism.

Widely publicized, his speech was castigated by U.S. government officials and major newspapers. It outraged most French leaders. Nonetheless, the speech earned him praise and affection in Third World countries. A few years later, the position he expounded was widely accepted, even by the French government, making Kennedy look statesmanlike.[12]

In 1930, when France celebrated its century-long possession of Algeria, it seemed the North African colony would always be a part of France. A million Europeans had settled there, apparently a guarantee that Algeria would develop along modern Western lines. All that remained was for native Algerians—Islamic Arabs—to embrace French culture and become French citizens.

But France's plan went awry. There gradually emerged among Algerian nationalists a revolutionary movement, the Front de Libération Nationale (FLN). On November 1, 1954, the FLN fired the first shots in their revolution, catching French leaders badly off guard. Branding the rebels irresponsible outlaws, French officials insisted that Algeria was part of France and would always remain so.

By 1957 the French had committed four hundred thousand troops to Algeria to crush the bloody uprising. France's widespread use of torture and terrorism, widely publicized in the French and foreign press, strengthened the resistance, alienated many in the world community, and badly damaged the reputation of the French army.[13]

In dealing with the Algerian crisis, the Eisenhower administration tried not to offend Asian and African nations, fervent supporters of the rebels, or France, our NATO ally. But in the United Nations the United States sided with France, claiming that the war was a French internal problem.

In Jack's speech of July 2 he argued that the most powerful single force in the world was neither communism, nor capitalism, nor even the H-bomb. What was most powerful was "man's eternal desire to be free and independent." The great enemy of that freedom was imperialism—"and today that means Soviet imperialism and, whether we like it or not, and though they are not to be equated, Western imperialism."

Kennedy disagreed with the notion that Algeria was wholly a matter of internal French concern, a provincial uprising, a crisis which would respond satisfactorily to local anesthesia. He considered Algeria a colony, not an integral part of France. The United States did have a stake in the war because the uprising had weakened France, and damaged NATO defense by tying down four hundred thousand French troops. Even worse, our country's "retreat from the principles of independence and anti-colonialism" had hurt "our standing in the eyes of the free world." It also damaged our "moral leadership" in the struggle against Soviet imperialism in the countries behind the Iron Curtain.

> If we are to secure the friendship of the Arab, the African, and the Asian—and we must, despite what Mr. Dulles says about our not being in a popularity contest—we cannot hope to accomplish it solely by means of billion-dollar foreign-aid programs. We cannot win their hearts by making them dependent upon our handouts. Nor can we keep them free by selling them free enterprise, by describing the perils of communism or the prosperity of the United States, or limiting our dealings to military pacts. No, the strength of our appeal to these key populations . . . lies in our traditional and deeply felt philosophy of freedom and independence for all peoples everywhere.

It might be too late to save the West from total catastrophe in Algeria. "But we dare not fail to make the effort." The United States should press for a solution under which Algeria would win political independence but France would keep some form of economic "interdependence." He called for Senate resolutions urging the Eisenhower administration to try to force a settlement through NATO or through Tunisian and Moroccan leaders; if that didn't bring substantial progress, the United States should support "an international effort" aiming at Algerian independence.[14]

As Jack had hoped, his speech drew massive press coverage, but most opinion was unfavorable. Of the editorials clipped by Kennedy's office staff, ninety criticized the speech and only forty-eight endorsed it. It brought public rebukes from President Eisenhower, Secretary Dulles, Dean Acheson, and French officials. Critics charged that the speech was superficial, inaccurate, and rash.

"A situation like this requires the most delicate exercise of diplomacy," said *The New York Times,* "and not a smashing public attack on the floor of the United States Senate." "The most telling argument against intervention is simply that Algeria is not our problem," wrote *The Wall Street Journal*.[15]

In Washington, French ambassador Herve Alphand implored Secretary of State Dulles "to do something to mitigate the effects of the speech and not let it go unanswered."

To the Eisenhower administration, Kennedy's address seemed like troublesome meddling, possibly a step in Kennedy's buildup to capture the Democratic presidential nomination in 1960. He would be "very sorry" to see the Algerian crisis, with its "great difficulty and complexity," become a U.S. problem, said Dulles. Anyone interested in attacking colonialism, Dulles added, need only aim at the Soviets for enslaving nations behind the Iron Curtain. President Eisenhower cited the complexity of the Algeria question. The "best role" for the United States was to "try to be understanding to both sides in any quarrel. . . . That means often you work behind the scenes because you don't get up and begin to shout about such things, or there will be no effectiveness." Adlai Stevenson privately called the speech "terrible," adding, "Algeria is a French problem."[16]

Washington's critique was mild compared to the bitter French reaction. France's defense minister, André Morice, accused Jack of encouraging Algerian rebels to prolong their bloody rebellion. "I don't know whether Mr. Kennedy has nights without nightmares," said the angry minister. "What I know well," he continued, "is that this will result in a great increase of innocent victims and the prolongation of a drama that would have been long ended if so many of our unthinking friends had weighed their words or their acts."

While the French sputtered, Jackie Kennedy wrote Joe and Rose a hilarious note. Rose could no longer attend the Bastille Day celebration in Boston, she advised. "Who cares if you never go to another ball at the French Embassy, and if Dior has you bounced out of the fitting room. We can always go and eat sheep's eyes with the Arabs."

Surprised at the virulence of the opposition, Jack clarified his position a week later. "Of course, Algeria is a complicated problem. Of course, we should not assume full responsibility for that problem's solution in France's stead. And, of course, the Soviet Union is guilty of far worse examples of imperialism."[17]

Kennedy's speech earned plaudits as well. Michigan governor G. Mennen Williams was highly impressed. So was Senator Hubert Humphrey, who declared that Kennedy had performed "a service to the cause of freedom." The prominent socialist Norman Thomas and the Protestant theologian Reinhold Niebuhr joined three others in an open letter of support to *The New York Times*.

The speech electrified Arab and African leaders. Historian Richard Mahoney observed:

> For African visitors in Washington, Kennedy became the man to meet. His dramatic speech on Algeria had coincided with the rush to independence in Black Africa. . . . President Moktar Ould Daddah of Mauritania remembered how thrilled he had been as a student in Paris to read the speech and how dramatic an impact it had made on all Africans living in Paris. Algerian guerrillas encamped on the thickly forested slopes of the Atlas Mountains received the news with a sense of amazement. An American correspondent who visited one camp later related to the senator his surprise at being interviewed by weary, grimy rebels on Kennedy's chances for the presidency.

Holden Roberto, the Angolan nationalist leader, journeyed to Washington to meet Kennedy because of his "courageous position" on Algeria.

Two prominent foreign correspondents, Alistair Cooke of the *Manchester Guardian* and Henri Pierre of *Le Monde,* praised Kennedy's understanding of Third World issues. In a letter to the editor of *The New York Times,* Pierre wrote: "Kennedy is more to be commended than blamed for his forthright, frank and provocative speech."

Cooke thought that Kennedy's speech had "brilliantly served its purpose of pitching him into center-stage. . . . It has nicely suggested to his newspaper supporters that the Senator is a statesman, something like Stevenson, of majestic disinterestedness."[18]

After Kennedy introduced his Algerian resolution in the Senate, a cynical veteran of the upper house observed:

> I'll probably have to vote against Kennedy on this, but his idea is refreshing. I've seen in my time hundreds of resolutions proposed on this Senate floor to give aid and/or undying sympathy to the Poles, the Irish, the Italians, the Jews and the Hungarians and a dozen other foreign groups, and every time I could figure about how many thousands of votes each Senator expected to get from these foreign blocs.
>
> I'll bet there aren't a dozen naturalized Algerian voters in Kennedy's Massachusetts and there probably aren't 100,000 registered voters in the United States who are devout followers of the Prophet.

Kennedy failed to persuade the Senate to adopt his resolution on Algeria, but his cause did attract the sympathy and backing of a number of senators whose criticism of the Eisenhower administration's handling of the Algerian problem embarrassed the White House and placed it on the defensive. In the wake of congressional criticism, led by Kennedy, the State Department shipped food and medical supplies through private institutions to Algerian refugees in the neighboring countries.

Afterward Kennedy had only one regret about his speech. He wished he had spoken about "permitting the Algerians to determine their relationship with France." The "use of the word 'independence' may have been unwise."

Time proved Jack right. A few years after his speech, the position he advocated in 1957 was seen as reasonable and statesmanlike. In March 1962, the warring parties signed an agreement in which France granted independence to Algeria.[19]

Kennedy also focused on Communist Poland. In 1944 the Red Army, pursuing the retreating German forces, rumbled into Poland. With Stalinists manipulating elections, Poland fell under complete Communist control by late 1948. Stalinists destroyed civil liberties and accused Catholic bishops of warmongering, spying, and acts of sabotage.

In September 1955, Jack and Jackie visited Poland. Deeply moved, Jack took astute notes on the dreary Communist state and later wrote a report—never published—on his observations. Subsequently he delivered several speeches about Poland.

The housing shortage in Poland was nearly intolerable, he discovered. "The government concentrates on building theaters, sport stadiums, and monuments rather than homes," he wrote. The most depressing site was the Warsaw ghetto, where the Germans had herded the Jews during the World War II occupation, systematically destroyed them, and then leveled the area. His notes were his first extended commentary on the Holocaust:

> The ghetto is now a great field near the heart of the city, with a few wooden shacks on it, bearing mute testimony to the most savage mass extermination in history. Of the 2½ million Jews who lived in pre-war Poland, only 80,000 survived. Of these a great proportion desire to go to Israel, but the Israeli Chargé d'Affaires told me the Polish Communist Government was granting visas to only about 8 Jews a month.

Communist control was rigid and unchecked. "When the Polish people are free to talk with visitors, when they can visit freely Western countries, when the Voice of America is no longer jammed, when free elections are held and a free press permitted, then it will be possible to say there has been a genuine change in the policy of the communists."[20]

Communists used several methods to force the Poles to conform:

Every youth must be certified as to his political reliability before he can take advance technical training in any field. Because his father worked at the American Embassy as a translator, one boy was denied permission to become a doctor. The type of housing a family will be given depends upon their political background. Taxes are made lighter for those who cooperate.

The only force resisting total domination of the population by the Communist government was the Catholic Church. But the Church, too, had been savagely attacked. Communists had assaulted seminaries and church organizations, throttled the Catholic press, closed Catholic schools, and denounced the hierarchy for reflecting the attitude of the pope. "In all this the Russians have played a prominent role," he noted. Nonetheless, he discovered Catholic churches in town after town crowded with people.

The fortitude of the Polish people in resisting their oppression impressed him. But the future looked bleak.

Time works against them. It is upon the youth who have no recollection of a free Poland that the communists concentrate their attention. Given control of the means of communication, given all of the weapons of a modern police state, given control over education, given a limitation of the power and influence of the Church, given time to consolidate their gains, the communists feel that they can remake Poland into an obedient instrument of Soviet policy.

The Poles wanted to believe that the West would not abandon the goal of a free Poland. Otherwise, Jack wrote, "their courageous struggle to maintain their freedom may cease."[21]

In June 1956, rioting broke out in Poznan, Poland, as workers went on strike to protest rising food prices and work quotas; their demands soon extended to include free elections. The government sent units of the Polish army to suppress the uprising, and in the ensuing fighting fifty-four people were killed. To cope with the challenge, the frightened Polish Communist leaders agreed to reinstate the country's only credible and popular leader, Wladyslaw Gomulka.

Gomulka was a Communist, but his rise to power was a hopeful sign in the West because a few years earlier he had stood up to Stalin and been imprisoned by the Stalinists. Inspired partly by Khrushchev's denunciation of Stalin in 1956, Gomulka led a rapid de-Stalinization movement in Poland which nearly provoked attack by Soviet forces—similar to the subsequent brutal Soviet assault on Hungary during that country's uprising in 1956.

Initially Gomulka's regime acted more humanely, flexibly, and independently than its predecessor. It curbed the power of the secret police, relaxed censorship, and allowed greater artistic expression. It released political prisoners and some members of the clergy from prison.[22]

Jack wanted the United States to exploit the favorable trends in Poland. In a letter to Secretary of State Dulles on March 12, 1957, and in speeches during the following two years, Kennedy called for a creative new strategy. Yes, the Communists retained control in Poland, but the Polish people themselves had made a determined and courageous fight to gain some freedom from Soviet domination. "They appear to have been at least temporarily successful in lessening the iron control that the Soviets have hitherto exercised over their lives," he wrote Dulles, "and their ability and willingness to turn to this nation for assistance for the first time should be encouraged, not castigated." There were risks, he conceded. "But hunger has never been a weapon of American foreign policy."

"If we fail to help the Poles," he later stated in a speech, "who else in [East] Germany, Czechoslovakia or anywhere behind the Iron Curtain will dare stand up to the Russians and look westward?"[23]

In the Senate, Kennedy attempted to amend the Battle Act, the law that prohibited U.S. aid to Soviet bloc countries, and urged the United States to sell agricultural surpluses to Poland. "He has not put forth more tiresome generalities," said an article in *The New Republic* about Kennedy's thoughts on Poland. U.S. laws then on the books saw only two categories of nations in the world: nations under the domination or control of the Communists, and "friendly nations." Judgments were either black or white. He wanted the United States to recognize shades of gray. Nations like Poland might not currently be U.S. allies or in a position to be friendly, but solicitations might lure them away from Soviet domination and control.

Polish Catholic opinion in the United States enthusiastically backed Kennedy's pro-Gomulka stand. The national Polish-American Congress, with a large Massachusetts contingent, lobbied for U.S. assistance to the new regime. On October 22, 1957, Roman Pucinski, president of the Polish-American Congress in Illinois, wrote to Sargent Shriver that "the Americans of Polish descent in this country are more and more looking to Senator Kennedy as the most outspoken defender of freedom for Poland."

Unfortunately, Kennedy and others who hoped Gomulka would continue to liberalize Poland were eventually disillusioned. After 1958 U.S.-Polish relations deteriorated as domestic reforms in Poland failed to materialize, and Poland resumed close identification with Soviet foreign policies.[24]

19

CIVIL RIGHTS AND
LABOR REFORM

Journalist and family friend Arthur Krock observed that the Kennedy boys, while displaying no racial prejudice, showed no interest in the plight of blacks. "I never saw a Negro on level social terms with the Kennedys in all my years of acquaintance with them."

Having grown up amid stories of discrimination against the Irish, John Kennedy knew about the sting of prejudice. But he didn't link his family's experience to prejudice against blacks in the United States. Except for the family's servants, he didn't rub elbows with blacks in Riverdale, Bronxville, Hyannis Port, or Palm Beach; nor did he mingle with them at Choate or Harvard. There were no blacks on PT boats; black sailors in the navy were usually cooks. He didn't read about racial problems, discuss them with his friends, or develop empathy for the problems of African-Americans.[1]

Unhappily in a Boston hospital in 1936, Jack referred to it as a "nigger place." He rarely mentioned blacks in his correspondence. During World War II he did tease Princeton graduate LeMoyne Billings about a mutual white friend who commanded "colored" troops. "Incidentally," he joked,

At the age of twenty-five, President Kennedy's father, Joseph P. Kennedy, became the president of the Columbia Trust Company of Boston. Circa 1914.

JFK baby pictures, 1918.

Joe Kennedy Sr., Joe Jr., and JFK, circa 1925. *(Royal Atelier)*

John F. Kennedy at about eight years old, circa 1925.

John F. Kennedy, circa 1929.

JOHN FITZGERALD KENNEDY

Born May 29, 1917, in Brookline, Massachusetts. Prepared at The Choate School. Home Address: 294 Pondfield Road, Bronxville, New York. Winthrop House. *Crimson* (2–4); Chairman Smoker Committee (1); St. Paul's Catholic Club (1–4). Football (1), Junior Varsity (2); Swimming (1), Squad (2). Golf (1). House Hockey (3, 4); House Swimming (2); House Softball (4). Hasty Pudding-Institute of 1770; Spee Club. Permanent Class Committee. Field of Concentration: Government. Intended Vocation: Law.

JFK and LeMoyne Billings in Europe, August 1937.

John F. Kennedy's Harvard College Class of 1940 yearbook photo.

Lt. John F. Kennedy
aboard the *PT 109*, 1943.

JFK and the crew of the *PT 109*, summer 1943.

The Kennedy family, Hyannis Port, 1948. *Left to right:* Eunice Kennedy, Robert F. Kennedy, Patricia Kennedy, Joseph P. Kennedy Sr., Rose Kennedy, Jean Kennedy, John F. Kennedy, and Edward M. Kennedy *(kneeling).*

John and Jacqueline Kennedy on their wedding day, September 12, 1953. *(Toni Frissel)*

Counsel to the McClellan
Committee, Robert F. Kennedy
questions an unidentified witness
during a May 1957 committee
hearing as his brother Sen. John
F. Kennedy listens.

President Kennedy.
Portrait distributed by the
White House, 1961–1963.

President Kennedy returns to the White House after attending the inaugural parade, January 20, 1961.

President and Mrs. Kennedy arrive at the inaugural ball.

President Kennedy in one of his famous rocking chairs in the Yellow Oval Room of the White House, March 19, 1962.

A pensive JFK.

Visit of Attorney General and Director of the FBI: President Kennedy,
J. Edgar Hoover, and Robert F. Kennedy in the Oval Office, February 23, 1961.

President Kennedy greets Peace Corps volunteers working in Ghana and
Tanganyika: President Kennedy, Director of the Peace Corps R. Sargent Shriver,
and others at the White House, August 28, 1961.

The first lady departs for a trip to India and Pakistan: Mrs. Kennedy and President Kennedy at National Airport's MATS Terminal, Washington, D.C., March 10, 1962.

Silver pitcher presented to the White House: Mrs. Kennedy in the Diplomatic Reception Room at the White House, December 5, 1961.

The President greets Peace Corps volunteers on the White House South Lawn, August 9, 1962.

The President addresses the AMVETS Convention in New York City by telephone from the Oval Office, August 23, 1962.

President Kennedy at a news conference in the State Department auditorium, November 20, 1962.

Signing of Commission for General Eisenhower in the Oval Office:
Press secretary Pierre Salinger, Secretary of Defense Robert S. McNamara,
and President Kennedy, March 24, 1961.

Watching the flight of astronaut Alan Shepard on television in the office
of the President's secretary: Vice President Johnson, Arthur Schlesinger,
Admiral Arleigh Burke, President Kennedy, and Mrs. Kennedy, May 5, 1961.

President Kennedy and his mother, Rose Fitzgerald Kennedy, at the first International Awards Dinner of the Joseph P. Kennedy Jr. Foundation, Statler Hilton Hotel, Washington, D.C., December 6, 1962.

John F. Kennedy Jr., Jacqueline Kennedy, Caroline Kennedy, and John F. Kennedy in Hyannis Port, Massachusetts, August 4, 1962.

A relaxed President Kennedy smokes a cigar as he reads the newspaper aboard the *Honey Fitz* off Hyannis Port, August 31, 1963.

President Kennedy delivers the State of the Union Address, January 14, 1963.

President Kennedy and John Jr.

President Kennedy and John Jr.

A huge crowd greets
President Kennedy in
West Berlin, June 1963.

The President's family leaves the Capitol: Caroline Kennedy, Jacqueline Kennedy, John F. Kennedy Jr. *(first row)*, Attorney General Robert F. Kennedy, Jean Kennedy Smith *(second row)*, and Peter Lawford, November 24, 1963.

Funeral procession for President Kennedy.

"there are some Princeton men stationed near here—they say they are doing very well under white officers."

When he began his political career in 1946, Massachusetts didn't have a large black population, only a few wards in Boston and other communities. Kennedy spoke before black audiences, but he knew few blacks intimately, hadn't penetrated the black infrastructure, and didn't attend their churches, weddings, or funerals. Herbert Tucker, a Boston leader in the NAACP, recalled that in the late 1940s Kennedy "had little or no contact with the Negro constituency." Kennedy gradually sought Tucker's assistance in establishing relationships with blacks in his congressional district.[2]

By seeking assistance from African-American leaders, Kennedy followed a Massachusetts tradition. Rather than fight for civil rights legislation, Democrats in Massachusetts traditionally looked to a few influential individuals to deliver the black vote. "You never had to say you were going to do anything on civil rights," observed Robert Kennedy. "It was mostly just recognition of [Negroes]." By winning the support of black leaders, a Democratic candidate could capture the black vote quite easily.

During the 1952 election, when John Kennedy spoke before black groups, he usually reminded them of the progress blacks had made during the Democratic administrations of Roosevelt and Truman. Republican leaders, he charged, had stymied progress. After Truman banned segregation in the armed forces, Kennedy told a black audience, General Douglas MacArthur, a Republican, "failed to integrate the Far East forces and integration was not developed until after MacArthur was forced out." The same was true in Europe and was not remedied until another Republican general, Eisenhower, resigned his NATO command to run for president. "This was the same man," Kennedy said of Eisenhower, "who in 1948 before the Armed Forces Committee in Washington opposed integration of troops."[3]

The demeaning, usually racist, portrayal of blacks in U.S. history influenced John Kennedy, just as it influenced millions of other white Americans. His view distorted his perception of blacks and made him reluctant to force racial change in the South. He had grown up at a time when historians harshly criticized the Reconstruction measures imposed on the South after the Civil War. Historians portrayed crafty, scheming white Northern carpetbaggers and degraded white Southern scalawags, joined by ignorant, lazy, and barbarous former slaves—all threatening to destroy Caucasian civilization in the South.

Running roughshod over the Constitution, Radical Republicans in Congress placed the South under onerous military occupation, granted the ballot to the unprepared blacks, and formed new state governments dominated by corrupt, selfish blacks and whites. Redemption for the South, the prevailing view contended, came in the mid-1870s, when Southerners organized and drove the blacks, carpetbaggers, and scalawags from power, replacing them with the honest, virtuous, natural white leaders.

In *Profiles in Courage,* Kennedy adopted the simplistic, biased, but pervasive view of Reconstruction. Oppressed by terror and corruption, the prostrate South was victimized after the Civil War by Radical Republicans. "The Reconstruction Period," he wrote, "was a black nightmare the [white] South could never forget."

By 1957, however, revisionist historians were drastically modifying our understanding of U.S. racial history, including our understanding of Reconstruction. Not that the old view of Reconstruction was pure fabrication— there was corruption, failure, and tragedy. But the historical view Kennedy and most Americans had been taught had overlooked a great deal. It had ignored the nobility, idealism, and humanitarianism of many carpetbaggers, scalawags, and blacks, and the idealism of Radical Republicans in Congress who pushed through two momentous constitutional amendments: the Fourteenth Amendment, granting blacks citizenship and the equal protection of the laws, and the Fifteenth Amendment, assuring them the right to vote.[4]

The "redemption" of the South following Reconstruction had disastrous effects on the black population. Sharecropping replaced the slave system, keeping blacks dependent and propertyless. Using subterfuge, coercion, deceit, spurious legalisms, and terror, Southern whites denied blacks the civil and political rights seemingly granted under the Fourteenth and Fifteenth Amendments.

A caste system replaced slavery, reducing blacks to second-class citizens, and race etiquette forced them to pay deference to all whites. The legend of Reconstruction had serious consequences because it influenced powerfully the political behavior of many whites, North and South.

Despite some improvement in conditions for blacks in the 1940s and 1950s, the results never approached full equality. Whites still excluded blacks from decent schools, restaurants, and public parks, confined them to the rear of buses and railroad cars, and denied them the vote.[5]

As a congressman and a senator Kennedy favored civil rights legislation as a matter of course rather than from deep conviction. Along with a growing number of Northern Democrats, he had supported a strong Federal Employment Practices Commission (FEPC), abolition of the poll tax, antilynching legislation, and restrictions on filibusters.

Those who discussed civil rights with Kennedy were impressed with his honesty and sincerity, but unlike many Northern liberals, he kept a low profile on civil rights, and his position on racial matters was not well known. He said most of the right things and cast the right votes, but he wasn't fervent on the issue or a leader of the cause. In the Senate his efforts were overshadowed by dynamic civil rights advocates like Senators Hubert Humphrey of Minnesota and Paul Douglas of Illinois. Kennedy led on other issues.[6]

By the late 1950s civil rights had become a serious political dilemma for Kennedy. How does a Democratic presidential candidate win African-American voters—and their supporters—without writing off all prospects for Southern white support? Civil rights strained the Democratic Party after World War II. Conservative white Southerners demanded the status quo; blacks, liberals, and organized labor in the North insisted on fundamental improvements for African-Americans.

In the absence of a meaningful two-party system in most of the South, Southern Democrats kept their seats longer and so accumulated decades of seniority, allowing them to control powerful committee chairmanships. The House and the Senate were bastions of Southern power.

Because Senate rules traditionally allowed almost unlimited debate, a minority could frustrate a majority by talking or threatening to talk a bill to death. A small group of Southern senators adroitly exploited the filibuster rule to block any civil rights legislation.

Racial tensions worsened when on May 17, 1954, in the case of *Brown v. Board of Education of Topeka,* the Supreme Court unanimously interpreted the Fourteenth Amendment to outlaw racial discrimination in public schools. "In the field of public education, the doctrine of 'separate but equal' has no place," said Chief Justice Earl Warren. "Separate educational facilities are inherently unequal." The following year the Court ordered the states to proceed "with all deliberate speed" to integrate their schools.

Bitterly resenting the school-desegregation order, Southern whites placed various obstacles in the way of its implementation, and denounced the Supreme Court. In March 1956, over ninety Southern officials, led by Senator Walter George of Georgia, presented Congress with the "Southern Manifesto" condemning the Court's decision and encouraging "every legal means" to resist it.[7]

Neither President Eisenhower nor Adlai Stevenson championed civil rights. Eisenhower wouldn't even commit himself publicly to supporting the *Brown* decision. Stevenson endorsed the Supreme Court's ruling, but he opposed the use of troops to enforce it. "We must proceed gradually, not upsetting habits or traditions that are older than the Republic," said Stevenson.

To reach the presidency Kennedy badly needed Southern support. No Democrat in the twentieth century had ever captured the presidency without winning a majority of the Southern vote. Democrats feared a repeat of 1948, when Dixiecrats bolted the party. President Harry Truman still won most of the South in 1948, but many judged his victory there a fluke.

With the Democratic Party split into two opposing camps on several major issues, maintaining fragile party unity was crucial. Because Southern

Democrats were so unyielding on civil rights legislation, some Northern Democrats believed compromises were necessary to prevent further division. Other Northern Democrats preferred to confront the South on the civil rights issue.[8]

Each Democratic presidential candidate found his every move on civil rights watched and reported. Taking a stand on civil rights was a painful decision. Stand up for civil rights and against the white Southern position and you lost backing in the South for the nomination and in the general election. Mute your support for civil rights and you alienated Northern blacks and their white supporters. Few politicians could successfully navigate those shoals.

The vice-presidential contest at the 1956 Democratic convention unexpectedly damaged Kennedy's civil rights image in the North. The surprising support he received in the South against Southerner Estes Kefauver made civil rights forces suspicious. Southern delegates detested Kefauver because he had refused to sign the "Southern Manifesto" and had openly supported the Supreme Court's 1954 desegregation ruling. "We'd be for anybody against that damned, nigger-loving Kefauver," said a Mississippi Democratic leader. Kennedy's profile on civil rights seemed so slender that Southern whites perceived him as a friend, or at least not their enemy. But if he was acceptable to white Southerners, then Northern blacks wondered if he might be inimical to their cause. Subsequently, during the 1956 campaign, when he made his first extended campaign tour of the South, civil rights forces suspected him of currying Southern favor.[9]

Jack preferred to keep civil rights out of the House and Senate because the issue disrupted the legislative process and severely divided the Democratic Party, making it more difficult to elect a Democratic President in 1960. Better to relegate the issue firmly to the federal court system. He planned no profile in courage, no rousing moral condemnation of the evils of racism, that would derail his drive for the White House.

As he had on the difficult McCarthy issue, Kennedy retreated to narrow legal arguments when quizzed on increasingly heated civil rights questions. Before the Democratic convention in 1956, reporters grilled him about civil rights on TV's *Meet the Press*.

Did he favor using federal funds for *segregated* schools? No, but he favored federal aid for schools, and if Congress added an amendment to exclude segregated schools, powerful Southern legislators would block the measure, hurting all schools. Consequently he opposed an amendment to exclude segregated schools. Besides, he said, school integration was being dealt with satisfactorily by the Supreme Court and the federal courts.

Was he endorsing gradualism? No, he insisted. He simply wanted the courts to exercise their judgment about the speed of school integration. "Fortunately, or unfortunately, I think fortunately we in the House and in the Senate have nothing to do with that decision. Whether we are in favor of it or against it, it is going to be carried out. It is the law of the land."

But shouldn't the U.S. attorney general move rapidly to enforce the Court's ruling? The Supreme Court, he responded, had used the words "deliberate speed," which "may sound like a paradox," but it actually wasn't. The lower federal courts could manage the problem.[10]

By the late 1950s many in Congress had become more responsive to civil rights advocates, and legislators were more sensitive to the damage that segregation inflicted on blacks and on the U.S. image abroad. In early 1957 President Dwight Eisenhower asked Congress for a civil rights act. While following a torturously slow and winding path through Congress, the bill was substantially weakened. It weathered conflicts between Northerners and Southerners, amendments and counteramendments, division between House and Senate, ambiguous administration policy, and complex backstage maneuvers.

The civil rights debate during 1957 was a nightmare for Kennedy. No matter what position he took he would antagonize one wing of his party. So he maneuvered independently, standing apart from both factions. He kept aloof from the caucuses of western and Northern liberals. "He was anxious not to offend the Southerners more than necessary," reflected liberal senator Paul Douglas. Although he stood aside, Kennedy supported major features of the bill and worked for a compromise to salvage some improvement for blacks. Nonetheless, two of his votes outraged civil rights advocates.[11]

Voting rights seemed the best path to advance civil rights because the Fifteenth Amendment to the Constitution did guarantee blacks the right to vote. The Constitution didn't say anything about segregation, social equality, or the right to a job, but it was unequivocal about voting. Since the amended Constitution guaranteed voting rights, and Southern legislators were constitutionalists, deprivation of voting rights was the weakest link in the Southern resistance to civil rights.

The heart of Eisenhower's bill, approved by the House on June 18, 1957, was Title III, which would enable the attorney general to protect through injunction *all* civil rights, including integrated schools, not just voting rights.

After the legislation passed the House, there was an uproar in the Senate. On July 2, Democratic senator Richard Russell of Georgia described the bill as "a cunning device" to force a "commingling of white and Negro children." During debate Southerners evoked the sordid memories of Reconstruction. Democratic senator Olin Johnson of South Carolina charged that the legislation would "destroy the Bill of Rights and create a modern American Gestapo state." Southern opponents tried to delay, defeat, or weaken the legislation. The longer they could prevent consideration, the more effective the South's ultimate weapon: the Senate filibuster.[12]

Following Russell's remarks, reporters quizzed Ike about the bill, forcing a startling admission. "I was reading part of that bill this morning," said the President, "and there were certain phrases I didn't completely understand. So, before I make any more remarks on that, I would want to talk to the Attorney General and see exactly what they do mean."

Eisenhower's admission was "a stunning confession of ignorance," said his biographer Stephen Ambrose. Ike had promoted the bill, and managed to get it passed in the House and considered by the Senate, but now conceded he didn't understand it. Eisenhower's confusion invited Southern senators "to modify, amend, [and] emasculate his bill, and they proceeded to do just that."[13]

Kennedy took almost no part in the Senate debate, but two of his votes won him unwelcome notice. Civil rights advocates hoped to save the bill from almost certain death in the Senate Judiciary Committee. James Eastland, Democrat from Mississippi, a tall, round-faced, cigar-chomping segregationist, ruled the Judiciary Committee with an iron hand. To Northern liberals Eastland was the archetype of the Southern racist, more inclined philosophically toward slavery than civil rights. Under Eastland's control the Judiciary Committee had for years been the graveyard for civil rights legislation.

When the House bill arrived in the Senate, Republicans used a novel and controversial parliamentary maneuver to save it from death in the Judiciary Committee. They proposed to bypass Eastland's committee entirely and place the bill on the Senate calendar, where it could be called up for consideration by majority vote at any time. Opponents could still filibuster, but at least the legislation avoided the dreaded clutches of Senator James Eastland. Many Democratic senators opposed the move—including the Senate majority leader Lyndon Johnson, Kennedy, and several liberal Northern Senators—but enough Northern Democrats joined the Republicans to carry the day, 45 to 39.[14]

In remarks to the Senate on June 20, Kennedy defended his controversial vote. Senate procedure took precedence. Yes, he shared the fear that the legislation might be slowly strangled before the Senate could vote, but he would not permit his "personal views on civil rights" to dull his "sensitivities to Senatorial rights." He wanted the bill to be considered "on its own merits," using normal procedures, not by a contrived parliamentary maneuver. "If the Senate is convinced at any time that a Committee has unfairly and undemocratically bottled up a bill favored by the majority," he said, "a motion to discharge the Committee, requiring only a majority vote, is the accepted remedy." He favored such a move if the Senate Judiciary Committee did not quickly report a bill.

Under pressure from Southern senators, Lyndon Johnson maneuvered to eliminate Title III, the heart of Eisenhower's proposal. On July 24, 1957, by a vote of 52 to 38, the provision was struck out, dealing a near-fatal blow to the legislation. Kennedy favored Title III and voted with civil rights forces.[15]

Title IV applied only to voting rights. Eisenhower's proposal would have allowed a federal judge to issue a criminal-contempt citation if a white Southern registrar, found to be denying voting rights, disobeyed a court injunction to stop.

Even the modest provisions in the remaining bill were too strong for Southern senators, who objected to the provision that anyone who violated a federal court order enforcing civil rights could be cited for criminal contempt. Surely the accused should be granted a jury trial.

Brilliantly the South had seized on a jury-trial amendment to confound the Northerners. They argued that the Constitution ensures a private citizen a jury trial when charged with a crime.

Having already lost Title III, most civil rights advocates insisted that the jury-trial amendment would cripple the remaining bill. No Southern white jury would ever convict a white registrar for refusing to allow a black to register to vote. There was no clear right to a trial by jury in such contempt cases anyway. When a person violated a valid court order—whether a matter of paying alimony, a labor-relations decree, or an antitrust order—the person laid himself open to conviction of contempt of court and punishment without a jury trial. "Southerners had never protested the fines and jail sentences meted out to the NAACP and its people without jury trials," argued Roy Wilkins, executive secretary of the NAACP. The American Civil Liberties Union also denounced the jury-trial amendment as a "contrived obstruction to defeat the desperately needed civil rights legislation."[16]

The right of an accused to a trial by a jury, however, was so deeply ingrained in the American tradition and so sacred that the amendment attracted support from such liberals as Joseph O'Mahoney of Wyoming and Frank Church of Idaho. Lyndon Johnson said, "The people will never accept a concept that a man can be publicly branded as a criminal without a jury trial."

With the threat of filibuster hanging over the Senate, Kennedy consulted two eminent legal scholars at Harvard, who advised him that the jury-trial amendment would not adversely affect the bill. Mark De Wolfe Howe, a renowned civil libertarian and a leader in Americans for Democratic Action, advised Kennedy to support the jury-trial amendment. "The issue has aroused more legal fuss than it deserves," said Howe, "and is certainly not a question which permits of too much dogmatic stubbornness." Paul Freund of Harvard Law School agreed that the amendment would not seriously weaken the bill. Armed with his legal advice, Kennedy announced on August 1, 1957, that he favored the jury-trial amendment.[17]

The civil rights bloc remained dead set against the amendment. At the same time, Southern senators threatened to filibuster the entire bill unless the amendment passed. Observed Kennedy biographer James MacGregor Burns: "Southern governors wired Kennedy urgent requests to vote for the amendment; one of them added, unsubtly, 'Still hearing good things about you and your future.' All factions were watching the Senator with a steely eye."

In the end Kennedy backed the compromise amendment which became part of the final bill. The "O'Mahoney amendment" upheld the right of a judge to rule without a jury in a case of *civil* contempt—that is, when the judge tried to secure compliance with or prevent obstruction of the court's rulings. Under certain conditions jury trials would be allowed in *criminal* contempt cases—those involving willful disobedience of the law on the part of the defendant.[18]

The Senate debate on the complicated legislation consumed over 121 hours. Democratic senator Strom Thurmond of South Carolina filibustered for a record 24 hours and 18 minutes, trying to impede a vote. Overall, though, Southern senators decided they would not employ the filibuster, because the weakened legislation was not so obnoxious to them as to warrant its use.

Finally a persistent coalition of liberal Republicans and Northern Democrats salvaged a bill which Kennedy supported. On September 9, 1957, President Eisenhower signed the first civil rights act in eighty-two years. Besides Title IV, the law created a six-person Federal Commission on Civil Rights with the power to hold hearings and subpoena witnesses and documents. A new Civil Rights Division replaced the Civil Rights Section in the Department of Justice. With more personnel and resources, the division was a much larger unit and in a stronger position to enforce federal civil rights laws.[19]

The new law brought meager results. Civil rights advocates, deeply disappointed, questioned whether they should even support the final bill. Senator Paul Douglas thought the law had as much substance as "soup made from the shadow of a crow which had starved to death." The law did little to increase voting by blacks and did nothing to protect other civil rights. Despite the act's mild features, though, it did reverse the federal government's traditional hands-off policy in the civil rights field.

Ironically, no evidence subsequently came to light that the jury-trial amendment weakened the bill in any way. "It hadn't hurt as badly as we had thought it was going to hurt, and there were some civil liberties aspects to it," reflected Joseph L. Rauh Jr., a prominent white labor lawyer, civil rights advocate, and cofounder of Americans for Democratic Action.[20]

Under severe pressure throughout the lengthy debate, had Kennedy acted cowardly? His support for Title III, his insistence that Eastland's committee report the bill, and his vote for final passage suggested no. "Certainly, however, he showed a profile in caution and moderation," concluded biographer Burns.

Constituent mail from Boston's black leaders, columns and editorials in black newspapers, and leaders of the NAACP castigated Kennedy for his willingness to send the legislation to Eastland's committee and his support for the jury-trial amendment. Cunningly political, they charged, Kennedy was attempting to convince Southerners that he was safe on civil rights while simultaneously trying not to antagonize Northerners.[21]

"At that time we were very exercised about it," said Clarence Mitchell, the NAACP's Washington lobbyist, "and when [Kennedy's] presidential ambitions began to flower a little more . . . there were some of us who tried to remind him of it. . . . We felt that this represented something less than a full commitment to the cause of civil rights."

The black *Chicago Defender* charged that while Kennedy spoke eloquently on behalf of freedom for Algerians, the "cat got his tongue" during the civil rights debate. He "cast his vote with the Southern block as the first installment toward Dixiecrat support come 1960." Another black newspaper charged that "Mr. Kennedy talks and votes like a Bostonian, who hasn't seen and doesn't understand the meaning of the Robert Gould Shaw and Crispus Attucks monuments on Boston Commons."[22]

Blacks in Massachusetts also rebuked their senator. A black newspaper condemned his "sorry performance," motivated by political ambition. In rationalizing his vote Senator Kennedy had said that he trusted Southern white juries because the attention of the world would be upon them. "In fact the Negro has always had to rely on public conscience rather than law to end discrimination. . . . We had hoped, however, that White America through law could give the Almighty an assist more quickly than it has."

In rebuttal Kennedy argued effectively—but only about tactics. The temporary advantage to be gained by bypassing Eastland's committee was not worth the dangerous break with tradition. "This is a precedent, after all, which can be used against the civil rights advocates in the future as easily as it was used against those who would block civil rights legislation." Several liberal senators—Morse, Anderson, Mansfield, Murray, Magnuson, and others—who had exemplary records on civil rights legislation had concurred with his position. "I favored letting the bill go to committee in the normal way and bringing it out by a discharge petition as the rules properly provided. In this way the bill would not have been permanently held in committee."

On the issue of the jury trial Kennedy plaintively wrote Herbert Tucker,

JOHNSTON PUBLIC LIBRARY
JOHNSTON, IOWA 50131

"I made every effort to consult people whose position on the extension and preservation of civil liberties is unquestioned and whose competence in the field of law is of the highest repute."[23]

Understandably, Kennedy was upset that many of his detractors neglected to credit his support for the key feature of the original bill. "You failed to mention completely my support of the strongest section of the bill, Title III," he complained to columnist Thomas Stokes, "certainly the section most repugnant to the South."

Frustrated with one letter-writing critic, Kennedy replied curtly: "Thank you for your letter of September twenty-ninth, which has reference to a statement I did not make, political allies I do not have and a Presidential nomination I do not seek."

During the tense period, battered by the criticism of civil rights advocates, Jack repeatedly insisted that he had "fought long and consistently" for civil rights and that "as in the past," he would be in the "forefront" of those battling for rights for African-Americans. In truth, while he had consistently *supported* civil rights, he had never *fought hard* for civil rights, nor been in the *forefront* of the struggle. He had displayed little empathy for long-suffering African-Americans.[24]

Ike had hoped to avoid any direct confrontation with the South over civil rights, but Orval Faubus, governor of Arkansas, forced his hand. On September 4, 1957, openly defying a court order, Faubus placed the Arkansas National Guard around previously all-white Central High School in Little Rock and instructed the troops to prevent black pupils from entering the school. In the following days crowds of racist whites gathered at the school to support the governor's defiance. Eventually Eisenhower had to send riot-trained units of the 101st Airborne Division to restore order and enforce integration. "Throughout the South," observed Stephen Ambrose of Eisenhower's action, "white segregationists were outraged by the 'invasion.'"

The Little Rock crisis complicated Kennedy's political prospects, creating another minefield for him to navigate. He endorsed the president's action in a brief, carefully worded statement. The Supreme Court's ruling on desegregation "is the law of the land," he said. "Neither mob violence nor the defiance of lawful court orders can ever be justified or condoned."[25]

Following Little Rock, Kennedy conceded that it would be tougher for the 1960 Democratic nominee to keep both the Northern and Southern wings of the Democratic Party together. Nonetheless, the politician must vote his conscience. "A person simply must vote each issue as he sees it month after month and that is his record," he said. "Voters take you or leave you."

Before federal troops entered Little Rock, Kennedy had accepted an invitation to speak at a convention of young Democrats in Jackson, Mississippi. After the tumultuous events at Central High School, some of his Southern friends had second thoughts about his visit to Mississippi and urged him to back out of the engagement. Any misspoken word about civil rights could do irreparable harm to his presidential candidacy. If he endorsed the Northern liberal view, he would alienate Southern supporters. If he tried to conciliate the South, civil rights supporters in the North would be angry. If he ducked the issue, he was weaseling. He seemed boxed in.

Nonetheless, Jack kept his commitment. After he landed in Jackson, he pored over the local newspaper and discovered that Wirt Yerger, Mississippi's GOP state chairman, had publicly challenged him to state his views on integration and segregation. Yerger had set a trap. While he kept an overflow reception crowd waiting in the Heidelberg Hotel, Kennedy hid out in his room, soaked in a warm bath, and revised his speech.[26]

That evening, as he was about to begin his address, the audience seemed suspiciously frigid. Kennedy tugged at his ear, tweaked his nose, ran a finger around the inside of his shirt collar, and announced, "I am particularly happy to be here tonight." The crowd sat silent, waiting. He continued: "It will be possible for us to disagree as Democrats within our party organization." The silence seemed heavier. Kennedy plunged ahead, reading the text of Republican Yerger's challenge. "I accept the challenge," said Kennedy.

> You who have been gracious enough to invite me here realize that we do not see eye to eye on all national issues. I have no hesitancy in telling the Republican chairman the same thing I said in my own city of Boston, that I accept the Supreme Court decision as the supreme law of the land. I know that we do not all agree on that issue, but I think most of us do agree on the necessity to uphold law and order in every part of the land.

There followed a desperate pause and more silence. Then he quickly resumed. "And now I challenge the Republican chairman to tell us where he stands on Eisenhower and Nixon!" Rising to its feet, the crowd burst into thunderous applause, roaring and stomping its approval.

"Jack Kennedy had won it by his own display of courage and by turning all good Democrats against the odious Republicans," *Time* concluded. "He was still a long, hard way from the Democratic nomination, but he had broken through a major roadblock."

Awed by Kennedy's display, a Mississippi congressman said, "I never thought I'd see anybody in Central Mississippi speak up for integration and get a standing ovation." The state's influential governor, James P. Coleman, seemed won over: "I think he is our best presidential prospect for 1960, and I am all for him."[27]

Kennedy's remarks in Mississippi aroused some anger in the South, but what was perceived as his audacity and flair muted most responses. The

Shreveport Times thought that "Kennedy's true political philosophies . . . were . . . quite unacceptable to the South on the issue of integration. . . . He certainly is far far from being a conservative politically."

The *Mobile Press* disagreed with his endorsement of desegregation, but added: "One thing can be said for Kennedy. He wasn't mealy mouthed about the matter. He had the courage to stand before a group known to be segregationists and state his position." The *New York Times*'s Arthur Krock reported from Texas that nearly every politician spoke favorably about Kennedy's speech. It heartened those Southern Democrats who wanted to remain loyal to the party.

Remarkably, Kennedy's handling of his stern test in Mississippi earned praise in the North as well. He had displayed "courage," "candor," and "intellectual honesty." A black newspaper in his home state marveled at his "courageous denunciation of school segregation" before a convention where blacks were not present as delegates to hear his declaration.[28]

Roy Wilkins, though, remained unappeased. In late April 1958, with Kennedy preparing for his reelection, Wilkins addressed an NAACP audience in Pittsfield, Massachusetts, and denounced Kennedy's recent civil rights record and flirtation with the South. The senator had happily rubbed elbows with white Southern segregationists, Wilkins charged. Newspapers, he said, carried photos of a smiling Kennedy with his arm around Governor Marvin Griffin of Georgia. "No pal of Griffin's can possibly be a pal of mine," Wilkins charged. "Griffin thinks I'm an animal." Kennedy's attitude might improve, said Wilkins, "but a man's record is a man's record . . . and when Kennedy voted, he was wrong."

Kennedy was furious. A week later he fired off a letter to Wilkins which demolished much of the argument of the NAACP leader. A historian of the Wilkins-Kennedy confrontation found Kennedy's comments "disingenuous," but if anyone had been less than straightforward it was Wilkins.

Kennedy correctly pointed out that Wilkins had not mentioned the senator's support of Title III, the meat of the original 1957 bill, its most controversial section. Nor had Wilkins told his audience that Kennedy supported reform of Rule 22 (the filibuster rule) and had consistently voted for civil rights legislation.

Instead you stated that I was no friend of yours because I was a friend of Governor Griffin of Georgia, your having seen a picture of me with my arm around the Governor. I have never seen such a picture, and can recall no time when my picture was taken with my arm around the Governor or anyone else. I have seen Governor Griffin only twice in my life—once at the 1956 Democratic Convention, and again last year when I was invited to deliver the University of Georgia Commencement Address.

He shrewdly linked Wilkins's charges with the specter haunting Kennedy himself: the issue of McCarthyism. "To assert that anyone who appears in a picture [is] a friend of someone else in the picture whom you dislike is an old and recently discredited political device—but I would never have thought from your outstanding record on behalf of individual rights and democratic principles that you would be applying it in this fashion."[29]

Wilkins's response was evasive and inaccurate. He incorrectly stated that while Kennedy had supported Title III of the bill, he had opposed Title IV. In any case, Wilkins's speech on Kennedy's civil rights record was not intended to be exhaustive.

> As for the expression about a picture with Governor Griffin, that was a figure of speech and was not intended to be a report of an actual photograph. There is no such photograph to my knowledge. Your friendly reception by Deep Southerners easily conjures in the minds of Negro citizens a picture of you arm in arm with them. It was this picture—figuratively—that I was calling up.

Kennedy had disturbed blacks because "you are hailed by the Dixiecrat leaders of South Carolina, Georgia and Mississippi, which, with Alabama, are the 'worst' states on the Negro question."

Unappeased, Kennedy shot back another blistering letter, pointing out persistent distortions in Wilkins's position.

> Are you under the impression, as you state, that I voted against Part IV of the Civil Rights Bill? I did not. Are you under the impression that I favored jury trial for those accused of civil contempt under the Bill (as opposed to criminal contempt), as you implied?. . . .
>
> Are you under the impression that you gave only a figure of speech about my being pictured with Governor Griffin? According to the *Berkshire Eagle* account of April 28: "Mr. Wilkins said newspapers carried pictures of a smiling Kennedy with his arm around Griffin."
>
> You state that you did not pretend to be exhaustive in regard to my voting record, in explaining why you neglected to mention my votes on Rule 22 and my long record of support of civil rights measures. But the newspaper quotes you as stating: "A man's record is a man's record . . . and when Kennedy voted, he was wrong." You state in your letter that I have been hailed by the Dixiecrat leaders of South Carolina, Georgia and Mississippi. I have never appeared at a Democratic dinner in either South Carolina or Georgia—my only appearance in Mississippi was the speech in which I endorsed the Supreme Court desegregation decision and called for law and order in every part of the land.

Kennedy claimed he was not trying to curry favor with the South for a presidential bid; he was "simply running for reelection as the senator from Massachusetts."[30]

In mid-July, in a third letter, Kennedy reminded Wilkins that the jury-trial amendment applied only to criminal—not civil—contempt. Nothing in the events since the bill's passage, he told Wilkins, indicated that the amendment had any importance in weakening the bill, "although it was clear at the time that it did help facilitate passage of the bill without a filibuster." He also complained to Wilkins that the NAACP's Clarence Mitchell had a "close association" with Richard Nixon, and had been "quite outspoken against" Kennedy at a recent NAACP convention. Kennedy thought it was "urgent" that he, Wilkins, and Mitchell sit down and discuss their differences.

Wilkins retreated. In mid-October 1958, barely in time for Kennedy's reelection bid, the civil rights leader composed a carefully crafted public letter supporting Kennedy's reelection. Wilkins still regretted Kennedy's decision to support the jury-trial amendment, but the "Senator's record, taken as a whole . . . must be regarded . . . as one of the best voting records on civil rights." The headlines the next day were predictably favorable for Kennedy. "It was a nasty, destructive interlude," Wilkins reflected in his autobiography, but he and the senator subsequently patched up their differences during several luncheon meetings.[31]

Kennedy won the tactical battle with Wilkins, but he hadn't won the war for the hearts of civil rights advocates. To win them over, though, risked losing white Southern support for the Democratic nomination. In the future, whatever positions he took on civil rights needed to be carefully stated and artfully finessed.

The battle over the 1957 Civil Rights Act taught another sobering lesson. If he ever won the presidency, Kennedy knew, he would have to find alternative means, besides new federal legislation, to advance the cause of civil rights. The legislative route was too perilous and unproductive. New legislative initiatives would merely cause another uproar in Congress, aggravate tensions within his own party, risk a long filibuster, block the President's entire legislative program, and proceed tortuously and slowly toward enactment. Then, most likely, after opponents had emasculated the legislation, it would end up with no more substance than soup made from the shadow of a crow which had starved to death. Other approaches—executive action, enforcement of existing federal laws—were the only realistic ways for the federal government to improve the lives of African-Americans.

"Senator Kennedy's role in the Senate is like that of the visiting literary professor," said a writer in the *Progressive,* "the glamorous young man who wows the students, makes a hit with the faculty wives, and stays aloof from the dull grind of the campus. This exasperates some of Kennedy's colleagues. They see him running about the country making headlines and reaping political hay while they attend to the chores."

Jack sensed that one of his main problems in winning the Democratic presidential nomination was the perception that he had not been a Senate leader on tough issues. Because he hadn't successfully managed any major legislation, he lacked stature in the Senate.

Was he skilled enough, mature enough, to bring together dissimilar legislators and contending groups to pass legislation in the national interest? Kennedy badly needed to establish a reputation for legislative competence.[32]

He decided to stake his reputation on forging a new labor-reform law. Why labor reform? Why would a senator, campaigning for the presidency with an absolute singleness of purpose, embroil himself in a controversy so complicated and fraught with political danger? "The early odds were such that he could gain only a little, perhaps lose a great deal," remarked one pundit.

In both the House and the Senate, Jack had served on Labor Committees, and union leaders viewed him as a friend and ally. They appreciated his opposition to the Taft-Hartley Act and his fight for a higher minimum wage, medical care under Social Security, and other legislation.

He could have evaded the floor leadership of the labor-reform legislation, but he knew that his experience and personal knowledge of the issues made him the logical choice for the job. He didn't want to be accused of shirking a tough responsibility; yet it did take courage to accept the assignment. Between 1957 and 1959, during the labor-reform battle in Congress, his relationship with his labor friends was severely tested. That he emerged from the battle having won their affection and deep respect testified to his superb leadership.[33]

The need for labor reform grew out of the hearings of the McClellan committee (nicknamed the Rackets committee). In January 1957, the Senate formed the Select Committee on Improper Activities in the Labor and Management Field, chaired by Senator John McClellan, Democrat from Arkansas. Jack was one of eight members.

Robert Kennedy became the committee's chief counsel, directing an investigative staff of sixty-five. For almost two years he guided the investigation through sensational televised and headlined hearings, exposing shocking fraud, gross mismanagement, and abuses of trust in unions.

The rackets investigation shaped the public's early perception of Robert Kennedy. Television showed a relentless interrogator dedicated to exposing corruption, but also an overzealous interrogator badgering recalcitrant witnesses.[34]

Although the committee found corruption in only a small percentage of unions, the hearings disclosed that organized crime had penetrated the labor movement, and had engaged in racketeering, kickbacks, violence, and strong-arm tactics. The worst abuses were discovered in the International Brotherhood of Teamsters, and millions of people were transfixed by one man: the sinister, arrogant, and belligerent president of the Teamsters, Jimmy Hoffa.

Mostly because of his nationwide speaking engagements, Jack missed many sessions of the McClellan committee hearings. But Robert Kennedy made sure his brother was present whenever television covered the testimony. Bobby had perceptive questions ready when Jack entered the committee room, normally at midafternoon. "Usually, they were the most pertinent questions of the day," said one observer. "They made the headlines. They got on television."[35]

Genuinely outraged by the revelations uncovered by the McClellan committee, Jack said privately of Hoffa, "I have never met a worse man. I look across at this fellow at the hearings, and reconstruct the motives for what he is doing, and they are evil."

While preparing legislation to curb union abuses, Jack emphasized that the labor movement needed to rid itself of corrupt and gangster elements. The federal government did not bear primary responsibility for labor reform. "That rests with the union members themselves," he said. Members should police their own union affairs by attending meetings, reviewing carefully the use of their dues, selecting their own leaders wisely, and throwing out of office those who reneged on their trust.[36]

To assist him in drafting new labor legislation, Jack recruited as his consultant one of his own constituents, Harvard Law School professor Archibald Cox. Five years older than Jack, Cox was the nation's foremost expert on the arcane field of labor law and had experience writing labor law. For two years Cox provided invaluable assistance, coaching Jack and drafting legislation.

The senator never suggested to Cox that the Harvard professor modify his own judgment to advance Kennedy's presidential ambitions. "No, categorically," Cox would later say. Nonetheless, "no one had any doubt that he would be a major contender in 1960."

Cox's impression of Kennedy was entirely favorable. His "instincts were right," Cox reflected; he was "highly intelligent," and "really interested" in the substance of labor policies "quite apart from or in addition to their political impact."

Cox told a story of the time the two of them flew to Boston from Washington. Each pulled out a book. "The politician was reading Proust," Cox recalled with a smile, "and the professor was reading Perry Mason."[37]

The Republicans on the committee detested Cox. "He was too damn good," said Stewart McClure, chief clerk of the Senate Committee on Labor, Education, and Public Welfare. With Cox coaching him, Kennedy held the Senate floor, answered difficult questions, and seldom faltered, treating each point with the "precision of a skilled surgeon."

In drafting a bill to curb the union corruption and thug rule exposed by the McClellan committee, Jack had to walk a tightrope. If he tilted too far against unions, he would outrage labor; if his bill seemed too soft on labor, he would outrage conservatives.

During hearings Kennedy clashed with George Meany, president of the AFL-CIO. While defending an early draft of his labor legislation, Jack claimed it couldn't possibly be antilabor because the legislation was drafted by Archibald Cox and other "experts friendly to labor."

Meany glowered at Kennedy. "My only comment is," he shot back, in a much-quoted reply, "God save us from our friends."

Kennedy replied quietly, "I say that too, Mr. Meany."[38]

On June 10, 1958, Jack brought the Kennedy-Ives bill to the Senate for consideration. Republican cosponsor Senator Irving Ives of New York paid tribute to Kennedy for his bipartisan approach in drafting the legislation. "Some persons may talk all they want about his being a candidate [for the presidency]," Ives declared, "but I say now that he is about the most bipartisan person I have seen around here."

Kennedy-Ives covered thirty major items dealing with union reform. Provisions required detailed reporting of all union financial transactions; mandated full reports by union officers on personal conflicts of interest; gave the secretary of labor broad investigative powers; provided criminal sanctions for embezzling of union funds, failure to make reports, false entry in books, and destruction of union records; and allowed union members the right to sue for recovery of embezzled or misappropriated funds.[39]

Kennedy-Ives was one of the most controversial measures of the entire 1958 session. The *Congressional Quarterly Almanac* reported that it "produced one of the year's longest Senate debates (five days), with the greatest number of floor amendments (53) and roll call votes (23) of any bill considered by Congress in 1958."

To most dispassionate observers the bill seemed reasonable: tough on labor bosses, but not too tough on labor in general. Jack was shocked, therefore, when both labor and management condemned it. The National Association of Manufacturers and the U.S. Chamber of Commerce criticized the bill for not going far enough in curbing labor's powers; the United Mine Workers, the Teamsters, and the steelworkers union criticized it for going too far. Only the AFL-CIO supported the measure as necessary to rid unions of racketeering.[40]

Shortly after the bill was introduced, the Eisenhower administration and its Senate allies suddenly attacked it, saying it wasn't tough enough on labor. Secretary of Labor James Mitchell claimed the bill was "full of imperfections, omissions or loopholes" and would be almost impossible to administer.

At a press conference the next day Kennedy and Ives made a point-by-point rebuttal of Mitchell's objections. Mitchell's remarks were "completely inaccurate and irresponsible," said Kennedy. Senator Ives agreed and added a dig at his own party. "It looks to me as though somebody is trying to make a Republican thing out of this, when we were trying to make it bipartisan."[41]

Many Republicans did want to disparage Kennedy's labor-reform efforts, maybe even keep his name off the legislation, to undermine his presidential chances. *Newsweek* reported on a secret meeting of GOP leaders at which Senator John Sherman Cooper remarked: "Kennedy is stealing the ball away from us on labor reform. I won't vote for anything that will help Kennedy." Senator Barry Goldwater phoned the White House and, while talking to the president's legislative aide, said, "This is a rotten bill. Kennedy's going to get all the credit for putting through labor reform. I want to see the President and recommend that he take a strong position against the bill as it now stands."

Because conservatives could offer no alternative to the bill, on June 17, 1958, Kennedy-Ives passed the Senate by an overwhelming vote of 88 to 1. *The Christian Science Monitor* commented: "It is a good bill and, for the purposes its sponsors set for it, a strong bill."

Despite nearly unanimous passage in the Senate, the Eisenhower administration, claiming the bill was too lenient on labor, successfully managed to tie up the legislation in the House, stalling until the Eighty-fifth Congress ended.[42]

For two legislative sessions Kennedy patiently worked for labor reform. When Senate majority leader Lyndon Johnson began scheduling night sessions, Jack napped a few hours in the afternoon. Evelyn Lincoln kept pillows and sheets in the office and woke her boss for roll calls.

He didn't pressure colleagues or engage in arm-twisting, the approach often used by Lyndon Johnson. When he judged his position correct, he wanted to carry the day through reasonable debate and discussion. "Kennedy has a technique of taking a hot issue, drawing the fire out of it, and calmly and dispassionately introducing a moderate reform," said one observer.[43]

On the Senate floor Jack's comments on his labor legislation were concise, accurate, and remarkably informed. "An amendment would be offered and he would spend a minute, maybe two minutes, answering it," marveled Senator Mike Mansfield, "while the proponent of the amendment would spend 15 or 20 minutes or a half-hour or an hour. [Kennedy] had a gift for getting right to the heart of the matter."

Wires and letters poured into his office congratulating him for winning almost unanimous Senate approval of Kennedy-Ives. "His fellow Senators gave him the sincerest form of flattery by asking him to make tape recordings explaining the bill for use in their states," said Evelyn Lincoln.

However, after Eisenhower attacked the bill, mostly disapproving letters flooded the senator's office. Late one evening he came back to his office, sat down at a desk, and started reading letters. Suddenly he started swearing and kept it up for several minutes. "Why do they bother to write when they don't understand what's going on?" Then he pulled himself up short and said, "Oh, well, it's worth it anyway."

He talked to fellow senators in elevators, corridors, and the cloakroom, and paid formal visits to their offices. On the days of Senate floor debate he entered the Senate chamber well in advance, armed with his documents. At the end of every session he huddled in his office with labor experts and labor representatives to gather ammunition for the next day's debate. "While they were working he would walk from one office to another like a panther in a cage," Evelyn Lincoln later recalled. "When he passed the conference table, he would stop and listen to the discussion and perhaps add a word or two." In the evening he often phoned his brother Robert and consulted with him.[44]

"You can't suggest any kind of a change in labor laws without getting a lot of influential people sore at you," a Democratic senator observed. "Kennedy gets jumped on by Barry Goldwater and the big business people and by the White House and he also gets himself called a traitor by the labor unions when he tries to make a compromise with the Republicans. But still he has stayed in there with both feet, trying to push labor reforms. It is hardly a field of endeavor that a cute and cautious candidate would care to get into."

After listening to Kennedy expound on the secondary boycott, a field of bewildering complexity, Senator Paul Douglas was impressed. The way his Massachusetts colleague discussed the issue "was a combination of politician and Ph.D. . . . After that no one could doubt his ability."[45]

On March 24, 1958, the McClellan committee issued an interim report while it continued its investigations. The report charged that Hoffa had "grossly misused union funds," and ran a hoodlum empire; it accused his union of wielding nearly "incalculable power over our country," since Teamster disapproval could stop the nation's economy.

President Eisenhower's repeated calls for a tough antiunion bill, and the exposure of corruption by the McClellan committee, incited an ever-increasing demand for labor reform. A Gallup poll conducted in 1958 asked voters what legislation they thought the new Congress should pass. The chaotic school-integration crisis in the South ranked first, followed closely by the desire to "clean up corruption and racketeering in unions."

After Senator Irving Ives retired in 1958, Kennedy secured the cosponsorship of a slightly amplified new bill from Senator Sam Ervin of North Carolina. Kennedy's staff thought that Senate majority leader Johnson, his own eyes on the White House, attempted to sabotage Kennedy's bill in the Senate. "He would schedule important votes deliberately on Friday afternoon, when JFK was not there," said Ralph Dungan. "There was absolutely no doubt that LBJ snookered [him] at every chance he got, along with a friendly 'ha ha' and a big arm around his shoulder."[46]

Following Democratic successes in the 1958 congressional elections, labor leaders grew overconfident. Why should they meekly accept any labor reform without prolabor "sweeteners"? "If organized labor was going to swallow a bitter anti-union pill, it wanted some quid pro quo built into the legislation now," observed Ken Gormley, Archibald Cox's biographer. "Otherwise, no deal."

In 1959 Kennedy reluctantly agreed to inject prolabor sweeteners directly into the heart of the bill. (Both Jack and Cox preferred to place these provisions in a separate piece of legislation.) Senator Ervin then angrily disavowed his own bill. What's more, Senator McClellan successfully pushed through an amendment he labeled the "Bill of Rights," containing harsh antilabor provisions strongly favored by management. The move was a "grave defeat" for Kennedy, said *The New York Times*.[47]

The numerous amendments sufficiently appeased some senators, and probably confused others. On April 25, 1959, Kennedy's revamped bill, a hodgepodge of pro- and antiunion features, raced through the Senate by a margin of 90 to 1. Once again, though, powerful forces prevented Jack's victory. President Eisenhower, determined to secure a more stringent bill, supported a new piece of legislation in the House that rivaled the Senate version. The Landrum-Griffin bill, much harsher on labor than the Senate's bill, passed the House. (Congressional experts reported that the key 229-to-201 roll-call vote on Landrum-Griffin was the largest House vote ever taken. Only 5 of the 435 Representatives did not vote.)

Landrum-Griffin gave the state courts wide injunction powers to control labor matters (the "no-man's-land" provision); permitted unrestrained transactions with struck firms (secondary boycott and hot cargo contract bans); and made union organization of new plants more difficult by restricting organizational, recognition, and informational picketing.[48]

Starting on August 18, 1959, and proceeding for twelve grueling days, the House-Senate Conference Committee, with Kennedy as chairman, met in the Foreign Relations Room of the Capitol. With a crisis on his hands, Kennedy tried to salvage the best bill possible.

Nerves frayed. During one session, observed Gormley,

Congressman [Graham] Barden suddenly turned on Cox, seated in the chair beside Kennedy, and lashed out that he was tired of "these intellectual outsiders nitpicking and scratching for little holes." A grim-faced Kennedy shot back, "And I'm sick and tired of sitting here and having to defend my aide time and time again from your attacks." The conferees sat back in stunned silence.

At another session a shouting match broke out after Congressman Landrum pointed his finger at Cox and accused him of being a "Communist." "Senator Kennedy pummeled Landrum with a stinging defense of Cox, one of the few times Cox ever saw JFK's Irish temper take over," said Gormley.

On September 3 and 4, 1959, the House and Senate finally approved a single piece of legislation. On the issues of the boycott and picketing, the conference version was closer to the Republican Landrum-Griffin bill than to Kennedy's Senate version. "Yet most of the internal union reform provisions, representing a critical contribution to American labor law, had come from the Kennedy camp," Gormley reported.

"Compromises are never happy experiences," Kennedy told the press after the patchwork legislation won approval. "I think it's the best bill we can get—and get a bill."[49]

Democratic congressman Richard Bolling thought Kennedy had provided "courageous and infinitely determined guidance" during the House-Senate conference. When the AFL-CIO issued a statement, it condemned the conference bill, but praised Kennedy for softening the blow.

Over the course of the labor-reform controversy Kennedy earned the respect of union leaders, who appreciated his effort to protect their interests. Before the McClellan hearings started, UAW president Walter Reuther considered Kennedy "a lightweight opportunist." But the senator's management of labor legislation completely changed Reuther's attitude. He would support Kennedy in 1960, rather than one of his former favorites, Adlai Stevenson and Hubert Humphrey.

"He wanted to know everything there was to know about a subject," reflected George Meany, who also changed his mind about Kennedy during the labor-reform process. "I don't recall a member of Congress that applied himself any more diligently to his work than did Senator Kennedy." It took longer for rank-and-file union members to appreciate Kennedy's role. Afterward many remained suspicious of him.[50]

Joseph Rauh a leader of the Humphrey-for-President camp, thought he could enthusiastically support Kennedy for president if he won the nomination. "Kennedy has grown immensely since 1954," Rauh told reporters. "He handled himself magnificently in the labor reform fight. He stood up to both management and Hoffa. I didn't see a single other presidential hopeful take on Jimmy Hoffa."

With the Democratic convention of 1960 now only a year away and taking center stage in his thoughts, Jack judged it best to accept praise for his leadership and workmanship during the labor-reform effort, but not to identify himself closely with the final law. "JFK's principal goal," said Gormley, "to demonstrate that he was mature enough and savvy enough to forge a major bill and steer it through Congress, had now been achieved."[51]

In the midst of forging his legislation on labor reform, Kennedy stood for re-election in 1958. With expert planning and organization minimizing the need for the candidate's personal presence, Kennedy toured Massachusetts for only seventeen days of intensive campaigning, freeing himself for important national appearances.

Everyone knew he would win. The only question was if it would be an overwhelming victory, one that would "send a message" to skeptics about his presidential chances in 1960. He not only needed to defeat his opponent, he needed to slaughter him. "Even a 2-to-1 margin, which most politicians up for office in November would hail as a delirious landslide if it happened to them, would make certain Democrat leaders wonder if Jack is losing his touch," said one pundit.

Republicans were expected to charge that Kennedy was only a part-time senator, using Massachusetts voters to propel himself into the presidency. But, *Newsweek* observed, "competent observers report that the voters realize this and are, by and large, delighted; nothing would please them more than a Massachusetts boy in the White House."

Unfortunately for state Republicans, their strongest potential candidates were happily ensconced in the Eisenhower administration. Henry Cabot Lodge, U.S. representative to the United Nations, didn't hanker for a return bout with Kennedy; Christian Herter was undersecretary of state; and Robert Cutler was special assistant to the president.[52]

For a while, Massachusetts Republicans thought they had a suitable candidate, onetime state Republican chairman Charles Gibbons, fifty-six, a businessman and former speaker of the state House of Representatives. But in June 1958, Gibbons bowed out to run for governor instead, believing he might have a chance to become governor but not to beat the incumbent senator.

The candidate Republicans finally roped in as their sacrificial lamb was an unknown lawyer, Vincent J. Celeste. Thirty-four years old, the son of Sicilian immigrants, Celeste had already lost once to Kennedy—by better than a three-to-one margin in the House race of 1950.

During his campaign Celeste charged that Jack had appeased the South in his civil rights votes, destroyed the Port of Boston by voting for the St. Lawrence Seaway, and allowed Walter Reuther to dictate to him during the labor-reform battle. But Celeste always returned to the issue of the Kennedy family's wealth. "I'm running against that millionaire, Jack Kennedy," Celeste repeatedly told voters on his handshaking tours.[53]

While Jack and Jackie traveled in Europe, Larry O'Brien and Ken O'Donnell devised the campaign schedule. When the two showed Joe Kennedy their plan, the senior Kennedy exploded. The rigorous schedule would ruin Jack's health. "It's crazy," he screamed. "You're going to kill him. You don't have to run him all over the state, just put him on television."

"I responded, as tactfully as I could, that Vincent Celeste's main campaign issue was Kennedy's wealth and that a massive television campaign would only support his argument," O'Brien later explained. "Thus, I said, we had to minimize television and maximize personal contact with the voters."

O'Brien and O'Donnell excused themselves and raced to meet Jack at the dock as his boat returned from Europe.

"It looks all right to me," Jack said of the schedule.

"Your father doesn't like it," O'Brien warned.

Jack shrugged. "We'll see what happens," he said.

When they all gathered at the elder Kennedy's Park Avenue apartment, Joe was still mad. "[Jack] was trying to be diplomatic, trying to keep his father happy without angering me," O'Brien said.

"Suppose I try the first day or two and see how it goes?" Jack suggested. "Let's give it a fair try, Dad."

His father reluctantly consented.

Subsequently, after Jack started campaigning, O'Brien and O'Donnell had another confrontation with Joe Kennedy about the campaign schedule.

"Don't argue with him," Jack instructed his two assistants.

Joe complained of having a dead senator on his hands. As O'Brien started to respond with a sarcastic remark, Jack quickly pulled him aside.

"Don't," he ordered. "Just ride with it. Your point is valid, but just don't make it."

O'Brien bit his tongue, and nothing more was said about canceling the tour.

The two incidents, O'Brien thought, illustrated Jack's respect for his father and his dad's affection and total commitment to his son. But they also illustrated Jack's independence.[54]

Young Ted Kennedy's political career began in the 1958 election. Six years earlier, when his brother defeated Lodge, Ted was serving in the army in Europe. While Jack challenged for the nomination for vice president in 1956, Ted was touring Europe and North Africa.

Although given the title of campaign manager, he actually managed nothing because he didn't have the experience or skill to run the operation. "Ted was really just window-dressing," said Thomas Winship; "he was put there to start exposing him." The main goal was to prepare Ted to run for political office himself one day. Larry O'Brien and Kenny O'Donnell actually directed Jack's campaign. But Ted was useful, charming voters at factory gates, firehouses, and police stations.[55]

Potential threats to Jack's reelection—Italian-Americans bitter about his feud with Furcolo, longshoremen upset about his vote for the St. Lawrence Seaway, Teamsters resentful of his labor-reform efforts, blacks angered by his votes on the Civil Rights Act—all received special material which emphasized Kennedy's efforts on their behalf and his endorsement by their leaders.

Up early each morning, Jack crisscrossed the state by auto, shaking the hands of thousands of voters and speaking as often as fifteen times a day. Sometimes Jackie campaigned with him. She stood at Jack's side and shook hands with farmers, tradesmen, and textile workers. She also accompanied her husband to political gatherings in Miami, Atlantic City, Cincinnati, and Cleveland. Between trips, she checked on baby Caroline. "She is simply invaluable," Jack told a reporter.

Private polls showed Kennedy so far ahead, said one wit, "that one suspects they were taken at a Democratic picnic." Kennedy was able to please both liberals and conservatives. A week before the election he won the endorsement of the Massachusetts chapter of Americans for Democratic Action; shortly thereafter he landed the editorial support of the staunchly Republican *Boston Herald,* a paper that often condemned the ADA.[56]

On election night, Jack racked up a huge victory, winning by 874,000 votes, a four-to-one margin over Celeste. "These are the figures that will impress political prognosticators and potential Democratic convention delegates across the country," reported one newspaper of Jack's smashing victory.

During a roaring celebration at his downtown Boston headquarters, and later when he toured the city's newspapers and radio and TV stations, Jack was repeatedly hailed as "our next President."

Although no member of the Kennedy family or Jack's managers would discuss publicly Jack's plans for the presidential nomination, they did privately. "Here's to 1960, Mr. President, if you can make it," Ted Kennedy toasted his brother. Jack returned the toast: "And here's to 1962, *Senator* Kennedy, if *you* can make it."[57]

"John Kennedy was not one of the Senate's great leaders," Sorensen later stated in assessing Kennedy's eight-year Senate career. No law of national importance bore Kennedy's name. Stewart McClure didn't think Jack was much of a senator. "He was kind of lazy," said McClure, referring to Jack's absenteeism.

Laziness wasn't the problem, however. Kennedy's national campaigning after 1956 caused many of his absences. His back surgery and other health problems kept him away from the Senate for over seven months. In addition, his womanizing adventures with George Smathers, Bill Thompson, and others distracted him from his Senate duties.

Kennedy did have solid legislative achievements to his credit. He sponsored an aid bill for India, tried to use foreign economic assistance to divide the Soviet Union from its satellites, fought for expanded unemployment compensation and an increase in the minimum wage, spearheaded the economic program for New England, delivered several forceful speeches on foreign policy, and made a sterling effort on behalf of labor reform.[58]

Senator Wayne Morse admired Kennedy's desire "to get the facts" on issues before taking a position. "In other words, if the facts were going in the opposite direction from partisan politics, that's just too bad for partisan politics," Morse observed. "Once you could satisfy him as to what the facts were on a given issue, you didn't have to worry then as to what his judgment was going to be. He was going to make a judgment on what he thought the facts were."

"He was a well-respected, well-liked man," said colleague Mike Mansfield. "A little cool, a little reserved on the surface, but very friendly and warm-hearted, kind, generous, understanding and tolerant underneath." While the aging Senator Ralph Flanders sat in a subcommittee meeting chaired by Kennedy, the Vermont Republican became confused, but Jack handled the situation with aplomb. Said Flanders: "My assistant here is uh is uh—well, to tell you the truth I can never remember whether his name is Hayward Carlton or Carlton Hayward." Without batting an eyelash, Jack responded "Senator, both Mr. Hayward and Mr. Carlton can remain."[59]

Although well liked by his colleagues, Kennedy's national popularity bewildered some of his associates on Capitol Hill. They privately shook their heads and asked: "What does this fellow have that I don't have?" He wasn't part of the Senate's inner circle. He didn't run with the liberals, the moderates, or the conservatives. Most of the time he stood by himself. "He felt himself in the Senate but not of it," said Senator Joseph Clark. The office of the secretary of the Senate was a favorite watering hole for senators escaping from long legislative sessions. But Jack never showed up there.[60]

Jack didn't speak often in the Senate except on the bills he was handling. "His speeches," Hubert Humphrey perceptively observed, "were all designed to be statements of public policy, not necessarily something that was current in the deliberations of the Senate."

Humphrey's remark is crucial for understanding Kennedy's Senate career.

Kennedy did not fit the mold of a traditional senator who focused primarily on legislation. Kennedy viewed himself, as historian Alonzo Hamby noted, "as a public leader, concerned with campaigning, getting elected, educating the people on the issues, and exercising his informed, independent judgment on important matters."

No matter how Kennedy is judged as a senator, most observers noticed a major change and improvement in his attitude and ability. Columnist Joseph Alsop lived and worked abroad from December 1956 until March 1958. When he returned home, he was struck by the great change in Kennedy. Quite suddenly he had matured, said Alsop. "The inward seriousness was now easy to detect beneath the surface wit and charm. The old casualness had now given way to a passionate absorption in every national problem; and his detailed knowledge of our problems was now combined with an equally detailed knowledge of the national political map, such as every serious politician needs."[61]

A lot had happened to John Kennedy since 1952. After his Senate election he married, had a child, and established a home of his own; endured life-threatening back surgery and many months of sober reflection and convalescence; helped produce an award-winning, bestselling book; narrowly missed the vice-presidential nomination of his party; emerged as a popular national figure; and crisscrossed the country campaigning, speaking, and learning.

As a congressman he complained and joked about the ponderous hierarchy in the House and the elderly leadership. As a senator he venerated Senate traditions and wanted the respect of his colleagues.

He understood issues far better than he had as a congressman. In 1949 he had blamed the Truman administration for the loss of China; eight years later a more mature Kennedy announced that "underlying revolutionary conditions" had "lost" China.[62]

He was more self-confident, a better public speaker, more punctual, and better organized in his Senate duties. He read far more than most senators, knew more history, and was more candid, informal, and relaxed.

"I never in my life have ever seen [such] a transformation," said George Smathers. Smathers judged Kennedy's improvement on a ten-point scale. "When he started out [as a congressman], he would be a four. After he got to be senator he moved up to a six. After he ran for vice president and missed that he moved up to a seven. When he started out to be a presidential candidate he moved up to ten and he stayed at ten."[63]

20

LIBERAL DOUBTS

Liberal Democrats wondered if Kennedy was one of them. Was he a liberal? "Some people have their liberalism 'made' by the time they reach their late twenties," he stated. "I didn't. I was caught in cross currents and eddies. It was only later that I got into the stream of things." Indeed, there were crosscurrents and eddies.

Kennedy had a strong independent streak. The son of a domineering father, he came to disagree with Joe Kennedy on most political issues. Raised and elected to Congress amid machine politics, he didn't align himself with an urban machine. Although the St. Lawrence Seaway was against the parochial interests of his own state, he endorsed it. He usually followed a liberal line in Congress, but refused to be labeled a liberal. His book *Profiles in Courage* honored the independence of political leaders under pressure.

Jack didn't express any fundamental dissatisfaction with the capitalist system, and neither did liberals. Both advocated moderate reforms, and neither sought, as author Allen Matusow noted, "to revive the old crusade against concentrated economic power," or "to stir up class passions, redistribute the wealth, or restructure existing institutions."[1]

Jack was brought up in the tradition of the Irish Catholic political machine of Boston, represented by both of his grandfathers. The pragmatic machine operated on the assumption that people responded to politics based on their immediate interests—food, clothing, shelter, employment, and self-respect. The goal was to further the interests of individuals and the group as a whole, not to advance some grand design. This meant working with the system as one found it, seeking practical immediate success as one could. Based on the old country and neighborhood ties, the Irish machine emphasized loyalty and personal leadership. William Shannon noted that "[T]his tradition acted as a barrier for [Kennedy] . . . against the ideological, issue-oriented politics that began to emerge in the 1930's."

Fifteen when Franklin D. Roosevelt became President, Kennedy admitted that the New Deal had little intellectual or emotional impact on him. What was Jack to make of his father's meandering politics? Initially his father supported Franklin Roosevelt, even administering two of FDR's agencies, but he ended up repudiating the New Deal and fraternizing with anti–New Deal conservatives Robert Taft, Herbert Hoover, and Joe McCarthy.[2]

For the most part John Kennedy adopted his convictions by rational reflection and enlightened self-interest. He had no firsthand experience with the loss of civil liberties, unemployment, labor exploitation, racial discrimination, or making ends meet during the Depression. In 1946 he began with little more than a tenuous link to the Democratic Party allegiance he had inherited. Living in fashionable suburbs and attending elite private schools were not conducive to making him a liberal Democrat.

There was pressure from his father toward conservatism. "Only Kennedy's aloofness and cherished sense of personal independence saved him from this reactionary fate," observed Shannon. He entered politics for the reason the Irish often did: It was a profession in which he could build a career.

Shannon captured the dilemma of Kennedy's early legislative record:

Entering the national scene comparatively young, being a member of the House of Representatives at twenty-nine, he had not yet defined himself as a public man or formed his body of political convictions. Since he had to vote on every issue as it came along, the hesitancies, inconsistencies, and odd lapses that naturally occur over a period of years if a man is trying to make up his mind on fundamentals and think (and feel) his way to a coherent philosophy were, in his case, spread on the public record by his votes in Congress and by his chance remarks.

The composition of Jack's congressional district, though, almost demanded that he support bread-and-butter, New Deal–Fair Deal measures like federal housing, minimum wage, Social Security, and prolabor legislation. By experience, he found that he agreed with his liberal colleagues more often than with conservatives.

After the New Deal a fairly rigid definition of the liberal "line" emerged. "Although independence of thought and political dissent were admired in the abstract," wrote Shannon, "deviations were not, in practice, welcomed or even readily tolerated." This was true in foreign policy as well. Under President Truman the liberal Democrat was expected to support the Marshall Plan, the NATO Treaty, the Berlin airlift, and the war in Korea. "He would protect Roosevelt's reputation by rejecting attacks on the wisdom of the Yalta agreement and uphold Truman by defending the rightness of his China policy," Shannon observed. Since Republican reactionaries like Joe Mc-Carthy smeared Dean Acheson, the liberal would also steadfastly praise the secretary of state's conduct of foreign affairs and condemn McCarthy.[3]

As Kennedy campaigned for the Democratic presidential nomination, liberal Democrats worried about Joe Kennedy, about Jack's choice of friends, but mostly they worried about his temperament and his positions on issues important to liberals. His father had made millions through financial manipulation and ruthless predatory practices, and was close to prominent conservatives and isolationists. To what degree was Jack influenced by his father? Why did Jack speak kindly of Nixon and McCarthy? Why was he such a close friend of conservative senator George Smathers of Florida (who defeated the liberal Democrat Claude Pepper in 1950)?

Why did Kennedy place the blame for the fall of China on Truman's State Department, criticize Dean Acheson, and doubt the wisdom of the U.S. intervention in Korea? Yes, Kennedy had worked hard for public housing, but, as Shannon noted, "he also expressed a recurring interest in the subject of economy in government expenditures, a question that in the postwar folklore of politics had become almost exclusively an issue for conservatives."[4]

Kennedy hadn't taken positions that liberals expected a liberal senator to have. He wasn't anti-McCarthy or a leader on civil rights. The "true" liberals, those influenced by Eleanor Roosevelt and Adlai Stevenson, thought Jack was too detached, too cool, too devoid of commitment. He seemed to have no deeply rooted principles, and always operated in a moral vacuum. "Where is the heart in the man?" asked an observer on Capitol Hill.[5]

Even when he voted "correctly," liberals felt he didn't care as they cared. He didn't have the moral fervor of Senators Wayne Morse, Paul Douglas, or Hubert Humphrey. "He looks like a young man who has carefully calculated what it takes to be a success in politics and is moving deliberately and intelligently along that road," said one commentator. "He does not allow strong emotions to pull him off course."

Shannon thought the difficulty was that Kennedy "was really being asked, not to commit himself on this or that specific issue, but to commit himself to a more crusading spirit, a more abstractly intellectual and idealistic view of politics, and a more dogmatic temper of mind." An outlook and a habit of mind natural for most liberals were unnatural for Kennedy. "Most liberals felt they had found in John Kennedy a strong ally and a prudent field marshal, but not a hero."

A statement Kennedy made in the *Saturday Evening Post* in June 1953 irritated liberals. Why did he resist efforts to label him a liberal? Because, he said, he was annoyed by those who chided him for not being a "true liberal." "I'd be very happy to tell them that I'm not a liberal at all. I never joined the Americans for Democratic Action or the American Veterans Committee. I'm not comfortable with those people." (He never specifically indicated what bothered him about "those people.")[6]

Kennedy thought that liberals wanted to institutionalize liberalism, and he didn't. Some were unreasonable and too doctrinaire for him. They wouldn't compromise. They had an orthodoxy, and he didn't. "They knew the answers and he was still trying to ask questions," wrote Shannon.

In 1949 Kennedy had suggested that both John Fairbank and Owen Lattimore had been part of the pro-Communist influence in the State Department which lost China to the Reds. Ten years later, journalist Theodore White, a former student and admirer of Fairbank, questioned Kennedy about the wisdom of his attack on the Harvard professor. The reminder mortified Jack. Putting his head down in his hands, shaking his head, he said to White: "Don't beat up on me. I was wrong. I know I was wrong. I didn't know anything then—you know what a kid congressman is like with no researchers, no staff, nothing. I made a mistake." White felt that Kennedy's remorse was sincere.[7]

Several other statements and events came back to haunt Kennedy. During the 1952 election, John P. Mallan, a teaching fellow at Harvard, reported in *The New Republic* on a seminar at Harvard that Kennedy had addressed two years earlier on November 10, 1950. According to Mallan, Congressman Kennedy told the gathering that he could see no reason why the United States was fighting in Korea; thought that sooner or later we would "have to get all these foreigners off our backs" in Europe; supported the repressive McCarran Internal Security Act which threatened traditional liberties; felt that not enough had been done about Communists in government; respected Joe McCarthy and thought he "knew Joe pretty well, and [McCarthy] may have something"; had no great respect for Secretary of State Dean Acheson or almost any other member of Truman's Fair Deal administration; and was personally very happy that liberal Democrat Helen Gahagan Douglas had been defeated in 1950 in the California Senate race by Republican Richard Nixon.

Based on a subsequent conversation with "the disarmingly frank and charming Mr. Kennedy," Mallan wrote that Kennedy's views were not so much ideological as a matter of casual, intuitive feeling. His liking for Mc-

Carthy seemed to be on a personal basis, as was his feeling that Congress-woman Douglas was "not the sort of person I like working with on committees."[8]

At the time the article appeared, Kennedy categorically denied saying that he could see no reason for fighting in Korea, that sooner or later we would have to get all the foreigners off our backs in Europe, or that he respected Joe McCarthy. That left his critical remarks about Acheson and Douglas and his support of the McCarran Act. Mallan, though, continued to insist that Kennedy had made *all* the comments described in the article.

At Kennedy's urging, Arthur Holcombe, Jack's former teacher and the director of the seminar Mallan had attended, wrote a letter to *The New Republic* claiming Mallan's article was full of "false and misleading statements" and was a violation of classroom confidence. But Holcombe's defense was vague; he didn't deny the specific statements so disturbing to liberals.[9]

Helen Gahagan Douglas, an actress and liberal political activist, had married actor Melvyn Douglas in 1931. From 1944 to 1950 she served as the Democratic representative from California's Fourteenth Congressional District. In 1950 she battled Republican Richard Nixon in California's U.S. Senate contest. Nixon spent a large part of his campaign claiming that Douglas was the "Pink Lady," who had "consciously fought to prevent the exposure and control of Communists in this country." If she won the Senate seat, Nixon told voters, it would be a signal to Joseph Stalin that his influence in America was on the rise. In the campaign's final days, Nixon's campaign blitzed California voters with postcards reading, "Vote for our Helen for Senator. We are with her 100%," and signed, "Communist League of Negro Women."

Nixon won, and because of the smear campaign against Douglas, she became a liberal hero and Nixon a liberal villain. In the Mallan article Jack praised the villain and disparaged the hero. (At the time of his remark, Kennedy may not have been fully aware of Nixon's smear tactics.)

The Mallan article caused no damage to Kennedy in 1952, but seven years later it resurfaced. In a letter to Kennedy on July 7, 1959, Arthur Schlesinger warned of an upcoming bombshell. "Pretty soon, someone will dig up the John Mallan piece which appeared in *The New Republic* in October 1952."[10]

Even before Schlesinger's warning, Kennedy was preparing his defense. Once again he asked Arthur Holcombe for assistance. "It seems to me it would be helpful if you could write me a letter indicating the falsehoods contained in this article, and its contradictions with my actions, votes and conduct as a representative and a senator. . . . This is part of the same old idea that I was somehow 'soft' on McCarthyism."

In June 1959, Milwaukee's Democratic congressman Clement Zablocki warned Kennedy that influential Paul Ringler of the *Milwaukee Journal* had been given the Mallan article. Planning to enter the Wisconsin primary the following year, Jack wrote to Ringler and told him that the article had "long-since" been discredited. "This is a kind of 'reverse twist' McCarthyism—and it may be helpful for you to have Professor Holcombe's letter for your files."

In 1959 liberals who read the Mallan article took Kennedy's random criticisms and dissents as proof of his conservatism. He only voted liberal for opportunistic reasons. Shannon countered that the Mallan article had misjudged Kennedy. In 1950 Kennedy was neither conservative nor liberal but "independent, skeptical, and sometimes undecided." Shannon should have added, "and, in a few instances, thoughtless."[11]

No issue caused Kennedy more problems with liberal Democrats than his attitude toward Joe McCarthy. It became a litmus test of the depth of his liberalism. His apparent evasion of the McCarthy issue raised doubts about his courage, his judgment, his concern for civil liberties, and his independence from his pro-McCarthy father.

To liberal Democrats McCarthyism was a moral issue, and Kennedy's insensitivity was deeply troubling "This has given rise to concern among doubting Thomases over Kennedy's possible lack of sensitivity to moral issues that are still over the horizon but which some day will have to be met head-on," said a writer in the *Progressive*.

Journalist Ronald May quoted a Democratic senator in reference to Kennedy's absence from the McCarthy censure vote. "He said he was sick in bed. Well, he was only sick a few months. Furthermore, he claims to have used his bed time writing a book."[12]

Kennedy had sat silently as McCarthy accused Democrats of being the party of treason, attacked great national leaders such as General George Marshall, and undermined constitutional freedoms. Ironically, it was on the issue of courage that Kennedy was found most wanting by many liberals.

Every time reporters questioned Kennedy about Joe McCarthy, a tone of annoyance crept into his voice, ruffling his normally flawless composure. In November 1957, when journalist Martin Agronsky grilled him during a TV interview about his view of McCarthy's censure, Kennedy expressed his irritation to Agronsky after the program.

When constituents questioned him about McCarthy, he avoided a direct answer. There was no pending matter related to McCarthy in the Senate, he would say, and because of his long-standing policy against commenting on the personality or actions of other senators, "I must decline to reply to your queries."[13]

In the summer of 1959, political observers waited eagerly after *The Washington Post* announced that Kennedy would write a review of Richard Rovere's new biography, *Senator Joe McCarthy*. The review, written by Jack himself, not Sorensen, proved disappointing. For one thing, Kennedy focused his criticism not on McCarthy but on Senator Robert Taft for his cynical strategy in manipulating the Communist issue to benefit Republicans. (This was the same Robert Taft who three years earlier Kennedy had given a place of honor in *Profiles in Courage*.)

In the early 1950s, Jack wrote in his opening remarks, Joe McCarthy was "Topic A" in Washington. "At every dinner table, throughout every cocktail party, he was discussed, analyzed, cursed, praised, feared and mocked." Jack praised the book and did not question Rovere's damning indictment of the Wisconsin red-hunter.

Kennedy worried that Rovere may have been "overly optimistic in his estimate of how swiftly and fully the nation has recovered its health" since McCarthy's decline and death. "Many who were directly affected—who lost jobs or friends or status—will neither forget nor forgive. And the indirect effects—in our educational system, our foreign service, our image abroad and scores of other areas—may well be with us for at least the duration of the 'Cold War.' "

"The review of the Rovere book was OK so far as it went," Schlesinger bluntly advised Kennedy immediately after it appeared. "But it didn't go far enough and, I fear, only raised in the minds of many the (alas, relevant) question: fine, but where the hell was he at the time all these dreadful things were going on?" The McCarthy issue was the "great talking-point against you," Schlesinger continued, "the one thing which has caused most doubt about you (and which, indeed, is hard to defend)."

For the present, Schlesinger suggested, Kennedy should "make clear that you believe in civil freedom, defend it where it is under current attack, talk as little as possible about the McCarthy period, and, if forced into saying something, say that the nation as a whole—you among them—learned from the experience and what you learned accounts for your determination now to fight for the Bill of Rights."[14]

Kennedy wondered aloud why he was being targeted for not speaking out on McCarthy when only a handful of his Senate colleagues had. Other possible presidential aspirants in 1960—Senators Lyndon Johnson, Stuart Symington, and Hubert Humphrey—had not boldly confronted McCarthy either, keeping their distance from the Wisconsin demagogue.

"If they want to say that Kennedy didn't speak out against McCarthy, I can be indicted for that," Kennedy contended. "But I stand to be indicted along with ninety others. Why not include the others? Why just Kennedy?" The most obvious answer was that Kennedy was the most prominent challenger for the Democratic nomination for President, and had written a book about political courage.[15]

Kennedy's recurring problem with McCarthy was one that politicians often face with issues close to home. Lyndon Johnson of Texas didn't condemn the oil depletion allowance; William Fulbright of Arkansas fell in with racial segregation; and John Kennedy didn't take a stand against Joe McCarthy.

In 1959, during an interview with James Burns, Kennedy conceded that his sensitivity to abuses of civil liberties had not been sufficient to recognize the real menace of McCarthy. "That's a reasonable indictment and I don't mind accepting it," he said. But liberal Democrats seemed to want to burden Kennedy with positions acceptable to them but unacceptable to everyone else. They were, said Herbert Parmet, "making his nomination impossible, a dilemma that already plagued Hubert Humphrey, who faced continuing southern opposition because of his advanced views on civil rights and unions. . . . [Kennedy] was already having enough trouble with the issues of youth and Catholicism." Still, in order to win the nomination in 1960, Jack realized, he had to cultivate a more liberal image because liberals would dominate the Democratic National Convention.[16]

Beginning in 1958, Kennedy often praised Franklin D. Roosevelt and the New Deal at Democratic dinners. He also kept affirming his support for liberal principles. Writing the fiercely anti-McCarthy and liberal William T. Evjue, editor of the *Capital Times* of Madison, Wisconsin, he stated "once again" his "devotion to the principles of due process and civil liberties which represent our best assurance for obtaining justice. In my devotion to these principles, and my record in support of them during 12 years in Congress, I yield to no man."

Liberal groups did approve of Kennedy's voting record during his final years in the Senate. The ADA rated him one of the top liberals in the Senate, giving him a 100 percent for voting "right" on thirteen crucial roll calls in the first session of the Eighty-sixth Congress. The AFL-CIO reported that he voted "right" on fifteen of sixteen key issues.[17]

While not sterling, Jack's record on civil-liberties issues was reasonably solid. Early in his legislative career he warned against "indiscriminate wire tapping." Any plan to investigate federal employees with Communist sympathies or affiliations should be conducted with the utmost care, he said.

In 1959 Kennedy made a strong effort to appease the liberal academic community by defending civil liberties during debate on the loyalty oath. The National Defense Education Act of 1958 had authorized a variety of federal aid programs, including loans to college students and grants for graduate fellowships. One small section of the act, a vestige of the McCarthy era slipped in almost unnoticed, provided that applicants for loans must take an oath of loyalty and sign a vague anticommunist affidavit.

Together with Senator Joseph Clark, his liberal Democratic colleague from Pennsylvania and a leader in Americans for Democratic Action, Kennedy sought to eliminate the provision. Action was urgent, he claimed. "At least 9 colleges and universities have refused to accept any benefits under the [act] . . . because of the oath and affidavit requirement," he wrote Lyndon Johnson.

Why did Congress single out recipients of federal loans for educational purposes and not those who received old-age benefits, crop loans, or other payments? The affidavit would not keep dangerous Communists out of the program anyway. "Card carrying members of the Communist Party will have no hesitancy about perjuring themselves in the affidavit," Kennedy argued.

Those excluded from loans might be nonconformists and dissenters, but our country needed to attract the best talents for science and could not afford to exclude talented nonconformists and dissenters. Besides, he continued, as Jefferson prescribed for the University of Virginia, colleges should be "based on the illimitable freedom of the human mind."

On July 23, 1959, on the key Senate roll call vote, Jack's bill was recommitted (by 49 to 42) to committee, in effect killing it. But his effort won approval from liberal Democrats.[18]

Jack's sharpest and most persistent critic was Eleanor Roosevelt, still revered by liberal Democrats; her barbs led to an exchange of letters with Kennedy. Much as he had in his acrimonious exchange with Roy Wilkins, Kennedy clearly gained the upper hand.

Mrs. Roosevelt had long despised Joe Kennedy. In the late 1930s she asked her husband why he had ever appointed that "awful" man as ambassador. Joe's attitude toward Jews, Nazis, and the war repulsed her, as did his criticism of the Roosevelt White House. His crude remarks about her in 1940, during an interview by Louis Lyons, simply increased her hostility. And there was another matter: "For all her magnanimity," observed historian William Leuchtenburg, "Mrs. Roosevelt was not altogether free of hostility toward the Catholic Church."[19]

Three times in nine months during 1958 Mrs. Roosevelt publicly challenged the senator's fitness to be President. In March, in a *Saturday Evening Post* article, she complained that Kennedy had avoided taking a stand on McCarthyism. In her autobiography, *On My Own,* she returned to the subject of Kennedy and McCarthy. "A public servant," she wrote, "must clearly indicate that he understands the harm that McCarthyism did to our country and that he opposes it actively, so that one would feel sure that he would always do so in the future."

On Sunday, December 7, 1958, during a television interview, she didn't specifically allude to McCarthy, but her words packed a powerful punch. Except for Adlai Stevenson, she was not impressed with any of the possible Democratic presidential candidates for 1960. What would she do, asked the interviewer, if she had to choose between a "conservative Democrat like Kennedy and a liberal Republican [like Nelson] Rockefeller"? She hoped the problem would not arise, she responded. "I would do all I possibly could . . . to have us nominate someone at least for President who we felt did not have any of the difficulties that possibly might come up if Senator Kennedy were nominated." In a caustic, often-quoted reference to Kennedy's *Profiles in Courage,* she added that she would hesitate to place difficult presidential decisions in the hands of "someone who understands what courage is and admires it but has not quite the independence to have it." What's more, she deplored the influence of Joseph Kennedy, who had been "spending oodles of money all over the country" to secure his son the Democratic nomination "and probably has a representative in every state by now."[20]

That was too much for Kennedy to ignore. Four days after the television interview, Jack responded to the weakest portion of Mrs. Roosevelt's comments. Unwilling to challenge her aspersion on his courage, he attacked her facts about his father's financial assistance. Alluding to her well-known hatred for McCarthyism, he slid a dagger in her back:

Because I know of your long fight against the injudicious use of false statements, rumors or innuendo as a means of injuring the reputation of an individual, I am certain that you are the victim of misinformation; and I am equally certain that you would want to ask your informant if he would be willing to name me one such representative or one such example of any spending by my father around the country on my behalf.

On December 18, Eleanor responded weakly that "many people" had told her about the money Kennedy's father spent "in your behalf." This was "commonly accepted as a fact. Building an organization is permissible but giving too lavishly may seem to indicate a desire to influence through money."

Jack persisted. He was disappointed that she would repeat rumor and allegation as fact. "My father has not spent any money around the country, and has *no* 'paid representatives' for this purpose in *any* state of the union." He demanded that she ask her informants to furnish more than gossip and speculation. If they were unable to produce concrete evidence to support their charges, "I am confident you will, after your investigation, correct the record in a fair and gracious manner."

The correspondence continued through January 1959. "People will, of course, never give names as that would open them to liability," Eleanor replied. To appease the senator and to be fair, she enclosed a copy of her recent newspaper column which included Jack's rebuttal.[21]

Still not satisfied, Jack continued to badger his nemesis. "While I appreciate your courtesy in printing my denial of the false rumors about my father and me, neither the article nor your letter to me deals with whether the rumors are true," he wrote her on January 10. "In view of the seriousness of the charge, I had hoped that you would request your informants to give— not their own names—but the name of any 'paid representative' of mine in any State of the Union. Or, if not the name, then mere evidence of his existence. I knew that your informants would not be able to provide such information because I have no paid representative." The fairest course of action would be for Mrs. Roosevelt to admit she had no evidence to justify the rumors. Again he alluded to McCarthyism, implying that Mrs. Roosevelt had acted hypocritically: "I am familiar with your long fight against the use of unsubstantiated charges and the notion that merely because they are repeated they attain a certain degree of credibility."

In the end Eleanor conceded she didn't have the facts. "My informants were just casual people in casual conversation. It would be impossible to get their names because for the most part I don't even know them."

Having made his point, Jack responded that he appreciated her "very gracious letter," and had decided not to pursue the matter any further "for the present."[22]

During the fall of 1960, in a book comparing Kennedy and Richard Nixon, Arthur Schlesinger praised Kennedy's liberalism and open-mindedness. "Can anyone imagine Nixon opening up his files for unrestricted use by a distinguished and independent-minded scholar in the preparation of a biography, as Kennedy did?"

Schlesinger was referring to James MacGregor Burns's *John Kennedy: A Political Profile* (1960), which several decades later many still regarded as "the most penetrating biography of a president-to-be that has ever been written." Intended for liberal readers, praised for its honesty and objectivity, the book was the first major study to conclude that Kennedy should be taken seriously as a presidential candidate. He had displayed impressive legislative competence and political judgment as a national leader, and had far more intellectual depth and steadfastness than many supposed.

What readers and reviewers, both then and now, did not know was that behind the scenes the book's highly respected author, under severe pressure, had agreed to many concessions favorable to Kennedy—some of them major. In fact, the book was significantly less objective than it appeared.

During 1958 Ted Sorensen and Kennedy quietly searched for a prominent author willing to write a serious biography of the senator. The goal was to have the biography completed in time to advance Kennedy's campaign for the Democratic presidential nomination in 1960.[23] They considered several authors—John Gunther, Marquis Childs, and John Hersey—but eventually settled on James Burns. In early November 1958, Sorensen approached Burns about writing the biography, and Burns eagerly agreed. "I am tremendously excited by the prospect of going to work for Jack," he wrote Sorensen. "There is no person I would rather work for or whose political prospects I am so interested in."

Burns, a distinguished professor of political science at Williams College in Williamstown, Massachusetts, was a specialist in American politics, comparative government, and political thought; his books and articles, particularly his biography of Franklin D. Roosevelt, *Roosevelt: The Lion and the Fox* (1956), had been praised for their engaging literary quality and academic integrity. Several reviewers judged his biography of Roosevelt to be the best study of FDR to date, and it had earned major awards. (Indeed, it was a top contender for the Pulitzer Prize in biography in 1956, the same year Kennedy won for *Profiles in Courage*.)

A liberal Democrat, Burns was active in the Berkshire County Democratic organization, and had been a member of the Massachusetts delegation to the Democratic National Conventions in 1952 and 1956. He deeply admired Kennedy and had supported him for the vice-presidential nomination in 1956. In 1958 Burns ran unsuccessfully as the Democratic candidate for the House of Representatives from Massachusetts's Republican-dominated First Congressional District, in the westernmost portion of the state. His campaign for Congress strengthened his relationship with Kennedy, who spoke on his behalf, while the senator coasted to reelection.[24]

Burns brought to the book project his outstanding reputation for integrity, objectivity, and scholarship. In short, he brought credibility. Because of his stature, his biography was expected to be several cuts above the usual books about candidates for President.

Before beginning the project, Burns wrote Kennedy setting down guidelines that he hoped would avoid any misunderstanding. He intended to write "an independent, disinterested, factual biography that will be of special interest to an academic, liberal, intellectual audience." The biography would not be an ordinary campaign "puff," but would live up "to the requirements of good scholarship." Burns presumed that Kennedy's office would cooperate by allowing him full access to needed information and files. He expected to interview the senator and his associates, observe nonsecret staff meetings, and travel with Kennedy on several speaking tours. Ultimately, Burns concluded, "the great value of this project may be in demonstrating that a presidential candidate was courageous enough and confident enough of his record that he wanted the full story presented to the public in a campaign year."[25]

For the most part, Kennedy fulfilled his part of their understanding. Granted extraordinary access to Kennedy's personal papers, Burns spent months combing through files in Kennedy's office. He spoke with Jackie and other members of the Kennedy family, former teachers, reporters, staff assistants, friends, political supporters, and political opponents. With the senator's assistance, he gained access to Kennedy's grades and some of his correspondence at Choate and Harvard, a remarkable concession for a presidential aspirant. He traveled with Kennedy to several appearances, and in the summer of 1959 he had a long interview with the senator.

Unlike many political leaders, Kennedy never suggested that the campaign biography glamorize him. "I don't think really in his own mind he thought it should," said Burns. Kennedy did hope that Burns's scholarly reputation and standing among liberal intellectuals would give the biography unique stature in the liberal community. "He felt," Burns recalled, "that an honest statement of his life, as any of us might feel, would be an asset to him."

"[Burns] was very carefully given no instructions concerning attitudes he should take," said Kennedy aide Myer Feldman. "We didn't even ask for any right to review or veto what he had written."[26]

In mid–August 1959, Burns informed the senator that the manuscript was substantially completed and had been sent to Burns's publisher, Harcourt Brace. "The work has gone well and I am rather pleased with how things have come along." He sent a copy of the nearly finished study for Kennedy's inspection, hoping that the senator would correct minor errors.

During the year since Burns had started his project, though, much had changed in Kennedy's life. His campaign for president had mushroomed, but critics were watching for missteps, competitors yapped at his heels, pundits gauged every utterance—and the early primaries were only a few months away. Under the circumstances, Kennedy had grown extremely sensitive about his public image.

About the third week of September, as Burns's manuscript was going into galley form, Sorensen phoned the author with bad news. While on a campaign trip out west, he and JFK had read the manuscript on the plane and didn't like it. In fact, the senator wanted Sorensen to inform Burns that if published in its current form, the book would be a catastrophe for Kennedy's campaign for the presidency. A week later the three of them met at the Waldorf–Astoria in New York to discuss the problems. "For at least four solid hours without interruption we went over the manuscript," Burns recalled. Sorensen was very upset, and the senator's critique was "about as strongly worded as anything I have ever seen from him."[27]

After the meeting, Kennedy let Sorensen try to jawbone Burns into amending his offending passages. "What disturbs me most about the book is the omissions," Sorensen wrote Burns on October 6, 1959.

> Nothing is said about his proposals on India, his speeches on the Eisenhower Mideast doctrine, Latin America, the missile gap and, somewhat earlier, Indo-China; or his fight to stop the "new look" reduction in our Armed Forces. These and others have been determined by some Washingtonians the only real new ideas in foreign policy since 1952. Nor is there any mention of this year's fight on the loyalty oath bill and minimum wages; or last year's bills on health, education and welfare funds.

The word "detachment" was considerably overworked in the manuscript, Sorensen complained. "It is important to refer to his analytical powers, his objective reasoning, his ability to coolly keep prejudices, whims and unreliable emotions out of the way when making a hard, tough decision and sticking to it. But the impression should never be given that he does not believe deeply in what he says or will not fight fiercely for the causes in which he believes."

Sorensen wasn't finished. On October 27, he sent Burns a long list of specific objections. Burns should not "charge" in two places that Kennedy was not deeply religious, because that "is not true," and "certainly unverifiable." There was too much emphasis on the dreadful Mallan article, the one with the bizarre account of Kennedy's statements in Arthur Holcombe's seminar. Kennedy's alleged reference to Helen Gahagan Douglas in particular gave a completely misleading impression, said Sorensen.[28]

"The whole McCarthy matter is not fairly or accurately presented. . . . It is not put in its proper perspective—and it is tied into his 1952 campaign, his book, his race for the Vice Presidency and the Presidential nomination in a way that implies it is a much larger issue in his life than it actually has been."

Worried that the senator might be perceived as physically weak, Sorensen seriously distorted the truth by insisting to Burns that Kennedy was *not* plagued by illness at Choate.

These and other errors, Sorensen reiterated, made the book, in its present form, a potential disaster for Kennedy's campaign and a powerful weapon in the hands of opponents. Sorensen continued: "I am at a loss to understand your motives for producing such a work unless you have decided on the basis of your studies that you are against Kennedy's nomination. We do not want the book to be a 'campaign puff'; but we did hope it would be fair, accurate and balanced."

"Burns seems to feel that unless somebody overstates or shouts to the top of their voice they are not concerned about a matter," Jack complained to Sorensen. If he heard the word "detachment" one more time, he would burst.[29]

Some of Kennedy's aides had the same reaction. "We felt that [Burns] had incorrectly described the Senator," said Feldman. "The part we objected to more than anything else was the description of Kennedy as 'cold and unfeeling.' Senator Kennedy was anything but cold and unfeeling. I think he was very warm."

Sorensen's letter of October 27 ingeniously concluded in capital letters: "PLEASE LET ME KNOW WHAT CHANGES YOU WILL BE MAKING ON THESE ITEMS—FOR, IF YOU DISAGREE ON THE NECESSITY FOR CHANGING THEM, IT COULD ONLY BE THAT I HAVE NOT MADE MY POINT AND THE REAL FACTS CLEAR." The meaning of Sorensen's brutal conclusion was obvious: Sorensen was right; Burns was wrong; and if Burns didn't agree, Sorensen would explain the "facts" to him again.[30]

Burns was shocked by the angry reaction. Pleading for understanding, he argued that reviewers and the public would surely perceive the book as a pro-Kennedy book, one that would "strengthen [Kennedy's] standing with liberals and voters generally." To talk in terms of "disaster," as Sorensen had done in a telephone call, made Burns feel that "we won't be able even to communicate . . . unless you can divest yourself for a moment of your intense loyalty to Jack."

Historian Michael Beschloss, a former student of Burns, claims that the Sorensen-Burns correspondence "shows no effort to pressure the author, only Sorensen's vigorous championship of his candidate in the dialogue that Burns had invited." In fact, Burns felt plenty of pressure. Sorensen didn't just suggest changes; he insisted upon them. What if Kennedy repudiated the book, claiming it was a hatchet job? Burns was under his own, internal pressure as well—to be objective and truthful. Finally, Burns was under pressure from his publisher, insisting that he meet its deadline.[31]

Worried that his labor might come to naught, Burns made nearly two dozen changes—some of them major. For example, in his draft the author had made two references to Jack's personal religious practice. The first quoted a letter Jack had sent home from Canterbury, followed by Burns's comment:

> "I received the prayer-book and would you please send me a puff because it is very cold . . ." But he was not deeply religious then, as he is not today.

In the book a crucial line was omitted:

"I received the prayer-book and would you please send me a puff because it is very cold. . . ."

Later in his draft Burns returned to the subject of Jack's religious practice:

John Kennedy spent only one year in a Catholic school—and even that school was taught by laymen. He was never deeply religious, though he observed the formalities.

In the book it appeared this way:

John Kennedy spent only one year in a Catholic school—and even that school was taught by laymen. He never made a display of his religion, though he observed the formalities.

Burns altered the account of Kathleen Kennedy's death because Jack did not want readers to know that Kathleen had an illicit affair with a married man. Burns intended to say:

Kathleen . . . was killed in a plane crash on a vacation trip to the Riviera with . . . British aristocrat, Lord Fitzwilliam.

In the book the offending—but truthful—passage was removed:

Kathleen . . . was killed in a plane crash on a vacation trip to the Riviera.

At Jack's insistence Burns deleted a critical reference to Joe Jr. Burns's draft read:

. . . asked whether anything really bothered him as a child, Kennedy can think only of his big brother: "He was rather a bully. He had a pugnacious personality. Later on it smoothed out but it was a problem in my boyhood."

The version that appeared in the book stated:

. . . asked whether anything really bothered him as a child, Kennedy can think only of his big brother: "He had a pugnacious personality. Later on it smoothed out but it was a problem in my boyhood."

In his draft Burns described Drew Pearson's allegation that Sorensen wrote *Profiles in Courage,* and explained Kennedy's counterclaim. Then Burns offered his own conclusion:

The truth seems to be that [Kennedy] had more help in preparation of his book than authors customarily have but that nonetheless in the end he wrote his own book.

In the book version the entire sentence—Burns's conclusion—was omitted.[32]

Burns's draft made two important references to John Mallan's article in *The New Republic* in 1952. Kennedy worried that the startling references would now be very offensive to liberals. Burns eliminated entirely from the book one long description of Kennedy's remarks. The author insisted that a second reference to Mallan's article be included, but he deleted several statements galling to liberals—and therefore to Kennedy. Burns's draft accurately summarized Mallan's article, but the book deleted references to the McCarran Act, Helen Gahagan Douglas, and getting "foreigners off our back."

The biggest concession Burns made related to Kennedy's health, specifically to his Addison's disease. In June 1959, Burns read a brief item in the *Boston Post* about a rumor that Jack had Addison's. (Apparently Burns had heard other rumors as well.) "It seems that it would be desirable from every standpoint to have the full record of your health background in the book, as part of the narrative and without overemphasizing it," Burns wrote the senator on June 30. "This would give the information that people want without overplaying it." Instead of referring Burns to the doctors who had treated the disease—Dr. Elmer Bartels at the Lahey Clinic and the New York doctors who operated on his back—Burns was referred to Dr. Janet Travell, currently Kennedy's primary physician.

Beschloss has said that Dr. Travell gave Burns information that "allowed him to write with some authority" on the senator's Addison's disease. In fact, the opposite was true. Travell distorted the nature of Kennedy's illness; despite having evidence that Travell was lying, Burns accepted her version and inserted the misinformation into his book.

Travell had personally collected Kennedy's medical files at nearly all the hospitals and clinics Kennedy had ever visited, and therefore she knew that he had been diagnosed with Addison's disease. To ingratiate herself with the leading Democratic presidential contender, however, she intentionally disguised the malady, insisting publicly that the illness was only a mild adrenal insufficiency.[33]

Travell sent Burns a statement which erroneously traced the Addison's disease to Kennedy's PT boat accident in 1943. The crash subjected him to "extraordinarily severe stress in a terrific ordeal of swimming to rescue his men. This, together perhaps with subsequent malaria, resulted in a depletion of adrenal function from which he is now rehabilitated."

A characteristic of Addison's disease, she wrote, was "deep pigmentation or tanning of the skin. Pigmentation appears early and it is the most strik-ing physical sign of the disease. Senator Kennedy has never had any abnor-mal pigmentation of the skin," and no discoloration of the skin or gums.

"Senator Kennedy has tremendous physical stamina," concluded Travell. "He has above-average resistance to infections, such as influenza."

Travell's statement was a masterpiece of deception. She didn't deny that Kennedy had Addison's disease, but she strongly suggested that to call him an Addisonian was a misdiagnosis. She claimed that Kennedy was "rehabili-tated" from a "depletion of adrenal function," but never mentioned that he was receiving treatment of both DOCA implants and cortisone. Kennedy currently had no pigmentation of the skin, she said, but she failed to indicate that Kennedy's cortisone treatment cleared up some of the abnormal pig-mentation. "Her statement that Kennedy never had any discoloration of ei-ther his skin or his gums is, at best, an exaggeration since there were frequent references [in the past] to Kennedy's 'jaundiced' or 'Atabrine-yellow' com-plexion," said Kenneth Crispell and Carlos Gomez, in their book *Hidden Ill-ness in the White House* (1988).[34]

Dissatisfied with Travell's vague and upbeat response, Burns sought advice from a physician friend, Dr. Alexander Preston of Middletown, New York, who in turn consulted two medical experts.

"I am plagued with the thought that the Senator is not coming clean to you with all of the facts with regard to his medical picture," Preston grimly reported to Burns on August 21, 1959. "I would think it would be fairly im-portant to verify the authenticity of this rumor and if it is true, certainly Kennedy has been less than forthright with you. I might think it almost im-portant enough to face him with the question directly."

Preston described Dr. Travell's letter as "rather loose medical terminol-ogy with a political orientation." It was not credible. "For instance, it could hardly be true that stress of swimming to rescue his men in conjunction with the malaria would have resulted in a depletion of adrenal function."

"It would seem to me that if it were true that Kennedy were taking DOCA, he could not hope that this would not come out in the campaign and he should tell you all about it forthwith. If he has been taking it, his ad-renal insufficiency is not 'slight.'"[35]

After further thought, Preston warned Burns a month later to nail down the rumors because Travell's letter was "inadequate as a medical statement, unconvincing, and was politically inspired." Burns should insist upon a re-port from whoever was evaluating or treating the problem, and a "clear and positive statement as to the treatment he has received or is receiving for his adrenal insufficiency."

Burns, though, never followed up on Preston's advice, never confronted Kennedy about Travell's unconvincing explanation. Pressured by his publisher to meet deadline, worried about further antagonizing Kennedy, he agreed to a misleading explanation of Jack's adrenal problem, one that influenced a generation of Kennedy observers.

On November 19, Burns explained to Sorensen his watered-down version of the health issue. He would write:

> While Kennedy's adrenal insufficiency might well be diagnosed by some doctors as a mild case of Addison's Disease, it was not diagnosed as the classic type of Addison's Disease, which is due to tuberculosis. Other conditions, often not known, can cause malfunctioning of the adrenal glands. As in Kennedy's case, this can be fully controlled by medication taken by mouth and requires a routine endocrinologic checkup as a part of regular physical examinations once or twice a year.[36]

By using the phrase "classic type of Addison's Disease"—meaning tubercular destruction of the adrenals—Burns misled readers. Crispell and Gomez observed:

> Although Thomas Addison himself was convinced that the etiology of the illness was tuberculosis, subsequent research clearly showed that other diseases could cause adrenal atrophy and precipitate an Addisonian crisis. As early as the 1920s, for example, epidemiologists had found that at least 50 percent of Addisonians in the United States lost their adrenal function from some malady other than tuberculosis. . . . Burns' point, finally, is irrelevant. Whatever the origins of Kennedy's disease, he was still an Addisonian requiring daily medication in order to survive.

In the end, Burns rationalized that his many concessions to Sorensen and Kennedy actually brought "balance" to the book. "For example," he wrote Jack, "on the Mallan episode I have quoted another student who was [in the seminar] who feels, interestingly enough, that what you said was good shock treatment for the stereotyped liberal mind and that you were way ahead of your time." In truth, Kennedy's bizarre comments before Arthur Holcombe's seminar had no "shock" value and didn't fairly represent the liberal mind. That was the reason Kennedy wanted to obliterate all references to the incident.

Trying hard to appease, Burns also wrote: "I realized that I had not carried through to its logical conclusion the point that in each job you have taken you have moved into it and through it and grown bigger in it, and since the Presidency is notably an elevating office, I brought in this point toward the end."

In the book's conclusion Burns questioned whether Kennedy had all the important ingredients for great leadership. Could Kennedy move his party, the country, and the world? "What great idea does Kennedy personify? In what way is he a leader of thought? How could he supply moral leadership at a time when new paths before the nation need discovering?"[37]

Still, Burns supplied ample reasons for voters to support Kennedy:

> Kennedy as President would mobilize traditional tools of presidential power and use them with force, astuteness, and tenacity. He would show a flair for personal influence and manipulation, perhaps some of the flair Roosevelt had. He would drive hard bargains, forming alliances with Republicans when necessary, but compromising, too, when he lacked the votes.

John Kennedy: A Political Profile appeared in January 1960, and won effusive praise by prominent reviewers. They thought it was gracefully written, objective, and scholarly. It told a "thrilling story" of a glamorous and dramatic life. Nearly every commentator was impressed that the front-runner for the Democratic nomination for president had allowed a respected scholar free access to intimate material. That Burns found a few disturbing traits in Kennedy gave greater credence to his mostly admiring portrait.[38]

"This excellent biography presents a very charming and intelligent young statesman," wrote the eminent theologian Reinhold Niebuhr. "Burns has certainly served the young senator well in his sympathetic but fair biography."

"The book will do [Kennedy] much more good than harm in the thinking of most people," wrote Erwin D. Canham in *The Christian Science Monitor*.

In an ironic twist, Sidney Hyman, commenting in *The New York Times Book Review*, praised Burns for having been "swayed by no consideration except his own perceptions."[39]

21

THE CATHOLIC
DILEMMA

As youngsters in church, the Kennedy children were expected to be perfect little gentlemen and ladies. One day, a neighbor girl, Helen Leahy, approached Jack in church while he served as an altar boy. "Hi, Jack," she said sweetly. "You shouldn't say anything to me in church, Helen," Jack scolded. "It's wrong to speak in church and you shouldn't do it."

Like the rest of his family, John Kennedy recited grace at every meal, said the Rosary with the family, and prayed on his knees before entering bed at night. He listened while Rose taught her children the meaning of Shrove Tuesday and Palm Sunday.

The Kennedy girls, though, were far more devout and received far more Catholic education than John and the other Kennedy boys. John attended only one year of a Catholic school taught by laymen. He learned little about Catholic theology. His education at mostly private and public schools, including Protestant-influenced Choate and Harvard, didn't expose him to scholasticism, the St. Thomas Aquinas–inspired system fundamental to Catholic beliefs. At Harvard he joined St. Paul's Catholic Club, but he mixed mostly with non-Catholics.[1]

"It was a bit difficult for Jack to buy a lot of the miracles which we were shown in Rome [in 1937]," said LeMoyne Billings, "for instance Veronica's veil or the steps down which St. Peter's head is supposed to have fallen." Kennedy assured the non-Catholic Billings that it wasn't necessary to believe those miracles in order to be a good Catholic. Kennedy rarely discussed religion with Billings. "I don't think he was a dedicated Catholic like his mother and his sisters, but he was a good Catholic. I cannot remember in my life when Jack Kennedy didn't go to Church on Sunday. . . . He always went to confession when he was supposed to," added Billings. Inga Arvad thought her paramour believed in life after death.[2]

During World War II, though, Kennedy seemed on the verge of renouncing his Catholic faith. While at Stanford, he talked about religion with his friend Henry James. "He found great difficulty in believing most of the tenets of the Catholic faith," said James. "Church bored him! He hardly ever went. Religion didn't interest him. He was all for being au courant, very much up to date with the things that were going on at the time, but not eternal verities."

Kennedy had little interest in the Catholic dogmatic tradition, and cared less about encyclicals. "It is hard for a Harvard man to answer questions in theology," he wrote privately before the 1960 election. "I imagine my answers will cause heartburn at Fordham and B.C. [Boston College]." "His social thought hardly resulted from a determination to apply the principles of *Rerum Novarum* to American life," observed Arthur Schlesinger. "He felt an immense sense of fellowship with Pope John XXIII, but this was based more on the Pope's practical character and policies than on theological considerations."[3]

Kennedy didn't applaud the most frequently praised Catholic virtues of piety and obedience; nor did he treasure the traditional Christian virtues of humility, penance, mortification, chastity, and poverty. What he did praise were the traditional American values of independence, freedom, and achievement.

Kennedy believed in the capacity of people to master their fate, overcome circumstances, and mold their environment. Lawrence Fuchs, an authority on Kennedy's Catholicism, found him attracted to "assertive and individualistic virtues." He loved William Ernest Henley's poem "Invictus." Henley thanked

> . . . *whatever gods may be,*
> *For my unconquerable soul*

and concluded:

> *It matters not how strait the gate,*
> *How charged with punishments the scroll,*

I am the master of my fate;
I am the captain of my soul.

Kennedy did not show a preference for Catholics on his staff; nor did he care about staff members' religious beliefs. He sprinkled quotations from the Protestant version of the Bible throughout his speeches. During the eleven years Sorensen worked for him, "I never heard him pray aloud in the presence of others, never saw him kiss a bishop's ring and never knew him to alter his religious practices for political convenience."[4]

He and Jackie detested gaudy displays of religiosity. When Robert and Ethel Kennedy presented each of their children with religious holy pictures to hang on their bedroom walls, Jack and Jacqueline confided to friends that they "wouldn't be caught dead with those pictures in their house." Jackie Kennedy laughed as she told Arthur Krock, "I think it is so unfair for Jack to be opposed because he is a Catholic. After all, he's such a poor Catholic. Now, if it were Bobby: he never misses mass and prays all the time."[5]

Still, politics in America required deference to God. Spiritual symbols and stories occasionally crept into Kennedy's statements and speeches. In June 1955 he spoke at the commencement of Assumption College in Worcester, Massachusetts, which had presented him with an honorary doctor of laws degree. He called for an emphasis on "spiritual and ethical goals in our foreign relations" rather than on the material goals the Communists stressed. "We point with pride to the great outpouring of our factories and assume we have therefore proved the superiority of our system," he said. "We forget the purpose of life is the future and not the present." Communists feared Christianity, he said. "They have no room for God. The claim of the state must be total and no other loyalty, and no other philosophy of life can be tolerated."

After World War II Kennedy had consistently attended Mass each Sunday, even in the midst of exhausting campaign trips when the public or the media wouldn't know if he had. Several friends witnessed him drop to his knees to say a brief prayer before he slipped into bed at night.

Boston's Archbishop Richard Cushing, who introduced Jack at charity and church functions, called him his "nearest and dearest friend—the most cherished personal friend I ever had." Kennedy enjoyed Cushing as well. He "felt closer to him than to any other clergyman," said Robert Kennedy.[6]

"He was just as good a Catholic as I am," said Cushing (surely exaggerating). "He spent more time in private prayer than many people know." Cushing claimed that before 1960 Kennedy occasionally stopped by the archbishop's home in Boston and joined in the evening Rosary Cushing was broadcasting on the radio. Kennedy never kissed Cushing's ring or genuflected when greeting the church leader, but Cushing didn't expect him to.

Kennedy personally gave Cushing hundreds of thousands of dollars for Catholic charities and for missions in Latin America, including four hundred thousand dollars in royalties from the television production of *Profiles in Courage.* "I know a lot of people whom he helped through me," said Cushing, "but he said nothing about it." Nonetheless, as most people discovered, Kennedy never had money in his pocket when he dined with the venerable churchman. "If you had a cup of coffee and a doughnut with Jack, you'd pick up the tab," Cushing said.[7]

Having a Catholic in the White House seemed revolutionary because of the Protestant roots of American democracy. Al Smith was the only Catholic ever nominated for President, and his defeat by Herbert Hoover in 1928 created a huge challenge for any Catholic presidential candidate. During Smith's campaign anti-Catholic zealots distributed ten million handbills, leaflets, and posters with titles like "Popery in the Public Schools," "Convent Life Unveiled," "Convent Horrors," and "Crimes of the Pope." The nondenominational *Christian Century* tersely summed up Protestant fears: "[Protestants] cannot look with unconcern upon the seating of the representative of an alien culture, of a medieval Latin mentality, of an undemocratic hierarchy, and of a foreign potentate in the great office of the President of the United States."

The attacks bewildered Smith. He believed in personal freedom and the separation of church and state. Why was he being held accountable for papal bulls and encyclicals he had never even read? He attended Mass, prayed the Rosary, and made his confession all his life, but that never prevented him from living up to his oath of office or being an excellent governor of New York.[8]

Not only bigots worried about Catholic political power in America. Many thoughtful people did as well. The most incisive and widely read critic was Paul Blanshard, a Unitarian lawyer and author, who after World War II chastised Catholic power in various liberal magazines. His first book, *American Freedom and Catholic Power* (1949), received favorable reviews, went through twenty-six printings, and sold 240,000 copies. (A second edition in 1958 also sold well.)

Blanshard rooted his critique in his study of canon law, encyclicals, pastoral letters, and other Catholic documents. The problem with Catholicism was not the ordinary Catholic layperson; it was the powerful Catholic hierarchy. "The American Catholic *people* have done their best to join the rest of America, but the American Catholic hierarchy . . . has never been assimilated. It is still fundamentally Roman in its spirit and directives. It is an autocratic moral monarchy in a liberal democracy."

Censorship by the Catholic Church in the United States was neither spasmodic nor intermittent, said Blanshard, but a highly organized system of cultural and moral controls applied to books, magazines, plays, and movies, and to persons and places, too. Blanshard summarized what he thought was the attitude of most non-Catholic Americans toward public support for Catholic schools:

> The Catholic people have been offered the same free, democratic schools that have been offered to everybody else. If they don't wish to join the rest of the American community, that is their affair. Methodists, Baptists, Jews, and nearly everybody else belong to the great fraternity of American public education. The Catholic people have not been blackballed; they have been elected to full membership, but their priests have persuaded them to stay away from the meeting. They should not pretend that they are being discriminated against. Methodists, Baptists, and Jews cannot collect public funds for their schools. Neither can Catholics. We must treat everybody alike.[9]

America had a settled tradition of separation of church and state, Blanshard stressed, and with the help of the Supreme Court the concept had come to stand for three basic policies: "complete freedom for all faiths, complete equality of all churches before the law, and freedom of the taxpayer from all general assessments to support a church which he does not endorse."

"There is no alternative for champions of traditional American democracy except to build a resistance movement designed to prevent the hierarchy from imposing its social policies upon our schools, hospitals, government, and family organization," Blanshard concluded.[10]

In campaigning for President Kennedy used a different approach than Smith. The New York governor tried to ignore the issue, claiming it wasn't worthy of a response. Too impatient and unwilling to deal with the issue methodically over a period of time, Smith didn't familiarize voters with the novelty of a Catholic running for President. When Smith did reply, he hurled insults at his critics. Occasionally Kennedy also downplayed the issue, hoping it would disappear, but usually he faced it squarely. Unlike Smith, Kennedy responded deliberately with logical appeals to pride, fairness, and patriotism. He made his arguments earnestly, but above all, he remained unfailingly courteous, patient, and good-tempered.

As a congressman Kennedy spoke before many different Catholic groups, but, unlike Smith, he lived apart from the world of Holy Name Societies, the Knights of Columbus, and Communion breakfasts. Nor did Kennedy embody the Irish Catholic stereotype personified by Smith—the brown derby, the big cigar, and the East Side, New York accent.[11]

Kennedy was much closer to the enduring Protestant image of the President. "If the tradition which has kept Catholics out of the White House is to go," wrote Catholic writer John Cogley, "the image Kennedy projects will provide a fairly painless transition. The stereotype of the Irish Catholic politician, the pugnacious, priest-ridden representative of an embittered, embattled minority, simply does not fit the poised, urbane, cosmopolitan young socialite from Harvard."

Ironically, Kennedy's Catholicism helped bring him to prominence. If he had been just another Protestant, the media would have paid less attention to him. "But being a Catholic," observed Schlesinger, "Jack is a controversial figure. That's why everybody is interested in him."[12]

After the 1928 election, efforts to reduce intolerance created an improved religious climate in America. The National Conference of Christians and Jews and the Anti-Defamation League of the B'nai B'rith had become effective protolerance organizations. "Almost any *public* reference to a politician's religion has come to be considered improper," noted a writer in *The New Republic* in 1957. Moreover, as waves of Catholic students flocked into non-Catholic universities after World War II, they weakened the once-formidable intellectual divide by assimilating into American intellectual and political circles.

In the 1958 election Catholic Democrats captured the governorships of seven states. Several big states, with large blocks of electoral votes, had Catholic governors—Edmund Brown in California, David Lawrence in Pennsylvania, and Michael DiSalle in Ohio. Eight Catholic Democrats, including four freshmen, won election to the U.S. Senate, making a total of twelve Catholic Democrats in the Senate.

Still, serious doubts remained about electing a Catholic president. "Protestants might elect a Catholic to the Senate or as governor, but would they elect one to the highest office of the land?" observed Lawrence Fuchs. "For many Americans, the Al Smith defeat in 1928 provided a resounding negative answer. The statehouse yes; but the presidency no!"

In running for President, Kennedy needed to strike a balance between his personal identification with Catholicism and his public separation from Catholicism. He needed to disqualify the religious issue, but he couldn't disqualify himself as a Catholic.[13]

Of all the church-state issues he had to face, federal aid to parochial schools was the most controversial. The Supreme Court had ruled that no tax funds could be used for the central activities of parochial schools, but provided no clear definition of what was central. Public funds could be used to pay for transportation of students to parochial schools, but other issues remained unresolved. Could states provide free textbooks and lunch for parochial students? Could funds be used for buildings?

In the late 1950s, with the financial burden on Catholics increasing as parochial-school populations exploded, federal aid to education emerged as an issue with high stakes. Powerful Catholic groups opposed legislation for federal aid to schools that omitted assistance to parochial schools. Since students at Catholic colleges had received benefits after World War II under the GI Bill, Catholic officials urged that the government view aid as assistance to children, not institutions.[14]

Initially, when Kennedy entered Congress, he hadn't developed well-defined views or convictions on church-state issues. As a young congressman he supported federal aid to education programs in which parochial-school students would share in funds for bus transportation, nonreligious textbooks, and health services. But a decade later he had changed his mind. In 1958 he introduced a bill for federal aid to education limited to public schools. When Senator Wayne Morse amended the bill to include nonpublic schools, Kennedy was the only presidential hopeful to oppose the amendment.

In 1958 Senator Joseph Clark discussed the birth-control issue with Kennedy. Catholics believed that the rhythm method—abstinence during the few days in twenty-eight that a normal woman was fertile—was the only morally acceptable method of contraception. Most Jews and Protestants believed that artificial contraception was equally moral. The liberal Clark wanted family-planning information made available within the United States and abroad. As a Catholic, what did Kennedy think about the issue of birth control? "It's bound to come," Kennedy responded; "it's just a question of time. The Church will come around. I intend to be as brave as I dare."[15]

On November 15, 1959, American bishops declared in stern, disapproving language that Catholics could not support any public assistance by the United States or the UN to promote "artificial birth prevention, abortion or sterilization." The bishops' statement and the reaction to it threatened to plunge the issue of population control into the 1960 presidential campaign. Reporters asked several potential candidates—Adlai Stevenson, Stuart Symington, Hubert Humphrey, and Nelson Rockefeller—for their reaction. All four diplomatically disagreed with the bishops. Governor Rockefeller of New York thought the United States "would want to cooperate" with a country seeking assistance.

Of all the potential candidates surveyed, Kennedy's statement most closely paralleled the bishops' position. It would be a "mistake" for the United States to advocate birth control in underdeveloped countries, he said. Such a policy might be resented by those people. He made it clear, though, that if he were president, and if Congress enacted a law at variance with the bishops' statement, he would decide whether to sign it solely on the basis of what he deemed to be best for the United States, irrespective of religious considerations.[16]

Kennedy's statement alarmed Arthur Schlesinger, who thought it conformed too closely to the views of the Catholic bishops. "I am sure you will not underestimate the importance of the birth control problem," Schlesinger advised the senator on November 30, 1959.

> A lot of people are looking for a quasi-legitimate pretext for raising the Catholic issue. They want to prove that a Catholic can't take disinterested decisions on some significant problems of public policy. The bishops unfortunately handed them an issue. Every adult in the United States knows about birth control, and most of them care about it. Most Americans would be appalled by the thought of a society where birth control was illegal. From the viewpoint of your own political future and of keeping religion out of this election, I think you should put this issue out of politics as quickly and efficiently as you can.

Schlesinger wanted Kennedy to say, simply, that birth control was a question of personal morality, not of public policy, that while Kennedy personally disapproved of birth control, he understood that others might adopt a different position. "I deeply believe that the lid ought to be nailed back on this Pandora's box as fast as possible," Schlesinger warned. Thereafter Kennedy nailed down the lid. The church didn't seem to be coming around, and, deciding he couldn't dare to be brave, he learned to finesse the touchy issue.[17]

For the most part, Kennedy forthrightly explained his views on issues involving religion and the Constitution. Indeed, at times he seemed too forthright for his political good. His theme was that religion is personal, politics is public, and they need never meet or conflict.

On March 3, 1959, *Look* magazine published Fletcher Knebel's article "Democratic Forecast: A Catholic in 1960." In expressing his candid views, Kennedy sparked full-blown controversy about his religion. He opposed the appointment of an ambassador to the Vatican, and reiterated his position against aid to parochial schools. "There can be no question of federal funds being used for support of parochial or private schools," he said; "it's unconstitutional under the First Amendment as interpreted by the Supreme Court." He made a distinction between extending support "to sustain any church or its schools" and "fringe matters [such as] buses, lunches, and other services," which he saw as primarily a social and economic problem. But his third statement, on conscience and the officeholder, caused an unexpected uproar.

> Whatever one's religion in his private life may be, for the office holder nothing takes precedence over his oath to uphold the Constitution in all its parts, including the First Amendment and the strict separation of church and state. Without reference to the Presidency, I believe that the

separation of church and state is fundamental to our American concept and heritage, and should remain so.[18]

Kennedy had tried to allay Protestant fears about his potential candidacy, but zealous Catholic critics objected to his argument that *nothing* took precedence over the officeholder's oath to uphold the Constitution. The Jesuit weekly *America* thought Kennedy "doesn't really believe that. No religious man, be he Catholic, Protestant or Jew, holds such an opinion. A man's conscience has a bearing on his public as well as his private life." "No man may rightfully act against his conscience," *Ave Maria* agreed.

Catholic critics wondered why only the Catholic Kennedy had to express his allegiance to the Constitution in order to satisfy Protestants. Why should Kennedy have to submit to a loyalty test for Catholics only? Such groveling was not required for candidates of other religions. No one asked the Baptist president, or the Presbyterian president, or the Episcopalian president to declare his stand on the Constitution or the First Amendment. Kennedy was going overboard merely to "placate the bigots," observed the *Catholic Review* of Baltimore.[19]

Some friendly Protestant leaders took a different slant, arguing that Kennedy had gone too far in the direction of secularism. James Pike, a former Catholic and the Episcopal bishop of the diocese of California, thought the issue of Kennedy's religion had little to do with Catholicism. Rather, Kennedy's position suggested a different problem. Kennedy's statement seemed to "represent the point of view of a thoroughgoing secularist, who truly believes that a man's religion and his decision-making can be kept in two watertight compartments." Robert McAfee Brown wrote in *Christianity in Crisis* that Kennedy had demonstrated "that he is a rather irregular Christian." The associate editor of the *Christian Century*, Martin Marty, judged Kennedy as "spiritually rootless and politically almost disturbingly secular."[20]

Kennedy's chief Catholic defender was John Cogley, a consultant for the liberal Center for the Study of Democratic Institutions in California, and a regular contributor to *Commonweal*, a weekly magazine published by Catholic laymen. Cogley argued that the religious beliefs of the political leader are his private affair, and he should feel no obligation, "as a political leader," to make these beliefs public. True, a special problem arises when the public beliefs are thought to derive from the private religious views. "If it is felt—as some people feel about Catholic candidates—that because they hold this or that 'private' view they will inevitably hold a consequent 'public' view, certain political questions become a serious concern." Cogley contended that in the *Look* article, Kennedy was not denying the primacy of conscience. "He was saying . . . that there is no necessary conflict between his conscience—or the conscience of any American Catholic—and the Constitution of the United States."

Kennedy responded that he had not intended his remarks in *Look* as a full exposition of his views on the role of conscience. "I should have thought it self-evident that all men regard conscience as an essential element in all human decisions."

The *Look* magazine controversy had two long-term effects. The strong reaction of Catholic periodicals reinforced Protestant fears that there was a Catholic monolith hostile to traditional democratic ideas, that Catholic leaders were attempting to reassert ecclesiastical control over a rebellious son. It also inspired Kennedy to rethink his position on the religious issue, and await an opportune moment to redefine his views.[21]

While Kennedy campaigned for the Democratic presidential nomination, an obscure incident in his past was exhumed, arousing Protestant suspicions. In December 1947, Congressman Kennedy at first accepted, then rejected, an invitation to speak at a dinner for the ecumenical Chapel of Four Chaplains in Philadelphia. Dr. Daniel Poling, a Republican and an editor of the *Christian Herald Magazine,* spearheaded the fund-raising dinner for the chapel, and had invited Kennedy. The chapel commemorated a dramatic incident during World War II involving four military chaplains—two Protestants (including Poling's son), a Catholic priest, and a Jewish rabbi—aboard an American troop ship, the *Dorchester.* On February 3, 1943, the ship was torpedoed off the coast of Greenland, killing seven hundred men. The four chaplains heroically gave up their life jackets to soldiers and then, joining together in prayer, went down with the ship. Poling had located the chapel in the lower level of Philadelphia's Grace Baptist Temple, where he placed a separate altar for each faith.

When he accepted the invitation, the newly elected, inexperienced Kennedy didn't know that the Catholic Archdiocese of Philadelphia opposed the project because the memorial chapel was located in a Protestant church and canon law prohibited such an arrangement. Kennedy later explained that he initially thought he was being invited as a "public officer," but then learned he actually received the invitation as an "official representative of a religious organization." After learning of the opposition of the archdiocese, Kennedy declined the invitation.[22]

Prominent newspaper columnist Drew Pearson was involved in the invitation to Kennedy and resented the congressman's "last minute" decision to decline. In his personal diary Pearson noted that Kennedy stated "that the Church had forbidden him to speak. He said he must follow the dictates of the Church. I am wondering," Pearson wrote, "if he also does in regard to legislation."

Kennedy had prepared a speech, and forwarded it to Poling for the dinner occasion. At the time, Poling didn't publicly express anger at Kennedy. On the contrary, in early January 1948, Poling profusely praised the congressman's undelivered speech in a syndicated newspaper column. Kennedy spoke "in his own right," wrote Poling, and was an "American of great promise." His message to the interfaith dinner was a "clear call to American unity." Kennedy, "this loyal and dynamic Roman Catholic," said Poling, concluded his message with a quotation from an eloquent declaration of World War II, the address of Rabbi Roland Gittelsohn. In April 1945, the rabbi spoke at the cemetery on Iwo Jima, and Kennedy quoted his ecumenical address: "Here lie officers and men, Negroes and whites, rich and poor . . . [H]ere are Protestants, Catholics and Jews . . . [H]ere no man prefers another because of his color. Here there are no quotas of how many from each group are admitted or allowed . . . Theirs is the highest and purest democracy."[23]

But thirteen years later Poling reopened the issue in the pages of his magazine. In retrospect, Poling claimed, what mattered was that Congressman Kennedy decided not to attend after learning that the Catholic Archdiocese of Philadelphia opposed the chapel drive. Poling had a point. On its face the chapel incident made it difficult for Kennedy to deny that there was a problem for him, as a Catholic, to take part in an interfaith gathering.

Commonweal rejected Poling's argument. It was clear that Kennedy had been invited primarily as a well-known Catholic rather than as a public official.

> What would the purpose of his presence have been except to symbolize Catholic participation in the project—a project in which Catholics did not in fact participate and from which they felt deliberately excluded by the initial decision to build the chapel in a Protestant church? . . . The fact that efforts to build a memorial chapel could arouse so much bitterness undoubtedly says something important about the state of Protestant-Catholic relations in this country. We cannot see that it says anything about Senator Kennedy's position on Church and State.

Whenever possible Kennedy added a light touch of humor to the touchy religious issue. As he awaited questions from reporters following a talk to the Los Angeles Press Club, a reporter asked amid laughter, "Do you think a Protestant can be elected President in 1960?" Kennedy grinned. "If he's prepared to answer how he stands on the issue of the separation of church and state," he answered, "I see no reason why we should discriminate against him!" The reporters howled.[24]

Kennedy enjoyed quips at the expense of the clergy. "He discussed the princes of the American Church with the same irreverent candor with which he discussed the bosses of the Democratic party," said Schlesinger.

While speaking at a dinner with an overweight monsignor, he called it an "inspiration . . . to be here with . . . one of those lean ascetic clerics who show the effect of constant fast and prayer, and bring the message to us in the flesh." At a dinner in New York, he said: "I sat next to Cardinal Spellman at dinner the other evening, and asked him what I should say when voters question me about the doctrine of the pope's infallibility. 'I don't know, Senator,' the Cardinal told me. 'All I know is he keeps calling me Spillman.' "[25]

22

GEARING UP
FOR 1960

For many years the annual Gridiron Dinner in Washington, D.C., stood as a critical test for politicians. Since President Benjamin Harrison's day, the dinner has lampooned Presidents and prominent politicians. "In this off-the-record setting, before a large number of journalists, other politicians, and businessmen from around the nation, politicians have often found ways to establish or reshape their images or reputations," noted Clark Clifford, a longtime participant. Kennedy viewed his Gridiron speech in 1958 as a major opportunity, one that would help launch his presidential campaign.

The elaborate preparations Kennedy made for his appearance illustrated the manner in which he would approach the entire 1960 campaign. For weeks in advance Ted Sorensen solicited ideas from advisers and friends, and arranged meetings to discuss various jokes. (At one session they voted on 112 jokes and humorous stories.)

A week before the 1958 event Joe Kennedy advised Jack that "to be terribly successful, you must get yourself plenty of laughs." Tell each joke "very slowly, with accent on the point and give them all a chance to laugh before passing on to the next one." And, finally, Jack should "keep smiling whenever you take a crack."

The big event occurred on March 15, 1958. Nearly every important official, politician, and journalist from Washington was present. Ironically, before Kennedy stepped to the rostrum, the preceding sketch had lampooned Jack's father for trying to buy the election for his son.

When it was Jack's turn, he reached into his breast pocket and pulled out a "telegram" from his "generous daddy." "Dear Jack," he read, "Don't buy a single vote more than is necessary—I'll be damned if I'm going to pay for a landslide." The audience howled.

Jack also delivered a political joke submitted by Clifford:

> I dreamed about 1960 the other night, and I told Stuart Symington and Lyndon Johnson about it yesterday. I told them how the Lord came into my bedroom, anointed my head, and said, "John Kennedy, I hereby anoint you President of the United States." Stu Symington said, "That's strange, Jack, because I had a similar dream last night in which the Lord anointed me President of the United States and outer space." Then Lyndon Johnson said, "That's very interesting, gentlemen, because I, too, had a similar dream last night—and I don't remember anointing either one of you!"

Clifford concluded of Kennedy's performance: "Watching the enthralled reaction of the Gridiron audience that night, I knew a new star had begun to rise in Washington."[1]

A lame-duck President, Dwight Eisenhower was barred by the Constitution from running again. Democrats hoped to lure back the millions of voters who had defected to Ike. After Democrats won a smashing victory in the congressional election of 1958, it seemed likely, said *Time*, "that the strong Democratic winds of 1958 might blow at gale force in 1960."

Americans weren't ready for sweeping changes in domestic policy. In January 1960, *Look* magazine, relying on a special Gallup poll, found most Americans "relaxed, unadventurous, comfortably satisfied with their way of life and blandly optimistic about the future." Few whites thought that race relations constituted a serious problem.[2]

The Cold War did worry Americans. On October 4, 1957, the Soviet Union amazed the world when it launched *Sputnik,* the first artificial earth satellite, gaining a huge propaganda victory. In America the event caused intense anxiety and ignited a national self-examination. The Soviet satellite seemed to cast doubt on America's superiority over the Soviet Union. *The New York Times* worried that the country was in a "race for survival."

The Soviets' success with *Sputnik* had military implications. "Both the United States and the Soviet Union were trying to perfect an intercontinental ballistic missile (ICBM)," noted historian Robert Divine, "a rocket powerful enough to hurl a hydrogen warhead some 5000 miles across the earth's surface." *Sputnik* seemed to prove that the Soviets were more technologically advanced in rocketry than the United States.[3]

Shortly after the shock of *Sputnik,* the press leaked the contents of the alarming Gaither Report. Rowan Gaither, director of the Ford Foundation, chaired a blue-ribbon panel to study the nation's defense, and the report to the National Security Council claimed that the Soviets could soon surpass the United States in nuclear striking power, perhaps even have a first-strike capability by 1959. Simultaneously, a Rockefeller Brothers report was equally pessimistic about America's defenses and urged a $3 billion increase in defense spending over the next ten years.

Columnist Joseph Alsop warned that by 1962 the Soviets would have 1,000 ICBMs to only 130 for the United States. Democrats pounced on the new evidence of weakness to accuse the Eisenhower administration of allowing a dangerous "missile gap." Kennedy joined in the partisan assault.

"Eisenhower refused to take these estimates seriously," noted Divine. "He knew from American U-2 reports that the Soviets had stopped testing ICBMs after the first one in 1957, and he knew that there had been no actual missile deployment in Russia, which suggested that the Soviets had run into unexpected difficulties in their program."

Eisenhower proved correct in his judgment. By the time he left the White House, no gap had opened up. But Ike failed to communicate effectively with the nation about the wisdom of his defense policies as a growing sense of insecurity and anxiety spread throughout the country. Assuming that people would trust his judgment in national-security matters, unwilling to reveal the secret U-2 flights, he did not give adequate assurances to Americans.[4]

In September 1959, Soviet premier Nikita Khrushchev's tour of the United States chilled Americans. He repeatedly expressed his confidence that his country would outpace the United States. *Time* judged Khrushchev "the embodiment of the elemental challenge" of communism, a man who had a "naked drive for world power no less sustained than that of the late Joseph Stalin." "Over and over," *Newsweek* reported, Khrushchev claimed in one way or another, " 'We will bury you.' Watching his face freeze with purpose, his little eyes flash, no one could doubt that he meant it."

After Khrushchev's visit, Walter Lippmann, one of America's most eloquent and thoughtful columnists, reflected on the Soviet challenge. "The critical weakness of our society is that for the time being our people do not have great purposes which they are united in wanting to achieve. . . . The public mood of the country is defensive, to hold on and to conserve, not to push forward and to create. We talk about ourselves these days as if we were a completed society, one which has achieved its purposes and has no further great business to transact." The Soviet Union's strength and success, Lippmann continued, derived from the fact that it was "above all else a purposeful society in which all the main energies of the people are directed and dedicated to its purposes."

Kennedy shared Lippmann's concerns and would make them a central theme of his campaign. He blamed Eisenhower's weak leadership, arguing that Ike had taken a narrow view of his obligations and duties, and that his umpirelike leadership was unsuited to the modern world. "A free society," Kennedy said, reflecting the position he took twenty years earlier in *Why England Slept,* "is at a disadvantage in competing against an organized, monolithic state such as Russia. We prize our individualism and rightly so, but we need a cohesive force. In America that force is the presidency. The President of the United States has an obligation to develop the public's interest in our destiny to the highest level of vigor that can be sustained."[5]

Kennedy's goal was a first-ballot victory at the Democratic convention to be held in Los Angeles in July 1960; he couldn't see himself winning the nomination any other way: "I'll be the last guy to come out of a smoke-filled room."

Starting in 1957 he privately told friends and a few journalists that he didn't see any other Democratic prospects noticeably more qualified for president than himself. "Nobody else is more able and nobody else has any more chance than I do to get it," he told Rowland Evans. "Therefore, since I am going to work harder than anybody else, I know I am going to be nominated."

When his father asked him why he wanted to assume the appalling burden of the presidency, he responded, "These things have always been done by men, and they can be done by men now."[6]

If Kennedy expected to win support in the Midwest, he needed to change his position on one issue: farming. He had no personal knowledge of farming; nor had he developed an understanding of farm problems as did legislators from predominantly rural states.

In 1954 he broke with Northern Democrats to vote for President Eisenhower's flexible-price-support program. He opposed any farm program "calling for high price supports fixed at 90 percent of parity," he said. "I shall vote against such programs in the future, particularly until such time as the flexible support program has had a sufficient opportunity to prove itself."

His opposition to high price supports didn't hurt him in Massachusetts, but it cost him Midwestern support during his vice-presidential nomination bid at Chicago. So he changed his position. "The President and Secretary of Agriculture Ezra Taft Benson misled those of us who live in the east," Kennedy told two thousand Iowa Democrats in March 1958, at their annual Jackson Day dinner in Des Moines. "But never again," he vowed. "The last five years have torn away any illusion about Mr. Benson and his efforts. I voted this week to freeze price supports at 1957 levels until Congress can enact a more effective long-range bill." Kennedy conceded he was a "city boy who never plowed a furrow," and didn't pretend to know the "long-range answer to farm problems."[7]

He never felt comfortable delivering his farm speeches. He delivered them only because they were a compulsory exercise for every presidential candidate. During the 1960 campaign speechwriter Richard Goodwin prepared the Farm Speech for the annual South Dakota Plowing Contest. It was a "doomed exercise," Goodwin recalled. "No eloquence of his or mine could persuade the skeptical, deeply conservative tillers of the soil that this slick, sophisticated urban youth with the strange accent and foreign faith knew the pains of their labor."

Goodwin asked Kennedy if he wanted to address his farm program. "Do I have one?" Kennedy smiled, and said, "Give them the whole thing from our position on parity to Food for Peace. They may get a little bored listening, but not as much as I will saying it. They're not the jolliest bunch in the world." The next night Goodwin showed him the speech. After he finished reading it, Kennedy commented, "Just think, Dick, here we are, a couple of Brookline farmers, preparing policy for the entire country. Isn't politics wonderful?" Following the speech, Kennedy said to Goodwin, "Fuck the farmers after November."

"They loved it," Goodwin teased.

"They've got a funny way of showing it," Kennedy answered. "Now where's my speech on how peace can be maintained?"[8]

Joseph Kennedy hosted the first strategy meeting of the 1960 campaign at his Palm Beach estate on April 1, 1959. Besides the senior Kennedy, and John and Robert Kennedy, those present were Stephen Smith (who had married Jack's sister Jean), pollster Lou Harris, political organizer Robert Wallace, Ted Sorensen, Ken O'Donnell, and Larry O'Brien. Holding most of their sessions next to the swimming pool, they discussed Kennedy's strengths and weaknesses, organizational priorities, potential allies, the makeup of state delegations, and the primaries Kennedy might enter.

At the meeting someone brought up the subject of money. "By golly, we've come this far," declared Joe Kennedy. "We're not going to let money stand in our way now. We're going to get this thing if it takes every dime I've got." With that Bobby Kennedy turned to his father and teased, "Wait a minute now. There are others in the family."[9]

During the rest of 1959, Larry O'Brien traveled about half the time; he and other Kennedy organizers discovered that they had the field almost entirely to themselves. No one representing other candidates preceded O'Brien to the statehouses and union halls. Kennedy campaigned unopposed for many months while his opponents underestimated him.

In the spring of 1959 Stephen Smith rented space in the Esso Building near Capitol Hill. Scattered in a nine-room suite on the top floor, the offices became the official national campaign headquarters. By the spring of 1960, ten men, about as many female secretaries, and assorted other volunteers operated in the bare, mangy complex of rooms.[10]

The Kennedy team were "brilliant improvisers," not "systematic calculators," said Arthur Schlesinger. Robert Kennedy's genius as campaign director "lay in his capacity to address a specific situation, to assemble an able staff, to inspire and flog them into exceptional deeds and to prevail through sheer force of momentum." When the approach worked, the Kennedy organization, said Harris Wofford, the campaign's civil rights coordinator, "released energy in a lot of directions."

Bobby made decisions quickly and crisply. One volunteer remarked, "You went in and you said, 'I would like to do boom, boom, boom, boom.' And he'd say, 'Do this, do this. Don't do this. And do this.'"

Answerable only to his older brother, Robert directed everything except the speechwriting, Sorensen's domain. He prodded, motivated, challenged, and energized the entire Kennedy team. Because he also whipped the recalcitrant into line, was blunt, rude, and insulting, those outside the Kennedy entourage often reviled him. "Little Brother is Watching You," said critics. "He has all the patience of a vulture," a Washington journalist acidly commented, "without any of the dripping sentimentality."[11]

Political adviser and organizer, the dour and taciturn Ken O'Donnell had no ambitions except to advance the interests of John Kennedy. While talking with a journalist, Kennedy said, "You see Kenny, there. If I woke him up and asked him to jump out of this plane for me, he'd do it. You don't find that kind of loyalty easily." Dave Powers, Jack's friend and companion since 1946, went along on many campaign trips, keeping Kennedy amused with his wisecracks.

Kennedy's press secretary, Pierre Salinger, adopted an almost clownlike amiability with the traveling media. Since covering a presidential candidate was inconvenient and exhausting, Salinger created an ambience of warmth and respect for the traveling reporters.[12]

Dedicated was not a strong enough term for Ted Sorensen's attitude. As one observer put it: "When Jack is wounded, Ted bleeds." During the campaign of 1960, though, Sorensen had to adjust to a new reality—he was no longer the only major adviser to Kennedy. Robert Kennedy was on board full-time, and so were O'Donnell, O'Brien, and Salinger. Apparently Sorensen resented the newcomers, igniting minor feuds and infighting—mostly between Sorensen and the others.

"Do you think you can get on with Ted Sorensen?" Kennedy asked his academic adviser, Archibald Cox. "Ted is very jealous of anyone who seems to have contact with me or a relationship with me threatening his."

When Kennedy learned from contacts in several states that Sorensen didn't relate well with local political officials, the candidate relied on more personable staff members to meet state officials. Kennedy realized that Sorensen was overly serious, too stiff for backslapping and small talk, not good at relaxing with potential delegates in the nearest bar.

Despite Sorensen's insecurities and testiness, everyone understood his critical role. "I just don't think Kennedy would have ever become President if he hadn't [hired] Sorensen," said campaign worker Robert Wallace. "Sorensen had that special something which matched Kennedy's special something and made it possible."

None of the squabbling affected the candidate's single-minded approach to winning. Kennedy's aides must have sensed that their boss would not tolerate serious clashes and might fire the offenders. Therefore, the staff tried to cooperate.[13]

Women played a subordinate role in Kennedy's campaign hierarchy. "There was really no room for women in the hierarchy," said Barbara Coleman, a Kennedy press aide. "We were all sort of a class of secretaries. You didn't necessarily do secretarial work, but [you were] still in that role."[14]

In 1959 four potential opponents emerged as Kennedy's most likely challengers for the Democratic nomination. Minnesota Democrat Hubert Humphrey, forty-eight, had been elected to the Senate in 1948. A fiery liberal with an ebullient personality, and an outstanding orator, Humphrey supported organized labor, civil rights, and programs for the less privileged. But he had two liabilities: He was too liberal to win in the conservative South, and he lacked strong financial backing. The hard-pressed Minnesota senator had to devote precious time and energy raising money while Kennedy focused on campaigning.[15]

Handsome and athletic, Missouri senator Stuart Symington, fifty-eight, had held several federal posts, including secretary of the air force (1945–1952), before being elected to the Senate in 1952. As a Protestant, with experience in business and government, and identified with the key issue of national defense, he held several advantages as a presidential candidate.

Symington was the first choice of Harry Truman, but the ex-President no longer had much influence. As the candidate who had made few enemies, Symington was the second choice for the nomination on many Democrats' list. If Symington had given no one reason to be against him, neither had he inspired much enthusiasm. "The greatest danger for Stu Symington is that someone like Jack Kennedy or Hubert Humphrey will walk away with the nomination before anybody gets around to second choice," said *Time*.[16]

Fifty-two years old in 1960, Lyndon Baines Johnson had been elected to the Senate from Texas in 1948. Because of his hard work and genius for persuasion and compromise, Democrats elected him their floor leader in 1953. Although he suffered a severe heart attack in July 1955, he seemed to have recovered well. As a moderate Democrat and consensus builder, he thought he could most effectively hold the nation together. His style in the Senate, though, led critics to call him autocratic.

LBJ deluded himself into believing that if he announced his bid for the presidency, he would immediately become the front-runner and opponents would gang up on him. Nor could he take Kennedy seriously. He often disparaged him to friends, saying Kennedy was a "playboy," a "lightweight," and a laggard in the Senate. Most often Johnson referred to Kennedy as "the boy," as in "I'll take this state from the boy," and "I'll lick the boy here," and "The boy isn't getting off the ground." He thought Kennedy needed "a little gray" in his hair.

Johnson couldn't decide if he should run or not. He let his staff draw up campaign plans, but then forbade any action. He authorized a campaign headquarters, then refused to allow it to do anything.

Eventually Lyndon decided to work hard in the Senate, build a record of legislative accomplishment, and let the other candidates knock each other out of the race. There would be no overt campaign, only an indirect effort. If others blocked Kennedy, LBJ could become the choice of a divided party.[17]

Following his second defeat by Eisenhower in 1956, Adlai Stevenson stated that he had no intention of actively soliciting a third Democratic nomination, nor did most Democrats want him to. He wouldn't run in the 1960 primaries, form a campaign organization, or buttonhole possible delegates. Still, his renunciation of a third nomination was partly a cunning tactical maneuver, a strategy of capturing the nomination without actively seeking it. He would remain aloof, but keep himself in the public eye, waiting—secretly hoping—for Democrats to turn to him again.[18]

Kennedy's opponents never imagined his campaign would be so organized and dynamic. Of course, money posed no problem. Organizer Robert Wallace was paid from Joe Kennedy's office in New York. The credit and airline travel cards he was given said "Joseph P. Kennedy." Wallace felt the need to be prudent in his spending, "but if I wanted to talk to a group of [Democratic] party leaders, it was very simple for me to invite them out to dinner. And I could have dinner with steak."

More effectively than any previous candidate in American history,

Kennedy conducted scores of opinion polls—to probe issues, the weaknesses and strengths of his candidacy and his opponents—and used the information to decide his schedule and tactics. The campaign's pollster, Lou Harris, became a member of the campaign's inner policy group. Harris's polling helped decide which issues to stress, which primaries to enter, and which ones to avoid. His service was expensive, costing about three hundred thousand dollars.

Polls indicated a rising Kennedy tide. "Other Democratic contenders showed strength in their own areas," noted Sorensen. "Kennedy showed strength in all areas."[19]

In the Washington, D.C., headquarters Kennedy's staff sent out letters, Christmas cards, invitations, and autographed copies of Kennedy's books. The staff compiled a file of fifty thousand people, listing them all on three-by-five index cards—supporters and potential supporters, farm and labor officials, black leaders, officeholders, volunteers, fund-raisers, and "key Kennedy contacts." Besides listing the person's address, state, and first choice for presidential nominee, each card also described the person's importance and the circumstances in which Kennedy had met the individual. Larry O'Brien wrote a "Kennedy Organization Manual," which instructed every state and local Kennedy organizer in the method for giving away stickers, picking volunteers, and directing mass telephone calls.[20]

Details mattered; the personal touch mattered. As Kennedy was about to visit Minnesota in early June 1960, Sorensen reminded him that Governor Orville Freeman "is very friendly," and added, "If you can spend some extra time with him, he wants to feel that he 'knows you better.'"

If Jerry Bruno, Kennedy's aggressive advance man, forgot a detail, Kennedy was sure to spot it when he surveyed arrangements for a campaign stop. Bruno forced himself to anticipate the problems Kennedy would notice: "How did I know there'd be a loudspeaker there? Who was making telephone calls to tell people about a stop? Where was the band coming from? Who else or what else was going to be in town at the same time? All these details got to be second nature, because I always felt John Kennedy was looking over my shoulder."[21]

Editorials appearing in small-town newspapers disappointed Kennedy. Aware that most of the newspapers in small towns didn't write their own editorials but got them from editorial services like the North American Newspaper Alliance, Kennedy's staff befriended one of the chief editorial writers for NANA. "He became a very strong supporter of John F. Kennedy, and the editorials began reflecting this," observed Feldman. "He'd write an editorial, and we'd see the same editorial appear in fifty or sixty papers."

The Kennedy camp, assisted by Joe, courted old-time party bosses, like Mayor Richard Daley of Chicago. "Illinois would likely be a critical swing state, and Daley's machine could deliver about a half-million votes, including some from the graveyard," observed Evan Thomas. "Joe Kennedy, who owned the single largest retail operation in Chicago, the Merchandise Mart, had been cozying up to the mayor for years."[22]

Kennedy insiders scoffed, though, at pundits who portrayed the Kennedy organization as a "well-oiled machine." It seemed well oiled only because the campaigns of Kennedy's opponents were so creaky. "All I can say is that the stuff that oiled most of my work was chaos and panic," said Jerry Bruno. Sorensen pointed out that local Kennedy leaders made wrong assessments or didn't deliver on promises. "Letters and telegrams of invitation sent to unknown names in our massive files sometimes garnered eccentrics, children and Republicans."

Yet, despite problems and mistakes, the campaign gained powerful momentum. "I would appreciate it if you would start sending me a weekly progress report on your organizational activities," Robert Kennedy wrote a dozen key campaign workers in November 1959.[23]

A collection of Kennedy's speeches, mostly on foreign policy, was published as a campaign book in 1960 with the title *The Strategy of Peace*. Taken together, Kennedy's speeches portrayed America's foreign policy as fraught with crisis and adrift. It lacked a sense of mission, purpose, and character commensurate with the "lessons" of history. This suggested a lack of leadership at the top, he charged. Leadership in foreign policy required a mission and purpose consistent with traditional American character.

Throughout *The Strategy of Peace* Kennedy offered dire warnings, some modeled after Winston Churchill's. There were parallels in the book between Churchill's effort in the 1930s to warn a complacent Britain of the Nazi threat and Kennedy's efforts to arouse Americans to the sacrifices needed to overcome the Soviet challenge. In his speech on the "missile gap," Kennedy quoted Churchill during England's darkest time: "Come then—let us to the task, to the battle and the toil—each to our part, each to our station. . . . Let us go forward together in all parts of the [land]. There is not a week, not a day, nor an hour to be lost." As Churchill had done for the British in the late 1930s, Kennedy wanted to awaken his countrymen from their complacency and softness and summon them to demonstrate "nerve and will in the face of a global challenge."

In the book Kennedy addressed a host of foreign and domestic problems, implicitly indicting the Eisenhower administration for not handling them well. But Kennedy was better at criticism than viable alternatives.

He advocated a stronger nuclear weapons program and an upgrading of conventional forces so the United States could intervene "effectively and swiftly in any limited war anywhere in the world." He urged the "rebuilding" of NATO, insisted on idealism in American foreign relations, condemned discredited colonialism, and proposed spending more of America's foreign aid on constructive economic development in the Third World.[24]

"Kennedy's formula of strength plus idealism was not a bad general approach to foreign policy during the volatile Khrushchev era," historian Alonzo Hamby observed. But it also was facile and deceptive. "Intentionally or otherwise, its 'hard side' overstated American military vulnerability. Its 'soft side' assumed too easily that the new, uncommitted states of the world could be won over by economic aid accompanied by protestations of friendship and understanding. On some matters he offered generalities that were vague but farsighted." Hamby thought that the "force of his foreign policy critique came not from his specific positions but from his youth, vigor, and receptivity to new approaches; to a large extent, his style was as important as his substance."

The Strategy of Peace was the largest single effort by Kennedy's campaign to beguile the intellectuals and opinion leaders. The campaign sent "personal" copies of the book to editors, scientists, columnists, educators, reporters, authors, publishers, labor leaders, clergymen, and Democratic politicians. The book enormously impressed Michigan's governor G. Mennen Williams. It reflected "a wide breadth of understanding," and contained "tough-minded analysis" and "courageous answers."[25]

The word "sacrifice" often appeared in Kennedy's speeches and articles throughout the 1960 election. To solve America's problems, "we must accept in our public life what we know is true in our private life—that nothing is achieved without effort and sacrifice."

Kennedy did not try to evade the unpleasant prospect that taxes would probably have to be increased. That was part of the sacrifice that must be made. "I think we will have to begin by deciding what is essential for the security of this country, and then determine in what way we are going to finance that agenda. These decisions will require sacrifices."[26]

Kennedy needed new speeches for his 1960 campaign. He wrote Arthur Holcombe in October 1959, requesting "the kind of material necessary to add some color, humor and interest to the speeches—particularly historical anecdotes, illustrations, quotations and verses."

Sorensen solicited speeches from several contacts as well. For a speech before Democratic audiences he sought "introductory material containing some color and sparkle, but emphasizing real thought content instead of slogans—and a concluding part which is not partisan or statistical but emphasizes more the 'call to greatness' kind of approach." He also needed a new college speech, "saying something substantial and at the same time witty and inspiring, presumably also following the theme of urging them to wake up to the challenge of our times." "The Senator's crowded speaking schedule makes necessary a continuous flow of new material," Sorensen wrote a prospective speechwriter, "and the well easily runs dry here in the office."

Rather than complete speeches, Sorensen wanted help with speech sections which could be adapted to different occasions. There were three kinds. In the first, Kennedy criticized the deficiencies of the Republicans and praised the Democratic Party—its majestic principles and noble heritage. The second was a "substantive" section addressing an issue of the day—agriculture, aid to Third World countries, arms control, health policy. The final section invoked American greatness, the glorious prospects of our nation, its obligation to uphold the torch of freedom. "We are in great need of speech sections—of three or four pages—in categories one and three," Sorensen explained to a contact in February 1960.[27]

Sorensen and the senator auditioned nearly a dozen potential speechwriters. To a speechwriting prospect Sorensen wrote: "In fairness, I must repeat my warning that our past experience would indicate that the chances of satisfying the Senator's standards are slim." One full-time writer, young Richard Goodwin, was eventually hired, along with several part-time writers.

In hundreds of speeches attacking the Republican Party, the Republican record, and Vice President Nixon, Eisenhower wasn't mentioned. Ike was still too popular to attack personally. Nonetheless, Kennedy implicitly indicted the president when he called for new leadership to arouse America from its corrosive complacency.[28]

When Goodwin handed Jack a draft of a speech castigating the Republicans for losing Cuba, Kennedy silently read the speech, then remarked, "Of course, we don't say how we would have saved Cuba." Handing the speech back to Goodwin, he added, "What the hell, they never told us how they would have saved China."

His prepared speeches, particularly before university audiences, were studded with quotations and historical anecdotes. On a three-day tour of the Midwest in 1959 he quoted Disraeli, Thomas Carlyle, Thoreau, Benjamin Franklin, Aristotle, Bismarck, T. S. Eliot, House Speaker Tom Reed of Maine, Ireland's Henry Grattan, Queen Victoria, Woodrow Wilson, Churchill, Jefferson, and Andrew Jackson.

He often linked his campaign to the American past. One of his favorite stories concerned the Connecticut legislature of 1789. Colonel Davenport, its speaker, refused to suspend a legislative session for an eclipse of the sun. "The day of judgment is either approaching or it is not," said Davenport. "If it is not, there is no cause for adjournment. But if it is, I choose to be found doing my duty. I wish, therefore, that candles may be brought." Kennedy told the Davenport story from coast to coast and received great applause. "His campaign," it sometimes seemed to journalist Theodore White, "was a transcontinental lecture in American history; the stories not only entertained but gave a lift to his audiences, making them see their connection with America's past."[29]

Reaction to his speeches varied. Some judged him slightly dull, slightly professorial, perhaps too serious. Wisconsin's Patrick Lucey criticized the speech he usually delivered before university audiences. "It had a lot of literary references in it," said Lucey. "It was a sort of a speech that a valedictorian might give." Robert Wallace agreed, and complained to Sorensen that the standard university speech was a "bunch of *Bartlett's* quotations strung together." (Sorensen was livid.) Later, however, when Kennedy delivered the speech at a university, Wallace was amazed at the audience reaction. "They just loved it."

When Kennedy answered questions from his audience or from reporters, all agreed he was invariably sharp, sparkling, and supremely confident. He struck most people as articulate without being glib. "Jack Kennedy somehow manages to be an intellectual without being an egghead," said one newspaper. "He makes no apology for having read a book—or for having written a couple." "Kennedy's [speeches] had . . . real substance," thought Carroll Kilpatrick of *The Washington Post*. "He was appealing to the higher instincts of people."[30]

"I'm getting a lot better on speeches," Jack commented during an interview. "I've got a control over the subject matter and a confidence so that I can speak more and more off the cuff, and I know how much better that is than the prepared speech. Maybe when I get enough control and even more confidence, then I'll be able to make my speeches less declamatory and more emotional. We need more jokes, too, I know, and I'm always looking for them."

In his hotel room after a day of campaigning, Kennedy turned on the television and watched intently a news segment about a speech he had made earlier in the day. Observing his own mannerisms, he critiqued himself. As he watched himself refer to the Democratic "Pawty," he pointed at the screen and said, "Party not pawty, party." "I don't think he did it just because he liked to hear himself talk or because he enjoyed seeing himself on the screen," said Feldman. "I think he did it in an effort to improve himself."[31]

Looking presidential mattered. He shunned silly hats and kissing babies. On his campaign stops he swiftly descended from the speaker's platform and darted into the crowd to shake hands. He liked maximum exposure to voters with a minimum amount of exposure of himself—a well-attended luncheon where he would make a brief address, shake hands, and then be off to meet another large group.

Throughout the campaign, as Cabell Phillips of *The New York Times* noted, Kennedy radiated a gentle, honest warmth, making people comfortable with him. His quick wit beguiled an audience or defused an awkward situation. "I am here to express my gratitude," he said over and over on the campaign trail, "to the Democrats of Missouri [or Tennessee or Minnesota or Pennsylvania]. If I'd gotten your vote for vice president at Chicago, I would have beaten Estes Kefauver—and my political career would now be over."[32]

During a question-and-answer session, he asked for one final question, and was rewarded with a long, rambling discourse from an incensed woman. Kennedy looked stunned, then responded, with a wry smile, "I should have stopped a minute sooner."

Ken O'Donnell told a hilarious story illustrating Kennedy's unpretentiousness:

> One night during the 1960 campaign he was speaking to a crowd of farmers in Sioux City, Iowa, where his clipped Cape Cod accent, with its broad and flat *a* sounds and no rolling *r's*, seemed comically out of place. He reached a climax in his oration on agricultural depression with a shouted question, "What's wrong with the American fah-mah today?" He stopped for a momentary dramatic pause, and down from the balcony loud and clear came a reply from a comical listener in a perfect imitation of the New England accent, "He's *stah*-ving!"
>
> The hall rocked with laughter, but nobody in the crowd was laughing harder than Jack Kennedy himself. He was doubled up and stamping around on the platform.

In an article under JFK's byline, "Keep Your Sense of Humor," Sorensen vividly described some of the ludicrous situations the candidate faced:

> My words were drowned out in the Indianapolis Armory by a train whistle; on a Brattleboro street corner by the noon-day traffic; and at the Laredo airport by a jet squadron overhead. I have traveled in an open-car motorcade in 30 degree Idaho temperature—looked out the plane windows for a Maine landing strip the pilot couldn't find—and landed one night in Reno in a little single-engine plane to find the welcoming committee, Mayor and band greeting a more luxurious, larger executive craft at the other end of the field.[33]

Kennedy usually remained unruffled as his plane bounced through storms. While everyone else aboard recited prayers or held on to their stomachs, Kennedy sat calmly writing his speech, checking his schedule—unconcerned with the elements. But occasionally, even he was unnerved. In October 1959, while flying out of Midway Airport in Chicago, the small, chartered

Apache airplane encountered high winds and stormy weather. "We were bucking like hell and the wind was knocking us up and down," recalled Robert Wallace. After perilously landing in a muddy field, the plane taxied up to a small, wet crowd of waiting politicians. As Kennedy poked his pale face out the door, he said under his breath, "Fellow Americans, it's good to be here."[34]

At first Kennedy traveled on regular commercial airlines. But in 1959 he began using a private plane. The Kennedy family formed Ken-Air Corporation, which bought a Convair 240 propeller plane—redesigned to carry eighteen passengers—for $385,000. The plane was then leased to the candidate at the rate of $1.75 a mile. The aircraft logged 110,000 miles in 1959 and 1960. The plane was comfortable and convenient, with a staff of three, complete with desk, galley, and bedroom; he named it the *Caroline* after his daughter.

For nearly two years the stewardess aboard the *Caroline* was Janet Des Rosiers, formerly the trusted secretary and secret mistress of Joseph P. Kennedy. Her prime focus was John Kennedy. She took dictation, provided his favorite food, massaged his head, combed his hair, and rubbed his back and neck. She was his "girl Friday." When Kennedy called, "Miss Janet!" she came immediately.

"One of my functions as stewardess, which could not have pleased Jackie very much, were the neck and shoulder massages I gave JFK every day. Give somebody a massage and people automatically assume there's something going on. But somebody had to do it. He worked himself into knots, toiling interminable hours, rising at 4 A.M. to shake hands at some remote airplane gate in sub-zero weather."

"I wouldn't call it affection," she said of her relationship with John Kennedy. "I would say mutual respect. He was extremely intelligent, courageous, responsive and very humorous, and I think underneath all this charm was a durable strength and a strong conviction."[35]

Advance arrangements for a Kennedy visit included a board under his hotel mattress; a lectern at the proper level for him to read his text; maximum media coverage; and meetings arranged with local Democratic officials, editors, students, and labor and farm leaders.

"To save time for rest and the strain on his back," Sorensen said, "he avoided the cocktail receptions held in his honor preceding dinner until only enough time was left to meet everyone personally without getting bogged down in small talk while constantly standing."

Kennedy would husband his energy. Shortly after an evening speech, he was aboard the plane and sound asleep. "I don't think he could have gone for more than a few days if he had not had that remarkable ability to take his rest where he found it," Evelyn Lincoln observed.

During a grueling campaign tour Kennedy wanted an hour or an hour and a half of free time prior to the dinner hour, and also an hour free at noon. He wanted to look fresh and energetic at all his public appearances. Also, the free time gave him a chance to telephone his Washington office for updates. Other than the rest periods, observed Wisconsin's Patrick Lucey, "he was a bear for punishment and just would resent it if there was any kind of a lull in his schedule."[36]

Normally he maintained a good disposition, but the tension of the long campaign sometimes made him testy. Evelyn Lincoln endured two angry outbursts in one week. She wrote about them in her diary:

> I told him that a couple newsmen were waiting to see him. He wanted to know what they wanted and who made the appointments. I told him Pierre had made the first one. He called Pierre—gave him the dickens. Then he blew his stack with me. Said "I don't want to see anyone—Why do you make these appointments?" Boy, was he mad!

A few days later she wrote:

> He blew up again and wanted to know why he was wakened. I told him I had nothing to do with it. Whew what a day. He called again before he went out to the plane and he was his usual self, but golly I was glad he was leaving.[37]

In January 1960, Kennedy asked Harvard law professor Archibald Cox to coordinate an academic advisory group to assist him with speeches and issues. "I have come to the conclusion that you would be the ideal man to head up my efforts this year to tap intellectual talent in the Cambridge area," Kennedy wrote Cox on January 18.

Cox agreed, and on January 24, about twenty college professors filed into the meeting room at the Harvard Club on Commonwealth Avenue. Most of the professors came from MIT and Harvard Law School. Kennedy introduced Cox as the person who would act as his representative to the intellectual community.

Kennedy sat absolutely alone in the center of the room, legs crossed, and spoke without notes. Guests were arranged in a semicircle. Kennedy's opening remarks captivated the academicians. "I have announced my candidacy for the Democratic nomination. This will be difficult, but it is possible. If I get the nomination, I believe I can defeat Mr. Nixon. In that case I will be the President of the United States. From the present forward, therefore, I wish to speak to the issues seriously conscious that I may be President."

He had only a limited amount of time to study the myriad issues, he told the professors. "I need people who know about issues, who will be honest and will criticize things truthfully."[38] Each professor was asked to speak a few minutes on a serious problem in his area of expertise and to offer suggestions as to how the senator could address it. "All of us were absolutely tremendously impressed with the speed at which Kennedy picked up whatever was said and with the penetrating quality of the questions he asked," recalled Harvard's Carl Kaysen.

While discussing one issue, a guest muttered, "Politically [this] might not work." Kennedy immediately interrupted, saying, "I don't want any of you to worry about the politics of the situation. You don't have that skill. Forget it. I'll do that." The professors were stunned. "You just worry about the substance," Kennedy declared. He wanted their suggestions only on policy formulation, not on politics.

"What amount of trimming or modifying or compromise he would have to do was a judgment that he wanted to make," said Abraham Chayes. "He didn't want us to make it for him and then give him a doctored version based on our judgment of what he could take politically."

The professors gave Kennedy high marks for understanding their ideas. "I've never met anyone more eager to pick the brains of people," marveled one professor.

A Stevenson supporter, Harvard economist Paul Samuelson detested old Joe Kennedy, disliked the senator's nonaction on the McCarthy issue, and was leery of a Catholic handling birth-control policy. But the meeting changed his mind. The young senator in front of him absorbed Samuelson's comments like a "sponge"; he seemed to want honest advice. "I decided that whatever Joe Kennedy was," Samuelson said later, "and whatever JFK's inner beliefs were, his colors were nailed to the liberal side of the centrist spectrum." Samuelson reached the conclusion that Kennedy was "more promising material" for the presidency than Adlai Stevenson.[39]

Cox was assisted by Deirdre Henderson, a bright young assistant in Kennedy's Boston office, who picked up the papers and memoranda from the professors and took notes on their ideas. Kennedy felt he needed academic contacts partly to woo intellectuals away from Adlai Stevenson, and partly to enhance his image. "He wanted to make the liberal elite of the country, who exerted great influence in newspapers, magazines, and television, feel as if they had access to the candidate," said Ken Gormley, Cox's biographer. Kennedy also wanted his campaign infused with fresh ideas. He hoped Cox's group could generate a stream of new position papers to last until election day.[40]

Jackie accompanied her husband on some trips, but grew exasperated with the burdens of the campaign, especially the intrusions on her family life, the personal questions fired at her, and the rude photographers who pursued little Caroline. While on the campaign trail in the spring of 1960, she penned a note to her father-in-law: "Factory gates tomorrow morning at 5am. You can't beat this life can ya!"

Publicly, of course, Jackie didn't complain. She was probably sincere when she told a reporter that "Jack is very considerate of me on these trips, very warm and tender. When he thinks I'm too tired, he'll suggest I skip things." While Jack took a boat trip from Duluth, Minnesota, to Superior, Wisconsin, he sent Jackie back to the hotel for a hot bath and rest.[41]

The public knew nothing about Jack's womanizing, and he wanted to keep it that way. He had to protect his public image as a fine husband, a doting father, and a candidate with outstanding moral character. On one occasion, George Smathers arranged for a group of beautiful women to pose with the Florida senator for a photo taken by the Senate photographer on the Senate subway tram. Smathers collared Kennedy to pose with them too. Shortly after the photo session, though, Kennedy thought better of his consent and demanded that the negative be destroyed. "Okay," said the Senate photographer, "don't worry, none of those will get out."

During a campaign stop a young college girl jumped into Kennedy's automobile. Photographers rushed to get a snapshot, including Stanley Tretick, who recalled Kennedy saying, "When I saw Stan and the others running toward my car, I got the girl out as quickly as I could."[42]

During the fall 1960 campaign, Kennedy briefly suffered from laryngitis and had to scrawl notes to his aides. While on the *Caroline,* he wrote on a manila envelope, in a clear, expansive style, "I suppose if I win—my poon days are over" ("poon" being an old navy expression for sexual activity). "I suppose they are going to hit me with something before we are finished," he also wrote, apparently a reference to the possibility that his adultery might be exposed before the election. To one of his aides—probably Dave Powers or Ken O'Donnell—he penned, "I got into the blondes." (The sentence might also be read, "I got into the blonde.")[43]

Despite his precautions, one sexual encounter nearly did ruin his drive for the presidency. The bizarre story involved an outraged woman and her husband who tried unsuccessfully for five years to expose Kennedy's sexual relationship with one of his aides.

During the summer of 1958, the senator made a late-night visit to his pretty staff member Pam Turnure, who rented a second-floor apartment in the Georgetown home of Mr. and Mrs. Leonard Kater. "We were up late one night, and heard someone outside throwing pebbles at Pam's window about one A.M.," Florence Kater recalled. The Katers looked out and saw

Senator Kennedy standing in their garden yelling, "If you don't come down, I'll climb up your balcony." So Turnure let him in.

Intrigued and outraged, the Katers placed tape recorders at two locations in their home, including a basement air vent leading to Pam's bedroom. The next time Kennedy came over, the Katers turned on the recorders and listened to the upstairs conversation and lovemaking.

Slim, dark-haired Pamela Turnure was a twenty-one-year-old ex-debutante. Although more petite, she bore a striking resemblance to Jackie Kennedy in both appearance and bearing. A receptionist in Kennedy's Senate office, she later joined his presidential campaign team and the White House staff (ironically, as Jackie Kennedy's press secretary).[44]

After kicking Turnure out of her apartment, the Katers, both strict Catholics, decided to expose the immorality of their nocturnal guest. "I was so enraged that this Irish Catholic senator, who pretended to be such a good family man, might run for President that I decided to do something about it," said Florence Kater. "I was very innocent and naïve in those days and had no idea of the power I was going up against. I knew no one would believe my story unless we had actual proof, so in addition to the tape recordings, we decided to get a photograph."

On the evening of July 11, 1958, the Katers drove to where Pam was currently living and waited in their car. At about 1:00 A.M., as the senator came out, Leonard Kater waited for him on the sidewalk. Kater yelled, "Hey, Senator," and as Kennedy turned, he took his picture. But Kennedy had covered his face with his hand. "What in the hell are you doing here?" Kennedy demanded. "How dare you take my picture!" Florence Kater then jumped out of the car and exclaimed, "How dare you run for President under the guise of a good Christian?" JFK apparently jotted down their license number.

The next day Florence Kater phoned Joe Kennedy and related her story. But he was leaving for Europe and didn't seem interested. A few nights later the Katers drove to John Kennedy's Georgetown home on N Street, where they sat and waited. Florence later claimed that when JFK spotted them, he made a threat. "I want you to know that I know all about you and your job," JFK allegedly said to Leonard Kater. "You're doing very well, so why don't you keep it that way. If you ever bother me or my father again, I'll see to it that you never work in Washington as long as you live."[45]

Florence Kater jumped out of her car and yelled at him, "I have a tape recording of your whoring. You are unfit to be the Catholic standard bearer for the presidency of this country." She thought JFK looked horrified at news of her evidence.

Before Mrs. Kater began her one-woman crusade to discredit the senator, she received a call from Ambassador Kennedy's attorney, James McInerney, who formerly worked for the Criminal Division of the FBI. According to Mrs. Kater, McInerney asked the Katers to hand over the photograph and tape recordings and forget the whole matter. "He told me if I went public with my information it would be political suicide for the senator and economic suicide for my husband. . . . He visited us about nine times." The Katers may well have been engaging in extortion. At one point in their negotiations with McInerney, the art-loving Katers admitted they were willing to forget the incident if Joseph Kennedy gave them an expensive painting to add to their collection; McInerney never delivered the painting.

Next the Katers took their campaign to the streets, showing up at JFK's political rallies with hand-fashioned signs denouncing him. They marched in front of Harry Truman's residence in Independence, Missouri, when Kennedy called on the former President. They even went to Boston to visit Richard Cardinal Cushing. Later, when all else failed, Florence picketed the White House.[46]

The Katers, especially Florence, became obsessed with the matter. They sent letters to over thirty newspapers and magazines, damning Kennedy for his adultery and his threat to have Leonard Kater fired. "I have personal knowledge and proof that Miss Pamela Turnure, press secretary in the White House to Mrs. John F. Kennedy, has an illicit sexual relationship with President John F. Kennedy," Florence wrote J. Edgar Hoover in April 1963. "Under the circumstances I feel it is in the national interest to call this matter to your attention as a very possible security risk." Hoover refused to meet with them or investigate (although he added the material to his bulging file on John Kennedy).

Only the *Washington Star* took her story seriously and started investigating. Some allege that the Kennedy family threatened a lawsuit if the *Star* published the Katers' charges. For whatever reason, the newspaper stopped pursuing the story.[47]

Florence Kater's credibility suffered because she seemed so eccentric. The photo she distributed didn't clearly identify the senator because his hand covered his face. Besides, without context, what did the photo prove? Her crusade was also undermined when the *Thunderbolt,* a vicious racist publication of the National States Rights Party, became the only publication to print her charges.

"I had told the truth but no one would listen to me," reflected Florence. "The press wanted Kennedy to be President and that was that."[48]

23

---·---

CAPTURING THE
NOMINATION

On January 2, 1960, Jack announced his candidacy. Beforehand he
was nervous, walking from room to room in his office complex,
sifting through papers, reading a little. Evelyn Lincoln later described his demeanor: "Then he would sit down at his desk, move the papers
around, lean back in his chair, stare up into the ceiling, then thump his fingers on the arm of his chair and look at the clock. He was like a thoroughbred racing horse waiting for the starting gate."

At 12:15 P.M. Myer Feldman, Ted Sorensen, Ted Reardon, and Mrs. Lincoln entered his office. "I just took a poll in the office and I have good
news," said Reardon. "They are all for you." That brought a smile to the
senator's face.

In announcing his candidacy, he said the presidency must become more
"vital" in addressing foreign and domestic problems.

For it is in the Executive Branch that the most crucial decisions of this
century must be made in the next four years—how to end or alter the
burdensome arms race, where Soviet gains already threaten our very

existence—how to maintain freedom and order in the newly emerging nations—how to rebuild the stature of American science and education— how to prevent the collapse of our farm economy and the decay of our cities—how to achieve, without further inflation or unemployment, expanded economic growth benefiting all Americans—and how to give direction to our traditional moral purpose, awakening every American to the dangers and opportunities that confront us.[1]

Favorite-son candidates posed a special dilemma in Kennedy's campaign strategy. He wanted to run in the Ohio primary, but the Democrats had two potential favorite sons, Governor Michael DiSalle and Senator Frank Lausche. Most likely Governor Edmund Brown would be California's favorite son, and several other state delegations might be tied up in the same way for at least the first ballot. Delicate negotiations were needed to capture delegates in those states.

With no serious opposition, Kennedy easily swept the New Hampshire primary on March 8. A much bigger test lay a month later, when Hubert Humphrey planned to challenge him. Wisconsin's primary commanded special attention because it was held in the first week of April 1960, early in the primary season. The primary was unusual because voters were free to "cross over" and vote for whichever ticket they preferred.[2]

In three years, from 1957 to 1959, Kennedy visited Wisconsin about ten times, establishing his organization and making many speeches and appearances. Several Wisconsin groups had serious doubts about him. Farmers were upset that he had voted against high rigid price supports; union officers judged him antilabor; blacks criticized his two votes on the Civil Rights Act of 1957; and many Democrats thought he had ducked the McCarthy issue.

Kennedy's campaign staff debated whether Jack should enter the Wisconsin primary. Minnesota senator Hubert Humphrey championed farmers and organized labor, and had won many friends in the state. (State Democrats called him Wisconsin's third senator.) "However," noted Larry O'Brien, "the polls looked good and we had some solid people committed to us." These included Ivan Nestingen, the influential mayor of Madison, and Patrick Lucey, a tireless organizer and forceful aggressive leader, who chaired the state Democratic Party (and later served as governor).[3]

In January 1960, while waiting for a plane to fly him from Wisconsin to Nebraska, Kennedy teased Lucey, who had pleaded with Kennedy to enter the state's primary. Jack had just announced he would. "Well, now that you've conned me into this thing, how do you feel about it?" said Jack. Then he grinned and continued, "As of today, my chances of getting the nomination are a lot less than 50-50. If I win the Wisconsin primary, they'll be just slightly better than 50-50. So if you look at it that way, I'm not gambling very much."

In mid-February Joseph Kennedy wrote a friend that Humphrey was "getting a great deal of money" but was "always crying poor mouth." Joe was wrong. Humphrey didn't raise much money. John Kennedy easily outspent him, but Kennedy also outmanaged and outorganized him.

"Disorder was a bigger Humphrey handicap than was his thin purse," said one of Humphrey's biographers. At the start of Humphrey's Wisconsin campaign, he showed up at a Milwaukee hotel to speak to a group of black leaders only to find that his supporters had not reserved a room for the occasion. Aides at Humphrey's national headquarters squabbled, and his Minnesota backers detested his chief Washington staffer. Orville Freeman, Minnesota's governor, thought Humphrey's campaign was "poorly handled, poorly organized, and poorly administered."[4]

On issues only subtle differences existed. "[We] had come to a position where our differences were really negligible," Humphrey recalled. "It was only the past that I could refer to." When Senator Humphrey made several harsh allusions to the Kennedys buying the election, Kennedy didn't respond or retaliate. "I thought that showed a very honorable position on his part," said one reporter.

Not able to give all his time to Wisconsin, Kennedy campaigned simultaneously in other primaries as well, and tried to capture delegates in nonprimary states. From the beginning of January to the April 5 primary, he spent twenty-nine days campaigning in Wisconsin. Usually traveling by motorcade, scheduled tightly, he made about eight speeches per day.

In some towns, especially in northern Wisconsin, voters seemed apathetic. On March 17, 1960, he entered a tavern, approached a couple in a booth, and introduced himself. "My name is John Kennedy and I'm running for President." The man turned toward Kennedy, studied him for a moment, and replied, "President of what?" The same evening, while Kennedy climbed into a car for a fifty-mile drive on empty roads to visit a factory in frigid Ashland on Lake Superior, he said to Dave Powers, "What a hell of a way to spend Saint Patrick's Day."[5]

Normally Kennedy disliked emotional scenes, but Gino Frinzi, a Kennedy volunteer worker in Milwaukee, saw tears in Kennedy's eyes at one appearance. As Kennedy walked into the Badger Home for the Blind, a man at a piano started playing "Anchors Aweigh," and a group stood to sing in tribute to Kennedy the World War II naval hero. Frinzi commented, "Kennedy's eyes were very wet." After leaving the building, the senator took out a handkerchief and wiped his eyes. "He looked like he didn't want anyone to see him do it."

Everywhere Kennedy campaigned, groups of Catholic nuns cheerfully greeted him. He responded warmly, but grew leery of media coverage of the scenes. On the outskirts of Ladysmith, the Kennedy motorcade passed a group of adoring nuns and postulants, waiting for him by the roadside. Kennedy ordered a halt, jumped out of the car, and talked with them. But when photographers' bulbs started popping, he looked nervous. Shortly after, while visiting a nearby convent, he barred photos. "I think not," he said.[6]

With university audiences he emphasized the need for fresh ideas and a new respect for the intellectuals who provided them. Before Democratic groups he stressed New Deal–style programs: broader minimum-wage coverage, better unemployment compensation, increased federal housing, medical care for the elderly, and high subsidy payments for farmers.

Pat Lucey thought Kennedy's most remarkable feature was his ability to be objective about his own campaign. Lucey had assisted several campaigns and discovered that each candidate, cool-headed and objective about everything else, lost objectivity during the heated campaign. That was never true of Kennedy. "He just seemed to be able to stand off, as though he were another person, totally disinterested in what was going on, and assess the effect of various elements of the campaign and make studious judgments about what they ought to do next."[7]

Humphrey could staff only two offices in Wisconsin; Kennedy had eight. Nor was the Kennedy staffing primarily paid personnel; most were volunteers. Robert Kennedy, Ted Sorensen, Larry O'Brien, and Ken O'Donnell worked diligently in the state. Kennedy's friends poured into Wisconsin to volunteer their time. Writer-artist Bill Walton, Lem Billings, and Charles Spalding helped organize in various districts. All the members of the Kennedy family except Jack's father (and, of course, the institutionalized Rosemary) worked in the primary too. Eunice, Pat, and Jean flew in and out of Wisconsin, attending scores of coffees and teas, speaking mostly to women. Eunice gave rousing stump speeches explaining Jack's position on issues.

The staff debated whether Rose Kennedy should appear in Wisconsin. Bobby Kennedy worried that his mother might say something damaging. When Rose did come to the state, she told audiences, "Bobby didn't want me to come, but here I am. Jack said I could."[8]

Since nearly every major labor-union leader in the state supported Humphrey, one of Kennedy's goals was to neutralize their pro-Humphrey efforts. It helped, Pat Lucey noted, "that the union leaders knew, in many instances, that the rank-and-file were not with them." Jack personally talked with every major labor leader in the state. "Just charmed the pants off of them," one labor official commented. "The opposition [to Kennedy] sort of quieted down a little bit."

In Wisconsin, and later in West Virginia, Sorensen flattered prominent liberal college professors by requesting their advice on state issues—much as the Cox group functioned in Kennedy's Washington headquarters. Sorensen sought advice from Professor Leon Epstein of the University of Wisconsin–Madison, a prominent political scientist, about Wisconsin's natural resources, housing needs, transportation problems, and attitude toward the St. Lawrence Seaway. All of the memoranda Epstein could furnish should be buttressed with "specific facts and needs," wrote Sorensen, "and the specific shortcomings of present plans and programs. Where there are deficiencies, the memoranda should contain suggestions for a specific plan of Federal action—if possible, a new and progressive plan." The state advisory groups, though, were too hastily assembled to be of much substantive benefit.[9]

That one-third of Wisconsin residents who identified with a church were Catholic was simply too intriguing a circumstance for the media to ignore. Time and again reporters reminded voters that the Wisconsin primary would determine if voters would accept a Catholic as President. Kennedy tried to avoid the religious issue, but to no avail.

Historian Mark Massa observed that "pictures of Kennedy greeting groups of nuns were printed across the nation, while other pictures were left on the newsroom floor; frequent questions from student audiences regarding his religion were invariably and extensively reported, while other questions about labor and agriculture went unnoticed." Kennedy pointed out afterward that at his rallies reporters quizzed potential voters about their religion, "not their occupation or education or philosophy or income, only their religion." One newspaper mentioned the word "Catholic" twenty times in fifteen paragraphs of analysis. Two days before the primary, the *Milwaukee Journal* published a demographic map of Wisconsin showing three clusters of voters: Democrats, Republicans, and Catholics.[10]

On April 5, election night, as the results poured in, Kennedy nervously paced and bit his fingers. Almost half of the state's eligible voters voted, the largest turnout for any of Wisconsin's primaries after World War II. Most independents voted in the Democratic primary, and so did many Republicans. Kennedy defeated Humphrey, 476,024 to 366,753—garnering slightly more than 56 percent of the vote. He carried six of the state's ten congressional districts, and earned twenty of Wisconsin's thirty delegates to the national convention.

"There was . . . every indication of a strong 'religious vote,' Catholics voting for Kennedy, Protestants voting for Humphrey (or against Kennedy)," said Robert Thompson in his history of the state. "On balance, Kennedy gained by the exchange." Three of the districts Humphrey won were Protestant areas in northern and western Wisconsin. Four of the six districts Kennedy won contained significant Catholic populations, making it appear that Protestants had simply voted for the Protestant Humphrey, and Catholics for the Catholic Kennedy. Both *The New York Times* and the *Milwaukee Journal* reported that most of Kennedy's winning margin came in three districts that were heavily Catholic, and two of those were normally Republican. Kennedy hadn't proved that he could attract non-Catholic voters, said pundits.[11]

Actually, the religious voting pattern was exaggerated in the post-election analysis. The three "Protestant" districts Humphrey won shared a common border with Minnesota, were influenced by the pro-Humphrey media centered in the Twin Cities, and were rural areas supportive of Humphrey's farm record. Kennedy did not lose these districts simply because he was a Catholic; other complex issues and impressions had emerged during the primary. This set of considerations, "posed against the varied economic, ethnic, religious, social, and political background of the electorate," Thompson concluded, "suggests that religion was only one of many factors, and not necessarily the most important one." A very large number of voters did not "simply vote their rosaries or their hymnals."

Because Kennedy won only six of the ten districts, analysts judged the results indecisive. At Kennedy's headquarters in Milwaukee there was an awful sense of gloom. On television Humphrey claimed a moral victory.

What did the election results mean? asked one of Jack's sisters. "It means," Jack answered quietly but bitterly, "that we have to do it all over again. We have to go through every [primary] and win every one of them— West Virginia and Maryland and Indiana and Oregon, all the way to the Convention."[12]

After the Wisconsin primary the senator took a few days off to vacation in Jamaica. Then he was back on the campaign trail in West Virginia for a month of strenuous campaigning before the state's critical May 10 primary.

Kennedy badly needed a victory over Humphrey in West Virginia to prove that he could win without the aid of a Catholic crossover. A victory would eliminate Humphrey as a rival and would demonstrate that Kennedy was "a winner," ending speculation that his religion was an insurmountable obstacle.

An impoverished rural state with a declining population and a sagging economy, West Virginia lay within the blighted region known as Appalachia. Falling demand for coal as fuel and increasing automation in the mines had left the state with high unemployment and nearly empty towns. In a third of its counties one out of six people received surplus commodities.[13]

During the year before the West Virginia primary Robert McDonough, the volunteer chairman of Kennedy's state campaign, and Matt Reese, former assistant to a West Virginia congressman, had quietly recruited chairmen for volunteer organizations in most of West Virginia's fifty-five counties. Once again, Kennedy's family, friends, and aides would follow the candidate into the state.

A Lou Harris poll in late 1959 had shown Kennedy beating Humphrey easily in West Virginia—by a 70-to-30 margin. But to Kennedy's dismay, in a second poll a month before the primary, Harris showed Humphrey leading. The pollster lamely explained that the first poll was taken before most West Virginians knew Kennedy was a Catholic.[14]

Now Kennedy seemed to be in trouble. On some days he campaigned from four-thirty in the morning until one-thirty at night with only a few rest periods. Like Patrick Lucey in Wisconsin, Robert McDonough was impressed with Kennedy's stoic determination. "He was most cooperative, and regardless of the time, how long he had been working, or how tired he was, if there was still something else to be done, he'd do it. And he would do it without grumbling."

West Virginia had the most sordid election system of any state in the country. It practically invited corruption. Each candidate had to "buy in" with a slate. Dan Fleming, the historian of West Virginia's 1960 primary election, explained that a "slate was a printed list of candidates that the poll worker employed by a candidate or faction recommended that the voter vote for." The list could include two, three, or a dozen candidates. In counties where different factions contested, two or more slates of candidates were presented to the voter.

Candidates paid money for election day drivers and poll watchers—and gave away bottles of liquor. A Charleston reporter noted that "putting a man on the election day payroll may assure the votes of a dozen relatives." (Normally drivers on election day were paid twenty-five to fifty dollars.)[15]

The county organization raised money by assessing each candidate a fee to be placed on its slate. If the candidate refused to pay his share, he could be left off the slate and could lose, depending on the machine's power.

Because there had been no presidential primary races in recent years, county leaders eagerly awaited a financial bonanza from the campaigns of Kennedy and Humphrey. Kennedy's campaign had no alternative but to buy in with county political machines. Critics later charged that Kennedy "bought votes." The truth is that everyone who ran for office in West Virginia bought votes. Both presidential candidates doled out the money, but Kennedy was in a better financial position to do it than Humphrey. West Virginia's politics, concluded Theodore White, was "squalid, corrupt and despicable."

Kennedy tried to be slated with the strongest faction in each county. "We were willing to pay our way, both in manpower from our volunteer organization and for legitimate Election Day expenses," observed Larry O'Brien. "At no time did I think we were being 'taken' for our money. We paid our fair share, which was always less than that of candidates for sheriff and the other more 'important' offices."[16]

The Kennedy camp viewed Humphrey as a spoiler. He couldn't be nominated, but by winning in West Virginia he could ruin Kennedy's chances and open the nomination for Johnson, Symington, or Stevenson. Stuart Symington had untactfully joked that Lyndon Johnson and he would still be in the race for President as long as there was a breath of air in the body of Hubert Humphrey. Kennedy accused Humphrey of being the "front man" for the gang-up strategy of Stevenson, Symington, and Johnson—all of whom refused to campaign in open primaries.

In West Virginia none of the state's leading politicians would endorse Kennedy or campaign for him, and he faced labor opposition from the United Mine Workers Union. Then there was the Catholic issue. In Wisconsin the vote had supposedly broken on strictly religious lines. The media reported that Kennedy's religion would severely damage him in West Virginia, where Catholics made up only 5 percent of the population.[17]

Except for politely answering hundreds of questions about his religion, Kennedy hadn't emphasized the issue in Wisconsin; now he felt he had to modify his approach. He adopted a dual strategy: He would reemphasize his independence from the church's hierarchy while putting doubters and bigots on the defensive.

First, he changed the topic of an upcoming speech at a national meeting of newspaper editors to the subject of religion. Second, his staff recruited nationally known Protestant ministers to issue a public statement urging an end to religious bigotry and "insinuation" in political ads. Finally, instead of trying to avoid the religion issue as he had mostly done in Wisconsin, he would face the issue directly and openly in West Virginia and call for fair play.[18]

On April 21, 1960, he addressed the religious issue before the American Society of Newspaper Editors (ASNE) in Washington. "There is no religious *issue*," he told the editors, "in the sense that any of the major candidates differ on the role of religion in our political life." Each of the presidential contenders was dedicated to the separation of church and state and to the preservation of religious liberty; each opposed religious bigotry, and favored the total independence of the officeholder from ecclesiastical dictation. Nor, he continued, "is there any religious *issue* in the sense that any candidate is exploiting his religious affiliation." In particular, "I am not 'trying to be the first Catholic President,' as some have written. I happen to believe I can serve my nation as President—and I also happen to have been born a Catholic."

The media had not created the religious issue, but reporters and editors "will largely determine whether or not it does become dominant—whether it is kept in perspective—whether it is considered objectively—whether needless fears and suspicions are aroused." To date the issue had not been kept in perspective. In Wisconsin, Kennedy told the group, he had spoken on farm legislation, foreign policy, defense, civil rights, and several other topics, but "I rarely found them reported in the press—except when they were occasionally sandwiched in between descriptions of my handshaking, my theme song, family, haircut and, inevitably, my religion." For the most part, his plea fell on deaf ears. The media continued to feature his Catholic religion.[19]

Four days later on April 25, before a crowd of 350 people gathered around the post office steps in Charleston, someone in the crowd asked him about the religious issue. He replied differently than he ever had before. "I am a Catholic," he responded, "but the fact that I was born a Catholic, does that mean that I can't be the President of the United States? I'm able to serve in Congress, and my brother was able to give his life but we can't be President?"

Standing nearby, Kennedy's state coordinator, Robert McDonough, felt the crowd's empathetic response. The incident convinced Kennedy that he should aggressively bring up the issue himself, rather than waiting for the question to arise.[20]

The Kennedy staff was split on the emphasis to place on the religious issue. In the last days of April, Robert Wallace wrote a flurry of memos to Sorensen and Robert Kennedy urging that less emphasis be placed on religion. "We have made our point on the religious issue," Wallace contended. "Can we proceed now to the positive, and let it alone?"

"Having gotten into the ring with the bull," Wallace said, "I don't think [Kennedy] should wave a red flag at it. . . . As a matter of fact, the Humphrey people could charge that we are the ones who are fanning it."

Wallace wanted Kennedy's speeches to "show a heart-feeling for the people" of West Virginia, combined with assurance that President Kennedy would help them overcome unemployment, hunger, hopelessness, malnutrition, and rickets in children. Kennedy must convey the message—"with *feeling, compassion, sympathy* and *understanding*"—that he could help the people of West Virginia.[21]

It turned out that Kennedy did develop empathy for the problems of impoverished West Virginians. Aside from life in the Solomon Islands during the war, Kennedy had never experienced hunger or deprivation. But as he started campaigning in West Virginia, the high unemployment and the number of people living on federal food packages appalled him. "Imagine, just imagine kids who never drank milk," he said privately one night.

On one campaign day he descended into the shaft of a coal mine and chatted with the miners. Richard Goodwin later described the scene:

> He was direct, his discussion stripped of rhetoric—he used words they could understand and answer; and he was curious, seemingly more interested in their way of life, the rigors of their job, even the mechanics of mining, than in trying to persuade them of his own merit. It was Kennedy at his best, because it was, in part, the real Kennedy. I never met a man so able to make an individual or a small group feel as if they and he were alone together, confined by the contours of a tiny world, bound by his quest to know, to understand, what others were like.

In the middle of the campaign, as he walked into his Senate office, he said to no one in particular, "You can't imagine how those people live down there. I was better off in the war than they are in those coal mines. It's not right. I'm going to do something about it. If we make it." Then he added, "Even if they are a bunch of bigots."[22]

The Kennedy campaign stressed Jack's war record because in West Virginia, with its reverence for war heroes, the courage of Kennedy in the Solomon Islands struck a responsive chord. ("To listen to their stuff," said an angry Humphrey supporter, "you'd think Jack won the war all by himself.")

A "state with a dozen Congressional Medal of Honor winners, and almost as many veterans' organizations as schools, could identify with Kennedy as a decorated combat veteran," said one observer. In the Charleston area, Kennedy volunteers distributed forty thousand copies of reprints of the *Reader's Digest* article on Jack's PT boat heroism.

One way the Kennedy camp hoped to arouse apathetic lower-income groups was to portray Kennedy as a dedicated New Deal Democrat. To foster this strategy, Franklin D. Roosevelt Jr. was recruited to stir memories of his popular father. "Of all the former President's sons, FDR Jr. looked the most like his father, and when he flashed a smile, he was the very image of him," said historian William Leuchtenburg. His voice, Humphrey would say, "seemed a precise echo of fireside chats heard on crystal sets and Emerson radios." Wherever he campaigned in West Virginia, FDR's namesake drew large crowds and received the most applause when he mentioned "my father." In FDR Jr., Leuchtenburg wrote, "Kennedy had the patriarch of liberalism incarnate." What's more, the Kennedy campaign mailed thousands of letters with FDR Jr.'s signature to West Virginia's voters. Ingeniously, the letters had been shipped north to receive the proper postmark: President Roosevelt's home, Hyde Park, New York.[23]

Frustrated, Humphrey struck out with personal attacks on Kennedy. "I don't have any daddy who can pay the bills for me," Humphrey bitterly asserted. "I can't afford to run around this state with a little black bag and a checkbook." Sometimes he resorted to sarcasm. "I trust it is not against the law to win against Senator Kennedy. I hope it is not un–American, indecent or illegal to run against him." On another occasion, he remarked: "Poor little Jack. That's a shame. . . . I wish he would grow up and stop acting like a boy. . . . What does he want, all the votes?"

On May 3 Sorensen privately listed for key staff members all the nasty things Humphrey had recently said about Kennedy. Picking up a theme in James Burns's recently published biography, Humphrey claimed Kennedy lacked emotional commitment to liberalism. "If you can't cry a little in politics, probably the only thing you can do is hate." Kennedy's shift to a more liberal position, said Humphrey, "can be credited less to a change in philosophy and more to the politics of a campaign to win the Democratic Presidential nomination."

Kennedy replied with an unaccustomed public complaint: "I have never been subject to so much personal abuse."

For the staff Sorensen contrasted Humphrey's nasty remarks with praise for Kennedy's statesmanlike campaign. In *The New York Times* James Reston had recently written that Kennedy "has made no charges against Humphrey, either on the local shows or from the stump. . . . And at no time has he lost his self-possession."[24]

The blackest mark on Kennedy's 1960 campaign came when it did retaliate against Humphrey's barbs. From an anonymous source in Minnesota, the Kennedy camp received alleged copies of correspondence between Humphrey and his draft board during World War II. Humphrey had maintained that he did not enter military service during the war because the army and the navy rejected him because of color blindness and a double hernia; but the anonymous material seemed to indicate that Humphrey sought a deferment and was actually a "draft dodger."

On May 6, Roosevelt charged that Humphrey had sought deferment from military service several times during the war, and claimed he had documents to prove it. "There's another candidate in your primary," Roosevelt said. "He's a good Democrat, but I don't know where he was in World War II." Humphrey had busied himself seeking deferments, Roosevelt said, while Kennedy heroically performed his duty in the Pacific. When the media prominently featured Roosevelt's comments, the Humphrey camp exploded. Subsequently, both Roosevelt and Kennedy apologized to the Minnesota senator.[25]

The question remains: Who was responsible for the smear of Humphrey? "We agreed that if Humphrey hit us with some extremely low blow," said O'Brien, "we might use the material to retaliate. We determined that if retaliation was decided upon, it would come from Frank Roosevelt, not directly from us, and we turned the material over to Frank." O'Brien claimed the incident was one of his "few regrets," and had happened "inadvertently."

Actually it was not inadvertent. "I knew that Franklin was going to make that speech before he delivered it," said Myer Feldman, who claimed he discussed the decision with Ken O'Donnell and Robert Kennedy.

According to FDR Jr., the person most responsible for the draft-dodging smear was Robert Kennedy. Robert had given Roosevelt the documents on Humphrey and urged Roosevelt to raise the issue. Bobby insisted, "We've got to do it." Roosevelt claimed he held off for about ten days. "Nightly I received calls from Bobby asking me, 'When will you lower the boom.' Then "Larry O'Brien and others all put the pressure on me to attack." Finally, Roosevelt delivered the smear.

When Kennedy learned by telephone of Roosevelt's statements, he commented, "Why did he do that? He didn't need to do that." Although he blamed Robert Kennedy for the incident because of the younger Kennedy's desire "to win at any cost," FDR Jr. didn't think that "Jack had anything to do with [it]." Myer Feldman agreed. "I honestly don't think that John F. Kennedy knew Franklin was going to use it."

"John F. Kennedy believed in a pretty high-level kind of campaign," Feldman maintained. "I don't know of any other politician that stuck as rigidly to principles of fair campaigning as John F. Kennedy. . . . I often had material that was nasty, was personal, and John F. Kennedy always decided against using that kind of material. He didn't believe that he could improve his chances by tearing down the personal character of the opposition."[26]

When Humphrey confidently challenged Kennedy to a televised debate, Kennedy upstaged him. Sorensen carefully cautioned his boss not to attack Humphrey directly, "particularly on his war record." Kennedy should make it clear that he was the victim of "unfair attacks," "gang-up," and "bigotry." Always state the victim charge in the passive tense: "I have been called . . . it has been suggested that . . . people are being asked to vote against me because." Dwell on "human interest" issues: the hardships of the unemployed, poverty, food, and the aged. "Simple words, short sentences and calm dignity are essential," Sorensen advised.

At the debate, held on May 4, Kennedy visually underscored his concern for the state's poor by displaying for television viewers the meager contents of a government's food-ration package, including the powdered milk given to the unemployed poor. By using the prop, Kennedy showed more concern than Humphrey about the plight of the state's poor. Afterward, state newspapers noticed voters switching their support from Humphrey to Kennedy.[27]

On May 8, two days before the primary, the Kennedy campaign purchased thirty minutes of television time. The show's format had Franklin Roosevelt Jr. asking Kennedy questions. Sorensen scripted the program, suggesting Roosevelt's questions and Kennedy's answers. What are your plans for this state when you reach the White House? FDR Jr. was to ask. Kennedy would respond that he wanted emergency help for those people suffering from a shortage of food, better unemployment compensation, better Social Security and medical care. He hoped to provide special help for areas of heavy unemployment by proposing a stronger depressed-areas bill and seeking defense contracts for the state. He would also support vocational-education retraining of workers for new jobs, and a Youth Conservation Corps, using unemployed youths to improve parks and forests to enhance the state's tourist industry.

The program raised the issue of religion. "Kennedy did not direct his answer to Roosevelt or focus on him," observed historian Mary Ann Watson. "He looked directly into the lens of the camera, into the eyes of the voters, as he delivered an impassioned statement of principle on the separation of church and state." He would take no orders from a pope or the Catholic hierarchy. To take any directive from a pope would violate the Constitution and make him liable to impeachment. Voters of Catholic Boston had supported Baptist Harry Truman in 1948, he pointed out; he wanted the same fairness that was shown to Truman.[28]

As the May 10 primary approached, most of the media assumed that the results would derail Kennedy's nomination bid or at least severely damage his chances. *The New York Times* saw evidence of "conflicting political trends" but was still certain of Kennedy's defeat. Humphrey was "setting the pace," wrote *Time* magazine. *The New Republic* assumed "Humphrey's style of campaigning would overcome Kennedy's organization."

On the evening of election day, the Ben Bradlees, neighbors of the Kennedys in Georgetown, were asked to wait out the primary returns with Jack and Jackie. To pass the time the two couples decided to attend the movie *Suddenly Last Summer*, but they arrived late and the film's publicity included a warning that no one would be admitted after the show started. So they walked several blocks to the Plaza Theater, then specializing in X-rated movies. "Not the hard-core stuff of later years," said Bradlee, "but a nasty thing called *Private Property*."[29]

When Jack returned from the movie about 11:30 P.M., he found a message from their maid to call Bobby in Charleston. A smile split his face when he learned of his triumph. "As he put the telephone down," reported Theodore White, "he burst out with a very un-Senatorial war whoop." Receiving 60.8 percent of the votes, Kennedy won by 236,510 to Humphrey's 152,187. Immediately he flew to Charleston, arriving at 3:00 A.M., where he thanked West Virginians over TV, and accepted Humphrey's concession. (Humphrey also withdrew from the presidential race.)

Kennedy won for several reasons: his efficient and well-funded organization; his extensive television campaign; his success in addressing the religious issue; the many alliances with local political leaders who agreed to slate him; the support of Franklin D. Roosevelt Jr.; and Kennedy's pledge to help the distressed areas of the state. West Virginia's United Mine Workers failed to bolster Humphrey's campaign as expected. With mines shut down and workers scattered, the union was weak, and its support never materialized.[30]

Religion played a high-profile role, but the media exaggerated when they warned that Kennedy would be awash in anti-Catholic, hillbilly prejudice. West Virginians had elected a host of Catholics to high office in recent years—a U.S. senator, a state attorney general, members of the legislature, and several supreme court judges. "The press publicized the state's tiny Catholic population without noting that only a little more than a quarter of the populace belonged to Protestant denominations," said one expert. "Church membership in West Virginia was among the lowest in the nation."[31]

There were vague accounts that the Kennedy campaign had paid Protestant ministers to persuade their co-religionists to back Kennedy. One Kennedy organizer was quoted as saying that a Protestant minister "was paid to support us."

Congressman Tip O'Neill described a wealthy Boston real estate man, an avid admirer of Kennedy's, who filled a suitcase with cash, drove through West Virginia in a Cadillac, and distributed thousands of dollars to powerful sheriffs who agreed to help Kennedy win. O'Neill insisted these kinds of payoffs happened—"although Jack didn't always know about them." In addition, said O'Neill, Joe Kennedy "made his own arrangements over and above the campaign staff."

Exactly how much each candidate spent in the primary is unknown. The best estimate is that Kennedy outspent Humphrey by about a four-to-one margin in funds publicly disclosed.[32] Investigative reporter Seymour Hersh accused the Kennedy family of spending upward of $2 million in bribes and payoffs. In fact, the few West Virginia officials Hersh actually named merely speculated on how much was spent.

Several writers have charged that the Mafia assisted Kennedy in West Virginia. In *The Kennedys: Dynasty and Disaster*, John Davis asserted, "In December 1961, FBI listening devices picked up evidence of large Mafia donations to the West Virginia campaign that had apparently been disbursed through Frank Sinatra. It was this under-the-table money, used to make payoffs to key election officials, that was to be the deciding factor in the contest." Mafia funds were supposedly channeled through Skinny D'Amato, a shadowy underworld figure with ties to gambling in West Virginia.

No link has ever been established between D'Amato and the 1960 West Virginia primary; he has never been interviewed or even located. "Several illegal gambling clubs operated in 1960 near the lavish Greenbrier Hotel," observed Dan Fleming, but "contacts with club workers at that time failed to uncover any recollection of D'Amato."

Shortly after the primary, Republicans, sensing an explosive issue with which to bludgeon Kennedy in the general election, investigated allegations of illegal campaign contributions; the FBI searched for violations of federal voting laws; and West Virginia's attorney general also investigated, as did the *Charleston Gazette*. None of the probes uncovered any noteworthy evidence of wrongdoing by Kennedy's campaign.[33]

Ed Folliard, a reporter for *The Washington Post,* also investigated the rumors of bribery in the presidential race and concluded that the allegations were nonsense. The editor of the *Logan Banner* wrote, "There was a hell of a lot of vote-buying here, the worst I've ever seen, . . . but it was among local, not Presidential candidates."

Humphrey's aides conceded that giving money to local officials for slating and for poll watchers was "common practice"—part of playing the political game in West Virginia. They only regretted that they couldn't afford to give as much money as the Kennedys. "At this degraded level," Theodore White concluded, "all were evenly matched."

With the West Virginia primary offering impressive proof of Kennedy's appeal, hesitant Democratic leaders in Michigan, New York, and Pennsylvania were now convinced that Kennedy was their best candidate.

Shortly after the primary, Joe Kennedy talked about Jack with Charles Spalding. Joe was astonished at what his son had achieved. "He's so different from me," said Joe. "I couldn't have done what he's done. I don't know how he did it."[34]

Kennedy was less successful in winning support in other Southern states. He wanted to placate the fears of Southern whites about his civil rights views; at the same time, he faced increasing pressure from Northern liberals and blacks to make stronger commitments to civil rights. Consequently, tension on the race issue permeated the Kennedy campaign. Historian Guy Land, who studied Kennedy's Southern strategy, observed that the senator sought "to court white Southern support by appearing to Southern Democrats as the kind of 'safe' candidate they had known in the past, offset by the awareness that a move too far to the right would sacrifice critical Northern and liberal support."

In several tours of the South since 1956, Kennedy had usually addressed nonpartisan forums—chamber of commerce dinners, college graduations— but he had also met informally with prominent Democrats. Sorensen wrote the organizer of one appearance that Kennedy would "like to have an opportunity to meet the state's leading Democrats, office holders, party leaders, and others who will be influential in the future from the Governor on down."

He developed friendships with moderate Democrats in the South, like Mississippi governor James P. Coleman and Louisiana's national committeeman, Camille F. Gravel. "All the major Kennedy contacts in the South were committed to maintaining the southern practices of segregation," observed Land, "but each hoped that the area's political problems could be solved within the Democratic party through calm, open dealing with national party officials."[35]

In the South Kennedy focused on safe, innocuous issues: the foreign-policy weaknesses of the Eisenhower administration, labor racketeering, the misuse of union funds, and the patriotic theme of America's call to greatness. He continued to support the *Brown* decision as the law of the land, but he added that implementation of the ruling would take time. For the most part, he was silent on civil rights during his Southern appearances. The subject arose only during his press conferences, where Kennedy jocularly evaded the question. Asked in Alabama how he would vote on what became the Civil Rights Act of 1957, he replied, "That bill is still in committee and for that reason I am not going to answer that question. After all, I am enjoying myself down here in Alabama. Let's keep it that way."[36]

In mid-December 1959, Sorensen cynically advised Robert Kennedy that when he toured the South on behalf of his brother, he should remind Southerners of the senator's two pro-Southern votes on the Civil Rights Act of 1957. He compared Kennedy's votes with those of Symington and Humphrey. In each case it was Kennedy who was a "friend" of the South:

> There have been two votes on civil rights . . . on which northerners divided into men of reason and men of anti-Southern prejudice:
>
> (a) The Russell challenge to the Nixon ruling which sent the House-passed civil rights bill directly to the Senate Floor without consideration by the Judiciary Committee; and
>
> (b) The jury trial amendment, permitting those convicted of criminal contempt under the Civil Rights Act of 1957 to the protection of trial by jury.

Kennedy supported both motions; Symington and Humphrey voted against them. At the same time, Kennedy told Northern liberals and blacks that his two votes did *not* signal his support of the pro-Southern attitude on race.[37]

At first Kennedy's Southern strategy seemed to be working. By 1959, however, two events had seriously undermined his approach. The federal government's efforts to enforce school desegregation, most notably in the Little Rock crisis of 1957, led to massive Southern resistance and brought to power reactionary Southern politicians, such as the firebrand Ross Barnett in Mississippi. "The Kennedy moderates went down to defeat at the hands of these rabid segregationists, and with their defeat the glow of the Kennedy regional plan changed to gloom," said Land. Moreover, the gradual emergence of Texan Lyndon Johnson as a presidential candidate dimmed Kennedy's prospects in the South. On the eve of the 1960 Democratic convention Kennedy had to scrounge for any votes available in the South.[38]

On Jack's forty-third birthday, May 29, 1960, following his victory in the Oregon primary, Kennedy landed at O'Hare Airport in Chicago. From there Adlai Stevenson's aides Bill Blair and Newton Minow drove him to Stevenson's home in Libertyville, Illinois. Kennedy was seeking Stevenson's support. On the drive Minow advised Kennedy not to bring up the prospect of Stevenson being appointed secretary of state in a Kennedy administration, and Jack agreed. "Why doesn't [Stevenson] come out for me?" Kennedy asked. Because the former governor wanted to remain neutral, came the reply. Kennedy wasn't convinced. "Don't kid me. That means he wants to get it himself."

Because Stevenson remained an uncommitted but potential candidate for a draft at the convention, some of his backers had participated in the covert "Stop Kennedy" effort. The New York Stevenson group gave Humphrey campaign funds; other Stevenson supporters worked for Humphrey in Wisconsin and West Virginia. Once Kennedy was prevented from mustering a majority at the Democratic convention and deadlock ensued, Stevenson's supporters thought, they might stampede the convention into nominating their hero.

By winning in West Virginia Kennedy not only destroyed Humphrey's presidential campaign; he also shattered Stevenson's strategy. It was no longer possible for Stevenson to remain aloof until the Democratic convention in July. "His maneuver had been based on the theory that the front-runner would fall considerably short of the needed majority, and after the first ballot or two had revealed that fact, Kennedy's delegate support would begin to melt away," noted Bert Cochran, one of Stevenson's biographers. Now it was likely that Kennedy would have enough delegates to win on the first ballot. Although it was useless for Stevenson to remain impassive and uninvolved, he still would not endorse Kennedy.[39]

"My difficulty is that I don't think he'd be a good president," Stevenson confidentially told one visitor early in 1960. "I do not feel that he's the right man for the job; I think he's too young; I don't think he fully understands the dimensions of the foreign dilemmas that are coming up, and I cannot in conscience throw my support to someone whom I do not really think is up to it." He added, "I admire him; I think he's a fine young man; I don't see him as a President." For their part, John and Robert Kennedy had come to judge Stevenson as weak and indecisive. Surely, he didn't deserve a third nomination. In public, though, John Kennedy diplomatically tried not to anger Stevenson.

Stevenson gave drastically different accounts of his private meeting with Kennedy in Libertyville. Shortly afterward he telephoned George Ball and ranted about Kennedy's language and demeanor. "Kennedy behaved just like his old man," Ball recalled Stevenson saying. Kennedy said, "I have the votes for the nomination and if you don't give me your support, I'll have to shit all over you. I don't want to do that but I can, and I will if I have to." An angry Stevenson told Ball, "I should have told the son of a bitch off but, frankly, I was shocked and confused by that Irish gutter talk." In truth, while Kennedy might speak caustically in private about Stevenson, he was too diplomatic to talk that way in Stevenson's presence.[40]

Stevenson gave a more accurate account of the meeting in a letter to Arthur Schlesinger on the day of his meeting with Kennedy. The meeting had been cordial, and "was entirely satisfactory from my point of view." Kennedy didn't seem surprised or disappointed by Stevenson's neutrality. "I think—and hope—that I left him with a feeling of great good will, determination not to hinder, and no doubt about my preference and anxiety to help in any way if he is nominated."

But following their meeting in Libertyville, Kennedy became more disillusioned with the former Illinois governor. Stevenson would never be his secretary of state, Jack told Charles Bartlett.[41]

Meanwhile, the Kennedy juggernaut rolled into Los Angeles. Arriving early for the Democratic National Convention, Kennedy's campaign staff was the first to survey the facilities in the Biltmore Hotel and the Los Angeles Convention Center. Were there enough typewriters, pencils, carbon paper, additional secretarial help? Those minute details, in the pressurized atmosphere of a political convention, could make or break a candidate.

Throughout the convention liaison volunteers in each delegation submitted daily written reports to Larry O'Brien. The Kennedy organization established a twenty-four-hour telephone service so the liaison officials could call any time a delegate appeared to be wavering.

Kennedy occupied a suite on the ninth floor of the Biltmore Hotel, one floor above his main campaign operation, staffed by Bobby Kennedy, Larry O'Brien, Pierre Salinger, and Ken O'Donnell. Jack also had a secret retreat for rest and relaxation at 522 North Rossmore Avenue, a small three-floor stucco apartment home owned by the comic actor Jack Haley. Jack's staff installed four telephone lines and stocked the refrigerator with food.[42]

Kennedy's youth remained a persistent problem right up to the convention until he lanced it with a deft blow. On July 2, shortly before the convention opened, former President Truman resigned as a delegate and lashed out at Kennedy during a remarkable press conference in Independence, Missouri. "Senator," he asked in his statement, "are you certain you are quite ready for the country, or that the country is ready for you in the role of President in January 1961?

"May I suggest you be patient."

The seventy-six-year-old Truman urged Kennedy to "put aside" his personal ambitions because of the troubled world situation. Democrats needed to nominate "someone with the greatest possible maturity and experience."

Truman's assault backfired and was widely condemned. Columnist James Reston reproached Truman for his "savage and vindictive" statement. Former advisers to Truman were embarrassed. "Such an attack was misguided in substance, and could only help the Republicans," thought Clark Clifford. Kennedy privately muttered that he wished "old men," long retired from politics, would not mix in the politics of a new generation. Still, Kennedy realized that Truman's attack offered him an opportunity to put to rest the dangerous, submerged issue of his youth.[43]

At a crowded televised news conference two days later, Kennedy brilliantly rebutted Truman. Courteous and serene, he said he would stay in the race. He had been a congressman and a senator for fourteen years. "If we are to establish a test for the Presidency whereby fourteen years in major elective office is insufficient experience. . . . all but a handful of our Presidents since the very founding of this nation should be ruled out, and every President elevated to that office in the twentieth century should have been ruled out, including the three great Democratic Presidents, Woodrow Wilson, Franklin Roosevelt and Harry Truman himself."

Most memorable was Kennedy's defense of the contributions made by Americans under forty-four years of age. "To exclude from positions of trust and command all those below the age of 44 would have kept Jefferson from writing the Declaration of Independence, Washington from commanding the Continental Army, Madison from fathering the Constitution, Hamilton from serving as Secretary of the Treasury, Clay from being elected Speaker of the House and Christopher Columbus from even discovering America."[44]

While defending himself from Truman's remarks, Kennedy mentioned that the new president needed to have "the strength and health and vigor of . . . young men." The paranoid Johnson camp fumed at the comment, thinking it a reference to Lyndon Johnson's heart attack in 1955. India Edwards, cochair of Citizens for Johnson, charged at a press conference on July 4 that Kennedy had Addison's disease.

"Doctors have told me he would not be alive if it were not for cortisone," she said. Her reference to Kennedy's illness came because she "objected to his muscle flexing in boasting about his youth." John B. Connally, director of

Citizens for Johnson, added that he would be happy to make public Johnson's medical record, and have it compared with Kennedy's.

Furious at the accusation, the Kennedy camp immediately snapped back that the Johnson forces were employing "despicable tactics," a sure sign of their "desperation." Kennedy's staff immediately prepared a medical statement quoting from the physicians Janet Travell and Eugene Cohen. Similar to the statement submitted to James Burns, it was reworked and issued by Robert Kennedy:

> John F. Kennedy does not now nor has he ever had an ailment described classically as Addison's disease, which is a tuberculose destruction of the adrenal gland. Any statement to the contrary is malicious and false. . . . In the postwar period [he had] some mild adrenal insufficiency. This is not in any way a dangerous condition. . . . Doctors have stated that this condition he has had might well have arisen out of his wartime experiences of shock and continued malaria.

The statement was another remarkable piece of political double-talk. The media reported the story the following day, but didn't investigate further, and the issue died quickly. The media downplayed the story partly because Edwards's accusation was vague, partially inaccurate, and reeked of political smear. She didn't identify the doctors who gave her the information, admitted her informants had not personally treated Kennedy, and defined Addison's disease as "something to do with lymph glands."[45]

Publicly Johnson took the high road after the charges by Edwards and Connally, saying none of the candidates would be running without medical clearance. But, as Robert Dallek has pointed out, Johnson had been savaging Kennedy in private. "Did you hear the news?" Johnson asked Republican congressman Walter Judd of Minnesota before the Democratic convention. "What news?" Judd replied. "Jack's pediatricians have just given him a clean bill of health!" To Peter Lisagor of the *Chicago Daily News,* Johnson described his opponent as a "little scrawny fellow with rickets."

Ironically, one reason Kennedy disguised his Addison's disease was because in 1960 he had the disease under control. "His Addison's was under beautiful control," said Dr. Elmer Bartels. "The fact that Jack was as active as he was shows we had him under good control. We always saw to it we kept him in perfect balance. I saw him about every two or three months [in the late 1950s]."[46]

Lyndon Johnson formally announced his candidacy on July 5. The issues before the convention, he said, were experience and the capacity to lead. Johnson brought to the convention his broad experience with national issues and his reputation as an astute majority leader. But he was too closely identified with the South. Northern liberals, blacks, and organized labor were either cool or hostile to him, and many Northern Democrats doubted he could carry their states in the general election.

The Democratic convention opened on Monday, July 11. The day before, the newspapers were filled with news about the powerful Kennedy juggernaut. Four governors, including Governor Edmund Brown of California, declared for Kennedy. In addition, Mayor Richard Daley of Illinois caucused his delegation, and said he had nailed down 59.5 votes for Kennedy.

In a last-ditch attempt to defeat Kennedy, Johnson challenged him to a debate, and Kennedy accepted. It was held on the afternoon of July 12 before the Texas delegation and about twenty members of the Massachusetts delegation. Johnson apparently assumed he could demolish his young opponent in a direct confrontation.[47]

At the debate Johnson focused on Kennedy's Senate absenteeism during recent round-the-clock debates on the 1960 civil rights bill. (The watered-down law allowed judges to appoint federal voting registrars, but only under very selective conditions. It passed under Johnson's leadership and was signed on May 6.) As majority leader, he said, he had answered all fifty quorum calls during the six-day session and voted in all forty-five roll calls on the bill and its amendments. But "some Senators," he asserted, answered none of the quorum calls and missed thirty-four of the voting roll calls. (He obviously meant only one senator: Kennedy.)

Kennedy listened, smiled, and when his turn came masterfully deflected Johnson's accusation, stating that he assumed Johnson had been talking about "some of the other candidates and not about me." He and Johnson agreed on the issues, Kennedy said. He praised Johnson's "wonderful record in answering those quorum calls," and said he was "strongly in support of him for majority leader and . . . confident that [with LBJ] in that position we are all going to be able to work together." Jack's aplomb carried the day.[48]

On Wednesday morning, July 13, still campaigning hard, Kennedy visited six caucuses before returning to his hideaway to settle in for the evening nomination session. When the media finally discovered the hideaway, he and Dave Powers slipped down the rear fire escape, climbed the back fence, and were driven to the Beverly Hills villa his father had rented, where he could swim and relax.

A minor scare arose when Adlai Stevenson edged into the contest for the nomination. On July 8, he had made his most explicit indication of his availability, saying he would accept a draft and "do my utmost to win."

On Wednesday evening, a rousing nominating speech for Stevenson by Senator Eugene McCarthy of Minnesota set off a wild, emotional, twenty-five-minute demonstration. "Chanting, placard-waving demonstrators jammed the aisles while the galleries suddenly came alive with thousands of placards and hundreds of demonstrators going round and round in a deafening din," reported *The New York Times*. But the surprising demonstration was mostly contrived. Stevenson supporters with entrance badges had passed them back outside after gaining entrance so that more backers could crowd onto the floor and the galleries.

Following the massive Stevenson floor demonstration, Governor Luther Hodges of North Carolina ran into Bobby Kennedy in the corridor of the convention hall and asked, "Aren't you worried about what they are going to do?" Bobby replied, "Not at all, Governor. We've got it all sewed up. Everything is going to be all right."[49]

Kennedy needed 761 votes to win. When Wyoming came through with enough votes to surpass the mark, Jack threw his score sheet in the air in celebration. After various delegations switched, Kennedy's final total stood at 806 votes. (Lyndon Johnson was second with 409 votes.)

In winning the nomination the Kennedy for President organization—a mixture of intellectuals, relatives, friends, politicians, and technicians—had produced a very professional performance. Like the candidate himself, the key members of the victorious team were young: Ted Sorensen was thirty-two; Harris Wofford, thirty-four; Pierre Salinger, thirty-five; Ken O'Donnell, thirty-six; Robert Wallace, thirty-nine; and Myer Feldman, forty-four.

Kennedy's wealth had been a huge advantage in his drive for the nomination. Money bought radio, television, and newspaper ads; financed his staff; paid for headquarters, meeting halls, and leaflets; and provided an airplane to convey him quickly to campaign stops. Jack's handsome features, personality, charm, and intelligence all contributed to his success. But his dogged, unrelenting effort was the heart of his long campaign. He felt that his hard work earned him the nomination. "I worked like a bastard ever since 1956," he told a reporter. "Take Utah, I've been there five times, [made] six trips to Indiana, and always in the end the hard work pays off. . . . Sooner or later you make a breakthrough."

Kennedy was a gifted young man, wrote James Reston, "experienced well beyond the normal expectation of his years, at home in both the intellectual and political institutions of the nation, articulate particularly in the give and take of modern television discussion and debate, industrious, energetic, and above all courageous."[50]

In the anxious, hectic weeks before the convention, Kennedy had little time to reflect on the selection of his vice-presidential running mate. Thrilled by their first-ballot victory on the evening of July 13, but exhausted and short of sleep, Kennedy and his advisers had difficulty focusing on the vice-presidential announcement expected the next day.

On the morning after the nomination, hordes of political officials and re-porters waited in the hallway outside Kennedy's suite at the Biltmore, all wanting a word with the candidate. At one point, retreating from the hassle, Kennedy looked out his bedroom window and said to no one in particular, "You'd think you'd have a little time to enjoy your nomination." It was "ter-rible," Kennedy told Bobby, that he had only "twenty-four hours to select a vice president."[51]

Three weeks earlier, on June 29, Sorensen had written a memo, "Possible Vice Presidential Nominees," outlining the choices. Lyndon Johnson headed the list. He bolstered the ticket with "farmers, Southerners and Texas," and would be "easier to work with in this position than as Majority Leader." The other possibilities Sorensen listed were Senators Humphrey and Symington, both Midwesterners. Governor Orville Freeman of Minnesota and Senator Henry "Scoop" Jackson of Washington State were also mentioned but were "handicapped by being young and too much like JFK (we don't want the ticket referred to as 'the whiz kids')."

Kennedy had talked privately to various associates about the vice-presidential prospects, but had kept his deepest thoughts close to his vest. If he prematurely disclosed his preference, the announcement might embitter other aspirants and damage his presidential bid. Before the nomination, key political figures, led to believe they might be under consideration for vice president, could be more supportive.[52]

Hubert Humphrey had eliminated himself from consideration on the Tuesday of the convention when he retracted his commitment to Kennedy and endorsed Stevenson. Three other prominent prospects—Symington, Jackson, and Freeman—were all acceptable to the liberals and labor. After Kennedy's nomination, *The New York Times* assumed that Symington was at the top of the vice-presidential list.

The one name that liberal and labor delegates never mentioned was Lyn-don Johnson. "The labor people had warned me repeatedly that they did not want Johnson on the Kennedy ticket," Ken O'Donnell later wrote. "I had promised them that there was no chance of such a choice. We had given the same assurance, with Kennedy's knowledge, to wavering liberal delegates."

Kennedy's staff was incensed when Edwards and Connally revealed Kennedy had Addison's disease, and when Johnson publicly implied that Joe Kennedy had been a Nazi appeaser before World War II. "I was never any Chamberlain umbrella policy man," Johnson told a group of delegates before the balloting, a remark printed in the press. "I never thought Hitler was right."

John Kennedy, though, seemed to be the only person in his entourage not resentful of Johnson's barbs. Such mudslinging was a part of the game of politics, something that had to be endured. Overall he admired and respected Johnson.[53]

Conventional wisdom assumed that Johnson would decline a vice-presidential offer because of the power he wielded in the Senate. Robert Dallek, however, judged that Johnson's best days as majority leader were over. "If Kennedy won the presidency, the White House would set the legislative agenda and Lyndon would be little more than the President's man in the Senate."

On July 5, while Johnson was announcing his candidacy for president, he signaled his availability and surprised reporters during the question-and-answer session when he passed up an opportunity to rule himself out as a possible vice-presidential selection. He would "serve my country in any capacity where my country thought my services were essential."

Why Kennedy might want the Texan on the ticket is obvious. As the leader of the Democrats in the Senate, runner-up in the balloting for President, spokesman for a large state that would be difficult for Kennedy to carry, Johnson was the strongest potential running mate. He provided excellent balance for the ticket: Southerner and Northerner, maturity and youth, moderate-conservative and moderate-liberal, Protestant and Irish Catholic. (There were precedents for Kennedy's decision. In 1928 New York Catholic Al Smith had selected the Protestant Southern senator Joe Robinson. Twice New York's Franklin Roosevelt picked Texas congressional leader John Garner as his running mate.)[54]

Behind the scenes, key individuals were lobbying for the selection of Johnson. Pennsylvania's Governor David Lawrence, columnist Joe Alsop, *The Washington Post*'s Philip Graham, and Jack's father—all told Kennedy that they wanted the Texan.

Following Kennedy's nomination various Southern political leaders agreed that if the Democrats were to win the general election, they needed to carry the South. To carry the South, the Democrats needed a prominent Southerner on the ticket. Southerners wanted Johnson.

Up until Kennedy's nomination, Sam Rayburn, the wise and powerful congressman from Texas, speaker of the House, and close adviser to Johnson, was opposed to LBJ accepting the second spot on the ticket. After Kennedy's nomination, though, several influential Southern Democrats changed Rayburn's mind and convinced him that only a Kennedy-Johnson ticket could defeat the Republican Richard Nixon. Hale Boggs, congressman from Louisiana and vice chairman of the Democratic National Committee, helped convert Rayburn. Rayburn asked Boggs, "What do you think about [LBJ as the vice-presidential nominee]?" Boggs replied, "Well, do you want Nixon to be president of the United States?" "You know I don't want that to happen," Rayburn replied, adding, "Well, that's right. [LBJ's] got to do it."[55]

Conflicting perceptions make it difficult to reconstruct the exact sequence of events that led to the selection of Johnson. On the chaotic morning after Kennedy's nomination, at about eight o'clock on July 14, he phoned Johnson and asked to see him. He arrived at Johnson's room at about ten.

What happened in Johnson's room has been the subject of intense speculation. Johnson apparently had expected an offer, wanted an offer, and perceived that Kennedy did extend him a firm offer, which Johnson immediately accepted. But as historian Jeff Shesol has shown, Kennedy "appears to have wanted only to determine LBJ's state of mind and to make a final choice shortly thereafter; but found, to his discomfort, he had inadvertently committed himself to a running mate he was not certain he wanted, a running mate who might inspire a revolt by liberals and labor. JFK was trapped."

Robert Kennedy later claimed that Jack merely wanted to flatter Johnson by asking him. LBJ would then decline, and Kennedy was free to ask someone else. Kennedy never dreamed Johnson would take the nomination, according to the younger Kennedy. Bobby later described his brother as shocked. "We spent the rest of the day alternating between thinking it was good and thinking that it wasn't good that he'd offered him the vice presidency—and how could [we] get out of it," Bobby said.

Bobby's version of events is probably inaccurate. Several people had already told Kennedy that LBJ had a serious interest in taking the vice presidency. Kennedy must have been confident that Lyndon would accept. Moreover, Kennedy had earlier told several key politicians that he strongly desired a Kennedy-Johnson ticket.

Robert Kennedy subsequently visited Johnson's suite three times. Clumsily trying to convince Johnson not to accept the nomination, he stirred up a hornet's nest each time. Although accounts are jumbled and contradictory, each visit clearly generated more confusion and irritation.

At about 4:00 P.M., Bobby Kennedy returned for his third visit to Johnson's suite. Bobby recalled, "I went down to see if I could get him to withdraw." Jeff Shesol observed:

> Johnson himself was extremely agitated, "about to jump out of his skin," ranting to [Phil] Graham that Bobby Kennedy was trying to pry him off the ticket. "Call Jack Kennedy and straighten out this mess!" [Sam] Rayburn barked at Graham.
>
> "Jack," Graham said into the phone, "Bobby is down here and is telling the speaker and Lyndon that there is opposition and that Lyndon should withdraw."
>
> "Oh," Jack replied serenely, "that's all right; Bobby's been out of touch and doesn't know what's happening."

Kennedy calmly read over the phone a press release about the vice presidency to the agitated Johnson. "Do you really want me?" Johnson asked.

Kennedy replied, "Yes." Johnson said, "Well, if you really want me, I'll do it."[56]

When Johnson's selection was announced, many Northern liberal delegates were irate. Michigan's Governor G. Mennen Williams told the press that he thought it was a "mistake" and a "disappointment." Joe Rauh called it a "double cross." But Kennedy's forces at the convention maneuvered behind the scenes, preventing an uproar on the floor, and Johnson's nomination was ratified.

Without Johnson on the ticket, Southerners might have reacted to the convention results with sullenness and resentment. What with the liberal, pro–civil rights platform and a Massachusetts Catholic presidential nominee, the convention was nearly a total defeat for Southern conservatives. Johnson's selection helped soothe their frayed nerves. *The New York Times* judged the selection a "swift, bold stroke," a "bridge to the South."

Afterward, together with Joe Kennedy at his Beverly Hills villa, Robert Kennedy was gloomy. "Yesterday was the best day of my life," he said, "and this is the worst day of my life." Jack was exhausted. "He had no animation in his face at all," said Charles Bartlett, who was also with the three Kennedys. "I remember old Joe Kennedy in his velvety dressing coat and slippers with fox heads on the toes. He was looking out at the sunset and said, 'Jack, in two weeks they will be saying this is the smartest thing you ever did.' "[57]

On Friday, July 15, fifty thousand spectators listened to Kennedy's acceptance speech in the huge Los Angeles Coliseum. The crowd was disappointing; the stadium, built for the 1932 Olympic Games, could seat over one hundred thousand. Speaking from the platform in the vast stadium, Kennedy had little empathy with the crowd scattered far away; helicopters hovering overhead proved a distraction. Under the circumstances, the haggard Kennedy found it nearly impossible to deliver a forceful call to arms. With little sleep, his reflexes stretched to the breaking point, he operated on reserve strength.

In his speech he warned that the national road to a "New Frontier" called for more sacrifices, not more luxuries. "Woodrow Wilson's New Freedom promised our nation a new political and economic framework," he said. "Franklin Roosevelt's New Deal promised security and succor to those in need. But the New Frontier of which I speak is not a set of promises—it is a set of challenges."

On July 17, a crowd of fifteen thousand supporters turned out to greet the new Democratic nominee at Logan International Airport in East Boston. From there Kennedy headed for Hyannis Port, where he spent the next two weeks resting and conferring with advisers.[58]

24

NIXON VS. KENNEDY

Both of the 1960 presidential candidates were young—Kennedy was forty-three; Richard Nixon, forty-seven. But Kennedy seemed much younger. "Kennedy could have passed for a man in his mid-thirties," noted Nixon's biographer Stephen Ambrose. "Nixon, for a man in his mid-fifties." Kennedy appeared vigorous and athletic, and the family's love for touch football and baseball games was widely known. As much as he loved sports, Nixon had no athletic grace or ability.

Both loved politics, competed intensely, and drove themselves to exhaustion. Nixon campaigned in all fifty states; Kennedy, in forty-five. Kennedy was able to conceal his exhaustion, to relax occasionally, and always looked vigorous and fresh in his appearances.

Kennedy was far more gregarious, enjoying the company of reporters and fellow politicians, swapping stories and wisecracks. Nixon was a loner, who socialized because he had to, not because he wanted to. "Kennedy had a marvelous sense of humor; Nixon, almost none at all. Kennedy delighted in poking fun at himself, while Nixon took himself with the utmost seriousness."

Nixon's style was folksy. Introducing his wife to the crowd came naturally. "I told you I'd bring Pat out to see you, and here she is," the vice president said. "Now I ask you, isn't she wonderful? Wasn't she worth waiting for?" Kennedy would never parade Jackie on stage; it took him three weeks of campaigning before he blurted out, "My wife's home, having another baby."

Nixon flashed a broad smile at his audience; Kennedy's was more diffident and hesitant. Nixon waved vigorously to the crowd, and often pointed to someone leaning out of a top-story window. Kennedy's wave, like his smile, was tentative, seldom reaching shoulder height.[1]

Well briefed, Nixon often praised the valor of the local football team. A polished orator, he knew how to generate applause and usually had at least a half dozen applause lines—remarks carefully designed to elicit shouts of approval and hand clapping. His timing was excellent. Kennedy used few oratorical tricks, seldom made homespun references to the local community, didn't try to elicit applause, and seldom even acknowledged it.

"A Nixon speech is well paced and carefully balanced; it builds as it goes and rises to a crescendo with the kind of emotional peroration that his audience will find ringing in their minds as they head homeward," *Newsweek* reported. "Kennedy plunges into his speech, with almost messianic fervor, delivers his message, and ends with an abruptness that often seems anticlimactic."

As the vice president under Ike, candidate Nixon was compelled to defend the Eisenhower record; Kennedy was free to exploit its shortcomings. He charged that the administration had failed to keep pace with the Soviets in education, technology, and ballistic missiles. America's prestige had declined in the world, particularly among the newly emerging nations of Africa and Asia, and the administration had lost Cuba to the Communists.[2]

Shortly after the Democratic convention, Kennedy asked Archibald Cox to gather a group of economic scholars to brief him on economic issues in preparation for the fall campaign. When they met on August 3, 1960, on the Kennedy family's yacht off Hyannis Port, Jack told the group, "Tell me the best thing to do."

While cruising around for several hours, they discussed several economic problems, which, Cox recalled, "was all an eye-opener to him." Kennedy told the scholars that he had taken "Economics A" at Harvard with Professor Russ Nixon, a Communist Party sympathizer, and received only a C. "I had Russ Nixon for my teacher, so don't omit anything," Jack said. The professors smiled knowingly.

The economists explained that faster growth depended on getting businessmen to increase their rate of investment in new plants and equipment. Lower interest rates would reduce the cost of borrowing investment

capital. But cheap money posed its own danger: inflation. "To avoid inflation, Kennedy would have to offset increased business spending with decreased spending either by the government or private consumers; that is,
he would have either to put a brake on the federal budget or raise taxes on
individuals."[3]

Harvard economist Seymour Harris, who had advised Senator Kennedy
earlier on Massachusetts's economic problems, later remarked, "I think this
was the first real education he had in modern fiscal policy." Harris spoke on
protecting the dollar and preventing inflation. "I was really quite surprised at
how much the Senator picked up inside of one hour on this really crucial,
very highly technical problem," he remembered.

Kennedy was particularly impressed by MIT economist Paul Samuelson,
who forcefully addressed the problem of the international balance of payments. He asked Cox to get Samuelson more closely involved as an adviser in
the campaign.

After the briefing, Kennedy served lunch aboard the yacht. Samuelson
had looked forward to a gourmet lunch. "The chef took out frankfurters and
beans. That wasn't my idea of a gourmet outing on Nantucket Sound."

Ted Sorensen wanted Cox's group to generate only raw material, not
speeches. Group authorship could never replace one speechwriter with a pen
or typewriter. But Cox's academic writers had little experience with political campaigns. Worried, Arthur Schlesinger Jr. wrote Cox, criticizing a proposed speech on defense policy written by Walter Rostow. "The speech is
heavy, prosy and boring," Schlesinger cautioned. "Conceivably it might be
okay for the Senate, but it would be death before the American Legion."[4]

"Most of the intellectuals who tried their hand at speech drafts came up
with rather dead prose more suited to articles in learned journals than delivery from the stump," observed James Sundquist, who worked with Cox for
part of the campaign. "And Cox was not an expert editor who could trans-
late them into usable speeches."

On September 5, before a huge Labor Day audience in Detroit, Kennedy
hacked partway through a speech written by Cox on the economy, then gave
up and ad-libbed the rest. Cox's text, filled with facts, figures, percentages,
and average annual rates of interest, did not inspire the crowd. The *Detroit
News* described the address as "booby-trapped with clumsy figures of
speech." Upset with Cox, Kennedy was less willing to use his material. For
his part, Cox complained that Kennedy didn't use his group's work.[5]

Chronic tension emerged between Sorensen and Cox. In a letter to his
wife, Cox described Sorensen as "haughty." During the fall Cox and
Sundquist flew to Minneapolis to hash out differences with Sorensen. From
there they flew with Sorensen to Duluth. In midflight the conflict boiled

over. Sorensen angrily disparaged Cox's efforts, saying his material "read like magazine articles instead of speeches delivered from the stump." Cox's Washington operation was virtually useless, he said.

At a luncheon in New York on October 11, 1960, Kennedy discussed his staff problems with Schlesinger. He regretted the tension between Cox and Sorensen, but added emphatically, "Ted is indispensable to me." Everyone would have to adjust and tolerate the situation.

Cox's group did enjoy some success. During a speech in Denver, using a paper by Professor Robert C. Wood of MIT, Kennedy spoke on urban renewal. "In those days," Wood recalled, "just to have a politician talk about urban problems was very rare." Ultimately the Cox group did provide an infusion of raw material for Sorensen and Goodwin. Goodwin appreciated having access to the group's studies. "I don't know what the hell we would have talked about without it."[6]

Some leading liberal Democrats remained unenthusiastic about the party's nominee. On August 26, Arthur Schlesinger complained to Kennedy that the candidate still had not won over a crucial group of traditional Democrats: the liberals, the reformers, and the intellectuals. Schlesinger admitted that their numbers were small. "But these are the kinetic people, and their participation or non-participation profoundly affects the atmosphere and drive of a Democratic campaign." As a result, the historian concluded, "the campaign thus far lacks much sense of crusading urgency."

Four days later, after returning from the meeting of the national board of Americans for Democratic Action, Schlesinger was even more alarmed. The board had endorsed the Kennedy-Johnson ticket, but did so tepidly. "I am now convinced that the situation is more serious than I supposed," he wrote Kennedy.

"As someone put it, 'We don't trust Kennedy and we don't like Johnson; but Nixon is so terrible that we have to endorse the Democrats.'" A paragraph was eliminated from the board's endorsement of Kennedy: "In the critical fields of human concern—foreign affairs, economic and social policy, civil rights—he has shown himself the aggressive champion of creative liberalism." The majority of the board "simply refused to believe these things about you," Schlesinger reported. He strongly urged Kennedy to move quickly to reassert himself with the kinetic liberals.

Schlesinger exaggerated the potential influence of the "kinetic" liberals, whose dynamic energy didn't extend very far—as Adlai Stevenson learned twice. Their impact—and the impact of the ADA—was much less than he supposed. If Kennedy had tried to appease liberal ADA members, he would have lost more votes than he gained. Besides, as Schlesinger indicated, for kinetic liberals and the ADA the alternative to Kennedy was the hated Richard Nixon.[7]

In late July, after his grueling speaking regimen at the Democratic convention, Kennedy began suffering from laryngitis. The problem lasted about two months, and occasionally unnerved him. One day in his Senate office, recalled Evelyn Lincoln, "He paced the floor, brushed his hair back a hundred times, and kept hitting his fist on the table."

David Blair McCloskey, a Boston University speech therapist recruited to help the candidate, gave him exercises to strengthen his vocal cords and ordered him to keep quiet on board the *Caroline,* to scratch his thoughts on notepads instead.

When his voice was at its worst, Kennedy scrawled hundreds of notes, using a ballpoint pen or felt-tip marker, writing on yellow-lined legal pads or on the back of envelopes. "I am exhausted," he wrote as he careened from state to state. "My voice is about to go completely."

"How long the rest?" he penned Des Rosiers. "I want to use the inhalator. Will you be at the hotel—I want my neck rubbed."

"It's all a matter of breathing," McCloskey explained. He wanted Kennedy to use his voice like a singer would, breathing from the diaphragm, but Kennedy never mastered the technique. Gradually, though, his throat healed.

"The problem of my voice is an old one," Kennedy wrote Eleanor Roosevelt after the election. "I attempted to improve it with voice instructions, but I have relaxed my efforts since then. It is difficult to change nature, but I will attempt to nudge it."[8]

After vacationing on the Riviera, Joe Kennedy returned to the United States in early September to a campaign he hadn't expected. "I came home to find the campaign not between a Democrat and a Republican, but between a Catholic and a Protestant," he wrote a friend. "How effectively we can work against it, I do not know."

John Kennedy's nomination rekindled anti-Catholic agitation. At the end of August a Minnesota Baptist convention declared that Catholicism posed "as serious a threat to America as atheistic communism." A few days later the general presbytery of the Assemblies of God, with over a half a million members, accused the Catholic Church of bigotry "as reflected in its position of infallibility of its leadership."[9]

Anti-Catholic sentiment peaked on September 7, 1960, with a formidable attack by a new group of prominent clergymen, the National Council of Citizens for Religious Freedom. Composed of 150 ministers and laymen, the group represented mostly evangelical conservative Protestants organized primarily in the National Association of Evangelicals. Their two-thousand-word manifesto contended that Kennedy's religion was "one of the most significant issues" of the 1960 campaign because, no matter what the senator claimed, "his church insists that he is duty-bound to submit to its direction."

The most prominent member of the group was Dr. Norman Vincent Peale, longtime Republican, friend of Vice President Nixon, and the best-selling author of *The Power of Positive Thinking*. Other members were L. Nelson Bell, editor of *Christianity Today;* Harold J. Ockenga, former president of the National Association of Evangelicals; and Kennedy's antagonist Daniel Poling.

Kennedy was unacceptable as President, the manifesto said, because no Catholic could be free of the hierarchy's "determined efforts . . . to breach the wall of separation of church and state." *Time* reported that Peale told the group that it was "a good thing to have this crisis forced upon us; it will bring us together. . . . Our American culture is at stake." At a press conference Peale and Ockenga charged that it was inconceivable "that a Roman Catholic President would not be under extreme pressure by the hierarchy to accede to its policies with respect to foreign relations . . . including representation to the Vatican."[10]

No Catholics, Jews, or liberal Protestants had been invited to join Peale's group; no details were given out on who organized it, who financed it, or who drafted its declaration. The group's pronouncement largely discounted Kennedy's legislative record and public statements and ascribed to him the political positions of the Catholic Church (positions the manifesto often distorted). Its propaganda stated that "spokesmen for the Vatican in the United States have repeatedly urged the establishment of diplomatic relations with the Roman Catholic Church," but it said nothing about the fact that Kennedy had repeatedly declared his opposition to diplomatic relations. Nor did the group mention that Presidents Franklin D. Roosevelt (an Episcopalian) and Harry Truman (a Baptist) had favored establishing diplomatic relations.[11]

An avalanche of criticism descended on the Peale group. Dr. John Bennett and Dr. Reinhold Niebuhr of Union Theological Seminary denounced the organization as unrepresentative of Protestant thought, reflecting "blind prejudice." Adlai Stevenson quipped, "I find Paul appealing and Peale appalling." Rebukes of Peale appeared in Catholic, Presbyterian, and Methodist publications. *The Philadelphia Inquirer* dropped Peale's weekly column.

Battered by the criticism, Peale retreated. Resigning from the National Council of Citizens for Religious Freedom, he declared that the people have a right to elect a man of any religion to the presidency. "I was not duped, I was just stupid," he later told a reporter.[12]

On the heels of the Peale group controversy came one of Kennedy's most dramatic campaign appearances. At 8:55 on the evening of Monday, September 12, 1960, he sat down on the dais in the ballroom of the Rice Hotel in Houston, Texas. Three hundred evangelical clergymen waited for his 9:00 P.M. speech to be broadcast on Texas television.

In early September the Greater Houston Ministerial Association had asked to meet with him during his forthcoming trip to Houston. Discussion among Kennedy's advisers was spirited and divided on whether to accept the invitation. Sorensen and Robert Kennedy pressed for the meeting, while Ken O'Donnell, Lyndon Johnson, and Sam Rayburn were cool to the idea. Kennedy decided to attend and address the religious issue one more time.

Worried about the upcoming speech, Johnson sulked. Rayburn told Kennedy, "These are not ministers. These are politicians who are going around in robes and saying they're ministers, but they're nothing but politicians. They hate your guts and they're going to tear you to pieces, and you shouldn't have done it."[13]

John Cogley and James Wine, both special assistants on religious issues for Kennedy's campaign, made the arrangements in Houston, and agreed there would be no screening of questions beforehand. That would seem too contrived. Sorensen was furious when he learned that Kennedy could be asked any question from the floor. This was putting too much pressure on the candidate. "They can ask him anything, and he's on television!" Sorensen screamed. Kennedy, however, accepted the arrangement without complaint. "He seemed to take it as one more ordeal he had to go through," Cogley recalled. While on the plane to Houston, Cogley grilled the candidate with questions the ministers were likely to ask.

It turned out that Kennedy's nervous advisers underestimated his improved ability to handle questions about his religion. The *Look* interview, the West Virginia campaign, the ASNE speech, and the Democratic convention had prepared him well. During his Houston appearance Kennedy was polished, relaxed, and polite; the ministers, on the other hand, appeared tense, apprehensive, and some even hostile. "In short," said one historian, "viewers witnessed a confrontation between Olympian grace and training, and sandlot ineptitude."[14]

In his opening remarks, Kennedy pointed out that issues far more critical than his religion should be stressed in the campaign. Among them were

> the spread of Communist influence, until it now festers ninety miles off the coast of Florida; the humiliating treatment of our President and Vice-President by those who no longer respect our power; the hungry children I saw in West Virginia, the old people who cannot pay their doctor bills, the families forced to give up their farms; an America with too many slums, with too few schools, and too late to the moon and outer space.

Nonetheless, with all the controversy about his religion, he needed to state again "not what kind of church I believe in, for that should be important only to me—but what kind of America I believe in."

I believe in an America where the separation of church and state is absolute—where no Catholic prelate would tell the President (should he be Catholic) how to act, and no Protestant minister would tell his parishioners for whom to vote—where no church or church school is granted any public funds or political preference—and where no man is denied public office merely because his religion differs from the President who might appoint him or the people who might elect him.

I believe in an America that is officially neither Catholic, Protestant, nor Jewish—where no public official either requests or accepts instructions on public policy from the pope, the National Council of Churches, or any other ecclesiastical source—where no religious body seeks to impose its will directly or indirectly upon the general populace or the public acts of its officials—and where religious liberty is so indivisible that an act against one church is treated as an act against all.

The finger of suspicion was currently aimed at Catholics, but someday it might be pointed at Jews, Quakers, Unitarians, or Baptists. "Today I may be the victim—but tomorrow it may be you."

Finally, I believe in an America where religious intolerance will someday end—where all men and all churches are treated as equal—where every man has the same right to attend or not attend the church of his choice—where there is no Catholic vote, no anti-Catholic vote, no block voting of any kind—and where Catholics, Protestants, and Jews, at both the lay and pastoral level, will refrain from those attitudes of disdain and division which have so often marred their works in the past, and promote instead the American ideal of brotherhood. . . .

This is the kind of America I believe in—and this is the kind I fought for in the South Pacific, and the kind my brother died for in Europe. No one suggested then that we might have a "divided loyalty," that we did "not believe in liberty," or that we belonged to a disloyal group that threatened the "freedoms for which our forefathers died."

Since Kennedy was to speak at the Alamo on his way to Houston, he insisted that his staff research the history of the shrine of Texas independence, searching for Catholics who may have fought there. The staff learned that some who had died had Irish-American names, so in one line of his speech Kennedy cleverly remarked, "[S]ide by side with Bowie and Crockett died

McCafferty and Bailey and Carey, but no one knows whether they were Catholics or not. For there was no religious test at the Alamo."

He wanted to be judged on the basis of his record during fourteen years in Congress, on his declared stands against a U.S. ambassador to the Vatican and against aid to parochial schools, not on the basis of scurrilous publications "that carefully select quotations out of context from the statements of Catholic leaders, usually in other countries, frequently in other centuries." These were his own views, he stressed,

> for, contrary to common newspaper usages I am not the Catholic candidate for President. I am the Democratic Party's candidate for President who happens also to be a Catholic. I do not speak for my church on public matters—and the Church does not speak for me.
>
> Whatever issue may come before me as President—on birth control, divorce, censorship, gambling, or any other subject—I will make my decision in accordance with these views, in accordance with what my conscience tells me to be the national interest, and without regard to outside religious pressures or dictates. And no power or threat of punishment could cause me to decide otherwise.

Kennedy deliberated carefully about the next passage, which he knew would be controversial. He said he would resign his office should the time come when the presidency would require him to violate his conscience or the national interest, but he didn't think any conflict "even remotely possible." He warned that "if this election is decided on the basis that forty million Americans lost their chance of being President on the day they were baptized, then it is the whole nation that will be the loser, in the eyes of Catholics and non-Catholics around the world, in the eyes of history, and in the eyes of our own people."[15]

Afterward the ministers asked pointed questions which he answered with confidence and poise. If a meeting or service was held in a Protestant sanctuary, would he attend? Yes, said Kennedy, he would attend any service that had any connection with his public office, and in the case of a private ceremony—weddings, funerals—he would participate and had already participated.

If elected President, would he use his influence to stop the persecution of Protestant missionaries in Catholic-dominated countries in South America and Spain? Of course, he replied; he would encourage freedom everywhere. He strongly supported "the right of free speech, the right of assembly, the right of free religious practice, and I would hope that the United States and the President would stand for those rights all around the globe without regard to geography or religion."

Would Kennedy ask Richard Cardinal Cushing to present to the Vatican Kennedy's statements on the separation of church and state so that the Vatican might officially authorize such beliefs for all Catholics in the United States? Kennedy responded:

I do not accept the right of any ecclesiastical official to tell me what I shall do in the sphere of my public responsibility as an elected official. I do not propose to ask Cardinal Cushing to ask the Vatican to take some action. I do not propose to interfere with their free right to do exactly what they want. There is no doubt in my mind that the viewpoint that I have expressed tonight publicly represents the opinion of the overwhelming majority of American Catholics.[16]

In concluding, the senator thanked the association for its invitation. He said he didn't regard reasonable questions about his religion as prejudiced or bigoted. His only objection was if someone voted against him *solely* because of his religion.

I would consider that unreasonable. What I would consider to be reasonable, in an exercise of free will and free choice, is to ask the candidate to state his views as broadly as possible, to investigate his record to see whether what he states he believes, and then to make an independent, rational judgment as to whether he could be entrusted with this highly important position.

When Kennedy began, the audience seemed sullen, almost hostile. But as he spoke, the ministers warmed up, and some applauded. The speech was powerful and eloquent, his best of the 1960 campaign and one of the most important in his political career.

Kennedy was pleased, as he often was when he met a crisis with effective action. He knew he had passed a difficult test. In the days following Houston, he was noticeably more relaxed and confident.[17]

"I didn't take an actual poll of the correspondents," said journalist Edward P. Morgan of the Houston appearance, "but I didn't need to. We were all so enormously struck and impressed." For the first time Sam Rayburn thought that Kennedy had defused the religious issue. "As we say in my part of Texas," said the delighted Rayburn, "he ate 'em blood raw!"

After Houston, the *Christian Century* switched from opposing Kennedy to being neutral. The nondenominational *Christianity in Crisis,* a liberal journal focused on modern theology and world affairs, became more supportive. Still, most Protestant periodicals remained skeptical or hostile. Two Presbyterian publications, *Presbyterian Life* and *Christianity Today,* argued that it was not enough for Kennedy to state his position; the Catholic Church itself must announce that it accepted his views.

For the next seven weeks the Kennedy campaign organization saturated the nation with edited television tapes of the speech. The program played in forty states.[18]

After intense negotiations, both candidates agreed to four one-hour debates to air simultaneously on the three television networks and all four radio networks. They would be held on September 26, October 7, October 13, and October 21. The first would originate in Chicago. The debates had the potential for reaching a huge audience. In 1960 forty-six million American homes had televisions, 25 percent more TV households than only four years earlier.

Unlike Kennedy, Nixon had participated in debate while in school. Beforehand Nixon was better known nationally, and was viewed as the more mature and experienced candidate. By confidently agreeing to debate, Nixon risked building an audience for Kennedy. He also underestimated his foe. Kennedy had performed well debating Lodge in 1952 and Humphrey in West Virginia, and, observed Sorensen, "He had, in a sense, been preparing for this moment for years, in hundreds of rapid-fire question-and-answer sessions with newsmen, college audiences, [and] TV panels."[19]

It turned out that Nixon could not be at his best during the first debate because of illness. He had bumped his knee getting into a car, and twelve days later the knee had become infected and intensely painful. He spent two weeks in bed at Walter Reed Hospital taking penicillin and other antibiotics. Instead of quickly seizing the initiative in the general election, as he had planned, he was losing it to Kennedy and missing precious campaign time. Now he had to debate his nemesis while still not fully recovered from his illness.

Kennedy's television adviser, J. Leonard Reinsch, was a longtime communications consultant for Democrats, including Presidents Roosevelt and Truman. Reinsch had recently arranged logistics for the Democratic convention. After winning the nomination, Kennedy asked him to assist with television during the fall. "Television may be the most important part of the campaign," Kennedy told him. "It may decide the election. Will you handle my TV arrangements?" Reinsch agreed.[20]

On the eve of the first debate a Gallup poll underscored its importance and dramatic tension. The country was evenly split: 47 percent for each candidate.

In Chicago Reinsch carefully inspected every detail of the setting and lighting. The day before the event Kennedy looked over the set design and shooting angles; Nixon received the same invitation but declined, rejecting an opportunity to inspect the television venue.

CBS offered Nixon the services of its professional makeup artist, but Nixon refused. Instead, he had a nonexpert adviser apply a pancake makeup designed to conceal his stubble of beard. Kennedy, looking fit and tanned, needed only a small amount of makeup. Kennedy's dark blue suit provided a crisp contrast with the bleak gray background. By comparison, Nixon's light gray suit blended blandly with the set.

Kennedy rearranged his schedule to provide enough time for briefing and rest. Reinsch coached him to watch Nixon while Nixon was speaking, but to talk directly to the television viewer. Kennedy should use each question as a springboard to rebut an earlier Nixon remark.

Before the program aired, Nixon was nervous, pacing up and down, mopping his brow. After brief introductory remarks, moderator Howard K. Smith introduced Kennedy, who confidently presented his eight-minute opening comments. He concluded by saying, "I think it is time America started moving again."[21]

Nixon startled his supporters by opening with a lame, conciliatory statement. Apparently hoping to persuade voters that he was no longer just a partisan "gut-fighter," but a statesman, Nixon began by agreeing with Kennedy's goals: "The things that Senator Kennedy has said, many of us can agree with. . . . I subscribe completely to the spirit that Senator Kennedy has expressed tonight. . . . I know Senator Kennedy feels as deeply about these problems as I do, but our disagreement is not about the goals for America but only about the means to reach those goals." After one of Kennedy's answers, Nixon weakly replied, "No comment." Kennedy aggressively carried the fight, correcting a questioner's assertion, taking the time to effectively refute earlier Nixon statements.

"Mr. Nixon was debating with Mr. Kennedy as if a board of judges were scoring points," Theodore White pointed out; "Nixon was addressing himself to Kennedy—but Kennedy was addressing himself to the audience that was the nation."[22]

The one question on everyone's lips was why did Nixon look so haggard, so worn, so grim? His facial muscles tensed, sweat appeared on his brow and cheeks; sometimes he forced a smile unrelated to his words. His eyes shifted and darted. By contrast Kennedy appeared fresh, vibrant, relaxed.

Seventy-five million viewers watched the first debate. The next day few could recall what the candidates had said. But Kennedy had certainly enhanced his image—and image won out over content. Newspaper editorials mostly gave Kennedy the edge, as did public opinion polls. In *The Atlanta Constitution* Eugene Patterson wrote, "The [television] medium is good to

Kennedy and most unkind to Nixon. It makes Kennedy look forceful. It makes Nixon look guilty."

The first TV debate was Kennedy's best answer to the Republican charge that he was immature. "Kennedy did not show that he was Nixon's master," noted *Newsweek*, "but he did show that he was Nixon's match." Following the debate ten Southern governors, earlier lukewarm toward Kennedy, announced their full support. Overnight, it appeared to Theodore White, crowds "seethed with enthusiasm and multiplied in numbers, as if the sight of him [on TV] . . . had given him a 'star quality' reserved only for television and movie idols."[23]

In the next three debates Nixon became more aggressive and improved his image, taking precautions not to look so wan. He was rested, ate better, and made sure to carefully apply his makeup. In the second, the viewing audience plunged from seventy-five million to sixty-one million; viewership held steady during the entire hour of the first debate, but dropped off sharply during the final half hour of the second.

But the final three debates were anticlimactic. All three were judged to be very close, but they had less impact than the first. The debates as a whole, said most poll surveys, were won by Kennedy.[24]

To win the black vote the Kennedy campaign felt that certain pragmatic— some would say cynical—steps needed to be taken. At the suggestion of Mayor Richard Daley of Chicago, Kennedy named Congressman William Dawson as chairman of the civil rights section of the campaign. Dawson was a "well-known shakedown artist from Chicago's notoriously corrupt Second Ward," noted Evan Thomas. The black congressman "was given a specially constructed office known among the staffers as Uncle Tom's Cabin and rarely spoken to again."

Congressman Adam Clayton Powell of Harlem requested three hundred thousand dollars from the Kennedy campaign to establish a nationwide get-out-the-vote drive. Kennedy's wary black adviser Louis Martin knew Powell's real intention was to pocket the money. Robert Kennedy finally agreed to pay Powell fifty thousand dollars for ten speeches.

In early August Sargent Shriver reported to Sorensen on the arrangements being made with Dawson, Powell, and black ministers, saying, "If Kennedy can take care of Dawson and we can take care of Powell and the ministers, I think we will have the Negro situation well in hand."[25]

Often quoted as evidence of Kennedy's cynicism about civil rights was his remark to Harris Wofford in August 1960. While driving to his Senate office, Kennedy saw Wofford waiting for a taxi. "Jump in," he said. Then, with his left hand tapping the window of his convertible, Kennedy said, "Now, in five minutes tick off the ten things a President ought to do to clean up this goddamn civil rights mess." Rather than cynicism, his remark actually reflected his flippant, offhand wit.

Marjorie Lawson, Boston's NAACP leader and a secondary adviser to Kennedy on civil rights during the campaign, didn't think Kennedy's campaign staff knew how to handle black voters, at least initially. "I think particularly Sarge [Shriver] thought . . . that he could flimflam through it all with people promising much and giving nothing."

At the urging of Lawson and other leaders, Kennedy spoke at African-American luncheons and dinners, attended meetings with African-Americans, and graciously posed for hundreds of photos. "This made the kind of pictorial record that we could use in the campaign," said Lawson. "We were always able to get out a wonderful brochure because we had all these very heartwarming pictures of President Kennedy and of Mrs. Kennedy."[26]

On February 1, 1960, four black students at North Carolina Agricultural and Technical State University sat at the lunch counter of the Woolworth store in downtown Greensboro to protest its "whites only" policy. Their action inspired thousands of young black and white activists to engage in similar sit-in demonstrations throughout the South. Kennedy publicly supported the student sit-in movement, saying it was "in the American tradition to stand up for one's rights—even if the new way is to sit down."[27]

Kennedy was extraordinarily successful in private, personal discussions with black leaders. Until the spring of 1960, the Kennedy camp hadn't appreciated the power of Dr. Martin Luther King's personality and vision and the sway he held over the black community. "The depth of [his] pull was certainly not appreciated by any of us," said an aide to Robert Kennedy. Most of Kennedy's contacts had been with local leaders of the NAACP.

Dr. King, thirty-one, had led the dramatic and successful Montgomery bus boycott in 1955–1956. Influenced by Gandhi's philosophy of nonviolent resistance and the power of redemptive love, King was emerging as the pre-eminent spokesman for human rights. In 1957 he and other black leaders had founded the Southern Christian Leadership Conference (SCLC), which would rock the foundations of the segregated South. Scholarly, passionate, deeply committed to civil rights, an extraordinary orator, King regarded imprisonment for breaking unjust laws as a badge of honor.

Before meeting Kennedy, King had not been impressed by the senator's record on civil rights. The senator was too focused on becoming president, King thought, and would compromise basic principles to reach the White House. After their initial meeting, on June 23, 1960, King changed his mind. Over breakfast Kennedy agreed with King that strong presidential leadership on civil rights was crucial, especially on voting rights. In a letter to Chester Bowles the next day, King expressed pleasure with their ninety-minute conversation. "I was very impressed by the forthright and honest manner in which he discussed the civil rights question. I have no doubt that he would do the right thing on this issue if he were elected President."[28]

On July 20, a few days after the Democratic convention, Michigan's Governor G. Mennen Williams and a delegation of blacks from his state met for breakfast and an all-morning discussion at Kennedy's Georgetown home. Most of the black leaders were skeptical of Kennedy, and some were hostile.

Kennedy emphatically stated that civil rights was "of overwhelming moral significance to him," Williams recalled, and "if elected President he would use the full prestige and weight of his office to completely eliminate second-class citizenship in America."

One issue particularly irritated the black leaders. When Kennedy endorsed the sit-ins, he always qualified his statement by saying, "If they act peacefully . . ." The Michigan black leaders judged the qualifier demeaning and condescending. Williams thought the blacks were not getting their point across to Jack, so the governor interjected:

> I tried to sum the situation up for Jack, and I said, "Well, as I understand my Negro friends, what they're trying to say to you is that your insisting on including this 'by peaceful means' in your statement, although they indicate they have no intention of anything except acting peacefully—they feel that it's as if you issued an invitation to them for dinner and said, 'Please come to dinner, but wash your hands before you sit down.' Obviously you would expect your guests to wash their hands before you sat down and you would be insulting them if you said that. And by saying this 'by peaceful means' you're doing the same thing."

Kennedy understood and came up with a statement that satisfied all present. What's more, he won over the group. Every guest left wearing a Kennedy PT boat pin, and many drifted out to Kennedy's front stoop and made enthusiastic pro-Kennedy remarks to the waiting media.

Next, in September, Kennedy charmed Roy Wilkins during a discussion in Kennedy's home. "Negroes did not make him uncomfortable," Wilkins later wrote. "I was impressed with the candidate I had seen that evening. In the three years since our difference over the jury trial amendment he seemed to have grown a great deal."[29]

When challenged about his record on civil rights, Kennedy defended it against all comers. His office issued a six-page outline of all the civil rights legislation and programs he had supported.

The Democratic platform had staked out an advanced liberal position on civil rights: Eliminate the poll tax and literacy tests, end discrimination in education, establish a strong federal Fair Employment Practices Commission, stop discrimination in federal housing, and provide the attorney general with the power to seek court injunctions against violations of civil rights laws. The emphasis was firmly on the need for new legislation, implying that previous legislation passed by Congress was inadequate.

On September 1, during a speech officially kicking off his campaign, Kennedy called upon Senator Joseph Clark of Pennsylvania and Congressman Emanuel Celler of New York to "prepare a comprehensive civil rights bill, embodying the commitments of the Democratic platform," and have it introduced early in the next session of Congress.[30]

By the beginning of October, though, he had clearly shifted his emphasis away from legislation to the potential for executive action. He must have realized that he was promising too much, that Congress would undoubtedly block civil rights legislation in the next session. In reply to a question in Minneapolis on October 1, he said, "There is a great deal that can be done by the executive branch without legislation. For example, the President could sign an executive order ending discrimination in housing tomorrow." Two weeks later he stated that the powers to guarantee voting rights were already available but had not been effectively used. "The Executive has full power to provide the right to vote. I don't think there is any legal limitation now, any lack of weapons by the Attorney General or the President to compel the right to vote if a major effort is made." His comments during the final five weeks of the campaign, therefore, showed less commitment to sweeping civil rights legislation.[31]

Throughout the campaign Harris Wofford's primary advice to Kennedy was to show "personal concern and understanding" on the race issue. Lawson echoed Wofford's admonitions, telling Kennedy that "warmth has to be added to [your] image of intellectual liberalism."

Before the first television debate with Nixon, Wofford sent a memo to Kennedy, urging him to dramatize the issue of human dignity by citing the burdens ahead for a Negro child. While Nixon dodged the subject of civil rights, Kennedy used Wofford's memorandum almost verbatim during the debate, presenting a powerful and vivid description of racial injustice:

> The Negro baby born in America today . . . has about one-half as much chance of completing high school as a white baby born in the same place on the same day, one-third as much chance of completing college, one-third as much chance of becoming a professional man, twice as much chance of becoming unemployed, about one-seventh as much chance of earning $10,000 a year, a life expectancy which is seven years shorter, and the prospects of earning only half as much.[32]

On one famous and dramatic occasion late in the campaign, when Kennedy displayed his personal concern about racial injustice, his symbolic action helped carry him to victory.

Nixon expected sizable support from blacks. They were mostly Protestant fundamentalists, and the vice president had supported civil rights over the years and had developed a good relationship with Martin Luther King Jr.—better than Kennedy's. King voted Republican in 1956, and his father had endorsed Nixon in 1960.

But Nixon abandoned King at a critical moment, and Kennedy seized the opportunity. On October 19, 1960, police arrested King for picketing an Atlanta department store. Three days later, on October 22, he was released from jail, but immediately rearrested for violation of a parole agreement growing out of a trumped-up charge—driving with an Alabama license while a Georgia resident. For this offense he was sent to a remote Georgia prison for a four-month term at hard labor. Coretta Scott King, having every reason to believe that her husband was in mortal danger, called her friend Harris Wofford and, crying, said, "They're going to kill him. I know they are going to kill him." Wofford immediately phoned Sargent Shriver in Chicago, where Kennedy was campaigning, and told Shriver of the near-hysteria of the pregnant Mrs. King.

The two concocted a plan. Shriver should rush over to O'Hare Airport and try to persuade Kennedy to make a reassuring telephone call to Mrs. King. To avoid staff members who might think such a call too controversial and risky for the candidate, Shriver waited to talk with Kennedy alone.

When the two were alone, Shriver said, "Jack, I have an idea that might help you in the campaign: Mrs. Martin Luther King is sitting down there in Atlanta, and she is terribly worried about what is going to happen to her husband. I suggest that you pick up the phone, say hello, and tell her you hope that everything works out well."

Kennedy listened intently and replied, "That's a good idea. Why not? Do you have her number? Get her on the phone." In another minute, while everyone else was still out of the room, he was talking, warmly and reassuringly, with Mrs. King. Afterward she phoned Wofford and expressed her gratitude. She quoted Kennedy as saying, "I want to express to you my concern about your husband. I know this must be very hard for you. I understand you are expecting a baby, and I just wanted you to know that I was thinking about you and Dr. King. If there is anything I can do to help, please feel free to call on me."

At headquarters in Washington Robert Kennedy was furious when he learned about the phone call. With fists clenched tightly, his blue eyes cold, he turned on Wofford. "Do you know that three Southern governors told us that if Jack supported Jimmy Hoffa, Nikita Khrushchev, or Martin

Luther King, they would throw their states to Nixon? Do you know that this election may be razor close and you have probably lost it for us?"

Wofford and Louis Martin explained that the judge had refused to allow King to make bail, that King had been sent to prison for violating his probation on an earlier minor offense and was in great danger. Kennedy listened and asked, "How could they do that? You can't deny bail on a misdemeanor." "Well, they just did it," said Martin.

Later, after thinking about the matter, RFK changed his mind and decided to help King. "It was disgraceful," he later explained. "It just burned me up . . . the more I thought about the injustice of it." According to most accounts, Robert Kennedy phoned the judge and bawled him out, and the judge agreed to release King. "I called him because it made me so damn angry to think of that bastard sentencing a citizen to four months of hard labor for a minor traffic offense."[33]

In his biography of Robert Kennedy, Evan Thomas claims that this conventional version of the story, related by Wofford and Robert Kennedy, omits important facts. When King was sentenced to four months of hard labor, Jack and Bobby Kennedy secretly used a back channel to free him, Thomas contended.

A few days after King's imprisonment, Senator Kennedy telephoned Governor Ernest Vandiver of Georgia to see if the governor would take action to release King. Thomas noted: "Vandiver, awakened at the executive mansion by JFK's call, said he couldn't do anything publicly—he was a segregationist himself and needed political cover. But he wanted Kennedy to win the presidency, and he understood and appreciated the political embarrassment of sentencing King to the rock pile over a traffic ticket."

Vandiver directly or indirectly contacted the DeKalb County judge in the King case, Oscar Mitchell, who consented to release King. But Mitchell also needed political cover. "Judge Mitchell had to be able to say that he let King out of jail only after being called on the phone by Senator Kennedy or his brother," wrote Thomas.

Vandiver relayed all of this information to John Kennedy, who, in turn, instructed Bobby to call the judge. RFK did not act impulsively, as conventional accounts allege; nor was he operating on his own initiative. He was carrying out his brother's orders. "Following a brief cordial conversation with RFK, the judge released King," wrote Thomas. "That intricate chain of events, long kept secret, is the more nuanced story behind Kennedy's impulsive blow for justice."

The impact of the two Kennedys' back channel to Governor Vandiver is probably exaggerated. The chronology of their contacts is vague. More important, both Kennedys acted surprised when they learned from their own staff of King's imprisonment, indicating that any earlier back-channel contacts must have been inconsequential.[34]

Whatever the process that freed King, JFK's call to Mrs. King and RFK's intervention with the judge had a huge impact. Martin Luther King's father, an influential Baptist preacher, publicly changed his endorsement from Nixon to Kennedy.

> I had expected to vote against Senator Kennedy because of his religion. But now he can be my President, Catholic or whatever he is. It took courage to call my daughter-in-law at a time like this. He has the moral courage to stand up for what he knows is right. I've got all my votes and I've got a suitcase and I'm going to take them up there and dump them in his lap.

Black newspapers in the North picked up the story and lavished praise on the Democratic candidate. They quoted Martin Luther King Jr. as saying that "it took a lot of courage for Kennedy to do this, especially in Georgia. For him to be that courageous shows that he is really acting upon principle and not expediency."

"Mr. Nixon, in his refusal to comment or to take a stand on the civil rights issue that Rev. King's arrest symbolized," said a black editor, "merely extends the say-nothing, do-nothing rule by golf-club philosophy of President Eisenhower regarding this moral issue."

The Kennedy campaign was careful not to publicize the Kennedy-King connection in the mainstream press for fear of angering white Southern voters. But Shriver, Wofford, and Martin brilliantly exploited Kennedy's phone call and the release of King with Northern black voters. "We've got to use these wonderful quotations of Mrs. King, Martin Luther King, Jr., and his father," said Shriver. "That's not propaganda, it's just reporting what has been said."

Ultimately two million pamphlets describing the incident were distributed at black churches and bars in the North. The pamphlet, *The Case of Martin Luther King, Jr.,* featured on the cover page the headline " 'No Comment' Nixon versus a Candidate with a Heart, Senator Kennedy." This improvised public relations offensive helped tip the balance in the election.[35]

Several years afterward, Martin Luther King Jr. perceptively analyzed the entire incident. True, Kennedy had hoped to sway black voters, but there had been more to his intervention.

> He did something that expressed deep moral concern, but at the same time it was politically sound . . . He didn't know it was politically sound.

It was a risk because he was already grappling with the problem of losing the South on the religious issue. He had to face the fact that this would even make his situation worse in the South. And there was no assurance that he would pick up in the North as a result of this, so it was a risk that he took.

On the other hand, King seethed over Nixon's silence. "He had been supposedly close to me, and he would call me frequently about things, getting, seeking my advice. And yet, when this moment came it was like he never heard of me, you see. So this is why I really considered him a moral coward."

Privately, John Kennedy later remarked of King's father, "He said he was going to vote against me because I was a Catholic, but that since I called his daughter-in-law he will vote for me . . . That was a hell of a bigoted statement, wasn't it? Imagine Martin Luther King having a bigot for a father." Then Kennedy smiled and added, "Well, we all have fathers, don't we."

For eight years President Eisenhower had practiced a steady indifference to blacks and to civil rights. Because blacks were desperate for attention and consideration, Kennedy's symbolic act, his expression of personal concern, fulfilled an important need in the black community.[36]

At about 2:00 A.M. on October 14, Kennedy arrived at the University of Michigan. Exhausted, he had just flown in from New York after completing the third debate with Nixon. On his arrival at Ann Arbor he was dumbfounded to discover ten thousand students waiting for him in the middle of the night.

In his little-noticed, extemporaneous speech, he focused on the essence of what later became the Peace Corps. "How many of you are willing to spend two years in Africa or Latin America or Asia working for the U.S. and working for freedom?" he asked. "How many of you [who] are going to be doctors are willing to spend your days in Ghana? . . .

"On your willingness, not merely to serve one or two years in the service, but on your willingness to contribute part of your life to this country, I think will depend the answer whether we as a free society can compete." The audience was wildly enthusiastic. Afterward, as the weary candidate made his way to bed, he told an aide that he thought he had "hit a winning number."

Kennedy had not actually mentioned a "Peace Corps" at Michigan, but his remarks embraced the spirit of the idea. Sorensen described the Peace Corps as a "lake" into which a number of Kennedy's "streams of interest" flowed. One was Kennedy's empathy with the aspirations of the world's poor and oppressed, and those trying to throw off the chains of their colonial oppressors. Having traveled extensively in Europe, Asia, and Latin America, he had been disturbed by the wretched conditions and abject poverty in many countries. He also remembered stories about the miserable experiences of his paternal ancestors in colonial Ireland.[37]

In the Senate Kennedy chaired the Senate Subcommittee on African Affairs and was a member of the Subcommittee on Latin American Affairs; both assignments enlightened him about conditions in the Third World.

Another stream, noted Peace Corps historian Gerard Rice, "was his desire to reinvigorate U.S. foreign assistance programs." The Foreign Service, "elite and out of touch with grassroots opinion in the countries which it served, was too much preoccupied with tennis and cocktails." Kennedy complained that "men who lack compassion . . . were sent abroad to represent us in countries which were marked by disease and poverty and illiteracy and ignorance, and they did not identify us with those causes and the fight against them."

America had a global mission, and must share its democratic virtues with the poverty-stricken people in the Third World. "The mantle of leadership has been placed upon our shoulders not by a nation nor by our own government or citizens but by destiny and circumstance," he said, "by the sheer fact of our physical and economic strength . . . and by what [George] Washington termed 'the sacred fire of liberty.'"

The Peace Corps would help win the hearts and minds of the developing countries, and advance U.S. interests in the Cold War. America's "ambassadors of peace," Kennedy said, would be competing in the Third World against "Castro-type or Communist exploitation."

In the late 1950s the American volunteer who worked in villages and jungles of the Third World became a folk hero. The exploits of Dr. Tom Dooley, who practiced medicine on behalf of the peoples of Southeast Asia, were dramatically publicized. Kennedy was struck by Dooley's "selfless example."

The idea of the Peace Corps had percolated among Kennedy's staff since early 1960. "We are considering a proposal dealing with increased use of American technicians in the underdeveloped countries," Richard Goodwin wrote to Archibald Cox in March. The idea would involve "several thousand American college graduates, primarily in technical and scientific fields," whom the government would sponsor to go overseas for a program of work and education. The program would appeal to the "imagination and interest of college graduates, give them an opportunity to make a real contribution to world *peace* and to receive valuable training and responsibility. Also," wrote Goodwin, "the idea of a 'Youth for Peace' program might have propaganda advantages."[38]

Subsequently Professor Samuel P. Hayes of the University of Michigan prepared a memo entitled "A Proposal for an International Youth Service," dated September 30, which Cox then forwarded to Kennedy. (While various people, including Senator Hubert Humphrey and congressman Henry Reuss, could claim some part in suggesting the Peace Corps, none of them were able to transform the idea into political reality. Henry Reuss conceded that "if it had been left to us, the Peace Corps idea would still be cluttering up the legislative corridors.")

On October 21 Kennedy started his day in Los Angeles and continued on to San Diego, San Jose, and Oakland. His final stop was San Francisco's Cow Palace auditorium, where a huge crowd of thirty-five thousand people crammed the hall.

The main theme of his eloquent address was the impact that talented young Americans could have in the Third World, "building goodwill, building the peace." He suggested a new government organization, the Peace Corps, that would help impoverished nations help themselves:

> There is not enough money in all America to relieve the misery of the underdeveloped world in a giant and endless soup kitchen. But there is enough know-how and enough knowledgeable people to help those nations help themselves. I therefore propose that our inadequate efforts in this area be supplemented by a Peace Corps of talented young men willing and able to serve their country in this fashion for three years as an alternative to peacetime selective service—well-qualified through rigorous standards; well-trained in the language, skills, and customs they will need to know.

The following day *The New York Times* prominently headlined: "Kennedy Favors U.S. 'Peace Corps' to Work Abroad." The national media followed suit, praising the concept.

President Eisenhower derided the idea of the Peace Corps as a "juvenile experiment," while Nixon denounced it as a form of "draft evasion." But by the end of 1960 Kennedy had received more letters on his proposal for the Peace Corps than on any other subject.[39]

After the first televised debate, mob scenes greeted Kennedy's car as it passed by on the way to his next appearance. Theodore White analyzed the phenomenon:

> The jumpers were, in the beginning, teen-age girls who would bounce, jounce and jump as the cavalcade passed, squealing, "I see him, I see him." Gradually over the days their jumping seemed to grow more rhythmic, giving a jack-in-the-box effect of ups and downs in a thor-

oughly sexy oscillation. Then, as the press began to comment on the phenomenon, thus stimulating more artistic jumping, the middle-aged ladies began to jump up and down too, until, in the press bus following the candidate, one would note only the oddities: the lady, say, in her bathrobe, jumping back and forth; the heavily pregnant mother, jumping; the mother with a child in her arms, jumping; the row of nuns, all jiggling under their black robes, almost (but not quite) daring to jump.[40]

Reporters also described double leapers, clutchers, and runners. The double leapers were women who jumped together while holding hands. Clutchers crossed their arms, hugged themselves, and screamed, "He looked at me! He looked at me!" The runners were women, sometimes carrying infants, who broke through police barricades to run after Kennedy's car.

A Nixon crowd was far more sedate. As the vice president's convertible passed by, onlookers cheered and applauded, but there were no jumpers, double leapers, clutchers, or runners.[41]

The media clearly preferred to travel with the Kennedy entourage. While aboard the *Caroline,* columnist Marquis Childs felt engulfed in consideration and kindness. "On a short run between campaign stops, I was invited aboard the *Caroline* . . . for a chat with Jack. I was received with warmth and candor. Part of this, to be sure, was careful calculation, but he liked reporters." While traveling with the Nixon entourage, Childs assessed the atmosphere as "correct and frigidly formal."

In October columnist Walter Lippmann told his readers that it was "truly impressive to see the precision of Mr. Kennedy's mind, his immense command of the facts, his instinct for the crucial point, his singular lack of demagoguery and sloganeering . . . his coolness and courage." Kennedy, he wrote, was a "natural leader, organizer and ruler of men."[42]

On October 21, Larry O'Brien reported on the status of the campaign in a memo for John and Robert Kennedy. There was good news and bad news. At least six million new voters had been registered, and the race in New York had improved from "even" to Kennedy "ahead." The bad news? California was "even." Moreover, the religious issue was "[g]etting hot. Many states report trouble spots . . . It is hurting in many states—some badly."[43]

Nixon and Kennedy vied for the honor of being the most aggressive cold warrior. They squared off on the best policy to adopt toward Castro's Cuba, but neither candidate enlightened voters on the subject.

In 1959 Fidel Castro overthrew the Cuban government of Fulgencio Batista, one of the worst dictators in Latin America. At first Americans sympathized with Castro, hoping for a more democratic leader, but sentiment turned against him when he exacted brutal vengeance on Batista's followers and drifted into the Soviet orbit in foreign policy. As Castro became more and more truculent, the Eisenhower administration and Congress cut back the Cuban sugar quota. "Castro responded by embracing the Soviets," noted diplomatic historian Robert Divine, "who supplied both economic assistance to his regime and the promise of rocket support in case of American attack."

Tension escalated. In June 1960, when U.S. oil companies in Cuba refused to refine Soviet petroleum, Castro forcibly took over the companies at the end of the month. On August 24, addressing the Veterans of Foreign Wars in Detroit, Nixon implicitly threatened to invade Cuba. There was "no question," he said, about America's determination to prevent "a foreign-controlled Communist dictatorship in Cuba." He warned that "the United States has the power—and Mr. Castro knows this—to throw him out of office any day that we would choose."[44]

At first Kennedy tried to outflank rather than confront Nixon's tough position on Cuba. He aimed his salvos at past Republican policy. Castro's Cuba was another clear symbol of American decline under Eisenhower. When Kennedy had visited Cuba in 1957, he "was informed that the American Ambassador was the second most powerful man in Cuba. . . . Today," Kennedy continued, "the Soviet Ambassador is." He reminded voters that "in 1952 the Republicans ran on a program of rolling back the Iron Curtain in Eastern Europe. Today the Iron Curtain is 90 miles off the coast of the United States."

Throughout the summer and fall of 1960, Nixon urged the CIA to push forward with its secret plan to train Cuban exiles for an invasion of Cuba—the plan that eventually led to the Bay of Pigs. But the CIA's plans were incomplete, the exiles were not yet properly trained and equipped, and, under those circumstances, Eisenhower would not grant his approval. "Nixon still hoped for a CIA-sponsored invasion before the election," noted Stephen Ambrose.

On October 14, Castro announced that Cuba would nationalize 382 American-owned firms in his country—banks, sugar mills, and other industrial and commercial operations. The next day, Kennedy taunted Nixon, who had complained that Kennedy had not been tough enough in insisting on defending the tiny islands of Quemoy and Matsu off the coast of Taiwan. "The people of the United States would like to hear [Nixon] discuss his views on an island not 4 miles off the coast of China [Quemoy], but 90 miles off the coast of the United States—Cuba."[45]

Two days before the fourth and final television debate, on October 19, the Kennedy campaign issued a statement which has been disputed ever since. To some it seemed to foreshadow the Bay of Pigs invasion. "We must attempt to strengthen the non-Batista democratic anti-Castro forces in exile, and in

Cuba itself, who offer eventual hope of overthrowing Castro. Thus far these fighters for freedom have had virtually no support from our government." *The New York Times* seized on the comment and ran an article headlined "Kennedy Asks Aid for Cuban Rebels to Defeat Castro: Urges Support of Exiles and 'Fighters for Freedom' Already on Island." The dramatic coverage guaranteed that the issue of communism in Cuba would be featured in the upcoming debate.

Nixon was convinced that Kennedy had abused classified information for political gain. "I knew," he later wrote in his autobiography, *Six Crises* (1962), "that Kennedy had received a CIA briefing on the administration's Cuban policy and assumed that he knew, as I did, that a plan to aid the Cuban exiles was already under way on a top-secret basis. His statement jeopardized the project, which could succeed only if it were supported and implemented secretly."

Certain the issue would be raised in the debate, claiming he needed to protect the secrecy of the planning and the safety of thousands of people involved in the operation, Nixon decided to lie about his real beliefs. He would take a completely opposite stand and attack Kennedy's advocacy of open intervention in Cuba.

During the debate Nixon delivered a brazen frontal assault, describing Kennedy's Cuban policies as "probably the most dangerously irresponsible recommendations that he's made during the course of this campaign." Assisting anti-Castro Cubans would violate several treaties, "lose all of our friends in Latin America," invite censure in the United Nations, and encourage Khrushchev "to come into Latin America."[46]

Nixon was furious about the awkward position Kennedy had placed him in. "For the first and only time in the campaign, I got mad at Kennedy *personally*. I thought that Kennedy, with full knowledge of the facts, was jeopardizing the security of a United States foreign policy operation. And my rage was greater because I could do nothing about it." Nixon bitterly recalled, "Kennedy conveyed the image—to 60 million people—that he was tougher on Castro and communism than I was."

Nixon's stand succeeded in stirring up opposition to Kennedy's Cuban proposal from several prominent journalists. In *The New York Times* James Reston criticized Kennedy's statement as "a clear violation of the Inter-American treaty" and "probably the worst blunder of the campaign." Shortly after his glowing endorsement of Kennedy, Walter Lippmann reproached him for his "mistake," one reminiscent of the loose talk about liberating Eastern Europe in 1952.

After the debate, while rebutting Nixon's charges, Kennedy denied that he had ever endorsed an approach to Cuba that violated existing U.S. treaties. His Cuban policy, he explained, sought nothing more than a propaganda campaign "to let the forces of freedom in Cuba know that we believe that freedom will again rise in their country."[47]

"Cuba failed to have a crucial impact on the 1960 election," historian Kent Beck concluded, "because the campaign produced no clear-cut difference between Kennedy and Nixon." There was no strong sentiment for American intervention in Cuba in 1960, and the candidates avoided a serious discussion of policy toward the island.

Following the election, the publication of *Six Crises* ignited a squabble about Kennedy's knowledge of the CIA's preparations to invade Cuba. Nixon insisted that Kennedy had been briefed by the CIA's director, Allen Dulles. By calling for American support for Cuban exiles, Kennedy had endangered "the security of a United States foreign policy operation."[48]

Both Dulles and Kennedy insisted that Dulles had not briefed Kennedy in detail about Castro in the preelection briefings. Still, Kennedy had uncovered some evidence that an invasion plan was in the works. One source was John Patterson, the Democratic governor of Alabama, who had learned of the CIA's secret plan, and rushed to inform Kennedy that the invasion was imminent. "If it occurred before the election," Patterson remembered telling Kennedy, "I believed Nixon would win. I recall watching him very closely. I couldn't read him. He heard me out and thanked me."

Kennedy, though, was not fully informed of the invasion plan, as Nixon later alleged, and did not learn the details of the proposed large-scale attack until after the election. Nixon exaggerated the provocative nature of Kennedy's statement on October 19 about strengthening democratic anti-Castro forces.

Kennedy and his campaign staff undoubtedly worried about a preelection invasion of Cuba, a crisis that could propel Nixon into the White House. Perhaps Kennedy's general support for Cuban exiles was designed to preempt any last-minute invasion crisis. Indeed, Nixon was hoping for just such a crisis.[49]

For the final weekend before the election, Kennedy had asked Ken O'Donnell to change the schedule so he could campaign in California, still a doubtful state, rather than New York and Connecticut, where he was ahead.

"I'll be wasting my time in New York," Jack said. "I've got New York and I've got Connecticut. But I haven't got California. Give me those two days in California and I'll win there." But O'Donnell's schedule was too inflexible to change. "You and your damned schedule," Kennedy angrily hollered at O'Donnell. "If we lose California, it will be your thick-headed fault." (Nixon would win narrowly in California.)

Near the end of the campaign Nixon made a series of sensational headline-grabbing proposals. On consecutive days, starting on October 25, he promised a manned flight around the moon by the end of the decade, a summit conference with Khrushchev, and a tour of Eastern Europe to "carry the message of freedom into the Communist world."

The grueling pace of the campaign took its toll; yet, like Nixon, Kennedy persevered. "He doesn't eat, he doesn't sleep, he doesn't do anything to keep fit," Jackie Kennedy observed of her husband, "but he thrives on it." "He found it increasingly hard to rise at dawn," noted Sorensen, "even when Dave Powers would rouse him with a cheery 'What do you suppose Nixon's doing while you're lying there?'"

Six days before the election, while Kennedy was campaigning in San Francisco, his friend Paul "Red" Fay found him soaking in a hot bath. His face looked drawn but his mind was still keen. "Redhead, come on in," Jack called. "This body which so heroically weathered the trials of the great war and has once again answered the call of the campaign trail is taking a good soaking before again responding to the call." The enthusiasm of his growing crowds also helped to renew and refresh him.[50]

Despite Eisenhower's personal appeal and two successive victories, the Democratic Party was still the country's majority party. In 1960 an energetic registration drive brought nearly seven million more people to the polls than four years earlier and over four million of them were Democrats; 63.8 percent of eligible voters cast ballots in 1960, the highest percentage since 1908.

Kennedy won comfortably in the electoral college, capturing 303 votes to Nixon's 219. But in the razor-thin popular vote, he barely edged Nixon, winning by fewer than 120,000 votes of over 68 million cast. Kennedy earned 49.7 percent of the total to Nixon's 49.6 percent, the smallest popular-vote margin of any presidential race in the twentieth century.[51]

No single factor explained Kennedy's victory. Winning the first debate was important. So were his personal attractiveness, effective campaign style, and phone call to Mrs. King. President Eisenhower's tepid efforts on behalf of his vice president hurt Nixon's campaign. Lyndon Johnson's presence on the ticket probably inched Texas into the Democratic column.

The African-American vote was a major reason that Kennedy carried the crucial states of Illinois, Michigan, New Jersey, New York, and Pennsylvania. In 1956 Adlai Stevenson won 60 percent of the Negro vote; in 1960 Kennedy captured 80 percent.[52]

Kennedy's religion both helped elect him and very nearly defeated him. He collected 78 percent of Catholic votes, propelling him to victory in urbanized northeastern states with large electoral votes. But he won only 38 percent of the votes of Protestants.

The religious issue hurt Kennedy most in the South, where about 17 percent of the normal Democratic vote defected. Fortunately, the South was so overwhelmingly Democratic that Kennedy still won 81 of the region's 128 electoral votes. In the Protestant farm states of the Midwest, his religion hampered him as well, but those states were traditionally Republican anyway. Despite the millions of Protestant voters he lost nationwide, the religious issue directly cost him the electoral votes of only two states, Tennessee and Oklahoma.[53]

Nowhere was the vote closer than in Illinois, which Kennedy carried by a mere 8,858 votes out of over 4,657,000 cast. In Chicago Kennedy won by the overwhelming margin of 456,000. The powerful and notoriously corrupt Cook County Democratic machine, directed by Chicago mayor Richard Daley, had thrown its potent resources behind Kennedy. On election night, as the Illinois results teetered in the balance, the mayor phoned Kennedy. "Mr. President, with a bit of luck and the help of a few close friends, you're going to carry Illinois."

Critics contend that a devilish bargain arranged by Joe Kennedy gained the election for his son in Chicago. Behind the scenes Joe Kennedy had promoted Jack's candidacy the way old Democratic pols, like Jim Farley and Ed Flynn, had done for Franklin Roosevelt. "If Jack had known about some of the telephone calls his father made on his behalf to Tammany-type bosses during the 1960 campaign, Jack's hair would have turned white," observed Ken O'Donnell.

One of the bosses Joe Kennedy may have contacted was Chicago's crime boss, Sam "Mooney" Giancana, one of America's worst criminals. According to Seymour Hersh's investigation, the senior Kennedy made an agreement with Giancana to ensure victory in Illinois and other states where the syndicate had influence. Joe turned for help to a friend, William J. Tuohy, chief judge of the Circuit Court of Cook County. Joe asked Judge Tuohy to set up a secret meeting with Giancana. Tuohy agreed, and asked a former protégé, Robert J. McDonnell, one of the mob's leading attorneys, to set up the meeting.

"The deal," Hersh claimed, "included an assurance that Giancana's men would get out the Kennedy vote among the rank and file in the mob-controlled unions in Chicago and elsewhere, and a commitment for campaign contributions from the corrupt Teamsters Union pension fund."

"There was no ballot stuffing," McDonnell told Hersh. "I'm not suggesting that. They just worked—totally went all out. He [Kennedy] won it squarely, but he got the vote because of what Mooney had done."

When John Kennedy assumed the presidency, so the story goes, he was therefore indebted to organized crime and to Giancana for securing the victory in Chicago.[54]

What are we to make of this allegation? Along with his virtues, Joe Kennedy had an infinite capacity for poor judgment and immoral, unethical activity. Perhaps Hersh's description of their meeting is correct, since similar meetings were taking place elsewhere. Joe Kennedy met with scores of big-city bosses in his attempt to elect his son. What's most important, though, is there isn't evidence of any campaign activity that Giancana used to elect Kennedy. He commanded few votes. Mayor Daley, not Giancana, managed the huge and potent Democratic organization in Chicago.

Giancana controlled only two wards, and both were heavily Democratic anyway. Chicago's First and Twenty-eighth wards, the crime syndicate's strongholds in the city, produced *low* recorded vote counts for Kennedy compared to the maximum turnout in nine other automatic Democratic wards. In other words, if Giancana and the crime syndicate campaigned for Kennedy, they did a poor job of turning out their voters. John Kennedy felt no obligation to return a favor to Sam Giancana.

Edmund Kallina, the preeminent authority on the Chicago election in 1960, concluded that Hersh's "hearsay" evidence was not convincing. In any case, "Nixon was deprived of votes but the number of votes involved is not enough to make a convincing case that Nixon was cheated of the Illinois electoral votes."

If Daley and the Cook County Democratic machine did steal the election for Kennedy, and the evidence points in that direction, it would not, by itself, have changed the national results. Kennedy would have won in the electoral college even if Illinois had gone Republican.[55]

After giving serious thought to challenging the presidential results in Illinois, Nixon decided against it. "The Vice President ran the race and accepts the decision of the voters," his press secretary, Herbert G. Klein, announced on November 11. "The decision made on Tuesday stands."

Kennedy had won "a victory without a verdict and a majority without a mandate," wrote the *Washington Evening Star*. He ran behind the Democratic ticket more often than he ran ahead of it. "Senator Kennedy's lack of a personal mandate will make it more difficult for him to strike out for the new frontiers he has pledged himself to reach," concluded columnist Richard Rovere.[56]

25

LET US BEGIN ANEW

On Sunday, January 1, 1961, in Palm Beach, Evelyn Lincoln listened to the jocular breakfast conversation between the President-elect and his longtime friend Lem Billings.

Was Billings thrilled to be eating breakfast with the President of the United States?

Not really, Billings responded.

Jack asked Mrs. Lincoln, "Are you thrilled to be working for the President?"

"I am overjoyed."

"See there," Jack said, "she is thrilled and you, Lem, don't feel a thing." With a twinkle in his eye, he said to Billings, "It is a privilege for you to be eating with the President."[1]

On the day after the election, Kennedy was amazed at what had to be accomplished in the short span of time until his inauguration—only seventy-two days. Not much time, Sorensen later noted, "to form an administration, staff the White House, fill some seventy-five key Cabinet and policy posts, name six hundred other major nominees, decide which incumbents to carry over, distribute patronage to the faithful and fix personnel policies for the future." Kennedy also had to liaise with Eisenhower, prepare for the inauguration, shape his domestic and foreign policies, and plan his legislative program.

On November 14, Kennedy shocked many of his supporters by visiting Richard Nixon in Florida. Nixon publicly praised the visit as a "very gracious act" and an excellent example of "how our American system works." Ken O'Donnell later recalled, though, that Nixon dominated the discussion, and that Kennedy wasn't impressed. "Kennedy studied him quietly, as if he was saying to himself, how did I manage to beat a guy like this by only a hundred thousand votes?" As Kennedy climbed into the helicopter to return to Palm Beach, he said to O'Donnell, "It was just as well for all of us that he didn't quite make it."

In the two months after his election, the President-elect maintained a bustling schedule, flying nearly fifteen thousand miles back and forth between Washington, Palm Beach, and New York, with side trips to Boston and Texas. He gained fifteen pounds. "He weighed now close to 190 and was considering dieting," recalled *Time*'s reporter Hugh Sidey.[2]

Thanks to the farsightedness of the Brookings Institution, an independent think tank in Washington, Kennedy had completed more advance planning than previous presidential transitions. Concerned by the casualness and problems of the 1952 transition from Truman to Eisenhower, the Brookings Institution had established committees to study the transition. One result was an invitation to both presidential candidates after the nominating conventions to send representatives to consult with the Brookings group for several months before the election. Kennedy selected Clark Clifford, whose informed advice the Kennedy team constantly sought during the transition.

Kennedy read *Presidential Power: The Politics of Leadership*, a new book by Richard E. Neustadt, a Columbia University government professor and a major presidential scholar. He asked Neustadt to outline his views on the personnel problems Kennedy would face if elected, but he did not want Neustadt to coordinate his efforts with Clifford. "I simply cannot afford to have just one set of advisers," Kennedy told him.[3]

At the same time Kennedy's aides coordinated various task forces on policy and organizational issues. Kennedy studied over twenty reports, somberly observing that "they don't make very pleasant reading." The task force reports did not arrive until after Kennedy had established his initial course. Nonetheless, as historian Carl Brauer noted, "the task forces in several areas, such as education, set future agendas, and they also proved useful in uncovering talent or lack of it in prospective appointees."

In the end, the transition from Eisenhower to Kennedy proved to be smoother than the Hoover-Roosevelt (1932) and Truman-Eisenhower

(1952) changeovers. At Ike's orders his cabinet and aides cooperated with Kennedy and the incoming appointees. "I don't think we have asked for anything that they haven't done," said the President-elect.[4]

After visiting the LBJ Ranch in Texas and working for a week in Palm Beach, Kennedy returned to Washington to spend Thanksgiving with Jackie and Caroline. Following a pleasant Thanksgiving dinner at their Georgetown home, Kennedy flew back to Palm Beach aboard the *Caroline*. The press contingent trailed behind on a chartered DC-6. During the flight Kennedy relaxed until he received an emergency message on the radio: Jackie had been rushed to the hospital.

The baby was not due until late December. Having already lost two babies, she was being extremely careful. She had seemed fine as Kennedy left Georgetown that evening to fly to Palm Beach. But shortly after his flight took off, an ambulance sped to their home. Jackie suddenly was in danger of a miscarriage. "Will I lose my baby?" she imploringly asked her obstetrician, Dr. John W. Walsh.

Meanwhile, on the plane Jack was a bundle of nerves, stricken with remorse. "I'm never there when she needs me." When the *Caroline* landed in Palm Beach, he talked by phone with Dr. Walsh, who informed him that Jackie was in the operating room and about to undergo cesarean surgery.

Kennedy decided to return to Washington immediately. Instead of using the *Caroline,* he boarded the press plane, the bigger, faster DC-6. After it took off, he moved to the cabin, clamped on radio earphones, and waited anxiously for news. At 1:17 A.M. he learned that John F. Kennedy Jr. had been born safely and that Jackie had experienced no serious problems. Pierre Salinger announced to reporters, "We have just been advised that Mrs. Kennedy has given birth to a baby boy. Both mother and son are doing well." The correspondents on the plane, quietly sweating out the delivery themselves, applauded and yelled wildly. The President-elect waved cheerfully at them and took a bow.[5]

For the next two weeks, Kennedy remained close to his wife and two children in Georgetown, visiting Jackie and John Jr. in the hospital several times a day. He took Caroline for walks and for pony rides at the estate of his mother-in-law, Mrs. Hugh Auchincloss.

In the hospital Jack and Jackie talked mostly about family matters, not cabinet appointments or world events. "Jack, are you taking time out for regular meals?" Jackie wondered. "How much sleep did you get last night? What does Caroline say about the baby?"

On his daily arrival at the hospital, Jack always looked in at his son. As he left he inquired, "Do you think it would be all right if I asked the nurses to show him to me again?" What was John Jr.'s weight? How much formula was the baby taking? "He was absolutely jubilant," said Louella Hennessey, who assisted Jackie.[6]

On December 6, Kennedy met with Eisenhower at the White House, hoping to find out Ike's thoughts on Berlin, the Far East (especially China), and Cuba. For an hour and forty-five minutes the two men met alone, and then for further discussion joined Eisenhower's three senior cabinet officers—Secretary of State Christian Herter, Secretary of Defense Thomas Gates, and Secretary of the Treasury Robert Anderson—plus Ike's chief of staff, Wilton Persons, and Clark Clifford.

Afterward Persons phoned Clifford to say that President Eisenhower, who had previously referred to Kennedy as a "young whippersnapper," had been "overwhelmed" by the President-elect. "What impressed the President most," said Persons, "was your man's understanding of world problems, the depth of his questions, his grasp of the issues, and the keenness of his mind."

Senator Kennedy, though, was not impressed with Eisenhower. He still regarded him as a "non-President." But he did gain a greater appreciation of Eisenhower's personality, and told Clifford he better understood the secret of Ike's success and popularity.[7]

Kennedy wanted a "ministry of talent," but his political career had left him with limited contacts in his hunt for the best. Shortly after the election he huddled with Dean Acheson to discuss possible cabinet appointments. He told Truman's secretary of state that one of his problems was that he had spent so much time in the past few years coming to know people who could help *elect* him President that he now found he knew few people who could help him *be* President. Acheson judged Kennedy's dilemma "both true and touching."

Kennedy knew people in politics, journalism, labor, and New England universities; he had not met many industrialists, bankers, scientists, military officers, diplomats, or foundation executives. He consulted with older and more experienced former government officials—Clark Clifford, Dean Acheson, John McCloy, and especially Robert Lovett. None of them wanted jobs for themselves. He also sought advice from members of the press—Joseph Alsop, Philip Graham, and Walter Lippmann.

Sargent Shriver headed a small search committee that sought out potential appointees. Kennedy did most of the work and made all of the final decisions on about forty top positions. He studied résumés, checked references, and personally interviewed dozens of candidates. He had excellent instincts for sizing up prospects, and motivated them to want to join his administration.[8]

Kennedy could work congenially with different types of people, but he didn't want to bring on board prospects who were too ideological, too earnest, too emotional, too talkative, or dull. He sought people with qualities like his own, an outlook more practical than theoretical and more logical than ideological.

The criteria that attracted the most attention in the media was toughness. "We even had people telephoning to say, 'I'm tough,'" said one of Shriver's assistants. By tough, they meant people who could withstand intense pressure, and would pursue long-range objectives in the face of obstacles.

Kennedy told Clifford that he wanted to dismiss political party affiliation as a consideration. A bipartisan administration was congenial for him, since as Walter Lippman pointed out, "by temperament and instinct and association, he has never been a partisan Democrat of the Roosevelt or the Truman persuasion."

"Henry Stimson was one of those New York Republicans, and Roosevelt was glad to get him," Kennedy told Ken O'Donnell. "If I string along exclusively with [John Kenneth] Galbraith, and Arthur Schlesinger and Seymour Harris and those other Harvard liberals, they'll fill Washington with wild-eyed ADA people. . . . I can use a few smart Republicans. Anyway, we need a Secretary of the Treasury who can call a few of those people on Wall Street by their first names."[9]

Two of his early appointments retained prominent government officials. J. Edgar Hoover, who had headed the FBI since 1924, was reappointed as the FBI's director. A master bureaucrat, Hoover had carefully molded his reputation as a model public servant and archenemy of communism and crime. "So great was his reputation and power that it is hard to imagine any Presidentelect in 1960 relieving him of his duties," observed historian Carl Brauer.

"[Hoover's] reappointment seems a matter of course," Richard Neustadt advised Kennedy in a memorandum; "you might as well make the most of it by an early announcement, particularly since you may well find some things you would like him to do for you, quite confidentially before Inauguration." Kennedy didn't want to create a political ruckus by firing Hoover, and thought it prudent to end any speculation about the director's future. Kennedy's father intensely admired Hoover, and Jack may have feared that firing Hoover would lead to the disclosure of all the derogatory information the director had collected in his files about his womanizing.

Kennedy reappointed Allen Dulles, the brother of Eisenhower's late secretary of state, as director of the Central Intelligence Agency. As with the reappointment of Hoover, Kennedy wanted to avoid a messy firing, end speculation about Dulles quickly, and reassure the nation.[10]

Some of his appointments paid off political debts. With the endorsement of his brothers Robert and Edward, Kennedy named Stewart Udall as secretary of the interior. A young and capable Arizona congressman, Udall was one of the few prominent western politicians to support Kennedy during the 1960 election. By appointing Luther Hodges, the governor of North Carolina, to head the Commerce Department, Kennedy rewarded his Southern constituency and encouraged its future support.

Governor Abraham Ribicoff of Connecticut had supported him since 1956, and Kennedy wanted to reward his loyalty. At first he offered Ribicoff the attorney general slot, but the governor turned it down, saying it would be politically awkward for an Irish Catholic President and a Jewish attorney general to enforce civil rights in the Protestant South. Instead, Ribicoff accepted Health, Education, and Welfare. Ribicoff had the reputation as a prudent financial manager, which Kennedy hoped would give him credibility with Congress.

The position of secretary of labor went to Arthur Goldberg, a friend and supporter, whom John and Robert Kennedy had known since they worked together on labor legislation and labor racketeering. A lawyer for labor unions, Goldberg earned respect for his intelligence, energy, and independence. For secretary of agriculture Kennedy selected Orville Freeman; he hoped the former Minnesota governor would take the burdensome problems of agriculture off his shoulders. The postmaster general's job went to J. Edward Day, an associate of Adlai Stevenson and an insurance executive in California.[11]

Kennedy devoted far more energy on his appointments to the State, Defense, Justice, and Treasury departments than he did on the other six cabinet positions.

Robert Lovett provided the best advice on three of the major posts. A Republican and an international investment banker on Wall Street, Lovett had nonetheless served as undersecretary of state and as secretary of defense under Truman. Because of ill health he declined to accept any appointment from Kennedy. "Since Kennedy was dealing constantly with people ambitious for office themselves or promoting the candidacy of others, Lovett's combination of disinterestedness and experience magnified his influence," noted Brauer.

For Treasury Kennedy settled on Douglas Dillon, the board chairman of a prominent Wall Street brokerage firm. He expected Dillon to provide public assurance that the administration would be fiscally responsible. Dillon had profitably managed his company's domestic and foreign holdings, and his recent government experience, as Eisenhower's undersecretary of state for economic affairs, offered an attractive credential for the key cabinet position that handled financial and trade issues.[12]

Kennedy knew that he didn't want Adlai Stevenson as his secretary of state. The party's presidential nominee in 1952 and 1956, Stevenson regarded himself as an expert in foreign affairs. He craved the top State Department position, and among his followers in the Democratic Party, he was the sentimental choice. But Kennedy no longer liked him and considered him indecisive; neither Lovett nor Acheson endorsed Stevenson. Instead, Kennedy named Stevenson to a lesser diplomatic post, U.S. representative to the United Nations.

In the end Kennedy selected the secretary of state by a process of elimination. McGeorge Bundy, the brilliant forty-one-year-old dean at Harvard, was mentioned, but advisers judged him too young and inexperienced. Foreign-policy expert Chester Bowles had wide government experience and had supported Kennedy in the 1960 election, but Kennedy thought the former Connecticut congressman was too idealistic and verbose, and not tough enough to negotiate with the Soviets. Kennedy considered David Bruce, an experienced diplomat and the undersecretary of state in the Truman administration, but Bruce lacked key qualities.

Arkansas senator William Fulbright, chairman of the Senate Foreign Relations Committee, was Kennedy's first choice. As a Senate colleague, Kennedy knew him well, and admired his intellect, common sense, and wisdom. Fulbright was also popular with Congress. But Robert Kennedy persuaded his brother that Fulbright carried too much baggage. As a segregationist and a signer of the hated Southern Manifesto, Fulbright had alienated civil rights leaders, who bitterly complained when his name circulated as a possible selection.

As a goodwill gesture, Kennedy invited Fulbright to Palm Beach to discuss personnel matters and the new administration's foreign policy, and to apologize for not appointing him to head the State Department. "I don't think I've ever seen a man of such importance, with more consideration, more sympathy for another politician, than this man was," said Fulbright, who claimed he didn't want the position anyway.[13]

After Dean Acheson and Robert Lovett both endorsed the little-known Dean Rusk, Kennedy appointed the Georgia native as secretary of state. A Rhodes scholar and professor of government, Rusk had served in the army in the Far East during the Second World War. Following the war he entered the State Department, working as an aide to Acheson and Lovett from 1946 to 1953. When Eisenhower entered the White House, Rusk left the federal government and became president of the Rockefeller Foundation, which did extensive work in developing countries.

Kennedy didn't know Rusk, but was impressed by an article in *Foreign Affairs* in 1960 in which Rusk argued that the President should take the lead on foreign policy, but should not engage in negotiations, leaving diplomacy to the diplomats.

Gentle and gracious, intelligent and hardworking, Rusk remained exceptionally loyal to the President and committed to his policies and objectives.

Kennedy liked Rusk, and came to respect him as an intelligent negotiator and an experienced diplomat.

But Rusk had serious limitations and never fit well with the new Kennedy team. Bland, colorless, overly cautious, he had little interest in administering the State Department. Rusk's lack of assertiveness, his unwillingness to speak his mind openly at meetings with others present, baffled Kennedy. Their relationship remained strictly formal. Kennedy addressed his cabinet and aides by their first names, but Rusk was always "Mr. Secretary." Rarely did anyone on the White House staff call him "Dean."[14]

For secretary of defense Kennedy selected Robert McNamara, the new president of the Ford Motor Company. Besides his prowess as an administrator, the auto executive had ties to Michigan's academic community and participated in great-books seminars. "How many other automobile executives or Cabinet members read Teilhard de Chardin?" asked Sargent Shriver. That McNamara climbed mountains and skied also appealed to the Kennedys' admiration for vigor and daring.

McNamara delighted his new boss from the start. Kennedy "had never met a self-made big businessman so literate and so able to hold his own against academics, Congressmen, and the press," observed Michael Beschloss. "He was dazzled by McNamara's toughness, quickness, fluency, competence, incorruptibility, freedom from political cant, and force of personality." Kennedy appreciated that his defense secretary clearly stated options and expressed his own judgment. McNamara would "come in with his twenty options and then say, 'Mr. President, I think we should do this.' I like that. Makes the job easier."

McNamara quickly moved to build up nuclear forces, enlarge conventional forces, increase military flexibility, and reduce costly interservice rivalries. Scientific management must be applied to defense planning, he believed; systematic quantitative analysis would enhance the quality of America's strategic decisions.[15]

McNamara, remarked Senator Barry Goldwater, was "an IBM machine with legs." Fast legs. "He really runs rather than walks," observed Secretary of Agriculture Orville Freeman of McNamara's energy; he even ran "up and down the escalator steps."

The aggressive McNamara carefully avoided giving the impression that he was encroaching upon the terrain of the mild-mannered secretary of state, but it was part of his nature to fill a void. "Whether in a debate behind closed doors or in public with his ferociously articulate Pentagon counterpart, Rusk could not compete," noted Beschloss.

Hidden by his enormous energy and competence were McNamara's serious weaknesses. Naive politically, he had no sense of history and minimal ability to understand people. Brushing aside anything not quantifiable, he could "not account for the intangibles, the depth of human spirit, motivation and morale," State Department official George Ball believed.[16]

The most controversial cabinet appointment turned out to be attorney general. Jack's father insisted that Robert Kennedy be given the post, but the President-elect resisted. Not that John didn't think his brother had major attributes. "I don't even have to think about organization," he had remarked about Robert during the campaign. "I just show up. Bobby's easily the best man I've ever seen. He's the hardest worker. He's the greatest organizer." But appointing his brother invited charges of nepotism.[17]

In his autobiography Clark Clifford described his bizarre involvement in the Kennedy family's internal struggle over appointing Bobby. John Kennedy approached Clifford with a dilemma: Joe Kennedy demanded that the President-elect appoint his brother as attorney general. "My concern is that Bobby has never practiced law. Bobby says he does not want the job—he thinks it will hurt me. I would rather put him into the Defense Department as the number-two man, and then let him succeed to the top after a while—or keep him around the White House to help me out. I have told my father that Bobby would create a real problem as Attorney General."

Clifford listened in amazement as Kennedy continued in a grave and intense voice. "My father said, 'That doesn't make any difference. I want Bobby to be Attorney General. He's a lawyer, he's savvy, he knows all the political ins and outs and can protect you.'" Kennedy thought his father might listen to Clifford. "I'd like you to go to New York and talk to him about this. But don't tell anyone else about it."

Clifford agreed, but privately judged his assignment an exceptionally strange one: "the President-elect asking a third party to try to talk to his father about his brother. Only the Kennedys!"

A few days later, Clifford called on the former ambassador in New York.

"Mr. Ambassador, there is an important matter that the President-elect has asked me to raise with you," Clifford began. "That is the question of the appointment of Bobby to be Attorney General." Joe Kennedy remained silent but listened to Clifford with total concentration. Clifford argued that Bobby should not be given the post. "He is young. He has time—start him somewhere else, perhaps number two at Defense. Give him the chance to grow. He will be outstanding."

When Clifford finished, Joe Kennedy thanked him for coming. "I am so glad to have heard your views," Joe said. After a momentary pause, the senior Kennedy continued. "I do want to leave you with one thought, however—one firm thought." He paused again and looked Clifford straight in the eye. "*Bobby is going to be Attorney General.* All of us have worked our tails off for Jack, and now that we have succeeded, I am going to see to it that Bobby gets the same chance that we gave to Jack."

Reflecting on the encounter, Clifford said, "He did not resent my presentation or my opposition to the appointment, he was simply telling me the facts. For a moment I had glimpsed the inner workings of that remarkable family, and, despite my admiration and affection for John F. Kennedy, I could not say I liked what I saw."[18]

Pressured and convinced by his father, Jack changed his mind. Although Robert initially declined the offer, he could not refuse his older brother's earnest entreaty. With Robert Kennedy listening nearby, John Kennedy explained his predicament to Bobby's friend John Seigenthaler. "I'm in a difficult position because in this Cabinet there really is no person with whom I have been intimately connected over the years. I need to know that when problems arise, I'm going to have somebody who's going to tell me the unvarnished truth, no matter what he thinks, and Bobby will do that. And so I need him. . . . The truth of the matter is I believe McNamara will make a great contribution, but I don't know him. And Dean Rusk is going to be my Secretary of State. The truth of the matter is I had no contact with him."

He needed an absolutely reliable attorney general. "I can count on [Bobby] completely." He continued: "Now, if I can ask Dean Rusk to give up a career; if I can ask Adlai Stevenson to make a sacrifice he does not want to make; if I can ask Bob McNamara to give up a job as head of that company—these men I don't even know—if I can ask them to make this sacrifice, certainly I can expect my own brother to give me the same sort of contribution."[19]

In the end, Robert agreed to take the post. At thirty-five, he became the youngest attorney general since the early nineteenth century.

When Ben Bradlee of *Newsweek* asked John Kennedy how he planned to announce the appointment, the President-elect said, "Well, I think I'll open the front door of the Georgetown house some morning about 2:00 A.M., look up and down the street, and, if there's no one there, I'll whisper, 'It's Bobby.' "

RFK's appointment was met with outrage. *The Nation* called it "the greatest example of nepotism this land has ever seen"; *Newsweek* described it as a "travesty of justice." But the criticism soon diminished.[20]

Of Kennedy's ten department heads, seven remained in their positions until his death; one of the other three, Arthur Goldberg, he appointed to the Supreme Court. Altogether, fifteen Rhodes scholars were named to major posts. "From Eisenhower to Kennedy," observed a Harvard professor, "is a shift from the 'gentleman's C' boys to the Phi Beta Kappas." A young cabinet, the average age was forty-seven, compared to Eisenhower's fifty-seven. Fewer members came from business backgrounds (four to Eisenhower's seven).

The cabinet balanced interests and sections. Three of his selections would have felt ideologically comfortable in the Eisenhower administration, but liberals like Freeman and Udall provided counterweight. (The President-elect told Walter Heller, his new chairman of the Council of Economic Advisers, "I need you as a counterweight to [Dillon]. He has conservative leanings, and I know your leanings are liberal.") "Few were ideologues," noted historian James Giglio, and "most were confident managers who emphasized efficiency, order, and, above all, results."

Robert Lovett thought Kennedy's reaction to his advice on cabinet choices had been extraordinary. "His thirst for information was so strong that he invited frankness and did not seem at all impatient with views which ran counter to those given him by others."[21]

The major positions on the White House staff all went to longtime, loyal members of Kennedy's Senate and campaign staff—with one exception. Initially Kennedy barely knew his special assistant for national security affairs, McGeorge Bundy, frequently calling him "McBundy."

The offspring of two of Boston's first families, the Lowells and the Bundys, the national security adviser was self-confident, usually considerate, but sometimes abrasive and flippant. Above all, Bundy possessed dazzling clarity and speed of mind. Arthur Schlesinger had watched as Dean Bundy operated masterfully at Harvard: "I had seen him learn how to dominate the faculty of Harvard University, a throng of intelligent and temperamental men; after that training, one could hardly doubt his capacity to deal with Washington bureaucrats." Although a Republican, Bundy had voted for Kennedy in 1960.[22]

A man of tremendous zest and verve, Bundy organized process at the White House, once describing his job as getting "to the bare bones of the problem as cleanly and clearly" as possible and then stating "the alternatives as sharply as possible." He insisted that his staff come to him with recommendations for action. He didn't want aimless discussion about a problem with China; he wanted to know what could be done about it given the political constraints. Bundy, remarked George Ball, had "extraordinary facility to grasp an idea, summarize or analyze it, and produce an orderly response as fast as a computer."

With the exception of his friend David Ormsby-Gore, Kennedy told associates, Bundy was the most intelligent person he had ever known. "Damn it, Bundy and I get more done in one day in the White House than they do in six months at the State Department." Kennedy remarked to Ben Bradlee, "You can't beat brains, and with brains, judgment. . . . [Bundy] does a tremendous amount of work. And he doesn't fold or get rattled when they're sniping at him."[23]

Kennedy appointed his former legislative secretary Evelyn Lincoln as his White House secretary. Pleasant, efficient, and loyal, Lincoln had no influence over policy in the way that Missy LeHand had with Franklin Roosevelt.

She typed, admitted visitors, and relayed messages, but Kennedy never asked her advice.

For press secretary Kennedy selected the man who had functioned in that capacity during the campaign. Reporters thought Pierre Salinger was inefficient, but he was so amiable and hardworking that he kept the media contented. Like Lincoln, Salinger exerted little influence on major policy decisions.

Kennedy had great confidence in his longtime aide, the hardworking Larry O'Brien, and named him as special assistant to the President for congressional relations. O'Brien had the daunting task of mobilizing all the resources of the White House to persuade Congress to enact the legislative program of the New Frontier. Because of his lack of experience in this area, O'Brien started slowly, but within a short time he proved exceptionally able in his role.[24]

Ted Sorensen's new title, special counsel to the President, was meaningless because he did almost no legal work for the President. His duties included preparing the legislative program, planning domestic policy, and writing speeches. Preparing speeches gave him important entreé into foreign policy as well.

Sorensen's balanced judgment most impressed David Bell, the administration's budget director. "He seemed to me almost uncannily able to weigh violently conflicting advice, extremely complicated substantive arguments, extraordinarily controversial issues, and cut through to recommendations for action which . . . averaged higher than the recommendations of anybody else I have ever seen in government."[25]

Sorensen accepted his White House position with more grace than he did his role during the campaign. He controlled his suspicions of newcomers and potential rivals. After the 1960 election, Kennedy apparently had a candid conversation with him about his insecurities. "Ted Sorensen, for a period of time, was far more interested in himself than he was in the President," reflected Robert Kennedy, "but I think they got that straightened out and Ted Sorensen was much better the last few years than he had been earlier."[26]

Of his exceptional dedication to Kennedy, Sorensen later remarked, "I had given eleven years of my life to John Kennedy and for those eleven years he was the only human being who mattered to me." Indeed, Sorensen's preoccupation with Kennedy's career probably caused his divorce in 1963 after fourteen years of marriage. (He remarried, but that marriage also ended in divorce in 1967.)

Sorensen explained the artificial dichotomy in his relationship with the President. "I was totally involved in the political, governmental, substantive side of his life and almost totally noninvolved in the social and personal side of his life. Except for a few formal banquets, we never even ate dinner together while I worked at the White House."[27]

Ken O'Donnell became one of the president's most trusted advisers. He acted as a liberal influence on Kennedy. "To hell with balancing the budget and keeping the conservatives happy," O'Donnell would say, in effect; "let's spend some money and help people."

O'Donnell was one of the "Irish Mafia," the media's label for Kennedy's Irish advisers from Massachusetts—Lawrence O'Brien, David Powers, and O'Donnell. Officially O'Donnell was appointments secretary to the president, but his actual duties were far-ranging. He planned the President's White House schedule, mapped out trips, and served as a sounding board for Kennedy's ideas. At Kennedy's request, he attended all meetings and listened. Kennedy often phoned him after dinner to compare observations. The President valued his advice—and often asked for it—because his aide was frank and honest.[28]

O'Donnell decided who could visit Kennedy and for how long. Because he was rude, abrasive, and blunt, and because he also decreed who could use limousines, helicopters, office space, and other amenities, his disposition made life unpleasant for some members of the staff and cabinet. He rarely bothered with civility, even with powerful cabinet members. "There were those who felt that he did not make things easy for them," said Tazewell Shepard, the President's naval aide. "But the point was that in the instance at hand O'Donnell thought the applicant was self serving rather than acting to serve the President."

After Pierre Salinger angered the appointments secretary, O'Donnell reacted furiously. "Listen, you son of a bitch, I'll put you out on Connecticut Avenue with a tin cup!" O'Donnell's swearing bothered some administration officials. "You talk about street language!" said one.

Despite the enemies he made, observed writer Patrick Anderson, who studied Kennedy's staff, it was O'Donnell's "very single-mindedness, the peculiar fierceness of his loyalty, his proud indifference to the opinions of anyone except the Kennedys, that made him so immensely valuable to them."[29]

Ebullient and elfish, Dave Powers became Kennedy's constant companion in the White House years. As they grew to know each other, the pair discovered that they enjoyed each other's wit and love of sports and politics. "Kennedy found in Powers an ethnic identity that he had not experienced in his cosmopolitan upbringing," said one observer.

With the official title of assistant appointments secretary, Powers worked closely with O'Donnell to keep the President on schedule during the day. Usually he was the first member of the staff to see the President in the morning and the last one to see him at night. He met visitors and dignitaries, greeting presidential callers in an uninhibited way—"Hi, pal"—and ushering them into the president's office or to a waiting room.

He swam with the President, and often dined with him in the evening when Jackie Kennedy was away. He accompanied the President to church and traveled with him, and in the evening they sometimes watched television in the President's living quarters or a motion picture in the White House theater.

"If you see the President with Dave," remarked a White House aide, "you know he is at ease." Powers assumed another, very private, role during Kennedy's presidency. Along with several others, he procured women for the President's sexual satisfaction.[30]

Arthur Schlesinger was asked to join the administration because Kennedy intended to be a great President, and thought it prudent to have a great historian in attendance. A distinguished Harvard professor, Schlesinger had won the Pulitzer Prize in 1946 for his history of America during the age of Andrew Jackson, and had recently completed the third volume of his majestic history of Franklin Roosevelt's presidency.

Schlesinger became Kennedy's ambassador to liberals and to the intellectual world—the world of writers, historians, and college professors. A gadfly, several responsibilities gravitated to him because of his special interests. Kennedy asked him to keep an eye on Latin American affairs because of the historian's longtime interest in the area. He served as Kennedy's informal channel of communication to Adlai Stevenson at the United Nations because Kennedy disliked talking to Stevenson. Jackie Kennedy treated Schlesinger as an ally, as her "minister of culture," and bombarded the historian with handwritten memos about her special projects.[31]

Kennedy's staff in the West Wing, though, never considered Schlesinger one of the inner circle of advisers. He did not have operating responsibility for anything. "He was at the ball park, but he wasn't in the ball game," remarked a White House aide.

"[The President] liked Arthur Schlesinger, but he thought he was a little bit of a nut sometimes," Robert Kennedy later remarked. More charitably, Robert added that Schlesinger "used to stimulate people all around the government by writing them memos, what they should be doing and what they should be thinking of, and frequently made a lot of sense. I think he was a valuable addition."[32]

Except for secretaries and his personal physician, Dr. Janet Travell, Kennedy didn't appoint any women to the White House staff or the cabinet or to head an independent agency. The highest position given to a woman went to Esther Peterson, appointed director of the Women's Bureau and assistant secretary of labor for labor standards.

There was plenty of talent in the new Kennedy administration, but as Harris Wofford observed, toward what end? There would be adventure, but "where would the adventure lead, and by what compass?"[33]

At Kennedy's request, on January 19, 1961, the day before the inauguration, he met again with Eisenhower at the White House. Alone at first, Eisenhower showed Kennedy how to use the codebook and the small computerlike device, always close to the President, for launching a nuclear attack. Ike also demonstrated the machinery at the president's disposal for evacuating the White House in case of emergency. When he spoke a few words into a phone, five minutes later an army helicopter hovered over the White House.

After forty-five minutes, the two men stepped into the Cabinet Room, where they joined Secretary of State Herter, Secretary of Defense Gates, Secretary of the Treasury Anderson, and their three counterparts in the new administration, Rusk, McNamara, and Dillon. Persons and Clifford also attended.

In a memo written to himself shortly after the meeting Kennedy indicated he had been eager to visit Eisenhower for two reasons: to reassure the public "as to the harmony of the transition," thereby "strengthening our hands," and to deal with the exploding crisis in Laos. Exactly what Eisenhower said about U.S. intervention in Laos, though, has been a subject of major contention.[34]

In Laos, which had gained its independence in 1954, the Communist Pathet Lao were winning their struggle against the U.S.-backed forces of Phoumi Nosavan for control of the country. President Eisenhower stated unequivocally that Laos was the key to the entire region of Southeast Asia; a Communist victory there would bring unbearable pressure on Thailand, Cambodia, and South Vietnam.

Afterward Kennedy requested memos from Rusk, McNamara, Dillon, and Clifford, asking for their recollections of what Ike said. Kennedy dictated his own thoughts to Evelyn Lincoln on the same day as the meeting:

> I asked the Secretary [Herter] as to whether in his opinion we should intervene if the SETO [sic] was invoked by the government. He said very directly that he felt we should. It was the cork in the bottle. If Laos fell, then Thailand, the Philippines, and of course Chiang Kai Shek [sic] would go. I turned to the President. He stated also that he felt we should intervene. When I asked him whether he felt that the communists could intervene with greater force, he said it was a question as to whether they would be willing to see the war spread.

Secretary Gates thought the United States would have sufficient military strength to land troops in Laos. Kennedy concluded that the Eisenhower administration supported intervention, feeling it was preferable to a Communist victory.

Clifford recalled that Eisenhower considered Laos so important that if it reached the point where the United States could not persuade our allies to act with us, then he would be willing, "*as a last desperate hope, to intervene unilaterally* [emphasis in original]." Dean Rusk's recollection tended to support Clifford's version.[35]

McNamara and Dillon, however, thought that Eisenhower delivered a mixed message. McNamara had the impression that Eisenhower was deeply uncertain about the proper course. "President Eisenhower advised against unilateral action by the United States in connection with Laos," McNamara wrote five days after the meeting.

Almost everything Eisenhower and Herter said about Laos was extremely pessimistic. Kennedy seemed to have no viable options. The Communists were winning; a coalition government would eventually lead to a Communist takeover; our allies England and France wouldn't intervene; and whatever supplies and troops the United States sent to the Royal Laotian Government, the Sino-Soviet bloc would more than match on behalf of the Communist Pathet Lao. When Kennedy asked, "What action can be taken to keep the Chinese Communists out of Laos?" Ike had no answer.

Dillon later told an interviewer that "Eisenhower and Herter both got a certain inner satisfaction from laying a potentially intractable problem in Kennedy's lap." McNamara agreed: "Eisenhower did not know what to do in Southeast Asia and was glad to leave it to the Democrats."

"What I do know is that we received no thoughtful analysis of the problem and no pros and cons regarding alternative ways to deal with it," McNamara wrote in his memoir. "We were left only with the ominous prediction that if Laos were lost, all of Southeast Asia would fall. By implication, the West would have to do whatever was necessary to prevent that outcome. The meeting made a deep impression on Kennedy and us all. It heavily influenced our subsequent approach to Southeast Asia."[36]

Kennedy hoped his inaugural on January 20, 1961, would set the tone for his presidency. He wanted to heal the lingering wounds inflicted during the 1960 campaign, to remind Americans of their common heritage and purpose, to set forth generally the policies and objectives of his administration, and to reassure the international community.

Presidential inaugurals usually focused on broad, undeveloped principles, policies, and promises. Kennedy asked Sorensen to study past inaugural addresses, and the secret of Lincoln's Gettysburg Address. "Lincoln never used a two- or three-syllable word where a one-syllable word would do," Sorensen discovered, and "never used two or three words where one word would do."

Kennedy wrestled with what to say about domestic policy. "Let's drop out the domestic stuff altogether," he finally told Sorensen. "It's too long anyway." It would inevitably sound too partisan, too divisive, more like the campaign.

His inaugural should be brief. "It's more effective that way and I don't want people to think I'm a windbag." He settled for one of the shortest in U.S. history—only 1,343 words.[37]

Sorensen wrote most of the address although the ideas and some of the phrases originated with Kennedy. On January 18 Sorensen consulted with Walter Lippmann at the columnist's home and brought along a draft of the speech. Lippmann suggested one change: cutting out an implicit reference to the Soviet Union as the "enemy" and substituting instead the word "adversary."

Stewart Udall suggested that Kennedy feature the eminent poet Robert Frost during the inaugural ceremony. Kennedy reacted favorably. Long an admirer of the eighty-six-year-old Frost, Kennedy often quoted the poet, concluding his speeches with the idealistic "But I have promises to keep, / And miles to go before I sleep." Frost's appearance would enhance the prestige of the inaugural and highlight Kennedy's desire to promote the arts.

Kennedy added one fascinating caveat about Frost's appearance. "He's a master of words and I'm going to be sure he doesn't upstage me. Let's not have him give any kind of a speech, or they'll remember what he said and not what I said. Maybe we can have him recite a poem."[38]

At noon on the day before the inaugural, snow began to fall in Washington; soon it strangled traffic throughout the city. For agonizing hours the huge inaugural event seemed destined to become a fiasco. "Foul-ups, fumbles and failures fell upon one another in a tangled heap," *Time* reported. It appeared that all the festivities might have to be rescheduled.

"Absolutely hopeless," Washington officials described the traffic mess at the peak of the blizzard. That evening, at the National Symphony's Inaugural Concert at Constitution Hall, two-thirds of the sellout audience couldn't make it because of the storm. Jack and Jackie managed to attend only after cutting short earlier engagements.

After the concert the couple took in Frank Sinatra's Hollywood-style gala at the cavernous National Armory. (Only two-thirds of the ticket holders turned up because of the blizzard.) Leonard Bernstein, Ethel Merman, Milton Berle, Nat King Cole, Mahalia Jackson, Juliet Prowse, Sir Laurence

Olivier, Jimmy Durante, and brother-in-law Peter Lawford put on the entertainment. Joe Kennedy hosted a big bash at a downtown restaurant following Sinatra's gala. Exhausted, Jackie Kennedy went home. It was 4:00 A.M. before Jack climbed into bed.[39]

Thousands of men, using seven hundred plows and trucks, worked through the night to remove tons of snow from Washington's main streets. Finally, after dropping nearly eight inches, the snow stopped.

Inauguration morning opened sunny but frigid. Kennedy began his day by attending Mass at Holy Trinity Church; next he and Jackie drove to the White House for coffee with Dwight and Mamie Eisenhower and other dignitaries. Then President Eisenhower and President-elect Kennedy emerged from the White House in top hats, climbed into the bubble-top presidential limousine, and drove to the inaugural platform on the steps of the Capitol's East Portico.

Kennedy waited in a small chamber near the Rotunda, whistling softly to himself as the ceremony ran behind schedule. With everything ready, he walked out onto the windswept platform and sat down next to Ike while the Marine Band struck up "America the Beautiful."

While Richard Cardinal Cushing intoned a long invocation, wisps of smoke curled from the lectern. Seconds after the cardinal's "Amen," secret service agents and Capitol custodians rushed down the crowded aisle to douse a smoldering electric motor used to adjust the height of the lectern.[40]

When Robert Frost was called forward, he ambled slowly to the podium, and fumbled momentarily with his papers. Haltingly, the bareheaded poet, his white hair whisking in the wind, began to read his new poem, "Dedication." Then he faltered. Embarrassed titters spread through the audience. The reflection of the bright sun and snow blinded the old New Englander; the wind whipped his manuscript. Lyndon Johnson leaped from his seat to shade Frost's manuscript with his hat, but to no avail.

Frost saved the day by reciting from memory a poem he had written two decades earlier, the finely chiseled "The Gift Outright," which he had planned to read after the new poem to Kennedy. In the end Frost's misadventure provided one of the most moving moments of the ceremony.[41]

Finally, at 12:51 P.M., Kennedy stepped forward with Chief Justice Earl Warren, put his left hand over a family Bible, and with his breath frosty in the twenty-two-degree temperature, raised his right hand and pronounced, "I do solemnly swear . . ."

Then, in a clear, crisp voice, with his jabbing finger, he delivered his inaugural oration.

> We observe today not a victory of party but a celebration of freedom—
> symbolizing an end as well as a beginning—signifying renewal as well as

change. For I have sworn before you and Almighty God the same solemn oath our forebears prescribed nearly a century and three quarters ago.

The world is very different now. For man holds in his mortal hands the power to abolish all forms of human poverty and all forms of human life. And yet the same revolutionary beliefs for which our forebears fought are still at issue around the globe—the belief that the rights of man come not from the generosity of the state but from the hand of God,

We dare not forget today that we are the heirs of that first revolution. Let the word go forth from this time and place, to friend and foe alike, that the torch has been passed to a new generation of Americans—born in this century, tempered by war, disciplined by a hard and bitter peace, proud of our ancient heritage—and unwilling to witness or permit the slow undoing of those human rights to which this nation has always been committed, and to which we are committed today at home and around the world.

Let every nation know, whether it wishes us well or ill, that we shall pay any price, bear any burden, meet any hardship, support any friend, oppose any foe, to assure the survival and the success of liberty.

He pledged loyalty to old allies, supported freedom for new nations, and promised to assist those "struggling to break the bonds of mass misery."

The United Nations was still "our last best hope in an age where the instruments of war have far outpaced the instruments of peace." He mentioned no countries and no leaders, but at times, the urgency of his message seemed to be aimed directly at Nikita Khrushchev:

Finally, to those nations who would make themselves our adversary, we offer not a pledge but a request: that both sides begin anew the quest for peace, before the dark powers of destruction unleashed by science engulf all humanity in planned or accidental self-destruction.

We dare not tempt them with weakness. For only when our arms are sufficient beyond doubt can we be certain beyond doubt that they will never be employed.

But neither can two great and powerful groups of nations take comfort from our present course—both sides overburdened by the cost of modern weapons, both rightly alarmed by the steady spread of the deadly atom, yet both racing to alter that uncertain balance of terror that stays the hand of mankind's final war.

So let us begin anew—remembering on both sides that civility is not a sign of weakness, and sincerity is always subject to proof. Let us never negotiate out of fear. But let us never fear to negotiate.

Let both sides explore what problems unite us instead of belaboring those problems which divide us.

Let both sides, for the first time, formulate serious and precise proposals for the inspection and control of arms—and bring the absolute power to destroy other nations under the absolute control of all nations.

Let both sides seek to invoke the wonders of science instead of its terrors. Together let us explore the stars, conquer the deserts, eradicate disease, tap the ocean depths, and encourage the arts and commerce.

Let both sides unite to heed in all corners of the earth the command of Isaiah—to "undo the heavy burdens [and] let the oppressed go free."

And if a beachhead of cooperation may push back the jungle of suspicion, let both sides join in creating a new endeavor, not a new balance of power, but a new world of law, where the strong are just and the weak secure and the peace preserved.

All this will not be finished in the first one hundred days. Nor will it be finished in the first one thousand days, nor in the life of this administration, nor even perhaps in our lifetime on this planet. But let us begin.

In your hands, my fellow citizens, more than mine, will rest the final success or failure of our course. Since this country was founded, each generation of Americans has been summoned to give testimony to its national loyalty. The graves of young Americans who answered the call to service surround the globe.

Now the trumpet summons us again—not as a call to bear arms, though arms we need—not as a call to battle, though embattled we are—but as a call to bear the burden of a long twilight struggle, year in and year out, "rejoicing in hope, patient in tribulation"—a struggle against the common enemies of man: tyranny, poverty, disease, and war itself. . . .

In the long history of the world, only a few generations have been granted the role of defending freedom in its hours of maximum danger. I do not shrink from this responsibility—I welcome it. I do not believe that any of us would exchange places with any other people or any other generation. The energy, the faith, the devotion which we bring to this endeavor will light our country and all who serve it—and the glow from that fire can truly light the world.

Finally, his powerful conclusion:

And so, my fellow Americans: ask not what your country can do for you—ask what you can do for your country.

My fellow citizens of the world: ask not what America will do for you, but what together we can do for the freedom of man.

Finally, whether you are citizens of America or citizens of the world, ask of us here the same high standards of strength and sacrifice which we ask of you. With a good conscience our only sure reward, with history the final judge of our deeds, let us go forth to lead the land we love, asking His blessing and His help, but knowing that here on earth God's work must truly be our own.[42]

"It was soaring," Jackie later remarked of her husband's oration. "I knew I was hearing something great. I was so proud of Jack. There was so much I wanted to say! But I could scarcely embrace him in front of all those people. So, I remember I just put my hand on his cheek and said, 'Jack, you were so wonderful!'"

He had masterfully distilled the themes he had presented in the campaign, but without seeming partisan. "Reaction to the speech was immediate," *Time* wrote. "From all shades of political outlook, from people who had voted for Kennedy in November and people who had voted against him, came a surge of congratulations. . . . The speech set forth few concrete proposals, but its broad, general imperatives stirred the heart."

A review in *The New Yorker* hoped Kennedy's success would "revive a taste for good oratory—a taste that has been alternately frustrated by inarticulateness and dulled by bombast. . . . We find it hard to believe that an Athenian or Roman citizen could have listened to it unmoved, or that Cicero, however jealous of his own reputation, would have found reason to object to it."[43]

The speech had emphasized the values of peace and freedom. Of its twenty-seven paragraphs, eleven focused on peace, and eight on freedom. Scholars of a later generation were struck by its martial tone: "Let every nation know, whether it wishes us well or ill, that we shall pay any price, bear any burden, meet any hardship, support any friend, oppose any foe to assure the survival and the success of liberty." But even though he promoted military strength and global commitment, he also stressed peace through negotiation, cooperation, and arms limitation. "Civility is not a sign of weakness," he said.

Without being too heavy-handed, he had sprinkled religious references throughout the speech. The same is true of historical references, especially to revered American values and forefathers. He claimed that the "same revolutionary beliefs for which our forebears fought are still at issue around the globe," specifically "the belief that the rights of man come not from the generosity of the state, but from the hand of God." As in Lincoln's Gettysburg Address, archaic diction occasionally crept into the speech: "anew," "asunder," "writ," "forebears" (twice).

"There is almost no word that a moderately intelligent high-school graduate would have to look up in a dictionary," said one observer. In fact, 71 percent of the words were monosyllabic.[44]

The oration is stylistically remembered for its antitheses—thirty altogether. He compared opposites: end-beginning, old-new, rich-poor, friend-foe. The most famous lines ("ask not what your country can do for you—ask what you can do for your country") and the second most famous ("Let us never negotiate out of fear. But let us never fear to negotiate") both exemplified the abundance of antitheses.

A few trite phrases and metaphors probably should have been excised with an editor's blue pencil: "those who foolishly sought power by riding on the back of the tiger ended up inside" and "the beachhead of cooperation may push back the jungle of suspicion." Some of the metaphors—"the torch," "bonds of mass misery," "the chains of poverty," "corners of the earth," "the trumpet," "the glow from that fire"—were rather hackneyed. Kennedy achieved more freshness with subtle metaphors: "iron tyranny," "destruction unleashed," "twilight struggle," "forge."[45]

After the inaugural ceremony the new President and the new first lady drove to the reviewing stand near the White House to watch the inaugural parade. "With a steady thump-de-thump of the drums and a silvery splash of cymbals and brass, the marchers tootled endlessly down the avenue," *Time* reported. "Trundling along, interspersed with the 32,000 marchers, were more than 40 huge floats."

Thoughtful and considerate, Kennedy requested that various dignitaries be brought to the front of the reviewing stand with him and Mrs. Kennedy. (He was particularly concerned that Chief Justice and Mrs. Earl Warren not feel neglected.) He signaled for his military aide, Chester V. Clifton. "There must be more that we can do up here," he whispered. "Why don't you think of something?" Clifton suggested bringing prominent persons—cabinet members, the secretaries of the army, navy, and air force, the Joint Chiefs of Staff—to the reviewing stand. "Why don't I bring them up one or two at a time to stand with you and review some of the sections of the parade?" Kennedy agreed. "That's a great idea, and then they'll get their pictures taken, and they'll all feel a part of this." For the next two hours Clifton kept rotating dignitaries into the President's box.[46]

That evening Jack was in an exuberant mood, but Jackie, emotionally depleted and overwhelmed by her new burdens, didn't join her husband for the receptions and parties in the early evening. Instead she stayed at the White House until Jack picked her up at ten-thirty. "I had been in my room for days, not getting out of bed," Jackie recalled. "All the details were getting too much."

She attended the first few inaugural balls but became exhausted; shortly after midnight she asked to be taken back to the White House.

After Jackie went home, Jack was about to hook up with Red Fay, who had been asked that evening to escort the beautiful actress Angie Dickinson. Kennedy wanted the couple to tag along and accompany him as he party-hopped. Fay asked if the rest of his group—actress Kim Novak and architect Fernando Parra—could join them. At that juncture Kennedy reconsidered. "I can just see the papers tomorrow," he told Fay. "The new President concludes his first day speeding into the night with Kim Novak and Angie Dickinson while his wife recuperates from the birth of their first son." With a tone of resignation, he continued, "Well, Redhead, for a moment I almost forgot I was President of the United States. It has its advantages and its restrictions, and this is one of the restrictions. Good night."

The new President stopped briefly at each of the massive balls, finding the halls so jammed that nobody could dance. To one crowd he cracked: "I hope we can all meet here tomorrow at the same place at 1 o'clock and do it all over again."[47]

At about 2:00 A.M., Kennedy left inaugural festivities at the Statler-Hilton, entered his limousine, and with Secret Service agents and press corp in tow, churned through Washington streets to a party at the Georgetown home of columnist Joe Alsop. "Shortly thereafter," said Robert Merry, Alsop's biographer, "hearing a loud knock at his door, Joe opened it to find a jaunty Jack Kennedy standing on his portico, flecks of snow scattered about his thick hair and overcoat." Alsop's party guests included Peter Lawford and a bevy of Hollywood actresses.

"The President was hungry," the columnist recalled. "So I fed him terrapin." Kennedy stayed at the party for an hour and a half, returning to the White House at about three thirty.[48]

What lay ahead was uncertain, but one feature of the new presidency was clear. Kennedy's youth and freshness "seemed to stand in contrast to the other men who had for so long dominated the world scene," wrote David Halberstam. Kennedy was twenty-seven years younger than Eisenhower. West Germany's Konrad Adenauer was eighty-five; Israel's David Ben-Gurion, seventy-four; India's Jawaharlal Nehru, seventy-one; and England's Harold Macmillan and the USSR's Nikita Khrushchev, both sixty-six. At age forty-three, President John F. Kennedy represented a startling generational change.

26

THE PERFECT FAILURE

On his first full morning as President, Kennedy arrived at his newly painted office at 8:50. As his first order of business, inspired by the poverty he had witnessed during the West Virginia primary, he signed an executive order doubling the five-cent allotment of grain and dried milk distributed daily to four million needy people in depressed areas.

At 10:00 A.M. he received his first White House visitor: Harry S. Truman. The day before, the former president had mentioned that he wanted to see the changes in the White House since he had left office. With tears in his eyes, Truman told an aide: "Isn't it nice of him to want to bother with an old farmer like me on his first day?"

The President was giddy about his new role. "There was this wonderful and exhilarating sense that all things were possible," said Charles Bartlett. "He was just bursting with all the things he could do. There was an enormous amount of goodness in his spirit then."

That evening, as the Kennedys dined with the Bartletts, when the men had taken off their jackets and lit their cigars, Kennedy said, "I slept in Lincoln's bed last night." Bartlett: "Any strange dreams?" Kennedy: "No, I just jumped in and hung on."[1]

A few days later, on a tour of the upstairs of the White House with Kenneth Galbraith, Kennedy pointed to where Ike's golf shoes had poked holes in the office floor. As they left the office in the West Wing for the house proper, Kennedy directed them headlong into a closet.

In mid-February the public gave Kennedy a 72 percent favorable approval rating. "The Kennedy buildup goes on," wrote James Burns, Kennedy's biographer, in *The New Republic*. "The adjectives tumble over one another. He is not only the handsomest, the best-dressed, the most articulate, and graceful as a gazelle. He is omniscient; he swallows and digests whole books in minutes; he confounds experts with his superior knowledge of their field. He is omnipotent." Burns worried that Kennedy and his family would soon suffer ill effects from public overexposure. "The buildup will not last. The public can be cruel, and so can the press."[2]

In the *New York Journal-American* Ruth Montgomery concluded that "the current reaction to Kennedy's Cabinet appointments, his Inaugural address, State of the Union message and general conduct has been so lopsidedly favorable that he would probably win a run-off election today by a landslide." Die-hard Republicans were still waiting for the first "real Kennedy blooper."[3]

A drastic blooper was right around the corner, but even that didn't dampen his popularity.

Initially Kennedy had been sympathetic to Fidel Castro's revolution. Early in 1960, in *The Strategy of Peace,* he described the Cuban leader as "part of the legacy of Bolivar." He questioned if Castro might have adopted "a more rational course" had the United States not supported Batista "so long and so uncritically," and had it granted Castro a warmer welcome on his trip to Washington. Later he stated that "the brutal, bloody, and despotic dictatorship of Fulgencio Batista" had caused its own downfall.

But as Castro became more stridently anti-American and cozied up to the Soviets, a sympathetic approach to Castro's Cuba became impossible for any American politician. In the last half of 1960, Kennedy adopted the standard U.S. view that Castro was a Communist who had "betrayed the ideals of the Cuban revolution" and transformed Cuba "into a hostile and militant Communist satellite."

In January 1960, the Eisenhower administration made the top-secret decision to overthrow Castro. By the following March the Central Intelligence Agency had developed a plan. The CIA's model and inspiration was a successful coup in Guatemala in 1954. In only one week the agency had helped to topple the leftist government of Jacobo Arbenz Guzmán using a force of 150 exiles and a few World War II P-47 fighters flown by American pilots. Both of the CIA's senior field operators during the Guatemalan operation held major posts in developing the Cuban plan.[4]

Established in 1947, the CIA correlated and evaluated intelligence data, advised the National Security Council, and engaged in espionage and sabotage under the guidance of the NSC. Besides overthrowing the Arbenz regime, the CIA claimed credit for gathering advanced information on the British-French-Israeli invasion of Suez in 1956, and for directing the U-2 flights over the Soviet Union which provided the United States with excellent intelligence. The CIA had won the reputation as the government's covert-action specialists, the agency that arranged quick fixes for awkward foreign predicaments.

The CIA's director, sixty-eight-year-old Allen Dulles, was the amiable and scholarly younger brother of John Foster Dulles, Ike's secretary of state. Dulles's deputy, the CIA official directly in charge of the Cuban operation, had been at the center of the CIA's most exciting adventures, a larger-than-life figure who could have walked out of a James Bond fantasy. A graduate of Groton and Yale, Richard Bissell shared the same background as Washington's policymaking elite. (As a young economics professor at Yale, he had taught McGeorge Bundy.) He had earned the reputation as a formidable administrator, managing shipping during World War II and helping to implement the Marshall Plan. In 1954 he joined the CIA as a special assistant to Dulles, and he gained extraordinary success and prestige by managing the U-2 reconnaissance program. Energetic and brilliant, hardworking and high-strung, Bissell was the CIA's director of plans. Impressed, Kennedy earmarked Bissell as eventual director of the CIA after Dulles retired.[5]

In thirteen months, from the time the CIA first presented the Cuban operation to President Eisenhower (March 17, 1960) to the invasion actually carried out under Kennedy's direction (April 17, 1961), the CIA radically changed its concept. Originally the plan called for a long, slow, clandestine buildup of guerrilla forces in Cuba, all recruited, trained, and infiltrated into Cuba by the CIA. Thirteen months later the agency advocated an overt amphibious landing of 1,400 combat-trained, heavily armed Cuban-exile soldiers. Most were not trained for guerrilla warfare. The assault force would administer a "shock" to Cuba which, the CIA hoped, would trigger an uprising against Castro.

At the White House meeting on January 19, 1961, President Eisenhower told Kennedy that "it was the policy of this government" to help the Cuban exiles "to the utmost." The invasion plan should be "continued and accelerated."

Unfortunately for Kennedy, the supposedly covert plan was becoming an open secret. On January 10, 1961, *The New York Times* exposed it on the front page. "U.S. Helps Train an Anti-Castro Force at Secret Guatemalan Air-Ground Base" screamed a three-column headline. Subheadings proclaimed "Clash with Cuba Feared" and "Installations Built with American Aid."[6]

Meanwhile, Allen Dulles told senators privately that Cuba was rapidly falling into the Soviet bloc. The Soviets were sending Cuba large amounts of arms, and Cuban pilots trained in Communist Czechoslovakia would return shortly to fly jets provided by the Soviets. Making rapid progress in controlling the entire Cuban population, Castro was creating a Communist totalitarian state. Castro supported revolutionary movements in Panama, Nicaragua, the Dominican Republic, and Haiti, Dulles contended; one or more of those countries might "go like Castro in the next few months."

President Kennedy's first official briefing on the Cuban plan took place on January 28, 1961; other meetings followed. At each one the President received an updated account of the preparations, but did not authorize any military action.[7]

Kennedy hoped to rid Cuba of Castro without suffering serious political consequences. A champion of the world's emerging nations, he didn't want to begin his presidency by openly destroying Castro's government, casting himself and the United States as the traditional imperialist. Committing full American military force to a Cuban invasion would be a propaganda disaster—like the Russian invasion of Hungary in 1956—with horrifying pictures of Cuban bodies in the streets of Havana. What's more, a full-scale U.S. invasion might spark Soviet retaliation against West Berlin.

If he didn't proceed with some action against Castro, though, Republicans would accuse him of being soft on communism, a coward, a traitor, a weakling. Nixon would say he had betrayed Eisenhower's commitment to liberate Cuba.

The project already had momentum, and Eisenhower backed it. Even though many of Kennedy's senior officials were neophytes, unseasoned and unaccustomed to working together, a decision needed to be made soon. "The few responsible officials who drove the project forward exuded enthusiasm and confidence," observed historian Lawrence Freedman. Especially Bissell, who was well organized and persuasive, blending analysis and advocacy with a "salesman's sense of the telling phrase."[8]

Kennedy had come to believe that unless the United States overthrew Castro the Cuban Revolution would infect other Central American countries, and dangerously expand Soviet influence. Since Central America was the United States' natural sphere of influence, any Communist foothold was a dangerous affront. "When the foothold was Cuba, so close to the coast of Florida, and personalized by such a charismatic and bombastic figure as Fidel, the affront was all the greater," noted Freedman.

The CIA's intelligence claimed extensive anti-Castro resistance on the island. As many as three thousand rebels, supported by twenty thousand sympathizers, actively engaged in resistance in Cuba; probably 25 percent of the Cuban people would welcome an organized, heavily armed force that could establish a stronghold on the island.

Not everyone agreed that the Cuban people were so disaffected with Castro or so ripe for counterrevolution. The *New York Herald Tribune* reported on a recent visit to Cuba by Senator-elect Claiborne Pell of Rhode Island. "The people of Cuba that I saw and spoke to during three or four days of quiet observation were not sullen or unhappy or dissatisfied," Pell stated. "They were still tasting the satisfaction of Castro's land reform, of his nationalization of United States companies and of the other much-touted reforms put into effect by Castro. The dispossessed and disgruntled were in jail or in exile."[9]

On March 11, 1961, the first of two critical meetings took place in the Cabinet Room. Arthur Schlesinger found the assembled group "intimidating." The president was there, along with Rusk and McNamara, CIA officials, and General Lyman Lemnitzer, chair of the Joint Chiefs of Staff, and the two other chiefs, all three in their uniforms and decorations. Schlesinger "shrank" into a chair at the far end of the room.

Sounding an ominous note of urgency, Dulles warned that the United States had a "disposal problem" with the U.S.-trained Cuban Brigade. "If we have to take these men out of Guatemala, we will have to transfer them to the United States, and we can't have them wandering around the country telling everyone what they have been doing." The political repercussions of canceling the invasion would be nasty. The petulant, bridled invasion force would spread word that the United States had turned tail. Republicans would call Kennedy a chicken.

At the meeting Bissell presented his plan, code-named Operation Trinidad (named after the invasion site, the Cuban town on the south-central coast of Cuba). He recommended an amphibious and airborne assault with tactical air support. The force would seize a beachhead adjacent to terrain suitable for guerrilla operations. The Trinidad site had several advantages: It was far from Castro's known troop locations, it permitted reversion to guerrilla operations in the Escambray Mountains if the invasion failed, and the local population had shown past sympathy toward anti-Castro guerrillas.

After lengthy discussion, the President stated that he would take the chance of going ahead, but could not endorse a plan that "put us in so openly, in view of the world situation." Trinidad was "too spectacular," too much like a "World War II invasion."

Kennedy told Bissell to revise the plan in two ways. The invasion must be an unspectacular landing at night in an area with a minimum likelihood of opposition. And, if ultimate success depended on tactical air support, that support should appear to come from a Cuban air base, meaning the landing site must have a suitable airfield nearby.[10]

From March 13 to March 15 the paramilitary staff of the CIA worked feverishly to devise a plan that addressed Kennedy's concerns. On March 15

Bissell presented his revised plan: an attack at the Bay of Pigs (Bahía de Cochinos), a site also known as Zapata. "The area selected is at the head of a well protected deep water estuary on the south coast of Cuba," Bissell reported. "It is almost surrounded by swamps impenetrable to infantry in any numbers and entirely impenetrable to vehicles, except along two narrow and easily defended approaches." As Kennedy had requested, near the beachhead was an airstrip (and possibly two) adequate to handle B-26s. The area had been the scene of resistance activities "for over a hundred years."[11]

At the meeting on March 15 nobody questioned the extraordinary fact that in only a few days Bissell had made huge changes in the plan. The Kennedy team was impressed when they should have been incredulous. Bundy wrote Kennedy that the CIA had "done a remarkable job of reframing the landing so as to make it unspectacular and quiet, and plausibly Cuban in its essentials. . . . I have been a skeptic about Bissell's operation, but now I think we are on the edge of a good answer."

The Zapata plan had been prepared so quickly that the Joint Chiefs could give it only a cursory evaluation. Nonetheless, they endorsed the Zapata plan as the best alternative, never indicating at the meeting that they still preferred the Trinidad plan. The chiefs assumed that the new plan included air support, and accepted the CIA's assurances that thousands of Cuban insurgents would immediately join the invasion forces and that, in the event the battle went against them, the invaders would at once "go guerrilla" and take to the hills. The endorsement by the Joint Chiefs, Dean Rusk later observed, "tended to encourage President Kennedy to make the decision to go ahead with it."[12]

At a meeting with the President the following day the CIA made further revisions. After the landing at night, there would be air drops at first light. All the ships would withdraw from the beach by dawn. Pleased with the changes, Kennedy directed the planners to proceed with the Zapata preparations although he still withheld final approval.

At none of the meetings about the Zapata plan was Kennedy or Bundy or McNamara or the Joint Chiefs made to understand that, unlike the Trinidad plan, the new one lost what Kennedy considered vital: the guerrilla option for the invaders. The President and his team still believed that the invasion force could "melt into the mountains." Nobody clearly explained that the mountains were now too far away.

To control the political risks, Kennedy had insisted, above all else, that the invasion carefully allow the United States to claim deniability. The CIA should not involve U.S. planes, ships, weapons, facilities, or personnel. Use nothing that could serve, if captured, as proof of U.S. participation. Bissell consented, but neglected to tell the president that "deniability" might affect the "viability" of the project. It might be impossible to disguise U.S. involvement in an invasion of the size now contemplated. "As D-day approached, presidential input into the planning process was largely driven by Kennedy's misconceived preoccupation with deniability," noted Freedman.

At the end of March Kennedy requested the CIA to ask the brigade leaders whether they believed the operation would succeed even though U.S. strike forces would not participate in any way. Did they still want to proceed? Brigade leaders responded that they wanted to go ahead.[13]

Opposition to the Cuban venture emerged, but supporters of the invasion muffled the voices of critics. Undersecretary of State Chester Bowles, who learned in late January of an imminent invasion, strongly opposed it. Senator William Fulbright, chairman of the Senate's Foreign Relations Committee, also dissented. On March 30 Fulbright hitched a ride with the President aboard *Air Force One* as Kennedy headed to Palm Beach for a long Easter weekend. Beforehand, Fulbright had instructed his aide, Pat Holt, to draft a memo critical of a U.S.-backed invasion. On the plane he handed his broadside to the President.

The proposed invasion was an "open secret," Fulbright charged. "To give this activity even covert support is of a piece with the hypocrisy and cynicism for which the United States is constantly denouncing the Soviet Union in the United Nations and elsewhere." Cuba would become for the United States what Hungary was for the Soviets in 1956—a propaganda disaster. To conceal U.S. involvement was impossible, and the invasion would violate several U.S. treaties and laws. Better to tolerate and isolate Castro, who was a "thorn in the flesh," not a "dagger in the heart."[14]

On the evening of April 4, Kennedy met at the Department of State with senior officials involved in planning the Zapata operation. He invited Fulbright to attend. After listening to Bissell explain the details of the operation, Fulbright realized the gravity of the situation. He had not expected the operation to be so large and complex or the planning to be so advanced.

Irritated and defiant, Fulbright denounced the entire operation. If it succeeded, Cuba would inevitably become a dependency of the United States, and the world would brand the United States brutal imperialists. If it failed, America would look weak and ineffective. Bissell's briefing did not convince Fulbright that the CIA's scheme was foolproof. In any case, an invasion clearly violated America's treaty obligations, and compromised the nation's moral position in the world. Despite Fulbright's eloquent plea, most of the meeting's participants remained unmoved. His comments did not even elicit discussion.

The President asked everyone, "What do you think?" He wanted yes-or-no answers. When Adolf A. Berle, the venerable State Department specialist in Latin American affairs, began a long reply, Kennedy cut him off and insisted on his vote. Whereupon Berle snapped, "I say, let 'er rip!" The consensus was to move ahead with the operation.[15]

On April 10 Schlesinger wrote Kennedy arguing that the operational planning for the invasion was much further advanced than the political, diplomatic, and economic planning which should ideally accompany it. Kennedy's excellent start in conducting foreign relations could be sullied by the Cuban operation. "In the days since January 20, your administration has changed the face of American foreign policy," Schlesinger contended. "The soberness of style, the absence of Cold War cliches, the lack of self-righteousness and sermonizing, the impressive combination of reasonableness and firmness, the generosity to new ideas, the dedication to social progress, the tough-minded idealism of purpose—all these factors have transformed (to use that repellent word) the 'image' of the United States before the world."

Cuba didn't present a threat grave or compelling enough to justify action "which much of the world will interpret as calculated aggression against a small nation in defiance both of treaty obligations and of the international standards we have repeatedly asserted against the Communist world. . . .

"An invasion of Cuba was made to order for Soviet propagandists," Schlesinger continued. "The objective will be to portray the Soviet Union as the patron and protector of nationalists, Negroes, new nations and peace and to portray the Kennedy Administration as a gang of capitalist imperialists maddened by the loss of profits and driven to aggression and war."[16]

Kennedy ignored the critics and decided to proceed. "I really thought they had a good chance," he told Sorensen afterward. Ideally the Cuban exiles, without overt U.S. participation, would succeed in establishing themselves on the island, proclaim a new noncommunist government, and rally the Cuban people to their cause. If they could oust Castro, all Latin America would feel more secure. Already armed and trained, the Cuban exiles could not be contained much longer. They wanted to return to Cuba. If the invasion failed, they could always flee to the mountains and fight as guerrillas, still a net gain. The CIA and the Joint Chiefs had the experience, the know-how. Evidently Eisenhower trusted them. Why shouldn't the new President rely on their judgment? The invasion plan must be feasible. Besides, it had worked in Guatemala.

"He was particularly impressed by the fact that three members of the Cuban Revolutionary Council had sons in the Brigade," Schlesinger later wrote; "the exile leaders themselves obviously believed that the expedition would succeed."[17]

Several reporters had sniffed out details about the Cuban Brigade, their training, and the impending invasion. "I can't believe what I'm reading!"

Kennedy exclaimed after scanning a newspaper account. "Castro doesn't need agents over here. All he has to do is read our papers. It's all laid out for him."

Gilbert Harrison, the publisher of *The New Republic*, sent Schlesinger the galleys of an article, "Our Men in Miami," and asked whether there was any reason not to publish it. Schlesinger judged the article to be "careful, accurate and devastating." It exposed the invasion plan. Uncomfortable having the government request an editor to "suppress the truth," he nonetheless showed the galleys to the President. Kennedy quickly read the article and suggested Schlesinger derail it. After contacting Harrison, Schlesinger happily reported back that the publisher had accepted the suggestion with "no questions." At Kennedy's request *The New York Times* also played down an article about the pending operation.

A week before the invasion, Kennedy let Charles Spalding in on the secret. He didn't expect any problems. "Everybody's gone over it. They're pretty sure that they can make this work."[18]

In a communiqué issued in Havana on Saturday, April 15, 1961, Cuban prime minister Fidel Castro charged that at six o'clock that morning B-26 bombers from the United States had simultaneously bombed several Cuban cities. The air assault, actually carried out from a secret CIA air base in Nicaragua, had begun. In New York the cover story issued by Miró Cardona, president of the Cuban Revolutionary Council, contended that the bombing of Cuban airfields that morning had been conducted by "certain members of the Cuban Air Force," an action the Revolutionary Council had encouraged. On the afternoon of April 15, the UN General Assembly began considering the conflict developing in Cuba. Castro's UN delegate, Raul Roa, accused the United States of aggression against Cuba, and the Soviet representative, Valerian A. Zorin, warned that "Cuba has many friends in the world who were ready to come to its aid, including the Soviet Union."

Adlai Stevenson, poorly briefed, believed the cover story. He defended the American position, replying that the air raids had been carried out by defectors from the Cuban air force who had subsequently landed in Florida and had asked for political asylum. When this was quickly proven false, Stevenson was embarrassed and furious.

On Sunday evening Stevenson telegrammed Rusk and Dulles: "Greatly disturbed by clear indications received during day in process developing rebuttal material that bombing incidents in Cuba on Saturday were launched in part at least from outside Cuba."[19]

Battered by propaganda at the UN, under instruction from the President, at 9:30 P.M. on Sunday McGeorge Bundy ordered the CIA to cancel the air strikes scheduled for dawn the next morning unless they could be conducted from an airstrip inside Cuba. Any further consultation on the matter should be taken up with Secretary of State Rusk.

Early on Monday morning, April 17, the fourteen-hundred-man Cuban Brigade landed at the Bay of Pigs. Although tactically surprised, Castro's forces reacted quickly and powerfully. At dawn Cuban airplanes attacked the beaches and the shipping, sinking two freighters, the *Houston* and *Rio Escondido*, which together carried a critical ten-day supply of ammunition for the brigade, plus medical supplies, food, and communications equipment.

Almost everything went wrong for the invaders. Their landing craft floundered among the unanticipated coral reefs. When portable radios got wet, they didn't function. Men landed at the wrong locations, several miles from comrades, and others reached shore without adequate supplies.

On the morning of April 18 the outlook was grim. The situation was "not good," Bundy reported to Kennedy; "the Cuban armed forces are stronger, the popular response is weaker, and our tactical position is feebler than we had hoped."[20]

On April 18, at lunch with James Reston of *The New York Times* and Arthur Schlesinger, Kennedy appeared poised. Retaining Allen Dulles had probably been "a mistake," he candidly stated. The veteran director was a legendary figure, but "it's hard to operate with legendary figures." Kennedy couldn't assess the director's remarks when Dulles spoke. "Bobby" should have the job, the President mused, because Bobby was "wasted" as attorney general. The Cuban debacle was "a hell of a way to learn things," but Kennedy needed to face the problems with the CIA.

Some of the President's comments at lunch appear roseate, not reflective of his true feelings. Ultimately, defeat at the Bay of Pigs would be judged as merely an "incident, not a disaster." Would American prestige suffer? "What is prestige?" he responded, downplaying a theme he had emphasized throughout the 1960 campaign. "Is it the shadow of power or the substance of power?" He would stress substance. The administration would be "kicked in the can for the next couple of weeks," but it wouldn't be deflected from its purpose. He told his guests that his primary concern was for the brave men on the beaches.[21]

That evening the President interrupted his grim preoccupation with the Cuban disaster to don white tie and tails and host a lively White House reception for 450 members of Congress and their spouses. At 10:15 P.M. the President and Jackie, looking radiant, descended the stairs to the entrance hall as the Marine Band struck up "Mr. Wonderful." Acting as gracious hosts, the president stood at one end of the ballroom greeting guests while Jackie danced with a succession of partners. At 11:45 P.M. he left the gala to meet with his key advisers.

Peter Wyden, an expert on the Bay of Pigs operation, described the scene: "It was a most extraordinary session. Nobody present would ever forget it. It began at 11:58 and lasted until 2:45 A.M. Like the President, Vice President Johnson, Rusk and McNamara were in white tie. General Lemnitzer and Admiral [Arleigh] Burke were in dress uniform, medals gleaming."

It was "a moment of desperation," Bissell felt. He argued that the operation could still be salvaged if the President authorized using jets from the aircraft carrier *Essex*. Admiral Arleigh Burke, chief of staff of the navy, agreed.

"Let me take two jets and shoot down the enemy aircraft," he pleaded.

The President said, "No." He reminded Bissell and Burke that he had warned them "over and over again" he would not commit U.S. forces to combat.

Burke suggested that unmarked jets be permitted to fly over the beaches as a show of strength with orders not to fire.

The President didn't like the idea. He pointed out that there always was the possibility that the jets would be attacked and fired at after all.

The admiral next suggested bringing in a destroyer. It could arrive in less than two hours. "One destroyer opening fire could have knocked the hell out of Castro's tanks," he said later. "It might have changed the whole course of battle."

The President got angry. "Burke, I don't want the United States involved in this," he said sharply.

Burke said, "Hell, Mr. President, we *are* involved!"

The two sides argued from entirely different perspectives. "Bissell and Burke still hoped to make the operation succeed," Wyden observed. "The President, seconded by Rusk, hoped only to minimize the damage."[22]

Several people in the room assumed that the brigade could still escape "into the hills." Rusk asked about "the hills." It was "time for this outfit to go guerrilla," said General Lemnitzer. Bissell shocked them when he explained that the invaders couldn't "go guerrilla," and were captives of the swamp.

Kennedy approved a compromise: Six unmarked jets from the *Essex* would fly over the Bay of Pigs for an hour to protect B-26s flying in from Nicaragua for an airdrop.

But this operation turned into a fiasco, like everything else about the invasion. Incredibly, the two air forces didn't coordinate their time zones: The B-26s arrived an hour earlier than their American escorts. Without proper defense, the Cubans drove away the supply flights and shot down two B-26s.

Ken O'Donnell thought that the President was about to weep. Robert

Kennedy murmured, "We've got to do something." Following the meeting the tearful attorney general put his hands on the President's shoulder and said, "They can't *do* this to you!"

"Without a jacket, the President opened one of the French doors and walked out into a gentle breeze on the South Grounds," Michael Beschloss observed of the scene. "Secret Service men kept their distance as he strolled until almost three in the morning by himself through the damp grass, his head bent, his hands thrust in his pockets."

After three days of fighting, the battle ended and the brigade forces surrendered. In the end 1,189 were taken prisoner; 140 died.[23]

Before news of the disaster arrived, about fifteen thousand wives, mothers, relatives, and friends of brigade members gathered in Miami's Bayfront Park for a "Thank Kennedy" rally. But after learning the extent of the tragedy, the women, faces wet with tears, screamed instead, "Kennedy! Help!"

Khrushchev denounced the invasion as "fraught with danger to world peace" and urged the United States to act to stop the "conflagration" from spreading. He promised the Cuban people and their government "all necessary assistance in beating back the armed attack." The president shot back a message to Moscow defending the U.S. actions and warning the Soviets not to use the situation in Cuba as a pretext "to inflame other areas of the world."

On April 19, Rose Kennedy wrote in her diary that Joe was "trying to bring up Jack's morale after the Cuban debacle." The same evening, after dinner at the White House, Jackie told Rose that Jack had been upset all day. Rose wrote: "Had practically been in tears, felt he had been misinformed by CIA and others. I felt so sorry for him. Jackie so sympathetic and said she had stayed with him until he had lain down that afternoon for a short nap. Said she had never seen him so depressed except at time of his operation."[24]

"I have had two full days of hell," Kennedy told Clark Clifford as the invasion force surrendered. "I haven't slept—this has been the most excruciating period of my life. I doubt my Presidency could survive another catastrophe like this." He continued, using precise, biting, angry words: "The decision I made was faulty because it was based upon the wrong advice. The advice was wrong because it was based upon incorrect facts. And the incorrect facts were due to a failure of intelligence."

In Rio de Janeiro, Bogotá, La Paz, Caracas, Mexico City, and Buenos Aires, mobs of students and workers protested "Yankee imperialism." In Mexico City, students shouted, "Castro sí. Kennedy no!" Mobs stoned American embassies in Warsaw, Cairo, and New Delhi.[25]

The debacle dismayed friends of the United States as well. "Bad show," reported the London *Daily Mail;* "a shocking blow to American prestige."

"Great nations are always criticized when they appear aggressive," wrote *Time* afterward. "They are despised when they seem weak. By backing an inadequate and mismanaged invasion attempt, President Kennedy achieved the unhappy feat of making the U.S. seem both aggressive and weak at the same time."

"Why we ever engaged in this asinine Cuban adventure, I cannot imagine," Dean Acheson wrote former president Truman. "The direction of this government seems surprisingly weak. . . . Brains are no substitute for judgment. Kennedy has, abroad at least, lost a very large part of the almost fanatical admiration which his youth and good looks had inspired."[26]

At a press conference on April 21, Kennedy took full personal responsibility. "There's an old saying, that victory has a hundred fathers and defeat is an orphan." Shell-shocked, McGeorge Bundy offered his handwritten resignation: "I wish I had served you better in the Cuban episode." (Kennedy refused to accept it.) Robert McNamara offered to publicly accept blame. "Mr. President, I know where I was when you made the decision to launch the invasion," McNamara told the President in the Oval Office. "I was in a room where, with one exception, all of your advisers—including me—recommended you proceed. I am fully prepared to go on TV and say so."

Kennedy heard him out. "Bob," he said, "I'm grateful to you for your willingness to assume part of the responsibility. But I am the President. . . . I am responsible, and I will not try to put part of the blame on you, or Eisenhower, or anyone else." McNamara later concluded: "I admired him for that, and the incident brought us closer. I made up my mind not to let him down again."

Although Kennedy admitted his own huge miscalculations, he let the story leak to the media that he was upset with the Joint Chiefs of Staff and the CIA. The Kennedy brothers also vented their wrath on Chester Bowles.[27]

Bowles took notes at a cabinet meeting on Thursday, April 20, and an NSC meeting on Saturday, April 22. Thursday's meeting, wrote Bowles, substituting for the State Department in Rusk's absence, was about as "grim as any meeting I can remember in all my experience in government." President Kennedy looked shattered. Reactions among cabinet members "were almost savage, as everyone appeared to be jumping on everyone else." Robert Kennedy was furious. Discussion "simply rambled in circles with no real coherent thought." After forty-five minutes the President rose and walked to his office.

Bowles and several others followed the President. "Bobby continued his tough, savage comments, most of them directed against the Department of State. . . . When I took exception to some of the more extreme things he said by suggesting that the way to get out of our present jam was not to simply double up on everything we had done, he turned on me savagely."[28]

On Friday, April 21, the newsmagazines and the morning papers reported "inside" stories about the Cuba decision. An instinct for self-preservation had tempted some of the officials in the planning meetings to, in Schlesinger's words, "put out versions of the episode ascribing the debacle to everyone but themselves." Schlesinger was among a half dozen aides invited to breakfast at the White House:

> The President remarked acidly that the role of the Joint Chiefs of Staff was notably neglected in several stories—an omission which, by Washington exegesis, pointed to the Pentagon as the source. The best way to turn off the speculation, he said, was to tell the truth: that all the senior officials involved had backed the operation but that the final responsibility was his own. Then he added with unusual emphasis. "There is only one person in the clear—that's Bill Fulbright. And he probably would have been converted if he had attended more of the meetings."

Thirty-five people attended the NSC meeting on Saturday. "Again Bob Kennedy was present," wrote Bowles, "and took the lead as at the previous meeting, slamming into anyone who suggested that we go slowly and try to move calmly and not repeat previous mistakes."

The atmosphere was almost as emotional as the meeting two days earlier, except the group focused on specific proposals to harass Castro in the future. On two or three occasions, Bowles claimed, he suggested that the

> greatest mistake we could make would be to pit the United States with its 180 million people in a contest against a Cuban dictator on an island of 6 million people. I stressed that while we are already in a bad situation, it would be a mistake for us to assume that it could not disintegrate further and an almost sure way to lose ground was to reach out in ways that would almost surely be ineffective and which would tend to create additional sympathy for Castro in his David and Goliath struggle against the United States.

According to Bowles the "various fire eaters who were present" brutally brushed aside his comments.

Others remembered more details about the NSC meeting on April 22. Beforehand *Time* had reported that Bowles opposed the invasion and, "somewhat deviously," was "leaking to the press stories of sharp conflict within the Administration." This report and others like it infuriated both John and Robert Kennedy.

Many years afterward Dean Rusk stated that Bowles "went around Washington after the Bay of Pigs, telling reporters, 'Oh this was a terrible mistake . . . a great mistake. . . . I tried my best to prevent it.' When this got back to the President, it cooked Chester Bowles's goose with John Kennedy. He deeply resented any lack of solidarity in his own administration over this debacle."[29]

Evan Thomas thought that Robert Kennedy took "vindictive pleasure in berating Bowles." The Stevensonian Democrat favored diplomacy over force, he was "soft" and "ladylike"—a "talker, not a doer." On April 22, Bowles presented a State Department white paper on Cuba. He concluded his tedious, generality-laden presentation by saying that nothing short of an invasion could now topple Castro.

When Bowles finished, Robert Kennedy exploded: "That's the most meaningless, worthless thing I've ever heard. You people are so anxious to protect your own asses that you're afraid to do anything. All you want to do is dump the whole thing on the President. We'd be better off if you just quit and left foreign policy to someone else." During Bobby's tirade, Richard Goodwin later wrote, the President sat calmly, "outwardly relaxed, only the faint click from the metallic pencil cap he was tapping against his almost incandescently white, evenly spaced teeth disrupting his silence—a characteristic revelation that some inner tension was being suppressed." Goodwin continued: "I became suddenly aware—am now certain—that Bobby's harsh polemic reflected the President's own concealed emotions, privately communicated in some earlier, intimate conversation. I knew, even then, there was an inner hardness, often volatile anger beneath the outwardly amiable, thoughtful, carefully controlled demeanor of John Kennedy."

Following Robert Kennedy's verbal assault, the President limited himself mostly to asking questions—"questions," thought Bowles, "which led in one direction"—about the best ways to harass Castro and topple his regime. Revenge was the order of the day.

"I left the meeting with a feeling of intense alarm," Bowles concluded, "tempered somewhat with the hope that this represented largely an emotional reaction of a group of people who were not used to setbacks or defeats and whose pride and confidence had been deeply wounded."[30]

The Bay of Pigs invasion has been aptly described as "the perfect failure." Afterward two major studies documented the reasons for the disaster. Kennedy asked retired general Maxwell Taylor to chair the Cuba Study Group, hoping to learn lessons from the failure. The CIA's inspector general, Lyman Kilpatrick, also investigated the invasion and issued a devastating secret report.

What had gone wrong? Everything about the operation was marginal or inadequate. The small landing force couldn't control the thirty-six-mile beachhead or repel the enemy counterattack. Air support over the beaches did not include enough high-quality planes and pilots; too many restrictions hampered bombing runs against the Castro airfields; and the invaders had no fighters to fend off Castro's planes, particularly three devastatingly effective T-33 jet trainers.[31]

An amphibious landing against a hostile enemy shore is one of the most difficult of all military maneuvers, requiring surprise, air superiority, and exceptionally good logistics. "Our Government had expected that an amphibious landing on a hostile shore by amateur soldiers directed by U.S. amateurs could succeed under the circumstances of the landing at the Bay of Pigs," observed Maxwell Taylor. "In all the staff schools of the Armed Services we are taught that such an operation is the most complicated and difficult operation in war. Yet we turned the Bay of Pigs Operation over to the CIA—we expected them to organize and train covertly Cuban volunteers capable of carrying out the landing plan."

Everything was small in relation to the needs, so everything had to work perfectly to assure success. The CIA entered the project without adequate boats, bases, training facilities, and Spanish speakers. It had no disaster plan and only vague plans for action following the landings.

Castro effectively removed any chance of an upheaval at the start of the invasion by arresting thousands of potential dissidents. What's more, the CIA never informed the leaders of dissident groups inside Cuba that an invasion was imminent.[32]

The changing ground rules, established for political reasons—for "deniability"—imposed serious restrictions and ensured failure. The original plan called for two air strikes, one on D-1 and another on D-day. When the D-1 strike created international noise at the United Nations, the President, on Rusk's recommendation, canceled the air strike on the morning of D-day. McGeorge Bundy had delivered the message to CIA officials and given them the opportunity to appeal the decision to Rusk. But Rusk stood firm. He offered them the opportunity to speak to the President, but they declined. The indispensable air strike for D-day morning, therefore, was never flown, eliminating the last good opportunity to destroy the Cuban air force on the ground.

Rusk later testified that while the CIA officials had insisted that the D-day strikes were important, they did not insist they were vital. Therefore Kennedy went to bed without knowing the full implications of the decision. No one even informed the Joint Chiefs of Staff that the bombing attack on D-day had been canceled.[33]

Several crucial misunderstandings between the White House and the CIA damaged the operation. The President clearly stated that he wouldn't allow the operation to turn into an American one. But CIA officials didn't believe him. They assumed that if the invasion was about to fail, Kennedy would change his mind and insert American forces.

In Guatemala in 1954, when the coup seemed likely to collapse, Eisenhower openly rushed airplanes to the rebels. The CIA expected Kennedy to react the same way. "We felt that when the chips were down, when the crisis arose in reality, any action required for success would be authorized rather than permit the enterprise to fail," said Dulles. The military and the CIA *assumed* the President would order American intervention; the President *assumed* they knew he would refuse to exceed his original limitation.

In case of failure, the President believed, the guerrilla option was still available to the exiles. The CIA never informed him that most of the exiles were untrained for guerrilla warfare, or that the eighty-mile escape route to the Escambrays was too far away and blocked by swamps and Castro's troops.

The greatest CIA failure was its incompetent intelligence. Its estimate of domestic discontent in Cuba and potential dissidents proved wildly optimistic. All allied intelligence reports showed Castro completely in command and supported by most of the Cubans on the island. Cuban resistance to Castro lay mostly in Miami.

Prior to the invasion, the CIA had disparaged the Cuban air force, describing it as "entirely disorganized," one that relied on "obsolete and inoperative" aircraft with "almost non-existent" combat efficiency.[34]

The Joint Chiefs, entrusted with the responsibility of evaluating the military feasibility of the operation, did not oppose the final plan, and their mild assent gave others the impression of approval. "You always assume that the military and intelligence people have some secret skill not available to ordinary mortals," Kennedy later remarked.

Overall, though, Kennedy's bitter feeling against the Joint Chiefs was misguided. It wasn't their plan. How could they know the President would cancel the second air strike? The chiefs' advice had assumed the accuracy of the CIA's intelligence estimates of widespread discontent with Castro in Cuba; the chiefs thought the invaders could convert to guerrilla warfare. Bundy later stated that the Joint Chiefs didn't deserve severe censure. They had also been reluctant to criticize another agency's plan in an open meeting. "If we had been more sophisticated and more experienced, we would have discounted things accordingly," said Bundy.[35]

The Bay of Pigs was a textbook example of the problems inherent in the covert method of conducting foreign policy. "Planned by a small, closed group, lacking exposure to the press, Congress, bureaucracy, and other institutions that monitor, criticize, and thus improve other government initiatives, the Cuban operation had defects that remained largely undetected," noted historian Michael Beschloss.[36]

All the key officials were unaccustomed to working with Kennedy and with each other. This hampered communication and circumscribed responses. McNamara's inexperience and deference to the CIA led him to accept the plan uncritically. He had listened to all the briefings leading up to the invasion, and had passed along to the President, without comment, the assessment of the Joint Chiefs. "The truth is I did not understand the plan very well and did not know the facts," McNamara reflected. "I had let myself become a passive bystander."

Secretary of State Rusk provided weak leadership. He had serious reservations about the invasion, but he didn't speak out forcefully at the various meetings where his influence might have mattered.

"Above all, the enormous shadow of Eisenhower seemed to cover the room," noted James Giglio. "No one wished to challenge 'the greatest military man in America,' least of all an inexperienced President who had criticized Ike for not confronting Castro."[37]

By publicly taking full blame, Kennedy earned respect from both career servants and the public, and avoided a partisan investigation. Sorensen thought his boss's assumption of responsibility was not just a political device or a constitutional obligation. He felt it strongly. "How could I have been so far off base?" he asked himself out loud while walking with Sorensen on April 20. "All my life I've known better than to depend on the experts. How could I have been so stupid, to let them go ahead?"

Dean Rusk rejected the view later expressed by Kennedy partisans that the president merely carried out an operation conceived and developed by Eisenhower. "We had a full opportunity to look at the operation and make a judgment of our own about it," said Rusk. "Kennedy never tried to export responsibility for the Bay of Pigs to President Eisenhower; he accepted the responsibility for it himself, as did I, because we had a clear chance either to go ahead with it or to call it off, and we made the wrong decision."[38]

Afterward, nearly everyone on the Kennedy team criticized the tactics used in the Bay of Pigs operation, but not its goals. Kennedy never apologized for his intentions. No one in a key position asked whether the United States should have sponsored an invasion of a small Latin American nation whose government it disliked.

As is often the case, the tragic failure was the foundation for future success. Kennedy no longer accepted conventional wisdom or bureaucratic momentum without intense questioning and scrutiny. Robert McNamara, disenchanted with the military advice he had received, insisted on examining the facts himself before he passed on his advice to the President. "We all learned from it," said McNamara. "It was a horribly expensive lesson, however."

Kennedy made several significant changes. The distinguished General Maxwell Taylor was asked to come out of retirement to be Kennedy's military adviser; later Kennedy appointed him chairman of the Joint Chiefs of Staff. Kennedy reactivated the Foreign Intelligence Advisory Board to monitor and control the CIA. He quietly asked both Dulles and Bissell to leave, though he did not reprimand either one. While acknowledging his own responsibility for the debacle, Kennedy told Bissell, "If this were the British government, I would resign, and you, being a senior civil servant, would remain. But it isn't. In our government, you and Allen have to go, and I have to remain." He told Bissell there was no hurry.[39]

After the Bay of Pigs, Bundy moved his operation from the Executive Office Building into the basement of the West Wing of the White House, where he established a communications center and took on added responsibility for security matters. He set up, in effect, a little State Department, directing his own area specialists: Michael Forrestal for Far Eastern affairs, Robert Komer for the Near East, and Carl Kaysen for Europe. Neither Robert Kennedy nor Ted Sorensen had taken part in the meetings on the Bay of Pigs. Afterward Kennedy gave both a broad mandate to advise him on foreign policy.[40]

In public President Kennedy accepted the blame for the failure with his usual poise and grace; in private he was distressed and guilty. "He hates to read the newspaper editorials," LeMoyne Billings wrote in his diary on April 30. "When he saw a recent copy of *Time* magazine, he threw it into the fire to avoid reading it." He wasn't interested in a second term as President, he told Billings. When they mused about a postpresidential library, Kennedy predicted it would never be built. His administration would be viewed as too tragic.

For several months afterward his thoughts often turned to the brigade prisoners. One morning when he came to his desk he remarked to O'Donnell that he hadn't slept. "I was thinking about those poor guys in prison down in Cuba," he said. "I'm willing to make any kind of a deal with Castro to get them out of there."

When a Gallup poll conducted two weeks after the failed invasion showed that support for the President had gone up to an unprecedented 82 percent, Kennedy dismissed it. "It's just like Eisenhower. The worse I do, the more popular I get."[41]

27

BERLIN AND VIENNA

More than any other foreign-policy dilemma, Kennedy's policy toward troubled Berlin was conditioned and restricted by historical circumstances. At the end of World War II the victorious Allies agreed to temporarily divide Germany into four zones—controlled by the British, French, Americans, and Soviets—and established a similar four-power control over the city of Berlin. The allies hoped to negotiate a final peace settlement with a new German government, but that prospect vanished with the onset of the Cold War. The Americans, French, and British converted their zones into West Germany (the Federal Republic of Germany), and the Soviet Union transformed its zone into East Germany (the German Democratic Republic). Berlin was left as an enclave far inside East Germany, 110 miles from West Germany. "Situated in the midst of the Soviet zone, West Berlin, with its independent administration and its allied garrison, was now the last democratic outpost on the communist side of the Iron Curtain," noted Schlesinger.

In effect, Berlin became two separate cities: East Berlin under Communist East Germany (which the Soviet Union dominated), and democratic West Berlin a part of West Germany. Access between East Berlin and West Berlin, nonetheless, remained mostly open.

In June 1948 the Soviets suddenly blocked the highways leading to West

Berlin. To maintain a lifeline to the city, President Truman ordered a massive airlift that frustrated the stranglehold and led Stalin to cease the blockade in May 1949. The heroic Berlin airlift had prevented the brave West Berliners from being "sucked into the yawning jaws of the communist monolith."[1]

The West wanted an undivided Berlin with open access and an undivided Germany. "The East feared the reunification of Germany under capitalism," noted Lawrence Freedman; "the West feared the reunification of Berlin under communism." The open city of Berlin threatened the viability of the Communist state, since discontented citizens could simply march to the western sector to escape Communist domination.

Since the end of World War II, applying the lesson of Munich, the United States had believed that any concession, any weakness on West Berlin, invited conquest by the Soviets. The status quo must be maintained. Public opinion in the United States overwhelmingly supported the defense of West Berlin, even to the point of going to war if the Soviets or the East Germans again cut off access routes.

The leader of West Germany, Konrad Adenauer, born in 1876, had been a lawyer and a rising political figure in Germany until Hitler came to power in 1933. Imprisoned twice by the Nazis, he resumed his political career after Germany's defeat in 1945, and worked to form the new Federal Republic of Germany. Elected chancellor in 1949, he was credited with bringing stability and prosperity to West Germany.[2]

Adenauer's "rigidity" in defending his position of no compromise on the issue of Berlin frustrated Eisenhower, who thought the elderly leader showed signs of "senility." Despite the public appearance of unity, West German–American relations were prickly throughout Kennedy's presidency. The West Germans remained loyal but very suspicious allies. The President was less at ease with Adenauer, less able to establish rapport, than with most of the major leaders with whom he dealt. "The two men literally and figuratively came from different centuries," noted one historian.

The Soviets held the advantage in Berlin. The Western powers had no viable way to prevent the Soviets from asserting their control. The only hope was to threaten the Soviets with nuclear weapons if they tried to change the status quo. But the nuclear threat did not seem entirely credible. Would the United States actually go to nuclear war to save West Berlin? Kennedy had to make the nuclear threat believable while at the same time doing everything possible to avoid unleashing a nuclear war.[3]

In May 1961, Kennedy and Khrushchev agreed to meet at a summit in Vienna early the following month. Their meeting was to be informal and agenda free. The White House announcement of the summit carefully restrained optimism. The meeting was "not for the purpose of negotiating or reaching an agreement" on major international problems.

Unfortunately, Kennedy was going to the summit weakened by the Bay of Pigs fiasco and humiliated by the Soviet Union's success with its first manned orbital flight. The atmosphere would not be promising for an important agreement, but he felt he needed to size up Khrushchev and establish a rapport that might later prove valuable. "I would rather meet him the first time at the summit, not the brink," he said.[4]

Kennedy prepared meticulously, searching for clues to Khrushchev's character, personality, and thoughts. He trimmed appointments, creating more time for solitude and study. What subjects should he raise? What matters should best be left for Khrushchev to initiate? Did logic work with the Soviet leader? How should he respond to his adversary's blustering? Impressions were important. He didn't want to say anything that might lead Khrushchev to miscalculate. "This is a game," said a Kennedy aide, "this mental combat; it's a hell of a challenge, and he likes it."

Kennedy read Khrushchev's speeches and studied the minutes of earlier summits between Eisenhower and the Soviet premier. He consulted with journalists Walter Lippmann and James Reston, asking for their assessments, and questioned Senator Hubert Humphrey about his eight-hour conversation with Khrushchev in 1959. He sought the guidance of former ambassador to the USSR Charles Bohlen, Secretary of State Dean Rusk, and former secretary of state Dean Acheson. Arthur Dean, the nuclear-test-ban expert, flew back from Geneva to offer his advice. The Harvard scholar Henry Kissinger presented his ideas on Berlin. Some assume that the President's staff poorly briefed him on the Berlin issue, but he actually prepared well for what the Soviet leader would demand.[5]

The picture that emerged of Khrushchev was of a crude, opinionated peasant. Often deliberately unpredictable, he was "a mischievous charmer one moment and a loud bully the next," an expert in the use of power with an inclination to gamble. Although a doctrinaire Marxist, he willingly bargained.

On Laos, Khrushchev would cooperate, but not on anything else. He hoped to force the young and inexperienced Kennedy to yield, particularly on the issue of Berlin. On the other hand, Kennedy planned to be tough but reasonable and hoped to charm and impress his counterpart.[6]

On his way to Vienna the President met in Paris with Charles de Gaulle. Austere and aloof, de Gaulle had become the President of the Fifth Republic in 1959. A glamorous war hero, General de Gaulle had escaped to England in June 1940 as the Germans overran his country. There he formed the Free French Army, and he triumphantly returned to Paris in August 1944 following the German retreat. As president of France he restored economic stability and tried to restore the nation's prestige and power. France had recently joined the United States, Great Britain, and the Soviet Union in the nuclear club, having tested its first nuclear bomb. Suspicious of the Anglo-Saxons, de Gaulle irritated the United States and Great Britain by his criticism of NATO and his unwillingness to cooperate in a common policy toward the Soviet Union.

Starting off on common ground, de Gaulle and Kennedy devoted their first session to Berlin, agreeing that they must firmly resist a Russian demand for a change in the city's status. Their second meeting dealt with Laos and Southeast Asia. Both agreed on the need for a cease-fire in Laos and hoped to unify and neutralize the country. De Gaulle made clear, though, that France would not send troops to Laos.

A leadership tip he received from the French President impressed Kennedy: "You can listen to your advisors before you make up your mind, but once you have made up your mind then do not listen to anyone."[7]

Subsequent sessions with de Gaulle, while still polite and cordial, dealt with far more sensitive issues. When Kennedy raised the touchy question of NATO, de Gaulle responded that he wanted to talk in detail about the subject. He intended to disengage from the organization. NATO had become obsolete. After World War II, France and other Western European nations had been so weakened that they had lain open to Communist aggression. Thankfully the United States, with its massive nuclear threat, had stepped in to fill the vacuum, and in the process the Americans had assumed control of NATO. But the world had changed. France was strong again, and the United States no longer enjoyed a nuclear monopoly and had assumed other "far-flung" commitments.

De Gaulle was not convinced that the United States would actually use its nuclear weapons to defend Western Europe. With the issue critical to France, he quizzed Kennedy carefully "as to where, when, how and to what extent American nuclear weapons would be employed to defend the continent." In de Gaulle's view America would use its nuclear weapons only if directly threatened. "I could only reaffirm France's determination to become a nuclear power," de Gaulle reflected, "since it was her only means of ensuring that no one could attempt to destroy her without the risk of self-destruction."[8]

Kennedy responded that the United States would use nuclear weapons rather than allow Western Europe to fall into the hands of the Soviets. The defense of Europe and the defense of the United States, he declared, were one and the same. This was the reason the United States stationed troops in Europe.

De Gaulle remained unconvinced. He doubted that the United States would strike the first blow against the Soviets if war threatened Western Europe. "I know you mean that," he told Kennedy, but France would still develop its own nuclear weapons.

Wanting to contain nuclear power, Kennedy warned of the grave danger of nuclear proliferation. In a misguided attempt to gain security and status, less-developed countries might sacrifice their own economic development to gain a nuclear arsenal, putting themselves in a position to engage in nuclear blackmail. The spread of these weapons also made an accidental nuclear war far more likely. "You can't blame him for wanting France to be as strong as the other world powers," Kennedy later told Ken O'Donnell. "But I had to argue against him. Too many of us have nuclear power as it is."[9]

The United States, Kennedy suggested, might be willing to give up some of its unilateral control of nuclear weapons and share the control, through NATO, with France and Great Britain, particularly in the case of Polaris submarines. De Gaulle rejected the suggestion. Handing a few Polaris submarines over to NATO would simply mean transferring them from one American command to another dominated by the United States, leaving the decision to launch the rockets still in the hands of the U.S. President.

De Gaulle wanted absolute equality with the United States and Britain in shaping world policy. The United States should speak for "the Western Hemisphere, Britain for the Commonwealth, and France for Europe and much of Africa." France would defend herself by herself, and would not end its nuclear-testing program.[10]

After the discussion Kennedy flew to Vienna. Fifteen hundred reporters and photographers attended the summit meeting between Kennedy and Khrushchev on June 3 and 4, 1961. It would be the only face-to-face confrontation between the two leaders. When they met, Kennedy carefully inspected the Soviet premier. With his hands in the pockets of his jacket, Kennedy "continued to stare at Khrushchev, not unpleasantly, but, with that deep curiosity of his, sizing him up," O'Donnell later wrote.[11]

The first session began on June 3 at 12:45 P.M. at the American ambassador's residence. Kennedy told the Soviet leader he wanted to avoid any "miscalculation" by either country. Miscalculation should be replaced by "precision in judgments." But Khrushchev hated the way Kennedy used the word "miscalculation," and wouldn't concede that he might ever miscalculate.

The premier briefly turned the session into an ideological harangue, putting Kennedy at a disadvantage. Kennedy wanted the Soviet Union to stop supporting nationalist movements. The United States supported "free choice," the President said.

> In some cases minorities seize control in areas associated with us, minorities which do not express the will of the people. Such groups associate themselves with the USSR and act against the interests of the United States. . . . This brings in conflict the USSR as center of Communist

power and the U.S. as center of our power. Thus the problem is how to conduct this disagreement in areas where we have interests without direct confrontation of the two countries and thus to serve the interests of our people.

The United States, retorted the Soviet leader, did not appreciate the aspirations of people to overthrow their oppressors. He lectured Kennedy about communism and Marxism, going as far back as the French Revolution. "Did the President want to say that Communism should exist only in those countries that are already Communist and that if Communist ideas should develop the U.S. would be in conflict with the USSR? Such an understanding of the situation is incorrect."

Conflicts were inevitable; ideas did not belong to any one nation. Once born, ideas would continue to develop: "If Communist ideas should spread in other countries, the USSR would be happy, just as the U.S. would be glad if capitalist ideas were to spread. In any event, the spread of ideas should depend on peoples alone. Ideas should not be borne on bayonets or on missile warheads."

When Kennedy weakly interjected that "Mao Tse Tung had said that power was at the end of the rifle," Khrushchev accused him of misunderstanding the Chinese leader. "Mao Tse Tung is a Marxist and Marxists have always been against war."[12]

Khrushchev's belief in the inevitability of the spread of communism was well known, the President replied as he maneuvered to change the subject. Khrushchev should try to understand the U.S. view on the development of the world so that the chances of peace could be increased.

In the afternoon session Kennedy did better. When Khrushchev remarked that the United States supported undemocratic governments, specifically in Spain and Iran, the President brought up Soviet-dominated Poland. If given a free choice, the people of Poland probably would not support the current Communist government. "People in the United States had a choice, whereas in Poland there was only one group. Mr. Khrushchev replied that parties in the United States were only for the purpose of deluding the people, since there was no difference between the parties. . . . In any event, no one should interfere in the Soviet Union's internal affairs."

The President then zeroed in on the crisis in Laos. He suggested that the two superpowers use their influence to create a cease-fire and an independent, neutral Laos; Khrushchev agreed.[13]

By the end of the second session, the two had not yet focused on Berlin or disarmament.

Several times during the summit Kennedy backed Khrushchev into a corner, forcing the Soviet premier to change the subject. Kennedy's immersion in previous American-Soviet discussions and his careful preparation allowed him to handle some of Khrushchev's bluster. While Khrushchev demanded the withdrawal of Allied troops from Germany, he argued that President Roosevelt had promised to make such a withdrawal within two to four years after the war ended. "President Roosevelt said we would withdraw our troops if Germany was reunited under one government," Kennedy countered. Khrushchev had no response.

At another point in a heated debate, Kennedy asked, "Do you ever admit a mistake?"

"Certainly," Khrushchev said. "In a speech before the Twentieth Party Congress, I admitted all of Stalin's mistakes."

"Those were Stalin's mistakes," Kennedy countered. "Not your mistakes." Again, Khrushchev didn't respond.

During a break from a rough session, Kennedy asked Llewellyn Thompson, the United States Ambassador to the Soviet Union, "Is it always like this?" Thompson assured him it was "par for the course."[14]

The third session, held at the Soviet embassy, began at 10:15 A.M. on June 4. Kennedy refocused on Laos, making certain both parties agreed, but the Soviet leader went on a tangent about U.S. "megalomania" and "delusions of grandeur." Kennedy listened patiently then refocused on Laos, confirming the premier's agreement in the previous session.

Khrushchev steered the subject from Laos to disarmament. Referring to the U.S. demand for twenty annual on-site inspections of nuclear tests, Khrushchev insisted that the Soviet Union would accept only three; any more would endanger Soviet sovereignty and facilitate U.S. espionage. Khrushchev linked the issue of nuclear tests with disarmament. As he had stated repeatedly, the USSR wanted general and complete disarmament.

The President couldn't agree to only three inspections. The U.S. Senate would never accept a test ban unless there was a foolproof control system to prevent violations. Moreover, the President pointed out, "How can we inspect events in the Soviet Union if any such inspection would be subject to Soviet approval? Under such an arrangement any party that might have tested clandestinely would simply refuse to accept inspection in the area where the test had occurred."[15]

The test ban alone was not very important, Khrushchev contended. What was needed was general and complete disarmament.

The President said that he agreed that a nuclear test ban would not of itself lessen the number of nuclear weapons possessed by the USSR and the U.S. Nor would it reduce the production of such weapons. However, a test ban would make development of nuclear weapons by other countries less likely. . . . If we fail to reach agreement on a nuclear test ban then other countries will undoubtedly launch a nuclear weapons program.

But if there was general and complete disarmament, Khrushchev said, then nuclear weapons would be eliminated altogether. The Soviet proposals provided for disarmament in stages and for control in stages. If both sides accepted general and complete disarmament, the President inquired, and agreed to reduce their armed forces, would the Soviet Union accept inspection anyplace in the USSR?

Contradicting his earlier expression of fear of espionage, Mr. Khrushchev answered in the affirmative, saying "Absolutely."

> In other words, the President inquired further, if general and complete disarmament were accepted as a commitment of national policy and a nuclear test ban were included in the first stage, would that mean that the test ban would be subject to inspection without a veto?
>
> Mr. Khrushchev replied that in that event he would try to persuade the President not to start with this measure because it is not the most important one.

The President disagreed. A nuclear test ban would be a very significant step and would facilitate a disarmament agreement. "There is a Chinese proverb saying that a thousand-mile journey begins with one step. So let us make that step."[16]

The premier returned to his previous objection to a test ban. "If the U.S. refuses to accept general and complete disarmament then the Soviet Union cannot agree to accept such [a test-ban] arrangement," he stated. Again, Kennedy countered effectively: "If controls should turn out to be prejudicial to the national interest of any of the parties to an unreasonable degree, the treaty could be abrogated."

The President inquired about U.S.-Soviet cooperation in space exploration, but Khrushchev rejected the idea. Cooperation in outer space was impossible without disarmament.

When the discussion turned to Berlin, Khrushchev displayed intense animation. He confronted Kennedy with an ultimatum and a dilemma. They could sign a treaty accepting the existence of two Germanys, or Khrushchev would be forced to sign a separate treaty with East Germany no later than December 1961.

Sixteen years had passed since the end of World War II; the USSR had lost 20 million people in the war, the premier said.

Now Germany, the country which unleashed World War II, has again acquired military power and has assumed a predominant position in NATO. Its generals hold high offices in that organization. This constitutes a threat of World War III which would be even more devastating than World War II. The USSR believes that a line should be drawn under World War II. There is no explanation why there is no peace treaty 16 years after the war.

Only the West German militarists—the revanchists—gained from further delay. He wanted to reach agreement with the West on a treaty, Khrushchev said, but if the United States refused, the Soviet Union would sign a treaty with East Germany by itself.[17]

Kennedy knew that the treaty would cancel all existing commitments, including occupation rights, administrative institutions, and rights of access. The German Democratic Republic would control West Berlin's communications, and agreement on access would have to be reached with the Democratic Republic, an intolerable situation for the West. West Berlin, in effect, would gradually be devoured by Communist East Germany.

The Western Allies remained in Berlin not because of someone's sufferance, Kennedy replied.

> This is an area where every president of the U.S. since World War II has been committed by treaty and other contractual rights and where every president has reaffirmed his faithfulness to his obligations. If we were expelled from that area and if we accepted the loss of our rights no one would have any confidence in U.S. commitments and pledges. U.S. national security is involved in this matter because if we were to accept the Soviet proposal U.S. commitments would be regarded as a mere scrap of paper.

The Soviet leader responded that he "was very sorry but he had to assure the President that no force in the world would prevent the USSR from signing a peace treaty. Sixteen years have passed since World War II and how long should the signing of a peace treaty be delayed? Another sixteen years, another thirty years? No further delay is possible or necessary."

Khrushchev's argument was transparently insincere. If only the Berlin issue could be resolved, "the road would be clear for the development of our mutual relations." Why didn't the President accept the Soviet Union's "good intentions and motivations?"

It was one thing for the Soviets to transfer their rights to the GDR, Kennedy said; it was an altogether different matter for the USSR to give away U.S. rights which it had on a contractual basis.

The Soviet Union would probably sign a peace treaty at the end of the year, Khrushchev insisted, with all the ensuing consequences. He continued: "If the U.S. should start a war over Berlin there was nothing the USSR could do about it. However, it would have to be the U.S. to start the war, while the USSR will be defending peace."

It wouldn't be the United States that precipitated the new crisis, Kennedy stated; Khrushchev was doing so by seeking to change the existing situation.

"Mr. Khrushchev replied he did not understand how the signing of a peace treaty could worsen the world situation. Peace is always regarded as something beneficial while the state of war is regarded as something evil."

Simply signing a peace treaty was not the crucial issue, the President repeated. The matter of a peace treaty with East Germany was a matter for Mr. Khrushchev's judgment and was not a belligerent act. "What is a belligerent act is transfer of our rights to East Germany. . . . If we accepted Mr. Khrushchev's suggestion the world would lose confidence in the U.S. and would not regard it as a serious country. It is an important strategic matter that the world believe the U.S. is a serious country."[18]

After the last scheduled session, Kennedy insisted on one more opportunity to reach an understanding with Khrushchev. "No," he barked at his staff. "We're not going on time. I'm not going to leave until I know more."

The United States wanted to humiliate the USSR and this could not be allowed, Khrushchev told him in their extra session.

> He would be glad if the U.S. were to agree to an interim agreement on Germany and Berlin with a time limit so that the prestige and the interests of the two countries would not be involved or prejudiced. However, he said, he must warn the President that if he envisages any action that might bring about unhappy consequences, force would be met by force. The U.S. should prepare itself for that and the Soviet Union will do the same.
>
> The President inquired whether under an interim arrangement forces in Berlin would remain and access would be free. Mr. Khrushchev replied that would be so for six months. In reply to the President's query whether the forces would then have to be withdrawn, the Chairman replied in the affirmative.

Kennedy reiterated that it was the chairman, not he, who wanted to force a change. Khrushchev replied that a peace treaty would not involve any change in boundaries (avoiding reference to the change in who controlled West Berlin). His decision to sign a peace treaty was firm and irrevocable; the Soviet Union would sign it in December if the United States refused an interim agreement. "If that is true," Kennedy responded, "it is going to be a cold winter."[19]

At 4:35 P.M. on June 4, Kennedy and Khrushchev walked down the stairs and out the front door of the Soviet embassy. They didn't speak. "The frigid effect of their final words clung to them," wrote Hugh Sidey. "Kennedy thrust his hands into his pockets. On the steps the two men paused for photographs. They forced a final smile and handshake." Then they departed.

"He just beat hell out of me," the stunned President told James Reston shortly after the last session. "I've got a terrible problem. If he thinks I'm inexperienced and have no guts, until we remove those ideas we won't get anywhere with him. So we have to act."

Arthur Schlesinger observed that the President "had never encountered any leader with whom he could not exchange ideas—anyone so impervious to reasoned argument or so apparently indifferent to the prospective obliteration of mankind. He himself had indicated flexibility and admitted error, but Khrushchev had remained unmoved and immovable. . . . The test ban seemed dead. Berlin held the threat, if not the certitude, of war."[20]

On the gloomy flight from Vienna to London, Kennedy talked quietly with Ken O'Donnell about his doubts and forebodings. "All wars start from stupidity," he said.

> God knows I'm not an isolationist, but it seems particularly stupid to risk killing a million Americans over an argument about access rights on an Autobahn in the Soviet zone of Germany, or because the Germans want Germany reunified. If I'm going to threaten Russia with a nuclear war, it will have to be for much bigger and more important reasons than that. Before I back Khrushchev against the wall and put him to a final test, the freedom of all of Western Europe will have to be at stake.

Kennedy's usual detachment crumbled when he talked with his brother Robert. "We've had a good life," he said; "we're adults. We bring these things on ourselves." Beginning to tear up, he continued, "The thought, though, of the women and children perishing in a nuclear exchange. I can't adjust to that."

In London Harold Macmillan quickly realized Kennedy's troubled state and knew that the President's back ached. Rather than force Kennedy to endure a formal meeting with key advisers of both countries, Macmillan canceled the session. "I said, 'Mr. President, you have had a tiring day, don't let's have this. . . . Why not come up to my room and we will have a little chat?' He seemed rather relieved, and he came up at about half past eleven, and we sat down till about three in the afternoon. I gave him some sandwiches and whisky, and that was all. He just talked."

That Kennedy let his hair down surprised Macmillan. He found the President "rather stunned—baffled would perhaps be fairer" and "impressed and shocked." Kennedy later expressed his deep appreciation for Macmillan's thoughtfulness. "I value our open and friendly conversations more and more," he wrote the British leader, adding a scribbled postscript, "Many, many thanks." Kennedy subsequently told a British journalist, "I feel at home with Macmillan because I can share my loneliness with him. The others are all foreigners to me."[21]

On the plane flight back to the United States, Kennedy was painfully uncomfortable. "His eyes were red and watery, dark pockets beneath them," observed Hugh Sidey. "He shifted stiffly in his seat to ease the back pain, occasionally reached to touch the spot that ached, as if such action might dispel it."

Back in Washington, Kennedy briefed congressional leaders and delivered a television report to the nation on June 6, emphasizing the seriousness of West Berlin's predicament but not mentioning Khrushchev's ultimatum.

After a few nights' sleep Kennedy felt better about his encounter. It had been a sobering experience but not shattering. "He seemed in excellent spirits," Sidey discovered a few days after the President returned home. "He seemed quite confident. . . . I think his morale was pretty good."[22]

The President had made an obvious mistake at the summit by allowing himself to be drawn into an abstract ideological debate on Marxist theory and the role of historical inevitability. The Soviet premier, an experienced dialectician, could not be convinced. With his superficial understanding of Marxism, the President played to Khrushchev's advantage. Kennedy did much better staying with his pragmatic arguments.

Accounts differ on Kennedy's performance at the summit. Yuri Barsukov, the Washington correspondent for *Izvestia,* contended the Soviet leader was surprised to find "in John Kennedy such an inexperienced politician." Viktor Sukhodrev, Khrushchev's interpreter, thought the Soviet leader came away from Vienna with a poor impression of Kennedy, a feeling that "the guy was inexperienced, perhaps not up to the task of properly running a country such as the United States."

Kennedy had been tongue-tied and permitted Khrushchev to make statements that Kennedy should have immediately challenged, said George Kennan. "I think Khrushchev . . . thought that he'd gotten away with many of these talking points; that he had placed President Kennedy in a state of confusion where he had nothing to say in return."[23]

The notion that Kennedy was weak, confused, and humiliated at Vienna is wrong. "That judgment comes mostly from Kennedy's own gloomy view of the meeting, and the way he backgrounded James Reston instantly after the meeting and the way [Reston] reported that," McGeorge Bundy stated. Kennedy was upset because the Soviet leader refused to bend. Except for

Laos, the President found no area of accommodation. Their conversation didn't suggest weakness or humiliation; nor did the premier confuse or intimidate. Kennedy did what he always did and did well—he listened.

Most of the time Kennedy was in good form—precise, logical, and informed. Both leaders were unyielding and vigorous in argument. "Kennedy carried the conversational initiative, introducing topics, keeping them specific, bringing straying discussions back to the question and pressing Khrushchev for answers," Sorensen accurately summarized. "Khrushchev usually talked at much greater length. Kennedy usually talked with much greater precision."[24]

Except for being drawn into ideological debate, Kennedy performed "excellently," thought the State Department's Charles Bohlen. Llewellyn Thompson agreed. "I think the President handled the thing exceedingly well. I think he made a great impression on Mr. Khrushchev."

Kennedy himself insisted that the confrontation had been "invaluable," giving him "a clearer idea of the intensity of the struggle we are in." What's more, despite their differences, he and Khrushchev had established rapport, making it easier to communicate in their future correspondence.[25]

For weeks afterward the Vienna confrontation preoccupied Kennedy. "He carried excerpts from the official translation of his talks with Khrushchev around with him wherever he went," said Ben Bradlee, "and read chunks of them to me several times." Kennedy decided to get tough. "The State Department is a bowl of jelly," he complained privately. "It's got all those people over there who are constantly smiling. I think we need to smile less and be tougher."[26]

He took personal charge of the planning discussions to meet the Berlin crisis. At times the work consumed him. Secretary of the Interior Stewart Udall, who had been working diligently on conservation issues, had difficulty securing an appointment with the President. "He's imprisoned by Berlin," Udall lamented. "He has a restless mind that likes to roam over all subjects, but ever since Europe, Berlin has occupied him totally."

Sorensen described the President's preparation:

He reviewed and revised the military contingency plans, the conventional force build-up, the diplomatic and propaganda initiatives, the budget changes and the plans for economic warfare. He considered the effect each move would have on Berlin morale, Allied unity, Soviet intransigency and his own legislative and foreign aid program. He talked to Allied leaders, to Gromyko and to the Germans; he kept track of all the cables; [and] he read transcripts of all the conferences.[27]

Kennedy asked veteran diplomat Dean Acheson to present his recommendations for handling the crisis. The former secretary of state's powerful presentation, delivered to the President on June 28, 1961, argued that Khrushchev was testing American resolve. "Berlin was not a problem but a pretext." The Soviets would interpret any attempt to negotiate as a sign of American weakness. They hoped "to neutralize Berlin as a first step and prepare for its eventual takeover by the German Democratic Republic." In addition, the Kremlin desired "to weaken if not break up the NATO Alliance." Finally, Khrushchev wanted "to discredit the United States or at least seriously damage its prestige," allowing the Soviets to extend their influence throughout Europe. The United States must be willing to use nuclear weapons rather than allow Khrushchev to get away with his demands. Acheson urged the President to call up reserves, move more troops and aircraft to Europe, increase defense appropriations, resume nuclear testing, and declare a state of national emergency.[28]

In the end Kennedy overruled Acheson on several points. "We have nothing to fear from negotiations," he said, "and nothing to gain by refusing to take part in them." He slashed the proposed supplemental military budget request from $4.3 billion to $3.2 billion. Instead of immediate mobilization, Kennedy would ask Congress for standby authority to call up the reserves and triple draft calls. Nor would he declare a state of national emergency. That was too drastic and could be effective only once. Better to wait and see if the Soviets actually signed a treaty or blocked access to West Berlin. The U.S. embassy in Moscow advised that the Soviets would be more impressed by a substantial but quiet buildup that didn't frighten our allies.

Nonetheless, to impress the Soviets with America's resolve, Kennedy called for a major military buildup. The United States would develop the capacity to send six new divisions to Europe by the end of the year. He would request that Congress give him standby authority to triple draft calls and to call up reserves. A civil defense program would construct fallout shelters to reduce the number of Americans killed in a Soviet nuclear attack. He increased naval strength and the number of bombers on ground–alert status.[29]

On July 25, in a nationally televised speech from the Oval Office, Kennedy delivered a firm and urgent message but steered clear of threats. Expressing resolution and commitment, he explained his new policies and his intention to continue negotiations. "If we and our allies act out of strength and unity of purpose—with calm determination and steady nerves—using restraint in our words as well as our weapons—I am hopeful that both peace and freedom will be sustained."

U.S. rights in Berlin were clear and deep-rooted, he stated. "But in addition to those rights is our commitment to sustain—and defend, if need be—

the opportunity for more than two million people to determine their own future and choose their own way of life."

West Berlin tested Western courage and will:

> It would be a mistake for others to look upon Berlin, because of its location, as a tempting target. The United States is there; the United Kingdom and France are there; the pledge of NATO is there—and the people of Berlin are there. It is as secure, in that sense, as the rest of us—for we cannot separate its safety from our own.
>
> I hear it said that West Berlin is militarily untenable. And so was Bastogne. And so, in fact, was Stalingrad. Any dangerous spot is tenable if men—brave men—will make it so.

American families would need to sacrifice and bear the burden: "Studies or careers will be interrupted; husbands and sons will be called away; incomes in some cases will be reduced. But these are burdens which must be borne if freedom is to be defended. Americans have willingly borne them before, and they will not flinch from the task now."

The United States would combine military proposals with diplomatic measures. We wanted to negotiate, to talk, to listen, but only about reasonable proposals:

> If they have proposals—not demands—we shall hear them. If they seek genuine understanding—not concessions of our rights—we shall hear them. We have previously indicated our readiness to remove any actual irritants in West Berlin, but the freedom of that city is not negotiable. We cannot negotiate with those who say, "What's mine is mine and what's yours is negotiable." But we are willing to consider any arrangement or treaty in Germany consistent with the maintenance of peace and freedom, and with the legitimate security interests of all nations. . . . There is peace in Berlin today. The source of world trouble and tension is Moscow, not Berlin. And if war begins, it will have begun in Moscow and not Berlin.

The United States must never be placed in the same impotent position England faced at Munich in 1938. "If we do not meet our commitments to Berlin, where will we later stand? If we are not true to our word there, all that we have achieved in collective security, which relies on these words, will mean nothing. And if there is one path above all others to war, it is the path of weakness and disunity."[30]

Some scholars later branded the speech "provocative" and "hard line." One claimed Kennedy used "apocalyptic rhetoric" and alarmed "the nation in a speech that was moralistic, specious, and jingoistic."

In fairness, Kennedy designed the speech to meet a serious threat, and it was moderate compared to Acheson's extreme proposals. A thousand telegrams flooded the White House by the next morning, running twenty to one in favor of his speech. A Gallup poll "showed 85 percent of Americans ready to risk war to keep U.S. troops in Berlin." On July 28, no senator voiced opposition as the Senate unanimously approved Kennedy's defense buildup.[31]

After Vienna, events turned sour for Khrushchev. Instead of retreating, Kennedy held firm. The Soviets were spending a fortune subsidizing the collapsing East German economy. The GDR's leader, Walter Ulbricht, had few options as refugees took flight to the West, including physicians, engineers, teachers, and other professionals. Between 1945 and 1960 nearly 4.3 million Germans had fled the German Democratic Republic, and the problem was getting worse.

In July 1961, over thirty thousand East Berliners—"voting with their feet"—fled to West Berlin. East Germany was hemorrhaging. "I don't understand why the East Germans don't close their border," Senator William Fulbright mused publicly in early August 1961. At about the same time the President told Walt Rostow, "Khrushchev is losing East Germany. He cannot let that happen. If East Germany goes, so will Poland and all of eastern Europe. He will have to do something to stop the flow of refugees—perhaps a wall. And we won't be able to prevent it. I can hold the Alliance together to defend West Berlin but I cannot act to keep East Berlin open."[32]

Khrushchev decided to fall back on Ulbricht's earlier suggestion to erect a wall. Beginning after midnight on August 13, 1961, the East Germans constructed a physical barrier along the boundary with West Berlin using obstacles and barbed wire; construction of a concrete wall started six days later.

At Hyannis Port, the President and his guests were cruising on the *Marlin* when a messenger arrived at the Kennedy compound. "This looks important," he told Chester V. Clifton, handing over a brown envelope. Clifton read that the East German regime had just cut Berlin in two and was starting to build a barrier. Clifton contacted the *Marlin,* and Kennedy immediately returned to shore.

Kennedy scanned the message, then made phone calls. It surprised the President that no Soviet soldiers were seen in the streets; nor was there interference with access to West Berlin. The measures taken did not threaten vital interests of the Allies in West Berlin.

Some demanded that the Western Allies tear down the wall. Although Kennedy briefly pondered the suggestion, he realized it was impractical. "We could have sent tanks over and knocked the Wall down," he mused. "What then? They build another one back a hundred yards? We knock that down, then we go to war?"

Kennedy quickly realized that the wall was less a problem than a solution. "Why would Khrushchev put up a Wall if he really intended to seize West Berlin?" he said privately to his aides. "There wouldn't be any need of a Wall if he occupied the whole city. This is his way out of his predicament. It's not a very nice solution, but a Wall is a hell of a lot better than a war."[33]

A few days after the East Germans started constructing the wall, Bundy offered three thoughts for the President: "(1) This is something they have always had the power to do; (2) it is something they were bound to do sooner or later, unless they could control the exits from West Berlin to the West; (3) since it was bound to happen, it is as well to have it happen early, as *their* doing and *their* responsibility."

On August 14, Kennedy urged Rusk to take steps "to exploit politically propagandawise" the closing of the border: "This seems to me to show how hollow is the phrase free city and how despised is the East German government, which the Soviet Union seeks to make respectable. . . . It offers us a very good propaganda stick which if the situation were reversed would be well used in beating us. It seems to me this requires decisions at the highest level."

"Vibrant with emotion," recalled Donald Wilson, Kennedy urged the U.S. Information Agency to exploit the propaganda advantage of the wall to the "maximum." "It was an enormous plus for the West," said Wilson, the agency's deputy director, "an enormous minus for the Communist nations. [Kennedy] recognized it as such. In effect, what he said was everything must be done in terms of pictures—pictures particularly . . . to describe what a dreadful thing this was in terms of bottling up a whole nation and preventing them from leaving."[34]

At first Kennedy's quiet public reaction to the wall didn't redress West Berlin's sagging morale. Subsequently he dispatched Vice President Johnson to demonstrate U.S. concern and resolve, and ordered 1,600 American troops to travel down the autobahn. Worried that something might go wrong with the high-risk move, he insisted on being kept informed of every detail of the convoy's progress. The troops arrived safely "to great popular acclaim."

The Berlin wall, viewed with some reason as a crisis in West Berlin and West Germany, did not turn into one for Kennedy. Republicans were not critical, nor were the media, and hard-line columnists mostly supported the President.

As Kennedy and his advisers discreetly reconciled themselves to the benefits of the Berlin wall, American policy on Germany broke loose "from what was, in effect, West Germany's domination of it," noted historian John Gaddis. The wall transformed the Cold War. "From this point on it is possible to trace the start of the European détente, based upon a shift in West Germany's foreign policy to a tolerance of the territorial status quo and a readiness to open up lines of communication to the East," wrote Lawrence Freedman. "Almost casually, Kennedy tended to write off East Berlin, paying little attention to allied rights there. The communists were in control and nobody was suggesting a direct challenge. Though he had obligations to the whole city, it was already divided in Kennedy's mind." Most U.S. political leaders agreed.[35]

Kennedy narrowly defined American goals in Germany: the presence of Allied forces in West Berlin, physical access and security for West Berlin, and the security of West Germany against attacks from the east. He would not use force to end the "de facto division of Germany" or the "de facto absorption of East Berlin into East Germany."

When the President learned that neutral nations questioned the U.S. policy on Berlin, he was incredulous. "There seems to be a general feeling that they wish us to agree to compromise our position along the lines suggested by the Soviet Union, even at the expense of the people of West Berlin," he wrote Adlai Stevenson and two others on August 20, 1961. "We seem to be caught between two unsatisfactory alternatives. If we respond vigorously to Khrushchev's pressure, we are regarded as belligerent and saber-rattling and we lose support. If we attempt to work out our difficulties by negotiation, as in Laos, we are regarded as weak and on the decline."[36]

Kennedy wanted to take a stronger lead in negotiations over Berlin, even if U.S. allies disagreed. He informed Rusk on August 21: "I no longer believe that satisfactory progress can be made by Four-Power discussion alone. I think we should promptly work toward a strong U.S. position in both areas and should make it clear that we cannot accept a veto from any other power. We should of course be as persuasive and diplomatic as possible, but it is time to act."

He outlined his specific thoughts. Make the framework of proposals as "fresh as possible." Protect U.S. support "for the *idea* of self-determination, the *idea* of all-Germany, and the *fact* of viable, protected freedom in West Berlin." Do not insist on maintaining occupation rights if other strong guarantees could be developed: "Occupation rights are a less attractive base, before the world, than the freedom and the protection of West Berliners." Consider parallel peace treaties: "Khrushchev would have to look at what we say, because he has invited just this course." Examine all of Khrushchev's statements for a way to peg the U.S. position. Khrushchev "has thrown out quite a few assurances and hints here and there, and I believe they should be exploited." Do not put too much distance between the initial U.S. proposals and the fallback position: "Indeed it may be well not to have any fall-back position. Our first presentation should be, in itself, as persuasive and reasonable as possible."[37]

In mid-September Kennedy sent General Lucius Clay to Berlin as his special adviser. An aggressive, tough hard-liner, popular in West Berlin for his leadership more than a decade earlier in the Berlin airlift, Clay added an unyielding presence to encourage the West Berliners and to discourage the Soviets.

But the general had the reputation of being difficult to control. "Clay is a soldier, but opinion is sharply divided on his ability to carry out a policy set by others, unless he fully agrees with it," Bundy had advised the President while considering Clay's appointment. "You want no risk of setting up another MacArthur-Truman affair." On the other hand, if Clay agreed with the President's policy in Berlin, "he can be a major political protection."

Clay's propensity for violent initiatives caused Kennedy uneasiness. In late October the general initiated, with glee, a tank confrontation at the border. American tanks faced Soviet tanks for three days, conjuring up fears of nuclear war.[38]

Kennedy phoned Clay to compliment him on his nerve during the standoff. The general wondered if Washington officials had lost their nerve. "I don't know about those of my associates," Kennedy replied, "but mine are all right." Actually Kennedy's nerves were probably frayed as Freedman observed: "This was the sort of situation Kennedy dreaded: a contrived incident over a secondary issue that could lead to a tank battle in the middle of Berlin with who knew what consequences to follow." A flurry of backstage messages led to the withdrawal of the tanks of both sides, ending the showdown.

After the three-day crisis, anxious to avoid any escalation of tensions, Kennedy discreetly placed rigid limitations on Clay's discretionary powers until the general was eventually retired. The President's masterful use of Clay during the tense period impressed Foy Kohler, assistant secretary of state. The President managed to keep the violent initiatives of General Clay reasonably in check, and satisfied Clay as to his firmness. "In retrospect," Kohler concluded, "Clay's presence there . . . certainly played a useful role in demonstrating our determination and the firmness of our purpose, and I am sure had a considerable influence on Soviet reactions."[39]

For McGeorge Bundy there was never a specific day on which it seemed likely that war would break out over Berlin. But almost every day there were nagging problems to solve; or there were worries about "what one or another of our allies would or would not support, or whether morale in West Berlin itself was holding up."

Kennedy grew exasperated with the West German and French attitude. He preferred to have the West Germans make direct contact with the Soviets. "This was one of the ways he thought of forcing the [West] Germans to come up with some sort of ideas of how they might do a deal with the Russians which would prevent us all being brought to the brink of a crisis about once every two years," David Ormsby-Gore recalled of Kennedy's attitude. But the West Germans wouldn't respond.[40]

The United States had gotten itself into an absurd situation. West Berlin was not defensible with conventional forces; yet it was almost unthinkable to start nuclear war over it. How could Kennedy persuade the Soviet Union to keep its hands off West Berlin "when the price of retaliation to a Russian move might be a global nuclear war?" Both the West Germans and the French demanded that the United States hold firm, be tough, but offered meager military assistance and no ideas for a solution. The French irritated Kennedy the most, thought Ormsby-Gore, because "they were always encouraging everybody to take a tough line, [but] he knew perfectly well that if it came to a showdown they would be the first to run up the white flag."

In the spring of 1962, Dean Rusk obtained clearance from Great Britain and France to present a proposal to the Soviets. Two important features were agreement on nuclear nonproliferation, aimed at mollifying Soviet fears that West Germany might someday acquire nuclear weapons; and an International Access Authority—composed of the four occupying powers, the two Germanies, and several neutral countries—to monitor travel in and out of Berlin.[41]

When Chancellor Adenauer suddenly became aware of the proposal for the International Access Authority, he arranged for calculated leaks to the press, creating a synthetic crisis and leading the German press to accuse Kennedy of weakness.

The deliberate campaign to sabotage an already exceedingly difficult and delicate diplomatic initiative irritated Kennedy. Thereafter he continued to monitor events in West Berlin, always trying to put the problem into cold storage. Stave off a crisis for ten years until the world situation changed, he concluded.

For the most part, Kennedy carried out statecraft of the highest order during the Berlin crisis. Unlike the Bay of Pigs misadventure, he wisely managed the crisis by combining power with creative negotiations. He had been tempered and measured in the way he used the nation's nuclear capacity as a diplomatic weapon. "In referring to Kennedy as a 'Cold War monger' over Berlin, revisionist historians have surely overstated the case," concluded James Giglio. "Kennedy had not instigated the conflict, nor could he have ignored the Khrushchev ultimatum at Vienna." Kennedy's combination of firmness and negotiations helped to resolve the Berlin crisis, put it on ice, and reduce its explosive potential.[42]

28

NO MANDATE

In the 1960 campaign Kennedy promised to provide dynamic leadership in dealing with Congress, saying the President should "fight for legislative programs and not be a casual observer of the legislative process." As it turned out, Kennedy had precious little political capital with Congress when he came into office. The close margin of his election victory did not justify a mandate for any of his initiatives, nor did the outcome of the congressional elections. The Democrats retained control of both houses, but Republicans took two seats from the Democrats in the Senate and gained twenty-one seats in the House. One after another, congressmen said, "[Kennedy's] a fine man, and I'm for him, but he's no help to me because I ran ahead of him in my district. President Eisenhower would run ahead of me in my own district."[1]

Immediately after his inauguration Kennedy found himself locked in a major procedural battle over reform of the House Rules Committee. The twelve-member committee, composed of eight Democrats and four Republicans, usually created a 6-to-6 tie vote because two conservative Southern Democrats sided with the four conservative Republicans. Unless the committee was diluted with liberal members, Kennedy's domestic program would be stymied.

Courtly, shrewd, and ruthless, seventy-nine-year-old Howard "Judge" Smith of Virginia chaired the House Rules Committee and was a leader of the conservative Southern Democrats. Without the consent of the Rules Committee, it was nearly impossible to get legislation to the floor of the House for a vote. Southern newspapers pressured Southern representatives to back Smith, portraying the Rules Committee as the last bastion against socialism and civil rights legislation. Journalist Tom Wicker explained the Rules Committee's powerful sway:

> The Committee held the immense power to decide what bills, of the thousands introduced each session by zealous members, would go to the House floor for a vote. A measure studied for months in a legislative committee, perfected to the last whereas by experts in its subject matter, supported by hundreds of members of the House—to say nothing of the President—could in an hour's time be killed by the Committee on Rules' refusal to send it to the House floor for a vote.

A tie vote was enough to block a measure from going to the full House.[2]

At a meeting at Palm Beach five days before Christmas, 1960, Kennedy convinced House Speaker Sam Rayburn to take the lead in diluting membership on the Rules Committee. They agreed to enlarge the committee by adding three more members, two Democrats and one Republican—ensuring, they assumed, a favorable 8-to-7 vote on most proposals.

Rayburn told Kennedy, "Mr. President, I'm not going to say anything to you about the Rules Committee fight. It's a legislative fight. The Administration has nothing to do with it, and we're going to handle it ourselves in our way." Reassured, Kennedy didn't worry about the problem for the next month. He assumed that the powerful Rayburn would win the battle.[3]

On Tuesday, January 24, four days after the inauguration, while Kennedy hosted his first breakfast meeting with Democratic leaders at the White House, Rayburn dropped a bombshell. "Mr. President," the Speaker announced, "I don't believe we have the votes to expand the Rules Committee."

Kennedy was stunned. Larry O'Brien, the special assistant to the President for congressional relations, recalled, "We were astounded to hear Rayburn report that the expansion plan would probably lose by a handful of votes."

"We can't lose this one, Larry," the President told O'Brien. "The ball game is over if we do. Let's give it everything we've got." During the next few days the White House lobbied furiously to win the battle in the House. "Victory," observed Wicker, "would mean opportunity—control of the House, political power, a lesson to opponents that Kennedy was not to be taken lightly. Victory, above all, would not be defeat and defeat was simply unacceptable."

Kennedy won the Rules Committee fight, but only by the narrow margin of 217 to 212. "Our majority included twenty-two Republicans, virtually the high-water mark of our Republican support, and thirty-four southern Democrats or about a third of the Southerners," said O'Brien. Sixty-four Democrats voted against the President. "With Rayburn's own reputation at stake, with all of the pressure and appeals a new President could make, we won by [only] five votes," Kennedy lamented many times in the next few months. "That shows you what we're up against."[4]

The Eisenhower administration had created the White House Office of Congressional Relations, but Larry O'Brien centralized the operation and made it systematic and aggressive. The amiable O'Brien was the primary lobbyist for the White House on Capitol Hill. A bartender's son, he was different from many of those who surrounded the President. "I don't know what I'm doing in this crowd," he mused. "I didn't go to Harvard and I'm not athletic. I don't even play touch football."

Tom Wicker thought that O'Brien's enemies could meet in a telephone booth; he was popular with members of Congress and enjoyed excellent relations with the media. Some judged him the ablest man in the administration. "Frankly," confided a cabinet officer, "he is the very best of the White House pros. There are always a hell of a lot of idea guys available but the Larrys are hard to find. He knows that ideas are fine, but that they're no damn good unless they can be translated into action."

Pierre Salinger marveled at O'Brien's ability to count votes. "Even before legislation went to the Hill, he could tell you almost exactly who would be for it, who would be against it, whose vote could be changed, and whose could not."[5]

The Kennedy-O'Brien operation encountered nearly insurmountable obstacles. With no national depression, no mass unemployment making constituents clamor for government action, the New Frontier operated in a vastly different environment than Roosevelt's New Deal. "Except for racial minorities," said one observer, "spiritual disquietude floated about without commitment to issues." In 1962 Majority Leader Mike Mansfield blamed the "strangely quiescent" mood of the country for the inability to pass the President's major programs. "It isn't stirred to any degree. It isn't demanding much of this or that." "President Kennedy today," Richard Rovere perceptively noted, "is attempting to meet a challenge whose existence he and his associates are almost alone in perceiving."[6]

Democrats in both houses had new and less potent leadership. In the Senate the powerful, skilled, and experienced Lyndon Johnson was succeeded by easygoing Mike Mansfield of Montana. A man of outstanding integrity, Mansfield was respected by members of both parties, but proved too mild-mannered as majority leader during the Kennedy administration to press hard for the administration's program. "Mansfield is generally conceded to be too nice a fellow to engage in the arm-twisting tactics his job requires," said *Time* in 1963. With Lyndon Johnson no longer the dominating presence, power reverted to several "feudal lords"—the senators who chaired major standing committees.

Over his long career, House Speaker Sam Rayburn had accumulated many IOUs from members, and he used them to dominate the House. But Rayburn died in the fall of 1961. Massachusetts's John McCormack replaced him as Speaker, and, while loyal to Kennedy, he did not have nearly the clout of the powerful Texan.

Charles Halleck, the abrasive, highly partisan congressman from Indiana and the Republican House leader, proved another major barrier to enacting Kennedy's domestic program. Halleck had deposed the aging and genial Joseph Martin of Massachusetts, whom Republicans accused of providing ineffective leadership. Larry O'Brien found it virtually impossible to work with Halleck, and the Republican opposition to Kennedy's domestic program plagued his presidency.

By 1962, said O'Brien, "we were lucky to pick up four or five Republican votes on most bills and often we got none." One study found that under Halleck's leadership "the Republicans gave Kennedy less support than any opposition party has given any President between 1954 and 1970." Halleck and his Republican forces, however, did cooperate with the President on defense and military appropriations, guaranteeing easy passage of those measures.[7]

Since Republican support was negligible on nondefense issues, Kennedy needed to win at least fifty conservative Southern Democrats to enact administration bills. To appease the South, Kennedy omitted civil rights legislation from his agenda for two years and remained aloof from the struggle in the Senate to eliminate the filibuster. "He was hardly in office before he increased cotton support prices," noted Tom Wicker. "He channeled ample patronage southwards, provided defense contracts in profligate supply, permitted a disproportionate share of area redevelopment funds to be made available for Southern projects, and spread flattering attention on Southern leaders."

When Senator Harry Byrd hosted a large luncheon for friends at his country estate in the spring of 1961, Kennedy arrived at the gathering by helicopter, shocking the old Virginia gentleman. "Don't jump to conclusions," a liberal senator later warned. "Harry Byrd still opposes us. We'll never get his vote. But he's not sitting up nights now figuring out ways to be mean."

Kennedy risked alienating liberals who supported him in order to gather votes from conservatives who opposed him. Liberals on the Hill sometimes resented his strategy. After one bitter debate, Senator Hubert Humphrey wearily told Arthur Schlesinger, "It's hard for us down here to keep on defending the things we think the White House believes in when the White House seems to spend its time saying nice things about the other side."[8]

When Myer Feldman pointed out another promise Kennedy had made during the 1960 campaign, the President jocularly exclaimed, "Jesus Christ, Mike, you've got me into a hell of a lot of trouble. Every time I want to do something, I'm faced with something I said during the campaign." One of those promises was to raise the minimum wage.

In 1938 Congress enacted the first minimum-wage law, placing a floor under the wage of certain categories of workers. When Kennedy took office, the minimum wage was a dollar an hour, a disgrace he thought. "I find it difficult to know why anyone would oppose seeing somebody, by 1963, paid $1.25," he said. He proposed an increase to $1.25 and to extend its coverage to an additional four million Americans.

During the 1960 campaign Kennedy had been particularly eloquent on the need for a minimum wage to alleviate the plight of 150,000 laundry workers, but that extension of coverage met strong Southern resistance. "We've got to hold with $1.25," O'Brien advised the President. "We'll have to cut back on the coverage."[9]

The administration backpedaled, agreeing to drop about a half million of the four million workers it intended to cover, a difficult but necessary concession. "Those to be dropped included [150,000] laundry workers, people who had come to be a symbol of underpaid workers in America," O'Brien stated. "But the cold political fact was that we knew of four or five votes in opposition, because of intense pressure from the laundry lobby, that would be gained by dropping the laundry workers."

Despite the concession and extensive lobbying by O'Brien's team, the House defeated the measure by a vote of 186 to 185. O'Brien immediately phoned the President with the bad news.

"One vote! I can't believe it!" Kennedy exclaimed. In his frustration, he plunged a letter opener into the top of his desk.

But the minimum-wage struggle had a mostly gratifying conclusion. The Senate subsequently passed the administration's proposal, and the House approved a version granting a minimum wage of $1.15. In the House-Senate conference, the administration agreed to a two-step increase: The minimum wage would start at $1.15, then rise to $1.25 in two years. The House endorsed the conference report, 230 to 196, "giving us," noted O'Brien, "substantially what we wanted and involving no real compromise with the $1.25 minimum."

Tom Wicker subsequently criticized the administration for "washing out" the laundry women in a "vain effort at conciliation," and thought Kennedy's compromise had weakened him in the eyes of the House. In fact, there was no alternative to compromise, and there is little evidence that it weakened the President in the House.[10]

"Of our defeats, none was more bitter than our inability to pass the bill to provide federal aid to elementary and secondary education," O'Brien reflected. With eighty million Americans born between 1945 and 1965, the population explosion was overwhelming American schools. Yet no general federal legislation to aid education had been passed after the war, primarily because of the power of entrenched interests. The most sensitive problems centered on whether aid should go to segregated and religious schools and whether the wealthier states should subsidize poorer ones.

After the Soviet Union launched *Sputnik* in 1957, embarrassing Americans, Congress passed the National Defense Education Act (NDEA) to promote education in science, engineering, foreign languages, and math. But as Hugh Graham observed in his history of federal aid to education, "attempts to enact more general-aid programs foundered on constitutional objections, the church-state issue, fear of loss of local control, partisan wrangling, and, beginning in the 1950s, the controversy over school desegregation."

In 1949, Congressman Kennedy endorsed legislation providing federal funds for buses, health services, and textbooks for private and parochial schools. After his 1952 Senate victory, Senator Kennedy avoided the controversial federal aid clashes until late in the decade. He was changing his mind. In the 1960 election campaign, he came out forcefully for federal aid to education—but for public schools only, not parochial schools.[11]

Three days before Kennedy's inauguration, Francis Cardinal Spellman of New York savaged the recommendations of Kennedy's task force on education, which had urged federal aid only to the public schools. The proposal was "unfair," "blatantly discriminating," and "unthinkable," Spellman charged; it made Catholic children "second-class citizens."

Kennedy had no choice but to try to fulfill his campaign pledges. On February 20, 1961, he recommended $2.3 billion over three years for general federal aid for public elementary and secondary classroom construction and teachers' salaries, but did not include parochial schools because of "the clear prohibition of the Constitution." Under his proposal states would control the allocation of grants, and segregated school districts could receive federal funds with no restriction.[12]

In early March, Kennedy proposed two major programs for higher education: $2.8 billion in loans over five years for academic facilities and $892 million for over two hundred thousand four-year-college scholarships based on merit and need.

With its headquarters in an eight-story building less than a mile from the

White House, the National Catholic Welfare Conference (NCWC) was the seat of Catholic power on social and economic issues. On March 1 the NCWC announced its opposition to any federal aid program that excluded children in private schools. Such exclusion was discriminatory, a denial of "equal protection of the laws." The bishops did not seek grants, said spokesman Archbishop Karl Alter, but "we hold it to be strictly within the framework of the Constitution that long-term, low-interest loans to private institutions could be part of the federal aid program."

Kennedy was irritated with the Catholic hierarchy, judging it insensitive to the unique problems of the country's first Catholic president. Larry O'Brien noted the irony: "The first Catholic President was being frustrated on one of his top-priority legislative proposals by leaders of his own Church; they, for their part, had come to feel that the Church's interest in education might be better served by a non-Catholic President and indeed they were right."[13]

By concentrating on acquiring federal *loans* rather than outright grants, the Catholic hierarchy had shrewdly placed Kennedy in an awkward position. The unconstitutionality of grants was clear, but the legal status of loans was uncertain. With most of the Catholic hierarchy opposing Kennedy's bill, tension mounted in the House. There was no consensus and seemingly no way to reconcile differences. One group preferred no bill to one that aided parochial schools; another wanted no bill rather than one that "discriminated" against parochial schools; a third opposed any bill.

Because of the mounting pressure, Kennedy sought a compromise acceptable to the Catholic hierarchy. At a presidential press conference on March 8, he announced that if the members of Congress wished "to address themselves to the problems of loans, which is a separate matter, we will be glad to cooperate in every way." But he insisted that the loan issue be kept separate from the grant issue. "I definitely believe that we should not tie the two together."

Following behind-the-scenes negotiations, the White House agreed to an amendment to a bill extending the life of the NDEA, which provided loans to parochial schools for constructing science, mathematics, foreign-language, physical-fitness, and lunch facilities.[14]

Kennedy tried to keep a low profile. Sorensen closed a confidential memo to the President with the stipulation that "there was to be no mention or indication that the Administration had played any role or taken any position on this amendment or course of strategy." The loan amendment would appear to be merely a matter of congressional discretion, with the President maintaining at his press conferences that he was not a party to the congressional maneuvers.

Despite Kennedy's denials, noted Hugh Graham, the "strategy of using NDEA revision to smuggle in aid to parochial schools was transparent." *The New York Times* charged that the NDEA revisions were "now being used as a cover under which there is an attempt to slip through large-scale Federal aid to non-public schools."

In July 1961, the House Rules Committee was considering three of Kennedy's education bills: the divisive public school bill, NDEA expansion, and a college aid bill. There the bills met an unexpected fate.[15]

The crucial problem involved one congressman, Democrat Jim Delaney, a Catholic from Queens, New York, who had a large Catholic constituency. Delaney normally voted with the administration, but he decided on principle that he could not support aid to public schools and not to Catholic schools as well. On July 18, the Rules Committee, with Delaney joining the opposition, voted 8 to 7 to table all three of the education bills, destroying Kennedy's education program for the year.

"Nothing could change Delaney's mind," O'Brien sadly recalled. "Ribicoff and I talked to him, many times, to no avail. The President had at least two long off-the-record talks with him in which he tried desperately to bring Delaney around, but Jim was adamant."

Critics of Kennedy's education strategy think he botched the job, particularly by initially standing so firm, only to retreat so swiftly. "Kennedy's decision to acquiesce privately in what he had repudiated publicly was unquestionably political," said historian Lawrence McAndrews. "He recognized that the bishops' power base coincided with his own—the urban North—and feared that to offend the NCWC was to jeopardize his support among Catholic Congressmen and the representatives of largely Catholic constituencies."

Wicker wondered why the administration allowed Delaney "to sink the final knife" into the President's education program and "escape unscathed." Why didn't Kennedy "bludgeon or wheedle" that single vote in the Committee on Rules? Why was Delaney never "punished"?[16]

Kennedy had no intention of bludgeoning or punishing members of Congress. "Had [Delaney] been bargaining, holding out for some patronage plum, we might have done business, but the only thing he wanted was the one thing Kennedy could not give—federal aid to Catholic schools," said O'Brien.

On October 6, 1961, Abraham Ribicoff sent President Kennedy a five-page memo analyzing the reasons for the defeat of the administration's education bills and the prospects for the future. "I am convinced that there is not a full commitment to [federal aid to] education in this nation," Ribicoff wrote. "People are concerned about the education of their own children, but there is very little realization throughout the land that increased financing for education, shared by the Federal Government, is urgently needed to improve education throughout the country."[17]

Medical care for the aged—Medicare as it was later called—was another major domestic goal. Throughout the 1950s, Congress had debated the issue. Organized labor, a few Republicans, liberal Democrats (including Kennedy), Northern urban legislators, and Americans for Democratic Action supported a compulsory health insurance program for people over sixty-five, financed through the Social Security payroll tax. Opponents included most Republicans and Southern Democrats in Congress, business and insurance groups, and the influential American Medical Association (AMA). They pushed for a voluntary system and a narrower federal role. "Their proposals centered on various reinsurance schemes to help private insurance companies offer voluntary coverage at a moderate cost for high-risk groups such as the elderly and the chronically ill," observed Anne Hodges Morgan in her biography of Senator Robert Kerr of Oklahoma. In 1960 they enacted the Kerr-Mills Medical Assistance for the Aged (MAA) program.

When Eisenhower left office, health insurance remained a major political issue, largely because the Kerr-Mills solution was piecemeal and ineffective. After three years only twenty-eight states had set up programs, and only four had comprehensive ones. Of the 18 million elderly citizens in the nation, only 148,000 received assistance in the month of July 1963. The program also generated exceptionally high administrative costs, and wealthier states disproportionately received the federal matching funds.[18]

On February 9, 1961, Kennedy sent Congress a message calling for the extension of Social Security benefits for fourteen million Americans over sixty-five to cover hospital and nursing-home costs (but not surgical expenses). A small increase in Social Security taxes would finance the benefits. "The program," Kennedy stated, "is not socialized medicine. . . . It is a program of prepayment for health costs with absolute freedom of choice guaranteed. Every person will choose his own doctor and hospital."

The AMA discovered that the most effective technique to combat the administration's bill, known as King-Anderson, was to label it "socialized medicine," and to link socialized medicine with poor-quality health care, impersonal service, overcrowded hospitals, and the specter of the Soviet Union. The AMA sponsored advertisements predicting that a "new bureaucratic task force" would enter "the privacy of the examination room," deprive patients of the "freedom to choose their own doctor," and take away the doctor's freedom "to treat his patients in an individual way."[19]

The fate of the Medicare proposal lay with the House Ways and Means Committee, chaired by Democrat Wilbur Mills of Arkansas, who had cosponsored Kerr-Mills. The influence of Mills within Ways and Means was crucial, and the administration's lobbyists concentrated on persuading him to support the President's program. If convinced, he could carry the committee with him.

The administration was in an awkward position with its Medicare legislation because Mills's Ways and Means Committee also had jurisdiction over other high-priority administration legislation—tax-revision, trade, and anti-recession measures. Chairman Mills had a "sizable chunk" of the administration's legislative program in his "hip pocket," said a White House aide. It seemed unwise to press Ways and Means too hard.

In 1962 the administration still did not have a majority in Ways and Means to report out its bill. Only eleven members out of twenty-five favored the legislation. The impasse continued.[20]

Unable to arouse great enthusiasm for Medicare within the Ways and Means Committee, at the urging of organized labor and the National Council of Senior Citizens for Health Care, Kennedy agreed to appeal over the head of Congress directly to the American public. Larry O'Brien opposed this approach: "I believed that, in dealing with Congress, Kennedy could try to work with Congress or he could declare war on Congress. The latter course was more dramatic but less productive. For the most part, Kennedy chose a strategy of conciliation."

Nonetheless, on May 20, 1962, Kennedy appeared before 17,500 supporters at Madison Square Garden and a national television audience and delivered an extemporaneous speech without his usual clarity and grace. Even supporters of the President rated his performance poor. The speech failed to arouse grassroots pressure on Congress, and annoyed Mills. "To get a vote on Medicare in the House, we had to persuade Mills, and you don't persuade Mills with a rally in Madison Square Garden," O'Brien maintained. "Kennedy understandably wanted to take his case to the people, but in this particular instance that approach didn't work." The approach favored by O'Brien, HEW Secretary Ribicoff, and Assistant Secretary Wilbur Cohen was to negotiate a compromise bill acceptable to three or four more members of the Ways and Means Committee.[21]

The President also urged Senator Harry Byrd, chair of the Senate Finance Committee, to report the Medicare bill, but Byrd refused. "It had been the Finance Committee's policy to wait for the House Ways and Means Committee to act before they did anything," noted Senator Mansfield. Later, on his own initiative, Mansfield bypassed the Finance Committee and brought the Medicare bill to the Senate floor for a vote. Despite extensive lobbying by the White House, the administration lost another close vote, 52 to 48.

Senate committee chairmen adamantly opposed bypassing a Senate committee, believing the same thing might happen to them. "[The Senate defeat] was not the President's fault," said Mansfield. "That was my own fault. Bypassing [a] committee was a tactic I tried once or twice. I failed both times."

In 1963 the President put Medicare on hold. He wrote to the new secretary of HEW, Anthony Celebrezze, that "events will not permit legislative action in 1963," but that "we should proceed on the assumption that we are attempting to secure it." *The New York Times* described Medicare as "the most forgotten of all forgotten issues of 1963." The President told the media that he would get a bill out in 1964.[22]

Congress did support Kennedy's call for a major new space program. If President Dwight Eisenhower had had his way, there might not have been a space race. He rejected the notion that spectacular space achievements had any effect on the strength of the country. In 1958, though, reacting to the Soviets' success with *Sputnik* the year before, Eisenhower did approve the creation of the National Aeronautics and Space Administration (NASA), and the agency brought together the resources for the U.S. space program.

On April 12, 1961, three months after Kennedy's inauguration, Moscow announced that cosmonaut Yuri Gagarin had completed an orbital flight around the earth, becoming the first human in space. Jubilant Soviet leaders used Gagarin's flight to promote themselves and the Communist system. While greeting the cosmonaut at the Moscow airport, Khrushchev remarked: "This victory contains a new triumph of Lenin's ideas, a confirmation of the correctness of Marxist-Leninist teaching. . . . Victory will be ours, and it will be the most noble, this most radiant victory."

Kennedy congratulated the Soviets for the accomplishment, but he said of the Soviets' lead in space: "The news will be worse before it is better, and it will be some time before we catch up." Gagarin's adventure was inspiring, wrote *Time,* but "the Soviet achievement could be seen only as a victory for Communism and a defeat for the free world as led by the U.S."[23]

On the evening of April 14, 1961—two days after Gagarin's triumph—the President assembled his science and budget advisers to discuss the space program. He asked *Time*'s Hugh Sidey to sit in during the discussion, and the correspondent later described the meeting.

"What can we do now?" Kennedy asked, rocking back and forth on the legs of his chair.

Presenting a discouraging picture, the experts thought the Soviets were far ahead of the United States. Kennedy frowned, Sidey reported, and ran his hands agonizingly through his hair. "We may never catch up," he muttered.

"Now let's look at this," Kennedy later interjected. "Is there any place where we can catch them? What can we do? Can we go around the moon before them? Can we put a man on the moon before them?" Budget Director David Bell suggested it might cost forty billion dollars. Science adviser Jerome Wiesner doubted that the United States could catch up to the Soviets in ten years.

"The cost," Kennedy pondered. "That's what gets me."

During the discussion Kennedy tapped the bottoms of his upper front teeth with the fingernails of his right hand. At one point he said quietly, "There's nothing more important."

Suddenly the President was out of his chair and on his feet. "Thank you for coming by." Afterward, Sidey concluded, "Kennedy thought about the curious dilemma further. The cost was frightening. Yet the threat was there, and Yuri Gagarin's name still lingered in the headlines to emphasize it."[24]

In early May the President worried that astronaut Alan Shepard's impending space flight might result in disaster—while millions watched on television. Was there a way to stop television from covering the event? he anxiously queried Dean Rusk and NASA's director, James Webb. "He is afraid of the reaction of the public in case there is a mishap in the firing," Evelyn Lincoln scribbled. Later the same day Webb advised him that everything had been done that could be done to assure the success of the venture.

On May 5, after Shepard's successful flight, Kennedy phoned to congratulate him. The astronaut later remarked that the President seemed "personally moved" by his success.

Gagarin's achievement ignited the President's intense competitive spirit. In the six weeks after the Soviets' success, he gathered recommendations, and then he presented his case to a joint session of Congress on May 25, 1961. "I believe we should go to the moon," he stated. An American should set foot on the moon "before this decade is out. . . .

"I am asking the Congress and the country to accept a firm commitment to a new course of action—a course which will last for many years and carry very heavy costs: 531 million dollars in fiscal '62—an estimated seven to nine billion dollars additional over the next five years."[25]

The President's goal struck a responsive chord. Within a few months Congress increased NASA's budget by 89 percent, and another 101 percent increase came the following year. "Between 1961 and 1963 NASA's payroll swelled from 16,500 people to more than 28,000, and the number of contractors working on the space program grew from fewer than 60,000 to more than 200,000," noted historians John Logsdon and Alain Dupas.

The President peppered John Glenn with questions after the lieutenant colonel became the first American to orbit the earth on February 20, 1962. What control did Glenn have over the booster during the launch? Did he drive the spacecraft like an airplane or was he controlled by guidance systems? What did Glenn see? How did he feel during reentry? Kennedy wanted the astronauts to visit high schools and colleges to promote the space program and inspire young people.[26]

Liberal critics argued that the space program drained money from housing, education, and other domestic programs. Senator William Fulbright urged the President to spend less on the space race and more on education and urban renewal. "Bill, I completely agree with you," the President responded. "But you and I know that Congress would never pass that much money for education. They'll spend it on a space program, and we need those billions of dollars in the economy to create jobs." If the space program's budget was cut from five billion to three billion, for example, the President had no illusions that Congress would take the two-billion-dollar difference and spend it on domestic programs.

Ironically, the Soviets lost their preeminence in space exploration while the American effort was enjoying strong support. "Personal rivalries, shifting political alliances and bureaucratic inefficiencies bred failure and delays within the Soviet lunar-landing program," observed Logsdon and Dupas. "The dissipation of the Soviet Union's lead in space during the 1960s tarnished the image of socialist competence and diminished Soviet standing in world affairs."

The space program enhanced America's prestige. "It harnessed American technological and organization skill, showed what government could do, and harmed nothing," said Carl Brauer. "Some people argued that it drained funds from more pressing objectives, but Kennedy was almost certainly right to observe that Congress would not have appropriated funds for *those* objectives."[27]

Kennedy often stated that America should demonstrate its concern for the welfare of the hundreds of millions of people on the edge of starvation. The day after his inauguration, the new President phoned Sargent Shriver and asked him to form a presidential task force on the feasibility of the Peace Corps. Shriver recommended that Kennedy issue an executive order granting the new organization life through its first year while awaiting congressional approval. Kennedy agreed, and signed the order on March 1.[28]

Busy with other legislative issues, Larry O'Brien worried about waging another legislative battle in Congress. "I think I probably [fit] in the category of the fellow saying, 'Hey, I think it's great. It's just as impressive as the devil. Marvelous idea. But now, how do you get it into formulation?' And what are the priorities here?"

Originally the administration planned to place the Peace Corps within the new Agency for International Development (AID), an approach that allowed the President to request only one congressional appropriation. Shriver, though, convinced his wife, Eunice, to lobby her brother for an independent agency and also solicited the backing of Lyndon Johnson.

Johnson reminded the President that Congress disliked foreign-aid programs, and argued that the Peace Corps be established as a unique, independent entity. Under the bureaucratic umbrella of AID, the agency would lose appeal among young people and become snarled in red tape, "just another box in an organizational chart, reporting to a third assistant director of personnel for the State Department." The President agreed, but not wholeheartedly.

After talking with the President, Eunice Shriver told her husband: "Jack feels that you and Lyndon Johnson demanded that the Peace Corps be separate and that therefore the two of you ought to get your damn bill through Congress by yourselves."[29]

After four months of brilliant lobbying, Shriver succeeded in convincing the Congress to permanently establish an independent Peace Corps. "And then we ran the Peace Corps without ever asking permission or getting clearance for anything from the White House," he later said. Kennedy praised Shriver's astonishing success with Congress, calling him "the most effective lobbyist on the Washington scene."

At age forty-four, the charismatic Shriver was handsome, intense, creative, and caring. He insisted that no other government agency interfere with the Peace Corps. "I'm getting rather suspicious over here that . . . despite your instructions . . . some of our friends over in the Central Intelligence Agency might think that they're smarter than anybody else and that they're trying to stick fellows in the Peace Corps," he informed the President. Agreeing that "we don't want to discredit this whole idea," Kennedy instructed Shriver to call Richard Helms, the CIA's deputy director, and tell him that the President didn't want "anybody in there. . . . And if they are there, let's get them out now."[30]

Because of his other responsibilities and Shriver's competence, Kennedy seldom focused on the Peace Corps. One exception was his attempt to nudge Shriver in a different direction: "I note that you have plans of increasing the number of Peace Corps volunteers in various parts of the world, such as North Borneo," Kennedy wrote in August 1962. "I would like for you to keep in mind the importance of Latin America, which I think should be the primary area. At the present time do we not have as many in the Philippines as we have in all of the Latin American countries?"

Shriver used the President mainly to publicize the agency. Kennedy cared about the Peace Corps, and never turned down Shriver's requests. "Whenever he was requested to greet Volunteers in the Rose Garden, announce a new program, or sign a letter of congratulations to those serving abroad, Kennedy willingly complied," observed Gerard Rice in his history of the Peace Corps. When Ambassador John Kenneth Galbraith returned from his post in India, Kennedy asked, "How are Sarge's kids doing?"[31]

At a meeting with Peace Corps officials in Washington in June 1961, the President praised Shriver and the new agency:

I don't think it is altogether fair to say that I handed Sarge a lemon from which he made lemonade, but I do think that he was handed and you were handed one of the most sensitive and difficult assignments which any administrative group in Washington have been given almost in this century. You have brought to government service a sense of morale and a sense of enthusiasm and really commitment which has been absent from too many governmental agencies for too many years.

Kennedy said on other occasions that the Peace Corps was "the most immediate response that the country has seen to the whole spirit which I tried to suggest in my inaugural." The volunteers had responded to the challenge to "ask not. . . ."

Although the Peace Corps failed to stimulate economic growth in host countries, it succeeded in other ways. It brought an understanding of Third World nations, improved the lives of poor people, and showed the idealistic side of America.[32]

Little in Kennedy's life suggested he would become a leader in conservation. He didn't hunt, fish, tent, backpack, or slip away alone into the wilderness. He was interested, though, in the seashore, and as senator had cosponsored a bill to establish Cape Cod National Seashore.

During Kennedy's presidency Americans increasingly demanded additional wildlands and a cleaner environment. Historian Thomas Smith, who studied Kennedy's conservation record, observed:

Aggressively pursuing preservation and the "greening of America," groups such as the Sierra Club, Wilderness Society, and Audubon Society gained in size and influence. The publication of Rachel Carson's *Silent Spring* gave a sense of urgency to environmental protection by pointing out the potential health hazards of indiscriminate pesticide use.

Secretary of the Interior Stewart Udall consistently lobbied the President on behalf of conservation. He had barely known Kennedy before 1961, but, impressed with his mind and ability, had become an early supporter of his presidential nomination.

The President endorsed the protection of seashores at Cape Cod; Point Reyes, California; and Padre Island, Texas, and sponsored the first Conservation Conference in fifty years. On March 1, 1962, he announced an ambitious program to give "priority attention" to wilderness protection, seeking to set aside fourteen million acres of unspoiled public land. The New Frontier adopted measures to control water pollution, studied rivers that should be left in a free-flowing state, and issued a report on the dangers of pesticides.[33]

Prodded by Udall, in mid-August 1962 the President made a Western conservation tour, visiting South Dakota, Colorado, and California. Kennedy dedicated dams, delivered speeches, mingled with politicians, and visited Yosemite National Park in California. "He lacks the conservation-preservation insights of FDR and TR," Udall inscribed in his journal during the trip. "And it will take some work to sharpen his thinking and *interest.*"

Overall, however, Udall was delighted with the tour. "A good trip—good for the country, an eye-opener for the Pres—a master stroke for us and our conservation program." The best part was that Kennedy and the media "have started making the golden word—conservation—part of our common dialogue again. We may succeed in our revival yet."[34]

In September 1963 Kennedy embarked on a major five-day, eleven-state Western tour. Only part of the tour was to be devoted to conservation, but Udall was disappointed by the "lousy" speeches the President delivered and was disheartened by Kennedy's lack of passion for the land and the outdoors. "I can hardly, with fairness, complain that my man does not have a streak of Thoreau or Robert Frost in his New England makeup, but I long for a flicker of emotion, a response to the out of doors and overwhelming majesty of the land." The President was not indifferent, Udall thought. He had environmental instincts, "but he doesn't feel the indignation the two truly great conservation presidents felt for the despoilers, and he doesn't respond to the land with their warmth or excited interest."

Historian Smith described one example of Udall's frustration:

> On September 24 the presidential party traveled to northern Wisconsin to visit the Apostle Islands of Lake Superior. Senator Gaylord Nelson [of Wisconsin] had recommended those islands as a national recreation area. As the helicopter passed over the islands, two bald eagles rose from the marshland and glided along side the presidential aircraft. It was a "rare, exciting sight," but Kennedy seemed disinterested.

At Grand Teton National Park in Wyoming, Udall arranged with park officials to have the President take a half-hour early-morning walk to see the moose, deer, and other wildlife. "I found out later that O'Donnell and these fellows laughed behind my back that I'd even suggested it," Udall recalled. "I went ahead and did it myself. A lot of the press corps went with me. It was a lot of fun. But, you know, the fact that I couldn't even get the President to take a little walk bothered me." Udall added: "Imagine a conservation trip where the leader never gets out of his suit or steps off the asphalt."

After reflection, Udall thought he had entertained unrealistic expectations about the western tour and had been too harsh on Kennedy. The trip was primarily political, and Kennedy's natural reserve made it difficult for him to show passion about conservation.[35]

Generally, the Kennedy administration dealt tentatively with the emerging ecological movement. It never developed a coherent conservation policy; nor did it match the conservation records of Theodore and Franklin Roosevelt. Still, there were notable successes. With the exception of Lyndon Johnson's Great Society, Smith judged Kennedy's administration the most conservation-minded since 1945. "They helped bring national attention to environmental issues, reinvigorated a traditional conservation program, and produced a substantial record of accomplishment. Sometimes overlooked, the conservation program must be considered one of the successes of the Kennedy presidency."[36]

Three other important programs initiated modestly during the Kennedy administration bore fruit after the President's death. In 1962 Eunice Kennedy Shriver decided to be frank about her sister Rosemary's retardation, exposing for the first time Rosemary's real condition. With the President's permission, she wrote an article for the *Saturday Evening Post,* published in September 1962. Rosemary "was slower to crawl, slower to walk and speak than her two bright brothers," Eunice wrote. "My mother was told she would catch up later, but she never did. Rosemary was mentally retarded."

"It was a historic moment in the history of mental retardation in America," observed Lawrence Leamer. "It was not simply the coming out of the Kennedys, but an attempt to use Rosemary's condition to further the evolution of concern about the developmentally disabled and their treatment. By any measure, the article represented the Kennedys at their most exemplary, taking this deep family tragedy and turning it into activities of the highest social usefulness." (However, the article didn't mention Rosemary's lobotomy.)

Eunice pressed the President relentlessly to take action on behalf of the mentally retarded. "Jack, this group interested in mental retardation is coming to Washington," she insisted. "Could I have them at the White House for a reception?" The President usually agreed.

"If [Eunice] hadn't nagged the hell out of Sarge Shriver and her brother, there wouldn't be a mental retardation program," reflected Wilbur Cohen. "The drive came from Eunice, not from Jack." His attitude was that "if Eunice wanted it, for God's sake . . . do it! Get her off my back!"

The President assigned Myer Feldman as his special assistant to oversee mental retardation legislation and to keep him informed. At the request of his sister, the President attended receptions and spoke to several groups concerned with the issue. He appointed the twenty-six-member President's Panel on Mental Retardation. After reviewing the panel's report, with its 112 recommendations, he addressed Congress on February 5, 1963, clearly outlining the challenge:

> We as a Nation have long neglected the mentally ill and the mentally retarded. This neglect must end, if our Nation is to live up to its own standards of compassion and dignity and achieve the maximum use of its manpower.
>
> This tradition of neglect must be replaced by forceful and far-reaching programs carried out at all levels of government, by private individuals and by State and local agencies in every part of the Union.
>
> We must act.

Over the next twenty years, Congress passed 116 laws or amendments providing support for the mentally retarded and their families. By 1976, federal agencies administered 135 special funding programs.[37]

Women played little role in the Kennedy administration. Not much effort was made to solicit women appointees, and few joined the Kennedy team. The administration "looks to me like the biggest stag party in the history of the U.S. Government," complained a female writer in *Harper's* in 1962. There were scores of secretaries, undersecretaries, assistants, and deputies. "But they are all men."

President Kennedy appointed only ten women who needed Senate confirmation; Truman had appointed fifteen and Eisenhower fourteen. Only 2.4 percent of all Kennedy's appointive positions went to women, a percentage about equal to the two previous administrations.

A month after the inauguration, Emma Guffey Miller, the Democratic National Committeewoman from Pennsylvania, angrily wrote Kennedy: "It is a grievous disappointment to the women leaders and ardent workers that so few women have been named to worthwhile positions." (Referring to the appointment of women, Robert Kennedy said privately in 1961, "I think a woman's place is in the home.")

From 1953 to 1960 Katie Louchheim had been the director of women's activities for the Democratic National Committee, and she had vigorously campaigned for Kennedy's election in 1960. But the only job Kennedy officials offered her was a lowly position in the State Department escorting female visitors. Although pleased to have a job, she disliked the one offered. "I was sensitive . . . that I was tagged and ticketed for life with this role." Angry, she complained to two of Kennedy's aides, "What am I supposed to do with my brains?" Patting her on the back, the aides said, "We are certain you will make something of the job."[38]

"None of the Kennedy women lobbied their brother or brother-in-law in the name of their sex," noted Lawrence Leamer. "None of the Kennedy women identified with their own sex as a political entity. None of them pushed for the advancement of women within the administration."

Kennedy was not likely to find women appointees in the places he was looking: in the elite universities, among the executives and on the boards of large corporations, and in prestigious law firms—all places that harbored few women. "It was the Kennedy search method, rather than an overt Kennedy intention, that excluded women more completely than in previous administrations," contended historian Cynthia Harrison.[39]

Appointments for women fell by the wayside partly because Kennedy preferred another route. He supported the agenda of the Women's Bureau coalition of liberal and labor organizations led by Esther Peterson. "The implementation of the Women's Bureau program constituted a New Frontier for women," said Harrison. "Unlike token appointments, the new plan directly addressed the problem of women's status in American society, and its impact was far-reaching."

Kennedy knew Peterson from his earliest days in the Congress, when she lobbied for the Amalgamated Clothing Workers. A capable advocate of labor's position, Peterson had joined Kennedy's campaign before the primaries, working to build labor support for him. To reward her efforts during the campaign, Kennedy offered her a choice of several administration jobs. She selected the Women's Bureau in the Department of Labor. In that position she strove to implement two programs long supported by women in the labor movement: legislating equal pay and creating a national commission on women.[40]

Because of the dearth of women in his administration, Kennedy came under fire at news conferences from May Craig, a persistent White House reporter known for her tough questions. On November 9, 1961, she asked Kennedy what he had done for women in accordance with the Democratic Party's platform. Recognizing a loaded question, Kennedy smiled broadly and responded, "Well, I'm sure we haven't done enough, Mrs. Craig," arousing laughter from other reporters. But Craig had raised a valid issue, one Kennedy acknowledged on February 12, 1962, when he explained why he created the President's Commission on the Status of Women. "One [reason] is for my own self-protection: every two or three weeks Mrs. May Craig asks me what I am doing for women!"

Kennedy recognized the problems women faced in the workplace, particularly discrimination in wages and hiring. He charged the commission to "review progress and make recommendations as needed for constructive action" relating to almost every aspect of female employment. It was the first time that a study of the status of women had received national focus. To highlight its significance, Kennedy wisely selected Eleanor Roosevelt as chairperson. Much of the work, though, fell to Peterson.

Peterson thought President Kennedy was "genuinely interested" in the commission's work, and she was delighted to have easy access to him. His "door was always open" to her. "It was just so splendid because you could get a reaction from the President without knocking down walls," she said.

In 1963 feminist writer Betty Friedan praised the commission for creating "a climate where it is possible to recognize and do something about discrimination against women, in terms not only of pay but of the subtle barriers to opportunity."[41]

With the support of the President, Peterson and the Women's Bureau successfully broke an eighteen-year legislative stalemate when the Equal Pay Act was signed in 1963. Narrow and limited, it applied only to women doing the same work as men, while ignoring the majority of women stuck in sex-segregated jobs. Despite its limitations, the Equal Pay Act was a milestone, marking the entrance of the federal government into the field of safeguarding the right of women to hold employment on the same basis as men. The program Peterson laid out for Kennedy, said Harrison, "had greater potential to affect the lives of American women than had all the female appointments of the previous fifteen years."[42]

During the 1960 campaign Kennedy made only a few references to poverty. He talked more about the need to find jobs. Nor did he focus on poverty during the first two years of his presidency, partly because there was no strong public demand for an antipoverty program. That the poor were not more angry and politically insistent perplexed Kennedy. "In England," he said, "the unemployment rate goes to two per cent, and they march on Parliament. Here it moves up toward six, and no one seems to mind."

Although there was no public outcry about poverty, it was attracting the attention of academics and social critics. In *The Affluent Society* (1958) John Kenneth Galbraith warned that the poor were a demoralized, invisible, inarticulate minority, ignored by politicians. In *The Other America* (1962), Michael Harrington maintained that poverty was hidden, "disguised by inexpensive clothing and concealed by beltways and interstate highways that no longer required driving through decaying inner cities and blighted rural areas." Puerto Ricans in New York, Mexican-Americans in the Southwest, blacks in ghettos, Indians on reservations, the elderly, and many rural people made up the "other America." In *The New Yorker* in January 1963, Dwight MacDonald vividly analyzed all the recent literature about poverty.[43]

Kennedy read the books by Galbraith and Harrington and MacDonald's essay. He also sensed "a greater public concern because of recent studies on poverty—including a TV documentary—and a spiraling civil rights movement that exposed black deprivation," noted Giglio.

There was another factor. The tax reduction Kennedy pushed would stimulate the entire economy, but would not assist people too poor to pay income taxes. A poverty program might offset the accusation that the administration's tax cut favored only the middle and upper classes.

In December 1962, during their year-end review of economic conditions, the President said to Council of Economic Advisers Chairman Walter Heller: "Now, look! I want to go beyond the things that have already been accomplished. Give me facts and figures on the things we still have to do. For example, what about the poverty problem in the United States?" The suggestion set in motion the staff work needed to formulate a war on poverty.

Later Kennedy told Heller that "if he could get sufficient *substance* in a program to deal with poverty, he would like to make a two- or three-day trip to some of the key poverty-stricken areas to focus the spotlight and arouse the American conscience on this problem from which we are so often shielded."[44]

Heller endorsed Kennedy's suggestion. He was strongly influenced by Wisconsin economist Robert Lampman, whose statistics indicated that the rate at which economic growth was attacking poverty was slowing down. The percentage of the poor who were elderly, female heads of families, and minorities had increased. There was a "dramatic slowdown in the rate at which the economy is taking people out of poverty," Heller told Kennedy in May 1963. Poverty had to be attacked by the government.

At a cabinet meeting on October 29, 1963, the President wrote, encircled, and underlined the word "poverty" on a yellow pad several times. He told Schlesinger, "The time has come to organize a national assault on the causes of poverty, a comprehensive program, across the board," and indicated that it would be "the centerpiece in his 1964 legislative recommendations."

On November 5, 1963, Heller wrote department heads requesting that they submit proposals ten days later. Their recommendations should "concentrate on relatively few groups and areas" where problems were most serious and solutions most feasible. They should focus on a coordinated attack in a few areas, and should minimize handouts, maximize self-help, and emphasize the prevention of poverty.

Kennedy did not make the final decision to proceed publicly with an antipoverty program until mid-November 1963, a few days before his trip to Dallas. Before leaving on the trip, Kennedy told Heller to continue his antipoverty planning. "First, we'll have your tax cut; then we'll have my expenditures program."[45]

In the end Congress failed to pass Medicare or Kennedy's education bills, but Larry O'Brien proudly listed many other legislative successes: the four-year,

$451 million Area Redevelopment program; a major trade bill; a tax-reform bill; the International Wheat Agreement treaty; the Communications Satellite Act; the $435 million Manpower Development and Training Act, providing job training for the unemployed; $400 million in special accelerated public works funds; a drug-labeling act; a poll-tax constitutional amendment; a $32 million program of assistance to educational television; the Institute of Child Health and Human Development; a mass immunization bill; and increased disability compensation to two million veterans.

Many historians, critics, and frustrated supporters of the Kennedy program emphasize the President's limitations for his failure to pass major liberal proposals. "Kennedy did not really have his heart in his congressional relations," Hugh Sidey maintained. "Kennedy at times appeared to be going through motions only."

Kennedy had been a relative neophyte in the Senate, a junior member not in the power structure, and didn't know his fellow senators intimately. "There was a slight reticence," conceded Larry O'Brien. "He would not attempt to put them on the hook." At the same time some elder statesmen in the Senate were skeptical of this youngster Kennedy who had spent only eight years in the Senate, then parachuted into the presidency.[46]

"Congressmen liked Kennedy, but they did not feel close—or personally obligated—to him," said James Giglio. In his conferences with members of Congress Kennedy was not good at the small talk most congressmen enjoyed. Still, the President amazed visitors with his knowledge of legislation.

Some legislators thought Kennedy's efforts were too timid; they expected more arm-twisting and pressure rather than reason and persuasion. "There was something lacking in this business of persuading them to do what he thought was in the public interest," thought William Fulbright. The White House didn't work hard enough for measures that the President had recommended, critics charged. "A hard-driving President would apply pressure to get his program passed," said a Democratic senator.

"He was not very deft with Congress," liberal senator Joseph Clark contended. "He was too willing to compromise on a good many occasions . . . I thought the liberal bloc, in the Senate at least, got rather short shrift."[47]

Kennedy used several rationalizations for not fighting harder for his legislative programs. "Why fight if you are not sure to win?" he would say. Or he would quote Thomas Jefferson's dictum, "Great innovations should not be forced on slender majorities."

Columnist Walter Lippmann blamed much of the domestic impasse on Kennedy, claiming the President had failed to educate the country and persuade it of the importance of his program. Despite his popularity, Kennedy had "not yet won over the minds of the people," Lippmann said, "because he ha[d] not yet conquered their hearts by opening his own." In a May 1963 television interview, Lippmann accused Kennedy of being cautious to a fault. "He does not want to be unpopular anywhere—anywhere—with anyone; and I think that a public leader, at times, has to get into struggles where somebody gets a bloody nose, and Kennedy doesn't want that ever."[48]

Kennedy had limitations in dealing with Congress, but he was concerned and did try hard. Lippmann's accusation riled Kennedy's advisers. They countered that the President sold himself and his policies in a subtle but more effective way. "Everyone yells about the need for more education on the President's program," one Kennedy lieutenant declared. "We feel they are out of touch, not we. Everything the President does sells his program." He was, in fact, an active publicist, discussing his ideas and programs in speeches and press conferences and in conversations with opinion makers.

Because he regarded legislative liaison as extremely important, he wanted Larry O'Brien to have direct and frequent contact with him. He made absolutely clear to everyone that O'Brien was his personal representative for legislation and contact with legislators. When anyone, even prominent members of Congress, made legislative proposals to him, his reply was: "Have you discussed this with Larry O'Brien?"[49]

The President invited congressmen in groups of fifteen to the White House to socialize, and the liaison staff brought individual congressmen to visit the President for off-the-record chats. On Tuesday mornings Kennedy met with Democratic legislative leaders over breakfast. Informal but businesslike, the breakfasts focused on the President's thoughts about legislation. "He was always courteous to us," said Mansfield. "He asked us for our views and he gave them consideration. He was not averse to calling us down at other times besides the breakfast period, either singly or in groups, and he kept us very well informed of events as they were developing overseas."

In 1961 Kennedy hosted thirty-two Tuesday morning leadership breakfasts and held about ninety private conversations with congressional leaders. "Coffee hours brought five hundred members of the House and Senate to the White House, and bill-signing ceremonies brought in the same number," O'Brien recalled. "All in all, Kennedy had about 2,500 separate contacts with members of Congress during his first year in office."[50]

Kennedy instructed that a hand-delivered letter be sent to each member on a birthday. He told Ted Reardon to study the *Congressional Record* every day and prepare a letter of congratulations and appreciation whenever a legislator commented favorably on the President's program. "That way all the members of Congress will feel that we are watching their work," the President said. He wanted to personally sign all the letters.

While seeking additional foreign aid, he talked to key Democrats by telephone or in his office. "I know your district, Sam, and this won't hurt you there. . . . This is a tough one for you, Mike, I realize, but we'll go all the way with you this fall. . . . Vote with us on recommittal, where it's close, Al, and then you can vote 'no' on final passage."

O'Brien believed that the President should not be overly involved. "I'm cautious about overextending him," O'Brien said. Only at critical times did he turn to the President for assistance. "Here is the situation," he would tell the President. "I've tried and failed. Either we have to try something else or you have to get involved." He rarely asked Kennedy to phone legislators to secure their vote, because all the members would then expect to be called by the President personally.[51]

With the exception of Medicare, the President didn't appeal over the heads of Congress to the people, believing that the approach would arouse animosity against the administration. Only occasionally did the liaison unit go behind the back of legislators and use their constituents to pressure them.

O'Brien and his four lieutenants were the core of the lobbying operation, but he also enlisted the support of congressional relations coordinators of forty federal departments and agencies. "In the past, these agencies had often negotiated directly with their friends in Congress with little regard for the President's legislative priorities," noted Patrick Anderson. O'Brien welded their efforts into a single operation that focused directly on the President's program, not their own vested interests. O'Brien met with them at weekly meetings and required them to report to him on their dealings with Congress.[52]

Most of O'Brien's "social" life during Kennedy's presidency involved entertaining members of Congress. Using the presidential yacht, the *Sequoia,* he invited fifteen or twenty legislators and their spouses for an evening cruise, complete with drinks, dinner, and entertainment. "In the summers, when the weather was best, we sometimes took the *Sequoia* out two or three times a week," said O'Brien. "Cruising down the Potomac . . . was also the most effective lobbying device I ever found." On many Sunday mornings O'Brien and his wife served brunch to political figures and legislators at the O'Brien home.

O'Brien tried to establish personal relationships with members of Congress. Senator Mansfield did not favor arm-twisting as a means of getting senators to go along with the President's program. O'Brien agreed, preferring gentle persuasion. The O'Brien team, noted Sorensen, "pumped far more arms than they twisted and brandished far fewer sticks than carrots." O'Brien provided advance notification of federal contracts, special White House tours, detailed data about legislation, and assistance with speeches and press releases.[53]

At a critical moment O'Brien dangled a favor: an invitation to a White House dinner, a seat in the presidential box for the baseball opener, coffee with the President. Influential legislators received special treatment. "For certain powerful members, such as Senators Russell of Georgia and Byrd of Virginia, and Congressmen Mills of Arkansas and [Carl] Vinson of Georgia, there was careful, continual cultivation," observed Patrick Anderson.

O'Brien managed the day-to-day responsibility of granting patronage favors, mainly postmasterships and judgeships. He dangled or withheld patronage, saying his efforts would never have been successful without using it. The White House occasionally turned a deaf ear to patronage requests or would refuse to expedite matters for uncooperative legislators.

When persuasion failed, O'Brien played tough. *Time* reported on one instance:

> When Louisiana's penny-pinching Representative Otto Passman decided to block a $600 million request for Latin American aid money in his House appropriations subcommittee, O'Brien's operatives went quietly behind his back, lined up enough votes to pass the bill over the chairman's objection; Passman eventually voted for the appropriation himself, rather than have it known he could not control his committee.

(A few of Larry O'Brien's liaison efforts backfired. A New York Democrat publicly accused the White House of trying "to twist his arm"; and a Southern Democrat complained of being bombarded with ten White House calls in one week.[54])

For the most part, there was close cooperation and mutual respect between Kennedy and Congress. "If you will look at the record of his recommendations, you will find that by far the great majority of them were agreed to by the Congress and most especially by the Senate," argued Senator Mansfield. "The few defeats which were suffered in the Congress were not the fault of the President but were in some instances, as a matter of fact, my fault, because I tried to bypass committees on various proposals."

Kennedy tried to respect the line which divided the executive from the legislative, and seldom crossed it. "No President ever treated the Congress with greater respect, in my opinion, and with more understanding than did President Kennedy," said Mansfield.

The primary reason the President couldn't enact more of his program was simply arithmetic. After the 1960 election Democrats controlled the House, 263 to 174, and the Senate, 64 to 36, but the numbers mislead because many of the members were part of the anti–New Deal coalition of conservative Southern Democrats and conservative Republicans. "Some Democrats," the President observed in 1962, "have voted with the Republicans for twenty-five years, really since 1938 . . . so that we have a very difficult time, on a controversial piece of legislation, securing a working majority."[55]

The conservative coalition held 285 of the 435 seats in the House and 59 out of 100 in the Senate. Conservative Southern Democrats controlled two-thirds of Senate committees, including Armed Services, Judiciary, Foreign Relations, and Finance. The same situation existed in the House. Southern Democrats had twelve of the twenty chairmanships, including Armed Services, Ways and Means, and Rules.

Congress failed to enact Kennedy's major domestic programs primarily because the voters who elected him did not vote in enough members of Congress to support the New Frontier. In 1964, with Barry Goldwater heading the Republican ticket, Democrats gained thirty-nine additional seats in the House. The election gave President Lyndon Johnson the luxury of a working majority, enabling him to pass major legislation in the congressional sessions of 1965 and 1966. In the 1966 midterm elections, Johnson lost most of that majority, and his Great Society stalled. Had he lived, Kennedy would undoubtedly have had a working majority after the 1964 election as well, and would have been able to enact his program.[56]

"There's no question in my mind that we would have put through exactly the same sort of a program under Kennedy that we put through under Johnson," said Congressman Tip O'Neill. Congressman Hale Boggs challenged the notion that President Kennedy was not active in contacting members of Congress, as President Johnson subsequently was. "President Johnson, having been reared in Congress, is of course in many ways more adept at that sort of thing than President Kennedy was, but the idea that President Kennedy didn't do this is just completely, totally wrong. He did it all the time."

"A myth has arisen that [Kennedy] was uninterested in Congress, or that he 'failed' with Congress," Larry O'Brien lamented. O'Brien contended that Kennedy's legislative record in 1961–1963 was "the best of any President since Roosevelt's first term." Even when Kennedy's program failed, it was building toward the future. "We could not pass Medicare in 1961–63, but we raised the issue, we forced our opponents to go on record against it, and we paved the way for its eventual passage in 1965," said O'Brien, adding, "I would take nothing from Lyndon Johnson's brilliant and tireless performance with Congress, but I believe that, had Kennedy lived, his record in his second term would have been comparable to the record Johnson established."[57]

29

MISSING THE MORAL
PASSION

At first Kennedy's primary impulse was to control the civil rights
movement: moderate its tactics, channel its demands toward voting,
and limit the social instability it caused in the South. This proved a
daunting task because he underestimated the passion of the movement.

Two weeks after Kennedy's inauguration Martin Luther King Jr. set forth
an ambitious but unrealistic civil rights agenda for the new President. Writing in *The Nation* on February 4, 1961, he contended that the "intolerably
slow pace of civil rights" progress was due "at least as much to the limits
which the federal government has imposed on its own actions as it is to the
actions of the segregationist opposition."

King wanted President Kennedy to emulate Franklin Roosevelt's action
in the 1930s. The New Deal provided ample precedent for the dynamic action the federal government should take now on civil rights. In a bewilder-
ingly brief period the federal government had created unemployment
insurance and relief agencies, and had passed regulatory legislation covering
banking, the stock market, and trade-union organization.

The country needed Roosevelt-style leadership from Kennedy on civil rights. "First, there is the legislative area. The President could take the offensive, despite Southern opposition, by fighting for a really far-reaching legislative program. With resolute Presidential leadership, a majority in both houses could be persuaded to pass meaningful laws."

A "vigorous" President could significantly influence Congress in the area of voter registration by eliminating the obstacles to black voting in the South—the legal impediments, administrative obstacles, and fear of economic reprisal and physical harm. "A truly decisive President would work passionately and unrelentingly to change these shameful conditions. He would take such a creative general proposal as that made by the Civil Rights Commission of 1959 on Federal Registrars to insure the right to vote, and would campaign on the Hill and across the nation until Congress acted."

Kennedy could also advance racial progress by using moral persuasion. "The President is the embodiment of the democratic personality of the nation," said King. "His own personal conduct influences and educates. If he were to make it known that he would not participate in any activities in which segregation exists, he would set a clear example for Americans everywhere, of every age, on a simple, easily understood level."

In recent years the power of the executive order has not been exploited, King charged.

> Historically, the Executive has promulgated orders of extraordinary range and significance. The Emancipation Proclamation was an Executive order. The integration of the Armed Forces grew out of President Truman's Executive Order 8891. Executive orders could require the immediate end to all discrimination in any housing accommodations financed with federal aid. Executive orders could prohibit any contractor dealing with any federal agency from practicing discrimination in employment.

Finally, the attorney general could use his power to ban school segregation. "There are existing laws under which the Attorney General could go into court and become a force in the current school struggles," wrote King.[1]

So there was the agenda. To achieve it, the nation needed courageous, resolute, vigorous, determined, and decisive leadership. Quite a challenge, one that President Kennedy would eventually face, but not immediately. Formidable political obstacles blocked the way; political considerations took precedence.

Kennedy faced his first civil rights crisis four months after the inauguration. In early May 1961, a band of six whites and seven blacks set out by bus to ride from Washington to New Orleans. Sponsored by the Congress of Racial Equality (CORE), a nonviolent civil rights organization dedicated to breaking down Southern racial barriers, the group called themselves Freedom Riders and hoped to prove that Southern interstate travel remained segregated in fact, although integrated by law. The Freedom Riders encountered little fuss as they passed through Virginia, North Carolina, South Carolina, and Georgia. At each stop the blacks marched into white restrooms and sat at white lunch counters.

But once they entered Alabama, they ran into more trouble than they wanted. Near Anniston a white mob hurled an incendiary bomb through a bus window, setting the bus afire. As it filled with black, acrid smoke, the frightened riders tried to escape, only to be beaten up by white toughs.

Before the bus burning in Anniston, the Freedom Riders hadn't caught the attention of John or Robert Kennedy (or of most Americans). Dismayed and exasperated, the White House desperately wanted to avoid a confrontation with white Southern authorities. The timing was crucial. The President, embarrassed by the disaster at the Bay of Pigs only a few weeks earlier, was about to confront Nikita Khrushchev at the summit conference in Vienna. The violence the Freedom Riders provoked focused unwanted international attention on U.S. racism. The Freedom Rides clearly showed that civil rights protests were not being controlled by the White House.[2]

When a second bus arrived at Birmingham's Trailways terminal another white mob attacked the riders with fists, blackjacks, and pieces of pipe. The terminal was only two blocks from Birmingham's police headquarters, but the police purposely stayed away, letting the blood flow. Nor was Alabama's Governor John Patterson any help: "I cannot guarantee protection for this bunch of rabble-rousers." News coverage reported the savagery to the world.

"Battered and bruised," said *Time,* the original Freedom Riders discontinued their trip. When the first group gave up, others resumed the ride, generating more confrontations and violence in Montgomery, Alabama, and at several stops in Mississippi.

In Montgomery the Freedom Riders were met with a fusillade of bottles, rocks, and stones. Again the local police stayed away. While trying to protect a black girl from being beaten, Robert Kennedy's aide John Seigenthaler was clubbed from behind. Whites poured a flammable liquid on a black's clothes and set him on fire. "One Montgomery [white] woman held up her child so that he could reach out and beat on a Negro with his fists," *Time* reported.[3]

Although frustrated with the Freedom Riders, Robert Kennedy believed that if Alabama officials shirked their duty to protect the riders in the peaceful pursuit of their constitutional rights to travel and speak, the federal government must ensure those rights. On May 21, he dispatched a force of four hundred federal marshals to Montgomery. "The situation which has developed in Alabama is a source of the deepest concern to me," President Kennedy declared in a White House statement. "I hope that state and local officials in Alabama will meet their responsibilities. The U.S. Government intends to meet its."

From the pulpit in Montgomery, Dr. King thundered that the "ultimate responsibility for the hideous action in Alabama . . . must be placed at the doorstep of the Governor of the state. We hear the familiar cry that morals cannot be legislated. This may be true, but behavior can be regulated. The law may not be able to make a man love me, but it can keep him from lynching me."

Robert Kennedy wanted to move the Freedom Riders out of Alabama quickly. "I thought that people were going to be killed," he later said, "and they had made their point. What was the purpose of continuing with it?" He urged a "cooling-off" period. James Farmer, CORE's national director, responded sharply, "We [have] been cooling off for 100 years. If we got any cooler we'd be in a deep freeze." When the attorney general stated that the disruption would embarrass the President during his meeting with Khrushchev, Ralph Abernathy, King's associate, replied, "Doesn't the Attorney General know that we've been embarrassed all our lives?"[4]

In a long telephone conversation King refused the attorney general's plan to release the Freedom Riders from jail in Jackson, Mississippi. King said they would remain in jail as "part of the philosophy of this movement."

"It's a matter of conscience and morality," King explained. "They must use their lives and their bodies to right a wrong. Our conscience tells us that the law is wrong and we must resist, but we have a moral obligation to accept the penalty."

"The fact that they stay in jail is not going to have the slightest effect on me," Robert Kennedy replied coldly.

"Perhaps it would help if students came down here by the hundreds—by the hundreds of thousands," King said.

"The country belongs to you as much as to me," Robert responded sharply. "You can determine what's best just as well as I can, but don't make statements that sound like a threat. That's not the way to deal with us."

King restated his case. "It's difficult to understand the position of oppressed people," he said, trying to make the attorney general understand. "Ours is a way out—creative, moral and nonviolent. It is not tied to black supremacy or Communism, but to the plight of the oppressed. It can save the soul of America. You must understand that we've made no gains without pressure and I hope that pressure will always be moral, legal and peaceful."

"But," RFK argued, underestimating the power of King's movement and overestimating his own, "the problem won't be settled in Jackson, Mississippi, but by strong federal action."

"I'm deeply appreciative of what the Administration is doing," King replied. "I see a ray of hope, but I am different than my father. I feel the need of being free now!"

"Well, it all depends on what you and the people in jail decide," the attorney general said. "If they want to get out, we can get them out."

"They'll stay," said King.[5]

Meanwhile, Alabama segregationists were angry that the Kennedys assisted the Freedom Riders. Governor John Patterson bitterly blamed the Kennedy administration, particularly Bobby Kennedy, for the violence. "I'm getting tired of being called up in the middle of the night and being *ordered* to do this and *ordered* to do that."

"He has no idea of conditions here," Patterson argued. "God Almighty, what he's trying to do is provoke a civil war. They try and get you to admit you can't or won't guarantee law enforcement, and then they twist your words because the [federal] marshals are on the way anyway. That Bobby Kennedy is just treacherous, that's what he is. I don't trust him and he don't trust me."

During the chaos Harris Wofford kept badgering the President with memos, hoping to nudge him to take a strong moral stand in support of the Freedom Riders, to exert moral leadership. "What Eisenhower never did was to give clear moral expression to the issues involved," Wofford wrote the President on May 29. "The only effective time for such moral leadership is during an occasion of moral crisis. This is the time when your words would mean most. . . . Despite your criticism of Eisenhower on this score, you have not chosen yet to say anything about the right of Americans to travel without discrimination."

In early June, after Kennedy returned from Vienna and was about to present his televised speech to the nation on the summit, Wofford again urged him to mention the Freedom Riders. "Is your speech tonight not the time for you to say a few stout words about the racial and constitutional crisis through which we are still passing?" But the President ignored Wofford's advice.[6]

Unlike Wofford, assistant attorney general Burke Marshall attended meetings with the President about the Freedom Riders and was impressed with the President's approach. Marshall witnessed "a real intelligence at work on gathering all this data and understanding it, weighing it, and accepting it." President Kennedy didn't usually complain about Governor Patterson or the Freedom Riders. "He didn't say I wish it hadn't come about or anything like that; he accepted it. And all of the discussion was not on how terrible it was or how bad it was, or, 'why don't they all stay home and stop stirring things up,' but on what he should do about it."[7]

Public opinion mostly opposed the Freedom Riders. "Nonviolence that deliberately provokes violence is a logical contradiction," stated a *New York Times* editorial. A Gallup poll in June found 63 percent disapproval of the rides; but Kennedy's action in sending marshals to protect the riders earned 70 percent approval.

The Freedom Rides did move the administration to take action. Under heavy pressure from Robert Kennedy, the Interstate Commerce Commission brought an end to all segregation signs in railroad, airport, and bus terminals. The coercive signs saying "Waiting Room for Colored Interstate Passengers" were outlawed. For the most part, segregation in interstate travel ended.

"The Freedom Riders do not seem to have hurt President Kennedy much," wrote the political expert Samuel Lubell. "It is 'brother Bobby' in the Attorney General's office, rather than president Jack, who has been blamed [by Southern whites]." When Lubell asked a Mississippi woman to name the biggest problem in the country, she replied: "Kennedy has too many brothers."

Most leaders in the civil rights movement appreciated Robert Kennedy's aggressive attempt to protect the Freedom Riders. "We thank Jack, Bob, and God!" exclaimed Fred Shuttlesworth, the Birmingham civil rights leader and colleague of King's. The Reverend Wyatt Walker, executive director of the Southern Christian Leadership Conference, nominated the attorney general for "American of the Year in 1961." A Freedom Rider, recalling a harrowing bus ride, stated, "Bobby Kennedy saved my life."[8]

Kennedy's narrow victory over Nixon made him hesitant to strike out boldly for new civil rights legislation. The Democratic platform he endorsed during the campaign firmly supported new legislation: more voting rights, an end to discrimination in education and housing, establishment of the Fair Employment Practices Commission, and more power for the attorney general to seek court injunctions against violations of civil rights law. Early in the general election campaign Kennedy announced that Senator Joseph Clark and Congressman Emanuel Celler had agreed to prepare a comprehensive civil rights bill "embodying the commitments of the Democratic platform," and would introduce it early in the next congressional session. While chiding Eisenhower for his callousness, Kennedy promised to exert "great moral and educational" force on behalf of civil rights. In the last month of the campaign, though, sensing he had promised too much, Kennedy redirected his emphasis away from new legislation to the potential for executive action. That part of his campaign promise he fulfilled admirably.

Immediately after his inauguration Kennedy mobilized the full powers of the executive branch to advance civil rights through executive action: litigation, negotiation, persuasion, appointments, directives, and an executive order.

"Next to Eisenhower, Kennedy seemed a breath of fresh air to many blacks," observed James Giglio. "Symbolic gestures abounded." At the inauguration parade the President noticed the all-white Coast Guard unit. Afterward he pressured the academy to integrate. The President withdrew from the Cosmos Club after it had rebuffed Carl Rowan, a black State Department official. Kennedy invited more African-Americans to White House meetings and social functions than any previous President.

The administration filled key positions with believers in civil rights and racial equality: Dean Rusk, Chester Bowles, and G. Mennen Williams in the State Department; Burke Marshall, John Seigenthaler, and Robert Kennedy in the Justice Department; Harris Wofford in the White House; and Sargent Shriver in the Peace Corps.[9]

Kennedy also appointed forty blacks to prominent administration posts. Robert C. Weaver was selected administrator of the Housing and Home Finance Agency; Andrew Hatcher, the associate White House press secretary; and Carl Rowan, the deputy assistant secretary of state for public affairs.

Up to 1961 only one black had held a federal judgeship; Kennedy appointed five black lawyers to the federal bench, including Thurgood Marshall, who during Lyndon Johnson's presidency became the first black Supreme Court justice. Dr. James Nabrit, president of Howard University, praised Kennedy's appointment of blacks to high office, saying; "President Kennedy has done more in a few months to increase the respect and give prestige to Negroes than any President in my lifetime."

At his first cabinet meeting Kennedy asked each member of the cabinet to study the employment and advancement practices in their departments, giving special attention to the status of blacks. Thereafter several executive departments vigorously recruited African-Americans into government service. From June 1961 to June 1963 the number of blacks holding positions in the highest ranks of the civil service increased by 88.2 percent. Delighted by the President's approach, Roy Wilkins remarked that "Kennedy was so hot on the department heads, the cabinet officers, and agency heads that everyone was scrambling around trying to find himself a Negro in order to keep the President off his neck."[10]

In his first days in office Robert Kennedy and John Seigenthaler toured the Department of Justice. "Did anything occur to you as strange in our visit around to these offices?" Kennedy asked. Everyone seemed to be working hard, Seigenthaler replied. "Yes," Kennedy said, "but did you see any Negroes?" Afterward, a study Kennedy ordered found that of the 955 lawyers in the Washington office, only 10 were African-American. At his first staff meeting the attorney general ordered "thorough integration" of all the Justice Department's offices everywhere in the country.

In May 1961, Robert Kennedy sent letters to the deans of forty-five law schools requesting that they recommend their most promising black graduates, but stressing that ability was still the "primary consideration" for appointment. In two years the department added ninety black attorneys to the staff. "Ashamed that his men's club, the Metropolitan, refused to take blacks, he quit in protest," noted Evan Thomas.[11]

On March 6, 1961, the President issued an executive order establishing the Committee on Equal Employment Opportunity (CEEO) and named Lyndon Johnson as chairman. The new committee replaced two older, ineffective committees, one on employment within the government and the other on private employment under government contracts. Kennedy charged the CEEO to end racial discrimination in government employment and in work performed for the government, because federal money "should be spent in such a way that it encourages the national goal of equal opportunity."

Nondiscrimination clauses had been attached to government contracts for years, but the Kennedy administration's enforcement placed greater demands on contractors. It published the names of violators, discontinued contracts, and required government agencies to refrain from recontracting with companies breaking the agreement until they had corrected the deficiencies. "Surveys of businesses made in 1964 and 1965 indicated a gradually changing attitude in racial policies," said one expert. The government's policy of barring discrimination on federal projects was usually cited as the major reason.

Another successful initiative was a subcabinet group on civil rights, chaired at first by cabinet secretary Fred Dutton, then by Harris Wofford. Key deputies from the executive departments met regularly to survey the civil rights aspects of public programs within the federal agencies.[12]

When his department had clear legal authority, Robert Kennedy aggressively applied federal power to extend civil rights. He enforced court orders desegregating schools with no prompting by civil rights organizations.

Abandoning Eisenhower's policy of engaging in litigation only after a judge's invitation to protect the integrity of a court order, Robert Kennedy brought the federal government into two Louisiana school cases without invitation and acted as amicus curiae to attack new state statutes.

"I want to move on voting," the attorney general told an assistant in the first hours of the new administration. Legal authority on voting rights was stronger (though still limited) than any other civil rights field. The Civil Rights Act of 1957 granted the Justice Department the power to file civil suits on behalf of those denied their right to vote or who were prohibited from registering to vote on account of race or color. The Civil Rights Act of

1960 mandated that local officials keep voting records and permit federal officials to inspect and investigate those records. Using the new laws, Kennedy's Department of Justice brought fifty-seven voting suits, thirty of them in Mississippi.[13]

Emphasizing voting rights was primary in Robert Kennedy's view because the federal government had more legal authority, and the effort would accomplish the greatest amount of good and would create less civil strife and less opposition. What he didn't mention was that the approach also paid valuable political dividends: Most of the new black voters would be Democrats.

Some civil rights leaders suspected the administration's focus on voting rights aimed to sidetrack other civil rights efforts. Lonnie King of the Student Non-violent Coordinating Committee (SNCC) charged the administration with trying to "kill the Movement, but to kill it by rechanneling its energies." Vincent Harding, the black historian, agreed: It was all an attempt "to get the niggers off the street."[14]

Because the legislation passed in 1957 and 1960 was limited, action based on it had only limited success. Each suit required an enormous effort. The lawyers in the Civil Rights Division felt compelled to prepare meticulously, not wanting to lose a single case for lack of proof. "We faced tough judges," said John Doar. "We wanted the proof to be so overwhelming so as to lock up the trial judge . . . and to convince the country as well."

Enforcing voter-registration laws was an incrementalist approach, and the lawsuits usually moved along at a snail's pace. The South had a genius for delaying litigation. Robert Kennedy himself became increasingly frustrated by the inadequate legal framework. Successful litigation seemed to take forever after all the appeals. "Once you got all the appeals done and won the case five or six years had passed, and then they would say the circumstances are different, you really ought to try all over again," observed Nicholas Katzenbach.[15]

Containing communism far outweighed civil rights action among John Kennedy's priorities. He grew frustrated with both sides in the racial conflict because neither seemed to focus on the ultimate prize: winning the Cold War. Indeed, both civil rights organizers and their opponents believed that race relations at home were far more important in their daily lives than a crisis in the Cold War.

The civil rights movement could get John Kennedy's undivided attention, though, when protests embarrassed the United States in the eyes of other nations. Dean Rusk instructed U.S. ambassadors to counter the "extremely negative reactions" racial incidents in America elicited "from all parts of [the] world."

African diplomats were leery of being assigned to Washington, D.C., a Southern city with a strong Jim Crow tradition. Would they find decent housing, or be assaulted on the streets of Washington? "Most African diplomats came to Washington by car from New York, and once they crossed the Delaware River on Route 40, they quickly discovered how unwelcome they were," observed one historian. "In Delaware and Maryland they were regularly refused service in restaurants, humiliated, and harassed."

Prompted by the State Department, the administration initiated a plan to desegregate public facilities in Maryland and Washington, D.C., where African diplomats traveled and lived. The State Department had difficulty finding homes or apartments for the staffs of embassies from African countries. "African diplomats did not know where they could go to have dinner without running into embarrassment," said Dean Rusk, "and one African diplomat told me that he didn't even know where he could go to have a haircut in Washington."

The department worked with real estate boards, city officials, police authorities, hotels, homeowners, and apartment owners, and the effort partially succeeded. Gradually, said Rusk, they "made some headway." The State Department also tried to orchestrate the diplomats' visits to the Deep South to prevent racial incidents. But that effort was awkward: preferential treatment for a special group—the diplomats—while American blacks were bloodied struggling for their civil rights.[16]

After John Kennedy's death, several of his private comments came to light, and their insensitivity earned condemnation. Most often the comments were sparked by fear that racial confrontations would cause international embarrassment. During the Freedom Rides the angry President phoned Harris Wofford and yelled, "Stop them! Get your friends off those buses!" Martin Luther King, James Farmer, and the riders embarrassed him and the country just as he entered the world spotlight for his meeting with Khrushchev in Vienna. "He supported every American's right to stand up or sit down for his rights—but not to ride for them in the spring of 1961," Wofford later observed.

As an African ambassador drove on Route 40 between Washington and New York, he was refused service, even a glass of water. The incident made headlines in the Washington newspapers and around the world. "Can't you tell them not to do it?" the embarrassed President asked Angier Biddle Duke, the State Department's chief of protocol. When Duke started to explain the progress made in integrating Route 40, Kennedy interrupted to say, "That's not what I'm calling about. Can't you tell these African ambassadors not to drive on Route 40? It's a hell of a road—I used to drive it years ago, but why would anyone want to drive it today when you can fly? Tell these ambassadors I wouldn't think of driving from New York to Washington. Tell them to fly!"[17]

On these occasions the President seemed impervious to the daily humiliation of racism. Freedom Riders judged their cause to be as important as

Kennedy's visit with the Soviet premier; white Americans drove on Route 40 without suffering embarrassment.

After his election Kennedy created task forces to make recommendations on pressing national problems, but he didn't appoint one for civil rights. Except for brief, innocuous references, Kennedy didn't mention civil rights in his inaugural or his first State of the Union address—a bad omen for civil rights supporters avid for new legislation.

A month after the inauguration Kennedy invited Dr. King to the White House for a visit. To King's dismay the President announced he was putting civil rights legislation on the back burner. "Nobody needs to convince me any longer that we have to solve the problem, not let it drift on gradualism," he said. "But how do you go about it? If we go into a long fight in Congress, it will bottleneck everything else and still get no bill." Kennedy gave a similar explanation to other supporters of civil rights.

Many critics, then and now, blame Kennedy for not seeking civil rights legislation during the first two years of his presidency. He vacillated, equivocated, and retreated. Roy Wilkins thought he made a "tactical error" and was acting with "super-caution." He wanted the new President to "charge the opposition."[18]

In early March 1962, in another article in *The Nation,* Martin Luther King critiqued Kennedy's first-year efforts on civil rights. It was mostly a record of caution and fumbling, King wrote. True, the administration "conceived and launched some imaginative and bold forays." More creatively than its predecessors, it blazed new trails, particularly in voting registration.

> Moreover, President Kennedy has appointed more Negroes to key government posts than has any previous administration. One Executive Order has been issued which, if vigorously enforced, will go a long, long way toward eliminating employment discrimination in federal agencies and in industries where government contracts are involved. So it is obvious that the Kennedy Administration has to its credit some constructive and praiseworthy achievements.

Overall, though, the administration's efforts were inadequate, incomplete, and superficial. Its strategic goals had narrowed. "Changes in depth and breadth are not yet in sight, nor has there been a commitment of resources adequate to enforce extensive change." The sad fact was that "the Administration is aggressively driving only toward the limited goal of token integration."

The President feared that Southerners might stymie his legislative program if he moved boldly on civil rights. But King disagreed:

For years, Abraham Lincoln resisted signing the Emancipation Proclamation because he feared to alienate the slaveholders in the border states. But the imperatives of the Civil War required that slavery be ended, and he finally signed the document and won the war, preserved the nation, and gave America its greatest hour of moral glory. President Kennedy may be tormented by a similar dilemma, and may well be compelled to make an equally fateful decision—one which, if correct, could be found a century later to have made the nation greater and the man more memorable.

Why weren't civil rights higher on the President's priority list?

Should Americans favor the winning of the welfare and trade programs in Congress at the cost of the Negro citizen's elementary rights? . . .

The President has proposed a ten-year plan to put a man on the moon. We do not yet have a plan to put a Negro in the State Legislature of Alabama.

King told Harris Wofford, "He's got the understanding and he's got the political skill . . . but the moral passion is missing."[19]

At the time, though, even Harris Wofford endorsed the strategy of minimum legislation, maximum executive action. "The Democrats had lost twenty-one seats in the House of Representatives and two in the Senate," he later noted, and "on most controversial social and economic issues, the Republican-conservative Southern Democratic coalition could probably muster a majority in the House, and successfully invoke a filibuster in the Senate." As much as Wofford wanted comprehensive new legislation, the strategy he proposed to Kennedy early in 1961 did not call for any major new legislative initiatives. Since the powers given by Congress in the civil rights legislation of 1957 and 1960 had not been fully tested, why not use them first? "If after a year of bringing many varied voting suits throughout the black belt no real breakthrough on Negro voting has occurred, then it would be the time to go to Congress to ask for [new] legislation," Wofford contended.

"It didn't seem to me sensible that the Kennedy Administration should come right into office and immediately precipitate a filibuster in the Senate and get all tied up," observed Tom Wicker of *The New York Times*. "I thought the executive approach was good politics."[20]

The President thought his decision was eminently reasonable given the harsh political realities. Southerners controlled two-thirds of the standing committees in the Senate, including the powerful Judiciary Committee, still in the iron grip of archsegregationist James Eastland of Mississippi. In the House, Southerners also dominated the chairmanships.

Larry O'Brien worried that pushing civil rights legislation would derail the rest of the President's legislative program. It would become "a single-effort legislative struggle focused totally in one area." The Rules Committee fight had shown how precarious Kennedy's congressional majority was. "We needed the Southerners to have any majority at all," said O'Brien, "and we would lose them if we pushed for a civil rights bill."

Although unstated publicly, election politics, not just legislative politics, probably motivated the President's reluctance to push civil rights legislation. "Where can they go to?" one of the President's liberal domestic advisers allegedly remarked when asked whether blacks might be alienated by the administration's failure to redeem specific campaign pledges. He meant that since blacks could not be expected to vote Republican, their discontents could safely be ignored.

What's more, the once solid Democratic South was no longer as solid. Kennedy had won only six of the eleven Southern states in 1960, and might lose them all in 1964 if he made civil rights legislation a priority. "It was morality against math," commented one observer. "It was yearning to lead against yearning to win. Winning won."[21]

The American people were not sufficiently aroused by civil rights, the Kennedys insisted, were not demanding new legislation. Nor were newspapers, radio, or television. John Seigenthaler later observed:

> There is a time warp that is almost impossible to understand unless you realize that a segregated Southern society was legal in the eyes of the nation, and that Martin Luther King and the demonstrators—in the eyes of most of the nation—were law violators who were trying to change the law. Most of the nation, for much of the time, was unsympathetic to that. Certainly, massive numbers of people in the South were unsympathetic to that, and most of the people in the Congress did not give a damn about that.

Kennedy often looked awkward and uncaring when confronted with civil rights supporters in Congress. Senator Joseph Clark and Representative Emanuel Celler, having waited patiently for the President to request the bills he had asked them to draft during the 1960 election campaign, finally introduced them in May 1961. But Press Secretary Pierre Salinger bungled the White House's response. Kennedy made it clear he would not seek their passage in 1961, but he didn't want to disavow them either. On the day after their introduction Salinger clumsily disassociated the administration from the bills, saying in partial justification that there had been "very little pressure" for new civil rights legislation. "Since the President and many of us had done our best to persuade civil rights groups *not* to press for legislation, this was a low blow," thought Wofford.[22]

Political posturing caused problems for the White House. After a few Northern liberal Republicans pushed for civil rights legislation, Northern liberal Democrats felt obligated to support the measures. The focus would then turn to the White House. Would the President endorse the measures? The administration would have to say no. "He had to say no," Burke Marshall claimed,

> because he knew perfectly well that what was going on was political posturing and that there was no chance, given the cloture requirement in the Senate at that time and the lack basically of national public support, that any of these bills would pass. So that if he said yes then he would do one of two things: he would either engage himself in the political posturing or he would get himself involved in a terrible fight in the Congress that would consume a whole year of Congress without anything coming out of it.

Past attempts by liberals to enact civil rights legislation had been a sham, Robert Kennedy believed. "You showed you were for civil rights by sending up legislation—whether the legislation passed or not—and made a public speech." This allowed liberals to claim they supported civil rights, even though their efforts always failed. "My brother and I thought what mattered was *doing* something. . . . But until the people became interested and brought pressure in Congress, you weren't going to get legislation."

In 1962 Congress shackled a mild administration civil rights bill. With the President's backing, Senator Mike Mansfield floated a trial balloon. He introduced a literacy-test bill, making a sixth-grade education the only standard necessary for voters in presidential and congressional elections. A civil rights historian described the result:

> When the Judiciary Committee refused to take any action on the bill, Mansfield brought it back to the floor of the Senate by attaching it as an amendment to a minor bill already passed by the House. Inevitably, the southern Democrats responded with a filibuster and two cloture petitions were filed. The first attempt on 9 May was defeated 53–43 with 30 Democrats supporting the filibuster. The second cloture vote one week later was defeated 52–42.

This was a clear indication of the hopelessness of the situation. Kennedy and Mansfield were not only short of the necessary two-thirds majority, they had been six votes short of a simple majority.[23]

The failure reinforced Kennedy's belief that cutting off a filibuster on any civil rights bill was currently impossible. Kennedy might be excused for not pushing new legislation. Less excusable was his failure to take another action he had promised.

Several times during the 1960 election campaign Kennedy had promised to sign an executive order ending racial discrimination in federal housing. He would do so with the "stroke of a pen." Presidents often used the executive order to bypass Congress, as President Truman famously did when he ordered the armed forces integrated.

After he returned to Washington in August 1960, following his triumph at the Democratic convention, Kennedy indicted President Eisenhower for failing to promote civil rights, including the integration of housing. Presidential leadership was crucial, he said, but Eisenhower hadn't furnished it:

> Let me give one example of an important immediate contribution that could and should be made by the stroke of a Presidential pen.
>
> Eleven months ago the Civil Rights Commission unanimously proposed that the President issue an executive order on equal opportunity in housing.
>
> The President has not acted during all this time. He could and should act now. By such action, he would toll the end of racial discrimination in all federal housing programs, including federally-assisted housing.
>
> I have supported this proposal since it was made last September. The Democratic platform endorses it. A new Democratic Administration will carry it out.[24]

The first time President Kennedy seriously considered signing the executive order on housing occurred in the fall of 1961, eight months into his presidency. But he decided to wait, say his supporters, because he needed Southern backing to get Congress to support a new department of urban affairs. Arthur Schlesinger explained:

> He intended to appoint Robert C. Weaver, an eminent black economist, as secretary. Legislative leaders made it clear that Congress would not create the new department if he issued the housing order. He agreed to postpone the order. The House Rules Committee, hating the idea of the first black cabinet member in history, killed the reorganization bill anyway.[25]

Civil rights supporters deplored the delay. They constantly reminded the President of his "stroke of a pen" pledge. Sarcastically inundating him with pens, they started an "ink for Jack" drive. Critics charged that he was afraid to be daring. "He has 'gone along' with too many things in an apparent effort to hoard his popularity figures in the Gallup polls," columnist James Wechsler wrote in December 1961. "The President cannot indefinitely tell us executive action is an adequate substitute for civil rights legislation, and then postpone so limited a measure as the housing order to help his deals on other legislation. That circle is too vicious." Advisers who told Kennedy it was "inexpedient" would have new reasons for not acting in six months. "John F. Kennedy effectively stated the case against Mr. Eisenhower in August, 1960. Has he lost touch with the President of the United States?"

JFK teased Sorensen about writing the "stroke of a pen" speech in 1960. When Sorensen claimed he'd had nothing to do with writing it, Kennedy remarked that nobody would take responsibility for it. "The stroke of a pen," the President kept muttering to himself. "Who put those words in my mouth?" (Actually, Richard Goodwin wrote it.)

On a trip to Philadelphia with the President, Pennsylvania's Governor David Lawrence acted as the straight man for Kennedy's version of a popular joke, reflecting the chilling effect new black neighbors had on white home-owners:

"Knock, knock," said the President.

"Who's there?" Lawrence responded.

"Iza."

"Iza who?"

Kennedy's punch line: "I's ya next-door neighbah!"[26]

The delay continued through most of 1962, with political considerations still paramount. The executive order generated new opposition from Northern liberal Democrats, particularly before the midterm congressional elections in 1962. "There were an awful lot of people running for reelection," recalled Lee White, "who let it be known to the White House that, if the President signs that order, tell him he'd better plan on someone else representing my district besides me."

The hostility was so intense that on September 11, 1962, Lawrence O'Brien reported to White that two liberal representatives were "vehement in opposing any housing order as they insist it would be devastating in their respective districts." One was the liberal Democrat Martha Griffiths, who represented the Seventeenth Congressional District of Michigan, which included a white suburban area of Detroit. She thought the housing order could cost her reelection. "If such an order is to be issued, it should not be issued immediately preceding an election," she wrote O'Brien. "No Democratic Congressman, from suburbia, to whom I have talked, believes he is in any danger of losing colored votes; but he does feel such an order could cost white votes."[27]

In the end the President issued a low-key announcement after the 1962 election, hoping to cause as little divisiveness as possible. He intentionally settled on the evening of November 20, 1962, the night before he and the rest of the country closed shop for the long Thanksgiving weekend. He sandwiched the announcement between a long, dramatic, and widely hailed statement about Soviet bombers leaving Cuba and another major statement about the border conflict between India and China. For the moment the clever ploy toned down damaging publicity, but it incurred the wrath of civil rights advocates and the disdain of future historians. What's more, because it excluded private financial institutions, the housing order applied to less than 3 percent of existing housing and only 20 percent of new construction.[28]

Kennedy administration blunders on federal judicial appointments also irritated advocates of civil rights. Although President Kennedy nominated more African-Americans to the federal bench than all of his predecessors combined, he also named five segregationists to the bench in the South. The five became notorious for their hostility toward blacks and their white civil rights allies. "The Kennedy Justice Department was forced to devote thousands of man hours, hundreds of thousands of dollars, untold energy, imagination and brilliance, all to counter the obstructionist tactics of its own appointees," concluded Victor Navasky.

Judge William Cox of Mississippi was the most notorious. "He no sooner got on the bench than he denied the Department of Justice the right, granted in the 1960 Civil Rights Act, to inspect public voting records in a Mississippi county where no black had registered for thirty years," observed Schlesinger. In a subsequent case Cox referred to blacks, in open court, as "a bunch of niggers . . . acting like a bunch of chimpanzees."[29]

Several factors explain these terrible appointments. Each judge received the endorsement of the American Bar Association, a key link in the appointment process. (Judge Cox was rated "Extremely Well-Qualified" by the ABA.) Because Cox was a close friend of Senator Eastland, and the Judiciary Committee chairman favored his appointment, Robert Kennedy thought it unwise to alienate the powerful Mississippi senator. "The appointment of a judge which is recommended by a chairman of a committee or a key figure on a committee can make the . . . difference on [President Kennedy's] whole legislative program," observed Robert Kennedy. Shortly after Kennedy's inauguration Congress created seventy-one new judgeships, giving the President an inordinately large number of judicial posts to fill. Navasky points out that "the administrative burden of processing such an extraordinary volume of judgeships took its toll in a failure to focus on the damage these men might do." The FBI's background investigations of the appointees didn't touch on the individual's racial views. (Burke Marshall described the investigations as "worthless.")

John Seigenthaler thought that RFK was firm and clear with Cox during a prenomination interview. RFK asked Cox if he thought everybody was "entitled to equal justice" and if he would respect blacks' right to go to integrated schools. Cox answered yes.

The five segregationist appointments occurred during the early months of the Kennedy administration. Afterward the administration used better judgment. Besides the five segregationists, President Kennedy named eight integrationists to the same Southern circuit, as well as three moderates.[30]

In the 1960 campaign John Kennedy had criticized President Eisenhower for sitting back in 1957 and allowing the Little Rock crisis to explode, then needing paratroopers, in combat gear with fixed bayonets, to integrate the high school. The incident had humiliated the United States throughout the world and provided ammunition for Soviet propaganda.

Expert planning and behind-the-scenes negotiation would help to manage a civil rights crisis, President Kennedy thought. The Justice Department's civil rights team functioned as the President's civil rights crisis management force. Not adept at forming policy or innovative strategies, the team focused on preserving law and order, on "reacting to situations created by others, conjuring clever solutions for containing trouble, negotiating compromises, and placating truculent actors on either side," observed historian James Hilty. When racial confrontations threatened violence, the team first tried to stabilize the situation. The use—or the threat—of U.S. troops should always be the last resort.

Robert Kennedy managed the team. He later said, "I wouldn't have to bother [the President] with [a civil rights matter], nor would he have to think about it." This changed in late September 1962, when for the first time John Kennedy became personally involved. The President, his brother, and the Justice Department team had to use all their skills to enroll a single black student at an all-white university.[31]

In January 1961, James Meredith quietly applied for admission to the University of Mississippi in Oxford. (He later stated that he had been inspired to apply by Kennedy's inaugural address.) A twenty-eight-year-old air force veteran, Meredith was transferring to all-white Ole Miss from all-black Jackson State.

Needing legal assistance, Meredith contacted Medgar Evers, Mississippi field secretary of the NAACP, who helped arrange legal help from the national civil rights organization. After a tortuous legal battle, the NAACP obtained a federal court ruling in 1962 ordering Meredith's admission, and a series of subsequent court rulings enjoined Mississippi officials from interfering. But Mississippi governor Ross Barnett claimed he would rather go to jail than let "that boy," backed by the "Communist" NAACP, get into Ole Miss.

Governor Barnett "combined the soft-spoken demeanor of the southern planter with the overheated rhetoric of the southern populist." When he spoke on the telephone with the Kennedys, he acted conciliatory and seemed to want a way out of the impasse. But the governor also made demagogic appeals to Mississippians. To the delight of forty-six thousand fans attending an Ole Miss football game, he said, "I love Mississippi. I love our people. I love our customs." A critic likened the spectacle to "a big Nazi rally."

Barnett's overt defiance presented President Kennedy with difficult choices. Meredith had the legal right to enroll, and civil rights forces backed his enrollment. But how should it be accomplished? To arrest and imprison a sitting governor would make Barnett a hero in Mississippi. Yet Kennedy could not allow Barnett to get away with his defiance. That would invite defiance all over the South. Using military force must be a last resort, for it would be deeply resented throughout the South.[32]

Barnett's strategy was clear: Make Robert Kennedy back down all the way or make him exert extraordinary force to enroll Meredith. "Either way the governor would have done his duty in the eyes of the people of Mississippi," noted James Hilty. Any public conciliation or public compromise with the Kennedys would bring disaster for Barnett.

The Kennedys' strategy was also clear, though difficult to implement successfully: Avoid the approach Eisenhower had followed in the Little Rock imbroglio. Instead, make an elaborate effort to find a peaceful solution by using quiet and patient action in the courts, prudent public statements, personal telephone appeals to the governor, and behind-the-scenes negotiation.

Several times in late September 1962, Barnett blocked Meredith's path when he attempted to register at the Oxford campus. By retreating, straining to avoid using force, the administration looked weak and hesitant.[33]

The world watched as events unfolded in Mississippi. Remarking on the rival efforts of the Soviet Union and the United States to make friends in Africa, a black diplomat from a nonaligned African country remarked, "We are waiting to see what President Kennedy will do in Mississippi." The racial barrier "made nonsense of United States claims to be the custodian of the free world in opposition to Communism," he said. "Action by the President will be welcomed by Africans. It will strongly demonstrate whether his use of the words 'free world' is merely a propaganda phrase."

The Soviet news media prominently featured the Mississippi racial dispute, particularly when it appeared that the federal government would not use force. "Washington Surrenders to Racist Onslaughts," headlined *Pravda*.

During a phone conversation at 2:00 P.M. on Saturday, September 29, the President tried to reason with the governor:

BARNETT:	You know what I am up against, Mr. President. I took an oath, you know, to abide by the laws of this state—
PRESIDENT KENNEDY:	That's right.
BARNETT:	—and *our* constitution here and the Constitution of the United States. I'm, I'm on the spot here, you know.
PRESIDENT KENNEDY:	Well, now you've got . . .
BARNETT:	I, I've taken an oath to do that, and you *know* what our laws are with reference to . . .
PRESIDENT KENNEDY:	. . . the problem is, Governor, that I got my responsibility, just like you have yours . . .
BARNETT:	Well, that's true. I . . .
PRESIDENT KENNEDY:	. . . and my responsibility, of course, is to the . . .
BARNETT:	. . . I realize that, and I appreciate that *so much*.
PRESIDENT KENNEDY:	Well, now here's the thing, Governor. I will, the Attorney General can talk to Mr. Watkins tomorrow. [Watkins was the governor's assistant.] What I want, would like to do is to try to work this out in an amicable way. We don't want a lot of people down there getting hurt.[34]

Less than an hour later, the President talked with Barnett again, this time about providing police protection when Meredith enrolled.

BARNETT:	They'll, they'll take positive action, Mr. President, to maintain law and order as best we can.
PRESIDENT KENNEDY:	And now, how good is . . .
BARNETT:	We'll have 220 highway patrolmen . . .
PRESIDENT KENNEDY:	Right.
BARNETT:	. . . and they'll absolutely be unarmed.

Kennedy stumbled over Barnett's remark: "I understa—"

"Not a one of them'll be armed," Barnett said proudly.

The problem was, continued the President, what could the highway patrolmen do to maintain law and order? ("Kennedy wanted the state forces armed to the teeth when it came to quelling the mob," noted Taylor Branch, "and nonviolent only in confronting Meredith, but Barnett refused to be so discerning."[35])

On Sunday afternoon, September 30, the Justice Department sent three hundred deputy marshals by helicopter to Oxford. The plan was to have Meredith peacefully register at the Lyceum Administration building on Monday. At 6:30 P.M. Sunday Meredith picked out a room at deserted Baxter Hall, and federal marshals were posted to guard him.

A large crowd had assembled on campus, angry about Meredith's anticipated enrollment. As word spread that federal marshals were on campus ringing the Lyceum, 2,500 people surged toward them. Some chanted, "Go to hell, JFK!" Roughnecks carried clubs, rocks, pipes, bricks, bottles, bats, and rifles.

A Molotov cocktail—a Coke bottle filled with gasoline—burst into flame near the marshals. After one of the lawmen was hit by a lead pipe, the chief of the marshals, Jim McShane, ordered his men to fire tear gas. The governor's representative on campus withdrew the Mississippi patrol officers who had provided a semblance of calm to the campus for several days. Now the marshals faced the angry mob alone.[36]

Assuming that Meredith's successful registration was imminent, President Kennedy appealed for calm and reason during a special Sunday evening television address. "If this country should ever reach the point where any man or group of men, by force or threat of force, should long deny the commands of our court and our Constitution, then no law would stand free from doubt, no judge would be sure of his writ and no citizen would be safe from his neighbors." He didn't criticize the Mississippi segregationists; nor did he endorse Meredith's cause. In a conciliatory spirit he praised Mississippi as the home of Lucius Lamar, a hero depicted in *Profiles in Courage,* who "placed the national good ahead of sectional interest"; mentioned the state's "four Medal of Honor winners in the Korean War"; and invoked the great tradition of Ole Miss, "a tradition of honor and courage, won on the field of battle, and on the gridiron, as well as the university campus."

Unknown to the President, while he spoke the situation was deteriorating in Oxford. When he finished the speech, RFK arrived in the Cabinet Room and announced that rioters outside the Lyceum were "throwing iron spikes."

During a riotous night, both Kennedys worried they might be facing another Bay of Pigs. In the Cabinet Room the President was joined by the attorney general, Sorensen, O'Donnell, Marshall, and Larry O'Brien. Two or three talked on telephones at once, pausing to relay new information to the others. "They're throwing Coke bottles, and they're throwing rocks," Robert Kennedy reported.[37]

At midnight in Washington the news from Oxford seemed desperate. "They're storming where Meredith is," announced RFK, reacting to an incorrect bulletin that rioters had found Meredith in his dormitory. "You don't want to have a lynching," Ken O'Donnell said anxiously.

Showing astonishing persistence, the rioters used a bulldozer, then a car, and sent them crashing toward the Lyceum like a battering ram. During the tumult the FBI detected 150 Mississippi troopers sitting in their cars watching.

Shortly after midnight, the President was on the phone with Barnett:

PRESIDENT KENNEDY:	Yeah, well, you see, we got to get order up there, and that's what we thought we're going to have.
BARNETT:	Mr. President, please. Why don't you, can't you give an order up there to remove Meredith?
PRESIDENT KENNEDY:	How can I remove him, Governor, when there's a riot in the street, and he may step out of that building and something happen to him? I can't remove him under those conditions. You . . .
BARNETT:	Uh, but, but . . .
PRESIDENT KENNEDY:	Let's get order up there; then we can do something about Meredith.

Moments later Robert Kennedy said, "I can't get him out. How am I going to get him out?"[38]

As the grim siege watch continued, President Kennedy, anguish on his face, paced impatiently from Evelyn Lincoln's office to the Cabinet Room and back. "He sat at my desk," Lincoln recalled, "he sat in the rocking chair in my office, he used the other telephone in my office. He would go into the Cabinet Room, then come right back into my office." The President slept only three hours.

Shortly after midnight, the Pentagon was ordered to airlift a force of MPs from Memphis to Oxford. Army officials promised that they could complete the operation in two hours and suppress the riot. Actually, it took them four and a half hours. "Damn army!" exclaimed RFK at about 1:00 A.M. "They can't even tell if the MPs have left yet." O'Donnell interjected, "I have a hunch that Khrushchev would get those troops in there fast enough."

Guilt-ridden, Robert Kennedy felt responsible for the deteriorating situation. "It was a nervous time for the President," he reflected, "because he was torn between, perhaps, an Attorney General who had botched things up and the fact that the Attorney General was his brother." His brother had placed him in charge, and everything was going wrong. "The call for troops was itself a confession of failure," noted Schlesinger. "Still worse, the troops had not come."

As the hours dragged on, John Kennedy phoned Secretary of the Army Cyrus Vance in the Pentagon and General Creighton Abrams in Memphis demanding to know what was delaying the progress of the troops. He could visualize marshals being killed and Meredith being lynched. "Even after the troops arrived in Oxford, there was inexplicable delay," observed Schlesinger. "At the Lyceum, the marshals had finally run out of tear gas. At the airport, half a mile away, the field commander, operating by the book, waited for his whole force to disembark and fall in before moving. Agonizing moments passed." The President was furious.[39]

The troops finally arrived on the campus at 4:30 A.M. and quickly restored order. RFK would later say the evening was "the worst night I ever spent." Two died in the rioting, and 375 were injured, including 166 federal marshals.

Within a few days twenty-three thousand army troops—three times the town's population—had taken up positions in Oxford. "Scorned by classmates and surrounded by marshals, Meredith attended classes and ate in lonely isolation," noted Evan Thomas.

Officials throughout Mississippi echoed their governor in blaming "trigger-happy marshals" and federal intruders for the riot. The marshals had "provoked the students and others," charged Senator James Eastland. The Mississippi senate expressed its "complete, entire and utter contempt for the Kennedy Administration and its puppet courts." A grand jury indicted Chief Marshal McShane for inciting the riot. "The Mississippi legislature's official report, oozing with self-pity and trampled virtue, charged the marshals with 'planned physical torture' and other atrocities against Ole Miss students," observed Taylor Branch.[40]

The University of Mississippi crisis left an enduring intellectual impact on John Kennedy, leading him to reevaluate his traditional beliefs about Reconstruction after the Civil War. The President told his brother that because of the lies and distortions trumpeted by Mississippi officials, he would never again believe the old view of Reconstruction, particularly the "terrible tales" about the Northern troops. "If they can say these things about what the marshals did and what we were doing during [the Meredith crisis], and believe it, then they must have been doing the same thing a hundred years ago."

The attorney general subsequently exposed the President to a new perspective on Reconstruction by inviting the distinguished history professor David Donald to a White House seminar. "Donald more charitably interpreted the motivations of Radical Republicans such as Senator Charles Sumner and House Speaker Thaddeus Stevens and more critically assessed Southern reaction to Reconstruction," noted Giglio, "an analysis that challenged Kennedy's earlier views in *Profiles in Courage*."[41]

Some civil rights leaders were disappointed by the way the Kennedys managed the crisis. Dispirited, Martin Luther King complained that President Kennedy's speech had done nothing more than summon the nation to obey the law. King was particularly irritated by Kennedy's lack of moral conviction and by his patronizing and political references to Mississippi heroes in war and football. Why didn't Kennedy praise Meredith's goal and courage? By negotiating privately with Barnett, the Kennedys had "made Negroes feel like pawns in a white man's political game."

But most of the public approved the administration's actions. It made a "deep impression" on black diplomats in Washington, Dean Rusk reported. "The Mississippi affair seemed from here to have been superbly handled," Ambassador John Kenneth Galbraith wrote from India. "Without question it greatly raised our stock in this part of the world. Not even the Communists now seriously accuse us of evasion."

"President Kennedy's handling of the crisis has impressed the capital," James Reston wrote in *The New York Times*. "The general feeling here is that he has handled this one with a surer touch than he showed in any other major crisis except Berlin. . . . He struck a good balance between conciliation and force."[42]

For all the Kennedys' good intentions and executive actions, their efforts in 1961–1962 disappointed most civil rights supporters and subsequently most historians. They had refused to call for much-needed legislation, failed to protect civil rights workers in the South, engaged in interminable litigation over voting rights, appointed racist Southern justices, and postponed—and finally limited—the stroke of the pen.

Critics charged that the Kennedys wouldn't abandon their strict-constructionist views of federal power, wouldn't concede Southern electoral votes in 1964, and didn't develop empathy for the victims of Southern racism. John Kennedy wasn't fulfilling his campaign promises on civil rights or his promise to be an assertive executive, willing to do the right thing even at the risk of incurring momentary displeasure. Always waiting for a change in circumstance or public opinion, he didn't try to educate the public to be more receptive to civil rights.[43]

The President should have embarked on a public education crusade to arouse the nation to the need for civil rights, much as President Franklin Roosevelt had done with his fireside chats during the Depression. By making the public more receptive, Congress would have become more receptive.

Even though it seemed impossible to get a strong civil rights bill passed by Congress, critics have argued, Kennedy should have pushed for the legislation anyway as a matter of principle. A strong effort would have bolstered the morale of the civil rights movement and maintained President Kennedy's moral and liberal credibility. Instead, he responded to the moral crisis, one that transcended the ordinary boundaries of American politics, not with moral conviction, but with "politics as usual."[44]

Robert Kennedy was inordinately interested in gaining exclusive control over civil rights. "Astonishingly," said James Hilty, "[the Kennedys] thought their control should extend beyond the government and into the movement itself, that their timing should dictate when the civil rights leadership should act."

The attorney general unfairly disparaged the highly respected U.S. Commission on Civil Rights. It was going over "old ground," he charged, "investigating violations of civil rights in areas in which we were making investigations." He had "no confidence" in the commission because it did not conduct "objective investigations." Acting like a "runaway grand jury," the commission approached its work "almost like the House Un-American Activities Committee investigating Communism." Most unbiased observers praised the commission's objectivity, tactics, and integrity.

Father Theodore Hesburgh, president of the University of Notre Dame and a leader of the Civil Rights Commission, was initially impressed by the Kennedy brothers' knowledge and incisiveness. Subsequently Hesburgh felt that "the civil rights issue really imposed itself upon them, rather than they imposing themselves on civil rights." Hesburgh had begun "with great optimism," but after the first year "I felt rather pessimistic."[45]

Despite their differences with Kennedy, many civil rights leaders respected the President, enjoyed his personality, and believed he was committed to their cause. He was accessible, candidly explained his strategy, assured them of his long-term commitment, and, as a civil rights leader commented, "won them with charm."

Those who dealt personally with the Kennedys did not share the bitterness felt by some black leaders. "Something about them—their openness, interest, the alertness of their sympathy—redeemed the hesitancy of their policy and offered hope for the future," Arthur Schlesinger observed. In July 1961, sixty-five leaders of the NAACP visited the President in the White House. "He was his usual charming and courteous self," Wilkins recalled. "The first thing he did was to see that all the women there got seats and he was getting chairs himself for them—not clapping hands and having somebody bring in chairs." The President listened intently to a five-minute presentation on the need for civil rights legislation to supplement his executive action. "[Kennedy] didn't gaze out the window," said Wilkins. "He didn't fiddle around. He listened." After the presentation the President responded, "We remain convinced that legislation is not the way. At least, it's inadvisable at this time." Despite the rebuff, Wilkins recalled, "everyone went out of there absolutely charmed by the manner in which they had been turned down."[46]

Unlike the President's easy relations with civil rights leaders Whitney Young and Roy Wilkins, tension pervaded those with Martin Luther King. The Atlanta preacher annoyingly spoke in moral terms, had his own agenda, and was difficult to control. King was a troublemaker. On March 6, 1961, when Robert Kennedy invited major civil rights leaders to a meeting in his office, he didn't invite King. "King himself asked for an appointment with the President ten days later and was rebuffed," noted Evan Thomas, "informed that the chief executive was too busy with the press of the 'present international situation.'" Despite the early snubs and continuing tension, over the next two and a half years King and the two Kennedys mostly engaged in cordial discussions.

On reflection, King understood—though he didn't agree with—Kennedy's reluctance to push boldly for civil rights:

> He was feeling his way, and he wasn't quite sure that he had the backing of the nation. He was afraid politically to go too far. . . . I think he was committed all along. I think he was very sincere when he said he felt that there was a need for strong moral leadership from the executive head of the nation, and I think he was sincere when he criticized Eisenhower for not giving this leadership. But in 1961 and 1962 he did vacillate a bit, and this was because he felt that he did not quite have the backing of the nation and because of this narrow margin of victory that made him . . . reluctant to move.[47]

Kennedy's defenders argue he did not promise as much on civil rights in the 1960 election as critics claim he did. What's more, they insist his assumption that Congress wouldn't pass civil rights legislation during 1961–1962 was absolutely correct.

It is naive to assume that the Roosevelt style of fireside chats could have generated public support for civil rights. "The sense of urgency that accompanied the New Deal was missing from the New Frontier and that made the public appeal over the heads of Congress a much less viable tool of Presidential leadership," observed civil rights historian John Hart.

Critics underestimate the significance of the Kennedy administration's executive action and often ignore the depth of white Southern opposition and hatred of the Kennedys for promoting civil rights. "Some political jokes and slogans that developed across the South are not heard today and not read in anything that is written and the depth of hostility for the administration somehow has been missed as a result of what I call revisionist history," John Seigenthaler reflected.

Kennedy "prepared the ground" through his effective executive action, said Arthur Schlesinger. "He had quietly created an atmosphere where change, when it came, would seem no longer an upheaval but the inexorable unfolding of the promise of American life."[48]

In August 1962, as Harris Wofford was leaving the administration for a position with the Peace Corps, Kennedy said to him very seriously, with un-usual gentleness and warmth, "It will take some more time, but I want you to know that we are going to do all these things," referring to the agenda of civil rights proposals. "As we parted," Wofford recalled, "he smiled reassur-ingly and repeated, 'You will see, with time I'm going to do them all.' "[49]

30

A LIMITED
COMMITMENT

In Laos, the first major crisis President Kennedy faced, he confronted a precarious situation. Laos was a small, impoverished, landlocked country with a population of about two million. Together with Vietnam and Cambodia, Laos emerged out of French Indochina after the Geneva Conference of 1954. It was of little strategic importance except that its border with North Vietnam furnished a route for Communist insurgents to travel to South Vietnam.[1]

Soon after the Geneva Conference, an intense civil war broke out between the Communist Pathet Lao and the American-supported royal government. In an attempt to bring peace, Laotian prince Souvanna Phouma established a neutral government in 1957 with the aid of his half brother, Prince Souphanouvong, leader of the Pathet Lao. But the Eisenhower administration regarded neutrality as "accommodation with evil" and rejected the coalition arrangement. With U.S. backing General Phoumi Nosavan, the right-wing leader of the royal army, staged a coup, forcing the Pathet Lao and Souvanna to flee to the hills, where they conducted successful guerrilla warfare against Phoumi. Sustained by North Vietnam and a huge Soviet airlift of supplies, the Pathet Lao won several military victories in 1961, bringing them precariously close to swallowing all of Laos.

"Will the Laotians fight for their country?" Kennedy inquired of his experts. "What kind of soldiers are they?" On several occasions he muttered to himself, "This is the worst mess the Eisenhower administration left me." He studied biographies of Phoumi and Souvanna Phouma. Phoumi, he learned, had a reputation as an incompetent military officer and a crooked administrator who stole American aid.

In February 1961, Kennedy consulted with Winthrop Brown, the U.S. ambassador to Laos. Kennedy wanted Brown's personal impressions of events in Laos, particularly whether the President could trust Souvanna. When Brown began to explain official policy, Kennedy interrupted him. "That's not what I asked you. I said, 'What do you think,' you, the Ambassador?" Brown then answered candidly, criticizing past American policy. Phoumi wasn't the answer; only Souvanna could unite Laos.[2]

On April 20, 1961, the day after the fighting ended in Cuba, the President told Richard Nixon, "I just don't think we ought to get involved [in Laos] particularly where we might find ourselves fighting millions of Chinese troops in the jungles. In any event, I don't see how we can make any move in Laos, which is thousands of miles away, if we don't make a move in Cuba, which is only ninety miles away." On other occasions he expressed skepticism about his military advisers. "Thank God the Bay of Pigs happened when it did," he said. "Otherwise we'd be in Laos by now—and that would be a hundred times worse."[3]

"You want to read something fantastic?" he asked Ben Bradlee at a White House dinner party in May 1961. He pulled from his pocket a two-page cable, probably from a U.S. Army officer in Laos. Summarizing the cable himself, he described the performance of the Royal Laotian Army as "just plain gutless." While a battle raged, Royal Laotian forces swam in a nearby stream. "General Phoumi is a total shit," the President said indignantly.[4]

On May 1, 1961, the President discussed the Laotian problem with the Joint Chiefs of Staff, who had urged sending ten thousand U.S. troops. Kennedy remained skeptical of the chiefs' recommendations and asked pointed questions. How many airstrips were there in Laos? the President asked. Only two, came the response, and these were unusable in poor weather or nighttime and were vulnerable to attack. If the Communists attacked and the United States did not use nuclear weapons "would we have to retreat or surrender in the face of an all-out Chinese intervention?" The United States would have to retreat or surrender, came the answer. Kennedy was stunned to learn that sending only ten thousand troops to Laos would dangerously lower American strategic reserves. The meeting was "unforgettable for all present," Walter Rostow recalled. "It was chaos."

The following day McNamara and his deputy, Roswell Gilpatric, sent the President a chilling memorandum setting forth options. U.S. intervention might lead to massive military assistance for the Pathet Lao from North Vietnam, China, and the Soviet Union. In that case the United States "must promptly counter each added element brought against our forces with a more than compensating increment from our side. If the Pathet Lao keep coming, we must take any military action required to meet the threat. If North Vietnam attacks, we must strike North Vietnam. If Chinese volunteers intervene, we will have to go after South China."[5]

Since Kennedy had lost confidence that Laotian or American military forces could win a victory in Laos, he supported reconvening the Geneva Conference. The conference met in 1961 and 1962. Meanwhile, he sent five thousand American troops to Thailand to signal U.S. resolve to the Communists.

Kennedy instructed Averell Harriman, the U.S. representative at Geneva, to attempt to negotiate a reliable neutral government in Laos, an exceptionally delicate and complex task. "Operating against heavy odds, Harriman worked a series of near-miracles at Geneva," noted historian Edmund Wehrle. "These included maintaining a cease-fire, eliciting Soviet support for Laotian neutrality, and persuading the American-supported, anticommunist royal government of Laos to cooperate."

The Geneva negotiations finally succeeded. On June 11, 1962, Souvanna announced the final arrangements for a neutralist coalition government. Souvanna would be prime minister and Phoumi and Souphanouvong the vice premiers. On July 23, fourteen nations signed the final Geneva accords. The Geneva settlement temporarily ended the crisis and provided relative stability until the Vietnam War undermined the coalition government.[6]

Most historians minimize Kennedy's diplomatic accomplishments in Laos, insisting that he only intended to neutralize Laos so that he could focus aggressively on stopping communism in South Vietnam. Dean Rusk confirmed that view. "President Kennedy made the decision that if we had to make a fight for Southeast Asia, we should do it in Vietnam where air and sea power could be brought to bear and where lines of communication were much more favorable to us than they might have been in Laos."

Still, Kennedy had displayed restraint, skill in negotiations, and a willingness to compromise. "In his support for Souvanna," noted Wehrle, "Kennedy showed an understanding of the importance of finding leaders with popular legitimacy."[7]

The facts startle. In 1969, at the height of U.S. involvement in the Vietnam War, the United States had 540,000 troops stationed in that tragic Southeast

Asian nation. Fifty-eight thousand Americans died in the war; 313,000 were wounded. About 2.1 million Vietnamese soldiers and civilians perished. The United States spent roughly two hundred billion dollars in its search for victory. Bombs and defoliation scarred the Vietnamese countryside; cities and towns were heavily damaged. The war stirred contentious debate in the United States and widespread cynicism. In the end the United States and its ally South Vietnam lost the war.

From 1950 through 1975 both Democratic and Republican Presidents supported the U.S. intervention in Vietnam; in Congress most leaders of both parties backed the U.S. effort.

Under the 1954 Geneva accords the French had been allowed to station 685 military advisers in South Vietnam. Although the United States did not sign the accords, it took over the French allocation, and the Eisenhower administration had stuck with the ceiling of 685. Since the North Vietnamese were thought to be violating the accords, Kennedy didn't feel bound by the ceiling.[8]

At the time of Kennedy's death the number of U.S. advisers stood at 16,900. Kennedy had also escalated the rhetoric and the rationale for a strong U.S. presence. Off the record he had serious reservations about fighting there, and hoped to find a way of holding South Vietnam with the minimal use of American troops. But he never expressed his private doubts in public—except to express doubt about the regime of Ngo Dinh Diem. Kennedy's successor inherited not his inner doubts, but his deeper commitment and his forceful public statements stressing the importance of saving South Vietnam.

Before 1954 Kennedy had castigated the French colonial regime, but after the Geneva accords he endorsed the installation of the anticommunist Diem. At the end of the 1950s the attempt to build a cohesive nation in South Vietnam had failed. Political discontent, economic disruption, corruption, and insurgency undermined Diem's control of the country.

In May 1959, from the North's capital in Hanoi, Ho Chi Minh called for the unification of Vietnam. In December 1960, the Communists formed the National Liberation Front of South Vietnam—the Vietcong—and soon Communist guerrillas were disrupting Diem's control in the countryside.[9]

President Kennedy justified U.S. assistance to Diem on idealistic principles. South Vietnam was one battleground in the broader conflict between freedom and communism. "We face a relentless struggle in every corner of the globe that goes far beyond the clash of armies or even nuclear armaments." He warned of "the Communist conspiracy," "the Communist tide," "Communist efforts," and "the Communist advance." The United States must "bear the burden . . . of helping freedom defend itself" in South Vietnam. Kennedy's key advisers agreed. Robert McNamara believed the United States should assist South Vietnam "to protect our security, prevent the spread of totalitarian Communism, and promote individual freedom and political democracy."

"The slide into Vietnam was so deceptively slow," observed James Reston, "and explained with such heroic purposes, that we scarcely noticed it until the body bags came home."[10]

Kennedy worried that nuclear weapons could not deter Communist aggression in places like South Vietnam because those conflicts were too limited to justify nuclear warfare. Nuclear weapons could not be used in "so-called brush-fire wars," he said. The United States needed military flexibility. "Flexible response" would counter a variety of threats without resorting to nuclear devastation, he argued.

On January 6, 1961, in a few paragraphs buried in a lengthy review of Soviet policies, Khrushchev endorsed wars of liberation in underdeveloped countries. "The Communists support just wars of this kind wholeheartedly and they march in the van of the peoples fighting for liberation." Kennedy pounced on the Soviet leader's words, coming as they did after a long series of verbal provocations by Khrushchev. Sensitive to Communist-inspired insurgencies in Laos and Vietnam, where Communist guerrillas used baffling techniques, Kennedy insisted on new U.S. countermeasures. Cuba, then in the forefront of his attention, also showed the trouble guerrilla warfare caused. "The reasons for his concern were serious ones and that concern was shared by most of the community qualified and informed in foreign affairs," noted Douglas Blaufarb, an expert on the history of counterinsurgency.[11]

"We can prevent one nation's army from moving across the border of another nation," Kennedy explained to Ben Bradlee. "We are strong enough for that. And we are probably strong enough to prevent one nation from unleashing nuclear weapons on another. But we can't prevent infiltration, assassination, sabotage, bribery, any of the weapons of guerrilla warfare." He had recently learned new and discouraging math: One guerrilla could pin down twelve conventional soldiers, and the United States had nothing comparable to meet the threat.

Kennedy ordered the Special Warfare School at Fort Bragg, North Carolina, to prepare troops for the unique skills necessary for guerrilla warfare in underdeveloped countries. In May 1961, he instructed McNamara to divert one hundred million dollars from his budget to retrain U.S. forces for "paramilitary and sub-limited or conventional wars."

JFK insisted that all of his major advisers read Khrushchev's speech, and he encouraged them to study the works of Mao and Ernesto "Che" Guevara, the ideologue of the Cuban Revolution. The President and his brother Robert also pored over counterinsurgency training manuals and equipment.

"Almost overnight, a new and faddish weapon was added to the Cold War arsenal: counterinsurgency," noted Evan Thomas. "If the communists were going to lead guerrilla uprisings, then the West would have to learn how to fight back. Unconventional warfare became the rage among New Frontiersmen: Special Forces, wearing rakish green berets, were trained to fight 'people's war.'" The United States must win the "hearts and minds" of the people in places like South Vietnam.[12]

Counterinsurgency was not a euphemism for counterrevolution; the Kennedy administration did not intend to suppress popular revolutions around the world. "It is clear that the original concept was at the opposite pole," said Blaufarb. They hoped to encourage the inevitable changes—even violent changes—taking place in underdeveloped countries to move in a democratic direction. "What we wished to combat was letting small groups of native communists confiscate the revolutionary process and convert it to their own ends," noted State Department official U. Alexis Johnson.

Supporters of counterinsurgency argued that the approach had worked in the past, pointing to the suppression of insurrections in the Philippines in the early fifties and in Malaysia only recently completed. The President aimed to use the fighting in Vietnam to study and test new counterinsurgency techniques and equipment. To expose promising military officers to experience with counterinsurgency, he insisted that they rotate through Vietnam for short tours. Nonetheless, the program had evolved so quickly that the concept confused those who had to implement it.[13]

Counterinsurgency required responsive, honest government and professional behavior by the host country's armed forces. Unfortunately, in South Vietnam the very government the United States wanted to assist was often the biggest obstacle to progress and lacked the support of its own people.

The campaign by the two Kennedys for a new approach to combat insurgency was "bold, determined, and energetic," Blaufarb concluded, "but it was also superficial and, responding to the perceived urgencies of the threat, too hasty."[14]

After the Vienna summit, Kennedy shocked and perplexed James Reston by stating that the only place in the world that there was a real challenge at the moment was Vietnam. "We have a problem in trying to make our power credible, and Vietnam looks like the place."

If the United States needed to take a stand, South Vietnam seemed more promising than its neighbor. Unlike Laos, Vietnam could be supplied by sea, and appeared to be a functioning nation with an army that would fight. Besides, Republicans would hold Kennedy responsible for any retreat in Southeast Asia. The loss of South Vietnam would be political dynamite, comparable to Truman's "loss of China" in 1949.

"There are limits to the number of defeats I can defend in one twelve-month period," the President told Galbraith, an opponent of escalation. "I've had the Bay of Pigs and pulling out of Laos, and I can't accept a third."[15]

Kennedy had little choice but to work with Diem, but this proved prickly because of Diem's personality and his controversial advisers. "Diem was an enigma to me," McNamara later said, "and, indeed, to virtually every American who met him. I did not understand him. He appeared autocratic, suspicious, secretive, and insulated from his people."

Ngo Dinh Nhu, Diem's chief adviser and younger brother, served as the regime's ideologue and brutally directed the police services. Cynical and devious, he systematically used corruption and terror to maintain Diem in power. U.S. officials repeatedly urged Diem to remove or exile Nhu, but he refused.

Madame Nhu, the wife of Ngo Dinh Nhu, was the "first lady" of the Diem regime. Intelligent, energetic, and beautiful, she wielded power because of her influence with the bachelor Diem and her husband, and because of her organizational skills. But her lack of tact and grace antagonized Washington officials by 1963.[16]

Kennedy hoped South Vietnam's leader would engage in reform, but the President was reluctant to push too hard. Diem worried that in a crunch the United States might back out of its commitment to him. Rather than press Diem to engage in needed reform, Kennedy made it his main priority to convince Diem that the United States supported him.

Soon after assuming office, Kennedy established a task force to prepare recommendations on Vietnam, and in late April and early May of 1961, administration officials debated the recommendations. In the end Kennedy approved a modest program that tripled the small contingent of American military advisers, increased logistical support, and provided funds to increase the size of South Vietnam's own military forces. To show his support for Diem and to obtain an independent firsthand report on conditions, in May Kennedy dispatched Vice President Johnson to meet with Diem.[17]

Kennedy strongly preferred an efficient counterinsurgency effort in South Vietnam rather than a large influx of U.S. combat forces. With the Berlin crisis boiling, with the United States contemplating sending six divisions to Europe, it was not a propitious moment to fight a war in South Vietnam.

Walter Rostow repeatedly advised the President that political leverage in Vietnam depended on U.S. willingness to use force. "Our political leverage had to be enlarged. The situation on the ground was so bad that I didn't see how diplomacy, by itself, was going to work."[18]

But the President received contrary advice as well. On July 20, 1961, Kennedy met with retired general Douglas MacArthur, who strongly advised against sending U.S. ground forces to Vietnam. Communists were experts in guerrilla warfare; Americans were not. Maxwell Taylor thought that MacArthur's comments made "a hell of an impression" on Kennedy. When the Joint Chiefs or Taylor urged expanding U.S. military intervention in South Vietnam, Kennedy often responded, "Well, now, you gentlemen, you go back and convince General MacArthur, then I'll be convinced.'"[19]

While the White House debated alternatives, made plans, and recommended action, Congress remained out of the decision-making process. The Senate Foreign Relations Committee mostly ignored the nation's involvement in Vietnam during Kennedy's presidency. "Senator Fulbright raised no particular problems," recalled Dean Rusk. "There were no doves and hawks in those days—that didn't come along until after we had put in substantial forces in South Vietnam."

Congress conceded management of the Vietnam policy to the White House, agreed with U.S. intervention, and raised few objections. Congress acted out its role as the "silent partner" of the President in foreign policy, a role it had played since World War II. Senator Mike Mansfield believed that in all cases of foreign policy and military command "the responsibility for the direction of the nation's course rests with the President." The primary role of Congress for Southeast Asian policy was to serve as a forum for public discussion of the issues.[20]

"Although at times . . . I have been rather troubled by Berlin," Galbraith wrote Kennedy in early October 1961, "I have always had the feeling that it would be worked out. I have continued to worry far, far more about South Vietnam. This is more complex, far less controllable, far more varied in the factors involved, far more susceptible to misunderstanding."

Kennedy worried too. In his autobiography, journalist Arthur Krock recalled a luncheon conversation with the President on October 17, 1961, during which the President expressed serious doubts about the prospect of sending U.S. combat forces to Southeast Asia. Kennedy told him that

United States troops should not be involved [in combat] on the Asian mainland, especially in a country with the difficult terrain of Laos and inhabited by people who don't care how the East-West dispute as to freedom and self-determination was resolved. Moreover, said the President, the United States can't interfere in civil disturbances created by guerrillas, and it was hard to prove that this wasn't largely the situation in Vietnam.[21]

In late October, in preparation for a major presidential review, Kennedy sent a top-level mission to Vietnam, headed by Maxwell Taylor and Walt Rostow. Before Rostow left for Vietnam, the President spoke to him alone. Rostow recalled:

> He kept coming back to the fact that the French put in more than 250,000 good troops, and were run out. . . . He wanted my judgment on whether the Viet Cong had nationalism on their side. Did the people of South Viet Nam really want Ho Chi Minh? We can't commit as many troops as the French, the South Vietnamese must fight this themselves— can they? Do they want to see it through?

The delegation arrived in Saigon on October 18, and spent ten days reviewing the situation and conferring with Diem and his associates. After stopping briefly in Thailand, the group returned to Washington on November 2. They sent their full report to the President on the following day, sparking two weeks of intense high-level debate within the administration.[22]

The report portrayed the Vietcong insurgency as one facet of the global Communist threat. It recommended a "quick U.S. response . . . to help save Vietnam rather than to disengage in the most convenient manner possible." The commitment "must include the sending to Vietnam of some U.S. military forces." The United States needed to change its relationship with South Vietnam from simply giving advice to a "limited partnership." Soon the United States must declare the intention "to attack the source of guerrilla aggression in North Vietnam and impose on the Hanoi Government a price for participating in the current war," Taylor wrote JFK in his cover letter for the report.

The most controversial portion of the Taylor Report recommended dispatching eight thousand U.S. combat troops to South Vietnam. More might be needed later. The job could not be done without them. Nothing would be as reassuring to the South Vietnamese government and the people of South Vietnam as the introduction of U.S. troops. American forces would build morale, and could also serve a humanitarian purpose by working as flood-relief crews, helping to stop flooding in the Mekong Delta. The recommendation for combat troops essentially abandoned the concept of counterinsurgency in favor of a large conventional force, like the United States had used in Korea.[23]

Kennedy's closest advisers endorsed the report. Anything less than 8,000 troops would fail to restore Diem's confidence, McNamara wrote on November 8. In fact, 8,000 troops would probably not be enough. In the future, he stated, "I believe we can safely assume the maximum U.S. forces required on the ground in Southeast Asia will not exceed six divisions, or about 205,000 men."

"General Taylor's proposals are, in my view, conservative proposals for action on our side of the Cold War truce lines," Rostow advised the President on November 11. Implementing them would "buy time and permit negotiation to take over for an interval, under reasonably favorable circumstances." If the United States moved energetically, Rostow wrote, "I believe we can unite the country and the Free World; and there is a better than even chance that the Communists will back down and bide their time."[24]

"The other day at the swimming pool you asked me what I thought and here it is," Bundy wrote Kennedy on November 15.

> *We should now agree to send about one division when needed for military action inside South Vietnam.* . . . This conclusion is, I believe, the inner conviction of your Vice President, your Secretaries of State and Defense, and the two heads of your special mission, and that is why I am troubled by your most natural desire to act on other items now, without taking the troop decision . . .
>
> I believe South Vietnam stands, internally and externally, on a footing wholly different from Laos. Laos was never really ours after 1954. South Vietnam is and wants to be. . . . South Vietnam troops are not U.S. Marines, but they are usable.[25]

A few critics disagreed, but the dissenters were not among Kennedy's closest advisers. On November 7, at the end of a meeting on another subject, George Ball, then undersecretary of state for economic affairs, informed the President of his fear of military escalation. "Within five years we'll have three hundred thousand men in the paddies and jungles and never find them again," Ball exclaimed. "That was the French experience. Vietnam is the worst possible terrain both from a physical and political point of view."

Kennedy dismissed Ball's pessimistic scenario as pure fantasy. With a gesture of impatience, he replied, "George, I always thought you were one of the brightest guys around there, but you're just crazier than hell. That just isn't going to happen." Kennedy's response perplexed Ball. Was the President convinced that future events would not require escalation? Or was Kennedy determined to halt escalation before it got out of control?[26]

On November 13, Galbraith sent the President a missive denouncing the Taylor Report. He had just finished reading all of it. ("I am advised," he noted, "that few others have done so.") Galbraith focused on extracts from the appendixes of the report, which provided damning evidence of the failures of the South Vietnamese. He quoted some:

> . . . there appears to be no driving determination to find, fix and kill the VC. On the other hand, it is generally conceded that the VC are completely indoctrinated in their purpose and will undergo privations, personal hardships and anything required to defeat the SVN.
> . . . The performance of the Army Republic Vietnam is disappointing and generally is characterized by a lack of aggressiveness and at most levels is devoid of a sense of urgency.
> . . . Many men of intelligence and ability have been kept out of government or been forced to resign if their complete loyalty to [Diem] came in doubt. The National Assembly has become a rubber stamp for the President's measures. Elections are a meaningless exercise that can only produce contempt for the democratic process.[27]

Senator Mike Mansfield also warned the President to proceed with caution. "On several occasions we have made commitments to use our own troops, while the Russians have carefully avoided using theirs." That would be the case in Vietnam as well. What's more, the United States would be engaged without the support of significant allies. South Vietnam could become quicksand for the United States. "Where does an involvement of this kind end even if we can bring it to a successful conclusion? In the environs of Saigon? At the 17th parallel? At Hanoi? At Canton? At Peking?" U.S. intervention could be interpreted by Southeast Asians "as a revival of colonial force." The responsibility of defending the country rests "on the shoulders of the South Vietnamese, whose country it is and whose future is their chief responsibility."[28]

Kennedy remained leery about introducing U.S. combat troops. "They want a force of American troops," the President told Arthur Schlesinger in early November. "They say it's necessary in order to restore confidence and maintain morale. But . . . the troops will march in; the bands will play; the crowds will cheer; and in four days everyone will have forgotten. Then we will be told we have to send in more troops. It's like taking a drink. The effect wears off, and you have to take another."[29]

At a dramatic meeting of the National Security Council on November 15 the President expressed grave concern about introducing American combat troops, far greater concern than his primary advisers ever expressed during his entire presidency. He said he feared becoming involved simultaneously on two military fronts—Berlin and South Vietnam—on opposite sides of the world. The wisdom of becoming more involved in Vietnam was not completely clear to him. By comparison, he noted that the Korean War had involved a case of clear aggression, opposed by the United States and other members of the UN. In South Vietnam the aggression was more obscure and less flagrant. The United States needed the support of allies in South Vietnam to avoid sharp domestic partisan criticism as well as objections from other nations. Kennedy said he "could even make a rather strong case against intervening in an area 10,000 miles away against 16,000 guerrillas with a native army of 200,000, where millions have been spent for years with no success." The United States could not expect support from the French. (And Rusk interrupted to say that the British were tending more and more to take the French point of view.)[30]

Kennedy compared the obscurity of the issues in South Vietnam to the clarity of the U.S. position in Berlin. Rusk remarked that the Berlin problem showed that firmness and resolve might also work in Vietnam without causing full-scale war. Kennedy disagreed, saying that "the issue was clearly defined in Berlin and opposing forces identified whereas in Vietnam the issue is vague and action is by guerrillas, sometimes in a phantom-like fashion."

General Lemnitzer stated that without U.S. action in South Vietnam "Communist conquest would deal a severe blow to freedom and extend Communism to a great portion of the world." When Kennedy questioned how the United States could justify sending troops into South Vietnam when we didn't send them into Cuba, Lemnitzer countered that the Joint Chiefs of Staff still wanted to send U.S. troops "into Cuba."

"It was pretty clear [Kennedy] did not like the situation," recalled McNamara of the meeting.[31]

In the end Kennedy decided to endorse most of the recommendations, but not the call for eight thousand troops. He was most comfortable with compromise, with a middle way. There would be no U.S. combat troops, no dramatic action that would rile the American people, but enough expertise from additional U.S. advisers and enough firepower to get the job done and avoid political crucifixion at the hands of Republicans.

Ironically, the middle way still meant escalation. Kennedy's decisions in November marked a major turning point in American involvement in South Vietnam. "Rejecting the extremes of negotiations on the one hand and the dispatch of combat troops on the other, Kennedy settled on a limited commitment of aid and advisers," said George Herring. The President made a serious mistake in not demanding that Diem reform his government. Such insistence "would probably not have compelled Diem to change his ways, but it would at least have forced the issue before American prestige became more deeply involved," Herring said, adding, "By deferring to Diem, the United States encouraged his intransigence and opened the way for conflicts that would make a mockery of the word 'partnership' and would have tragic consequences for all concerned."[32]

Within two years the small American contingent in South Vietnam would escalate to 16,900 advisers, making a future decision to withdraw much more difficult.

Before the fall of 1961, Kennedy's verbal commitment to South Vietnam, expressed in speeches, press conferences, and the like, had been relatively mild. But now, David Halberstam observed, Kennedy would "have to escalate the rhetoric considerably to justify the increased aid, and by the same token, he was guaranteeing that an even greater anti-Communist public relations campaign would be needed in Vietnam to justify the greater commitment."

Shortly after their arrival in South Vietnam, the new contingent of U.S. advisers engaged in combat operations. They accompanied Vietnamese pilots on missions, flew helicopters carrying Saigon's troops into battle, and returned fire in "self-defense"—all critical steps in the Americanization of the war.[33]

On February 12, 1962, Kennedy established the Military Assistance Command, Vietnam (MACV) to direct the expanded military effort. Maxwell Taylor personally selected his protégé, General Paul Harkins, as commander. But Harkins was not widely respected. Observed Halberstam: "His two main distinctions during his years of service in Vietnam would be, first, that his reporting consistently misled the President of the United States, and second, that it brought him to a point of struggle with a vast number of his field officers who tried to file realistic (hence pessimistic) reports."

Kennedy tried to conceal the combat role of U.S. advisers so as not to upset the American public. He also disguised the fact that the United States had violated the Geneva accords at a time when his administration had charged North Vietnam with violations.[34] Nevertheless, based on newspaper stories that U.S. advisers were engaging in combat, questions began to be raised. "Mr. President, are American troops in combat in Vietnam?" a reporter asked on January 15, 1962. Kennedy answered in one word: "No."

Two days before the President made his statement, the first U.S. air combat support mission, code-named Farm Gate, flew to support a South Vietnamese combat unit under attack. By the end of January 1962, Farm Gate crews had flown 229 combat sorties.

In mid-February, after eight American advisers were killed in a plane crash, a *New York Times* editorial criticized the administration for concealing the facts about America's deepening military involvement. On the same day the *Times* carried a column by James Reston, who flatly declared that "the United States is now involved in an undeclared war in South Vietnam. This is well known to the Russians, the Chinese Communists, and everyone else concerned except the American people."

Occasionally criticism was trenchant. "There may be places in the world where the new counter-guerrilla squads now in training can be profitably fielded," wrote *The New Republic* on March 12, 1962. "Vietnam isn't one of them, for the North can literally carry on the war forever." The "active sanctuary" provided by North Vietnam "exposed Saigon in a manner quite without precedent in the Malaya, Greek, and Filipino cases."

"Who is the man in your administration who decides what countries are strategic?" Galbraith sarcastically wrote the President on March 2, 1962. "I would like to have his name and address and ask him what is so important about this real estate in the space age. What strength do we gain from alliance with an incompetent government and a people who are so largely indifferent to their own salvation?"[35]

Criticism was the exception, though, not the rule. During 1962 the strategic-hamlet program became the centerpiece of the administration's counterinsurgency plan. Gather Vietnamese peasants into compact enclaves, protect them with barbed wire and mines, and provide them with radios to contact military forces. Homes, schools, a community center, and other services were to be built inside the hamlets. Used successfully by the British in Malaysia, the hamlets were supposed to create a secure zone and protect vulnerable peasants from unfair tax collection, pillaging, and coercion by Communist guerrillas. Supporters hoped that the program would bring the countryside into close alliance with the Diem regime.

Diem put his brother Nhu in charge of construction, and by the end of the summer of 1962, Nhu bragged that he had constructed 3,225 hamlets, and relocated over four million peasants into them.

During 1962 the conflict seemed to take a turn for the better. U.S. advisers accompanied South Vietnamese army units into battle; American helicopters shuttled South Vietnam's soldiers to attack guerrillas; American pilots flew missions against Vietcong concentrations; and, in Washington's view, the strategic hamlets thrived.

Ambassador Frederick Nolting and General Harkins issued glowing reports on the war. "There is no doubt we are on the winning side," Harkins told McNamara in July 1962. "If our programs continue we can expect Vietcong actions to decline." Nolting reported "substantial progress in pacification and stability."[36]

Historian Herring criticized the pervasive optimism, particularly the views of Nolting and Harkins:

Their confidence was clearly misplaced, and in time they appeared at best fools, at worst dissemblers. But the flaws in the program were more apparent later than at the time. Strangers in an unfamiliar country, the Americans were to a large extent dependent for their information on the South

Vietnamese government, which produced impressive statistics to back its claims of progress. Nolting and Harkins erred badly in accepting these figures at face value, but the conflict did not lend itself to easy analysis.

In Washington, Kennedy, who had many issues on his mind, cheerfully accepted the optimistic reports from men in whom he had confidence. For eighteen months after the debate on the Taylor Report, he put aside the Vietnam problem. He assumed that the strategic-hamlet program was being effectively implemented and that U.S. assistance would help defeat the insurgency.[37]

One serious dissent raised questions in Kennedy's mind about the rosy picture his advisers presented, but did not convince him to change course. In late 1962, Senator Mansfield visited Saigon at Kennedy's request. He had been to Vietnam several times and was an early Catholic sponsor of Diem. Unlike most Washington visitors to Saigon, Mansfield cut short his official briefings. Instead he spent four hours talking with American journalists. Upon returning to Washington he issued a mild report for public consumption, but a harshly critical assessment for the President. The deterioration of Diem's regime, his growing isolation, and the detrimental influence of Nhu and his wife deeply disturbed Mansfield.

"Going to war fully ourselves against the guerrillas" and establishing "some form of neocolonial rule in South Vietnam . . . is an alternative which I most emphatically do not recommend," Mansfield wrote the President. After receiving billions of dollars in U.S. aid, Saigon's government was still weak.

> Vietnam, outside the cities, is still an insecure place which is run at least at night largely by the Vietcong. The government in Saigon is still seeking acceptance by the ordinary people in large areas of the countryside. Out of fear or indifference or hostility the peasants still withhold acquiescence, let alone approval of that government. In short, it would be well to face the fact that we are once again at the beginning of the beginning.

Mansfield urged negotiations rather than military escalation. Vietnam was only desirable for our national interests, not "vital" or "essential." He urged that Kennedy concentrate on "vigorous diplomacy" to "lighten our commitments without bringing about sudden and catastrophic upheavals in Southeast Asia."

Kennedy invited Mansfield to Palm Beach on December 26, 1962, where the senator spent two hours reviewing the private report with the President. Kennedy studied it closely and asked questions. Upset at the unexpected bad news, Kennedy snapped, "Do you expect me to take this at face value?"

Mansfield responded, "You asked me to go there." Kennedy looked at him icily and said, "Well, I'll read it again!"

Afterward Kennedy told O'Donnell, "I got angry with Mike for disagreeing with our policy so completely, and I got angry with myself because I found myself agreeing with him."[38]

Mansfield's version of the situation in South Vietnam was much closer to the truth than the optimistic reports of key officials responsible for the administration's policy. Policymakers badly underestimated the nationalism of Ho Chi Minh's movement, seeing him primarily as a Communist and only secondarily as a Vietnamese nationalist. They underestimated the determination and perseverance of the enemy, their organizational skills, and their superior strategy. Not just terrorists, the insurgents were close to their nation's pulse, deep believers in their cause, and would endure monumental sacrifices to gain victory.[39]

Conversely, U.S. officials overestimated the strength and cohesiveness of South Vietnam. To most Washington officials the Army of the Republic of Vietnam (ARVN) seemed viable. They were well equipped with radios, airplanes, artillery, and fighter planes, while the enemy had only light infantry. ARVN forces had uniforms; the Vietcong wore only black pajamas. The ARVN needed only a little prodding, "an adviser or two, a few people to help the soldiers with map reading; a more vigorous leadership by the better officers, trained by Americans," noted Halberstam of Washington's attitude.

Diem ran a dictatorship. He imprisoned, tortured, and killed his opponents. He rigged elections and controlled the press, radio, and television. Paranoid, worried about a military coup, he stationed his finest troops near Saigon, where they could protect him, leaving the countryside more open to the Vietcong. General Harkins wanted the ARVN to "take the war to the enemy," but Diem remained cautious.[40]

Diem ruined the most promising counterinsurgency measure by placing his dreadful brother Nhu in charge. Nhu's decision to establish hamlets in remote areas to "show the flag" disregarded U.S. advice. "Of the eighty-six hundred strategic hamlets claimed by the Diem government, only 20 percent met U.S. standards," observed James Giglio. "Most would be overrun within a year, enabling the Vietcong to capture thousands of American weapons." Nor did Nhu provide the crucial social, political, and economic reforms that might have made the strategic-hamlet program effective. "Money the United States allocated for such purposes never reached the peasants," said Giglio. "Nhu clearly tried to use the strategic-hamlet system to extend his control over the countryside, and as a result the hamlet program heightened the peasants' hostility." Kennedy, his Washington advisers, Nolting, and Harkins remained oblivious of the failure.

Uncertain how to gauge results in a war without traditional battle lines, U.S. military leaders tried to monitor progress with quantitative measurements: enemy casualties (body counts), weapons seized, prisoners taken, and sorties flown. Only later did they learn that these measurements were misleading or wrong. "I think we were given a good deal of wishful thinking in the reports we were getting from the South Vietnamese," Dean Rusk later stated.[41]

Because Rusk and the State Department backed away from U.S. policies in Vietnam, McNamara and the Pentagon filled the void. "When all is said and done the fact is that McNamara, by sheer force of energy, personality, and a very aggressive staff, tended to take charge," observed Chester Cooper, liaison officer to the NSC staff from the CIA. That meant the military priorities dominated political priorities.

McNamara tried to quantify the unquantifiable. Although he pored over pages of data, what his numbers couldn't quantify proved more important than physical resources. These included, noted one observer, "the history of Southeast Asia, the élan of the opposition, the impact of racial differences, Hanoi's hatred of colonial powers and its ability to mobilize its people to fight and die, and the identification of the American forces with their French predecessors."

"Like most Americans, I saw Communism as monolithic," McNamara recalled in his Vietnam apologia, *In Retrospect: The Tragedy and Lessons of Vietnam* (1995). "I believed the Soviets and Chinese were cooperating in trying to extend their hegemony. In hindsight, of course, it is clear that they had no unified strategy after the late 1950s." Moreover, few Washington officials appreciated the long history of enmity between China and the nations of Indochina.[42]

Kennedy's advisers—McNamara, Bundy, Taylor, and Rostow—knew little about the region's history, languages, cultures, or values. Rostow thought in terms of "capital flow, national savings, engineering know how, infrastructures, stages, takeoffs." McNamara later realized that he and his associates were "setting policy for a region that was terra incognita."

Misjudgments and mistakes occurred partly because the Kennedy administration lacked high-level experts on Southeast Asia, like those—Llewellyn Thompson, Charles Bohlen, George Kennan, Dean Acheson—who had spent decades studying the Soviet Union. "We were flying blind," McNamara recalled, because "we had no counterparts" to the State Department's Soviet experts.[43]

The quality of debate on Vietnam did not approach the quality of those on Berlin or during the Cuban missile crisis. "Kennedy, beset by the missile crisis, congressional elections, de Gaulle, Latin America, the test ban negotiations and the civil rights fight, had little time to focus on Southeast Asia," noted Arthur Schlesinger. "His confidence in McNamara, so wholly justified in so many areas, led the President to go along with the optimists on Vietnam." McNamara agreed. "We faced a blizzard of problems, there were only twenty-four hours in a day, and we often did not have time to think straight."[44]

In the last six months of Kennedy's life the inattention, mistakes, misjudgments, and faulty illusions returned to haunt his presidency.

31

ECONOMICS 101

Sluggish economic growth, slack consumer demand, and a high rate of unemployment (6.7 percent) faced Kennedy when he assumed the presidency. During the Eisenhower era the nation experienced three recessions in seven years. "The present state of our economy is disturbing," Kennedy asserted in his first State of the Union address. "We take office in the wake of seven months of recession, three and one-half years of slack, seven years of diminished growth, and nine years of falling farm income."

Yet people seemed complacent and not amenable to changes in economic policy. "The major barrier to getting the country's economy moving again lay in the economic ignorance and stereotypes that prevailed in the land," contended Walter Heller, chairman of the Council of Economic Advisers (CEA). "The copybook maxims of private finance misapplied to federal finance threatened to strangle expansionary policy."[1]

John Maynard Keynes, the brilliant British economist, had convincingly argued during the Great Depression that governments did not have to sit idly by while "imperfect markets inflicted misery on mankind." A government had two methods to rationally control the economy. It could regulate the money supply (monetary policy) and had the power to tax and spend (fiscal policy). "Using these tools to manipulate aggregate demand, political leaders could make capitalism work properly," noted author Allen Matusow.

After World War II liberal economists in Europe and in American universities contended that it was not necessary to redistribute the wealth of the rich in order to improve the condition of the poor. By applying the proper economic measures, the total amount of wealth could be increased, benefiting everyone. Keynesian ideas, continually updated and modified, became the new academic orthodoxy. Nonetheless, by 1961 few politicians had learned the Keynesian lessons; nor had much of the public been converted.[2]

All the members of Kennedy's Council of Economic Advisers—Heller, James Tobin of Yale, and Kermit Gordon of Williams College—were widely respected Keynesian economists. They hoped to teach the President modern economics. A budget surplus, they contended, though needed to cool down an inflationary economy, was a "fiscal drag" on recovery from a recession and would result in another economic downturn before the country reached full employment. High tax levels drained needed purchasing power and caused expansion to stop short of full employment. Merely to end a recession and initiate a recovery was inadequate. Expansive measures should not stop with the beginning of recovery, because the recovery might not lift the economy all the way to full employment.

The President should concentrate on full employment and willingly accept substantial federal deficits even during an economic recovery. A large pool of potential workers far exceeded the supply of jobs. "Unless the economy grew fast enough to create new jobs as rapidly as the manpower tide increased, there would be no end to recurring recessions, or even to high unemployment in the midst of prosperity," Sorensen reflected. Not overly worried about inflation, Heller and the CEA were confident they could control its consequences if it became a problem.[3]

As a congressman and then senator from Massachusetts, Kennedy had wrestled with several thorny economic problems—declining industries, unemployment, area redevelopment, labor, and trade—but he didn't understand modern economics. An unbalanced budget might be necessary in an emergency, but he couldn't accept its desirability under normal circumstances. The low point for the CEA came in the summer of 1961, when President Kennedy planned a tax increase of three billion dollars to finance the Berlin military buildup. Initially the council was shut out of the deliberations. Only Ken O'Donnell's sympathetic intercession gave Heller access to the President to try and reverse the planned move. "Another strategically placed ally, Paul Samuelson, helped the cause with a timely visit to Hyannis Port on the weekend just before the final decision," Heller recalled.

A tax increase was "bad economics," Heller warned the President on July 21, 1961:

There is plenty of room in the economy for defense spending of the magnitude now contemplated. With an important assist from the Federal Budget, the recovery has started well. But it has a long way to go, and inflation has never been more dormant since the war. We have all been worrying—publicly as well as privately—that the tax system may choke off full recovery.

In the end Kennedy's economic advisers persuaded him that a tax increase would hinder the recovery then in progress.[4]

Kennedy would have liked to stimulate economic expansion by increasing government expenditures, but opposition to new spending programs in Congress blocked this route. The traditional liberal Democratic agenda was impossible to enact. Within a month of taking office, former New Deal economist Robert R. Nathan, the spokesman for Americans for Democratic Action, proposed a huge expenditure plan that would have increased the federal deficit by fifty billion dollars. "The difficulty with your proposal," Kennedy told Nathan, "is that 93 percent of the people in this country are employed. That other 7 percent isn't going to get enough political support to do it. The difference between me and Roosevelt is that he could get these things done."

The conservative-dominated Congress would support large increases in federal spending only for defense and space programs; it would never support increased spending for federal aid to education, "socialized medicine," or other social measures. And Congress insisted on a balanced budget.[5]

The President and his advisers needed a program that was not only economically workable but politically marketable. Kennedy doubted that tax cutting was politically marketable. In his inaugural address he had stressed the need to sacrifice; a tax cut was inconsistent with that message. His theme of sacrifice, his narrow victory margin, and the demand for "fiscal responsibility" hemmed him in. Kennedy told his economic advisers that congressional conservatives would "piss all over" a big tax-cut proposal; the White House would be "kicked in the balls by the opposition."

"Suppose that I ask for [a] bold program and don't get it, I'm turned down?" Kennedy asked his economic advisers. "Then you've fought the good fight," he was told. Kennedy disagreed. "If that jeopardizes other programs, that's pure vanity." Paul Samuelson came to appreciate Kennedy's dilemma and judged him an insightful political strategist. "Had President Kennedy come out boldly for the sizeable deficit which objective economic analysis called for, he would have run into severe opposition in the divided Congress; and by becoming tarred with the asinine label of an 'irresponsible spender,' the President might have put all his new programs in jeopardy."[6]

Popular myths about the economy could not be changed overnight, and until people were better informed, Kennedy thought, it was political suicide to push the CEA's approach. Nonetheless, he showed a willingness to learn. Surrounded by brilliant economists, he soaked up information and asked incisive questions. He lingered longer on the newspapers' financial pages and studied *The Economist*, the British weekly focused on economic issues.

He insisted on seeing economic reports as quickly as possible; memos and letters from economists should immediately be brought to his attention. "Mr. Heller," Evelyn Lincoln informed the economist, "President Kennedy read every memorandum you ever sent him from cover to cover."

He wanted facts and perceptive analysis. "We were often amazed at his capacity for understanding a particular set of relationships in economics," said Heller, who added proudly that Kennedy was "the best student" he ever had.[7]

Kennedy encouraged Heller and CEA members to take their message to the public. "I can't say that yet, but you can," he told them. They should educate the public on the virtues of a federal deficit in a recession, adding quickly, "but always make clear that the recession started last year," that is, during Eisenhower's administration. When critics accused the administration of being fiscally irresponsible, the President teased Heller: "Walter, I want to make it perfectly clear that I resent these attacks on *you*."

In the fall of 1962, James Tobin engaged the President in a half-hour discussion of economic issues. "[Kennedy] wanted to ask me some questions, but it turned out he wanted to give his own answers to them too and see if I agreed," Tobin recalled. One topic was the budget deficit. "Is there any economic limit to the deficit?" the President asked. "I know of course about the political limits. But is there any economic limit on the size of the debt in relation to national income? There isn't, is there? That's just a political answer, isn't it?" Tobin replied that the only limit was inflation. "That's right," Kennedy eagerly interjected. "The deficit can be any size, the debt can be any size, provided [it doesn't] cause inflation. Everything else is just talk."

Because he sometimes couldn't remember when to apply the terms "fiscal" and "monetary," he devised a system for distinguishing them. The M in monetary stood for Martin—William McChesney Martin, chairman of the Federal Reserve Board—and everything else was fiscal. "If Martin leaves," he joked to Heller, "we will have to get somebody with a name beginning with 'M'."[8]

Heller's effort to educate the President was finally rewarded in the summer of 1962. When Treasury Secretary Douglas Dillon also saw the benefit of a massive stimulant for the slack economy, Kennedy agreed to seek a major tax reduction. Although the economy had been clearly improving in 1961, it was doing so at a low level. In 1962 there was a danger of a decline, which critics would surely label a "Kennedy recession." By mid-1962 the economic outlook seemed dire. Even conservatives feared another recession, or at least a drawn-out failure to achieve prosperity. This frightening scenario softened opposition to the expansive measures the CEA sought.

Again the issue arose: Why a tax cut instead of an expenditure program? Liberals, such as John Kenneth Galbraith, favored the Keynesian alternative to a general tax cut: a large increase in federal spending to improve housing, schools, hospitals, and welfare programs. "I am not sure," Galbraith told Kennedy, "what the advantage is in having a few more dollars to spend if the air is dirty, the water is too polluted to drink . . . the streets are filthy, and the schools so bad that the young . . . stay away."

"The glories of the Kennedy Era will be written not in the rate of economic growth or even in the level of unemployment," Galbraith wrote from New Delhi on July 10, 1962, "[but] will be from the way it tackles the infinity of problems that beset a growing population and an increasingly complex society in an increasingly competitive world. To do this well costs the money that the tax reducers would deny."[9]

Heller conceded that the nation badly needed federal social programs. But there were two problems with Galbraith's approach. First, even if Congress would appropriate the added billions for social programs, how could the money be spent—in time? "Attempts to enlarge spending at the rate required to do the economic job would lead to waste, bottlenecks, profiteering, and scandal," Heller argued.

The second problem was political. An expansion of spending would bring charges of "fiscal irresponsibility" the same way tax cuts would. "But on top of this would be all of the opposition to expansion of government, to overcentralization, to a 'power grab' and a 'take-over' of the cities, the educational system, the housing market. . . .

"A vigorous economy, stimulated by tax cuts," Heller concluded, "will provide a broader economic base and an atmosphere of prosperity and flushness in which government programs can vie much more successfully for their fair share of a bigger pie."[10]

Kennedy agreed with Heller and made a major effort to sell Keynesian economics during his commencement address at Yale University on June 11, 1962. Sorensen and several others contributed, but Kennedy wrote more of his speech than usual. Attired in a purple-trimmed LL.D. hood, he attacked the "myths," "truisms," "clichés," and "stale phrases" which obscured truths about U.S. economic life. "The great enemy of the truth," he said, "is very often not the deliberate, contrived, and dishonest—but the myth—persistent, persuasive, and unrealistic. Too often we hold fast to the clichés of our forebears. We subject all facts to a prefabricated set of interpretations. We enjoy the comfort of opinion without the discomfort of thought."

The myth persisted that federal deficits created inflation and budget surpluses prevented it. Actually, large budget surpluses after World War II had not prevented inflation, and recent deficits had not upset basic price stability. "Obviously deficits are sometimes dangerous—and so are surpluses. But honest assessment plainly requires a more sophisticated view than the old and automatic cliché that deficits automatically bring inflation."

Conventional wisdom assumed that the federal debt was growing at a dangerously rapid pace. In fact, the "national debt since the end of World War II has increased only 8 percent, while private debt was increasing 305 percent, and the debts of state and local governments . . . have increased 378 percent." Public and private debts were neither good nor bad, in and of themselves. "Borrowing can lead to overextension and collapse—but it can also lead to expansion and strength. There is no single, simple slogan in this field that we can trust." We needed fewer labels and clichés.

The national interest lay in high employment and steady expansion of output, he concluded, in stable prices and a strong dollar. "The declaration of such objectives is easy; their attainment in an intricate and interdependent economy and world is a little more difficult. To attain them, we require not some automatic response but hard thought."[11]

Heller judged Kennedy's speech to be the most "literate and sophisticated dissertation on economics ever delivered by a President." At Yale, in his two annual economic messages, in two television addresses urging the tax cut, and in press conferences and statements, Kennedy put presidential economic discussion on a much loftier level.

But Kennedy was deeply disappointed that his speech didn't seem to resonate, didn't garner much praise. "I don't think I ever saw him more depressed than a few days after it," said David Ormsby-Gore. "He just felt that this weight of prejudice against any new move on the financial front was so heavy that you just couldn't break through."[12]

A subsequent speech on the economy did win acclaim. On December 14, 1962, Kennedy addressed businessmen at the Economic Club of New York. He explained his rationale for a tax cut. The best way to strengthen demand among consumers and business, he said, was to reduce the burden on private income and the deterrents to private initiative imposed by the current tax system. It siphoned out of the private economy too much personal and business purchasing power and reduced the financial incentives for personal effort, investment, and risk taking.

Any new tax legislation enacted next year should meet the following three tests: First it should reduce net taxes by a sufficiently early date and a sufficiently large amount to do the job required. . . . Too large a tax cut, of course, could result in inflation and insufficient future revenue—but the greater danger is a tax cut too little or too late to be effective.

Second, the new tax bill must increase private consumption as well as investment. . . .

Third, the new tax bill should improve both the equity and the simplicity of our present tax system. This means the enactment of long-needed tax reforms, a broadening of the tax base and the elimination or modification of many special tax privileges.

Only full employment could balance the budget, and tax reduction would pave the way for that employment. "The purpose of cutting taxes now is not to incur a budget deficit, but to achieve the more prosperous, expanding economy which can bring a budget surplus."

Galbraith described the address as the most "Republican speech since McKinley," and a newsmagazine thought the President sounded like an official in the National Association of Manufacturers.

When business praised the tax speech, though, Kennedy was delighted. He phoned Heller to say, "I gave them straight Keynes and Heller, and they loved it." From then on, Heller recalled, "Kennedy moved steadily ahead on the tax-cut course and the educational job needed to put it across."[13]

In December 1962, Heller advised the President that the cost of a slack economy in 1962 was thirty to forty billion dollars—"almost equal to the total GNP of Italy." Now was the time to push for the tax cut. "Congress may be lukewarm, but powerful groups throughout the country are *ready for action*. When the Chicago Board of Commerce, the AFL-CIO, the CEA, and the U.S. Chamber are on the same side—when repeated editorials in *Business Week* are indistinguishable from those appearing in *The Washington Post*—the prospect for action cannot be wholly dim."[14]

Kennedy agreed. Privately he told key advisers: "If this policy is right it will pay off in the long run; that is what interests me, not the ephemeral day-to-day popularity that is readily available by simply giving in to any and all demands for special spending programs." He added, "This is the right thing to do and it's going to work. Let's do it. If it works, people will like what the final result is even if it takes two or three years."

In January 1963 Kennedy asked Congress to reduce taxes by $13.5 billion. The tax cut would stimulate the economy as consumers spent more money. Then, explained economist Robert Heilbroner, "tax revenues would also rise, and in the end the budget would be balanced at a higher level of national output than if there had been no cut in the first place."[15]

The tax-cut legislation passed the House on September 25, 1963. The Revenue Act, eventually enacted under President Johnson in 1964, had the effect Kennedy had hoped. The Kennedy "boom," begun unspectacularly in the spring of 1961, became the longest peacetime period of prosperity in modern U.S. history. In 1966 nearly five and a half million more people were employed than in 1961. Corporate earnings soared; profits after taxes improved by almost 70 percent between 1961 and 1965. The growth of real per capita income—which had risen 5.9 percent between 1946 and 1950, and another 15.2 percent in the 1950s—rose spectacularly by 31.7 percent in the 1960s.[16]

Kennedy's efforts to stimulate the economy occurred while he was also trying to reduce the nation's chronic balance-of-payments deficit. The problem weighed heavily on him. Unlike the consensus of modern economists about the need for compensatory fiscal policy, there was no consensus on what to do about the balance of payments.

More dollars were leaving the United States than were coming in, because of rising U.S. imports, increasing foreign investment, expenditures abroad, and the military buildup in Europe. A country was only as strong as its currency, Kennedy believed, and the deficit would weaken the U.S. dollar. Foreign countries might turn nearly all of their dollars in for gold held by the United States, drastically drawing down the nation's gold reserves.[17]

It irritated him that European countries that benefited from U.S. military protection used the payments deficit as a "stick" to beat his administration. Because Treasury Secretary Douglas Dillon shared his view of the seriousness of the problem, the President relied heavily on Dillon's recommendations. Dillon and Robert Roosa, undersecretary of the Treasury for international monetary affairs, warned of the collapse of the international monetary system unless the administration quickly restored confidence in the dollar.

To stem the gold outflow, Kennedy instituted mild controls, enticed foreign tourists and investments, promoted exports, and bargained for lower tariffs. He tied aid loans and grants to procurement in the United States. "Instead of making dollars available which would be spent wherever in the world competitive price and quality factors would indicate," observed David Bell, the administration by and large arranged for "the exportation from the United States of goods and services."[18]

The Council of Economic Advisers emphasized economic growth at home over balancing payments overseas. Heller believed that a more productive economy would automatically solve the balance-of-payments problem. To the dismay of his Keynesian advisers, though, Kennedy stuck to his defense of the dollar, making it more difficult to attain the domestic objectives of faster growth and full employment. "There was, for example, the matter of easy money," said Matusow. "If the government lowered American interest rates for domestic reasons, dollars would flee the country in search of higher interest rates elsewhere, and the deficit in the balance of payments would worsen."

Carl Kaysen and George Ball worried about Kennedy's obsession with the balance of payments. The President's action threatened to produce serious distortions in U.S. economic policy, and to drive the United States toward restrictions and protectionism. "The duty-free allowance for goods brought back by returning tourists was drastically reduced," noted Ball, "and 'Buy America' provisions were tightened to the point where domestic goods had to cost 50 percent more than similar imports before the Defense Department could buy abroad."

Kennedy cut overseas military expenditures partly by bringing home the families of troops stationed in Germany; he also seriously considered reducing the size of U.S. troop deployments in Europe. "That was fodder for Europe's neutralists, who questioned the firmness of our defense commitments," noted Ball.[19]

"He spent more time on it in some ways than he spent on subjects that might have been equally important," observed Kaysen. In part Kennedy's attitude reflected the views of his father, who had an inordinate fear of the payment deficit and the outflow of gold from the United States. Those who wanted to keep the problem in perspective grew apprehensive every time the President visited his father on a weekend. "Whenever the President returned from Hyannis Port, we braced ourselves for a sermon on gold and the hellfire awaiting us if we did not promptly correct the balance of payments deficit," George Ball recalled. Twice when Ball argued with the President about the problem, Kennedy replied ruefully, "All right, George, I follow you, but how can I ever explain that to my father?"[20]

In June 1962, the President excitedly phoned James Tobin about an issue with the balance of payments. To crack down on the nation's spending abroad he wanted Tobin to tabulate the foreign outlays of various federal departments and agencies. Tobin agreed to gather the data, but he told the President, "I don't think further cracking down on federal outlays abroad is a good approach to the problem." Taken aback, Kennedy asked why. "We've already gone a considerable distance in that direction at some cost to the effectiveness of our foreign policy," Tobin answered, "especially foreign aid, and at extra dollar cost to the budget."

The federal government had already borne more than its share of belt-tightening for the balance of payments, Tobin pointed out. "Something is wrong when we have to cut back on important national programs and private citizens can travel, send money abroad, [and] buy imports, as they please." In any case, the balance of payments problem wasn't that serious. There were other ways to deal with it.

Tobin later recalled: "I was impressed with the man, that he would stop to listen calmly to a dissent to something he was headlong bent upon when he picked up the phone." Kennedy claimed that he hadn't known of Tobin's point of view. "Walter and I had been trying to say this sort of thing to him in memos for a long time, but they hadn't sunk in. This time we got his attention, and he studied the memo he had invited, and we had a good talk about it." Kennedy agreed that it made no sense for the federal government to hamstring important national programs while banks, businesses, and tourists did what they pleased. Gradually he placed less emphasis on the payments problem.[21]

Kennedy initially pushed legislation for tax reform. It was unfair, he sincerely felt, that many wealthy people paid almost no taxes because of loopholes and inequities in the tax laws. But conservatives in Congress objected to closing tax loopholes, forcing Kennedy to abandon his tax-reform proposals.[22]

More successful was another major economic innovation, the Trade Expansion Act of 1962. With the trade law enacted in the New Deal era about to expire in the summer of 1962, the United States desperately needed new legislation. If the United States hoped to benefit from the economic opportunities afforded by the new European Economic Community, tariff negotiations had to start soon, before the countries of the EEC instituted their new tariff structure.

Anticipating a difficult struggle in Congress, Kennedy vigorously lobbied for his measure. Between his State of the Union message in January 1962 and the final signing of the trade bill on October 11, 1962, he promoted the measure at ten press conferences.

The House passed the Trade Expansion Act by 298 votes to 125, and the Senate followed by the overwhelming vote of 78 to 8. For the next five years, the President was given the power to reduce U.S. tariffs to half their current levels. While signing the legislation, Kennedy called it "the most important piece of international legislation affecting economics since the Marshall Plan."[23]

Newspaper editorials praised the legislation as "the crowning achievement of the Kennedy Presidency in domestic legislation." The "Kennedy Round" of tariff negotiations lasted from January 1963 to June 1967. In the end, tariffs were lowered on 6,300 items by an average of 35 percent—encouraging, but not as successful as hoped or expected.

Still, the President had skillfully molded a political consensus at home on the trade issue, and made the greatest advance in trade legislation since 1934. That he "convinced other nations, namely the Europeans, to join with America to lower trade barriers attested to his success as a leader in the world economy," contended one expert.[24]

"I just don't see how Eisenhower sat around evening after evening with all those businessmen," Kennedy told a friend. Eisenhower had enjoyed socializing with leaders of the business world; Kennedy regarded them as narrow and boring.

Yet he wanted the support of business for all his economic initiatives. Several of the administration's actions were favorable to business; private ownership of the Communications Satellite Corporation, more liberal depreciation allowances, trade expansion, and lower taxes. He wanted business expansion and modernization. "The clear answer," recalled Heller, "though un–Democratic in tradition, was to offer special tax incentives for investment in machinery and equipment." Kennedy did manage to convince Congress to enact a 7 percent tax credit for business investment in new machinery and equipment.[25]

Getting along with business proved difficult, however. The Business Advisory Council, created in 1933, offered the business community's advice and assistance to the federal government. The organization, composed of about 160 prominent corporation executives, met privately at least twice annually with government officials, usually at elite resort hotels. Secretary of Commerce Luther Hodges, the administration's liaison with the council, wanted to make the organization less exclusive and more open to the public. He pressured the BAC to open its ranks to small businessmen and allow the news media to attend all its meetings with government officials.

In early July 1961, the council, fed up with Hodges and his pressure to change, revolted. The group announced that it would disaffiliate from the federal government and operate as a private group. Kennedy immediately reconciled with the council, in the process undermining Hodges. Press secretary Pierre Salinger announced that the President had assured the council that its new "private" status was a fine idea. Cabinet officers would cooperate with the reorganized group. Hodges's efforts to put together a new Business Advisory Council received no backing from the administration. Bitter, Hodges later concluded, "I did not get Mr. Kennedy's backing because he took the position, very erroneously, that [the council] was now a different organization."[26]

Kennedy's acquiescence grew out of his fear that the BAC's divorce from the government might worsen his relations with business. He had enough problems without a "whispering campaign" against him coming out of corporate boardrooms. He wanted the support of big business in all his efforts to improve the economy.

Walter Heller met several times with delegations from the new Business Advisory Council. Always diplomatic, Heller nonetheless privately expressed exasperation with the group's ultraconservative attitudes. Meeting with a delegation in the summer of 1962, Heller detected a clear "party line" on several points, such as "confidence uber alles" and "cut taxes and expenditures." He told the President:

> They were insistent on the need to hold down—and even cut back—Federal expenditures in order to improve "confidence." . . . All suggested, or endorsed, an *immediate* tax cut, and stressed that the cut must be *permanent*. . . . The form of the tax cut was stressed as all-important. Highest priority went to a substantial cut in the top brackets of the personal income tax. Second priority was placed on a reduction in the corporate rate. . . . They consistently wanted the President to act like a conservative Republican. It was strongly suggested that the President should drop support of Medicare, school aid, and the 1962 tax bill. Only thus could one restore business *confidence,* the central theme of the whole discussion.

It took "some forbearance" for Heller to remain cordial with the delegation, he told Kennedy, because of the "unrelenting ultra-conservative cast of their recommendations—by far the most conservative stance they have taken with us."[27]

Ideally the interplay of market forces established wages and prices without government intervention. During World War II and the Korean War the federal government had imposed wage and price controls. In the absence of wartime controls the Council of Economic Advisers sought another method to restrain inflation. Economic historian Kim McQuaid observed that Kennedy wanted to control the process "whereby powerful unions forced higher and higher costs upon industry and equally powerful industrial combines then passed such increased costs on to the public in the form of ever higher prices."

Modern economists had designed wage and price guidelines to equate price and productivity levels. They calculated the average annual productivity increase in American industry after World War II, a figure initially set at 3.2 percent per year. McQuaid explained:

> If . . . workers in an industry where productivity had been growing at the average 3.2 percent rate wanted a wage increase, they could obtain up to a 3.2-percent hike without their employer's having to raise prices to recoup the profits lost to increased production costs. In this situation, prices

would remain stable and neither management nor labor would lose anything.[28]

In its *Annual Report* of January 1962, the CEA established voluntary informal guidelines for the first time. With published guidelines, it was hoped, public opinion and presidential persuasion could counteract the market power of strong unions and strong businesses. The guidelines were used to bring to the bargaining tables and boardrooms "a sense of the public interest in noninflationary wage and price behavior," said Heller. To be noninflationary, wage and price decisions had to be geared to productivity increases. All wage and price decisions should be measured against the CEA's published wage-price guidelines.

The White House stayed in close contact with the labor-management talks in several major industries, but one in particular: the steel industry. In late March 1962, when negotiators led by Secretary of Labor Arthur Goldberg managed to convince both sides to agree on a noninflationary pact, Kennedy was delighted. The settlement protected worker job security, and cost only 2.5 percent, well within the wage-price guidelines put forth by the CEA. Because the agreement seemed to make unnecessary a price increase by steel companies, the settlement was a major victory for collective bargaining and for the President's intense desire to control inflation. Neither side complained about the settlement. The Steelworkers' Union, which in previous contracts had received raise hikes as high as 8 percent, settled for much less.[29]

Then, on April 10, 1962, during an appointment at the White House, U.S. Steel's chairman, Roger Blough, handed Kennedy a memo stating that his company would immediately raise prices on its products by 3.5 percent or six dollars a ton. Nearly every other major steel company immediately followed suit.

Stunned, Kennedy told Blough he was making a mistake. Dismayed, Arthur Goldberg tendered his resignation, insisting he had lost credibility with labor because of Blough's action. (Kennedy did not accept his resignation.) "You kept silent and silence is consent," Goldberg told Blough. "One thing you owe a President is candor."

Kennedy viewed Blough's action as a personal affront. He phoned David McDonald, president of the Steelworkers' Union, and said, "Dave, you've been screwed and I've been screwed." Blough's decision would undermine Kennedy's prestige with labor and his program to control inflation. "Since he had concentrated his greatest effort for price-wage stability on the steel negotiations, his failure seriously weakened his position with all other industries and unions," noted business historian Jim Heath.[30]

"They kicked us right in the balls," Kennedy angrily told Ben Bradlee. "Are we supposed to sit there and take a cold, deliberate fucking. . . . They fucked us, and we've got to try to fuck them."

At his next press conference the President pointed out the simultaneous and identical actions of U.S. Steel and other major steel corporations. Increasing steel prices by six dollars a ton was totally unjustified and an irresponsible defiance of the public interest.

In this serious hour in our nation's history, when we are confronted with grave crises in Berlin and Southeast Asia, when we are devoting our energies to economic recovery and stability, when we are asking reservists to leave their homes and families for months on end and servicemen to risk their lives . . . and asking union members to hold down their wage increases, at a time when restraint and sacrifice are being asked of every citizen, the American people will find it hard, as I do, to accept a situation in which a tiny handful of steel executives, whose pursuit of power and profit exceeds their sense of public responsibility, can show such utter contempt for the interests of 185 million Americans.

During the press conference Kennedy rarely smiled, and he walked out of it as unsmiling as when he had entered.

Robert Kennedy later explained that the administration needed to play "hard ball" with the steel executives. The attorney general immediately convened a grand jury to investigate whether the steel companies had violated the law. "We were going to go for broke—their expense accounts and where they'd been and what they were doing. I picked up all their records. . . . I told the FBI to interview them all—march into their offices the next day. . . . All of them were subpoenaed for their personal records and . . . their company records. . . . .Under the circumstances we couldn't afford to lose."[31]

The White House produced facts and figures to prove that U.S. Steel did not need to raise prices. Armed with subpoenas, FBI agents barged into the offices of steel-firm executives, hunting for incriminating evidence.

At a Bethlehem Steel stockholders' meeting in Wilmington, Delaware, on the same day Blough had announced his price increase, the company's president, Edmund Martin, had allegedly commented that because of competition, particularly from foreign countries, American steelmakers needed to cut prices. (There was confusion about Martin's exact words.) If Martin had been quoted correctly about the need to reduce the price of steel, and the next day had gone along with the price increase, that was evidence of illegal administered prices. Or at least that was the judgment of Robert Kennedy. Bethlehem was in lockstep with U.S. Steel's price rise regardless of competitive or market conditions. Therefore, the attorney general ordered the FBI to contact reporters to confirm Martin's remarks at the stockholders' meeting.

Assistant Attorney General Nicholas Katzenbach cautioned the FBI to interview the steel executives at their offices, not at their homes. No one thought to give similar instructions to the FBI about interviewing reporters who had covered Bethlehem's stockholders' meeting. At 5:00 A.M., an FBI agent phoned John Lawrence of *The Wall Street Journal* and said, "The Attorney General asked us to call you." At about the same time, agents showed up at the door of two other journalists. When news broke of the early-morning visits, the media clamored for an explanation. (Later Robert Kennedy issued a brief statement accepting "full responsibility" for what had happened.)[32]

Shortly after, U.S. Steel and the steel companies that had followed its lead rescinded their price increases. Kennedy had forced a capitulation, but the administration's tactics led critics to scream "Gestapo," "secret police," "middle-of-the-night tactics." "After this display of naked power," wrote Erwin D. Canham in *The Christian Science Monitor,* "whatever its provocation or justification, how free will the American economy be?" *The Wall Street Journal* complained that the federal government had set the price of steel "by naked power, by threats, by agents of the state security police."

Writing in *The New Republic,* Charles Reich, a law professor at Yale, lambasted the administration for violating civil liberties. Normally, summoning a grand jury took place only after careful preliminary inquiry and preparation. "Why the middle-of-the-night calls by the FBI, to gather evidence of 'criminal' activities which for years have been the subject of leisurely and tedious law review articles? One would think the companies were holding a baby for ransom," Reich wrote. "Why did the administration lose its prosecutorial zeal just as soon as the companies capitulated? Can acts or conditions that are criminal on Tuesday become less criminal by the following Monday?" It was dangerous for an angry President to "loose his terrible arsenal of power for the purpose of intimidating and coercing private companies and citizens."[33]

To friends who congratulated him on his victory, Kennedy said he was pleased, but "now it has been done and we want to give them every bit of help we can. If they don't prosper, the whole economy is in trouble." He desperately needed to cooperate with business to avoid a "Kennedy recession." "I don't want [political advantage]," he said privately. "We want the support of business on trade. We want them on the tax bill. I've been breaking my ass trying to get along with these people."

At a news conference on April 18, 1962, Kennedy claimed he harbored "no ill will against any individual, any industry, corporation, or segment of the American economy." A few days later, though, a reliable report circulated that Kennedy had privately used an extremely derogatory reference in refer-ring to businessmen shortly after the price increase had been announced. His father had always told him that all businessmen were "sons-of-bitches," but he never believed it until Blough had double-crossed him. The story first ap-peared in *The New York Times* on April 23, 1962. (A few days later, he re-marked to Adlai Stevenson and Arthur Schlesinger, "They are a bunch of bastards—and I'm saying this on my own now, not just because my father told it to me.") Two weeks later, questioned about the remark, Kennedy awk-wardly declared that his statement was not meant to apply to "all" business-men, but he did not deny having said it. Once it became public, Kennedy's "sons-of-bitches" remark further alienated the business community.

Robert Kennedy later reflected on his brother's and his family's attitude toward businessmen: "[The President] never liked them. I mean, he just al-ways felt . . . that you couldn't do anything with them and there's no way to influence them. I suppose the fact [was] we were brought up thinking that [way]. . . . My father thought businessmen didn't have any public responsi-bility."[34]

Shortly after the steel crisis, a brief but drastic slump in the stock market dropped Kennedy's popularity with businessmen to a new low. Business at-tributed the stock collapse to lack of confidence in the administration. "When the market went down, it's the Kennedy stock market," the Presi-dent remarked sarcastically; "when it goes up, it's the free enterprise sys-tems."

On May 29, the day after the market's sudden collapse, Kennedy held meetings with his key economic advisers. What should be done to restore business confidence and ward off recession? The President could address the problem on national radio and television, but his advisers rejected this possi-bility as too alarming. "I am strongly against a TV speech from you now on the stock-market flap," McGeorge Bundy wrote Kennedy. "What we have at the moment is panicky selling. . . . If you take to the TV, the market will surely go on down, and you will surely get the blame."[35]

All in all, the Kennedy administration's "coercion" of the steel companies scared the business community and severely strained relations. The damage was "irreparable," wrote *Business Week*. A survey of six thousand business ex-ecutives in June 1962 found that 52 percent described the administration as "strongly anti-business," and 36 percent as "moderately anti-business." The crisis also reinforced the image of Robert Kennedy as a ruthless prosecutor riding roughshod over individual rights, using any means to an end.[36]

Shortly after the crisis Ted Sorensen warned his boss that if businessmen felt, *"however incorrectly,"* that the national climate was one hostile to them, "in which their profits are frowned upon, their labor costs increased, their views rejected and their every move subject to litigation," the consequences would severely damage the economy. Business would not risk new invest-ments, the stock market would drop further, and voters, "influenced by the articulate voice of business that dominates their Main Street and their press," would blame their market losses and the next recession on the Kennedy ad-ministration.

Little could be done to change the attitude of business, Sorensen wrote. "Businessmen have a natural dislike for the President, his party, his advisers and his program." Nonetheless, a few new approaches might alleviate the hostility. Small groups of business leaders should be invited to presidential luncheons or black-tie stag dinners. Each cabinet member should host simi-lar gatherings for businessmen affected by his operations. "Can the President, or the Attorney General, or the Special Counsel, meet quietly and individu-ally with the heads of the regulatory agencies, the anti-trust division [and] emphasize that there are times to steam ahead, to pursue, to be zealous, and there are times to be cooperative and understanding (and the latter is more appropriate now)[?]" Perhaps the SEC could tone down its investigations, Sorensen suggested. "Is the anti-trust division encouraging treble damage suits? Has the NLRB given public emphasis to those of its decisions that fa-vor management? Are there broad new areas of investigation planned that can be postponed?"[37]

Kennedy's friendly gestures toward business did increase after the steel cri-sis. He invited more businessmen to social events and for private talks at the White House. He asked for their assistance in securing a tax cut. He did not oppose a steel-price increase in 1963, and no longer emphasized the guidelines on price and wage policy. "Businessmen who are seeing the President in growing numbers report that he is a sympathetic listener," reported U.S. News and World Report on June 3, 1963. During his last year in office Kennedy dis-cussed business problems far more knowledgeably. Many businessmen still dis-agreed with his prescription for prosperity—the large budget deficit plus a large tax cut—but they conceded that he argued his case well.

By early 1963, some business circles looked more favorably on Kennedy. Criticism continued, "but it was neither as pervasive nor as harsh as it had been during the preceding eighteen months," noted Jim Heath. A financial columnist wrote, "The Kennedy Administration is cooperating and trusting U.S. business to a degree unprecedented in modern times." Indeed, Kennedy did try to cooperate with business. They needed each other.[38]

32

MONGOOSE AND THE CUBAN MISSILE CRISIS

Mongoose was poorly conceived and wretchedly executed," concluded Arthur Schlesinger, normally a champion of Robert Kennedy. "It deserved greatly to fail. It was Robert Kennedy's most conspicuous folly." Operation Mongoose was folly for President Kennedy as well.

In 1975 the Senate established the Select Committee to Study Government Operations with Respect to Intelligence Activities, commonly known as the Church committee. Relying on sworn testimony and written records, the committee investigated illegal and improper activities by the CIA and FBI. In the course of the investigation spectacular evidence emerged about Kennedy's presidency, including reports on assassination plots and covert operations to overthrow Fidel Castro.[1]

Because of Eisenhower's affinity for covert action, U.S. operatives during his administration overthrew what they considered procommunist governments in Iran (1953) and Guatemala (1954). The Church committee discovered that in 1960 the CIA intended to assassinate Patrice Lumumba, the Congolese firebrand, and planned to overthrow and murder Fidel Castro. Because Eisenhower used covert operations, Kennedy probably assumed that the secret approach was acceptable presidential conduct. Unlike his traumatic public failure at the Bay of Pigs, covert action permitted Kennedy to act without being held accountable. If covert action failed against Castro, nobody would know, and it wouldn't hurt him politically. Neither Congress, the public, nor the media could fault the President.

Fidel Castro had lost America's goodwill with tirades against U.S. imperialism and his execution of several thousand dissidents. Historian Robert Weisbrot observed, "It was his hard left turns—appointing Marxists like his brother Raul to key government posts, seizing U.S. businesses with scant compensation, and inviting Moscow to offset Cuba's dependence on its giant neighbor to the north—that magnified his menace to Americans intent on stopping the Red Tide from poisoning the Western Hemisphere."

Many U.S. officials assumed that most Cubans didn't support the tyrannical Castro regime and would revolt if given the opportunity. Alarmingly, Castro set up training facilities for revolutionaries and welcomed Latin American Communists to Cuba to train for revolutionary activity in their own countries. Castro's Cuba symbolized Khrushchev's boast that communism was successfully on the march.

Overthrowing Castro was also a very personal matter for the Kennedys. Having absorbed their father's admonitions, the two brothers competed fiercely and detested losing. "Both Jack and Bobby were deeply ashamed after the Bay of Pigs, and they became quite obsessed with the problem of Cuba," explained Ray Cline, deputy director of intelligence at the CIA. "They were a couple of Irishmen who felt they had muffed it, and they vented their wrath on Castro for the next two years."[2]

After the Bay of Pigs, President Kennedy established a secret committee—the Special Group—to bring order and discipline to decision making in intelligence matters. Subsequently, he authorized two additional powerful secret committees: the Special Group (CI), which focused on counterinsurgency, and the Special Group Augmented (SGA), which planned specifically to subvert Castro's rule in Cuba.

The SGA had a staff and a permanent membership that included its chairman, General Maxwell Taylor; Robert Kennedy; CIA director John McCone; McGeorge Bundy; U. Alexis Johnson of the Department of State; Roswell Gilpatric of the Department of Defense; and the chairman of the Joint Chiefs, General Lyman Lemnitzer. The SGA acted like "a circuit breaker," said the CIA's Richard Helms, so that "things did not explode in the President's face . . . [and so] that he was not held responsible for them."

Robert Kennedy played an active role in all three committees. So did General Taylor, who recalled that the groups met consecutively each Thursday from 2:00 P.M. to about 6:00 P.M. To prepare the agenda and follow-up actions resulting from the three committees, Taylor estimated that he devoted two days each week to the meetings.[3]

In November 1961, General Edward Lansdale, the CIA's deputy director for plans, was appointed to coordinate the SGA's activities. A counterinsurgency expert with experience in both the Philippines and Vietnam, Lansdale hoped to overthrow Castro by October 1962. The SGA designated its secret war on Castro Operation Mongoose, named for the ferret-sized mammal known for its ability to kill rats and other small animals. U.S. officials considered Castro a rat.

At the weekly meetings Robert Kennedy was the dynamic force, displaying, in the words of Evan Thomas, "his scorn for the bureaucracy, his zest for covert action, his misplaced idealism and identification with the underdog, his restless insistence on action as well as his carelessness about the consequences." On January 19, 1962, while addressing the SGA, Robert Kennedy conveyed the President's desire to get rid of Castro. It was "the top priority in the U.S. government—all else is secondary," he declared. "No time, money, effort, or manpower is to be spared."[4]

Meanwhile, a major independent assessment expressed pessimism about the prospect of overthrowing Castro. In January 1962, the CIA's Board of National Estimates, operating separately from the Directorate of Plans, prepared a study entitled "The Situation and Prospects in Cuba." Castro's regime had sufficient popular support and repressive capabilities to cope with any internal threat, the report said, and "[Castro's] loss now, by assassination or by natural causes, would have an unsettling effect, but would almost certainly not prove fatal to the regime. . . . [I]ts principal surviving leaders would probably rally together in the face of a common danger."[5]

The SGA ignored the warning. The CIA quickly spent from fifty to one hundred million dollars on Mongoose. With its huge nerve center on the campus of the University of Miami, and with four hundred CIA officers, Mongoose was the agency's largest operation in the world outside its Langley, Virginia, headquarters. The officers controlled thousands of Cuban agents, purchased exotic weapons, and ran a secret fleet of ships and aircraft.

The SGA gathered intelligence data on possible Cuban targets, infiltrated the island with guerrilla teams, recruited agents, and tried to isolate Cuba economically and diplomatically. "A substantial propaganda effort was made in Latin America with movies, comic books, broadcasts, and other media to discredit Castro's brand of communism," said U. Alexis Johnson. Mongoose also arranged the sabotage of a large Cuban copper mine and blew up bridges and production plants.[6]

Still, Mongoose made meager progress. Castro was too entrenched. On August 17, 1962, Taylor conceded that Mongoose had been disappointing. The SGA "does not feel that the information obtained has been adequate to assess accurately the internal conditions," Taylor wrote the President. From what the group could gather, "we perceived no likelihood of an overthrow of the [Castro] government by internal means and without the direct use of U.S. military force."

Despite all the meetings, studies, proposals, memos, and raids, not much was accomplished. "Agents were infiltrated, raids took place, bombs went off, Cuban exiles were killed or captured, but Mongoose never seriously threatened Castro," wrote Thomas Powers, who studied the operation.

"Operation Mongoose wasn't worth a damn," concluded Robert McNamara. "All it accomplished," contended Ray Cline, "was to make Castro beholden to the U.S.S.R."[7]

Operation Mongoose had one more exceptionally controversial feature. Between 1960 and 1965 the CIA concocted eight plots to assassinate Castro. A few did not advance beyond planning and preparation; one used Mafia figures to recruit Cubans with the intention of poisoning the Cuban dictator; another planned to use a high-powered rifle; still others employed bizarre assassination devices: poison pills, poison pens, exploding exotic seashells, and deadly bacterial powders.

Political assassination has gone on for centuries. During World War II, Allen Dulles, the top agent of the OSS (the wartime predecessor of the CIA), was authorized to encourage German generals to try to kill Hitler, an effort most people would later commend. "During the Cold War, the CIA, under Dulles, made the same case for the elimination of anti-American dictators," observed Harris Wofford. "A quick killing would be more effective and more humane, CIA planners argued in the inner circles of the 'intelligence community,' than letting people suffer all the casualties of a civil war or revolution."

Few now believe that Castro's murder would have solved America's quandary over Cuba. It probably would have made him a martyr, further entrenched Communist control of the island, and aroused intense anti-American sentiment throughout Latin America.[8] Nonetheless, debate has raged for several decades about whether the Kennedys did try to murder Castro. Did President Kennedy know about the plots? Did he authorize them? What was the role of Robert Kennedy?

In August 1960, during Eisenhower's presidency, Richard Bissell, then the CIA's chief of covert action, made the astonishing decision to hire the Mafia to assassinate Castro. Later, claiming that he acted without orders from any-

one, Bissell contended that since Eisenhower wanted to get rid of Castro, organized crime, with its professional killers and its desire to resume control of
lucrative Havana gambling casinos, had the best men to do the job. Using
gangsters to murder Castro was the "ultimate cover" with "very little
chance" that anything the Mafia attempted would be traceable. Bissell
claimed he vaguely informed CIA director Allen Dulles that he had hired the
mob, and when Dulles did not object, he proceeded with his scheme.[9]

In the summer of 1960, searching for an assassin, the CIA's director of security, Colonel Sheffield Edwards, approached Robert Maheu, a former FBI
agent who had done freelance work for the CIA in the past and who had
contacts with organized crime. When Edwards offered $150,000 for Castro's
assassination, Maheu contacted the West Coast Mafia figure John Roselli,
who agreed to sign up. Roselli in turn recruited Sam Giancana, the disreputable organized-crime boss of Chicago, and Santos Trafficante, the Miami
gangster who at one time controlled the mob's gambling business in Havana.

Because of a complex, ridiculous screwup, in the course of working with
the mob the CIA got entangled in a wiretapping violation involving Giancana. Since wiretapping was a federal offense, the FBI began investigating. As
the FBI was closing in and about to expose the incredible fact that the CIA
had been working with the Mafia, including the notorious Sam Giancana,
CIA officials were trapped and mortified.[10]

On May 7, 1962, the CIA's general counsel, Lawrence Houston, had the
unenviable assignment of meeting with Attorney General Kennedy to plead
with him to drop the FBI's investigation because the CIA had contracted
with the Mafia figures to assassinate Castro. He claimed that national security
was at stake. Now Robert Kennedy was horrified. "Whatever question there
may be about his general attitude toward assassinating Castro, no one can
doubt Kennedy's deep and abiding hatred of organized crime," noted Wofford. Houston thought the Mafia assassination scheme had ended—actually
it was still ongoing—and assured the attorney general that the Mafia plot had
been called off. Kennedy only needed to respond to a completed situation.[11]

Describing the attorney general's anger, Houston later testified: "If you
have seen Mr. Kennedy's eyes get steely and his jaw set and his voice get low
and precise, you get a definite feeling of unhappiness." Kennedy told Houston, very specifically, that "if we were going to get involved with Mafia personnel again he wanted to be informed first."

Robert Kennedy hadn't expressed surprise or anger at the plot to kill
Castro, only that the killers being used were gangsters. Plotting with the
Mafia would jeopardize his goal of putting Giancana and Roselli in prison.
(Most likely Giancana never did any work for the CIA or made any attempt
to kill Castro, but only pretended to go along with the agency, hoping to
sidetrack the Justice Department's effort to put him in prison.)

In 1967 Drew Pearson and Jack Anderson revealed that the CIA may have contracted with the Mafia to murder Castro, but they mistakenly reported that Robert Kennedy took part in the planning. "I didn't start it," Robert told aides after the column appeared. "I stopped it. . . . I found out that some people were going to try an attempt on Castro's life and I turned it off."[12]

The key figure in the assassination plots was Richard Helms, chief of operations in the Directorate for Plans until February 1962, after which he succeeded Bissell as deputy director for plans. Helms testified before the Church committee that the extraordinary pressure forced on him by the Kennedy administration to overthrow Castro had led him to conclude that the CIA was acting within its authority by trying to assassinate Castro, even though assassination was never directly ordered. "I believe it was the policy at the time to get rid of Castro and if killing him was one of the things that was to be done in this connection, that was within what was expected." No member of the Kennedy administration ever told him that assassination was ruled out. He claimed he never informed the SGA or any of its members about the plots to kill Castro. Nor did he tell any officials in the White House or even his own boss, CIA director John McCone.

The Church committee asked Helms if President Kennedy had been informed of any assassination plots. Helms sidestepped the question. "I think any of us would have found it very difficult to discuss assassinations with a President of the U.S.," he testified. "We all had the feeling that we're hired out to keep these things out of the Oval Office." Nobody wanted to embarrass the President of the United States "by discussing the assassination of foreign leaders in his presence."[13]

Every major surviving member of the Kennedy administration stated under oath that he thought the assassination of Castro was improper without a direct order from the President, and that assassination was outside the range of the anti-Castro program. What's more, they were certain the President never gave such an order. Secretary of State Dean Rusk testified that he "never had any reason to believe" that "any active planning of assassination [was] underway"; Robert McNamara agreed, stating that he had "no knowledge or information about . . . plans or preparations for a possible assassination attempt." McGeorge Bundy, who worked closely with the President every day, found the notion that the two Kennedys "separately, privately encouraged, ordered, or arranged efforts at assassination totally inconsistent with what I knew of both of them."

General Maxwell Taylor insisted that he had "never heard" of an assassination attempt against Castro, and that the SGA never raised the subject of assassination. The President and the attorney general, Taylor said, "would never have gone around" the SGA to deal with Helms or other CIA officials in planning an assassination.[14]

Still, two incidents reveal that the assassination of Castro was on President Kennedy's mind. According to Senator George Smathers, in late March 1961, during a stroll on the White House grounds, President Kennedy asked him what reaction there would be throughout South America if Fidel Castro was assassinated. Smathers responded that he did not think it would be a good idea because no matter who did it or how it was done, the United States would be blamed throughout Central and South America. "I disapproved of it, and [Kennedy] completely disapproved of the idea," Smathers recalled, adding, "He was just throwing out a barrage of questions—he was certain it could be accomplished. . . . But the question was whether or not it would accomplish that which he wanted it to, whether or not the reaction throughout South America would be good or bad."[15]

Then on November 9, 1961, the President discussed the Cuban situation in the Oval Office with journalist Tad Szulc of *The New York Times*. An expert on Cuba, Szulc had interviewed Castro several times after the Bay of Pigs. The President asked Szulc, "What would you think if I ordered Castro to be assassinated?" Szulc told the President it wouldn't work, and that the United States should not engage in such an action. Kennedy replied that he and his brother agreed. Szulc's notes of the meeting, made the same day, read:

> JFK then said he was testing me, that he felt the same way—he added "I'm glad you feel the same way"—because indeed U.S. morally must not be part [sic] to assassinations.
>
> JFK said he raised question because he was under terrific pressure from advisers (think he said intelligence people, but not positive) to okay a Castro murder, sed [sic] he was resisting pressures.

Was the President merely sending up a trial balloon with Szulc to see how the media would react? Szulc's notation that the President was being pressured puzzled the Church committee. Who was pressuring him? Everyone else questioned by the committee denied ever discussing assassination with the President, let alone having pressured him to consider it.

Richard Goodwin, the only other person present during Kennedy's discussion with Szulc, recalled the President saying, "Well, that's the kind of thing I'm never going to do." Several days later, when Goodwin referred to the previous discussion with Szulc, President Kennedy responded, "We can't get into that kind of thing, or we would all be targets."[16]

Defenders of both Kennedys deny that their heroes authorized assassination plots. With both Smathers and Szulc, President Kennedy clearly rejected assassination on practical and moral grounds. The Church committee never discovered a written order to kill Castro; nor did any of the testifying witnesses admit to having received such an order.

The Kennedys' most zealous defender, historian Arthur Schlesinger Jr., makes a strong case that neither Kennedy was aware of what the plotters were doing. The Kennedys were too noble and, particularly Robert, too Catholic to plot murder. "The record shows that the only assassination plot disclosed to Robert Kennedy involved Sam Giancana—and that Kennedy did his best thereafter to put Giancana behind bars."

The historian cited the testimony of all the people who worked closely with the President—all agreeing they never heard of assassination plots. There is no evidence that any CIA official ever mentioned assassination to President Kennedy; nor were the plots ever submitted to the SGA. "Rusk, McNamara, Bundy, Taylor, Gilpatric, Goodwin, Rostow, all testified under oath that they had never heard of it (nor had Kenneth O'Donnell, nor, for that matter, had I)."

No one in the Kennedy administration told Helms to kill Castro, Schlesinger insisted. Yet because no one ever specifically ruled it out, the CIA believed it could work toward Castro's overthrow as it thought best. "It appears that the CIA regarded whatever authorization it thought it had acquired in 1960 as permanent, not requiring review and reconfirmation by new presidents or, even more astonishingly, by new CIA directors. For neither Bissell nor Helms even told John McCone what his own Agency was up to."[17]

In the final analysis, the defense of the Kennedys is not convincing. That there was no paper trail did not necessarily mean that the two brothers were not involved. As James Hilty has observed, covert action could have been initiated by a "nod of the head or with vague verbal instructions that later could be refuted under the doctrine of plausible deniability."

If President Kennedy did not know about the CIA's murder plots, then he was a grossly negligent administrator, blind to what his subordinates were doing in his name. Shortly after Lyndon Johnson entered office in 1963, he discovered what Kennedy supporters claimed the two Kennedys never knew: that the CIA was directing assassination plots. Johnson told the writer Leo Janos that he had discovered in late November 1963 that the CIA was "operating a damned Murder, Inc. in the Caribbean." "Evidently Johnson was more adept at securing intelligence information from the CIA than Kennedy was," one pundit commented sarcastically.

"The available evidence leans heavily toward a finding that the Kennedys did, in fact, authorize the CIA to make an attempt on Castro's life," contended Thomas Powers. That evidence is circumstantial. Powers and others cite the conversations the President had with Smathers and Szulc. "Why would [the President] discuss the possibility of the assassination of Castro with two friends if such a possibility did not in fact exist?" noted one critic. Also, the briefing Robert Kennedy received from Lawrence Houston elicited only a very narrow response from the attorney general. Using the Mafia was wrong, but the attorney general didn't rule out other assassination plots.[18]

In his oral history for the Kennedy Library, Robert Kennedy disavowed any involvement with plots to kill Castro, but his perfunctory denial is unconvincing.

Did he know of any attempt to assassinate Castro?

"No," responded the attorney general.

None tried?

"No."

Contemplated?

"No."[19]

If Helms lied before the Church committee, the entire controversy becomes clear. Robert Kennedy met secretly with Helms and verbally ordered him to try to assassinate Castro, and both of them maintained the secret. Helms had a record of lying. In 1973, during testimony before the Senate Foreign Relations Committee, Helms swore under oath that the CIA had neither tried to overthrow the government of Chile's Marxist President Salvador Allende nor funneled money to political enemies of Allende. Later, Senate investigators discovered that the CIA had run a secret operation in Chile that gave more than eight million dollars to Allende's opponents. Allende died during a military coup in 1973.

"I had found myself in a position of conflict," Helms explained to a federal judge during his trial for perjury. "I had sworn my oath to protect certain secrets. . . . I didn't want to lie. I didn't want to mislead the Senate. I was simply trying to find my way through a difficult situation in which I found myself." The judge found Helms guilty of two misdemeanor charges of perjury.

Helms probably lied to the Church committee as well, finding himself in a "position of conflict," trying to find his way through "a difficult situation." The pressure on Helms, particularly from Robert Kennedy, had been intense. Several times Helms had said privately, "My God, these Kennedys keep the pressure on about Castro." It was "white heat." Perhaps the "pressure" President Kennedy felt about approving the assassination plots came from his own brother, the attorney general.[20]

Helms's testimony before the Church committee was filled with evasions and lapses of memory. He "did not recall" or "doubted" or had "no knowledge" or "could not remember." He sounded "like an amnesia victim," Thomas Powers concluded. "When investigators nailed him with a piece of paper, he answered as he could. All the rest he had forgotten. It is said men begin life with a *tabula rasa;* Helms ended it that way."

During the Church committee's investigation there was talk of prosecution. "Helms was asked about his role in murder plots, burglaries, wiretaps, secret medical experiments, and other allegedly illegal acts," noted Powers. "In keeping quiet, Helms was protecting himself." He knew there was not a single written document, not a single piece of paper, that anyone could cite that could link him with the Kennedys and the assassination plots.

General Maxwell Taylor was probably wrong to assume that the President and the attorney general would never have gone around the SGA to deal with Helms. Robert Kennedy did go around the SGA, and kept the secret from all of the President's advisers and aides. Even Helms's boss, CIA director John McCone, wasn't told, primarily because he was a devout Roman Catholic, worried about his immortal soul, and personally opposed to assassination.[21]

If we assume that Robert Kennedy directed the assassination plans, it is certain he discussed them with the President. The brothers were so close and the matter was too important. President Kennedy must have authorized the plots.

Unaware of Operation Mongoose, news stories constantly harped on the Kennedy administration's "weakness" in handling Castro. Communists were "getting away with murder" in Cuba while the United States did nothing. "Castro's arrogance and resilience, the failure at the Bay of Pigs, and a growing Soviet presence all mocked the administration's promise to show a new vigor in world affairs," observed historian Weisbrot. Republican National Chairman William Miller charged that the President's "irresolution" about Cuba would be the dominant issue in the November elections in 1962.

By late summer 1962, growing Soviet arms shipments to Cuba led several Republicans to expand their attacks on the administration. Beginning on August 31, New York's Republican senator Kenneth Keating repeatedly warned that the Soviets were placing offensive missiles in Cuba. Keating referred to the lessons of Munich:

> Remember, too, what happened before the outbreak of the Second World War. Had Hitler been stopped decisively when he marched into the Rhineland, into Austria, or even when he went into Czechoslovakia, the Second World War would probably never have occurred. . . . If we do not act decisively in Cuba, we will face more—not less—trouble in Berlin and elsewhere in the world.[22]

Kennedy's critics accused the Soviets of violating the Monroe Doctrine, used by the United States for over a hundred years to bar European nations from interfering in the Western Hemisphere. *Newsweek* and *U.S. News and World Report* indicted Kennedy for not upholding the doctrine.

The President and his advisers worried. On September 13, in preparation for Kennedy's news conference, Sorensen informed the President that "the Congressional head of steam [about Cuba] is the most serious that we have had. . . . The immediate hazard is that the Administration may appear to be weak and indecisive." Three weeks later Louis Harris, the President's pollster and adviser, warned Kennedy that tension was peaking on the Cuban issue. "In Michigan, within the past week, a majority of 82–18 percent wanted a blockade on Cuba, although a majority of 68–32 percent oppose going to war there."[23]

Few U.S. officials believed that Khrushchev would ever place offensive nuclear weapons in Cuba. Such a bold move would be too risky; besides, the Soviets had never placed offensive missiles outside their country. In fact, the Soviets planned to deploy in Cuba thirty-six SS-4 medium-range ballistic missiles (MRBMs) and twenty-four SS-5 intermediate-range ballistic missiles (IRBMs). The blast from a single SS-4 was equivalent to one million tons of TNT. (By comparison, the bomb that leveled Hiroshima in 1945 equaled only fourteen thousand tons of TNT.) Cuba also bristled with forty-two thousand Soviet troops—far more than U.S. intelligence estimated—forty MiG-21 planes, surface-to-air missiles, six IL-28 bombers, twelve Luna missiles, and eighty cruise missiles capable of short-range nuclear strikes.[24]

Why had Khrushchev acted so rashly? Protecting Cuba was one reason. Soviet assistance allowed Cuba to survive "right in front of the open jaws of predatory American imperialism," he proudly claimed afterward. Communist Cuba was terrific propaganda for the Soviets and might encourage other Latin American countries to follow the country's example.

U.S. military maneuvers and covert operations convinced the Soviets and the Cubans that the United States intended to invade the island. Long after the crisis, Robert McNamara conceded, "If I had been a Cuban leader at that time, I might well have concluded that there was a great risk of U.S. invasion."

Inserting offensive missiles into Cuba was also a shortcut to gaining nuclear parity with the United States. Anatoly Dobrynin, the Soviet ambassador in Washington, thought that Khrushchev had a "sincere" desire to defend Cuba, but that the move was primarily "part of a broader geopolitical strategy to achieve greater parity with the United States that would be useful not only in the dispute over Berlin but in negotiations on other issues."

Khrushchev confidently believed that the installation of the missiles could be kept secret until they became fully operational following the November off-year elections. Once they were deployed, the burden of changing the status quo would fall on Kennedy. "If we installed the missiles secretly and then if the United States discovered the missiles were there after they were already poised and ready to strike, the Americans would think twice before trying to liquidate our installations by military means," Khrushchev stated in his memoirs.[25]

At 8:30 P.M. on Monday, October 15, 1962, McGeorge Bundy was notified that a U-2 reconnaissance aircraft had discovered medium-range ballistic missiles in Cuba. They were offensive missiles, the kind the Soviets had promised never to install there. Bundy waited until the following morning to notify the President because blowups and other technical data would not be ready before morning. He also feared that assembling high officials for a meeting that Monday evening would alert the media about the secret discovery. Moreover, Bundy later explained to the President, "I had heard that you were tired" from strenuous campaigning. "So I decided that a quiet evening and a night of sleep were the best preparation you could have in the light of what would face you in the next days."

"Well, what are we going to do?" the President responded to Bundy's news the next morning. "We have to do something." Kennedy's initial reaction was to "take them out" with an air strike. "What we have to decide right now is what we are going to do." He ordered a meeting as soon as key officials could be brought together.[26]

Instead of assembling the National Security Council or the cabinet, Kennedy gathered around him those advisers and experts whose judgment he trusted. The group, subsequently labeled the Executive Committee of the National Security Council (ExComm), consisted of Dean Rusk, Ted Sorensen, Robert Kennedy, McGeorge Bundy, Robert McNamara, Douglas Dillon, Maxwell Taylor, John McCone, Undersecretary of State George Ball, Deputy Undersecretary of State U. Alexis Johnson, Assistant Secretary of State for Latin American Affairs Edward Martin, Ambassador Llewellyn Thompson, Deputy Secretary of Defense Roswell Gilpatric, and Assistant Secretary of Defense Paul Nitze. A few others, including Lyndon Johnson and Adlai Stevenson, occasionally attended. ExComm needed to operate under extreme time constraints. "We had to force the issue before any missiles were fully installed or we risked their being fired," George Ball pointed out.

The Soviet action infuriated ExComm partly because it was surreptitious and deceitful. The Soviets had repeatedly stated that they had no plans to place offensive weapons in Cuba. The United States had openly installed its missiles in Turkey. "The intensity of the American reaction in October was very largely a function of the deception," Bundy later said.[27]

No U.S. President could politically survive if he allowed the Soviet Union to brazenly enter the Western Hemisphere and establish missile bases ninety miles off the U.S. coast. It would have undermined NATO's confidence in the will and determination of the United States and disturbed all the nations in North and South America.

During the Cuban missile crisis only Robert Kennedy knew that the President was secretly taping the discussions. (Such taping was legal at the time.) In the summer of 1962, ostensibly to preserve records of his administration for the memoir he would write after he left the presidency, Kennedy installed the taping system. Concealed microphones were placed in unused light fixtures in the Cabinet Room; another was hidden in the kneehole of the President's desk in the Oval Office. The microphones transmitted to a reel-to-reel tape recorder in the basement of the White House. The President had only to flip a switch to activate the tapes. The ExComm deliberations displayed remarkable candor partly because the participants, except for the two Kennedys, didn't know they were being taped most of the time.[28]

The ominous crisis could escalate to nuclear war. Dismayed by Khrushchev's decision, Kennedy said on October 16, the first day of the Ex-Comm meetings: "He's initiated the danger, really, hasn't he? He's the one that's playing at God, not us." Later the same evening he remarked, "I don't think there's any record of the Soviets ever making this direct a challenge ever, really, since the Berlin blockade" of 1948–1949.

After consulting with the Joint Chiefs, at the evening meeting McNamara judged that even a limited air attack on Cuba would need to be formidable—not just twenty sorties or fifty sorties or one hundred sorties, but probably several hundred sorties. "And to move from that into the more extensive air attacks against the MiGs, against the airfields, against the potential nuclear storage sites, against the radar installations, against the SAM sites, means . . . possibly 700 to 1,000 sorties per day for 5 days." An invasion following the air attack meant using up to 150,000 men.[29]

Still obsessed with Castro, RFK impulsively searched for a pretext to invade the island. Perhaps the United States could fabricate a Cuban attack on the Guantánamo Bay naval base or "sink the *Maine* again or something." He calmed down after it became obvious that the overriding problem was not Castro or Khrushchev, but the danger of slipping into a nuclear confrontation with the Soviet Union.

It took a day's reflection before President Kennedy and the ExComm members got over their initial shock and anger. "On the first day of deliberations, most advisers felt it urgent to bomb the missile sites and perhaps other Cuban military bases, even to invade the island, before the nuclear missiles could become operational," observed Weisbrot. "After that, they feared, an attack would risk retaliation by surviving missiles against American cities." Kennedy later expressed relief that there had been time to reconsider. "If we had had to act in the first twenty-four hours," he said, "I don't think . . . we would have chosen as prudently as we finally did."[30]

Despite his burden, on Wednesday, October 17, the President maintained a full schedule while ExComm members pondered options. Early in the afternoon, while driving to a luncheon, he asked Dave Powers to accompany him to St. Matthew's Cathedral. "We're going in here to say a prayer," the President said. Powers, who knew nothing about the missiles in Cuba, was surprised, but stopped for a visit with the President at the almost empty cathedral.

On Thursday morning, October 18, U.S. intelligence analysts, having studied photos from recent U-2 flights over Cuba, reported evidence of IRBM sites in addition to the MRBM sites discovered earlier. IRBMs had more than twice the range and yield as MRBMs, and could devastate the entire United States except the Pacific Northwest.

At Thursday's meeting President Kennedy discussed the problem of the U.S. missiles in Turkey. In late 1957 the Eisenhower administration had publicly offered to deploy intermediate-range Jupiter missiles in Turkey, a U.S. ally; installation began in 1961. In the fall of 1962, with the installation completed, the United States turned them over to the Turks. Inaccurate, vulnerable, and outdated, the liquid-fueled Jupiters were useful only for a first nuclear strike, and were therefore provocative. Several Turkish governments had wanted the Jupiters. "They added prestige, emphasized Turkey's key role in NATO, and exaggerated the warmth of relations with a great power, the United States," observed historian Barton Bernstein. (The United States also had missiles in Italy, and they were mentioned during ExComm deliberations, but played a smaller role during the October crisis.) The President judged that the only negotiating ploy the United States could offer would be to withdraw the Jupiters from Turkey, in return for the Soviets withdrawing their missiles from Cuba.[31]

By October 18 ExComm had focused on two major options: an air strike coupled with a possible invasion, or a blockade. The hard-liners thought it was imperative to destroy the missiles immediately. If the United States warned Cuba of an attack, Castro would disperse or hide the missiles. But the air-strike option raised several serious difficulties. A "surgical" strike was an illusion. With so many targets, massive bombardment would be needed to demolish them all. Even then there was no assurance that all the missiles and other targets could be destroyed or that some of the missiles would not fire first, landing devastatingly on American soil. Most of ExComm's air-strike advocates agreed that their route would ultimately end in an invasion. But an invasion, with all its consequences, the President would not approve.

The problem of advance warning proved impossible to resolve. As the attorney general passionately phrased it, a surprise attack would be "a Pearl Harbor in reverse" and would "blacken the name of the United States in the pages of history" as the great power who ravaged a tiny neighbor.

Furthermore, the air strike would undoubtedly kill Russians as well as Cubans, and therefore risked Soviet military retaliation. Sorensen pointed out that "any Cuban missiles operational by the time of our strike might be ordered by Khrushchev to fire their nuclear salvos into the United States before they were wiped out—or, we speculated, the local Soviet commander, under attack, might order the missiles fired on the assumption that war was on."

At first the blockade option received little support; it appeared irrelevant to getting the offensive missiles out of Cuba. And the blockade alternative had drawbacks. "If Soviet ships ignored it," said Sorensen, "U.S. forces would have to fire the first shot, provoking Soviet action elsewhere." Perhaps the Soviets would move against Berlin. In addition, the United States could not be certain that the blockade option was even possible. Without getting a two-thirds vote in the Organization of American States (OAS)—which appeared doubtful—many countries might regard it as illegal, a violation of the UN Charter and international law. Finally, the blockade was likely to be a prolonged and agonizing approach, allowing Soviet missiles to become operational.

But despite the disadvantages, the blockade route gained adherents because the alternative seemed worse. Unlike the air strike, it was a limited, low-key military operation. Khrushchev could avoid a direct military clash by simply keeping his ships away. "It could at least be initiated without a shot being fired or a single Soviet or Cuban citizen being killed," Sorensen pointed out. If a naval engagement became necessary, having the confrontation just off U.S. shores was a major advantage. "To avoid a military defeat Khrushchev might well turn his ships back, causing U.S. allies to have increased confidence in our credibility and Cuba's Communists to feel they were being abandoned."

The blockade would signal Khrushchev that the United States was adamant; yet it wouldn't be sudden or humiliating and would probably avoid casualties. Beginning at the lowest level of action was least likely to alienate U.S. allies. What's more, the blockade only applied to offensive weapons, not defensive ones or food and supplies that would affect innocent Cubans. "This delineation helped relate the blockade route more closely to the specific problem of missiles and made the punishment more nearly fit the crime."[32]

"I think it's very highly doubtful that the Russians would resist a blockade against military weapons," said Llewellyn Thompson in an influential statement on October 18, "particularly offensive ones, if that's the way we pitched it before the world."

Blockade supporters also pointed out that their course did not exclude subsequent options. The United States could still expand the contraband list, launch an air strike, or invade if the blockade failed. By Thursday, October 18, the President secretly favored the blockade option.[33]

Early in the evening of October 18, President Kennedy hosted a regularly scheduled meeting with Andrey Gromyko. Unaware that Kennedy knew about the offensive missiles in Cuba, the Soviet foreign minister stressed the need to settle the Berlin issue. Although the Soviets would not make any threatening move before the U.S. elections, they intended to take action later in November. The Western military presence in Berlin was a "rotten tooth which must be pulled out." As for Cuba, Soviet specialists were only training Cubans in defensive armaments which posed no threat to the United States.

Silently marveling at Gromyko's hollow assurances, Kennedy restated U.S. policy toward the Soviet presence in Cuba, including the warning against installing offensive missiles. Following Gromyko's departure, Kennedy welcomed Bundy and Robert Lovett, the defense secretary during the Truman administration. Lovett recalled the discussion: "[Kennedy] grinned and said, 'I ought to [tell] you about Gromyko, who, in this very room not over 10 minutes ago, told more barefaced lies than I have ever heard in so short a time. . . . I had the low-level pictures in the center drawer of my desk, and it was an enormous temptation to show them to him.' "[34]

Late in the evening Kennedy entered the Oval Office to tape-record his thoughts. (The most recent ExComm meeting had not been recorded.) "During the course of the day," he dictated, "opinions had obviously switched from the advantages of a first strike on the missile sites and on Cuban aviation to a blockade." He continued:

> Everyone else felt that for us to fail to respond would throw into question our willingness to respond over Berlin, [and] would divide our allies and our country. [They felt] that we would be faced with a crunch over Berlin in 2 or 3 months and that by that time the Soviets would have a large missile arsenal in the Western Hemisphere which would weaken our whole position in this hemisphere and . . . face us with the same problems we're going to have in Berlin anyway.
>
> The consensus was that we should go ahead with the blockade beginning on Sunday night. Originally we should begin by blockading Soviets against the shipment of additional offensive capacity, [and] that we could tighten the blockade as the situation requires. . . .
>
> It was determined that I should go ahead with my speeches so that we don't take the cover off this, and come back Saturday night [October 20].

Then he shut off the tape recorder.[35]

Robert Kennedy prodded, questioned, and kept the discussions specific and moving ahead. Initially he mostly listened. He spoke more often after the lines were drawn. He effectively critiqued the air-strike option. Skeptical about precision bombing and surgical air operations, he steered the group toward a blockade. "Throughout the thirteen days, he was an effective prod and synthesizer who, for the most part, showed instinctive good judgment about how hard to push the Soviets and when to ease up," Evan Thomas observed. "Robert Kennedy surprised me," George Ball recalled. "Until then I had not had much respect for his judgment; he had seemed to me . . . immature, far too emotional, and inclined to see everything in absolute terms with too little sensitivity to nuance and qualification. But during the Cuban missile affair he was a stabilizing influence. Aware of the gravity of the situation, he was a force for caution and good sense."[36]

Articulate, logical, and forceful, Robert McNamara also consistently urged the blockade alternative and tended to draw hard-line ExComm members away from extreme solutions. "McNamara unintentionally silenced less articulate men," Sorensen concluded.[37]

Dean Rusk did not assume a leadership role, remaining reticent. Often he was absent. At first he favored an air strike; then he endorsed negotiation, a role for the United Nations, and a peaceful resolution of the crisis. Since he seldom spoke, several members didn't know where he stood.

The State Department's Soviet expert, Llewellyn Thompson, proved to be one of the most perceptive members of ExComm. The former ambassador to Moscow, he understood Khrushchev better than anyone in ExComm, quickly appraised Soviet moves, and skillfully recommended U.S. countermoves.[38]

President Kennedy received extreme advice from the Joint Chiefs of Staff, who kept clamoring for large-scale air strikes without warning and an invasion to destroy any surviving missiles. The generals chafed at what they thought was irresolution on the part of the commander in chief. On October 19, the President met with them and urged them to ponder the risks of attacking the missiles. "We would be regarded as the trigger-happy Americans who lost Berlin," he said. "We would have no support among our allies." If the Soviets countered by taking West Berlin, Kennedy was left with only one alternative: to fire nuclear weapons—"which is a hell of an alternative"— and begin a nuclear exchange.

General Curtis LeMay responded that the United States should simply tell the Soviets that if they moved against Berlin, "we're going to fight." As for Cuba, "This blockade and political action, I see leading into war. I don't see any other solution. It will lead right into war. This is almost as bad as the appeasement at Munich. . . . I just don't see any other solution except direct military intervention *right now*."

Kennedy rebuffed LeMay's urgings. A blockade was not a weak response, and the Joint Chiefs' alternative was "unsatisfactory." The President was "a bit disgusted" after meeting with the Joint Chiefs, Sorensen recalled.[39]

President Kennedy knew he had to act soon to stay ahead of major newspapers, which might soon get wind of an impending crisis. Resuming his regular schedule, he was in Chicago on Saturday morning, October 20. While Pierre Salinger was briefing newsmen, outlining Kennedy's schedule for the day, Kennedy summoned him to the President's suite. Unshaven, still in his pajamas, Kennedy told his press secretary, "I have a temperature and a cold." Salinger should tell the media that the President was returning to Washington on the advice of his doctor. Salinger called the reporters back from their buses and read them the "medical bulletin." None of the newsmen raised questions.

On the flight back to Washington Salinger remarked to the President that he didn't look sick. Kennedy responded, "That's true; you'll find out why I'm going back to Washington when we get there, and when you do, grab your balls!"

Before leaving Chicago, the President phoned Jackie and requested she return to the White House with Caroline and John. In case of a sudden emergency he wanted his family nearby.[40]

Early in the crisis, George Ball had argued that a great power should never violate its own tradition or it would lose its moral authority in the world. A surprise air strike by the United States on Cuba would undermine that moral authority. Robert Kennedy restated Ball's argument more powerfully to ExComm on October 20. A surprise air strike on Cuba was analogous to the Japanese sneak attack on Pearl Harbor. "My brother is not going to be the Tojo of the 1960s." Thousands of Cubans and Russians would die. It was a telling argument, thought Ball, "and I thought at the time that it altered the thinking of several of my colleagues."

Indeed, it did. "The way Bob Kennedy spoke was totally convincing to me," said Douglas Dillon. "I knew then that we should not undertake a strike without warning." "Bobby Kennedy's good sense and his moral character were perhaps decisive," added Alexis Johnson.

ExComm finalized the decision. It would be a blockade, now renamed a "quarantine" to overcome legal objections. During his evening swim in the pool with Dave Powers, the President talked about the danger of a nuclear war in almost the same words he used after the Vienna summit. "Dave, if we were only thinking of ourselves, it would be easy, but I keep thinking about the children whose lives would be wiped out."

Kennedy sent emissaries to explain the U.S. action to U.S. allies. Before delivering his speech to the nation on Monday evening, October 22, the President met with congressional leaders. Senator William Fulbright, an opponent of the Bay of Pigs invasion, surprisingly favored an invasion of Cuba rather than a blockade. "I think a blockade is the worst of the alternatives," he said, "because if you're confronted with a Russian ship, you are actually confronting Russia. This way, if you have the invasion against Cuba, this is not actually an affront to Russia. . . . I'm in favor, on the basis of this information, of an invasion, and an all-out one, and as quickly as possible."

Kennedy's prudence annoyed Richard Russell, the crusty, influential Democratic senator from Georgia and chair of the Armed Services Committee. A blockade signaled weakness. War with the Soviets would come someday. Would it ever be under more auspicious circumstances?

"If they want this job, fuck 'em," a frustrated Kennedy said after wrangling with his former Senate colleagues. "They can have it. It's no great joy to me."[41]

That Monday evening he addressed the American people on national television. Within the past week, he announced, "unmistakable evidence has established the fact that a series of offensive missile sites is now in preparation on that imprisoned island. The purpose of these bases can be none other than to provide a nuclear strike capability against the Western Hemisphere." The secret, sudden, and extraordinary buildup "is a deliberately provocative and unjustified change in the status quo which cannot be accepted by this country, if our courage and our commitments are ever to be trusted again by either friend or foe."

He announced a strict quarantine on all offensive military equipment under shipment to Cuba. In case the Soviet Union misunderstood, he added a clarification: "It shall be the policy of this nation to regard any nuclear missile launched from Cuba against any nation in the Western Hemisphere as an attack by the Soviet Union on the United States, requiring a full retaliatory response upon the Soviet Union."

"My fellow citizens," he concluded,

> let no one doubt that this is a difficult and dangerous effort on which we have set out. No one can foresee precisely what course it will take or what costs or casualties will be incurred. Many months of sacrifice and self-discipline lie ahead—months in which both our patience and our will will be tested—months in which many threats and denunciations will keep us aware of our dangers. But the greatest danger of all would be to do nothing.[42]

The quarantine would go into effect on Wednesday, October 24. After Kennedy's speech a Gallup poll indicated that 84 percent of Americans supported the blockade and only 4 percent opposed it. Thousands of telegrams flooded the White House, running twelve to one in the President's favor.

The media's outpouring of faith was exceptional. Kennedy had acted "magnificently," "with wisdom, with courage and with reason," "wisely and unemotionally," in a manner "properly tough and forthright." Kennedy's "resolve" could prove "one of the decisive moments of the twentieth century," wrote *Time*.[43]

The day after the speech Americans stocked up on food, gasoline, and other supplies. "In homes and in bars, television watchers saw footage of airplanes taking off and troop trains moving tanks and soldiers," wrote historians Ernest May and Philip Zelikow. Although tension was pervasive, there was no panic.

In a surprising and gratifying decision, on October 23, the Organization of American States condemned the missiles in Cuba as a threat to the peace and insisted on their removal. The unanimous vote was far better than Washington had expected.

Still, the crisis seemed ominous. "It looks really mean, doesn't it?" the President said to his brother on the evening of October 23. "But, on the other hand, there wasn't any other choice."

"There isn't any [other] choice," Robert Kennedy responded. "You would have been impeached."

The President agreed. "I think I would have been impeached."[44]

After a private dinner the President discussed the crisis with David Ormsby-Gore, who suggested that Kennedy change the quarantine line from eight hundred miles to five hundred miles off the Cuban coast, giving Soviet ships more time to react, and more time for Khrushchev to ponder. Kennedy immediately phoned McNamara, who made the change. The British ambassador also realized the propaganda value of Kennedy immediately releasing to the media the U.S. photographs of the missile installations in Cuba. "This was done, with telling effect," said one observer.[45]

President Kennedy insisted on keeping track of every detail. Each morning he reviewed the location of every ship approaching the quarantine line and the instructions given to U.S. commanders. "It is not the first step or the second step that concerns me," he said in the midst of the crisis. "It's the fourth or fifth and the fact that there will be nobody left to take the sixth."

The President's worst nightmare was that the Soviets might decide that since total war was inevitable, they should launch a preemptive nuclear strike against the United States. He occasionally lightened the atmosphere. "I hope you realize," he said to Sorensen, "that there's not enough room for everybody in the White House bomb shelter."

The quarantine went into effect at 10:00 A.M. on October 24. American ICBMs and nuclear submarines, and almost every available bomber—about 1,400—were on alert. "Scores of bombers, each loaded with several nuclear weapons and carrying folders for preassigned targets in the Soviet Union, were kept continuously in the air around the clock, with shifts, refueled by aerial tankers, taking turns hovering over northern Canada, Greenland, and the Mediterranean Sea," observed May and Zelikow.[46]

During an ExComm meeting, as McNamara explained the dangerous procedure of forcing a Soviet submarine to the surface, Robert Kennedy, sitting across from the President, scribbled notes:

The danger and concern that we all felt hung like a cloud over us all. . . . These few minutes were the time of greatest worry by the President. His hand went up to his face and covered his mouth and he closed his fist. His eyes were tense, almost gray, and we just stared at each other across the table. Was the world on the brink of a holocaust and had we done something wrong?. . . . I felt we were on the edge of a precipice and it was as if there were no way off.

As Kennedy had hoped, on October 25 Khrushchev ordered Soviet missile-carrying ships to turn back. So far, the quarantine had not sparked any shooting. But the major problem remained: How to get the Soviet nuclear missiles out of Cuba? Kennedy resumed contingency plans for an air strike and an invasion.

At the UN Adlai Stevenson famously and dramatically defended the U.S. position before the Security Council. He challenged the Soviet ambassador, Valerian Zorin, to state clearly whether Soviet missiles were in Cuba. "Yes or no—don't wait for the translation—yes or no!" Stevenson would have to wait for his answer, said Zorin. "I am prepared to wait for my answer until hell freezes over," Stevenson retorted. Watching the confrontation on television, Kennedy remarked, "Terrific."[47]

On Friday evening, October 26, there arrived at the White House a long, confidential letter from the Soviet premier, appearing to have Khrushchev's handwritten notations on it, indicating he had personally written it. The letter suggested a deal: a pledge by the United States not to invade Cuba in exchange for the Soviet withdrawal of their missiles from Cuba.

The letter delighted ExComm. A resolution of the crisis seemed near. That hope evaporated on Saturday morning, and events seemed to spin out of control. Shortly after ExComm met at 10:00 A.M., news arrived that a second letter from Khrushchev was being broadcast on Radio Moscow. Different in tone and substance from the personal message of the previous night, it seemed to have been written by a committee.[48]

In addition to the no-invasion pledge, it proposed a missile swap: The United States would take its Jupiter missiles out of Turkey; in return, the Soviets would withdraw their missiles from Cuba. ExComm members were outraged. The day before, Khrushchev had suggested only an American pledge not to invade Cuba. Now the Soviets demanded a second condition.

ExComm's anxiety increased after news that a Soviet ship was heading for Cuba, and that feverish work on the missile sites continued. Almost all the Soviet MRBMs were ready to fire. Most alarming, a Soviet SAM in Cuba had shot down a U-2 reconnaissance plane, killing the U.S. pilot, the first death of the crisis. Earlier ExComm had firmly agreed that if a U-2 was shot down, the U.S. would send planes to destroy the SAM site. If another U-2 was attacked, the U.S. would take out all the SAM sites. "The more blood-thirsty members of the ExComm were insisting that we act Sunday morning," recalled George Ball. But the President refused to panic. To avoid escalation, he postponed the decision to destroy the SAM site; he also ordered the Jupiters in Turkey defused.[49]

In the early afternoon ExComm learned that a U-2 plane, conducting atmospheric tests near the North Pole, was missing near Alaska. Additional reports indicated that the plane had strayed off course into Soviet airspace and Soviet MiGs were attempting to intercept it. American fighter planes in Alaska scrambled to protect the U-2 when it reentered U.S. airspace, which it soon did. A close call.

The plans for an air strike and an invasion, perhaps as early as Monday, October 29, called for an air attack of 1,080 sorties on the first day. An invasion force of 180,000 troops stood ready.[50]

Meeting continuously all day on Saturday, ExComm members thought nuclear war a distinct possibility. Sorensen recalled the fear: "If the Soviet ship continued coming, if the SAMs continued firing, if the missile crews continued working, and if Khrushchev continued insisting on concessions with a gun at our head, then—we all believed—the Soviets must want a war and war would be unavoidable."

"It was unmistakably Black Saturday," echoed George Ball; "one might reasonably infer from the evidence that the Soviets really intended war and were simply stalling until they were better prepared."[51]

The Saturday ordeal may well have been Kennedy's greatest day as president. He remained calm and analytical. "He seems more alive to the possibilities and consequences of each new development than anyone else," said May and Zelikow. "He is the only one in the room who is determined not to go to war over obsolete missiles in Turkey." He took Khrushchev's second proposal seriously, telling ExComm how "reasonable" the offer would appear to most of the world. The Soviets had stationed missiles in Cuba near the United States; the United States had stationed missiles in Turkey near the Soviet Union. Both countries should remove their missiles.

The United States didn't need the Jupiters. Technologically advanced Polaris submarines could patrol in Turkish waters and be far more effective. Removing the missiles from Turkey was better than bombing Cuba for a week, mounting an invasion, and risking nuclear war. "We all know how quickly everybody's courage goes when the blood starts to flow," he said, "and that's what's going to happen in NATO." When the United States bombs and invades Cuba, when the Soviets grab Berlin, "everybody's going to say: 'Well, [the Turkey missile trade] was a pretty good proposition.'"

"We can't very well invade Cuba, with all the toil and blood it's going to be, when we could have gotten [the Soviet missiles] out by making a deal on the same missiles in Turkey," he argued. "If that's part of the record, then I don't see how we'll have a very good war."

Still, the President didn't want to appear "to sell out" the Turks. NATO, especially Turkey, would deeply resent bartering away the Jupiters to appease an enemy.[52]

A few ExComm members proposed disregarding the Soviets' Saturday letter and responding only to the first offer, the one on Friday. Llewellyn Thompson judged that Khrushchev was simply upping the ante. The Soviet leader would back down, Thompson thought, if Kennedy simply insisted on accepting his original proposal—the American pledge not to invade Cuba. "The important thing for Khrushchev, it seems to me," Thompson pointed out, "is to be able to say: 'I saved Cuba. I stopped an invasion.'" Kennedy agreed.

"New information from Soviet sources indicates that Thompson was right," observed historian Robert Divine. "Khrushchev was bluffing on the Turkish missiles, trying to see if he could force Kennedy to make additional concessions. The missiles in Turkey were just a useful bargaining chip for the Russians, not a primary concern."

On the evening of October 27, operating as the President's personal emissary, Robert Kennedy met privately in his office at the Justice Department with Ambassador Dobrynin. The ambassador needed to know that the situation was urgent; time was running out. If the Soviets refused to remove their missiles, then the United States "would remove them." If the Soviets retaliated, then "before this was over, while there might be dead Americans, there would also be dead Russians." If the Soviets agreed to remove the missiles, the United States would agree not to invade Cuba. In addition, while the United States could not agree publicly to remove the Jupiter missiles from Turkey, he assured Dobrynin that they would be removed in four or five months.[53]

Impressed by U.S. resolve and the ominous prospect of war, the Soviet leader had decided to withdraw the missiles from Cuba even *before* he learned of Dobrynin's conversation with Robert Kennedy. It turned out that the pledge not to invade Cuba had been enough to cause Khrushchev to back down.

If all else failed, Kennedy had been prepared to remove the Jupiters and agree not to invade Cuba, in return for the Soviet agreement to remove their missiles—all brokered by the UN. This was his secret backup position, arranged by Dean Rusk. Ineffective for most of the ExComm deliberations,

Rusk secretly devised the contingency plan at the end of the crisis. UN Secretary-General U Thant would publicly request the withdrawal of missiles from both Turkey and Cuba. By prearrangement the President would agree. "Had Khrushchev not accepted an earlier American offer, Rusk's idea might have served as the basis for a settlement under UN auspices," noted Robert Weisbrot.

On October 30, after Khrushchev sought to formalize the withdrawal of missiles from Turkey, Robert Kennedy told Dobrynin that the White House would not formalize the accord with confidential letters or any correspondence. The subject was too sensitive. "Very privately," Dobrynin wrote in his memoir, "Robert Kennedy added that some day—who knows?—he might run for president, and his prospects could be damaged if this secret deal about the missiles in Turkey were to come out."[54]

The Cuban missile crisis was over. Kennedy emerged from it as a national hero, an almost "Lincolnesque" figure. "This country, and free peoples everywhere," lauded the *New York Herald Tribune*, "may well be grateful for the firmness and skill he has displayed in this crisis, aware of the risks, under pressure from the fainthearted and the impatient, yet holding to the course he had set."

Walter Lippman praised Kennedy for having shown "not only the courage of a warrior, which is to take the risks that are necessary, but also the wisdom of the statesman, which is to use power with restraint." In *The New Yorker* Richard Rovere judged Kennedy's achievement to be "perhaps the greatest personal diplomatic victory of any President in our history."[55]

After the crisis Kennedy modified his no-invasion pledge. At his November 20 press conference, he tightened his conditions: There would be "peace in the Caribbean" only if there were no more offensive weapons in Cuba, "adequate verification and safeguards" were ensured, there was "no export of revolution" from Cuba, and there were no Cuban violations of the UN Charter or the Rio Treaty of 1947 in which the United States and Latin American countries joined in common concern against aggression. Castro's influence in Latin America dropped dramatically following the crisis. "Castroism as an exportable commodity from Cuba to the rest of the Americas seemed a dead issue," said Dean Rusk.

U.S. allies, including Turkey, subsequently accepted a plan to replace the Jupiters with nuclear-armed Polaris submarines. The United States had dismantled the Jupiters by the end of April 1963.

For years after the crisis Robert Kennedy, McNamara, Rusk, Bundy, and several others repeatedly lied when questioned about the informal deal to remove the missiles in Turkey, preserving the secret. Despite persistent rumors, they insisted there was no deal. They apparently wanted to protect JFK's reputation for gaining an uncompromised victory, avoid offending U.S. allies, and protect Robert Kennedy's future presidential ambitions. Remarkably, Soviet leaders, who had a vested interest in making the deal public, never did so.[56]

Khrushchev later rationalized that his missile gambit was a success because he won his primary goal: a U.S. promise not to invade Cuba. "For the first time in history," he stated in his memoirs, the "American imperialist beast was forced to swallow a hedgehog, quills and all . . . I'm proud of what we did."

"This was an effort to put the best face on failure," observed Michael Beschloss. "The billion dollars earmarked for moving eighty MRBMs and IRBMs, related equipment and troops in and out of Cuba was a high price to pay for a flimsy no-invasion pledge that could be revoked at any time."[57]

Khrushchev had relied on flawed intelligence reports and poor assessments of the potential U.S. reaction. Naive, he expected to deploy the missiles secretly. He surely knew that the many warnings Kennedy had issued to the Soviets included not installing offensive weapons in Cuba. "Otherwise why did he feel compelled to proceed secretly and by deceit?" observed George Ball.

While badly underestimating America's potential reaction, Khrushchev failed to seek the advice of his ambassador in Washington and other Soviet experts. He had "grossly misunderstood the psychology of his opponents," Ambassador Dobrynin later commented. "Had he asked the embassy beforehand, we could have predicted the violent American reaction to his adventure once it became known." He also rejected the advice of Soviet foreign minister Gromyko, who claimed he warned the Soviet premier privately that "putting our missiles in Cuba would cause a political explosion in the United States."

"Khrushchev's failure to insist on a public pledge by Kennedy cost him dearly," Dobrynin added. "Kennedy was proclaimed the big winner in the crisis because no one knew about the secret deal."[58]

Although Kennedy made extraordinary efforts to limit risks, several miscues and malfunctions could have escalated the confrontation, indicating the harrowing difficulties in managing a major crisis. During the crisis the air force tested a long-range missile in California, which, noted Barton Bernstein, "could have looked to Soviet observers like the beginning of an American ICBM attack." On October 22, General Thomas Powers, the commander of the Strategic Air Command, had dangerously conducted the U.S. nuclear alert "in the clear," meaning he purposely did not use the customary encryption. Kennedy wasn't told that U.S. destroyers may have damaged a Soviet submarine with depth charges close to the quarantine line, an incident that could have escalated into a major naval clash.[59]

Kennedy's conduct during the crisis, some critics allege, was irresponsible and reckless. Driven by his machismo, his hatred of Castro, his rage over the Soviet deception, his selfish concern for political advantage, Kennedy exaggerated the missile danger, rejected a possible diplomatic solution, and insisted on a dangerous public showdown. He should have confronted Gromyko privately and negotiated a settlement, giving Khrushchev the chance to save face. While pursuing his foolish policy, Kennedy risked nuclear war "to satisfy his own psychic and political needs." Moreover, after the crisis the Soviets reacted by vastly improving their nuclear arsenal, leading to a dangerous nuclear arms race.

Kennedy's deceitful final settlement—with the secret Jupiter exchange—allowed him to misrepresent the agreement. "Secrecy . . . meant that the President, as well as the administration and the Democratic party, did not have to face problems with voters," Barton Bernstein contended. "The claims of a great triumph, as opposed to the reality of a victory with compromise, greatly helped the President and his administration both at home and abroad." The crisis encouraged Americans to believe in easy victory, not compromise, "and to conclude that toughness and resolution were the guides to success in their nation's foreign policy."

The strategic arms race did intensify following the missile crisis. But as historian John Gaddis pointed out "it was conducted within an increasingly precise set of rules, codified in formal agreements like the Limited Nuclear Test Ban Treaty of 1963, the Non-Proliferation Treaty of 1968, and the Strategic Arms Limitation Treaty of 1972, as well as the equally important informal understanding that both sides would tolerate satellite reconnaissance."[60]

Actually, Kennedy had shown remarkable restraint. If he had tolerated the missiles in Cuba, he would have encountered intense opposition from the military, hard-liners in the State Department and the CIA, most Republicans in Congress, and some Democrats, and the public.

At each stage of the crisis he chose the moderate and prudent course. Observed Tony Judt: "Instead of an invasion he favored an air strike on missile bases; instead of a blanket air strike he favored selective strikes only; he insisted that no strikes, however selective, should happen until warning had been given. He opted for a naval blockade over immediate military action, and a partial naval quarantine over a blanket blockade on all shipping."

He rejected pleas to retaliate when the reconnaissance plane was shot down over Cuba on October 27. At every stage of the crisis Kennedy gave Khrushchev time to reflect and reappraise. He was willing to use the Jupiter missiles in Turkey and Italy as a secret bargaining strategy and even authorized Dean Rusk to have the United Nations broker a deal.

"It seems especially odd," noted historian Alonzo Hamby, "that he has been criticized for impulsiveness when he sought the advice of an executive committee composed of most of the major foreign policy authorities of the United States or that he has been accused of playing out irrational machismo impulses when he accepted the most pacific alternatives seriously offered to him."[61]

Judging from the tapes of the ExComm meetings, Kennedy played a mostly wise and prudent role. "Though he would often use a word, then check himself and substitute another, and would frequently leave sentences unfinished, [Kennedy] was usually both precise and clear," said May and Zelikow.

The shared experience of the Kennedy brothers during the ordeal "sealed forever" a common bond. On the last night of the crisis, JFK said to Dave Powers, "Thank God for Bobby."

The ExComm meetings were far superior to the deliberations during the Bay of Pigs. Kennedy himself was far better informed, and far more perceptive. ExComm's "intellectual interchange," George Ball recalled, "was the most objective I ever witnessed in government—or, for that matter, in the private sector."

Arthur Schlesinger was mostly correct when he concluded, several decades ago, that the combination of Kennedy's "toughness and restraint, of will, nerve and wisdom, so brilliantly controlled, so matchlessly calibrated, . . . dazzled the world."[62]

A small but ugly controversy, played out in the media, marred Kennedy's triumph and damaged his reputation among historians. Following the missile crisis Charles Bartlett teamed with Stewart Alsop, the *Saturday Evening Post*'s Washington editor, to write an article about the dramatic encounter. When the article appeared in the *Saturday Evening Post* issue of December 8, 1962, one section branded Adlai Stevenson an appeaser. "Only Adlai Stevenson, who flew down from New York on Saturday, dissented from the ExComm consensus," the key portion stated. "There is disagreement in retrospect about what Stevenson really wanted. 'Adlai wanted a Munich,' says a nonadmiring official who learned of his proposal. 'He wanted to trade the Turkish, Italian and British missile bases for the Cuban bases.'" Many years later the "nonadmiring official" was identified as Michael Forrestal, a staff member in Bundy's operation at the National Security Council.[63] However, since Bartlett was a close friend of the Kennedys'—having introduced Jack to Jackie, ushered at their wedding, and spent many weekends with the Kennedys—the media assumed that the President himself had supplied the two newsmen with the information to embarrass Stevenson and nudge him out of the UN.

Stevenson took part in the inner-circle discussion for the first time on Saturday, October 20, after ExComm had already reached consensus on the quarantine option. Little had been done to prepare the political and diplomatic side of U.S. strategy, he pointed out. The United States should consult the NATO allies, seek approval from the Organization of American States, and call an emergency meeting of the UN Security Council—all helpful suggestions.

But Stevenson's suggestion for negotiations with the Soviets sparked controversy. His remarks were not tape-recorded, unfortunately, making it difficult to know exactly what he said. Based on notes of the meeting, he argued against a surprise air strike and supported the quarantine alternative. The United States should offer to withdraw missiles from Turkey and Italy and evacuate the Guantánamo naval base.[64]

The President sharply rejected the suggestion of withdrawing from Guantánamo because it would seem to the world that the United States had been frightened into abandoning the base. Withdrawing missiles from Turkey and Italy was an option, but the United States should only make such a proposal, if necessary, in the future.

Some ExComm members interpreted Stevenson's remarks to mean that Kennedy should initiate discussions on withdrawing the missiles even *before* the outcome of the quarantine became clear. They emphatically objected to his willingness to bargain away the important Guantánamo naval base. According to George Ball, Stevenson's proposals set off a furor.

> Though the President was courteous but firm [in rejecting Stevenson's ideas], some of the others present were outraged and shrill. Dillon [former secretary of defense Robert] Lovett, and McCone violated the calm and objectivity we had tried to maintain in our ExComm meetings when they intemperately upbraided Stevenson. The attack was, I felt, quite unfair, indicating more the state of anxiety and emotional exhaustion pervading the discussion than any reasoned reaction. . . . I felt protective of Adlai, embarrassed for him, and exceedingly annoyed with my colleagues.

Apparently Stevenson intended his suggestions as a bargaining ploy in future negotiations.[65]

During the crisis Kennedy found several of Stevenson's suggestions useful. On Stevenson's recommendation Kennedy postponed his speech from Sunday to Monday to better prepare the diplomatic groundwork. He agreed to the suggestions regarding the UN and the OAS, and strengthened the political passages in his speech.

Ken O'Donnell recalled that after Stevenson's presentation on the twentieth, Robert Kennedy was furious. "He's not strong enough or tough enough to be representing us at the UN at a time like this," Bobby advised his brother. "Why not get him out of there?"

"Now wait a minute," O'Donnell remembered the President responding. "I think Adlai showed plenty of strength and courage, presenting that viewpoint at the risk of being called an appeaser. It was an argument that needed to be stated, but nobody else had the guts to do it. Maybe he went too far when he suggested giving up Guantánamo, but remember we're in a situation here that may cost us millions of lives, and we should be considering every side of it and every way to get out of it. I admire him for saying what he said."[66]

On Saturday, December 1, President Kennedy informed Arthur Schlesinger about the upcoming Bartlett and Alsop article. "You had better warn Adlai that it is coming. . . . Everyone will suppose that it came out of the White House because of Charlie. Will you tell Adlai that I never talked to Charlie or any other reporter about the Cuban crisis, and that this piece does not represent my views."

The article caused a media frenzy. Speculation mounted that Kennedy had plotted with Alsop and Bartlett to embarrass Stevenson and force his resignation. The President must not be backing Stevenson, since the first White House statement defending the UN ambassador was released through Press Secretary Pierre Salinger instead of being issued in the President's name. Nor did the statement set the record straight about Stevenson's real position during the crisis.

Most pundits defended Stevenson. "The reaction was so intense and so strongly in Mr. Stevenson's favor," *The New York Times* observed, "that the President had to keep him on, even if he had wanted otherwise."[67]

In a letter on December 5, Kennedy expressed his deep regret to Stevenson about the "unfortunate fuss." He praised Stevenson's performance at the United Nations, specifically during the Cuban crisis. "The fact that Charles Bartlett was a co-author of this piece has made this particularly difficult for me," the President conceded. "I did not discuss the Cuban crisis or any of the events surrounding it with any newspapermen—and I am certain that the quotations in the *The Saturday Evening Post* article with respect to your role did not come from the White House." Kennedy claimed to have known when Bartlett started writing the article that everything controversial "would be laid at my door, whether I talked to him or not." Still, "I did not feel I could tell him or any other friend in the press what subject to write or *not* write about." After the release of the letter, the furor died down.[68]

Historians have since castigated Kennedy for deceitfully using Bartlett to embarrass Stevenson. Most accounts assume Bartlett's revelation pleased the President. One account described a conversation between Bartlett and Kennedy: " 'Oh, you got that, huh?' replied Kennedy with a smile. 'I wasn't sure you'd get that.' Bartlett described the President's reaction as 'confirmation by indirection.'"

Evan Thomas claims that Michael Forrestal was recruited as an "agent of disinformation" and that Stevenson's enemies within ExComm "slandered Stevenson at the direction of the President." By creating a stir over Stevenson, some believe, Kennedy hoped to distract skeptics who might inquire too closely about the Jupiter missile trade. Historian Robert Divine wrote that Kennedy "permitted his close friend Charles Bartlett to portray Stevenson as an appeaser."

> Kennedy's failure to defend Stevenson publicly, while remarkably ungracious, is now at least understandable. The President in fact pursued privately the course of action Stevenson recommended but was able to force Khrushchev to agree without making the Jupiter concession public. The last thing Kennedy wanted the American people to learn in 1962 was that he had made a missile swap with the Russians. And so he allowed Stevenson to be pilloried in public while Kennedy received all the public acclaim.

Only after the attempt to embarrass Stevenson backfired and appeared to be damaging the President's reputation, critics allege, did Kennedy release his laudatory letter of December 5.[69]

The Bartlett-Alsop article had been unfair to Stevenson. The authors never interviewed the UN ambassador to learn his side of the story; nor did they mention Stevenson's strong endorsement of the quarantine. On October 20, Stevenson never mentioned "British missile bases."

Although Kennedy strongly disliked Stevenson and was occasionally mean to him, the President appreciated Stevenson's suggestions and admired his forthrightness during the Cuban crisis. The accusation that Kennedy conspired with Bartlett to undermine Stevenson, while perhaps partly true, is mostly distorted.

Stevenson was consulted about the statement issued by Pierre Salinger and approved it. In his oral history for the Kennedy Library, Bartlett stated that Kennedy "very clearly" told Bartlett "that he had no intention of being a source for my article." The President said, "My role, I've decided, in all these articles will be not to talk to the writers who are doing them. After all, I would just be putting credit on myself." From that point on, said Bartlett, "I never had any inclination to go to him on any point of the article. It seemed to me [he had] made it very clear he didn't want to be a part of my article or anybody else's."[70]

However, after Bartlett ran into the story "about Adlai Stevenson having proposed to give up the Guantánamo Naval base, plus the missiles in Turkey, plus the missiles in Italy," he mentioned this information to the President in the course of a dinner. Bartlett recalled: "He had that sort of wary look you know but he said, 'Did you hear about that?' I said, 'Yes, we got it.' He said, 'Are you going to put it in the article?' I said, 'Yes.' He sort of shook his head. That was the only real comment that he made.

The President "shook his head," said Bartlett; he didn't "smile" as if delighted to know that Stevenson was about to be pilloried.

Stevenson seemed satisfied with Kennedy's support. "I am sure you know full well how grateful I am for your most kind letters and statements in connection with the recent unpleasantness," he wrote Kennedy after the furor.[71]

The 1962 midterm election followed closely on the heels of the Cuban missile crisis. From 1902 to 1958 the opposition party had increased its congressional representation in midterm elections fourteen of fifteen times, gaining an average of forty-five seats. In 1962 Republicans confidently predicted a gain of twenty seats in the House.

One contest held special interest for the President. His brother Edward was running for the vacant Senate seat in Massachusetts. In the Democratic primary, Ted faced Eddie McCormack, the nephew of the new Speaker of the House, John McCormack, reviving stories of bad blood between the two families.

Initially, the President had thought Ted should consider a lesser statewide office—state treasurer or secretary of state—as a stepping-stone. But both the President and Robert Kennedy soon changed their minds.[72]

"My brother is carrying this campaign on his own," the President said publicly, a claim that was mostly true. Behind the scenes, though, the President did aid Ted's campaign. He "summoned all the White House aides with Massachusetts connections to a secret meeting on April 27, 1962," said Adam Clymer, Edward Kennedy's biographer. "He even had politicians from Boston fly to Washington under assumed names." Sorensen sent quotations for Ted to use in his speeches; William Hartigan, a White House staff assistant, took a leave of absence to help Ted.

When an aide presented the President with a critical assessment of Ted's performance in a debate with McCormack, the President wanted to deemphasize anything negative. "Don't give [Ted] a dispassionate analysis [of his debate performance]," the President responded. "He's the candidate. He's the one under the gun. You've got to make him feel good." Buoying Ted's spirit was critical.

James Reston of *The New York Times* repeatedly disparaged Ted's candidacy, claiming it was an "affront and a presumption." "One Kennedy is a triumph, two Kennedys at the same time are a miracle, but three could easily be regarded as an invasion."[73]

Meanwhile President Kennedy campaigned extensively for Democratic candidates, advocating medical care for the aged and federal aid to education. On October 13, he castigated the Republican Party for opposing progressive social programs since the New Deal:

Can you tell me one piece of progressive legislation of benefit to the people of this country that the Republican party has sponsored in years? Because if you can't, I can tell you one hundred pieces of legislation that they've opposed—from the beginning of the right of labor to organize, and social security and minimum wage, and housing legislation, and all the rest that make it possible for us to produce a better life for our people.

The election results were stunning, a "dramatic triumph" for Democrats, said *Newsweek*. Instead of losing many seats, Democrats gained four in the Senate, and lost only four in the House. Cuba turned out to be the decisive issue. "It cost the Republicans heavily," *Newsweek* observed. "They had decided to make Cuba the issue; when President Kennedy removed the issue, the Republicans who had used it were dead." But the election did not change the basic composition in Congress. Conservative Democrats and Republicans continued to block Kennedy's domestic programs.[74]

Edward Kennedy was one of the Senate victors. After defeating young McCormack in the primary, he beat George Lodge in the general election. At Ted's first public Washington address following the election, he brought down the house after a reporter asked if he was going to be "independent." "I'm independent," he responded. "I've been helping [the President] for a number of years, and I think it's time he stood on his own feet."

As senator, Ted Kennedy saw more of the President than he had earlier. He frequently swam at the White House, then afterward had dinner and a cigar. "Sometimes Jack wanted the conversation light or focused on the family," observed Clymer. "But sometimes he wanted to talk about what was happening"—the civil rights movement, Khrushchev's current thinking, or the House Rules Committee's attempts to block legislation.

"Some pipeline I have into the White House," the new senator joked to Ben Bradlee at a White House dinner dance. "I tell him a thousand men are out of work in Fall River; four hundred men out of work in Fitchburg. And when the Army gets that new rifle, there's another six hundred men out of work in Springfield. And do you know what he says to me? 'Tough shit.'" The President roared with laughter.[75]

Kennedy pursued an aggressive policy toward Cuba after the missile crisis. Although attempts to overthrow Castro looked unpromising, the raids and the sabotage continued. "The political consequences of open efforts at rapprochement were more than Kennedy felt he could risk a year before his reelection campaign," noted historian Robert Dallek.

Nonetheless Kennedy secretly explored ways to improve relations with Cuba's Communist leader. "Stripping the Republicans of the Cuban matter by 'neutralizing Cuba on our terms' had considerable appeal to Kennedy," Dallek observed. "It would also eliminate international embarrassment over the image of a superpower America bullying a weak island country. If rapprochement included the removal of all Soviet forces from Cuba, an end to Cuba's hemisphere subversion, and Havana's commitment to nonalignment in the Cold War, Kennedy believed he could sell it to the American public."[76]

The White House used several intermediators to suggest a rapprochement with Castro: William Attwood, former ambassador to Guinea and a deputy to UN Ambassador Adlai Stevenson; Jean Daniel, a French journalist; and Lisa Howard, a correspondent for ABC News were enlisted in the effort.

In the spring of 1963, the NSC suggested using "the sweet approach . . . enticing Castro over to us," as potentially more rewarding than the CIA's covert operations to overthrow the regime. Castro seemed interested in improving relations, telling correspondent Howard in May 1963 that negotiation with Washington was "possible if the United States government wishes it."[77]

During a secret meeting with Daniel, Kennedy conceded that the United States deserved some of the responsibility for the tyranny inflicted on the Cubans by Batista. "I believe that we created, built and manufactured the Castro movement out of whole cloth and without realizing it," he said.

In early November 1963, Kennedy and McGeorge Bundy discussed the possibility of a secret meeting in Havana in which Attwood would engage in secret talks with Castro to improve relations with Washington. Kennedy approved the plan if it could be plausibly denied.

Any agreement between the two nations, though, still seemed remote. Bundy once said that it was fine to talk with the Cuban leader but "things would have to get rougher for Castro before he would consider any deal with us which we could accept."[78]

33

CONNOISSEUR OF
THE SEXUAL GAME

Kennedy told his friend Charles Bartlett that he intended to curb his womanizing in the White House. He would keep the White House "white." In fact, the presidency never stopped Kennedy from pursuing attractive women. He was confined by the White House and restricted by the media's glare; but the aura of his office, his constant travel, Jackie's frequent absences, solicitous procurers, and the discreet attitude of the Secret Service enabled him to continue his extramarital affairs. Several members of the White House staff—Arthur Schlesinger, Myer Feldman—knew little if anything about the President's womanizing; others, like Dave Powers and Ken O'Donnell, helped arrange Kennedy's sexual dalliances.[1]

Occasionally people noticed that Kennedy was easily distracted by beautiful women or that his conversation turned to sex. In March 1963 Richard Goodwin accompanied the President to Costa Rica for a summit meeting with leaders of Central America. In his hotel room the President chatted with his aides about Latin American problems. Momentarily distracted as he stood at the hotel window, Kennedy motioned for Goodwin to join him.

"Look down there, Dick . . . no, near those cars. Now that's one hell of a woman. . . . Why don't you . . ." Then his voice trailed off.[2]

In the middle of a working lunch on nuclear arms with British prime minister Harold Macmillan, Kennedy's attention wandered. He turned to Macmillan and said, "I wonder how it is with you, Harold? If I don't have a woman for three days, I get a terrible headache." The sixty-seven-year-old, monogamous prime minister was baffled. Late in life Macmillan showed rare impatience with Kennedy, excoriating him for "spending half his time thinking about adultery." President Kennedy, though, did far more than just *think* about adultery.[3]

One of his adulterous affairs burst onto the national headlines on December 17, 1975. A month earlier the Senate Select Committee to Study Government Operations with Respect to Intelligence Activities (the Church committee), in its report on CIA assassination attempts, had discreetly stated that a "close friend" of President Kennedy had also been a close friend of mobsters John Roselli and Sam Giancana. Shortly after, *The Washington Post* leaked the person's identity. The friend was a woman, Judith Campbell Exner. On December 17, sitting next to her second husband, Dan Exner, a golf pro, and hiding behind large sunglasses, Exner, then forty-one, held forth at a press conference and denied any knowledge of underworld activities.

Two years later, in her sensational autobiography, *My Story,* Exner recounted her sexual tryst with JFK and her simultaneous relationship with Giancana, plus her friendship with Roselli.

Of all the Kennedy sex scandals, the Exner story may be the one that troubles his admirers most. It is also a tale that remains clouded with uncertainty. Exner changed it several times, amplifying her original confession of an affair into bizarre claims about her role in a conspiracy involving Kennedy and the Mafia. The first accusations were bad enough; the later ones would seriously injure Kennedy's reputation as President, if true. For that reason, it's important to be clear about which of Exner's claims we should believe, and which appear to be fantasy.[4]

Exner's friend Sam Giancana, a short, dour, homely Sicilian, held court at the Armory Lounge in Forest Park, Illinois, ordering murders and managing his crime empire. An extraordinary criminal, Giancana had murdered more than two hundred men up to 1960. "Some of the victims were simply shot," said one authority, "while others were hung on meat hooks and tortured with electric cattle prods, ice picks, baseball bats, and blowtorches."

A leading member of La Cosa Nostra, the national crime syndicate, Giancana was Chicago's Mafia boss, the successor to Al Capone. He controlled all the "protection rackets, pinball machines, prostitution, numbers games, narcotics, loan sharks, extortioners, counterfeiters, and bookmakers in the Chicago area." He had served time in prison and been arrested more than seventy times, including three times for murder. Giancana's friend and associate, John Roselli, represented the Chicago mob on the West Coast.[5]

Born Judith Immoor, Exner grew up in Pacific Palisades, California, where her father worked as an architect. The family was financially well off, but when Judith was fourteen, her mother nearly died in an auto accident. Traumatized by the experience, Judith withdrew from high school and was privately tutored. At eighteen, she married the alcoholic actor William Campbell, but after an unhappy marriage they divorced in 1958. Stunningly beautiful, she resembled actress Elizabeth Taylor and became a regular at Hollywood parties. One evening in 1959 she met singer Frank Sinatra, and they engaged in a brief affair.

Then on the evening of February 7, 1960, Campbell met Senator John Kennedy and his entourage at Sinatra's table at the Sands Lounge in Las Vegas. After perfunctory introductions, Kennedy conversed with all the women at the table, but focused on Campbell. When he listened to her, she recalled in her autobiography, "it was as if every nerve and muscle in his whole body was poised at attention. As I was to learn, Jack Kennedy was the world's greatest listener."

The next day Kennedy invited her for lunch on the patio of Sinatra's suite. Again, he acted insatiably interested in Exner's life. They talked for three hours. When Campbell revealed that the night before, young Ted Kennedy (who was married) had tried to seduce her, Jack Kennedy laughed hilariously. "That little rascal," he said, shaking his head. "You'll have to excuse his youthful exuberance. He's still quite a kid in many ways, but his heart is in the right place. He's a little immature, but time will cure that."[6]

After their Las Vegas encounter, Kennedy often phoned her, telling her how much he missed her and wondering when they could meet again. They finally rendezvoused on March 7, 1960, at the New York Plaza Hotel, where they had their first sexual encounter. At first Campbell resisted:

> By this time, he had maneuvered me over to the bed, and had gently pushed me on my back. His kisses were more passionate now and my head was beginning to reel. Suddenly, I pushed at him and said, "No, Jack."
>
> He couldn't believe it. "What do you mean, no?"
>
> I just can't do this right now," I said. "I haven't seen you for a month."
>
> "But we've talked on the phone every day. What's the matter?"

Annoyed, Kennedy picked up his jacket, apparently ready to leave. Exner recalled her thoughts: "I wanted to be with him, but it was so abrupt, so cold and calculated."

She changed her mind and asked him to stay, and they made love. She learned then the pattern their lovemaking would take: "His attitude was that he was there to be serviced. Partly this was due to his back problem, and partly I think he had been spoiled by women. There is a world of difference between a man who expects to be made love to and two people making love to each other."

In Florida in late March 1960, Sinatra introduced Campbell to a man named "Sam Flood." It took a while for Campbell to learn that the man who had befriended her in Florida was actually Sam Giancana. Was it just a coincidence, critics wondered, that within a two-month period Sinatra's introductions had sparked Exner's romances with a future President and a notorious criminal? Was Giancana using Exner because she was Kennedy's girlfriend? In her autobiography Exner dampened such speculation. It "never occurred to me that Sam's interest in me was simply because of my association with Jack Kennedy." She added, "Sam never asked me for anything."

On April 6, 1960, Kennedy invited her to his Georgetown home while Jackie was away. Exner recalled the visit:

> We wandered through various rooms until we came to the master bedroom, which was upstairs at the front of the house. There were twin beds with pale green spreads, very filmy and delicate.
>
> He put his arms around me and we sat on one of the beds. We kissed and he was almost immediately amorous. I went to the bathroom to undress, and when I came back into the room, the lights were very low and Jack was already in bed.
>
> "I've missed you so much," I said, as I went into his arms.
>
> We kissed passionately, and he said, with his lips still on mine, "Do you think you could love me?"
>
> "I'm afraid I could," I whispered, and it was so true.

As she would on several future occasions, Campbell worried about his recklessness, worried that the servants had seen them together.[7]

On Monday, July 11, 1960, the opening day of the Democratic National Convention in Los Angeles, she met him in the evening in his hotel suite and waited as he took care of political business. There were six or seven men in the room and one woman, "a tall, thin, secretarial type in her late twenties."

After the men left, Kennedy took Campbell into the bedroom, where they sat on the edge of the bed. Exner described what happened next:

As I looked up, I saw that the tall, thin woman was standing at the other end of the room. She gave me a little smile and went into the bathroom, closing the door. While I was trying to figure out what she was doing there, I heard Jack say something about the three of us going to bed together. . . .

I think I said something like, "Oh God, Jack, how could you?" He said, "But it's all right, don't be afraid, I know you'll enjoy it." I thought, "Oh Lord, what's wrong with me?" He tried to kiss me and I pulled away. There was an anxious look on his face and I could see that he was puzzled by my rejection. . . . He assured me the girl was safe, that she would never talk about it to a single soul, that there was nothing wrong with a *ménage à trois,* that it was practiced widely, and, over and over again, that I would enjoy it—"I know you, I know you'll enjoy it."

Realizing the gravity of his mistake, Kennedy shifted gears, sent the other woman away, and tried to make amends. He put his arm around Campbell. "I hope you're not angry with me," he said.

"I can't tell you how disappointed I am in you," she replied. "You didn't have to present this the way you did. You could have first asked me about it."

"I'm really sorry," he said. "It was a stupid mistake."

She continued. "If you cared as much about me as you say you do, how could you have put me in this position?"

She insisted on going home.

He shook his head and stood up. "I really did it, didn't I?" he said.

"You puzzle me," she said. "I would think you had enough on your mind without cooking up something like this."

He forced a smile. "It wasn't easy."[8]

Nonetheless, throughout the fall of 1961 and the winter and spring of 1962, she continued seeing Kennedy in the White House. Their routine seldom varied. Evelyn Lincoln made reservations for her at the Mayflower Hotel. In the evening the White House car drove her to the East Gate, the one tourists used in the daytime. "Either Jack would meet me in the entrance hall near the door or an aide would escort me to the little elevator and Jack would be waiting in the family quarters." After her arrival at about 7:30 P.M. she and the President usually had frozen daiquiris and then dinner.

During their White House lovemaking the President acted as if time wasn't a problem. But it was a problem for Campbell, who worried she was imposing on the busy President. "Time was the only enemy," she said. "I was the one who watched the clock." They never spent the entire night together.

"I didn't want to discuss his wife and from all indications the feeling was mutual," she said. "The whole time I knew Jack Kennedy, he never once mentioned another woman in my presence. Nor did he criticize Jackie. The most he ever said was that their marriage was not a happy one."

She claimed that the President had no qualms about asking her to accompany him on *Air Force One*. "It wasn't maybe it could be done this way or that way—he had it all worked out." She refused the offer, judging it reckless. "I think he just loved intrigue," she said.

Gradually, she began to sense a change in his attitude. "He wasn't as happy-go-lucky, not as relaxed and cheerful. He was somber, sometimes downright solemn. He would drift off into his own private world, and I could feel him a million miles away. He had more important things on his mind."

By late spring 1962, their romance had cooled off. He phoned her infrequently, and she returned his calls less often.[9]

Was Exner's story true? By the time she wrote her autobiography in 1977, Kennedy, Giancana, and Roselli were all dead. Had she concocted all or most of her story in order to sell a book?

Exner had told the Church committee that her relationship with Kennedy was only personal and that she had no knowledge of any relationship between Giancana and the President. She made the same denials in her press conference in December 1975 and in her autobiography. At her press conference she accused the media of "wild-eyed speculation" for suggesting that she was an intermediary between JFK and Giancana and was simultaneously having affairs with both men.

Kennedy's advisers Ken O'Donnell and Dave Powers both denied even knowing Exner, then known as Judith Campbell. "The only Campbell I know," Powers told the press in late 1975, "is chunky vegetable soup." But both of them were lying. So was Evelyn Lincoln, who claimed Campbell was merely a campaign volunteer. The dates in the gate logs of Campbell's White House visitations generally coincided with her own recollections. O'Donnell and Evelyn Lincoln personally authorized some of Campbell's visits. White House telephone logs show Exner called Lincoln more than eighty times, and there were also calls from Lincoln to Exner. Exner's autobiography convincingly listed fifteen telephone numbers where she had reached both Lincoln and Kennedy from 1960 to 1962.

Reviewers found Exner's autobiography to be credible. The evidence she offered—addresses, telephone numbers, descriptions of White House décor—made "the defensive protestations of the keepers of the Kennedy flame somewhat dubious," said a review in *The New York Times*.[10]

But eleven years after her book was published, Exner began telling another, very different story. In 1988 *People* magazine published an article by Kitty Kelley, based on the author's interviews with Exner. "I lied when I said I was not a conduit between President Kennedy and the Mafia," Exner told

Kelley. "I lied when I said that President Kennedy was unaware of my friendships with mobsters. He knew everything about my dealings with Sam Giancana and Johnny Roselli because I was seeing them for him. I wouldn't have been seeing them otherwise."

Why had she lied before the Church committee, during her 1975 press conference, and in *My Story*? She needed to protect herself, she said. "If I'd told the truth, I'd have been killed. I kept my secret out of fear." Exner's fear seemed well founded. Senate investigators were about to call Giancana to testify before the Church committee when on the night of June 19, 1975, he was shot seven times in the head in the kitchen of his Oak Park, Illinois, residence. The killer was never found, but it was a Mafia-style murder. Days later Roselli testified before the Senate committee about the CIA's attempts to kill Castro, including Giancana's role. A year later, Roselli's dead body was found in a fifty-five-gallon oil drum weighted with heavy chains floating in Dumfoundling Bay near Miami.

Exner claimed that her first assignment as a courier was suggested by JFK at the dinner in his Georgetown town house on April 6, 1960. That evening had not just focused on dinner and lovemaking, as she had stated in her autobiography. A third person, a lobbyist named Bill [Bill Thompson], was at dinner with them. He and Jack spent the entire evening discussing strategy for the upcoming West Virginia primary on May 11.

During the conversation Jack turned to her and said, "Could you quietly arrange a meeting with Sam [Giancana] for me?" Pleased to be of help, Exner claimed she called her new friend Giancana the next morning and said she'd like to talk to him in Chicago. "I arrived at 8:30 A.M. on April 8th and talked to Sam at a Chicago club," said Exner. "I told Sam that Jack wanted to meet with him because he needed his help in the campaign." Giancana agreed, and the meeting was set for four days later at the Fontainebleau Hotel in Miami Beach. "I called Jack to tell him, then I flew to Miami because Kennedy wanted me to be there."

On April 12 Kennedy met with Giancana at the Fontainebleau. "I was not present," Exner said, "but Jack came to my suite afterward, and I asked him how the meeting had gone. He seemed very happy about it and thanked me for making the arrangements." Apparently in gratitude, Kennedy gave her a present of two thousand dollars in cash.

Kitty Kelley speculated that the meeting between Kennedy and Giancana on April 12 concerned the West Virginia primary. Giancana was to assist Kennedy's campaign by using fifty thousand dollars to bribe key election officials in the state.[11]

Even after becoming President, Exner contended, JFK continued to use her as a courier. A few days after the bungled Bay of Pigs invasion in April 1961, Kennedy called Exner in California and asked her to fly to Las Vegas, pick up an envelope from Roselli, and deliver it to Giancana in Chicago. Then she was to arrange a meeting between the President and the Mafia boss, one that took place in her suite at the Ambassador East on April 28, 1961.

"It was a short meeting early in the evening," Exner claimed. "Sam arrived first and then Jack, who put his arms around me and said, 'I'm sorry I can't stay and see you for the evening.'" (He was in town to address a Democratic Party dinner.) After the President and Giancana shook hands, JFK asked Exner to stay in the suite while he and Giancana talked. "To give them privacy, I then went into the bathroom," she told Kelley, "sat on the edge of the tub and waited until they were finished."

On April 29, Exner maintains, she flew to Florida at Kennedy's request, where she met with Giancana and Roselli, picked up another envelope from them, and returned to Washington on May 4. "We were scheduled to have lunch at the White House on Saturday, May 6," she said, "but [Kennedy] said the envelope couldn't wait, so I took it to him late Friday afternoon." The following day, May 6, she lunched at the White House, where Kennedy gave her another envelope for Giancana.

Meanwhile the FBI was hounding Exner and Giancana; she was terrified, but when she told Kennedy, he seemed unconcerned. "Don't worry," he told her. "They won't do anything to you. And don't worry about Sam. You know he works for us." According to Exner, "He told me that over and over. 'Don't worry. Sam works for us.'"

For eighteen months in 1960 and 1961, Exner claimed, she served as the President's link with the mob. At Kennedy's request, she crisscrossed the nation carrying envelopes between the President and Giancana, and arranged about ten meetings between the two, one of which, she thought, took place inside the White House.

"They were sealed but not taped," Exner said of the plain nine-by-twelve-inch manila envelopes. "They weighed about as much as a weekly magazine and felt as if they contained papers, but I don't know for sure because I never looked inside . . . I didn't know what they contained." Not until 1975, when the Church committee made its report, did Exner become convinced that she "was probably helping Jack orchestrate the attempted assassination of Fidel Castro with the help of the Mafia."[12]

In 1997, however, eighteen years after the publication of *My Story,* Exner significantly changed her account again. In separate interviews with journalists Liz Smith (for her article in *Vanity Fair*) and Seymour Hersh (for his book *The Dark Side of Camelot*), Exner unveiled sensational new allegations.

On April 6, 1960, at the dinner and lovemaking session at JFK's Georgetown home, JFK not only asked her to deliver an envelope to Giancana, he revealed to her the contents of the envelope. "I want you to know what's in it," Kennedy told her. He opened it and showed her the money, perhaps as much as $250,000 in hundred-dollar bills.

To buttress his story that Campbell delivered money to Giancana in Chicago, Hersh produced a witness: Martin Underwood, a former political operative for Mayor Richard Daley, and a Kennedy campaign worker in 1960. According to Hersh, in April 1960 Ken O'Donnell asked Underwood to take the overnight train from Washington to Chicago and keep an eye on Judith Campbell. Underwood claimed he watched her on the train and saw her deliver the envelope to the waiting Sam Giancana.

JFK also revealed to Campbell the contents of envelopes she subsequently delivered to Giancana and Roselli. "I knew what [the documents] dealt with. I knew they dealt with the 'elimination' of Castro and that Sam and Johnny had been hired by the CIA. That's what Jack explained to me in the very beginning."

For the first time Exner implicated Robert Kennedy in the CIA-Mafia-Castro story. "I used to be at the White House having lunch or dinner with Jack, and Bobby [Kennedy] would often come by," she told Liz Smith. "He'd squeeze my shoulder solicitously and ask, 'Judy, are you O.K. carrying these messages for us to Chicago? Do you still feel comfortable doing it?' "

Exner also told Hersh that she was a conduit for payoffs to Kennedy from a group of California businessmen who desperately wanted defense contracts. Her close friend Richard Ellwood, a neighbor and vice president of a small electronics company in Culver City, California, introduced her to "two senior Pentagon procurement officials." She began socializing with all of them during her frequent trips to Washington.

Eventually, Exner told Hersh, "I took payoffs" from the California businessmen to Kennedy in the White House. "I didn't want to go to Jack" with the payoff money, she said. But "I asked Jack about it and he thought it was a good idea." She recalled three separate contract proposals for which she brought payoffs into the White House.[13]

"What I want to tell you is my very last secret—an extremely personal one," Exner dramatically told Liz Smith in 1997. The secret was the abortion she had as a result of her last sexual encounter with the President. She had been "too ashamed" to tell it earlier. "But now, before I die, I think the Camelot myth should also be demystified, and the Kennedy legend examined for its reality. I don't have a single, solitary thing to hide."

Jack begged her to come back and talk, to try again, Exner said. She went to see him one last time in late December 1962. "I said I wouldn't see him anymore; it was too painful. But we were intimate that one last time, in the White House." Shortly after, she realized she was pregnant. "I hadn't been with anyone but Jack—not ever during the whole time."

By her calculations she was "almost two months" pregnant. Because abortion was then illegal, the President said, "Do you think Sam would help us? Would you ask Sam? Would you mind asking?" Giancana agreed to assist her.

The same evening she told Giancana she needed an abortion, she was sexually intimate with him. "It was the one time with Sam. . . . I would hardly say that that was having a simultaneous affair with two men." Exner claims she had her abortion at Chicago's Grant Hospital, and left the hospital on January 28, 1963.[14]

Exner's autobiography had been convincing because her key contentions could be documented with FBI reports, Secret Service logs, White House telephone records, witnesses, and evidence in her own possession. But the same is not true for her revelations after 1977. Her supporters, mainly Liz Smith and Seymour Hersh, have tried to bolster her recollections, but their evidence is not compelling. Her sensational charges—that money and documents were directly exchanged between JFK and Giancana; that Robert Kennedy colluded with Giancana as well; that the President welcomed payoffs from California defense contractors; and, finally, that Exner aborted a child conceived by JFK—all rely primarily on Exner's sole testimony.

Several serious weaknesses cast doubt on Exner's post-1977 allegations. Secret Service agents who candidly testified about the President's womanizing do not confirm any of Exner's contentions about JFK's relations with Giancana. "Ms. Exner has, like all of us, read about the CIA's attempt to use Giancana to assassinate Castro," noted Garry Wills of Exner's revelations to Hersh, "so—sure enough—Kennedy relied on her to send messages and documents to Giancana dealing with this explosive matter. What documents? Hersh might have asked himself at this moment."[15]

Exner's post-1977 observations defy logic. Why would JFK select Exner as his courier to the Mafia? She thought she was the perfect choice because Kennedy didn't trust the CIA. She was the "one person around him who didn't need anything from him or want anything. He trusted me."

But John Kennedy had plenty of aides—and Joe Kennedy, plenty of retainers—who could have performed the role of courier far more safely and capably than Exner. When Kennedy supposedly selected Exner to be his courier to Giancana, he had known her for only two months, and she had been introduced to "Sam Flood" only a week earlier.

Would JFK really have used a "none-too-bright girlfriend to handle something so incredibly sensitive as passing bribes to the Mafia?" asked Evan Thomas in *Newsweek*. "Surely Father Joe taught his sons a few tricks about keeping secrets. Using emotionally fragile lovers as bagmen could not have been one of them." Added Thomas: "It also stretches credulity to suggest that Giancana, the all-powerful don, would have been waiting around on a station platform in Chicago to meet the train."

Hersh's account of the train ride Campbell took on Kennedy's behalf in April 1960 to deliver money to Giancana has unraveled because the key witness recanted his original story. Martin Underwood denied that he followed Judith Campbell on the train, and claims he had no knowledge about her alleged role as a courier.[16]

If the FBI "hounded" Exner and Giancana, wouldn't the G-men have trailed or wiretapped Giancana when he supposedly had all these meetings with Kennedy in Chicago, Florida, and the White House? Finally, why did Exner wait until 1997 to reveal that she had met Attorney General Robert Kennedy and that he colluded with the President and Giancana? She would not have risked her life by mentioning that fact a decade earlier.

In her autobiography Exner stated: "I saw Jack in March and April [1962] and the calls did not stop until sometime in June [1962]." (White House logs indicate her last call was August 6, 1962, and Kennedy refused to take the call.) Twenty years later Exner said she engaged in lovemaking with Kennedy in "late December" of 1962, became pregnant, and aborted his child in January 1963. She claimed she had receipts and the doctor's name for her abortion at Chicago's Grant Hospital, but these do not prove Kennedy was the aborted child's father. By the fall of 1962, Exner said in *My Story,* she was "deeply involved" with Giancana. If this was true, and her abortion story was true, perhaps the aborted child was Giancana's. Or someone else may have been the father.[17]

In critiquing Exner's abortion story, as she told it to Hersh, Garry Wills noted the incongruity of it all: "When she became pregnant with Kennedy's child, she and the President decided she must have an abortion. Where did Kennedy turn for that? By now you expect it: 'Would Sam help us?' The President wants to incur a debt that gives precious knowledge of a scandal to the Mafia boss." It is impossible to believe.

Even conservative critics, who might have been expected to treat Exner's later revelations more favorably, were unimpressed. After reading Exner's 1977 autobiography, columnist William Safire severely criticized Kennedy. But Exner's subsequent revelations left him cold. "She's changed her story too often over the decades," Safire concluded.[18]

Exner had a long history of instability, making her an exceptionally unreliable witness. She admitted to lying repeatedly and changed her story several times. Traumatized as a youth, she couldn't finish high school. She became addicted to alcohol and amphetamines, suffered from depression and paranoia, seriously contemplated suicide, endured two divorces (one from an alcoholic), was hounded and harassed by the FBI, feared death at the hands of the Mafia, underwent an abortion, gave up a child to adoption, had several major operations, and was told her cancer was terminal. Her background and problems do not inspire confidence in her veracity.

Exner deeply resented critics of *My Story* who portrayed her as a vapid party girl, the mistress of the President and a Mafia don. She referred to it as her "stupid" book. She wasn't a "tramp, a slut," she said. "I was never anybody's kept woman." Probably to counter her image as simply a scarlet woman who sexually serviced two famous people, she probably invented a role, concocted fanciful tales, trying to re-create her image into a serious, sympathetic, and important person.

She reveled in the drama and intrigue of her post-1977 stories. She was dying of cancer, she dramatically told Kelley, Smith, and Hersh. "For that reason, I must now tell the truth." She played a "secret" role as courier between the President and Giancana, received the personal backing of Robert Kennedy as well, took payoffs from businessmen directly to the President, and had one "last secret"—her abortion.

As if she had just tumbled out of a spy novel, she breathlessly explained her techniques for arranging contacts between Kennedy and Giancana. "As a rule I would just call Sam," she said. "I learned to almost speak in a kind of code. I would usually say, 'Have him call the girl from the West.' And if something was happening in Florida, it was, 'Can you meet him in the South?' Sam always knew that 'him' was Jack. I really became very adept. I think that I was having a little bit of fun with this also." The fifty thousand dollars *People* magazine paid Exner in 1988 for telling her amplified story to Kitty Kelley may also have stimulated her imagination.[19]

Historians may never prove or disprove Exner's assertions. Scholarship on the Mafia and on the presidents' private lives, observed historian Michael Beschloss, "is not subject to the same precision as the study of diplomatic history, for which there are official documents drafted and preserved according to professional standards in public archives." Perhaps evidence will emerge in the future to bolster Exner's recent contentions.

Until then, we should assume that the first story, regarding the affair, because it was supported by White House logs and other evidence, was true; but that her later claims about her role in an alleged Giancana-Roselli-Kennedy triangle, because they are not supported by other sources, are fantasy.[20]

A young White House intern, Mimi Beardsley, performed sexual favors for the President during two summers. Two young White House employees, Fiddle and Faddle, also regularly had sex with the President. Fiddle was Priscilla Wear; Faddle was her close friend Jill Cowen. Both were in their early twenties and recent graduates of Goucher College. Fiddle had nicknamed herself as a child because she couldn't pronounce Priscilla; Kennedy's staff naturally tabbed her sidekick Faddle.

Fascinated with politics and enamored of Kennedy, they had showed up wearing similar dresses to volunteer for the 1960 campaign. Quickly promoted, they worked at the 1960 Democratic convention in Los Angeles, and posted election returns in Hyannis Port.

After the election Wear went to work as Evelyn Lincoln's assistant, and Cowen was the girl Friday to Pierre Salinger in the press office. Though not classic beauties, the pair were comely and fun-loving—"full of dash and vigor." And because they were also sexually accommodating, it was easy to see why they pleased the President.[21]

Kennedy partied with the two women in the White House swimming pool, a focal point for his sexual activity. Sometimes a pitcher of daiquiris would be prepared and chilled in a portable refrigerator and hors d'oeuvres warmed in a portable heater. The waiters, household staff, and Secret Service were told to stay away from the swimming pool. Then Fiddle and Faddle skinny-dipped in the pool with the President and male guests. Later the President had sex with them in a small adjoining room. "It was common knowledge in the White House," said Secret Service agent Larry Newman, "that when the President took lunch in the pool with Fiddle and Faddle, nobody goes in there."

When Jackie Kennedy left for their home in Glen Ora, the President gulped his bowl of soup, then hit the pool with Fiddle and Faddle. "When [Jackie] was there, it was no fun," said Newman. "He just had headaches. You really saw him droop because he wasn't getting laid. He was like a rooster getting hit with a water hose."[22]

A few White House reporters soon noticed that both women were available to the President at all hours, accompanied him on his trips, and were assigned quarters near his room. "Since the women did not have highly developed secretarial skills," Hugh Sidey of *Time* recalled of the plane trips, "imaginations were inflamed, particularly since one or the other often returned to her quarters physically spent."

Once, while a male reporter was eating a late dinner with Fiddle in Palm Beach, she was suddenly called to the phone. "It's the President," she explained on her return. "He wants me. Right now." She shrugged her shoulders apologetically and said, "I've got to go."

Newman thought the two young ladies were "very intelligent" but "over their heads. I felt sorry for them. I thought they were being used."[23]

An old flame remained in Kennedy's life as well. Flo Pritchett had become the second wife of Earl E. T. Smith, the U.S. ambassador to Cuba under Eisenhower, and they lived next door to the Kennedys in Palm Beach. There were reports of secret rendezvous between Jack and Flo, feverish interludes on the beach connecting their respective homes.

Flo occasionally visited the President alone in the White House, and sent him notes. "It was wonderful seeing you in Palm Beach looking so well and being so gay," she wrote in April 1961. "I know we have the smartest President in the world, but it is reassuring to have it confirmed again that we also have the most attractive President in the world."[24]

Television and movie star Angie Dickinson met Kennedy in 1960 and continued seeing him in the White House. Although Dickinson has never publicly confirmed a relationship with Kennedy, she has made suggestive and coy comments. "He's the only presidential candidate who has ever turned me on," she said. "Naturally it was said, printed, that we were lovers. Even if I deny it now, I won't be believed."

A famous older actress visited the White House as well. On September 10, 1963, Evelyn Lincoln confided in her diary: "At 3:45 [P.M.] today Marlene Dietrich came in to see the President. She looks mighty good—leggy—for 62."[25]

A shocking headline in a sleazy tabloid first alerted the nation to John Kennedy's White House relationship with Mary Meyer. The *National Enquirer* trumpeted their affair on March 2, 1976, with the bold front-page headline "JFK 2 YEAR WHITE HOUSE ROMANCE." The Mary Meyer revelation stunned even veteran observers of the White House scene. "It was a bombshell," said one, "not because it happened but because nobody I know ever heard a whisper."[26]

Mary Meyer was a descendent of a prominent American family, the Pinchots of Pennsylvania. Her uncle Gifford Pinchot was a well-known conservationist and two-term governor; her father, Amos Pinchot, was a radical lawyer and a leading isolationist opponent of FDR before World War II. The Pinchot's family fortune reached into the millions.

Mary graduated from Vassar in 1942; three years later she married Cord Meyer, a Yale graduate and World War II hero. In the 1950s Cord Meyer became chief of the covert action staff at the CIA. Partly because Cord drank too much and provoked arguments, the Meyers divorced in the mid-1950s; Mary moved to Washington, D.C., and became an artist. Lovely, vibrant, and poised, Mary was one of Kennedy's most worldly lovers. Rebellious and a sexual adventurer, she was a "blue blood with a wild streak." Mary's sister, Tony Bradlee, was the wife of Kennedy's journalist friend Ben Bradlee of *Newsweek*. (The Bradlees later divorced.)[27]

Kennedy had known Mary slightly, having met her at a dance during his senior year at Choate. Their paths crossed again when Mary was at Vassar and Kennedy dated her classmates, and in 1945 in San Francisco during the organizing convention of the UN.

Together with the Bradlees, Mary Meyer was invited to many of the big White House dances and smaller dinners arranged by Jackie Kennedy. The dance of the moment was the twist, danced to the tune by Chubby Checker. (At one party *The Washington Post*'s publisher Phil Graham split the seat of his pants doing a particularly energetic version.) "The twist represented youth and the end of the dreary 1950s," observed Nina Burleigh, Mary Meyer's biographer. Perfect for the White House parties, Mary "could do the twist, drink and smoke, keep up with the action, and above all, get the joke."

On the fall evening of November 11, 1961, Jackie and the President hosted a dinner dance for more than eighty in honor of Jackie's sister, Princess Lee Radziwill. Burleigh described the party atmosphere:

> The candlelight did wonders for female guests such as Anne Chamberlin and Mary Meyer, nearly twenty years out of Vassar and suddenly glowing regulars at the hottest parties in the nation. Fashion designers, journalists, politicians, and diplomats tippled and danced until the wee hours, serenaded by strolling musicians and escorted through the corridors of the White House by solicitous men in uniform. The guests dined on duck and did the twist to the Marine Corps Band and Lester Lanin's orchestra.[28]

That evening President Kennedy made his first sexual advance to Meyer. Mary confided this to a friend, James Truitt, an executive at *The Washington Post,* who kept notes and became the primary source about Mary's relations with the President. Mary refused Kennedy's advance on November 11, according to Truitt, but ten weeks later, on January 22, 1962, with Jackie away at Glen Ora, the President's offer to send a White House limousine to Mary's town house proved irresistible. That evening Mary Meyer was signed in at the White House by Evelyn Lincoln to see the President at seven-thirty.

During the next year, Mary was frequently logged in at the White House—particularly when Jackie was away. The routine was always the same. She usually arrived at around 7:30 P.M., often delivered by a White House driver, then was ushered into a private dinner with the President. Sometimes other guests, usually Ken O'Donnell or Dave Powers, were present for dinner as well. After dinner the men retired, leaving Mary alone with the President.

Mary Meyer was not a surreptitious guest at the White House. "She was never as hidden as some of Kennedy's other girlfriends, whose names were not even entered in the official logs," observed Burleigh. "But discretion was always observed when Mary visited the White House. The true nature of her relationship with the President was not obvious to the other dinner guests."

Kennedy's aides concede that Meyer was one of the President's favorite women and were not surprised to see her in the private residence. Kennedy "had a great attachment to her," Myer Feldman said, though he saw no indication they were lovers. "Around eight-thirty, when the day was over, often I'd walk over to the residence and she'd be sitting there," said Feldman.[29]

On the evening of July 16, 1962, according to Jim Truitt, Kennedy and Mary smoked marijuana together. The White House was hosting a conference on narcotics in two months, and Kennedy joked about it to Mary. (Truitt claimed he himself provided Mary with the pot.) "The President smoked three of the six joints Mary brought to him," Burleigh wrote. At first he felt no effects. Then he closed his eyes and refused a fourth joint. "Suppose the Russians did something now," he said. Kennedy allegedly told Mary that the pot "isn't like cocaine," and informed her that he would get her some cocaine.

During her affair with Kennedy, Mary visited Harvard's Timothy Leary, the high priest of the hallucinogenic drug LSD. There is no confirmation that Kennedy tried LSD with Mary, but, said Burleigh, "the timing of her visits to Timothy Leary do coincide with the dates of her known private meetings with the President." If Kennedy did experiment with LSD, his aides knew nothing about it.

Kennedy's relationship with Meyer began to cool early in 1963. One reason may have been an outgrowth of an alarming incident in January 1963 when Phil Graham, suffering from alcoholism and manic depression, publicly mentioned Meyer's affair with the President at a convention of American newspaper editors in Phoenix. "Graham had attended the convention without being invited to speak," wrote Burleigh. "In the middle of the proceedings he stumbled to the podium, grabbed the microphone, and began a rambling tirade that included a story about the President's 'new favorite,' Mary Meyer." So astonishing was the outburst by the consummate Washington insider that the White House itself provided a government jet to bring Graham's doctors to him quickly. (Graham was committed to the care of a private mental institution, and subsequently committed suicide.)[30]

President Kennedy viewed Hollywood star Marilyn Monroe as an exceptionally desirable notch to add to his belt. He managed to add the notch, but many accounts of their relationship are exaggerated. Some allege that secret FBI records, wiretaps, tape recordings, photographs, sworn depositions, and police reports all prove that Kennedy and Monroe had a long-standing intimate—often salacious—relationship, including liaisons in the White House. But the authors of these sensational tales never produce documentation for independent experts to study.

No responsible biographer maintains that Monroe and JFK were partners in a love affair. "Accounts of a more enduring affair with John Kennedy, stretching anywhere from a year to a decade, owe to fanciful supermarket journalists and tales told by those eager for quick cash or quicker notoriety," commented Monroe biographer Donald Spoto.[31]

Traphes Bryant, a White House employee who saw or heard almost everything, never saw Marilyn Monroe around the White House and never heard talk of her being there. "I personally never saw Marilyn Monroe in the White House," agreed Secret Service agent Larry Newman. "I never heard [from others] that she was in the White House."

JFK and Monroe were together on four occasions and one time had a sexual encounter. Kennedy met Monroe for the first time on Sunday, November 19, 1961, at the Santa Monica home of the Peter Lawfords. (Peter Lawford, said Gore Vidal, was "Jack's Plenipotentiary to the Girls of Hollywood.")

Peter Lawford arranged another meeting two weeks later. The President was the guest of honor at the awards dinner of the National Football Foundation and Hall of Fame at the Waldorf-Astoria in New York. Following the dinner he went to a party at the Park Avenue apartment of Mrs. John "Fifi" Fell, the wealthy socialite widow of a prominent investment banker. Lawford had arranged for Monroe to fly in for the occasion.[32]

By 1962 Monroe, then thirty-six, was often despondent and disoriented. Hooked on dangerous barbiturates, besotted with alcohol, unable to work regularly on her films, she was an emotional wreck. But President Kennedy didn't care about Monroe's health; he was only anxious to bed America's reigning sex symbol.

Their tryst finally occurred on Saturday, March 24, 1962, while both the President and Monroe were houseguests at Bing Crosby's home in Palm Springs, California. Before their rendezvous Kennedy met twice with Peter Lawford, presumably to coordinate his weekend at Crosby's home. (On the Monday following the weekend he huddled privately with Lawford two more times.)[33]

Their last meeting was at a huge Democratic Party function at Madison Square Garden on Saturday, May 19, 1962. Intended to raise money to wipe out the party's deficit from the 1960 election, the gala was billed by organizers as a forty-fifth-birthday salute to President Kennedy.

Ella Fitzgerald, Peggy Lee, Jack Benny, Maria Callas, Bobby Darin, Harry Belafonte, and other stars preceded Monroe. Her song was to be the finale. She slithered onstage in a dress Adlai Stevenson described as looking "like flesh with sequins sewed onto it." (She had literally been sewn into the gown she wore that evening.)[34]

One of Monroe's biographers, Barbara Leaming, described the scene: "Marilyn began to sing. She closed her eyes. She licked her lips. She ran her hands up her thighs and stomach, aborting the gesture at her breasts. The

Broadway columnist Dorothy Kilgallen, commenting on the telecast, described Marilyn's act as 'making love to the president in the direct view of forty million Americans.' "

Hugging herself, Monroe began purring, "Happy Birthday, Dear Mr. President." When she finished her sexy performance, the President hopped onstage and said, "I can now retire from politics after having had 'Happy Birthday' sung to me by such a sweet wholesome girl as Marilyn Monroe."

After the Madison Square Garden gala, Kennedy put an end to his relationship with Monroe. People were gossiping about the President and the movie star. He worried that some publication such as *Time* or *Newsweek* might print a story linking them.

When Marilyn phoned the White House, the President refused to accept her calls. "He wanted to stop it," said Senator George Smathers, "because it got to be to a point where it was somewhat embarrassing." Refusing her calls seemed to work. "She stopped bothering him," said Smathers, "because he quit talking to her."[35]

Dark suspicions purport to prove that Robert Kennedy also had a passionate affair with Monroe. When the romance soured, the story goes, with the connivance of the FBI, the CIA, or Communists, RFK arranged to have Monroe murdered, and then orchestrated an elaborate cover-up. None of these allegations have been substantiated.

Robert Kennedy first met Monroe in October 1961, at a party at the Lawfords' home in Santa Monica. They met on several other occasions as well, usually with RFK's aides or friends present. Because Monroe supported civil rights, she questioned the attorney general about the issue, and they exchanged phone calls. Suggestions that they enjoyed anything but a polite social relationship are unfounded, as are the scurrilous reports that he was somehow involved in her death.[36]

On August 6, 1962, the day after Monroe committed suicide, her death was the banner headline in all the newspapers. That day was also one of the most bizarre in the private life of John Kennedy. Nina Burleigh related the day's events:

> Telephone records indicate mob moll Judith Campbell called for the President from Los Angeles in midafternoon and was told no by Evelyn Lincoln, indicating Kennedy was not taking her calls. "Mrs. Mary Myer [*sic*]" called a little later and left her number. Judith Campbell called again that evening shortly before Mary Meyer was logged in, and phone records indicate Mrs. Lincoln again put her off, telling her the President was in a conference. That evening, while Mary was with Kennedy at the White House, Mrs. Kennedy called from New York at 7:50 and was told the President was out. At quarter to nine, Peter Lawford, in the thick of the

suicide story by virtue of having spoken with Marilyn just before she died (reports claim he was talking to her when she passed out), called Kennedy from Beverly Hills and got through. At 11:28 Kennedy called for a car to be sent to the South Gate, presumably to take Mary home.[37]

The President's clandestine womanizing created frightful problems for the Secret Service. The agents' stories add a new dimension to our understanding of Kennedy's reckless behavior. Agent Larry Newman was assigned to the presidential detail in the fall of 1961, and his first assignment—protect the President in Seattle in November 1961—proved traumatic, his "baptism by fire." Agents had sealed the President's floor at the Olympic Hotel, and Secret Service protocol dictated that access be limited to those with special clearance.

Suddenly a local Democratic sheriff came out of the elevator with two prostitutes and was bringing them down toward the President's suite. "I stopped the man," said Newman, but he loudly proclaimed that the "two girls were for the President's suite." Several policemen were there, as well. Before long, Dave Powers came out of the suite, thanked the sheriff for bringing the women, and ushered them into the President's suite.

Newman was embarrassed. Before leaving the floor, the sheriff had warned the two women, "If any word of this night gets out, I'll see that you both go to Stillicoom [a state mental hospital] and never get out."

"I couldn't believe he said this, but he did," Newman recalled. One of the policemen, a lieutenant, asked Newman, "Does this go on all the time?" Not knowing how to respond, Newman sputtered, "Well, we travel during the day. This only happens at night."

Later that evening Newman discovered six police officers, who had left their guard posts, peering through a window at the President's party. In a room next to the President, two young women on the White House staff, probably Fiddle and Faddle, were engaging in a three-way sexual romp with Ken O'Donnell, who had drawn the window's gauze curtains but not the heavier blinds. The policemen passed a pair of binoculars back and forth— binoculars they were supposed to be using to survey the streets outside to protect the President. "They were waiting in turn so they could watch," Newman said.[38]

What Newman and other agents experienced in Seattle became commonplace. Tony Sherman served two years on the Kennedy detail. "It was just not once every six months, not every New Year's Eve, but was a regular thing," Sherman said of the President's womanizing.

"Dave Powers was the interface on these occasions, and he would find the women or bring the women along," said Newman. The women would remain in the President's suite for three or four hours. "This became a matter of great concern," Newman said, "because we didn't know who these people were and we didn't know what they had on their person. You would just look up and see Dave Powers mincing down the hall and saying 'Hi pal.' " The agents had no way to stop it, and were told by their superiors not to interfere.

Powers angered the Secret Service agents because he prevented them from conducting even a cursory security check of the women. "He knew we were trying to protect the President," Newman complained. "We didn't know if these women were carrying listening devices, if they had syringes that carried some type of poison, or if they had Pentax cameras that would photograph the President for blackmail." Security was only as good as its weakest link, and Powers was the weak link.

"A procurement is illegal," agent William McIntyre observed. "And if you have a procurer with prostitutes paraded in front of you, then as a sworn law enforcement officer you're asking yourself, 'Well, what do they think of us?' When that occurs, the agent would feel that his authority and his reason for being there is nullified."

Powers also arranged for ambitious Hollywood starlets to fly into Washington to service the President. In one case, Newman said, "I saw Dave Powers bring in two starlets who were easily recognizable. [Powers] had one [of the women] put a scarf over her head. They had a White House car go out and pick her up at the airport, and Powers met her at the car and walked her up to the second floor."[39]

Agent McIntyre speculated that a public scandal was inevitable. "It would have had to come out in the next year or so. In the [1964 presidential] campaign, maybe."

In December 1962, Newman was on duty during a raucous party at Bing Crosby's huge estate in Palm Springs. (The absent Crosby let the President stay at his home several times.) At one point Secret Service agents rescued a young airline stewardess from Peter Lawford's drunken advances, leaving him sprawled in the desert, near Crosby's home.

From Newman's point of view the Crosby weekend was the nadir of presidential partying. Some of the women at the pool were stewardesses from a European airline, their names unknown to the Secret Service. Because of the shouts and shrieks of the partygoers, Newman intruded on the President's privacy by going poolside for a look. What Newman saw was Powers "banging a girl on the edge of the pool. The President is sitting across the pool, having a drink and talking to some broads. Everybody was buckass naked.

"We loved the man," concluded Newman of his Secret Service duty. "By the same token, we grieve that he would conduct himself in such a way as to make us so vulnerable and make the country so vulnerable."[40]

The President's penthouse suite at the Carlyle Hotel in New York provided spectacular views of New York City. But the reporters, always waiting in the hotel lobby, constricted JFK's freedom. The Secret Service, however, discovered a series of underground passageways running beneath the hotel that connected to nearby apartment houses and other hotels. The tunnels allowed the President to attend small parties with intimate friends nearby without the media ever knowing about it. "It was kind of a weird sight," Charles Spalding recalled. "Jack and I and two Secret Service men walking in these huge tunnels underneath the city streets alongside those enormous pipes, each of us carrying a flashlight. One of the Secret Service men also had this underground map and every once in a while he would say, 'We turn this way, Mr. President. . . . ' "[41]

The Kennedy White House was a man's world, an atmosphere that Walter Rostow described as "tremendously suppressed affection on both sides," like the atmosphere in a highly motivated unit at war. Myer Feldman believed that at least a half dozen of the President's loyalists would have taken an assassin's bullet meant for the President, throwing themselves across his body.

"Kennedy's was a phallocentric world," Nina Burleigh contended. "He and the men around him discussed events in terms of the relative safety of their testicles." Burleigh exaggerated, but Kennedy did refer to "nut-cutter" situations and "castrating" events. Unfair criticism he likened to being "kicked in the balls." The timid and fearful were said to be "grabbing their nuts." He privately used words like "prick," "fuck," "nuts," and "bastard" with "an ease that belied his upbringing," said Ben Bradlee.[42]

Uneasy with women in politics, he said to New York's Democratic leader Marietta Tree, "I don't know how to treat women politicians—as women or as politicians." Tree was stunned. "I knew lots of women in politics," she said, "and I think they just thought of themselves as people involved in politics and the issues of the day and would like to be treated like people."[43]

At times the normally charming President was privately crude and vulgar in the presence of women. Nurse Rita Dallas took care of Joseph P. Kennedy after his stroke. One evening the President summoned her to the White House. A valet guided her to a closed door, knocked politely, and led her into a bathroom, where the president lay placidly in the tub, his hands locked behind his head. Dallas recalled her bathroom meeting:

> "Nice of you to come, Mrs. Dallas," he said.
> What else could I answer except "Nice of you to have asked me"?
> He went on in his most polished Harvard manner, telling me that he and his wife were terribly anxious about his father. . . .

JOHN F. KENNEDY / 702

I was listening to him, of course, but all I could really think of was what in heaven's name does one say to a naked President.

But with the Kennedys, you could not survive with a middle-of-the-road attitude, so I took a washcloth off the rack, tossed it in the tub, and said, "For heaven's sakes, cover up."

He splashed the water with his hands like a gleeful boy, then with an appealing look of mock contrition, made a fair attempt to cover up by ceremoniously draping the cloth over himself. He grinned and motioned for me to sit down—on the toilet.

I could not bring myself to do it.

"Thank you," I said, "but I'd rather stand."

As the President of the United States lay stretched out in a bathtub, clutching at a floating rag, I gave, in my most professional tone, my opinion of his father's health.

We talked back and forth for about ten minutes, and then he started to get out of the tub. I asked quickly, "Is that all, Mr. President?"

He sat back down, fished for the washcloth, and said, with great dignity, "Why, yes, Mrs. Dallas . . . and thank you for coming."

Grappling for protocol, I muttered something like, "Thank you for asking me, Mr. President."

I recall passing the valet and frowning at the twinkle in his eye.[44]

The President's crude comments flabbergasted Laura Bergquist, a reporter for *Look*. When she interviewed him on one occasion, he was dressed only in his shorts. "And he's sitting around scratching himself in various places and the first thing he says to me is, 'Hi, Laura, getting much?' "

Bergquist had traveled to Cuba several times on reporting assignments, and she visited the President to inform him about her findings. Instead of listening carefully, as he did with most male journalists, he teased her about Castro and about her interviews with Che Guevara. "Something gives me the feeling you've got the hots for Che," the President said. Reacting angrily, Bergquist protested. Hadn't the President seen the photo of her and Che arguing during an interview? "Yeah," said Kennedy, "but that kind of hostility often leads to something else." In the President's view Che had simply bedazzled her, his beguiling male charm muddling her judgment.

He also quizzed her about Castro's love life, asking, "Who does he sleep with? I hear he doesn't even take his boots off." Bergquist responded that such questions were not of overwhelming importance to her. JFK continued, "He runs around making those long speeches, but where are the dames?"

Bergquist had wanted to give Kennedy a serious report, one more sympathetic to Castro's revolution than the President received from his male foreign-policy advisers. "I came away wondering, does this man really know what it's like to be poor and hungry and revolutionary and angry and nationalistic?"

Bergquist may indeed have had important information about Cuba and Cuban leaders, but the President wouldn't take her seriously. (The Bergquist incident was not typical, however, only because few women reporters covered foreign affairs.)[45]

British economist and author Barbara Ward was one of the few women whose advice President Kennedy took seriously and whose counsel he actively solicited. Three years older than Kennedy, the vivacious Ward was respected for her lucid, informed, and tough-minded writing. She had written several books on the relationship between the newly independent nations of the Third World and the industrialized West. Western nations should correct injustices at home and share a greater part of their enormous wealth with developing countries. Closing the gap between the industrialized West and the economically deprived Third World was essential for world peace and stability. Kennedy agreed with her and with her view that intelligence and will could stimulate progress in underdeveloped countries.

Ward often lectured in the United States, and Kennedy invited her to his Senate office and later to the White House. Although they became friends, Kennedy's inability to look beyond a woman's sex bothered Ward. "President Kennedy . . . had little empathy for the trained, intelligent woman," she said. "I don't think he would have been happy in a team that had included women at an operating level."[46]

Some White House staff members knew nothing about the President's sexual liaisons. "We simply never saw a thing," said Letitia (Tish) Baldrige. "The President's dalliances were kept hidden. That was just not part of our working lives in the White House."

Barbara Gamarekian, an aide to the assistant press secretary, had a different, more complex perspective. There was "underlying sexual tension," making the West Wing a "titillating" place to work. "It was a discreet, but sexually charged White House," she thought. As much as she disapproved of infidelity, she relished the vicarious thrill of being "an insider," privy to "rumors of presidential escapades," a recurring topic of gossip among the White House press corps and staff.

Still, the media never exposed the President's escapades, and she didn't discuss the subject at home or among friends. "Perhaps it was because no woman ever went public with charges of sexual misbehavior . . . and we could remain protective, in denial, rationalizing that circumstantial evidence and gossip best be kept within the White House family."[47]

Kennedy seemed to believe that his philandering was in no danger of exposure by the media. Once he supposedly said, "They can't touch me while I'm alive. And after I'm dead, who cares?" He had cheated fate by winning the presidency in spite of his sexual behavior, reinforcing his sense that his private life was unlikely to become a public embarrassment.

Despite whispers, gossip, and bits of evidence, the media did not buck tradition by investigating and publicizing the President's personal conduct. Unwilling to be the skunk at the garden party, reporters didn't go out of their way to find something nasty about the very popular President. Kennedy served before the courts weakened the libel laws, and the threat of legal action deterred publication of anything scandalous. Michael Beschloss speculated that "[John Kennedy's] lawyers, his father, and his brother Robert evidently used financial payoffs, legal action, and other kinds of threats to silence women who had been involved with Kennedy and, for breach of promise or other reasons, threatened to go public."[48]

In any case, it was exceptionally difficult to prove that two people were having an affair; proof of misbehavior—the kind that convinces editors to print a story—was hard to obtain. Journalist Maxine Cheshire noted, "In Washington, women all too often lie about their relationship with famous men—to get publicity, to even a score, to enhance their power."

Since the Franklin Roosevelt era the media had adhered to a gentleman's understanding not to pry into the President's personal life. As much self-protective of the press corps as protective of the President, the attitude was, "If we're going to blow the whistle on this guy, are we going to start telling about each other?" Some male reporters who covered Kennedy were hardly in a position to cast stones at a President who was fooling around with women. "They, too, got lonely, with so much traveling away from home," Cheshire observed. A few reporters simply grew too close to Kennedy. They liked him and agreed with his political views, and several reveled in their acceptance by him.

Some reporters later claimed they knew about the President's womanizing. In fact, most did not. The primary reason the media didn't expose Kennedy's philandering is that most reporters were oblivious of his private behavior. Columnist Betty Beale claimed that "the press was totally in the dark. I mean totally. The idea of the President having an affair with Marilyn Monroe or anyone else . . . well, it was just inconceivable." UPI White House correspondent Helen Thomas agreed. "I was right there every day," Thomas said, "and I didn't know a thing. Period."[49]

Only rarely did journalists get a glimpse of Kennedy's womanizing. Robert Pierpoint claimed that he witnessed a liaison in March 1962, while Kennedy visited Palm Springs. On an early Sunday evening Pierpoint and another reporter, Douglas Cornell, waited in a car in the driveway of the estate where the President was staying. (The pair were the designated pool cor-respondents assigned to accompany Kennedy back to Washington aboard *Air Force One.*) Suddenly the front door opened and JFK emerged with a woman on his arm. "Kennedy pulled her along toward the limousine, and then, opening the door, laughingly shoved her into the back seat. As the light went on inside the car, we got a brief glimpse of his young friend just before she disappeared into the President's arms. Then the light went out again."

A few minutes later the front door of the house opened again and another woman, one of Kennedy's sisters (probably Pat), emerged. She climbed into a fancy open convertible parked nearby and cruised up beside the motorcade to the President's limousine.

> "Come on, Mildred," she shouted, and as the light went on again in the car we could see "Mildred" (whom Cornell and I never identified more fully) disengaging herself from the President of the United States. After a brief farewell kiss she got into the other woman's car and they drove away. A moment later the motorcade headed for the airport.

Neither Pierpoint nor Cornell, however, ever published the Palm Springs story during Kennedy's presidency.[50]

Ironically, the only personal scandal involving President Kennedy that re-ceived media scrutiny turned out to be fabricated. Amateur genealogist Louis Blauvelt, a retired toolmaker who lived in East Orange, New Jersey, spent three decades compiling entries for his family's history. *The Blauvelt Family Genealogy,* published privately in 1957, would have remained obscure except for two factors. First, the lengthy history was available in the Library of Congress; and second, of its thousands of entries, one referred mysteriously to John F. Kennedy. Item number 12,427 stated:

> DURIE, (Kerr), MALCOM . . . She was born Kerr, but took the name of her stepfather. She first married Firmin Desloge, IV. They were di-vorced. Durie then married F. John Bersbach. They were divorced, and she married, third, John F. Kennedy, son of Joseph P. Kennedy, one time Ambassador to England. There were no children of the second or third marriages.[51]

Had John Kennedy been married and divorced before he married Jacque-line Bouvier? There was, in fact, evidence that Durie Malcolm and Kennedy dated in 1947. On January 20, 1947, the *New York World-Telegram's* society writer, Charles Ventura, reported that Congressman Kennedy was on the verge of being given Palm Beach's "annual Oscar for achievement in the field of romance." The article cited Kennedy, pictured in the column, for giving Durie Malcolm "the season's outstanding rush. . . . Only the fact that duty called him to Washington as a Congressman from Massachusetts kept Jack from staying around to receive his Oscar in person, so it may be awarded to Durie. The two were inseparable at all social functions and sports events. They even drove down to Miami to hold hands at football games and wager on the horses."

Blauvelt's book attracted no attention until mid-1961, when rumors about the entry mentioning the President began circulating among Kennedy's political opponents. The word soon passed to newspapermen, and Blauvelt's book became a popular item at the Library of Congress. A report first appeared in a small Greenwich Village magazine in March 1962, under the headline "The Story Behind the Rumor About President Kennedy's First Marriage."

It next showed up in an anti-Semitic, racist Alabama hate sheet, *The Thunderbolt*. Under the headline KENNEDY'S DIVORCE EXPOSED! IS PRESENT MARRIAGE VALID? EXCOMMUNICATION POSSIBLE, the "official White Racial organ of the National States Rights Party" claimed the President was "secretly divorced" before he married Jacqueline Bouvier.[52]

On September 2, 1962, the story reached a national audience when the Sunday supplement *Parade* published a letter from a reader asking "once and for all, will someone please tell me the truth" about reports of a previous marriage by the President. *Parade* claimed the rumors were false but also put them into wide circulation. The British press then placed the story on its front pages. In mid-September, the aging gossip columnist Walter Winchell reprinted the *Parade* item in his syndicated column and asked: "Why hasn't the White House debunked it?"

While the rumors were circulating, Sam Rayburn showed up in Robert Kennedy's office. "We've got documented proof that the President was [previously] married!" exclaimed the alarmed House Speaker. Suddenly the FBI began receiving reports about the genealogy as well. On November 22, 1961, after alerting Robert Kennedy, J. Edgar Hoover wrote a memo for his personal file: "The Attorney General stated the newspapermen come in and he tells them he hopes they print it because then 'we' could all retire for life on what 'we' collect."

The President contemplated legal action as well. When Daniel Mich, editorial director of *Look,* visited the President about an unrelated story, Kennedy said, "I understand that [Fletcher] Knebel and some of the other people . . . at *Look* . . . are digging into a silly report that I was secretly married once. I just want to tell you Mr. Mich that if . . . you all print that I'll sue you and wind up owning *Look* magazine."[53]

Earlier, in January 1962, Kennedy had requested the assistance of Clark Clifford to contain the story. "You won't believe this one," the President told Clifford. When Clifford asked him for the facts, Kennedy replied, "All I know is that some years ago, I knew very briefly a young woman named Durie Malcolm. I think I had two dates with her. One may have been a dinner date in which we went dancing. The other, to my recollection, was a football game. Those were the only two times I ever saw her. My brother Joe also dated her a few years earlier. I remember that she was quite attractive."

Ironically, Clifford had known Malcolm for a long time, and phoned her in Palm Beach.

"Did you know John F. Kennedy?"

"Yes, I knew him and his brother Joe," said Durie (then Mrs. Thomas Shevlin). "He was young and attractive. . . . My recollection is that we had two dates. We may have had dinner in New York and the other time we went to a football game."

"Durie, we are old friends. Let me ask you the sixty-four-dollar question. Was there anything serious between you and John F. Kennedy?"

"Absolutely not," she replied emphatically. "We hardly even knew each other. There were those two casual dates. . . . I come from the Blauvelt family, but the genealogy is wrong." Clifford asked if she would sign an affidavit stating that she had never been married to John F. Kennedy, and she readily agreed.[54]

The President also convinced his close friend Ben Bradlee of *Newsweek* to come to his rescue. Having gotten "the complete story from the President himself," Bradlee later said, he was fully convinced the tale was false. Bradlee arranged through Pierre Salinger for temporary use of FBI documentation about the character of the organizations and people involved in spreading the Blauvelt rumor. In return, Bradlee gave the President the extraordinary right of approval and clearance of the story before publication. But the story was so favorable to the President that Kennedy could have had no problems with the piece.

In the September 24, 1962, issue of *Newsweek* Bradlee and his coauthor, Charles Roberts, flatly discounted the poisonous "sensation" and attributed its spread to "hate groups and gossip columnists." One Blauvelt relative described the Malcolm entry in the genealogy as "just one colossal mistake," and speculated "that the old man formed the idea in his head, seeing that [1947] clipping, and the family hadn't had anyone famous for a long time."

The *Newsweek* story exposed several major errors in Blauvelt's amateurish account. Malcolm's maiden name was spelled "Malcom." She first married Bersbach, then Desloge, not vice versa. She married Shevlin on July 12, 1947—five months after divorcing Desloge, and ten years before the Blauvelt genealogy was published. Nonetheless, the Shevlin marriage was not even noted in the genealogy. *Newsweek* helpfully concluded: "The President and Mrs. Kennedy—who celebrated their ninth wedding anniversary last week—are philosophical about the 'Blauvelt campaign.' They recognize that it is motivated by extremist groups and circulated for political purpose."

As the Kennedys had hoped, once the *Newsweek* article appeared, the story of Kennedy's "other wife" seemed destined to be a curious footnote in the Kennedy legend. "I remain to this day convinced that the entire affair was nothing more than the result of an error made by an old man who was not careful in checking his facts," Clifford recalled in 1991.[55]

Rumors about Kennedy's "other wife" languished until Seymour Hersh revived the story in 1997 in *The Dark Side of Camelot*. Hersh interviewed Charles Spalding, who claimed that Kennedy *did* marry Durie Malcolm in 1947. "I went out there and removed the [marriage] papers," Spalding told Hersh, presumably from the Palm Beach courthouse. "It was Jack who asked if I'd go get the papers." Spalding said he retrieved the marriage documents with the help of a lawyer in Palm Beach.

Spalding described Kennedy's marriage as a lark, "a high school prank, a bit of daring that went too far." Getting married with no advance notice, he told Hersh, "was the kind of joke that Durie would go for"—a spur-of-the-moment decision that lasted only twenty-four hours.

In 1947 couples applying for a marriage license had to wait three days for the license to be issued. "If Jack Kennedy and Durie Malcolm followed the law," Hersh contended, "their wedding was planned at least three days in advance and thus was more than a spur-of-the-moment 'prank,' as Charles Spalding claimed."

Spalding, the main source for Hersh's contention, was seventy-nine years old when Hersh interviewed him and suffered from what Hersh described as "short-term memory" loss. (Hersh also relied on a priest, Father James J. O'Rourke, who claimed that he once overheard Richard Cardinal Cushing discussing Kennedy's marriage to Malcolm.)

Spalding's account raises several important questions. Why hadn't he mentioned his role earlier during the many occasions when he'd been interviewed about his friendship with John Kennedy? Who was the lawyer that assisted him in Palm Beach? Exactly what process did he use to retrieve the documents from the courthouse?[56]

Hersh's allegation is probably untrue. It is unlikely that Kennedy would send Spalding to Palm Beach on such a delicate assignment. The Kennedy family had access to plenty of investigators, lawyers, and retainers who could have performed the task far better than Spalding.

Spalding talked about destroying the marriage record. Did he also find and destroy the record of the license being issued? "Both Kennedy and socialite Durie Malcolm were high-profile people in Palm Beach society," Garry Wills has observed. "The dates they did have were reported in the press. How could the two acts—taking out the license and getting married— not have been reported by any of the people handling the ceremonies, and spread by word of mouth?"

Since 1962 Durie has consistently and repeatedly denied ever marrying John Kennedy. A handwritten letter she sent him, probably in early 1947, gave hint of a friendship but not of a marriage. "I was so sorry and disappointed that you couldn't be with us last night," she wrote. "You were so sweet to send over those lovely gardenias." And in a reference to his poor health, she added, "Do so hope you'll feel better soon."[57]

The story of John Kennedy's "other wife" didn't cause public scandal because the tale was exposed as fantasy. But in the fall of 1963 the President came within an eyelash of having his own sensational "Profumo scandal" because of his links to the roguish Bobby Baker and the prostitutes Maria Novotny and Ellen Rometsch. Only luck and adroit political maneuvering saved him from public disgrace.

Dashing John Profumo, minister of war in Harold Macmillan's government, had an affair with Christine Keeler, who had also had a sexual relationship with Yevgeny Ivanov, the Soviet naval attaché in London. Dr. Stephen Ward, a London procurer of high-class prostitutes, had arranged Keeler's relationship with Ivanov. At first Profumo denied that he had a sexual relationship with Keeler, but he resigned in disgrace in June 1963 after admitting he had lied. A subsequent investigation concluded that Profumo had not divulged national secrets, but the scandal embarrassed and damaged Harold Macmillan's government.

Shortly after Profumo resigned, the anti-Kennedy, Hearst-owned *New York Journal-American* linked Kennedy to the scandal in an article in late June 1963. The coauthors, Don Frasca and James Horan, the managing editor and a Pulitzer Prize winner, charged that one of the "biggest names in American politics"—who held "very high" elective office—had had a sexual affair with Suzy Chang, a model and an aspiring London actress linked to Stephen Ward.[58]

Forty-eight hours later, a Saturday afternoon, while Robert Kennedy was supposed to be on a family holiday at Hyannis Port, he met in his office with Frasca and Horan. Although the reporters had requested a private meeting, the attorney general insisted on the presence of the FBI's Courtney Evans. Frasca and Horan claimed they had information that linked John Kennedy in 1960 and 1961 with Suzy Chang and Maria Novotny, both connected to Stephen Ward of the Profumo scandal.

Robert Kennedy asked if the reporters had further corroboration, grilled them with questions, and then coolly dismissed them. "Although far from disproving the allegations," said RFK's biographer James Hilty, "Kennedy had put the *Journal-American* on notice: He would not tolerate the further publication of such accusations and, by insisting that all 'information' be turned over to the Justice Department, he would invoke the powers of his office to deal with them." For whatever reason—lack of concrete evidence, fear of a lawsuit—the *Journal-American* never followed up on its original story.[59]

It turned out that Kennedy had indeed been involved with Suzy Chang and Maria Novotny. In 1960 Chang had been seen several times with Kennedy, once at New York's posh restaurant "21."

Kennedy's indiscretions with Novotny could have threatened his presidency. In December 1960, at a party in New York, Peter Lawford introduced the nineteen-year-old Novotny to the President-elect. She and Kennedy wandered off to one of the bedrooms to have sexual relations.

"Jack and I got on well together from the word 'go,'" Novotny recalled. "He was charming and amusing."

Subsequently they rendezvoused at the apartments of friends in New York and Washington. "I would get a telephone call inviting me to tea or to cocktails, and then I would be picked up in a car by one of Jack's aides. . . . There were always other people there. It was all very natural. . . . Then, gradually the others would leave and Jack and I would be left alone. There would be security men around, but they were never obvious."

Kennedy's relationship with Novotny could have endangered national security—like John Profumo's affair—because she shared an apartment with TV producer Harry Towers, whom the FBI suspected of being a Soviet agent. (Towers fled the country in 1962.)[60]

Bobby Baker, a native of Pickens, South Carolina, started as a Senate page and rose to become secretary for the Democratic majority in the Senate and a protégé of Lyndon Johnson. In his autobiography, *Wheeling and Dealing,* Baker called himself "a Capitol Hill operator." Accused of influence peddling in 1963 for taking payoffs in return for steering federal contracts to his friends, Baker resigned from his Senate position on October 7, 1963. He eventually served eighteen months in a federal prison for fraud and tax evasion.

Baker not only brilliantly guided the Senate's legislative process, he did personal favors for senators, congressmen, lobbyists, and friends. The favors included providing them with women. He helped found the Quorum Club, a private suite in the Carroll Arms Hotel in Washington patronized by legislators and lobbyists on Capitol Hill. There beautiful Ellen Rometsch served as a hostess and a high-priced call girl. Bill Thompson, always on the lookout for beautiful women to take to the President, spotted Rometsch and arranged through Baker to bring her to the White House.

"She had good manners and she was very accommodating," Baker said of Rometsch. "I must have had fifty friends who went with her, and not one of them ever complained. She was a real joy to be with."

Kennedy understood, said Baker, that Rometsch would have to be paid. "President Kennedy did not want a date with somebody for social purposes. It was clearly understood when [Thompson] took girls to the White House they were going to be party girls."[61]

But the FBI, worried that Rometsch was a security risk, had been keeping tabs on her. As a youth in East Germany she had belonged to two Communist Party organizations. After defecting to the West, she married a sergeant in the West German air force and accompanied him on his assignment in Washington. Rometsch, twenty-seven, met Kennedy in the spring 1963. Baker estimated that she visited the President at least ten times in the spring and summer of 1963.

On July 3, 1963, Hoover informed Robert Kennedy that the FBI believed Rometsch was having illicit relations with highly placed governmental officials. Ominously, the FBI thought she came from East Germany and had formerly worked for Walter Ulbricht, the Communist dictator of East Germany.

Fearing that Rometsch worked for the Communists and was gathering incriminating information on U.S. government officials, the FBI, with Robert Kennedy's approval, arranged to have her and her husband quietly sent back to West Germany in August 1963. She would be denied a visa if she attempted to reenter the United States. (She may have been given money to remain quiet.) President Kennedy didn't know about Rometsch's background and didn't realize that she might be a Communist spy.[62]

The Rometsch story remained quiet until October 26, 1963, when the investigative reporter Clark Mollenhoff published a dispatch in the *Des Moines Register* revealing that the Senate Rules Committee studying the Bobby Baker scandal was also planning to hear testimony about Ellen Rometsch and her abrupt expulsion from the United States. "The evidence also is likely to include identification of several high executive branch officials as friends and associates of [Rometsch], the part-time model and party girl," Mollenhoff wrote.

Mollenhoff's story horrified President Kennedy. In an exceptionally unusual entry in her diary Evelyn Lincoln wrote on October 28, 1963: "The President came in all excited about the news reports concerning the German woman and other prostitutes getting mixed up with government officials, Congressmen, etc. He called Mike Mansfield to come to the office to discuss the playing down of this news report."[63]

To stave off a security scandal like the Profumo affair that might destroy the Kennedy presidency, Robert Kennedy hustled behind the scenes to prevent the Senate investigation of Baker's influence peddling from disclosing Baker's use of call girls such as Rometsch. The Republicans on the Senate Rules Committee might publicly demand to interview Rometsch and insist she be given a visa to return to Washington.

After Mollenhoff's article appeared, the White House phone lines burned up between RFK, O'Donnell, and JFK. President Kennedy's phone log, Evan Thomas noted, showed calls "from the Attorney General at 4:26, O'Donnell at 4:42 and 5:24, the Attorney General at 5:25 and 5:45, O'Donnell at 5:50, . . . and the Attorney General at 6:50."[64]

The attorney general's aides repeatedly asked the FBI to dissuade other journalists from picking up the story. Thomas noted that on the fifth request, one of Hoover's assistants wrote that an aide "told me the President was personally interested in having this story killed."

Usually, when Robert Kennedy wanted to talk with Hoover, they met in the attorney general's office. But on Monday morning, October 28, Kennedy appeared, "an uneasy supplicant," at Hoover's office. "He had a very big favor to ask," Thomas observed. He told Hoover that the President "urgently wished the FBI director to brief the Senate leadership on the dangers of the Rometsch case. If word got out that senators and executive branch officials were carrying on with a woman suspected by the FBI of spying, the integrity of the country would be damaged."

Robert Kennedy had to implore Hoover to help contain a sordid scandal that might easily entangle the President. Thomas observed:

> Hoover let Kennedy squirm. The whole matter was distasteful to him, he said. Why shouldn't Kennedy speak to the Senate leaders himself? RFK was obliged to say aloud what Hoover wanted to hear: that only the legendary FBI director had the independent stature and authority to impress upon the senators the gravity of the situation. Outwardly reluctant, no doubt inwardly triumphant, Hoover agreed.

The same day, Hoover met secretly with Senator Mike Mansfield and the Republican minority leader, Everett Dirksen, at Mansfield's home. He told them that Rometsch was not a spy, had not been involved with anyone at the White House, but that the FBI had the names, dates, and places where Bobby Baker's girls had entertained U.S. senators.

The strategy worked. Fortunately for the Kennedy presidency, most senators, particularly the Democrats, wanted to handle the Baker matter discreetly. The Senate had a longtime reluctance to police its own members, and therefore the investigation was not very searching. It ignored Baker's and the senators' link to Rometsch and other women—and President Kennedy's sexual relationship with Rometsch.[65]

Why did John Kennedy engage in such behavior with women? As a model for his womanizing JFK had an example of somebody whom he admired, respected, and loved all his life: his own father. Joe Kennedy apparently never cautioned his son to abandon the models, stewardesses, actresses, and prostitutes. "Given Joe's record as a husband," said Charles Spalding, "he was in no position to tell Jack to clean up his act and he knew it."

Biographer Nigel Hamilton blamed much of JFK's sexual behavior on Rose Kennedy's inadequacies. Consequently, according to Hamilton, John Kennedy developed twin obsessions: "sexual revenge against his mother and, quite simply, the need for a quality of physical touching denied him from infancy." Hamilton's simplistic Freudian interpretation slanders Rose and ignores the prevailing child-care advice Rose—and millions of other mothers—adopted. Joe Kennedy's awful example deserves far more responsibility than his well-meaning wife.[66]

Lem Billings recalled Jack saying that "getting it off with beautiful people was sort of reaffirming the life-force and escaping life's pressures all at the same time." Billings added, "It was part of Jack's cynical, lonely, don't-give-a-damn attitude." Escape from boredom was also a factor, Billings thought. Kennedy believed in living "for the moment, treating each day as if it were his last, demanding of life constant intensity, adventure, and pleasure."

Perhaps Kennedy had a hereditary or physiological predisposition toward womanizing, or a prodigious sexual drive, an exceptional libido. His chronic ill health may also have contributed to his obsession with women. As Garry Wills suggested, his sexual performance was "a way of cackling at the gods of bodily debility who plagued him, as if to say, 'I'm not dead yet.'"

Several women referred to Kennedy as a "boy" in terms of his sexual interest, indicating an immature sexual identity:

"Jack was a very busy boy" (Lundberg).

He was a "little boy" (Von Post).

He "was like a little boy who wouldn't grow up" (Storm).

He splashed in the tub like a "gleeful boy" (Dallas).

He acted like a "fourteen-year-old high school football player on the make" (Coit).[67]

Whatever the causes of his behavior, John Kennedy pursued women with an urgency and single-mindedness that made ordinary courtship seem casual and desultory, and with a recklessness that jeopardized his marriage, his career, his health, and the health of his partners. After all, he may have reasoned, his father's public career seemed undamaged by womanizing. Joseph P. Kennedy was one of America's wealthiest businessmen, had served in the New Deal and as ambassador to Great Britain—yet he simultaneously held his family together and avoided public scandal.

Chasing women was just one of several aspects of John Kennedy's life which he carefully compartmentalized. "There was a niche for each one," observed Judith Exner, "his career, his Presidency, his political party, his family, his children, his wife, . . . me, his cronies." His sexual liaisons were all momentary pleasures, "diversions walled off" from the complex world of politics, legislative strife, and the Cold War.[68]

Unburdened by conscience or guilt, he didn't think of himself as a contemptible sneak or an adulterer. He rationalized that because Jackie didn't satisfy all his emotional and sexual needs, he would enjoy companionship and sex with other women. Besides, if he didn't act on his urges, he remained horny, suffered headaches, and grew restless.

After a while, though, sex with the same woman proved disappointingly pallid, and he sought new excitement, fresh conquest. He approached sex in a mechanistic way, measuring satisfaction in quantitative terms, accumulating lovers like belt notches. He engaged in sexual escalation, urging his partners to perform a succession of erotic variations, leading to sex with multiple partners. The pleasure of the variations derived from their novelty.[69]

His sexual gamesmanship required concentration, self-control, persistence, and persuasiveness. Through repetition and practice, he mastered the game's rules and techniques and integrated them into a body of learned reflexes. The game shored up his ego and reinforced an inner sense of potency, attractiveness, and power.

A connoisseur of the sexual game and a habitual deceiver in his courtship, he assumed a seductive mask, keeping his genuine feelings deeply hidden from his partners. His exceptional charm and sensitivity appeared natural, spontaneous, and sincere, but was usually calculating, deliberate, and manipulative. By adroit questioning and probing, he induced a woman to talk about herself and flattered her in the process.

His relationships had an air of transience and improvisation. When separated from Jackie or a lover, he didn't seem to suffer from genuine disappointment; he simply looked for a new partner. No loss was unbearable, no woman irreplaceable.

His relationships began quickly with an instant of physical attraction. He didn't question his passion or analyze his sexual urges before acting on them. Nor did he practice birth control, and he seemed indifferent to the dangers of sexually transmitted disease or of causing pregnancy.

Because he was handsome, charming, wealthy, and powerful, he became accustomed to getting what he wanted from women and retreated further into his narcissism, into a world in which his wish for endless sexual gratification was usually satisfied. Occasionally women rejected him. Although annoyed, he remained mostly unfazed. The blow wasn't mortal, and he quickly resumed his normal seduction routine.

In some ways his compulsive pursuit of women resembled addictions to drugs and alcohol, but not completely. One proponent of the controversial theory of sexual addiction observed that "sex addicts, like alcoholics and other addicts, are virtually helpless to resist it. They want to stop. Time and again, they promise to stop. They even try to stop, but they cannot." In Kennedy's case, however, there is almost no evidence that he *wanted* to stop, or *promised* to stop, or *tried* to stop. Addicts go through a personal hell, but Kennedy never indicated that his sexual escapades made his life a personal hell. (*Exposure* of his escapades, though, could make his life a personal hell.) He showed no desire to be cured. Of course, one need not admit to addiction to be addicted.[70]

JFK's personal life did affect his performance as President, though; his retention of Hoover as director of the FBI, for example, can partly be explained by his womanizing. Hoover's bulging file on the President's sexual encounters went back to Kennedy's affair with Inga Arvad during World War II. Kennedy may have kept Hoover in his post because the President feared that Hoover would make incriminating information public.

The link between JFK's private life and his presidential performance, though, should not be exaggerated. He disconnected his personal life from his work. "He was as consistently cautious in his policy-making as he was reckless in private," historian Mark White accurately observed. Kennedy didn't send American soldiers into Cuba during the Bay of Pigs debacle or deploy combat troops in Vietnam, and preferred the blockade option rather than the dangerous air-strike alternative during the Cuban missile crisis. "If Kennedy had displayed the machismo and recklessness in his political life that he exhibited privately, he would have fought in Vietnam and over Cuba," said White.[71]

Nonetheless, Kennedy's sexual liaisons were damaging, or potentially damaging, in several ways. They exposed him to blackmail from scorned women, the Mafia, the FBI, the Teamsters, the Soviets, or some hostile foreign intelligence service. Fortunately for him, none of his lovers objected to being used and discarded. None complained and found the ear of a brave reporter or editor. "Women could be especially dangerous if they became emotional about being treated in the casual, unfeeling style," observed Nina Burleigh.

There was always the chilling possibility that Sam Giancana would threaten to publicize evidence of Kennedy's sexual relationship with Judith

Campbell Exner. Then, suggested Michael Beschloss, the President "could have been faced with a choice between giving in to whatever demands Giancana made or allowing himself to be driven out of office. What President could survive the revelation that he had knowingly slept with the mistress of a Mafia chief?" J. Edgar Hoover could have indefinitely held his secret information as a threat over John and Robert Kennedy.[72]

The Secret Service lacked the resources or the mandate to investigate the background of every woman discreetly slipped into the White House or the President's hotel suites around the country. Some of the women were strangers and could easily have had a sinister purpose. LeMoyne Billings observed that "it never occurred to Jack that some of the women might be considered dangerous. They were never searched, never questioned in depth."

"We were told that the Soviets had women who were very good agents," said Larry Newman. Distressed and annoyed, the Secret Service felt powerless to intervene. Agent Joseph Paolella adored Kennedy but worried that one of the President's women might be a Communist spy. Agent Tony Sherman agreed. "I never knew the name of the outsiders, where they came from, where they were, or anything," said Sherman. "I opened the door and said good evening and they said good evening. And in they went and the door shut. And when I reported for my next shift the next day, the President was still alive."[73]

Using a standard espionage technique, Soviet-bloc intelligence during the Cold War made a serious effort to sexually compromise Western officials. In 1958, for instance, the Soviet's KGB enticed Maurice Dejean, France's ambassador in Moscow, into an affair in order to put him in their debt. Kennedy's relations with Ellen Rometsch could have erupted in scandal like Profumo's in England. What if Mary Meyer had been a spy with a Soviet handler? "If she were an agent, she'd have been a terrific one," said Myer Feldman.[74]

Given Kennedy's acute sensitivity in most aspects of his political career, his reckless philandering is almost incomprehensible. He must have convinced himself that the media and the Republican opposition would continue to be discreet. "He seemed to have an aristocratic view of public leaders and their private sexual adventures," historian James Giglio correctly observed. "Kennedy felt sorry for [John] Profumo, without thinking that the same thing could happen to him."

John Kennedy might not have survived a second term without a devastating exposé. Herve Alphand, the French ambassador in Washington, confided in his diary that Kennedy's "desires are difficult to satisfy without raising fears of scandal and its use by his political enemies. This might happen one day, because he does not take sufficient precautions in this Puritan country."

Had the American people known the full extent of Kennedy's womanizing, or even a fraction of it, they would surely have objected to using public funds, facilities, and personnel for illicit affairs. From the White House to *Air Force One* to suites in hotels, his aides scheduled and facilitated the President's meetings with women.

The mind-altering drugs he may have received from Mary Meyer could have affected his judgment, an exceptionally foolhardy presidential transgression in the nuclear age. Finally, the stunning scandals about Kennedy's personal life later contributed to the public's alienation from politics, providing additional evidence that political leaders cannot be trusted.[75]

34

THRIVING ON PRESSURE

The author Garry Wills, a severe critic of John Kennedy, sarcastically observed that the "official Kennedy literature is drearily joyful in repeating how much fun Kennedy had being President." But it was true—he did enjoy it. "John F. Kennedy was a happy President," said Sorensen. "He liked the job, he thrived on its pressures." Stewart Udall agreed, saying the President showed a great capacity to grow and thrive under pressure. "You could watch him almost grow before your eyes. . . . The more intense the pressures, the more he tended to try to be dispassionate and wise."

When he assumed the presidency, Kennedy had almost no executive experience. "It is a tremendous change to go from being a Senator to being President," he said. "In the first months it is very difficult." Indeed, the first months produced the chaos of the Bay of Pigs.

White House staff meetings and weekly cabinet meetings were a thing of the past under Kennedy. Nor would he employ an "assistant president," the role played in the Eisenhower White House by Sherman Adams. He abolished the NSC Planning Board and the Operations Coordinating Board because he thought they engaged in needless paperwork and blocked the President's contact with his responsible officers. Eisenhower wanted his aides to present him with a consensus, an agreement on a course of action by all relevant parties with the arguments neatly summarized. Then he would say yes or no.[1]

Unlike Ike, Kennedy wanted to participate in the process of decision making. Documents presented to him should be vivid and forceful and offer opposing points of view. "He was not interested in unanimous committee recommendations which stifled alternatives to find the lowest common denominator of compromise," said Sorensen.

Kennedy's cabinet and NSC meetings were largely symbolic, conducted to satisfy the public's desire for order and regularity. President Eisenhower, a military man, noted Arthur Schlesinger, was "accustomed to a relatively rigid, orderly, hierarchical structure with firm assignments and obligatory channels, all ruled by detailed organization charts. President John F. Kennedy was a political man, accustomed to a far more flexible, informal, and untidy system, hoping thereby to stop others from defining his choices and enabling him to question information and recommendations rising upward through the ordained channels."[2]

In mid-May 1961, McGeorge Bundy composed a long memo to the President outlining problems and setting down ways that Kennedy could improve his administrative performance:

> Centrally it is a problem of your use of time and your use of staff. You have revived the government, which is an enormous gain, but in the process you have overstrained your own calendar, limited your chances for thought, and used your staff incompletely. You are altogether too valuable to go on this way; with a very modest change in your methods you can double your effectiveness and cut the strain on yourself in half.

The President should set aside a regular time each day for national security discussion and action. Several weeks earlier the President had asked Bundy to meet with him first thing in the morning. "I have succeeded in catching you on three mornings, for a total of about 8 minutes," Bundy wrote. "Moreover, 6 of the 8 minutes were given not to what I had for you but what you had for me from [journalists] Marguerite Higgins, David Lawrence, Scotty Reston, and others. The newspapers are important, but not as an exercise in who leaked and why."

Bundy also urged the President to run closer to his schedule. "When you start a big meeting half an hour late and let it go an hour overtime, you have not only disrupted the schedules of 30 men, but you have probably set 100 men under them to still greater trouble." This wasted executive energy, a precious commodity. "The White House is a taut ship in terms of standards—but not in terms of schedules," Bundy continued. In the end, the President did improve, setting down a regular time for national security discussion and keeping closer to his schedule.[3]

Orville Freeman thought the White House was well organized, with the lines of authority for staff people clear. "The result was that the working relationships were generally very good," said Freeman.

Maxwell Taylor, though, was surprised at the lapses in organization at the time he entered the White House in the spring of 1961. "There was little perceptible method in the assignment of duties within the staff, although I had to admit that the work did get done, largely through the individual initiative of its members."[4]

The President gathered information from a wide assortment of sources: magazines, books, television, radio, elder statesmen, friends, politicians, experts, polls, and especially newspapers. "Ken," he said, "have you seen the corn-surplus story on page fourteen of the *Times*? No? Well, read it and ask Freeman to stop in to see me around ten." Or he called Sorensen. "Ted, have you read the Gromyko speech in Leningrad? Well, it's on page four of *The Washington Post* and I wish you would check it out with Rusk and Kohler and find out if it represents a change of view on Cuba."

His procedure for gathering information was quick. Pick up the phone and call Rusk; pick up the phone and ask McNamara a question. He telephoned an assistant desk officer—not a desk officer—in the State Department and asked him a question. Before the President hung up, he told the assistant to inform Secretary Rusk about the call. "I never heard of a President who wanted to know so much," said one longtime career servant.[5]

"There were some things he was extremely careful about and knew exactly whom he wanted to do [the assignment]," said Carl Kaysen. "But with many things, perhaps unimportant things, it was simply a question of handing them to the first fellow who walked in."

Usually Kennedy's written messages were terse, understated, almost polite. Rather than demand, he "suggested" or "appreciated." He was always seeking more facts, documents, or evidence. "I would like to have more information on the progress of the negotiation with the Germans on increasing their participation in foreign aid to the underdeveloped countries and to defense."

Usually the President entered a conference room rapidly, moved quickly to his chair, and started the meeting. Once he announced a decision at a meeting, he grew impatient with further discussion on the subject. Additional dialogue was unnecessary, he would curtly point out to those who continued to argue. His mind was made up. Normally, said Sorensen, "he would gather up all his papers as a sign that the meeting was over and, if this hint was not taken by persistent conferees, suddenly rise to his feet to say good-bye."[6]

Often Kennedy made his decision on the spot. But if the issue was complicated, or if the meeting included the secretary of defense, the chairman of the Joint Chiefs of Staff, or others of high stature, and if there had been disagreement over a significant matter, Kennedy ended the meeting without a formal decision.

During meetings Ken O'Donnell stood with his back to the Oval Office, looking at his watch. "Freeman has been in there thirteen minutes," O'Donnell said. "I'll give him one more." Asked about the best method for getting visitors out of the President's office, O'Donnell grinned. "When I think the time is up," he answered, "I just walk in. Usually the visitor takes the hint and says good-bye to the President."

O'Donnell prevented some people from seeing the President too often. "We only isolated him when we knew that he didn't value very highly advice he might be getting from [a person]," said Ralph Dungan. "A couple of times Stewart Udall was hot on some conservation issue, which basically bored Kennedy—he was no Theodore Roosevelt—and when the decision was made, he didn't want to hear any more pleadings."[7]

Kennedy understood that aides and cabinet members found it intolerable to have to ask O'Donnell's permission every time they wanted to see the President. Because O'Donnell had the reputation for being overly protective, the President arranged an informal system that bypassed his appointment secretary and allowed visitors to see the President via Evelyn Lincoln's office.

O'Donnell wasn't happy about the arrangement, but visitors found it convenient and easy. They lined up at Lincoln's door to the Oval Office, which the President purposely left slightly ajar at certain times, most often on weekdays at 1:15 P.M. and 6:30 P.M. "Whoever had some business would simply line up at Evelyn's desk and stand around there," said Carl Kaysen. The President would spot them and invite them in.[8]

Kennedy had extraordinary zest for his work. He might start off the day with only five scheduled appointments neatly spaced. But as the day progressed he filled in the gaps, resulting in a busy twelve-appointment day. "A man lacking zest for his job does not deliberately and even joyously fill in gaps in his work load," said one observer. Although he didn't like to be bothered by verbose visitors, whiners, or insignificant details, he was very accessible. Staff, cabinet members, or legislators with important business could see him alone.[9]

He occasionally apologized for misdirected anger, forgave officials who committed an unusual lapse in judgment, and extended kindness. After the politically naive Robert McNamara prematurely announced that there was no missile gap, he was embarrassed by the public outcry, and offered to resign. McNamara recalled Kennedy's response: " 'Oh, come on, Bob, forget it,' said Kennedy without the slightest hint of anger. 'We're in a helluva mess, but we all put our foot in our mouth once in a while. Just forget it. It'll blow over.' It eventually did, but I never forgot the generous way he forgave my stupidity."

"I would hope that you would take a few days off," the President wrote Dean Rusk in early May 1963. "You and Secretary McNamara work much too hard and it gives me a guilty feeling.

"It seems to me that after a long trip like you have had that it really would be wise for you to take three or four days in the sun.

"I would be delighted if you would use Camp David."[10]

He took very seriously his responsibility to uphold high standards of government service even on subjects some might judge minor. When an architectural magazine devoted an entire issue to Washington, D.C., one problem it focused on was the dreadful appearance of public parks, such as the trash and poor housekeeping near the Washington Monument. Kennedy read the article and contacted Conrad Wirth, the director of the National Park Service, and asked him to acquire attractive trash baskets and clean up the areas near the monuments, particularly the Washington Monument. Wirth immediately took measures to remedy the problem.

In early November 1963, Kennedy was shocked to learn of the spread of polio in the United States Trust territories. "It seems to me that this is inexcusable," he wrote Stewart Udall.

I would like to have an investigation made into why there were inadequate funds in 1958 for administering preventive medicine and why no action was undertaken between 1958 and 1963 when the spread of the disease again became acute. How much would it have cost to have taken precautionary steps?. . . . I would like a complete investigation into the reason why the United States government did not meet its responsibility in this area. Would you expedite this matter?[11]

He wrote two cabinet secretaries about reports on the facilities for visitors who arrived at the port of New York. The docks were "cold and drafty, the custom inspectors are cold and the whole appearance is rather bleak. In fact, the image of America is not advanced during the first two hours the visitors are in this country." He concluded: "Do you think you could have a look at this and give me a report?"

"I would like to be kept up to date on the plans that are being made for the American exhibits at the World's Fair," he wrote Luther Hodges in early September 1962. "Who is in charge of our exhibits? Do we have an effective advisory group which can assure that the American section will be imaginative, original and successful?"[12]

The White House staff was exceptionally talented and maintained excellent spirit. There was minor tension within the group—between O'Donnell and Sorensen, between O'Donnell and O'Brien—but almost no intrigues, personal vendettas, bureaucratic paranoia, or competing fiefdoms.

Asked by a reporter to draw up a chart of the White House staff, a presidential assistant said he couldn't do it. "Draw a circle instead," he replied, "and put the President in the center with the lines running out to the assistants on the rim of the circle." Kennedy maintained bilateral relations with an astonishingly large number of people. "These men have managed the deliberate overlapping of their work and their bilateral relations with the President in remarkably self-disciplined fashion," observed Richard Neustadt.[13]

Cabinet meetings bored Kennedy. He made no important decisions at the meetings. He reluctantly summoned the cabinet to inform them, to help maintain esprit de corps, and to ward off the accusation that he ignored the cabinet. The issues he did bring up at cabinet meetings had broad impact and were almost entirely on the domestic side: the national economy, budgetary policy, government personnel, congressional relations.

The cabinet meeting was not an effective forum to discuss important issues, Kennedy believed. "He hasn't downgraded the Cabinet," said a White House aide. "He has a great deal of respect for the members personally and he works with all of them." But each had his specific responsibilities, his separate problems. When several of them had a common problem, he brought those individuals together for discussion.

Why should the postmaster general sit through a meeting on the problems in Laos? Kennedy asked. Others agreed. "I can't imagine," commented one cabinet officer about the President's approach, "why the President would want to hear Bob McNamara talk about price supports on cotton or Orville Freeman talk about sending troops to Vietnam."[14]

Cabinet officers often didn't want to burden the President with their problems, preferring instead to talk with the White House staff. The staff, said Myer Feldman, "could get the answer for them quickly or, in many instances, could give them the answer themselves and take care of the matter in the President's name."

Orville Freeman took it as a compliment that he rarely needed to meet with the President. He dealt with Sorensen and Feldman, "both of whom are very able, and I could usually get a decision from them on most things. When I needed some help the President would give it to me, and when he had a question he would call me, but I really felt that he had enough to do."

Over two-thirds of the interactions the President had with cabinet members were with four key people: Dean Rusk, Robert McNamara, Douglas Dillon, and Robert Kennedy. The rest of the cabinet was peripheral. Twice a week Fred Dutton received an eight- or nine-page synopsis of activities from each cabinet member, which he then summarized. Kennedy would usually read them the same day, scribbling in the margin: "I want more information from [Arthur] Goldberg on this" or "Tell him I don't want that." Anything urgent or important prompted the President to phone the cabinet member or arrange a meeting.[15]

Instead of regular cabinet and National Security Council meetings, Kennedy established small interagency task forces to gather facts, isolate issues, and make recommendations. There were task forces on Laos, Cuba, Vietnam, NATO, minimum-wage policy, and integration in federal employment.

In addition, Kennedy usually held three or four small daily meetings, more often on foreign policy than on domestic matters. Several times Orville Freeman went to the President with issues which also involved half a dozen other important people who had a direct interest in the matter.[16]

The President granted cabinet officers free rein to run their own departments and seldom meddled. "He knew what you were doing and he followed it closely, and he was very alert," observed Freeman. "This was quite a difference from working [later] with [President] Lyndon Johnson, because when you were up on the Hill doing something you were supposed to do, all of a sudden you found out the president was up there changing it and didn't get around to telling you. Well, nothing like that happened under Kennedy."

Some cabinet members believed that Kennedy should have encouraged free-wheeling discussions. Freeman wanted to discuss fiscal policies at a cabinet meeting. Stewart Udall was particularly upset. "I don't think either of the presidents that I worked for understood the degree to which cabinet officers were eyes and ears for them. After all, we got around the country a great deal more," said Udall, who also worked under President Lyndon Johnson. "Some of us were politically astute, some were not, but all of us had a finger on the country's pulse." Udall wanted wide-ranging, open discussion on issues, such as national priorities, giving cabinet members the opportunity to argue that money for domestic programs was being cut back to pay for military and space programs.

Robert Kennedy held the same view. In a confidential memorandum to the President in early 1963, he observed:

> The best minds in Government should be utilized in finding solutions to . . . major problems. They should be available in times other than deep deep crisis and emergencies. . . . You talk to McNamara but mostly on Defense matters, you talk to Dillon but primarily on financial ques-

tions. . . . These men should be sitting down and thinking of some of the problems facing us in a broader context. I think you could get a good deal more out of what is available in Government than you are at the present time.

On reflection, Arthur Schlesinger also agreed that the President should have taken his cabinet more seriously as a general sounding board. Kennedy didn't think Freeman or Udall knew anything about Laos and Vietnam. What could they contribute? "In point of fact," said Schlesinger, "his secretary of agriculture and secretary of the interior were both experienced men whose judgment on Laos and later on Vietnam was a lot wiser than the judgment of his secretary of state."[17]

The National Security Council had been established in 1947 primarily to provide the President with expert advice on foreign policy and military affairs. Eisenhower set up a ponderous bureaucratic system of boards, staffs, and interdepartmental committees through which national security policy was supposed to function, but instead of strengthening the NSC, the elaborate machinery produced stagnation. In 1960 Senator Henry Jackson's Subcommittee for National Security Staffing and Operations issued a series of thoughtful Senate reports criticizing Eisenhower's approach, giving Kennedy the justification for using a different, more comfortable one.

After the Bay of Pigs, Kennedy and Bundy decided to solve the information problem with a full-blown crisis center in the basement of the White House. "It would routinely receive copies of all the relevant cables and have the capability to inform the President and NSC staff when trouble broke out anywhere," noted writer John Prados. With this move Bundy became a trusted confidant of the President.[18]

Kennedy cut the NSC's meetings back to about once every three weeks, and used them mostly as briefing sessions or to rubber-stamp decisions already made. The NSC staff became a "little State Department," with its own area specialists. Harvard professor Carl Kaysen studied nuclear disarmament; Michael Forrestal oversaw Far Eastern affairs; Robert Komer specialized in Near Eastern problems. They were Kennedy's eyes and ears. Each member had his own portfolio, not just ad hoc assignments. Bundy and his staff kept in touch with every aspect of foreign affairs—from disarmament negotiations to NATO troop levels, from the aid program in India to conditions in Yemen.[19]

Unlike the State Department, Bundy gave the President quick, clear, intelligent responses. A facilitator, he managed the flow of business, knowing and coordinating everything to do with foreign policy. He was also a troubleshooter and an adviser. An example of his advice is the memo he wrote the President in July 1962: "Here is the basic paper for tomorrow's testing—disarmament meeting. . . . It puts the main issues clearly. The position relating to the general disarmament treaty [is] easy—and unanimously agreed. The testing scenario is the hard one. My belief is that you will want to listen hard, and *not* decide, tomorrow morning."

Bundy's staff often duplicated the State Department's responsibilities, but Kennedy didn't care. Since he had little faith in the State Department and didn't know most of its personnel, he felt more confident receiving information and opinions from Bundy's staff because he knew the issue would be carefully studied.[20]

The President insisted that in letters to foreign leaders the NSC staff use excellent written style and present logical arguments. "These letters were instruments of diplomacy," observed Robert Komer. "These were diplomatic demarches, and he insisted they get rewritten five or six times."

There was always the potential for tension between the NSC and the State Department, but because of the attitude of the two principals in charge, it never developed. "One person or another, either in the department or in the White House, might not be tactful, or might not share information at a useful point, and there is likely to be something that will go wrong as a result," Bundy recalled. "I think basically that Rusk and I understood it and tried to see to it that the rest of our people did."

Rusk deeply respected Bundy's ability, the precision of his mind, his comprehensive grasp of information, and his skilled draftsmanship. He also appreciated Bundy's cooperation and courtesy. "I always found him to be a very honorable man in his relations with me and in his relations with the President that affected me. I never had the feeling that he was cutting my throat or that he was running behind me to the President to get policies changed without my knowledge."[21]

Earlier in his career, while serving under Truman and Acheson, Dean Rusk had specialized in problem solving and had excelled. But as secretary of state under Kennedy, he had too many new roles. "No one could perform them all well," noted biographer Warren Cohen. "Rusk lacked the time for some of the chores assigned and the skill for others."

Kennedy became discouraged with the State Department almost immediately. He may have been influenced by his father's long-standing antipathy for the department; Joe Kennedy had despised professional diplomats, had mocked the "striped-pants set." The President deplored the department's built-in inertia and its inability to report anything on time. Because of the State Department's bureaucracy, "its labyrinthian system of clearances," a statement about the Congo had to be cleared by the African Bureau, the

United Nations Bureau, the Public Affairs Bureau, the undersecretary for political affairs, and Rusk.[22]

Rusk communicated poorly with his subordinates. Some never knew his goals or how he assessed their work. "Others lacked information necessary to perform their duties," said Cohen. "One assistant secretary claimed to have developed a way of interpreting facial expressions and another found direction listening carefully to Rusk's interviews with foreign ambassadors."

Robert Kennedy complained that the President seldom received "an original idea" from the department. "I believe the proposed answer prepared for Lyndon Johnson by the State Department is hopeless," the President wrote Bundy in July 1961. "I am shocked that it could be approved by them. . . . It indicates how careful we must be with their proposals." Other departments gave the President timely, coherent answers; why couldn't the State Department? Since Kennedy wouldn't tolerate the poorly written memos and documents coming out of the State Department, Bundy and his staff rewrote many of them.[23]

"If a problem arose, the White House staff might have a proposed solution hours, days, weeks—even months—before the State Department presented the President with a recommendation," noted Cohen. "On occasion the Department might match Bundy's bunch in competence or brilliance, but never in speed. So the President invariably had an answer before Rusk came to whisper in his ear."

Rusk believed it was wrong for the secretary of state to debate the President in front of others, partly because he didn't want to lose and have it be known that Kennedy followed someone else's advice. During meetings on foreign policy he presided over debate and discussion, summarized issues, but didn't express his own opinion; afterward, alone with the President, he gave his assessment. "Few, if any, in the Department, certainly no one in the press, would ever be aware of disagreement between the President and his Secretary of State," Cohen observed. "And the surest way to prevent leaks about disagreement, about the President overruling the secretary, was to keep the views of the secretary secret."[24]

Some of the problems were not Rusk's fault. The President had appointed Rusk, Bowles, Ball, and Stevenson without considering whether they knew each other or could work together as a team. Rusk had to tolerate outsiders meddling in foreign policy. Schlesinger and Richard Goodwin both dabbled in Latin American affairs, and Robert Kennedy expressed strong convictions on foreign policy and had direct access to the President.

If the President thought a country desk officer could solve a problem, he issued instructions, leaving four or five levels of higher-ranking officials in the dark. "That made problems for us, but President Kennedy did not seem to mind," said U. Alexis Johnson.

New to public administration, Kennedy and his team had never negotiated anything with a foreign government. They needed to learn, said Rusk, "the importance of diplomacy, the rules of protocol, the process of negotiation, the role of the United Nations and international law."[25]

Many who frequented Robert Kennedy's Hickory Hill seminars—informal monthly lectures and discussions at Robert Kennedy's home—prodded Bobby to urge the President to have Rusk removed as secretary of state. In their view Rusk was too stolid, too passive, and too indifferent about managing his department. The President briefly considered replacing Rusk with Robert McNamara or the experienced diplomat David Bruce. One day after talking with Robert Kennedy, the President said to Ken O'Donnell, "Don't you think we ought to get somebody in the State Department with a little more pep?" O'Donnell gave him all the arguments for keeping Rusk, and added, "Do you want somebody like Dean Acheson over there? Somebody who would be fighting everything you want to do, and antagonizing the Congressmen on the foreign policy and appropriations committees, and talking to the newspapers?"

"Thanks for reminding me," the President responded. "I'd be foolish to get rid of Rusk."

Kennedy never came to grips with the problems at the Department of State, believing that they were endemic to the institution. But he did reach an accommodation with his secretary of state. By the end of 1961 the President had a better appreciation of Rusk's strengths and weaknesses. The secretary had performed well in developing the U.S. negotiating position on Berlin. "Rusk carried out Kennedy's directives with no arguments and no second-guesses," O'Donnell observed. "He was always discreet, well respected by Congress, and not a flashy publicity-seeker, all of which qualities Kennedy valued highly."

Their relationship was not all that either man wanted, said Cohen, but "the tensions and frustrations of the previous spring were gone."[26]

Kennedy's relationships with Chester Bowles and Adlai Stevenson were exceptions to the generally warm and respectful bonds he established with his advisers and cabinet. A former advertising executive, the idealistic Bowles believed the greatest danger in the world was not so much the Soviets as poverty and hunger, and his ideas for solving the problems of the poor in underdeveloped nations had captured the imagination of many liberals.

But because of his verbosity and disorganization, he antagonized the Kennedy team. Rusk, constantly pressed for time, grew impatient with Bowles's long, wide-ranging visionary memos. "He needed a man who could run the Department for him, a man of sound judgment and assured loyalty to him, and Bowles, though he tried, was not that man," observed Cohen. Bowles allowed important letters and other papers to pile up on his desk where they remained for weeks, irritating Rusk and the President's staff.[27]

"I like Bowles," Galbraith cleverly wrote the President. "His only trouble is an uncontrollable instinct for persuasion which he brings to bear on [the] persuaded, the unpersuaded and the totally irredeemable alike." Robert Kennedy despised Bowles, complaining about the undersecretary's "whiny voice," his tendency for not getting to the point and "all the long sentences and the big words." When Bowles disagreed with the President, he committed the mortal sin of talking to the press about his differences.

Bowles had a reputation for fuzzy and woolly-headed thinking, which made him a major target for hard-liners in the media and in Congress. He wasn't tough enough, the President told John Sharon, a friend of Bowles. "What I need over here to make this government run is ten or twelve sons of bitches. One of the reasons that McNamara and Ball and Doug Dillon are so effective is that they are tough bastards."[28]

Bowles had important assets, Schlesinger reminded the President in a letter:

> He has considerable gifts for persuasive public presentation. His personal idealism inspires great devotion on the part of many who work for him. He has labored loyally for the President. He is more responsible than anyone else for the distinguished series of ambassadorial appointments. He is identified both in the U.S. and through the world with the generous and affirmative aspects of American foreign policy.

On November 26, 1961, the administration announced a major shakeup. Bowles would, in effect, be demoted, replacing Averell Harriman as roving ambassador; Harriman became assistant secretary for Far Eastern affairs; George Ball, a good administrator, assumed Bowles's position as undersecretary; and George McGhee replaced Ball as junior undersecretary.

Ignoring his own weaknesses, Bowles thought that Kennedy and his team simply disparaged his kind. "They looked on people like Stevenson and myself as traitors to our class. We were 'liberals'—a horrible thing."[29]

Adlai Stevenson and Kennedy had little sympathy for each other and even less respect. Stevenson had not thrown his support to the President at the Democratic convention, and had only halfheartedly campaigned for him. It didn't help their relationship when FBI director J. Edgar Hoover privately leaked to the President the false story that Stevenson was a notorious homosexual.

Stevenson was not happy with his UN job and seemed uninterested. He left meetings early and was a disappointing administrator.[30]

Both Kennedys detested his whining. Robert Kennedy privately expressed his own venomous attitude toward Stevenson, who he thought "acted like a girl, looked like a girl, complained like a girl, cried like a girl, moaned, groaned, whined like a girl. Every time he'd talk on the phone, he whined about something."

The President grew contemptuous of Stevenson. "He loved to hear jokes made about him," said Joe Alsop, "and I was only too eager to make them. He saw him as a self-regarding, posturing fellow."[31]

In his autobiography Oleg Cassini reported an instance of the President's cruelty toward Stevenson. Kennedy was spending a summer holiday at the Auchincloss house in Newport, Rhode Island. The sky was dark and threatening as the President said to Cassini, "I'm going to get that Adlai to fly out here today."

"Mr. President," Cassini said, "look at the skies."

"Good," he said, "he'll be airsick."

Stevenson landed at a nearby air force base. From there he proceeded to Newport by helicopter. Cassini recalled: "I remember seeing that helicopter, which seemed to stand still in the sky, fighting the winds and rain, gradually growing larger until it plopped down on the lawn and Stevenson emerged, wiping his brow, a little green at the gills."

"Adlai," the President said, with a charming smile, "how good to see you. Let's go and talk."

"Wonderful, Mr. President. There are a lot of things I want to talk to you about."

"We'll go out for a sail on my boat."

"The boat?" Stevenson replied. "I could see the horror in his eyes," Cassini said.

The wind was up, and the seas were treacherous. It was threatening to pour; lightning flashed in the distance. "The President, who, of course, was quite a good sailor and used to such things, insisted Adlai sit out back with him in the two captain's chairs," said Cassini. "I could see the President sitting there with no coat on, though. Stevenson, who wasn't going to wear a coat if the President wasn't, was attempting—unsuccessfully—not to shiver in the wind and rain."

When the boat returned to shore, the President said, "Well, Adlai, there's your helicopter waiting."

The little helicopter struggled against the storm. "Mr. President," Cassini said, "that is truly cruel and unusual punishment."

"He could use it," the President responded. "It's good for his health."[32]

Kennedy was sensitive to Vice President Lyndon Johnson's awkward predicament. Unable to command or dominate, feeling trapped and isolated,

Johnson withdrew psychologically during his vice presidency. "From time to time, he displayed acute symptoms of inferiority about what he perceived as his cultural deficiencies and lack of social graces," observed historian Alonzo Hamby.

To Kennedy's dismay, Johnson made only a halfhearted attempt to lobby legislators on behalf of the administration's programs. At White House meetings he gloomily sat in virtual silence, offering no suggestions. "Kennedy tried to draw Johnson into the debate," observed Jeff Shesol, "but as a matter of principle and political instinct, Johnson remained silent, providing no fodder for rumors of a split between himself and the President." If he felt strongly about a matter, he spoke privately with Kennedy, but he did so rarely.[33]

Kennedy insisted that Johnson be invited to meetings. During a session on Laos, the President looked around the Cabinet Room and said, "Where's the vice president?" Someone said, "He's circling Washington; the weather is bad." Kennedy replied, "We will take some other item up; I want him here when we discuss Laos." When his aides forgot to notify Johnson of another meeting, Kennedy angrily repeated an earlier injunction. "Don't let this ever happen again. You know what my rules are, and we will not conduct meetings without the vice president being present."

Kennedy asked several people to pay special attention to Johnson. "I just want you to know one thing," the President told Ken O'Donnell.

> Lyndon Johnson was majority leader of the United States Senate, he was elected to office several times by the people, he was the number one Democrat in the United States elected by us to be our leader. I'm President of the United States. He doesn't even like that. He thinks he's ten times more important than I am, he happens to be that kind of a fellow. But he thinks you're nothing but a clerk. Just keep that right in your mind. You . . . are dealing with a very insecure, sensitive man with a huge ego.

JFK ordered O'Donnell to take care of the vice president. "I want you literally to kiss his fanny from one end of Washington to the other." According to Shesol, O'Donnell did a poor job: "As a custodian of the vice president's well-being, O'Donnell was indifferent and offhandedly cruel. He demanded that every request LBJ made of the Pentagon, however mundane, be cleared first by the White House. He had no time for Johnson whatsoever, 'wouldn't give him the time of day,' said another presidential aide."[34]

Robert Kennedy and Johnson loathed each other. "He lies all the time," Robert Kennedy said in 1964. "In every conversation I have with him, he lies. He lies even when he doesn't have to lie." At Robert Kennedy's Hickory Hill seminars Johnson was the object of nasty jokes and mean-spirited stories. It was "just awful . . . inexcusable, really," recalled Hugh Sidey.

Robert Kennedy's animosity stemmed partly from his ambition to run for president in 1968. The scenario he worried about went like this: President Kennedy would win reelection in 1964, but couldn't seek a third term in 1968. If Johnson remained as the vice president in JFK's second term, the Texan would have the inside track for the Democratic nomination in 1968. In an interview in 1964, Robert Kennedy claimed that both he and the President brooded about the scenario.

> We were going to have to come up with a new president in 1968, we discussed it quite frequently, and I think I can say that he thought that Lyndon Johnson was better as a vice president than the other ones that were being considered at Los Angeles [in 1960]. . . . But as the days passed, he felt stronger and stronger that he shouldn't be president.

Then RFK let slip his real motivation: "It was always a question what I was going to do in [1968]."[35]

For his part Johnson privately referred to the attorney general as "that snot-nosed brother," "that son of a bitch Bobby," "that little shit-ass," "little runt," "punk kid," or "little bastard."

Although the President gently poked fun at Johnson, he treated him with dignity and tried to keep him busy. He appointed the vice president to chair the President's Committee on Equal Employment Opportunity, the Peace Corps advisory board, and the National Aeronautics and Space Council, and sent him on eleven foreign trips. Johnson attended the legislative breakfasts, campaigned for Democratic candidates, and spoke at fund-raisers. Kennedy kept Johnson informed on issues, made sure he was invited to ceremonies and parties, and granted him easy personal access to the Oval Office.

Composing a birthday telegram to his paranoid, supersensitive vice president, Kennedy told a reporter, was like "drafting a state document." Yet the vice president appreciated the personal kindness. After the President sent LBJ a birthday cake, Johnson responded, "I am constantly amazed, amid all you have to do, that you never overlook the extra kindnesses."[36]

The President's kindly approach was partly cold pragmatism. "I can't afford to have my vice president who knows every reporter in Washington going around saying we're all screwed up, so we're going to keep him happy," he said privately.

Many noticed the President's efforts. "President Kennedy," *Time* reported in early 1962, "is tireless in his efforts to keep Lyndon Johnson busy—and happy." George Reedy, Johnson's aide, thought President Kennedy was "generous" to the vice president. "I saw no signs that he resented LBJ as previous presidents had resented their vice presidents. . . . I do not know whether he was aware of the antagonism between Lyndon Johnson and his brother Bobby."

Johnson, though, remained withdrawn and morose. "He looks so sad," Kennedy told George Smathers. "I don't know what to do about him. I've tried to do everything we could to make him happy—I've put him up front whenever I can."

Reflecting on his days as vice president, Johnson recalled "trips around the world, chauffeurs, men saluting, people clapping [and] chairmanships of councils, but in the end, it is nothing. I detested every minute of it."[37]

At a dinner shortly after the inaugural the President joked that he saw no harm in naming his brother attorney general to give him "some legal experience before he goes out to practice law." Everyone laughed, except Bobby. Afterward, his face blue, his fists clenched, he complained, "Jack, you shouldn't have said that." The President responded, "Bobby, you don't understand. In politics you've got to make fun of your vulnerable points in order to make people laugh with you. If you poke fun at yourself then you get the people on your side." Not satisfied, Bobby said, "Yeah, but you weren't poking fun at yourself, you were poking fun at me."

Eight years younger than the President, the attorney general stood five feet ten inches, weighed 150 pounds, and retained his boyish face and an unruly shock of hair. In appearance, mannerisms and voice, the brothers were similar. So were their backgrounds. Both had attended excellent schools and traveled extensively. But they differed in temperament, personality, and outlook. Arthur Schlesinger, who studied both men, described John Kennedy as "urbane, objective, analytical, controlled, contained, masterful, a man of perspective." Robert, while very intelligent and increasingly reflective, was "more open, exposed, emotional, subjective, intense, a man of commitment."[38]

More than any of the other Kennedy children, Bobby resembled his father. "Both were high-strung and hyperactive; direct and outspoken; highly temperamental and sometimes tempestuous," observed Joe's biographer David Koskoff. Congressman Tip O'Neill, who detested Bobby, claimed that Joe Kennedy told him that Jack was too forgiving. "You can trample all over him," Joe said, "and the next day he's there for you with loving arms. But Bobby's my boy. When Bobby hates you, you stay hated."

Robert Kennedy also hated incompetence, laziness, stupidity, and pretense. He earned a bad reputation in the bureaucracy for his explosive temper—he once stormed into a meeting, expressed his displeasure, and slammed a chair on the floor of the State Department. He chastised bureaucrats in front of their peers, not seeming to care whom he offended. Many resented his rudeness and intimidation, but found it difficult to complain about the President's brother.[39]

Self-righteous, accusatorial, and abusive, Robert could also be kind and tender, caring deeply for children, the disadvantaged, and the victims of injustice. "At times during his brother's presidency his softer side emerged, but most remembered the tougher, uncompromising side," said James Hilty.

Robert attacked his responsibilities as attorney general with energy and dedication. He recruited an excellent staff of talented and idealistic lawyers from top law firms and universities, and his team remained exceptionally loyal to him. Under his direction the Justice Department's Organized Crime Section and the Tax Division convicted 96 racketeers in 1961, 101 in 1962, and 373 in 1963.

He turned a huge, slumbering, bureaucratic department into a vibrant and effective organization. Influenced by his contagious enthusiasm, his staff willingly worked overtime on holidays and weekends. One of his aides recalled:

> He had a gym built on the roof and he brightened up the dreary courtyard with an outdoor lunch stand and tables sheltered by multi-colored umbrellas. He had parties for employees' children and welcomed an endless stream of young people to his office. He ordered the Department and FBI to hire more Negro attorneys and agents. In the evenings he met with section after section until he had met every employee in the Department. After each session, he would ask if there was anyone who did not have enough work or who wanted something more challenging to do. Those who came forward were assigned to the more demanding areas such as organized crime or civil rights. The whole place came alive.[40]

Robert refused to allow his office to be tarnished by political favoritism. The absence of political scandal during his tenure was partly a matter of his strict moral and ethical code, but it also stemmed from his and his brother's refusal to make political deals. "Unlike their father, the Kennedy sons (particularly Robert) were reluctant to engage in the traditional quid pro quo of patronage-based politics," Hilty observed, adding, "His achievements as attorney general were offset by his failure to constrain the excesses of FBI director J. Edgar Hoover and by his troubling indifference toward the protection of civil liberties."[41]

After the failure of the Bay of Pigs, Bobby became his brother's informal deputy on foreign policy, playing a major role in everything from Vietnam to Cuba. He managed the negotiations for the ransom of prisoners taken by

Castro's forces after the Bay of Pigs, and handled delicate American negotiations during the Cuban missile crisis. He embraced the use of counterinsurgency forces in Third World countries menaced by Communist rebels. "Bobby fell in love with the notion of counterinsurgency, and the Green Berets were his kind of fighters," noted Ron Steel in his biography. "He brought them to the Kennedy family compound at Hyannis Port, where they swung from trees, scaled walls, and emitted such fierce noises that brother-in-law Sargent Shriver forbade his children to be around them."

Bobby's intervention in foreign affairs rankled Dean Rusk, but he tolerated the arrangement at the President's urging. "My understanding with President Kennedy," Rusk subsequently explained, "was that we would try to find ways" to let Bobby express his "considerable interest in foreign policy . . . but that there would be no confusion about who was Secretary of State."[42]

Away from work the two brothers had different interests. At the end of a long day the President found his brother too demanding, insistent, still too wrapped up in issues. The President seldom invited Bobby and Ethel to social events at the White House. At leisure JFK wanted diversion, not nagging by his younger brother. The President did not find Bobby to be relaxing company, and their wives had little in common. "JFK had little patience with RFK's boisterous and too-numerous offspring," noted Evan Thomas. "At a rare family gathering, he stood at the head of the stairs as various Robert Kennedy children squealed and squabbled below, and declared: 'I am the president of the United States and I say, 'Out! Out!' "

In 1963 Ben Bradlee asked John Kennedy why he thought Robert was so outstanding. "First, his high moral standards, strict personal ethics," the President responded. "He's a puritan, absolutely incorruptible. Then he has this terrific executive energy. We've got more guys around here with ideas. The problem is to get things done. Bobby's the best organizer I've ever seen."[43]

"Kidding remained the favorite Kennedy form of communication," said Schlesinger. When a magazine listed the attorney general as the number two person in Washington, the President said darkly, "That means there's only one way for you to go, and it ain't up!" Their communication was cryptic, as if in secret code. "One would start a sentence; the other would finish it," said John Seigenthaler. "They could talk about somebody for five minutes on the telephone without mentioning the name. It was as close to one heartbeat, one pulse beat, as you could get."

Bobby was fiercely loyal to his brother—like "a tigress protecting her cubs." "He would have taken a bolt of lightning for Jack," Seigenthaler later said. Instead of the normal relationship of the older brother looking after the younger one, Bobby looked after John. He gauged each delicate situation and seemed to ask himself, "How can this affect Jack? How can it hurt Jack?"

JOHN F. KENNEDY / 736

His duties included acting as the family's sexual policeman, trying to "keep John in line, and, when that failed, cleaning up the debris," observed Hilty.[44]

Bobby was the only person in the administration who could be absolutely candid with the President. "That is a terrible idea," he would declare. Bobby realized that one of his most important roles was to speak frankly, to contradict his brother at times, and to nudge him onto the right course.

In a crisis, with his older brother dependent on his advice and support, Bobby was usually wise, calm, restrained, and realistic in getting the facts at the heart of a problem. The President trusted his judgment, and relied on him to handle problems. But it was John Kennedy who weighed alternatives and made decisions. "*Nobody* told President Kennedy what to do," said Ken O'Donnell. "The President was much the toughest of the Kennedy brothers."[45]

J. Edgar Hoover and the Federal Bureau of Investigation were important elements in American myth, making the director difficult to manage. Arthur Schlesinger observed that they were "symbols of perfection in detective methods, wholesome anti-Communism, ruthless pursuit of gangsters and spies, . . . the nation's watchdog, and the President's counsellor."

Entranced by the myth, Joseph Kennedy had tried to cultivate Hoover, writing him many flattering letters and volunteering to be a special contact for the bureau. The FBI was "the greatest organization in the Government and you have performed the greatest public service of any man that I know," he gushed to Hoover in 1958.

Actually Hoover was an aloof, smug, narrow-minded martinet with an imperial ego, who had molded the FBI into his private empire and ruled it with an iron hand. He had held his position for thirty-six years. Kennedy was the first President who was younger than Hoover—younger by twenty-three years; Hoover's new boss, Robert Kennedy, was thirty-one years younger. The FBI director maintained power through his professionalism, his astute dealings with Congress, and excellent public relations. He also instilled fear of blackmail throughout Washington, shrewdly passing along juicy gossip to the Presidents he served, a practice raising a question in each President's mind: "What did Hoover know about him?"[46]

At first the attorney general and Hoover tried to be cordial, but they soon drifted apart. Hoover detested the new arrangement. Since Franklin Roosevelt's administration, Hoover's practice had been to go over the attorney general's head to report directly to the president. Now he had to report to the inexperienced thirty-five-year-old brother of the President.

Their different personal styles sparked resentment. "The FBI director was a deeply conservative man who insisted that his agents keep their hair short, be clean-shaven, and never take off their suit jackets in the office," noted

Ron Steel. "He was deeply shocked to serve under an attorney general who came to the office with a huge dog, worked in shirtsleeves, put his feet on the desk, and threw darts at a target on his wood-paneled walls."[47]

When Robert Kennedy took over the Justice Department, the FBI was lily-white, and Hoover responded angrily when Robert Kennedy pressured him to hire black agents. Hoover was also reluctant to involve the bureau in protecting the rights of blacks to vote. Also, he had long denied even the existence of a "Mafia." When the attorney general asked about the FBI's files on organized crime in New York, he received mostly newspaper clips. "The New York office had four hundred agents out looking for communists and ten devoted to the mob," observed Evan Thomas.

Robert Kennedy tried to contain Hoover, but was reluctant to impose his will on the FBI's director. Hoping to keep Hoover content, every two months or so he set up a luncheon meeting with JFK and Hoover. "It was important, as far as we were concerned, that he remain happy and that he remain in his position, because he was a symbol, and the President had won by such a narrow margin," RFK recalled after his brother's death.[48]

The attorney general attended dinners and luncheons in Hoover's honor, showed up at FBI ceremonies, and generally made himself available whenever the director requested. But Hoover did not reciprocate, noted Hilty, "conspicuously absenting himself from department social gatherings, declining invitations to Hickory Hill, and sending emissaries to department functions." Trying to mediate between the two strong-willed men "was the hardest job I've ever had," said the FBI's Courtney Evans.

Hoover was particularly dangerous for the Kennedy brothers. "Every month or so," Robert Kennedy recalled, Hoover would "send somebody around to give information on . . . a member of my family, or [made] allegations in connections with myself." Hoover wanted "to find out what my reaction would be." In January 1961 Hoover started a secret file on Robert Kennedy that eventually mushroomed to more than three thousand items— detailing his public appearances, private contacts, physical movements, and rumors alleging sexual misconduct.[49]

The Kennedys greatest worry, though, was the burgeoning file Hoover had accumulated on John Kennedy. They probably suspected that Hoover knew about the President's sexual liaison with Inga Arvad in 1942, and about other sexual intimacies that could destroy Kennedy's presidency if made public. They had good reason to worry. Shortly before the 1960 election, when told by an aide that the FBI files showed that John Kennedy had romanced Inga Arvad, Hoover dismissed the evidence. "You have the wrong Kennedy. You got the one that was killed in the early part of the war." The aide replied, "No, I haven't." Hoover said, "Yes, you have. You go back and review those files again, and you will find out that you've made a mistake."

The aide insisted, "I have not made a mistake," and produced the file. It was John F. Kennedy who was cross-referenced in the file. Hoover exclaimed, "Well, I'll be damned!"[50]

The type of information and misinformation deposited in John Kennedy's file included a memorandum of July 13, 1960, from an agent to Hoover's top aide, Cartha DeLoach. "As you are aware, allegations of immoral activities on Senator Kennedy's part have been reported to the FBI over the years." The allegations included "data reflecting that Kennedy carried on an illicit relationship with another man's wife during World War II; that (probably in January, 1960) Kennedy was 'compromised' with a woman in Las Vegas; and that Kennedy and Frank Sinatra have in the recent past been involved in parties in Palm Springs, Las Vegas and New York City. Regarding the Kennedy-Sinatra information, 'Confidential' magazine is said to have affidavits from two mulatto prostitutes in New York."

"You can't fire God," the President remarked about Hoover. The Kennedys intended to wait until after the 1964 election, when Hoover would reach his seventieth birthday, the mandatory retirement age. "They expected the law to take its course," said Courtney Evans.[51]

35

---•◆•---

WHITE HOUSE, PERSONAL LIFE, AND HEALTH

On December 19, 1961, while playing golf in Palm Beach, Joe Kennedy, then seventy-three years old, suffered a severe stroke. He became an invalid, and could not control his speech (but continued to understand what was said to him). Most words came out garbled. His "no" was a long, loud noise: "NNNnnnooooo!" He said it over and over again. His family pretended to understand. "Thanks, Dad," the President would say, "I'll take care of it. I'll do it your way."

Shortly after the stroke, Jack questioned the family's chauffeur, Frank Saunders, about his father's condition.

"Do you think he's getting the best of care, Frank?" the President asked.

"Yes I do."

"I talk with him and I wonder if he really understands."

"He understands."

"But I don't understand *him,*" said the President. "I just had a talk with him. I couldn't understand a single thing he said. And he didn't seem to know that he wasn't making one damn bit of sense."

The President shook his head, bewildered by his father's condition. "Frank, if you ever think that he's not getting the attention he should, I want you to come right to me with it. Understand?"

"Yes sir."

"I miss him, Frank."[1]

Joe Kennedy was occasionally brought to the White House for dinner and afterward sat in his wheelchair, remaining within the circle of conversation. At the White House gatherings Jackie hovered over him, wiping his mouth when he drooled, touching and kissing him. When his caretaker, Ann Gargan, announced that "Grandpa is going to bed," everybody came to shake his hand or kiss his head. "It was all so touching and simple and moving," recalled Ben Bradlee. "The Kennedys are at their best, it sometimes seems, when they are family, and forthright and demonstrative, and they were at their best tonight."[2]

The President enjoyed one glorious moment with his ailing father. While hospitalized in a private institution, Joe learned the President would visit. Before the news, Joe had been grumpy, but now he excitedly insisted on putting on his leg brace. He maneuvered his chair adjacent to a supporting pole and settled down expectantly.

When the President burst through the door, Mr. Kennedy grabbed the pole and pulled himself to his feet, balancing himself perfectly, without assistance.

Joe's private nurse, Rita Dallas, described the scene:

> His son, seeing this, ran toward him. There were tears in the President's eyes on seeing his father stand alone. Mr. Kennedy, with great pride, raised his hand in a silent salute. When he reached his father, the President stood very straight and applauded him. Mr. Kennedy stood erect and proud accepting his son's acknowledgement. . . .
>
> The President then came to him, wrapped both arms around his shoulders in a tight embrace, and kissed him. He cupped his hands under his father's elbow and gently helped him back to his chair. Neither man made an effort to hide his emotions. Speaking for the first time, the President choked, "Oh, Dad."[3]

The President quickly learned everyone's name on the White House staff and something about their families. "Whenever he saw you, he always smiled and spoke to you," said Joseph Karitas, the White House painter; "he always called me 'Joe.' " Jackie appreciated each of the maids and showed affection toward them. When the large number of Secret Service agents made it difficult for the President to remember their names, he asked Jerry Behn, head of the White House detail, to send him photos with each agent's name underneath.

The White House was divided into three sections: the Mansion, the East Wing, and the West Wing. The first family lived on the second floor of the Mansion. In the East Wing were the offices of Jackie Kennedy and her staff, plus those of the Secret Service, Arthur Schlesinger, the White House police, and the President's military aides. In the West Wing were the offices of the President and his key aides, the pressroom, and the swimming pool.[4]

A complement of domestic staff—maids, cooks, butlers—came with the White House, but the President and Mrs. Kennedy also brought with them several of their personal employees. The nanny Maud Shaw continued to attend to the mundane needs of John and Caroline. George Thomas, the President's black manservant, took care of JFK's clothes and personal needs. A jack-of-all-trades, John "Muggsy" O'Leary, a longtime Kennedy retainer, chauffeured guests and ran errands. Providencia Parades, a native of the Dominican Republic, served as Jackie's personal maid and took care of her clothes.[5]

The President blundered in instructing employees of the White House to sign a confidentiality pledge. After Pierre Salinger let news of the pledge slip out at a press conference, the media lambasted the President for muzzling employees. Shortly after the uproar, the President visited chief usher J. B. West and made an ignoble request. "I want you to help me, Mr. West," he began. "This 'pledge' business is causing a lot of trouble. Would you take the blame for it?"

"I did ask the staff to sign it, Mr. President," West answered.

"Good. We'll put out a statement saying it was your idea, and you initiated it. It will look more official, and less of a personal thing coming from you." The ploy worked, and the small crisis passed.[6]

John Kennedy's daily regimen began when George Thomas whispered, "Mr. President. It's close to seventy thirty."

After being awakened, Kennedy collected his wits quickly. Not needing a second rap on the door, he was out of bed at once.

Propped up by pillows on the bed, wearing a robe over his nightshirt, collecting the newspapers delivered to him, he began searching for important stories in *The New York Times, The Washington Post,* the *St. Louis Post-Dispatch,* and *The Wall Street Journal.*

Normally Chester Clifton and McGeorge Bundy arrived at his bedroom between seven-thirty and eight o'clock with briefings from the CIA, the State Department, and the Joint Chiefs of Staff, and any special information from an agency. Clifton, the President's military aide, found these early-morning sessions to be challenging. He described the dynamics:

Usually he was surrounded by all the morning newspapers as well as by letters and papers that Mrs. Lincoln may have put there for early morning reading and answering. . . . You'd give him a piece of intelligence on the Congo, and there would be a scramble through the newspapers, and a big rip, and he'd hand you the clipping, saying, "Well, read this on the Congo. We'd better find out who's right, our report or their reporter." You got a constant play between intelligence reports, affairs of state, the local press, last night's baseball scores, and his interrogation on your opinion of this man or that man. . . . It was lively and it was rapid, but it wasn't chaotic. He never got mixed up; he knew exactly what had been done and the instructions he had given you when you left there.[7]

Before breakfast Kennedy shaved in the hot bath prepared by George Thomas. Still reading in the bathtub, Kennedy often annotated memos, which later arrived at an aide's desk slightly moist.

At 8:50 he had his breakfast in bed, again propped up with a pillow. His breakfast tray consisted of fresh orange juice, two poached eggs, bacon, toast, and a cup of coffee with sugar and cream. While eating, he continued his reading or entertained Caroline and John, who had entered the bedroom to say good morning.

At about 9:30 A.M. Kennedy left the second-floor family quarters, often with Caroline and John in tow, took the elevator to the first floor, and walked down the corridor to his West Wing office.

Kennedy usually limited his appointments to fifteen minutes. In addition to his official calendar of appointments, he had many off-the-record meetings and brief conferences in the hallway. Throughout the day and night the President made phone calls and dictated terse memoranda—inquiring, requesting more information, suggesting an approach. Usually he was on the phone more than fifty times a day.[8]

"This is precisely what I want done," he said during meetings with staff members, all the while tapping a pencil on his desk; or "I want an answer on this by afternoon," he instructed on the phone. "Action was always expected as soon as possible," said Sorensen.

At about one-thirty each afternoon, the President left his office and swam for thirty minutes in the pool. Located between Kennedy's office and the mansion, the pool had been built for Franklin Roosevelt because swimming was an important therapy for FDR, a polio victim. With the temperature set at ninety degrees, the pool gave JFK relief from his back pain. Ambassador Kennedy paid for major improvements in the pool area, commissioning a huge mural on three walls surrounding it. The mural re-created the harbor at St. Croix in the Virgin Islands. Large mirrors covered the fourth wall of the pool. "When the President swam at noon," said Salinger, "the waterfront and the landscape beyond were lit with bright sunlight. When he swam after dark, there were lights twinkling around the harbor and a moon and stars in the sky."[9]

After his swim, Kennedy entered an adjoining room, the White House gym, where he did prescribed exercises. The routine was presided over by one of the two physical therapists assigned to the White House dispensary, and supervised by New York back expert Dr. Hans Kraus. The simple exercises were designed to strengthen his back. Periodically he had his scalp massaged, and a manicurist "fixed" his toenails and fingernails. After showering he entered the elevator, which took him back upstairs. He ate lunch in bed—a hamburger or a glass of the diet drink Metrecal.

After lunch George Thomas drew the drapes and said: "Mr. President, what time do you want me to call you?" "Three-thirty, George." Briefly he read papers he had brought with him, then quickly fell asleep. Jackie dropped everything she was doing to join her husband at nap time. "If she had visitors in tow, they would be left for me to entertain," said J. B. West. "During those hours, the Kennedy doors were closed. No telephone calls were allowed, no folders sent up, no interruptions from the staff. Nobody went upstairs, for any reason."[10]

After his nap, he took another hot bath, dressed, and returned to the office shortly after 3:30 P.M. for more appointments and meetings, usually working until 7:30 or 8:00 P.M. After completing his evening work, he stopped again at the pool to swim, then changed clothes for dinner. (He wore at least three separate suits of clothes every working day of his presidency.)

Wherever Kennedy traveled, the White House switchboard linked him to a telephone. A platoon of Secret Service agents followed him everywhere, along with an army warrant officer carrying the black case with the secret codes the President would need to order a nuclear retaliation.[11]

Kennedy relished the comfort and privacy of *Air Force One*. "He had a big bed back there," said Vernon "Red" Shell, his favorite flight steward. "On a short trip, say to Cape Cod, a one-hour flight, he'd skim through two or three newspapers real fast, maybe have a cup of fish chowder, then take a little nap. . . . Kennedy enjoyed that plane more than anybody I ever saw."

The White House sponsored a successful series of outdoor concerts, giving talented young amateurs—students of music and dance—a chance to perform. In a brief welcoming address Kennedy tried to inspire each group. One chilly spring day in 1962, the Greater Boston Youth Symphony Orchestra played on the South Lawn for an audience of children. He apologized for not being able to stay for the entire concert, but he promised to leave his office door open so he could listen. "The children kept looking back, and sure enough, the French doors of the Presidential office were kept open through-out," said Tish Baldrige, "as they were for every children's concert there-after."[12]

Baldrige recalled that she and a tour guide took a group of "spastic" children on a private tour of the mansion. (The childrens' wheelchairs would have been blocked by the masses of people during the regular visiting hours.) While the wheelchair brigade stopped near the Rose Garden, the President, who was late for an appointment, spotted them. Baldrige recalled:

> He crossed the lawn to us, insisted on being introduced to each child, and either picked up each limp, paralyzed hand to shake it, or touched the child on the cheek. He had a different conversation with each child. . . . He could comprehend what the spastic children said to him. Their speech had been so affected by their affliction, I could not understand one word. He knelt down by the side of a young boy and held a long conversation with him. Then he dashed back into his office, returned with an old PT boat skipper's hat he had used in the war, and plopped it down on the boy's head.
>
> The child's face radiated a joy totally impossible to describe. I will never forget the look in his eyes.
>
> "His father was in PT boats, too," the President said to me by way of explanation. "His father is dead."[13]

In June 1961, during his trip to Paris, Vienna, and London, Kennedy was enormously impressed with the lush lawns and exquisite gardens surrounding the official residences. The White House grounds and flowers looked humdrum by comparison.

"Mrs. Lincoln, do you see that brown spot out there on the lawn?" he asked. "Will you tell them to have that fixed?" But the lawn didn't improve. Salinger visited the President's office one day and found him looking gloomily out the window. "Isn't that damned lawn ever going to grow?" The White House gardeners told the skeptical President that helicopter landings caused the brown and bare spots. In any case, the lawn was blighted. As a stopgap, he ordered the gardeners to spray the bare spots with green paint before the arrival of distinguished visitors.

JFK feuded with the White House gardeners. Salinger recalled: "He was convinced his crew was twice as large as necessary and that the budget for maintenance of the grounds could be cut in half."[14]

The lawn remained blighted, but fortunately Mrs. Rachel "Bunny" Mellon of Upperville, Virginia, a friend of the Kennedys and a master gardener, learned of the President's unhappiness with the gardens and volunteered to help devise a plan of improvement. In late November 1961, she and her husband attended a dinner honoring the cellist Pablo Casals. When the President spotted her, he said "Bunny, where is my garden plan?"

"I'm afraid it is still in my head, Mr. President, not yet down on paper, but I will finish it and send it to you soon."

"That's the story of my administration," he said with a twinkle in his eye.

In the spring of 1962 Mellon started working on the garden, and she completed the project by the end of the year. Kennedy had studied the gardening notes written by Thomas Jefferson, and requested the same kind of flowers that bloomed during Jefferson's presidency.

Occasionally, as Mellon surveyed the area, the President spotted her and rushed out of the Oval Office to greet her. "What do you think can be done?" he asked. "Have you any ideas?" "Although I had no thoughts of what to do at that moment, President Kennedy's enthusiasm and interest were so contagious that I felt I must certainly find him a good solution," said Mellon.[15]

After the President approved her blueprints, she began clearing out the vegetation and planted four full-grown magnolia trees. "What I want is blooming flowers on the three sides, and especially along the portico where I receive groups," Kennedy told her. "And I would like to look at those flowers as I walk from the mansion to my office. And I would like them changed from season to season."

Caroline's horse was a problem. "Mrs. Lincoln, get Macaroni out of my garden." Lincoln would rush out and chase the pony away.

When Mellon completed the project, the proud President took heads of state for walks by the garden. "I would watch him coming around the corner from the mansion, enjoying every minute of the walk as he surveyed his garden," said Lincoln.[16]

By the end of 1961, through the various trusts Joe Kennedy had established over the years, each of the seven Kennedy children was worth about ten million dollars. Each received from five hundred thousand to one million dollars a year in pretax income. John Kennedy also earned one hundred thousand dollars a year in salary, an additional fifty thousand dollars a year as an expense account, and forty thousand dollars a year for travel.

The key person who handled the Kennedy family finances in Joe Kennedy's New York office was Thomas Walsh, an accountant and tax expert. (Stephen Smith also closely supervised the Kennedys' financial affairs.) Walsh periodically explained to the President his current financial status.

He'd come into the office with me, sit down, close the door and just say, "Well, are we making money?" with a smile on his face. Fortunately, we always seemed to be making money. . . . I'd point out certain areas where I thought he might be going overboard, and he'd say, "Well, let me have the details on that, and I'll find out why." . . . He thought he should remain within his income; there is no doubt about that.[17]

Since 1947 John Kennedy had donated his entire legislative salary to charities. (Had he not turned the money over to charities, his high income-tax bracket would have forced him to pay most of it in taxes anyway.)

In consultation with Walsh, the President decided which charities to donate his presidential salary to. "I want to make sure," Kennedy said, "that there is no publicity on this. Now when you send these checks out, make sure the recipient knows that fact." The New York office tried to maintain confidentiality, but shortly after Kennedy's death the news did become public.

While his book *Why England Slept* was being reprinted in 1961, the President wrote Richard Cardinal Cushing: "The publishers tell me the book will bring in royalties somewhere between $5000 to $10,000. I would appreciate your telling me of a specific charity in which you are interested to which I can assign the royalty. Naturally, I would like to have this matter held in confidence."[18]

Usually he divided his donations among Protestant, Jewish, and Catholic organizations, and such groups as the Boy Scouts and the Girl Scouts. In late December 1962, he signed checks giving ten thousand dollars to the United Negro College Fund and sixteen thousand dollars to the Cuban Families Committee.

Kennedy sporadically watched over the spending of the White House staff and of his own family's spending. He complained about the waste of having six ineffective gardeners on the White House payroll. To save money at receptions he ordered butlers not to open additional bottles of champagne until the opened ones were empty. "Don't have five open at the same time. Don't go out filling guys' glasses when they are half-full."[19]

Being wealthy allowed him to enjoy his leisure in splendid, if not luxurious, residences. Normally he escaped the White House and relaxed for at least twenty-four hours on a weekend, for the entire weekend in the summer, and for an occasional longer holiday. In the summer the President still preferred going to Hyannis Port. He flew to Otis Air Force Base and from there boarded a helicopter for the twenty-two-mile flight to the Kennedy compound. Anticipating his arrival, a mob of Kennedy grandchildren gathered in the driveway. Usually a few close friends gathered as well.

"Then Bobby's children would run to him, or the Shrivers' or Lawfords' or Smiths' or Teddy and Joan's—whoever was there," Rose recalled. "Jack then would come up onto the front porch where his father was sitting so proudly in his wheel chair. They would embrace, say a few words; then Jack would come and hug me too and let me kiss him on the cheek. And Jack would always have a big, all-embracing smile."[20]

Before the inauguration, the artist William Walton assisted Jackie in renting Glen Ora, forty miles west of Washington, located in the horse and hunt country near Middleburg, Virginia. Owned by Walton's friend Gladys Tartière, Glen Ora was the President's concession to Jacqueline. A French villa with French furnishings and decor, the home had six bedrooms and five baths. The four-hundred-acre estate included stables, pastures, a guesthouse, and an Olympic-size swimming pool.

At Glen Ora, Jacqueline rode horses and the children played happily. But the President preferred the ocean, not the countryside. "Horses bored him, and Jackie's horsy friends were not a part of his world, but he understood his wife's need for escape and physical exercise," noted Jackie's biographer Sarah Bradford.[21]

Until December 1961, the President often journeyed to his father's oceanfront home in Palm Beach, but after Joe Kennedy's stroke, the President needed new quarters. Colonel C. M. Paul, a New York and Palm Beach businessman, loaned the Kennedys his oceanfront home, about two miles closer to the center of Palm Beach. There the President swam in the ocean or in a large heated pool nearby. In New York the President and Jackie stayed at the Kennedys' penthouse suite at the Carlyle Hotel at Seventy-sixth and Madison. The beautiful apartment had a large two-story living room with a magnificent view of the city.[22]

A few weeks before Christmas 1962, the White House announced that the Kennedys were starting to build a new home; also in the hunt country near Middleburg. To please her husband, Jackie christened it Wexford, a bow to the Kennedys' roots in County Wexford, Ireland. The home contained fifteen rooms on one floor.

Jack never liked Wexford, never felt comfortable there. "Wexford epitomized the differences in their taste," observed Ralph Martin. "He liked the open sea and she loved the sweeping forest and mountains." She could ride her horses in privacy. But the house had no swimming pool for the President. "To him, it provided no beach to walk, no ship to sail, nothing he truly liked to do. Wexford excited her and bored him."

Wexford caused a budget quarrel between the President and his wife. Furnishing and decorating it was expensive and occurred simultaneously with the expense of returning Glen Ora to its original condition, as Mrs. Tartière insisted.[23]

In the spring of 1963, with Wexford under construction, the first couple spent weekends at Camp David, the presidential retreat in the Catoctin Mountains of Maryland. Because the old-fashioned Eisenhowers had loved Camp David, the Kennedys, without even looking at it for two years, assumed they wouldn't enjoy it.

To their surprise they fell in love with it as well. A mountaintop retreat surrounded by woods, Camp David was miles from civilization. With beautiful scenery, comfortable living quarters, guesthouses, stables with horses, bowling alleys, a movie theater, a heated swimming pool, a three-hole golf course, and complete and secure privacy, it resembled a splendid resort. "If only I'd realized how nice Camp David really is, I'd never have rented Glen Ora, or built Wexford," Jackie wistfully told J. B. West.

In the summer of 1963, the Kennedys rented a weathered-shingled home on Squaw Island, Massachusetts still close to Hyannis Port, but far enough away to escape the chaos at the Kennedy compound.[24]

The President's friends came in layers. There were, noted Arthur Schlesinger, "the Choate and Harvard friends, the friends from the Navy, the social friends from Palm Beach and Newport, the Irish friends, the senatorial friends, the intellectual friends." Jackie Kennedy attracted a new set of people and interests for the President—designers, choreographers, painters, and photographers. For the most part, Kennedy socialized separately with each group.

Reporter Fletcher Knebel studied eight of Kennedy's closest friends in 1962 and summarized their traits. Kennedy had been pals with them an average of twenty years. Five were Catholics and two were Protestants. All had served in World War II and had gone to college.

At leisure the President wanted distraction, a change of pace, stimulating conversation. Designer Oleg Cassini discovered that spending time with the President was the conversational equivalent of athletic competition. Cassini had to be prepared, and always on his toes. He perceived that Kennedy was bored by those who tried to impress him with their seriousness. "I hoped to entertain, not impress," said Cassini. "I knew that if the entertainment was sophisticated enough, he would be impressed as well." Cassini played word games with the President. "He enjoyed my ability to mimic others; I did my Chaplin walk for him."[25]

At small dinners and luncheons the President often had sport at the expense of his friends. "Oleg Cassini will now show us how to do the twist," he would say. Or he would announce, "Okay . . . Speech! Speech! Oleg?" And Cassini would have to hold forth on a topic the President selected and try to entertain.

David Ormsby-Gore first met JFK in England before World War II. In a masterful decision, the British sent him to Washington as ambassador during the Kennedy presidency. The Ormsby-Gores (later Lord and Lady Harlech) were often guests of the Kennedys. Some friends, like David Ormsby-Gore,

Jack greatly admired. Others he didn't particularly admire, but they were nonetheless extremely close to him. LeMoyne Billings and Red Fay were in the latter category. Neither was an intellectual giant or notably successful. Yet in both cases, noted Ormsby-Gore, "he knew that these people would go through fire and water for him and this, of course, quite naturally made him feel very close to them."[26]

A bachelor, Billings worked in advertising in New York, and was the Kennedys' most frequent guest. Like Dave Powers, he acted as the court jester, providing comic relief. "When the Kennedys first moved into the White House, Lem came down every weekend, and just moved into his room without anybody ever knowing he was coming," said J. B. West. On a Friday, as Jackie was about to leave for Virginia for the weekend, West mentioned that Billings had arrived. "Oh, Mr. West," she whispered in mock despair. "He's been a house guest of mine every weekend since I've been married."

At Glen Ora, Jacqueline went horseback riding while Jack and Lem ambled around the grounds. Before dinner, the two longtime friends played backgammon, always wagering small amounts, accumulating debts they never would pay. After dinner they enjoyed quiet evenings of conversation and laughter.

In August 1963, as Billings was about to embark on a trip to Europe, he relayed a plaintive phone message for the President through Evelyn Lincoln. "If for any reason you would like for him to come up here—he couldn't care less about going to Europe. Wants you to know he would be very happy to come if you say so."[27]

Paul B. Fay Jr., a navy friend and owner of a San Francisco construction company, was appointed undersecretary of the navy and lived in the Washington, D.C., area. He and his wife, Anita, were frequent guests on weekends. Tall, handsome, athletic, Charles Spalding had been a friend since before World War II. James Reed, whom Jack had known in Massachusetts, was brought to Washington as assistant secretary of the Treasury.

There were newspaper friends: Ben Bradlee, then bureau chief of *Newsweek* magazine, and Charles Bartlett, the columnist for the *Chattanooga Times*. Bill Thompson, Peter Lawford, and Dave Powers had a special relationship with the President partly because they procured women for Kennedy's voracious sexual appetite.

Other guests and friends of the President included Franklin D. Roosevelt Jr. and his wife, Sue, and the artist Bill Walton. By the time Kennedy entered the White House his friendship with Senator George Smathers had cooled, and they no longer socialized.[28]

Jackie carefully managed the selection of friends for weekends. For a vacation in Newport in 1961 the guest list included the following:

Friday, September 22nd through Sunday 24th, the Charles Spaldings.
Monday, September 25th and Tuesday 26th, Bill Walton.
Wednesday 27th and Thursday 28th, Oleg Cassini.
Saturday a.m. 30th through Sunday, Oct. 1, the
Charles Bartletts.[29]

The five or six small dinner dances that Jackie arranged during the presidency were gala occasions. "Jackie was the producer of these parties," said Ben Bradlee. "Jack was the consumer." She "conceived them as a means of restoring a larger social gaiety to her husband's life," said Schlesinger. After several months of pressure on her husband, Jackie decided it was time for another dancing party. She devised a pretext to give one, "whether to say hello or farewell to the Radziwills, welcome Kenneth Galbraith or honor Eugene Black." About twenty guests were invited, mostly close friends. "The President seemed renewed by them and walked with a springier step the next day," Schlesinger thought.[30]

One friendship was too controversial to continue. As a congressman and senator, Kennedy spent much of his leisure time in Hollywood romancing movie stars and other women. After his sister Patricia married the actor Peter Lawford in 1954 and bought a home in Santa Monica, Kennedy attended parties and get-togethers there. Through Lawford, Kennedy became close friends with Frank Sinatra, who introduced Kennedy to numerous women.

Shortly before becoming President, Kennedy stayed at Sinatra's Palm Springs home and accompanied the singer to nightclubs in Las Vegas. Sinatra personified "the sleek, swinging, emancipated male who can do anything he wants and never pay the consequences," noted Kitty Kelley, Sinatra's biographer. "Let's just say that the Kennedys are interested in the lively arts and that Sinatra is the liveliest art of all," added Peter Lawford.

But Sinatra had unsavory friends, including Chicago mob boss Sam Giancana, former Al Capone gang members Joseph and Charles Fischetti, and New Jersey mobster Willie Moretti. (Despite Sinatra's associates, there is no evidence that he engaged in criminal acts for the mob.)[31]

Sinatra, a longtime Democrat, developed a particular fondness for John Kennedy. He raised funds for the 1960 election campaign and orchestrated the inaugural ball in January 1961.

Kennedy's continued friendship with Sinatra, though, brought severe public condemnation from critics who objected to the President's socializing with a person with such disreputable associates. Bobby repeatedly warned his brother about Sinatra's companions. The President may have remained friends with Sinatra partly to bolster the marriage of his sister Patricia. "Everybody complains about my relationship with Sinatra," he told Charles Bartlett. "Sinatra is the only guy who gives Peter Lawford jobs. And the only way I can keep this marriage going is to see that Peter gets jobs. So I'm nice to Frank Sinatra."

But the President finally decided that his friendship was too controversial. Shortly before a trip to California in the spring of 1962, Kennedy told Lawford that he could not stay at Sinatra's Palm Springs home. "I can't go there," he said, "not while Bobby is handling this [Giancana] investigation." Sinatra was incensed by the rejection.[32]

John Kennedy's alleged connections with Sam Giancana and other Mafia figures have been grossly distorted. True, his imprudent friendship with Frank Sinatra and his very imprudent sexual affair with Judith Exner *indirectly* tied him to Giancana and the mob. But there is no reliable evidence that Kennedy was *directly* tied to them. He didn't consort with Mafia figures or perform favors for them, and most likely he never met Sam Giancana or communicated with him.

The CIA recruited mobsters to kill Castro during the Eisenhower administration, but when Robert Kennedy found out, he tried to stop it. John Kennedy didn't know that Sam Giancana shared intimacy with Judith Campbell until Hoover told him. If the Kennedy brothers conspired with mobsters, why were they so diligent in investigating and prosecuting them? Robert Kennedy and leading Mafia figures hated each other. Giancana, in particular, complained of being constantly hounded by the Justice Department. Both before and after JFK became President, RFK made organized crime his national priority. "As attorney general, RFK pushed the very limits of the law (and some would say beyond) to harass and prosecute leading figures in the mob, as well as Teamsters leader Jimmy Hoffa," noted one authority.

It is true, though, that Robert Kennedy never prosecuted Giancana. Part of the reason may have been that the attorney general learned that the President had foolishly exposed himself to blackmail by sharing Judith Campbell with Giancana. But even if she had never existed, said Evan Thomas, "the FBI's main evidence against Giancana—his own admissions that he had murdered, bribed, and extorted—was unusable in a court of law. It had been gathered by illegal wiretapping."[33]

Because of the criticism leveled at President Eisenhower for golfing too often, Kennedy seldom golfed during his campaign for the presidency. His golfing ability was one of his best-kept secrets. Only after his inauguration did he permit photographs to be taken of him on a golf course. "Even then," said *Time,* "the President declined to pose with a club in his hands, and reporters were allowed to witness only the first tee-off." When he resumed golfing, he initially swung cautiously, worried about reinjuring his back. As he gained confidence, his game improved.

Kennedy approached golf with enthusiasm but little dedication. He seldom completed a full eighteen holes, generally quitting after nine or eleven. He golfed in a hurry, never bothering to study his shots.[34]

He normally hit his drives between 225 and 250 yards, excelled with his short irons, was erratic with his long irons, and was deft around the green. "He had an extremely graceful swing, got his club head back well and hit the ball a country mile when he hit it," said Senator Stuart Symington. "He wouldn't score too well but he hit magnificent shots." Walter Hall, the pro at the Kennedy' home course in Hyannis Port, thought the President could easily have shot in the seventies if he had concentrated.

"The smoothest part of his game," said Salinger, "was not his swing but the 'con' he gave his fellow players." He never began a round of golf without negotiating a complicated system of bets with his playing partners. Wagering was half the fun. "He works out the best possible arrangement before he makes a move," said singer Bing Crosby, who golfed with him in Palm Beach.[35]

Boating relaxed him the most, even on overcast and chilly days. "The guests would huddle together against the cold," noted Schlesinger, "while the President sat in the stern in a black sweater, the wind blowing his hair, blissfully happy with a steaming bowl of fish chowder." Or an all-beef hot dog. Once, while Jackie served the hot dogs to guests, the President teased, "This is history in the making: 'The First Lady with the elegance and dignity of the White House hostess she is, serving the humble hot-dog to her distinguished guests at sea.' "

When he sailed, he sat at the bow, clinging to the forestay. "He loved the view from there and seemed to listen to the sound of the water being parted by the bow into a rush of surging white that swept aft along both sides," reported the sailing expert Julius Fanta. A naval aide recalled seeing him "gazing over the sea, lost in thought, and idly chewing on the frame of his sunglasses."[36]

Kennedy often cruised on the *Marlin* and the newly christened presidential yacht the *Honey Fitz.* He used both boats to entertain heads of state and other distinguished visitors. The informal atmosphere took a "lot of the starch out of a formal meeting," recalled Tazewell Shepard. When there was a mechanical problem with the *Honey Fitz,* the President said, "Well, we've got to do something because that means an awful lot to me." The yacht was moved to wherever the President was staying: Palm Beach for the winter, and Newport or Hyannis Port in the summer. While sailing or yachting the President read books, chatted with family and guests, waved at passing boats, or watched Jackie water-ski.[37]

Private screenings of films were a frequent pastime at the White House, but unless the movie was very dramatic the President walked out after the first twenty-five minutes, usually to read or work. Movies he ordered while in the White House included *Cimarron, Where the Boys Are,* and *The Sundowners.* His favorites were *The Guns of Navarone* and *Spartacus.*

The artist William Walton thought all the Kennedys had terrible taste in films. "Essentially, Jack preferred action movies," said Walton. Sometimes Walton would "con him" and try to stimulate his interest in more artistic movies, such as films by the French director François Truffaut. But the con didn't work. "He'd yawn and get up and leave," said Walton. "He just didn't dig it at all."[38]

Kennedy enjoyed meeting outstanding athletes, watching championship boxing matches on television, and performing his annual ceremonial duty of throwing out the first pitch to open the professional baseball season. He especially enjoyed college and professional football.

He couldn't stand cigarettes, smelly pipes, or most cigars. But he loved an occasional small cigar. Chester Clifton recalled:

Whenever he would say, "Anybody got a cigar?" if you didn't have his cigar and pulled out one of your own, he just shook his head and said, "Oh no, thanks." That meant it wasn't the kind he was used to. He directed his aides to go to Mrs. Lincoln, get three or four of his cigars and carry them in their pockets. But he wanted the cigars wrapped in tinfoil, so they wouldn't get soggy or bent. So occasionally I would go around with his cigars in my pocket, wrapped in foil, in case he asked for one.[39]

On National Prayer Day Kennedy slipped away from the White House unnoticed and went to St. Matthew's Cathedral. Undetected, he sat in a dark rear pew and prayed. "To many who had watched him through nine months of crisis, it seemed that his church attendance and the reference in his talks to prayer had become less mechanical and more meaningful," reporter Hugh Sidey thought.

Speaking at a large gathering in Constitution Hall in Washington shortly after Kennedy's inauguration, Paul Blanshard, the nemesis of the Catholic Church, warned the new President to keep his pledges on church-state issues. "We are watching you," he said, "and we want to say this to you, Mr. Kennedy. If you so much as crook your little finger in the direction of a single public dollar for Catholic schools, you will not return to the White House in 1965." He described the Catholic Church as the "most unashamed, most absolute dictatorship in the world."

Nonetheless, Ted Sorensen treated Blanshard as a friendly adviser, and invited him to the White House to discuss confidentially his point of view. Sorensen successfully sought Blanshard's agreement on including private colleges in the administration's education bill.[40]

Kennedy displayed no religious favoritism in his appointments and no fear of ecclesiastical pressure. He sent no ambassador to the Vatican. He vetoed a bill that would have censored obscene publications in the District of Columbia because he thought it violated the Constitution. "With his support," Sorensen reported, "the Federal Government quietly but extensively increased its activities in the area of birth and population control—increasing its research grants, supporting an expansion of UN efforts and offering to help make more information available to other countries requesting it."

On Good Friday afternoon before Easter, 1963, the President, Paul Fay, and a large contingent of the Secret Service went to confession at the Catholic church on Ocean Boulevard in Palm Beach. On an earlier occasion, Kennedy had entered the confessional and was startled to be met with the priest's greeting, "Good evening, Mr. President." Kennedy replied, " 'Good evening, Father,'" and politely but quickly left.

This time Kennedy tried to make certain the priest didn't know who was in the confessional. Fay recalled the President's strategy:

"Now here in Palm Beach, he had the Secret Service men who were going to confession line up ahead of him. After the first of the agents had gone to confession, Jack slipped in ahead of the remaining three men. By changing his place in line, I'm sure he kept that a day of anonymous sinners."[41]

Kennedy attended Mass every Sunday. Although he opposed prayer in public schools, he encouraged prayer: "We can pray a good deal more at home, we can attend our churches with a good deal more fidelity, and we can make the true meaning of prayer much more important in the lives of all our children."

Broadly ecumenical, Kennedy praised Pope John XXIII for his farsighted encyclicals and for promoting peace "across the barriers of sect and creed." After Pope John's death, Kennedy lauded "his concern for the human spirit," which "transcended all boundaries of belief or geography."

In general, though, as Paul Fay observed, for Kennedy "life was full and demanding and the need for religion generally seemed remote." He was still mostly a Catholic in name only.[42]

After his inauguration Kennedy appointed Dr. Janet Travell as his White House physician, the first woman ever to hold the post. He also inherited Admiral George C. Burkley, who had worked in the Eisenhower administration.

Burkley was asked to direct the military support medical unit at the White House. By having on staff two primary doctors, Kennedy invited friction.

Medical attention was a regular part of Kennedy's daily routine. As Robert Dallek noted, "He was under the care of an allergist, an endocrinologist, a gastroenterologist, an orthopedist, and a urologist, along with that of Janet Travell [and] Admiral George Burkley."

In the first six months of his presidency, "Kennedy suffered stomach, colon, and prostate problems, high fevers, occasional dehydration, abscesses, sleeplessness, and high cholesterol, in addition to his ongoing back and adrenal ailments." His physicians administered large doses of so many drugs that Travell kept elaborate records. The medications included

> injected and ingested corticosteroids for his adrenal insufficiency; procaine shots and ultrasound treatments and hot packs for his back; Lomotil, Metamucil, paregoric, phenobarbital, testosterone, and trasentine to control his diarrhea, abdominal discomfort, and weight loss; penicillin and other antibiotics for his urinary-track infections and an abscess; and Tuinal to help him sleep. Before press conferences and nationally televised speeches his doctors increased his cortisone dose to deal with tensions harmful to someone unable to produce his own corticosteroids in response to stress.

Dr. Travell brought in Dr. Paul F. de Gara to deal with the President's allergies. A shoe box full of freshly vacuumed dust from the White House's living quarters was used to create an "autogenous environmental vaccine." Injections of the vaccine apparently helped the president tolerate exposure to dogs and dust.[43]

"I treated him several times for stiff neck and we worked a great deal of this stiffness out," said Travell. He also had muscular pain in his right shoulder which Travell claimed she also treated. Every spring, before he threw out the first ball at the opening of the professional baseball season, he had doctors check his right shoulder. He "wanted me to be sure that his shoulder was in A-1 condition to throw out that ball," said Travell.

"His growing intolerance to milk also aggravated a gastric disorder," noted Giglio. "Doctors placed him on a bland diet and restricted his alcoholic intake to an occasional beer, daiquiri, or Bloody Mary. . . . He needed glasses for prolonged reading, and by 1963 he required larger type script for speeches." The President smilingly asked Travell not to tell Jackie about his medical problems. "I don't want her to think she married either an old man or a cripple."[44]

Lying about Kennedy's medical condition continued in the White House, even about minor illness. His Addison's disease, managed well in the White House, caused no serious problem for him during his presidency. But the disease was still referred to as an "adrenal insufficiency." When he had a throat infection, Travell responded and took his temperature. It had risen to 103 and would rise to 105. By morning it was down to 101. "That was what I gave in the press release, that it was 101," Travell later said. "I skipped the whole intermediate period of the night."

Kennedy's painful back remained a major cause of concern. During his state visit to Canada in May 1961, he took part in a tree-planting ceremony in Ottawa. While shoveling spadefuls of dirt, he felt a twinge in his back. During the next several days the pain worsened, and he hobbled about on crutches. Dr. Travell described the problem as "a lumbosacral strain," and treated it with procaine injections and hot packs. Before the President retired for the evening, his valet occasionally had to help him remove his shoes and trousers.[45]

Dr. Travell tried to provide him with comfortable seating to reduce his back strain. A rocking chair was brought over from his former Senate office and installed in the Oval Office, and additional rockers were purchased. "He asked me to tackle this problem for his Executive Office, the Cabinet room, the boats that he often used, ... his helicopters, and *Air Force One,* the bubble-top presidential limousine, and his personal home furnishings." White House carpenters and upholsterers designed new chairs according to Dr. Travell's specifications.

Whenever the President traveled, two specially designed chairs went with him, used for his platform appearances. "Two were required because many times the President's engagements were close together in time but not proximate, requiring a leap-frogging of the chairs to have a chair in place when he arrived," noted Tazewell Shepard.

After their meeting in Bermuda in December 1961, Harold Macmillan commented in his diary about the President's back problem:

> He is very restless owing to his back. He finds it difficult to sit in the same position for any length of time. I noticed the difficulty he had in picking up a piece of paper that had fallen to the floor. . . . It is really rather sad that so young a man should be so afflicted, but he is very brave and does not show it except, as I say, by his unwillingness to continue to talk for any length of time without a break.

The President discussed his back pain with his doctors, but seldom complained about the pain even with his closest associates. "They knew he was in pain and would sometimes try to offer comfort," commented Pierre Salinger. "He would usually smile them off with an assurance that everything was well.

Occasionally, he would direct a bit of profanity toward his back, and then the subject would be forgotten for weeks."

In the summer 1961, Dr. Edwin Cave, an outside orthopedic consultant, was asked to analyze the X-rays of Kennedy's back. In his report on July 4, Cave attributed the President's back pain to "the scar in the region of his previous operation[s]." He never mentioned compression fractures or osteoporosis, major contentions of historian Robert Dallek.[46]*

On X-rays in 1962 there was evidence that JFK had osteoarthritis—facet joint degeneration and loss of articular cartilage, narrowing of the disk space, and spur formation around the joints. Kennedy showed such changes, noted Dr. Robert Boyd, the orthopedic consultant for this study, "at the L5-S1 interspace noted as narrowing of the disk space, and thinning if not almost obliteration of the L5-S1 facet joints." Dr. Boyd agreed with Dr. Cave's assessment that the degenerative arthritis was caused by the trauma of the 1944 operation and the two operations in 1954 and 1955.

Conflict erupted over the proper method to treat the President's back pain. Travell's solution was to numb it with injections of procaine, a local anesthetic. Burkley strongly objected, arguing that procaine did not improve the basic condition; once the numbness wore off, the back pain returned. Burkley advocated more conventional treatment: exercise and physical therapy. Gradually the President came to accept Burkley's judgment and Travell's influence diminished. Not wanting to fire her, Kennedy kept her in the White House, but quietly assigned her to take care of Jackie and the two children.

Of the many orthopedic surgeons Kennedy had seen for his back pain, he received the most sensible advice from Dr. Hans Kraus of New York. In the fall of 1961, Dr. Burkley brought in Dr. Kraus to implement exercise therapy.

---

* Early in 2002 a small committee composed of Kennedy administration friends and associates opened a collection of John Kennedy's Papers for the years 1955–1963. Historian Robert Dallek was the first person granted access to the newly released materials, which had been gathered by Dr. Janet Travell, one of Kennedy's primary physicians. Documenting Kennedy's health, the Travell files include valuable X-rays, correspondence, and prescription records.

Using the medical records, Dallek and his medical consultant discovered that Kennedy suffered from far more ailments than previously known. He was also in greater pain and took more medications than anyone realized.

Dallek's pioneering study disclosed that Kennedy took "painkillers, antianxiety agents, stimulants and sleeping pills, as well as hormones to keep him alive, with extra doses in times of stress." Dallek contended that Kennedy's multiple ailments still didn't incapacitate him. Transcripts of tape-recorded conversations during critical periods of his presidency, like the Cuban missile crisis in 1962, show he was lucid, articulate and in firm command.

Dallek published his findings in the *Atlantic* in December 2002, and in his bestselling book,

Kraus thought Jack had weak abdominal, hip, and lower back muscles and recommended gradually increased strengthening exercises for weak muscles and limbering and stretching exercises for stiff muscles. (Kraus disdained Travell's procaine injections.)

Three times per week Kennedy followed Kraus's regimen, exercising in the small gymnasium next to the White House swimming pool. Kraus reported steady progress in the strength and flexibility of the President's back, and Kennedy's pain diminished.

"In very good shape, no complaints," Kraus noted on July 16, 1962. "Given very heavy workout."

"No stiffness, no tenderness of the back muscles," Kraus wrote in early March 1963. "Doing quite well."

"Patient told me that he had now had a good back for over three weeks," wrote the delighted Kraus in early April 1963.

"In two years, Dr. Kraus built Jack up until he could do [exercises] that I can't do," recalled LeMoyne Billings.[47]

Conflict continued between Burkley and Travell. "There has been a squabble over the treatment that should be given to the President," Evelyn Lincoln penned in her diary on December 27, 1961, referring to the conflict between Burkley and Travell. "Dr. Burkley called and said things were all straightened out about the treatment for the President and that Dr. Kraus was going to be in charge. We all sighed a sigh of relief."

Almost exactly a year later there was more friction. Lincoln jotted in her diary: "Dr. Kraus explained to me that if Dr. Travell was going to continue making suggestions and innuendos concerning the President's health he was going to get out of the picture. He said it had to be 'Yes' or 'No'—that he

_____

An Unfinished Life: John F. Kennedy, 1917–1963 (2003). He shows that Kennedy went to great lengths to conceal his ailments, and exposes the truth underneath Kennedy's public image as a vigorous man.

In June 2003, I arranged to meet at the Kennedy Library with three medical experts, and the four of us studied the same Travell records. We also studied the recently opened and important medical file on JFK in the Joseph P. Kennedy Papers. (The latter material was not available when Dallek conducted his research.) My committee of medical experts comprised Edwin Cassem, professor of psychiatry at Harvard Medical School and consulting psychiatrist at Massachusetts General Hospital; Gilbert Daniels, endocrinologist, associate professor of medicine at Harvard Medical School, and physician at Massachusetts General Hospital; and Robert Boyd, retired, formerly assistant clinical professor of orthopedic surgery at Harvard Medical School and chief of the Orthopedic Spine Service of Massachusetts General Hospital.

My team of doctors disagree with several of Dallek's major contentions.

Dallek claims that in the late 1930s the first clinical use of corticosteroids—compounds derived from adrenal extracts that reduce tissue inflammation—were made available. Doctors

was not interested in half way tactics." A short time later Burkley and Kraus emerged the winners. "[Dr. Burkley] said Dr. Kraus had talked to the President and everything had been cleared up. The President called Dr. Burkley in and told him he was in charge of the medicine from here on."[48]

There was one more feature about Kennedy's health history. Clearly he had serious ailments and real pain: Addison's disease, allergies, and back pain. But there was a host of other ailments for which there was no laboratory confirmation. Joe Kennedy's fear, expressed in 1938, that his son was becoming a hypochondriac proved very close to the truth. As President, John Kennedy became overly preoccupied with his health, concerned that his stomach was going to act up, that his voice would not be strong, or that he was about to catch a cold.

Over many years scores of doctors, nurses, and school officials had focused on his ailments. His many visits to doctors and hospitals led him to focus extraordinarily on *imagined* as well as real health problems.

James Giglio has found that the President's doctors micromanaged his health, "adjusting medication on a daily basis and often over medicating for virtually every minor problem." Kennedy often sought treatment for minor illnesses: colds, discomfort in his eye, mild diarrhea, constipation, and insomnia. His knee bothered him "a little bit," he said. Burkely gave the President several medications because Kennedy "was having some cramping." A bowel movement, while "not actually diarrhea," was "loose following the cramping."

In his notes, Dr. Burkley reported that President Kennedy had discomfort in his right eye. Examination of the eye proved normal. But a few hours later, when the President complained of an itching sensation in the right eye,

---

began to administer DOCA (desoxycorticosterone acetate) in the form of pellets implanted under the skin. Historians know that doctors treated Kennedy with DOCA beginning in 1947 after his Addison's disease was diagnosed, but Dallek maintains that Kennedy was taking DOCA as early as 1937 for his colitis. "Early that year," Dallek writes, "in a handwritten note to his father after a family vacation, Jack worried about getting a prescription filled in Cambridge, Massachusetts, where he was a freshman at Harvard College. 'Ordering stuff here very [illegible word],' he wrote to his father. 'I would be sure you get the prescription. Some of that stuff as [sic] it is very potent and he [Jack's doctor] seems to be keeping it pretty quiet.'" Dallek thinks "it is reasonable to hypothesize that the prescription Jack asked for was DOCA."

The second bit of evidence is the story told by Jack's friend Paul Fay, who claimed that in 1946, one year before Jack was diagnosed with Addison's disease and is known to have begun taking DOCA, he watched Jack implant a DOCA pellet in his leg. "In short," Dallek writes, "it appears that Jack was on steroids—still an experimental treatment, with great uncertainty as to dosage—for his colitis well before the Addison's disease diagnosis."

Dallek argues that Jack paid a price for taking DOCA early and for many years. Cortico-

a Bethesda ophthalmologist was summoned. Again, the examination revealed nothing.

On one occasion Dr. Burkley began to suspect that the President's stomach problem might stem from anxiety. On August 13, 1963, he discussed Kennedy's gastrointestinal ailment with another physician. "We should stress the fact that emotional tension rather than food could be the cause of the [President's] distress and that no actual organic change was taking place," Burkley reported.

What would the President's diagnosis be by the diagnostic criteria of the early twenty-first century? Because of the many bodily symptoms that were not confirmed by physical findings or abnormal test results, the most obvious diagnosis is somatization disorder. To qualify under the definition of the disorder the patient must have (1) pain in four different sites or functions; for JFK it was cervical spine, lumbar spine, abdomen, and joints; (2) two gastrointestinal symptoms; for JFK it was constipation and diarrhea; (3) one "neurological" symptom; for JFK it was weakness in his legs; (4) one sexual symptom, such as erectile/ejaculatory trouble; JFK apparently did *not* have this symptom. The disease had to begin before the patient was thirty years old—certainly true of JFK. Finally, the patient must not feign the symptoms, and has no insight into the psychiatric nature of his symptoms—both mostly true in JFK's case.[49]

"The President received no other treatments that were not authorized or indicated by me or by someone that I had asked to see him," Burkley later stated, seemingly oblivious of the now famous intervention of another doctor who was injecting Kennedy with dangerous compounds.

---

steroids have deleterious long-term effects, "including osteoporosis of lower-back bones and increased incidence of serious infection (owing to suppression of the body's immune system). Kennedy would suffer from all these problems, including outright degeneration of his lumbar spine. In addition, the long-term use of corticosteroids suppresses normal adrenal function; it may have been the cause of Kennedy's Addison's disease. . . .

"Navy medical records indicate that back surgery Kennedy underwent in 1944 had revealed clear evidence of osteoporosis." The surgeon, Dallek contends, removed "some abnormally soft disc interspace material" and predicted additional problems if Kennedy continued to suffer bone loss.

Dallek asserts, finally, that the X-rays in the Travell records, which he examined with the help of a physician, "show that the fourth lumbar vertebra had narrowed from 1.5 cm to 1.1 cm, indicating collapse in the bones supporting his spinal column. By March of 1951 there were clear compression fractures in his lower spine."

In fact, the evidence that Kennedy began taking corticosteroids in 1937 is extremely weak. The story about young Kennedy filling a prescription in 1937 is vague and unconvincing.

In the fall of 1960, during the presidential campaign, Kennedy mentioned to his friend Charles Spalding that he felt fatigued, his muscles "weak." Spalding arranged a confidential consultation for Kennedy with Dr. Max Jacobson, who injected the candidate with what was apparently his standard concoction: amphetamines, steroids, calcium, placenta, and vitamins. "After his treatment," said Jacobson, "he told me his muscle weakness had disappeared. He felt cool, calm and very alert."

Dark haired, with horn-rimmed glasses, Jacobson was sixty years old when he first treated Kennedy. "Dr. Feelgood," as he was known, continued to treat Kennedy for the next three years. Born in Germany, where, he claimed, he had earned his medical degree, Jacobson emigrated to the United States in 1936, and set up a medical practice in New York. Denied hospital privileges since 1946, he conducted his practice out of his office, located at 56 East Eighty-seventh Street in New York. Brusque and forceful, dogmatic and funny, he was a compulsive diagnostician who relied on his intuition rather than on medical studies. Some patients visited him once a month, some weekly, some every day.[50]

Amphetamine (also known as speed) is a powerful stimulant once widely and carelessly prescribed. In the early 1960s the drug was used to treat depression and to prevent fatigue. Amphetamine was not illegal at the time, and the drug's dangers and addictive properties were not widely known. Amphetamine can cause nervousness, impaired judgment, and overconfidence. Jacobson claimed that the dose levels of amphetamine he prescribed were too small to lead to dependence when administered in the quantities he directed. Besides, Jacobson said during an interview, "Amphetamine is not an addictive drug. Heroin is. Morphine is." Now most experts would strongly disagree with his opinion.[51]

The witness who recalled decades afterward that Kennedy implanted pellets in his leg in 1946 probably had the wrong date. It is difficult to believe he was taking DOCA while he served in the Solomon Islands.

Osteoporosis leads to spontaneous fractures usually of the spine or hips, or fractures resulting from minimal trauma. JFK had none of those problems. In the report of his operation in 1944, Dr. Poppen's finding of soft IV disc material suggests that he removed normal disc material from the nucleus pulposis of the fifth lumbar disc space. It was not a sign of osteoporosis. In addition, the many orthopedic surgeons Jack consulted after 1944 never diagnosed him as having osteoporosis.

Dr. Robert Boyd, the orthopedic surgeon who assisted on this study, found no evidence in the newly released health records to suggest that Kennedy had osteoporosis. Nor do the X-rays show collapse in the bones supporting his spinal column or compression fractures in his lower spine.

Historian James Giglio of Southwest Missouri State University, a longtime Kennedy scholar, has also studied the recently opened Travell medical records and the medical file of

An investigative report by *The New York Times* in 1972 found that "most of Dr. Jacobson's patients use the stimulant in dosages below that required to produce severe symptoms. They appear to use amphetamine only from time to time to get 'up' for special occasions or to get through difficult periods."

Jacobson gave some patients 30-cubic-centimeter vials of his concoction and a number of disposable needles, and taught them to inject themselves. Prominent patients of the doctor included writer Truman Capote, filmmakers Cecil B. DeMille and Otto Preminger, singer Eddie Fisher, playwright Tennessee Williams, Congressman Claude Pepper of Florida, and actor Anthony Quinn. Many of his patients swore by his compound and insisted that his shots gave them boundless energy, allowing them to lead more productive and pleasurable lives. One of his most devoted fans was lyricist Alan Jay Lerner, who claimed he visited Jacobson only a few times a year for sinus headaches and considered him a "great man." Other patients quit seeing Jacobson, complaining of adverse reactions and enslaving addictions. At least one of Jacobson's patients died from what a medical examiner termed "acute amphetamine poisoning."[52]

In his ramshackle office, which doubled as an unauthorized drug laboratory, the unkempt Jacobson didn't maintain quality control or sterility standards. He treated patients while wearing bloodstained surgical garb. Finally, in 1975 the New York State Board of Regents revoked his license to practice medicine.

In late May 1961, after the President hurt his back during the tree-planting ceremony in Canada, Jacobson was invited to the White House to treat the President's pain. The doctor first explained his ground rules. "(1) No alcohol, neither beer nor wine; (2) No Codeine nor opiates; (3) Follow my instructions to the letter; and (4) Report any change immediately." Then he administered his first treatment. Immediately after receiving his shot, Kennedy stood up and walked back and forth several times. "I feel very much better."[53]

The President convinced Jacobson to accompany him to Europe for the Vienna summit. "Khrushchev is supposed to be on his way over," Jacobson said the President told him before Kennedy's first informal meeting in Vienna. "The meeting may last for a long time. See to it that my back won't give me any trouble when I have to get up or move around." Jacobson gave him a shot. (As it turned out, Khrushchev arrived later than expected.) On the plane trip back from Europe, Eunice Shriver seemed suspicious of Jacobson. So did Robert Kennedy. "Bobby didn't trust us," Jacobson later wrote.

JFK in the Joseph P. Kennedy Papers. Assisted by Dr. Bert Park, a neurosurgeon and the author of *The Impact of Illness on World Leaders* (1986), Giglio confirmed the major findings of my medical team: no evidence of osteoporosis, no compression fractures in Kennedy's lower spine, no cortisone taken by Kennedy in the late 1930s that later damaged his back and caused his Addison's disease. Giglio, "Why Another Kennedy Book?" 648.

In late September 1961, Jacobson received an emergency phone call to report to the Carlyle Hotel in New York, where Kennedy was preparing to speak to the United Nations General Assembly. Suffering from laryngitis, the President welcomed him in a whisper. "What are you going to do about this?" "Mr. President, what I'm going to do hasn't been done before," Jacobson claimed he said. The President replied, "Do what's necessary. I don't give a hoot." Then the doctor gave him a shot in the neck near the larynx. Five minutes later the surprised President could speak normally, Jacobson stated. "Later on I have done that with many singers at the Metropolitan."[54]

According to gate logs, Jacobson visited the White House more than thirty times, and also treated Kennedy at Palm Beach, Hyannis Port, and Glen Ora. He claimed that his treatments helped Kennedy through the Vienna summit, the Cuban missile crisis, a threatened steel strike, and the James Meredith affair in Mississippi.

In her oral history and in her published autobiography, Dr. Travell never mentioned Jacobson; nor did Dr. Burkley in any of his public comments. Both were privately suspicious of him. Burkley probably spied on Jacobson, but was helpless to stop his White House visits. At 7:12 P.M. on Sunday, March 25, 1962, Jacobson marched in for his appointment with JFK; at 7:28 P.M. Dr. Burkley checked on the President. On several other occasions, Burkley followed up on Jacobson's visit.

Although Secret Service agents inspected Jacobson's medical bag, they didn't know what the hypodermic needles contained. Larry Newman and other agents referred to Jacobson's concoctions as "bat wings and chicken blood." Newman added: "We didn't know in those days the definition of speed and amphetamines like [we] know now." The agents couldn't bar Jacobson because, like the unknown women paraded to the President, the doctor's visits had Kennedy's blessing.[55]

Robert Kennedy remained suspicious of Jacobson, and demanded that his brother tell the doctor to turn over samples of his drugs to be tested. Jacobson agreed. "Bobby sent several vials to the FBI labs," Evan Thomas explained. "Noting the attorney general's 'intense personal interest,' the Justice Department aide passing along the request speculated that the drugs were for RFK's father. . . . The FBI lab reported back that the sample was too small to thoroughly analyze. The sample did not test positive for narcotics, but then Jacobson never used opiates. The FBI apparently did not test for amphetamines." The President told Jacobson that his injections were now "government-approved." Thereafter, Kennedy rebuffed his brother's attempted intervention. "I don't care if it's horse piss. It works."

Jacobson's treatment of the President remained secret until long after Kennedy's death. But Frank Saunders, the Kennedys' chauffeur, claimed that staff members at Hyannis Port knew about Jacobson. "Anybody at the

Kennedy place [in Hyannis Port] could have had a shot from Dr. Jacobson. The nurses even asked me, 'Dr. Jacobson's here, Frank. Do you want a vitamin shot?' "[56]

There is no evidence that Jacobson's treatment affected Kennedy's behavior at Vienna or during the Cuban missile crisis or at any other time. He never appeared to have symptoms of excessive amphetamine usage. Nor did illness or pain seem to diminish his competence. "When he was in agony during periods of international tension," observed George Ball, "he bore that burden with gallantry and with no perceptible loss of alertness."

One doctor who treated the President later claimed he warned Kennedy to stop seeing Jacobson. "I said that if I ever heard he took another shot, I'd make sure it was known. No President with his finger on the red button has any business taking stuff like that."[57]

That Jacobson intervened in managing Kennedy's health care replicated a long-term problem. For most of his life Kennedy received fragmented medical care from too many physicians, with no one doctor in charge of his overall management having all the available information. No single physician coordinated all the drugs he received. In addition, the problems of secrecy and the need to present a political image of robust health further complicated the quest for accurate and reliable medical information to allow precise analysis and conclusions.

Although Kennedy's handling of major crises after Jacobson had treated him remained adroit and cautious, even the possibility that his thinking and judgment might be impaired at crucial moments is chilling.

Despite his ailments and treatments, Kennedy appeared to the public to be in excellent health—young, trim, and vigorous. During his entire presidency, he missed work only one day because of illness. He overcame his medical problems partly through his remarkable will and fortitude. "Therein, perhaps, lies his real profile in courage," observed Giglio.[58]

36

WHITE HOUSE
PRINCESS

Asked to describe his wife's greatest contributions to his presidency after the first two years, John Kennedy didn't hesitate. "Her emphasis on creative fields, her concentration on giving historical meaning to the White House furnishings, and her success as an ambassador on the trips she has made with me abroad." At the same time, he added, she was doing a fine job of carrying out her "primary responsibility to support her husband and care for her children."

Jackie was thirty years younger than the three earlier first ladies that chief usher J. B. West had served, requiring him to be flexible in his approach to her. West thought she had the most complex personality of them all. "In public, she was elegant, aloof, dignified, and regal," he recalled. "In private, she was casual, impish, and irreverent. She had a will of iron, with more determination than anyone I have ever met. Yet she was so soft-spoken, so deft and subtle, that she could impose that will upon people without their ever knowing it."

Her teasing, joking, and wit were a daily delight for West. "Relaxed and uninhibited, she was always popping up anywhere, wearing slacks, sitting on the floor, kicking off her shoes, her hair flying in every direction. We all had fun along with her. Yet she also drew a line against familiarity which could not be crossed.

"It was only with the cameras grinding or guests coming in the front door that the seriousness, the poise, the coolness that were also part of her, began to appear," said West.[1]

The Vienna summit in June 1961 provided an example of Jackie's sensitivity and generosity. At a luncheon for Madame Khrushchev and Mrs. Kennedy the crowd outside kept calling for "Jacqueline." Letitia Baldrige told the story:

> So Mrs. Kennedy walked to the open window and smiled and waved briefly and the crowd erupted and the noise was terrific. Then she realized that Mrs. Khrushchev, after all, was co-guest, and she was very embarrassed by the fact that nobody was calling Mrs. Khrushchev. . . . She went over to Mrs. Khrushchev and said, "They want to see you too," and took her to the window and Mrs. Khrushchev waved and the two women stood there together.

"I was astounded by the organization of her mind," said Oleg Cassini. A remarkable master of endless details, she didn't hold herself to a schedule, yet was highly organized. "For others, she insisted upon order; for herself, she preferred spontaneity," said West. "She took advice readily, but only when she asked for it, and she strongly resisted being pushed."[2]

She had few female friends. Her Kennedy sisters-in-law never stopped by for lunch; nor did she seek the companionship of other women, except her sister Lee Radziwill and a few others. She had no independent friendship with the women who joined their husbands for the private evenings with the President and first lady. "She seemed to enjoy being in the company of men far more than she enjoyed women, and often invited men, usually older men who were involved in the arts, to tea in the mansion," noted West. The same was true when she hosted large functions: She socialized with the men but not their wives.

Frank Saunders recalled talking to Jackie as he chauffeured her to Hyannis Port. "She said that sometimes it just overwhelmed her—all the Kennedys and their foolish lawn games. . . . She said she didn't know how many more summers like this one she could take at Hyannis Port."

When the first lady wanted to escape the chaos of the Kennedy compound in Hyannis Port, she convinced the captain of the *Marlin* to take her to the sheltered waters of Chappaquiddick, an island near Edgartown, where she could water-ski away from prying eyes.

In her triumphant trips abroad with her husband, Jackie captivated foreigners with her youth, beauty, poise, clothes, and brief speeches in French or

Spanish. In June 1961 she was the star in Paris. Her knowledge of France, her fluency in the subtleties of French, and her entertaining conversation captivated Charles de Gaulle.[3]

"On her first night in Paris Jackie was dressed, coifed and made up as elaborately as any princess," *Time* reported. "When she emerged from her bedroom at the Palais des Affaires Etrangères, she was magnificent in a narrow, pink-and-white straw-lace gown and a swooping 14th century hairdo with a fake topknot."

Seated on his right during an intimate luncheon at the Élysée Palace, Jacqueline zeroed in on de Gaulle, flashing her smile and speaking in French. The glacial Charles de Gaulle "promptly melted," said *Time*.

> The same thing happened all over again in Vienna, Jackie literally stopped traffic wherever she went. Nikita Khrushchev seemed smitten: at a banquet, he edged his chair closer to hers and, eyes twinkling, told her funny stories. Next day, as Jackie and motherly Nina Khrushchev lunched together in Pallavicini Palace, a crowd outside chanted, "Jacqueline, Jacqueline, Jacqueline." . . . Paris and Vienna had a new goddess. The U.S. had a queen, and not from Hollywood.

At a Paris press conference, the President said, "I do not think it altogether inappropriate to introduce myself to this audience. I am the man who accompanied Jacqueline Kennedy to Paris, and I have enjoyed it."[4]

The media in Latin America, France, Poland, India, Pakistan, and England praised her "chic and charm" and her attention to art, literature, and the theater, and lauded her independent mind, and her recognition of American intellectuals. She had brought a new "tone and style" to the West.

She received about seventy-five hundred letters a week from throughout the world, mostly fan mail, requiring thirteen people to process. A girl in Indonesia wrote: "I've seen pictures of you. I am studying English because I admire you so much." A letter from a young Japanese girl stated: "My mother tells me not to slump so that I will grow up to be tall and queenly like you."

In March 1962, John Kenneth Galbraith wrote the President that Nehru was "deeply in love [with Jackie] and has a picture of himself strolling with J.B.K. displayed all by itself in the main entrance hall of his house."[5]

Five weeks after the 1960 election Jackie laid out for fashion designer Oleg Cassini her plans for clothes:

> I seem to be all set for evening. Now would you put your brilliant mind to work for day—Coats—dresses for public appearances—lunch and afternoon that I would wear if Jack were President of FRANCE. . . . I am counting on you to be a superb Wardrobe Mistress—every glove, shoe, hat

etc.—and all delivered on time. You are organized for that—being in New York—better than I—If you need to hire another secretary just for me do it and we'll settle the financial end together.

One reason she was so happy to be working with Cassini, she wrote, was that "I have some control over my fashion publicity which has gotten so vulgarly out of hand—I don't mind your saying now the dresses I have chosen from you—as I am so happy if it has done you any good—and proud to have you, a gentleman, doing clothes for the wife of the President. I will never become stuffy—but there is dignity to the office which suddenly hits one."

Cassini should make sure no one had an exact copy of her dress. "I want all mine to be original and no fat little woman hopping around in the same dress."

1) Forgive me for not coming to you from the very beginning. I am so happy now.
2) Protect me—as I seem so mercilessly exposed and don't know how to cope with it (I read tonight I dye my hair because it is mousy gray!).
3) Be efficient—by getting everything on time and relieving me of worry about detail.

Oleg Cassini described the physical features of the woman he was to clothe:

Jackie reminded me of an ancient Egyptian princess—very geometric, even hieroglyphic, with the sphinx-like quality of her eyes, her long neck, slim torso, broad shoulders, narrow hips, and regal carriage. One can never underestimate the importance of good shoulders. Good shoulders and a long waist are a great asset when it comes to wearing clothes, and Jackie had both. She was the perfect model for very simple lines—a minimalist *par excellence*.[6]

With her Paris visit making her an international superstar, Jackie was now news twenty-four hours a day. "*Women's Wear Daily* could have been rechristened *What Jackie Wears Daily*," said Sara Bradford. Department-store mannequins now looked like Jackie; ladies' coiffed their hair in Jackie's characteristic bouffant bob.

In order to quell fashion gossip and inaccurate information, at Jackie's urging Letitia Baldrige wrote a letter to John Fairchild, the publisher of *Women's Wear Daily*. "For the next four years Mrs. Kennedy's clothes will be made by Oleg Cassini. They will be designed and made in America. She will buy what is necessary without extravagance. . . . Should you receive a report that Mrs. Kennedy has ordered clothes not made by Mr. Cassini, I would appreciate it if you would call me and I will give you a prompt and accurate answer."[7]

"Suddenly, this enormous adulation was showered on her, and it changed her," said Cassini of Jackie's life after her visit to Paris. "Outwardly, no. The voice was the same, the mannerism the same. But she became different. Because when the entire world constantly lauds you, it would take a tremendously disciplined mind not to fall a little bit in love with yourself. She knew she had a fantastic hook into her husband, who as a good politician realized that she was a huge asset. Until Paris," Cassini continued, "Jackie was nothing but a little housewife."

With amused recollection Princess Grace of Monaco (formerly Grace Kelly) described meeting the President at a luncheon. JFK turned to her suddenly and asked: "Is that a Givenchy you're wearing?"

She said, "How clever of you, Mr. President! However did you know?"

"Oh," he replied, "I'm getting pretty good at it—now that fashion is becoming more important than politics and the press is paying more attention to Jackie's clothes than to my speeches."[8]

Television enhanced her celebrity. Several television programs dwelled on her pillbox hats and bouffant hairstyles. The youngest first lady since the 1890s, she was frequently photographed with her two little children. She was a new model of womanliness. "Here was a First Lady who seemed acquainted with Europe, informed about literature and the arts, yet attractive enough to compete with movie actresses and sex symbols," said writer Betty Caroli.

Women everywhere asked for her beauty secrets; mothers thanked her for improving their daughters' self-image. She had an uncanny knack of intriguing the country. "By remaining aloof—but glamorous and confident in her aloofness," said one observer, "she stirred up more interest than if she had mingled with the crowds and hugged every child in sight."

"Jackie felt she couldn't do anything, say anything, go anywhere, without public knowledge," said Cecil Stoughton, official White House photographer. "To her, the White House signified losing control of her life, becoming the butt of political comment and political gossip."[9]

Unknown to her adoring public, Jackie warred with the media, especially with female reporters. Part of her reticence came from her naturally retiring nature. Mobs of reporters and photographers made her extremely uncomfortable. "She is constantly torn between her public role and her desire for absolute privacy," observed writer Marianne Means. "She cannot accept the fact that the First Family, as well as the President, is an object of total interest to the nation." The President usually did not pressure her to make more public appearances than she felt she could comfortably handle.

Shortly after the inauguration, she instructed aide Pam Turnure:

I feel so strongly that publicity in this era has gotten so completely out of hand—and you must really protect the privacy of me and my children . . . just know you can't discuss us—JFK, me and infants. . . . I have suddenly realized what it means to completely lose one's privacy. . . . My press relations will be minimum information given with maximum politeness— you are great at that anyway. I won't give any interviews—pose for any photographs, etc. for next four years.

There were exceptions. She intended to invite in photographers from *Life* and *Look*. In addition, she agreed to other photo sessions or interviews, but only if she initiated them and remained in control. Once in a while she filtered stories and photographs to the media through Turnure. Jackie also allowed releases about the White House restoration project and state entertainments. But news or photos about the family life and the children were strictly forbidden.

"The inner workings of Jackie's East Wing would be as difficult to penetrate as the Kremlin," said Sara Bradford. Pierre Salinger had a difficult dilemma. "Jackie had a running battle going with Pierre over keeping the children out of the press, even though they were always in the press," observed Stoughton. "The President understood the political advantages of having the children photographed, whereas Jackie saw it as an invasion of their privacy." With the President's permission Salinger would schedule photo sessions for the children when Jackie was away from the White House; then she would be irate with Salinger when she later found out.[10]

She was protected and protected herself. In February 1962 NBC thought it had an agreement to film interviews for a program on Jackie's work in the White House. Letitia Baldrige, Oleg Cassini, and Pam Turnure were scheduled to be interviewed. But JFK (perhaps reflecting Jackie's wishes) nixed the interviews. Instead, he selected people who barely knew the first lady— Margaret Mead, Eleanor Roosevelt, and the wife of Senator John Sherman Cooper. NBC and Pam Turnure, the coordinator for the program, were livid. Turnure wrote the President to protest:

NBC's feeling now is that they gave us the right [to] clear all portions of the program to protect Mrs. Kennedy, and that we have now overprotected her to the point where the program will be a compilation of stock film clips and interviews with persons who know her in the most limited way and will give no view of her and the work she actually does at the White House.

In short, they feel that they gave us the right to clear a program which they could have produced anyway without any prior permission.[11]

Shortly after the Bay of Pigs disaster, the White House hosted its first reception for the president of Tunisia, Habib Bourguiba, and his wife. Several female reporters were in attendance. "The President noticed [Jackie] giving us dirty looks," recalled reporter Esther Van Wagoner Tufty. "He went over to her and took hold of her very hard by the left arm. He marched her over to us and in his most charming voice told her to 'say hello to the girls, darling.' After she whispered hello, he released her arm and you could still see the imprint of his hand in her flesh."

The public's appetite for stories about Jackie was insatiable. "A picture of Jackie on the cover of a magazine, a word or glimpse of family life in the White House, sent circulation soaring," observed *Time*'s Hugh Sidey. United Press International's Helen Thomas thought Jackie did a great service to the women reporters. "Her elevated profile meant we were covering front-page news every day."[12]

That Jackie found the reporting preposterous, a grotesque invasion of her privacy, was understandable. Thomas bragged that she interviewed Jackie's hairdresser, her caterer, the pianist she hired for parties, and "even made good" by "interviewing the owner of the diaper service the family used."

Jackie hated Helen Thomas. She once told Traphes Bryant, the White House dog keeper, not to tell "Helen Thomas or the rest of those witches anything about how I keep fit—not even that I walk the dogs." On another occasion, she heatedly told the dog keeper, "Bryant, don't give Helen Thomas any information about the dogs. Not a damn thing!" She continued: "I am sick of her stories and I don't want you to give Helen Thomas a damn thing."

"We were the thorn in her crown," observed Thomas, adding that "Jackie was charmingly at ease with men, children, and animals" but "was constantly on guard with women of the press."

"The working press in the White House, particularly, had a great deal of resentment for Mrs. Kennedy," said Laura Bergquist. "She wouldn't even recognize their existence, which was, I thought, unnecessary. You don't have to give them big exclusive interviews, but you can be polite."[13]

Jackie contributed substantially to her husband's presidency, vastly improved the beauty of the White House, encouraged the performing arts, and, with assistance, took care of her two children. At the same time she hated many of the traditional duties of the first lady and was often uncooperative.

After he entered the White House, the first thing JFK said to Angier Biddle Duke was to lay down some guidelines, some rules, for the public appearances of the first lady. Would Duke go over this with Jackie and work out arrangements?

Duke made the appointment with Mrs. Kennedy, and asked about her public appearances. How many did she want to make? She replied, "Let's start right away with that—as little as possible." She had responsibilities for her young children, she said. They came first. "But I will do my duty, and I will do what is required of me." Duke pointed out that when the head of state brings his wife to an official Washington visit, protocol required that the President's wife attend official functions. Jackie replied, "Can you fix it up with the ambassadors as much as you can to tell the heads of state not to bring their wives?"[14]

Often moody, easily fatigued, and naturally shy, she found excuses for avoiding traditional responsibilities of the first lady. She detested many of the rituals: attending luncheons, or meeting ambassadors' wives or foreign leaders she thought were unimportant. She refused to meet with major charitable organizations such as the Muscular Dystrophy Association and the American Red Cross.

She asked Letitia Baldrige to represent her at a Congressional Wives' Prayer Breakfast, saying, "I can't bear those silly women." She mimicked them, Baldrige later said, "making fun of their dowdiness and their slobbering devotion to their husbands' political careers." She thought all those events were "tacky."[15]

When the prime minister of Italy, Amintore Fanfani, visited the White House, the President relayed a message through Evelyn Lincoln, requesting that Jackie entertain the prime minister for five minutes while the President finished another appointment. Jackie said to Lincoln, "All that time? What will I talk to him about?" Lincoln said she would try to get the President to come earlier. Jackie responded "Oh. I wish you would."

She sometimes embarrassed her husband by canceling an appearance because of illness, only to have the media report she was seen in New York or water-skiing at Hyannis Port. "She had almost as many excuses as she had invitations, and she avoided all but the most public and important functions," observed Lawrence Leamer.[16]

"Jackie's regal mask concealed a personality subject to great strain and periods of collapse," said her biographer Sara Bradford. "There were times when she felt inadequate and unable to cope, leaning heavily on Jack." She would cry, "Oh, Jack, I'm so sorry for you that I'm such a dud," and the President would attempt to reassure her: "I love you as you are."

Criticism of her during Kennedy's presidency was mild and infrequent, focusing mainly on her smoking, foxhunting, waterskiing, penchant for French fashion designers, and allegedly undignified appearance—wearing a bikini, attending church in sandals.

On reflection, after her husband's death, more substantial criticism surfaced, especially from reporters. "She was a very odd woman," said Evelyn Lincoln. "You couldn't get close to her." In her memoir Mary Gallagher, Jackie's personal secretary, described her boss as "a terrible-tempered petty tyrant whose personal maid was required to change her sheets for an afternoon nap and iron her stockings."[17]

Reporter Van Wagoner Tufty thought the image of Jackie as an outstanding mother and first lady was a myth. "I don't see what distinguishes her as a mother from 50 million other American moms, except that she had more cash, employees and elitist tendencies than any of them."

As for Caroline and John-John, how many children are fortunate enough to grow up in the White House, ride an elevator to school, have their own ponies galloping about on their front lawn, own large enough wardrobes to clothe half the children of Harlem, never have to sit in a doctor's or dentist's waiting room, never have to ride a public bus or subway, know that they can have anything, go anywhere, do practically whatever they want in life? Those kids were treated like royalty. They wanted to meet Bozo the Clown, they met Bozo the Clown. They wanted to pet Lassie, they got to pet Lassie. Am I supposed to feel sorry for them? Must I regard Jackie as Mother-of-the-Year because she read them an occasional bedtime story or once in a while watched their nanny give them a bath?

George Herman, a veteran of CBS News, was disgusted with Jackie's attitude toward her responsibilities and thought both Kennedys were fortunate that the media neglected to stress the awful way she deported herself:

For instance, Jackie would skip out on a White House dinner and the word would be that she was ill or that she had other responsibilities. And the next day the New York newspapers would show pictures of her dancing at a ball in New York or water-skiing while the president was entertaining some head of state that she wasn't anxious to meet. And yet everybody was talking about what a wonderful first lady she was. Baloney, she was one of the worst first ladies. She didn't want to bother with many duties. She only came to a dinner or took part in a thing when it was something she liked.[18]

Before his marriage, Jack Kennedy acted indifferent to the children of his friends. Why were they always raving about their children? He said to Paul Fay, "I don't understand how you can get such a big kick out of your children, particularly when they are only about one and three years of age. Certainly nothing they are going to say is going to stimulate you. You're not going to discuss with them any of the problems down at the plant."

He changed his mind after he had his own children. During his time in the White House, raising children became one of his favorite topics of conversation. "He was very affectionate and attentive to his children," said Secret Service agent Larry Newman. "No matter how pressing his duties were," said Maud Shaw, "he always found time to listen to the children."

Occasionally the President listened at the bedroom door for a few moments before saying good night to the children. Once he listened as Maud Shaw taught the children a new evening prayer.

"That's a lovely prayer, Miss Shaw," he said after she finished. "Is it an English one?"

"Yes, Mr. President," she said.

"Well, I like it. I hope they learn it."[19]

While he sat in his rocking chair, Caroline and John would climb all over him. "I'll race you over to the pool," he would say, and the two children were off like a shot. Caroline and John walked with him to his office almost every morning. Five or ten minutes later Maud Shaw would take John back to the mansion and Caroline to her school.

John was captivated by the President's helicopters. During a visit to Camp David, the President and his son briefly disappeared, only to be found later inside a parked helicopter. "John was sitting in the pilot's seat, fingering the control instruments and steering an imaginary flight to rescue survivors of a sinking PT boat in the South Pacific," observed Dave Powers. The President was acting as copilot.[20]

There was always teasing and joking. Young John was very proud of having the same first name as his father. But the President would tease him, calling him "Sam." The flustered boy would shout, "Daddy, you *know* my name is John!"

The President told the children imaginary stories such as the one about the white shark that distinguished itself by eating people's socks. During a summer cruise near Cape Cod, while Caroline sat on the deck of the *Honey Fitz* with her father and Franklin D. Roosevelt Jr., the President said, "I just saw the white shark." He ordered Roosevelt to take off his socks and feed them to the shark, and Roosevelt immediately complied. Caroline was impressed.

Loose in the West Lobby of the White House, Caroline chatted with reporters. One asked her what her father was doing. "Oh, he's upstairs with his shoes and socks off, not doing anything." Salinger said it was the young girl's last press conference.

The President's magnificent old desk in the Oval Office, one Jackie unearthed from a storeroom in the White House basement, had a hinged panel in the front that opened outward like a door. Dave Powers observed: "John would crawl under the desk and hide behind the panel, making scratching and growling noises. The President would exclaim, 'Is there a rabbit in there?' Then the panel would swing open and out would pop John, rolling on the rug and screaming with laughter."[21]

Robert McNamara told the story of the time the President accosted Caroline just before her supper hour. "Caroline," he said, "have you been eating candy?" She ignored him. He repeated the question, but she still ignored him. Finally, he insisted. "Caroline, answer me. Have you been eating candy—yes, no or maybe?"

Dean Rusk waited in the Oval Office one morning before Kennedy had finished breakfast. As he sat there, Caroline emerged from behind a screen in the room and said, "Mr. Secretary, what is the situation in Yemen today?" Rusk heard tittering behind the screen. "It was John Kennedy," said Rusk. "He had put her up to it."[22]

Underneath the trees near the President's West Wing office, following Jackie's design, carpenters built a treehouse, a rabbit hutch, a barrel tunnel, a swing, and a slide. Later, they added a pen for the lambs, another for the guinea pigs, a stable for the ponies, Macaroni and Tex, and several doghouses.

"The President could look out on the play-yard from his office, and he often stepped out to shrieks, hugs, quacks, barks, cackles, bleats, and all sorts of commotion," said J. B. West. "He seemed to delight in the mad scene."

Mrs. Kennedy laid out a nursery school for Caroline on the third floor of the Mansion, complete with sandbox, rabbit cages, guinea pigs, goldfish, plants, books, and bookshelves. There were ten pupils. "The first year it was a cooperative nursery school with the mothers, and Mrs. Kennedy included, taking turns as teachers and helpers each week," said Pamela Turnure, "and then next year it became more formal and they got regular nursery school teachers and kindergarten teachers. It went into two classes while it was there."

As in her life before the inauguration, Jackie wasn't burdened in the White House by the daily routine of child care. She didn't change diapers, give baths, mend jackets, or wipe noses. Caroline and John Jr. had Maud Shaw attend to their mundane needs. Still, Jackie attended to their major ones. "She took care of those children like a lioness," said Larry Newman.

While J. B. West watched Jackie attentively play with the children, he thought this was the "real" Jacqueline Kennedy. "She was so happy, so abandoned, so like a little girl who had never grown up," he observed. "Many times, when she was performing with such grace and authority the role of First Lady, I felt she was just pretending. 'She really longs for a child's world,' I thought, 'where she can run and jump and hide and ride horses.' I thought of her as an actress—constantly playing a role."[23]

West had a unique vantage point from which to compare the Kennedys with their predecessors. "They were not knit-from-the-same-cloth and mirror-close like the Trumans; they were not openly sweethearts, like the Eisenhowers; but neither was their relationship formalized and 'official,' like the Roosevelts."

The White House staff was discreet with the first couple, attuned to their intimacy. Their early-afternoon nap was spent in absolute privacy. "Quite often, music was heard floating out into the hall, from the stereo that Mrs. Kennedy had installed in the passageway between her bedroom and her husband's," recalled West. "And many a morning, when George Thomas, whose job it was to wake Mr. Kennedy, would find him absent from his bedroom, the valet would tiptoe into the room next door, and gently shake the President—so as not to awaken the President's wife."

Janet Auchincloss thought Jack and Jackie were "very close to each other and understood each other wonderfully. He appreciated her gifts and she worshiped him and appreciated his humor and his kindness, and they really had fun together."[24]

Jackie often wrote clever, humorous notes to her husband and left them around the mansion. "He'd read one of these little notes and burst out laughing," said Baldrige. "It was their private joke."

One evening Jackie playfully decided to dazzle her husband at dinner with a complicated political question. Robert Kennedy suggested a dandy: "Ask him whether it isn't true that confirming Albert Beeson to membership on the National Labor Relations Board has the effect of wrecking the Bonwit Teller clause of the National Labor Relations Act."

Rita Dallas recalled a tender moment: "The First Lady would be sitting on the couch, outlined by a gentle halo of light, and then the President would step from the elevator that opened onto the living room. He would stand very still, waiting, while his wife rose from the couch to come to him. He would rest his hand on her cheek and then take her in his arms for a quiet embrace."

They did not air their marital problems in front of the White House staff. All their arguments were behind closed doors. After a heated argument with her husband Jackie would leave the White House for a while. "She simply disappeared to Glen Ora and rode horses when she got mad," said Baldrige.[25]

"In the first year or so in the White House, Jackie and Jack related to each other like professionals," Angier Biddle Duke observed. "They were coworkers. But then, after the Cuban missile crisis, they became more personal with each other. . . . Jackie started to talk about him in a more personal way. Like, 'Angie, the President is tired; lay off him, okay?' She seemed more concerned about him as a person. I could see them working more closely together." By 1963, holding hands, Jacqueline would walk with the President to *Air Force One*, heedless of the spectators watching them.

Overall, Jacqueline Kennedy was a major asset for her husband's presidency. "Opinion polls gave her high approval ratings," noted James Giglio, "and she soon headed the list of 'most admired women' (Mamie Eisenhower had never reached the top position)."

Robert McNamara thought Jackie was acute politically and that the President consulted her on several issues. "I don't mean in the sense of long anguished discussions, but certainly she was informed of what was going on and expressed her views on almost everything." General Clifton recalled that the President asked his wife's advice during times of crisis: Berlin, the Cuban missile crisis, the Bay of Pigs. "He would talk with her about it and she would talk with him. She wouldn't advise his staff, she would advise him—that's why nobody knew about it."

In general, though, Jacqueline Kennedy was not like Eleanor Roosevelt, who had an overdeveloped social conscience and nagged her husband about moral questions. "In their time together," noted Harris Wofford, "Kennedy's wife tried to divert him from politics and stir his underdeveloped artistic tastes, but probably not very often his conscience."[26]

In early August 1963, while the Kennedys vacationed on Squaw Island, Jackie was pregnant, due in mid-September. The pregnancy was her fifth. (Her first ended in a miscarriage in 1955; the following year she delivered a stillborn baby by cesarean; and Caroline and John Jr., also came by cesarean.) This time Jackie planned to give birth by cesarean at Walter Reed Army Hospital in Washington. But on Wednesday morning, August 7, five and a half weeks early, she felt birth pangs. "Extraordinary measures had been taken for just such an emergency," noted Lawrence Leamer. "Eight minutes after her physician, Dr. John Walsh, made his request, a helicopter landed on Squaw Island to fly her to a special ten-room suite at Otis Air Force Base hospital."

The baby boy, four pounds ten and one-half ounces, was christened Patrick Bouvier Kennedy after Jack's grandfather. Patrick had difficulty breathing and was immediately baptized, but at first the problem didn't seem serious. The President proudly took Patrick into Jackie's room, and she held the child for a few minutes.[27]

Shortly after, doctors diagnosed Patrick as having hyaline membrane disease, and rushed the child to Boston Children's Hospital later in the afternoon. With the disease, most common in premature infants, a membrane coated the air sacs in the lungs, hindering the baby's ability to pass oxygen into the bloodstream. It was inoperable, and didn't respond to antibiotic drugs. The only hope was that normal body functions would eventually dissolve the membrane.

The President had returned to the house on Squaw Island to check on Caroline and John Jr. That evening he flew to Boston, and went by motorcade to the hospital, where he learned that the baby's condition was stable.

That evening the President stayed at the Ritz-Carlton Hotel. On Thursday, August 8, he visited the hospital four times, as the baby's condition remained stable. That evening he flew back to Squaw Island. He hadn't been there long when he was called back to Boston. The baby's condition had turned critical. He spent the night near Patrick in a bed on the fourth floor of the hospital.[28]

At 4:04 A.M. on Friday, August 9, less than forty hours after his birth, Patrick Bouvier Kennedy died. Robert Kennedy, Dave Powers, and Pierre Salinger were with the President. "He walked away from us through a door into the hospital's boiler room," Salinger later wrote about the President, who rarely displayed emotional outbursts. "There, he wept for ten minutes, finally coming back to the three of us where Bob put his arm around his brother's shoulders."

"He put up quite a fight," the President said quietly. "He was a beautiful baby."

Only thirteen people were invited to attend the Mass of the Angels presided over by Cardinal Cushing in Boston the next day. (Jackie was unable to attend.) After the other mourners left for the cemetery, Kennedy remained behind. Cushing watched him circle "the tiny coffin with his arm, as if he wanted to take it with him." He placed a St. Christopher medal inside the casket next to the baby's body. The President was weeping and so was Cushing. "My dear Jack, let's go, let's go. Nothing more can be done." Patrick was buried in Brookline's Holywood Cemetery in a new family plot marked by a single headstone, reading "Kennedy."[29]

Jackie later told her mother of the wise counsel the President gave her shortly after the burial. "You know, Jackie, we must not create an atmosphere of sadness in the White House because this would not be good for anyone—not for the country and not for the work we have to do."

"I know he wanted another boy," Jackie said. "John was such pure joy for him. He was the kind of man who should have had a brood of children. . . . He felt the loss of the baby in the house as much as I did."

After Patrick's death the Bradlees were surprised by the change in the Kennedys' relationship. Jackie "greeted JFK with by far the most affectionate embrace we had ever seen them give each other. They are not normally demonstrative people, period." Several others noticed a change in their marriage. "They seemed to spend more time together," said Secret Service agent Larry Newman. "They would walk arm in arm to the mansion" from the Oval Office. "He seemed much more attentive to her."

After the tragedy, the President flew to the Cape several times each week to visit Jackie. "Each time he wanted to take her something that would let her know he had been thinking about her and to share with her something of his life in Washington," Lincoln recalled. "Sometimes he would ask that a bouquet of flowers be gathered from those blooming in his garden or on the White House lawn."[30]

Two months after Patrick's death, O'Donnell and Powers accompanied the President to the Harvard–Columbia football game at Harvard Stadium. Near the end of the first half, Kennedy turned to O'Donnell and said, "I want to go to Patrick's grave, and I want to go there alone, with nobody from the newspapers following me." O'Donnell organized the maneuver:

> We made our way out of the stadium to his car, with Pierre Salinger and his entourage of reporters hurrying to their cars behind us. I said a few words to a Secret Service agent, who spoke to the Boston Irish police officer in charge of the parking lot. The policeman saw to it that Salinger and the reporters did not move until the President's car was safely out of sight.

At Patrick's grave, the President prayed quietly for a few moments, then laid a yellow chrysanthemum bouquet by the tombstone.[31]

37

RENOVATION AND
CULTURE

In December 1960 Mamie Eisenhower led Jackie Kennedy on an inspection tour of the White House. Afterward the new first lady told friends that the Mansion looked like a hotel "decorated by a wholesale furniture store during a January clearance." The bedroom curtains were "seasick green," the ground-floor hall a "dentist's office bomb shelter." She railed against the "Pullman car ashtray stands" and the "eyesore ornamentation."

Past presidents and their wives had never refurbished the entire White House. Instead, they merely altered a wall or two to suit their own taste, never blending the modifications with the rest of the decor. "The result is that the White House was one of the most badly decorated mansions in the world," commented author Jim Bishop. "The rooms were green or blue or red or white, and the paintings were hung willy-nilly, wherever a suitable space of wall could be found to hang them. The storage area was full of antique treasures—some rare and fine, some assorted bric-a-brac."[1]

Jackie started her renovation with the family residence—the falling plaster, torn drapes, spotted carpets, and peeling wallpaper. She enlisted the help of the prominent New York decorator Mrs. Henry Parish II, or "Sister," as she was known. After two weeks Jackie had exhausted the entire fifty-thousand-dollar appropriation for White House remodeling, and she had only redecorated the family living quarters. "I know we're out of money, Mr. West," she said, "but never mind! We're going to find some way to get real antiques into this house." She needed benefactors.

On February 23, 1961, she launched a historic renovation project by appointing a twelve-member Fine Arts Committee chaired by Henry Francis du Pont, the multimillionaire from Wilmington, Delaware, and the finest historic collector in the country. The formidable experts on the committee were mostly wealthy, influential Republicans.

Jackie correctly assumed that the well-connected committee members would be able to find donors of money and furnishings, making unnecessary the need to ask Congress for appropriations. Besides Henry du Pont, the most significant adviser was the Frenchman Stéphane Boudin, who had directed the restoration of numerous European palaces.[2]

Jackie worked subtly to smooth the ruffled feathers of the two experts. "When she walked Boudin and duPont from room to room together for the first time, she realized they must never again meet if the restoration was ever to be completed," noted writer Christopher Andersen. "Dealing with each separately, she catered to their outsized egos, praising, cajoling, and coaxing until she got both men to agree to what *she* wanted."

The President was cautious, worried when critics questioned the new color scheme. "For God's sake, Jackie," he exclaimed while his wife repainted the Blue Room walls white, "shouldn't the Blue Room be *blue?*" The President took seriously his responsibility to care for the White House, but at the same time fretted about any departure from tradition that would be politically harmful.

Eventually Jackie's project captured his imagination. He had never expressed any interest in furniture, wall painting, curtains, or rugs, but now he gave tours to guests, pointing out all the aesthetic atrocities. "Look," he said, crawling on his hands and knees to examine a table. "It's not even a good *reproduction.*"[3]

Jackie carefully explained that her project was a "restoration," not a mere "redecoration." "Everything in the White House must have a reason for being there," she stated. "It would be sacrilege merely to redecorate it—a word I hate. It must be restored, and that has nothing to do with decoration. That is a question of scholarship."

The work of the Fine Arts Committee between 1961 and 1963 was impressive. Observed James Abbott and Elaine Rice in *Designing Camelot: The Kennedy White House Restoration* (1998), "Committee members' collective efforts yielded over five hundred new acquisitions for the White House, including 129 chairs, 82 tables, 50 lighting fixtures, and 7 mantels." Equally significant was the change in public perception. The committee's professional approach generated public support and enthusiasm and set a precedent for future improvements in the White House.

On November 3, 1961, Jackie's efforts created a permanent protective umbrella, the White House Historical Association. To raise money for the organization Jackie came up with the brilliant idea of publishing a White House guidebook. "They don't even have a brochure for all the tourists who go through here," she exclaimed to J. B. West. "But if we could sell one, we could finance the restoration!" At first President Kennedy opposed the idea, worried about unfavorable publicity if the public judged it smacked of commercialism, but he changed his mind.

Jackie oversaw every stage in the production of *The White House: An Historic Guide,* which became a best seller. It has now sold eight million copies, helping to fund the historical association's acquisition of furniture and pieces of art.[4]

On February 14, 1962, Jacqueline Kennedy welcomed the nation into the restored White House during a CBS television tour. Network officials later bragged that the show was the "greatest sight-seeing trip in history." Forty-six million viewers, three out of every four people with their TV sets on, watched the program. Jackie looked awkward, but the audience overlooked any shortcomings. "Here was an example of television at its best," said a reviewer for the *Chicago Daily News.*

A few critics panned her performance, most notably the novelist Norman Mailer in an article for *Esquire.* He asked his readers, "Do you remember the girl with the magnificent sweater who used to give the weather reports on television in a smarmy singsong tone?" With her "manufactured voice," Jackie strolled through the tour "like a starlet who is utterly without talent."[5]

Always vigilant, Jackie wanted nothing to spoil the beauty and elegance of the White House. She dictated the following memo to legislative liaison Larry O'Brien:

> I was passing by Mrs. Lincoln's office today and I saw [Congressman Aspinall] being photographed in the Rose Garden with an enormous bunch of celery. I think it is most undignified for any picture of this nature to be taken on the steps leading to the President's office or on the South grounds. If they want their pictures taken they can pose by the West Lobby. This also includes pictures of bathing beauties, etc.

Proud of his wife's success, the President delighted in taking people on tours. "How are the crowds holding up?" he often asked White House policeman Kenneth Burke. "Did we have any special tours today? How many of the public went through today?"[6]

Jackie also took a serious interest in preserving the distinct federal-style buildings surrounding Lafayette Park, the square facing the White House across Pennsylvania Avenue. Before Kennedy's inauguration, the decision had been made to tear down the historic buildings and replace them with modern government office buildings. "When the new First Lady heard about this, she was appalled," noted author Marianne Means. "She loved the peaceful, picturesque view the park afforded, and she thought it should be protected for future generations."

"The wreckers haven't started yet, and until they do, it can be saved," she told a friend. She discussed the problem with Bernard Boutin, the administrator of the General Services Administration, who hastily revised his agency's blueprints to come up with a compromise. The old buildings would be retained; new buildings would be built in the rear of the old ones.

"Jackie wanted to look out on a world of beauty," noted Lawrence Leamer. Indeed, her musicales and her efforts on behalf of renovation, preservation, and other cultural activities encouraged historical awareness, excellence, and beauty.[7]

During his presidency, Kennedy played host to sixty-six heads of state. Traditionally there had been three major dinners for state visits: one presided over by the President, another hosted by the secretary of state, and the last given by the visitor at his country's embassy. To lessen the time spent on empty formalities, Kennedy eliminated the dinner hosted by the secretary of state. He wanted to preserve more time for personal interaction. He made it clear he wanted effective personal interaction with the guest and fewer tedious ceremonial events.[8]

The White House social secretary was Letitia Baldrige. Exceptionally capable, statuesque, a congressman's daughter, and a veteran of American embassies in Europe, Baldrige had joined Kennedy's staff before the 1960 election. But in arranging the first official White House reception, Baldrige blundered. On a Sunday evening, the President played host to administration appointees and their spouses. Hard liquor, never permitted during the Eisenhower administration, was served at bars in the reception rooms.

The following day the President summoned Baldrige into his office. She expected to be patted on the back for arranging an outstanding reception.

"Tish," he said, "why didn't you tell me there had never been hard liquor at a party like this before?"

"What do you mean, Mr. President?"

Several delegations from the Women's Christian Temperance Union had been trying to see him, and congressmen from the Bible Belt had phoned to protest.

"But—but," Baldrige sputtered, not quite knowing what to say.

To make matters worse, the reception had been held on a Sunday. "We had to break all precedents, and do it on a Sunday!" He showed her a pile of evening newspapers with headlines, "Liquor on Sunday at the White House Draws Criticism" and "Never On Sunday at JFK's House says Baptist Congressman." The President should have been notified of the tradition and been left to make his own decision. Baldrige had no right to make that decision herself.

Later the same afternoon he phoned her to apologize. He had been "a little rough" that morning; she should understand that he had a lot of things on his mind. Afterward the White House continued to serve liquor, but the bars disappeared. "Drinks were mixed in the butler's pantry and passed on trays," said Baldrige.[9]

The President remained wary of any departure that might arouse criticism. When Baldrige wanted to pay the travel expenses of performers who volunteered to appear at the White House, Kennedy agreed. The air force could fly the performers to Washington "as long as we do it exactly the same way the previous administration did, and as long as we minimize the publicity."

He wanted a diversified group invited to receptions—political figures, businessmen, African-Americans, labor leaders, artists, writers. "Make sure that Hubert Humphrey and his wife are invited to one of our State dinners," he advised. "We ought to . . . make sure that everybody in the Senate gets invited rather than just the same old names."

Kennedy's sensitivity with guests at the receptions impressed Senator William Fulbright. "Every time I went to a White House dinner, or any kind of ceremony, I was very proud of the way he represented me and my country." Fulbright always found the President in good humor at the receptions. "I've never seen him surly, or glum, or depressed."[10]

Initially Kennedy chafed at ceremonial protocol. "He would charge off by himself, eager to get the action going, and find the flag-bearers, his wife, honored guests and military aides far behind," said Baldrige. At his first official luncheon, he ignored Baldrige's warning to turn left. "He charged straight ahead with his guest by the arm, opened a door, and startled eight footmen, the butler and the chef, all working in the pantry on the drink trays and hors d'oeuvres platters." He made a superb recovery. "And this, Mr. President," he said smoothly to his guest, "is one of the historic rooms of the mansion, too. Now I'll show you some others."

After that mistake Kennedy promised to follow Baldrige's signals. "One day," she recalled, "when I passed him in the ground floor corridor, he introduced me to his visitor as 'Miss Push and Pull' and called me that often ever after."[11]

The quality and style of entertaining at the White House dramatically changed. "All the rooms were decorated with casual Flemish-inspired arrangements of fresh flowers, as opposed to the large, static selections of previous White House occupants," noted Baldrige. Fireplaces were lit; candlelight provided most of the illumination.

In the spring of 1961, the White House hired a new French chef, René Verdon, ushering in an era of culinary excellence. Jackie selected menus and shortened them from the traditional seven courses to five or fewer, preserving more time for the entertainment, the focal point of the evening. "Elegance was the word," commented one observer. "The right wine, the right crystal, the right china." The Women's National Press Club's cookbook referred to the White House as the "best French restaurant in town."

Baldrige explained another major change: "Everyone violently disliked using the traditional U-shaped table. . . . In the Eisenhower regime the President and First Lady sat side by side, and no guests sat opposite them. The Kennedys used both sides of the U, and sat in the middle opposite each other, so that each one of them could be blanked by two honored guests, instead of just one."

Instead of greeting guests in a long receiving line, the President and Jackie mingled among the guests. Most observers thought the tone of a Kennedy reception was lighter, gayer, and more fun than those during the Eisenhower presidency.[12]

For after-dinner entertainment Jackie invited esteemed performing artists: cellist Pablo Casals, violinist Isaac Stern, and pianist Eugene Istomin. There were also performances of ballet, chamber music, opera, and Shakespearean drama. Most of the ideas originated with Jackie; Baldrige followed through and made the contacts.

Arthur Schlesinger Jr., an ally of Jackie's in pushing for cultural activities, wrote the President two weeks after the inauguration, urging him to take advantage of the opportunity to stimulate "a sense of genuine cultural concern." Kennedy could "launch a new image of America as a land which deeply values artistic and cultural achievement." A number of specific possibilities existed, such as "receiving leading artists and scholars at the White House; [and] the appointment of a serious commission on government and the arts." Two days later JFK invited Schlesinger to discuss with him how the White House could communicate "a sense of genuine cultural concern." The discussion proved fruitful.[13]

"After-dinner musicales in the East Room of the White House have been rather distressing in recent years," *Time* reported. "During the Eisenhower occupancy there were the schmalzy tunes of Hildegarde and Lawrence Welk." That changed on the evening of November 13, 1961, when the White House invited 153 guests to a musicale in the East Room to hear cellist Pablo Casals, eighty-four, one of the world's greatest performing musicians. The evening's music, declared *Time,* "sent shards of rapture through the world of serious music."

Casals had banished himself from his native Spain in 1939 to protest the rule of fascist Francisco Franco. Since then he had refused to play his cello in any country that recognized the Franco government. But when President Kennedy learned that Casals approved of his administration, he asked him to play at the White House, and Casals accepted.

The nation's finest conductors—Leonard Bernstein, Eugene Ormandy, Leopold Stokowski, and others—were all invited, as were music critics from New York and Washington. Said one guest: "The composers acted and talked like poor country cousins who had at last been let in the front door."

At the end of the concert the audience, led by the President, gave Casals a standing ovation. Leonard Bernstein, his head buried in his hands during most of Casals's performance, said afterward, "I was deeply moved by the entire occasion, not merely by the music of Casals but by the company in which it was played."

"It's all like having dinner with friends," Bernstein added about the evening. "The food is marvelous, the wines are delicious, there are cigarettes on the table, people are laughing, laughing out loud, telling stories, jokes, enjoying themselves, glad to be there."[14]

Because he didn't understand classical music, on several occasions Kennedy clapped at the wrong time, thinking the concert was over. The different movements within a composition confused him. Baldrige worked out a code system for a concert by Isaac Stern. When Stern had almost finished his last piece, said Baldrige,

> I was to open the central door of the East Room from the outside about two inches—enough for him to glimpse the prominent Baldrige nose structure in the crack. It worked beautifully that night and for all future concerts. When the President noticed the door slightly ajar, that meant the last piece was in progress. He would await the applause; then, clapping heartily, he would take Mrs. Kennedy by the arm, and escort the honored guests to the stage to congratulate the musicians.

Since Kennedy did not know prominent American composers, he requested background information about them and their compositions. Then, when he met the composer, he would say, "Oh, you're the famous composer of . . ." "They would just be absolutely flattered to death," said Baldrige.[15]

"The Casals evening has had an extraordinary effect in the artistic world," Schlesinger wrote the President shortly after the performance.

You probably saw John Crosby's column this morning ("President Kennedy is the best friend culture . . . has had in the White House since Jefferson"). All this is of obvious importance, not only in attaching a potent opinion-making group to the Administration, but in transforming the world's impression of the United States as a nation of money-grubbing materialists. And it is notable that all this has taken place without any criticism, so far as I am aware.

Schlesinger urged the President to go "a step further" and appoint a special assistant for culture. The assistant could survey

areas of actual or possible government impact on culture (from airport construction to tax policies to honors lists to direct government sponsorship or subsidy) and to come up at the end of six months with a report and, hopefully, a program.

The mere existence of this White House inquiry would do a good deal to generate concern through the bureaucracy for the government's cultural responsibilities. At the end, we would have a much better idea of the resources, possibilities and problems in the area.

Schlesinger suggested August Heckscher as the man to do the job. Heckscher was the director of the Twentieth Century Fund, a nonprofit research institution that subsidized studies of economic, political, and social issues. The President acted immediately. In early December he asked Heckscher to join the White House team to work on cultural matters. "I have in mind an inventory of the variety of public activities which impinge on cultural matters," the President wrote in his charge to Heckscher,

from the construction of post offices to the imposition of taxes. Such an inventory would give us an idea of the resources, possibilities and limitations of future policy in the cultural field. Obviously government can at best play only a marginal role in our cultural affairs. But I would like to think that it is making its full contribution to this role.[16]

For many politicians the arts were a laughing matter, certainly nothing to be subsidized. A Virginia congressman contended that playing poker was "an artful occupation." It "was as logical to subsidize poker players as artists."

The President emphasized to Heckscher his desire for a "quiet inquiry, without fanfare." Over the next year and a half, serving as the administration's cultural liaison, Heckscher gathered volumes of information. In the process, noted author John Wetenhall, he brought "to the administration the expectations and good will of the arts constituency." Kennedy remained cautious, Heckscher recalled, but "if he could be convinced that [an idea] would receive a good public reception . . . [and] would not involve undue expenditure of funds, he would say, 'Go ahead with it.'"

According to Heckscher, "The President would take a step and then if the reaction was good, he would be encouraged and would be willing to take another." Heckscher's report criticized governmental design standards—for coins, stamps, federal buildings—and urged the government to use independent panels of experts for aesthetic advice. The report also "called attention to the inadequate condition of America's cultural facilities, suggested educational reforms, decried the run-down appearance of the national capital, and even offered tax reforms." In consultation with Heckscher the President issued an executive order on June 12, 1963, establishing the President's Advisory Council on the Arts.[17]

On a beautiful fall Saturday, October 26, 1963, Kennedy delivered a personal manifesto on government and art. He spoke at Amherst College in honor of Robert Frost, who had died the previous January. Stressing the theme of "poetry and power," Kennedy focused on the need for the free artist in society:

> The men who create power make an indispensable contribution to the nation's greatness, but the men who question power make a contribution just as indispensable, especially when that questioning is disinterested, for they determine whether we use power or power uses us.
>
> Our national strength matters, but the spirit which informs and controls our strength matters just as much.

Robert Frost had linked poetry and power, seeing poetry as the means of saving power from itself: "When power leads man toward arrogance, poetry reminds him of his limitations. When power narrows the areas of man's concern, poetry reminds him of the richness and diversity of his existence. When power corrupts, poetry cleanses. For art establishes the basic human truth which must serve as the touchstone of our judgment." Kennedy linked art with the creation of national values. Government must not dictate those values to the artist; instead it should examine its own values by the standards of art:

> The artist, however faithful to his personal vision of reality, becomes the last champion of the individual mind and sensibility against an intrusive society and an officious state. The great artist is thus a solitary figure. He has, as Frost said, a lover's quarrel with the world. In pursuing his perceptions of reality, he must often sail against the currents of his time. This is not a popular role.

Kennedy offered his vision for the future:

> I look forward to an America which will reward achievement in the arts as we reward achievement in business or statecraft. I look forward to an America which will steadily raise the standards of artistic accomplishment and which will steadily enlarge cultural opportunities for all of our citizens. I look forward to an America which commands respect throughout the world not only for its strength but for its civilization as well. And I look forward to a world which will be safe not only for democracy and diversity but also for personal distinction.[18]

Referring to the White House appearances by Isaac Stern and Pablo Casals, critic Richard Schickel contended that any sugestion that "these gestures had any substantial effect on the national cultural climate is nonsense. . . . They helped keep the intellectual and artistic community in line on the cheap, and they may have offered a certain amusement to the culturally aspiring middle class. But the White House musicales were the equivalent, on a grandish scale, of a Book-of-the-Month Club subscription for the occupants."[19]

Schickel's view is cynical. Despite the limits of Kennedy's own artistic talent and taste, he appreciated cultural excellence and sincerely wanted to promote the arts. Culture may have served as ornamentation in the Kennedy administration, wrote author Gary Larson, but "the arts served as something more substantial as well—something to strive for, an aspect of life worth seeking out, a part of the larger American environment, finally, that the federal government had an obligation to protect and promote."

Although completely unfamiliar with an artistic concept, Kennedy still appreciated "the merit of that concept with all the enthusiasm of an impressed critic," said Baldrige. "He simply understood the *quality* of greatness." When Kennedy embraced the performing arts, observed Dore Schary, the average person was "bound to change his mind about such things being effete."[20]

In terms of governmental policy, the Kennedy administration made only incremental progress. The White House dinners were mostly symbolic, Heckscher's report merely a beginning. Still, as Wetenhall contended, Kennedy's effort displayed "sensitivity to the rising concerns for culture in America." The New Frontier formed practical recommendations and endowed the cultural agenda with a "vocabulary of idealism that left a legacy of national values to the legislation that would follow."[21]

38

MIND AND
PERSONALITY

"If I were drawing him," Jackie Kennedy famously remarked, "I would draw a tiny body and a big head."

Among Kennedy's salient qualities of mind were flexibility, breadth of interest, curiosity, wit, and detachment. His mind was analytical but not creative; skeptical but not original or imaginative. With the significant exception of his attitude toward women, he was remarkably free from bias and prejudice, allowing him, thought Charles Bohlen, to approach "any problem with a clarity that was certainly a pleasure to behold in operation."

He preferred ideas he could use. When told something, he wanted to know how he could put it into practice. "His was a directed intelligence," said Sorensen, "never spent on the purely theoretical, always applied to the concrete. He sought truth in order to act on it."[1]

Quick and retentive, he absorbed information swiftly. Edward R. Murrow returned from meetings at the White House full of admiration. "Golly, that guy—he'll look at a piece of paper for about thirty seconds—it's *remarkable* how quickly he can absorb and play back at you, almost verbatim."

He hated the wordiness endemic in political life. "He never, at least in his adult life, opened his mouth without having something to say," John Kenneth Galbraith stated. Kennedy enjoyed an affinity with Britain's Harold Macmillan partly because neither could tolerate verbosity.[2]

Kennedy developed short-range plans, but not grand designs. In a private talk at Hyannis Port, James Reston asked him to describe his long-range plans. "He looked at me as if I were a dreaming child," Reston recalled. "I tried again: Did he not feel the need of some goal to help guide his day-to-day decisions and priorities? Again a ghastly pause. Only after Reston turned the question to an immediate specific problem did Kennedy roll off "a torrent of statistics about the difficulty of organizing nations at different levels of economic development." Reston concluded that he had so many day-to-day problems that "he didn't think much about what lay ahead. Maybe this was all to the good."

He loved history, particularly dramatic moments and great people. During a visit to the battlefield at Gettysburg, Kennedy displayed a knowledge about the Civil War that amazed Paul Fay. "When we came to a certain area where a Boston or Massachusetts unit had fought, he recounted the battle with such detail that I could almost see it taking place." He ruminated about Civil War battles. Did Confederate general George E. Pickett make the right decision when he ordered the famous charge at Gettysburg? Was it a suicidal attack, one for which he deserved to be court-martialed? "These kinds of moments in history, when individual people had to make a very difficult judgment, always fascinated him," said Ormsby-Gore.[3]

The President had no aptitude for foreign languages. He grew impatient waiting for translations; when he had to use an interpreter and couldn't communicate directly, he had a less successful relationship with the individual.

While Jacqueline Hirsh taught French to Caroline in the White House, the President briefly became interested in learning the language himself, but his aptitude didn't match his enthusiasm. "I think it's time I learned French," he told Hirsh. "If you gave me a French lesson, how would you do it?" (He teased: "You have five minutes to think about it.") She suggested he read *Profiles in Courage* in French so he didn't have to worry about understanding the contents.

They held four sessions together. "He seemed extremely self-conscious, extremely," said Hirsh. He kept fiddling with his tie and getting up and sitting down. But he was anxious to learn. "I can't wait to really surprise the world," he said. "It's always good to improve anything."

Each time he tried to speak in French he hesitated. After he spat out a phrase, he asked Hirsh, "How was it?" She replied, "Well, technically it's good, but your accent doesn't sound good at all." Kennedy agreed.

"Do you think I can manage to sound like a French person?" he asked.

"You sound like an American right now when you say something in French," she replied.

"Well, I want to be able to do it just perfectly."[4]

He was curious and a superb listener. In a ten-minute interview, said one visitor, Kennedy listened for nine and a half minutes. He tried to find the area of another person's expertise and to keep the dialogue on that subject. He gathered facts and took assessments from people he respected.

"He would lean forward, his eyes protruding slightly, concerned with using the occasion not to expound his own thoughts but to drag out of the talker whatever could be of use to him," said Arthur Schlesinger. "In this way he ventilated problems in great detail without revealing his own position and without making his visitors conscious that he was holding back."

After meeting Kennedy, the British philosopher and author Isaiah Berlin remarked, "He exhausts you by listening." He was the best listener George Kennan ever knew in high position. "He was able to resist the temptation, to which so many other great men have yielded, to sound off himself and be admired. He asked questions modestly, sensibly, and listened very patiently to what you had to say and did not try, then, to tell jokes, to be laughed at, or to utter sententious statements himself to be admired."[5]

Barbara Ward felt that his intellectual curiosity was exceptionally strong and utterly disinterested. "He simply wanted what was accurate, what reflected the truth, and what could be given to him in a completely unbiased way."

Kennedy's interest in science amazed Jerome Wiesner, his science adviser. "He often asked about obscure stories concerning science buried in *The New York Times* or the London *Observer* or any one of the dozens of papers and periodicals he somehow found time to read."

Kennedy gathered information effectively from listening, but he retained more when he read. "His mind didn't seem to want to hold on to things he heard quite as much as it did with things he had read," thought Senator George Smathers, who therefore put his most important proposals in writing.[6]

Kennedy preferred written briefings. If Fred Dutton sent the President a forty-page memo, Kennedy returned it within thirty-six hours, with editorial notes all over the margins. "It was incredible—his ability to consume paper, to read it, [and] make intelligent comments."

While reading a newspaper, the front page received his first attention. "He scanned the headlines, skimmed through pieces of marginal interest, took a moment or so longer with the vital stories while he sucked out their juice," noted Hugh Sidey. He browsed the editorial page, taking most interest in the columnists. (He especially admired columnists Walter Lippmann and Joseph Alsop.) He skimmed the rest of the paper—the movie reviews, sports, and financial page—and skipped the comics and the society section.

The magazines he regularly scanned were *Time, Life, Newsweek, U.S. News* and World Report, Business Week, Nation's Business, Saturday Review, The New Yorker, Harper's, Atlantic Monthly, The Spectator, The New Republic, History Today, Foreign Affairs, the Manchester Guardian Weekly, and the London Economist.

He often wandered into Pierre Salinger's office, where he read a clipping or picked up a book off Salinger's desk and disappeared with it. Salinger would have to call George Thomas and ask if the book was on the President's nightstand. Sure enough, it was there, and Salinger would get it back. "Nothing was really safe," said one of Salinger's aides.[7]

History, biography, and current events dominated his leisure reading. He relished notable writing, and since 1945 had collected examples of great prose, putting them in a bound book. Many of his insights about leadership came from his study of great men. He read almost every book by the prolific Winston Churchill. He admired Churchill's gracefully written memos, and often read them to savor their craftsmanship.

He quoted Churchill and inscribed in his post–World War II notebook a statement by Churchill with special meaning to him: "The whole history of the world is summed up in the fact that, when nations are strong, they are not always just, and, when they wish to be just, they are often no longer strong. . . . Let us have this blessed union of power and justice."

"He roots around in a book looking for what he wants," James Burns wrote of Kennedy's utilitarian approach. "He might start in the back, then go to the parts that can help him." He searched for something of specific value. "What good are ideas unless you make use of them," he told a friend.[8]

He learned valuable lessons from Barbara Tuchman's The Guns of August (1962), which won the Pulitzer Prize. Absorbing, beautifully written, the book explored the immediate background of World War I and the first month of the fighting. Although Europe sat on a powder keg, divided into two armed alliances, no one expected a war to begin. Kennedy often cited Tuchman's book as evidence that the rigid mobilization plans, both of the Triple Alliance and of the Triple Entente, made it impossible for the diplomats and politicians to avert a world war in 1914.

Flexibility, preserving options, were critical in the nuclear age. "He had read The Guns of August with great interest," observed Maxwell Taylor, "and frequently turned to me and commented on the dull generals who never had more than one solution and hence governments were bound to call a levee en masse—massive mobilization—and depend on the execution of a single war plan at the time of the outbreak of World War I." Kennedy insisted that Taylor and other military officials read the book and learn the lesson.[9]

He read most of Hemingway, and a few other novels, but fiction rarely appeared on his reading list. Critics believe that the President spent evenings immersed in the fantastic tales of Ian Fleming's British secret agent, James Bond, and that Fleming's stories encouraged Kennedy to engage in espionage. "JFK was such an aficionado of Fleming's novels that, by enthusing about them, he helped make the British thriller writer a top bestseller in the United States," said Evan Thomas. Of the film version of Fleming's *From Russia with Love,* Ben Bradlee observed that Kennedy "seemed to enjoy the cool and the sex and the brutality." But suggestions that the Bond book and the movie were favorites, that they stimulated his support for covert action, that Bond typified his personal style, or that he had an intimate friendship with Ian Fleming are all exaggeration.[10]

Kennedy invited the novelist William Styron and his wife aboard the presidential yacht. "There are introductions all around," Styron later wrote; "the President's smile is broad, honest, and Irish, his handshake firm, and he plainly relishes his embrace with Sue, who is a looker and who calls him, yes, 'Jack.' "

While the President chewed on the end of his small cigar, he asked Styron about his current writing project. The novelist was in the midst of writing his powerful fictionalized autobiography of the black slave who led an uprising in Virginia in 1831. Fifty-five whites and two hundred blacks died in the rebellion. Published in 1967, *The Confessions of Nat Turner* won the Pulitzer Prize.

Kennedy was fascinated. "Tell me about it," he said. The President had never heard of Nat Turner. "Outside of a few historians specializing in American slavery," Styron recalled, "no one is aware of this rebel Negro, and that includes most Negroes."

> Afraid to bore, wary of becoming too wound up in his own obsessions, the Writer tries to abbreviate his account, but the President is plainly captivated and probes for more detail, more information. His questions are searching and pertinent, as if he shares—or at least wants to share— the Writer's involvement with that mysterious and catastrophic event.

Flattered by the President's close attention, Styron was "very much impressed by the bright and persistent nature of the interrogation. . . . Time disappears."

Like other guests invited on the presidential yacht, Styron thought the food had to be eaten to be believed: "Ice cold hot dogs in buns so soggy from some steam bath that the bread sinks like paste beneath thumb and fingers. An attempt at *oeufs en gelée,* but the yolks either hard as a rock or running out in a horrible goo. The Filipino mess steward all aquiver with nervousness and dropping spoons in everyone's lap, including Numero Uno."

Despite Kennedy's power and super-matinee-idol appearance, "one does not sense the preening vanity of the movie star," Styron concluded of the President's demeanor. "He has a beguiling and self-effacing modesty which comes out in the really funny little remarks he makes about himself, and that is one of his nice charms."[11]

Kennedy often told friends about his two favorite books. "*Pilgrim's Way* is a book of great beauty and strength," wrote a reviewer of John Buchan's newest book, published in 1940. John Kennedy read the book shortly after it appeared.

Of Scottish Puritan background, modest, with a genius for friendship, John Buchan journeyed to South Africa early in his career to serve in a minor British administrative capacity under Alfred Milner at the end of the Boer War. Following a brief career practicing law in London, he went into publishing for ten years. The longest period of his life, though, he spent writing scores of books—fiction, biography, and history. He was best known for his novels, particularly *The Thirty-nine Steps*. At the end of his career he was elevated to the peerage and became the governor-general of Canada.[12]

In *Pilgrim's Way,* usually described as an autobiography, Buchan recorded only a "few selected experiences." Actually the book was not about John Buchan at all, but about the outstanding men whom he had known and loved: Alfred Milner, Aldous Huxley, Rudyard Kipling, H. G. Wells, Ramsay MacDonald, T. E. Lawrence, George V, Arthur Balfour. (Buchan's portraits were exclusively about men; no woman appeared on his pages except his wife.)

"We are presented with a wonderful exhibition of portrait sketches," observed one reviewer. "The brilliant contemporaries of the author's young days live again. . . . The portraiture, though not uncritical, is always as kindly as it is arresting."

"Public life is the crown of a career," Buchan wrote, "and to young men it is the worthiest ambition. Politics is still the greatest and most honorable adventure."

"A statesman's first duty," Buchan continued, was to "see facts clearly and to make the proper deductions from them." Using that standard, Buchan judged Arthur Balfour to be the greatest British statesman in the first quarter of the twentieth century. "The most remarkable union of opposites was his devotion to what was old and his aliveness to what was new. . . . He saw the long descent of the most novel problems. Like [Edmund] Burke, he would not destroy what many generations had built merely because some of the plaster-work was shaky. At the same time he was wholly in tune with his age and aware of every nuance of the modern world."[13]

Buchan knew T. E. Lawrence—the famous Lawrence of Arabia—the British soldier who in 1916 was assigned to advise Prince Faisal, the leader of the Arab uprising against the Turks, one of Britain's enemies in World War I.

After gaining Faisal's confidence, Lawrence organized the Arabs into an effective military force which, astonishingly, captured the Red Sea port of Aqaba, and subsequently achieved other military successes. Lawrence later wrote about his experiences in his classic *Seven Pillars of Wisdom* (1926), a book Kennedy read in the 1940s. A complex, tortured individual, emotionally scarred by his war experiences, Lawrence died in a motorcycle accident in 1935.

"I do not profess to have understood T. E. Lawrence fully," Buchan wrote, "still less to be able to portray him; there is no brush fine enough to catch the subtleties of his mind, no aerial viewpoint high enough to bring into one picture the manifold of his character."

> It is simplest to say that he was a mixture of contradictories which never were—perhaps could never have been—harmonized. His qualities lacked integration. He had moods of vanity and moods of abasement; immense self-confidence and immense diffidence. He had a fastidious taste which was often faulty. The gentlest and most lovable of beings with his chivalry and considerateness, he could also be ruthless.

Buchan thought Lawrence's life in 1920 was in grave disequilibrium. "You cannot in any case be nine times wounded, four times in an air crash, have many bouts of fever and dysentery, and finally at the age of twenty-nine take Damascus at the head of an Arab army, without living pretty near the edge of your strength."

Buchan claimed he was not given to hero worship,

> but I could have followed Lawrence over the edge of the world. I loved him for himself, and also because there seemed to be reborn in him all the lost friends of my youth. If genius be, in Emerson's phrase, a "stellar and undiminishable something," whose origin is a mystery and whose essence cannot be defined, then he was the only man of genius I have ever known.[14]

Buchan's most memorable portrait, the one John Kennedy found most inspiring, described Raymond Asquith. Young Asquith was the son of Herbert H. Asquith, the eminent British politician and prime minister (1908–1916). "There are some men whose brilliance in boyhood and early manhood dazzles their contemporaries and becomes a legend," Buchan wrote. "They march on into life with a boyish grace, and their high noon keeps all the freshness of the morning. Certainly to his cradle the good fairies brought every dower. They gave him great beauty of person; the gift of winning speech; a mind that mastered readily whatever it cared to master; poetry and the love of all beautiful things; a magic to draw friends to him; a heart as tender as it was brave. One gift only was withheld from him—length of years."

Even as a young man Asquith's great mind was evident to all:

> In sheer intellectual strength he may have had his equals, and there were limits to his imaginative sympathies; but for manifold and multiform gifts I have not known his like. He was a fine classical scholar, at once learned and precise; he was widely read in English literature; he wrote good poetry, Greek, Latin, and English; he had the most delicate and luminous critical sense; he had an uncanny gift of exact phrase, whether in denunciation or in praise.

Despite his gifts Asquith was not necessarily popular: "His courtesy was without warmth, he was apt to be intolerant of mediocrity, and he had no desire for facile acquaintanceships."

Asquith fought in World War I:

> He disliked emotion, not because he felt lightly but because he felt deeply. He most sincerely loved his country, but he loved her too much to identify her with the pasteboard goddess of the music-halls and the hustings. War meant to him the shattering of every taste and interest, but he did not hesitate. It was no sudden sentimental fervour that swept him into the army, but the essential nature of one who had always been shy of rhetorical professions, but was very clear about the real thing. Austerely self-respecting, he had been used to hide his devotions under a mask of indifference, and would never reveal them except in deeds.

While leading his military unit, young Asquith was killed in 1915.[15]

In Kennedy's post–World War II notebook, he inscribed Buchan's final testimony to Asquith: "He will stand to those of us who are left as an incarnation of the spirit of the land he loved. He loved his youth and his youth has become eternal. Debonair, brilliant and brave, he is now part of that immortal England which knows not age or weariness or defeat."

With friends, Kennedy often talked about Raymond Asquith. "I remember him saying over and over that there was nobody in our time who was more gifted," Ormsby-Gore recalled. "Whether Jack realized it or not, I think he paralleled himself after Asquith."

While Kennedy wrote *As We Remember Joe,* he intentionally emulated Buchan's lucid, graceful, and moving style. "I thought [*Pilgrim's Way*] was a first-class book during my post-college time," Kennedy told James Burns in 1959. "It was beautifully done. I thought his . . . character studies were damn good."[16]

Kennedy's other favorite book was a distinguished biography. In 1939, David Cecil published *The Young Melbourne,* a study of William Lamb, who became Lord Melbourne, and the prime minister of Great Britain from 1834 to 1841. The book explored Melbourne's life up to the time he became prime minister. Cecil had intended to cover Melbourne's entire life in one volume, but World War II disrupted his plan; he published what was completed, hoping he could later finish his study. The book was praised as an unusually fascinating portrait; Cecil treated his subject as a human being, not just a figurehead.

In 1954 Lord David Cecil, now professor of English literature at Oxford and renowned for his sensitive, stylized biographies, completed his study and published the two parts in one volume, *Melbourne.* Although the parts were completed fifteen years apart, Cecil gracefully fused the two sections.[17]

One fascinating aspect of *Melbourne* was Cecil's brilliant portrayal of British Whigs. For years the Whigs had controlled Great Britain and felt they could do as they pleased. Wealthy landowners, they lived the life of the ordinary Englishman, but on a grander scale. The Whigs, wrote Cecil, believed in "the Renaissance ideal of the whole man, whose aspiration it is to make the most of every advantage, intellectual and sensual, that life has to offer. . . . All believed in ordered liberty, low taxation and the enclosure of land; all disbelieved in despotism and democracy. Their only concern was to restate these indisputable truths in a fresh and effective fashion."

At twenty-one William Lamb fell in love with the beautiful, dynamic, but wildly eccentric fourteen-year-old Caroline Ponsonby, who was to make his life miserable until she died in 1828. Caroline fell in love with Lord Byron, the handsome English Romantic poet and satirist, who had enthralled Europe with his poetry and personality. Their public affair scandalized Whig society until Byron left her.

When the eighteen-year-old Victoria suddenly became queen in 1837, Melbourne was prime minister. He developed a platonic and sentimental attachment to the young queen, becoming her political tutor during the first three years of her long reign.[18]

Melbourne was more intelligent than most Whigs, and less profligate. He was outspoken, sometimes intentionally shocking, charming, handsome, and kind. Everyone liked him. But he was not a great man, not one to be emulated by John Kennedy. Indecisive, he much preferred to put off decisions than make them. He was indolent and cynical. Reform movements were dangerous, he said, because they aroused expectations that government and society could actually be improved. He opposed popular education because "[y]ou may fill a person's head with nonsense which may be impossible ever to get out again."

In his description of Melbourne's mind, Cecil displayed his graceful style and penetrating insight:

> To be a thinker one must believe in the value of disinterested thought. William's education had destroyed his belief in this, along with all other absolute beliefs, and in so doing removed the motive force necessary to set his creative energy working. The spark that should have kindled his fire was unlit, with the result that he never felt moved to make the effort needed to discipline his intellectual processes, to organize his sporadic reflections into a coherent system of thought. . . . This lack of system meant . . . that he never overhauled his mind to set its contents in order in the light of a considered standard of value—so that the precious and the worthless jostled each other in its confused recesses; side by side with fresh and vivid thoughts lurked contradictions, commonplaces and relics of the conventional prejudices of his rank and station. Even his skepticism was not consistent; though he doubted the value of virtue, he never doubted the value of being a gentleman.[19]

Reviewers heaped praise on *Melbourne*. "A classic," said the *Chicago Tribune;* "superb," wrote reviewer John Lukacs; "a work of art," penned George Dangerfield in the *Saturday Review*. In his review in *The New York Times* Orville Prescott praised Cecil as a "consummate prose stylist," who had composed "one of the finest biographies of our time." The book was listed briefly on the bestseller list of *The New York Times*.[20]

While reading *Melbourne* during his recuperation from back surgery in 1955, Kennedy scribbled a few notes about a small item in the book. The notes exposed Kennedy's simplistic view of women. As Lawrence Leamer observed, "[Kennedy] found European women such as Lady Melbourne and Mary Queen of Scots interesting because they were 'women of leisure' but in America 'women [were] either prostitutes or housewives [and] do not play much of a role in [the] cultural or intellectual life of [the] country.' "

Historians, biographers, and other students of Kennedy's life mistakenly assume that Kennedy read *The Young Melbourne*. Kennedy never mentioned the early version; he read *Melbourne* shortly after it appeared. Some also assume that Kennedy was attracted by the rakish character of Lord Byron. In fact, while Kennedy enjoyed his poetry, Byron was a minor figure in *Melbourne*.[21]

Closer to the truth was journalist Hugh Sidey's view that Kennedy enjoyed *Melbourne* because it portrayed a "society of young, wealthy aristocrats who devoted themselves honorably and tirelessly to service to their queen and empire—and on their weekends to themselves and their pleasures."

More insightful was Kennedy's friend David Ormsby-Gore. "He liked the way [the book] was written, he liked the style of the writing and he was interested in the period. I think these were all elements which gave him great pleasure rather than the fact that he was a particular admirer of a certain character which I am sure he wasn't. . . . He certainly never talked about Melbourne as being one of the great figures of the 19th century."[22]

Exquisite prose style, captivating narrative, brilliant portraits—these were the primary attractions of *Pilgrim's Way* and *Melbourne*.

Kennedy's attempt to cultivate intellectuals set him apart from other modern Presidents. "He is far from being the best educated of Presidents," noted Richard Rovere, "even if one leaves out of account those who were children of the Enlightenment—the Adamses, Jefferson, and Madison. His background in literature does not match that of Theodore Roosevelt, who enjoyed the company of poets, read Dante in Renaissance Italian, [and] could rattle off long passages in French from the *Chanson de Roland*." Still, no other President ever tried to identify the White House with a wide range of intellectual life, or regarded intellectuals as a national treasure whom the government should recognize and cultivate.

In 1961 Arthur Schlesinger arranged for several prominent intellectuals to visit with the President, among them D. W. Brogan, the British historian; Raymond Aron, the French sociologist; and Alfred Kazin, the prominent American literary critic. Each had a White House luncheon and discussion with Kennedy.[23]

Afterward, Kazin, the author of *On Native Grounds* (1942), expressed his disappointment with Kennedy in his essay "The President and Other Intellectuals," published in the *American Scholar* (autumn 1961). The President possessed mental agility, Kazin conceded, a passion for learning, respect for intellectual achievement, and good taste in books and ideas. Unfortunately, Kennedy lacked one crucial intellectual trait: conviction. What were Kennedy's intellectual convictions? What did he believe? Following his discussion in the White House, Kazin claimed he still didn't know.

Kazin cited recent examples of what he thought was exaggerated praise of Kennedy's intellectual ability. Walter Lippmann, Kazin claimed, "must have carried many votes for Kennedy by certifying his faith in Kennedy as a thinking politician who promised to be a statesman." In his book on the 1960 election campaign, *The Making of the President, 1960,* Theodore H. White had described Kennedy as one "who enjoys words and reading, is a Pulitzer Prize winner himself and a one-time reporter; he has an enormous respect for those who work with words and those who write clean prose."

Kazin disagreed. Kennedy was merely slick and cool, a calculating pragmatist who lacked vision. He criticized *Profiles in Courage*. An unworthy Pulitzer winner, the book reminded Kazin "of those little anecdotes from the lives of great men that are found in the *Reader's Digest,* Sunday supplements, and the journal of the American Legion. It is the kind of book that reads like a series of excerpts even when you read it through; and indeed it seems composed of excerpts—excerpts of reading, excerpts of anecdote."[24]

About Kennedy, wrote Kazin, "one *has* to make psychological guesses."

> His most essential quality, I would think, is that of the man who is always making and remaking himself. He is the final product of a fanatical job of self-remodeling. He grew up rich and favored enough not to make obvious mistakes or to fall for the obvious—he has been saved from the provincial and self-pitying judgments that so many talented Americans break their teeth on. He has been saved, not merely from the conventional, but from wasting his time on it. Even now there is an absence in him of the petty conceit of the second-rate, and a freshness of curiosity behind which one feels not merely his quickness to utilize all his advantages, but also his ability to turn this curiosity on himself. He turns things over very quickly in his own mind; he gets the angle. Yet all the while he stands outside, like a sculptor surveying his work.

Switching themes, Kazin thought Kennedy had badly misjudged the Cuban invasion. "Castro was far too popular to be overthrown with a small landing at the Bay of Pigs," he charged. "Yet faced by so many conflicting and in a sense mutually canceling bodies of advice, Kennedy allowed the gun to go off. And nothing has been said by him since, or by his advisers, that indicates it was anything but the failure of the Cuban invasion that they regret. It has given a 'bad mark' to the Administration that wants so much to succeed." What was "immoral" and "downright stupid" about the invasion Kennedy and his advisers never considered.[25]

After Kennedy read Kazin's essay he quipped, "We wined him and dined him. . . . Then he went away and wrote that piece!"

When William Styron talked with the President aboard the presidential yacht, Kennedy asked his guest if he had read the article by Kazin. Styron nervously replied that he had. (Styron privately thought Kazin had made "a fairly good case for the fact that the President, while enchanting and certainly anything but a dumbbell, was not charged with the "intellectual high voltage" claimed for him by some admirers.) What did Styron think of the piece? the President asked.

> The Writer flushes, feeling as if he were being forced to catch a smoking, red-hot cinder. But he is saved immediately by another question, spoken

in a kind of angry petulance and so naive, really, as to validate rather strongly Kazin's judgment: What qualifies a critic to make an assessment of a work if he himself has never created one? Boy, thinks the Writer, Alfred's really got Kennedy's goat.[26]

In a personal letter of protest to Kazin, Schlesinger chided the literary critic for his "untypically unfocused piece. . . . What you are saying is contained more in the tone of faint derision and frustration rather than in explicit analysis."

Kennedy has not advertised himself as an intellectual. He has not regarded his inclination toward books, ideas and the product of the mind as an expedient instrument of his political rise. He has spoken of his feelings about books, used quotations and brought intelligent men around him because he wanted to. It is the intellectual himself who has advertised these things and now, the final irony, views them as a symbol of the fact that it is fashionable and politically good to be intellectual.

Kennedy, wrote Schlesinger, possessed outstanding qualities of mind, rare enough anywhere, especially among politicians.

He has a capacity to view a problem with detachment free from petty prejudices. He is not only freely open to a wide range of argument and gifted with a respect for facts but he has the capacity to understand the arguments and the facts. In addition, he has an enormous, instinctive capacity for the relevant, for the critical aspect of a problem on which decision must turn. This is a faculty which is notably lacking in most of the intellectual commentators on affairs. His advisers respect him not because he is more tireless than they, but because he is smarter.

Schlesinger blasted Kazin's facile accusation that the U.S. intervention in Cuba was "immoral."

Does the Soviet Union threaten our security in this hemisphere? Is it moral to attack their forward military and propaganda base in the Caribbean? Why not? Because we have not declared war? . . . Would it have been moral to go to the aid of the Hungarians? What is the difference between this case and Cuba's? . . . I don't know all these answers. But you must if you so blithely call the Cuba invasion immoral.

Schlesinger's generally effective rebuttal failed, though, to address Kazin's major point—that Kennedy lacked intellectual conviction. In the end the

Harvard historian could identify only one obvious Kennedy conviction. "Implicit in all decisions are convictions and ideas" which guide political leaders, Schlesinger stated vaguely. Facing "alternative courses of action" required the leader to have some "larger idea" or "concept." But Schlesinger could offer no examples of Kennedy's ideas or convictions except anticommunism.[27]

As President, Kennedy rarely had time to write his own speeches. One estimate is that Sorensen composed about 60 percent of Kennedy's addresses. "The evidence still is that the President's best efforts are more nearly his own than are those of most public figures," concluded one study of his speeches.

Rather than speak on multiple topics, Kennedy preferred to tailor his remarks for a specific audience or situation. While studying a draft, he scribbled almost illegibly on the margin. An excellent editor, he altered phrases, eliminated verbal excess, and added new ideas. "He loved pungent expressions," said Schlesinger. David Bell listened as Kennedy instructed Sorensen to make changes. "Sorensen would seemingly catch them on the fly and in the next draft they would be there word for word as the President had uttered them, even though he had not dictated them in the formal sense to a secretary," said Bell. "The interplay between the two men was a beautiful thing to watch."

After Sorensen, Richard Goodwin was Kennedy's best speechwriter, followed by Arthur Schlesinger. "The President somewhat mistrusted my efforts," said the Harvard historian. They were "too Stevensonian," meaning too complicated in syntax and too fancy in language. "He felt that his voice had too narrow a range to permit rhetorical flight and used to envy Stevenson his greater inflection of tone."

Most observers marveled at Kennedy's eloquence. "For a man without much obvious passion, he could arouse an enormous passion in others," said journalist Ralph Martin. "He had a special ability to handle the fluent phrases of the English language, combining poetry with power to evoke a tremendous vibrancy."[28]

Kennedy never manifested much interest in metaphysical, abstract, or moral questions. He valued courage, learning, excellence, freedom, rationality, competition, and style.

"The characteristic that he admired the most was courage," said Robert Kennedy. In *Profiles in Courage* he had honored the courage of senators who risked their careers by resisting their constituents and defying their colleagues in order to serve a broader national good. Nonetheless, he did not make an absolute value even of courage. As Richard Rovere noted, he honored "compromise almost as much—even on matters of principle—and h[eld] that there are times when the most courageous of senators should not risk their careers." A senator—or a president—who went down to defeat in a defense of a single principle would not be around to fight for any other principle in the future.

Kennedy once defined himself politically as "an idealist without illusions." It was his duty to strive for excellence in all his activities—in the administration of his office, in his speeches, programs, and appointments, in the arts—but this goal had to be tempered by realism and must not unduly risk his political defeat.[29]

His definition of happiness, paraphrased from Aristotle, was the maximum expression of a man's capacities, set against standards of excellence. He inspired people to excel. Journalist Peter Lisagor "always had the feeling that [the President] had a high standard. If he picked up something of yours and read it, you wanted it to be good."

The President was riveted by the lives of great men—Winston Churchill, Ray Asquith, Jefferson, Lincoln, Napoleon, Lenin. When he talked about them, Isaiah Berlin concluded after a discussion with Kennedy, "his eyes shone with a particular glitter, and it was quite clear that he thought in terms of great men and what they were able to do, not at all of impersonal forces. A very, very personalized view of history." He respected distinction in many fields and tried to foster it, dotting his conversation, as well as his formal speeches, with the sayings of great men.[30]

Kennedy "loved being President and at times he could hardly remember that he had ever been anything else," said Schlesinger. He didn't complain about the "awesome burdens" he faced or the "terrible loneliness" of his position. When events didn't go his way, he might briefly complain, but he didn't indulge in self-pity. "He took success and failure in equal stride," Dean Rusk thought. "I was as impressed with his performance after the fiasco of the Bay of Pigs as by any of his accomplishments."

Kennedy developed a highly refined political "persona." "As in the case of most people who are on the political stage, he was acting his part in a way most of the time," George Kennan observed. In his work he was self-controlled and self-disciplined. Hardly anyone, including Rose Kennedy, ever saw him in raging anger or uncontrollable tears. Some judged him indifferent and unfeeling because he seemed in command of his emotions. "Jack had a total lack of ability to relate, emotionally, to anyone," said Betty Spalding. "Everything was so surface with him in his relationships with people." Spalding's view, though, mostly applied to the women he was trying to seduce.

"How can anybody call Jack cold?" Jackie Kennedy reflected. "He's warm, he's attentive, he has such a sense of humor and he's so considerate of people." People often asked Rose Kennedy if Jack was emotional. "I suppose the reason for the question is that he always seemed so self-possessed, unruffled, equable, with a certain air of 'detachment' as though he were in the scene and living it fully and yet observing the scene with himself in it. I think by and large this was true. He did have an even temperament."[31]

"Passion" was not a word one used to describe Kennedy's approach to government. He believed that hysterical or overly excited people usually did not have good judgment. To be emotionally committed was to be captive. When he acted immoderately, he regretted it. If he overstated his case, people would think he was not thoughtful or rational. He expressed exasperation, but usually because other people allowed their passion to overcome their reason.

Arthur Schlesinger noted that Kennedy "was embarrassed on the rare occasions when he succumbed to public emotion himself, as he did when the Cuban Brigade, freed from Castro's prisons, presented its flag to him at Miami in December 1962."

"I don't think I ever react emotionally to a problem, but that doesn't mean I'm not emotional," Kennedy mused. "It simply means I reason problems out and apply logic to them. . . . I probably have as many emotions as the next person. I have emotional feelings about my family."

The President didn't like anyone probing his intimate feelings. When a reporter's question became too personal, the President responded sharply, "Now don't bother with those couch questions because they simply don't mean anything to me."

Ormsby-Gore thought his friend had deep emotions and strong passions underneath, and "when his friends were hurt or a tragedy occurred or his child died, I think he felt it very deeply. But somehow public display was anathema to him."[32]

Kennedy usually maintained objectivity even under pressure. He had an exceptional capacity for detachment. "I felt as if his mind had left his body and was observing the proceedings with a detached, almost amused air," said Clark Clifford. He seemed to have an "extra eye," outside of himself, which surveyed a scene. "It was a very eerie thing to see this, and feel it, but there it was," said Chuck Spalding. "You always had the feeling that to some extent he was standing in the corner kind of looking at all of this with something of an air of detachment," agreed Orville Freeman.

In her diary Evelyn Lincoln noted several occasions in which the President was edgy or irritable. (She seldom knew the cause of his ill humor.) Few people, though, ever saw him hotly angry. "I've never seen him exhibit real anger," said Senator William Fulbright. He didn't bang his desk, wave his arms, and usually didn't shout loudly. "Jeezus Christ!" he bellowed when something went wrong or someone made a mistake. But he calmed down quickly.[33]

Kennedy sought intense experiences. "The routine, the ordinary, the merely average displeased and bored him," observed Joe Alsop. "He wanted to live intensely, meaningfully, to the utmost limit of his powers." He rebelled from the tedium of the House of Representatives, walked out on undramatic films, and quickly tired of many of the women he courted.

He hated to be bored. "It made him rather exhausting to be around for a long period of time," said Charles Bartlett. "As you got to know him, you went to some pains not to bore him."

He was impatient with people who talked too much. "I learned to speak precisely to the point at hand, then shut up and go back to my office," said Dean Rusk. When a cabinet officer phoned and talked at great length, Kennedy placed the receiver down and signed a letter while the caller rambled. "Bobby would just tell him to cut the crap," Kennedy said to his office guest. "I'm more polite." The President listened patiently to Chester Bowles's long explanation of world problems. Afterward Kennedy told Ambassador Galbraith, "Chet tells me there are six revolutions going on in the world. One is the revolution of rising expectations. I lost track of the other five."[34]

Boredom led to irritation and restlessness. When he was irritated, said Lincoln, "his left eye would get a little askew and sort of droop a little, as if there was an irritation behind it." At other times he smoothed his hair, adjusted his tie, fiddled with his belt, or thrust his hands in and out of his pockets.

"He was a hard man, casually cruel," concluded Richard Reeves in his study of Kennedy:

> I did not like the man who jabbed a needle into his buddy Red Fay's leg to show the pain of his own daily medical regimen. . . .
> I did not like the man who refused to talk to his friend Ben Bradlee for months to punish him for a small criticism. . . . And I did not like the man who ran meetings from the bathtub, giving the orders of the day to assistants sitting on toilets and leaning on sinks.

Reeves's specific examples are true, and there were others, but the author exaggerated. For the most part, Kennedy was not a vindictive man and did not harbor grievances. "There was no 'Kennedy treatment' comparable to the 'LBJ treatment,'" noted Dean Rusk.[35]

Kennedy generated repressed but powerful affection from many people who worked closely with him. "The whole atmosphere in the White House and in his entourage was one of unspoken but very powerful affection—going both ways—always under control," said Walt Rostow. "It was all amusing and dry and understated. . . . It was much the kind of spirit and feeling that grows in a first-rate, small military unit that has been through a lot."

Richard Reeves also judged Kennedy egocentric, a person who used his charm to manipulate people for his own selfish ends. Kennedy was "an artist who painted with other people's lives. He squeezed people like tubes of paint, gently or brutally, and the people around him—family, writers, drivers, ladies-in-waiting—were the indentured inhabitants serving his needs and desires." This was true in some cases, particularly with ladies-in-waiting, but he was seldom brutal with anyone. He brandished his charm and squeezed people primarily because that was what politicians did. He turned on his charm to convince Congress and the American people to support his programs; he turned on his charm so he could be reelected in 1964 and continue to push his programs.

Others had a different impression of Kennedy's ego. "He did not fall victim to the pervading virus of vanity which so frequently seems to attack the holders of great positions of power in any government," said Robert Lovett.[36]

"The fascination of politics to me," Kennedy once said, "is that it's so competitive with this tremendous sense of excitement and challenge." He always wanted to win, and fought hard to win. "But he was also a very gracious loser," said Charles Bartlett; "he was not a bitter-ender, and it didn't undo him to lose a game of Monopoly, or a game of tennis or golf."

Some friends, though, thought that at times he was indeed a poor loser. Sitting at a very small table, the checkerboard supported partly by their knees, Paul Fay played checkers with the President. Fay later reported:

> I was winning the first game, when I noticed a warning look in his eyes. He coughed suddenly, and the checkerboard bounced, sending the checkers onto the floor or helter-skelter across the checkerboard.
>
> "One of those unfortunate incidents of life, Redhead," he said with a touch of a smile. "We'll never really know if the Under Secretary was going to strategically outmaneuver the Commander in Chief."

But to say, as one chronicler has, that Kennedy "absolutely had to always win, win, win to maintain his self-esteem," and that "when he lost at something, he would sulk, and pout, often get mean, and sometimes not even talk" was wild exaggeration.[37]

He had an insatiable appetite for gossip. One of the unexpected pleasures of being President was reading the FBI reports on his appointees. Theodore White recalled Kennedy's "amused, almost pickpocket like skill of filching impressions or memories."

Frank Sinatra fed him juicy gossip about Hollywood celebrities. Kennedy enjoyed gossip about Sinatra's own romances as well. "Oh, but he loved gossip," said Judith Campbell Exner. "He adored it. That was something he was always asking me about on the telephone and in person. He would say, 'Who's Frank seeing now?' or 'I heard Frank is seeing so-and-so and isn't she married?' "[38]

"All three Presidents I served—Truman, Kennedy, and Johnson—had lively senses of humor, but Kennedy's was the best," said Dean Rusk. Kennedy used humor, sardonic wit, and teasing on everyone, including himself. His laugh was usually restrained and seldom boisterous; his face crinkled, and eyes twinkled as he broke into a broad grin.

The public saw him display his humor at press conferences. "The press saw more of it at their various annual dinners, where he invariably stole the show," said Sorensen. "Around the White House we saw it every day, on every subject. It flowed naturally, good-naturedly, casually. It was dry, wry, ironic and irreverent."

Asked what he enjoyed best about being President, Kennedy replied, "The work, the traveling conditions, and the White House switchboard."[39]

"I've been back in touch with my constituents and seeing how they felt," the President announced after a brief respite in Florida. "And, frankly, I've come back to Washington from Palm Beach, and I'm against my entire program."

As the President talked with friends about the threat of nuclear war, he expressed serious doubts about military technology. In the first nuclear exchange, Kennedy predicted, "The Soviets will shoot off their missiles and hit Moscow, and we will respond and take out Miami or Atlanta."

As Kennedy and Dave Powers drove by the house where Powers was born, Kennedy remarked, "Dave, you're always talking about your humble origin. This house is a much nicer house than the one I was born in on Beals Street in Brookline. I came up the hard way."

"Oh, sure," Powers shot back. "You came up the hard way. One morning they didn't bring you your breakfast in bed." Jack collapsed in laughter, and told the story for many years afterward.

While Kennedy hosted a meeting aboard the *Honey Fitz,* moored in Newport, he introduced all the distinguished guests to a navy captain, the officer of the deck. "This is the secretary of state, Mr. Rusk; the secretary of defense, Mr. McNamara; General Taylor, the chairman of the Joint Chiefs of Staff . . ." Then the President announced seriously, with no change in tone, "This is Lieutenant Junior Grade Billings."[40]

While talking to a guest, the President was told that Robert Kennedy was on the phone. A few days earlier a magazine had rated the attorney general as the second most powerful man in the country. Picking up the phone, the President paused, muffled the speaker, and said to his guest with mock sarcasm, "This is the second most powerful man in the nation calling. Do you want to tell him anything?" After some phone conversation, the President laughed. "Bobby wants to know who No. 1 is."

His most remembered witticisms were original, as when he hosted a large group of Nobel Prize winners at the White House: "This is the most extraordinary collection of talent, of human knowledge, that has ever been gathered together at the White House, with the possible exception of when Thomas Jefferson dined here alone."

Having been born into wealth and privilege, very successful in his political career, and immensely attractive, Kennedy could have been "insufferable in his pretensions," said one historian. But he didn't appear to take himself too seriously and used his wit "to puncture the pomposity" that usually accompanies power and in that way created "an enormously appealing memory."[41]

From the time he recovered his health in the late 1950s, Kennedy no longer had a morbid fascination with the subject of death. Still, there were moments when his own possible assassination or death entered his mind. One afternoon in Palm Beach, as he sat by the pool, he asked Dr. Travell, "What do you think of the rule that for the last hundred years every president of the United States elected in a year divisible by twenty died in office?"

Travell replied that she had never heard of the rule.

Kennedy quickly named them and the years of their election: "William H. Harrison 1840, Lincoln 1860, Garfield 1880, McKinley 1900, Harding 1920, and Roosevelt 1940."

Just a coincidence, said Travell.

Kennedy dropped the subject.

On another occasion, Dr. Travell reported that while the President was reading the newspaper in his limousine, he glanced up and saw a boy in the backseat of a sedan ahead of him holding a large motion-picture camera against the back window with its lens pointed at the President. Instantly Kennedy's muscles tensed.

"It's only a child with a movie camera," Travell assured him.

The President took a deep breath and said, "I will not live in fear. What will be, must be."[42]

39

IMAGE AND THE MEDIA

Kennedy cultivated and protected his public image. He avoided being photographed eating food or wearing his glasses. He was impatient with photographers who tried to take "corny" photographs of him, such as wearing a silly hat. In Sioux Falls, South Dakota, his hosts crowned him with an Indian warbonnet, but the bonnet remained on his head only a split second before he slipped it off.

No one was to know about his health problems, even minor ones. On one occasion, while the President met with aides in his office, Evelyn Lincoln handed him two cold pills. He quickly stuffed them into his pocket, and later instructed her not to advertise his illness. In late summer 1963, he apparently pulled a muscle in his groin. "Now listen, Pierre," he instructed Salinger, "I don't want to read anything in the papers about my groin. We can attribute it all to the back. If I'm not playing golf, I'm still having trouble with my back. I don't want the American public thinking that their President is falling apart: 'Now he's got a bad back, now his groin is going.' The next thing the Republicans will be claiming, 'Now it's his brain.' "[1]

His attractive personal style offset his mistakes, masked ineptness, and enhanced his popularity. Much of Kennedy's image focused on his family life with his two adorable children and glamorous wife. "Photographers captured the Kennedys happily leaving Mass together or aboard the family boat with a vibrant president at the helm," noted Giglio.

"He just naturally looked good," said one photographer. "If you took him as he was, natural, and when he wasn't aware of the camera, he looked better than any other President." According to another photographer, "You couldn't miss with him. It was just like French cooking. No matter what you did, you always came up with something fine."

"President Kennedy had very few rules about what could and couldn't be done," said a third photographer. "He paid very little attention to the camera. He didn't worry whether you shot him from the right side or the left side, or from the floor, or from standing on a chair, or from behind his ears or anything else. He knew enough about the business to know that photographers strive to make meaningful photographs, and that giving them freedom of action was probably the most cooperative thing he could do."[2]

A national poll of college students in the spring of 1962 disclosed that coeds thought that President Kennedy had more sex appeal than anybody, including the movie star Rock Hudson. Together with Jackie Kennedy, the President was a trendsetter, "slavishly followed" in Washington. *Time* reported: "Cigar sales have soared (Jack smokes them). Hat sales have fallen (Jack does not wear them). Bureaucrats . . . avoid button-down shirts (Jack says they are out of style). The more eager New Frontiersmen secure their striped ties with PT boat clasps—and seem not the least bit embarrassed."

David Halberstam judged Kennedy an artful manipulator:

> The Kennedys were perceived as exciting and different from ordinary people. They were star-crossed. They were handsome and had handsome wives. Actors and actresses and great athletes and astronauts wanted to be around them. Theirs was like a great dramatic novel being played for the entire nation, being played out, as it were, on television. All of this began with Jack Kennedy; he was so good, so smart, so fresh, so intuitive, as he manipulated from the very first with a powerful new weapon without seeming to manipulate. That was his real skill. Manipulation *au naturel.*

Journalist Tom Wicker was more sympathetic. "For all his charm and fire and eloquence, [Kennedy] was a straightforward political man, who listened to his own rhetoric, contrived his 'image' in the comforting faith that a statesman had to get elected before he could do anyone any good, and believed sincerely that his causes were not only right but actually offered solutions to human problems."[3]

Creating a favorable image for himself and his policies was a daunting challenge, one every President must cope with. John Kennedy met the challenge by using television as Franklin Roosevelt used radio: to give him direct, instantaneous, and unmediated access to the public.

On January 25, 1961, only five days after his inauguration, President Kennedy stood before the cameras for the first-ever live televised presidential news conference. The luxurious new State Department Auditorium, a cavernous chamber with thick beige carpeting and orange-and-black padded seats, hosted the unprecedented event. With a New York television consultant directing the staging, cameras were arranged to give minimum interference to print journalists (who would ask the questions); special phones were installed in a hall outside the auditorium, and a reporting service provided instant transcripts for the correspondents. More than four hundred reporters had gathered for the President's debut.[4]

The 6:00 P.M. broadcast was an enormous popular success, with an estimated television audience of sixty-five million. "His performance was almost flawless," said reporter Charles Roberts; "I sensed from the moment the President walked on stage that the presidential press conference would never be the same again." Indeed, Kennedy had opened a new era in political communications.

President Eisenhower's press conferences had been taped for radio since 1953 and filmed since 1955. But in each case they were broadcast later, usually long after prime time. "Sometimes they aired just before the national anthem, they got so dull," said one reporter. Moreover, Jim Hagerty, Eisenhower's press secretary, could edit the films, much different from a live TV news conference.

Questions about the news-conference format came up frequently at staff conferences after the 1960 election. Pierre Salinger had urged Kennedy to hold his conferences live on television, but the suggestion met stiff opposition from within the Kennedy circle. McGeorge Bundy and Ted Sorensen thought it was too dangerous. So did Dean Rusk when he joined the new team. Nor was Ken O'Donnell enthusiastic about the new format.[5]

But JFK sided with Salinger. He wasn't worried and gave little weight to the possibility that a foreign-policy question might catch him off guard. "He was absolutely confident of his ability to handle himself," said Salinger. Besides, the publishers of seven out of ten daily newspapers had endorsed Nixon in 1960. Eventually many of them could be expected to oppose Kennedy's legislative program before Congress. "This is the right thing," Kennedy told Salinger. "We should be able to go around the newspapers if that becomes necessary. But, beyond that, I don't know how we can justify keeping TV out if it wants in."

Kennedy had been interviewed on television many times and had grown comfortable with the new technology. During the West Virginia primary he had used TV with devastating effect to address the religious question; his TV debates with Richard Nixon had helped him win the November election. "It was through TV that the Kennedy profile, the sincere Kennedy tones, the Kennedy thoughts could get to the people," observed Hugh Sidey. "He did not have to run the risk of having his ideas and his words shortened and adulterated by a correspondent."

Still, the President seemed to be taking an enormous risk. He would be communicating instantaneously with tens of millions of Americans in their homes—and watchful Communist diplomats in their embassies could scribble down every indiscretion. He could accuse no one of misquoting him.[6]

The change to a large auditorium had been forced upon the White House by the march of events. The huge increase in the number of correspondents could not be ignored. Only a hundred correspondents had been accredited to the White House in FDR's first term; Salinger had to deal with more than twelve hundred, many of them television correspondents.

The official announcement came on December 27, 1960, at Salinger's daily briefing in Palm Beach. Print journalists reacted with a storm of protest. But Salinger remembered informing the group, "It was the President's news conference—not theirs—and he would run it his own way. The decision was final. They could take it or leave it."

The week before a press conference, Salinger met with the information officers of major departments, gathering their materials on current issues. The State Department prepared a large briefing book, listing possible questions and answers on issues of foreign policy; the Council of Economic Advisers did the same for major economic developments. All the various reports were gathered for the President to study.[7]

On the morning of the press conference Kennedy had breakfast with key advisers, usually Salinger, Walter Heller, Myer Feldman, Ted Sorensen, Dean Rusk, Lyndon Johnson, and McGeorge Bundy. As they grilled him with questions, the President replied, "I can handle that one—let's move on." Usually he gave answers and invited comments and suggestions. Before one early press conference a State Department memo had suggested evasion on two or three questions. "I can evade questions without help!" exclaimed the President; "what I need is answers!"

He always asked for more specific information on some issues. How many tons of wheat? How much American traffic over the German autobahn? How much foreign aid to the Congo this year as compared with two years ago? Salinger and others spent the next five hours after breakfast digging up answers. The President napped after lunch to increase his alertness. Awake about 3:00 P.M., he reviewed the new information while he dressed. He arrived at the State Department ten minutes before 4:00 P.M., the usual starting time, where State Department officials would brief the President again with the latest information off the department's Teletype.[8]

JFK was quicker and far more articulate in his responses to news-conference questions than his predecessor. Ike's syntax was obscure and convoluted; Kennedy's was clear and direct.

Kennedy occasionally felt that correspondents failed to ask questions on subjects he wanted to discuss. At an early press conference, he expected to reaffirm his opposition to seating China in the United Nations. When no one asked the question, the White House had to issue a lame statement the next day. Thereafter Salinger planted a few questions. A presidential pronouncement often appeared more newsworthy if the press drew it out of the President than if he volunteered it himself. When Salinger tipped ABC's William Lawrence that a question might get an interesting response, Lawrence obligingly asked about the relative power of U.S. and Soviet nuclear tests. With his answer neatly prepared and organized on paper, Kennedy responded effortlessly.[9]

If he had time, the President eagerly appraised his performance afterward. A Washington TV station taped the news conference and ran it later in the evening. The President critiqued himself and the staging. "I could have done better with that one" or "That's lousy lighting" or "That camera angle murders me" were typical comments.

"I was blessed during President Kennedy's Administration with the fact that President Kennedy himself was superb in his press conferences," said Dean Rusk; "that greatly eased the problem of the Secretary of State in having press conferences about some of the same subjects."

The news conferences kept the President's mind razor sharp, like preparing for a final exam. Ted Sorensen detected a greater sense of direction and pride throughout the executive branch after an impressive news conference. They allowed him to speak directly to Congress and foreign governments, and to dominate the front pages. "Above all," Sorensen contended, "the televised press conferences provided a direct communication with the voters which no newspaper could alter by interpretation or omission." "We couldn't survive without TV," remarked the President as he watched a re-broadcast of that day's conference.[10]

Some print journalists detested the new format. The State Department Auditorium was too formal and cold, they said. Eisenhower had stood level with the press, an arrangement so informal that those in the first row could almost lean out and touch him. President Kennedy stood on a step-high podium, the press spread out before him in upholstered seats, "like a college class about to hear a lecture." Under the Kennedy format the critical "follow-up" question, designed to draw out the President on an issue he had only briefly discussed, was difficult to put. "We were props in a show," complained Peter Lisagor. "I always felt that we should have joined Actors Equity."

Nevertheless, the new format mostly won critical praise and popular acclaim. Public opinion surveys gave Kennedy exceptionally high approval ratings for his performances. James Reston noted wonderingly, "How Kennedy knew the precise drop in milk consumption in 1960, the percentage rise in textile imports from 1957 to 1960, and the number of speeches cleared by the Defense Department is not quite clear, but anyway, he did. He either overwhelmed you with decimal points or disarmed you with a smile and a wisecrack."[11]

Kennedy's live news conferences were almost virtuoso performances. He set the standard by which following Presidents were often judged.

Besides sixty-four news conferences, Kennedy went on television nine other times to issue important statements about a single subject or crisis. First came the report on his return from Europe, then the Berlin crisis. Others dealt with nuclear tests and disarmament, the state of the national economy, and the crises over integration in Mississippi, Soviet missiles in Cuba, integration in Alabama, the successful negotiation of a test ban treaty, and tax legislation.

He held informal television interviews. The most memorable occurred in late 1962, when the three television networks teamed up to make available an hour of prime time for a review of Kennedy's first two years as President. All parties agreed that ninety minutes would be taped and thirty minutes edited from the conversation; slow sections or less interesting comments would be deleted, resulting in a better program. *After Two Years: A Conversation with the President*—the "Rocking Chair" interview—aired on Monday, December 17, 1962.[12]

A vast audience, tens of millions of viewers, watched as the President—relaxed in his White House rocking chair, with three correspondents in a cozy cluster near him—spoke candidly about his views of the presidency, his problems, and his prospects. "Kennedy displayed a range of admirable qualities," said television historian Mary Ann Watson. Clever, funny, and contemplative, "He would occasionally interrupt himself and change course in mid-sentence. He was, viewers had to conclude, the genuine article."

The President's graceful command of language was another impressive trait as he looked back at the first half of his administration. Referring to the Bay of Pigs catastrophe he said, "Success has a hundred fathers and defeat is an orphan." There was no sense, he said, "in having the shadow of success and not the substance." In a candid self-assessment he admitted, "Appearances contribute to reality."

The most memorable and penetrating answer about the President's attitudes and feelings came in reply to a question from ABC's Bill Lawrence, who asked: "As you look back upon your first two years in office, sir, has your experience in the office matched your expectations?"

"Well," Kennedy, responded,

> I think in the first place the problems are more difficult than I had imagined they were. Secondly, there is a limitation upon the ability of the United States to solve these problems. We are involved now in the Congo in a very difficult situation. We have been unable to secure an implementation of the policy, which we have supported. We are involved in a good many other areas. We are trying to see if a solution can be found to the struggle between Pakistan and India, with whom we want to maintain friendly relations. Yet they are unable to come to an agreement. There is a limitation, in other words, upon the power of the United States to bring about solutions.

He continued, saying that the

> responsibilities placed on the United States are greater than I imagined them to be, and there are greater limitations upon our ability to bring about a favorable result than I had imagined them to be. . . . There is such a difference between those who advise or speak or legislate, and between the man who must select from the various alternatives proposed and say that this shall be the policy of the United States. It is much easier to make the speeches than it is to finally make the judgments, because unfortunately your advisers are frequently divided. If you take the wrong course, and on occasion I have, the President bears the burden of the responsibility quite rightly. The advisers may move on to new advice.

Reporter Mary McGrory judged the telecast to be "the most effective appearance of his entire presidency—it was perfectly delightful." Journalist Max Ascoli thought "the viewer sensed in him the human being, the person . . . the quiet smile sometimes dimly but gently lighting up his features—all this contributed to inspire a sense of confidence and respect."[13]

To avoid overexposure he held the "fireside chat" format—inspired by FDR—to a minimum, on the theory that citizens wearied of too much speechmaking. After finding that FDR held only thirty fireside chats in twelve years, Arthur Schlesinger informed the President of the surprising tally. "All this shows the unreliability of memory. Many of your critics seem to suppose that FDR took to the microphone every couple of weeks."

The networks' televised evening news intrigued the President. When the Huntley-Brinkley or Walter Cronkite shows aired, he insisted that no one disturb him. An aide could watch with him but could not talk; these shows were too important. "Perhaps it was not reality and perhaps it was not even good journalism," observed David Halberstam, "but it was what the country perceived as reality and thus in a way was closer to reality than reality itself."

Except for the news programs, JFK seldom watched television. An exception was a late-night movie about himself—the screen version of *PT-109*. Like many Americans, the commercial breaks infuriated him. His wartime heroism was now selling deodorants, foot powders, and digestive aids. Unlike his fellow citizens, though, he could call up the head of the Federal Communications Commission the next day to complain. "Why do you let them put so many commercials on?" he demanded of Newton Minow. "It's cheap! Cheap! Cheap!" He was very angry. "I want a rule that limits the number of commercials," he told Minow. But Minow ignored Kennedy's impulsive instruction.[14]

Kennedy once teased his friend, print journalist Ben Bradlee, "When we don't have to go through you bastards we can really get our story to the American people." Indeed, television gave Americans a familiarity with Kennedy unlike with any President before him. They saw him at work, in his office, presenting speeches, meeting foreign dignitaries, standing up to the Russians, playing with Caroline and John-John, escorting his beautiful wife, sailing leisurely, joking, reflecting, impassioned, in triumph and disaster. What they saw was not the traditional notion of a politician or even a president. "J.F.K. was forceful, decisive, knowledgeable, the very image of a dynamic young executive effortlessly on top of things," observed Tom Wicker. "Image it was, of course, but powerfully effective."[15]

Kennedy's success on television contrasted sharply with the pale image of the opposition. Republicans tried, pathetically, to counter the President. Two Republican congressional leaders, Senator Everett Dirksen and Congressman Charles Halleck, held a weekly television press conference. "The only problem was that Dirksen and Halleck were not primarily designed for television," observed Halberstam. The "Ev and Charlie Show" was "like watching two burned-out Shakespearean actors playing the role of the tired if not loyal opposition." Kennedy himself could not have cast them better.

The President's news conference in March 1962 was typical of the opposition's dilemma:

President Kennedy's news conference yesterday was attended by 391 persons. For this morning's "Ev and Charlie Show," the authorities of the

Capitol press gallery had set up facilities for seventy-five reporters. Seventeen showed up.

After the President's news conference yesterday afternoon, all the major television and radio networks had tapes immediately available for unabridged reproduction across the country. 'Ev and Charlie' drew four screen-film cameras to record fragments that may, or may not, yield the Republicans a few seconds of canned film in some of the nation's living rooms tonight.

Despondent about their show, the Republican leadership cut off funds for its continuance in 1963.[16]

Press secretary Pierre Salinger conferred with the President five to ten times per day, and was one of the few White House staffers who had "barging-in" privileges. (On important issues, though, the President was his own best press secretary. He made the decisions and informed Salinger.) "The President likes people who don't cry gloom and doom every time something goes wrong—and Pierre is no cry-baby," said a White House staffer. "The President also likes people who don't buckle under fire—and Pierre is a stand-up guy."

Salinger occasionally felt the wrath of the President, as he did shortly after the inauguration, when he let slip that the domestic help at the White House had been asked to swear never to write memoirs of their experiences under Kennedy. Kennedy scathingly dressed down his press secretary for his mistake.

Reporters often found misspellings and garbled titles in Salinger's handouts. But the rotund, witty, and personable press secretary was popular with most of the media, who realized he worked under exceptional pressure.

The Kennedy administration opened itself to the press. Each day scores of printed handouts flowed out of Salinger's office. The White House released everything that could be safely released—task-force reports, the toasts at the state dinners and official lunches, speeches the President made in the Rose Garden. Hugh Sidey observed: "Whenever possible, Salinger routed official visitors through the lobby, so that reporters could talk to them after they had seen the President. Much of this great, youthful churning . . . was open to be watched and written about. Often just the sights and sounds were more than a reporter could handle in a day."[17]

The President was receptive to Salinger's suggestion to remove many of the traditional obstacles standing between the President and the media. The rule against live television at his press conferences was the first barrier to go. Salinger described other innovations:

His greater availability for exclusive interviews on TV and in all other media was another advance. He was also to surpass all other Presidents in the number of briefings, or backgrounders, he held in his office with large numbers of reporters—both foreign and American. Many of his comments were off-the-record, but they gave the press a clear reading of his attitudes and objectives. Because of such briefings, he was able to reduce substantially the publication or broadcast of false or misleading speculation that could react to his disadvantage both at home and abroad.

Under President Eisenhower reporters could rarely interview any White House staff member—except Sherman Adams—without first clearing it with Jim Hagerty. Under Kennedy correspondents could visit the administration's top advisers in their offices or at lunch—including Sorensen, Bundy, O'Brien, Rostow, Schlesinger, O'Donnell, Heller, and Salinger. "This was a great break for correspondents who didn't want to live only on handouts and news distributed at Pierre Salinger's daily briefings," said Charles Roberts. "There was hardly anybody in the White House who wasn't accessible," said Edward P. Morgan. "And I used them quite frequently."

That the President let key aides talk to the media on delicate subjects shocked General Maxwell Taylor. "Fortunately, they were able men and usually knew what to say," Taylor observed, "but I thought at the time that he was really inviting trouble. . . . I think looking back on it again that [Kennedy] got by well."[18]

Edward P. Morgan was president of an overseas writers group during most of JFK's presidency. The group consisted of correspondents from mostly noncommunist European countries. "We got an awful lot of very informative and interesting meetings because the Kennedy people . . . would come to [our] meetings. . . . The contrast between that and what we'd gotten during the Eisenhower Administration was absolutely vivid."

Kennedy courted prominent newspaper columnists because millions of people read them daily. These included James Reston, Walter Lippmann, Joseph and Stewart Alsop, Marquis Childs, Doris Fleeson, William S. White, Rowland Evans, Robert Novak, and Joseph Kraft. Because of their stature these columnists received special treatment. "A request from one of them to see the President personally was usually honored," explained Salinger, and "White House staff members at the policy level like Ted Sorensen and McGeorge Bundy made sure that they had the administration's views on prevailing problems."

Because of the huge readership of *Life, Look, McCall's, The Saturday Evening Post, Ladies' Home Journal, Good Housekeeping,* and *Redbook,* their reporters also had special access to Kennedy. The popular weekly newsmagazines, especially *Time* and *Newsweek,* received special attention as well.

At the end of each year of his presidency, while the President relaxed in Palm Beach, reporters gathered to listen to Kennedy furnish inside details about his policies. Most of the sessions were "backgrounders," meaning that the reporters had to use the clumsy disclaimer "a close friend of the President said today . . ."

Tom Wicker hated the disclaimer but praised the quality of the information revealed at the background briefings:

> He was very good at least at the impression of candor. . . . I say at the impression of candor because you came away feeling you had been told a lot and that you knew a lot. . . . He was much freer than in the news conferences. It wasn't helter-skelter. Reporters would follow up other reporters' questions more than they do in news conferences. . . . I thought the stories that came out were pretty good.[19]

The guest list for major White House social and cultural spectaculars was sprinkled with media representatives. On November 13, 1961, when cellist Pablo Casals played at the White House dinner, guests included the editors of the *Atlantic Monthly* and *Reporter* magazines, the executive editor of *The Saturday Evening Post,* both the editor and the publisher of the *New Bedford* [Mass.] *Standard Times,* the editor of the Spanish daily *La Prensa* in New York, and the board chairman of the Columbia Broadcasting System.

Kennedy originated the idea of inviting the country's leading publishers to lunch at the White House, twenty-five such lunches on a state-by-state basis. Usually invitations went out to about twenty of the largest papers in the state. To complete the guest list, the officers of the state's weekly press association would also be invited, giving the President a good cross section of the state's press.

At one luncheon a publisher criticized Kennedy's spending policies; a little later the same publisher asked why the President wasn't supporting a major federal building project in his state. The President seized the opportunity to make a point. "On the one hand," he told the publisher, "you ask me to cut back the domestic spending of the government and on the other hand you ask me for special treatment for your state." The publisher couldn't have it both ways. "Everybody is for less government spending and less taxes. And everybody has some pet project they would like to see made an exception. That's what makes life so interesting around here."[20]

At the gathering for Texas publishers in October 1961, the *Dallas Morning News*'s publisher, Edward Musgrove Dealey, read a bristling statement. Claiming he represented grassroots sentiment in Texas, the archconservative publisher said: "We need a man on horseback to lead this nation and many people in Texas and the Southwest think that you are riding Caroline's tricycle. The American people are aroused and rightly so. They are, as a body, way ahead of Washington. If you don't believe this, read the letters from the readers' columns in most United States newspapers. The general opinion of the grass-roots thinking in this country is that you and your Administration are weak sisters." Kennedy listened quietly, and later dismissed the statement with one curt comment: "I don't subscribe to that paper. I'm tired of reading its editorials."

By and large the publishers seemed honored and flattered to be invited to the White House, and found the sessions informative and stimulating. "I came to Washington quite critical of foreign aid," said a Republican publisher. "I had the feeling that the money was not getting to the people who need it and that we were not doing enough to insist that other well-to-do countries bear their share. I spoke to the President about this. He gave me some good answers. I must say that he convinced me we are doing right." Another Republican publisher remarked that the President "asked us for our opinions on a number of matters. He told us that he liked to have as much background as possible before making a decision. The President speaks so frankly about things that you get a feeling he trusts you and that he is taking you into his confidence." Still another publisher observed: "I was amazed. He did not dodge a single question."[21]

President Kennedy avidly read major newspapers, a batch of them in the early morning, others in the late afternoon. "He was constantly beating all of us who were around him to the news," said Maxwell Taylor. "He would usually greet you as you walked into the room with 'Have you seen so-and-so on something,' and usually I had not." This made Taylor improve his reading habits. "But I never caught up with the President." Pierre Salinger woke up extra early in the morning so he could read the papers before the President phoned him about a story. Quite often, though, he was still caught uninformed.

Reporters were shocked that the President had read their article or column. Tom Wicker, recently assigned to cover the President, had written a column contending that Kennedy was a good speaker extemporaneously, but that he read speeches poorly. "I was shown into his office," said Wicker about his initial interview. "The first thing he said to me after we shook hands [was] 'You know, you're right. I can't read a speech worth a shit.' "[22]

Kennedy was a journalist's president, interested in the politics of the media—its personalities, internal rivalries, gossip, rising stars, and profits. He dumbfounded Wicker. "What are the prospects for a merger in the New York newspaper field?" the President inquired. "I didn't have the faintest notion," Wicker later said.

The President asked Hugh Sidey detailed questions about *Time*. "He wanted to know the deadlines," said Sidey. "He wanted to know how they did a cover story, how the selection of cover art was made, how they chose the people to go on the cover. He wanted to know how much employees were paid. Was it really true that we paid more than other magazines? He wanted to know about the writers and researchers. . . . It was incredible."

Kennedy had early copies of *Time* and *Life,* airlifted from the Chicago printer, hand-delivered to his office a day ahead of publication. Henry Luce once complained that Kennedy saw a copy of *Time* before he did. After reading his advance copy, Kennedy often called Hugh Sidey on a Sunday evening to complain, "in cheerfully profane style," about some choice of phrase or photo.[23]

Kennedy overreacted to what he considered careless or biased reporting, leading critics to accuse him of whining about picayune matters. Merriman Smith of United Press International, the dean of White House correspondents, marveled at the President's close attention to everything written about him. "How they can spot an obscure paragraph in a paper of 3,000 circulation 2,000 miles away is beyond me. They must have a thousand little gnomes reading the papers for them." Fletcher Knebel of *Look* magazine wrote: "Never before have so few bawled out so many so often for so little."

Part of Kennedy's sensitivity stemmed from the universal desire to be liked and admired. At a party at the home of California's Democratic senator Clair Engle, Kennedy asked the wife of humor columnist George Dixon, "Why doesn't your husband like me?"[24]

In February 1962, Kennedy angrily blasted Sidey after *Time* published a gossipy story stating that the President had modeled a "trimly tailored dark gray suit" for a cover photo of *Gentlemen's Quarterly. Time* also reprinted the photo from the male fashion magazine. (Sidey knew nothing about the story or photo.) In the midst of John Glenn's historic return from space, the President summoned Sidey to the White House, slammed the open magazine down on his desk, and insisted on knowing what *Time* was trying to do to him. "This goddam magazine is just too much. Where did you get this ridiculous item about me? I'll be the laughing stock of the country. . . . People always remember the wrong things, they remember . . . Coolidge for wearing those hats and they'll remember me for this. It's just not true. It never happened." Then the President simmered down.

The President was both right and wrong. The photographer for *Gentlemen's Quarterly* did take part in a photo session with several other photographers; JFK wasn't aware that one of the photographers represented the magazine. "That was without a doubt the loudest and most direct . . . conflict [with] *Time,* or at least myself and the President," said Sidey.[25]

The scribe who wrote that JFK's sailboat, the *Victura,* ran aground with JFK as the skipper also incurred the President's displeasure. Kennedy telephoned

UPI's Hyannis Port reporter, who had witnessed the embarrassing incident. Kennedy didn't deny the story's accuracy but asked plaintively, "Have you thought just what the Republicans will say about the Commander-in-Chief of the armed services running a little sailboat aground?"

After the steel crisis, the Huntley-Brinkley television news program interviewed a business leader who criticized the President. Afterward Kennedy complained to Newton Minow, his appointee as chairman of the Federal Communications Commission. "What about these guys, [Chet] Huntley and [David] Brinkley? Are they trying to load the news against me?" Minow replied, "No, sir, those are very fair-minded reporters." "Well," the President continued, "I want you to look into [them]. It's bad enough for me with the newspapers. If I can't get a fair shake on television, I'm cooked." Minow said he'd look into it, but he never did, because if "I had, it would have been to no purpose and could have hurt the President."[26]

Because of his long experience and broad knowledge of contemporary issues, many regarded columnist Walter Lippmann as America's foremost political philosopher and commentator. JFK admired Lippmann's ability to write lucidly about an obtuse subject. During a television broadcast Lippmann was asked to describe Kennedy's weaknesses. He replied that the President was not a good "teacher," that he had no instinct to teach about what he was trying to accomplish and didn't explain himself. He was failing to communicate adequately with the people. Afterward, the President didn't complain to Lippmann about the broadcast, but Kennedy's military aide, General Chester Clifton, telephoned CBS and vigorously protested "[He] never protested to me, but after that [my relationship with the President] was over," Lippmann recalled.[27]

On September 5, 1961, the President dictated this memo to Evelyn Lincoln:

> Tell Fred Dutton to compose a letter to a fellow called Daniels, Reader's Digest (copy to the president of the Reader's Digest) challenging his statistics in the September Reader's Digest on unemployment that the program presented this year would cost the taxpayer 18 billion dollars annually in a few years. It is wholly untrue and we ought to make him eat it.[28]

The most publicized incident of the President's anger at newspaper criticism occurred in 1962, when Kennedy canceled twenty-two White House subscriptions to the Republican *New York Herald Tribune* for its alleged biased reporting. During the feud Traphes Bryant, the White House electrician and dog keeper, lined a box for new puppies with the newspaper, leaving the *Herald Tribune*'s masthead visible so the President would be sure to see it. "Sure enough, he grinned from ear to ear and nodded approval," recalled Bryant. "He said not a word until he was walking away, and then he called back, 'It's finally found its proper use.'"

The media were not to intrude on Kennedy's privacy and leisure. He didn't want reporters around when he skippered the *Victura*, or when he cruised on the *Honey Fitz*, the President's yacht, or in the *Marlin*, the family yacht. He deliberately turned away when he sighted the press boat. "He demanded privacy," observed Helen Thomas, "and, like all other Presidents, he got angry with reporters who ignored his wishes."[29]

Every President, from Washington to Eisenhower, had been accused of censorship, managing news, manufacturing news, or blacking out news. The media insisted on their right to report everything happening in government; the President insisted on his right to conceal or withhold information whose publication might damage the national security. Furthermore, the President and his aides tried to make the President look outstanding and obfuscate or minimize his reverses and setbacks. Normally the media deferred to the government only in wartime. But was an actual declaration of war (or a national emergency) necessary before the President could invoke extraordinary controls on the flow of information? Salinger observed: "The press answers 'yes' there can be no justification for government secrecy in time of peace. The President answers 'no'—a democratic society, if it is to survive in today's world, must be able to launch covert actions against its enemies."

Kennedy thought the media had responsibilities as well as rights—they had to get the facts correct, to consider the national interest, and to place their opinions on the editorial page. The Cold War was only an instant away from flaring into a hot war, and therefore the administration needed to conceal some operations and sometimes maneuver secretly. If prevented from concealing critical maneuvers, the administration would lose a key tactic in the Cold War: keeping the enemy unknowing.[30]

After the Bay of Pigs defeat, Kennedy spoke to the American Society of Newspaper Editors, presenting his views on the free press–national security dilemma. The government should not cover up its mistakes, suppress dissent, or withhold from the press and the public facts they deserve to know. Then, changing his focus, he criticized the press for its poor judgment in publishing pre–Bay of Pigs stories about the covert operation. He stressed the need for greater official secrecy:

> I do ask every publisher, every editor, and every newsman in the nation to re-examine his own standards, and to recognize the nature of our country's peril. . . . It requires a change in outlook, a change in tactics, a

change in missions—by the government, by the people, by every businessman or labor leader, and by every newspaper. For we are opposed the world around by a monolithic and ruthless conspiracy that relies primarily on covert means for expanding its sphere of influence.

Editorial pages throughout the country promptly lambasted his remarks. In retrospect, Ken O'Donnell and Dave Powers thought the speech ill-advised, partly because the President sounded petulant. "Coming on top of the failure in Cuba, such a criticism of the press seemed to be a childish attempt to shift the blame." Kennedy himself regretted the speech and privately admitted his mistake. "I should have realized," he said, "that there is no way of keeping a clandestine operation like this one a secret in a free democracy. And that's as it should be."[31]

After the Cuban missile crisis, Arthur Sylvester, the assistant secretary of defense for public affairs, fueled the news-management controversy when he told reporters that "news generated by the action of the government as to content and timing are part of the arsenal of weaponry that a President has." Sylvester argued that it was "the government's inherent right to lie if necessary to save itself when faced with nuclear disaster."

Critics then and later have charged that the Kennedy administration engaged in suppression, distortion, and outright lies. They cited the three reporters questioned in the early-morning hours by the FBI during the steel controversy.[32]*

A few reporters were cut off from all news sources at the White House because an item they wrote did not win approval at the White House. Correspondents whose papers criticized the President sometimes received the silent treatment; presidential aides refused to answer questions or give information to them. "If you want to be an insider, the best thing to do is to let Ted Sorensen write your stories for you," said one detractor.

Critics also accused the administration of making every effort to bend the news its way. "They remind me of the ballplayer who yells at the umpire after the strike call," said a veteran reporter. "The batter has no hope of changing the ump's decision, but he hopes to soften him up on the next pitch." Said another, "They mean it when they take you to the woodshed. They're not Victorian in their choice of language when they get mad."

The Cuban missile crisis intensified the charges of news management. The Pentagon lied by disclaiming knowledge of offensive missiles in Cuba; the President invented a cold to abandon his speaking tour. It wasn't just the lies that spawned controversy. It was the silence. "Nobody outside the Ad-

* For Kennedy's tense relations with journalists covering the war in South Vietnam, see Chapter 41.

ministration knew what was happening," *Newsweek* observed. "No comment. No answer. No news. Reporters damned suppression, damned the silence."[33]

The most prominent critic of the President was, surprisingly, an old friend of the Kennedy family. A native of Kentucky, Arthur Krock first covered Washington politics when William Howard Taft was President. He joined *The New York Times* in 1927, and, as chief of the *Times* Washington bureau from 1932 to 1953, he earned two Pulitzer Prizes. After 1953 he focused on his *Times* column of news commentary, "In the Nation."

During the New Deal, Krock became a close friend of Joseph P. Kennedy, with whom he shared conservative views, and he had assisted Jack Kennedy in converting his 1940 Harvard thesis into *Why England Slept.*

Krock's exclusive interviews with Roosevelt in 1937 and Truman in 1950 had caused press envy at a time when exclusives were rare. A racial segregationist, his relationship with John Kennedy soured during the election of 1960, when Kennedy endorsed civil rights. By 1962, in his mid-seventies, Krock was an outsider, no longer privy to inside tips from high officials that columnists rely on.

President Kennedy respected Krock, but he didn't like him. When angry at Krock, the President encouraged Ben Bradlee to criticize the columnist in *Newsweek.* "Tuck it to Krock. Bust it off in old Arthur. He can't take it, and when you go after him he folds."[34]

In the March 1963 issue of *Fortune* magazine Krock leveled a widely publicized broadside against the President for attempting to manage the news. "A news management policy not only exists but . . . has been enforced more cynically and boldly than by any previous Administration in a period when the U.S. was not in a war." President Kennedy "was prone to turn loose the FBI in a search for the official source of any published information that appeared in a form displeasing to him for one reason or another, especially when the publication was in the nature of an unmanaged leak." (Managed "leaks," wrote Krock, were everyday occurrences on the New Frontier.)

More sinister was the administration's "indirect but equally deliberate action" to manage news—more sinister "because it has been employed with subtlety and imagination for which there is no historic parallel known to me."

By indirectly managed news Krock meant "social flattery" of Washington reporters and commentators. "In the new Administration, the quotable exclusive interview has ceased to be a rarity," Krock claimed. "Mr. Kennedy prefers the intimate background briefings of journalists, and the publishers, on a large scale, from which members emerge in a state of protracted enchantment evoked by the President's charm and the awesome aura of his office."

Krock was partly right; the President did try to "manage" the news—

especially about U.S. involvement in South Vietnam—and did employ "social flattery" with persons in the media. Some reporters were inordinately enchanted by his charm and the awesome aura of his office.[35]

Photographer Stanley Tretick and reporter Laura Bergquist of *Look* enjoyed the Kennedys' confidence and received special treatment in securing photos of the Kennedy children. They brought their photos to the President and allowed him to choose which ones to publish. "You talk about news management," said a White House staff member; "this falls in the same category: picture management."

One category of information that Kennedy did not reveal to Congress, the media, or the public was the covert actions in foreign policy, especially in Cuba after the Bay of Pigs. Operation Mongoose avoided media exposure because only a select few within the administration knew about the secret program.

During the 1960 election campaign, *Time*'s Henry Luce admitted privately that he was a victim of the Kennedy charm. "I don't agree with Kennedy on most things. But I like him." Later Luce added: "Dammit, why am I so attracted to Jack Kennedy?" Still later he admitted, "He seduces me!" President Kennedy knew how to play on Luce's feelings. After discovering that Luce had recently visited Washington, the President promptly sent him a note: "Harry, how can you be in town without coming to see me?"[36]

Kennedy had several close friends in the media, but his two closest were Charles Bartlett and Ben Bradlee. Five years younger than the President, Bartlett had for sixteen years been the Washington correspondent of the *Chattanooga Times*. He earned the reputation as a solid Washington interpreter and won a Pulitzer Prize in 1956 for disclosing a conflict-of-interest scandal involving Harold Talbott, then Eisenhower's secretary of the air force. "He knows all the President's thinking, much, much more than he can ever tell," a columnist said. "He's a tomb of secrets."

While writing stories and columns about the Kennedy administration, Bartlett also privately advised the President on a wide variety of subjects. For instance, he sent Kennedy the draft of a book by Roy Hoopes on the steel crisis. "I asked [Hoopes] to let me see it and keep it for a few days with the idea that without involving you, I could pass it along to you to discover if any changes should be made," Bartlett wrote the President. "If you see any changes that you want made, I believe that I can get him to accept them— again without involving you or putting him in a position to say that you have seen the manuscript."[37]

Ben Bradlee, a reporter and bureau chief for *Newsweek* during the Kennedy administration, was, like Kennedy, a product of Boston and Harvard and a veteran of World War II. Before the 1960 election Bradlee lived on the same Georgetown street as Kennedy. (Later Bradlee won fame as the editor in charge of *The Washington Post*'s brilliant coverage of the Nixon administration's Watergate scandal.)

During the 1960 election campaign, newsman Bradlee furnished intelligence to Kennedy about Lyndon Johnson's campaign. In May 1959, he privately reported to JFK on a recent Johnson speaking engagement, concluding that Johnson could never make it to the presidency:

> The image is poor. The accent hurts. Even if we assume many people would say they have no prejudice against a southerner, the fact is that in this country the Texan is partly a comic, partly a horse opera figure. He is hard to take seriously even when he is being desperately serious. More than that, in this particular case Johnson really does not have the requisite dignity. . . . He's somebody's gabby Texas cousin from Fort Worth. Friendly, relishing a good yarn, socially conspiratorial with the hand on the shoulder and the whispered pleasantry. None of it adds up to President.

Bradlee later wrote candidly about his friendship with Kennedy. "At issue, then and later," he said in the opening chapter of his memoir, *Conversations with Kennedy* (1975), "was the question that plagued us both: What, in fact, was I? A friend, or a journalist? I wanted to be both. And whereas I think Kennedy valued my friendship—I made him laugh, I brought him the fruits of contact with an outside world from which he was now shut out— he valued my journalism most when it carried his water."

Indeed, it seemed Bradlee's desire for the President's friendship sometimes undermined his journalistic standards. The President wanted loyalty and favors. "The President asked if we were going to take a look at [Governor Nelson] Rockefeller's war record," Bradlee wrote in his memoir. "It is interesting how often Kennedy referred to the war records of political opponents." Bradlee quoted Kennedy as saying, "Where was old Nels when you and I were dodging bullets in the Solomon Islands? How old was he? He must have been thirty-one or thirty-two. Why don't you look into that?"

Bradlee's memoir is littered with potential news stories—CIA intrigues, wiretaps, underhanded tactics—that the journalist ignored because of his intimate friendship with Kennedy.[38]

Bradlee felt the sting of the President for a brief and mildly critical comment he made for a feature story in *Look* magazine in August 1962. "It's almost impossible," Bradlee said, "to write a story they like. Even if a story is quite favorable to their side, they'll find one paragraph to quibble with."

For this remark Kennedy ostracized Bradlee for almost three months. "I wanted to be friends again," Bradlee said in *Conversations with Kennedy*. "I missed the access, of course, but I missed the laughter and the warmth just as much. What I couldn't and wouldn't do was send a message over the stone wall, saying I had learned my lesson." He and the President subsequently reconciled and resumed their social contact. During his banishment Bradlee wondered how "a friendship like ours" could have been derailed by such an innocuous remark in *Look* magazine.[39]

Several wise news correspondents mused about the problem of socializing with the President. The special relationships enjoyed by Bartlett and Bradlee irritated some correspondents not close to the President who feared they would be frozen out. "But this did not happen often," said Robert Pierpoint, "and I don't think I missed any major stories because I lacked the proper social connections."

Edward P. Morgan enjoyed social contact with the President but didn't feel it warped his professional approach to his job. "I could produce commentaries that were highly critical of something that the Administration did." Still, Morgan found something insidious about his social relations with the President. "It's very difficult to go to a man's house for dinner and have a hell of a good time in the process—let alone to the White House for dinner and enjoy an intimate relationship with the President and the First Lady of the land—and then go off . . . and be enormously critical."

"It is hard," agreed James Reston, "to go into that House that means so much to us historically and not be impressed with it and the terrible burdens that the President has to carry. How could you help but be sympathetic? Once you become sympathetic it becomes increasingly difficult to employ the critical faculties."

In sum, Kennedy attempted to manage the news in a few instances, and by his social flattery of journalists and close friendship with several, he hoped to influence news coverage. But detractors exaggerated when they claimed his actions seriously compromised the independence and freedom of the media. Kennedy's attempts at management and social flattery applied to only a tiny segment of the news industry, and his attempts often had little impact. "Kennedy has committed no serious offenses against press freedom," said *Time*.[40]

Not many journalists agreed with Arthur Krock that the Kennedy administration managed the news "cynically and boldly." The opportunities for getting news from responsible officials was greater than they had been at any time in the previous twenty years. President Eisenhower had a firm rule never to receive correspondents in his office; rarely did a week go by in which Kennedy did not talk with two or three. James Reston pointed out that one of the most effective ways for public officials to "manage the news" was to "announce what they want to announce and then make themselves scarce."

"I thought [Krock's allegation] was a completely phony issue," said *The Washington Post*'s Carroll Kilpatrick. "We had our squabbles with Salinger many times, and we fought. We were no doubt misled, as everyone is, on some occasion. [But] the President was always remarkably candid, I thought, in his talks with us."

"I don't deny that the Kennedy Administration did try to manage the news; every administration tries to manage the news to a certain extent," said Edward P. Morgan. "I just don't think that charge holds up to the extreme to which . . . Mr. Krock seems to make it."[41]

Krock had enjoyed access to both Roosevelt and Truman, access not accorded to other reporters. (Krock had special individual briefings with President Kennedy himself up to 1962, the same kind he later criticized.) Reminded that he had earlier been favored with exclusive interviews, the imperious Krock awkwardly explained the difference between an interview with him and an interview with just anyone. His exclusives had "served [these Presidents'] purpose," Krock said. "And they were doing me no favor." Roosevelt and Truman considered *The New York Times* the "best and most effective medium" for the dissemination of their ideas, so the interviews granted Krock were "not illegitimate." But when President Kennedy selected other media for the dissemination of his ideas, Krock implied, he was doing something illegitimate.[42]

Kennedy's supporters argued that he had the right to expect that his administration would speak with one voice and support his policies, and that the coordination and clearance he demanded of sensitive information was nothing new. In moments of crisis, one official should not contradict what another was saying or, most important, what the President was saying. At his press conference on November 20, 1962, the President asked: "Are we suggesting that any member of the Defense Department should speak on any subject to any newspaperman? That the newspaperman should print it or not print it as he sees fit without any effort to attempt to limit the printing of news which may deal with intelligence information?"

The President's defenders wondered if his critics would have had the President reveal his suspicions about the Soviets in Cuba, the confirmation of those suspicions, and his strategy to confront the Soviets with the facts. Writing in the *Saturday Review,* Lester Markel argued that "such a procedure would probably have enabled the Communists to cover their tracks and would surely have removed from the enterprise the element of surprise which was so important psychologically." Markel added that it was a "curious business that the very newspapers which applauded the President for having brought Khrushchev to heel proceeded then to criticize him for the way he performed the deed."

"Beyond any reasonable doubt, the Kennedy Administration has deliberately sought to magnify each of its accomplishments and minimize its shortcomings," concluded *Newsweek*. "But here's the rub. Virtually every government in history has done the same thing."[43]

The President dissolved some of the tension with his wit. At the annual Gridiron Club dinner in Washington in 1963, he opened his talk with a wry comment: "Fellow managing editors . . ."

Despite whining about picayune matters, and occasionally trying to manage segments of the news, for the most part Kennedy respected press freedoms. Early in 1962, after Kennedy had been in office slightly more than a year, a reporter asked him at his press conference to comment on his relations with the media. "Well, I am reading more and enjoying it less," he replied, to laughter. "I have not complained nor do I plan to make any general complaints. I read and talk to myself about it, but I don't plan to issue any general statement to the press. I think that they are doing their task, as a critical branch, the fourth estate. And I am attempting to do mine. And we are going to live together for a period, and then go our separate ways," he concluded, and the reporters laughed again.

40

A MORAL ISSUE

I sensed . . . greater warmth on the part of the President, greater understanding," said James Farmer after attending a reception at the White House. "Maybe it was because it was in a social gathering rather than in the cold walls of the meeting room. But there was greater warmth, and he seemed much more human to me."

The President and Mrs. Kennedy were remarkably successful at social gatherings with African-Americans. "Here the contrast between Kennedy and his predecessor, Eisenhower, was stark," observed Taylor Branch. "In no other aspect relating to race did he compare more favorably."

Carl Rowan and his wife were invited to President Kennedy's first state dinner, a white-tie-and-tails affair for President Bourguiba of Tunisia. Rowan recalled:

> That night in the East room of the White House blacks and whites danced together, reveling in the twist, waltzes, and the jitterbug.
>
> From that party forward, even the most benighted hostesses knew that integration was in and Jim Crow was out. It became de rigueur to have one of Kennedy's top blacks at your party if you still wanted to qualify as the "hostess with the mostest."[1]

On February 12, 1963, President Kennedy sponsored an unprecedented White House reception for eight hundred black leaders and their spouses to celebrate Lincoln's birthday and the one-hundred-year anniversary of the Emancipation Proclamation. Although Martin Luther King Jr. extended his regrets, almost every other black leader was there. The affair was a political triumph—except for one sour note brought to light long afterward.

The reception was going well until the President noticed Sammy Davis Jr. among the guests. Kennedy was aghast. Davis, a talented song-and-dance performer, had married the white Swedish actress May Britt, scandalizing Americans who disapproved of any interracial marriage. Kennedy worried that a photograph of Davis with Britt could spell political disaster.

That Davis ever got invited was remarkable. "The President was absolutely feathered," a White House official recalled of the invitation to Davis. "He didn't give a damn about all the others, but how did that guy get there? It was as though the whole [reception] was a flop, and you never saw more people hiding under the table because nobody, absolutely no one had anything to do with Sammy Davis getting invited."

Kennedy kept buttonholing aides, furtively insisting they keep Davis away from photographers. He finally settled on the strategy of having Jackie pull Davis aside for a private discussion just as photographers were admitted to the reception. Richard Reeves observed: "Jacqueline Kennedy refused. She was so angry at the suggestion she did not want to go downstairs at all, and the formal reception began without the President and his wife. He was still upstairs trying to talk her into going down."

She finally did agree to come downstairs and sit for group photos. Then she stood up and left.

In the end Davis and Britt were not photographed. At Lincoln's Birthday celebrations throughout the country, Republicans, without access to prominent blacks, were upstaged by the White House.[2]

When Congress met early in 1963 no one foresaw that within a few months the nation's racial crisis would become America's paramount domestic issue. Kennedy didn't intend to offer major proposals on civil rights; the issue remained dormant to retain the backing of Southern Democrats for the President's major tax bill. Still, small legislative forays might relieve pressure.

Pressure from civil rights groups "make it clear that a message [on civil rights] would be most desirable," Lee White advised the President on February 25, 1963, but White doubted that the new proposed legislation would pass Congress. In addition to proposing modest legislation, White recommended that the President "recount achievements through executive action."

Three days later, on February 28, the President sent Congress the first civil rights message since he entered the White House. For those who thought he hadn't done enough for civil rights, he summarized the administration's ac-complishments: the executive action, litigation, persuasion, and private initia-tives. In addition, he recommended extending the life of the Civil Rights Commission, and proposed a bill with four timid measures to secure blacks their voting rights: proposed appointing temporary voting referees to register blacks in counties where voting-rights suits were filed and less than 15 per-cent of the voting-age blacks were registered; expediting treatment of voting-rights suits in federal courts; making a sixth-grade education pre-sumptive of literacy (because of discrimination in applying literacy tests); and providing federal technical and financial assistance to school districts in the process of desegregating. He didn't advance the bold legislation most desired by civil rights advocates—on jobs, housing, and public accommodations.[3]

These modest proposals immediately met opposition and the promise of strong resistance from Southern members of Congress, while Northern liber-als complained that the President hadn't gone far enough. Robert Kennedy testified on behalf of the new measures, but later complained, "Nobody paid the slightest bit of attention to me." The public didn't seem to care.

Eventually Southern senators were able to filibuster the measures to death because, claimed RFK, there was no "public outcry." This explanation ig-nored the President's own inaction on the measures, leaving the impression that he was indifferent to the outcome. Biographer Hilty concluded, "If the President did nothing after sending up the legislation because nothing he could have done would have made a difference, then it seems hard to escape the conclusion that they sent up the bill for appearances' sake only."

The administration's attitude changed in the spring. Beginning on April 3, 1963, Martin Luther King led a series of demonstrations in Birmingham, Alabama. He hoped to break the city's solid wall of racial segregation. Dur-ing April and May hundreds of blacks marched through downtown Birm-ingham and staged sit-ins to protest discrimination at lunch counters and in department stores, and in hiring practices. King selected Birmingham be-cause it was the symbol of segregation. In the previous six years there had been fifty cross burnings and so many racial bombings that blacks had taken to calling the city "Bombingham." Schools, restaurants, drinking fountains, and toilets were all segregated. Birmingham gave up its minor-league profes-sional baseball team rather than allow it to play integrated teams. The Met-ropolitan Opera took the city off its tour because local officials refused to integrate the municipal auditorium. For twenty-three years the city's arch-segregationist public safety commissioner Eugene "Bull" Connor had cowed blacks with loud threats and club-swinging police.

On May 2 hundreds of black schoolchildren staged protest marches and were arrested and jailed. During the next few days Bull Connor ordered the use of fire hoses and police dogs to break up demonstrations.

"Some Negroes stood their ground, began flinging stones and bottles at the police," *Time* reported. "One waved a knife at an officer. But the dogs, held on long leashes, lunged at those who retreated slowly. There was some scuffling; then the crowd broke for the church—chased by snarling dogs and club-waving cops." "Look at those niggers run," shouted the delighted Connor.

"We're through with tokenism and gradualism and see-how-far-you've-comism," said King during the protest. "We're through with we've-done-more-for-your-people-than-anyone-elseism. We can't wait any longer. Now is the time."[4]

The injustice, lack of opportunity, and meanness shocked the President. He also viewed the struggle in a worldwide context. Battered and bloody black children in the streets badly tarnished the nation's image. At the founding conference of the Organization of African Unity (OAU) in Addis Ababa, Ethiopia, Uganda's prime minister, Milton Obote, sent notice to the President that the "ears and eyes of the world are concentrated on events in Alabama." A Nigerian newspaper accused the United States of becoming "the most barbarian state in the world."

During the crisis Donald Wilson, the acting director of the United States Information Agency, wrote to the President, "Most attention was given to the use of brutality and especially dogs against the Negro demonstrators. Many papers, particularly in Europe and India, showed unusual sympathy and understanding of the race issue, but the failure of the Federal Government to intervene caused considerable questioning."

Moscow's propaganda predictably exploited the Birmingham events and beamed the story to Africa. "Moscow tried to convert developments into a mass indictment of U.S. democracy," Wilson informed the President. "As *Pravda* wrote recently, 'One day in Birmingham gives the world a much clearer idea of the American way of life than years of propaganda about U.S. freedom.' "[5]

The administration swung into action, organizing a behind-the-scenes campaign to contact Alabama business executives to urge them to push for a settlement. Cabinet members, including Treasury Secretary Douglas Dillon and Defense Secretary Robert McNamara, were assigned businessmen to phone.

Burke Marshall was dispatched to Birmingham to mediate. On May 18 Governor George Wallace met Kennedy at Muscle Shoals, Alabama, where the President made a speech; then the governor jumped into Kennedy's helicopter for a thirty-five-minute ride to the Redstone Arsenal at Huntsville, Alabama.[6]

On the trip, Pierre Salinger took notes on their conversation. Kennedy pressed for progress in integrating Birmingham. "The Governor replied that he thought he could keep things under control in Birmingham and the President reiterated the fact that things would never be under control in Birmingham until some progress was made." Kennedy wondered why blacks were not being hired to work in downtown stores. "He said that the very people who protested this action had Negroes serving their tables at home."

Wallace bitterly attacked Martin Luther King and his Birmingham associate Fred Shuttlesworth for vying with each other to see "who could go to bed with the most nigger women, and white and red women too. They ride around town in big cadillacs smoking expensive cigars."

Refocusing the discussion, Kennedy said progress was crucial. "Birmingham was getting an absolutely impossible reputation throughout the country and the world."[7]

During his 1962 election campaign Governor Wallace had promised "to stand in the schoolhouse door" and bar any black students from entering the University of Alabama. By 1963 Alabama was the only state which still had no blacks attending its state-supported university. Two black students, Vivian Malone and James Hood, both twenty, intended to register at the university on June 11. By detailed planning the Kennedy administration sought to avoid the tragic violence that had occurred the previous fall when James Meredith enrolled at the University of Mississippi.

Privately Wallace knew that integration of the university was inevitable, and he hoped it could be accomplished without violence. But Wallace, forty-three, a former state judge and amateur boxer, wanted the opportunity to express his disdain for the federal government in a face-to-face confrontation with its representatives. He wanted to make the federal government use overwhelming force, before which, as one journalist noted, Wallace "was determined to stand alone at center stage as the heroic defender of the rights of oppressed whites."[8]

President Kennedy hoped to enroll the students without using armed force and without arresting Wallace and making him a martyr. To resolve the problem peacefully the Justice Department worked secretly with the university president, Dr. Frank A. Rose; with the faculty; and with the state attorney general, Richmond Flowers, to prepare for the admission of the two blacks. "At the urging of Robert Kennedy," observed Hilty, "members of the cabinet telephoned prominent Alabama business leaders and encouraged them to accept integration. Burke Marshall personally contacted most of the leading newspaper publishers, ministers, and community leaders in the state. They, in turn, put pressure on Wallace."

To avoid repeating the problems at Ole Miss, where white Mississippians had bitterly resented the presence of "Yankee" troops on Southern soil, President Kennedy planned to federalize the Alabama National Guard in the event Wallace refused to step aside. "Because the guard commander and his troops were Alabamians, Kennedy believed it more likely that Wallace would peacefully capitulate," said Hilty.

Partly because of the administration's efforts, Wallace was deluged with pleas from religious leaders, businessmen, and educators to moderate his stand. Over two hundred Tuscaloosa civic officials signed a petition urging Wallace not to "carry out your announced intention of personally and physically interfering with the order of the United States Court."[9]

On June 11 Wallace arrived at the university campus at 10:00 A.M. and stood in the doorway of Foster Hall, where the students were to register. In Washington Robert Kennedy had rolled up his sleeves and turned his office into a command post. With him were his aides, maps of Tuscaloosa, a TV set, a radio, and a telephone line linking him with his team in Tuscaloosa: a group of U.S. marshals and Justice Department officials, headed by Deputy Attorney General Nicholas Katzenbach. At Fort Benning, Georgia, four hundred riot-trained army troops sat in helicopters, ready to respond to any emergency.

There were two separate confrontations with Wallace during the day. Late in the morning Katzenbach arrived at the campus and strode to the doorway of Foster Hall. Wallace stood waiting, a lectern in front of him.

Katzenbach asked Wallace to give "unequivocal assurance that you will not bar entry to these students." Wallace responded by reading a five-page statement charging that the "unwelcomed, unwanted, unwarranted and force-induced intrusion upon the campus of the University of Alabama today of the might of the central government offers a frightful example of the oppression of the rights, privileges and sovereignty of this state by officers of the Federal Government."

When Wallace finished, Katzenbach asked him to "step aside." Wallace simply stood there, glaring. "Very well," said Katzenbach. He turned away, and, by prearrangement, federal marshals escorted the two students to their dormitory rooms.

Katzenbach then telephoned Robert Kennedy, who called the President. At 1:34 P.M. President Kennedy signed an order federalizing the Alabama National Guard.

At the second confrontation, in midafternoon, Brigadier General Henry Graham of the Alabama Guard division walked up to Governor Wallace, saluted, and said, "It is my sad duty to inform you that the National Guard has been federalized. Please stand aside so that the order of the court may be accomplished." After a brief statement protesting the "trend toward military dictatorship," Wallace stepped back. The federal officials escorted Malone and Hood into the building, where they registered.

There had been no riot, no violence, and no need for troops. The only opposition was Wallace's empty gesture of defiance. When Wallace stepped aside, Robert Kennedy breathed a sign of relief and lit his cigar.[10]

On the evening of June 11, President Kennedy countered Wallace's media thrust. He decided to throw his prestige and the weight of his office behind the civil rights cause he had once tried to avoid. "In doing so, he went farther than any president before, took considerable risks in the bargain, and built most meaningfully upon the liberal tradition he had inherited," judged historian Alonzo Hamby.

Larry O'Brien and Ken O'Donnell advised against a speech, but Robert Kennedy endorsed it. Said Burke Marshall: "He urged it, he felt it, he understood it, and he prevailed; I don't think there was anybody in the Cabinet—except the President himself—who felt that way on these issues, and the President got it from his brother."

The President's sudden decision to address civil rights caught Sorensen off guard, making it impossible for the speechwriter to prepare a complete text. Robert Kennedy, who discussed ideas for the speech with his brother "for about twenty minutes," told the President not to worry about using a text; the speech would be better if he delivered it extemporaneously. The President busily outlined and organized his thoughts on the back of an envelope. Five minutes before airtime, he received Sorensen's partial draft.

His speech was blunt, eloquent, idealistic, and one of the most emotional he ever delivered. Earlier in the day, he explained, two clearly qualified blacks had been admitted to the University of Alabama despite threats and defiance by Alabama officials. "I hope that every American, regardless of where he lives, will stop and examine his conscience about this and other related incidents. This nation was founded by men of many nations and backgrounds. It was founded on the principle that all men are created equal, and that the rights of every man are diminished when the rights of one man are threatened."

Discrimination existed in all parts of the country, and was not primarily a legal or a legislative problem. In the speech's most memorable lines, he went on to say:

> We are confronted primarily with a moral issue. It is as old as the Scriptures and is as clear as the American Constitution.
>
> The heart of the question is whether all Americans are to be afforded equal rights and equal opportunities, whether we are going to treat our fellow Americans as we want to be treated. If an American, because his skin is dark, cannot eat lunch in a restaurant open to the public, if he cannot send his children to the best public school available, if he cannot vote for the public officials who represent him, if, in short, he cannot enjoy the full and free life which all of us want, then who among us would be content to have the color of his skin changed and stand in his place? Who among us would then be content with the counsels of patience and delay?

It was time for Congress to face the issue, and therefore he would shortly be asking for new legislation, including the right of all Americans to be served in facilities which were open to the public—hotels, restaurants, theaters, retail stores, and similar establishments.

Today there are Negroes, unemployed—two or three times as many compared to whites—with inadequate education, moving into the large cities, unable to find work, young people particularly out of work and without hope, denied equal rights, denied the opportunity to eat at a restaurant or lunch counter or go to a movie theater, denied the right to a decent education. . . . It seems to me that these are matters which concern us all, not merely Presidents or congressmen or governors, but every citizen of the United States.[11]

After watching the television speech in Atlanta, Martin Luther King rejoiced. He immediately wrote to compliment the President, and told reporters the speech was a masterpiece. A year later he stated that "[Ike] never spoke to the moral issue, and I think this is something that President Kennedy brought to the nation that . . . it desperately needed, the insistence on the morality of integration and the fact that the issue was more than a political or an economic issue, but that it was, at bottom, a moral issue." His speech, said King, was the "most eloquent, passionate, and unequivocal plea for civil rights . . . ever made by any President."[12]

Afterward the President complained wearily that "events are making our problems"; civil rights "has become everything." He worried that his speech may have been his "political swan song." A Gallup poll conducted after the speech found that 36 percent of Americans thought he was pushing integration "too fast"; 32 percent "about right"; and 18 percent "not fast enough." Yet when Luther Hodges pointed to the damaging fallout the civil rights effort might have on Kennedy's reelection, the President expressed deep commitment to the cause. "Governor, I may lose the legislation, or I may even lose the election in 1964, but there comes a time when a man has to take a stand, and history will record that he has to meet these tough situations and ultimately make a decision."

To many he appeared bold and statesmanlike. In *Newsweek* Walter Lippmann lauded his "momentous and irrevocable step." The President had "committed himself to lead the movement toward equality of status and opportunity for the American Negro. No President has ever done this before, none has ever staked his personal prestige and has brought to bear all the powers of the Presidency on the Negro cause. . . . I count very high the speed, the intelligence, the imagination, and the courage of the Kennedy reaction."

"If the President proves as good a politician in the next few months as he has . . . shown himself a statesman, who can tell what higher roads the Republic may be traveling before the year has ended," praised an editorial in *The New Republic*.

John Kennedy had become committed to the civil rights cause. "Sometimes you look at what you've done and the only thing you ask yourself is— what took you so long to do it?" the President confided to a friend. He remarked sadly to Arthur Schlesinger, "I don't understand the South. I'm coming to believe that Thaddeus Stevens was right. I had always been taught to regard him as a man of vicious bias. But when I see this sort of thing, I begin to wonder how else you can treat them."[13]

During the ferment in Birmingham, Robert Kennedy and his aides had been disturbed by the tiny number of black federal employees there—only fifteen out of two thousand. A wider investigation led Robert Kennedy to believe that the committee chaired by Lyndon Johnson was not doing its job. The Committee on Equal Employment Opportunity was supposed to review the employment practices of the federal government in terms of race, make recommendations for improvement, and establish antidiscrimination rules that all government contractors should follow.

For two years the CEEO had made moderate gains, but often it had exaggerated its success and misrepresented its statistics. When Robert Kennedy surveyed government-contracted firms, he discovered that the number with no black workers "was shockingly high." One study found that twenty-five thousand of thirty-five thousand companies with federal contracts still employed no blacks. The CEEO stressed *percentage* gains, but a 100 percent increase in the number of blacks in a large company sometimes meant a jump from only one to two.

Johnson's operation was merely spreading propaganda, Robert Kennedy believed. According to the attorney general, President Kennedy shared the view. "Oh, he almost had a fit. And he said 'That man can't run this committee. Can you think of anything more deplorable than him trying to run the United States? That's why he can't ever be president.' "[14]

At the committee's meeting on June 18, the attorney general was on the warpath. "Within a matter of three or four minutes," recalled Jack Conway, who represented the federal housing agency, "the Vice President found himself on the defense because Bob just tore in . . . and asked for facts and statistics."

"Bobby peppered the committee with questions about progress in Birmingham," observed historian Jeff Shesol, "about the city's defense industries, about employment patterns and compliance reports. What agencies had how many Negroes? How many vacancies were there? Who was doing what to improve the situation?"

Kennedy bitterly turned on James Webb, head of the National Aeronautics and Space Administration, because NASA had contracts of $3.5 billion, but had only one and a half men in Washington working on equal employment. This exchanged followed:

KENNEDY: I asked how many people you have got in your program and you said one and a half men.

WEBB: I am not sure. I can furnish you that, but with nine centers throughout the country we are putting a great deal of effort on it. . . .

KENNEDY: Mr. Webb, I just raised a question of whether you can do this job and run a center and administer its [$3.5] billion worth of contracts and make sure that Negroes and non–whites have jobs . . . I think that unless we can get down into the specifics, Mr. Webb, unless you get down to the specifics and the particular individuals and find out what they are doing and have them understand that . . . this Committee and the president of the United States are interested in this program, I don't see that the job will be done. . . .

WEBB: I would like to have you take enough time to see precisely what we do.

KENNEDY: I am trying to ask some questions. I don't think I am able to get the answers, to tell you the truth.[15]

As Bobby kept pressing, Webb grew more vague. A pall of embarrassment covered the room. RFK then turned on Hobart Taylor, LBJ's protégé and the panel's executive vice chairman. He asked about compliance reports:

A new form was being developed, Taylor assured him. "Where is the form?" Bobby snapped. It was being processed by the Budget Bureau. "Where in the Budget Bureau?" Bobby offered to expedite it—insisted, really. Taylor was becoming visibly upset now, straining to keep a level tone: "Mr. Attorney General," he protested, "I don't believe I need your help. . . . It really won't be necessary."

Mortified, Lyndon Johnson slumped grimly in his chair, his eyes mere slits. "It was," Conway remarked, "a pretty brutal performance, very sharp. It brought tensions between Johnson and Kennedy right out on the table and very hard. Everybody was sweating under the armpits."

More than "generalized statements" were needed, RFK told the committee. "Why hasn't somebody followed it up, what companies have you actually gotten in touch with, is anybody going to see any of the companies? . . . You have to go out and look for these people."

"Finally," Conway remembered, "after completely humiliating Webb and making the vice president look like a fraud . . . [Bobby] got up. He walked around the table . . . shook my hand . . . and talked to me for about thirty seconds about how things were going here, there, and every place, and then he went on out."[16]

On May 17, 1963, during a flight to Asheville, North Carolina, Robert Kennedy and Burke Marshall discussed the need for new civil rights legislation. The attorney general urged his brother to assume leadership of the cause. The problem needed to be faced. On May 31, after debating with himself and his aides for two weeks, the President agreed. He realized that the rest of his legislative agenda would probably be stalled while debate raged on civil rights.

It was a courageous stand. By committing themselves to full equality for African-Americans, Sorensen observed, "both brothers knowingly cut themselves off from this traditional Democratic source of electoral votes without obtaining—in view of their already commanding political position among black and other liberal voters—offsetting gains elsewhere."

The timing for new legislation was much better than a few months earlier. Because of the Birmingham demonstrations, the public was more concerned about the racial problem. "There was enough demand [for legislation] that we could get to the heart of the problem and have some chance of success," said Robert Kennedy.[17]

The Kennedys now did what they did best: meticulously organized and promoted, as they had done for the 1960 election. The President had intense consultations with members of Congress. "The attorney general and I," said Marshall, "met personally with every senator, including senators who were going to be dead set against this bill, and every member of the House—not individually—but every member of the House who was not from a state that is simply impossible, every member of the House, for example, from the border states."

Vice President Johnson was angry that he wasn't consulted or even shown a copy of the legislation, but he provided honest and thoughtful counsel. "I don't know who drafted it; I've never seen it," Johnson snapped to Ted Sorensen, displaying his wounded ego. "Hell, if the vice president doesn't know what's in it, how do you expect the others to know what's in it? I got it from *The New York Times*." Using his legislative mastery, he detailed the committee members to target and identified likely coalitions. He cautioned against moving too fast. Key legislative leaders should be consulted before a bill was introduced. It was critical, Johnson stressed, that President Kennedy make a strong public commitment to civil rights, using the moral power of the presidency. "I want to pull out the cannon," Johnson said. "The President is the cannon." Bobby Kennedy later conceded that Johnson had contributed "some good ideas" which the President heeded.[18]

To arouse public support for the new legislation the White House invited influential citizens—groups of business leaders, women, educators, labor officials, lawyers, religious leaders—to meetings at the White House. Kennedy conducted the meetings between June 4 and June 22, when the President left for Europe, and resumed them on his return. About 250 people attended each session; the President or his designated representative—usually Robert Kennedy or Lyndon Johnson—addressed the group, then turned it over to the floor for questions and comments.

The two Kennedys and Vice President Johnson addressed group after group in their contrasting styles, observed Arthur Schlesinger: "the President crisp and businesslike, the Vice President emotional and evangelical, the Attorney General blunt and passionate."[19]

On June 4, the President met with businessmen from twenty-six different states—owners and managers of businesses operating in Southern cities, mostly national chains of theaters, drugstores, and department stores. Before the meeting with religious leaders on June 17, Ralph Dungan reminded the President "to underscore again the moral position of the churches on the question of racial equality." Kennedy didn't need the reminder. During the meeting he stressed that the civil rights movement, determined to make substantial progress, would no longer tolerate blacks being "second-class" citizens. "Our job is to make that transition . . . as peaceful, as productive, as orderly as we possibly can."

> I would hope each religious group would . . . underscore the moral position of racial equality. . . .
>
> Then I would hope that we could attempt to establish as close a contact as possible—and I say this to the white members of the group—with the Negro clergy. They are [the] most responsible leaders, they have had the experience, they know their community better, they can offer the soundest judgment, they are local to the community, and I would think that the best way to prevent the most violent situations would be by the closest coordination between the clergy of both Negro and White in each community.

"What about racial intermarriage?" asked one minister.

"I am not talking about private lives," replied the irritated President, "but public accommodations, public education, and public elections."

Praising the meetings, the NAACP's Clarence Mitchell said, "It was almost as though the lobbying efforts of organizations like the NAACP were suddenly supplemented by a very helpful and benevolent sponsor. . . . That was a thing which undoubtedly got the country in the frame of mind to pass the legislation."[20]

A group of fifteen black physicians requested an audience with the President while Congress considered the civil rights legislation. They shocked the President with their stories of discrimination, particularly in the South, but in Northern communities as well. Hospitals would not permit black physicians to use their facilities, they explained. Often a rule required that only members of the local medical society could use the hospitals and admit patients, and the local medical society itself was the one that restricted black membership. "The President was aghast at the fact that some were not permitted to bring their patients into hospitals and [he] said that he wanted to see if he could meet with people from the American Medical Association," recalled Lee White. "He wanted to know who could he meet with to correct this kind of situation and encourage the opening up of hospitals."[21]

The President planned to introduce the bill in the House of Representatives rather than in the Senate because James Eastland chaired the Senate Judiciary Committee. The chairman of the House Judiciary Committee, however, was Emanuel Celler, a liberal and longtime champion of civil rights. Celler also presided over the House Judiciary Committee's Subcommittee no. 5, where the administration's bill would start its legislative journey. Because Celler's subcommittee was dominated by liberal Democrats, the bill would receive more favorable treatment than anywhere else in Congress.

Although all the supporters of the new legislation agreed that the bill must start in the House, the huge obstacle of a future Senate filibuster had to be considered long before the bill made its way to the Senate. Southerners were certain to filibuster, and the Senate had never imposed cloture against a civil rights talkathon. For the two-thirds vote (sixty-seven members) required for cloture, the administration would need the support of at least twenty Republicans.[22]

On June 18, Senate majority leader Mike Mansfield advised the President that there was only one practical way to assure passage of the legislation in the Senate: Count sixty-seven votes on cloture for whatever House bill was pushed. "Any phraseology in the legislation, any parliamentary tactic or political statement which subtracts from the total of votes obtainable for cloture is to be avoided. As it now stands, the short-side of sixty-seven lies in the public accommodations title."

To obtain the needed sixty-seven votes for cloture required "complete co-operation and good faith" with Republican Senate leader Everett Dirksen, Mansfield wrote. The Illinois senator's power to persuade "key Republicans to cloture will be lost if the impression develops that the Democratic Party is trying to make political capital." Bipartisan cooperation was crucial.[23]

The administration agreed to work with a bipartisan coalition. Among Democrats, though, two pro–civil rights groups disagreed on the scope of legislation and the wisest strategy to use. Congressman Richard Bolling of Missouri explained the division:

> One, which seemed to include most members of the Administration who were involved in the matter, seemed to feel that it would be impossible to pass a law that contained strong fair-employment-practices provisions, or one that would provide for the withholding of federal funds from any federally supported program in which there was racial discrimination. This group favored sending to Congress a fairly mild bill, of which the most controversial section would have been the one dealing with public accommodations.
>
> The other group, of which I was a member, included many middle-rank Democrats in both House and Senate, who, with support from the outside by civil rights and allied organizations, felt that the strongest possible measures should be proposed. We had three reasons for this: Objectively it was a matter both of conscience and of the actual need for strong legislation. From a legislative point of view, it seemed sensible for the House to pass the strongest possible bill to allow for the Senate whittling away some of it without making the final version worthless. And from our partisan viewpoint, we knew that if the Democrats proposed a weak bill, the minority of Republicans who were traditionally in favor of civil rights laws would quickly top it with a stronger bill of their own.[24]

In the House the administration's strategy sought to get bipartisan agreement on a bill right from the beginning, long before it ever came to the House floor.

Of the eight provisions in Kennedy's bill, one was particularly important and controversial—the heart of the bill. Title II prohibited discrimination in public accommodations, including all places of lodging, eating, and amusement and other retail or service establishments. The focal point of the Birmingham campaign had been the exclusion of blacks from lunch counters, restaurants, amusement parks, theaters, hotels, and other public places.

On the morning of June 20, Kennedy's bill began its tortuous journey through the intricate maze of the House and Senate. The administration's most powerful witness for the bill was the President's brother.

Robert Kennedy repeatedly testified with eloquence and passion. Public-accommodations legislation was needed, not just to stop disorder, but to prove "to millions of our fellow citizens the very premise of American democracy—that equal rights and equal opportunity are inherent by birth in this land." Local communities and states were not solving the problem.

> We believe therefore that the Federal Government has no moral choice but to take the initiative. How can we say to a Negro in Jackson:
> "When a war comes you will be an American citizen, but in the meantime you're a citizen of Mississippi and we can't help you."
> How, by any moral standards, can we tell our Negro citizens:
> "Our forefathers brought your forefathers over here against their will, and we are going to make you pay for it."
> Yet isn't that just what the argument boils down to?
> The United States is dominated by white people, politically and economically. The question is whether we, in this position of dominance, are going to have not the charity but the wisdom to stop penalizing our fellow citizens whose only fault or sin is that they are born.

According to two current tourist guidebooks, he told the Senate Judiciary Committee, there was only one place for a black to obtain overnight lodging in Montgomery, Alabama; there was none in Danville, Virginia. Yet dogs accompanying whites were welcome to stay in five places in Montgomery and four in Danville.[25]

President Kennedy occasionally had second thoughts about his decision. Every fourth day or so he would say to his brother, in a mostly jocular way, "Do you think we did the right thing by sending the legislation up? Look at the trouble it's got us in."

There were rumors in the legislative cloakrooms that the administration and the congressional leaders were about to scuttle the public-accommodations provision. "After a sham battle," *Time* reported, "the Administration would let the Southern Democrats kill off Title II, and the Southerners would let the Administration have the rest of the bill."

Several times Senator Mansfield discussed with the President the difficulty of securing passage of the public-accommodations section. "You've got to get it done," Mansfield recalled the President responding. "It's the heart of the matter. These people are entitled to this consideration, and I'm depending upon you to see that what I recommend is passed."[26]

At a meeting with civil rights leaders on June 22, Kennedy reacted to a recent announcement by civil rights groups that they were organizing a march on Washington to be held in late August. Anticipating the worst, the President thought it was a mistake to announce a huge march at the very moment Congress considered major new legislation. Legislators would be offended. "We want success in Congress," the President told them, "not just a big show at the Capitol. Some of these people are looking for an excuse to be against us; and I don't want to give any of them a chance to say, 'Yes, I'm for the bill, but I am damned if I will vote for it at the point of a gun.'" The march would only create an atmosphere of intimidation, and might be strongly resented by Congress.

Dr. King responded that the march could dramatize the issue and mobilize support. "It may seem ill-timed. Frankly, I have never engaged in any direct action movement which did not seem ill-timed. Some people thought Birmingham ill-timed."

"Including the Attorney General," the President quipped with RFK nearby. A few minutes later, during a discussion of police chief Bull Connor's brutal actions during the Birmingham demonstrations, Kennedy said, "I don't think you should all be totally harsh on Bull Connor. After all, Bull Connor has done more for civil rights than anyone in this room." Everyone chuckled.

"This is a very serious fight," Kennedy continued. "The Vice President and I know what it will mean if we fail. . . . A good many programs I care about may go down the drain as a result of this—so we are putting a lot on the line. What is important is that we preserve confidence in the good faith of each other."

The President's commitment impressed the civil rights leaders. "I liked the way he talked about what *we* are getting," said King. "It wasn't something that he was getting for you Negroes. You knew you had an ally."[27]

By August 2, Subcommittee no. 5 had completed twenty-two days of public hearings on the administration's bill. Chairman Celler announced that the subcommittee would now go into private session to mark up the bill, the process of rewriting it into final form for consideration by the full Judiciary Committee.

Actually Celler had been asked by President Kennedy to stall until the administration's tax legislation was voted out of the House Ways and Means Committee. He feared that the Southerners on Ways and Means would kill the tax bill in retaliation if the civil rights bill moved out of Subcommittee no. 5.

In the meantime the Kennedys courted Congressman William McCulloch of Ohio, an influential Republican member of the subcommittee whose support was crucial for winning over House Republicans. McCulloch met secretly with Justice Department officials to hammer out a bill that would pass the full Judiciary Committee.[28]

On August 28, a disciplined, law-abiding, and spontaneously enthusiastic crowd of over two hundred thousand marched slowly from the Washington Monument toward their symbolic destination, the Lincoln Memorial, in the

"March on Washington for Jobs and Freedom." It was the largest public demonstration ever held in the nation's capital. King brought the throng to tears with his brilliant visionary oration: "I have a dream. . . ."

At about 5:00 P.M. President Kennedy greeted the leaders of the march at the White House. "*I* have a dream," the President said kindly to King. When the President discovered that the group hadn't eaten since breakfast, he ordered sandwiches and coffee from the kitchen. Besides King, the group included Walter Reuther, A. Philip Randolph, Whitney Young, and Roy Wilkins. They took the opportunity to lobby the President for a stronger bill, but Kennedy was pessimistic about its chances. To make his point he ticked off a detailed, state-by-state analysis of House Democrats. "Alabama, of course, none," he began. "Alaska, one. Arizona, you've got one sure and one doubtful. Arkansas, nothing. California, ah, all the Democrats are right." He came up with about 160 Democrats. The rest, about 60 more votes, would have to come from the Republican side—and they would be "hard to get."[29]

"Congressman McClintock," said Kennedy, mispronouncing McCulloch's name, "indicated to the Department of Justice this week that he thought he could vote for our bill with some changes. He's the chief fellow. He won't vote for it unless he's got the green light from Halleck. If we can get him, we will get the 60 Republicans."

On the morning of September 10 Kennedy's tax bill passed a major test, winning approval by the House Ways and Means Committee by a vote of 17 to 8. Now Celler could proceed with the markup of Kennedy's civil rights bill.

In late September, however, Celler and strong civil rights advocates on his subcommittee outraged McCulloch and the administration by ramming through a much stronger bill without any attempt at bipartisan consultation. After intense lobbying by supporters of civil rights, Subcommittee no. 5 approved its own version of the bill, throwing a monkey wrench into the President's strategy. The new bill expanded the administration's package, adding a provision for a powerful Fair Employment Practices Commission (FEPC); expanding the public-accommodations section to include almost every establishment in a state offering goods and services to the public; augmenting the injunctive powers requested for the attorney general; and adding voting-rights guarantees to include not only federal elections but state elections as well.

The President was livid. The unrealistic provisions would ruin bipartisanship and kill the legislation. In a meeting with civil rights leaders he demanded to know how supporters of the strengthened bill proposed to get the legislation though the House. "Can Clarence Mitchell and the Leadership group deliver 3 Republicans on the Rules Committee and 60 Republicans on the House floor?" the President said. "McCulloch can deliver 60 Republicans. Without him it can't be done. McCulloch is mad now because he thinks that an agreement he had with us on the language of compromise has been thrown away by the subcommittee. So now he's sore. . . . I'll go as far as I can go, but I think McCulloch has to come with us or otherwise it is an exercise in futility."[30]

The administration tried to patch up the subcommittee bill. An angry Bobby Kennedy summoned Celler to the Justice Department and lambasted him for not following the agreed-upon strategy. RFK made amends with McCulloch. "Determined to bolster McCulloch's confidence in the administration, Kennedy gave orders that no one in the White House or the Justice Department would take credit for the bill if it was successful," observed Charles and Barbara Whalen in their history of the legislation. "All statements would say, 'Congressman McCulloch has done it . . . and Congressman Emanuel Celler.'"

Two clever Southerners, Virginia's Representative Howard Smith and Georgia's Senator Richard Russell, maneuvered to get their supporters to back the stiff bill. Since the strong bill had no chance of being enacted, its approval by the Judiciary Committee would probably kill civil rights legislation for the year.

Painfully aware that he would be castigated by civil rights leaders, on October 15–16 RFK went before the Judiciary Committee to plead that the subcommittee's bill be watered down to passable strength.[31] "He used no notes," said Republican James Bromwell of Iowa. "He had stacks of books in front of him and Katzenbach and Marshall behind him. He referred to neither. He had a complete grasp of the bill. Also, I was impressed with his forthrightness. There was no equivocation. He took full responsibility for the proposed cutbacks."

Afterward Celler promised to put aside his own feelings and "exert every effort" toward working for a compromise. Inevitably, civil rights leaders cried sellout. The Leadership Conference on Civil Rights, an association of top civil rights leaders, wrote Celler urging him to ignore Bobby's advice.

President Kennedy was determined not to lose control of the bill. Taking stock of the situation, he summoned Republican and Democratic leaders for a meeting at the White House on October 23. The next day Charles Halleck phoned. "Mr. President, we've got enough votes for you." Kennedy was delighted. "We couldn't have been more pleased," said Larry O'Brien. "It was a major, major breakthrough."[32]

In a series of votes on October 29, the administration's bill won approval. The Judiciary Committee rejected the subcommittee's bill 19 to 15; then by 20 to 14 the committee accepted Kennedy's bipartisan version.

It was a compromise—a bipartisan "unity bill." It forbade discrimination in hotels, motels, filling stations, movie houses, and restaurants. An equal employment opportunities commission would outlaw discrimination in industries employing twenty-five or more people and engaged in interstate commerce. The bill granted the attorney general more power to intervene in voting discrimination against blacks and to move against segregated public facilities. Literacy tests had to be given in writing, and a sixth-grade education was to be presumptive proof of literacy for registration.

The legislation still faced major hurdles. The House Rules Committee could stall the measure. If it passed the entire House, the bill faced a Southern filibuster in the Senate. Still, Kennedy's bill had overcome its first huge hurdle.[33]

Kennedy damaged his political fortunes by the stand he took with civil rights forces. In a major poll reported by *Newsweek* in late October 1963, the political impact of the racial upheaval was clear: "it has hurt John F. Kennedy, and it may have hurt him badly." The President had picked up 1 million black votes since 1960, but the *Newsweek* poll showed the racial issue had driven about 4.5 million white voters away from Kennedy. But the resulting loss of 3.5 million voters was something he could afford at the moment because of his commanding lead over potential challengers in 1964.

> In all, because of disenchantment on other issues as well, he has lost the support of some 6.5 million Americans who voted for him in 1960. But the *Newsweek* Poll also shows that for various reasons—his handling of foreign policy, the facedown over Cuba, his personal appeal, his family, the aura that surrounds every occupant of the White House—he has gained the support of some 11 million people who voted for Richard Nixon. The result: if the election were held today, President Kennedy could defeat any Republican by some 4.5 million popular votes.

Bitterness against Kennedy was strongest in the South. "Mr. Kennedy may lose between three and six of the seven states he won in 1960." No Democratic President in the twentieth century had been so widely disliked in the South. "A full 67 percent of the South's white voters are dissatisfied with the way President Kennedy has handled civil rights." A housewife from Raleigh, North Carolina, claimed that the President had "stirred up all the colored people to get their vote." A middle-aged carpenter in Jonesboro, Tennessee, said of Robert Kennedy, "He's a 'nigger' man."

Most white voters were unsympathetic to the methods and pace of the civil rights campaign. "Only one white American in three believes the Negro is ready to handle what he's demanding in jobs and housing and equal opportunity, and 74 percent say that the Negro is moving 'too fast.'"

Louis Harris, who directed the poll for *Newsweek* and analyzed its results, concluded that the 1964 election would be a landslide for Kennedy were it not for the racial issue. Civil rights held little opportunity and great danger. "The civil-rights issue represents a definite, distinct loss for Mr. Kennedy in 1964, and, if it grows into the overriding issue, it might just cost him the election."[34]

Dr. King came to believe that the Kennedys had responded "to creative pressure," not just political calculation and crisis management. Kennedy "frankly acknowledged that he was responding to mass demands" but had done so, said King, "because he thought it was right to do so. This is the secret of the deep affection he evoked. He was responsive, sensitive, humble before the people, and bold on their behalf."[35]

Historian David Garrow has described Robert Kennedy's decision, made on October 10, 1963, to approve FBI wiretaps on the phones of Martin Luther King "as one of the most ignominious acts in modern American history." Garrow's accusation is wrong. Considering the circumstances, there was nothing shameful or dishonorable about the decision. But what J. Edgar Hoover and the FBI did to King over the next five years was indeed ignominious.

On the surface the charge that Communists influenced King could be quickly dismissed as a right-wing, McCarthyite smear. But the story is more complicated and puzzling. In early January 1962, Hoover notified Robert Kennedy that two persons in King's circle had ties to the Communist Party, USA. One, Jack O'Dell, had a long public involvement as a party organizer, but his minor position with King's Southern Christian Leadership Conference never allowed him to become a close adviser to King. The other, Stanley Levison, provoked a storm of alarm within the FBI.

Stanley Levison, a white attorney and businessman from New York City, had been introduced to King in 1956. He soon emerged as King's closest white adviser. Beginning in 1957 Levison handled King's complicated financial affairs, evaluated labor and liberal leaders, wrote speeches, raised funds, and assisted with the production of King's first book.

Levison also had a hidden insidious past, and the FBI had good reasons to suspect his intentions in befriending King. The FBI had learned of Levison's extensive activities on behalf of the Communist Party, USA, from a major intelligence-gathering coup. The brothers Jack and Morris Childs—codenamed "Solo" by the FBI—were high-level party officials turned FBI informants. The FBI assumed that Levison had infiltrated King's inner circle and that he was actually a cunning party operator, still under Soviet direction.[36]

Levison was a secret Communist committed to one of the most evil and dangerous leaders of the twentieth century. Until his death in 1953, Joseph

Stalin had been the ruthless dictator of the Soviet Union for twenty-five years. Under his reign of terror, millions of Russians died during his forced collectivization of farming and in the Great Purge of the late 1930s, when he executed millions of his political opponents. He persecuted artists, writers, and intellectuals, and after World War II imposed brutal police states in Eastern Europe, managed by native Communists controlled by himself. Following World War II, the United States gravely faced the Stalinist threat in the Cold War.

In the early 1950s, and probably before then, Levison supported Stalin. He was a major fund-raiser for the party and managed its national finances. He bragged about "infiltrating" a Manhattan chapter of the American Jewish Congress, and delivered speeches following the party's political agenda. One notion he promoted was that the Eisenhower administration was rapidly moving toward fascism.

Levison regularly took precautions to avoid tails and surveillance by the FBI, using circuitous routes for secret rendezvous with other party members.[37]

Robert Kennedy thought that the FBI's information on Levison was dependable and that he was dangerous. Harris Wofford, John Seigenthaler, Burke Marshall, and the attorney general all spoke to King about the danger of associating with Levison. Still, King was incredulous. Where was the proof? (The FBI wouldn't reveal its secret source.)

On June 22, 1963, the attorney general brought the President into the matter. After meeting with civil rights leaders at the White House, the President invited King for a stroll in the Rose Garden. "I assume you know you're under very close surveillance," he told King. He warned the civil rights leader that Hoover regarded Levison as "a conscious agent of the Soviet conspiracy."

Then the President took another approach. "You've read about Profumo in the papers?" he asked. King said he had read the stories about John Profumo, the British secretary of state for war, who had become entangled in a sensational sex scandal. Such a scandal could ruin public leaders, the President stressed. "[Prime Minister Harold] Macmillan is likely to lose his government because he has been loyal to a friend [Profumo]," Kennedy told King. "You must be careful not to lose your cause for the same reason."

Later the President added, "If they shoot *you* down, they'll shoot *us* down, too. So we're asking you to be careful." It was a reasonable request.[38]

Robert Kennedy was not sympathetic to King. Shortly before the March on Washington in August 1963, at a Georgetown dinner party, the homophobic attorney general expressed contempt for Bayard Rustin, a homosexual and major adviser to King. "So you're down here for that old black fairy's anti-Kennedy demonstration?" he said to Marietta Tree. According to Mrs.

Tree, Kennedy said of King, "He's not a serious person. If the country knew what we know about King's goings on, he'd be finished."[39]

One way to find out if the FBI's information was accurate was to tap King's telephone, a possibility Hoover kept pressing. If Levison was a top Soviet agent, as the FBI believed, it was incumbent on RFK to act; otherwise Hoover would probably leak the information, causing irreparable harm to King, the civil rights bill in Congress, and the Kennedys. "If Robert Kennedy refused a tap on King and anything went wrong, Hoover would have a field day," noted Schlesinger. "On the other hand, a tap might end the matter by demonstrating King's entire innocence, even to the satisfaction of the FBI."

"Bobby Kennedy resisted, resisted, and resisted tapping King," said Hoover's deputy William Sullivan. "Finally, we twisted the arm of the Attorney General to the point where he had to go. I guess he feared we would let that stuff go in the press if he said no."

On October 7, 1963, citing "possible communist influence in the racial situation," Hoover asked the attorney general for permission to wiretap King's residence and the SCLC office in New York. Robert Kennedy signed the request on October 10. On October 21, he also approved an FBI request for coverage of the Atlanta office of the SCLC, but insisted that at the end of thirty days all the results should be evaluated. A month later the President was assassinated, and the distracted attorney general apparently forgot about the matter, leaving the FBI free to do as it pleased.[40]

Levison had lied to King about his extensive Communist past, telling King merely that he had "known" some Communists and had worked with some in Henry Wallace's 1948 presidential bid, but that those activities were history.

An outstanding moral leader, King was not a Communist; nor was he a Communist sympathizer. He was too independent. Still, his relations with Levison are particularly disturbing and raise an important question: Did Levison have an insidious hidden agenda in befriending King? The FBI and the Kennedy administration had good reason to suspect he might have. In "legal terms," Garrow has written, the FBI's case against Levison *after* 1955 was "so weak as to be virtually worthless." History, though, need not be judged strictly in "legal terms," and the grounds for harshly judging Levison should be his important, secret work for the party before he met King.[41]

Why did King continue his relations with O'Dell and Levison? Friendship and personal loyalty were part of the answer. Dr. King viewed Levison as indispensable. Besides, he never took seriously the warnings of the Kennedy administration officials, judging their evidence shallow and exaggerated. His continuing relations with Levison and O'Dell showed poor judgment. "After all," wrote Eric Breindel in *The New Republic*, "to associate

politically with men who had strong ties to Communism American-style—
i.e., Stalinism, which reigned supreme in the C.P.U.S.A.—seems more than
simply unwise, particularly as it was likely to offend King's most important
potential supporters, the Kennedy brothers."

In the final judgment, it is regrettable that King associated with the two
Communists. As Breindel noted, "Men who were involved with American
Communism, in all its Stalinist ugliness, as late as Levison and O'Dell were,
and who never repudiated that involvement, made for dubious political allies."[42]

What the FBI did with its new freedom was disgraceful. Hoover was intolerant of blacks and detested King. Starting in 1964, under the guise of
protecting national security, the FBI used counterespionage activities and vast
electronic surveillance—telephone taps at King's home and office, hidden
microphones in his hotel rooms—to denigrate King, treating him like a
Russian agent and countenancing inexcusable violations of his civil liberties.
The FBI scrutinized Dr. King's tax returns, monitored his financial affairs,
and leaked information to the press.

The bureau received a dozen reels of tape recordings from bugs placed in
King's room at the Willard Hotel in Washington, D.C. The tapes recorded an
exceptionally active sexual encounter involving King and several SCLC colleagues with two black women. Hoover privately castigated King's "obses-
sive degenerate sexual urges" and said he qualified for the "'top alley cat'
prize." In November 1964, the FBI surreptitiously mailed King a tape containing excerpts from recorded sexual encounters, and in an accompanying,
anonymous letter railed against his "incredible evilness." Hoping to intimidate King, the FBI's letter suggested the civil rights leader commit suicide.

Without the Levison problem, concluded David Garrow, "the Kennedy
and Johnson Administrations would most likely have embraced both King
and the entire southern black freedom struggle far more warmly than they
did."[43]

41

FRUSTRATING
COMMITMENT

In early 1963 Kennedy and his top advisers shared the illusion of growing success in South Vietnam. During a speech in New York in April, Dean Rusk expressed satisfaction with the military and political progress. He described a "steady movement [in South Vietnam] toward a constitutional system resting upon popular consent." The strategic-hamlet program had produced "excellent results," the "morale in the countryside ha[d] begun to rise," and to the peasants the Vietcong "look[ed] less and less like winners." Everything Rusk asserted turned out to be wrong.

At about the same time as Rusk's speech, the CIA provided a more realistic assessment. The tide had not yet turned in favor of Saigon. The Vietcong had expanded the size and effectiveness of their forces, and attacked more boldly. Nor had Diem made progress in political reform. "The number of government strikes has certainly increased during the past year," said the CIA report. "But all too frequently the Viet Cong are gone when the strike force arrives. Hence, a pure count of government-mounted operations may indicate a more determined government policy but not necessarily a weakened enemy."

The strategic-hamlet program, the CIA reported, had antagonized the peasantry. "Insensitivity to real or fancied popular grievances or to issues of popular interest such as corruption has done little to enhance the regime's internal image. On balance, the war remains a slowly escalating stalemate."[1]

Journalists also criticized the war effort, portraying a situation far different than Kennedy heard from his advisers. Beginning in 1962 and reaching a peak the following year, a small group of American correspondents in Saigon—David Halberstam of *The New York Times,* Neil Sheehan of United Press International, and Malcolm Browne of the Associated Press—disparaged Diem's regime and U.S. ineffectiveness.

The twenty-eight-year-old Halberstam kept American generals and U.S. intelligence agencies busy trying to refute and discredit him. In his history of the Saigon correspondents, *Once Upon a Distant War* (1995), William Prochnau described Halberstam as a "big, loud, loose cannon, with all the firepower of *The New York Times* in his armory," who "suddenly began careening through Kennedy's nonwar."[2]

Normally reporters recorded and interpreted events and didn't act as partisans for one viewpoint or another. But the three American journalists reported from an anti-Diem perspective. The Diem government, and particularly Diem's brother Ngo Dinh Nhu and his wife, developed a special hatred for the three Americans, which the correspondents fully reciprocated.

"What we were reflecting was reality as seen by American and Vietnamese officers who were fighting the war," Halberstam later claimed. "Our conflict was not with officers who were there; our conflict was with people who were in Saigon at the official level who reflected not what was happening in the field, but what they wanted to happen in the field."[3]

The correspondents accused the U.S. mission in Saigon of deliberately lying to them about the Diem regime and the progress of the war. The mission "became part of American policy to camouflage the shortcomings of the Diem oligarchy," wrote Stanley Karnow of *The Saturday Evening Post.* "The U.S. Embassy turned into an adjunct of dictatorship," said Halberstam. "In trying to protect Diem from criticism, the ambassador became Diem's agent." (What the reporters thought were lies were often exactly what the mission genuinely believed, and was telling Washington. The mission itself was unaware of how badly the war was going.)

The American reporters in Saigon refused to be controlled. Halberstam observed: "Diem controlled his press, his military, his legislature; [General] Harkins his reporting channels, and [Ambassador] Nolting his. The only people who could be candid were the American reporters."

Kennedy considered the correspondents unprofessional because their stories varied so much from the official, more optimistic reports. He didn't want Americans to think that the United States was even at war in Vietnam, much less that Kennedy's policies were failing.[4]

Embarrassed by correspondents who exposed the fact that U.S. advisers engaged in combat, on February 21, 1962, Kennedy issued restrictive and naive guidelines to Saigon on how to manage press relations. The U.S. mission should cooperate with reporters to maintain their "good faith." Nonetheless, reporters should be restricted from seeing military operations that would result in "undesirable dispatches," such as civilians who became the "unfortunate victims" of the operations. What's more, reporters should be advised to avoid "frivolous, thoughtless criticism" of Diem.

Pierre Salinger accused Halberstam, Sheehan, and several other correspondents of being political activists rather than traditional reporters. "They were actively trying to bring down the government of President Diem, . . . [and] would go to any lengths to discredit him in the United States . . . If they wanted to bring down the government of President Diem, they should have gotten outside of the press and gone about it as lobbyists or activists."

Maxwell Taylor accused the reporters of abandoning "any pretense of impartial reporting," and Bundy, who had known Halberstam at Harvard, described him patronizingly as "a gifted boy who gets all steamed up."

Their reporting was inadequate in one critical respect, Neil Sheehan thought. The correspondents never challenged the basic assumption that a military victory could be won. "We didn't have a very long view of American foreign policy." They didn't see that what the United States was trying to accomplish "was going to end badly. But no American had that perspective."[5]

Kennedy invited John Mecklin, the counselor for public affairs at the U.S. embassy in Saigon, to meet with him at the White House on April 29, 1963. "Why are we having so much trouble with the reporters out there?" the President inquired. Kennedy listened intently while Mecklin explained his perspective.

The newsmen in Saigon compared favorably with newsmen elsewhere, Mecklin contended; they were just frustrated and angry at the U.S. mission and the Diem regime. More favorable coverage, or at least sympathetic understanding, would come if U.S. officials gave reporters more latitude and more truth. Washington agencies and the mission in Saigon should stop issuing "excessively optimistic public statements," stop complaining about unfavorable stories, and take the newsmen into their confidence, particularly about events the newsmen would find out about anyway. Kennedy appeared skeptical but willing to try a different approach.[6]

After the meeting, Salinger recalled, "the President told me he had been deeply impressed with Mecklin's recital—but at the same time he did not feel that any new press policy in Vietnam would, in the long run, be successful because of the highly conflicting interests of the government and the press there." Nevertheless, Kennedy authorized Salinger to draft a new press guideline and deliver it to Harkins and Nolting. The more lenient guideline granted leeway to correspondents, including "wherever possible taking American reporters in Saigon further into our confidence, particularly on matters which they are almost certain to learn about anyway." A severe political crisis in South Vietnam immediately put the more liberal policy to the test.[7]

In May 1963, without warning, events in South Vietnam suddenly careened out of control. For years the Catholic-dominated Diem government had discriminated against Buddhists. One decree placed legal restrictions on Buddhist associations but not on Catholic organizations. Catholics could display the Vatican flag, but Buddhists could not fly their own flag.

Pent-up frustration by Buddhists exploded on May 8, 1963. When Diem prohibited Buddhists from flying their religious flag on the anniversary of the Buddha's birth, more than a thousand Buddhist protesters gathered at the radio station in Hue demanding revocation of the order. After they refused to disperse, government troops opened fire, killing eight people. The following day ten thousand Buddhists showed up to renew the protest.

Diem's government refused to accept responsibility for the deaths, blaming Vietcong agents for stirring up the crowd. In a private review of the crisis, the CIA disagreed. "There is still no evidence that the Buddhist protest was the result of Communist inspiration or influence on the Buddhist hierarchy."[8]

The U.S. mission in Saigon, like everyone else, was surprised by the Buddhist protest. On orders from Washington, one member of the mission "applied direct, relentless, table-hammering pressure on Diem" to repair his relations with the Buddhists, accept responsibility for the killings, indemnify the victims' families, and apologize. But Diem remained adamant.

The Buddhist crisis irritated and bewildered Kennedy. "How could this have happened?" he demanded of aides. "Who are these people? Why didn't we know about them before?"

The United States was handicapped in trying to improve the situation because it didn't have much influence over Diem. The crisis rattled American officials. "Although the United States will inevitably share in the outcome of the dispute between Diem and the Buddhists," reported Neil Sheehan, "it finds itself in the impotent position of having the Diem regime refuse its advice on the Buddhist issue, just as it has on so many other issues in the past."[9]

International outrage against Diem's regime reached new intensity on June 11. To protest the government's discrimination, a seventy-three-year-old Buddhist monk knelt on a major intersection in Saigon. After a colleague doused him with gasoline, the monk lit a match and immolated himself in front of a large crowd which included newsmen and photographers. The poignant picture of the monk, engulfed in flames, appeared on front pages and television throughout the world. Thereafter the Buddhists adroitly used immolations, demonstrations, and public statements to generate extensive and sympathetic media coverage.

When questioned about the immolation of Buddhist monks, Madame Nhu responded, "I would clap hands at seeing another monk barbecue show." This and other tactless remarks made her a pariah in the United States; many times Kennedy urged his advisers to pressure Diem to send her and her husband abroad. Diem steadfastly refused, however, because he felt he needed them.[10]

The Buddhist crisis ultimately destroyed Diem's government and seriously complicated Kennedy's policy. *The New York Times* criticized the administration for poor use of the leverage it commanded in Saigon. "American officials have not expressed objections to Diem's actions and policies with either force or consistency."

The awkward position of the United States troubled many newspapers. "Our soldiers are supposed to be only advisers, even though they keep getting killed in action, and disagreements with the Vietnamese military authorities are not infrequent," stated *The Wall Street Journal*. The United States "must decide at some point soon whether a victory is possible, how long it is likely to take, what changes have to be made to bring it about; or, if it appears victory is not feasible, what the U.S. then proposes to do."

The Diem government's image in the United States was now beyond repair. Even if Diem "succeeds once more in staying in power temporarily," said the *Milwaukee Journal* in a common complaint, "he has lost all claim to any confidence in his word or his future by the U.S."[11]

In August Kennedy appointed his old foe Henry Cabot Lodge to replace Frederick Nolting as ambassador to South Vietnam. When Dean Rusk suggested Lodge for the post, Kennedy liked the idea. A Boston blue blood, Harvard educated, fluent in French, widely experienced, Lodge seemed perfect. "Because of his gilt-edged Republican credentials, Lodge might deflect some of the right-wing criticism of the administration," observed James Olson and Randy Roberts in their chronicle of the Vietnam War, *Where the Domino Fell*. O'Donnell also remembered that for Kennedy "the idea of getting Lodge mixed up in such a hopeless mess as the one in Vietnam was irresistible."

When JFK asked Lodge to be ambassador, the President held up Malcolm Browne's photo of the monk's fiery suicide and sadly remarked, "I suppose these are the worst press relations to be found in the world today."[12]

On August 21, Nhu's Special Forces ransacked pagodas and arrested more than fourteen hundred Buddhists in Saigon, Hue, and other cities. Americans were outraged. After the attack, Lodge, who had just arrived at his Saigon post, requested guidance from Washington. In the afternoon of Saturday, August 24, Roger Hilsman drafted and Averell Harriman approved instructions to the new ambassador. In the sharpest language the Kennedy administration had ever used with the Saigon government, the message said to give Diem one final chance to remove his brother Nhu; otherwise, it suggested, Lodge should encourage a coup: "U.S. government cannot tolerate situation in which power lies in Nhu's hands," read the cable. "Diem must be given chance to rid himself of Nhu and his coterie and replace him with best military and political personalities available. If in spite of all your efforts, Diem remains obdurate and refuses, then we must face the possibility that Diem himself cannot be preserved." Lodge should make clear to dissident South Vietnamese generals that the United States would provide them with "direct support in any interim period of breakdown of central government mechanism."

The President, who had spent the weekend on Cape Cod, cautiously told Forrestal, Harriman, and Hilsman that they could proceed with the message provided they secured the necessary clearances. As it happened, McNamara, McCone, and Taylor, all opponents of removing Diem, were out of town for the weekend. So Forrestal, Harriman, and Hilsman convinced underlings in Defense, the CIA, and in the office of the Joint Chiefs of Staff to sign off on the message.

Two days later, when Kennedy met with his major advisers, he found them in an uproar, furious that subordinates had implemented a major change in policy over a weekend when they were not consulted.

Taylor later described the small group as "anti-Diem activists" who acted to "perpetuate an egregious end run." McNamara, who later attributed much of the Vietnam disaster to the cable of August 24, worried that overthrowing Diem meant putting the future of South Vietnam in the hands of an unknown. Disturbed as well, Kennedy thought that the tactics of the dissident group had aggravated the divisions within his government.[13]

Tense White House meetings over the next few days produced the most irate exchanges heard in the Oval Office during the entire Kennedy administration. Rudy Abramson, Harriman's biographer, described one meeting:

> [Harriman] sailed into Nolting for being too cozy with Diem. And when the former ambassador tried to defend himself, Harriman snapped that he should keep his mouth shut because no one cared what he thought. With that, Kennedy curtly interrupted. He was fond of Nolting, and he told Harriman that the President, for one, was interested in hearing what Nolting had to say.

The cable itself did not explicitly call for a coup, and no coup occurred immediately afterward. Still, the bitter debate on the cable revealed to Kennedy "a policy-making process in disarray."

Despite the recriminations, nobody urged that the cable be recalled. As long as the Nhus were aboard, support for the Diem government was "impossible to contemplate," said George Ball. "It put America in an odious position quite inconsistent with the principle on which we had based our Vietnam intervention in the first place."

In subsequent messages Kennedy advised Lodge to proceed cautiously, but he confirmed the instructions of August 24. "Lodge was authorized to repeat to the generals assurances that the United States would not assist a coup but that it would support a new government that appeared to have a good chance of success," observed George Herring. "And [Lodge] was authorized, at his own discretion, to announce publicly a reduction in American aid to Diem, the signal the generals had requested as an indication of U.S. support."[14]

Worried about U.S. embarrassment if a coup failed, JFK wrote Lodge on August 29, "Until the very moment of the go signal for the operation by the Generals, I must reserve a contingent right to change course and reverse previous instructions. . . . I know from experience that failure is more destructive than an appearance of indecision." (The last remark was an unmistakable reference to the Bay of Pigs.) Lodge concurred.[15]

During the last week of August 1963, Halberstam's articles reached the front page of *The New York Times* almost every day. "By one count," said Prochnau, "the President made twelve separate attacks on him that week." The minutes of meetings reflected Kennedy's frustration: "The President observed that Mr. Halberstam of *The New York Times* is actually running a political campaign; that he is wholly unobjective. . . . He stated that it was essential that we not permit Halberstam to influence our actions." Moments later, he added: "[W]hen we move to eliminate this [Diem's] government, it should not be as a result of *New York Times* pressure." On the evening of September 11, Kennedy ordered that an instruction be sent to Lodge "to hush up the press in Saigon."

Briefly, in mid-September, the President was in a more tolerant mood. In a letter to Diem, he asked the South Vietnamese leader to try to understand the media: "The only way to correct this difficulty is to allow more and not less reporting by Americans in your country. If there is one principle upon which my people are united, by Constitutional commitment, conviction, and tradition, it is that the way to get at the truth is to let people see for themselves." The only way to deal with press criticism was to get on with the job, the President told major advisers on September 23. "The way to confound the press is to win the war."[16]

By October Kennedy was angry again. Without his customary adroitness

JOHNSTON PUBLIC LIBRARY
JOHNSTON, IOWA 50131

and subtlety, he took the extraordinary step of seeking Halberstam's removal from Vietnam. He broached the subject on October 22, 1963, during a private meeting with *Times* publisher Arthur Sulzberger at the White House.

"What do you think of your young man in Saigon?" Kennedy asked Sulzberger.

"We like him fine," Sulzberger replied, somewhat taken aback.

"You don't think he's too close to the story?" the President asked.

No, said Sulzberger, he did not.

"You weren't," suggested the President, "thinking of transferring him to Paris or Rome?"

Sulzberger and the *Times* held firm and kept Halberstam in South Vietnam.

In the end peers honored the three correspondents. In the 1963 awards for journalistic excellence, Malcolm Browne and Halberstam jointly won the Pulitzer Prize for international reporting. Halberstam, Browne, and Sheehan earned the Louis M. Lyons Award for conscience and integrity in journalism.[17]

On September 2, 1963, during a major television interview with Walter Cronkite of CBS, Kennedy warned the South Vietnamese to improve their reform efforts, but he still thought the United States must continue to help them win. "I don't think that unless a greater effort is made by the [South Vietnamese] government to win popular support that the war can be won out there. In the final analysis, it is their war. They are the ones who have to win it or lose it. We can help them, we can give them equipment, we can send our men out there as advisers, but they have to win it." In the past two months, he said, "the government has gotten out of touch with the people. . . . But I don't agree with those who say we should withdraw. That would be a great mistake. . . . .We . . . made this effort to defend Europe. Now Europe is quite secure. We also have to participate—we may not like it—in the defense of Asia."

At his news conference on September 12, 1963, reporters peppered Kennedy with tough questions. In view of the "prevailing confusion," was it possible to state what the U.S. policy was toward the government of South Vietnam? Could the United States carry out any significant changes in its policy toward South Vietnam so long as Ngo Dinh Nhu remained as Diem's top adviser? Another questioner wanted Kennedy to respond to critics' charges that he was "operating on the basis of inadequate information."[18]

In Saigon, Lodge quickly grew frustrated trying to converse with Diem, adding to the ambassador's inclination to support a coup. "[Diem] would simply look at the ceiling and talk about his childhood or talk about Vietnamese history and would absolutely refuse to discuss the matters with me that President Kennedy wanted me to discuss with him," Lodge recalled.

Policy differences over South Vietnam ran deeper than on any other foreign-policy issue in the Kennedy administration. On one side were Roger Hilsman, Averell Harriman, and George Ball, who believed that the Diem regime was unpopular and corrupt, making it impossible to make progress in the war. On the other side were those in the Pentagon and at the highest levels of the CIA, and hard-liners in the State Department, who thought Diem represented stability and a commitment to anticommunism. The balance tipped in favor of the anti-Diem group when Lodge replaced Nolting in late August.

The policy choices for Kennedy were maddeningly complex; decisions needed to be made based on inadequate or conflicting evidence. On September 10, 1963, after a brief visit to South Vietnam, Major General Victor Krulak reported to the President that Diem's political problems were "not great." His traveling partner, Joseph Mendenhall of the State Department, foresaw "a large-scale movement to the Viet Cong" unless Nhu was forced out. Kennedy stared at both of them and remarked, "Did you two gentlemen visit the same country?"[19]

At meeting after meeting in the fall, Kennedy and his advisers discussed options. Should the United States back the Vietnamese generals? How strong were the coup plotters? What would happen if the coup failed? What effect would a coup attempt have on the military effort against the Vietcong? What if the coup attempt resulted in a stalemate or a prolonged civil war? Should the United States evacuate Americans?

On October 2, 1963, after McNamara and Taylor returned from an inspection tour in South Vietnam, they reported that the "military campaign has made great progress and continues to progress," but doubted that "pressures exerted by the U.S. will move Diem and Nhu toward moderation."

Most important, they recommended that Vietnamese be trained to replace U.S. military advisers. It should be possible to withdraw the bulk of U.S. personnel by the end of 1965. "In accordance with the program to train progressively Vietnamese to take over military functions, the Defense Department should announce in the very near future presently prepared plans to withdraw 1000 U.S. military personnel by the end of 1963."[20]

At a White House staff meeting on October 7, Bundy expressed surprise that "some people" regarded the recommendation to withdraw a thousand troops as too optimistic. They were taking as "pollyanna-ish" the statement that the United States could pull out of Vietnam in two years. Notes of the meeting reported that

> [Bundy] said what struck him was that two years was really a long time, considering that by then the war would have lasted four years—or longer than most wars in U.S. history. . . . The general line will be that in two

years the Vietnamese will be able to finish the job without U.S. military forces on the scene—a position considered reasonable by everyone around the table.

Taylor and McNamara concluded that the best course was to apply "selective pressures" on Diem's government, including cuts in foreign aid. On October 5 Kennedy approved their specific recommendations to cut off funds to Nhu's Special Forces and suspend shipments of several products under the commodity import program.[21]

Finally, on the morning of November 1, a group of South Vietnamese generals and their forces attacked the presidential palace in Saigon. The following day the White House learned that Diem and Nhu had been captured and murdered.

Having given little thought to the inevitable violence of any coup, Kennedy hadn't expected Diem and Nhu to be killed. Everyone in a meeting watched in silence as Kennedy was informed of the murders. He "leaped to his feet and rushed from the room with a look of shock and dismay on his face which I had never seen before," Taylor recalled. "He had always insisted that Diem must never suffer more than exile and had been led to believe or had persuaded himself that a change in government could be carried out without bloodshed."

A few days later Kennedy wrote Lodge praising the ambassador's efforts and urging him to place "primary emphasis" on "effectiveness rather than upon external appearance." He hoped the new government could "limit confusion and intrigue among its members" and concentrate on winning the war.[22]

The coup turned out badly for the United States as a series of ineffective military strongmen assumed control in Saigon; but it might have been just as bad or worse if Diem had remained in power and continued to alienate groups in his country.

Beginning in 1956 and lasting to the day he died, John Kennedy's public remarks expressed nothing but determination to support the South Vietnamese government and to defeat the Communist insurgents. In public he never hinted that the United States should withdraw. "What helps to win the war, we support; what interferes with the war effort, we oppose," he stated in September 1963. "We have a very simple policy in [Vietnam]. . . . We want the war to be won, the Communists to be contained, and the Americans to go home. . . . But we are not there to see a war lost."

Some argue that these public statements were merely a smoke screen to conceal the President's real intentions. Roger Hilsman later stated that

Kennedy told him "over and over again" that Hilsman's job was to keep American involvement at a minimum, so that the United States could withdraw at the first opportunity. Charles Bartlett claimed that Kennedy frankly told him, "We don't have a prayer of staying in Vietnam. We don't have a prayer of prevailing there. Those people hate us." Kennedy added, "They are going to throw our tails out of there at almost any point. But I can't give up a piece of territory like that to the Communists and then get the American people to reelect me."[23]

No one can know for certain what policy Kennedy would have followed in Vietnam had he lived longer, but that hasn't stopped people from speculating. Clark Clifford, who knew both President Kennedy and President Johnson, noticed profound differences in their personalities and styles, and believed that Kennedy would never have allowed U.S. involvement to escalate the way Johnson did.

> I often saw President Johnson personalize the actions of the Vietcong, interpreting them as somehow aimed personally at him. He reacted by thinking, *They can't do this to Lyndon Johnson! They can't push me around this way!* On the other hand, I believe President Kennedy would have treated the attacks strictly as an international problem—not something aimed at him personally. In reacting to the same events, I believe he would have thought, *I don't like the looks of this. I don't like the smell of it. Sending more troops may just increase the costs—let's hold off for a while and see what happens. I'm not going to get us more deeply involved.*

Arthur Schlesinger Jr., Ken O'Donnell, and Ted Sorensen have all claimed that Kennedy would have avoided further involvement in Vietnam. Ted Sorensen mused that it was simply not Kennedy's nature "to stubbornly throw division after division into a bloody, worsening struggle without reexamining the balance between cost and gains."[24]

After-the-fact reminiscences, though, might be only wishful thinking to protect JFK's reputation. The timing of the recollections is suspect. In Arthur Schlesinger's *Robert Kennedy and His Times* (1978) and Sorensen's *The Kennedy Legacy* (1969), the argument is advanced that Kennedy would have withdrawn from South Vietnam. But in earlier books by Schlesinger and Sorensen, both published in 1965, when policymakers still hoped to win the war, neither even hinted that Kennedy contemplated withdrawal. "Recollections by underlings dedicated to affirming their boss's reputation, while not without value, are weak reeds upon which to build an argument," said one observer.[25]

The most intriguing recollection involved Kennedy's conversation with Senator Mike Mansfield, whose integrity and probity are unquestioned. In the spring of 1963, Mansfield criticized the U.S. involvement in the Vietnam War at a congressional leadership breakfast at the White House. Afterward, according to Ken O'Donnell, the President invited Mansfield to his office for a private talk. (O'Donnell listened to the conversation.) The President told the majority leader that he had come to agree with Mansfield on the need for the United States to withdraw. "But I can't do it until 1965—after I'm reelected," Kennedy said. If he announced a withdrawal before the 1964 election, conservatives would castigate him during his reelection campaign.

After Mansfield left the office, according to O'Donnell, the President said to his aide: "In 1965, I'll become one of the most unpopular Presidents in history. I'll be damned everywhere as a Communist appeaser. But I don't care. If I tried to pull out completely now from Vietnam, we would have another Joe McCarthy red scare on our hands, but I can do it after I'm reelected. So we had better make damned sure that I *am* reelected."

Subsequently Mansfield confirmed O'Donnell's primary recollection, but denied there was any discussion of the 1964 election. "The only thing discussed at that meeting . . . was the President's desire to bring about a withdrawal but recognizing that it could not be done precipitantly but only over a period of months. The election was not even mentioned."[26]

Complicating the picture are several top advisers who dispute the notion that Kennedy would have withdrawn from Vietnam. Secretary of State Dean Rusk, for example, has insisted that Kennedy never mentioned disengaging from the war. "I talked with John Kennedy on hundreds of occasions about Southeast Asia," Rusk wrote in his memoir, "and not once did he suggest or even hint at withdrawal."

What seems peculiar, historian Gregory Olson has perceptively observed, "is that the President never discussed his plans for Vietnam with his brother, Robert. The President depended on his brother's advice on foreign policy. If Kennedy had really committed to withdrawal after reelection, it seems likely that Robert would have known." Asked in 1964 whether his brother gave any consideration to pulling out of Vietnam, Robert Kennedy answered, "No." The Kennedy administration thought "we should win the war in Vietnam."[27]

Still, in John Kennedy's uncertainty about sending troops to Vietnam, like his rejection of hard-line advice during the Cuban missile crisis, he acted more judiciously than his major advisers. Perhaps he would have recognized that the costs of fighting in South Vietnam outweighed the possible benefits. In any case, he had made the commitment to Diem without much enthusiasm and with grave misgivings.[28]

42

CRISIS IN
THE THIRD WORLD

The Eisenhower administration frowned on anticolonial zeal in Africa, fearing the nationalist movements would lead to Communist subversion. Supporting nationalism would also embroil the United States in disputes with European NATO allies in conflict with their colonies—France in Algeria, Belgium in the Congo, and Portugal in Angola. Eisenhower endorsed "order and stability" in the African decolonization process. In effect, the policy didn't sympathize with African nationalism and underwrote Western colonialism.

In May 1959, after the Senate Foreign Relations Committee had appointed Senator Kennedy to chair the new subcommittee on Africa, he asked the assistance of his British Africanist friend, Barbara Ward. "If . . . you know of any material which I could read or you have any ideas which you feel deserve attention over here, I hope you will send them to me. In this area it is so difficult to get expert advice that any counsel from you will be doubly appreciated."[1]

During the 1960 election campaign Kennedy mentioned Africa nearly five hundred times. He indicted the Eisenhower administration for losing ground in Africa. "We have neglected and ignored the needs and aspirations of the African people," he charged. "The word is out—and spreading like wildfire in nearly a thousand languages and dialects—that it is no longer necessary to remain forever poor or forever in bondage."

After his election Kennedy wrote to his task force studying Third World countries, asking, "What special proposals should we make in the winter of '61 in regard to raising the educational level, the fight against disease and improving the available food supply?" He also wanted to get "more Negroes into the Foreign Service."

Shortly after his inauguration Kennedy dispatched G. Mennen Williams, the new assistant secretary of state for African affairs, to meet with African leaders. "He wanted . . . the Africans to know that we wanted friendship with them, wanted to recognize their independence and to be friendly with them," Williams recalled.

When Williams made the public statement "Africa for the Africans," the remark sparked a furor in European colonial capitals. When reporters queried Kennedy about the statement, he replied dryly, "I don't know who else Africa should be for."[2]

Kennedy named highly respected diplomats to difficult ambassadorial posts in Africa—Edmund Gullion (Congo), William Attwood (Guinea), and Edward Korry (Ethiopia). He instructed his ambassadors to African nations to "stay in close, keep working, and wait for the breaks." The fact that the ambassadors had his backing occasionally led to small gains, and in some cases to major breakthroughs. "Sékou Touré's sudden exit from the Soviet embrace in 1963 was possible because Kennedy's ambassador, William Attwood, had kept the American door open," noted historian Richard Mahoney.

Twenty-eight African heads of state passed through Kennedy's White House, and he corresponded occasionally with a half dozen African leaders. After an Oval Office visit, almost every African leader would say, "It is incredible how much he knows about Africa. How did he learn all of this?" Attwood thought Kennedy understood "what the non-aligned nations wanted . . . and was able to make the leaders of these new nations feel that he was interested in them."[3]

Kennedy was exceptionally informed about Sékou Touré, the president of Guinea. He knew that Touré descended from an emperor in West Africa and that he had been a leader in a labor union, and in joking with him about Soviet assistance, Kennedy showed a profound understanding of Guinea and its politics.

"Although he never visited Africa, Kennedy sent his brothers, Robert and Edward, his brother-in-law Sargent Shriver, and Vice-President Lyndon Johnson there on diplomatic missions to underscore the importance of that continent," noted James Giglio.[4]

A prominent African leader he dealt with was Kwame Nkrumah of

Ghana, who in 1957 had led his country to independence. "Nkrumah regarded himself as the tribune of Africa's unemancipated and as the chosen agent of 'pan-African union,'" observed Mahoney. At the time Kennedy assumed office, Nkrumah was angry at the West, and had openly cozied up to the Soviets.

Kennedy intended to win him back. Nkrumah wanted financial aid for the Volta project, a complex six-hundred-million-dollar electrification undertaking debated for almost fifty years. The project envisioned a 2,100-foot-long earthen dam, a 3,275-square-mile lake, and a one-hundred-thousand-ton aluminum smelter. The smelter would purchase a large share of the electrical power, making the project economically viable. "We have to modernize," said Nkrumah. "Either we shall do so with the interest and support of the West or we shall be compelled to turn elsewhere," a veiled reference to the Soviet Union.

Kennedy's persistence kept Nkrumah neutral enough to justify the United States in helping to finance—with restrictions—the Volta project. "We have put quite a few chips on a very dark horse, indeed, but I believe the gamble is worthwhile," Kennedy wrote Barbara Ward after approving assistance for the project.[5]

The Angolan independence movement embroiled Kennedy with a NATO ally. In the late 1950s, while he chaired the African subcommittee of the Senate Foreign Relations Committee, African nationalist leaders called on him in Washington to plead their case after official protocol ignored them. One of them was Holden Roberto, leader of a large nationalist group in Angola. "I had been moved by his speech about Algeria," said Roberto. "It was a courageous stance. I talked to Kennedy for two hours about the nature of our fight in Angola." Sympathetic, Kennedy told him the United States should oppose the Portuguese regime that enslaved native Angolans. They also agreed that it was necessary to prevent Communists from controlling the Angolan liberation movement.

The Angolan nationalist revolt was one of several African conflicts that caused deep division in the United States after Kennedy became President. Africa was facing a whirlwind of nationalism. In 1960 eighteen colonies declared their independence. Unlike most European leaders, though, Portugal's Dr. Antonio de Oliveira Salazar, the nation's seventy-two-year-old autocrat, had no intention of granting independence to his country's colony in Angola. The first Europeans to colonize Africa four hundred years earlier, the Portuguese proudly proclaimed they had civilized the native Angolans. Rejecting democracy, Salazar didn't believe Angola's black population was capable of self-rule. In his view Angolan nationalism merely disguised the spread of communism.

After nationalist violence erupted in Angola early in 1961, Portuguese soldiers savagely slaughtered rebels and civilians. "Portuguese repression in Angola is even bloodier than has come to light," Dean Rusk reported. Yet Salazar expected his NATO partner, the United States, to be supportive. Surely the United States would abstain if the United Nations condemned Portugal.[6]

But as early as 1956 Senator Kennedy had urged that the United States "no longer abstain in the UN from voting on colonial issues"; it should stop trying "to prevent subjugated peoples from being heard." On the Angolan issue President Kennedy courageously detached himself from the African policies of his European allies. On March 15, 1961, the American delegation to the United Nations, joined by the Soviet Union and African and Asian nations, voted to condemn Portuguese policy in Angola. U.S. allies Great Britain and France abstained. In early June the United States again joined with the Soviet Union—Britain and France again abstaining—in demanding that Portugal end its repression in Angola. Salazar protested that American support for these resolutions fostered "communist revolution" in Angola; in Lisbon anti-American demonstrators stormed the U.S. embassy.

The Angolan issue split the Kennedy administration. General Maxwell Taylor, CIA director John McCone, Dean Rusk, Europeanists in the State Department, and the entire Defense Department urged assistance to Portugal in its war with the Angolan nationalists. They stressed Portugal's link to NATO, and warned of Communist influence in the rebel forces. "The Portuguese are allies and friends," pleaded Dean Acheson. "They have made available to us and NATO important military advantages. It is important that we play fair with them."[7]

Africanists in the State Department and American blacks focused on Portugal's brutal repression and endorsed independence. For them the U.S. alliance with Portugal was a moral embarrassment. Kennedy's friend Barbara Ward warned him that the "assumed" NATO support for Portugal seriously weakened Western influence in Africa. "The Communists, of course, are busy with the theme that the West doesn't give a damn about the massacre of Africans."

Besides supporting the UN resolutions, Kennedy slashed military aid to Portugal from twenty-five million dollars to three million. He approved a program that brought Angolan exiles to the United States and provided them with college educations. In July 1961, he authorized one million dollars for emergency medical and nutritional relief to Angolan refugees. The cost was slight, but the effort was highly successful.[8]

However, Salazar had one terrific trump card: the U.S. lease of the military base on the Portuguese-owned Azores. The Azores, nine islands in the North Atlantic, eight-hundred miles off the coast of Portugal, were critically important for U.S. dominance of the Atlantic. In 1951, Portugal had signed a defense treaty with the United States granting the Americans use of the La-jes base on the Azores, and the two countries had renewed the agreement in 1957. (Instead of paying rent, the United States granted military aid to Portugal in order for the country to play a strong role in NATO.) The United States used the base to shuttle troops and supplies to Lebanon in 1958 and to Berlin in 1961. The Joint Chiefs of Staff considered the Azores critical for military emergencies in Europe and the Middle East. Salazar now threatened to exact revenge and not renew the lease when it expired on December 31, 1962.

Fear of losing the base forced Kennedy to waver. In 1962 he ordered the United States to abstain on two UN resolutions involving Portugal. To lower the U.S. profile on the Angolan problem, Kennedy told Stevenson "to sit back and let others take the lead." John Kenneth Galbraith protested the change in policy: "We are trading in our African policy for a few acres of asphalt in the Atlantic." "Only the fear of not having the Azores agreement renewed moderated the New Frontier's sympathy with anticolonialist policy," recalled Pedro Pereira, Portugal's ambassador to the United States.[9]

What appeared to be a turn toward moderation, however, was actually a case of Kennedy biding his time. He never abandoned his goal of freeing Angola from Portugal's brutal control. Needing European support for the nuclear test ban treaty, Kennedy waited until it was nearly signed in Moscow. Then in late July 1963, he wrote confidentially to Robert McNamara: "I think we should develop a contingency for the loss of the Azores base." He would give up the base rather than permit Portugal to dictate his policy toward Angola. In August, when he sent George Ball as his emissary to Salazar, he instructed Ball not to link Angola and the Azores.

Despite a period of silence and moderation, Kennedy did more for Angolan independence than past or future Presidents. He succeeded in identifying nationalism as the "central reality of his age," Mahoney concluded. "Whatever failures existed were rooted in the dichotomy of the Cold War, which made it virtually impossible for the United States always to overturn past policies," noted James Giglio.[10]

The crisis in the Congo was a complicated challenge for the President. On June 30, 1960, Belgium granted independence to the Republic of the Congo. A period of chaos followed. In July, Moise Tshombe, primarily backed by Belgian mining interests, declared the independence of the mineral-rich Katanga Province. The UN authorized a military force, made up mostly of Africans, to reunite the country, and Kennedy supported the UN's action.

The anticommunist, pro–Western Tshombe won the support of many Europeans who eagerly sought Katanga's copper and cobalt. Tshombe had powerful white defenders in the United States as well. The American religious right, Southern congressmen, and Senators Thomas Dodd and Barry

Goldwater endorsed Tshombe, complicating Kennedy's ability to find a solution. What's more, the issue divided the State Department, with the pro-Tshombe European Bureau contending with the anti-Tshombe African Bureau.

"Though black himself, Tshombe's close ties to Belgium and especially his hiring of white mercenaries—including hated South Africans and Rhodesians—to preserve his control of an independent Katanga framed the Congo crisis in racial terms," observed writer Thomas Borstelmann. Africans, African-Americans, and antiracists everywhere condemned Tshombe as a stooge of the white Belgian mining interests.[11]

Breaking with Eisenhower's policy, Kennedy opposed Katangan separatism and chastised Tshombe as the Congo's "most determined agitator of racism." The power struggle in the Congo also created an opportunity for the Soviets to gain a foothold in the heart of Africa. While opposing Tshombe, Kennedy worried about a Communist takeover. He didn't want to get rid of a "Congolese Batista to facilitate the rise of another Castro."

"Kennedy feared that the further he traveled into the Congo, the more treacherous would be his path of extrication and the more the U.S. would become part of the problem instead of part of the solution," noted Mahoney. He rejected the proposals by the State Department and the Joint Chiefs of Staff to intervene with U.S. military forces. Agreeing with Adlai Stevenson's statement, Kennedy said that "the only way to keep the Cold War *out* of the Congo was to keep the UN *in* the Congo."

For two years Kennedy stuck with the UN. In 1963 its forces finally overran Katanga and forced Tshombe to surrender. Despite the complexity of the operation, the UN had won a huge victory. So did Kennedy. Afterward, he wrote personal letters of thanks to his aides who had persevered in working on the crisis. The task had been "extraordinarily difficult," he wrote the State Department's George McGhee, and now everyone was entitled to "a little sense of pride."

In the Congo crisis Kennedy achieved his goal by restraining his use of power. His approach avoided a superpower showdown and allowed the UN to maintain peace. "The President made containment in the Congo what it never was in Vietnam—a workable and constructive policy that was fundamentally in consonance with nationalist reality," observed Mahoney.[12]

In Latin America, Kennedy faced another difficult challenge. Animosity against the United States had peaked in 1958 when Vice President Richard Nixon received a rude, hostile reception there during his visit. Latin Americans often viewed the United States as a bully that didn't care about their social and economic well-being and that supported right-wing dictatorships.

Early in 1961, before the Bay of Pigs debacle, Kennedy discussed his idealistic goals for Latin America with Richard Goodwin.

I'd like to get a major statement on our Latin American policy soon. Next to Berlin it's the most critical area, and will be for a long time. The whole place could blow up on us. . . . We can't embrace every tinhorn dictator who tells us he's anticommunist while he's sitting on the necks of his own people. And the United States government is not the representative of private business. Do you know in Chile the American copper companies control about eighty percent of all the foreign exchange? We wouldn't stand for that here. And there's no reason they should stand for it. All those people want is a chance for a decent life, and we've let them think that we're on the side of those who are holding them down. There's a revolution going on down there, and I want to be on the right side of it. Hell, we are on the right side. But we have to let them know it, that things have changed.

Kennedy said he was willing to make a "big commitment."[13]

In a stirring speech on March 13, 1961, Kennedy pledged that the United States would lead a "vast cooperative effort, unparalleled in magnitude and nobility of purpose, to satisfy the basic needs of Latin American people for homes, work and land, health, and schools." He named the new effort the Alliance for Progress. No American President had ever proclaimed such lofty goals for the region. Kennedy studied Latin American issues and problems, consulted with aides, and welcomed scores of Latin American visitors to the White House. He was "an informed, intelligent leader who treated Latin Americans with dignity," noted historian Stephen Rabe.

Initially, optimism permeated the alliance programs. Progress was made in improving education, public health, and economic conditions; hospitals, roads, schools, low-income housing, and power plants were built. Venezuela, Chile, and Peru seriously attempted to improve social justice and democracy.

Latin America responded enthusiastically to the Catholic President's charisma, and to his elegant Spanish-speaking wife. But there was more. He "cared about the poor of Latin America and vowed to fulfill their yearnings for economic progress, social change, and democracy," Rabe observed.[14]

Overall, though, the alliance didn't succeed. There were multiple reasons for its failure. Kennedy conceived the program too hastily. "If anyone had any really detailed view of it, I don't know who it was," said Adolf Berle, who chaired Kennedy's postelection task force on Latin America. The alliance was also thwarted by the huge population explosion in Latin America, which impeded the effort to improve the region's annual per capita economic growth rate. In addition, Congress appropriated a billion dollars in aid for the alliance's first year, but the amount was far too small to alleviate the region's problems. Some of the funds Congress did appropriate stayed in the United States to defray Latin American debts. "The administration also insisted that some of the money be used to purchase United States commodities at United States prices," noted James Giglio.

There were also organizational and bureaucratic problems. "It is increasingly disappointing that a program which is sound in conception and historically right is operating at about one-half effectiveness," Goodwin complained to the President in September 1963. Goodwin placed major blame on the poor quality of the U.S. government's bureaucracy—the "complete lack of a good recruiting effort, impossible personnel procedures, a structure which discourages individual initiative and responsibility, a careerist mentality, and inability to recognize mediocrity when it is seen."[15]

Many Latin American government officials were content with the status quo; they welcomed U.S. financial aid but rejected social and economic reforms. Latin American rightists, protecting their vested interests, contended that the alliance was utopian and unrealistic; Marxist groups condemned it as imperialistic and worthless. Only a few Latin American countries engaged in significant agrarian reform, and major changes in the tax system never emerged.

Kennedy completely reversed his critical view of the influence of private business in Latin America. "I have received some complaints about the new land reform law in Honduras," he wrote the State Department's Edwin Martin on October 2, 1962. "It is alleged that this will adversely affect the American interests and that one of the justifications of its passage was the Alliance for Progress." In his reply, Martin assured the President that the United States was pressuring Honduran officials to "not adversely affect the legitimate interests of the present property owners, including United States corporations."[16]

As much as anything, Kennedy's growing obsession with Cuba undermined the idealistic goals of the Alliance for Progress. Often Kennedy and his advisers chose "security and stability over change and development," Rabe observed. "Their fear of Castro and communism tempered their zeal for democracy and reform." Kennedy judged Latin American leaders by the policy they adopted toward Castro, and by their willingness to sponsor anti-Castro resolutions at international gatherings.

On July 10, 1961, when Kennedy queried Robert Woodward, assistant secretary of state for inter-American affairs, he worried about evidence of Communist activity or "Castro activities" in the Dominican Republic. "We don't want to have another Cuba to come out of the Dominican Republic." If the United States "could not have a democracy with some hope of survival," the President continued, "I would rather continue the present situation than to have a Castro dictatorship. That is our policy and we want to make sure that in attempting to secure democracy we don't end up with a Castro-communist island."

A month later Kennedy urged Richard Goodwin to increase anticommunist activity in Latin America. "It is going to become increasingly difficult to get the money from Congress unless we can find some interest on the part of other Latin American countries to do something about Communism."[17]

In 1963, after coups brought right-wing, anticommunist dictatorships to power in Argentina, Guatemala, and the Dominican Republic, the Kennedy administration quietly resigned itself to the coups, and the new military governments continued to receive U.S. financial aid. Theodore Sorensen later wrote that Kennedy learned "that the military often represented more competence in administration and more sympathy with the U.S. than any other group."

"The Castro bogey also caused the administration to increase military aid to Latin America by 50 percent and to create an Office of Public Safety in AID to train Latino police officers in mob control and counterinsurgency," noted Giglio.

By November 1963, Kennedy knew that the alliance was failing. The economic numbers were dismal. He admitted that he had underestimated the degree of social and economic problems in the region.

The administration could boast that it had allowed no new Castros to emerge in Latin America, but it had also failed to prevent the rise of new dictatorships. Communism was stymied, but so was democracy. "What survived was as much a military as an economic aid program," wrote Giglio. "Kennedy had devoted too much attention to Castro and not enough time to the Alliance's lofty goals."[18]

Kennedy's Middle East policy was more innovative than critics have contended. His policy is "hard to square with the revisionist portrait of Kennedy as an inflexible cold warrior," said Warren Bass in his book, *Support Any Friend* (2003). At the end of the Eisenhower Administration Washington's Middle East policy was in shambles. Pro-Western Middle East defense organizations had collapsed; the Soviet Union had successfully entrenched itself in the Arab world; and American-Israeli relations were strained.

During Kennedy's presidency, Arab-Israeli tension simmered in the background. A Mideast war preceded Kennedy's election (the Sinai War in 1956) and war followed Kennedy's death (the Six-Day War in 1967). Preoccupied with Berlin, the Soviets, the Congo, Cuba, Laos, and South Vietnam, Kennedy had little time to focus on the Middle East. Nonetheless, he kept himself remarkably informed about the region, and encouraged a series of steps to put the Middle East on the road to peace. Trying to be evenhanded in his approach, he strengthened ties with Israel while he sought to befriend Egypt and accept the legitimacy of Arab nationalism.

Kennedy was the most informed person in his administration about the Middle East, devouring news stories, books and articles, intelligence reports, and the State Department's daily summaries. "He literally knew more about the matter than the Secretary of State," said Robert Komer, Middle East specialist on the National Security Council.

The more Israel and its Arab neighbors met and worked together, Kennedy believed, the more likely it was that they would take small steps toward peace. He encouraged Israeli participation with Arab countries in international organizations. "For instance," Myer Feldman observed of Kennedy's small-step approach, "with the international Atomic Energy Commission on which both Israelis and Arabs sat, [the United States should] see to it that they both were on the same committees."[19]

Kennedy inherited a State Department that was critical of Israel and sympathetic to Arab views and feelings. The State Department wanted Israel to absorb several hundred thousand Arab refugees. Herbert Druks stated that the "State Department officials were opposed to Israel's strong retaliatory measures against Arab infiltrators and terrorists; they opposed Israel's divergence of the Jordan River waters for its own agricultural programs; and they did not support Israel's desire to make Jerusalem the capital of Israel. Perhaps most of all they did not wish to see Israel become stronger militarily."[20]

In contrast, Kennedy, the son of an anti-Semite, had been an outspoken and early supporter of Israel. Throughout his career in the House and Senate he had been sensitive to Israel's security needs. His belief in America's moral commitment to Israel endeared him to Jewish voters in the United States. When Kennedy asked Myer Feldman, who was Jewish, to be the point man on Middle Eastern affairs, Feldman replied that he had an "emotional bias" in favor of Israel. Kennedy replied, "So do I. That's why I want you on the job." But he added that "I want all points of view fairly and forcefully represented."

Kennedy was the first American President to sell arms to Israel and to declare that the United States would guarantee Israel's security. In May 1961, he told Israeli prime minister David Ben-Gurion, "I was elected by the Jews. . . . I have to do something for them." He informed Israeli foreign minister Golda Meir in December 1962 that the United States had a "special relationship" with Israel comparable only to that which it had with Britain. Still, he informed her that he intended to cultivate friendships with Arab countries. If the United States "pulled out of the Arab Middle East and maintained our ties only with Israel this would not be in Israel's interest."[21]

That Myer Feldman was Jewish and strongly backed Israel was well known in the White House and the State Department and occasionally resented. "Mike Feldman played the role of lawyer for the Israelis," Komer candidly stated. "Feldman went too far in trying to change the balance of foreign policy efforts because of domestic political considerations," claimed State Department official Phillips Talbot. "[Feldman's] major interest was Israel rather than the United States," agreed Robert Kennedy. "But. . . . he did an awful lot of valuable, helpful, worthwhile work."

In turn, Feldman privately chastised State Department officials he thought were pro-Arab. "They'd send papers to the White House all the time saying our policy ought to be shifted toward the Arabs because the Arabs could do so much for us. Morality apparently didn't play much of a part in their thinking."[22]

In August 1962, Kennedy decided to sell a key weapons system to Israel. Eisenhower had refused to supply Israel with critical equipment to offset the military improvement of Israel's enemies. Kennedy thought that Israel needed American military aid in order to survive. The Hawk, a ground-to-air missile, was a defensive weapon designed to protect Israeli airfields. Until the deal Israel had never received weapons from the United States. On September 13, 1962, Kennedy met with twenty American Jews and announced the Hawk missile sale, occasioning a spontaneous cheering ovation. As Herbert Druks has noted, Kennedy believed that "it would be easier to live with an Israel that was getting weapons and was secure than an Israel that might undertake unpredictable adventures such as the 1956 Sinai War. Israel might even become an effective arm against Soviet expansionist ambitions."

Kennedy tried to revive the United Nations plan to solve the Palestinian refugee problem. "Here was the President's furthest-reaching scheme," noted one authority, "offering the refugees the choice between repatriation to Israel or compensation for lost property, with the understanding that the overwhelming majority would opt for the latter."

Kennedy's "special relationship" with the Israelis and his decision to sell them Hawk missiles did not give him leverage to change Israeli policy. He couldn't convince Israeli officials to begin even a modest repatriation plan. "State feels as I do that [Ben-Gurion's] conditional 'yes' on refugees is in fact a flat 'no,'" Komer wrote the President on January 23, 1963. "By making Israeli agreement to a refugee plan conditional upon prior working out of *a total, final solution which must be firmly accepted beforehand by the Arabs*, BG has posed impossible conditions."[23]

With time, Kennedy's Middle East policies became more nuanced. In the summer of 1962, Kennedy questioned the wisdom of his own policy: "Why isn't the status quo more preferable for both the Israelis and the Arabs?" After all, the U.S. paid the bill for the refugees, "and there is no compromise of principle." Two weeks later he asked: "Isn't one group going to be horribly disappointed—either the Israelis by a lot more than one out of ten [refugees] coming back, or by the Arabs when only one out of ten wants to go back? Isn't it going to blow up . . . ?"[24]

Kennedy vigorously expressed his personal concerns to Israel about nuclear proliferation in the Middle East. Israel claimed that it's nuclear reactor at Dimona was for peaceful purposes, but Kennedy remained suspicious.

Kennedy kept pressing Israel on the Dimona issue. He insisted on unannounced, unrestricted inspections by foreign experts, but Ben-Gurion resisted. Nuclear proliferation was one of Kennedy's top priorities, and couldn't be handled gently. "If Israel had to be pressed hard so that the United States could keep a watchful eye on a suspiciously constructed, dangerously located, and evasively concealed nuclear reactor, then Israel had to be pressed hard," said Bass. "To be sure, Kennedy failed to stop the weapons program at Dimona. But the intensity with which he pushed in 1963 suggests that he would probably have assertively revisited the issue."[25]

Kennedy hoped to channel Arab nationalism in constructive ways, to convince Gamal Abdel Nasser to stress Egyptian internal development instead of fomenting revolutions. Beginning in September 1962, however, a conflict in Yemen soured U.S. relations with Nasser.

Following the overthrow of King Farouk in 1952, Nasser seized power and became the dynamic leader of Egypt and a symbol of Arab nationalism. Since 1955 Nasser had been condemning Israel and his oil-rich conservative Arab rivals, and had accepted $600 million in military assistance from Soviet-bloc countries.

Nevertheless, Kennedy wanted Bundy and Komer to reappraise U.S. relations with Nasser and Arab countries. "We intend to pursue a reasonably balanced policy in the area," JFK told Komer in May 1961. "We want to work with the Middle East countries so they control their own destinies." To ostracize Nasser would be "an open invitation to the Soviet Union to exploit discontent and hunger" throughout the Third World. He viewed Nasser as an energetic young nationalist leader whom he might be able to sway with aid, quiet diplomacy, and a personal relationship.[26]

To improve ties with Nasser, Kennedy named John Badeau, the former president of the American University in Cairo, as the new United States ambassador to the United Arab Republic. An excellent choice, Badeau was fluent in Arabic, understood the Islamic world, and already knew high-ranking Egyptian officials. Badeau appreciated Kennedy's deep interest and probing questions about Egypt. "This made you feel that he had been following the situation, that he knew what he was talking about and he expected you to know what you were talking about."

Kennedy conducted a candid and warm personal correspondence with Nasser, writing him over a dozen letters. The correspondence addressed current issues and problems, and frankly stated the American position. "They were never condescending or peremptory," said Badeau. "To an unusual degree, President Kennedy was sensitive to the political problems faced by Arab leaders."

"I want to be certain that you and other Arab leaders have no misunderstanding of our attitude towards the Arab people," he wrote Nasser as he praised the Egyptian leader's dedication and statesmanship. Nasser responded by thanking Kennedy for his "appreciation of the problems of the countries aspiring to progress," and asserted that "mutual understanding will keep those differences between limits that will not be exceeded." Once, after an aide had drafted a letter to Nasser, Kennedy expressed strong disapproval. It needed to be more precise. "This will not do at all," he said. "I've got something very direct and slightly unpleasant to say to Nasser in the first paragraph. You didn't say it. You pussyfooted about it. . . . The second paragraph sounds like the end of a treaty. This isn't a treaty. This is a personal letter. Now, take this draft."[27]

When the State Department objected to his personal correspondence with Nasser, Kennedy explained: "Nasser's got his problems. I've got my problems. I'm not going to persuade him to act against his interests. I won't even try. But it can't hurt down the line if we understand each other a little better."

After the decision to sell the Hawk missile to Israel, Kennedy sent a special emissary to Cairo to inform Nasser. "There was no publicity given this at all," Badeau recalled. "This was done not to justify [the sale] or to argue about it, but simply because the President did not want him taken by surprise, realizing it would create a political problem for him." Nasser wasn't pleased, but replied, "I do appreciate the fact that I know what's going to happen." Kennedy's consultation with Nasser on the sensitive issue seemed effective. "We never had any trouble with the Egyptian government about it," said Badeau. Kennedy used his personal touch on other occasions as well, informing Nasser in advance when the United States decided to resume nuclear testing.[28]

American economic assistance to Egypt ballooned to $500 million. Washington planned a state visit for Nasser "complete with White House banquets and a coast-to-coast helicopter tour."

"We've made a score on relations with the key guy in the Arab world," an internal National Security Council memo proclaimed. "Let's keep nurturing it."

But events in tiny Yemen ruined Kennedy's promising new relationship with Nasser. Located at the mouth of the Red Sea and bordering on Saudi Arabia, Yemen was ruled by the aging Imam Ahmad. In September 1962 Ahmad died, and his son, Muhammad al-Badr, succeeded him. A week later

Colonel Abdullah Sallal, a young nationalist, overthrew al–Badr. The coup became an international crisis when Saudi leaders, fearing a successful revolution in Yemen might ignite a Nasserite revolt in their own country, funneled military supplies to al–Badr guerrilla forces. Nasser countered by endorsing Sallal and dispatching an expeditionary force of seventy thousand Egyptian troops to Yemen. As events escalated, the Yemeni conflict turned into a proxy war between radical and conservative Arabs.[29]

When Nasser resumed his fiery speeches condemning the United States, the "speeches made it politically difficult for us to maintain the support of the Congress for aid programs to Egypt," said Dean Rusk. In the end Kennedy's search for a rapprochement with Egypt failed. Nasser's shrill anti-American rhetoric alienated Congress, and when Nasser's military forces bombed royalist guerrilla camps inside Saudi Arabia, Kennedy grew more disenchanted.[30]

America's strong ties to Israel handicapped Kennedy's ability to persuade Arab countries to join the Western camp. "Our lack of leverage on the Israelis, more than anything else, made it impossible to achieve any kind of Arab-Israeli settlement," concluded Robert Komer.

Although too optimistic, Kennedy's Middle East policy was generally enlightened. "Kennedy came as close as any president during the past forty years to solving the riddle of American relations with the Arab world," said historian Douglas Little. Warren Bass agreed, saying that Kennedy's interventions in Middle East discussions were consistently "crisp, savvy, and skillful." His "raw talent, agility, and policy mastery remain impressive."[31]

Although sometimes superficial or flawed in execution, the Peace Corps, the Alliance for Progress, and Kennedy's endorsement of Third World aspirations gave U.S. foreign policy "a tinge of democratic altruism it had lacked under Eisenhower," in the words of Alonzo Hamby. "He made the Cold War seem a progressive crusade." His speeches, and the way he described his foreign policy, said another historian, "offered a vision of America that seemed to restore it to its historic position as the exemplary nation, a model for those countries that would aspire to liberty and wealth."[32]

43

❦

SEARCHING FOR
PEACE

On the first leg of his European trip in June 1963, President Kennedy's reception in West Germany was, in the words of *Time*, "almost beyond the bounds of reality." Huge crowds chanted "Ken-ah-*dee*! Ken-ah-*dee*! Ken-ah-*dee*!" Hundreds of thousands of hand-held flags fluttered in the air. "Women broke through the barricades, children grabbed for the President's coat, people threw torrents of flowers," *Time* reported.

Kennedy grew somber as he approached the Berlin wall. Mounting a platform at the Brandenburg Gate, he stared at the "stark, grey, Communist city." After viewing East Berlin from another site, Kennedy stepped down from the platform looking "like a man who had just had a glimpse of Hell."[1]

Kennedy normally avoided crowd-baiting, demagogic speeches, but on this day, as Michael Beschloss said, his "juices were flowing from the most responsive audience of his life, his admiration for the West Berliners' bravery, his eagerness to reassure them that he would not sell them down the river to Khrushchev as part of a détente." With his back to the Berlin wall, addressing a crowd of 150,000, Kennedy defined the difference between the Communist and the free worlds:

> There are many people in the world who really don't understand, or say they don't, what is the great issue between the Free World and the Communist world. *Let them come to Berlin.* There are some who say that communism is the wave of the future. *Let them come to Berlin.* . . . And there are some who say in Europe and elsewhere we can work with the Communists. *Let them come to Berlin.* And there are even a few who say that it is true that communism is an evil system, but it permits us to make economic progress. "Lass' sie nach Berlin kommen." *Let them come to Berlin!*
>
> Freedom has many difficulties and democracy is not perfect, but we have never had to put a wall up to keep our people in, to prevent them from leaving us. . . .
>
> All free men, wherever they may live, are citizens of Berlin, and, therefore, as a free man, I take pride in the words "Ich bin ein Berliner."

His powerful address exposed the dangers of spontaneous speeches on foreign policy. "He sounded as though he were rallying opposition to the very kind of collaboration with the Soviets he was then seeking on the Test Ban Treaty and other matters," noted Sorensen. In his next stop Kennedy toned down his rhetoric and called for the great powers to work together.

Still, it was a great day. Afterward Kennedy told Sorensen, "We'll never have another day like this one as long as we live." Actually, the next few days were also great days, a respite from the constant pressure.[2]

Before the trip, while Ken O'Donnell talked with the President about the travel plans, Kennedy told him, "I've decided that I want to go to Ireland, too."

"Ireland?" O'Donnell said. "Mr. President, may I say something? There's no reason for you to go to Ireland. It would be a waste of time. It wouldn't do you much good politically. You've got all the Irish votes in this country that you'll ever get. If you go to Ireland, people will say it's just a pleasure trip."

"That's exactly what I want, a pleasure trip to Ireland," Kennedy replied.

O'Donnell, not convinced, asked Bundy's advice. The resident expert on foreign affairs agreed that there was nothing to gain from just a sentimental visit. The next day O'Donnell informed the President of Bundy's judgment.

"Kenny, let me remind you of something," Kennedy said impatiently. "I am the President of the United States, not you. When I say I want to go to Ireland, it means that I'm going to Ireland. Make the arrangements."[3]

The trip would be personal and have nothing to do with foreign policy except to foster goodwill. Before the visit the President reviewed the genealogy of the Kennedys and the Fitzgeralds, and reexamined Irish history, literature, and poetry. He had always been inspired by Irish poetry and literature and its stories of tragedy and desperate courage. One passage of Irish verse that fascinated him he often quoted: "War battered dogs are we, gnawing a naked bone, fighting in every land and clime, for every cause but our own."

After setting the dates of the President's visit to Ireland, Thomas Kiernan, Ireland's ambassador to the United States, hoped Kennedy could "come and have a comfortable rest." But resting was not Kennedy's intention. "I don't want to rest in Ireland," he told Kiernan. "I want to go around and meet people. I want to meet plenty of people. I don't want to stay in Dublin. I don't want too many official receptions. I don't want any of the stuff shirt arrangements, if I can avoid it. . . . The more I can cover, the better it will be. That's what I call a rest."

Dublin burst with Gaelic pride when Kennedy arrived. "Men were holding small children above their heads to get a look at the President, women were screaming, 'Bless you!' and everybody seemed to have tears in their eyes," O'Donnell wrote. The President stayed at the elegant American embassy for three nights. Each day he eagerly sought new adventures.[4]

On the first morning he visited Dunganstown and the old Kennedy homestead. The President's third cousin Mary Ryan, her family, and cousins from miles around greeted him. "Cousin Jack came here like an ordinary member of the family," Mary Ryan later said. "He crouched at the fire and blew the bellows. He asked everything about the family and the farm."

The Ryans had set up tables with white linen tablecloths and served sandwiches, cold salmon, and tea. Kennedy raised his teacup and toasted "all the Kennedys who went and all the Kennedys who stayed." In his parting words the President told Mary Ryan that the next time he would bring Jackie and the children. As the President left, he kissed Mary on her cheek. Eunice and Jean, who accompanied their brother, were shocked; he seldom displayed such public affection.

He asked questions about the people he met, the landmarks he viewed, and the remarks he heard. "He wanted an explanation of everything," said Sean Lemass, Ireland's prime minister. "He was asking questions from an intense and lively interest." But he pointedly made no mention of the touchy issue of the island's partition.[5]

Relaxed, playful, and witty, Kennedy announced that in 1968 he would support whichever Democratic candidate promised to appoint him ambassador to Ireland. He introduced people in his entourage who had Irish ancestors, among them Monsignor Michael O'Mahoney, "the pastor of a poor, humble flock in Palm Beach, Florida." Everyone roared.

The Bunratty Singers, in fifteenth-century costumes, sang Irish songs. While the President listened, he whispered to Dave Powers, "Ask them to sing 'Danny Boy.'" As the Irish girls sang the song, the President joined in the singing. Another group enchanted the President with one of his favorite Irish tunes: "We are the boys of Wexford, who fought with heart and hand to burst in twain the galling chain and free our native land." As he listened to still another singing group, he "had the sweetest and saddest kind of look on his face," said Kennedy's friend James Reed. "He was standing by himself, leaning against the doorway, and just seemed transported into a world of imagination."[6]

He dotted his speeches with wit, graceful literary quotations, and acclaim for Ireland's courageous past, its literary and artistic genius, and its contributions to America. On Friday morning, June 28, he flew to Cork, where he addressed the combined houses of the Irish parliament. Ireland was "the first country to lead what was the most powerful tide in the twentieth century, the desire for national independence, the desire to be free. . . .

"This is an extraordinary country," he continued. "George Bernard Shaw, speaking as an Irishman, summed up its approach to life: Other people, he said, see things and say: 'Why?' . . . But I dream things that never were and I say: 'Why not?'"

At the airport, instead of saying he was flying to England, Kennedy told the crowd he was "going to another country." Everyone laughed. He would return "in the Springtime," he said, to see "old Shannon's face once again." As he left he told a friend that his visit had been the "happiest days I've ever spent in my life."

On the flight to England, the President's plane stopped briefly at Waddington Royal Air Force Base. There the President and his sister Jean made their way to the British hamlet of Edensor. No crowds followed them as they walked along a country lane to a tree-shaded cemetery, where they stopped at a headstone bearing the words JOY SHE GAVE JOY SHE HAS FOUND. Jack stood silently as Jean placed three bouquets of roses on the gravesite of Kathleen Kennedy.[7]

President Kennedy emphasized foreign affairs over domestic problems because he judged the issues more important. "The big difference," he remarked, "is between a bill being defeated and the country being wiped out." In foreign policy Kennedy could operate more independently of Congress and public opinion and make better use of his initiative and decision making. In foreign affairs he was more attentive to details, and to shaping alternatives.

The successful Soviet missile test in 1957, the launching of *Sputnik*, and Khrushchev's belligerence and boasts of nuclear superiority deeply worried U.S. officials. The United States had far more strategic bombers than the Soviet Union, but the Soviets had been quicker to perceive the advantage of the intercontinental ballistic missile (ICBM) as a delivery system for nuclear weapons, and they appeared to be ahead of the United States in developing them.[8]

The United States assumed that the Soviets' ICBM testing program was successful and that production in numbers would shortly follow. In January 1961, the best estimate was that by mid-1961 the Soviets would have 50 to 150 ICBMs, and the United States would have 36. By mid-1963 the numbers would be 200 to 400 ICBMs to 340. "Certainly Kennedy assumed for the first months of his presidency that there was little he could do about the retaliatory capability of the Soviet Union," noted Lawrence Freedman.

It wasn't until September 1961 that the National Intelligence Estimate destroyed any notion of a missile gap by dramatically lowering the estimated number of Soviet ICBMs from between 140 and 200 to between 10 and 25. (Even that estimate was too high.)[9]

Bolstered by the new intelligence estimate, Kennedy decided to end the missile-gap myth. To stop Khrushchev's nuclear bluster, reassure European allies, and comfort the American public, Roswell Gilpatric, deputy secretary of defense, was given the assignment of warning that the United States could absorb the Soviets' first strike and still devastate the Soviet Union with a retaliatory nuclear blow. (Gilpatric was a high-enough-ranked official to expose Khrushchev's bluff, but not high enough to seem overly provocative.)

In his speech on October 21, 1961, Gilpatric described his country's powerful nuclear assets: six Polaris submarines, dozens of intercontinental ballistic missiles, six hundred bombers. It was clear, he said, that

> the destructive power which the United States could bring to bear even after a Soviet surprise attack upon our forces would be as great as—perhaps greater than—the total undamaged forces which the enemy can threaten to launch against the United States in a first strike. In short, we have a second strike capability which is at least as extensive as what the Soviets can deliver by striking first. Therefore, we are confident that the Soviets will not provoke a major nuclear conflict.

Why hadn't the President spoken out himself? asked Hugh Sidey in a private conversation with the President. Kennedy shook his head and answered, "I don't want to get up against Khrushchev like we were last year [in Vienna]. . . . I want him to be able to get off the hook in this thing. I don't want to force him into anything. When I get up and say those things, it sounds too belligerent."[10]

Kennedy still worried that a genuine missile gap might emerge. In 1962, before the National Security Council, he said that to "be honest, we would probably be safe with less—but we believe in an ample safety factor." Besides, Congress and the military were constantly pressuring him to build a larger military.

"We arm to parley," he often said, quoting Churchill. A well-armed country had more bargaining power for disarmament talks. "Our arms," he said, should be "sufficient beyond doubt." At a cost of about seventeen billion dollars in additional appropriations, Kennedy vastly strengthened U.S. military power and made it far more versatile.[11]

It is not true, as some have argued, that in conducting foreign policy Kennedy purposely created an atmosphere of crisis. He much preferred seemingly pointless talks with the Soviets to direct confrontation. "You can't have too many of those [confrontations], because we are not sure on every occasion that the Soviet Union will withdraw." Peace was a long process— "the sum of many acts."

In response to a query by Luther Hodges on how to enforce export rules in trading with the Soviets, Kennedy endorsed the most lenient interpretation. Certainly the United States should not sell the Soviets anything that was detrimental to national security. But "there are so many major issues between ourselves and the Soviets, that I think it unwise to engage in actions which are likely to cause irritation out of proportion to their real significance."[12]

Kennedy needed to assure allies of his willingness to use nuclear weapons in a crisis, but he had deep forebodings about a nuclear confrontation. "Ever since the longbow," he told Hugh Sidey, "when man had developed new weapons and stockpiled them, somebody has come along and used them. I don't know how we escape it with nuclear weapons."

The prospect of a nuclear exchange was so horrible, he said, that "it would be preferable to be among the dead than among the quick." He worried that he might be required "to come up with a decision to launch our retaliatory effort almost without any warning whatsoever," recalled Lyman Lemnitzer.

Kennedy prudently ordered that electronic locks be placed on strategic nuclear weapons to prevent unauthorized use, and then intentionally leaked the technology to the Soviets so their weapons would also be more secure.

Kennedy wanted to redirect world affairs, Rusk thought, so that it moved "toward a period of consultation, negotiation, and agreement rather than a period of competition, hostility, and ideological opposition."

Sidey singled out Kennedy's horror of nuclear war as the most important feature in his thinking. Kennedy had "a total revulsion over the terrible toll that modern war had taken on individuals, nations and societies, and the even worse prospects in the nuclear age. . . . It ran even deeper than his considerable public rhetoric on the issue."[13]

Kennedy wanted strong conventional forces as well as nuclear forces in

Europe, and a higher nuclear threshold. "It was one thing to rely on nuclear weapons in the 1950s, when America had a new monopoly and faced little risk of retaliation," said one expert. "It was quite another in the 1960s, when the Soviets were in a position to respond in kind."

The President did not want to be confronted with the awful choice of having to use nuclear weapons or conceding territory to the Soviets. He insisted on a broader range of choices. Nonnuclear forces needed to be built up, including those of NATO allies, in order to avoid a rash move to nuclear weapons.

Europeans were deeply skeptical of Kennedy's "flexible-response" doctrine. During the Eisenhower administration they were told that U.S. deployment of nuclear weapons would offset the Soviets' huge superiority in conventional forces. Now the Kennedy administration seemed to be telling them the opposite. Europeans feared that any increase in conventional forces would only discredit the nuclear deterrent. The Soviets would be more effectively deterred if they assumed that the United States had only nuclear deterrence. Nor did Europeans want to use far more of their financial resources to pay their portion of the conventional buildup. They did not share Kennedy's sense of urgency. To counter the assumption that the United States was reneging on its commitment to use nuclear weapons in Europe, Kennedy continued to stress publicly that the United States would indeed strike with nuclear weapons if the Soviet Union was about to attack Europe.[14]

The British maintained a small independent nuclear deterrent, and France was developing an independent nuclear *force de frappe*. Kennedy was deeply concerned that West Germany might develop its own nuclear weapons and once again become a menace. To keep Germany aligned with the West, and hopefully prevent additional national nuclear deterrents, the Kennedy administration pushed the concept of the multilateral force (MLF).

The idea was to create a fleet of surface ships, run by a mixed crew from NATO forces, and armed with Polaris missiles jointly owned and operated by NATO nations. The decision to use the missile warheads would remain under U.S. control. The MLF would give NATO allies, specifically West Germany, a sense of participation in nuclear strategy, and so stop the proliferation of nuclear weapons. "This would forestall independent German action while leaving U.S. weapons under Washington's sole control," said historian Frank Costigliola. "By these means Americans hoped to channel German power into European political unification and Atlantic economic and military integration."

But the concept of the MLF was unwieldy and complicated—an "absurd diplomatic contraption." It won little support among NATO nations. "From a military standpoint, MLF was complete nonsense from the outset," said historian David Nunnerley; "it had no military value, there was no military need for it, and it carried almost insuperable technical complications." In a few years the concept was abandoned.[15]

Britain's Harold Macmillan was Kennedy's closest friend among foreign leaders. The pair developed a genuine fondness for each other, extraordinary considering the great difference in their ages. "I value our friendship," Macmillan wrote Kennedy. "I rejoice that relations between the United States and my country are so close and happy."

Altogether they met seven times—more frequently than Kennedy met with any other foreign leader—and they often exchanged letters and telephone calls. Their mutual trust inspired frankness and acceptance of honest differences.

One touchy issue did create a brief fuss. In March 1960, Eisenhower had offered to sell the Skybolt missile system to Britain in return for American use of the submarine base at Holy Loch, Scotland. A thousand-mile, two-stage ballistic missile, Skybolt was released from beneath the wing of a large bomber. The system was attractive to the British because it would extend the life of the country's 180 B-52 bombers. In the age of ground-to-air missiles, bombers were exceptionally vulnerable over enemy territory. But with Skybolt, a B-52 could hover one thousand miles away from its target and deliver its payload.[16]

But Robert McNamara wanted to scrap Skybolt and put the money saved into developing the more promising Polaris and Minuteman missiles. In the defense secretary's view, Skybolt had to be evaluated for its cost-effectiveness and in comparison with competing systems. The system had become too costly, while the development of the other two was proceeding well. McNamara concluded that Skybolt did not justify all the expense, and America didn't need it. In early December 1962, he announced publicly that five test flights of Skybolt had failed.

Communication about Skybolt's development was a disaster. Several British ministers complained that the United States had never informed them that Skybolt was in trouble and in danger of cancellation; American officials insisted that they had fully informed their British colleagues.

Late in December 1962, Kennedy and Macmillan met in Nassau for a "friendly wintertime parley" that turned into a minicrisis. The President had recently approved McNamara's decision not to develop Skybolt. The system had tested poorly and it was not worth continuing its expensive development, he told Macmillan, especially in light of more promising weapons.

After the Nassau meeting the tired President traveled with David

Ormsby-Gore to Palm Beach for the weekend. It was three days before Christmas. There news arrived that a sixth test of the Skybolt missile had proven successful. "The U.S. Air Force was jubilant, Macmillan was embarrassed, [and] Kennedy was furious," observed David Nunnerley.[17]

How could McNamara have allowed this to happen? How could he authorize the testing of Skybolt—at the same moment the President and Macmillan had just decided to abandon the missile system—and then claim the test was a perfect success? Luckily for McNamara, he was on a skiing holiday in Colorado. Poor Roswell Gilpatric received the full fury of Kennedy's wrath. "He got a hold of Gilpatric and did he read the [riot] act to him," Evelyn Lincoln wrote in her diary on December 22, 1962. "After hanging up he said 'I can't understand McNamara doing this. He is generally so good [at] everything. He must have been tired.'"

The British media were enraged. The *Daily Herald* called the long Skybolt history "a pretty rotten road." But the controversy soon died down.[18]

While Britain tried to sustain its role as America's favorite ally, the French kept their distance. In the French view, Britain's special relationship with the United States was merely a junior partnership, neither available to the French nor desired. Charles de Gaulle wanted supremacy in Western Europe, and to create for France a nuclear capability exclusively under French control. Why should France run the risk of becoming a battlefield but not have possession of nuclear weapons that would probably decide the outcome of the war? "Kennedy's determination to keep to himself the final responsibility for decision on the use of nuclear weapons was at least as strong as de Gaulle's desire to share it," McGeorge Bundy said on reflection.

De Gaulle feared that military integration with the powerful United States would make the French subordinate. Although he supported the concept of European unity and wanted the United States to come to the assistance of European nations in the event of attack, he opposed NATO. The United States should help defend Europe but should not interfere in Europe's affairs. De Gaulle also tried to maneuver Konrad Adenauer to distance West Germany from the United States and to look instead to Paris for its security.

The French and West Germans objected to Kennedy's willingness to negotiate with the Soviets. De Gaulle and Adenauer feared that negotiations would eventually lead to Western concessions, and might draw Washington and Moscow closer together.[19]

It irritated Kennedy that while the United States supplied most of the military forces in Europe to protect West Berlin, Charles de Gaulle received the most credit for taking the toughest line. On May 11, 1962, Kennedy vented his feelings when he met in Washington with André Malraux, the prominent writer, a leader of the French Resistance in World War II, and confidant of de Gaulle. Currently the French minister of cultural affairs, Malraux was visiting in conjunction with the *Mona Lisa*'s exhibition in the United States.

Kennedy reminded Malraux that the United States had engaged in a heavy military buildup in Europe and supported development of the Common Market. When there was trouble in Berlin in 1961, the burden fell on the United States. "We have called up 160,000 men while France brought in only two new divisions," he pointed out. It was the U.S. military effort which had led Khrushchev to back away from the showdown in Berlin at the end of 1961. "Yet General de Gaulle seemed to say it was his determination which had produced the results. . . . We find it difficult to understand the apparent determination of General de Gaulle to cut across our policies in Europe. If it is desired that we should cease to carry the load in Europe, nothing could be better from our point of view."

Malraux responded that France needed to re-create her nationhood and could not endure having her defense entirely in the hands of the United States, however friendly. The President asked why these French requirements made it necessary to oppose NATO and any diplomatic probes with the Soviets. Why did the two nations always wind up in such sharp disagreement? Given the dangers and the heavy responsibilities which it faced in Berlin, the United States must make an effort to talk to the Soviets. "Such talks might not work, but we ought to find out."

The feeling in Bonn and Paris seemed to be that the United States was not standing firm, and the President was getting tired of the carping. The United States felt like a man carrying a two-hundred-pound sack of potatoes, and others not carrying a similar load keep telling him how to carry the burden. "We have done most of the work and now we are carrying most of the burden of criticism."[20]

In early January 1963, de Gaulle took a major slap at the United States and Britain. He rejected the U.S. offer of a multilateral deterrent force, signed a treaty with West Germany, and vetoed Britain's entry into the Common Market. Allowing Britain to join the Common Market, he argued, would lead to a "colossal Atlantic Community under American dependence and leadership."

There was little Kennedy could do that didn't play into de Gaulle's hands. "Absolutely nothing is gained by criticism of de Gaulle in public," Bundy advised the President. "It simply builds him up."[21]

Fascinated by de Gaulle, Kennedy groped for an explanation of the French leader's behavior. "He was always trying to find out what made the man tick, why he acted the way he did," said Charles Bohlen, U.S. ambassador to France beginning in 1962. Bohlen recommended that Kennedy "avoid any open confrontation or row with de Gaulle." The United States should continue "to treat him with great courtesy; to recognize that there are many areas in which cooperation with France continues and should be maintained; not to permit the existence of differences in the nuclear and defense field and in the attitude towards Europe in the Atlantic Community to become embittered so that they adversely affect the entire relationship."

According to Bohlen, Kennedy "finally came to the conclusion that de Gaulle needed some form of friction with the United States for his own personal policies, domestic and otherwise, but Kennedy was equally determined that he was not going to oblige him."[22]

In the summer of 1963, Kennedy focused much of his attention on negotiations for a nuclear test ban treaty. A major impetus for the ban was his concern about the Chinese Communists. Kennedy had no mandate to change U.S. relations with Communist China. Before Dwight Eisenhower left office, he firmly told Kennedy that he would support the new President's foreign policy in general, but was adamantly against recognizing China or seating the Communist nation at the United Nations. To abandon Taiwan and normalize relations with China was far too sensitive for Kennedy to consider only a dozen years after Republicans had accused Democrats of losing China to the Communists. "I think we should get an up to date report on the Communist Chinese admission question," Kennedy wrote Bundy in August 1961 as the issue of Chinese admission to the UN was about to be considered. "We can't permit ourselves to get beaten."[23]

U.S. contacts with the Communist nation were not promising. Belligerent and uncompromising, the Chinese Communists displayed no interest in improving U.S.-Chinese relations. If Kennedy had made concessions to Communist China, he would have been "cut to ribbons politically by the China Lobby, the Republicans, and many members of Congress," said Dean Rusk. "Let's face it," Kennedy told Sorensen, about possible grain shipments to China, but referring to the entire China question, "that's a subject for the second term."

The ideological and political differences between China and the Soviets had widened considerably since the late 1950s. The Communist Chinese constantly criticized the Soviet Union, challenging its dominance of the international Communist movement, and accusing the Soviets of "revisionism" and submission to U.S. imperialism. In January 1963, the Central Intelligence Agency reported that Sino-Soviet relations had reached a new crisis. "In effect, a 'split' has already occurred. . . . The USSR and China are now two separate powers whose interests conflict on almost every major issue."[24]

Kennedy brooded about the possibility of China acquiring nuclear weapons, regarding the prospect as one of the most dangerous developments in the future. The Chinese "would be perfectly prepared to sacrifice hundreds of millions of their own lives" to fulfill their "aggressive and militant policies," he said privately.

Kennedy tried to exploit the tension between the Soviet Union and China. He hoped the Soviets might join the United States in taking military action against the Chinese nuclear facilities. He worried, Sorensen noted, that "the most populous nation in the world, under a Stalinist war-minded regime, was equipping herself with nuclear weapons and was accustomed in the past to dominating most of the weak nations adjacent to her." Ideally, Kennedy would have liked an unidentified airplane to fly over China and destroy its nuclear facilities. "They've only got a couple," he told aides, "and maybe we could do it. Or maybe the Soviet Union could do it."

Several administration officials later testified that such drastic action was only speculative contingency planning. It was only "talk, not serious planning or real intent," recalled McGeorge Bundy. Still, fear of Communist China's nuclear program remained at the forefront of Kennedy's thinking as he sought to curb nuclear testing.[25]

The danger of testing nuclear weapons first became a major concern to the world on March 1, 1954, when the United States detonated a hydrogen bomb at Bikini Atoll in the Pacific. The huge explosion showered radioactive debris on the crew of the Japanese tuna trawler *Lucky Dragon,* causing severe radiation sickness and one death. Radiation sickness spread to the Marshall Islands as well.

"Strontium-90 generated by tests in Nevada showed up in milk in New Jersey," noted Ernest May and Philip Zelikow. "*Newsweek* in 1957 devoted a special section to 'this insidiously invisible powder' of which 'a concentrated teaspoonful could kill 30 million people.'" World leaders, including Prime Minister Nehru of India, Albert Schweitzer, Pope Pius XII, and Albert Einstein called for a ban on nuclear tests.[26]

Many Americans believed that negotiations to ban nuclear tests were fruitless. Admiral Arthur Radford, Ike's chairman of the Joint Chiefs of Staff, expressed a common view: "We cannot trust the Russians on this or anything. The Communists have broken their word with every country with which they ever had an agreement." Nonetheless, since November 1958, the Soviet Union, the United States, and Great Britain had joined in a voluntary moratorium on future atmospheric tests.

Both the United States and the Soviets developed the ability to test underground, a more expensive method of testing, but much safer. Underground tests posed unique verification problems, however. American scientists could easily detect atmospheric nuclear explosions in the Soviet

Union, but had difficulty distinguishing underground tests from natural events like earthquakes.

To protect the United States from Soviet trickery, the U.S. negotiating position on banning underground testing called for twenty on-site inspections per year; the Soviets would accept only three. Khrushchev refused to accept more inspections, claiming the CIA only wanted to spy on his country. The Soviet leader complicated negotiations by insisting on adding new provisions, such as linking progress on a test ban to success in achieving "general and complete disarmament." Such a provision was too utopian for the United States to seriously consider but gained a propaganda advantage for the Soviets.

When Kennedy took office in January 1961, negotiations in Geneva were deadlocked. Kennedy managed to convince Congress to create the new United States Arms Control and Disarmament Agency. (He had complained during the 1960 campaign that fewer than one hundred scattered government officials worked on disarmament.)[27]

With negotiations deadlocked, for a while Kennedy's policy consisted of gaining propaganda advantage. The United States aimed "to win out over the Soviets . . . on the public opinion front," said a State Department report. Propaganda was not the only goal, but "at this time, in view of the intransigent Soviet attitude, it is the primary purpose."

On September 1, 1961, the Soviets broke the voluntary moratorium by exploding the first in a series of powerful tests in the atmosphere, climaxing with the explosion of a 58-megaton device, three thousand times more powerful than the bomb dropped on Hiroshima.

At first Kennedy reacted angrily. The Soviets had deceived him. "Their tests had obviously been under secret preparation even before Vienna and throughout the Geneva negotiations," said Sorensen. "His second reaction was one of deep disappointment—deeper, I believe, than that caused by any other Soviet action during his tenure."[28]

The President had to calibrate carefully the policy he could sell to the American people. The Soviet test series revived intense pressure from the military, Congress, and the Atomic Energy Commission to resume U.S. testing. The President refused to resume U.S. aboveground testing until early March 1962, and even then did so with great reluctance.

After the favorable outcome of the Cuban missile crisis, Kennedy used his increased stature and freedom to improve East-West relations. In a letter to Khrushchev on October 28, 1962, he urged that the two antagonists "step back from danger" and attempt to make "real progress" in disarmament. The most promising area, he suggested, was "the proliferation of nuclear weapons, on earth and in outer space." Kennedy hoped a test ban treaty would reduce the danger to health from radioactive fallout, put a brake on the arms race between the superpowers, stimulate additional arms-control agreements, and, most important from his perspective, control the proliferation of nuclear weapons.[29]

"Our last message from Khrushchev is absolutely categorical in its 'unequivocal and frank' rejection of any inspection," Bundy wrote the President on November 8, 1962. "This leaves us in a logical box, because there is no way that we can get Senate consent to a treaty covering underground tests that does not provide for inspections."

Another possibility, Bundy explained, was to raise with Khrushchev the question of Chinese Communist agreement to a test ban. "Without the Chicoms, after all, the agreement is not going to mean much, and there may be advantage in pressing with Khrushchev the inescapable relevance of this problem." The United States might tell the Soviets that concessions would be considered if the Chinese could be brought on board. "To put it another way, is it really worthwhile for us or the Russians to go around and around the test ban issue without facing squarely up to the question of Chinese Communist participation? A Red China nuclear presence is the great single threat to the status quo over the next few years."[30]

Kennedy kept negotiations moving ahead despite Soviet obstructionism. Delving deeply into the issue, he kept himself as well informed as any non-scientific person could be. He asked about technical details and encouraged discussion. William Foster, director of the Arms Control and Disarmament Agency, argued with the Joint Chiefs in front of the President. "He would let me carry the argument, then he would say: 'Well, all right, there is a basic question here, and let's have this looked at from both viewpoints.'"

The issue deeply disturbed the President. "We test, and then they test, and we have to test again," he said, "and then it becomes easier to use them on each other." On a rainy afternoon following a U.S. test, he quizzed Jerome Wiesner, the White House science adviser, about the contamination caused by nuclear explosions. How did fallout return to earth from the atmosphere?

"It comes down in rain," Wiesner replied.

The President stared out the window at the rain falling on his precious Rose Garden. "You mean there might be radioactive contamination in that rain out there right now?"

"Possibly," Wiesner said.

After Wiesner left the office, Kennedy quietly sat in his chair for several minutes, looking at the rain falling on the garden. "I never saw him more depressed," recalled Ken O'Donnell.[31]

During a visit to New Mexico to view a large crater created by an underground test blast, Kennedy listened to two nuclear scientists explain enthusiastically how they were building a smaller bomb that would yield a much more powerful explosion. Kennedy's face carried a puzzled frown. Later he said to O'Donnell, "How can they be so damned cheerful talking about a thing like that?"

"I don't care if I have no more than ten votes in the Senate," he said privately. "If I get an agreement I think is right, we are going to do our best to push it through. . . . I know it may sound a little corny, but our world doesn't matter much. But I think Caroline's world does matter, and I am prepared to take every conceivable step to bring about a nuclear agreement with the Russians."[32]

On June 10, 1963, one day before his eloquent speech on civil rights, Kennedy delivered another major address at American University in Washington. He sought to lessen Cold War tensions, limit nuclear weapons, and make an unprecedented appeal to Americans to understand the Soviet Union.

Unlike most of Kennedy's foreign-policy speeches, this address was drafted by a tiny group of trusted advisers without departmental input. Kennedy didn't want the speech diluted by the "usual threats of destruction, boasts of nuclear stockpiles, and lectures on Soviet treachery." He wanted to display his sincerity to the Soviets and to ready Congress and the American people to support the test ban treaty that he hoped would soon emerge.[33]

His speech addressed the "most important" topic on earth: "world peace."

What kind of peace do we seek? Not a Pax Americana enforced on the world by American weapons of war. . . . I am talking about genuine peace, the kind of peace that makes life on earth worth living, the kind that enables men and nations to grow and to hope and to build a better life for their children—not merely peace for Americans but peace for all men and women—not merely peace in our time but peace for all time.

The "new face of war" made no sense. A single nuclear weapon contained ten times more explosive force than all the Allied bombs delivered in the Second World War. Deadly poisons produced in a nuclear exchange "would be carried by wind and water and soil and seed to the far corners of the globe and to generations yet unborn."

True, Soviet leaders needed to be more enlightened. But Americans needed enlightenment as well. To many Americans, peace seemed impossible:

"But that is a dangerous, defeatist belief. It leads to the conclusion that war is inevitable—that mankind is doomed—that we are gripped by forces we cannot control.

We need not accept that view. Our problems are man-made— therefore, they can be solved by man.

With peace there would still be disagreement and conflicting interests. But "history teaches us that enmities between nations, as between individuals, do not last forever. However fixed our likes and dislikes may seem, the tide of time and events will often bring surprising changes in the relations between nations and neighbors."

Americans needed to reexamine their attitude toward the Soviet Union. Of course, "It is discouraging to think that their leaders may actually believe what their propagandists write." Nonetheless, Americans held distorted views of the Soviet Union:

> No government or social system is so evil that its people must be considered as lacking in virtue. As Americans, we find communism profoundly repugnant as a negation of personal freedom and dignity. But we can still hail the Russian people for their many achievements—in science and space, in economic and industrial growth, in culture and in acts of courage.

Kennedy graciously asked Americans to appreciate the horrific price the Soviet people paid during World War II:

> No nation in the history of battle ever suffered more than the Soviet Union suffered in the course of the Second World War. At least twenty million lost their lives. Countless millions of homes and farms were burned or sacked. A third of the nation's territory, including nearly two thirds of its industrial base, was turned into a wasteland—a loss equivalent to the devastation of this country east of Chicago.

"Let us not be blind to our differences," he warned; but we should also stress common interests. "For, in the final analysis, our most basic common link is that we all inhabit this small planet. We all breathe the same air. We all cherish our children's future. And we are all mortal."

Near the end of his address Kennedy made two important announcements. Great Britain, the United States, and the Soviets had agreed to high-level negotiations in Moscow toward agreement on a comprehensive test ban treaty. In the meantime the United States would not conduct nuclear tests in the atmosphere as long as other nations did not test.

The United States would do its part to build a world peace, he concluded, "where the weak are safe and the strong are just. We are not helpless before that task or hopeless of its success. Confident and unafraid, we labor on—not toward a strategy of annihilation but toward a strategy of peace."[34]

In Moscow, Khrushchev was deeply impressed with the address, saying it was "the best speech of any American president since Roosevelt." He even allowed his countrymen to hear it by not jamming the Voice of America broadcast. Humphrey Trevelyan, the British ambassador in Moscow, thought that "for the first time" Soviet leaders judged Kennedy as "someone who was genuinely working for a détente and with whom they could do business."

Confident, magnanimous, lacking in cant, the lyrical address was one of Kennedy's finest speeches. It differed sharply from the traditionally shrill anticommunist rhetoric of almost every American political leader since the end of World War II. Several references seemed to have been inspired by Pope John XXIII's recent "Pacem in Terris." "Pope John opened the door, and Kennedy stepped through," said one commentator.[35]

The President appointed Averell Harriman to represent the United States in negotiations in Moscow. If the existing nuclear powers could agree on a test ban, "they could pressure other countries to follow suit and sign," noted historian Gordon Chang. "The result would be the end of nuclear proliferation since, the thinking went, no additional country could develop a bomb without testing. The nuclear powers would also conveniently retain their monopoly."

Kennedy hoped to use the negotiations to explore the possibility of joint action with the Soviets to stop China's nuclear weapons program. On July 15, 1963, he cabled Harriman:

> I remain convinced that Chinese problem is more serious than Khrushchev comments in first meeting suggest, and believe you should press question in private meeting with him. I agree that large stockpiles are characteristic of US and USSR only, but consider that relatively small forces in hands of people like CHICOMS could be very dangerous to us all. Further believe even limited test ban can and should be means to limit diffusion. *You should try to elicit Khrushchev's view of means of limiting or preventing Chinese nuclear development and his willingness either to take Soviet action or to accept US action aimed in this direction.*

In Moscow Harriman never directly proposed a joint preemptive strike to the Soviets, and the Soviets flatly rejected the indirect proposals Harriman did suggest.[36]

Nonetheless, on August 5, Britain, the United States, and the Soviet Union signed the test ban treaty in Moscow. (Officially it was called the Treaty Banning Nuclear Weapons Tests in the Atmosphere, in Outer Space, and Under Water.) Because it applied only to aboveground testing, it lacked the complications of inspections and other control machinery.

Public opinion in the United States moved decisively in favor of the treaty. A Harris poll in early July reported 47 percent of the public offering unqualified approval; on September 1, 81 percent completely approved of the treaty. The dramatic change in public support made Republicans reluctant to criticize Kennedy's effort. "I don't see any political mileage in opposing the treaty," said a Republican senator.[37]

Kennedy carefully orchestrated the strategy to gain support in the Senate. He discussed the treaty with senators and convinced the wary Joint Chiefs of Staff to endorse the treaty when they testified before Senate committees. He approved newspaper and television advertisements. He also encouraged the Citizens' Committee for a Nuclear Test Ban. Norman Cousins, an officer in the lobbying group, recalled that Kennedy suggested the names of prominent businessmen and scientists to recruit. "He felt that religious figures, farmers, educators, and labor leaders all had key roles to play and he mentioned a half dozen or more names in each category," said Cousins. "Then he went down the list of states in which he felt extra effort was required."

In a shrewd political move Kennedy convinced the Senate's minority leader, Senator Dirksen, to announce his support in the Senate. The Republican Party's platform in 1960 had advocated such a treaty, the sixty-seven-year-old Dirksen said; "I should not like to have written on my tombstone: 'He knew what happened at Hiroshima but he did not take a first step. . . . If there be risks I am willing to assume them for my country." With every able-bodied legislator voting, on September 24, 1963, the Senate approved the treaty, 80 to 19.[38]

The agreement didn't fulfill all of Kennedy's goals. It decreased the amount of strontium 90 in the atmosphere but did little to end the pace of the superpowers' accumulation of nuclear weapons. Both China and France refused to sign it. Nor did the treaty stop underground nuclear testing.

Along with the treaty Kennedy found other areas of common interest with the Soviets. In the summer of 1963, the two superpowers signed the "hot-line" agreement, establishing a twenty-four-hour communications link to avoid a situation like the one they had encountered during the Cuban missile crisis, when critical messages took a long time to transmit. In October they reached agreement on the sale of American wheat to the Soviets.

Kennedy displayed intense interest and skill in negotiating the test ban accord and in securing Senate ratification. The treaty "opened the door to future agreements, a broadening of trade and exchanges, increases in American and Russian tourism, and a general lessening of Cold War tensions," concluded Dean Rusk. This was the legacy of what Kennedy believed was his greatest achievement.[39]

44

DEATH IN THE FALL

In the fall of 1963, Kennedy, now forty-six years old, had strands of gray on the fringes of his hair, furrows in the corners of his eyes, and the start of a second chin. In November he phoned a friend to say that he was sending a recent photo of himself, and added that it "shows my battle scars and wrinkles, although I don't see any warts. I'm not the skinny kid you once knew. In the picture I'm looking upward, watching eternity."[1]

In early November Kennedy dined with David Ormsby-Gore. A few months earlier he had spoken to his English friend about possibly visiting the Soviet Union. Now he had made up his mind. "One of the things that I really must do is to go to the Soviet Union. I believe that this would be in everybody's interest—whether I can do it before the Presidential election next year, may be a bit doubtful."[2]

After the 1962 midterm elections a small group of Kennedy loyalists—Robert Kennedy, Larry O'Brien, Ken O'Donnell, Ted Sorensen, John Bailey, Steve Smith—plotted the President's reelection in 1964. Politics was an ever-present reality in the Kennedy White House, Sorensen noted, used as a "criterion for trips, visitors, appointees and speeches, as an unspoken force counterbalancing the unrealistic, checking the unreasonable, occasionally deterring the desirable and always testing the acceptable." The staff automatically assumed they should weigh the political effect of every move and every statement on Congress and on public opinion. "Kennedy retained in the White House his unusually acute political antennae, with which he sensed the public mood both quickly and accurately," said Sorensen.

The South seemed lost for Kennedy in 1964. "There is no hope for Kennedy in this State," said a supporter in Jackson, Mississippi. White Southerners were angry about civil rights demonstrations and federal intervention. "Even the word 'Kennedy' is an epithet in some parts of the South," wrote *U.S. News and World Report*. On the other hand, the President's increased popularity among blacks, young males, and voters in the West, especially in California, more than offset Southern losses.

Kennedy had no intention of removing Lyndon Johnson as his running mate in 1964, and grew testy when anyone suggested otherwise. While Charles Bartlett swam with the President in the White House pool, he asked, "Why don't you get another vice-president in 1964?" Kennedy turned on him with fury, Bartlett recalled. "Why would I do a thing like that? That would be absolutely crazy. It would tear up the relationship and hurt me in Texas. That would be the most foolish thing I could do."[3]

Kennedy much preferred having conservative Republican Senator Barry Goldwater as his opponent in 1964. He feared, though, that Republicans might nominate a more dangerous candidate, either Nelson Rockefeller or George Romney.

Rockefeller, a liberal Republican, had been elected governor of New York in 1958. Glamorous and urbane, he won reelection easily in 1962. "I remember we were on the *Honey Fitz* one day," Jim Reed recalled, "and Kennedy kept talking about one subject during that whole trip—Rockefeller. Everybody there had to tell him everything they knew about Rockefeller. He was insatiable to know absolutely everything—his private world, his techniques, his staff, his philosophy, his women."

When Khrushchev asked columnist Walter Lippmann about the psychology for understanding Kennedy, Lippmann responded, "Rockefeller." But when Rockefeller divorced his wife in March 1962 and remarried two months later, he badly damaged his political career.[4]

"The one fellow I don't want to run against is Romney," the President privately said in the spring of 1963. The former president of American Motors Corporation, George Romney, had captured the governor's office in Michigan in 1962, the first Republican governor of the state in fourteen years. "He was always for God," Robert Kennedy remarked about Romney, "and he was always for [motherhood] and against big government and against big labor." Because of the President's concern that Romney might win the Republican nomination, he seldom mentioned Romney's name lest the suggestion "build him up."

Kennedy did ask his aides to mention Goldwater as having presidential stature. "We had worked with Goldwater and we just knew he was not a very smart man and [he was] just going to destroy himself," said Robert Kennedy. The President worried "that he would destroy himself too early and not get the nomination." "Give me good old Barry," the President said. "I'd never have to leave this Oval Office."[5]

Assuming he won reelection in 1964, what did Kennedy intend to do after his second term? "Oh, probably sell real estate," he joked. "That's the only thing I'm equipped to do."

He gave different answers as if he was musing about several alternatives. "He told me that he might be president of Harvard University," said Evelyn Lincoln. He would spend part of his time writing the history of his administration, adding with a smile that the challenge was to beat two members of his staff—Bundy and Schlesinger—to publication. To another person he indicated he might buy a newspaper.

"I'd run for the Senate," he told Paul Fay.

"But isn't it quite a comedown from being the President of the United States?" Fay responded.

"John Quincy Adams served in the House after being President. If a man came from the White House to the Congress, he could give a voice of judgment and authority to the legislative branch that would elevate the whole body."[6]

On September 24, 1963, the same morning the Senate ratified the test ban treaty, Kennedy left Washington for a five-day, ten-thousand-mile trip through eleven states, most of them in the West. Ostensibly it was a conservation tour, but its real purpose was political. Of the eleven states on the tour, Kennedy had lost eight in the 1960 election. "In ten of these states, there would be Senatorial elections in 1964, with nine Democrats trying to retain their seats," noted journalist Sander Vanocur, who wrote an article about the trip.

The first two stops went poorly. Unfamiliar with his conservation subject matter, he bored himself and his audience when he spoke of "the average number of meters to each mile of line in urban-based utility systems" and the "gasification of coal at the mine." One speech was "perfectly dreadful," Vanocur wrote, "one of the worst reporters could remember." It was "heavy listening," Ben Bradlee reported in *Newsweek*.[7]

In Billings, Montana, he praised the leadership of Senator Mike Mansfield and Minority Leader Everett Dirksen in helping to ratify the test ban treaty. As soon as he mentioned the treaty, the crowd erupted in loud cheering and applause. He appeared surprised by the reaction. With his carefully tuned political antennae, he sensed what his audience wanted and immediately began to embellish the peace theme, accelerating his tempo and intensity. "His right forefinger stabbed the air, and the strident tone of the campaign days returned to his voice," said Vanocur. He mentioned the dangerous confrontations in Berlin and Cuba. "What we hope to do," he said, "is lessen the chance of a military collision between these two great nuclear powers which together have the power to kill three hundred million people."

By the time the President left Billings and flew to Jackson Hole, Wyoming, he knew that people in the West wanted no more dry speeches about conservation. What interested them was war and peace.

To the thirty thousand people who heard him in Hanford, Washington, Kennedy stressed that "no one can say . . . with certainty . . . whether we shall be able to control this deadly [nuclear] weapon, whether we shall be able to maintain our life and our peaceful relations with other countries." He promised to try. "It is for this reason that I so strongly supported the test ban treaty, recognizing as I did its limitations, as a step on the long road to peace."

Kennedy returned to Washington, D.C., on September 30. "If John F. Kennedy ever had any doubts about his reelection—and I think he had none—they were dispelled by this trip," wrote Vanocur.[8]

President Kennedy devoted his final days to campaigning for reelection. He intended to waste little energy trying to capture the South in 1964, having alienated white voters there with his strong support for civil rights. But two large Southern states—Florida and Texas—he did not intend to write off.

On Monday, November 18, he spoke in Tampa and Miami Beach. That night he returned to Washington for two days of official business. On Thursday, the President and Jackie flew to Texas.

Jackie had told her assistant to inform the media that she was going to campaign alongside her husband. "Say I am going out with my husband on this trip and that it will be the first of many that I hope to make with him, and if they ask about campaigning, say yes that I plan to campaign with him, and that I will do anything to help my husband be elected president again."

The President hoped to raise money for the Democratic Party and improve his chances to win in Texas in 1964. Texan voters were increasingly attracted to Republicans who opposed Kennedy on civil rights. He also intended to placate warring factions in the state's Democratic Party. The party was split between conservatives led by Governor John Connally and liberals following the lead of Senator Ralph Yarborough.[9]

Thursday's warm and enthusiastic receptions in San Antonio, Houston, and Fort Worth encouraged him. But at the end of the first day, Kennedy realized he had a serious political problem. Vice President Johnson and Senator Yarborough had been feuding for some time over who controlled Texas patronage. When Yarborough refused to ride in the same car as Johnson, reporters prominently featured the story, overshadowing the President's visit. On Friday morning in Fort Worth, Kennedy ordered Larry O'Brien to end the Johnson-Yarborough feud. "I don't care if you have to throw Yarborough into the car with Lyndon," he said. "Get him in there."

He was next scheduled to appear in Dallas, a hotbed of extreme right-wing activists. The city had a recent history of ugly incidents. In the 1960 election campaign, a group of Dallas housewives had sprayed saliva on the Lyndon Johnsons, and in late October 1963, Adlai Stevenson had been roughed up by a crowd.

On Friday, November 22, 1963, the President began his day in Fort Worth by leaving his hotel to mingle with a friendly crowd in a nearby parking lot. "Where's Jackie?" someone yelled. The President smiled. "Mrs. Kennedy," he said, "is busy organizing herself. It takes a little longer, you know, but then she looks so much better than we do." When Jackie did emerge, she looked lovely dressed in a strawberry wool suit and a pillbox hat. After a breakfast appearance, sponsored by the Fort Worth Chamber of Commerce, the President and his entourage flew to Dallas.[10]

At 11:37 A.M. *Air Force One* touched down at Dallas's Love Field, where the official welcoming party presented Jackie with a bouquet of red roses. Although behind schedule, the President stopped to shake a few hands among the crowd of several thousand.

The President was nonchalant about his own security. In the Southern sunshine and warm temperature, he had the protective bubble top of his blue Lincoln limousine removed and the bulletproof side windows rolled down. That way people could see him wave and smile as he rode through the city. Kennedy's motorcade was to proceed on an eleven-mile route through downtown Dallas, where he would give an address at a civic luncheon at the Dallas Trade Mart.

In the backseat the President sat on the right, Jackie beside him; Governor Connally and his wife sat in front of them. As the twelve-car motorcade proceeded at twenty-five miles an hour, it took a sharp left turn and continued down an incline toward a triple underpass near a seven-story brick warehouse, the Texas School Book Depository. As Mrs. Connally turned, smiled, and said to the President, "You can't say that Dallas isn't friendly to you today," the President's reply was cut off.

Crack!

A rifle shot split the air.

Crack! Crack!

Two more shots followed.[11]

The second shot wounded the President, but not fatally. In his classic account of Kennedy's assassination, *The Death of the President*, William Manchester noted that it had "entered the back of his neck, bruised his right lung, ripped his windpipe, and exited at his throat, nicking the knot of his tie." Later, the controversial Warren Commission concluded that the same bullet continued its flight, passing through Governor Connally's back, chest, right wrist, and left thigh.

A third bullet, the fatal shot, tore through Kennedy's cerebellum, the lower portion of his brain. As the President lay unconscious on his back in the limousine, his head cradled in Jackie's lap, her suit splattered with her husband's blood, the presidential limousine dashed seventy-seven blocks to the emergency entrance of Parkland Memorial Hospital. "The news of the shooting crossed the nation like a shock wave," *Newsweek* reported. "For 30 agonizing minutes, Americans heard and waited and kept the death watch in unprecedented numbers."

In the emergency room doctors worked feverishly to revive the President. "It's too late," said a doctor monitoring an electrocardiograph. At 1:33 P.M., assistant White House press secretary Malcolm Kilduff met waiting reporters. Bleary-eyed, tremulous, he read a statement: "President John F. Kennedy died at approximately 1 P.M., central standard time, today here in Dallas. He died of a gunshot wound in the brain."[12]

Shortly after, aboard *Air Force One,* Lyndon Johnson was sworn in as the country's thirty-sixth President. Bearing Jackie and her husband's casket, the plane returned to Andrews Air Force Base near Washington.

On Saturday morning Kennedy's body lay in the flag-draped closed casket in the East Room of the White House, the same spot the murdered Abraham Lincoln had lain almost a century earlier. Shortly after noon the President's coffin was moved from the White House to lie in state in the Rotunda of the Capitol. On Sunday a huge crowd, at one point stretching forty blocks, stood in line to view the coffin. The same day, as Dallas police walked him through the basement of the Dallas police station, the alleged assassin, Lee Harvey Oswald, was shot and killed by Jack Ruby in full view of a national television audience.[13]

President Johnson declared Monday, November 25, a day of national mourning. Across the nation and the world millions watched the somber events on television. A columnist's description of the scene in San Francisco could just as well have portrayed any American community in the aftermath of the assassination:

It is less than 72 hours since the shots rang out in Dallas, yet it seems a lifetime—a lifetime of weeping skies, wet eyes and streets. . . . Over the endless weekend, San Francisco looked like a city that was only slowly emerging from a terrible bombardment. Downtown, on what would normally have been a bustling Saturday, the people walked slowly, as in shock, their faces pale and drawn, their mood as somber as the dark clothes they wore under the gray skies.

The Kennedy family, marching troops, and bands escorted the caisson from Capitol Hill to funeral services at St. Matthew's Cathedral, and from there to Arlington National Cemetery in Virginia. In the long processional came foreign dignitaries, including crowned heads of state and the magisterial Charles de Gaulle of France. The cadence of muffled drums throbbed throughout the march. Black Jack, a riderless horse, symbolizing a lost leader, was led behind the casket.[14]

When the funeral service at St. Matthew's was completed, the casket team carried the coffin slowly down the church steps. Jackie, Caroline, and John Jr., waited at the bottom of the steps. As the band struck up "Hail to the Chief," soldiers snapped from parade rest to present arms. Mrs. Kennedy leaned down and whispered to her son, "John, you can salute Daddy now and say good-bye to him."

"Of all Monday's images, nothing approached the force of John's salute," wrote Manchester. "His elbow was cocked at precisely the right angle, his hand was touching his shock of hair, his left arm was rigidly at his side, his shoulders were squared and his chin in." It was heart-wrenching.[15]

After the church service the mourners journeyed down Constitution Avenue, around the Lincoln Memorial, over Memorial Bridge, to Arlington Cemetery. A million people gathered to watch the procession.

During the playing of the national anthem at Arlington, fifty jet planes, one for each state, screamed over the cemetery in salute, followed by *Air Force One*. After the lighting of a perpetual flame, at 3:34 P.M. John Kennedy's body was lowered into the ground.

"It was a day of such endless fitness, with so much pathos and panoply, so much grief nobly borne," wrote columnist Mary McGrory.[16]

ON THE NOTES SECTION

Due to length and production constraints with the publication of *John F. Kennedy,* the publisher was unable to include the notes section for this book. However, the notes section can be downloaded and printed from the St. Martin's Web site at the following address: www.stmartins.com/jfk notes.pdf.

A hard copy of the notes section can also be requested from the John F. Kennedy Library. Contact:

Research Room
John F. Kennedy Library
Columbia Point
Boston, MA 02125

BIBLIOGRAPHY

MANUSCRIPTS

(Unless otherwise indicated, all manuscript collections are located at the John Fitzgerald Kennedy Library at Columbia Point, Boston, Massachusetts.)

Americans for Democratic Action Papers, State Historical Society of Wisconsin, Madison, Wisconsin

Edwin Bayley Papers, State Historical Society of Wisconsin, Madison, Wisconsin

Kirk LeMoyne Billings Papers

Clay Blair Papers, American Heritage Center, University of Wyoming, Laramie, Wyoming

Robert Coughlan Papers, Northwestern University, Evanston, Illinois

C. Douglas Dillon Papers

Paul Fay Papers

Federal Bureau of Investigation File on John F. Kennedy (Microfilm, Scholarly Resources, Inc.)

Federal Bureau of Investigation File on Robert F. Kennedy (Microfilm, Scholarly Resources, Inc.)

Myer Feldman Papers

Victoria Fullerton Papers, Los Osos, California

James Giglio Papers, Southwest Missouri State University, Springfield, Missouri

Kay Halle Papers

Nigel Hamilton Papers, Massachusetts Historical Society, Boston, Massachusetts

Walter Heller Papers

Dierdre Henderson Papers

Arthur Holcombe Papers

John F. Kennedy National Historic Site Papers, Brookline, Massachusetts

John F. Kennedy Papers

Joseph P. Kennedy Papers

Robert F. Kennedy Papers

David Koskoff Papers

Evelyn Lincoln Papers

Blair Moody Papers, Bentley Historical Library, University of Michigan, Ann Arbor, Michigan

Gaylord Nelson Papers, State Historical Society of Wisconsin, Madison, Wisconsin

Richard Neustadt Papers

Kenneth O'Donnell Papers

David Powers Papers

Ted Reardon Papers

Riverdale Country School Papers, Bronx, New York

Arthur Schlesinger Jr. Papers

Theodore Sorensen Papers

James Seymour Papers

Janet Travell Papers

U.S. Secret Service Records

Robert Wallace Papers

Theodore White Papers

Harris Wofford Papers

ORAL HISTORY INTERVIEWS

A. In the John Fitzgerald Kennedy Papers, John Fitzgerald Kennedy Library

Acheson, Dean
Aiken, Frank
Aiken, George
Akers, Anthony
Albert, Carl
Alphand, H.E.
Alsop, Joseph

Amory, Robert
Anderson, Clinton
Anderson, George
Auchincloss, Janet
Bailey, John
Baldrige, Letitia
Barbour, Walworth

Barboza, Joanne
Barnes, Donald
Barnett, Ross
Bartlett, Charles
Batt, William
Battle, Lucius
Behn, Gerald

Bell, David
Bell, Jack
Ben-Gurion, David
Bergquist, Laura
Berle, Adolf
Berlin, Isaiah
Biemiller, Andrew
Billings, Kirk LeMoyne
Bissell, Richard
Boggs, Hale
Bohlen, Charles
Bolling, Richard
Booker, Simeon
Bouck, Robert
Bowles, Chester
Brandon, Henry
Brown, Edmund
Burke, Grace
Bridge, Dinah
Broderick, Thomas
Bruce, Preston
Burke, Arleigh
Burke, John
Burke, Kenneth
Burkley, George
Burns, James
Busby, Horace, Jr.
Casey, Joseph
Cavanaugh, John
Celebrezze, Anthony
Chayes, Abram
Clark, Joseph
Clay, Lucius
Cleveland, Harlan
Cloherty, Peter
Cogley, John
Cohen, Wilbur
Coit, Margaret
Colbert, James
Coleman, Barbara
Collins, Leroy
Cooper, Chester
Council of Economic
    Advisers
Couve de Murville, Mau-
    rice
Crane, Edward

Curnane, Joseph
Cushing, Richard
Dalton, Mark
Daly, Charles
Davis, Mary
Dazzi, Andrew
Dempsey, John
Desautels, Claude
de Valera, Eamon
Disalle, Michael
Donelan, Paul
Douglas-Home, Alec
Douglas-Home, William
Douglas, Paul
Douglas, William
Droney, John
Duke, Angier
Dulles, Allen
Dungan, Ralph
Dutton, Frederick
Ellender, Allen
Evans, Rowland
Farmer, James
Farrell, James
Feldman, Myer
Flood, Richard
Folliard, Edward
Foster, William
Frankfurter, Felix
Freeman, Orville
Fraser, Hugh
Fulbright, J. William
Furcolo, Foster
Gallagher, Edward
Gallucio, Anthony
Galvin, John
Gamarekian, Barbara
Garabedian, Charles
Gatov, Elizabeth
Geoghegan, William
Gilpatric, Roswell
Glenn, John
Grace de Monaco (Grace
    Kelly)
Green, Edith
Grennan, Josephine
Gore, Albert

Grewe, Wilhelm
Guthman, Edwin
Gwirtzman, Milton
Hackett, David
Halle, Kay
Halleck, Charles
Hamilton Fowler
Hanford, Chester
Harlech, Lord (William
    David Ormsby-Gore)
Harllee, John
Harriman, Averell
Harris, Seymour
Harrison, Gilbert
Hartigan, William
Hatcher, Andrew
Hays, Brooks
Healey, Joseph
Hearst, William
    Randolph, Jr.
Heckscher, August
Heffernan, Roy
Helms, Richard
Hennessey, Louella
Herling, John
Hickenlooper, Bourke
Highley, David
Hillenbrand, Martin
Hilsman, Roger
Hirsh, Jacqueline
Hodges, Luther
Holness, Wilma
Holt, Pat
Holtz, Jackson
Hooker, John
Hopkins, William
Horsky, Charles
Horton, Ralph
Humphrey, Hubert
Hurwitch, Robert
Jackson, Barbara
Jacobson, Benjamin
Johnson, Lady Bird
Karitas, Joseph
Katzenbach, Nicholas
Kaysen, Carl
Keenan, Joseph

Kelly, William
Kelso, John
Kennan, George
Kennedy, Robert
Kennedy, Rose
Kiernan, Thomas
Kilpatrick, Carroll
King, Martin Luther, Jr.
Knebel, Fletcher
Kohler, Foy
Komer, Robert
Kraft, Joseph
Krock, Arthur
Lansdale, Edward
Laski, Fridda
Lawford, Peter
Lawrence, David
Lawrence, William
Lawson, Belford
Lawson, Marjorie
Leahy, Joseph
Lee, Robert
Lemass, Sean
Lemnitzer, Lyman
Lempart, Helen
Lester, Richard
Lewin, Charles
Lewis, Samuel
Lincoln, G. Gould
Lippmann, Walter
Lisagor, Peter
Lodge, Henry Cabot
Louchheim, Kathleen
Lovett, Robert
Luce, Henry
Lucey, Patrick
Macdonald, Torbert
Manatos, Mike
Mann, Thomas
Mannix, Jean
Mansfield, Mike
Marshall, Burke
Martin, Louis
McClure, Stewart
McCone, John
McCormack, John
McDermott, Edward

McDonald, David
McDonough, Robert
McGhee, George
McGill, Ralph
McNamara, Robert
McNaughton, John
McShane, James
Meany, George
Meyner, Robert
Mills, Wilbur
Minihan, Andrew
Minow, Newton
Mitchell, Clarence
Morgan, Edward
Morrissey, Francis
Morse, Wayne
Morton, Thruston
Mulkern, Patsy
Munroe, Patrick
Muskie, Edmund
Nestingen, Ivan
Nolting, Frederick
Norton, Clement
O'Brien, Lawrence
O'Connor, Frank
O'Donnell, Kenneth
O'Ferrall, Frank
O'Neill, Thomas
Orrick, William
Patterson, John
Peek, Scott
Pell, Claiborne
Pereira, Pedro
Peterson, Esther
Phillips, Vel
Pierce, Nelson
Poverty and Urban Policy
    Panel
Press Panel
Pusey, Nathan
Quigley, Thomas
Rauh, Joseph
Reed, James
Reese, Matthew
Reeves, Frank
Reinsch, J. Leonard
Rice, Willard

Roberts, Chalmers
Roberts, Charles
Rosetti, Joseph
Rostow, Walt
Rusk, Dean
Russell, Francis
Russo, Joseph
Salinger, Pierre
Saltonstall, Leverett
Sanford, Terry
Schary, Dore
Schlei, Norbert
Schlesinger, Arthur, Jr.
Schlesinger, Marian
Seigenthaler, John
Sharon, John
Shea, Maury
Shepard, Alan
Shepard, Tazewell
Shoup, David
Shriver, Eunice
Sidey, Hugh
Sitrin, Gloria
Smathers, George (two
    different interviews)
Smith, Bromley
Solomon Islanders
Spalding, Charles
Sparkman, John
Stahr, Elvis
Stedman, Donald
Sundquist, James
Sutton, William
Sylvester, Arthur (two
    different interviews)
Symington, Stuart
Taylor, George
Taylor, Hobart
Taylor, Maxwell
Thant, U
Thaxton, Cordenia
Tinker, Harold
Thompson, Llewellyn
Thompson, Robert
Travell, Janet
Tree, Marietta
Tretick, Stanley

Trimble, William
Tyler, William
Tubridy, Dorothy
Tucker, Herbert
Tuckerman, Nancy
Turnure, Pamela
Udall, Stewart
Ulen, Harold
Vance, Cyrus
Vogelsinger, Sue
Wagner, Robert

Wallace, Robert
Walton, William (two
    different interviews)
Watson, Thomas
Weaver, Robert
West, J. Bernard
Wheeler, Earle
White House Staff
    Reflections on the
    New Frontier
White, Lee

Wicker, Tom
Wild, Payson
Wilkins, Roy
Williams, G. Mennen
Williams, Irwin
Wilson, Donald
Wine, James
Winship, Thomas
Wood, Robert
Yarmolinsky, Adam
Zuckert, Eugene

B. In the Clay Blair Papers, University of Wyoming

Barclay, Thomas
Bartels, Elmer
Bartlett, Charles
Berndtson, Arthur
Billings, Lem
Brantingham, Henry
Christiansen, Glen
Churchill, Pam
Clayson, Pam
Cluster, Alvin
Coleman, John
Davis, Mary
Facto, Homer
Fay, Anita
Fay, Paul
Fullerton, Harriet
Gallucio, Anthony
Galvin, John
Gibson, Jack
Harris, Charles

Harris, Charlotte
Hersey, John
Hinckley, Jeanne
Horton, Ralph
Houghton, Charles
Keresey, Richard
Kernell, Joseph
Krock, Arthur
Lannan, Patrick
Macdonald, Torbert
Maguire, John
Marvin, Langdon
McCoy, Ronald
McLaughlin, Cis
McLaughlin, Ed
Menzies, Kay
Mitchell, John
Morse, Nancy
Nikoloric, Leonard
Powers, Dave

Reed, James
Reed, Jewel
Rhoads, Robert
Ross, Barney
Servatius, Edward
Shriver, Eunice
Shriver, Sargent
Smathers, George
Smith, Ben
Smith, Earl
Spalding, Betty
Timilty, Joseph
Walton, William
Warfield, Thomas
White, John
Wilson, Paige
Woods, James
Zinser, Gerard

C. In the Nigel Hamilton Papers, Massachusetts Historical Society

Cloherty, Peter
Fay, Paul
Finley, Thomas
Galvin, John
Greene, Angela

Hunter, S.A.D.
Iles, John
Lamphier, Timothy
Newberry, Cam
Pope, Ralph

Rousmanière, Jim
Smathers, George
Sutton, Billy
Thorn, George

D. Author Interviews

Cowen, Jill
Elwell, Mrs. Albert
    (Margaret Coit)
Hersh, Seymour

Kallina, Edmund, Jr.
Kessler, Ronald
McLaughlin, Edward
Newman, Larry

Paolella, Joseph
Sherman, Tony

BOOKS

Abbot, James A., and Elaine M. Rice. *Designing Camelot: The Kennedy White House Restoration.* New York: Van Nostrand Reinhold, 1998.

Abell, Tyler, ed. *Drew Pearson Diaries, 1949–1959.* New York: Holt, Rinehart and Winston, 1974.

Abramson, Rudy. *Spanning the Century: The Life of W. Averell Harriman, 1891–1986.* New York: William Morrow, 1992.

Aliano, Richard. *American Defense Policy from Eisenhower to Kennedy.* Athens: Ohio University Press, 1975.

Ambrose, Stephen E. *Eisenhower—Soldier and President.* New York: Simon and Schuster, 1990.

———. *Nixon: The Education of a Politician, 1913–1962.* New York: Simon and Schuster, 1987.

Andersen, Christopher. *Jack and Jackie: Portrait of an American Marriage.* New York: William Morrow, 1996.

Anderson, Patrick. *The President's Men.* Garden City, N.Y.: Doubleday, 1968.

Anthony, Carl S. *As We Remember Her.* New York: HarperCollins, 1997.

Archdeacon, Thomas J. *Becoming American: An Ethnic History.* New York: Free Press, 1983.

Badeau John S. *The American Approach to the Arab World.* New York: Harper and Row, 1968.

———. *The Middle East Remembered.* Washington, D.C.: Middle East Institute, 1983.

Baker, Bobby, and Larry L. King. *Wheeling and Dealing: Confessions of a Capitol Hill Operator.* New York: W. W. Norton, 1978.

Baker, Jean H. *The Stevensons: A Biography of an American Family.* New York: W. W. Norton, 1996.

Baldrige, Letitia. *Of Diamonds and Diplomats.* Boston: Houghton Mifflin, 1968.

Ball, Desmond. *Politics and Force Levels: The Strategic Missile Program of the Kennedy Administration.* Berkeley: University of California Press, 1980.

Ball, George W. *The Past Has Another Pattern: Memoirs.* New York: W. W. Norton, 1982.

Bass, Warren. *Support Any Friend.* New York: Oxford University Press, 2003.

Bealle, Morris. *The History of Football at Harvard: 1874–1948.* Washington, D.C.: Columbia Publishing, 1948.

Bennett, Judith. *Wealth of the Solomons.* Honolulu: University of Hawaii Press, 1987.

Bernstein, Irving. *Promises Kept: John F. Kennedy's New Frontier.* New York: Oxford University Press, 1991.

Berry Joseph P., Jr. *John F. Kennedy and the Media: The First Television President.* Lanham, Md.: University Press of America, 1987.

Beschloss, Michael R. *The Crisis Years: Kennedy and Khrushchev, 1960–1963.* New York: Edward Burlingame Books, 1991.

———. *Kennedy and Roosevelt: The Uneasy Alliance*. New York: W. W. Norton, 1980.

Beschloss, Michael R., and Thomas E. Cronin, eds. *Essays in Honor of James MacGregor Burns*. Englewood Cliffs, N.J.: Prentice-Hall, 1989.

Bethell, John T. *Harvard Observed: An Illustrated History of the University in the Twentieth Century*. Cambridge, Mass.: Harvard University Press, 1998.

Bill, James A. *George Ball: Behind the Scenes in U.S. Foreign Policy*. New Haven, Conn.: Yale University Press, 1997.

Birmingham, Stephen. *Real Lace: America's Irish Rich*. New York: Harper and Row, 1973.

Bishop, Jim. *A Day in the Life of President Kennedy*. New York: Random House, 1964.

Bissell, Richard M., Jr. *Reflections of a Cold Warrior*. New Haven, Conn.: Yale University Press, 1996.

Blair, Anne E. *Lodge in Vietnam: A Patriot Abroad*. New Haven, Conn.: Yale University Press, 1995.

Blair, Joan, and Clay Blair Jr. *The Search for JFK*. New York: Berkeley Publishing, 1976.

Blanshard, Paul. *American Freedom and Catholic Power*. 2nd ed. Boston: Beacon Press, 1958.

———. *Personal and Controversial*. Boston: Beacon Press, 1973.

Blaufarb, Douglas S. *The Counterinsurgency Era: U.S. Doctrine and Performance: 1950 to Present*. New York: Free Press, 1977.

Blauvelt, Louis. *The Blauvelt Family Genealogy*. Association of Blauvelt Descendants, 1957.

Bohlen, Charles E. *Witness to History: 1929–1969*. New York: W. W. Norton, 1973.

Bolling, Richard. *House Out of Order*. New York: E. P. Dutton, 1965.

Bowles, Chester. *Promises to Keep: My Years in Public Life, 1941–1969*. New York: Harper and Row, 1971.

Braden, Joan. *Just Enough Rope: An Intimate Memoir*. New York: Villard Books, 1989.

Bradford, Sarah. *America's Queen: The Life of Jacqueline Kennedy Onassis*. New York: Viking, 2000.

Bradlee, Benjamin. *Conversations with Kennedy*. New York: W. W. Norton, 1975.

———. *A Good Life*. New York: Simon and Schuster, 1995.

Branch, Taylor. *Parting the Waters: America in the King Years, 1954–63*. New York: Simon and Schuster, 1989.

Brandt, Willy. *My Life in Politics*. New York: Viking, 1992.

Brauer, Carl. *John F. Kennedy and the Second Reconstruction*. New York: Columbia University Press, 1977.

———. *Presidential Transitions: Eisenhower Through Reagan*. New York: Oxford University Press, 1986.

Breuer, William B. *Devil Boats: The PT War Against Japan*. Novato, Calif.: Presidio Press, 1987.

Brinkley, Douglas. *Dean Acheson: The Cold War Years, 1953–71*. New Haven, Conn.: Yale University Press, 1992.

Brinkley, Douglas, and Richard Griffiths, eds. *John F. Kennedy and Europe*. Baton Rouge: Louisiana State University Press, 1999.

Brown, Thomas. *JFK: History of an Image*. Bloomington: Indiana University Press, 1988.

Bronxville: Views and Vignettes, 1898–1973. New York: Bronxville Diamond Jubilee Committee, 1974.

Bruno, Jerry. *The Advance Man*. New York: Bantam Books, 1971.

Bryant, Traphes. *Dog Days at the White House*. New York: Macmillan, 1975.

Buchan, John. *Pilgrim's Way: An Autobiography*. New York: Carroll and Graf, 1984.

Bundy, McGeorge. *Danger and Survival*. New York: Random House, 1988.

Burke, Richard E. *The Senator: My Ten Years with Ted Kennedy*. New York: St. Martin's Press, 1992.

Burleigh, Nina. *A Very Private Woman: The Life and Unsolved Murder of Presidential Mistress Mary Meyer*. New York: Bantam Books, 1998.

Burner, David, and Thomas R. West. *The Torch Is Passed: The Kennedy Brothers and American Liberalism*. St. James, N.Y.: Brandywine Press, 1984.

Burns, James M. *John Kennedy: A Political Profile*. New York: Harcourt Brace, 1959.

Caroli, Betty Boyd. *First Ladies*. New York: Oxford University Press, 1995.

Cassini, Igor. *I'd Do It All Over Again*. New York: G. P. Putnam's Sons, 1977.

Cassini, Oleg. *In My Own Fashion*. New York: Simon and Schuster, 1987.

———. *A Thousand Days of Magic*. New York: Rizzoli, 1995.

Cate, Curtis. *The Ides of August: The Berlin Wall Crisis, 1961*. New York: M. Evans, 1978.

Catudal, Honoré M. *Kennedy and the Berlin Wall Crisis: A Case Study in U.S. Decision Making*. Berlin: Berlin-Verlag, 1980.

Cecil, David. *Melbourne*. Indianapolis: Bobbs-Merrill, 1954.

Chang, Laurence, and Peter Kornbluh, eds. *The Cuban Missile Crisis, 1962*. New York: New Press, 1992.

Chase, Harold W., and Allen H. Lerman, eds. *Kennedy and the Press: The News Conferences*. New York: Thomas Y. Crowell, 1965.

Cheshire, Maxine. *Maxine Cheshire, Reporter*. Boston: Houghton Mifflin, 1978.

Childs, Marquis. *Witness to Power*. New York: McGraw-Hill, 1975.

Claflin, Edward B., ed. *JFK Wants to Know: Memos from the President's Office, 1961–1963*. New York: William Morrow, 1991.

Clifford, Clark. *Counsel to the President: A Memoir*. New York: Random House, 1991.

Clymer, Adam. *Edward M. Kennedy: A Biography.* New York: William Morrow, 1999.

Cochran, Bert. *Adlai Stevenson: Patrician Among the Politicians.* New York: Funk and Wagnalls, 1969.

Cohen, Adam, and Elizabeth Taylor. *American Pharaoh: Mayor Richard J. Daley: His Battle for Chicago and the Nation.* Boston: Little, Brown, 2000.

Cohen, Warren I. *Dean Rusk.* Totowa, N.J.: Cooper Square Publishers, 1980.

Collier, Peter, and David Horowitz. *The Kennedys: An American Drama.* New York: Summit Books, 1984.

Cook, Blanche Wiesen. *Eleanor Roosevelt: Vol. 2, 1933–1938.* New York: Viking, 1999.

Cooper, Bryan. *The Battle of the Torpedo Boats.* New York: Stein and Day, 1970.

Corbett, Edward, *Classical Rhetoric for the Modern Student.* 2nd ed. New York: Oxford University Press, 1971.

Cornwell Elmer E., Jr. *Presidential Leadership of Public Opinion.* Bloomington: Indiana University Press, 1965.

Crispell, Brian Lewis. *Testing the Limits: George Armistead Smathers and Cold War America.* Athens: University of Georgia Press, 1999.

Crispell, Kenneth R., and Carlos F. Gomez. *Hidden Illness in the White House.* Durham, N.C.: Duke University Press, 1988.

Cronin, Thomas E., and Michael A. Genovese. *The Paradoxes of the American Presidency.* New York: Oxford University Press, 1998.

Curtis, John Gould. *History of the Town of Brookline, Massachusetts.* Boston: Houghton Mifflin, 1933.

Cutler, John Henry. *Cardinal Cushing of Boston.* New York: Hawthorn Books, 1970.

———. *"Honey Fitz": Three Steps to the White House: The Life and Times of John F. (Honey Fitz) Fitzgerald.* Indianapolis: Bobbs-Merrill, 1962.

Dallas, Rita. *The Kennedy Case.* New York: Popular Library, 1973.

Dallek, Robert. *Flawed Giant: Lyndon Johnson and His Times: 1961–1973.* New York: Oxford University Press, 1998.

———. *Lone Star Rising: Lyndon Johnson and His Times: 1908–1960.* New York: Oxford University Press, 1991.

———. *An Unfinished Life: John F. Kennedy, 1917–1963.* Boston: Little, Brown, 2003.

Damore, Leo. *The Cape Cod Years of John Fitzgerald Kennedy.* Englewood Cliffs, N.J.: Prentice-Hall, 1967.

David, Paul T., ed. *The Presidential Election and Transition: 1960–1961.* Washington, D.C.: Brookings Institution, 1961.

David, Sheri. *With Dignity: The Search for Medicare and Medicaid.* Westport, Conn.: Greenwood Press, 1985.

Davies, Norman. *God's Playground: A History of Poland*. Vol. 2. New York: Columbia University Press, 1982.

Davies, Richard O. *Housing Reform During the Truman Administration*. Columbia: University of Missouri Press, 1966.

Davis, John H. *The Kennedys: Dynasty and Disaster: 1848–1983*. New York: McGraw-Hill, 1984.

De Breffny, Brian, ed. *The Irish World*. New York: Harry N. Abrams, 1978.

Destler, I. M. *Presidents, Bureaucrats, and Foreign Policy*. Princeton, N.J.: Princeton University Press, 1972.

Dickerson, Nancy. *Among Those Present*. New York: Random House, 1976.

Divine, Robert. *Since 1945: Politics and Diplomacy in Recent American History*. 3rd ed. New York: McGraw-Hill, 1985.

Dobrynin, Anatoly. *In Confidence*. New York: Random House, 1995.

Donovan, Hedley. *Roosevelt to Reagan*. New York: Harper and Row, 1985.

Donovan, Robert J. *PT 109: John F. Kennedy in World War II*. New York: McGraw-Hill, 1961.

Douglas, Paul. *In the Fullness of Time: The Memoirs of Paul H. Douglas*. New York: Harcourt Brace Jovanovich, 1971.

Douglas, William O. *The Court Years, 1939–1975: The Autobiography of William O. Douglas*. New York: Random House, 1980.

Drudy, P. J., ed. *The Irish in America: Emigration, Assimilation and Impact*. Cambridge, England: Cambridge University Press, 1985.

Druks, Herbert. *The Uncertain Friendship: The U.S. and Israel from Roosevelt to Kennedy*. Westport, Conn.: Greenwood Press, 2001.

Dubbert, Joe. *A Man's Place: Masculinity in Transition*. Englewood Cliffs, N.J.: Prentice-Hall, 1979.

Dunleavy, Stephen, and Peter Brennan. *Those Wild, Wild Kennedy Boys*. New York: Pinnacle Books, 1976.

Earle, Dr. Ralph, and Dr. Gregory Crow. *Lonely All the Time*. New York: Pocket Books, 1989.

Ehrenreich, Barbara, and Deirdre English. *For Her Own Good: 150 Years of the Experts' Advice to Women*. Garden City, N.Y.: Anchor Press/Doubleday, 1978.

Ernst, Harry W. *The Primary That Made a President: West Virginia, 1960*. New York: McGraw-Hill, 1962.

Exner, Judith. *My Story As Told to Ovid Demaris*. New York: Grove Press, 1977.

Fairlie, Henry. *The Kennedy Promise: The Politics of Expectation*. Garden City, N.Y.: Doubleday, 1973.

Fanta, J. Julius. *Sailing with President Kennedy*. New York: Sea Lore Publishing, 1968.

Fay, Paul B., Jr. *The Pleasure of His Company*. New York: Harper and Row, 1966.

Fensch, Thomas, ed. *Top Secret: The Kennedy-Khrushchev Letters*. Woodlands, Tex.: New Century Books, 2001.

Final Report of the Assassination Records Review Board. Washington, D.C.: U.S. Government Printing Office, 1998.

Fleming, Dan B., Jr. *Kennedy vs. Humphrey, West Virginia, 1960*. Jefferson, N.C.: McFarland, 1992.

Fontaine, Joan. *No Bed of Roses*. New York: William Morrow, 1978.

Four Days. Compiled by United Press International and American Heritage Magazine. American Heritage, 1964.

Fox, Stephen. *Blood and Power: Organized Crime in Twentieth-Century America*. New York: William Morrow, 1989.

Franklin, John Hope. *From Slavery to Freedom*. 4th ed. New York: Alfred A. Knopf, 1974.

Freedman, Lawrence. *Kennedy's Wars: Berlin, Cuba, Laos, and Vietnam*. New York: Oxford University Press, 2000.

Fried, Richard M. *Nightmare in Red: The McCarthy Era in Perspective*. New York: Oxford University Press, 1990.

Friedman, Alan. *Agnelli: Fiat and the Network of Italian Power*. New York: New American Library, 1989.

Fuchs, Lawrence H. *John F. Kennedy and American Catholicism*. New York: Meredith Press, 1967.

Fursenko, Aleksandr, and Timothy Naftali. *"One Hell of a Gamble": Khrushchev, Castro, and Kennedy, 1958–1964*. New York: W. W. Norton, 1997.

Gaddis, John Lewis. *We Now Know: Rethinking Cold War History*. New York: Oxford University Press, 1997.

Galbraith, John Kenneth. *Ambassador's Journal: A Personal Account of the Kennedy Years*. New York: Paragon House, 1988.

Gallagher, Mary Barelli. *My Life with Jacqueline Kennedy*. New York: David McKay, 1969.

Gardner, Lloyd C. *Pay Any Price: Lyndon Johnson and the Wars for Vietnam*. Chicago: Ivan R. Dee, 1995.

Garrow, David. *Bearing the Cross: Martin Luther King, Jr., and the Southern Christian Leadership Conference*. New York: William Morrow, 1986.

Garthoff, Raymond L. *Reflections on the Cuban Missile Crisis*. Washington, D.C.: Brookings Institution, 1989.

Gentry, Curt. *J. Edgar Hoover: The Man and the Secrets*. New York: W. W. Norton, 1991.

Gerrard, Thomas. *Marriage and Parenthood*. New York: Joseph F. Wagner, 1911.

Giancana, Antoinette, and Thomas C. Renner. *Mafia Princess: Growing Up in Sam Giancana's Family*. New York: William Morrow, 1984.

Gibson, Barbara, and Ted Schwarz. *Rose Kennedy and Her Family*. New York: Birch Lane Press, 1995.

Giglio, James. *The Presidency of John F. Kennedy*. Lawrence: University Press of Kansas, 1991.

Giglio, James, and Stephen Rabe. *Debating the Kennedy Presidency*. Lanham, Md.: Rowman and Littlefield, 2003.

Gilbert, Robert E. *The Mortal Presidency: Illness and Anguish in the White House*. New York: Basic Books, 1992.

Gillon, Steven M. *Politics and Vision: The ADA and American Liberalism, 1947–1985*. New York: Oxford University Press, 1987.

Goldfarb, Ronald. *Perfect Villains, Imperfect Heroes*. New York: Random House, 1995.

Goldman, Eric F. *The Crucial Decade: America, 1945–1955*. New York: Alfred A. Knopf, 1959.

Goodman, Aviel. *Sexual Addiction: An Integrated Approach*. Madison, Conn.: International Universities Press, 1998.

Goodwin, Doris Kearns. *The Fitzgeralds and the Kennedys*. New York: Simon and Schuster, 1987.

Goodwin, Richard N. *Remembering America: A Voice from the Sixties*. Boston: Little, Brown, 1988.

Gordon, David C. *The Passing of French Algeria*. London: Oxford University Press, 1966.

Gorman, Joseph Bruce. *Kefauver: A Political Biography*. New York: Oxford University Press, 1971.

Gormley, Ken. *Archibald Cox: Conscience of a Nation*. Reading, Mass.: Addison-Wesley, 1997.

Graham, Hugh. *The Uncertain Triumph: Federal Education Policy in the Kennedy and Johnson Years*. Chapel Hill: University of North Carolina Press, 1984.

Graham Otis L., Jr. *Toward a Planned Society: From Roosevelt to Nixon*. New York: Oxford University Press, 1976.

Greeley, Andrew M. *The Irish Americans*. New York: Harper and Row, 1981.

———. *That Most Distressful Nation*. Chicago: Quadrangle Books, 1972.

Gunther, John. *Inside Europe*. New York: Harper and Brothers, 1937.

Guthman, Edwin. *We Band of Brothers*. New York: Harper and Row, 1971.

Guthman, Edwin O., and Jeffrey Shulman, eds. *Robert Kennedy in His Own Words: The Unpublished Recollections of the Kennedy Years*. New York: Bantam Books, 1988.

Halberstam, David. *The Best and the Brightest*. New York: Random House, 1969.

———. *The Powers That Be*. New York: Alfred A. Knopf, 1979.

Hamby, Alonzo L. *Liberalism and Its Challengers: From F.D.R. to Bush*. 2nd ed. New York: Oxford University Press, 1992.

Hamilton, Nigel. *J.F.K.: Reckless Youth*. New York: Random House, 1992.

Handlin, Oscar. *Boston's Immigrants: A Study in Acculturation*. Cambridge, Mass.: Belknap Press of Harvard University Press, 1959.

Harper, Paul, and Joann Krieg, eds. *John F. Kennedy: The Promise Revisited*. Westport, Conn.: Greenwood Press, 1988.

Harrison, Cynthia. *On Account of Sex: The Politics of Women's Issues, 1945–1968*. Berkeley: University of California Press, 1988.

Hart, Roderick P. *The Sound of Leadership*. Chicago: University of Chicago Press, 1987.

Hearst, William Randolph, Jr. *The Hearsts: Father and Son*. Niwot, Colo.: Robert Rinehart, 1991.

Heath, Jim F. *John F. Kennedy and the Business Community*. Chicago: University of Chicago Press, 1969.

Heilbroner, Robert, and Aaron Singer, eds. *The Economic Transformation of America: 1600 to the Present*. 4th ed. Fort Worth: Harcourt Brace College Publishers, 1999.

Heller, Walter W. *New Dimensions of Political Economy*. Cambridge, Mass.: Harvard University Press, 1967.

Hellmann, John. *The Kennedy Obsession: The American Myth of JFK*. New York: Columbia University Press, 1997.

Henderson, Deirdre, ed. *Prelude to Leadership: The European Diary of John F. Kennedy: Summer 1945*. Washington, D.C.: Regnery Publishing, 1995.

Hennessy, Maurice N. *I'll Come Back in the Springtime: John F. Kennedy and the Irish*. New York: Ives Washburn, 1966.

Herring, George C. *America's Longest War: The United States and Vietnam, 1950–1975*. 2nd ed. New York: Alfred A. Knopf, 1986.

Hersh, Seymour M. *The Dark Side of Camelot*. Boston: Little, Brown, 1997.

Hess, Stephen. *Organizing the Presidency*. Washington, D.C.: Brookings Institution, 1988.

Heymann, C. David. *A Woman Named Jackie*. New York: Carol Communications, 1989.

Higham, Charles. *Rose: The Life and Times of Rose Fitzgerald Kennedy*. New York: Pocket Books, 1995.

Hills, T. L. *The St. Lawrence Seaway*. New York: Frederick A. Praeger, 1959.

Hilsman, Roger. *To Move a Nation*. Garden City, N.Y.: Doubleday, 1967.

Hilty, James W. *Robert Kennedy: Brother Protector*. Philadelphia: Temple University Press, 1997.

Hoffman, Elizabeth Cobbs. *All You Need Is Love: The Peace Corps and the Spirit of the 1960s*. Cambridge, Mass.: Harvard University Press, 1998.

Hohenberg, John. *The Pulitzer Diaries: Inside America's Greatest Prize*. Syracuse, N.Y.: Syracuse University Press, 1997.

Holt, L. Emmett. *The Care and Feeding of Children*. 10th ed. New York: D. Appleton, 1920.

Holt, P. M., and Ann K. S. Lambton, eds. *The Cambridge History of Islam*. Vol. 2. Cambridge, England: University Press, 1970.

Holtzman, Abraham. *Legislative Liaison: Executive Leadership in Congress*. Chicago: Rand McNally, 1970.

Hopper, Bruce. *Pan-Sovietism: The Issue Before America and the World*. Boston: Houghton Mifflin, 1931.

Horne, Alistair. *Harold Macmillan*. Vol. 2, *1957–1986*. New York: Viking, 1989.

Horton, D. C. *Fire over the Islands: The Coast Watchers of the Solomons*. London: Leo Cooper, 1970.

Hourani, Albert. *A History of the Arab Peoples*. Cambridge, Mass.: Belknap Press of Harvard University Press, 1991.

Hoyt, Edwin. *The Glory of the Solomons*. New York: Stein and Day, 1983.

Hutchinson, Dennis J. *The Man Who Once Was Whizzer White: A Portrait of Justice Byron R. White*. New York: Free Press, 1998.

Javits, Jacob K. *Discrimination U.S.A.* New York: Harcourt, Brace, 1960.

———. *Javits: The Autobiography of a Public Man*. Boston: Houghton Mifflin, 1981.

Johnson, Richard Tanner. *Managing the White House: An Intimate Study of the Presidency*. New York: Harper and Row, 1974.

Johnson, U. Alexis. *The Right Hand of Power*. Englewood Cliffs, N.J.: Prentice-Hall, 1984.

Johnson, Walter, ed. *The Papers of Adlai E. Stevenson: Toward a New America, 1955–1957*. Volume 6. Boston: Little, Brown, 1976.

Joll, James. *Europe Since 1870: An International History*. New York: Harper and Row, 1973.

Kallina, Edmund F., Jr. *Courthouse over White House: Chicago and the Presidential Election of 1960*. Orlando: University of Central Florida Press, 1988.

Kaufman, Martin, John Ifkovic, and Joseph Carvalho, eds. *A Guide to the History of Massachusetts*. Westport, Conn.: Greenwood Press, 1988.

Kelley, Kitty. *His Way: The Unauthorized Biography of Frank Sinatra*. New York: Bantam Books, 1986.

———. *Jackie Oh!* Secaucus, N.J.: Lyle Stuart, 1978.

Kennan, George F. *Memoirs: 1925–1950*. Boston: Little, Brown, 1967.

———. *Memoirs: 1950–1963*. Vol. 2. Boston: Little, Brown, 1972.

Kennedy, Edward M., ed. *The Fruitful Bough: A Tribute to Joseph P. Kennedy*. Halliday Lithograph, 1965.

Kennedy, John F., ed. *As We Remember Joe*. Cambridge, Mass.: University Press, 1945.

Kennedy, John F. *Profiles in Courage*. Garden City, N.Y.: International Collectors Library, 1964.

Kennedy, Rose Fitzgerald. *Times to Remember*. Garden City, N.Y.: Doubleday, 1974.

Kenney, Charles. *John F. Kennedy: The Presidential Portfolio*. New York: Public Affairs, 2000.

Kent, Janet. *The Solomon Islands*. Harrisburg, Pa.: Stackpole Books, 1972.

Keresey, Dick. *PT 105*. Annapolis, Md.: Naval Institute Press, 1996.

Kern, Montague, Patricia W. and Ralph B. Levering. *The Kennedy Crises: The Press, the Presidency, and Foreign Policy*. Chapel Hill: University of North Carolina Press, 1983.

Kessler, Ronald. *Inside the White House.* New York: Pocket Books, 1995.

———. *The Sins of the Father.* New York: Warner Books, 1996.

Kimbrell, Andrew. *The Masculine Mystique: The Politics of Masculinity.* New York: Ballantine Books, 1995.

King, Larry. *Tell It to the King.* Thorndike, Maine: Thorndike Press, 1988.

Klein, Edward. *All Too Human: The Love Story of Jack and Jackie Kennedy.* New York: Pocket Books, 1996.

Kochavi, Noam. *A Conflict Perpetuated: China Policy During the Kennedy Years.* Westport, Conn.: Praeger, 2002.

Korda, Michael. *Male Chauvinism! How It Works.* New York: Random House, 1972.

Koskoff, David E. *Joseph P. Kennedy: A Life and Times.* Englewood Cliffs, N.J.: Prentice-Hall, 1974.

Kraft, Joseph. *Profiles in Power: A Washington Insight.* New York: New American Library, 1966.

Kramnick, Isaac, and Barry Sheerman. *Harold Laski: A Life on the Left.* Allen Lane: The Penguin Press, 1993.

Krock, Arthur. *Memoirs: Sixty Years on the Firing Line.* New York: Funk and Wagnalls, 1968.

Lamarr, Hedy. *Ecstasy and Me: My Life as a Woman.* Bartholomew House Publishers, 1966.

Landau, Ronnie S. *The Nazi Holocaust.* Chicago: Ivan R. Dee, 1994.

Lapomarda, Vincent A. *The Boston Mayor Who Became Truman's Secretary of Labor: Maurice J. Tobin and the Democratic Party.* New York: Peter Lang, 1995.

Larson, Gary O. *The Reluctant Patron: The United States Government and the Arts, 1943–1965.* Philadelphia: University of Pennsylvania Press, 1983.

Latham, Caroline, and Jeannie Sakol, eds. *The Kennedy Encyclopedia.* New York: New American Library, 1989.

Latham, Earl. *Massachusetts Politics.* New York: Citizenship Clearing House, 1956.

Lawford, Patricia Kennedy. *That Shining Hour.* Privately published, 1969.

Lawford, Patricia Seaton. *The Peter Lawford Story: Life with the Kennedys, Monroe and the Rat Pack.* New York: Carroll and Graf, 1988.

Lawson, Annette. *Adultery: An Analysis of Love and Betrayal.* New York: Basic Books, 1988.

Leamer, Laurence. *The Kennedy Women: The Saga of an American Family.* New York: Villard Books, 1994.

Leaming, Barbara. *Marilyn Monroe.* New York: Crown Publishers, 1998.

Lebow, Richard Ned, and Janice Gross Stein. *We All Lost the Cold War.* Princeton, N.J.: Princeton University Press, 1994.

Lee, R. Alton. *Eisenhower and Landrum-Griffin: A Study in Labor-Management Politics.* Lexington: University Press of Kentucky, 1990.

————. *Truman and Taft Hartley: A Question of Mandate*. Lexington: University of Kentucky Press, 1966.

Lerner, Alan Jay. *The Street Where I Live*. New York: W. W. Norton, 1978.

Leuchtenburg, William E. *In the Shadow of FDR*. Ithaca, N.Y.: Cornell University Press, 1989.

Lewis, Anthony. *Portrait of a Decade: The Second American Revolution*. New York: Bantam Books, 1971.

Lieberson, Goddard, ed. *John Fitzgerald Kennedy . . . As We Remember Him*. New York: Atheneum, 1965.

Lincoln, Evelyn. *My Twelve Years with John F. Kennedy*. New York: David McKay, 1965.

Lowe, Jacques. *Jacqueline Kennedy Onassis: The Making of a First Lady*. Los Angeles: General Publishing Group, 1996.

————. *Portrait: The Emergence of John F. Kennedy*. New York: Bramhall House, 1961.

MacMahon, Edward, and Leonard Curry. *Medical Cover-ups in the White House*. Washington, D.C.: Farragut Publishing, 1987.

Macmillan, Harold. *At the End of the Day: 1961–1963*. New York: Harper and Row, 1973.

Maheu, Robert, and Richard Hack. *Next to Hughes*. New York: HarperCollins, 1992.

Mahoney, Richard D. *JFK: Ordeal in Africa*. New York: Oxford University Press, 1983.

Manchester, William. *The Death of the President*. New York: Harper and Row, 1967.

Marable, Manning. *Race, Reform and Rebellion: The Second Reconstruction in Black America, 1945–1982*. Jackson: University Press of Mississippi, 1984.

Marmor, Theodore. *The Politics of Medicare*. London: Routledge and Kegan Paul, 1970.

Martin, John Bartlow. *Adlai Stevenson of Illinois: The Life of Adlai E. Stevenson*. Garden City, N.Y.: Doubleday, 1976.

Martin, Ralph G. *Henry and Clare: An Intimate Portrait of the Luces*. New York: G. P. Putnam's Sons, 1991.

————. *A Hero for Our Time: An Intimate Story of the Kennedy Years*. New York: Macmillan, 1983.

Martin, Ralph G., and Ed Plaut. *Front Runner, Dark Horse*. Garden City, N.Y.: Doubleday, 1960.

Matthews, Christopher. *Kennedy and Nixon*. New York: Simon and Schuster, 1996.

Matusow, Allen. *The Unraveling of America: A History of Liberalism in the 1960s*. New York: Harper and Row, 1984.

May, Ernest R., and Philip D. Zelikow, eds. *The Kennedy Tapes: Inside the White House During the Cuban Missle Crisis*. Cambridge, Mass.: Belknap Press of Harvard University Press, 1997.

Mays, Victor. *Pathway to a Village: A History of Bronxville*. Bronxville, N.Y.: Nebko Press, 1961.

McCarthy, Joe. *The Remarkable Kennedys*. New York: Popular Library, 1960.

McCaffrey, Lawrence J. *The Irish Catholic Diaspora in America*. Washington, D.C.: Catholic University of America Press, 1997.

McClintock, Michael. *Instruments of Statecraft*. New York: Pantheon Books, 1992.

McKeever, Porter. *Adlai Stevenson: His Life and Legacy*. New York: William Morrow, 1989.

McLellan, David S., and David C. Acheson, eds. *Among Friends: Personal Letters of Dean Acheson*. New York: Dodd, Mead, 1980.

McNamara, Robert S. *In Retrospect: The Tragedy and Lessons of Vietnam*. New York: Vintage Books, 1995.

McQuaid, Kim. *Big Business and Presidential Power: From FDR to Reagan*. New York: William Morrow, 1982.

McTaggart, Lynne. *Kathleen Kennedy, Her Life and Times*. Garden City, N.Y.: Dial Press, 1983.

Means, Marianne. *The Woman in the White House*. New York: Random House, 1963.

Mecklin, John. *Mission in Torment: An Intimate Account of the U.S. Role in Vietnam*. Garden City, N.Y.: Doubleday, 1965.

Medved, Michael. *The Shadow Presidents: The Secret History of the Chief Executives and Their Top Aides*. New York: Times Books, 1979.

Merrill, Dennis. *Bread and the Ballot: The United States and India's Economic Development, 1947–1963*. Chapel Hill: University of North Carolina Press, 1990.

Merry, Robert W. *Taking On the World: Joseph and Stewart Alsop, Guardians of the American Century*. New York: Viking Penguin, 1996.

Meyers, Jeffrey. *Robert Frost: A Biography*. Boston: Houghton Mifflin, 1996.

Miller, Nathan. *War at Sea: A Naval History of World War II*. New York: Oxford University Press, 1995.

Miller, William "Fishbait." *Fishbait: The Memoirs of the Congressional Doorkeeper*. Englewood Cliffs, N.J.: Prentice-Hall, 1977.

Mintz, Steven, and Susan Kellogg. *Domestic Revolutions: A Social History of American Family Life*. New York: Free Press, 1988.

Mitchell, Arthur. *JFK and His Irish Heritage*. Dublin, Ireland: Moytura Press, 1993.

Morgan, Anne Hodges. *Robert S. Kerr: The Senate Years*. Norman: University of Oklahoma Press, 1977.

Muller, Herbert J. *Adlai Stevenson: A Study in Values*. New York: Harper and Row, 1967.

Murphy, David E., Sergei A. Kondrashev, and George Bailey. *Battleground Berlin: CIA vs. KGB in the Cold War*. New Haven, Conn.: Yale University Press, 1997.

Murray, Donette. *Kennedy, Macmillan and Nuclear Weapons*. Houndmills, Basingstoke, Hampshire: Macmillan Press 2000.

Nash, Philip. *The Other Missiles of October*. Chapel Hill: University of North Carolina Press, 1997.

Nathan, James A., ed. *The Cuban Missile Crisis Revisited*. New York: St. Martin's Press, 1992.

Navasky, Victor S. *Kennedy Justice*. New York: Atheneum, 1971.

Nelson, Harold, ed. *Poland: A Country Study*. Washington, D.C.: American University, 1984.

Newman, John M. *JFK and Vietnam: Deception, Intrigue, and the Struggle for Power*. New York: Warner Books, 1992.

Newman, Michael. *Harold Laski: A Political Biography*. Houndmills, Basingstoke Hampshire: Macmillan Press, 1993.

Nitze, Paul H. *From Hiroshima to Glasnost: At the Center of Decision, A Memoir*. New York: Grove Weidenfeld, 1989.

Niven, David. *The Moon's a Balloon: Reminiscences*. London: Hamish Hamilton, 1971.

Nixon, Richard. *The Memoirs of Richard Nixon*. New York: Grosset and Dunlap, 1978.

Nunnerley, David. *President Kennedy and Britain*. New York: St. Martin's Press, 1972.

O'Brien, Lawrence F. *No Final Victories: A Life in Politics from John F. Kennedy to Watergate*. Garden City, N.Y.: Doubleday, 1974.

O'Brien, Michael. *Hesburgh: A Biography*. Washington, D.C.: Catholic University of America Press, 1998.

———. *McCarthy and McCarthyism in Wisconsin*. Columbia: University of Missouri Press, 1980.

O'Connor, Thomas H. *Bibles, Brahmins and Bosses*. Boston: Trustees of the Public Library, 1976.

O'Donnell, Helen. *A Common Good: The Friendship of Robert F. Kennedy and Kenneth P. O'Donnell*. New York: William Morrow, 1998.

O'Donnell, Kenneth P., and David F. Powers. *"Johnny, We Hardley Knew Ye": Memories of John Fitzgerald Kennedy*. Boston: Little, Brown, 1970.

Olson, Gregory Allen. *Mansfield and Vietnam: A Study in Rhetorical Adaptation*. East Lansing: Michigan State University Press, 1995.

Olson, James, and Randy Roberts. *Where the Domino Fell: America and Vietnam, 1945 to 1990*. New York: St. Martin's Press, 1991.

———. *Where the Domino Fell: America and Vietnam, 1945 to 1995*. 2nd ed. New York: St. Martin's Press, 1996.

O'Neill, Tip. *Man of the House: The Life and Political Memoirs of Speaker Tip O'Neill*. New York: Random House, 1987.

Orman, John M. *Presidential Secrecy and Deception: Beyond the Power to Persuade*. Westport, Conn.: Greenwood Press, 1980.

Oshinsky, David M. *A Conspiracy So Immense: The World of Joe McCarthy*. New York: Free Press, 1983.

Parini, Jay. *Robert Frost: A Life*. New York: Henry Holt, 1999.

Park, Bert E. *Ailing, Aging, Addicted: Studies of Compromised Leadership.* Lexington: University Press of Kentucky, 1993.

Parker, Robert. *Capitol Hill in Black and White.* New York: Dodd, Mead, 1986.

Parmet, Herbert S. *Jack: The Struggles of John F. Kennedy.* New York: Dial Press, 1980.

Parsons, Talcott, and Kenneth Clark. *The Negro American.* Boston: Houghton Mifflin, 1966.

Paterson, Thomas G. *Meeting the Communist Threat: Truman to Reagan.* New York: Oxford University Press, 1988.

Patterson, James T. *America's Struggle Against Poverty, 1900–1980.* Cambridge, Mass.: Harvard University Press, 1981.

———. *Grand Expectations: The United States, 1945–1974.* New York: Oxford University Press, 1996.

Pearson, John. *The Life of Ian Fleming.* New York: McGraw-Hill, 1966.

Perret, Geoffrey. *Eisenhower.* New York: Random House, 1999.

Pierpoint, Robert. *At the White House: Assignment to Six Presidents.* New York: G. P. Putnam's Sons, 1981.

Pollard, James E. *The Presidents and the Press: Truman to Johnson.* Washington, D.C.: Public Affairs Press, 1964.

Powers, Richard. *Secrecy and Power: The Life of J. Edgar Hoover.* New York: Free Press, 1987.

Powers, Thomas. *The Man Who Kept the Secrets: Richard Helms and the CIA.* New York: Alfred A. Knopf, 1979.

Prados, John. *The Hidden History of the Vietnam War.* Chicago: Ivan R. Dee, 1995.

———. *Keeper of the Keys: A History of the National Security Council from Truman to Bush.* New York: William Morrow, 1991.

Prescott, Peter S. *A World of Our Own.* New York: Coward-McCann, 1970.

Prochnau, William. *Once Upon a Distant War.* New York: Times Books, 1995.

Quirk, Lawrence. *The Kennedys in Hollywood.* Dallas: Taylor Publishing, 1996.

Rabe, Stephen. *The Most Dangerous Area in the World: John F. Kennedy Confronts Communist Revolution in Latin America.* Chapel Hill: University of North Carolina Press, 1999.

Ranelagh, John. *The Agency: The Rise and Decline of the CIA.* New York: Simon and Schuster, 1986.

Reedy, George. *Lyndon B. Johnson: A Memoir.* Kansas City: Andrews and McMeel, 1982.

Reinsch, J. Leonard. *Getting Elected: From Radio and Roosevelt to Television and Reagan.* New York: Hippocrene, 1988.

Reston, James. *Deadline: A Memoir.* New York: Random House, 1991.

Rice, Gerard T. *The Bold Experiment: JFK's Peace Corps.* Notre Dame, Ind.: University of Notre Dame Press, 1985.

Rice, Otis, and Stephen W. Brown. *West Virginia: A History*. 2nd ed. Lexington: University Press of Kentucky, 1993.

Riva, Maria. *Marlene Dietrich*. New York: Alfred A. Knopf, 1993.

Rorty, James, and Moshe Decter. *McCarthy and the Communists*. Boston: Beacon Press, 1954.

Rovere, Richard. *Final Reports*. Garden City, N.Y.: Doubleday, 1984.

Rowan, Carl. *Breaking Barriers: A Memoir*. Boston: Little, Brown, 1991.

Rusk, Dean. *As I Saw It*. New York: W. W. Norton, 1990.

Ryan, Dennis. *Beyond the Ballot Box: A Social History of the Boston Irish, 1845–1917*. East Brunswick, N.J.: Associated University Presses, 1983.

Sabato, Larry J. *Feeding Frenzy*. New York: Free Press, 1991.

Salinger, Pierre. *With Kennedy*. Garden City, N.Y.: Doubleday, 1966.

Saunders, Frank. *Torn Lace Curtain*. New York: Holt, Rinehart and Winston, 1982.

Scheerenberger, R. C. *A History of Mental Retardation*. Baltimore: Paul H. Brookes, 1983.

Schickel, Richard. *Intimate Strangers: The Culture of Celebrity*. Garden City, N.Y.: Doubleday, 1985.

Schlesinger, Arthur M., Jr. *Robert Kennedy and His Times*. Boston: Houghton Mifflin, 1978.

———. *A Thousand Days: John F. Kennedy in the White House*. New York: Fawcett World Library, 1965.

Schwab, Orrin. *Defending the Free World: John F. Kennedy, Lyndon Johnson, and the Vietnam War, 1961–1965*. Westport, Conn.: Praeger, 1998.

Seaborg, Glenn T. *Kennedy, Khrushchev and the Test Ban*. Berkeley: University of California Press, 1981.

Searls, Hank. *The Lost Prince: Young Joe, the Forgotten Kennedy*. New York: World Publishing, 1969.

Shannon, William. *The American Irish*. New York: Collier Books, 1974.

Shapley, Deborah. *Promise and Power: The Life and Times of Robert McNamara*. Boston: Little, Brown, 1993.

Shaw, Maud. *White House Nannie: My Years with Caroline and John Kennedy, Jr.* New York: New American Library, 1965.

Shesol, Jeff. *Mutual Contempt: Lyndon Johnson, Robert Kennedy, and the Feud That Defined a Decade*. New York: W. W. Norton, 1997.

Shipman, David. *Judy Garland: The Secret Life of an American Legend*. New York: Hyperion, 1992.

Sidey, Hugh. *John F. Kennedy, President*. New York: Atheneum, 1963.

Smith, Amanda ed. *Hostage to Fortune: The Letters of Joseph P. Kennedy*. New York: Viking, 2001.

Smith, Richard Norton. *The Harvard Century*. New York: Simon and Schuster, 1986.

Smith, Sally Bedell. *Reflected Glory: The Life of Pamela Churchill Harriman*. New York: Simon and Schuster, 1996.

Snyder, J. Richard, ed. *John F. Kennedy: Person, Policy, Presidency*. Wilmington, Del.: Scholarly Resources, 1988.

Solberg, Carl. *Hubert Humphrey: A Biography*. New York: W. W. Norton, 1984.

Sorensen, Theodore. *Decision-Making in the White House*. New York: Columbia University Press, 1963.

———. *Kennedy*. New York: Harper and Row, 1965.

———. *The Kennedy Legacy*. New York: Macmillan, 1969.

———, ed. *"Let the Word Go Forth": The Speeches, Statements, and Writings of John F. Kennedy, 1947–1963*. New York: Laurel, 1988.

Sperber, A. M. *Murrow: His Life and Times*. New York: Freundlich Books, 1986.

Spielvogel, Jackson J. *Hitler and Nazi Germany: A History*. Englewood Cliffs, N.J.: Prentice-Hall, 1988.

Spoto, Donald. *Marilyn Monroe: The Biography*. New York: HarperCollins, 1993.

Stack, John F. *International Conflict in an American City*. Westport, Conn.: Greenwood Press, 1979.

Stack, Robert. *Straight Shooting*. New York: Macmillan, 1980.

Stampp, Kenneth. *The Era of Reconstruction, 1865–1877*. New York: Alfred A. Knopf, 1966.

Starr, Blaze, and Huey Perry. *Blaze Starr: My Life As Told to Huey Perry*. New York: Praeger, 1974.

Steel, Ronald. *In Love with Night: The American Romance with Robert Kennedy*. New York: Simon and Schuster, 2000.

———. *Walter Lippmann and the American Century*. Boston: Little, Brown, 1980.

Stein, Herbert. *The Fiscal Revolution in America*. Chicago: University of Chicago Press, 1969.

Stein, Jean, ed. *American Journey: The Times of Robert Kennedy*. New York: Harcourt Brace Jovanovich, 1970.

Steinberg, Alfred. *Sam Rayburn: A Biography*. New York: Hawthorn Books, 1975.

Stivers, Richard. *Hair of the Dog: Irish Drinking and Its American Stereotype*. New York: Continuum, 2000.

St. John, George. *Forty Years at School*. New York: Henry Holt, 1959.

Stone, Ralph A., ed. *John F. Kennedy: 1917–1963*. Dobbs Ferry, N.Y.: Oceana Publications, 1971.

Storm, Tempest, and Bill Boyd. *Tempest Storm: The Lady Is a Vamp*. Atlanta: Peachtree Publishers, 1987.

Strait, Raymond. *The Tragic Secret Life of Jayne Mansfield*. Chicago: Henry Regnery, 1974.

Strober, Gerald, and Deborah Strober. *"Let Us Begin Anew": An Oral History of the Kennedy Presidency*. New York: HarperCollins, 1993.

Summers, Anthony. *Goddess: The Secret Lives of Marilyn Monroe*. New York: Macmillan, 1985.

Sundquist, James. *Politics and Policy: The Eisenhower, Kennedy, and Johnson Years.* Washington, D.C.: Brookings Institution, 1968.

Swanson, Gloria. *Swanson on Swanson.* New York: Random House, 1980.

Tanzer, Lester, ed. *The Kennedy Circle.* Washington, D.C.: Robert B. Luce, 1961.

Taylor, Maxwell D. *Swords and Plowshares.* New York: W. W. Norton, 1972.

Taylor, Richard. *Love Affairs: Marriage and Infidelity.* Amherst, N.Y.: Prometheus Books, 1997.

terHorst, J. F., and Colonel Ralph Albertazzie. *The Flying White House: The Story of Air Force One.* New York: Coward, McCann and Geoghegan, 1979.

Theoharis, Athan, ed. *From the Secret Files of J. Edgar Hoover.* Chicago: Ivan R. Dee, 1991.

Theoharis, Athan, and John Stuart Cox. *The Boss: J. Edgar Hoover and the Great American Inquisition.* Philadelphia: Temple University Press, 1988.

Theriot, Nancy. *Mothers and Daughters in Nineteenth-Century America.* Lexington: University Press of Kentucky, 1996.

Thomas, Evan. *Robert Kennedy: His Life.* New York: Simon and Schuster, 2000.

Thomas, Helen. *Dateline: White House.* New York: Macmillan, 1975.

———. *Front Row at the White House: My Life and Times.* New York: Charles Scribner's Sons, 1999.

Thompson, Kenneth W., ed. *The Kennedy Presidency.* Lanham, Md.: University Press of America, 1985.

Thompson, William. *The History of Wisconsin: Continuity and Change, 1940–1965.* Vol. 6. Madison: State Historical Society of Wisconsin, 1988.

Tierney, Gene. *Self-Portrait.* New York: Wyden Books, 1979.

Toscano, Vincent L. *Since Dallas: Images of John F. Kennedy in Popular and Scholarly Literature, 1963–1973.* San Francisco: R and E Research Associates, 1978.

Trachtenberg, Peter. *The Casanova Complex: Compulsive Lovers and Their Women.* New York: Poseidon Press, 1988.

Travell, Janet. *Office Hours: Day and Night, the Autobiography of Janet Travell, M.D..* New York: World Publishing, 1968.

Tregaskis, Richard. *John F. Kennedy and PT-109.* Eau Claire, Wisc.: E. M. Hale, 1962.

Trent, James. *Inventing the Feeble Mind: A History of Mental Retardation in the United States.* Berkeley: University of California Press, 1994.

The U.S. Government and the Vietnam War. Part 2, 1961–1964. Washington, D.C.: U.S. Government Printing Office, 1985.

Valeo, Francis R. *Mike Mansfield: Majority Leader.* Armonk, N.Y.: M. E. Sharpe, 1999.

Von Post, Gunilla. *Love, Jack.* New York: Crown Publishers, 1997.

Watson, Mary Ann. *The Expanding Vista: American Television in the Kennedy Years.* New York: Oxford University Press, 1990.

Weisbrot, Robert. *Maximum Danger: Kennedy, the Missiles, and the Crisis of American Confidence.* Chicago: Ivan R. Dee, 2001.

Weiss, Murray, and Bill Hoffmann. *Palm Beach Babylon.* New York: Birch Lane Press, 1992.

West, J. B. *Upstairs at the White House.* New York: Coward, McCann and Geoghegan, 1973.

Whalen, Charles, and Barbara Whalen. *The Longest Debate: A Legislative History of the 1964 Civil Rights Act.* New York: New American Library, 1985.

Whalen, Richard J. *The Founding Father: The Story of Joseph P. Kennedy.* New York: New American Library, 1964.

Whalen, Thomas. *Kennedy Versus Lodge: The 1952 Massachusetts Senate Race.* Boston: Northeastern University Press, 2000.

White, Mark, ed. *Kennedy: The New Frontier Revisited.* New York: New York University Press, 1998.

———. *The Kennedys and Cuba: The Declassified Documentary History.* Chicago: Ivan R. Dee, 1999.

White, Theodore H. *In Search of History: A Personal Adventure.* New York: Harper and Row, 1978.

———. *The Making of the President: 1960.* New York: New American Library, 1961.

Whitefield, Stephen J. *The Culture of the Cold War.* Baltimore: Johns Hopkins University Press, 1991.

Wicker, Tom. *JFK and LBJ: The Influence of Personality upon Politics.* New York: William Morrow, 1968.

———. *Kennedy Without Tears: The Man Beneath the Myth.* New York: William Morrow, 1964.

Wilkins, Roy. *Standing Fast: The Autobiography of Roy Wilkins.* New York: Penguin Books, 1982.

Williams, Paul Kelsey. *The Historic Homes of JFK.* Auburn, N.Y.: Topical Book, 1992.

Wills, Garry. *The Kennedy Imprisonment.* Boston: Little, Brown, 1981.

Wofford, Harris. *Of Kennedys and Kings: Making Sense of the Sixties.* New York: Farrar, Straus, and Giroux, 1980.

Wolpert, Stanley. *Nehru: A Tryst with Destiny.* New York: Oxford University Press, 1996.

Woods, Randall Bennett. *Fulbright: A Biography.* New York: Cambridge University Press, 1995.

Wright, Gordon. *The Ordeal of Total War, 1939–1945.* New York: Harper and Row, 1968.

Wright, Gordon, and Arthur Mejia, eds. *An Age of Controversy.* New York: Dodd, Mead, 1973.

Wyden, Peter. *Bay of Pigs: The Untold Story.* New York: Simon and Schuster, 1979.

Youcha, Geraldine. *Minding the Children.* New York: Charles Scribner's Sons, 1995.

SELECTED ARTICLES

Approximately 150 articles from *Time, Newsweek*, and *U.S. News and World Report* are not included in this listing.

"After the Election." *Commonweal*, November 18, 1960, 187–188.

Alkema, Ynze. "European-American Trade Policies, 1961–1963." In *John F. Kennedy and Europe*, edited by Douglas Brinkley and Richard Griffiths, 212–234. Baton Rouge: Louisiana State University Press, 1999.

Allison, G. T. "Cuban Missiles and Kennedy Macho: New Evidence to Dispel the Myth." *Washington Monthly*, October 1972, 14–19.

Alsop, Joseph. "The Legacy of John F. Kennedy: Memories of an Uncommon Man." *Saturday Evening Post*, November 21, 1964, 15–19.

Alsop, Stewart. "The Collapse of Kennedy's Grand Design." *Saturday Evening Post*, April 6, 1963, 78–81.

———. "The White House Insiders." *Saturday Evening Post*, June 10, 1961, 19–21, 91, 94, 95, 98.

Alsop, Stewart, and Charles Bartlett. "In Time of Crisis." *Saturday Evening Post*, December 8, 1962, 15–20.

Ambrose, Stephen E. "The Ups and Downs of Presidential Reputations." *Times Literary Supplement*, July 19, 1991, 9.

Antunes, José Freire. "Kennedy, Portugal, and the Azores Base, 1961." In *John F. Kennedy and Europe*, edited by Douglas Brinkley and Richard Griffiths, 148–165. Baton Rouge: Louisiana State University Press, 1999.

Ascoli, Max. "The Inaugural Address." *Reporter*, February 2, 1961, 10, 12.

Baldwin, Hanson W. "Managed News: Our Peacetime Censorship." *Atlantic Monthly*, April 1963, 53–59.

Ball, George W. "JFK's Big Moment." *New York Review of Books*, February 13, 1992, 16–20.

———. "Kennedy Up Close." *New York Review of Books*, February 3, 1994, 17–20.

Ball, Moya Ann. "Vacillating About Vietnam: Secrecy, Duplicity, and Confusion in the Communication of President Kennedy and His Advisors." In *Group Communication in Context*, edited by Lawrence Frey, 181–198. Hillsdale, New Jersey: Lawrence Erlbaum Associates, Publishers, 1994.

Barkaoui, Miloud. "Kennedy and the Cold War Imbroglio: The Case of Algeria's Independence." *Arab Studies Quarterly* 21 (Spring 1999): 31–45.

Bayley, Edwin R. "Kennedy Warms Up Wisconsin Democrats." *New Republic*, June 2, 1958, 9.

Beauchamp, Cari. "The Mogul in Mr. Kennedy." *Vanity Fair*, April 2002, 394–407.

Beck, Kent M. "Necessary Lies, Hidden Truths: Cuba in the 1960 Campaign." *Diplomatic History* 8 (1984): 37–59.

Bergquist, Laura. "Fiddle and Faddle." *Look*, January 2, 1962, 30–33, 35.

———. "Rose Kennedy." *Look*, November 26, 1968, 25–34.

———. "What Women Really Meant to JFK." *Redbook*, November 1973, 49–54.

Beschloss, Michael R. "A Tale of Two Presidents." *Wilson Quarterly* 24 (Winter 2000): 60–70.

Best, James J. "Who Talked with President Kennedy? An Interaction Analysis." *Presidential Studies Quarterly* 22 (Spring 1992): 351–369.

Bingham, Worth, and Ward S. Just. "The President and the Press." *Reporter*, April 12, 1962, 18–23.

Blagden, Ralph M. "Cabot Lodge's Toughest Fight." *Reporter*, September 30, 1952, 10–13.

Blumenthal, Sidney. "The Ruins of Georgetown." *New Yorker*, October 21–28, 1996, 221–237.

Borstelmann, Thomas. "Hedging Our Bets and Buying Time." *Diplomatic History* 24 (Summer 2000): 435–463.

Bostdorff, Denise, and Steven R. Goldzwig. "Idealism and Pragmatism in American Foreign Policy Rhetoric: The Case of John F. Kennedy and Vietnam." *Presidential Studies Quarterly* 24 (Summer 1994): 515–530.

Bostdorff, Denise, and Daniel J. O'Rourke. "The Presidency and the Promotion of Domestic Crisis: John Kennedy's Management of the 1962 Steel Crisis." *Presidential Studies Quarterly* 27 (Spring 1997): 343–361.

Bradford, Richard. "John F. Kennedy and the 1960 Presidential Primary in West Virginia." *South Atlantic Quarterly* 75 (Spring 1976): 161–172.

Bradley, John. "Blaze Starr's Showgirl Creation." *Washington Post Magazine*, December 10, 1989, pp. 25–30, 70–72.

Branch, Taylor. "The Ben Bradlee Tapes." *Harper's*, October 1975, 36–43.

Branch, Taylor, and George Crile III. "The Kennedy Vendetta." *Harper's*, August 1975, 49–63.

Brauer, Carl M. "Kennedy, Johnson and the War on Poverty." *Journal of American History* 69 (June 1982): 98–119.

Brinkley, Douglas. "Trading in a Hard-Won Reputation." *New Leader*, December 29, 1997–January 12, 1998, 7–8.

Burke, Vincent, and Frank Eleazer. "How Kennedy Gets What He Wants." *Nation's Business*, September 1961, 96–102.

Burns, James MacGregor. "The Legacy of JFK." *New Choices for Retirement Living*, October 1993, 42–47.

Burr, William, and Jeffrey T. Richelson. "Whether to 'Strangle the Baby in the Cradle': The United States and the Chinese Nuclear Program, 1960–64." *International Security* 25 (Winter 2000/01): 54–99.

Carleton, William G. "The Cult of Personality Comes to the White House." *Harper's*, December 1961, 63–68.

"The Candidates and the Arts." *Saturday Review*, October 29, 1960, 42–44.

Carty, Thomas. "The Catholic Question: Religious Liberty and JFK's Pursuit of the 1960 Democratic Presidential Nomination." *Historian* 63 (Spring 2001): 577–599.

Cassini, Igor. "How the Kennedy Marriage Has Fared." *Good Housekeeping*, September 1962, 68–69, 183–184, 187–188, 192, 195, 198.

Cater, Douglass. "The Cool Eye of John F. Kennedy." *Reporter*, December 10, 1959, 27–32.

———. "A New Style, a New Tempo." *Reporter*, March 16, 1961, 28–30.

———. "The Ways and Means of Wilbur Mills." *Reporter*, March 29, 1962, 24–27.

"Catholicism and the Campaign." *Commonweal*, September 23, 1960, 507–508.

"Catholic Editors and Senator Kennedy." *Commonweal*, June 10, 1960, 280–281.

Chang, Gordon H. "JFK, China, and the Bomb." *Journal of American History* 74 (March 1988): 1287–1310.

Chilcote, Ronald H. "Angola or the Azores?" *New Republic*, July 30, 1961, 21–22.

Childs, Marquis. "Bobby and the President." *Good Housekeeping*, May 1962, 80–81, 162, 164, 167, 169.

"The Closest Look Yet at JFK." *Life*, April 28, 1961, 35–38.

Coffin, Tris. "John Kennedy: Young Man in a Hurry." *Progressive*, December 1959, 10–18.

Cogley, John. "A Catholic for President?—I." *Commonweal*, March 20, 1959, 649.

———. "A Catholic for President?—IV." *Commonweal*, April 10, 1959, 53.

———. "Kennedy the Catholic." *Commonweal*, January 10, 1964, 422–424.

Collins, Frederic W. "The Mind of John F. Kennedy." *New Republic*, May 8, 1961, 15–20.

Colloff, Pamela, and Michael Hall. "The Conspiracy Theories." *Texas Monthly*, November 1998, 128+.

Costigliola, Frank. "The Failed Design: Kennedy, DeGaulle, and the Struggle for Europe." *Diplomatic History* 8 (Summer 1984): 227–251.

Coventry, Richard. "A Self-Made Patrician." *New Statesman and Nation*, August 31, 1940, 211–212.

Dallek, Robert. "The Medical Ordeals of JFK." *Atlantic Monthly*, December 2002, 49–61.

Dangerfield, George. "Queen's Minister and Friend." *Saturday Review*, October 9, 1954, 21.

Danner, Mark. "The Color of Truth." *New York Times Book Review*, April 4, 1999, 11–13.

Dean, Kevin W. " 'We Seek Peace—but We Shall Not Surrender': JFK's Use of Juxtaposition for Rhetorical Success in the Berlin Crisis." *Presidential Studies Quarterly* 21 (1991): 531–544.

Dean, Robert D. "Masculinity as Ideology: John F. Kennedy and the Domestic Politics of Foreign Policy." *Diplomatic History* 22 (Winter 1998): 29–62.

Dickson, David A. "U.S. Foreign Policy Toward Southern and Central Africa: The Kennedy and Johnson Years." *Presidential Studies Quarterly* 23 (Spring 1993): 301–315.

Diebold, William, Jr. "A Watershed with Some Dry Sides: The Trade Expansion Act of 1962." In *John F. Kennedy and Europe*, edited by Douglas Brinkley and Richard Griffiths, 235–260. Baton Rouge: Louisiana State University Press, 1999.

DiLeo, David L. "George Ball and the Europeanists in the State Department, 1961–1963." In *John F. Kennedy and Europe*, edited by Douglas Brinkley and Richard Griffiths, 263–280. Baton Rouge: Louisiana State University Press, 1999.

Divine, Robert A. "Alive and Well: The Continuing Cuban Missile Crisis Controversy." *Diplomatic History* 18 (Fall 1994): 551–560.

———. "Tale of the Presidential Tapes: A Review Essay." *Political Science Quarterly* 113 (Summer 1998): 307–312.

Dooley, Brian. "The Cuban Missile Crisis: 30 Years On." *History Today*, October 1992, 6–8.

Douglas, Susan J. "Back to the Future." *Progressive*, January 1994, 17.

"A Dreamer Wide Awake." *American Heritage*, October 1965, 77–81.

Eidenberg, Eugene. "The Presidency: Americanizing the War in Vietnam." In *American Political Institutions and Public Policy*, edited by Allan Sindler, 69–126. Boston: Little, Brown, 1969.

Erskine, Hazel Gaudet. "The Polls: Kennedy as President." *Public Opinion Quarterly* 28 (Summer 1964): 335–342.

Fedler, Fred, Ron Smith, and Milan D. Meeske. "*Time* and *Newsweek* Favor John F. Kennedy, Criticize Robert and Edward Kennedy." *Journalism Quarterly* 60 (Autumn 1983): 489–496.

Fenno, Richard F., Jr. "The Cabinet: Index to the Kennedy Way." *New York Times Magazine*, April 22, 1962, 13, 62–64.

Firestone, Bernard. "Kennedy and the Test Ban: Presidential Leadership and Arms Control." In *John F. Kennedy and Europe*, edited by Douglas Brinkley and Richard Griffiths, 66–94. Baton Rouge: Louisiana State University Press, 1999.

Fischer, John. "Hard Questions for Senator Kennedy." *Harper's*, April 1960, 21–23.

Fleming, Thomas. "Kennedy the Catholic." *Nation*, June 8, 1964, 571–572.

Fontaine, Andre. "Senator Kennedy's Crisis." *Redbook*, November 1957, pp. 49–51, 119–122.

"Four Who Would Be President." *New Republic*, April 13, 1959, 7–9.

Frankfurter, A. "Kennedy Pro Arte . . . et Sequitur?" *Art News*, January 1964, 23, 46–47, 60–61.

Fuchs, Lawrence. "JFK and the Jews." *Moment*, June 1983, 22–28.

Fuller, Helen. "Kennedy's Problem." *New Republic*, March 9, 1963, 12–14.

Garrow, David. "The FBI and Martin Luther King." *Atlantic Monthly*, July–August 2002, 80–88.

Gavin, Francis J. "The Gold Battles Within the Cold War: American Monetary Policy and the Defense of Europe, 1960–1963." *Diplomatic History* 26 (Winter 2002): 61–94.

Gelb, Arthur, and Barbara Gelb. "Culture Makes a Hit at the White House." *New York Times Magazine*, January 28, 1962, 10, 64, 66.

Gewen, Barry. "Profile in Caution." *New York Times Book Review*, October 19, 1997, 12–13.

Gibson, James William. "Revising Vietnam, Again." *Harper's*, April 2000, 78–83.

Giglio, James. "Why Another Kennedy Book?" *Reviews in American History* 31 (2003): 645–655.

Giglio, James. "John F. Kennedy as Domestic Leader: A Perspective on the Literature." In *Kennedy: The New Frontier Revisited*, edited by Mark White, 222–255. New York: New York University Press, 1998.

———. "Kennedy." *American Vision*, February/March 1995, 40–41.

———. "Past Frustrations and New Opportunities: Researching the Kennedy Presidency at the Kennedy Library." *Presidential Studies Quarterly* 22 (Spring 1992): 371–379.

Gilbert, Robert. "John F. Kennedy and Civil Rights for Blacks." *Presidential Studies Quarterly* 12 (Summer 1982): 386–392.

Gold, Victor. "Summer of '63." *Washingtonian*, May 1993, 27–35.

Goldzwig, Steven R., and George N. Dionisopoulas. "Legitimating Liberal Credentials for the Presidency: John F. Kennedy and *The Strategy of Peace*." *Southern Communication Journal* 60 (Summer 1995): 312–331.

Goodwin, Doris Kearns. "The Fitzgeralds and the Kennedys: Reflections of a Biographer." *Prologue* 22 (Summer 1990): 115–127.

Green, James F. "More Sleep Than Rest." *Saturday Review*, September 7, 1940, 20.

Greenberg, D. S. "John F. Kennedy: The Man and His Meaning." *Science*, November 29, 1963, 1151–1152.

Greenstein, Fred I. "Coming to Terms with Kennedy." *Reviews in American History* 20 (1992): 96–104.

Greenstein, Fred I., and Richard H. Immerman. "What Did Eisenhower Tell Kennedy About Indochina? The Politics of Misperception." *Journal of American History* 79 (September 1992): 568–587.

Haefele, Mark. "John F. Kennedy, USIA, and World Public Opinion." *Diplomatic History* 25 (Winter 2001): 63–84.

Hahn, Dan F. "Ask Not What a Youngster Can Do for You: Kennedy's Inaugural Address." *Presidential Studies Quarterly* 12 (Fall 1982): 610–614.

Halle, Louis J. "The Armies of Ignorance." *New Republic*, December 7, 1963, 16–17.

Harris, Eleanor. "The Senator Is in a Hurry." *McCall's*, August 1957, 44, 45, 118, 119, 123, 125.

Harris, Seymour. "Kennedy and the Liberals." *New Republic*, June 1, 1963, 15–16.

Harrison, Cynthia E. "A 'New Frontier' for Women: The Public Policy of the Kennedy Administration." *Journal of American History* 67 (June 1980): 630–646.

Harrison, Selig S. "Kennedy as President." *New Republic*, June 27, 1960, 9–15.

Hart, John. "Kennedy, Congress and Civil Rights." *Journal of American Studies* 13 (August 1979): 165–178.

Healy, Paul. "Galahad in the House." *Sign* 29 (July 1950): 9–11.

———. "The Senate's Gay Young Bachelor." *Saturday Evening Post*, June 13, 1953, 26, 27, 123, 124, 126, 127, 129.

Henkin, William A. "The Myth of Sexual Addiction." In *Clashing Views on Abnormal Psychology*, edited by Susan Nolen-Hoeksema, 198–205. Guilford, Conn.: Dushkin / McGraw-Hill, 1998.

Hennessey, Louella. "Bringing Up the Kennedys." *Good Housekeeping*, August 1961, 52–57, 115–119.

Henry, David. "Senator John F. Kennedy Encounters the Religious Question." In *Contemporary American Public Discourse*, 3rd ed., 177–193. Prospect Heights, Ill.: Waveland Press, 1992.

Herring, George C. "America and Vietnam: The Debate Continues." *American Historical Review* 92 (April 1987): 350–362.

Hersey, John. "Survival." *New Yorker*, June 17, 1944, 27–38.

Hershberg, James G. "Before 'The Missiles of October': Did Kennedy Plan a Military Strike Against Cuba?" *Diplomatic History* 14 (Spring 1990): 163–198.

Higgins, Marguerite. "Rose Fitzgerald Kennedy." *McCall's*, May 1961, 102–105, 192, 193, 195, 196, 197.

Hilsman, Roger. "McNamara's War—Against the Truth: A Review Essay." *Political Science Quarterly* 111 (Spring 1996): 151–163.

Hirshey, Gerri. "The Last Act of Judith Exner." *Vanity Fair*, April 1990, 162–167, 221–222, 224–225.

Hodgson, Godfrey. "Family as Destiny." *New Republic*, March 24, 1982, 31–33.

Holcombe, Arthur. "What Mr. Kennedy Said." *New Republic*, November 3, 1952, 2.

Holder, Calvin B. "Racism Toward Black African Diplomats During the Kennedy Administration." *Journal of Black Studies* 14 (September 1983): 31–48.

Holland, Max. "After Thirty Years: Making Sense of the Assassination." *Reviews in American History* 22 (1994): 191–209.

———. "The Docudrama That Is JFK." *Nation*, December 7, 1998, 25–32.

Hostetler, Michael J. "Gov. Al Smith Confronts the Catholic Question: The Rhetorical Legacy of the 1928 Campaign." *Communications Quarterly* 46 (Winter 1998): 12–24.

Hyman, Sidney. "How Mr. Kennedy Gets the Answers." *New York Times Magazine*, October 20, 1963, 17, 104–105.

————. "Presidential Popularity Is Not Enough." *New York Times Magazine*, August 12, 1962, 10, 64–66.

Jack, Peter Monro. "The Lives John Buchan Lived." *New York Times Book Review*, September 1, 1940, 1, 19.

Jeffries, John W. "The 'Quest for National Purpose' of 1960." *American Quarterly* 30 (1978): 451–470.

Judis, John. "Political Affairs." *New York Times Book Review*, January 3, 1999, 26.

Judt, Tony. "On the Brink." *New York Review of Books*, January 15, 1998, 52–59.

Just, Ward S. "The Scrapping of Skybolt." *Reporter*, April 11, 1963, 19–21.

Kallina, Edmund. "The State's Attorney and the President: The Inside Story of the 1960 Presidential Election in Illinois." *Journal of American Studies* 11 (1978): 147–160.

Kaplan, Fred. "JFK's First-Strike Plan." *Atlantic Monthly*, October 2001, 81–86.

Kaufman, Burton. "John F. Kennedy as World Leader: A Perspective on the Literature." *Diplomatic History* 17 (Summer 1993): 447–469.

Kay, W. D. "John F. Kennedy and the Two Faces of the U.S. Space Program, 1961–63." *Presidential Studies Quarterly* 28 (Summer 1998): 573–586.

Kazin, Alfred. "The President and Other Intellectuals." *American Scholar* 31 (Autumn 1961): 498–516.

Keefe, Robert. "On Cowboys and Collectives: The Kennedy-Nixon Generation." *Massachusetts Review* 21 (Fall 1990): 551–560.

Kelley, Kitty. "The Dark Side of Camelot." *People Weekly*, February 29, 1988, 106–114.

Kempton, Murray. "Sorensen's Kennedy." *Atlantic*, October 1965, 71–74.

Kennedy, John F. "America's Stake in Vietnam." *Vital Speeches*, August 1, 1956, 617–619.

Kennedy, John F. "A Democrat Says Party Must Lead—or Get Left." *Life*, March 11, 1957, 164–166.

Kennedy, John F. "Social Security: Constructive If Not Bold." *New Republic*, February 8, 1954, 14–15.

Kennedy, John F. "We Must Climb to the Hilltop." *Life*, August 22, 1960, 70, 72, 75–77.

Kennedy, John F. "What's the Matter with New England." *New York Times Magazine*, November 8, 1953, 12.

"Kennedy as Target." *New Republic*, June 1, 1963, 3–5.

"Kennedy and Poland." *New Republic*, September 2, 1957, 7.

"A Kennedy Runs for Congress." *Look*, June 11, 1946, 32–36.

"The Kennedys on Vacation." *Ladies Home Journal*, August 1961, 758–766.

"Kennedy Sought Dialogue with Cuba," November 24, 2003, <http://www.gwu.edu/~nsarchiv/NSAEBB/NSAEBB103/index.htm>.

Kilpatrick, Carroll. "The Kennedy Style and Congress." *Virginia Quarterly Review* 39 (Winter 1963): 1–11.

King, Martin Luther, Jr. "Equality Now: The President Has the Power." *Nation*, February 4, 1961, 91–95.

———. "Fumbling on the New Frontier." *Nation*, March 3, 1962, 190–193.

———. "It's a Difficult Thing to Teach a President." *Look*, November 17, 1964, 61, 64.

Knebel, Fletcher. "The Bishops vs. Kennedy." *Look*, May 23, 1961, 40–48.

———. "Can a Catholic Become Vice-President?" *Look*, June 12, 1956, 33–35.

———. "Democratic Forecast: A Catholic in 1960." *Look*, March 3, 1959, 13–17.

———. "Kennedy and His Pals." *Look*, April 25, 1961, 117–118, 120, 123–124, 126.

———. "Kennedy vs. the Press." *Look*, August 28, 1962, 17–21.

———. "Pulitzer Prize Entry: John F. Kennedy." In *Candidates 1960*, edited by Eric Sevareid, 181–215. New York: Basic Books, 1959.

———. "What You Don't Know About Kennedy." *Look*, January 17, 1961, 81–85.

Kochavi, Noam. "Limited Accommodation, Perpetuated Conflict: Kennedy, China, and the Laos Crisis, 1961–1963." *Diplomatic History* 26 (Winter 2002): 95–135.

Kraft, Joseph. "John F. Kennedy: Portrait of a President." *Harper's*, January 1964, 96, 98, 100.

———. "Kennedy and the Intellectuals." *Harper's*, November 1963, 112, 114–117.

Krock, Arthur. "Mr. Kennedy's Management of the News." *Fortune*, March 1963, 82, 199, 201, 202.

Kubricht, A. Paul. "Politics and Foreign Policy: A Brief Look at the Kennedy Administration's Eastern European Diplomacy." *Diplomatic History* 11 (Winter 1987): 55–65.

Land, Guy Paul. "John F. Kennedy's Southern Strategy, 1956–1960." *North Carolina Historical Review* 56 (1979): 41–63.

Lasch, Christopher. "The Life of Kennedy's Death." *Harper's*, October 1983, 32–40.

LeFebvre, Jeffrey A. "Kennedy's Algerian Dilemma: Containment, Alliance Politics and the 'Rebel Dialogue.'" *Middle Eastern Studies* 35 (April 1999): 61–82.

Lessard, Suzannah. "A New Look at John Kennedy." *Washington Monthly*, October 1971, 8–18.

Leuchtenburg, William. "John F. Kennedy, Twenty Years Later." *American Heritage*, December 1983, 50–59.

Levering, Ralph B., and Montague Kern. "The News Management Issue and John F. Kennedy's Foreign Policy." In *John F. Kennedy: The Promise Revisited*, edited by Paul Harper and Joann P. Krieg, 143–152. Westport, Conn.: Greenwood Press, 1988.

Lewis, Ted. "Kennedy: Profile of a Technician." *Nation*, February 2, 1963, 92–94.

———. "TV Press Conference." *Nation*, February 11, 1961, 112–113.

Licklider, Roy E. "The Missile Gap Controversy." *Political Science Quarterly* 85 (1970): 600–615.

"Life Goes Courting with a U.S. Senator." *Life*, July 20, 1953, 96–99.

Little, Douglas. "The New Frontier on the Nile: JFK, Nasser, and Arab Nationalism." *Journal of American History* 75 (September 1988): 501–527.

Logan, Andy. "JFK: The Stained-Glass Image." *American Heritage*, August 1967, 4–7, 75–78.

Logevall, Fredrik. "Vietnam and the Question of What Might Have Been." In *Kennedy: The New Frontier Revisited*, edited by Mark J. White, 19–62. New York: New York University Press, 1998.

Logsdon, John M., and Alain Dupas. "Was the Race to the Moon Real?" *Scientific American*, June 1994, 36–43.

Lukacs, John A. "An Autumnal Mood." *Commonweal*, December 10, 1954, 293–294.

Maga, Timothy P. "The New Frontier vs. Guided Democracy: JFK, Sukarno, and Indonesia, 1961–1963." *Presidential Studies Quarterly* 20 (Winter 1990): 91–102.

Malcolm, Donald. "The Man Who Wants Second Place." *New Republic*, July 30, 1956, 13–14.

Mallan, John P. "Massachusetts: Liberal and Corrupt." *New Republic*, October 13, 1952, 10–12.

Markel, Lester. "The 'Management' of the News." *Saturday Review*, February 9, 1963, 50–51, 61.

Marmor, Theodore R. "The Congress: Medicare Politics and Policy." In *American Political Institutions and Public Policy*, edited by Allan P. Sindler, 3–66. Boston: Little, Brown, 1969.

Massa, Mark S. "A Catholic for President? John F. Kennedy and the Secular Theology of the Houston Speech, 1960." *Journal of Church and State* 39 (Spring 1997): 297–317.

May, Ernest R., and Philip Zelikow. "Camelot Confidential." *Diplomatic History* 22 (Fall 1998): 642–653.

McAndrews, Lawrence. "The Avoidable Conflict: Kennedy, the Bishops, and Federal Aid to Education." *Catholic Historical Review* 76 (April 1990): 278–294.

———. "Beyond Appearances: Kennedy, Congress, Religion, and Federal Aid to Education." *Presidential Studies Quarterly* 21 (Summer 1991): 545–557.

McCartney, James. "Rallying Around the Flag." *American Journalism Review* 16 (September 1994): 40–46.

McGrory, Mary. "Flying Start and Notable Agility." *America*, February 4, 1961, 585.

McGreevy, John T. "Thinking on One's Own: Catholicism in the American Intellectual Imagination, 1928–1960." *Journal of American History* 84 (June 1997): 97–131.

Meagher, Michael E. " 'In an Atmosphere of National Peril': The Development of John F. Kennedy's World View." *Presidential Studies Quarterly* 27 (Summer 1997): 467–479.

Mellon, Rachel Lambert. "President Kennedy's Rose Garden." *White House History* 1 (1983): 5–11.

Michaelis, David. "The President's Best Friend." *American Heritage*, June/July 1983, 12–27.

Michelson, Edward. "Lodge Dislodged?" *Nation*, October 4, 1952, 297–298.

Miller, Helen Hill. "A Catholic for President?" *New Republic*, November 18, 1957, 10–13.

Montalva, Eduardo Frei. "The Alliance That Lost Its Way." *Foreign Affairs*, 45 (April 1967): 437–448.

Morgan, Edward P. "O'Brien Presses On with the 'Four P's.'" *New York Times Magazine*, March 25, 1962, 28, 29, 116, 118.

Morgan, Thomas B. "Madly for Adlai." *American Heritage*, 1984, 49–64.

Muheim, Harry. "When J.F.K. Was Rich, Young, and Happy." *Esquire*, August 1966, 65–66, 132–133.

Mullen, Jay Carlton. "West Virginia's Image: The 1960 Presidential Primary and the National Press." *West Virginia History* 32 (July 1971): 215–223.

Nash, Philip. "Nuclear Weapons in Kennedy's Foreign Policy." *Historian* 56 (Winter 1994): 285–300.

Nelson, Anna Kasten. "President Kennedy's National Security Policy: A Reconsideration." *Reviews in American History* 19 (March 1991): 1–14.

Neubauer, John. "The Camera and JFK." *Popular Photography*, November 1967, 88–102, 144–145.

Neustadt, Richard E. "Approaches to Staffing the Presidency: Notes on FDR and JFK." *American Political Science Review* 57 (December 1963): 855–862.

———. "Kennedy in the Presidency: A Premature Appraisal." *Political Science Quarerly* 79 (September 1964): 321–334.

Newhouse, John. "De Gaulle and the Anglo-Saxons." In *John F. Kennedy and Europe*, edited by Douglas Brinkley and Richard Griffiths, 32–48. Baton Rouge: Louisiana State University Press, 1999.

Nicholas, James, et. al. "Management of Adrenocortical Insufficiency During Surgery." *Archives of Surgery* 71 (November 1955): 737–742.

Nichols, John. "President Kennedy's Adrenals." *JAMA* 201 (July 10, 1967): 129–130.

Nobile, Phillip, and Ron Rosenbaum. "The Curous Aftermath of JFK's Best and Brightest Affair." *New Times*, July 9, 1976, 22–33.

"Notes and Comment." *New Yorker*, February 4, 1961, 23–24.

O'Brien, Michael. "Old Myths/New Insights: History and Dr. King." *History Teacher* 22 (November 1988): 49–65.

Oren, Michael. "Road Maps." *New Republic*, September 22, 2003, 42–45.

Parmet, Herbert S. "The Kennedy Myth and American Politics." *History Teacher* 24 (November 1990): 31–39.

Paterson, Thomas G., and William J. Brophy. "October Missiles and November Elections: The Cuban Missile Crisis and American Politics, 1962." *Journal of American History* 73 (June 1986): 87–119.

Pedroncelli, Rich. "JFK: A PT Skipper Remembers." *Naval History* 13 (December 1999): 24–27.

Phillips, Cabell. "How to Be a Presidential Candidate." *New York Times Magazine*, July 13, 1958, 11, 52, 54.

"Pre-presidential." *New Yorker*, April 1, 1961, 26–27.

"The President Who Loved Sport." *Sports Illustrated*, December 2, 1963, 20–21.

"Protestants in Politics." *New Republic*, September 19, 1960, 3–5.

Rabe, Stephen G. "After the Missiles of October: John F. Kennedy and Cuba, November 1962 to November 1963." *Presidential Studies Quarterly* 30 (December 2000): 714–726.

———. "Eisenhower Revisionism: A Decade of Scholarship." *Diplomatic History* 17 (Winter 1993): 97–115.

Reeves, Richard. "My Six Years with JFK." *American Heritage*, November 1993, 98–101.

Reich, Charles. "Another Such Victory." *New Republic*, April 30, 1962, 8–10.

Reston, James. "What Was Killed Was Not Only the President but the Promise." *New York Times Magazine*, November 15, 1964, 24, 25, 126, 127.

Riccards, Michael P. "Rare Counsel: Kennedy, Johnson and the Civil Rights Bill of 1963." *Presidential Studies Quarterly* 11 (Summer 1981): 395–398.

Romano, Renee. "No Diplomatic Immunity: African Diplomats, the State Department, and Civil Rights, 1961–1964." *Journal of American History* (September 2000): 546–579.

"Rose Fitzgerald Kennedy." *McCall's*, May 1961, 102–105, 192–196.

"Rose Kennedy Talks About Her Life, Her Faith and Her Children." *McCall's*, December 1973, 74–75, 118, 121.

Rose, Gideon. "Who Set Up the Dominoes?" *New York Times Book Review*, May 14, 2000, 10.

Ross, Irwin. "The Senator Women Elected." *Cosmopolitan*, December 1953, 81–85.

Rovere, Richard. "Kennedy's Last Chance to Be President." *Esquire*, April 1959, 61–67.

———. "Letter from Washington." *New Yorker*, November 19, 1960, 203–210.

———. "Letter from Washington." *New Yorker*, March 30, 1963, 163–169.

———. "Letter from Washington." *New Yorker*, June 1, 1963, 100–104, 107–108.

Russell, Francis. "Honey Fitz." *American Heritage*, August 1968, 28–31, 76–80.

Sanders, Marion K. "Nobody Here but Us Pompadours." *Harper's*, October 1962, 141–146.

Scheele, Henry Z. "Response to the Kennedy Administration: The Joint Senate-House Republican Leadership Press Conferences." *Presidential Studies Quarterly* 19 (Fall 1989): 825–845.

Schlesinger, Arthur, Jr. "Camelot Revisited." *New Yorker*, June 5, 1995, 33.

———. "Effective National Security Advising: A Most Dubious Precedent." *Political Science Quarterly* 115 (2000): 347–351.

————. "On JFK: An Interview with Isaiah Berlin." *New York Review of Books*, October 22, 1998, 31, 32, 34–37.

————. "What the Thousand Days Wrought." *New Republic*, November 21, 1983, 20–30.

Schram, Martin. "Goldwater-Kennedy Debates." *Journal of Commerce* 416 (June 4, 1998): 6A.

Schwartz, Thomas A. "The Berlin Crisis and the Cold War." *Diplomatic History* 21 (Winter 1997): 139–148.

Seligman, Daniel. "The Kennedy-Goldberg Labor Movement." *Fortune*, December 11, 1995, 236–237.

Sella, Marshall. "Hail to the Coif." *Gentleman's Quarterly*, June 1999, 178, 183.

"Senator Kennedy and His Critics." *Commonweal*, March 20, 1959, 645–648.

"Senator Kennedy and the Chapel." *Commonweal*, January 29, 1960, 479–480.

Shannon, William V. "The Kennedy Administration: The Early Months." *American Scholar* 31 (Autumn 1961): 481–488.

Sherrill, Robert. "The Power Game: George Smathers, the Golden Senator from Florida." *Nation*, December 7, 1964, 426–437.

Sidey, Hugh. "Departure of a 'Deputy President.'" *Life*, March 6, 1964, 105, 106, 108+.

————. "Joe Kennedy's Feelings About His Son." *Life*, December 19, 1960, 32.

————. "The President's Voracious Reading Habits." *Life*, March 17, 1961, 55–64.

Small, Melvin. "Kennedy Without Tears." *Diplomatic History* 14 (Spring 1990): 265–271.

Smith, Liz. "The Exner Files." *Vanity Fair*, January 1997, 30–43.

Smith, Thomas G. "John Kennedy, Stewart Udall, and New Frontier Conservation." *Pacific Historical Review* 64 (August 1995): 329–362.

Stark, Steven D. "The Cultural Meaning of the Kennedys." *Atlantic Monthly*, January 1994, 18+.

Steel, Ronald. "The Kennedy Fantasy." *New York Review of Books*, November 19, 1970, 3–12.

Steele, John L. "The Adlai Stevenson Affair." *Life*, December 14, 1962, 44–46.

Stern, Mark. "Eisenhower and Kennedy: A Comparison of Confrontations at Little Rock and Ole Miss." *Policy Studies Journal* 21 (1993): 575–588.

————. "John F. Kennedy and Civil Rights: From Congress to the Presidency." *Presidential Studies Quarterly* 19 (Fall 1989): 797–823.

Stern, Sheldon M. "What JFK Really Said." *Atlantic Monthly*, May 2000, 122, 124–128.

St. John, Seymore, and Richard Bode. "'Bad Boy' Jack Kennedy." *Good Housekeeping*, September 1985, 166–167, 236–240.

Stone, I. F. "The Test Ban Comedy." *New York Review of Books*, May 7, 1970, 14–22.

Strout, Richard L. "The Cool Mr. Kennedy." *New Republic*, January 11, 1960, 16.

———. "J.F.K. Remembered." *New Republic*, November 21, 1983, 24.

Styron, William. "The Short, Classy Voyage of JFK." *Esquire*, 124–126, 129, 130.

Summers, Anthony. "The Unmaking of a Myth." *Sunday Times* (London), October 6, 1991, 18–25.

"Their Finest Hour." *Nation*, February 2, 1963, 81.

Thomas, Evan. "Bobby Kennedy's War on Castro." *Washington Monthly*, December 1995, 24–30.

Thompson, Kenneth W. "John F. Kennedy and Revisionism." *Virginia Quarterly Review* 70 (Summer 1994): 430–443.

T.R.B. "Dr. Poling to Dr. Peale." *New Republic*, September 19, 1960, 2.

———. "Kennedy's Extemporizing." *New Republic*, September 19, 1960, 2.

Trilling, Diana. "A Visit to Camelot." *New Yorker*, June 2, 1997, 54–60, 62–65.

Tugwell, Rexford. "The President and His Helpers." *Political Science Quarterly* 82 (June 1967): 253–267.

Turner, Russell. "Senator Kennedy: The Perfect Politician." *American Mercury*, March 1957, 33–40.

"The Uses of Presidential Power." *New Republic*, May 14, 1962, 13–18.

Vanocur, Sander. "Humphrey v. Kennedy: High Stakes in Wisconsin." *Reporter*, March 17, 1960, 28–30.

———. "Kennedy's Voyage of Discovery." *Harper's*, April 1964, 41–45.

Vidal, Gore. "Coached by Camelot." *New Yorker*, December 1, 1997, 84–92.

Waldrop, Frank C. "JFK and the Nazi Spy." *Washingtonian*, April 1975, 89–91.

Walker, Gerald, and Donald A. Allan. "Jack Kennedy at Harvard." *Coronet*, May 1961, 82–95.

Walker, William O., III. "JFK, Democracy, and U.S. Security Policy in the Americas." *Diplomatic History* 25 (Winter 2000): 159–164.

Walsh, John. "John F. Kennedy: Policy and Legacy." *Science*, November 29, 1963, 1152–1153.

Ward, Geoffrey C. "Young Jack Kennedy." *American Heritage*, December 1992, 12, 14.

Warner, Geoffrey. "President Kennedy and Indochina: The 1961 Decisions." *International Affairs* 70 (1994): 685–700.

Warnick, Barbara. "Argument Schemes and the Construction of Social Reality: John F. Kennedy's Address to the Houston Ministerial Association." *Communication Quarterly* 44 (Spring 1996): 183–196.

Watson, Mary Ann. "How Kennedy Invented Political Television." *Television Quarterly* 25 (1991): 61–71.

"We Agree Mr. Kennedy." *Life*, August 25, 1952, 22.

Wehrle, Edmund F. "'A Good, Bad Deal': John F. Kennedy, W. Averell Harriman, and the Neutralization of Laos, 1961–1962." *Pacific Historical Review* 67 (August 1998): 349–377.

Weinstein, Lewis H. "John F. Kennedy: A Personal Memoir, 1946–1963." *American Jewish History* 75 (September 1985): 5–30.

Weis, W. Michael. "The Twilight of Pan-Americanism: The Alliance for Progress, Neo-Colonialism, and Non-Alignment in Brazil, 1961–1964." *International History Review* 23 (June 2001): 322–344.

Wenger, Andreas, and Marcel Gerber. "John F. Kennedy and the Limited Test Ban Treaty: A Case Study of Presidential Leadership." *Presidential Studies Quarterly* 29 (June 1999): 460–487.

Wetenhall, John. "Camelot's Legacy to Public Art: Aesthetic Ideology in the New Frontier." *Art Journal* 48 (Winter 1989): 303–308.

"What's He Up To?" *Nation*, February 2, 1963, 81–82.

"White House 'Lobby' Operates on Capitol Hill." *Congressional Quarterly Weekly Report*, June 30, 1961, 1181–1182.

White, Mark. "Behind Closed Doors: The Private Life of a Public Man." In *Kennedy: The New Frontier Revisited*, edited by Mark J. White, 256–276. New York: New York University Press, 1998.

———. "New Scholarship on the Cuban Missile Crisis." *Diplomatic History* 26 (Winter 2002): 147–153.

White, Theodore H. "For President Kennedy: An Epilogue." *Life*, December 6, 1963, 158–159.

Wicker, Tom. "Committed to a Quagmire." *Diplomatic History* 19 (Winter 1995): 167–171.

———. "Kennedy and Our Vanished Dreams." *New York Times Magazine*, November 20, 1983, 73, 124, 148, 149.

———. "A Theological War." *Diplomatic History* 20 (Summer 1996): 445–449.

———. "'A Total Political Animal.'" *New York Times Magazine*, April 15, 1962, 26, 128–130.

Wiesner, Jerome B. "John F. Kennedy: A Remembrance." *Science*, November 29, 1963, 1147–1150.

Williams, Robert J., and David A. Kershaw. "Kennedy and Congress: The Struggle for the New Frontier." *Political Studies* 27 (September 1979): 390–404.

Wills, Garry. "A Second Assassination." *New York Review of Books*, December 18, 1997, 4, 6, 8.

Witcover, Jules. "Unshining Moments." *Columbia Journalism Review* 36 (January–February 1998): 69–77.

Yarmolinsky, Adam. "Camelot Revisited." *Virginia Quarterly Review* 72 (Fall 1996): 652–662.

Young, Hugo, Bryan Silcock, and Peter Dunn. "Why We Went to the Moon." *Washington Monthly*, April 1970, 28–58.

Zane, Maitland. "Joan Hitchcock's Evenings with J.F.K." *Qui*, July 15, 1976, 77, 116.

Zeiler, Thomas W. "Meeting the European Challenge: The Common Market and Trade Policy." In *Kennedy: The New Frontier Revisited*, edited by Mark J. White, 132–159. New York: New York University Press, 1998.

Zoumaras, Thomas. "Plugging the Dike: The Kennedy Administration Confronts the Balance-of-Payments Crisis with Europe." In *John F. Kennedy and Europe*, edited by Douglas Brinkley and Richard Griffiths, 169–188. Baton Rouge: Louisiana State University Press, 1999.

THESES, DISSERTATIONS, AND ESSAYS

Anderson, Freddie W. "From Congressman to Senator: The 1952 Campaign of John F. Kennedy." Seminar paper, 1973. Author's Files.

Bender, Lynn Darrell. "U.S.-Cuban Relations, 1959–1972: An Examination of the Determinants, Implications, and Consequences of American Policy Toward the Revolutionary Regime." Ph.D. dissertation, George Washington University, 1972.

Berry, Fred, Jr. "Counterinsurgency: Kennedy's War in Vietnam, 1961–1963." M.A. thesis, University of Houston-Clear Lake, 1990.

Blanchard, B. Wayne. "American Civil Defense 1945–1975: The Evolution of Programs and Policies." Ph.D. dissertation, University of Virginia, 1980.

Blumenthal, Richard. "Community Action: The Origins of a Government Program." Honor's essay, Harvard University, 1967.

Bolles, Charles DeVallon Dugas. "The Search for an American Strategy: The Origins of the Kennedy Doctrine, 1936–1961." Ph.D. dissertation, University of Wisconsin–Madison, 1985.

Bowman, Stephen Lee. "The Evolution of United States Army Doctrine for Counterinsurgency Warfare: From World War II to the Commitment of Combat Units in Vietnam." Ph.D. dissertation, Duke University, 1985.

Burke, Mary Kathleen. "Liege Man at Camelot: The Role of David F. Powers in the Career of John F. Kennedy." Ph.D. dissertation, Providence College, 1987.

Coye, Beth Frances. "The Requirements of National Security Policy as Conceived by the Kennedy Administration." M.A. thesis, American University, 1968.

Davis, Amy Elizabeth. "Politics of Prosperity: The Kennedy Presidency and Economic Policy." Ph.D. dissertation, Columbia University, 1988.

Elliott, Derek Wesley. "Finding an Appropriate Commitment: Space Policy Development Under Eisenhower and Kennedy, 1954–1963." Ph.D. dissertation, George Washington University, 1992.

Felkins, Patricia Kay. "Perceptions of J.F.K.: Image and Myth." Ph.D. dissertation, University of Missouri–Columbia, 1975.

Kane, Paula Marie. "Boston Catholics and Modern American Culture, 1900–1920." Ph.D. dissertation, Yale University, 1987.

Kemper, Deane Alwyn. "John F. Kennedy Before the Greater Houston Ministerial Association, September 12, 1960: The Religious Issue." Ph.D. dissertation, Michigan State University, 1968.

Kennedy, John F. "Appeasement at Munich: The Inevitable Result of the Slowness of Conversion of the British Democracy from a Disarmament to a Rearmament Policy." Senior thesis, Harvard University, 1940.

Koger, Daniel Allan. "The Liberal Opinion Press and the Kennedy Years in Vietnam: A Study of Four Journals." Ph.D. dissertation, Michigan State University, 1983.

Kyes, Elizabeth Anne. "President Kennedy's Press Conferences as 'Shapers of the News.'" Ph.D. dissertation, University of Iowa, 1968.

Landis, Mark L. "Personality and Style in the United States Senate." Ph.D. dissertation, Columbia University, 1973.

Lemke, William Edgar. "The Political Thought of John F. Kennedy: To the Inaugural Address." Ph.D. dissertation, University of Maine at Orono, 1973.

Lisle, Teddy David. "The Canonical Impediment: John F. Kennedy and the Religious Issue During the 1960 Presidential Campaign." Ph.D. dissertation, University of Kentucky, 1981.

Machin, Maria A. "The Cuban Missile Crisis: An Analysis of a Quarter Century of Historiography." M.A. thesis, Florida Atlantic University, 1990.

Mahood, Harry Richard. "The St. Lawrence Seaway Bill of 1954: A Case Study of Decision-Making in American Foreign Policy." Ph.D. dissertation, University of Illinois, 1960.

Merchant, Jerrold Jackson. "Kennedy-Khrushchev Strategies of Persuasion During the Cuban Missile Crisis." Ph.D. dissertation, University of Southern California, 1971.

Nurse, Ronald. "America Must Not Sleep: The Development of John F. Kennedy's Foreign Policy Attitudes, 1947–1960." Ph.D. dissertation, Michigan State University, 1971.

Sarbaugh, Timothy J. "John Fitzgerald Kennedy, the Catholic Issue, and Presidential Politics, 1959–1960." Ph.D. dissertation, Loyola University, 1987.

Sather, Lawrence Arne. "Biography as Rhetorical Criticism: An Analysis of John F. Kennedy's 1960 Presidential Campaign by Selected Biographers." Ph.D. dissertation, Washington State University, 1974.

Sharp, Harry Wall, Jr. "The Kennedy News Conference." Ph.D. dissertation, Purdue University, 1967.

Smith, Gary Duane. "The Pulse of Presidential Popularity: Kennedy in Crisis." Ph.D. dissertation, University of California, Los Angeles, 1978.

Trotter, Richard Gordon. "The Cuban Missile Crisis: An Analysis of Policy Formulation in Terms of Current Decision Making Theory." Ph.D. dissertation, University of Pennsylvania, 1970.

Usowski, Peter Stanley. "John F. Kennedy and the Central Intelligence Agency: Policy and Intelligence." Ph.D. dissertation, George Washington University, 1987.

Walters, Ronald. "The Formulation of United States Foreign Policy Toward Africa, 1958–1963." Ph.D. dissertation, American University, 1971.

White, Mark Jonathan. "Approaching the Abyss: The Cuban Missile Crisis and the Men Who Made and Resolved It." Ph.D. dissertation, Rutgers University, 1992.

Wolfe, James Snow. "The Kennedy Myth: American Civil Religion in the Sixties." Ph.D. dissertation, University of California, Berkeley, 1975.

NEWSPAPERS AND PERIODICALS

(The Kennedy Library has microfilmed scrapbooks of news clippings kept by John F. Kennedy's congressional and presidential staffs from 1946 to 1963. This was the primary source for news clippings.)

Boston Herald American

The Christian Science Monitor

John Herling's Labor Letter

Newsweek

The New York Times

Time

USA Today

U.S. News and World Report

The Wall Street Journal

Washington Daily News

The Washington Post

REFERENCE WORKS

Book Review Digest

Columbia Companion to British History

Congressional Quarterly Almanac

Current Biography

Diagnostic and Statistical Manual of Mental Disorders, 4th ed.

Encyclopedia of the Vietnam War

Foreign Relations of the United States

New Encyclopaedia Britannica

Presidential Recordings: John F. Kennedy

Survey of Contemporary Literature

INDEX